WITHDRAWN

THE
BOWKER ANNUAL

308511

THE BOWKER ANNUAL OF LIBRARY & BOOK TRADE INFORMATION
1972

17th Edition
Janice Johnson, Managing Editor
Frank L. Schick, Consulting Editor
Sponsored by The Council
of National Library Associations

R. R. BOWKER, *New York & London*

Published by R. R. Bowker Co. (a Xerox company)
1180 Avenue of the Americas, New York, N.Y. 10036
Copyright © 1972 by Xerox Corporation
All rights reserved.
International Standard Book Number: 0-8352-0520-7
Library of Congress Catalog Card Number: 55-12434
Printed and bound in the United States of America

Contents

Preface ix

**PART 1   THE YEAR'S WORK IN LIBRARIANSHIP
AND PUBLISHING**

LIBRARY AND BOOK TRADE INFORMATION

News Report: 1971   KARL NYREN 3
Developments in Children's and Young Adults' Library Services
  during 1971   PATRICIA SCHUMAN 15
The State of Federal Libraries   FRANK KURT CYLKE 22
The Library of Congress in 1971 25
The National Library of Medicine   MARTIN M. CUMMINGS 31
The National Agricultural Library   LEILA P. MORAN 34
The Bureau of Libraries and Educational Technology in 1971
  BURTON E. LAMKIN 37
U.S. Office of Education Organizational Chart 41
The Council on Library Resources, Inc.   LEE E. GROVE 42
American National Standards Institute, Inc. Standards Committee Z39
  LINDA SCHNEIDER 45
National Commission on Libraries and Information Science
  FREDERICK BURKHARDT 50
The American Library Association   KEITH DOMS 51
The Special Libraries Association   F. E. MCKENNA 54
The ERIC Clearinghouse on Library and Information Sciences
  CHARLES W. HOOVER 58
The Committee on Scientific and Technical Information   MELVIN S. DAY 62
The Struggle for Intellectual Freedom in 1971   DAVID K. BERNINGHAUSEN .. 66
National Book Committee, Inc.   JOHN C. FRANTZ 71
Book Trade Mergers, 1971 74

LIBRARY AUTOMATION

Library Automation in the Federal Government   MADELINE M. HENDERSON 75
Automation in Technical Processing at the Library of Congress
  HENRIETTE D. AVRAM 80
Developments in Nonprint Media, 1971: The Year of Minimal Change
  GERALD R. BRONG 86

v

Library and Information Networks   DAN CLEMMER AND RUSSELL SHANK 90
The Library Technology Program   MARJORIE E. WEISSMAN 95

LIBRARY AND BOOK TRADE EVENTS
Calendar of Book Trade and Promotional Events, 1972 99
Library Association Meetings 101
Literary and Library Prizes and Awards, 1971 105
Basic Books and Periodicals for Librarians   FLORA D. COLTON 111
Basic Books for the Publisher and the Book Trade   JEAN R. PETERS 121
Best Sellers, 1971   ALICE PAYNE HACKETT 125
Best Children's and Young Adults' Books of 1971 125
Notable Books of 1970 and 1971 128

PART 2   NATIONAL LIBRARY AND BOOK TRADE DEVELOPMENTS

LIBRARY AND BOOK TRADE STATISTICS
Statistics of Libraries for the 1970s   DOROTHY M. GILFORD AND
   FRANK L. SCHICK 133
Plans for a Nationwide System of Library Statistics   RUTH R. FRAME 138
U.S. Office of Education Plans for a Survey of Public Libraries
   RUTH L. BOAZ 142
College and University Library Statistics   THEODORE SAMORE 144
Health Sciences Libraries in the United States: Survey and Statistical Profile
   SUSAN CRAWFORD 148
Characteristics of the U.S. Population Served by Libraries   GEORGE LIND . 154
Statistics on Libraries 156
Data on Public Library Budgets and Expenditures for Library Materials 157
Data on College and University Library Budgets and Expenditures for
   Library Materials 159
Public Library Data on Audiovisual and Microform Expenditures 161
College and University Library Data on Audiovisual and Microform
   Expenditures 162
Growth of the Bookstore Industry in the United States   WILLIAM S. LOFQUIST 163
Book Publishing Sales Statistics 171
American Book Title Output — 1971 176
Books in the Mails   ROBERT W. FRASE 179
Book Review Media 180
Book Publishing Stock Prices, 1971 181
Prices of U.S. and Foreign Published Materials   HUGH ATKINSON 183
Growth of U.S. Trade in Book Exports and Imports   WILLIAM S. LOFQUIST ... 190

LIBRARY AND BOOK TRADE STANDARDS

International Library Statistics Standardization Developments during 1971
  FRANK L. SCHICK 193
International Standard Serial Numbering (ISSN) EMERY I. KOLTAY 197
Standard for Title Leaves of a Book 200
Standard for Advertising of Books 201
Standards for the Bibliographic Control of Nonprint Media PEARCE S. GROVE.... 203

LEGISLATION AND GRANTS

Federal Legislation for Libraries during 1971 GERMAINE KRETTEK
  AND EILEEN D. COOKE 207
The Library Services and Construction Act during Fiscal Year 1971
  ELIZABETH H. HUGHEY 214
ESEA Title II Program Accomplishments, 1966–1972 HARRY L. PHILLIPS 220
Summary of Title II-A Grants for Academic Library Resources under
  the Higher Education Act of 1965 FRANK A. STEVENS 225
Higher Education Act of 1965, Title II-B: Library Education
  FRANK A. STEVENS AND FRANCES YVONNE HICKS 227
Higher Education Act, Title II-B: Library and Information Science Research
  PAUL C. JANASKE 233
Foundation Grants to Libraries or for Library Purposes, 1971 237
Federal Legislation Affecting Book Publishing in 1971 ROBERT W. FRASE 246

LIBRARY EDUCATION, MANPOWER, AND SALARIES

Placements of Library School Graduates for the Academic Years
  1967/68–1967/70 D. KATHRYN WEINTRAUB 253
Library Manpower Statistics 1969–1972 and the Outlook for the Future
  SARAH R. REED 260
Placements and Salaries 1970: The Year That Was *Not* What It Seemed
  CARLYLE J. FRAREY AND MARY R. DONLEY 269
Library Salaries and Vacancies As Reflected in Ads RUTH R. FRAME 278
Graduate Library Schools Accredited by the American Library Association 282
Library Scholarships and Fellowships 284
Library Fraternities 286
Trainee or Student Librarian Programs 289

LIBRARY BUILDING

Public Library Building in 1971 HOYT GALVIN AND BARBARA ASBURY 301
Academic Library Building 1967–1971 JERROLD ORNE 320
Two-Year Academic Library Buildings JOLEEN BOCK 357

PART 3 LIBRARY AND BOOK TRADE ASSOCIATIONS AND AGENCIES

National Associations 365
Chart of National Library Associations 412
State, Regional, and Provincial Associations 413
State School Library Associations 421
Directory of Federal Library Programs   FRANK KURT CYLKE 423
State Library Agencies... 424
State School Library Supervisors 427
Book Trade Associations 430

PART 4 INTERNATIONAL LIBRARY AND BOOK TRADE DEVELOPMENTS

International Book Year — 1972   EDWARD WEGMAN 439
International Relations Activities of the American Library Association
  in 1971   DAVID G. DONOVAN 443
The International Federation of Library Associations, Activities for 1971
  HERMAN LIEBAERS 445
Developments in Librarianship in Canada   KATHERINE H. PACKER 448
Library Developments in the United Kingdom in 1971   N. B. W. THOMPSON 456
Library Developments in the Soviet Union in 1971   L. I. VLADIMIROV 460
Library Developments in Finland in 1971   RITVA SIEVANEN-ALLEN 463
Library Developments in the Czechoslovak Socialist Republic during 1971
  MIRKO VELINSKY 466
Library Developments in the Federal Republic of Germany in 1971
  OTTO LOHMANN 468
International Book Production Statistics, 1968–1970 473
British Book Production 476
The State of Canadian Publishing   PATRICIA A. FARRELL 477
Book Publishing in the United Kingdom, 1971: A Cautious Year
  DAVID WHITAKER 486
International Book Programs 490
Frankfurt Book Fair, 1971 494
International Associations 495
Foreign Library Associations 501
Foreign Antiquarian, Booksellers, and Publishers Associations 509

APPENDIXES

A. Activities Index to Library Associations 515
B. Library Purchasing Guide 1972 537

Index 575
Library Addresses and Telephone Numbers

Preface

This 17th edition of the *Bowker Annual* continues the policy of updating essential features and adding new articles of current interest. In Part 1, in addition to our regular features, new articles have been included on children's and young adults' library services, the National Commission on Libraries and Information Science, the American Library Association, the Special Libraries Association, ERIC, and COSATI. Also in Part 1, a new section has been added on Library Automation, which includes articles on developments in this field on the state, regional, and federal levels.

In Part 2, particular emphasis has been placed on the Library Education, Manpower, and Salaries section, in which new and original surveys investigate the salary and placement picture for all types of librarians, including library technicians, and the employment outlook for the future. New to the Library and Book Trade Statistics Section are three articles covering the U.S. Office of Education — National Center for Educational Statistics plans for compiling library statistics on a nationwide basis. Also in this section, of particular interest to the book trade, are articles on the growth of the U.S. bookstore industry and the growth of U.S. trade in book exports and imports. The Library and Book Trade Standards section covers 1971 developments in new standards that are pertinent to both the library and the book trade world: ISSN, ANSI standard for title leaves of a book and standard for advertising of books, standards for the bibliographic control of nonprint media. New articles in the Legislation and Grants section give a roundup of federal legislation affecting libraries and book publishing in 1971. The Library Building section continues to report on public library building and includes this year a five-year review of academic library building, along with a separate article on two-year academic library buildings.

Part 3 again includes the latest information on state, regional, provincial, national, and federal associations and agencies. Appendix A, the Activities Index, lists by category the committees and committee chairmen of the many national and international library associations (located in Part 3 and Part 4, respectively), thus bringing to light the various library groups that are active in the same field. Two new lists have been added to Part 3 this year: a list of State School Library Associations, and a list of State School Library Supervisors.

Partly in observance of International Book Year and partly in the hope of bringing to international attention national developments in librarianship and book pub-

x / PREFACE

lishing, Part 4 has been expanded considerably to include for the first time articles on library developments in the Soviet Union, Finland, the Czechoslovak Socialist Republic, and the Federal Republic of Germany, and on book publishing in Canada and the United Kingdom.

We wish to thank our colleagues who, in spite of the demands of their professional careers, have been able to contribute articles on their special fields of expertise for the *Annual*. It is through their generous contributions that the *Annual* continues to bring together a wide range of information of interest to and for the mutual benefit of the library and book trade professions.

Mr. Lee E. Grove's article "The Council on Library Resources, Inc." is published posthumously. Mr. Grove passed away suddenly on December 17, 1971. He contributed the article on the Council of Library Resources to the 1968 through the 1972 editions of the *Annual;* the editors are most grateful for his contributions and are much saddened by his passing.

Special thanks must be given to two colleagues and long-time contributors to the *Annual* for their advice on new material for inclusion in this year's edition: they are Russell Shank of the Smithsonian Institution for his suggestions for the new Library Automation section, and Robert W. Frase of the Association of American Publishers for his counsel on book trade statistics. Mention must also be made of Chandler Grannis, Editor-at-Large, *Publishers' Weekly,* whose valued advice on various material in the Library and Book Trade Statistics section was greatly appreciated.

The editors welcome suggestions for new topics to be covered in subsequent editions of the *Annual* and comments, either favorable or critical, on data printed in this edition, with the hope that the *Bowker Annual* will continue to fill a basic need in library and book trade literature.

JANICE JOHNSON
FRANK L. SCHICK

PART 1 THE YEAR'S WORK IN LIBRARIANSHIP AND PUBLISHING

Library and Book Trade Information

NEWS REPORT: 1971*

by

Karl Nyren**

The year 1971 was unmistakably an *Annus Mirabilis* in the world — rather a more spectacular one than the one that proto-Alsop John Dryden memorialized some 300 years ago. It was the year that Red China ping-ponged its way into the United Nations and the Pirates rose up and smote the Orioles. It was the year of political paleontology, with a record catch of creatures from the tar pits marching on the Supreme Court. Rufus R. Rand, last surviving member of the Lafayette Escadrille (*pace* Snoopy) winged off to that great hangar in the sky. And in Japan, practically all the palm trees suddenly flowered and then died, as they did in the year Commodore Perry dropped in.

On Election Day, November 3, an old American custom vanished in New York and liquor was freely available at bars and package stores, and it could be coincidence, but a series of calls from *LJ* to librarians around the state on the following day found almost no one at work.

1971 was also the year when polls showed that the confidence of Americans in their institutions had dropped to a new low. The My Lai trials opened American eyes to an aspect of soldiering and war from which they had been miraculously shielded. The New York City police scandal taught an old history lesson: ever since Robert Peel the police forces of our cities have had as their primary function the regulation and protection of crime. They found that although teachers were getting paid more than ever before, they didn't seem to be able to teach children to read. And they found a Frenchman arguing — somewhat plausibly — that evolution is one of our worst afflictions, rather than something to be proud of.

On the other hand, 1971 was the year when Americans began to come back from Vietnam in large numbers — bringing with them (besides heroin and some exotic strains of V.D.) the hope of peace. It was the year in which someone at last did something to slow down the inflation elevator. It was a year in which it became clear that colleges and universities as we know them may well vanish like the dinosaurs, to be replaced by TV sets, learning corporations, and possibly even by library books.

LIBRARY WONDERS AND PORTENTS

As we look back on the past year in libraries, we can see that we too have

---

*Reprinted from *Library Journal,* January 1, 1972.

**Associate Editor, *Library Journal.*

had our share of three-headed dogs. Natural disasters included earthquake damage in the Los Angeles area, where library buildings and bookstacks fell down at a conveniently early hour when there was no one to be crushed by them. A library director in Connecticut refused a raise and another in Pennsylvania turned down an $85,000 grant. Some 700 librarians at the New York Public Library were told by a board notable for its patrician makeup that they had to join the AFL-CIO or be fired. The American Library Association began to raise its voice in indignation at people mistreating librarians by firing them for improper reasons — and at the same time condoned its own executive director's clobbering of *Choice* editor Peter Doiron. One librarian in Connecticut got fired for politicking, while another, in Minnesota, was busy being county Democratic chairman.

Librarians, like some other Americans, tried out the four-day work week, but the experiments seemed to have petered out. Too many new librarians were unable to find jobs, and also it looked as though there could be severe erosion in academic libraries of gains made so far toward faculty status.

Ex-Martinsville (Virginia) librarian Ellis Hodgin, fired ostensibly because his book orders got ahead of his budget, appealed the court ruling that okayed his dismissal and lost the appeal, brushing against the rough hide of contemporary history in the process: the judge was Clement Haynsworth, one of those strange people the President seems to be attracted to. As for Hodgin's alleged fiscal sins, by year end a number of reputable companies were urging upon librarians purchase plans that involved encumbering funds as much as four years in advance.

Farmingdale, New York finally lost its ex-Bircher trustee Carl Gorton, who did his best to push one good library into the tar pits. Some librarians worked hard to improve library service to prisoners this year, and others worked at a well-heeled scheme to improve information service for the police. Some libraries dropped fines, some started fines for the first time, and in New Jersey (it's always New Jersey) delinquent borrowers were threatened with jail sentences.

Women's Lib and Gay Lib had their library echoes, but no substantial progress was reported in either the granting of equal opportunities to women or the extension of tolerance to homosexuals. In the latter area, despite a very circumspectly worded ALA statement against discrimination for sexual reasons, the only case actually known about was going badly at the year's end. J. Michael McConnell, hired as a cataloger by the University of Minnesota, then unhired when he made waves by applying for a license to marry his buddy, won his court case and supposedly would be hired by the university. But Minnesota appealed and won the appeal. Meanwhile, those libraries which stock games may well be considering purchase of a recently announced board game designed to provide for heterosexual-homosexual interaction.

As in other years, the wonders and portents included such things as the successful call girl who gave the public library full credit for her success — and the library night watchman who walked off with a houseful of religious books. It included the grandmotherly librarian who zipped across the country to attend a library conference — on a motorcycle, and another one who smashed a swimming record in the over–45 athletic scene. Librarians frothed at the mouth when their image suffered at the hands of American Motors and Bayer Aspirin. Hot pants were a library issue here and there, as were short skirts. But no one had quite figured out what the impact on the image might be of the knowledge that not only was Mao Tse-Tung once a librarian, but the man who turned him on to that revolution stuff was one also.

THE REAL CHANGES

The foregoing is largely froth and vaporings, to be sure, although its importance in assuring us that we too are human and fallible and sometimes ridiculous — and even on occasion downright bad — is not to be underestimated. The really significant news of the library year is necessarily less colorful and sometimes it's almost invisible. We're talking now about the inching along of the wheels of history, something which can be made pretty exciting over a long enough time period, but hardly ever in the span of a year.

The task this year, however, is easier, because there is real change going on all around us — a very exhilarating thing to contemplate. From this point in the flow of library information, it looks as though we can categorize the changes as three: the changing role of the library institution; the growing stature of the librarian; and the intensifying of efforts to relate librarianship to vital current issues.

These seem to be the main currents of 1971, but there are others which also deserve mention: the turbulent situation in which library associations find themselves; the growing intricacy of the relationships between profit-making, non-profit, and government organizations in the information-handling business; the 1970s version of the old roadshow, The Library as a Cultural Center; the Literacy thing and the IBY hoopla; the possibility of a new international role for librarians; the still uneasy question of the role of computers in libraries; the looming, but still not quite clear vision of networks; the immediate budgetary crisis which is gripping libraries everywhere; the signs of life from that somnolent beast, the library trustee; and the ongoing civil war between the backers of the different varieties of intellectual freedom.

THE CHANGING INSTITUTION

The library — public, school, and academic — is changing at last. The changes have been fulminating away slowly for some years, but the sudden shock of the money drought, plus the restless climate of the early seventies, seem to have combined to cut in the afterburners on the slow process of change. Librarians are finally beginning to see how library service can come out from under the carapace of the library institution, exchanging that exoskeleton for a more modern inside job. In this case, the inner structure is provided by the new focus on the user.

It's something that librarians have known — and said — they wanted to do for quite a while. But the how of it all was not at all clear. They key words seem to have been "the library as an information center" and "service to minorities" — the latter proving to be as seminal a concept as the older "service to groups" was a dud. The trouble with the latter was that it was based on a sincere but naive arrogance. "Groups" were those sparse audiences watching 16mm films in the library or down at Moose Lodge; they were, to the public librarian, the sort of dumb people for whom one "planned programs." They were, to the academic librarian, the faculty and the student body, and one played storekeeper for them. To the school librarian they were classes to be taught "library."

In the last couple of years, a lot of librarians have learned that an institution can be mobilized, can be reshaped in protean fashion to perform the information function for the individuals who make up a specific group. Somehow, setting up library and information services for minorities like blacks, Indians, and scientists taught us a new pattern of behavior — one which can be applied to all the other minorities to which we all belong.

Right now, librarians are involved in a large number of promising new programs aimed at adapting institutions to the needs of people. The most ambitious and promising is the city-wide establishment of information centers at all branches of the New York, Brooklyn, and Queens Borough Public Libraries. If matching money can be found, this Social Security Act financed venture could make library history overnight. Iowa is planning a statewide project of similar nature.

In the meantime, large and small libraries everywhere are trying their hand at the game. The Memphis Public Library has added the words "and Information Center" to its name to signify its new direction — changing itself from an efficient marketer of entertainment to an organization geared to serving a broad spectrum of informational needs in Memphis and West Tennessee. Buffalo's Project RAM is one of several applications of SDI (selective dissemination of information) to ordinary citizens. The Toronto Public Library is the linchpin in a major Canadian social science data study; libraries in Coshocton and at the University of Pittsburgh have active programs serving business and industry; Ohio's Project OPRIS is demonstrating how libraries in a network can gather and package information for local government agencies.

Librarians are not the only people active in this area. In 1971 we saw information network initiatives involving government agencies, nonprofit firms, and profit-making firms. These initiatives ranged from the development of specific information products adaptable to many kinds of network distribution to the design and creation of networks themselves.

The Ohio OPRIS project mentioned previously is an interesting example: the library network is actually being designed by the Battelle Memorial Institute. In a major national effort aimed at developing information networks, Urban Information Systems Inter-Agency Committee, working with HUD (Department of Housing and Urban Development) money, is teaming up city governments, hardware/software firms, universities, and research organizations — but not libraries — in a two-year program. NASA is backing six STRC's (Science and Technology Research Centers), through which college students can obtain low-cost ($15) searches of masses of automated data.

In 1971, Canadian libraries were fighting against the Information Canada plan — or rather trying to maintain their claim of being the people in charge of information services. Info Canada would set up a separate agency to serve citizens.

For-profit information firms, nonprofit organizations, and government agencies have, for some time, found themselves linked in the ERIC (Educational Resources and Information Center) program of the United States Office of Education. ERIC/CLIS, the clearinghouse for libraries and information sciences, for example, is funded by the Office of Education, administered by the American Society for Information Science, and most of the actual work is contracted out to the Leasco Corporation. In 1971 the ERIC/CLIS team got a new opportunity: it will set up an information center for USOE itself.

Meanwhile, many new "information services" — generally best described as open-ended collections of data — were being marketed or otherwise disseminated in the areas of earthquakes, drugs, college selection, urban affairs, nutrition, and a host of other subjects.

HANDICAPPED AND AGED

Meanwhile, librarians are finding service to the handicapped, the aged, the poor, the ill, and the racial minorities to be a challenging and demanding business that is not by any means "charity" but is essential work that must be done if the human venture is to be kept afloat. In the library news this year, the bloody business at Attica came in the middle of a quiet drive by librarians to bring library service to prisoners. New libraries have been established in many prisons; others have been refurbished and restocked, often with the help of volunteers from nearby public library staffs; and in other places public libraries and systems have for the first time shouldered the responsibility of officially serving all those persons resident, however unwillingly, in their service areas.

The aged have also become suddenly more visible to librarians. The results range all the way from friendly gestures like the "no fines" policy of the Fairfax County (Virginia) Public Library, to a Rhode Island project which asked senior citizens to help select books for libraries, to Minot (North Dakota's) vigorous program for the rural aged, and to an unusual library education program specializing in gerontology.

For the handicapped, libraries have shown real concern, with the result that large-print books are widely available in library collections. The obvious interest of librarians has been a stimulus to the development of auxiliary reading aids, from magnifying lenses to high-fi opaque projectors and video adaptations. In 1971 librarians helped in the successful fight to hold down postage on recorded news "magazines" for the blind, and few libraries were built or remodeled without the special needs of the handicapped being taken into consideration. Many libraries instituted new service to housebound handicapped persons for the first time in 1971; and the Association of Hospital and Institution Libraries signalled a major shift in its aims away from concern with the institutionalized person to the person himself, to whom institutionalization is only one phase of his total experience. In England, Fred Thorpe passed a noble milestone: the 500th title in his large-print Ulverscroft series: Han Suyin's *A Many Splendored Thing*.

BLACKS

The public is probably unaware of it, since mostly librarians talk to other librarians about it, but concern for giving blacks their fair share of the action has been with librarians a great deal in the past year. It isn't all roses, however.

The 13 blacks fired by the Library of Congress for protesting what they called unfair treatment comes close to being the major atrocity of the year, although there are a few competitors for the title elsewhere in the library news. Similar protests in Los Angeles, New York, and Washington, D.C. brought no such spastic vengeance and seem to have been considered for what they are: a messy but necessary part of the process of straightening things out.

School Library Journal's exposé of the plight of black Southern librarians in integrated communities is another disheartening antidote for optimism (see Schuman's article, "Developments in Children's and Young Adults' Library Services during 1971," this volume.) And a third, possibly the most tragic setback, was the foundering of the Urban Information Specialist Program, a largely black library education program at the University of Maryland — a failure that leaves us back with a fragmented approach to the problem of developing black librarians and discovering their potential for black communities.

That's enough to hold down any overwhelming emotion of self-congratulation. Now the good things. Look around and see the black men and women who have quietly stepped forward from the ranks to positions of leadership: in library education, there's Milton Byam directing the library school at St. John's University and Robert Wright manning the critical post of Dean of Admissions, University of Maryland.

In federal and state government posts, there's Burt Lamkin, head of the Bureau of Libraries and Educational Technology (though maybe about to be torpedoed in the coming OE reorganization); there's E. J. Josey with the New York State Department of Education. Elsewhere around the country and increasingly prominent on the national library scene are Clara Jones, William Miles, Binnie Tate, Robert Wedgeworth, Ella Yates, Barbara Birthwright, and many more.

But in 1971 *LJ* newsgathering picked up word of only two more blacks moving into prominent positions. Charles W. Harris left Howard University to head an agency of particular interest to blacks — the Government and General Research Division of the Congressional Research Service of the Library of Congress, and the Urban League's Raymond R. Brown moved up from vice-president to president of the Ohio State Library Board.

The development of more — and better — library materials for blacks has been a problem in focus this past year. Minority publishing has received some, but still token encouragement; textbooks which fail to take minority groups into consideration are being eyed askance by growing numbers of librarians; books dealing with minority experiences are capable of roof-raising brouhahas (as with *Down These Mean Streets* and *Epaminondas*) in 1971.

Landmark efforts to develop real library service for blacks can be seen now in Chicago (housing project facilities); in Queens Borough, N.Y., where a black-run library branch is quietly pioneering; and in the District of Columbia, where community information centers are being set up in branch libraries — including the three brand new branches in black areas of the city.

Then there are all those little events which have only a symbolic or ceremonial meaning in the struggle to bring the black experience into phase with the American experience: a new Martin Luther King Library is going up in the District of Columbia — and it's the main library, not a storefront branch. The names of other great black men and women are going up on the facades of library buildings around the nation: Phillis Wheatley, Frederick Douglass, and Sojourner Truth are a few of them. Among the new collections set up in 1971 in libraries are the Frantz Fanon collection at the Countway Library of Medicine (Harvard) and Brooklyn College's collection of the works of four black American composers.

DAWNING OF THE NETWORK IDEA

Out of our experience in designing information services to our more obvious minorities should come the ability to provide—for the first time—widespread, efficient, and meaningful information service to all people, something which exists today only as a pious hope. It's going to be easier for librarians to move ahead here because of the new cluster of ideas and awarenesses developing under the hothouse stimulation of the network concept. And one of the clearest gains from this new construct seems to be the realization that even as no individual library can take all knowledge as its province, neither can it perform the Bunyanesque role of all-purpose social agency — a role which some have urged upon it. The local library, it seems clear, does not have to be the mental hospital or the gym or the legal aid society and a half-dozen other agencies rolled into one, any more than it needs to have an exhaustive collection of Carolingian manuscripts on the premises. But it must have the personnel and facilities to enable it to plug into any of these sources of information for the person needing them.

THE GROWING LIBRARIAN

There are village librarians today — thanks in large part to the heroic bootstrap efforts of public library systems in the last decade — who are more sophisticated about information than many a top library director — and even more sophisticated than some highly placed reference specialists. On one occasion last year, a man walked into a large science and technology department for help in locating a manual for a 25-year-old marine engine on which he was going to have to depend for a fairly long ocean passage. He drew a blank with the reference specialist at the big library, beyond finding out that the book wasn't in the collection. Just for kicks he asked the librarian of a tiny town library for help. It took her about a week to get him a copy of the needed manual from the Detroit Public Library.

The upgrading of the abilities of the men and women manning libraries at this community level is only one aspect of a general move toward the development of the librarian into a real pro. One of the places where a lot is happening is the library school.

True, some of the new courses and programs announced are new only in the sense that the same old glop has been given a sexy new name, and some of the messiahs of the new library education quite obviously are talking through their hats. But this is only the inevitable noise in a system which is going steadily up through the gears.

THE NEW LIBRARY EDUCATION

One reason why it took the library schools so long to get off dead center in the past decade was the existence of long-static faculties. In one library school three or four years ago, there had not been an important new full-time faculty appointment for 20 years. Then the surge of new federal money sparked the enlargement of classes and faculties, and schools ready for change were able to do something about it.

Looking back at the interesting news notes on library science curricula in just this past year, one is impressed by the many developments. There are new courses in library automation, in systems theory, in intellectual freedom, and a number of approaches to interdisciplinary education which could go a long way toward destroying the old provincialism. Let's tally a few noted this year in *LJ* news columns.

A sense of maturity was evident in the Kent State faculty-student appeal to Washington in support of employment legislation; Peabody added a course in automated systems; ALA accreditation came to three more schools, boosting the number of centers from which innovation can be expected. They are C. W. Post, Iowa, and Rhode Island.

Overhaul of curricula was seen in 1971 at Rosary, which is moving toward a new departmentalization in order to turn out more specialized librarians; at Pratt, where new goals were adopted; and at South Carolina, where a brand new library school is being planned from the ground up. The curriculum design will grow out of a study of the needs of the region.

Continuing education began to come into its own in 1971, with the City University of New York going into its second year of course offerings designed for the working librarian; Catholic University finished a study of the continuing education needs of federal librarians and launched courses to fill those needs; the University of Illinois started a Librarian in Residence program; and the Illinois Institute of Technology announced a program for an M.S. in Science Information.

The St. Louis Public Library and the Public Library of the District of Columbia are up to their ears in on-the-job education designed to upgrade staff abilities and to bring into the staff people who are needed but otherwise unqualified.

The last year or two has also seen the growth of student participation in library school planning and direction. This ranged from student evaluation of faculty to participation in the choice of a new dean, and the active participation of library school students in both state and national library organizations. Among these are the ALA's Students to Dallas program and the formation of the first student SLA chapter at Simmons.

LIBRARIANS IN A LANDSCAPE

The status of the librarian in relation to the institution has shown real change in this past year. One negative factor has been the sudden drying up of vacancies in all types of libraries. The consequent inability to move freely has had a chilling effect both on the student looking forward to his first job and the librarian who can be thereby dissuaded from asserting himself as a vigorous spokesman for change.

The placement picture grew steadily worse all year, as indicated by a drop in help-wanted ads and by the disappearance of all but a few notices in the Federal Library Committee's *Vacancy Roster*. In the latter publication, about the only positions open were those at upper levels and those calling for highly specialized talents. Similarly, medical librarians continued in fair demand throughout the year. *Special Libraries* offered free "position wanted" ads to any of its members out of a job. In many large libraries, accustomed to a regular annual turnover as people moved to better jobs elsewhere, almost no one was giving up the job he had.

VOLUNTEERS

Despite the lack of vacancies, libraries were still shorthanded and unable to do many of the things they knew they should be doing. In a few cases, as in

East Hartford, Connecticut, this led to appeals for and experiments with volunteers. Most librarians seem to disapprove of volunteers, possibly because it isn't all that long ago that library salaries were so low that librarians were practically volunteers themselves. Also, library administrators have had little or no experience in coordinating volunteers with professionals and other paid staff.

Despite this, volunteers are actively helping the Los Angeles Public Library with its shut-in service; and many a local public library has appealed for volunteer help. One Texas public library reports that it has been using volunteers with real success for the last few years, and promises a detailed report in a forthcoming issue of *LJ*. Another librarian, in Pennsylvania, has promised an equally detailed report on why volunteers don't mix with libraries.

EMERGENCY EMPLOYMENT ACT

Many libraries found at least temporary relief in staffing from the Emergency Employment Act program, which provides funding for public service jobs for unemployed people. Alert library administrators were among the first to take advantage of the new source of help, and the result was in most cases a restoration of reduced hours of service and of faltering outreach programs. The two-year program is supposed to terminate if the local employment index drops to a certain point, and there is no provision for what happens after the two years are up.

TRUSTEES

There seemed to be somewhat more of a stirring than usual in the placid waters of library trusteeship in 1971. In Groton, Connecticut, trustees backed librarian John Carey in a censorship battle that ended badly. Carey got through it without striking his colors, but the board was intimidated into pulling *Evergreen Review* out of circulation and their powers were sharply curtailed. Still, they did put up a good fight.

In Fairfax, Virginia, trustees came off a little better in a skirmish with superior authorities. Told that they should cancel a "meet the candidates" night scheduled in the library auditorium, they notified county authorities that they were no rubber-stamp board and they had no intention of cancelling the meeting — and they made it stick, too.

LJ picked up only one report in 1971 of a youth being seated on a library board, although several were foreseen a few months back, and the only fuss kicked up over representation was in Washington, D.C., where a do-nothing board has disgusted both librarians and citizens with its inability even to get to meetings — and its failure to represent the people of the city.

The formation of the Urban Library Trustees Council, a new association aimed at advancing the fortunes of urban public libraries, was announced in 1971. ULTC will have offices at the Chicago Public Library and will field a lobbyist in Washington.

ACADEMIC STATUS

Librarians in Rhode Island state colleges were assured faculty status by the Board of Regents in 1971, but New Jersey state college librarians were stripped of what seemed to be well-established faculty status. The New Jersey librarians are fighting back, and have the support of ALA and NJLA as they move toward a court test of their wholesale demotion. Elsewhere in the nation, librarians who had already achieved at least token faculty status managed to cling to it, but not to improve their positions. Then toward the end of the year, the AAUP (American Association of University Professors) liberalized the conditions under which librarians can join it. Previously, a librarian had to have been given faculty rank before he could be an AAUP member. But now, any college or university professional librarian can be a member. With top dues only $25 and beginning dues as low as $10, AAUP could divert a good many potential ALA members to its ranks.

UNIONS

The big news in library unions is the decision of the New York Public Library and the Brooklyn Public Library to grant "agency shop" to the AFL-CIO American Federation of State, County, and Municipal Employees, and to fire any librarian who refuses to either join the union or pay an equivalent fee to the union. The union also gets $175 this year and $250 per library member next year paid into its health fund. The 700-odd nonunion librarians at NYPL are appealing what they see as being sold down the river to the union, and the case may go to court in 1972.

There is no question but that a strong union can counter the more gross abuses of administrative power, but whether it can lead to improved standards of service is something else again. In the rhetoric of the teacher unions, "quality education" clearly means less work and more pay — a semantic bobble comparable to that great term the New York City firemen use to describe staying out on fake sick leave: "withdrawal of excess devotion."

But in 1971 we got at least one glimmer of hope: at Queen's University, Kingston, Ontario, library staff members won a union contract giving them three hours a week off with pay for attendance at classes in the University.

Also in 1971, the big public library unions based in New York City got their first chance to be statesmanlike — and they blew it. When asked to comment on the new state plan which could lead to all children's service being handled by the schools, they opposed the plan on the grounds that they hadn't been consulted in its development. The impression was strong that they hadn't bothered to do their homework.

TENURE AND DUE PROCESS

The issue of tenure, which is basically one of professional status, was a highly inflamed one in 1971. It's a question of status because it ultimately boils down to whether a librarian need or need not be treated with respect when his employer decides to terminate their relationship. That's from the librarian's point of view.

For the administrator, really stringent due process and tenure provisions could tie his hands and make it impossible to rid the organization of some highly destructive people. For example, if mental imbalance is what's wrong with an employee, the administrator had better never mention the fact unless he wants to lose his shirt in a lawsuit.

Still, we can't grow full-sized professionals and treat them like day laborers, so sentiment is growing for more restrictions on employers and more rights for employed librarians. In 1971, SCMAI, the ALA Staff Committee on Mediation, Arbitration, and Inquiry, took the field with a crowded calendar of cases to investigate, most of which involved librarians who claim to have been fired unjustly and improperly. At the same time, ALA itself was coming under heavy fire for allowing its executive director, David Clift, to fire *Choice* editor Peter Doiron without any satisfactory explanation — and for refusing to let Doiron have a hearing by the ALA Executive Board to plead his case.

The Rhode Island Library Association came angrily to the defense of Richard Waters early in 1971, when the latter was fired by East Providence city officials for not complying with the civil service residency requirement. RILA lashed the library board for delinquency in letting the city officials usurp their hire-and-fire responsibility, and an investigation was launched which could lead to legal action against the city.

There were two echoes of the bitterly fought San Jose State College case, which pitted library Director Stuart Baillie against several members of the library staff, one of whom was Robert Duman. In 1971, Duman was denied tenure by the college despite the fact that the outcome of the long quarrel would seem to have vindicated his actions. Baillie has asked ALA's SCMAI to investigate his case.

The Library of Congress was the scene of two of the thorniest cases, however. One was the firing of 13 blacks for their part in demonstrations against what they charged was systematic racial discrimination by LC. The other was the passing over of Barbara Ringer for the post of register of copyrights, for which Miss Ringer is in the process of lending new meaning to the old saw, "Hell hath no fury . . . ."

Besides being decorated with recommendations and qualifications for the promotion, Ringer had been much identified with the cause of blacks at LC. And on top of that, she is a woman in a year when almost all of us have finally realized that women have been badly treated and it's got to stop. Passed over for George Cary, who everyone says is a nice person but one who neither showed much interest in the job of register nor could claim anywhere near what she could in honors, Barbara Ringer took L. Quincy Mumford to court for treating LC personnel procedures in cavalier fashion. The judge agreed, told Mumford to unhire Cary and go back and do the whole thing over properly. Mumford did, but of course reappointed Cary. It's not over yet, and Miss Ringer still has some ammunition. For librarians everywhere, her case is a classic demonstration of the conflicting claims of traditional authority and the rising stature of the professional. The lesson: You've got a long way to go, baby.

TURBULENCE IN THE ASSOCIATIONS

This was an active, if often unpleasant year for library associations. The biggest one, ALA, faced loss of members and a financial crisis at the year's end, after having staved off incipient threats of secession by the big blocs of the school librarians and the academic librarians. Shaken by strife, the ALA Council voted to disband itself so that a more representative body could be elected. The list of nominees for the new Council promises to provide just that, for by and large they appear to be representative, not just of regions or library types, but of the deepest interests of today's librarians.

The Special Library Association, like a skittish old bachelor, finally refused the hand of the American Society for Information Science, and a long-pondered merger was at last off. But both SLA and ASIS say they'll remain good friends.

The Association of College and Research Libraries and the American Association of School Libraries both expressed discomfort last year with their roles under the ALA umbrella—as much a sign of their own growth and maturity as of their disenchantment with ALA. Their new strength made it all the more likely that ALA will one day be dismembered as a powerful central authority and be reconstituted as a rather more humble secretariat for a federation of associations.

The Medical Library Association showed signs of renewed strength in 1971, again a reflection of the growth in medical libraries and facilities like MEDLARS. The growing experience of medical librarians in international matters led to a strong expression of interest in greatly increased international activities and contact with medical librarians everywhere. ALA, taking a somewhat narrower view, raised nary an eyebrow at the report of its International Relations Committee which said in Dallas that its aim was to be active in those nations in which the United States has an interest — that is, those nations where AID (Agency for International Development) money is available for preserving democracy. But it looks as though international relations appears to ALA as just one place where it can save money by cutting support for the International Relations Office in Washington.

Two new associations commenced activity in the year 1971: the Urban Library Trustees Council and the Directors of Large Public Libraries. Both are relatively small, fairly well-heeled groups with a good amount of political muscle; both can be expected to work quietly behind the scenes for better library support; notably, neither shows any interest in publicizing its plans.

State library associations had a good year, showing more life than ever. California jacked up the radiator cap of the old CLA and built under it a completely new model which may be worth following by many associations — especially those in big states. The Rhode Island, New Jersey, and New York state associations were ready to do public battle for their members' concerns; squabbles ensuing involved civil service, academic status, and due process. New Jersey reared up and blasted ALA for its lack of responsiveness to the membership, and also cancelled its annual contribution for support of the Washington Office of ALA.

The Canadian Library Association was racked by increasing internal strains again in 1971, and may be heading for a major reorganization.

The International Federation of Library Associations was helped along last year by a substantial grant from the Council on Library Resources — this could be taken as a signal that CLR feels it's about time to get back to our neglected international duties. IFLA also made the news by rather sharply refusing to go along with a UNESCO proposal/ directive that it crack down on its South African affiliates.

The Library Association of the University of California moved closer to University recognition. Its potential size and the prestige of its members could make this fledgling academic association into an important power in librarianship. And the East Coast version, New York University's SUNYLA, found 1971 a good year in which to sum up its progress toward greater participation of its members in the huge academic enterprise of which they are a part.

LITERACY

Librarians clearly have a stake in the worldwide problem of literacy, which, like sin, seems to remain at a constant level, or perhaps to get a little worse all the time despite all the pronunciamentoes made against it, all the reading specialists created, all the inspiring missionary-type things announced from time to time (like "each one teach one" and all that) — and in 1971, the emergence of commercial firms offering to teach children to read for rather fancy prices, using Skinnerian bribes ranging from extra privileges to transistor radios. Also in 1971, Yemen ordered everyone in the country to learn to read — or else. In the coming year, much hoopla about literacy will be made in the name of the International Book Year, but no one really expects illiteracy to go away — not when our urban schools are turning out illiterates at their present prolific rate. Some libraries are involved in literacy programs, but compared to what the schools are doing for the other side, these programs seem likely to make little impact on American culture.

LIBRARY AS A CULTURAL CENTER

In both the public library and in the undergraduate academic library, there seem to be signs of a renewed interest in libraries sponsoring or being more closely associated with the arts. In Tulsa, a major grant made possible continuation of an effort begun a year or so before to bring people to the library for cultural programs. The Brooklyn Public Library mounted an impressive series of programs aimed at making manifest the many ethnic strata which have made this most provincial and most cosmopolitan of cities what it is. BPL took on one unusual venture which was a spinoff from the programs: assembly of a book of writings by (unpublished) Brooklyn residents. It just could be a prototype for dozens of similar local publications.

A really large number of libraries of all types now stock art reproductions as well as recorded music, and presumably will be lending videotapes in a few years. Some of them may find the nerve — and the ability — to grab the opportunities now offered by CATV. This last imponderable will doubtless be the greatest factor in determining to just what extent the library of tomorrow will be a cultural center.

COMPUTERS

Despite a great deal of rhetoric to the contrary, no one who can claim to be a disinterested observer can say that the place of the digital computer in libraries is either nonexistent or established. The controversy sparked some fine articles in 1971, notably by Ellsworth Mason in *LJ* and *College and Research Libraries,* saying computers should be stamped out; by Gerard Salton, writing in *LJ* for those who feel that Mason ought to be stamped out; and Anthony Ralston writing in *CRL,* making the suggestion that libraries be, if not stamped out, at least demoted financially, by being forced to compete annually with computer centers and other campus facilities for budget money. The big computer question still remains for administrators: what to do about automation to keep one's library from being behind the door when the networks get passed out — and how to keep this position without going broke. Libraries so far can't live with computers comfortably, but they can't live without them either.

But even though the great debate raged unslackened, a great deal was happening in the automation of libraries in 1971. *LJ* news pages noted a major automated reclassification project initiated at Western Kentucky University; a new automated circulation system at the University of Colorado; and a big computerized acquisitions program for state colleges run successfully by the University of Massachusetts. Meanwhile, Connecticut quietly abandoned its project for an automated union catalog for the libraries of the state.

While all this action was being reported on many fronts, long range building was going on as well as ever behind the lines. The work of developing standards for the wide range of procedures and activities in which libraries are involved was pushed ahead by the Z39 Committee of the American National Standards Institute. The Library of Congress came back to take a determined swing at a problem which had bloodied it once: Cataloging in Publication.

The Library of Congress also moved along the project of assigning ISBNs (International Standard Book Numbers) to a wide range of currently published books; and the Council on Library Resources put its bucks strongly behind continued research on preservation of paper and other library materials, and on support of IFLA.

The only thing wrong with all these good things being done at high levels is that they don't involve enough people in the library community. The well-meaning, but annoyingly patrician attitude of too many library leaders conceals a real weakness: unless they communicate a lot more and better with the community, they will have to do without the support — intellectual as well as otherwise — that could come to them from a more involved constituency. Take a painful example: at a recent meeting of New England librarians discussing acquisitions problems with publishers representatives, it was appallingly clear that many of those present had not heard of the ISBN.

LOOKING AHEAD

Despite the many negative indicators on the library scene today — failing budgets, lack of jobs for many young librarians, and a probably growing hostility to intellectual freedom — it looks from here as though, on balance, libraries have gained in 1971.

We have moved ahead in the development of more responsible and more expert librarians; we have moved ahead to a new skillfulness in adapting our institutions to new demands; and we have seen librarians, and all the other people who maintain a kind of symbiotic relationship with them, come closer to grips with the great issues of the day.

Our question, as we look toward 1972: can we keep these good currents moving? Will we have moved, a year from now, a step closer to the development of information service to all people at all levels?

(For a report on intellectual freedom, see Berninghausen's article, "The Struggle for Intellectual Freedom in 1971," this volume.)

DEVELOPMENTS IN CHILDREN'S AND YOUNG ADULTS' LIBRARY SERVICES DURING 1971*

by

Patricia Schuman**

The year 1971 may be remembered as one of recession, retrenchment, and inflation in the educational world, and for libraries in particular. Budget cuts, job freezes, and even layoffs were the rule, rather than the exception. Librarians serving children and youth found themselves cross-pressured by a national economy in trouble, reluctant taxpayers, and their recognition of the desperate needs for, and desire to render, innovative, effective patterns of service.

The year 1971 was also one of reevaluation. Accepted standards for the judgment of children's and young adult literature were up for question, particularly those books focusing on minority groups and women; censors hit hard in some areas; the merging of media had a few rough spots; and some new trends in education were revealed — especially in finance and in establishing new or projected programs which will have far-reaching effects on the services of librarians.

Some 30 percent of the U.S. population is made up of teachers, students, and educational administrators. Some $80 billion was spent on education in 1971, but due to inflation this amount bought 10 percent less.

TIGHT BUDGETS

School districts were hit hard. The opening of the school year saw Chicago with a $26 million deficit and Philadelphia schools caught short by $68 million. As of December 1971, almost 30 school districts in Ohio had applied for special audits — a first step toward legal school closing procedures.

A school district in Waldo County, Maine decided to adopt a four-day school week to cut down long-distance bussing costs.

School libraries and librarians were often the first — if not the last — to suffer. Elementary and junior high school librarians in New Rochelle, N.Y. found themselves "excessed," and in Island Park, Long Island, a tenured elementary school librarian, close to maximum salary, was replaced by a "civil service" librarian at beginning salary.

Even parents in affluent Great Neck, N.Y. were affected when they were sent bills of $25 each for library books and other instructional materials for each of their children in school because of an austerity budget in the district.

The finance problem may take on a whole new dimension because of a recent California Supreme Court decision ruling that reliance on local property taxes for school support discriminates against the poor, depriving them of their rights under the Fourteenth Amendment: "equal protection under the law," and by extension, equal education. State after state has been hit by similar suits since the California decision and a recent federal study would seem to back up the findings. Conducted by the National Education Finance Project, the survey found "great inequities" in school districts in every state, resulting in "unequal educational opportunities." Some school districts spend from two to four times as much per pupil as other school districts in the same state. The report, which favors a tripling or quadrupling of the portion of federal support for schools, also favors full state and federal funding of education.

Congress managed to appropriate an additional $4 million over the original education budget request, giving a 6 percent raise for ESEA and NDEA funds. The largest increase was for ESEA Title I (educationally deprived children), some $65 million over last year, for a total of $1,565 billion. Title II (library serv-

---

*Adapted from the article "SLJ News Roundup," *School Library Journal,* December 1971.
**Associate Editor, *School Library Journal.*

ices and materials) squeezed through with a $10 million increase, bringing total funds available up to $90 million. ESEA Title III (combined with NDEA Title V-A) was upped $3 million, providing $146.4 million for supplementary centers, guidance, and counseling.

But the specter of an administration revenue-sharing plan still hangs over federal aid to libraries and education. This concept, which would drastically change the shape of federal aid, is being particularly pushed in HEW to consolidate all educational grant-in-aid programs. The general area of support services discussed in an "Educational Special Revenue Sharing" proposal put forth by OE Commissioner Sidney P. Marland this spring would lump together some 75 categorical programs, including the NDEA and ESEA Titles into five blocks — aid for federally impacted areas, vocational education, education for the disadvantaged, education for the handicapped, and education support services — to be distributed directly through a state agency designated by the governor of each state. In the latter category are library programs, instructional materials, school lunches, equipment, supplementary education centers, and guidance counseling centers. Essentially, the states would have broad discretionary powers and almost a "no strings attached" mandate. With the exception of funds for the disadvantaged, states would be free to designate specifics within the five categories of aid, as well as to transfer up to 30 percent of the funds for one program to another.

Another proposed federal plan may also have grave implications for libraries. Marland has proposed a major "renewal" program in OE, which would include transferring technology from the present Bureau of Libraries and Educational Technology to a proposed "Office of Renewal," leaving the question of Bureau status for libraries — and federal commitment to them — unresolved.

The proposed office would handle all discretionary programs in OE, such as the Right to Read program, bilingual education, drug abuse education, environmental education, and innovations.

RIGHT TO READ

The "Right to Read," OE's "target for the 70s," does seem to be showing some progress. Workshops for parents and teachers have been conducted across the country, and $10 million has been allocated to set up over 100 reading renewal centers. Ruth Holloway, director of the national Right to Read effort, suggested several ways librarians could tie into these programs. During a speech at the ALA conference in Dallas, she said: "You can be the torchlight for the total educational reform we need by:

" 'Right to Read' corners in every school and public library, with motivational materials for children and adults; taking the lead in developing and implementing state programs; workshops for parents and teachers, teaching them storytelling; consulting with industry on both useful and needed materials."

PENDING LEGISLATION, NEW TRENDS

Two major bills which will probably have direct relevance to libraries are now pending before Congress. The Child Development Bill promises to be a major piece of social legislation, creating a vast network of day care centers and social services, including breakfast programs, free schools, and the like, for children of all economic levels. Services would be provided free to low-income families, while families of higher economic levels would be assessed for fee payments. Whether the bill is passed or not, libraries of all types will find themselves more involved in regular services to the youngest children. OE's Center for Educational Statistics survey shows that 40 percent of U.S. children three to five years old are now attending school, as compared to 25 percent seven years ago. (See also Krettek and Cooke's article, "Federal Legislation for Libraries during 1971," this volume, for further information on the Child Development Bill.)

The second bill would create a National Institute of Education to support research into innovative ways of teaching preschoolers through postgraduates. Its passage will probably be spurred on by an investigation recently conducted by the General Accounting Office which said USOE research contracts awarded to outside agencies have been mostly a waste of money.

Accountability and performance contracting, both being emphasized through OE and local school contracts, have so far not directly affected school libraries, being confined to more narrow, statistically measured programs like reading and mathematics. Professional teacher associations have been protesting the validity of the results of these, charging "teaching to the test" by private companies.

Another tack being investigated by OE is a teacher and parent bonus plan being tested in four cities. Schools in Oakland, California, and San Antonio, Texas are offering teachers and parents up to $1,000 per child and teachers up to $200 per child if students make strides in reading and arithmetic, while Cincinnati, Ohio, and Jacksonville, Mississippi are offering bonuses only to teachers.

EFFECTS OF FEDERAL FUNDS

Librarians have a possible reason to continue to fight for categorical aid to libraries, since the results of several surveys conducted by OE itself of the program from 1966–1968 revealed that Title II has had its own impact, and has stimulated state and local support for school libraries and the unified media concept — these funds have reached over 95 percent of eligible children. However, most school districts still fall far short of the AASL-NEA joint *Standards For School Media Programs*. Title II has generally encouraged schools to improve instruction through the multimedia approach, but there is an endlessly long way to go — particularly in the elementary schools, when large numbers of communities still provide no elementary school library.

Studies on the use of Title I funds, a portion of which support library and library-related programs for the disadvantaged, were not as favorable. The NAACP and OE, among others, published surveys which showed that many of these funds were not reaching disadvantaged children and further that they are often used to provide basic, not supplementary, services — including library services, bookmobiles, and programs. OE has taken several actions to correct this, setting up stringent regulations requiring school districts to prove they spend as much from state and local funds for disadvantaged students before applying Title I moneys. It moved this fall to ask for repayment of some $5 million of "unauthorized" expenditures from several states, and has announced plans to move against others. Greater involvement of parents of disadvantaged children in the disbursement of Title I funds is another move OE has announced — albeit under some legal pressure brought about by several parent suits.

COOPERATION?

The budget crisis and the job freezes do seem to augur well for cooperation between school and public libraries. Though the controversial Report of the New York State Commissioner's Committee on Library Development was hotly debated — particularly its recommendation that schools provide almost all service to children, preschool through grade six (the Author's Guild called this economy "not worth the harm it would cause to the development of independent young readers through public libraries") — we have been hearing encouraging reports of cooperation in recent months, though not necessarily along the lines of the CCLD recommendation.

Hawaii has taken several steps toward achieving a "total unified, integrated, statewide media network" — a master plan to furnish multimedia resources and equipment to the public as well as students and faculty. Its fourth and latest addition to the network will be the Ewa-Beach Community School Library, a $1,160,000 facility which will serve over 20,000 adults, 215 faculty members, and 7,000 students, and will remain open 65 hours a week.

The Aurora Hills Library of Arlington, Virginia, has announced plans to occupy an annex to an existing elementary school, combining the facilities of both institutions into a "community library" open to patrons of all ages. The public will have access to children's facilities, including audiovisual equipment and materials.

The Vancouver Island Regional Library in British Columbia is attempting to implement a centralized buying and cataloging service for schools, similar to that of Cuyahoga, Ohio, County Public Library.

With the aid of small federal grants, two Massachusetts libraries are also attempting cooperative projects. The Snow Library in Orleans is using $5,400 to set up a school-public library union catalog, and the Medford Public Library is implementing an instructional materials center for parents and professionals working with handicapped youth.

In Philadelphia a community library project began in September, separate from both school and public libraries, to serve the needs of children and youth.

The "Co-Plus" of Model Cities Program in Chicago is providing funds for the bussing of elementary school children to public library branches at least once a week for library orientation and programs. Chicago Public Library is also supplying books to schools and community centers through its extension services program, and running a number of tutoring programs for students with reading problems.

PROGRAMS

The direction of children's programs in public libraries and schools this year ranged from traditional story hours to puppet shows, from Detroit Public Libraries' "funmobile," providing game books and toys to children in the Model Cities area, to a "check-a-pet" project in Harrison, Indiana. The Canadian National Institute for the Blind is running a unique program geared toward helping blind adults read to children by pasting Braille texts in illustrated children's books.

Libraries in Maryland, California, and other states were tying their programs into "Sesame Street" television shows. Lima, Ohio Public Library was offering educational kits for the deaf for home teaching. San Antonio, Texas Public Library is using a "peer group" storytelling workshop for Spanish-speaking fourth graders, hoping the listening and telling aspects of the program will improve the children's reading and vocabulary skills.

Chicago Public Library is helping to keep alive a community-run independent library, serving children in the inner city, by lending several thousand books to them. Though the library is in dire need of funds and is attempting everything from famous speakers to chicken dinners to raise operating money, the Helen Robinson Library and Study Center has steadfastly refused to become a branch of the public library.

Among the more unique young adult programs were Chicago Public Library's "Young Filmmaker's Festival," a multimedia room in Mount Vernon, N.Y. Public Library, and the use of teen-age guides at Kansas City Public Library.

Librarians in Maryland were looking to the community when they sponsored a "Crisis Information Center" workshop for librarians and library school students in the area.

The picture for Young Adult Services in New Jersey is bleak, according to a recent survey by Jewel Melton of the Woodbridge Public Library. Melton found that specific budgets for young adults were limited and in some cases nonexistent, as were specific reference areas and recreational programs.

CENSORSHIP

William Steig's Cadecott Award-winning *Sylvester and the Magic Pebble* was still in the lead this past year in school and public library censorship cases, so much so that ALA's Office of Intellectual Freedom issued an advisory statement assuring librarians it is a "legitimate acquisition." Attacks on the book went from individual parent complaints all the way to organized efforts by state and national police associations, largely because of a single drawing of policemen — though friendly — as pigs. In Toledo, an individual policeman's complaint began the furor and eventually caused *Sylvester's* removal from school library shelves pending an "investigation and evaluation by teacher librarians." In Prince George's County Schools, however, authorities stuck to their guns, refusing to remove it though also ordering an evaluation, which eventually recommended that the book remain on the shelves. In Palo Alto, California, it was the librarians themselves who removed the book from the Unified School District because they felt the offending picture reinforced stereotypes and misconceptions.

Other attacks centered around Eldridge Cleaver's *Soul on Ice* in upstate New York, where a strong parents' group, PONY-U (Parents of New York United), has been organizing to fight obscene literature, sex education, bussing, the ecology movement, and various other current concerns the group considers "un-American."

Jerry Rubin's *Do It!* came under attack by the Philadelphia American Legion, but the library held out under strong pressure. Censors managed to cause the firing of a South San Francisco teacher for lending an eighth-grader his own copy of Eve Merriam's *The Inner City Mother Goose*. Teachers in Brick Township, N.J., made a partially successful effort to fight the removal of controversial books from school reading lists by staging a one-day walkout. *Goodbye Columbus* and *Black Rage* were reinstated, though *Soul on Ice* and *Manchild in the Promised Land* remained taboo.

In Groton, Connecticut, the library board took an exemplary — though temporary — stand by voting to keep periodicals such as the *Evergreen Review* and the *Los Angeles Free Press* available to borrowers of all ages, but later gave in to strong, probably improper pressure from municipal authorities.

A judge in Rochester, Michigan, ruled against Kurt Vonnegut's *Slaughterhouse Five*, removing it from Oakland County school library shelves. In New York, the local Civil Liberties Union (NYCLU) lost the first round in its attempt to fight a Queens' community school board's decision to remove Piri Thomas' *Down These Mean Streets*. NYCLU has already begun an appeal.

Montgomery County, Maryland, Public Schools banned not only the book *Little Black Sambo*, but all recordings and filmstrips of the story after receiving complaints of racism, while San Jose, California, refused to remove *Epaminondas and His Auntie* — or even to put it into the children's research collection at the NAACP's request. (See also Berninghausen's article, "The Struggle for Intellectual Freedom in 1971," this volume.)

MINORITY GROUP BIASES

The National Council of Teachers of English has charged that racism and bias result from many current educational materials (including audiovisual materials). Stating that most English and language aid materials were guilty of inadequate, inaccurate, demeaning, and biased representation of minority groups, they issued a set of 17 "Criteria for Teaching Materials in Reading and Literature," placing responsbility on educators and publishers to provide materials which "foster in the student not only a self-image deeply rooted in a sense of personal dignity, but also the development of attitudes founded in a respect for the understanding and diversity of American Society."

In an entirely different context, a recent survey of drug education films evaluated by the National Coordinating Council on Drug Abuse found almost half of those evaluated "scientifically inaccurate," although in wide use in libraries.

Problems involving racism, sexism, and chauvinism have been surveyed in a number of other studies this year, as they have been in the past, centering on the treatment in books and media accorded women, as well as blacks, Indians, and other minority groups. The studies have stirred some thought in the library world, but so far none have resulted in a definition of objectives for dealing with such texts.

The Indian Historian Press has issued a report charging most school texts with cultural chauvinism, distortion, and gross omission in the treatment of American Indians. The Feminists on Children's Media and the Princeton, N.J. chapter of NOW (National Organization of Women), among other women's groups, have examined books' highly recommended lists and found them sadly deficient in presenting a positive picture of women.

Both have issued detailed studies and prepared multimedia slide shows. The Feminists have also published "Little Miss Muffet Fights Back," a bibliography for girls of books they consider nonsexist. The SRRT Task Force on the Status of Women held their own "alternative Newbery-Caldecott" award dinner in Dallas, pointing up the need for a reconsideration of the criteria employed in awarding such prizes.

A study of the *Treatment of Black Americans in Current Encyclopedias*, by Irving Sloan for the American Federation of Teachers, points out that most encyclopedias contained serious omissions and distortions, despite efforts by publishers to correct faults. Though many had added sections on blacks, there was a general failure to "integrate" other American history entries.

The Council on Interracial Books for Children is attempting to support a minority publishers fund, a Social Responsibilities Task Force is in the process of setting up a parallel to the Greenaway Plan for minority publishers' books, and another SRRT Task Force is preparing a second edition of *Alternatives in Print*. Librarians in San Mateo County are writing publishers to tell them when and why they reject a title for sexist or racist content. The Los Angeles Public Library conducted a one-day institute on "Racism in Books for Children and Young People," which resulted in some practical suggestions and recommendations for the profession, including reappraisal methods of weeding out derogatory materials, expanding award committees, and exerting pressure on publishers. Hopefully, other libraries and professional associations will follow suit.

ALA's Black Caucus Resolution asking for censure of libraries providing service to white, segregated schools in the South is still pending, though ALA has finally passed a policy statement against discriminatory hiring practices in libraries and industries dealing with libraries. A survey done by the NAACP for the Black Caucus charging five public libraries with segregated patterns of service was turned over to ALA's Intellectual Freedom Committee, but no hard investigation has been done by ALA. The topic has simply been turned over to another new Staff Committee on Arbitration, Mediation, and Inquiry.

According to a number of studies released this year, school integration itself has resulted in the large-scale displacement and demotion of black teachers and principals. *SLJ* followed up on some of these surveys to determine if librarians were being similarly affected. We found demotions and transfers, rather than displacement, the rule. The black librarian, we discovered, was considered "safer" than teachers in the classroom, since he or she did not come into direct contact with whole classes at one and the same time. Most — though often more qualified than the white librarian — became "assistant" librarians in formerly segregated schools.

On a more hopeful note, though our survey documents many less successful cases, Carrie Robinson, the Alabama State School Library Consultant who charged that discriminatory practices had denied her a promotion, won her case in court with the assistance of the NEA Du Shane Fund, receiving both a promotion and a salary increase.

The Equal Rights Amendment — tied up in Congress for over 20 years — leaves discrimination against women as a problem still to be dealt with by society as a whole, as well as libraries in particu-

RESEARCH FINDINGS
Role

Work of the Federal Library Committee's Task Force on Role of Libraries in Information Systems culminated with the issue of a report by Alan M. Rees of Case Western Reserve University.[5] The report proposed that:

"A joint ad hoc, FLC–COSATI working group should be appointed to consider how libraries and extralibrary information programs may be best integrated into comprehensive information systems.

"FLC and COSATI should establish a long-term mechanism for a program of joint research and development for the creation of integrated national library-information networks.

"The administrative problems identified in the research investigation as requiring immediate attention should be studied in order to determine an appropriate course of action:

"1. Duplication of library functions by the extralibrary information programs studied.

"2. The appropriate administrative position of the extralibrary information program in relation to that of the library.

"3. The domination of the field of information collection, analysis, and dissemination by individuals trained in fields other than library science.

"4. A general disparity in the status of librarians and those of staff members of extralibrary information programs."

Implementation plans are being considered by the group established to address problems related to the President's Departmental Reorganizational Program.

Automation

The System Development Corporation, working under contract to the U.S. Office of Education,[6] in July 1971 issued a two-part report, *Automation and the Federal Library Community; Handbook on Federal Library Automation.* Both will be placed in the ERIC system for use by federal and nonfederal librarians.

In summary, the report noted that federal work should be addressed to five major objectives: (1) development of generalized system components; (2) selective development of centralized services; (3) extension of service to forgotten (disadvantaged) publics; (4) accelerated development of standards; (5) development of effective library communication mechanisms.

The *Handbook* provides automation guidelines, a detailed summary of automation projects, and extensive resource material.

Action plans are being drawn. Commercial publication is projected for the *Handbook* to permit dissemination to all those in the library community concerned with automation applications.

NATIONAL COMMISSION

The National Commission on Libraries and Information Science held the first of three meetings on September 20–21, 1971, in the Wilson Room, Library of Congress. The Executive Secretary of the Federal Library Committee represented the federal community as an observer and participant in the open session. Dr. Frederick Burkhardt, Chairman of the Commission, stated that he will be asking all library and informational organizations for their estimates of the nation's most important needs in serving users, as well as taking advantage of studies already in existence. The Commission also met on November 15–16 and December 9–10, 1971. Mr. Charles H. Stevens was appointed Executive Director, effective January 1972. (See also Burkhardt's article, "National Commission on Libraries and Information Science," this volume.)

---

[5] Alan M. Rees. *Interface of Technical Libraries with Information Systems.* Washington, D.C., Department of the Army, Office Chief of Engineers, March 1971.

[6] See 1971 *Bowker Annual,* pp. 264-265 and Henderson's article, "Library Automation in the Federal Government," this volume.

M. Oliver, report on a recently developed Evaluation System for Administrative, Professional, and Technological Positions. In brief, the System "has grouped Federal positions into six broad categories. Models for evaluating positions in these categories are in various stages of development and testing. The Administrative, Professional, and Technological category covers most nonsupervisory positions in the Federal Government that possess similar characteristics to those nonsupervisory jobs classified as exempt status employees in private industry. Other models under development are: Executive Evaluation System (EES), which will be available for agencies to use in ranking positions in the Federal Executive Service; Clerical, Office Machine Operation, and Technician Evaluation System (COMOT), applicable to production-oriented jobs requiring nonprofessional qualifications; Special Occupations Evaluation Systems (SOES), designed for ranking positions and personal competence of incumbents in occupations such as teachers, attorneys, doctors and nurses, scientists and engineers engaged in research and development work, and certain protective jobs; and Supervisor and Manager Evaluation System (SAMES), which is to be used in evaluating all such jobs regardless of occupation."[3]

The Task Force investigated various systems now in use in the federal government and those used by the more progressive state governments and major private employers to determine what methodology of job evaluation would best fit the current needs of the federal service. The factor ranking method with bench mark job descriptions and guide charts was found to utilize techniques which overcome the deficiencies of the present classification system. Findings, following agency investigation, will be submitted to Congress for consideration.

If adopted, there are obvious implications for federal librarians — and for the library community generally.

The Federal Library Committee and the Special Libraries Association both have assigned ad hoc groups responsibility for working with the Civil Service Commission, thus assuring professional library input in all deliberations.

WAGE AND PRICE FREEZE

On August 15, 1971 the President issued Executive Order No. 11615 which stabilized prices, rents, wages, and salaries. At the September 22 meeting of the Federal Library Committee,[4] Mr. Harold Drury, Program Manager of the Printing and Publishing Program, Bureau of Domestic Commerce, Department of Commerce, discussed the emergency price freeze and its implications for federal libraries. He explained that all complaints in the area of printing and publishing are handled by his office on a case-by-case basis, using the guidelines set up by the Office of Emergency Preparedness. Serials, new editions, raises in printing costs, and other technical problems were addressed by Mr. Drury in response to questions from the floor. He also noted that publishers are not affected, as some industries are, by "seasonality," so that the cost of some items which might be interpreted as seasonal, such as calendars, cannot be increased. The 10 percent tax increase on foreign goods does not apply to duty-free items — books, periodicals, and magazines — and should not be included in their costs. Mr. Drury explained that since he is aware of the many complications involved for both libraries and publishers during the freeze, his office will be glad to assist any librarian requiring clarification on specific cases. Extension of the freeze into 1972 heightens the importance of Mr. Drury's offer.

---

[3]Job Evaluation and Pay Review Task Force. *Evaluation System for Administrative, Professional, and Technological Positions.* Washington, D.C., U.S. Civil Service Commission, September 1971. 2 vols.

[4]*FLC Newsletter,* October 1971.

THE STATE OF FEDERAL LIBRARIES

by

Frank Kurt Cylke*

It is not possible to rank in order of priority the activity affecting federal libraries during 1971. However, preliminary planning for major reorganizational efforts, the wage and price freeze (economic stabilization regulations), research findings, and commencement of work by the National Commission on Libraries and Information Science shared the focus of attention.

REORGANIZATIONAL EFFORTS

On January 22, 1971, the President announced his intention to reorganize seven Executive departments and several independent agencies into four Executive departments.[1] On February 9, 1971, Federal Library Committee[2] representatives met with Office of Management and Budget officials to discuss how the federal library/information community might cooperate with the phased restructuring effort.

It was agreed that phase 1 activity, the drafting of legislation, was outside the scope of Federal Library Committee concern. However, FLC would be fully involved in phase 2, the development of guidelines for the placement of libraries and information services in the proposed restructuring, and in phase 3, implementation. A cooperative Federal Library Committee/Committee on Scientific and Technical Information (COSATI) 11-member work group was established by the FLC Chairman. It was immediately decided that operating libraries throughout the government need to interrelate with information services in order that information transfer in its broadest sense be conducted at the highest level of efficiency. Plans call for an examination of the problems in connection with the President's plan and the supply of specific answers to the questions about the most effective way to reorganize and relate executive branch libraries and information services, with models and guidelines developed for restructuring such library/information systems. A 12-month preliminary work schedule is anticipated.

This opportunity to design extensive and sophisticated model library systems for certain implementation is unparalleled within the federal environment. The results should serve as a guide to the library planning community. Specifically, this study will serve as a guide for:

1. The Office of Management and Budget in connection with its oversight of library/information resources in the federal government;

2. Heads of agencies and departments — especially those affected by proposed reorganization;

3. Governmental groups responsible for federal and national coordination of library/information resources (including COSATI, the Federal Library Committee, and the National Commission on Libraries and Information Science) and professional associations with a direct concern for national requirements.

The General Accounting Office implemented an examination of federal library operations and management programs. While it is not clear at the time of this writing what effect the resulting report will have, it may be assumed that high level administrative attention will be directed toward the federal library community. It is anticipated that study findings will be released in 1972.

The U.S. Civil Service Commission requested that its Job Evaluation and Pay Review Task Force, directed by Philip

---

*Executive Secretary, Federal Library Committee, Library of Congress.
[1]Papers Relating to the President's Departmental Reorganizational Program: A Reference Compilation, March 1971. Washington, D.C., U.S. Government Printing Office, 1971. $1.75.
[2]See 1967 *Bowker Annual,* pp. 113–114 and 1971 *Bowker Annual,* pp. 266–267.

lar. Though the library profession is 80 percent female, a recent ALA salary survey revealed that women earn an average of $3,400 less than men. The survey also reveals that school librarians — again, most are women — earn about $600 less than public librarians and from $800 to $7,500 less than college and special librarians. Advanced degrees make little difference, according to the statistics. School librarians in several states are running up against specific discrimination when placed in competition with male audiovisual specialists for head-of-media-center jobs. The problem involves sexism, professionalism, and paranoia.

The paranoid view was typified this year in a vanity press publication written by Doris Timpano, *Crisis in Educational Technology: A Critique of American Library Association-National Education Association Standards for School Media Programs*, a footnoted fantasy describing war between the "ed coms" and the "libs," with the latter out to take over *everything*.

The Association of Educational and Communications Technology (AECT) conference this spring showed some signs of hope. An attempt to recant their stand on the joint *Standards* failed, though a watered-down statement supporting a "variety of standards" succeeded. A more hopeful sign was the recognition of the need for merged state library and audiovisual associations. Some seven states, Alabama, Nebraska, New Hampshire, New Jersey, North Dakota, Oregon, and Vermont, have already taken this step.

Phase II of the Knapp School Library Manpower project, providing $100,000 each to six schools — Arizona State University, Auburn University, Mankato State College, Millersville State College, University of Denver, and the University of Michigan — is one cause for optimism, and another is a new statement of purpose adopted by the American Association of School Libraries (AASL) of ALA. It emphasizes social, moral, and professional support; encourages professionalism; and serves as both a code of ethics for the individual and the profession. It details 17 specific functions and defines AASL's responsibility to individual librarians, to the profession, and to society as a whole. Implementation will be the key.

The American Student Media Association, formed this summer, should also provide fresh insights and ideas. The Association plans to coordinate students working in media centers and has already formed a clearinghouse for the exchange of ideas, issuing a regular newsletter.

As of December 1971, the economic picture for 1972 is unclear. The effects — if any — of Nixon's wage-price freeze on public and school libraries, and on the fate of the impending legislation on day care, research, and desegregation are the unsettling questions.

The year ahead requires a redefinition of the librarians' role and the form our services will take, necessitated not only by the financial squeeze, but by the new approaches employed in the education of children and young adults. The answer to our most pressing problems demands the firm direction of political pressure to acquire adequate funding and a stronger voice in educational planning at every level. Foot-dragging on the part of library service in either of these problem areas can only result in professional goals never reached for lack of staff or money for necessary materials, and no role at all in shaping the conditions or policies under which we work.

THE LIBRARY OF CONGRESS IN 1971*

The Library of Congress, probably the world's largest library, is both the research arm of the U.S. Congress and the national library of the United States. Congress has traditionally shared the Library's resources and services with other government agencies, with readers and scholars who visit the Library, and with other research libraries through interlibrary loans.[1] As part of the legislative branch of the federal government, the Library is headed by L. Quincy Mumford, Librarian of Congress since 1954, and is organized into six departments. The Deputy Librarian is John G. Lorenz, and the Assistant Librarian, Mrs. Elizabeth E. Hamer. The six departments and their directors are Reference Department, Paul L. Berry, Director; Law Library, Carleton W. Kenyon, Law Librarian; Congressional Research Service, Lester S. Jayson, Director; Processing Department, William J. Welsh, Director; U.S. Copyright Office, George D. Cary, Register of Copyrights; and Administrative Department, Fred E. Croxton, Director. Mr. Kenyon, who had been Associate Law Librarian, and Mr. Cary, who had been Deputy Register of Copyrights, assumed their new positions during 1971.

The Library's comprehensive collections continued to grow in 1971.[2] By June 30, the total holdings had reached more than 64 million items — including more than 15,660,000 books and pamphlets on every subject and in a multitude of languages; almost 30,339,000 manuscripts; nearly 3,372,000 maps and views; 3,366,000 items of music; 3,137,000 photographic negatives and prints; nearly 750,000 reels and strips of microfilm (including approximately 230,000 reels of newspaper on microfilm); 323,000 recordings of music and speech on discs, tapes, and wires; 175,000 artists' prints and drawings; 158,000 motion-picture reels; 121,000 bound newspaper volumes; 1,200,000 braille books; 2,615,000 containers of talking books on disc and tape; and many other items such as posters, broadsides, and photostats.

The activities of the Reference Department were marked by a continued growth in both acquisitions and reference services, and by a significant increase in the use of the microform, manuscript, and music collections. The Department is responsible for the operation of 14 general and specialized reading rooms. Outside the Library itself, the Department's Loan Division issued nearly 240,000 pieces of material to Congressional, governmental, Library and other borrowers during fiscal year 1971.

The Department was also active in the preparation of bibliographies and other publications including *Periodical Literature on the American Revolution,* issued in 1971, and the 409-page *Sub-Saharan Africa: A Guide to Serials,* 1970, the largest bibliography prepared by the African Section. The Slavic and Central European Division completed for publication *The Federal Republic of Germany: A Selected Bibliography of English-language Publications with Special Emphasis on the Social Sciences.*

The bibliographic highlight of the year in the Science and Technology Division was the publication of *A Directory of Information Resources in the United States: Physical Sciences, Engineering.* The division continued its work on the application of data processing techniques to its current bibliographic and management procedures.

The Library's Rare Book Division acquired 985 items in fiscal year 1971, in-

---

*Prepared by the staff of the Library of Congress.

[1] The Library's functions as a national library have been described in the 1970 *Bowker Annual,* pp. 236-237.

[2] All statistics in this article are from the *Annual Report of the Librarian of Congress* for the year ending June 30, 1971. All other activities reported on occurred during calendar year 1971, except where noted.

cluding 24 illustrated volumes purchased through the Lessing J. Rosenwald Fund. Among the acquisitions were a circular letter from George Washington to Governor Green of Rhode Island in June 1783, a copy of Linnaeus' *Reflections on the Study of Nature* from Thomas Jefferson's last library, and four plates to add to the Library's second copy of John James Audubon's *The Birds of America*.

Among the Manuscript Division's acquisitions in 1971 were new papers for the Freud Archives, a series of correspondence between William Jennings Bryan and Woodrow Wilson, and unpublished letters of several Presidents. Gifts to the Manuscript Division, and to the Library in general, were limited, as they were in 1970, as a result of the Tax Reform Act of 1969.

The Geography and Map Division acquired several important items during the year, including a manuscript *Plan de West-Point du Nord,* believed to have been drafted in 1781 by Christian Deuxponts; 70 panoramic maps of American cities prepared by Thaddeus M. Fowler and his associates during the period from 1865 to around 1920; and four lunar maps from the Apollo XV Chart Kit used by the astronauts this past summer. The lunar maps were part of an exhibit entitled "Maps of the Moon."

The Prints and Photographs Division mounted several exhibitions during the year, including "The Performing Arts in 19th-century America," which coincided with the opening of the Eisenhower Theater in the John F. Kennedy Center for the Performing Arts. The outstanding acquisition of 1971 was the gift of the noted photographer, Toni Frissell, who presented to the Library her life work consisting of over 40,000 color transparencies and more than 270,000 negatives, together with a fund for their maintenance.

The Division's Motion Picture Section was the focus of one of the more important technical advances in the Reference Department during the year. The new motion picture printing laboratory, equipped with a highly sophisticated optical printer which has a special capability to handle shrunken nitrate film, now makes it possible to reprint these materials on safety (acetate) film. By June 1971 the laboratory had produced over 600,000 feet of finished acetate conversion, and it is expected that production in the coming year will exceed 2,000,000 feet.

The work in motion pictures was only one part of the response of the Reference Department to the Library's preservation problems. In the Serial Division, work continued on the program to replace current and noncurrent newspapers with microfilm. Long-range plans were prepared for retiring the bound newspaper holdings; one proposal is to complete the filming of all pulp-paper domestic newspapers within five years. An important Serial Division acquisition during 1971 was an original copy of the 3 A.M. special edition of *The New York Herald* of April 15, 1865, containing "The Latest News" account of the assassination of Abraham Lincoln.

The Orientalia Division sponsored a panel discussion at the Library on March 30 as part of the twenty-third annual meeting of the Association for Asian Studies in Washington, D.C., held in March. The Division also mounted an exhibit in honor of the celebration of 2,500 years of Persian monarchy, which was followed by a significant gift of nearly 1,000 items from the Ambassador of Iran.

A major event previously unreported was the Music Division's Fourteenth Festival of Chamber Music, presented by the Elizabeth Sprague Coolidge Foundation in the fall of 1970, for which 11 new works were commissioned. The Division's series of music programs, together with delayed broadcasts to other cities in the United States made possible by the Katie and Walter Louchheim Fund, continued through 1971.

Another significant event was the publication of a recording of Chilean poet Gabriela Mistral reading 18 selections from her poetry which she had recorded for the Music Division's Archive in 1950.

The record was announced simultaneously with the publication of *Selected Poems of Gabriela Mistral* for the Library's Hispanic Foundation.

Under the direction of the Poetry Office of the Manuscript Division, the Library's literary programs, sponsored by the Gertrude Clarke Whittall Poetry and Literature Fund, continued through 1971; a special program in October presented Russian poet Andrei Voznesensky. William Stafford, 1970–1971 Consultant in Poetry, was appointed in May to a three-year term as Honorary Consultant in American Letters, and Mrs. Josephine Jacobsen was appointed Poetry Consultant for 1971–1972.

Finally, the Department's work in the Division for the Blind and Physically Handicapped now extends through 50 regional libraries with the opening of libraries in Delaware and West Virginia in 1971. In fiscal year 1971 700 talking book titles were produced, along with 500 cassette and open-reel tape titles and 275 braille titles. In March, the Division celebrated the fortieth anniversary of the nation's program of free library service to the blind.

On December 30, 1970, the Ford Foundation announced a $500,000 eight-year grant to the Library to support an extensive revision and enlargement of the Burnett edition of *Letters of Delegates to the Continental Congress,* which will be edited by the Library's American Revolution Bicentennial Office.

On November 16, 1971, the Librarian of Congress announced the publication on behalf of the Oliver Wendell Holmes Devise of Volumes I and VI of *The History of the Supreme Court of the United States,* the first comprehensive survey of the development of the Supreme Court from its creation to modern times. The series was made possible by a bequest to the United States from the late U.S. Supreme Court Justice.

Late in 1971 the Library prepared two new traveling exhibits. Scheduled to open in January 1972, "Contemporary Photographs from Sweden" was based on a larger exhibition held at the Library during the winter and spring. An accompanying catalog was published in late 1971. The twenty-second National Exhibition of Prints, a biennial show on display at the Library during the summer of 1971, began its tour as a traveling exhibit in December. The exhibition is designed to display the character of the most recent work being done by artists residing in the United States. Two other major exhibits, celebrating the sesquicentennial of statehood of Maine and Missouri, opened at the Library this past year, and exhibit catalogs were also published to coincide with both of these events.

Major concerns in the Law Library in 1971 were the development and organization of the collections, preservation of materials, expansion of research coverage, and the rearrangement of the collections and other facilities of the department.

During fiscal year 1971, 39,400 volumes and pamphlets were added to the collections to bring the total to 1,232,000 bound volumes. In cooperation with the Processing Department, 19,000 retrospective and 8,400 new volumes were cataloged in classes K and KF, bringing the total cataloged since the beginning of the Class K Project to 78,700 volumes.[3] Subclass KD for Great Britain is expected to be completed, and the application of the class to cataloging legal materials begun, by the end of 1971. Work continued on the U.S. Supreme Court Records and Briefs Project, with the bound record set scheduled for completion early in 1972.

The condition and arrangement of the collections were carefully surveyed and, as a result, several restoration, preservation, and reorganization projects were established or expanded, including the microfilming of material in danger of irreparable deterioration. In order to use legal materials in microform more efficiently, the Law Library Microtext Reading Room was created — one of several

---

[3] The Class K Project is fully described in the 1970 *Bowker Annual,* p. 243. Additional information is contained in the 1971 *Bowker Annual,* p. 274.

realignments accomplished during the year to allow the Law Library to make the most effective use of its facilities.

To obtain direct current access to primary and secondary sources, several Law Library divisions undertook indexing projects to produce more sophisticated research tools. The work is to be patterned after the *Index to Latin American Legislation* begun in the 1940s. Other significant research guides completed in 1971 included the *Revised Guide to the Law and Legal Literature of Mexico* and *A Chinese Glossary of International Conference Terminology*. Four new legal specialists were added to the Department in international and comparative law, Greek law, Indian and Pakistani law, and Vietnamese law. These additions aided substantially in broadening the Law Library's research capability.

The Congressional Research Service (CRS), formerly the Legislative Reference Service, was renamed on January 3 pursuant to the enactment on October 26, 1970, of PL 91-150, the Legislative Reorganization Act of 1970. The Act improved and expanded the Service's research facilities to be available to the Congress and its committees. CRS, which exists solely for the use of Congress and serves as its primary research and information center, responded to nearly 181,000 reference and research inquiries from members and committees in fiscal year 1971. Other departments of the Library also assisted in meeting the needs of the Congress by answering additional requests for information or books.

On January 11, the Library's bookroom in the Rayburn House Office Building was transferred from the Loan Division to CRS and was converted into a CRS information center, enabling the Service to provide expanded in-person reference services to the Congress.

The American Law Division of CRS assumed responsibility in 1971 for the preparation of the revised edition of *The Constitution of the United States of America — Analysis and Interpretation*, last published in 1964. The law authorizing the revision, PL 91-589, also contemplates biennial supplements and subsequent revised editions every ten years. Known popularly as *The Constitution Annotated*, the work traces its antecedents to 1915 when the Senate published a work listing the sections of the Constitution along with the citations to Supreme Court decisions construing them.

One of the most significant events of 1971 in the Processing Department was the successful launching of the Cataloging in Publication (CIP) program, with the aid of a joint grant of $400,000 from the Council on Library Resources, Inc. and the National Endowment for the Humanities, which will support the program through June 1973. Under CIP, titles currently issued by American publishers will eventually contain within the books themselves the essential cataloging information needed by libraries. The program will benefit libraries large and small and all who use them, through a tremendous reduction in the cost of cataloging to individual libraries and through the earlier availability of publications to library users.

The National Program for Acquisitions and Cataloging[4] was successfully extended to Spain, Romania, Malaysia, Singapore, and Brunei.

Through the Public Law 480 Program,[5] 1,347,000 publications from Ceylon, India, Israel, Nepal, Pakistan, the United Arab Republic, and Yugoslavia were acquired and sent to over 300 American libraries.

The Processing Department cataloged 255,000 titles for printed catalog cards, a new record. The card distribution service completed its seventieth year. A reorganization of the Card Division, further application of automated techniques, and

---

[4] NPAC is described in the 1969 *Bowker Annual*, pp. 228-229; the 1970 *Bowker Annual*, p. 242; and the 1971 *Bowker Annual*, pp. 273-274.

[5] The PL 480 program is described in the 1969 *Bowker Annual*, pp. 227-228; the 1970 *Bowker Annual*, pp. 241-242; and the 1971 *Bowker Annual*, p. 273.

a broadened subscriber relations program significantly improved the quality and speed of the service to the 30,000 subscribers who purchased over 74 million cards; from the sale of cards and publications, the division returned $7,120,235 to the U.S. Treasury. In response to numerous requests from other libraries, the Library of Congress began including on its catalog cards for U.S. Government publications the classification numbers assigned by the Superintendent of Documents.

To meet other expressed needs, the Department expedited its cataloging of serials, analyzed and assigned separate classification numbers to an increasing number of monographs in series, gave wider dissemination to its cataloging interpretations and decisions through publication in *Cataloging Service,* and began the preparation of a guide to its widely used classification system.

The editing of the eighteenth edition of the *Dewey Decimal Classification* was completed and the volumes were published in December 1970 by the Forest Press. The editing of the 600-volume *National Union Catalog: Pre-1956 Imprints* passed the quarter mark.[6]

For the activities of the MARC Development Office of the Processing Department, see Henriette Avram's article reporting on "Automation in Technical Processing at the Library of Congress," this volume.

The U.S. Copyright Office registered 329,696 claims to copyright during fiscal year 1971, an increase of 4.2 percent over the previous year, and turned over to the U.S. Treasury in that period $2,045,458 in net fees. Of 530,933 deposits accompanying registrations, 316,972 were transferred to the Library's Processing Department for addition to the collections or other disposition.

S. 644, a bill for the general revision of the copyright law, was reintroduced in the 92nd Congress. Near the end of the year, acceptance by the interested groups of a proposal for settlement of the cable television (CATV) issue greatly enhanced prospects for action on the bill next year. In the meantime, because of the urgent need for legislation to cope with the growing practice of unauthorized reproduction of sound recordings, which are not subject to copyright under the present law, the substance of that portion of the revision bill dealing with sound recordings was incorporated in S. 646; the record antipiracy bill was signed into law (PL 92-140) by the President on October 15. Although the provision for copyright in sound recordings will not become effective until February 15, 1972, additional remedies, including criminal prosecution in certain cases, for infringement where copyrighted musical works are unlawfully used in sound recordings, became available immediately on enactment of the law.

The Senate passed on July 15, and the House on November 15, another interim extension bill, which extended certain renewal copyrights through December 31, 1972.

In addition to its obligations to the Library in such areas as finance, general services, and personnel, the Administrative Department is responsible for the Preservation Office, the Information Systems Office, and the Photoduplication Service.

The preservation program made great progress in 1971 with the installation of a modern restoration shop, the employment of a Restoration Officer, and the recruitment of other restoration specialists to form the core of the team of experts essential to the preservation of the Library's collections. A Research Officer was also appointed during the year and under his direction, work began on the establishment of the Preservation Research and Testing Laboratory, which is intended to create a better understanding of the deterioration and restoration processes of library materials. Additional staff was employed and the installation of the

---

[6] A full account of the National Union Catalog Publication Project can be found in the 1969 *Bowker Annual,* pp. 229-230.

laboratory was completed by the end of 1971.

A third computer was acquired by the Library in 1971. There are now two computers in the Computer Service Center of the Information Systems Office[7] and one dedicated to the work of the Card Division. During the year, additional computer terminals were installed throughout the Library and the computer became a more integral part of the functions of the Processing, Reference, and Administrative Departments and of the Congressional Research Service.

As it has done for many years, the Photoduplication Service furnished important support to the scholarly community and to the library world, particularly in the United States. In fiscal year 1971, more than 100,000 requests for service were filled by the Photoduplication Service, which was established in 1938 with the aid of a grant from the Rockefeller Foundation and which operates on a self-sustaining revolving fund rather than through federal appropriations. In 1971, the Service's business reached nearly $2,000,000.

In the Administrative Department, planning continued for the new James Madison Memorial Building — the third major facility on Capitol Hill for the use of the Library of Congress. Scheduled for completion in 1975, the building will have a gross floor area of over 50 acres and will relieve present crowded conditions. The contract for the excavation and underground concrete structure was let in April and work on this portion of the construction is expected to be complete in May 1972. Under appropriations to the Architect of the Capitol for fiscal year 1972, $71,090,000 was appropriated to the Library for the new building.

Appropriations for the operation of the Library in fiscal year 1972 under PL 92-51 totaled $68,053,250, an increase of $17,656,650 above funds appropriated for fiscal year 1971. Funds for the National Program for Acquisitions and Cataloging, which had previously been transferred to the Library by the Office of Education, Department of Health, Education and Welfare, were included in the Library's appropriation for the first time.

[7] The work of the Information Systems Office is more fully described in the 1971 *Bowker Annual*, pp. 275-276.

THE NATIONAL LIBRARY OF MEDICINE

by

Martin M. Cummings, M.D.*

The National Library of Medicine during 1971 observed both the 135th anniversary of its founding in 1836 by the Army's first surgeon general and the tenth anniversary of the dedication of its unique and functional building in suburban Washington, D. C., by continuing to expand its developing biomedical communications network of regional medical libraries and supporting programs.

The Library's major programs were reviewed by the Presidentially appointed Board of Regents under its statutory obligation "to advise, consult with, and make recommendations to the [HEW] Secretary on important matters of policy." The Board created a Scholars in Residence Program to encourage and recognize scholarly research requiring use of the Library's collection. William G. Anlyan, M.D., Vice-President for Health Affairs of Duke University, was elected Chairman of the Board to succeed Robert H. Ebert, M.D., Dean of Harvard Medical School.

Other regents are: William O. Baker, Ph.D., Vice President in Charge of Research, Bell Telephone Laboratories; Susan Crawford, Ph.D., Director, Archive-Library Department, American Medical Association; Mrs. Bernice M. Hetzner, Librarian, University of Nebraska Medical Library; Jack M. Layton, M.D., Dean, College of Medicine, University of Arizona; J. Stanley Marshall, Ph.D., President, Florida State University; Angelo M. May, M.D., physician, San Francisco, California; John P. McGovern, M.D., Professor and Chairman, Department of the History of Medicine, University of Texas Graduate School of Biomedical Sciences; Max Michael, M.D., Executive Director, Jacksonville Hospitals Educational Program; and George W. Teuscher, D.D.S., Dean, Dental School, Northwestern University.

Ex officio members are the Surgeons General of the Army, Navy, Air Force, and Public Health Service, the Chief Medical Director of the Veterans Administration, the Librarian of Congress, and the Division Director of Biological and Medical Sciences, National Science Foundation.

LIBRARY OPERATIONS

All of the 11 Regional Medical Libraries were operational and the network processed more than half a million requests for interlibrary loans during the year. More than 125,000 of these loans were filled by the Library from the MEDLARS data base, which now exceeds 1.4 million bibliographic citations. There was an increase of 26 percent in the number of demand literature searches conducted for domestic users.

Five new recurring bibliographies were initiated during 1971, bringing the total produced by the Library to 23. The monthly *Abridged Index Medicus* continues to be well received by physicians and hospital libraries. More than 2.7 million pages of deteriorating and irreplaceable material were microfilmed according to archival standards. New acquisitions raised the total of the Library's collections to 1,347,521 titles.

The success of the on-line, experimental, remote bibliographic service known as AIM-TWX (developed by the Library's Lister Hill National Center for Biomedical Communications), which is being used by over 50 institutions, has led to its further expansion. In a new contract, MEDLARS will be converted to third-generation hardware, and certain features will be added, including an expanded vocabulary, with the new system designed around the file structure and design of AIM-TWX. This contract followed the decision not to continue the MEDLARS II program as negotiated in June 1969.

---

*Director, National Library of Medicine, 8600 Rockville Pike, Bethesda, Md. 20014.

Planned as a prototype for other medical libraries, a basic multimedia resource area was completed in the Library's main reading room. The new facility includes soundproof viewing rooms, color television receiver with earphones, microfiche and microfilm readers, cassette recorder, conventional slide and film projectors, and a stereophonic tape recorder. More than 1,000 titles are listed in the card catalog of the multimedia collection.

LISTER HILL NATIONAL CENTER FOR BIOMEDICAL COMMUNICATIONS

The Center expanded the testing of an experimental two-way closed-circuit television link between Dartmouth Medical School's clinical facilities and the Claremont General Hospital about 30 miles apart. The project uses video technology to extend the consultation facilities of a university medical center to physicians somewhat isolated from major clinical resources. An auxiliary link is available three hours daily for transmission of electrocardiograms. An additional contract was negotiated to include the University of Vermont in the network.

The Center has continued the development of satellite communications experiments designed to improve health care services in Alaska. A two-level network between the Alaskan Native Medical Centers and Field Service Unit Hospitals will be extended from these units to the 26 villages selected for the experiment. The village sites are in areas with unreliable short-wave radio reception. The network will permit direct consultation between physicians, and also between physicians and health aides in the villages.

In October 1971 the Library inaugurated MEDLINE (MEDLARS On-Line), the expanded bibliographic search service developed by the Lister Hill Center for medical schools, hospitals, medical libraries, and research institutions. The initial data base consists of citations to all articles in the top 239 journals indexed for MEDLARS since January 1969 — over 130,000 citations. The base is being expanded to cover over 1,000 journals, with more than 300,000 citations. MEDLINE operates directly on NLM's 360/50 computer and can support up to 25 simultaneous users. The Library is installing a data communications network to facilitate access to the service; by 1972 it will be possible to reach the computer by a local call in at least 20 major cities.

SPECIALIZED INFORMATION SERVICES

The Toxicology Information Program has been expanded through access to several automated data banks and systems of the Food and Drug Administration and the Environmental Protection Agency that contain pesticide information. Through an agreement with the Atomic Energy Commission, a Toxicology Information Response Center has been established at the Oak Ridge National Laboratory. This will permit in-depth literature searches from multiple scientific disciplines represented at Oak Ridge and from most of the commercially available literature tape services. The new on-line, computer-based *Roster of Authorities in Specialized Subtopics of Toxicology and Related Fields* is operational.

NATIONAL MEDICAL AUDIOVISUAL CENTER

The Center is cooperating with a number of health science organizations in developing and producing pilot instructional units for medicine, dentistry, nursing, and related health professions, and in reviewing and evaluating other audiovisual media. One such group, the Association of Deans of Southern Medical Schools, initiated a program to develop modularly constructed teaching packages for cross-sharing among its 28 member schools. A slide/sound package on the team approach to dentistry was produced in cooperation with the Division of Dental Health of the Bureau of Health Manpower Education, and successfully used in training 12 key dental faculty members. The Bureau has established an Office of Audiovisual Educational Development in the Center.

In the first full year of a computer-supported distribution system, the Center processed about 120,000 requests and loaned 85,000 audiovisuals. In a review of the International Index of Medical Film Data, to maintain currency, its 25,000 citations were reduced to about 4,000. During the year ten specialized seminar/workshops were presented by the staff of the Center, and three others were cosponsored with national medical organizations.

EXTRAMURAL PROGRAMS

The Medical Library Assistance Extension Act of 1970 enabled the Library, through six assistance programs, to make 529 awards for $5,992,000. Specialized manpower training was supported through 17 active training programs, wherein 112 persons pursued studies in a variety of health information specialties. A conference of training program directors was held to consider manpower needs in the health communications field, and was supplemented by appropriate educational programs. Support was also provided for 21 research projects and 16 scientific publications.

The amended resource grant authority attracted 462 applications during the year as compared to 594 received during the entire five-year authority of the Medical Library Assistance Act of 1965. Although most of the resource grant funds were committed to the continuation of awards made under the initial authority, 84 new resource grants were awarded. Of these, 30 were resource project grants and 54 were resource improvement grants. In the Regional Medical Library Program, contracts were negotiated and awarded to seven of the eleven operating Regional Medical Libraries.

The Library serves as the principal resource within the Department of Health, Education, and Welfare for the improvement of international exchange of published biomedical information in the special foreign currency program (Public Law 480). The Library continued to sponsor a series of projects in Israel, Poland, and Yugoslavia. Eighteen new projects were activated in Israel under the Library's multicategorical Public Law 480 Agreement with the *Israel Journal of Medical Sciences*. A new agreement established a three-year Health Science Research Communications Program in Poland under the auspices of the Coordinating Commission for Polish-American Scientific Collaboration. (For historical material on the National Library of Medicine, see the 1971 *Bowker Annual*, pp. 278-283, and previous editions.)

SUMMARY OF EXTRAMURAL PROGRAMS

Program	New Grants FY 1971	Total Active Grants & Contracts
Regional Medical Library	0	10
Medical Library Resource Grants	84	469
Training Grants & Fellowships	3	23
Special Scientific Projects	1	6
Research Grants	6	51
Publication Grants	8	25
TOTAL	102	584
Special Foreign Currency Projects	34	76
GRAND TOTAL	136	660

HIGHLIGHTS OF NLM ACTIVITIES, 1971

Size of collections	1,347,521
Additions to collections	34,565
Reader requests filled	83,585
Reference services provided	20,286
Readers & visitors	23,782
Interlibrary loans	102,559
Serial titles received	22,161
Journal articles indexed	224,619
Literature searches distributed	23,717
Recurring bibliographies	23
Professional & technical staff	462
Projects supported by grants	548
Appropriations	$21,436,000

THE NATIONAL AGRICULTURAL LIBRARY

by

Leila P. Moran*

The National Agricultural Library is one of the principal agencies in the U.S. Department of Agriculture dealing with scientific and technical information. It provides information services in support of all Department agencies, as well as other governmental activities supporting Department missions. Moreover, it serves as one of three national libraries in the United States to provide researchers, other libraries, and the general public with specialized information in the fields of agriculture and related sciences.

NAL is engaged in a long-range program of building a responsive information system. Programs are designed to serve and support the rapidly changing and expanding interests of the national and international agricultural–biological communities.

Library activities are channeled into two basic organizational groupings: Resource Development (input functions) and Library Services (output functions). Responsibilities for collection of literature in agriculture and the allied sciences and dissemination of this information are assigned to Resource Development.

Currently the collection numbers approximately 1.5 million volumes and covers such related subjects as botany, chemistry, entomology, forestry, food and nutrition, law, water resources, and economics. All publications of the U.S. Department of Agriculture and all reports of research supported by Department funds are included in the collection. Additionally, the Library acquires works in some 50 languages and from more than 120 countries and governmental jurisdictions. A collection of approximately 6,000 rare volumes has been acquired over the years as a result of the Library's general acquisition program. Most of these volumes are in the field of botany and include fine specimens of lithographs, as well as a strong collection of the original works of Linnaeus.

A significant acquisition in 1971 was the donation of the James M. Gwin Poultry Collection. This is the first substantive collection to be accepted under the terms of legislation authorizing the Secretary of Agriculture to receive gifts for the benefit of the National Agricultural Library. The collection contains books on poultry from every state in the United States and from 42 foreign countries. Part of its uniqueness lies in the great amount of commercial and allied industry material. Other aspects of the collection are the many files covering the early breeders in the poultry industry, posters, signs, and other materials boosting the development of the poultry industry.

Dissemination of agricultural information is provided in three NAL-oriented publications. The *Bibliography of Agriculture* is published by and available from CCM Information Corporation (New York, N.Y.). This monthly index to the literature of agriculture and the allied sciences is computer-produced by CCM from magnetic tapes containing bibliographic data prepared by the Library. Each issue contains author and subject indexes. Literature received more than one year after publication is generally not indexed. Unsigned articles and those signed with pseudonyms or initials, editorials, letters to the editor, and columns appearing regularly are omitted. The *Bibliography* is divided into four sections: a main entry section, a checklist of new governmental publications, a subject index, and an author catalog. The current subscription rate is $85.00 per year.

The publication of the *Dictionary Catalog of the National Agricultural Library, 1862–1965* has been completed with volume 73. This massive publication project was begun in 1965 by Rowman and

---

*Information Officer, The National Agricultural Library.

Littlefield, Inc. (now Littlefield, Adams & Company, Totowa, N.J.), who photographed, edited, and prepared for publication over 1,700,000 cards. The *Dictionary Catalog* contains, in one alphabetic sequence, author, title, and subject entries for monographs, serials, and analytics as cataloged for the main collection of NAL, for its Bee Culture Branch, and for the former Beltsville Branch. All the cataloging information was reproduced as it appears on the original cards. The complete set is priced at $1,460.00 and is available from the publisher.

The *National Agricultural Library Catalog*, which has been published monthly since 1966 by the same commercial firm, contains entries for all books, serials, and analytics cataloged during the previous month by the Library. With the conversion to the CAIN (Cataloging-Indexing) system, NAL is able to supply the publisher with computer-produced camera copy for the *Catalog*. Now, for the first time, there are four indexes with each issue — Personal, Corporate Author, Subject, and Title — which will be cumulated semi-annually and annually. The subscription rate is $72.00 per year.

Further current awareness is provided by CAIN Data Tapes. CAIN is a complex and comprehensive computer system which has been designed to handle up to five simultaneous separate users who share the same controlled authority files. The basic intent in the development of computer applications at NAL is to make input and output simple and convenient for the users, with the computer assuming as much detail and data manipulation as is technically feasible. CAIN Data Tapes contain a store of bibliographic data encompassing the broad field of agriculture. Subject, author, bibliographic, and organizational indexes can be compiled from the tapes, as well as comprehensive bibliographies.

Utilization of documents is centered in the Library Services function. Three basic services are available in varying degrees to all libraries and agricultural science workers: extensive interlibrary loan, photocopying, and specialized reference service. Installation of telefacsimile transmission and teletype equipment provides rapid document and information delivery.

Code-A-Phones were installed late in 1971 to improve services and access to information resources for Library customers. During daylight operating hours the Code-A-Phone system automatically records a message when Telephone Inquiry lines are busy. A second Code-A-Phone is located in The Food and Nutrition Educational Materials Center at NAL to record messages during daylight operating hours when Center personnel are away from their desks. Neither of these two systems is available at night. A third system at the main switchboard in the Library records incoming messages from 5:00 P.M. to 7:30 A.M.

Continuing efforts in 1971 have been directed toward establishing and implementing an Agricultural Science Information Network with the objective of strengthening agricultural information communications among land-grant universities, the National Agricultural Library, and other library networks. The Agricultural Science Information Network (ASIN) has as its objectives enhancing the quality and quantity of literature, other forms of knowledge, information relating to agriculture, and dissemination on national and international levels. It will provide additional and improved services to scientists in agriculture and related fields, professional agriculturalists in both the public and private sectors, agencies and organizations of government at all levels.

The broad ASIN concept has been divided into five components. The primary function of the Library component is threefold: acquisition, indexing, cataloging, and classifying of reports of new agricultural scientific knowledge, wherever recorded, and the storage of this knowledge for use in both present and future time; provision for bibliographic access to and retrieval of this knowledge; and dissemination of vehicles — books, reports, and journals — containing this knowledge. This component will consist of agricultural libraries with interconnections to other repositories of scientific information.

The Information Analysis Center (IAC) component will define and establish an appropriate organizational framework for the agricultural IAC network at the national and international levels, identify and define current IAC programs, as well as additional areas of needed service, which can best be accomplished through an IAC network.

Integrated Knowledge Services will provide effective access to, and utilization of, specialized knowledge by researchers, management, and the general public. This approach requires maximum application of modern methods, especially computer and communications technology, to the collection, processing, and dissemination of information and data.

Research and Development Programs will experiment with information techniques and advanced technology, the development of information procedures, and the preparation of guidance documents and educational programs for information activities to provide more effective information support activities.

International Cooperative Programs will identify international efforts appropriate to the Network and additional areas requiring international cooperation.

A *Directory of Information Resources in Agriculture and Biology* was published July 1971 as a project of the Agricultural Sciences Information Network in cooperation with the land-grant colleges and USDA. The *Directory* brings together in one volume the resources of information in the many diverse fields of agriculture and biology. Included in the publication is information on federal organizations, units of land-grant colleges and universities and their campus affiliates. Research moneys available to agricultural experiment stations are identified and there are detailed descriptions of prime research areas for laboratories and information centers. Literature research collections at agricultural libraries are described in detail. The *Directory* is available only from the Superintendent of Documents, U.S. Government Printing Office, Washington, D.C. 20402, and is priced at $4.50.

NAL is deeply concerned with providing the highest level of professional development for its employees and at the same time providing for the education of agricultural librarians and technical information specialists in the United States and abroad. NAL and The School of Library and Information Services, University of Maryland are developing an educational process which provides training in research methodology for teams of graduate library students, librarians, and library school faculty by involving them in the analysis of important and current problems of a library system. The procedures thus developed can be used in several ways, including all of those generally taught in a library school or a continuing education curriculum.

A pilot project for developing a Food and Nutrition Information and Educational Materials Center was initiated in 1971. The project will seek to identify the sources of educational materials and nutrition information and to define information requirements of food and nutrition programs. The Center will first concentrate on a collection of vocational and instructional materials relating to the training of personnel, operational management of programs, and pertinent research. Depending on the interest and support of users, the Center will expand into other aspects of food and nutrition information as rapidly as possible.

The Associates of the National Agricultural Library were incorporated under the laws of the State of Maryland September 23, 1970. This is a group of "friends" interested in supporting and participating in the growth of the National Agricultural Library. Their purpose is to actively encourage donation of gifts and desirable collections to the Library and to sponsor programs designed to inform the agriculturally oriented community about the Library's services and problems. Membership in the "Associates" is open to all persons, institutions, and businesses interested in the development of agricultural information and the National Agricultural Library.

(For historical material on the National Agricultural Library, see the 1971 *Bowker Annual,* pp. 284–286, and previous editions.)

THE BUREAU OF LIBRARIES AND EDUCATIONAL TECHNOLOGY IN 1971

by

Burton E. Lamkin*

Fiscal year 1971 marked the Bureau of Libraries and Educational Technology's first full year of operation. For the library programs comprising the resources of the Bureau's Division of Library Programs (the Division of Educational Technology was the Bureau's other major administrative unit) fiscal year 1971 was a year of change.

During this period, program activities in the areas of library training and manpower, library resources, and library research were redirected so that their administration could more closely reflect such Office of Education priorities as service to the disadvantaged, the reduction of racial, cultural, and ethnic isolation, and the promotion of innovation in educational practice and administration. Although the state-administered Library Services and Construction Act was not subject to administrative change on the scale initiated for discretionary programs, program staff worked closely with state library agencies in developing plans for public library programs that were responsive to national goals such as the Right to Read and drug abuse education, as well as to local priorities.

PROGRAM REDIRECTION

The three Bureau programs redirected during the fiscal year were College Library Resources (Title II-A, Higher Education Act), Library Training (Title II-B, Higher Education Act), and Library Research and Demonstration (Cooperative Research Act and Title II-B, Higher Education Act).

College Library Resources was refocused during this period to better serve the Office of Education's overriding commitment to the equalization of educational opportunity. Briefly, the number of institutions assisted under this program was reduced from 2,201 in 1970 to 606 in 1971 in order to concentrate the funds available ($9.9 million) on smaller, needier institutions such as community and junior colleges, black colleges, and post-secondary vocational schools, since these schools either have markedly substandard collections or sizable enrollments of economically and culturally deprived students. Special-purpose grants under Title II-A were awarded to promote cooperative use of library resources at the academic level. In Minnesota, for instance, ten academic, public, and private libraries received support to form CLIC (Cooperating Libraries in Consortium), a cooperative program designed to make the resources of all ten of the libraries involved available to students and faculty of each participating school.

The Library Training Program was redirected to meet training priorities emphasizing service to the disadvantaged and the recruitment of minority persons into library work as professionals and paraprofessionals. Of the two activities previously funded under this program — library training institutes and. fellowships

---

*Associate Commissioner, Bureau of Libraries and Educational Technology, Regional Office Building, 7th and D Streets S.W., Washington, D.C. 20202.

to students of library science — the former was selected as the best format for achieving these training goals, and no new fellowships were awarded during 1971. Twelve of the 38 institutes funded in fiscal year 1971 recruited more than 175 chicanos, Indians, blacks, and Appalachian whites into the library and information science fields. Other institutes focused on retraining librarians to take leadership roles in developing programs responsive to minority groups and to such national priorities as the Right to Read, early childhood development, environmental education, and drug abuse education.

Typical of the new thrust in library training during 1971 was the formation of a Library Training Institute, comprised of a consortium of six black colleges in South Carolina, to train paraprofessionals for library work. The Institute, which is located at Voorhees College, has graduated 30 students who are now filling positions in their respective college libraries as well as in public school libraries in South Carolina and neighboring states.

In another Title II-B program, the Atlanta University School of Library Service is operating a two-year institute for 12 college graduates who are interested in careers that involve working with the disadvantaged in urban public libraries. In addition to library education, the course offers practical experience in programs dealing with drug abuse, legal aid services, consumer education, Right to Read efforts, and vocational guidance.

Redirection of the Library Research and Demonstration Program during 1971 resulted in a shift of program emphasis away from basic research toward support of studies to identify the information requirements of specific population groups and toward demonstrations of innovative, library-based projects designed to improve delivery of informational and instructional resources to disadvantaged neighborhoods and communities. Branch activities included:

Four separate studies were funded to identify the special informational needs of the urban poor, Spanish-speaking Americans, American Indians, and the aging, and to develop data concerning the extent and quality of present library services to these groups. In addition to these studies, the Branch also funded an evaluation of the operation and impact of the Albuquerque Model Cities Library Materials and Cultural Center, where innovative approaches to the provision of library and related services to minority groups in the Model Cities area are being tested.

In Philadelphia the Branch launched a major demonstration of a community-controlled library-learning center, where print and nonprint materials, special programs, and a large staff of paraprofessionals recruited from the disadvantaged target neighborhood will be combined in an attempt to increase library usage and educational progress on the part of previously "turned off" students and adults. Nearly $800,000 in funds from the Elementary and Secondary Education Act, Cooperative Research Act, and Library Services and Construction Act were targeted for the project (which is directed by a consortium of representatives of Philadelphia's public library, public and diocesan schools, and residents of the service area) during 1971.

The Branch supplied support for design of a model information system to provide administrators, teachers, and students in the Los Angeles Unified School District with computerized access to *all* instructional materials stocked by the district.

Support was continued for the development in Ohio of the first state-wide computerized library cataloging service for academic libraries. The system, which is being designed by the Ohio College Library Center as a prototype that might be adopted by other regions, has resulted in substantial financial savings for member libraries.

LIBRARY SERVICES AND CONSTRUCTION ACT (LSCA)

During fiscal year 1971, LSCA program officers worked closely with the various state library agencies to prepare for adoption of the 1970 amendments to the LSCA, which became effective at the beginning of fiscal year 1972. In addition to consolidating LSCA into three programs (Services, Construction, and Interlibrary Cooperation), the amendments call for increased emphasis on library programs for the disadvantaged and on long-range library planning efforts at the state level. The latter requirement led to the funding of a three-phase library training institute (sponsored under Title II-B, Higher Education Act, and conducted by the Ohio State University Evaluation Center) to acquaint state library officials with planning and evaluation techniques. In a related development, the Bureau and the Office of Education's planning and evaluation staff worked together to launch an intensive survey to identify LSCA projects which have been particularly successful in extending public library services to the poor and to minority groups. Results of this survey will be disseminated to the profession upon completion of the project.

ORGANIZATION AND FUNDING

All library programs administered by the Bureau are clustered within the administrative framework of the Division of Library Programs. Central staff located in the Division's Training and Resources Branch (Titles II-A and II-B, Higher Education Act), Research and Program Development Branch (Title II-B, Higher Education Act, and Cooperative Research Act), and Services and Facilities Branch (LSCA) were augmented by Regional Library Services Officers who, although assigned to the Office of Education's Office of Regional Office Coordination, are responsible for LSCA programs within their regions and provide consultative services on all library programs administered by the Bureau. (For fiscal year 1972 appropriations for library programs, see Table 1 in Krettek and Cooke's article, "Federal Legislation for Libraries during 1971," this volume.)

DHEW REGIONAL OFFICES

Region 1 (Connecticut, Maine, Massachusetts, New Hampshire, Rhode Island, Vermont): Arlene Hope, Library Services Program Officer, DHEW/Office of Education, John F. Kennedy Federal Bldg., Government Center, Boston, Mass. 02203. 617-223-6548

Region 2 (New Jersey, New York, Puerto Rico, Virgin Islands): Mrs. Eleanor T. Smith, Library Services Program Officer, DHEW/Office of Education, Federal Bldg., 26 Federal Plaza, New York, N.Y. 10007. 212-264-4417

Region 3 (Delaware, District of Columbia, Maryland, Pennsylvania, Virginia, West Virginia): Evelyn D. Mullen, Library Services Program Officer, DHEW/Office of Education, P.O. Box 12900, Philadelphia, Pa. 19108. 215-597-9014

Region 4 (Alabama, Florida, Georgia, Kentucky, Mississippi, North Carolina, South Carolina, Tennessee): Shirley A. Brother, Library Services Program Officer, DHEW/Office of Education, 50 Seventh St. N.E., Room 550, Atlanta, Ga. 30323. 404-526-3102

Region 5 (Illinois, Indiana, Michigan, Minnesota, Ohio, Wisconsin): Allen Sevigny, Library Services Program Officer, DHEW/Office of Education, 300 South Wacker Drive Building, Chicago, Ill. 60606. 312-353-1243

Region 6 (Arkansas, Louisiana, New Mexico, Oklahoma, Texas): S. Janice Kee, Library Services Program Officer, DHEW/Office of Education, 1114 Commerce St., Dallas, Tex. 75202. 214-749-2341

Region 7 (Iowa, Kansas, Missouri, Nebraska): Denny Stephens, Library Services Program Officer, DHEW/Office of Education, 601 East 12th St., Kansas City, Mo. 64106. 816-374-3070

Region 8 (Colorado, Montana, North Dakota, South Dakota, Utah, Wyoming): Henry A. Fontaine, Library Services Program Officer, DHEW/

Office of Education, Federal Office Bldg., 19th and Stout Sts., Denver, Colo. 80202. 303-837-4957

Region 9 (Arizona, California, Hawaii, Nevada, American Samoa, Guam, Trust Territory of the Pacific Islands): Helen Luce, Library Services Program Officer, DHEW/Office of Education, 50 Fulton St., San Francisco, Calif. 94102. 415-556-6928

Region 10 (Alaska, Idaho, Oregon, Washington): Robert Geiman, Library Services Program Officer, DHEW/Office of Education, Arcade Plaza Bldg., 1321 Second Ave., Seattle, Wash. 98101. 206-442-4962

DEPARTMENT OF HEALTH, EDUCATION, AND WELFARE
U.S. OFFICE OF EDUCATION

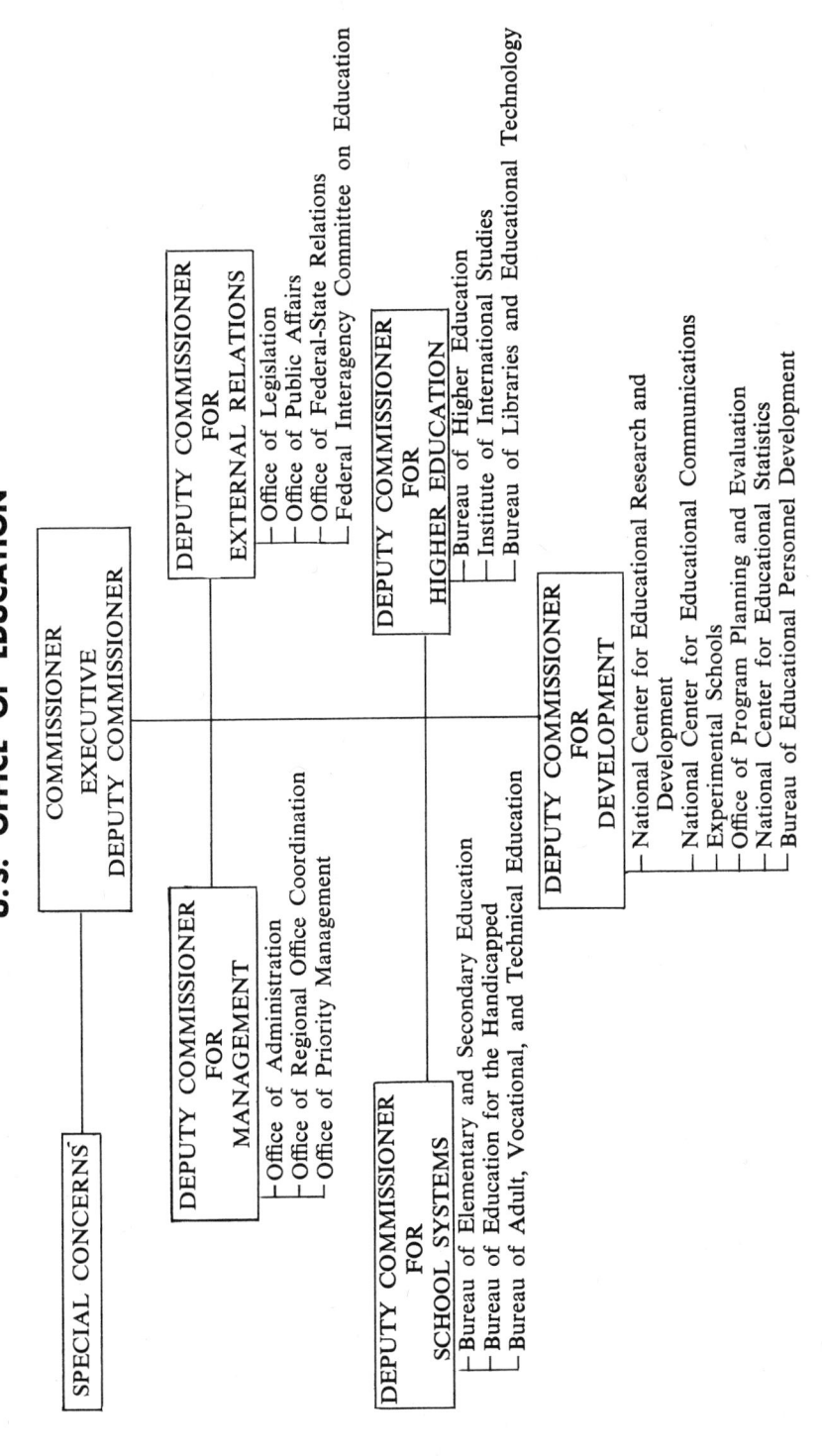

COMMISSIONER
EXECUTIVE DEPUTY COMMISSIONER

- SPECIAL CONCERNS

DEPUTY COMMISSIONER FOR MANAGEMENT
- Office of Administration
- Office of Regional Office Coordination
- Office of Priority Management

DEPUTY COMMISSIONER FOR SCHOOL SYSTEMS
- Bureau of Elementary and Secondary Education
- Bureau of Education for the Handicapped
- Bureau of Adult, Vocational, and Technical Education

DEPUTY COMMISSIONER FOR EXTERNAL RELATIONS
- Office of Legislation
- Office of Public Affairs
- Office of Federal-State Relations
- Federal Interagency Committee on Education

DEPUTY COMMISSIONER FOR HIGHER EDUCATION
- Bureau of Higher Education
- Institute of International Studies
- Bureau of Libraries and Educational Technology

DEPUTY COMMISSIONER FOR DEVELOPMENT
- National Center for Educational Research and Development
- National Center for Educational Communications
- Experimental Schools
- Office of Program Planning and Evaluation
- National Center for Educational Statistics
- Bureau of Educational Personnel Development

THE COUNCIL ON LIBRARY RESOURCES, INC.

by

Lee E. Grove*

In the spring of 1971 the independent, nonprofit Council on Library Resources, Inc., received a grant of $5 million from the Ford Foundation, at whose instance it was established in 1956. The new grant enables the Council to continue its program of research, development, and demonstration of new methods and techniques in library operation and service.

The renewed support came at a time of profession-wide concern about the austerity programs being forced upon libraries by rising costs and tightening purse strings with no decline in the demands for service. One way industry and government have obtained more for the dollar has been through improved management techniques. Aware of this, the Council made a grant to the Association of Research Libraries for a preliminary study of academic library management by a firm of management consultants with the guidance of a joint Association–American Council on Education committee.

The study resulted in a number of suggestions for further investigation. It also led to the establishment in the fall of 1970 of an Office of University Library Management Studies within the Association with the cosponsorship of the American Council on Education and funding from the Council on Library Resources. Shortly thereafter, a Council-funded case study of certain management aspects of a great research library was initiated as a step in the development of the overall program. The study of the organization and staffing of the Columbia University Libraries is being conducted by professional management consultants under the general direction of the Office of University Library Management Studies and its advisory committee of university administrators and librarians. Columbia's library system was chosen for study because it incorporates in representative portions the operational complexities, the service capabilities, and the financial problems characteristic of most large academic research libraries. Also, the project fitted into a management study of the whole university. The thrust of the study is not primarily aimed at cost reduction; it is to secure for the university maximum benefits from its library resources — funds, talent, collections, and space. While the project focuses on Columbia, it is felt that the findings will be of interest and use to other institutions.

Another aspect of library management — the economics — is the subject of work by Mathematica, Inc., Princeton, New Jersey, under contract to the Council. The study has been under the general guidance of an advisory committee of leading university librarians and is expected to assist academic libraries in their planning and to justify their need for a fair share of available funds.

Librarianship, in terms of financial remuneration, has always been an unrewarding profession for most of those in it. It has in consequence failed to attract as many able recruits as could be wished; further, it sometimes loses those in mid-career to other fields of endeavor. The Council therefore engaged Dr. Donald F. Cameron, Librarian Emeritus of the Rutgers University Library, and Dr. Peggy F. Heim, Director of the Planning Center for the South Carolina Independent Colleges and former staff economist with the American Association of University Professors, to make a study of the economics of librarianship in four-year university and college libraries. Following a statistical survey of 249 academic libraries during the academic year 1969–1970, they concluded that librarians did not fare nearly as well as their teaching colleagues. A major difference

---

*Director of Publications, Council on Library Resources, Inc.

was that less than 20 percent of the faculty were at the lowest rank, that of instructor, and moreover, nearly all of them held this rank for but a brief period. For most, the next higher rank, assistant professor, was passed before they were 40 years old. In contrast, roughly 50 percent of the professional librarians are classified in the basic rank from which many never advance, and of those who do advance, most rise no higher than department head or branch librarian. At the top of the hierarchy approximately 50 percent of the faculty are professors or associate professors, while directors, associate and assistant directors of libraries comprise only about 10 percent of the total. The report has been published by the Council and the authors retained for a second year to gather new statistics for purposes of comparison.

Because more needs to be known about the users of libraries, present and potential, the Council has made a grant to the library of the University of Lancaster in England for a study by its research unit. The study is seeking to discover and identify information about the factors that tend to encourage or discourage the use of available services and to learn how the impact of proposed changes in library and information services can be predicted.

The National Endowment for the Humanities and the Council have jointly provided funds for a study of users and nonusers in another environment — the crowded, predominantly black and Puerto Rican Bedford-Stuyvesant area of Brooklyn, New York. The study is being conducted by Hardy R. Franklin, librarian and student at the Rutgers Graduate School of Library Service.

The need of public libraries to redefine their role in a changed world is widely recognized. As a step in this direction, the American Library Association's Public Library Association is making a preliminary evaluative study of the goals and services of public libraries. The Council and the National Endowment for the Humanities have made matching grants for the purpose. The study is expected to lead to a full-scale inquiry in which the effect of altering urban and social conditions will be considered as well as that of broadening opportunities for higher education.

With grants from the Council, the National Endowment for the Humanities, and the College Entrance Examination Board, the Dallas Public Library in September 1971 began a two-year investigation of the effectiveness of the public library as a center for independent study directed toward a two-year college education. Information centers have been established at five branch libraries, serving different socioeconomic communities, to provide information, counseling, and study guides for use in the College Level Examination Program (CLEP). Depending on the examination scores he achieves, a student may earn up to two full years of academic credit at a participating institution. Southern Methodist University is taking an active part in the program.

It was in the belief that libraries should assume a more active role in the educational process that a joint Council on Library Resources–National Endowment for the Humanities College Library Program was established in mid-1969. Under the program, the Endowment and the Council make matching grants to selected institutions of higher learning whose libraries have proposed creative projects involving the library, faculty, and students in active participation. In 1971 grants were made to Howard University, Swarthmore College, and Washington and Lee University, making a total of eight colleges or universities to receive grants. Another college received a similar grant from the Council in independent action. An equivalent amount has been pledged by the institution in each case.

In the field of automation, the Council has continued to provide assistance to the National Libraries Task Force on Automation and Other Cooperative Services, formed in 1967 by the Library of Congress, National Library of Medicine, and the National Agricultural Library. Agreement has been reached on standards for some of the bibliographic information to be represented in automated systems, and

Task Force members are working on the coordination of present or future automation of the three libraries' acquisitions systems.

The program of Information Transfer Experiments (INTREX) at the Massachusetts Institute of Technology has as its objective the development of innovative methods, utilizing new technology or combinations of it, to bring under control and provide better access to an ever-increasing mass of books, periodicals, reports, and records. Work has now progressed to the point where the indexing necessary to bring the data base to 18,000 documents has been completed; more than 17,000 of these have been keyed and about 16,000 processed into the computer store. Work on an expanded and updated "Augmented Catalog" is in progress. A model transitional library developed by the project is now functioning within the engineering library with services based on the new technologies and new uses of old technologies alongside and integrated into traditional services.

The University of Chicago Library, which has developed an extensive computer-based bibliographic data processing system, is currently working on the control of book circulation with the support of matching grants from the National Endowment for the Humanities and the Council. The work is part of a five-year program, the major objective of which is the development of an efficient computerized system to handle large bibliographic data files, and application of the system to various library operations.

The Council has again given some assistance to two developing service networks. One is the New England Library Information Network (NELINET), which is sponsored by the New England Board of Higher Education and serves 22 academic libraries within the region with cataloging products. The other is the Ohio College Library Center, located at Ohio State University, which offers cataloging and other services as part of its developing computerized regional system.

Precise identification of serials is an essential, if confusion is to be avoided in their control. In this connection an important development has occurred as the result of the work of the American National Standards Institute's Sectional Committee Z39 (Standards in Library Work, Documentation and Related Publishing Practices). A system developed by Z39 for assigning an identifying Standard Serial Number (SSN) unique to each periodical or other serial has been approved by the parent institute and recommended for international adoption by Technical Committee 46 of the International Standards Organization. The work of Z39 is supported by the Council and the National Science Foundation.

Another important development for libraries is the establishment of the Cataloging in Publication (CIP) Program at the Library of Congress on July 1, 1971, for which the National Endowment for the Humanities and the Council have made matching grants for a two-year period. A similar project, then called "cataloging in source," was the subject of a Council-supported experiment in 1958–1959. CIP will provide participating publishers with cataloging data for publication in their books, preferably on the verso of the title page. It is anticipated that by the end of the two-year period CIP will be geared to provide data for 30,000 to 36,000 titles per year.

An experiment at the Tulane University Library for the computer-output-microfilm (COM) production of a short-title catalog and the testing of its acceptance by readers has been completed. The test revealed certain shortcomings, but the microfilm catalog was found to be quite acceptable to most users during the experiment. Also with Council support, an experiment is now underway at the New York Public Library to ascertain the feasibility of putting its catalogs on microfilm. Working in another direction, the Dartmouth College Library is experimenting with the micropublishing of rare scholarly materials in small editions, interest being too limited to justify letterpress printing.

In the field of preservation, the Council is continuing its support of the W. J. Barrow Research Laboratory in Richmond, Virginia. Currently, the laboratory, among various other projects, is executing a contract jointly for the Council and the Library of Congress for the revision of the 1960 specifications for permanent/durable book papers developed by the late Mr. Barrow. A history of permanent/durable book paper by Verner W. Clapp, consultant to the Council and its former president, has been published in three parts in the University of Toronto Press' quarterly, *Scholarly Publishing,* appearing in the January, April, and July issues.

Among publications resulting from the Council grants are: "Aging of Paper," a chapter by Ann M. Carlton, of the Barrow Laboratory, in *Handbook of Pulp and Paper Technology,* edited by Kenneth W. Britt (Van Nostrand Reinhold Company, 1970); *Library Systems Analysis Guidelines,* by Edward A. Chapman, Paul L. St. Pierre, and John Lubans, Jr. (Wiley-Interscience, A Division of John Wiley & Sons, 1970); *Library Lighting,* by Keyes D. Metcalf (The Association of Research Libraries, 1970); and *Reader for Archives and Records Center Buildings,* compiled by Victor Gondos, Jr. (Committee on Archival Buildings and Equipment, The Society of American Archivists, 1970).

The Council has continued its Fellowship Program. This year fellowships were awarded to 18 North American working librarians, bringing the total to 53 since inception of the three-year-old program. The awards are to enable promising mid-career librarians to familiarize themselves with new developments in their fields. The awards do not cover salaries — which are expected to be met by the parent institutions — but are for such items as travel, per diem living expenses, and supplies incident to a fellow's project while on leave of absence.

All told, during its fiscal year 1970–1971 the Council on Library Resources, of which Dr. Fred C. Cole is president and Mrs. Edith M. Lesser is secretary and treasurer, allocated $1,401,982 for the support of 32 new projects and continued or completed work on a number of others. Additionally, in a number of cases projects and programs were assisted directly by staff members. Annual reports may be obtained by writing to the Council at its headquarters in the National Center for Higher Education, One Dupont Circle, Washington, D.C. 20036.

AMERICAN NATIONAL STANDARDS INSTITUTE, INC. STANDARDS COMMITTEE Z39

by
Linda Schneider[*]

For Standards Committee Z39, 1971 was a fruitful year. Six standards, some of which had been in development for several years, were published by the American National Standards Institute. These are the ANS (American National Standard) for Bibliographic Information Interchange on Magnetic Tape, the ANS for Writing Abstracts, the ANS for Directories of Libraries and Information Centers, the ANS for the Advertising of Books, the ANS Identification Number for Serials Publications, and the ANS for Title Leaves of a Book. This brings the number of Z39 standards in the area of library work, documentation, and related publishing practices to twelve.

Two other standards were approved

---

[*]Research Assistant for Z39, University of North Carolina Library, Chapel Hill, N.C. 27514.

as American National Standards in late 1971, with their publication planned for 1972; they are Romanization of Arabic and Romanization of Japanese. The National Clearinghouse for Periodical Title Word Abbreviations, supported by Z39 funds, published the *NCPTWA Word-Abbreviation List, 1971 Edition*. This *List* of more than 7,000 word abbreviations was designed to supplement the ANS for the Abbreviation of Titles of Periodicals.

Three standards will be submitted to ANSI early in 1972 for approval. The standard for the Transliteration of Slavic Cyrillic Characters was originally approved by Z39 in 1970, but due to revisions suggested by the Library of Congress during the voting period, the proposal was resubmitted to Z39 members in 1971. It has been approved as revised and will be submitted to ANSI in 1972. The Preparation of Scientific Papers draft was submited to Z39 for voting in March 1971 and approved; at the end of the year, the subcommittee chairman was making final editorial changes suggested during the ANSI Public Review. The proposed ANS for Scientific and Technical Reports was also submitted to the membership for voting in 1971, but due to increased interest on the part of the American Society for Information Science membership, which may necessitate some changes, it was not forwarded to ANSI.

At the end of the year, the proposed ANS for Proof Corrections was being set in type; it will be submitted to the membership for a vote when it is available.

Two subcommittees submitted drafts for comment. Two drafts of the standard Guidelines for Thesaurus Structure, Construction and Use were submitted for comment and the final version will be submitted for voting in 1972. The Specialized Vocabulary of Information Dissemination, which is being prepared as one section of the International Organization for Standardization/Technical Committee 46 (ISO/TC 46) Working Group 3 — Vocabulary of Documentation, was circulated for initial comment.

Work continues on initial drafts for standards for library materials price indexes, identification codes, and conversion systems for Hebrew and Yiddish.

To continue standards work in other areas, several subcommittees were reorganized in 1971. The subcommittees on Bibliographic References and Publicity and Promotion were reorganized under new chairmen, and the Subcommittee on Periodical Title Arrangement was reactivated to review Z39.1–1967, the ANS for Periodicals: Format and Arrangement, in accordance with ANSI practice.

Three new subcommittees were organized in response to interest in standards for Bibliographic Entries for Microfiche Headers and Roll Microfilm Containers, Technical Report Numbering, and the Music Industry Code (a system for the identification of music industry products). The MIC group will concentrate its efforts on work with ISO/TC 46 Working Group 1, which has recently undertaken work in this area.

Plans are under way to reactivate Subcommittee 2, which prepared Z39.2–1971, to work on a standard for the interchange of bibliographic information on magnetic tape for specified data communication links.

Five members of Standards Committee Z39 (Jerrold Orne, Henriette Avram, Emery Koltay, Lawrence Livingston, and Ben H. Weil) attended the thirteenth Plenary Session of ISO Technical Committee 46: Documentation, in Lisbon from April 27 to May 7 as the U.S. (i.e., ANSI) delegation. Items discussed and acted upon at the meetings included the ISBN and ISSN systems, country codes, terminology, abstracts, thesaurus guidelines, conversion of languages, automation in documentation, and others. (Information regarding these particular areas may be obtained from the Z39 Office, University of North Carolina Library, Chapel Hill, N.C. 27514.)

The ISO Central Secretariat called a Co-ordinating Meeting of International Organizations on the Representation and Coding of Country Names in October.

Representatives of 11 international organizations (e.g., International Air Transport Association, Universal Postal Union, World Intellectual Property Organization, UNESCO) and members from four ISO Technical Committees (37, Terminology; 46, Documentation; 97, Data Elements and Their Coded Representations; and 104, Freight Containers) attended. Patricia Parker, Chairman of Subcommittee 27, and Jerrold Orne represented Z39 and TC 46. Subcommittee 27 has now accepted responsibility for completing the U.S. Country Code standard; Standards Committee X3's project in this area has been discontinued, and members of the X3L8 subcommittee will now work with SC 27.

The ANS Identification Number for Serial Publications (SSN) has been accepted as the basis for the numerical code for international use. A group of International Standard Serial Numbers were assigned to R. R. Bowker Company for use in its *Ulrich's International Periodicals Directory* and *Irregular Serials and Annuals* for 1972. Now being considered are the next steps, including coordination of national agencies with an international center. Lawrence Livingston and Jerrold Orne participated in several meetings during the year concerned with the establishment of this international center. (See table of contents, this volume, for individual articles on specific standards.)

Jerrold Orne also attended the UNISIST meeting in Paris in October as a representative of ISO/TC 46.

One general meeting of Z39 was held in Washington, D.C. in May. Membership continued to be the same as in 1970, with the few following changes: the American Association of University Presses was admitted to membership; the Joint Committee on Pharmacy College Libraries was disbanded; and the American Book Publishers Council and the American Educational Publishers Institute, both members of Z39, merged to form the Association of American Publishers, which will continue as a member organization. There are now 45 member organizations in Z39.

The Chairman of Z39, Jerrold Orne, was honored by the American Society for Information Science on November 10, 1971 in Denver as the 1971 recipient of the Society's Award of Merit, for his "outstanding work in the area of standardization for library and information work."

Officers for the first half of 1971 were Jerrold Orne, Chairman; James L. Wood, Vice-Chairman; and Harold Oatfield, Secretary-Treasurer. In May Harold Oatfield and Linda Schneider were appointed to three-year terms to begin in July 1971, as Vice-Chairman and Secretary-Treasurer, respectively. Stephanie Fennell and Israel Resnick served as ANSI staff liaison for the year. The Council of National Library Associations continued as Z39's official Secretariat. Standards Committee Z39 ended the year with renewed support from the National Science Foundation and the Council on Library Resources, Inc.

The member organizations and their representatives at the end of 1971 were as follows.

American Association of Law Libraries, Hugh Y. Bernard

American Association of University Presses, Marjorie Scal

American Business Press, Evelyn French

American Chemical Society, James L. Wood and Robert S. Tannehill

American Institute of Physics, A. W. K. Metzner and Arthur Herschman

American Library Association, Stephen R. Salmon and Frederick G. Kilgour

American Petroleum Institute, Ben H. Weil and E. H. Brenner

American Society for Information Science, Charles P. Bourne

American Society for Testing and Materials, Donald P. Hammer and Walter V. Cropper

American Society of Indexers, John Rothman

Association for Computing Machinery, R. E. Utman, George Patterson, and Jacques Vallee

Association of American Library Schools, Theodore C. Hines

Association of American Publishers, Robert W. Frase and M. Ann Heidbreder

Association of Jewish Libraries, Herbert C. Zafren

Association of Research Libraries, Jerrold Orne

Bio-Sciences Information Service, H. E. Kennedy and Phyllis Parkins

Book Manufacturers' Institute, Malcolm D. Gordon

R. R. Bowker Company, Emery Koltay

Catholic Library Association, Catherine M. Pilley

Center for Applied Linguistics, Frederick Bauman

Center for Computer Sciences & Technology, National Bureau of Standards, Madeline M. Henderson

Council of Biology Editors, Jerold A. Last

Council of National Library Associations, Robert W. Gibson

Council on Library Resources, Inc., Lawrence Livingston and Verner W. Clapp

Drug Information Association, Harold Oatfield and Oliver Buchanan

Engineering Index, Inc., Bill M. Woods and Carolyn Flanagan

Engineers Joint Council, Eugene B. Jackson and Frank Y. Speight

Information Industry Association, James Henderson

International Business Machines Corp., Stephen E. Furth

Library Binding Institute, Dudley A. Weiss

Library of Congress, William J. Welsh

Medical Library Association, Henry Lemkau, Jr.

Music Library Association, Jean Bowen and Fred Blum

National Academy of Sciences, James L. Olsen, Jr.

National Association of Home Builders, Karl A. Baer

National Federation of Science Abstracting and Indexing Services, Stella Keenan

National Security Industrial Association, Claude Gibson

Printing Industries of America, George Mattson

Shoe String Press, Frances Rutter

Society for Technical Communication, Helen Cressman

Special Libraries Association, Logan O. Cowgill

U.S. Dept. of Commerce, Hubert E. Sauter

U.S. Dept. of Defense, Walter B. Greenwood and Frederic R. Theriault

U.S. Dept. of Health, Education, and Welfare, Office of Education, Library Services Branch, Robert Klassen

U.S. Dept. of the Interior, Office of Water Resources Research, Raymond A. Jensen and Logan O. Cowgill

Liaison Representative to Standards Committee X3, David A. Weisbrod.

The subcommittees and their chairmen for 1970 were as follows.

SC/1: Program, Harold Oatfield, Route 3, Box 859, Gales Ferry, Conn. 06335

SC/2: Machine Input Records, Henriette D. Avram, Information Systems Office, The Library of Congress, Washington, D.C. 20540

SC/3: Periodical Title Abbreviations, James L. Wood, Chemical Abstracts Service, University Post Office, Columbus, Ohio 43210

SC/4: Bibliographic References, Ben H. Weil, Esso Research and Engineering Company, P.O. Box 121, Linden, N.J. 07036

SC/5: Transliteration, Jerrold Orne, University of North Carolina Library, Chapel Hill, N.C. 27514

SC/6: Abstracts, Ben H. Weil, Esso Research and Engineering Company, P.O. Box 121, Linden, N.J. 07036

SC/8: Proof Corrections, Bruce C. Young, University of Chicago Press, 5801 Ellis Avenue, Chicago, Ill. 60637

SC/9: Terminology, Patrick D. J. Rae, Washington State Library Network, Washington State Library, Olympia, Wash. 98501

SC/10: Arrangement of Periodicals, Anne J. Richter, 222 Valley Road, Montclair, N.J. 07042

SC/13: Trade Catalogs and Directories, Karl A. Baer, National Housing Center, 1625 L Street N.W., Washington, D.C. 20036

SC/17: Standard Book Numbers, Emery Koltay, R. R. Bowker Company, 1180 Avenue of the Americas, New York, N.Y. 10036; and Robert W. Frase, Association of American Publishers, 1826 Jefferson Place N.W., Washington, D.C. 20036

SC/19: Book Publishers Advertising, Ellis Mount, School of Engineering Library, Columbia University, New York, N.Y. 10027

SC/20: Standard Serial Coding, Fred Croxton, Administrative Department, The Library of Congress, Washington, D.C. 20540

SC/21: Title Leaves of a Book, Anne J. Richter, 222 Valley Road, Montclair, N.J. 07042

SC/22: Library Materials Price Indexes, William H. Kurth, Washington University Libraries, St. Louis, Mo. 63130

SC/24: Report Literature Format, Parmely C. Daniels, 5719 Third Street South, Arlington, Va. 22204

SC/25: Thesaurus Rules and Conventions, Frank Y. Speight, 725 Catalonia Avenue, Coral Gables, Fla. 33134

SC/26: Preparation of Scientific Papers, F. Peter Woodford, 22 Priory Gardens, Highgate, London N6, England

SC/27: Identification Codes for Countries, Languages, Publishers, Areas and Dates, Patricia E. Parker, MARC Development Office, The Library of Congress, Washington, D.C. 20540

SC/29: Publicity and Promotion, Harold Oatfield, Route 3, Box 859, Gales Ferry, Conn. 06335

SC/30: Identification Code for Libraries and Bookdealers, Joseph Eisner, ANYLTS, Roosevelt Field, Garden City, N.Y. 11530; and Russell Reynolds, National Association of College Stores, 55 E. College St., Oberlin, Ohio 44704

SC/31: Music Industry Code, Kenneth C. Schonberg, Billboard Publications, 164 E. 46 St., New York, N.Y. 10036

SC/32: Technical Report Numbering, Donald P. Hammer, Purdue University Libraries, Lafayette, Ind. 47907

SC/33: Bibliographic Entries for Microfiche Headers and Roll Microfilm Containers, Joseph H. Howard, Descriptive Cataloging Division, The Library of Congress, Washington, D.C. 20540

The following Z39 standards in the fields of library work, documentation, and related publishing practices are currently available from the American National Standards Institute, 1430 Broadway, New York, N.Y. 10018.

Z39.1–1967 Periodicals: Format and Arrangement, $2.75

Z39.2–1971 Bibliographic Information Interchange on Magnetic Tape, $5.00

Z39.4–1968 Basic Criteria for Indexes, $2.75

Z39.5–1969 Abbreviation of Titles of Periodicals, $2.75

Z39.6–1965 Trade Catalogs, Specifications for, $5.00

Z39.7–1969 Library Statistics, $4.50

Z39.8–1969 Compiling Book Publishing Statistics, $2.25

Z39.9–1971 Identification Number for Serial Publications, $2.75

Z39.10–1971 Directories of Libraries and Information Centers, $3.00

Z39.13–1971 Advertising of Books, $3.00

Z39.14–1971 Writing Abstracts, $3.00

Z39.15–1971 Title Leaves of a Book, $2.50

NATIONAL COMMISSION ON LIBRARIES AND INFORMATION SCIENCE

by

Frederick Burkhardt[*]

The National Commission on Libraries and Information Science was created by Public Law 91-345, 91st Congress S. 1519, which was signed by President Nixon on July 20, 1970.

In this Act the Congress affirms "that library and information services adequate to meet the needs of the people of the United States are essential to achieve national goals and to utilize most effectively the Nation's educational resources," and it gives the Commission responsibility for developing or recommending plans to assure optimum provision of such services. In carrying out that responsibility, the Commission is directed to:

"1. Advise the President and the Congress on the implementation of national policy by such statements, presentations, and reports as it deems appropriate;

"2. conduct studies, surveys, and analyses of the library and informational needs of the Nation, including the special library and informational needs of rural areas and of economically, socially, or culturally deprived persons, and the means by which these needs may be met through information centers, through the libraries of elementary and secondary schools and institutions of higher education, and through public, research, special, and other types of libraries;

"3. appraise the adequacies and deficiencies of current library and information resources and services and evaluate the effectiveness of current library and information science programs;

"4. develop overall plans for meeting national library and informational needs and for the coordination of activities at the Federal, State, and local levels, taking into consideration all of the library and informational resources of the Nation to meet those needs;

"5. be authorized to advise Federal, State, local, and private agencies regarding library and information sciences;

"6. promote research and development activities which will extend and improve the Nation's library and information-handling capability as essential links in the national communications networks;

"7. submit to the President and the Congress (not later than January 31 of each year) a report on its activities during the preceding fiscal year; and

"8. make and publish such additional reports as it deems to be necessary, including, but not limited to, reports of consultants, transcripts of testimony, summary reports, and reports of other Commission findings, studies, and recommendations."

On May 19, 1971 the President nominated the following persons to serve as the first members of the Commission, and their appointments were confirmed by the Senate on July 15, 1971. Upon confirmation, the President designated Frederick Burkhardt Chairman of the Commission.

For a term expiring July 19, 1971 (reappointed for a term expiring July 19, 1976): Andrew A. Aines, of North Springfield, Va., Technical Assistant for Scientific and Technological Information, Communication and Computers to the Director of the Office of Science and Technology, Washington, D.C.; Catherine D. Scott, of the District of Columbia, Head Librarian, Bellcomm, Incorporated, D.C.

For a term expiring July 19, 1972: Martin Goland, of San Antonio, Tex., President, Southwest Research Institute, San Antonio, Tex.; Louis A. Lerner, of Chicago, Ill., Publisher, Lerner Home Newspapers of Chicago; Charles A. Per-

---

[*]Chairman, National Commission on Libraries and Information Science, Washington, D.C. 20007.

lik, Jr., of Falls Church, Va., President, American Newspaper Guild, District of Columbia. (Mr. Perlik has since resigned.)

For a term expiring July 19, 1973: John G. Kemeny, of Hanover, N.H., President, Dartmouth College; Mrs. Bessie B. Moore, of Little Rock, Ark., Director of Economic and Environmental Education, State Department of Education, Arkansas; Alfred R. Zipf, of San Carlos, Calif., Executive Vice President, Bank of America, San Francisco.

For a term expiring July 19, 1974: Joseph Becker, of Bethesda, Md., President, Becker and Hayes, Inc., Bethesda; Carlos A. Cuadra, of Los Angeles, Calif., Manager of Library and Education Systems Department, Systems Development Corporation, Santa Monica, Calif.; John E. Velde, Jr., of Pekin, Ill., Vice President, Velde, Roelfs and Company, Pekin, Ill.

For a term expiring July 19, 1975: W. O. Baker, of Morristown, N.J., Vice President of Research, Bell Telephone Laboratories; Frederick Burkhardt, of New York, N.Y., President, American Council of Learned Societies, New York; Leslie W. Dunlap, of Iowa City, Iowa, Dean of Library Administration, University of Iowa.

In addition to those named above, the Librarian of Congress serves *ex officio* as a member of the Commission.

The Commission held its first meeting in Washington, D.C. on September 20–21, 1971; subsequent meetings have been held since. (See also Cylke's article, "The State of Federal Libraries," this volume.)

THE AMERICAN LIBRARY ASSOCIATION
by
Keith Doms*

Since 1876 the American Library Association has shaped its structure and activities toward the attainment of its basic objective: "to extend and improve library service and librarianship in the United States and throughout the world." While the founders of the American Library Association seem to have been extremely farsighted in most ways, they underestimated the future growth of the profession and the human desire and need for meetings and conventions. To be more specific, it has been reported that upon the occasion of the first ALA conference in 1876, the opinion was freely expressed that "while librarians might usefully come together once in a while for a conference, and print a periodical of occasional character, there could scarcely be enough to talk about to justify frequency or regularity in either meetings or publications."

Most organizations have priorities which they evaluate and reorder in keeping with professional goals and social change. The ALA is no exception. The Association's highest current priorities are intellectual freedom, social responsibility, manpower, legislation, planning, research and development, democratization, and reorganization.

The priority of intellectual freedom is managed through three different organizational components: the Intellectual Freedom Committee; the Office for Intellectual Freedom; and the Freedom to Read Foundation. The Committee was established in 1940 "to recommend such steps as may be necessary to safeguard the rights of library users, libraries and librarians, in accordance with the First Amendment of the United States Constitution and the Library Bill of Rights." The Office for Intellectual Freedom, es-

---

*President, American Library Association.

tablished in 1967, operates with the goal of educating librarians about the importance of the concept of intellectual freedom. Toward this end, the Office serves as the administrative arm of the Committee and bears responsibility for implementing ALA policies in intellectual freedom, as approved by the ALA Council. The Freedom to Read Foundation was incorporated in November 1969, in response to the increased interest of ALA members in having machinery to support and defend librarians whose jobs were jeopardized because they challenged violations of intellectual freedom. A primary objective is to set legal precedents for the freedom to read. The Foundation was established outside the structure of the ALA but is closely affiliated with ALA through its board of trustees and executive director, who also serves as the director of the Office for Intellectual Freedom. Through the combined efforts of the Intellectual Freedom Committee, the Office for Intellectual Freedom, and the Freedom to Read Foundation, the American Library Association carries on a total program to promote and defend intellectual freedom. (For information on ALA's activities in intellectual freedom, see Berninghausen's article, "The Struggle for Intellectual Freedom in 1971," this volume.)

Within the area of social responsibility the membership of the ALA has expressed deep concern for the inadequacy of library service to the disadvantaged of the country. The Social Responsibilities Round Table of the ALA has been a prime mover in pressing for response to the needs of the disadvantaged and unserved. At this point in U.S. history, there is widespread concern with relieving the poverty of a large number of our citizens and with upgrading the education and employment possibilities of those who have been discriminated against because of their race, color, or religious belief. Development of library service to the disadvantaged has been accepted by the ALA as a major goal for as long as it shall be necessary. The ALA Coordinating Committee on Library Service to the Disadvantaged is working with divisions and committees of the entire Association to bring their activities in this field into a unified program of significant impact. Further, in the development of such a unified program, it was recommended by the Activities Committee on New Directions that an ALA Office for Library Service to the Disadvantaged and Unserved be established. At the 1971 Annual Conference funds were appropriated to inaugurate a coordinated program of library service to the disadvantaged and unserved. The responsibility for the program has been assigned temporarily to the Executive Secretary of the Association of Hospital and Institution Libraries, who will act as a coordinator for these services until the new Office is fully funded and developed.

Another major priority of the ALA is manpower. This is defined not just in terms of personnel, but with regard to manpower activities in general. On the basis of recommendations made by the membership, plans are being made to establish an Office of Library Manpower to be responsible for programs relating to all aspects of library manpower including, but not limited to, recruitment, education and training, salaries, status, welfare, employment practices, tenure, ethics, and other personnel concerns. The Office will also be involved in the establishment of standards and the development of sanctions for enforcement of policies and standards. This new Office will bring together the functions of the present Office for Library Education and the Office for Recruitment, as well as certain action responsibilities now resting with other committees, divisions, and round tables. In addition, a committee known as the Staff Committee on Mediation, Arbitration, and Inquiry was appointed in December 1970 to handle complaints and conduct inquiries relating to tenure, ethics, fair employment practices and due process, ethical practices, and the principles of intellectual freedom as set forth in policies adopted by the Council of the American Library Association. This committee, which meets almost weekly, was established in response to the long-standing and intense concern of the membership regarding such matters. It functions as the action arm of the Committee on Policy and Implementation. This latter Committee was established to assure the ALA Council and the membership of full implementation of the program of mediation, arbitration, and inquiry.

Another major committee appointed as a result of the Association's self-analysis was the Committee on Planning. The statement of responsibility for this committee is as follows: "to provide to membership information and recommendations to assist in the periodic selection of goals; to provide the Association with a structured and identifiable feed-back mechanism for detecting future trends and needs by developing methods of involving individual members and units in the planning process; to provide the guidelines for program evaluation necessary to the Committee on Program Evaluation and Support in its budget-making process; to select and define long-range and short-range objectives; to plan and recommend to the Council projects designed to meet objectives, and to establish stated criteria and methods of evaluation of such projects; and to identify and involve the appropriate units of ALA for participation in specific projects to carry out the Association's objectives."

The priorities discussed here grew largely from membership action taken at the 1969 Annual Conference of the Association. Historically this process of restructuring and reordering of priorities has been a continuous process of the Association. Throughout its existence it has been rather constantly engaged in self-examination of its purpose and structure. These examinations have been conducted in several ways, usually by "activities" committees from the membership. There has been one comprehensive study by a management firm and separate studies of different units of ALA by members and outside firms. It could be said, then, that the American Library Association has rigorously examined itself on the average of about once every 15 years. The present Association has evolved from this continued study by members and by persons and agencies from outside the organization.

In the process of establishing its highest current priorities, the American Library Association reaffirmed in 1970 that it would continue to be an organization for both librarians and libraries, with the overall objective of promoting and improving library service and librarianship. This was a most important decision since it rejected the concept of reorganizing as an exclusively professional organization rather than maintaining ALA's traditional role of an educational association with membership open to institutions, trustees, and interested persons, as well as librarians.

Further, this decision established the base line for ALA's current self-analysis, which is focused mainly on reorganization and further democratization of the organization. The criteria that have been suggested in connection with further study of the organizational structure reveal rather sharply the current developments and the direction of development in the objectives, structure, and functions of the ALA. These criteria emphasize that the structure of the ALA should be oriented to program and to implement priorities acknowledged by the membership, and that any acceptable plan of reorganization should encourage and facilitate meaningful and productive membership participation. Further, there must be sufficient flexibility to provide for early budgetary response and for on-going evaluation of policy, program, and structure. Finally, any acceptable plan of reorganization must enable the staff of the ALA to work toward organization objectives, effectively and efficiently, using the highest level of their abilities. Clearly, responsiveness, membership participation, flexibility, and effective utilization of the ALA staff will continue to be central to the future growth and development of the American Library Association.

The current program of reorganizing and restructuring the ALA has included various actions, among which was a major step toward a democratization of the operation of the Association through its Council. The 1971 Annual Conference saw the Council vote itself out of existence following the 1972 Conference. The Council will be reconstituted in 1972 as a body of 100 members elected at large, plus one Councilor representing each chapter and elected for a term of four years by ALA members in the chapter. There will be no fewer than two candidates for each Council position; these candidates will be chosen by the nominating committee or by petition of the members.

The current status and direction of development of the American Library Association reflects the members' concerns for the people they serve and wish to reach with relevant library services. Nearly all of the membership's concerns are reflected with remarkable clarity in the current priorities of the American Library Association. Recent and current self-examinations of the ALA by its members and government suggest strongly that without the benefit of continuous reevaluation of purpose, goals, and mechanisms for achieving these goals, any professional organization can fall only too readily into a quagmire of self-satisfaction and smugness.

THE SPECIAL LIBRARIES ASSOCIATION
by
F. E. McKenna*

Special Libraries Association is an association of individuals and organizations with educational, scientific, and literary interests in library and information service and in information science and technology — especially as they apply to the selection, recording, and retrieval of knowledge. It is an international organization of approximately 7,000 professional librarians and information experts. Special libraries serve industry, business, research, educational and technical institutions, government, special departments of public and university libraries, newspapers, museums, and all organizations, both public and private, requiring or providing specialized information. The Association encourages and promotes the utilization of knowledge through the collection, organization, and dissemination of information.

Through its programs and publications the Association constantly encourages its members and others to increase their own professional capabilities and performance. Continuing education seminars keep members and other interested persons informed of new developments in techniques and sophisticated equipment. The Association seeks to stimulate research leading to improved and more sophisticated information services.

SLA facilitates communications among its members through the Association's unique information network of Chapters and Divisions. Soon after the Association was organized in 1909, its structure of Chapters and Divisions was initiated. This SLA network has been frequently updated in response to the needs of new informational requirements.

WHAT IS A SPECIAL LIBRARY?

A clear and distinct definition has not been developed for special libraries be-

---

*Executive Director, Special Libraries Association.

cause of the many and diverse subspecies of specialized libraries that exist. The following statements in italics attempt to define a specialized library:[1]

1. *A special subject collection.* This phrase defines the subject (or subjects) of the collection. One of the major misunderstandings about specialized libraries is the idea that each one is a special subject collection. A special subject can define a special collection, but a special subject alone is not sufficient to define a specialized library. Perhaps the subject approach was adequate 50 years ago; in 1972 it is a relatively naive approach.

2. *A special subject collection or a collection in a special format.* This second attempt at definition tries to incorporate the concept of nonbook materials such as maps, pictures, clippings, government documents, patents, research notebooks, musical scores, sound recordings, microforms, etc. The informational content is rarely dependent on the form of storage.

3. *A specialized collection organized for use by a specialized clientele.* This definition begins to recognize the user as an integral part of a specialized library. More importantly, it recognizes that the collection must be organized to meet the needs of specialized users.

4. *A specialized collection organized so as to anticipate the specialized services required by a specialized clientele.* An important operative factor enters the definition: the anticipation of the clients' needs by the library staff.

5. *A specialized service so organized as to anticipate — or to be quickly responsive to — the specialized needs of its specialized clientele.* By replacing "collection" with "service," this definition does not imply simply that a desk and telephone have replaced the collection. It recognizes that no collection (regardless of size) can have all necessary informational materials in stock. Here the specialized library is already acting as a switching point in a network to reach information located elsewhere. The operative and distinctive words in this definition are "quickly responsive."

Specialized service, anticipation of client needs, and quick response to such needs characterize the specialized library. An outstanding specialized library will have stretched the dimension of time still further. The library will have alerted its clients to the existence of new information before its clients know that new information exists.

SPECIAL LIBRARIES ARE A NORTH AMERICAN INVENTION

Historians of the library scene ascribe diverse beginnings to the concept of specialized libraries; a collection of clay tablets in pre-Biblical times and the monastic collections of the Middle Ages have both been cited. Our concept of specialized library services — especially when we include responsiveness to a need — can be recognized as a distinctly American phenomenon which began about the time of the Revolutionary War and has continued its evolution up to the present time. The concept has now been exported to every nation on earth.

Specialized libraries have been most frequently established to meet an unsatisfied need for information. Such changes in focus are often related to new areas of man's endeavors. Specialized libraries may be discontinued when a need no longer exists, or the library may completely reorient its objectives to meet new needs.

Examples of the changing needs of society can be traced in the terminology of the organic units of Special Libraries Association. In the early 1920s there were financial libraries, insurance libraries, newspaper, civics, technology, and advertising-industrial-commercial libraries. By the 1930s the civics libraries had been renamed social science libraries. Museum libraries had come into existence. In the 1940s the libraries of publishing companies were differentiated from newspaper libraries, and business

---

[1] The term "specialized library" rather than "special library" will be used to avoid confusion with the name of the Association and to emphasize an operational concept.

libraries were distinguished from libraries in financial institutions.

The advent of World War II created a real need for map and transportation libraries. With the development of the wonder drugs, pharmaceutical libraries were recognized as an urgent need.

The growth of commercial radio led to electrical communications libraries in the 1930s. With World War II, electrical engineering was emphasized in general, as well as the more sophisticated developments of radar, sonar, and television. In recent years the emphasis has moved once again to a different kind of engineering, that is, aerospace libraries.

During World War II, reports on government defense contracts generated a voluminous collection of documentary reports. Many, if not all, report libraries were in research installations where punched card equipment was available. The documents librarians began to experiment with machine indexing of these crucial reports. Almost all of today's know-how in computerized information storage and retrieval has its roots in the experimental investigations by the documents librarians of the 1950s. Information science, in its present state, is largely the outgrowth of the early experiments in specialized libraries where electromechanical equipment was then available.

The concept of specialized library services has been exported from the United States and Canada to virtually all parts of the globe. In 1924 visitors from England attended an SLA Conference. They were so impressed with these concepts that they returned home and organized ASLIB (Association of Special Libraries and Information Bureaus). In 1972, the Special Libraries Association of Japan observes its twentieth anniversary. In Germany, India, and Israel there are well-established organizations of special libraries. Sections for special libraries exist in almost all national library associations. It will be astonishing if specialized libraries are not found in the People's Republic of China when contacts are established during the coming years.

SLA DURING 1971

For SLA, 1971 was a year of consolidation and of organizational changes, many of which had been initiated in the past few years. Perhaps one of the most important changes was the amended Bylaws, which now simplify the admission requirements. For example, a library school graduate is now eligible to be a Member even if he is not employed in a special library. From December 31, 1970 to December 31, 1971 the number of members increased by 133, from 6,710 to 6,843. By December 31, 1971 there were already 369 new member applications processed for 1972.

The organization of Student Groups has been authorized by SLA's Board of Directors. Four Student Groups have already been formally organized, at Simmons College, the State University of New York at Albany, North Texas State University, and Southern Illinois University. Continuing inquiries from both faculty and student leaders indicate enthusiastic interest in student participation in SLA as a professional association.

The Association's fiscal year has been changed to coincide with the membership year (i.e., the calendar year), and the accounting has been changed from a cash basis to a more sophisticated accrual basis. Membership and subscription records have been converted from EAM to an IBM System/3 computer which is better able to cope with the details of SLA's Chapter and Division structure.

Continuing the consolidation efforts begun in 1970, additional committees which were no longer useful, or which did not contribute to the Association's total efforts, were discontinued. To insure greater relevance to committee activity, members of the Board of Directors have been assigned as proctors for each committee. Thus, Board intentions and committee actions are focused on the same objectives.

Since 1969 a joint committee of SLA and ASIS (American Society for Information Science) had discussed the possibility of a merger of the two organizations. Based on the results of a straw ballot in April 1971, the Board decided to accept the recommendations of the SLA members of the joint committee that "the discussion of merger of SLA and ASIS should be discontinued and the Joint Merger Committee should be dissolved." This decision was based on the following points. Twenty-nine percent of the questionnaires were returned (i.e., of the 6,624 mailed, 4,679 were not returned). Of the ballots received, 54 percent were in favor of merger; 38 percent were against merger; 7 percent were undecided. The total of those against or undecided is 45 percent, which is the most significant fact in the results of the tally because it shows there is no clear mandate to continue merger discussions. The Board acted after three years of discussion, during which time a specific merger plan was developed for consideration by the Advisory Council, the Chapters, and finally by the individual members through a straw ballot. No mandate for continuing negotiations was expressed by the membership and the Board has decided to discontinue further discussions. In July the ASIS Council adopted a similar act regarding the merger discussions.

The softening of the general economy in early 1971 affected special librarians. As manpower cutbacks occurred — especially in defense- and space-related industries, some special librarians were terminated. Although such terminations are a matter of real concern, there emerged one important optimistic observation. For the first time, the number of special librarians employed by any one organization had increased to such a point that they were furloughed or terminated in proportion to the engineers, technicians, scientists, etc. who were found to be surplus. Two free ads in *Special Libraries* were made available to unemployed members, but only 12 persons made use of this free service during 1971. SLA's annual Employment Clearing House was again in operation during the San Francisco Conference in June; more than 80 job openings were listed, but only about 50 job-seekers had registered. It is difficult to evaluate the unemployment picture from information available.

"Position Open" ads in *Special Libraries* had decreased in midyear, but had begun to build up again toward the year's end. SLA's most recent salary survey (*Special Libraries,* July/August 1970) gave important salary guidance to employers. Furthermore, no ads are accepted where the minimum is below $9,000 for positions in the United States or $8,500 in Canada.

In spite of the recession, Conference registration in San Francisco in June 1971 was 1,650. Although this figure was below the projected 1,800, it was well above the 1,450 registrants in Detroit in 1970. Even though exhibitor budgets were also adversely affected by the recession, more than 80 exhibitor booths were alive with active inquiries by registrants during the Conference.

SLA's Continuing Education Seminars were again an important attraction in the Conference program; 235 persons registered for the day-long seminars.

The official journal of the Association, *Special Libraries,* with its new editor, Janet D. Bailey, continued its broadened editorial policy. As a result, the journal attracted manuscripts from both members and nonmembers from all parts of the world. Two other periodical publications continue to provide important information to their subscribers: *Technical Book Review Index* (in its 37th year) and *Scientific Meetings* (in its 15th year). Beginning with the January 1971 issue, SLA ceased to be the publisher of *Translations Register-Index.* The publication of this semimonthly has been transferred to the National Translations Center at John Crerar Library (Chicago). SLA continues to be one of three sponsors of *Information Science Abstracts* (formerly *Documentation Abstracts*); the other two sponsors are the American Society for Information Science and the American Chemical Society/Division of Chemical Literature.

SLA's book publication program resulted in three new titles in 1971: *The Effective Echo: A Dictionary of Advertising Slogans,* Valerie Noble, 176 pp. $8.00; *A Basic Collection for Scientific and Technical Libraries,* Effie B. Lunsford and Theodore J. Kopkin, 288 pp. $12.95; *Map Collections in the United States and Canada: A Directory.* 2nd ed. David K. Carrington, 159 pp. $7.00.

The 1971 SLA Hall of Fame award was presented to Ruth S. Leonard, recently retired from the Simmons College faculty, and Herman H. Henkle, director of the John Crerar Library, Chicago, before his retirement. The SLA Professional Award was not presented in 1971.

Three $2,500 scholarships were awarded to outstanding students.

SLA continues its cooperation with other organizations through its membership in CNLA, IFLA, International Federation for Documentation, American Federation of Information Processing Societies, American Association for the Advancement of Science, and with representation or cross-representation with ALA, ANSI, ASIS, Federal Library Committee, Medical Library Association, National Microfilm Association, National Translations Center, Theater Library Association, U.S. Book Exchange, and the UN Non-Governmental Observers Organization.

THE ERIC CLEARINGHOUSE ON LIBRARY AND INFORMATION SCIENCES

by

Charles W. Hoover*

THE ERIC PROGRAM

The ERIC program, part of the National Center for Educational Communication in the Office of Education, is a national information system dedicated to furthering the progress of education through making information on education available to a wide variety of users. The ERIC system is decentralized, with a total of 19 clearinghouses scattered throughout the country. Each clearinghouse responds to the information needs of its professional clientele with appropriate services and acitvities. Basic functions of all clearinghouses include: (1) Acquisition of all significant documentary materials in the assigned field of specialization, with some emphasis on securing current "fugitive" materials such as reports, speeches, conference proceedings, and instructional materials. (2) Acquisition of documents which are evaluated and appropriate items selected for national subject control through listing in *Research in Education.* (3) Participation in the production of *Research in Education,* a monthly publication of the Government Printing Office (domestic subscription $21.00, foreign $26.25). All documents listed in this bibliography are indexed by personal author, institution, and subject, along with an informative abstract of approximately 200 words. Responsibility for copy preparation of *Research in Education* is contracted to Leasco Systems and Research Corporation, which receives copy from the clearinghouses, edits it, and prepares a camera-ready tape for printing. Unless subject to copyright restrictions, the documents are microfilmed and made available to the public through the ERIC Document Reproduction Service, contracted to Leasco Information Products,

---

*Chief, Educational Resources Information Center, U.S. Office of Education, Washington, D.C. 20202.

Inc., in either microfiche or hard copy form. (4) Participation in the production of the monthly publication *Current Index to Journals in Education*. Clearinghouses and the CCM Information Corporation cover approximately 575 education journals through indexing by personal author and subject, as well as annotations where considered necessary. Hard copy is furnished to CCM for preparation of camera-ready tape, printing, and distribution. The *Current Index to Journals in Education* also contains a Source Journal Index and a Journal Contents Index. (5) Dissemination of information, primarily in the form of publications such as newsletters, annotated and critical bibliographies, review articles, state-of-the-art reports, and other analytical publications. (6) Provision of reference and retrieval services. Because of the size of the clientele for ERIC services, it is not possible to respond to all individual requests for information. Individual clearinghouses, within available resources, may attempt to provide reference service on the scene, by telephone, and by mail. A major goal of the ERIC system is to anticipate major needs of the educational community through preparation of bibliographic and analytical information designed to meet those needs in advance.

ERIC/CLIS

The ERIC Clearinghouse on Library and Information Sciences (ERIC/CLIS) is one of 19 decentralized information centers which comprise the Educational Resources Information Center (ERIC) of the U.S. Office of Education. Originally established at the University of Minnesota in 1967, the Clearinghouse operation was transferred in 1970 to the American Society for Information Science.

ERIC/CLIS is responsible for information pertaining to all aspects of the information transfer process, through research, application, development, and education. Included in these concepts are such areas as the management, operation, and use of libraries and information centers; the technology used to improve their operations; and the education and training of librarians and information specialists.

ERIC/CLIS is dedicated to the development of various services and products to meet the information needs of the library, information science, and educational communities. It has responsibility for acquiring, indexing, abstracting, and making available copies of studies of current research and research-related work in the field of library and information sciences. ERIC/CLIS processes over 100 titles per month, of which 60 are announced in *Research in Education (RIE)*, and indexes articles from approximately 20 professional journals for *Current Index to Journals in Education (CIJE)*. Coverage is to be expanded in 1972.

Currently in preparation by the CCM Information Corporation is a "microlibrary" of titles which have been announced in *RIE* relating to topics in library and information science. The micro-library is composed of a printed index and microfiche copies of relevant documents, arranged in numerical sequence in a special case. This special package of materials will be available from CCM in 1972.

Also, beginning in January 1972, titles processed by ERIC/CLIS are included in a new NTIS (National Technical Information System) announcement publication. The publication, which began on a semimonthly subscription basis in January 1972, is a new section of the NTIS Government Report Topical Announcements (GRTA) and carries the subject title *Library and Information Sciences*. The new section provides a central source for announcing the availability of both government-sponsored documents (NTIS) and nongovernment or "fugitive" literature (ERIC/CLIS) on library and information science topics.

Acting in response to expressed needs of the professional community, the Clearinghouse program also includes activities focused on the repackaging and special analysis of information gathered.

Literature reviews, state-of-the-art reports, and specialized bibliographies are developed under the direction of ERIC/CLIS.

Over 20 information analysis publications have been completed thus far, and for 1972, 25 additional publications are planned, dealing with such topics as library services to specialized groups, networks, and professional education of library and information scientists. A list of ERIC/CLIS information analysis publications is available upon request.

ERIC/CLIS seeks two copies of any current documentary materials which represent important resources in library and information sciences — technical reports, conference proceedings, evaluation study reports, interpretive studies, and the like — for evaluation and possible inclusion in *Research in Education*. Documents for ERIC/CLIS may be sent to: ERIC Clearinghouse for Library and Information Sciences, 1140 Connecticut Avenue N.W., Suite 804, Washington, D.C. 20036.

ERIC CLEARINGHOUSES

Adult Education. Syracuse University, 107 Roney Lane, Syracuse, N.Y. 13210. Tel: 315-476-5541, ext. 3493. Adult education in public schools, colleges, and universities; activities carried on by national or community voluntary and service agencies; all areas of in-service training; fundamental and literary education for adults; correspondence study; continuing education in the professions.

Counseling and Personnel Services. Information Center, 611 Church Street, Room 3056, Ann Arbor, Mich. 48104. Tel: 313-764-9492. Preparation, practice, and supervision of counselors at all educational levels and in all settings; theoretical development of counseling and guidance; use and results of personnel procedures such as testing, interviewing, disseminating, and analyzing such information; group work and case work; nature of pupil, student and adult characteristics; personnel workers and their relation to career planning, family consultations, and student orientation activities.

Disadvantaged. Information Retrieval Center on the Disadvantaged, Teachers College, Columbia University, Box 40, 525 West 120 Street, New York, N.Y. 10027. Tel: 212-870-4808. Effects of disadvantaged experiences and environment, from birth onward; academic, intellectual, and social performance of disadvantaged children and youth from grade 3 through college entrance; programs and practices which provide learning experiences designed to compensate for special problems of disadvantaged; issues, programs, and practices related to economic and ethnic discrimination, segregation, desegregation, and integration in education; issues, programs, and materials related to redressing the curriculum imbalance in the treatment of ethnic minority groups.

Early Childhood Education. University of Illinois, 805 W. Pennsylvania Avenue, Urbana, Ill. 61801. Tel: 217-333-1386. Prenatal factors, parental behavior; the physical, psychological, social, educational, and cultural development of children from birth through the primary grades; educational theory, research, and practice related to the development of young children.

Educational Management. University of Oregon, Eugene, Ore. 97403. Tel: 503-686-5043. Leadership, management, and structure of public and private educational organizations; practice and theory of administration; preservice and in-service preparation of administrators, tasks, and processes of administration; methods and varieties of organization, organization change, and social context of the organization. Sites, buildings, and equipment for education; planning, financing, constructing, renovating, equipping, maintaining, operating, insuring, utilizing, and evaluating educational facilities.

Educational Media and Technology. Institute for Communication Research, Cypress Hall, Stanford University, Stanford, Calif. 94305. Tel: 415-321-2300, ext. 3345. Individualized instruction; systems approaches; film, television, radio; programmed instruction, computers in education, and miscellaneous audio-visual means of teaching. Technology in instruction and technology in society when clearly relevant to education.

Exceptional Children. Council for Exceptional Children, 1411 South Jefferson Davis Highway, Suite 900, Arlington, Va. 22202. Tel: 703-521-8820. Aurally, visually, mentally, and physically handicapped; emotionally disturbed, speech handicapped, learning disabilities, and the gifted; behavioral, psychomotor, and communication disorders, administration of special education services; preparation and continuing education of professional and paraprofessional personnel; preschool learning and development of the exceptional; general studies on creativity.

Higher Education. George Washington University, One Dupont Circle, Suite 630, Washington, D.C. 20036. Tel: 202-296-2597. Various subjects relating to college and university students, college and university conditions and problems, college and university programs. Curricular and instructional problems and programs, faculty, institutional research, federal programs, professional education (medical, law, etc.), graduate education, university extension programs, teaching-learning, planning, governance, finance, evaluation, interinstitutional arrangements, and management of higher educational institutions.

Junior Colleges. University of California, Powell Library, Room 96, 405 Hilgard Avenue, Los Angeles, Calif. 90024. Tel: 213-825-3931. Development, administration, and evaluation of public and private community junior colleges. Junior college students, staff, curricula, programs, libraries, and community services.

Languages and Linguistics. Modern Language Association of America, 62 Fifth Avenue, New York, N.Y. 10011. Tel: 212-691-3200. Instructional methodology, psychology of language learning, cultural and intercultural content, application of linguistics, curricular problems and developments, teacher training and qualifications, language sciences, psycholinguistics, theoretical and applied linguistics, language pedagogy, bilingualism, and commonly and uncommonly taught languages including English for speakers of other languages.

Library and Information Sciences. American Society for Information Science, 1140 Connecticut Avenue N.W., Suite 804, Washington, D.C. 20036. Tel: 202-659-3778. Various detailed aspects of information retrieval, library and information processing, library services, library and information systems, information utilization, publishing industry, terminology, library facilities and information centers, library materials and equipment, librarian and information science personnel, library organizations, and library education.

Reading. 200 Pine Hall, School of Education, Indiana University, Bloomington, Ind. 47401. Tel: 812-337-9101. All aspects of reading behavior with emphasis on physiology, psychology, sociology, and teaching. Instructional materials, curricula, tests and measurement, preparation of reading teachers and specialists, and methodology at all levels. Role of libraries and other agencies in fostering and guiding reading. Diagnostic and remedial services in school and clinical settings.

Rural Education and Small Schools. Box 3 AP, New Mexico State University, Las Cruces, N.M. 88001. Tel: 505-646-2623. Education of American Indians, Mexican Americans, Spanish Americans, and migratory farm workers and their children; outdoor education; economic, cultural, social and other factors related to educational programs in rural areas and small schools; disadvantaged of rural and small school populations.

Science, Mathematics, and Environmental Education. Ohio State University, 1460 West Lane Avenue, Columbus, Ohio 43221. Tel: 614-422-6717. All levels of science, mathematics, and environmental education; development of curriculum and instructional materials; media applications, impact of interest, intelligence, values, and concept development upon learning; preservice and in-service teacher education and supervision.

Social Studies/Social Science Education. University of Colorado, 970 Aurora Avenue, Boulder, Col. 80302. Tel: 303-443-2211, ext. 8434. All levels of social studies and social science; all activities relating to teachers; content of disciplines; applications of learning theory, curriculum theory, child development theory, and instructional theory; research and development programs; special needs of student groups; education as a social science; social studies/social science and the community.

Teacher Education. One Dupont Circle, Suite 616, Washington, D.C. 20036. Tel: 202-293-7280. School personnel at all levels; all issues from selection through preservice and in-service preparation and training to retirement; curricula; educational theory and philosophy; general education not specifically covered by Educational Management Clearinghouse; Title XI NDEA Institutes not covered by subject specialty in other ERIC Clearinghouses.

Teaching of English. 1111 Kenyon Road, Urbana, Ill. 61801. Tel: 217-328-3870. Skills of English, including speaking, listening, writing, and reading (as it relates to English instruction); content of English, including composition, literature, and linguistics; methodology of English teaching; speech and public speaking; teaching of English at all levels; preparation of English teachers; preparation of specialists in English education and teaching of English; teaching of English to speakers of nonstandard dialects.

Tests, Measurement, and Evaluation. Educational Testing Service, Princeton, N.J. 08540. Tel: 609-921-9000, ext. 2691. Tests and other measurement devices; evaluation procedures and techniques; application of tests, measurement, or evaluation in educational projects or programs.

Vocational and Technical Education. Ohio State University, 1900 Kenny Road, Columbus, Ohio 43210. Tel: 614-486-3655. Agricultural education, business and office occupations education, distributive education, health occupations education, home economics education, technical education, trade and industrial education, subprofessional fields, industrial arts education, manpower economics, occupational psychology, occupational sociology, and all matters related to the foregoing.

THE COMMITTEE ON SCIENTIFIC AND TECHNICAL INFORMATION

by

Melvin S. Day[*]

ORIGIN

On May 22, 1962, the Federal Council for Science and Technology, chaired by the President's Special Assistant for Science and Technology, established the Committee on Science Information (COSI) in response to the growing concern both within and outside the government over the problems in management and dissemination of information created by the rapid growth of scientific and technical activities. The Committee was charged with (1) coordinating federal agency scientific and technical information services; (2) examining interrelationships of existing information services,

---

[*]Chairman, Committee on Scientific and Technical Information, Office of Science Information Service, National Science Foundation, Washington, D.C. 20550.

both in and outside the government, and identifying gaps or unnecessary overlaps; and (3) developing government-wide standards and compatibility among information systems.

In 1964, the COSI charter was revised and the Committee was given its present name, The Committee on Scientific and Technical Information (COSATI).

CHARTER

The following is the charter of COSATI granted on February 11, 1964, by the Federal Council for Science and Technology.

"The Committee on Scientific and Technical Information (COSATI) is a committee of the Federal Council for Science and Technology. The primary objective of COSATI is the development among the Executive agencies, of a coordinated, but decentralized scientific and technical information system for scientists, engineers, and other technical professions. As a secondary objective COSATI will be concerned with coordination and cooperation with improved Federal and National systems for handling scientific and technical information.

"COSATI will, within the priorities indicated by the above objectives, carry out the following activities pertaining to scientific and technical information: (1) Identify the problems and requirements; (2) Review the adequacy and scope of present programs; (3) Devise or review new programs and other measures to meet the requirements and solve the problems; (4) Recommend standards, methodology, and systems for uniform adoption by the Executive agencies; (5) Identify and recommend assignments of responsibility among the Executive agencies; (6) Review and make recommendations concerning the resources assigned to the programs of the Executive agencies; (7) Recommend management policies to improve the quality and vigor of the information activities; (8) Generally facilitate interagency coordination at management levels.

"Appropriate provision will be made for the Committee to include in its deliberations both technical and operational personnel conversant with technical information requirements and problems of scientists and engineers. The Committee will be assisted as needed by task groups and panels of personnel selected from inside and outside the Federal Government. It will coordinate its efforts with other committees and groups whose programs may affect scientific and technical information."

THE ORGANIZATION OF COSATI

COSATI consists of members representing 12 federal departments and agencies, the largest scientific and technical information producers and users in the government. In addition, about two dozen observers represent many smaller agencies or subordinate components of the principal member agency. In recent years, the chairman and executive secretary have been staff members of the Office of Science and Technology, Executive Office of the President. In July 1971, administrative responsibility and operation of COSATI were transferred to the National Science Foundation's Office of Science Information Service.

Most of the work of COSATI is carried on by Panels and Work Groups, each assigned a specific task or mission. Membership in the Panels and Work Groups includes both federal agency representatives and nongovernment specialists in various aspects of information sciences and related fields. There are about 200 to 250 individuals who attend meetings and work on COSATI programs.

The membership in COSATI and its Panels and Work Groups changes from time to time to reflect changes in the organization of the federal government, the state of technology, and the general focus of information programs.

Panels are continuing bodies, charged with studying and reporting on an assigned subject area over an extended period of time. A Work Group is generally assigned a specific mission and is dissolved upon its completion. Ad Hoc Panels or Work Groups may be named to consider whether a more permanent group is needed, and, if so, to define its charter.

Presently active (1971) Panels and Work Groups consist of the following: Panel on Information Systems Management (includes former Panel on Operational Techniques and Systems and Panel on Management of Information Activities); Panel on International Information Activities; Panel on Information Analysis Centers; Panel on Legal Aspects of Information Systems; Panel on Library Programs; Ad Hoc Task Group on Chemical Information Systems.

Other Panels and Work Groups, no longer active, concerned themselves with information sciences technology, education and training, synoptic data, national systems, dissemination of information, and technology utilization.

SIGNIFICANT ACHIEVEMENTS

In the area of bibliographic control, COSATI developed and saw adopted a government-wide standard for descriptive cataloging of technical reports produced by the research and development agencies. A guideline for a standard format for technical reports was also developed. *Corporate Author Headings* (COSATI Panel on Operational Techniques and Systems, August 1970, COSATI — 70-7) is a tool for and a by-product of the implementation of the COSATI Guidelines for Descriptive Cataloging. The COSATI Subject Category List, first produced in 1964 as a uniform subject arrangement for distribution of scientific and technical reports issued or sponsored by Executive Branch agencies, has undergone extensive modification and is in use both within and outside the government. All of these actions have contributed to improved federal scientific information dissemination programs.

In 1965, COSATI produced the first federal microfiche standard, which called for a 20-to-1 size reduction. In 1971, COSATI agreed to revise the standard to 24-to-1 with a 98-image format, thus bringing the federal standard into conformity with the National Microfilm Association standard. It was agreed that the federal agencies would make the shift according to their own timetables and as their resources permit.

COSATI and its Panels and Work Groups have initiated a number of nationwide meetings as a means of stimulating better communication on information problems and of relating more effectively federal information activities to those information activities in the private sector. For example, the Panel on Library Programs, in cooperation with the Association of Research Libraries, the Federal Library Committee, and the U.S. Office of Education, has sponsored two conferences in 1970 and 1971 on Federal Information Resources. Other conferences have included a National Engineering Information Conference (1969), a Seminar on Foci for Progress in Scientific Publications (1969), and two Forums on Information Analysis Centers (1967 and 1971).

A government-wide policy on "page charges," designed as a general guideline for all federal agencies to assist in their handling of requests for financial assistance to nonprofit, extragovernmental scientific and technical publications, was recommended to and endorsed by the Federal Council.

At the recommendation of COSATI, the Federal Council for Science and Technology asked the National Bureau of Standards to establish the National Standard Reference Data System to coordinate the collection and evaluation of numerical data in the physical and engineering sciences and to ensure that evaluated data are readily available to all users.

In recognition of the need for a centralized program for announcement and dissemination of scientific and technical reports produced by federal agencies, and at the recommendation of the Federal Council, the Commerce Department's Office of Technical Services was transformed into the Clearinghouse for Federal Scientific and Technical Information, precursor organization of today's National Technical Information Service.

In the area of international exchange of information, COSATI and its Panel on International Information Activities have developed policies and guidelines governing the foreign dissemination of scientific and technical information, the utilization of special foreign currencies for international scientific communication, the exchange of magnetic tapes containing bibliographic information with foreign groups and countries by federal agencies, and the announcement and dissemination of translations.

During 1971, COSATI provided a national forum for the development of the U.S. position on the recommendations of the ICSU-UNESCO UNISIST study on the feasibility of creating a worldwide science information system. The forum assisted the development of the U.S. position from advice provided by representatives from both public and private institutions, reflecting the mutual involvement of government, profit, and nonprofit organizations that characterizes information activities in the United States.

On the legal aspects of information systems, a special bibliography on copyright, prepared in 1967, has been expanded into a comprehensive reference bibliography that will be published in late 1971. A major Conference on Legal Aspects of National and International Computerized Information Systems is planned for spring 1972 to present the culmination of a number of study efforts, including problems of right of privacy, antitrust, right of access, copyright, and proprietary rights.

With the transfer of the stewardship of COSATI to the National Science Foundation, at the end of 1971 a COSATI Review Group was organized to examine COSATI's goals, objectives and functions in light of the information challenges of the 1970s. It is expected that the problems facing the federal information community and the nation will receive even greater attention in the future at the highest levels of the federal government, so that information may be more effectively disseminated and utilized in the pursuit of major national and international objectives.

For complete information on COSATI activities over the past nine years, see the COSATI annual reports (a list of which follows) available from the National Technical Information Service, Springfield, Va. 22151. The COSATI Annual Report for 1970 contains a complete annotated bibliography of COSATI publications.

BIBLIOGRAPHY

Progress in Scientific and Technical Communications, Annual Report 1970. (COSATI 71-1) 146 pp. (PB 202 448).

Progress of the United States Government in Scientific and Technical Communications — 1969 (COSATI Annual Report for 1969). November 1970, 166 pp. (COSATI-70-3; PB 193 386).

Progress in Scientific and Technical Communications — 1968 Annual Report. October 1969, 99 pp. (COSATI-69-5; PB 186 400).

Progress of the United States Government in Scientific and Technical Communications — 1967 (COSATI Annual Report for 1967), 99 pp. (PB 180 867).

Progress of the United States Government in Scientific and Technical Communication — 1966 (COSATI Annual Report for 1966). October 1967, 39 pp. (PB 176 535).

Progress of the United States Government in Scientific and Technical Communication — 1965 (COSATI Annual Report, 1966), 48 pp. (PB 173 510).

"Summary Progress Report, September 1964." In Study Number IV, *Documentation of Research and Development Results; Report of the Select Committee on Government Research of the House of Representatives, 88th Congress, 2nd Session.* Appendix A, pp. 101-106, November 20, 1964.

Outline Scope of Activities of Committee on Scientific and Technical Information. Supplement No. 2. Committee on Scientific Information, January 1964.

Status Report on Scientific and Technical Information in the Federal Government. Committee on Scientific Information, June 1963, 27 pp. (PB 181 541; AD 411 939).

THE STRUGGLE FOR INTELLECTUAL FREEDOM IN 1971

by

David K. Berninghausen[*]

THE MAJOR BATTLE

The publication of the Pentagon Papers by the *New York Times* and other newspapers and the ensuing attempt by the administration to stop their publication was the major battle of 1971. These documents, variously classified as "Top-Secret Sensitive," "Top-Secret," and "Secret," consist of 47 volumes entitled *History of the U.S. Decision-Making Process on Vietnam Policy* (1945–67) and the one-volume *Command and Control Study of the Tonkin Gulf Incident* (1965).

On June 19, 1971, Judge Murray I. Gurfein, U.S. District Court, denied the U.S. Justice Department a permanent injunction to prohibit the *Times* from continuing to publish the series. Judge Gurfein concluded, "A cantankerous press, an obstinate press, an ubiquitous press must be suffered by those in authority in order to preserve the even greater values of freedom of expression and the right of the people to know."

In light of this decision we can still entertain the popularly held notion that we enjoy a "free press," yet it brings us up short to note that at various times the International Press Institute has surveyed the so-called "free" countries and disqualified the United States because of censorship barriers imposed by federal agencies which "over-classified" information.

Harold Lasswell, expert in communications, describes in his book *National Security and Individual Freedom* what happens when government officials become unwilling to risk releasing information, tending to classify almost everything:

"The continuing crisis gradually imposes a dimout on the sources and channels of public information. This is a result of the steady pressure of security consciousness in spite of the general admission that the public must have facts if it is to reach rational opinions on defense policy . . .

"If public information dries up, and the level of suspiciousness goes up, the first casualty is the man of independent mind. When the caliber of the news in the media is reduced, the honest man finds the ground slipping out from under his feet. He sees that he does not have the raw material of judgment. As the fog deepens from the progressive blackout of information, it is apparent to the citizen that he is less and less qualified for effective citizenship."

Fortunately for the man of independent mind, and for our still relatively free society, this battle in the struggle was won for free inquiry, and additional "raw material" on the Vietnam war is available to everyone.

Probably even some of the censors who get uptight about obscenity disapprove of the kind of overclassification described by Professor Lasswell. What is seldom if ever recognized by the censor focusing upon "lewd and filthy" literature or films is that censorship is contagious: if he is permitted to censor what he considers obscene and morally offensive, others will have license to censor what they consider politically or socially offensive.

ON THE OBSCENITY FRONT

There will always be attempts to censor "obscenity" (whatever that may be), and it seems important to re-emphasize the findings of the Report of the President's Commission on Obscenity and Pornography. Published in September 1970, this was the first major attempt to assess the reading of pornography in relation to behavior, but its recommendations were denounced before being effec-

---

[*] Director, Library School, University of Minnesota, Minneapolis; and former Chairman of the ALA Intellectual Freedom Committee 1948–1950, 1970–1971.

tively evaluated. (The President rejected its "morally bankrupt conclusions and recommendations"; only five members of the U.S. Senate refused to pass a negative judgment on a study that they had not read.) One of its major findings, however, that 60 percent of all adults believe that their own access to reading and viewing materials related to sex should not be restricted in any way, has already begun to influence public opinion. It seems probable that the conclusions and recommendations of this Report, especially the lack of evidence that there is a one-to-one causal relationship between viewing "obscenity" and "bad behavior," will eventually lead to more freedom for people of all ages to learn more about the sexual nature of the "naked ape." The work of William Lockhart, Chairman of the Commission, and the debate about the majority and the minority reports will help to dispel these erroneous notions we have held regarding obscenity and to free man to learn and understand more about himself.

H. L. Mencken seems to have provided a comment appropriate: "Human beings never welcome the news that something they have long cherished is untrue; they almost always reply to that news by reviling its promulgator. Nevertheless, a minority of bold and energetic men keep plugging away, and as a result of their hard labors and resultant infamy, the sum of human knowledge gradually increases."

It seems reasonable to predict that the majority report of the Commission, a voice of calm and reason on the passion-provoking subject of pornography, will in time be heard with the calm and reason it did not receive in 1970 and 1971.

THE AMERICAN LIBRARY ASSOCIATION JOINS IN THE OBSCENITY BATTLE

The ALA joined 30 other educational and professional groups in a statement emphasizing the importance of the Report, recommending it as material for serious study and debate. ALA also passed its own resolution in January 1971, urging all libraries to make the Report, including all its supporting volumes, available to all and to encourage people to read it and form their own private judgments.

ALA's Office for Intellectual Freedom followed up on the obscenity front by suggesting, in its October memorandum to chairmen of state intellectual freedom committees, that they write letters to their governors protesting against the current campaign of the Citizens for Decent Literature, who claim to have organized in 30 states. CDL urges the banning of various books and movies, most of which have never been found obscene in a court of law.

The ALA Committee on Intellectual Freedom moved into this fight by proposing at the Dallas Conference in June a new policy on challenged materials. Citing cases in Groton, Connecticut and New York, this policy, which was approved by ALA's Council, denies the authority of a local or state law enforcement agency to decree that a publication is obscene without an adversary hearing in a court of law, in accordance with well-established principles of law.

ON THE CIVIL RIGHTS FRONT

Although in 1971 the chief target of the censor was once again "obscenity," skirmishes flared up involving censorship in political and social issues — reminiscent of the McCarthy era.

In Ridgefield, Connecticut, 12 books were removed from classrooms and libraries due to complaints from "concerned parents" and a group calling itself the Ridgefield Taxpayers League. The books, used in English and social studies classes, were primarily anthologies dealing with controversial issues such as dissent, civil rights, religion, and women's rights. Authors included Carl Sandburg, George Wallace, and Malcolm X. The Ridgefield Teachers Association, with the support of the East Ridge Junior High PTA, objected to the removal of the books.

In New York William F. Buckley, Jr., challenged the constitutionality of a requirement that he join and pay dues to a private organization in order to appear regularly on television and radio.

Also in New York the state Civil Liberties Union (NYCLU) filed suit in federal court challenging the banning of *Down These Mean Streets* by the school board of District 25, Flushing, Queens. NYCLU lost its case, and has already begun an appeal.

In Danvers, Massachusetts, a resident charged in a letter to the editor of the local newspaper that the Danvers Public Library stocked books which advocated revolution. The more serious charge was that the library collection was unbalanced, representing primarily "left-wing books and newspapers" and anti-administration writings. The resident stated, "In summary: Granted, that with the funds at his disposal, a librarian must make a decision on what books he will order and what books he will not. My question is, why has this decision lately been in favor of extremist non-literature advocating violence and revolution and not well-written and well-recognized literature offering rational analysis and constructive solutions to the problems that confront us."

(In this case, the charges may be grounded on fact, or they may not be. The complainant could file a Request for Action with the American Library Association, which then might try to determine the facts. It is likely that in many cities library patrons will be distressed by the display of radical literature, especially underground newspapers, on the new book shelves. It is true that librarians are responsible for "balancing" the collection with representation of all points of view.)

BATTLES WON

Not all acts or attempts to restrict distribution of information were successful. For example:

In New York City's Washington Irving High School students were not permitted to distribute in the school the *Student Rights Handbook for New York City*, published by the N. Y. Civil Liberties Union. Alan H. Levine, director of the NYCLU student rights project, commented: "The suppression by school officials of free speech is a formula for explosion. If students cannot even work peacefully to distribute legal information, how can they work within the system." Fortunately, NYCLU's efforts to have student rights enforced in the school were successful (see September 1971 *Newsletter on Intellectual Freedom*).

In Sacramento a three-judge federal panel held unconstitutional and enjoined enforcement of part of the California education code which prohibits the unauthorized distribution of student publications on high school campuses. The court declared sections of the code to be overly broad and vague. It declared the regulation to be a "prohibition" rather than a "regulatory provision."

In Los Angeles two volunteer censors tried to impose their limited view of appropriate films in the public library. They tried, unsuccessfully, to ban 19 films that they did not like.

In Chapel Hill, North Carolina, a couple requested that *Black Like Me* be withdrawn from a junior high school because of the use of "offensive vocabulary." They also complained that the offer of one concerned parent to "proofread books" for the school and "clean up their library free of charge," was not accepted. Superintendent Wm. S. Cody said, "In view of the . . . way the material is handled by the teachers, the decision of the Junior High English Department to use *Black Like Me* in the program has my approval."

Another skirmish was won for intellectual freedom in Prince George's County, Maryland, where a special ten-member School Board panel ruled that *Sylvester and the Magic Pebble,* with its pictures of police as pigs, did not contribute to the "development of negative attitudes toward police officers." The panel ordered the book made available in all elementary school libraries.

CONSISTENCY VS. EXPEDIENCY

The objections of some police to *Sylvester* in various cities gave the American Library Association's Office for Intellectual Freedom an opportunity to do a saturation job of publicity on the crucial question of whether a library is ever justified in banning a book because it is considered offensive by a special group. Memoranda were sent to nearly 150 cities and to every state committee on intellectual freedom, advising librarians that the banning of *Sylvester* would violate the policies of ALA.

In a parallel case, *Little Black Sambo* was removed from the school libraries of Montgomery County, Maryland, raising the same crucial question, which was sharpened by the additional doubt as to whether librarians will hold to the principle of intellectual freedom in spite of pressures from police, but will bow to pressures from other groups in other cases. "An Ox of a Different Color," *American Libraries,* May, 1971, by James Harvey and Judith Krug, provides a penetrating and clarifying analysis of this subject.

"LET SLEEPING DOGS LIE" VS. "LET IT ALL HANG OUT"

Library administrators often face a choice — either to cover up a dispute over a controversial document or idea or to give it full publicity.

In the spring of 1971 in Brecksville, Ohio the Branch Librarian, Mrs. Wilmer, took the latter course, when she decided to encourage the airing of a variety of opinions, making the library a center for dialogue on controversial topics. A kiosk covered with bright felt was erected and library visitors were invited to express their opinions in a special exhibit of "graffiti." Samples included, "Fighting for peace is like screwing for virginity," "War is good for freedom," "I feel that the use of bad language in this experiment impedes its progress."

The librarian reported that suddenly the library and she were in the public eye. "There seemed to be no escape from people's glances as they approached me in the supermarket or the local restaurant either to 'chew me out' or to embrace me — one old woman really did embrace me and said, 'Please stay in our town. We need outspoken people like you.' "

In spite of some objections, the graffiti board was kept two and half weeks after it was scheduled to come down because people *did* want to see it, and because it was important to make everyone aware that the library would not give in to pressures. In Brecksville the library won the battle for freedom of dialogue on current controversies. Although there are always some groups and individuals so sure of their own values that they try to impose their limitations upon everyone, publicity can be, and usually is, a potent weapon against the censor.

ARTILLERY FOR DEFENSE IN ACTION

On June 18, 1971, the still young Freedom to Read Foundation announced its largest grant to date, $1,000 to the Rochester, Michigan Community Schools Appeal Fund, to help finance the appeal of an Oakland County Circuit Court decision limiting the use of Kurt Vonnegut's *Slaughterhouse Five* in Rochester schools. (This is reported in more detail in the Fall issue, Vol. 1, No. 1, of a new publication, *The Freedom to Read Foundation News.*)

Alex P. Allain, President of the Foundation, described a problem arising from the fact that many state penal codes prohibit distribution of so-called "harmful matter," without clear definitions of what the term means. Mr. Allain stated:

"To render librarians vulnerable to criminal prosecution for purchasing and disseminating works which have not previously been held illegal through adversary hearings is to require every librarian to reject the primary philosophical basis of his role in society. Under such an obligation, he either knowingly becomes a censor or unknowingly breaks a law. The Board believes this choice is inimical to the concept of intellectual freedom and a derogation of the professional responsibilities of librarians. Thus, the Foundation plans to challenge the constitutionality of those laws which can inhibit librarians from including in their collections and disseminating to the public every work which has not previously been ruled illegal."

ALA ACTIVE ON SEVERAL FRONTS

In the field of intellectual freedom 1971 was a busy year for the American Library Association. It firmly supported the right of the public to read the Pentagon Papers and the Report of the Commission on Obscenity and Pornography, it established a new policy on the importance of keeping confidential library circulation records that would identify what person reads what specific book, and it issued a new series of "Interpretations of the Library Bill of Rights" which elaborate on specific points in the brief, general statement. Interpretation 1, called "The Intellectual Freedom Statement," is a detailed elaboration of many points in the Library Bill of Rights. (See *American Libraries,* September 1971, pages 831-832.) Interpretation 2 is a revision of the old (1952) statement on labeling. (See *American Libraries,* September 1971, p. 833.) Interpretation 3 is a brand new policy statement against removal of challenged library materials, declaring that "as a matter of firm principle . . . no challenged library material should be removed from any library under any legal or extra-legal pressure, save after an independent determination by a judicial officer in a court of competent jurisdiction and only after an adversary hearing, in accordance with well-established principles of law." (See *American Libraries,* September 1971, p. 832.)

ALA's Office for Intellectual Freedom identified over 25 policies pertinent to intellectual freedom, none of which has ever been rescinded. Since these policies overlap and conflict with each other, they cause delays and prevent effective action. The case of J. Michael McConnell, an avowed homosexual who was refused an appointment in the University of Minnesota library by the Regents of the University, focused attention upon the overlapping jurisdiction of the Library Administration Division, the Association of College and Research Libraries, and the Intellectual Freedom Committee, each of which could point to ALA policy statements which seemed to give them the authority to act on such a case. Since there was a jurisdictional fuzziness and a dispute over which ALA agency should deal with this case (and other cases as well), the Intellectual Freedom Committee reported to Council (for information, rather than action) its opinion that Mr. McConnell's rights under the First Amendment had been violated. IFC proposed for action, and it was approved by the Council that the new Staff Committee on Mediation, Arbitration, and Inquiry should give high priority to the McConnell case.

The IFC also called attention to the conflict between the Library Bill of Rights and the 1970 Resolution on Library Service to Educational Institutions Established to Circumvent Desegregation Laws, and moved that the Council "remove its direct order to the Intellectual Freedom Committee for implementation of the (Black Caucus) Resolution, and that responsibility for its implementation be given to the new Staff Committee on Mediation, Arbitration, and Inquiry, with budget support of $10,000 for this purpose." (See IFC column in the September 1971 *American Libraries* for details.)

A NEW MECHANISM FOR DEFENSE

ALA's decision in June 1971, to establish a single agency with authority and responsibility to defend librarians whose jobs are in jeopardy because they fought for intellectual freedom, is a landmark in the history of ALA's efforts in this field. The IFC report to the Council in January stated:

"One desirable change in ALA policy, overdue since 1946, would be centralization in *one* agency of the responsibility and the authority for investigating all dismissal cases, whether or not they involve intellectual freedom. Almost always, until the investigation is well under way, it is impossible to determine whether LAD, ACRL, or OIF [Office for Intellectual Freedom] should be looking into the particular case. The costs of the investigation necessary for responsible action are heavy. There may be more cases than any office can afford to handle with present resources. If so, these resources should be increased."

In response, ALA President Lillian Bradshaw grasped the nettle firmly, calling the interested agencies together in Chicago on March 19, 1971. The result was the recommendation to the Council, presented on June 22 by James Richards, then President of the Library Administration Division, to establish a single agency with full authority over all investigations. Council members were overwhelmingly in favor of this proposal, and of the guidelines for action proposed.

TESTING THE NEW MACHINERY

This new committee, SCMAI—the Staff Committee on Mediation, Arbitration, and Inquiry, is now struggling with its many problems. It is to be expected that additional revisions in its procedures will be required.

It would be unreasonable to expect SCMAI to resolve *any* case to everyone's satisfaction. Inevitably, some parties to every dispute will be unhappy with the decision. But now, for the first time, jurisdictional disputes need no longer cause inaction on a case. SCMAI has all the authority needed to mediate and arbitrate. If these efforts fail, then it can proceed to conduct investigations concerning the facts in a case. When an impartial, documented report of the facts justifies censure, then, after observing all the necessary provisions of due process, ALA's influence through moral persuasion may still resolve a problem before a librarian takes his case into court.

In summary, some skirmishes were lost, some small battles won, and the major battle of the Pentagon Papers was won for journalists, publishers, librarians, and citizens of independent mind. The Freedom to Read Foundation, though hindered by a shortage of resources, has proved a useful form of defense, and a path has been cleared through the swamp of jurisdictional fuzziness. The struggle for intellectual freedom will continue.

NATIONAL BOOK COMMITTEE, INC.

by

John C. Frantz[*]

The National Book Committee is a nonprofit membership corporation of 200 individuals committed to the value of books and reading and to the importance of good library services for all. Its mission is to keep books and other library materials free, to make them widely and conveniently available, and to promote both the desire and the ability to read.

The activities of the National Book Committee are designed to reflect the public interest in books, reading, and the use of library materials. Activities are conducted in close cooperation with both the producers — authors and publishers — and with the profession — teachers, scholars, and librarians. The three priority program areas are reading and library development, encouragement of the literary arts, and the conduct of research and development.

The 1972 National Library Week program marks the fifteenth annual effort to promote library use by incorporating both the continuing importance of the "Right-to-Read" theme and the current U.S. observance of International Book Year. Calendar year 1972 was designated by the Member States of UNESCO as "International Book Year" with the general theme of "Books for All." Grants to the Book Committee from the U.S.

---

[*]Executive Chairman, National Book Committee, Inc.

Department of State and Council on Library Resources, Inc. made possible the establishment of a U.S. Secretariat to initiate and coordinate domestic activities in connection with IBY. The NLW-IBY programs promote the role of reading and libraries in helping to deal with urgent national priorities; early childhood education, drug abuse information, equal educational opportunities for the disadvantaged, and improved interracial and intercultural understanding. Throughout 1972, conferences, publications, and exhibit materials will call general public attention to the NLW-IBY objectives.

The basic objectives of IBY are to encourage authorship and translation; to improve book production and distribution, especially through free library services in the developing countries; to promote the reading habit and the reading aloud of books to children; and to strengthen the usefulness of books in the service of education, international understanding, and peaceful cooperation.

Early in 1972, a "Charter of the Book" was adopted by seven international nongovernmental organizations, setting forth the treatment to which books are entitled nationally and internationally. The initial adherents included the International Confederation of Societies of Authors and Composers, the International Federation for Documentation, the International Federation of Library Associations, and International P.E.N.

The Charter stresses the importance of the free flow of books across frontiers. Emphasizing the vital role of printed matter in education, the Charter points to ways in which books can promote improved relationships among the peoples and nations of the world. Among the ten articles of the Charter are the right to read, the educational functions of print, the obligations of society to creative writers, and the importance of book production and widespread distribution.

Late in 1971, the IBY Secretariat produced the 44-page *International Book Year 1972: A Handbook for U.S. Participation* to help libraries, schools, groups and organizations participate in the year's observances. The *Handbook* describes the goals and purposes of IBY, offers specific program suggestions, and suggests ways of adding an international dimension to ongoing activities. This publication and further information on IBY are available from Miss Esther J. Walls, Director, U.S. Secretariat, IBY, 1972, National Book Committee, Inc., One Park Avenue, New York, N.Y. 10016. (For international developments concerning IBY, see Wegman's article, "International Book Year — 1972," this volume.)

In its capacity as consultant to the National Reading Center, the Book Committee continues to aid in the authorship and editing of a wide range of public information materials. Local and regional conferences, many in cooperation with the regional offices of the U.S. Office of Education, are being conducted by NLW-NBC-IBY staff. A direct by-product of one such conference, funded by USOE, is a multimedia Kit containing two filmstrips and a tape cassette. This Kit presents the scope and effects of illiteracy and functional illiteracy and suggests a number of ways in which the goals of the Right-to-Read effort may be achieved.

Early in 1972, the Book Committee sponsored the publication of a second fully revised edition of *A Parent's Guide to Children's Reading*, by Nancy Larrick. This, together with G. Robert Carlsen's *Books and the Teen-Age Reader* (also sponsored by the Book Committee) offers parents, teachers, and librarians useful tools to encourage young people to become good readers. Other publications during 1971 and 1972 include *Outreach Reading Programs That Work* (tentative title of a guide to informal and innovative out-of-school reading programs) — *The Right-to-Read Resource Book*, and *International Book Year, 1972: A Handbook for U.S. Participation*, mentioned previously.

The National Book Committee administers the annual National Book Awards program which honors current books by American authors judged by writers and critics to be the most distinguished work in each of seven categories: Arts and Letters, Children's Books, Fiction, History and Biography, Poetry, Philosophy and Religion, The Sciences (these last two presented in alternate years), and Translation.

The National Book Committee sponsors the National Medal for Literature which since 1965 has honored a living American author for the excellence of his or her total contribution to literature. The award, $5,000 and a bronze medal designed by Leonard Baskin, is endowed by the Guinzburg Fund in memory of Harold K. Guinzburg, founder of The Viking Press and one of the organizers of the National Book Committee. The recipient in 1971 was E. B. White.

The most comprehensive research project now being conducted by the Book Committee is the Educational Media Selection Centers program founded by the U.S. Office of Education. The principal product of the second phase is the publication, in 1972, of a guide for the establishment of such centers with attention to the concept of media evaluation and selection, organization and operation, program, space, staff and budget. Phase III consists of the operation of a small number of model or demonstration centers in a variety of administrative and geographic settings.

Operational policy for the National Book Committee is established by an Executive Committee of 24 members. The 1972 Chairman is Roger L. Stevens; Vice-Chairmen are William Bernbach and Harrison E. Salisbury. Secretary-Treasurer is A. Edward Miller.

BOOK TRADE MERGERS, 1971

For a list of mergers 1962–1970, see the 1971 *Bowker Annual*, pp. 315-323; for mergers 1958–1961, see the 1961–62 and 1962–63 editions of *Literary Market Place*.

Aldine Publishing Co. merged with Atherton Press, became Aldine-Atherton, Inc. *PW* 1/25/71

Atherton Press. *See* Aldine-Atherton, Inc.

Auerbach Publishers, Inc. acquired Brandon/Systems Press, Inc. *PW* 9/21/71

Barnes & Noble, Inc. *See* Harper & Row, Publishers

Bradbury Press purchased from Prentice-Hall, Inc. by officers. Prentice-Hall will continue to distribute. *PW* 1/18/71

Brandon/Systems Press. *See* Auerbach Publishers, Inc.

Columbia Broadcasting System acquired assets of Popular Library, Inc. *PW* 10/11/71

Cowles Book Company. *See* The Henry Regnery Company

East-West Center Press. *See* University of Hawaii Press

Farrar, Straus & Giroux, Inc. acquired Hill & Wang, Inc. *PW* 10/4/71

Funk & Wagnalls, Inc., purchased by Standard Reference Library. *PW* 2/22/71

Harper & Row, Publishers acquired Barnes & Noble, Inc. *PW* 12/13/71

Hill & Wang, Inc. *See* Farrar, Straus & Giroux, Inc.

Oceana Publications, Inc. acquired Trial Lawyers Service Company. *PW* 11/22/71

Popular Library, Inc. *See* Columbia Broadcasting System

The Henry Regnery Company purchased The Cowles Book Company, a subs. of Cowles Communications, Inc. *PW* 3/8/71

Standard Reference Library acquired Funk & Wagnalls and adopted name Funk & Wagnalls, Inc. *PW* 2/22/71

Trial Lawyers Service Company. *See* Oceana Publications, Inc.

University of Hawaii Press merged with East-West Center Press forming a publishing organization called The University Press of Hawaii. *PW* 12/13/71

Library Automation

LIBRARY AUTOMATION IN THE FEDERAL GOVERNMENT

by

Madeline M. Henderson*

The Task Force on Automation of Library Operations (TFA), of the Federal Library Committee, has set four long-range objectives: (1) to review and report on the status of automation activities in federal libraries; (2) to encourage the development, whenever possible, of compatible automated systems; (3) to furnish guidance to federal librarians and administrators on problems of library automation; and (4) to provide liaison in the area of library automation between the federal library community and other segments of the library world.

In working toward these objectives, the TFA has undertaken three phases of its total program: it conducted a review of the literature on library automation for the purpose of defining trends and identifying gaps in such automation activities; it obtained support for a study in depth of the history and development of selected automated systems in federal libraries with special emphasis on the organizational and administrative factors affecting those systems; and it served in a technical advisory capacity for a broad survey of the current status of automated operations in federal libraries, conducted by System Development Corporation with the support of the U.S. Office of Education, Bureau of Libraries and Educational Technology. The Task Force is indebted to OE for its generous support of both the in-depth study and the broader survey of federal library automation activities.

The latter study was described in Frank Kurt Cylke's article, "The State of Federal Libraries," in the 1971 *Bowker Annual*, pp. 264-265. The survey was designed to accomplish three goals: (1) to define library operations susceptible to automation, whether such operations are now being automated or not; (2) to describe automation techniques of potential use in library operations, both those techniques now being applied and those of possible interest for library applications; and (3) to establish criteria for determining the feasibility of automation ("what to automate"), the types of hardware and software available for library automation, and the various factors to be taken into account in considering library automation possibilities.

This study, which was started in June 1970 and completed in July 1971, was under the capable direction of Barbara Evans Markuson. The work involved a questionnaire survey of the entire federal library community except the three Na-

---

*Chairman, Task Force on Automation of Library Operations, Federal Library Committee.

tional libraries (Library of Congress, National Library of Medicine, and National Agricultural Library) and preparation of both the *Handbook on Federal Library Automation* and a report analyzing and summarizing the data gathered in the survey itself. The facts and figures on library automation in the federal government presented in this article are based on the data contained in these two reports, scheduled for publication in the spring of 1972.

SURVEY OF THE FEDERAL LIBRARY COMMUNITY

The listing of federal libraries, *Roster of Federal Libraries, 1970*[1] served as the source of individual libraries to which the survey questionnaires were addressed. The total number of questionnaires sent out was 2,106; 1,012 were returned.

Of the responses received, 964 contained sufficient information to be included in the data base compiled and analyzed by the study team. Some replies showed that the respondents were not libraries, or were not federal agency libraries; others included insufficient data to be useful. One librarian apologized for not filling out the questionnaire: her library had just been demolished in the early 1971 Los Angeles area earthquake! The 964 replies included in the data base were studied carefully to confirm that they were indeed representative of the total community surveyed. The only skew apparent was the low percentage of replies from U.S. Information Agency libraries overseas, which perhaps can be explained by the fact that most of these are very small and manned by non-English speaking native staff.

CHARACTERISTICS OF THE COMMUNITY

The general picture of the federal library community shows that the community is widely dispersed within the United States and around the world. Most federal libraries are characterized as special or technical, including medical libraries. The majority of federal libraries are small or medium-sized, in terms of holdings, budget, and staff resources. In spite of their small size, many make use of machine-readable data bases in servicing the information needs of their clients. Federal librarians expressed a strong positive attitude toward automation, but not to the exclusion of other critical needs such as increased budgets, staff, and space. In the majority of cases, local facilities could not support library automation, so librarians favor programs of centralized support and services.

In more detail this survey of the community revealed the following facts:

Contrary to local belief, only 7 percent of all federal libraries are to be found within the metropolitan Washington, D.C. area. Perhaps even more surprising, only 60 percent are located within the continental United States. (These figures are based on the *Roster of Federal Libraries,* rather than on actual responses.)

Although more than 50 percent of all federal libraries are special libraries, the spectrum is complete and includes public, school, university, and archival libraries. The public and school libraries include those which serve the so-called "forgotten publics," such as Indian school children and institutionalized (prison and hospital) persons.

The size of the libraries was determined from a number of factors. For example, the median size of federal library collections is 16,500 total holdings. Books are the predominant type of material among these holdings, but there are also some less traditional materials such as audio recordings, maps, and films.

Budget figures also indicate the size of a library; the median respondent spent less than $27,000 for materials, staff, and equipment in fiscal year 1970. However, working with the figures that were submitted in the questionnaire responses and with supplementary budget figures supplied by the three National libraries, the study team compiled an estimated figure

---

[1]Mildred Benton. *Roster of Federal Libraries, 1970.* Washington, D.C., The George Washington University, November 1970. (Available from: Federal Library Committee, Library of Congress, Washington, D.C. 20540.)

TABLE 1   ESTIMATED TOTAL FEDERAL LIBRARY BUDGET

Category	Number of Libraries	Actual or Estimated Budget
Low-range: Assumes 2,100 libraries plus national libraries		
Survey respondents providing budget data	825	$60,640,208
USIA libraries	138	1,848,961[1]
All other federal libraries	1,139	31,830,100[2]
Library of Congress	1	57,483,814[3]
National Library of Medicine	1	20,321,259
National Agricultural Library	1	2,500,000
Estimated total		174,624,342
High-range: Assumes 2,500 libraries plus national libraries		
Estimated total for 2,100 libraries and national libraries	=	174,624,342
Estimated total for 400 unidentified federal libraries	=	10,918,020[4]
Estimated total		185,542,362

[1] Only 3 United States Information Agency libraries responded to the survey. Total materials and miscellaneous budget for the 138 USIA libraries, supplied by USIA headquarters, was $1,158,961. Most of these libraries are one-staff operations, manned by local nonprofessionals, and are budgeted by individual USIA posts. Total staff budget was estimated by SDC (System Development Corporation) to be $690,000 (at $5,000 average per staff).

[2] Since nonrespondents were largely the smaller libraries, estimate was based on the median for each budget category; for contract and "other" expenditures, estimates were based following the percentage of respondents reporting that category. Estimate includes $6,882,000 for materials, $22,940,000 for staff, $860,709 for equipment and supplies, $464,400 for contractual services (34 percent of total) and $147,390 for other (15 percent of total).

[3] The budgets for the three National libraries are as reported by the libraries to the SDC project team. The LC budget includes only federal funds.

[4] Based on medians for all budget categories. Includes $2,400,000 for materials, $8,000 for staff, $302,800 for equipment and supplies, $163,200 for contractual services (34 percent of libraries) and $52,020 for other (based on 15 percent of libraries).

for the federal library budget (Table 1). For the first time we have an idea of the total federal expenditures in support of libraries and library services.

Another indicator of size is staff: the majority of the responding libraries have fewer than three staff members. Typically, the federal library has one librarian who may or may not be a professional and who may or may not have supporting staff. The overall ratio of professional to nonprofessional staff is 1:1.3, far less than the recommended 1:3-5 ratio.

A series of questions was directed to the subject of cooperative networks, involving more than interlibrary loan and operating outside the parent agency. Only 10 percent of the respondents said that they were involved in such networks. These networks were rather small, involving ten or fewer libraries, but they covered extensive geographic areas, in some instances, and helped to augment the small staffs and collections already noted.

Interlibrary activities other than formally established networks tend to involve other local libraries rather than more distant ones, even to the extent of more cooperation with local nongovernmental libraries than with parent agency libraries outside the immediate area. This pattern held true for all but exchange of materials (see Table 2). These

TABLE 2 RESPONDENTS' INTERACTION WITH OTHER LIBRARIES, BY ACTIVITIES

	Respondents Interacting with	
Kind of Library	Libraries within Local Area	Libraries outside Local Area
INTERLIBRARY LOAN		
Other libraries in own agency	464	417
Other federal libraries	459	384
Nonfederal governmental libraries (e.g., state libraries)	375	278
Nongovernmental libraries	497	399
PHOTOCOPYING		
Other libraries in own agency	186	190
Other federal libraries	194	173
Nonfederal governmental libraries (e.g., state libraries)	134	115
Nongovernmental libraries	205	180
REFERENCE ASSISTANCE		
Other libraries in own agency	293	230
Other federal libraries	263	186
Nonfederal governmental libraries (e.g., state libraries)	181	121
Nongovernmental libraries	286	274
EXCHANGE OF MATERIALS		
Other libraries in own agency	281	231
Other federal libraries	186	142
Nonfederal governmental libraries (e.g., state libraries)	90	66
Nongovernmental libraries	122	80

activities, of course, also serve to augment the library's resources.

Federal librarians, in spite of the constraints on resources, do a creditable job of serving the needs and requests of their patrons. A relatively high proportion (27 percent) of the respondents said they use information retrieved from machine-readable data bases (e.g., MEDLARS, NASA, RECON, Chemical Abstracts) to answer some user inquiries. Of these respondents, 16 have terminals on-line to the data bases; the rest submit written, formatted search requests. Since these are not large libraries, they must be considered in the vanguard in library use of these tools.

In addition, many federal librarians are able to provide what are usually considered specialized services: preparation of subject bibliographies, current awareness devices, and selective dissemination of information (SDI) service, for example.

FEDERAL LIBRARY AUTOMATION ACTIVITIES

Of the 964 respondents included in the data base for this study, 133 libraries indicated some involvement with automation activity. These libraries then received a second questionnaire — or set of questionnaires — designed to elicit details about the development and operation of specific automated library functions. The sections of the questionnaire covered Acquisitions, Cataloging, Circulation, Serials, and Other Automated Functions. A first general section was sent to all of the 133 libraries to record their experiences in introducing automation; of the other questionnaire sections, the libraries received only those for which they had reported automation programs.

Ninety-one responded; of these, 59 actually have operational or definitely planned automation projects. Some of the others use automated systems maintained elsewhere and could not supply details of operation, maintenance, and the like.

The tabulation of answers from these questionnaires by location shows that the greatest number of automated libraries — 19 — are in the Washington, D.C. area, but these still constitute only a third of the total number. The only library overseas to report automation activity is a U.S. Air Force dependent schools media center in Japan, serving 30 schools.

When tabulated according to agency, the information showed that over one-half (57 percent) of the current automation activity is occurring in Department of Defense (DOD) libraries; however, these 33 libraries are only 2 percent of all DOD libraries, some 1,411 in number. On the other hand, the five automated Atomic Energy Commission (AEC) libraries represent about 38 percent of the 13 libraries in the AEC.

The types of applications that have been automated illustrate the emphasis on systems related to user services (Table 3). Many of the cataloging systems include book catalogs and specialized indexes; the serials systems emphasize serial holdings lists for distribution to users.

In terms of resources, automated libraries are among the "advantaged" federal libraries. One-half of the libraries reported automation of one or two applications, but two libraries reported six and seven, respectively.

Most of the automated systems were developed singly. More recently, however, there has been a trend toward integration of modules into a comprehensive system. As a matter of fact, when librarians were asked what they would recommend to others who are embarking on automation projects, they advised against the piecemeal systems approach.

The first part of the questionnaire (the general section) asked respondents to explore the general management factors that influenced them most in arriving at a decision to automate functions in their libraries. Responses indicate that the factor most influential was the need to improve services; other important factors include the need to improve control of operations, the availability of computer equipment and staff, and the support of both staff and supervisors. The responses indicate that the decision to automate is consistent with the overall objective of any library or information service: to provide the best, most efficient service to the users.

These survey data reflect guidance from the federal library community as

TABLE 3   AUTOMATED FUNCTIONS

Applications	Libraries Reporting Projects	Operational Systems
Acquisitions	10	7
Cataloging	32	27
Circulation	18	13
Serials	31	25
Information retrieval	18	14
Bibliographic publications	13	10
Selective dissemination of information	12	7
Abstracting and indexing	4	3
Indexes to special collections	9	6
Others	3	3

to needs and future programs. The community expressed its preferences for centralized automation planning, a stronger role for the Federal Library Committee in supporting local automation planning, centralized automated federal library networks or service centers, and standardized program packages for use in federal libraries.

Based on assumptions that library automation is desirable and would improve the ability to serve users, that library automation should be extended to as many federal libraries as possible and in the most efficient manner, and that it is in the national interest that federal libraries achieve maximum possible system compatibility within the community and with other segments of the library world, within a reasonable length of time, the study team proposed several alternative methods for accomplishing federal library automation. They recommended to the Federal Library Committee these objectives: (1) Development of generalized system components; (2) Selective development of centralized services; (3) Extension of service to the "forgotten publics" served by federal libraries; (4) Development of standards; (5) Provision of effective communication mechanisms.

In the *Handbook of Federal Library Automation*, one of the two products of this study, several guidelines were proposed for effective automation planning and development within a library. If this system approach is essential in automating one library, it will be even more necessary in planning for the entire community. Realizing the importance of its deliberations and decisions, the FLC Task Force on Automation is studying the recommendations made by the SDC study team as input to a proposed program of further action in support of the effective automation of federal libraries.

AUTOMATION IN TECHNICAL PROCESSING AT THE LIBRARY OF CONGRESS

by

Henriette D. Avram*

The MARC Development Office was established in the Processing Department of the Library of Congress in June 1970. The rationale leading to the creation of the office was to provide the climate to concentrate on automation in technical processing. The MARC Development Office "is charged with the development and implementation of systems for recording cataloging data in machine-readable form; for using those records to produce book catalogs, special listings, and other printed output; and for developing applications of these records to internal bibliographical control."[1]

Many of the office's activities are closely related to those of the MARC Editorial Office, the Technical Processes Research Office, and the Card Division, and some of the project descriptions in this report are the results of the combined efforts of these units and the MARC Development Office.

It is not possible to discuss all particulars of the work in progress in an article limited in length. This article provides the reader with a summary of the major activities in technical process-

---

*Chief, MARC Development Office, Library of Congress.
[1] U.S. Library of Congress. *Annual Report of the Librarian of Congress.* 1969/70. p. 13.

ing automation at the Library and references to other sources for those who desire more detailed accounts.

MARC

The MARC Distribution Service is in its third year of operation. The data base includes all English language material cataloged by the Library of Congress since 1968, and since October 1971, all records produced by the Cataloging-in-Publication program. At present, the data base contains approximately 175,000 records. It is planned to expand this coverage to motion pictures and filmstrips in fiscal year 1972 and if funds are available, to French language material in fiscal year 1973. Although the production of MARC records is the responsibility of the MARC Editorial Office and the duplication and distribution of tapes, the responsibility of the Card Division, the MARC Development Office maintains the MARC computer programs and interfaces with both the national and international library community on bibliographic and technical matters related to records in machine-readable form.

At present, there are 62 subscribers to the service. Considering the services offered by several regional organizations, such as the Ohio College Library Center and the Oklahoma Department of Libraries, the MARC data base is actually utilized by approximately 200 institutions.

In its efforts to promote standardization, the MARC Development Office, with other units of the Library and with the advice of pertinent authorities outside the Library, continues to develop formats for other forms of material. Published formats include ones for books, serials, films, and maps,[2] and in draft form, formats for manuscripts, music, and sound recordings.

The American National Standards Institute format structure[3] for bibliographic information interchange on magnetic tape is based on MARC, and this format has been recommended to the International Organization for Standardization for adoption.

RECON

The RECON Pilot Project came into existence as a result of a study conducted by a task force to investigate the problems of centralized conversion to machine-readable form retrospective catalog records and their distribution from a central source. The task force recommended the implementation of a pilot project at the Library of Congress to test empirically the techniques suggested in the feasibility study.[4] Funds were received from the Council on Library Resources, Inc. and the U.S. Office of Education for the pilot project and the continuation of the activities of the task force.

The pilot project included five major areas:

1. Techniques postulated in the RECON feasibility report were tested in an operational environment by converting

---

[2]*Books: A MARC Format; Specifications for Magnetic Tapes Containing Catalog Records for Books.* 5th ed. 1971. 106 p. [In press]. *Serials: A MARC Format.* 1970. 72 p. $.70 a copy (LC 1,2:M18/7). Addendum no. 1 [serials]. 1971. 31 p. $.35 a copy. *Maps: A MARC Format; Specifications for Magnetic Tapes Containing Catalog Records for Maps.* 1970. 45 p. $.50 a copy (LC 1.2:M18/6). *Films: A MARC Format; Specifications for Magnetic Tapes Containing Catalog Records for Motion Pictures, Filmstrips, and Other Pictorial Media Intended for Projection.* 1970. 66 p. $.65 a copy (LC 1.2:M18/8). These formats are distributed by the Superintendent of Documents, U.S. Government Printing Office, Washington, D.C. 20402.

[3]A format may be defined as composed of three elements: structure, content designators, and content. The structure can be compared to an empty container; it provides the basic framework to which are added the content designators (explicit identification of data for machine manipulation) and the content (the data itself).

[4]RECON Working Task Force. *Conversion of Retrospective Catalog Records to Machine-Readable Form: A Study of the Feasibility of a National Bibliographic Service.* Washington, Library of Congress, 1969. 230 p.

English language monographs cataloged in 1968 and 1969 but not included in the MARC Distribution Service.

2. Format recognition procedures and computer programs were developed.

3. Conversion techniques for processing older English language material and titles in foreign languages using the roman alphabet were analyzed.

4. The state of the art of input devices that might facilitate the conversion of a large data base was monitored. Keying devices were tested in a production environment and direct-read optical character readers were tested at the vendor's site. This phase of the work included an investigation of cathode-ray tube terminals and the use of a mini-computer on line for input functions.

5. Microfilming techniques and their associated costs were investigated in terms of providing source documents for a large-scale conversion activity.

The RECON Working Task Force assumed responsibility for the following tasks, some of which are complete and some of which are still in progress.

1. The feasibility of determining levels or subsets of the established MARC format that would allow a library using a less detailed version of the MARC format to be part of a future national network was investigated.[5]

2. Problems related to and the estimated cost of the production of a national union catalog consisting of Library of Congress entries and titles from other libraries (records in both machine-readable form and printed form) are being studied. The study assumes a bibliographic register (full bibliographic entries arranged by a sequential number) with indexes to the register by name, title, and subject, and a register of locations.

3. The possibility and the cost of using machine-readable data bases from a variety of institutions in a national bibliographic store to reduce costs and accelerate the conversion effort at the national level are being investigated. The aim of the task is to determine as definitively as possible, whether it is more efficient to add records from selected data bases to the MARC data base or whether it is more efficient to reinput these records at the Library of Congress. The study takes into account the requirement of consistency of the data content.

4. Alternative schemes for converting retrospective records to increase the timeliness of these records are being studied. Conversion in reverse chronological order by category of material and language as recommended in the RECON feasibility report may not be the most satisfactory method for all purposes.

Progress reports on the pilot project and the research of the RECON Working Task Force have appeared in the professional journals,[6] and the final report on the pilot project, describing the results of work done by both the Library of Congress and the RECON Working Task Force, is in preparation and should be available early in 1972.

FORMAT RECOGNITION

The MARC format employs tags, indicators, and subfield codes (referred to as content designators) for the explicit identification of data for computer manipulation. In addition, certain codes are assigned to the record to designate language of the text, country of publication, etc., or to indicate a particular condition, such as the existence of an index or a bibliography (referred to as fixed fields). The preparation of the data for conversion to machine-readable form (called editing) involves a human being assigning content designators and fixed field codes. This editing process is tedious and time-

---

[5]RECON Working Task Force. "Levels of Machine-Readable Records." *Journal of Library Automation*, v. 3, no. 2, June 1970. p. 122-127.

[6]Henriette D. Avram [and others] "The RECON Pilot Project: A Progress Report..." *Journal of Library Automation*, v. 3, no. 2, June 1970, p. 102-114; v. 3, no. 3, Sept. 1970. p. 230-251; v. 4. no. 1, Mar. 1971, p. 38-51; v. 4, no. 3, Sept, 1971, p. 159-169.

consuming and thus a costly activity. It appeared advantageous to develop a method to use the computer to examine character strings for certain keywords, significant punctuation, and other clues to replace this human function. This technique became known as format recognition.

The Library began its work on format recognition in the winter of 1968 with a feasibility study which was completed in February 1969. Based on the encouraging conclusions of the study, a decision was made to proceed with the development of this technique to accomplish machine editing of bibliographic records. Through a series of computer program modules, each field is fully identified (tags, indicators, and subfield codes assigned) and the data are then scanned for information needed for the fixed fields. For example, the date of publication are derived from the date subfield in the imprint statement; or if the Dewey number field contains the notation "[FIC]," the fiction indicator is set to "x" denoting a fictional title.

To date, approximately 16,000 RECON records have been processed by the format recognition programs since actual production began in May 1971. RECON records were used to test format recognition because they were not needed for a weekly production operation. The Library expects to use format recognition on current MARC records in the very near future. The machine processing time in format recognition is 1½ seconds per record as compared to 3 seconds per record for records processed by editors. Production rates of the editors, who now do proofing only instead of editing and proofing, have increased significantly.

Since the MARC Distribution Service will be expanded to include records in other roman alphabet languages, the library is analyzing the requirements to expand format recognition for these languages. The complete logical design for format recognition, including typing specifications, has been published by the American Library Association.[7]

PLAN FOR THE SYSTEMATIC AUTOMATION OF TECHNICAL PROCESSING

In order that automation of technical processing proceed in accordance with the priorities and requirements of the Processing Department and other departments in the Library, guidelines are being developed within the scope of the following criteria: 1) Automation of a function must be technically feasible (within the state of the art today); 2) the function must be capable of being automated in a reasonable period of time; and 3) the function must be of such scope that it has a significant impact on the operations of the Library of Congress.

The guidelines may be augmented and/or modified in light of any of the following conditions: research and development activities dictate a different solution; new hardware devices allow for greater flexibility; funding situations change, resulting in a reduction or expansion of the plans; or experience in an operational mode, serving as a learning mechanism, suggests another approach. The importance of the guidelines, in addition to providing a blueprint for allocation of staff, training, and funds, is the ability to proceed in as orderly a way as possible with some guarantee that modules of the system will fit together as the system expands.

The guidelines constitute the master plan or the core bibliographic system toward which all efforts are directed.

MULTIPLE USE MARC SYSTEM

Under development is the Multiple Use MARC System (MUMS), a software system that will provide the supporting services (message display, storage and retrieval functions) required in common by the whole array of bibliographic processing applications.

Instead of each application providing its own message display and storage and

---

[7]*Format Recognition Process for MARC Records: A Logical Design.* Chicago, American Library Association, 1970. 301 p. $10.00 a copy.

retrieval functions, MUMS maintains and controls a central pool of such services for use by all applications. Thus, a particular application provides the program modules needed to execute those tasks central to its purpose while MUMS provides the servicing modules. If any module is needed by a given application and is not already contained within MUMS, the module is developed according to the specifications provided by the application.

Once included within MUMS, a servicing module becomes available to any other applications which care to make use of it. In fact, the application modules themselves can be shared in this same manner, i.e., a routine originally developed as part of one application program may prove useful to a new application under development. In this case, the new application may make use of the routine through MUMS.

In addition, MUMS connects the servicing and application modules appropriate to a given application, defines their sequence of operation, and regulates their execution. MUMS is also responsible for determining, on a priority basis, the order in which the applications are to be processed in a multi-programming environment.

ORDER DIVISION PROJECT

Phase I of the Order Division Project, consisting of programs to handle regular orders and new continuation orders, is in progress. Phase I has been divided into three tasks. Task 1 covering the production of bibliographic records, such as the order file slip, purchase order, dealer slip, etc., has been operational since February 1971. Work is proceeding on Tasks 2 and 3, which deal with file management and control and the accounting subsystem, respectively. The machine-readable records produced in the Order Division will serve as input to the computer-based Process Information File when that project is operational.

PROCESS INFORMATION FILE

Preliminary investigation is underway to provide on-line input and access to the Library's Process Information File (PIF). The manual PIF has been a valuable tool for locating titles in the process of being cataloged, but its use has been hampered by access to the file by main entry only and numerous misfiled and unweeded cards which tend to inflate the size of the file. It is estimated that the PIF contains approximately 576,000 cards, but after redundant entries have been discounted, the actual size of the file is estimated to be approximately 357,000 cards. The machine file would eliminate this problem of maintenance, and the flexibility of the format for the machine-readable PIF records would allow multiple access to the file, provide accurate and up-to-date status information, build the foundation for the full MARC record, provide an improved selective dissemination of information service to LC staff members, and provide a prototype for a machine bibliographic file subject to heavy use for a variety of purposes. The automated PIF will be one of the largest applications of the Multiple Use MARC System.

AUTHORITY FILES

A processing system is being developed that will provide the capability for the Library to maintain the subject heading file in machine-readable form and to prepare the file for printing according to the specifications of the Government Printing Office for the Linotron. The first phase of the system consists of merging the machine-readable file for the seventh edition of the *LC Subject Heading List* with the tapes for the supplements, including all additions, corrections, and deletions, in order to produce the eighth edition of the list and to have one master machine-readable file in a MARC format. Long-range plans include using this file to extract the proper references for each subject heading recorded in a MARC bibliographic record for a computer produced book catalog and to link the records in this file to the MARC bibliographic records with which they are associated to aid in the subject cataloging process.

Since the advent of the MARC Pilot Project, the Library has recognized the importance of name reference information in machine-readable form to augment the MARC bibliographic records. In addition to the requirement for references for card and book catalogs, such data would aid in the searching of computer based files.

Preliminary investigation included selecting a sample of name authorities from the LC Official Catalog to determine the characteristics of that file. This information is important in order to determine an efficient file organization technique.

It is recognized that the name reference file alone or in conjunction with the automated Process Information File and the MARC bibliographic file will provide a valuable aid to cataloging. Although the Library is still in the early planning stages of this project, it has already held a meeting of a group of MARC users at which the problems associated with a distribution service for reference information were explored.

BOOK CATALOGS

Work is proceeding on several projects to produce book catalogs from machine-readable records. Book catalogs will be produced on the computer printer for the reference collections of the Main Reading Room and the Science Reading Room, respectively. The first book catalog to be printed on the GPO Linotron from MARC data will be *Library of Congress Catalog: Motion Pictures and Filmstrips*. Work on this photocomposition program is being done in cooperation with the Library's Information Systems Office.

FILING

An LC working document specifying a simplified filing arrangement for the Library of Congress catalogs has provided the foundation for a machine filing system. Programs are being written to implement these filing rules for computer-produced book catalogs and provide some of the following capabilities: ignore certain characters (i.e., initial articles such as "A," "An," or "The") at the beginning of certain title fields when filing; place fields beginning with numerals before those beginning with alphabetic characters with the digits in numerical sequence rather than the machine collating sequence; analyze the tags, indicators, or subfield codes for a particular field to achieve the proper filing order (e.g., Washington, George should file before Washington, D.C.). This machine filing program, called LIBSKED (Library Sort Key Edit) has incorporated the routines found in an earlier sort program, SKED (Sort Key Edit).[8]

CONCLUSION

The first three projects described, MARC, RECON, and Format Recognition, have a scope beyond that of automating technical processing functions at the Library of Congress. Although the techniques developed and the data base converted are used internally at the Library, the main thrust of these projects is the distribution of bibliographic data and the promotion of standards for the library community, both nationally and internationally. Sights have turned inward on the remainder of the projects. However, by-products of some of these projects, such as those dealing with name and subject authority files, have implications to the entire library community.

---

[8] John C. Rather and Jerry G. Pennington. "The MARC Sort Program." *Journal of Library Automation,* v. 2, no. 3, Sept. 1969. p. 125-138.

DEVELOPMENTS IN NONPRINT MEDIA, 1971: THE YEAR OF MINIMAL CHANGE

by

Gerald R. Brong*

Frustrating as it may seem to the reader, the events of 1971 in the nonprint media field taken singly were not of great significance. The audiovisual "field" is a difficult one to define, and before an examination of trends in this field, it is important to identify what audiovisual materials are and the role they play in a library collection.

Audiovisual materials can be warehoused like print material; they contain information, yet they are not dependent on the printed word to transmit this information.[1] All items in a library can be classed as media; audiovisual materials can be classed as nonprint media. Unlike print media, nonprint media usually require some sort of display device, such as a projector or record player, to extract the stored information. John Vergis clarifies the use of the term "media," indicating that "in its broad sense [it] is not a fixed characteristic of a class of materials or equipment — it is an operational term that can be applied to any of man's extensions of himself — whether they are words, films, brass bands, rubber bands or even paper clips. It is what one does to and with things purposefully that counts."[2] A library can be defined as an organized collection of information that allows for the transfer of that stored information from the storage unit to the patron. The storage medium used most frequently is the printed word, but information storage in media other than words is rapidly becoming more common.

TECHNOLOGICAL DEVELOPMENTS
Nonprint Media Software

No totally new developments occurred during 1971 in the audiovisual production or storage field; exciting trends, however, continued. The increased ease with which informational materials can be produced locally continues to expand the possibilities for libraries to become "proactive" information centers—centers that not only store information but also record information and apply it to effect sociological change or produce a new informational product.

Motion picture production is making inroads into libraries. Eastman Kodak introduced the XL super 8mm camera, designed to utilize a new 8mm cartridge load color film sensitive enough to produce usable images indoors without the use of additional light sources. Motion picture cameras continue to become more reliable and simpler to operate. In 1970 and 1971 new varieties of 8mm sound camera systems were introduced. Battery-operated electronic video recorders have continued to be developed and are now only a little more complex than a sophisticated 8mm camera. Combined with the increase in the local production of motion pictures is the increase in the availability of motion pictures for purchase, rental, or loan in all formats in storage.

Still photography has had minimal impact in libraries (although libraries a familiar with the storage and utilizatic of slides or photographic prints). Now, with other nonprint materials, availab quantities of photographic materials a rapidly increasing.

The standardization problem in audio recording field was compound this year with the introduction of m than one four-channel stereo sound s tem, the systems being not totally co

---

*Assistant Director, Audio-Visual Center, Washington State University Library, Pullman Washington.

[1] Robert S. Taylor, "Technology and Libraries." *EDUCOM*, 5 (May 1970), pp. 4-5.

[2] John Vergis, "An Open Forum — Together or Separate." *Audiovisual Instruction*, 1 (October 1970), pp. 22-29.

patible. Four-channel stereo recording is a significant development in the field of recorded sound on both disc and tape.

As with previous years, the trend is toward continued and increased production of nonprint informational units (materials) in the media we have today. Indicators of the future point to an increase in the variety of storage forms available. It is safe to predict that the specific nonprint media bandwagon of the past (and even 1971) will continue. Hopefully, work will continue on standardization of software formats.

Media Production and Display Equipment

Standardization within equipment types, especially in the video recording field, continues to be a problem. In 1970 a standardized half-inch video tape format was agreed to. This EIA-J format was available throughout 1971 and, for the most part, its results have been satisfactory. Equipment using this format allows for a tape produced on one brand of video recorder to be played on any other brand of recorder using the same format. New visual and audio production and display equipment continues to enter the marketplace, but quality of equipment continues, in some cases, to leave something to be desired.

The price freeze and the imposition of an import surtax, introduced in 1971, will have an impact on the pricing and availability of audiovisual equipment. Prices on domestically produced equipment have been increasing, as has the cost of imported equipment. In December the American dollar was devalued. Although the full economic impact of these events on the audiovisual equipment marketplace has yet to be seen, predictions indicate that prices will increase on imported equipment and the inflationary trend on domestically produced equipment will slow down. This is significant since nearly all audiovisual equipment is dependent on some sort of display device (projector, player, etc.) to extract the stored information, and 1972 appears to be another year of reduced library budgets.

Delivery Systems

With the development of alternative delivery systems for the physical checkout of a nonprint unit, libraries may become huge mechanisms for identifying what is wanted by the patron, reproducing or providing it from storage, and providing the patron with freedom of interaction with the information.[3] Here we shall concern ourselves with only two types of delivery — dial access information retrieval systems and community antenna television systems.

Dial access is not a new development in school and academic libraries, but discussions now center on dial access information retrieval systems (DAIRS) for other than just school libraries. The DAIRS allow a patron remote access to information stored in a central location. The switching technology employed to interconnect the patron with the information source is not unlike that used for telephone service. The first DAIRS were for audio delivery and were restricted to a dedicated system serving the institution where installed. Now audio DAIRS can be interconnected with electronically switched telephone systems (systems utilizing Touch-Tone dialing). At Washington State University automatic switching was not possible since the local telephone company continued to utilize the mechanical switching systems; instead, a library attendant would interconnect, in a matter of seconds, the patron calling in to any audio program source available through the library. In February 1970, the use of what is thought to be the first digital access color TV system began at Fullerton Junior College in Fullerton, California.[4] In Provo, Utah, the Brig-

---

[3] Nelson N. Foote, "The New Media and Our Total Society." *The New Media and Education: Their Impact on Society.* Ed. by Peter H. Rossi and Bruce J. Biddle. Garden City, N. Y.: Anchor Books (Doubleday and Co., Inc.), 1967.

[4] Shirley E. Bosen, "A Video Dial Select System That Works." *Educational Television*, 3 (September 1971), pp. 9-11.

ham Young University has operative a fully two-way closed circuit television system interconnecting 35 buildings on campus. The two-way system allows for full communication (audio/video) to take place between two or more points on campus.[5] The Brigham Young and Fullerton systems are examples of delivery capability that could be developed and operated by any type of library.

The year 1971 saw an increase in activity in planning for the use of community antenna television systems as full communication carriers. In November 1971, the Association for Educational Communications and Technology (AECT) Telecommunications Division released a "Position Paper on Community Antenna Television,"[6] reviewing community antenna television (CATV) developments and proposing a course of action to assure the educational community access to the capabilities of CATV. In regard to the 2,600 CATV franchises now in existence, there is minimal mention of "public service" uses of the system. There is a potential, however, of 15,000 more CATV systems and, by all indications, 1971 was the year when educators (including librarians) began to plan for CATV. With 17,000 to 20,000 CATV systems in operation a national network suddenly exists; and, when coupled with satellite communications, the prediction by Frank Norwood, Executive Director of the Joint Council on Educational Telecommunications, and Brigitte Kenney, Chairman of the ALA Information Science and Automation Division's Telecommunications Committee, that "... CATV will become perhaps *the* most important means for connecting libraries, as well as for connecting users to libraries," may prove correct.[7]

LIBRARY TECHNOLOGY – A MARC FORMAT FOR FILM AND CATALOGING RULES

In May 1971, the MARC Development Office of the Library of Congress distributed *Films: A MARC Format*, which presents specifications for machine-readable magnetic tapes containing catalog records for motion pictures, filmstrips, and other pictorial media intended for projection. The rules for entry follow the proposed revision of Chapter 12, "Motion Pictures and Filmstrips," in the *Anglo-American Cataloging Rules*. Libraries utilizing MARC records for print resources now can expand into the use of MARC records for nonprint resources as well.

Bibliographic control of nonprint library resources moved closer to reality in 1971 when the *Standards for Cataloging Nonprint Materials* was published by the AECT. These standards exist as the major reference source for cataloging procedures for the Joint Advisory Committee on Non-Book Materials, sponsored by the AECT, ALA, and Canadian Library Association. Further, these standards are compatible with the MARC formats for nonprint media now in existence. (See also Pearce Grove's article, "Standards for the Bibliographic Control of Nonprint Media," this volume.)

INDEXES AND REVIEW SOURCES FOR NONPRINT RESOURCES

Historically, we have developed the most usable information locating tools in fields in which the frequency of demand justified the production of reference tools for mass distribution and in areas where society has recognized the urgency of need, such as poison control and law enforcement.[8] The year 1971 saw the creation of the *Multi-Media Reviews Index* with Volume 1 covering

---

[5] Dean M. Austin, "Two-Way Education at Brigham Young University." *Educational Media*, 4 (August-September 1971), pp. 4-5.

[6] *Audiovisual Instruction*, November 1971, pp. 56-65.

[7] Brigitte L. Kenney and Frank W. Norwood. "CATV: Visual Library Service." *American Libraries*, 2 (July-August 1971), pp. 723-726.

[8] Ralph R. Shaw, "Using Advances in Technology to Make Library Resources More Available." In American Library Association. *Student Use of Libraries*. Chicago: American Library Association, 1964.

1970. The *Multi-Media Reviews Index* (published by Perian Press, Ann Arbor, Mich.) provides, as its name implies, an index to critical reviews of a wide variety of nonprint media. Supplements to *MMRI* appear in the journal *Audiovisual Instruction*. Also initiated in 1971 was the *Films Review Index*, published by Audio-visual Associates, Monterey, California.

Other indexes for nonprint media available include, but are not restricted to:

Educator's Purchasing Masters, Fisher Publishing Company, Englewood, Colo.

8mm Film Directory, Educational Film Library Association, New York, N.Y.

Index to 8mm Educational Motion Pictures, Index to Overhead Transparencies, Index to 16mm Educational Films, and *Index to 35mm Educational Filmstrips*, R. R. Bowker, New York, N.Y.

DEVELOPMENTS WITHIN PROFESSIONAL ASSOCIATIONS

Three associations (AECT, ALA, and American Society for Information Science) have experienced the following developments:

1. The AECT formed the Information Systems Division, which will study the processes of bibliographic control, information science, and information delivery technologies to meet patron needs.

2. The ASIS formed a Nonprint Media Special Interest Group.

3. The ALA spent time planning the 1972 convention to address the questions prompted by the increased utilization of audiovisual materials and technology.

4. The ALA Information Science and Automation Division planned a Telecommunications Applications Seminar for spring 1972.

5. The question of consolidation on the state level between audiovisual and library associations is heard with increasing frequency.

6. The ALA Library Administration Division has developed an active Nonprint Media Statistics Committee.

7. Fourteen states now certify media specialists, and 22 states are planning certification programs.[9]

8. The Association of College and Research Libraries of ALA and the AECT have been examining program standards for media programs.

THE FUTURE?

In 1971 there were no indications that trends toward inclusion of nonprint media as basic items in library collections would slow down or cease. On the other hand, there were no indications that 1972 would bring any major changes in nonprint media technology or in the ways nonprint media would be used in libraries. There are indications, however, that telecommunications technology will rapidly advance and that independent common carriers will increase their competition with Western Union and AT&T, thus stabilizing or possibly lowering costs for telecommunication services.[10] Indications are that rapid advances will continue in the development of instructional technology but that the adoption of these developments by the educational institutions will continue at a slow pace.

---

[9]William F. Grady, "Certification of Audiovisual Personnel: A Nationwide Status Report." *Audiovisual Instruction*, 16 (March 1971), pp. 8-12.

[10]Nelson F. Barry. "Data Transmission in Transition." *Datamation*, 17 (October 1, 1971), pp. 20-24.

LIBRARY AND INFORMATION NETWORKS

by

Dan Clemmer* and Russell Shank**

For many library and information networks operators and planners, 1971 was a year of assessing past performance, looking at costs of operation, and planning for the future. Title III (Interlibrary Cooperation) of the Library Services and Construction Act (LSCA) of 1966 was extended for another five years by Congress, and a sum of $2,640,500 was appropriated and funded for fiscal year 1972. The U.S. Office of Education, responsible for the distribution of the minimum $40,000 grants to each state, and the responsible state agencies devoted considerable effort toward looking for new directions for the next five years. Title VIII (Networks for Knowledge) of the Higher Education Act of 1968, however, has yet to be funded. Major progress was made by two of the leaders in the network field, the Ohio College Library Center and the National Library of Medicine; and continued favorable regulation of the telecommunications industry by the Federal Communications Commission provides hope for network planners who anticipate the application of new telecommunications technology to their network needs.

One of the major network evaluations appearing during the year was the study of the Colorado Statewide Reference Network (SWRN),[1] established in 1968 to connect public, school, and community college libraries with a State Communications Center at the Bibliographical Center for Research in Denver. A combination of mail, telephone, and teletypewriter exchange terminals (TWX) has been employed for the exchange of reference and bibliographic information, although virtually all the transactions have involved interlibrary loan requests. The study revealed that over 90 percent of the administrators at the system and state level were displeased with the administration of SWRN and that almost 50 percent felt that the cost of the network was not justified because (1) there were no standardized policies or written procedures, (2) the network was too little used and poorly publicized, (3) the service was poor, and (4) the hierarchical pattern of requesting information was cumbersome. They felt that the network should be administered by a representative body from all types of participating libraries rather than by the Colorado State Library. On the other hand, 63 percent of the administrators of smaller libraries were completely satisfied with the services available. Of those who were dissatisfied, 92 percent gave as their first reason the long delays involved in filling requests. Although almost 75 percent of all network requests originated from public libraries, only 52 percent of them used the network. The top-level administrators attributed the nonuse to the fact that smaller libraries had never heard of SWRN, or if they had, didn't know how to use it.

The underuse of network facilities noted in Colorado is not an uncommon occurrence. The Louisiana Rapid Communication Network which connects all libraries in Louisiana by means of WATS lines or TWX is reportedly underused.[2] One library, that of Louisiana State University, accounted for about

---

*Assistant to the Director of Libraries, Smithsonian Institution, Washington, D.C.
**Director of Libraries, Smithsonian Institution, Washington, D.C.
[1] Mary Sypert, *An Evaluation of the Colorado Statewide Reference Network*, Center for Communication and Information Research, Graduate School of Librarianship, University of Denver, Project No. 71-2, April 1971.
[2] Jane P. Kleiner, "The Louisiana Rapid Communication Network: A System for Improved Interlibrary Loan Service," *Louisiana Library Association Bulletin*, Vol. 33, No. 4, Winter 1971, pp. 103-108.

one-fourth of the 9,467 transmissions in the 1967–1968 year. The cost of operating networks in many cases has not been adequately analyzed, but in those that have, the networks have made policy and equipment changes. The New York State Interlibrary Loan Network (NYSIL), for example, has converted from TWX to dataphone teletype to be used on state tielines. As a result, network costs are stabilized, and stations with heavy traffic have a fixed monthly cost. NYSIL has also decided to restrict its requests by handling no in-print material costing less than $7.50, and will no longer supply copies of any periodical materials indexed in the *Reader's Guide to Periodical Literature* since 1940. As a result of a study made at the Denison Memorial Library at the University of Colorado Medical Center in Denver, it was determined that the use of TWX for interlibrary loan could not be justified unless there was a need to obtain the material on a rush basis. In other instances the conventional interlibrary loan process should be used.[3]

Network performance can be evaluated by the use of various methods, and the method used to evaluate the effectiveness of a Maryland network is somewhat unique. The Maryland Interlibrary Loan Network, a combination of county libraries, small college and special libraries, the Enoch Pratt Free Library in Baltimore, and the McKeldin Library at the University of Maryland, was studied in 1969 to determine the effectiveness of the network, that is, the degree to which it realized its goal measured in terms of output.[4] The analytical model employed compared the total system's output with that of the units within the system; it can be used for any network structured in a hierarchical manner in which requests are screened through successive levels.

The promise attending the advent of facsimile transmission is yet to be fulfilled. Facsimile transmission experiments have been tried and discarded time and again, and are being used very little today. In addition to the slowness of copying (generally six minutes per page) and poor reproduction, the major stumbling block to heavy utilization of the process is that material cannot be transmitted directly from a bound volume. Instead, each page must be copied on a standard format and then be fed into the transmitter, a very slow and expensive process. It is possible to have the receiving machines run unattended, but only at extra cost. In addition, few libraries have access to facsimile equipment; the directories of those which do have equipment are incomplete; only two manufacturers make compatible equipment; and copyright restrictions hinder the transmission of much material.

Virtually every state either has an operational network or a network in the planning stages; most of these are used almost exclusively to facilitate interlibrary loan among their members. Many states have developed union lists of holdings within the states' libraries. The Indiana Union List of Serials, for instance, is expected by February 1972. It will contain 95 percent of the serial titles held in the state and will serve as a data base for the Indiana Libraries Teletype Network. The Machine Readable Cataloging (MARC) information on magnetic tapes distributed by the Library of Congress since 1969 not only makes it possible to develop standardized union lists for states and regions, but can also be used to make centralized and cooperative cataloging networks a reality.

The MARC format is a standard for the transmission and recording of bibliographic information; it can be used by any library for these purposes. The cost

---

[3] Robert M. Braude and Nancy Holt, "Cost-Performance Analysis of TWX-Mediated Interlibrary Loans in a Medium-Sized Medical Library," *Bulletin of the Medical Library Association,* Vol. 59, No. 1, January 1971, pp. 65-70.

[4] Edward S. Warner, "A Tentative Analytical Approach to the Determination of Interlibrary Loan Network Effectiveness," *College and Research Libraries,* May 1971, Vol. 32, No. 3, pp. 217-221.

of buying the tapes and the cost of the hardware and software needed to implement a system that can take advantage of the work done by the Library of Congress is so considerable that cooperative use of the tapes is virtually mandatory. The Ohio College Library Center (OCLC) has provided the most successful example of what can be done cooperatively with the MARC information. Previously described in the 1970 *Bowker Annual,* p. 293, and the 1971 *Bowker Annual,* p. 301, OCLC has expanded its activities to include on-line cataloging, on-line location of materials for interlibrary loan, and on-line training of catalogers; by 1973 OCLC plans to have serials control, technical processing, and circulation control subsystems at work. All members of OCLC can participate on-line by means of cathode-ray tube terminals connected by telephone lines. The input cataloging subsystem, activated this year, provides immediate addition of a bibliographic record used for card production to the on-line bibliographic data base. The cards are produced off-line at night, and input record is available within seconds for another library to use. Whenever a bibliographic record appears on the screen, the holdings information by institution will be displayed too. OCLC produces about 500,000 cards every six weeks.

The MARC tapes are also used as the data base for the New England Library Information Network (NELINET), which is now expanding its membership to other libraries in the region. The University of Florida Libraries at Gainesville are now using the MARC tapes to provide, for a fee, current awareness searches, retrospective searches, and current and retrospective standard interest profiles. The Oklahoma Department of Libraries began in 1969 using the MARC tapes to provide selective dissemination of information (SDI) services to state agencies and soon expanded the service to subscribers. In 1971 the Department expanded MARC-O (MARC-Oklahoma) to make bibliographic records available to Oklahoma libraries which request them by LC card number. A second service to provide card sets and spine, book, and circulation card labels is scheduled for January 1972. The services available from MARC-O are being marketed to SLICE (Southwestern Library Interstate Cooperative Effort), a consortium formed by the Southwestern Library Association covering the states of Texas, Oklahoma, Louisiana, Arkansas, New Mexico, and Arizona. SLICE, formed late in 1971, plans to implement a regional educational program directed to the present and potential application of the MARC tapes and the SDI system.

Without doubt, the most sophisticated network bibliographic retrieval services in the nation are being offered to the medical libraries, chiefly the National Library of Medicine (NLM) in Bethesda, Maryland. Conceived as part of a larger Biomedical Communication Network, the National Medical Library Network is composed of eleven Regional Medical Libraries (RML), not branches of NLM but independent libraries receiving additional funds under the Medical Library Assistance Act. The National Library of Medicine serves as the RML for the mid-Atlantic states and backs up the other ten libraries with its resources. It has also served as the indexing and cataloging center for the nation since 1967. The Regional Medical Libraries are charged with the responsibility of improving their reference and interlibrary loan services to medical and hospital libraries in a broad geographic area. Prior to the establishment of the network, NLM handled interlibrary loan services nationwide; but after the RML structure was set up, interlibrary loan was decentralized and overall interlibrary loan activity increased while NLM's share decreased. The MEDLARS Centers were also decentralized, some of them established in the Regional Medical Libraries.

In cooperation with NLM, the Lister Hill National Center for Biomedical Communications, also in Bethesda, Maryland, began in April 1970 an experimental project designed to provide access to data from the *Abridged Index Medicus,* produced by NLM. The data base of AIM-TWX (*Abridged Index Medicus-TWX*) contains about 150,000 citations to over 100 English-language medical journals for the past five years and is stored on a computer at the System Development Corporation in Santa Monica, California. Access can be gained through TWX or teletype terminals on the telephone network by as many as 18 users simultaneously. After placing a call to the computer, the user is given simple instructions on how to search for the bibliographic information. Computer costs are paid by the Lister Hill Center, but the cost of terminals and toll calls are paid by the user. Costs run the user from $.20 to $.70 per minute for TWX and $.45 per minute for phone-system teletype. An average search runs about 20 minutes and may cost up to $14.00. Presently the service is available to a limited number of users as the system is still being evaluated. It is being used by over 50 institutions nationwide, and is of special value to hospital libraries and other smaller establishments. One particularly attractive feature of AIM-TWX is that very little training is required to use the system.

MEDLINE (MEDLARS On-Line) is similar to AIM-TWX, except that it provides access to a much wider data base. Initially, the top 239 medical journals indexed for MEDLARS since January 1969 will be available, but the base will be expanded to include over 1,000 journals. The system will be operated on an IBM 360/50 computer located at NLM which can support up to 25 simultaneous users. NLM is installing a data communication network that will make the computer available by a local call in at least 20 major cities. Special lines will be extended from these cities to the RMLs and the MEDLARS Search Centers. As with AIM-TWX, each user will pay for his own terminal and telephone costs. The system can be accessed by teletype, IBM 2741, and other terminals operating at 100, 148, or 300 words per minute. Each user institution must agree to provide bibliographic services to health professionals beyond their normal service responsibilities. The users will be able to gain access to the other computers on the network by dialing the same phone number as that used for MEDLINE.

The National Agricultural Library (NAL) in Beltsville, Maryland, has been proposed as the national coordinator for an Agricultural Sciences Information Network. The Network proposal includes (1) an Agricultural Libraries Network, (2) a research and development program in information science and services, (3) information analysis centers, (4) a national referral center, and (5) participation through NAL in programs of international cooperation. The first step in the network would be the immediate establishment of an Agricultural Libraries Network composed of the libraries of the land-grant universities and the U.S. Department of Agriculture. Membership could be expanded after the network has been established.

One of the more unique networks has been recently proposed by the City of New York. It may become the model for networks of its kind. Late in 1971 Deputy Mayor Timothy Costello announced to an assemblage of the New York Library Association that a library urban information network was to be formed in the boroughs of Manhattan, Brooklyn, and Queens, aimed at equalizing the balance of power between the social classes in gaining access to information. The project is seeking $9,000,000 from the Department of Health, Education, and Welfare to be matched with $2,000,000 in local funds for the establishment of 200 information centers in 200 library branches in the three boroughs. The centers will provide information concerning public services and facilities as well as provide access to public documents stored throughout the city. Each branch will increase its staff by one professional librarian and two paraprofessionals who will man the center. From the beginning of the project each library will have access to a printout containing information keyed to its needs. The network may eventually make use of remote terminals connected to the central memory bank, cathode-ray terminals capable of reproducing documents and microfiche copies of documents, and CATV outlets. Libraries were chosen as the base for the networks not only because of their present informational resources but also because new space would not have to be found and because such a location would remove the stigma attached to going to welfare centers to obtain information. At the beginning the network will focus on the needs of the disadvantaged and later attempt to carry the services to the rest of the public.

A June 1971 report[5] to the Department of Housing and Urban Development foresees the development of four CATV networks to help solve some of the problems of the cities in a number of areas, such as citizen-government interaction, education, health, pollution, transportation, and crime prevention. Four basic networks are envisioned: (1) a telephone network for pictures and voice and written communication; (2) a network based on existing CATV systems with information from a central facility to homes and offices, with a limited two-way capability; (3) a broadband communication highway, equal to 30 TV channels in both directions, interconnecting major public institutions and large city commercial enterprises; and (4) a multipurpose city sensing network to collect data on weather, pollution, traffic, vehicle location, power status, etc.

In 1971 the Federal Communications Commission (FCC) announced that it intended to adopt rules requiring CATV operators to build their systems so as to provide as much channel space for nonbroadcast services as is provided for the retransmission of signals from local and distant television stations. Channels must be set aside for education, municipal government, and public access, and educators and local government are to have access without cost for a five-year period. After this period the FCC will determine whether free channels should be terminated, expanded, or the experimental period extended. The FCC also intends to assure that additional channels will be available for lease at a relatively modest cost. The Commission will also propose that CATV systems be built with two-way capability so that return signals can be sent. Two CATV systems established in Manhattan have been required to provide free air time for city and public use; two additional channels are planned. One of the systems grants free use of its studios and equipment with restrictions on the amount of equipment used. The other system charges for any equipment used.

Very few libraries are concerning themselves, however, with the possibilities of CATV use, and often find that decisions have been made that preclude the possibility of their using it. At the national level, ALA is a member of both the Joint Council on Educational Telecommunications and PUBLICABLE, both of which are attempting to assure that the public will not be excluded from the use of CATV and that governmental units recognize an obligation to protect the interest of the public. The Chicago Public Library, the Rochester, New York Public Library, and the District of Columbia Public Library have been among the few actively concerned with CATV in libraries. Reported in the 1971 *Bowker Annual*, p. 302, was an experiment conducted by the Natrona County Public Library in Wyoming in which reference questions were answered via CATV. During the past year representatives of the District of Columbia Public Library (DCPL) appeared before the D.C. City Council in August of 1971 and drew a parallel between the founding of public libraries a century ago to provide citizens with free and equal access to books

---

[5]*Communications Technology for Urban Improvement: Report to the Department of Housing and Urban Development,* Washington, D.C. Committee on Telecommunications, National Academy of Engineering, June 1971 (PB200317).

which were relatively expensive at the time and the present opportunity to provide the citizenry with access to information transmitted on newer and even more expensive forms. DCPL would like to transmit cultural and educational programs based on its resources as well as on other resources in the area, and anticipates direct reference service with branch libraries and homes. The library proposed that it be assigned special responsibility for coordinating the programming of city government agencies; that meeting rooms in the system libraries be used as bases for a cable information system linking the citizens and government; that a representative of the library be included on the policy-making board of any executive agency operating CATV in the District; and that an intensive program be undertaken to educate the public to the potential of cable television.

The potential use for CATV in libraries is great. It could serve to extend traditional services provided by libraries: children's story hours, book talks, and cultural programs taking place in the library. With the use of videotape, libraries could generate special programs for specialized groups within the community. All of these services are possible now at relatively low cost. Other services possible with CATV, however, are considerably more expensive and, while technically feasible, are still in the experimental stage. For instance, it is possible to provide facsimile reproduction of newspapers, magazines, documents, etc. through CATV; computers can communicate with each other via CATV; a reader can request, read, respond, and even alter information with the aid of a light pen transmitting a signal which a TV screen can read. All of this is cheaper than a network based on existing telephone lines, which has far less communication capacity than one using cables.

In May 1971, the FCC accepted the recommendation of its Common Carrier Bureau to approve all applications to construct microwave links which meet basic technical and financial requirements. This decision followed an earlier groundbreaking decision to allow Microwave Communications, Inc. (MCI) to construct a microwave transmission system for specialized types of services along lines parallel to those constructed by AT&T. As of June 1971 there were some 1,700 applications. Two coast-to-coast networks are now expected, one by MCI and one by DATRAN. It is hoped that these new carriers will provide better services at less expense for communications among computers, but no new networks are yet in operation.

THE LIBRARY TECHNOLOGY PROGRAM

by

Marjorie E. Weissman*

In 1971 the Library Technology Program moved ahead in all its programs, with special emphasis on performance standards development and equipment research and evaluation projects. Significant progress was made in equipment improvement, while equipment surveys, consultations with manufacturers on library furniture, and equipment development received attention.

In basic, ongoing activities, the information service continued to answer inquiries from all over the world; information and articles about LTP continued to be disseminated regularly to the professional and business press and to profes-

---

*General Editor, Library Technology Program, American Library Association.

sional institutions and organizations; and *Library Technology Reports* enlarged its circulation.

PERFORMANCE STANDARDS DEVELOPMENT

LTP is represented on the American National Standards Institute Committee PH7 on Audiovisual Photographic Standards, concerned with setting standards for photographic systems, materials, apparatus, nomenclature, and test methods pertaining to audiovisual technology.

In connection with this committee, work continues on the drafting of performance standards for record players, tape recorders and playback units, 16mm motion picture sound projectors, and filmstrip and combination filmstrip/slide projectors. Sponsored jointly by LTP and the Association for Educational Communications and Technology, the work is being carried out by Dr. Raymond Wyman, Director of the Audiovisual Center at the University of Massachusetts, Amherst. It is anticipated that the proposed standards will be forwarded to the American National Standards Institute for adoption as ANSI standards. One of the benefits to be derived from the program is the provision of performance standards to manufacturers of audiovisual equipment, enabling them to produce equipment that will meet the requirements of librarians and media specialists.

The first drafts of two proposed performance standards, prepared two years ago, are undergoing slight technical revision: they are for bracket-type steel shelving and card catalog cabinets. Both programs are the responsibility of ANSI Committee Z85, which is sponsored by LTP.

ANSI Committee PH5 for Photographic Reproduction of Documents, on which LTP is represented, has been engaged in discussions regarding, among other subjects, the development of consumer standards for equipment, and performance standards for microform readers. LTP has a direct interest in both.

LTP has the chairmanship of, and represents the interests of the consumer on Storage Containers for Imaged Microfilm, a subcommittee of the National Microfilm Association Materials and Supplies Standards Committee. The parent committee is concerned with dimensions and methods of evaluation to determine quality, uniformity and life of materials used in the micrographics industry.

The director, representing LTP, has been active on the Government Printing Office Micropublishing advisory committee, which has been considering the GPO's proposal to publish federal government documents in microform.

LTP is also represented on the Illuminating Engineering Society Subcommittee on Library Lighting, which is revising the IES publication *Recommended Practice of Library Lighting*. The revision was scheduled to appear in 1971.

COMMITTEES

A subcommittee on Technical Processing Standardized Times, established in 1970, prepared a research proposal to carry out the first phase of the study. This phase is likely to include the identification of existing useful data of standardized times already established as well as the observation and timing of original cataloging. Future phases would establish standard times for tasks basic to library operations.

A Microfilm Cartridge Evaluation advisory subcommittee, initiated at the same time, and a subcommittee on Forms Standardization were discharged. A paper resulting from the work of the former committee was published in *Library Technology Reports* in January 1972.

EVALUATION PROGRAMS

An evaluative program, supported by LTP funds, for cassette tape recorders was completed. Eight heavy-duty models, specifically designed for institutional use, were tested, and results published in *Library Technology Reports*.

In another program, 24 top-of-the-line, 100 percent rag and permanent/durable purified wood pulp stocks from eight national distributors were tested to find out which, if any, met the ANSI Standard for Permanent and Durable Library Catalog Cards, Z85.1-1969. Only one stock was found to meet the standard in all respects. Further objectives of the program were to demonstrate how the performance standard might be used in place of specifications when ordering library catalog cards, and to encourage manufacturers to make available catalog card stock which meets or surpasses the requirements outlined in the standard. The program was supported by a grant of $3,322 from the Council on Library Resources, Inc.

A new program, supported by LTP funds, for the evaluation of eight microform readers was carried out, and results were published in *LTR*.

An extensive evaluation program of both arm and armless chairs suitable for general seating in libraries continued. Some 28 wood chairs were tested this year, and results were published in *Library Technology Reports*. Two wood samples remain to be tested in order to complete the entire program, in which a total of 50 wood or plastic chairs will be evaluated. The program is funded by the Council on Library Resources, Inc. Preliminary steps for producing a draft performance standard for general seating chairs are under way.

Four proposals for evaluation programs were submitted to a funding agency for its consideration of support. The programs were for performance testing of dry study carrels, evaluation of the effectiveness of film rejuvenation treatments, and performance testing of a new, low-cost card catalog cabinet constructed of particle board with a vinyl laminate finish. A companion proposal was made for testing plastic card catalog trays with wood fronts, a supplement to the work already carried on and completed this year by LTP on all-plastic trays. Results of those tests were published in *Library Technology Reports*. (Proposals had not yet been considered at time of writing.)

The feasibility of a user-evaluation program for microform readers is being explored. Such evaluation would follow laboratory testing of the devices.

SUBSCRIPTION SERVICE

Now in its seventh year of bimonthly publication, *Library Technology Reports* is subscribed to by libraries in every state in the Union and in some 39 countries. Although the year-end figure for subscriptions to *Library Technology Reports* showed a drop to 1,006 from 1,086 a year earlier, multiple subscriptions increased, raising the number of individual copies to 1,145 from 1,123 in the previous year. Of the total, 132 subscriptions are foreign.

In the past 12-month period, *LTR* published evaluations of the following: portable microfiche readers; bracket-type steel shelving; wood chairs and plastic-shell general seating chairs; cassette tape recorders; catalog card stock; card- and form-holding devices for electric and manual typewriters; record players and tape recorders; filmstrip and slide projectors; and a photocopier. Major market surveys were made of cassette tape recorders, study carrels, and card catalog cabinets. Each issue of *LTR* also contained abstracts from nonlibrary literature useful to librarians, a new products section, questions and answers on technical problems, and news about LTP.

BOOK PUBLISHING

The Evaluation of Micropublications: A Handbook for Librarians was published in June 1971 as No. 17 in LTP's numbered series of books. Written by Allen Veaner of Stanford University Libraries, its purpose is to instruct librarians and others responsible for the acquisition of micropublications on how to inspect and evaluate micropublications in the form of roll films, microfiche, and micro-opaques.

Two advisory committees were established, one for the publication of a manual on the organization of a library microtext reading room, and one for a manual on the organization and operation of library reprographic departments. The committees are preparing prospectuses and talking with potential authors.

CONSERVATION PROJECT

The Conservation of Library Materials project, Phase II, financed by a grant from the Council on Library Resources, Inc., plans to publish material by several experts in conservation. Subjects under consideration include the deacidification of paper, the support of weak and disintegrated paper, and the repair of leather bindings. Other papers will deal with treatment of fire- and water-damaged materials and with the restoration of vellum and parchment manuscript.

Restoration of Leather Bindings, the first manuscript in Phase II of the Conservation Series, has been sent to the typesetter for publication in early 1972. It deals with the restoration of leather bindings and was written by Bernard Middleton, a leading English independent book restorer and author of *A History of English Craft Bookbinding Technique.*

DEVELOPMENT AND MISCELLANEOUS ACTIVITIES

The Smyth Cleat Sewing Machine, developed through the efforts of LTP with the aid of funds from the Council on Library Resources, Inc., has undergone further modification by both the Smyth Company and a major library binder. Smyth will build ten production models of the latest version of the cleat sewer by May 1972, with the first machine being made available in March. The library binder is employing the prototype machine to sew all suitable materials having less than ½-inch margin. One innovation is the placing of hot-melt adhesive in each cleat, which results in securely locking the threads.

Significant advantages of the new machine are that a book sewn by it can be opened to lie flatter than one sewn by the standard method; and that, under normal circumstances, the method consumes about half the amount of paper from the inner margins as compared to the paper used by the oversewing method. It is also especially suitable for brittle materials. Testing has shown that the stitching is at least as durable as that of the oversewing machine generally used in binderies.

A further possible application of the machine is for the stitching of newspapers bound into volumes. Developmental work is going forward to modify the cleat sewer for edition binding.

The SE-LIN book labeling system has been further developed to operate with a computer-controlled typewriter for the production of multiple-copy labels. It had previously been adapted to operate on an automatic typewriter.

Numerous other activities have been explored during the year, with a view to ascertaining their feasibility for further work. Aids for the handicapped, with special attention to mouthstick page turners, a manual on library security, and ways to tackle the problem of informing new librarians of all past research in the field were among the subjects investigated.

As a result of the dissolution of the Institutional Research Council, of which LTP was a founder, and the distribution of its assets, ALA (LTP) owns two U.S. patents for a carpet wear tester. The tester was developed for the IRC under the auspices of LTP, which is now seeking means to make the device available to the market. Carpet manufacturers and others have evinced considerable interest in the tester, which, it is expected, will replace that long used by the industry and the National Bureau of Standards.

Library and Book Trade Events

CALENDAR OF BOOK TRADE AND PROMOTIONAL EVENTS, 1972

For additional information on book trade and promotional events, see *1972 Directory of Exhibit Opportunities; National, State, Regional,* published by the Association of American Publishers; *Chases' Calendar of Annual Events,* published by the Apple Tree Press, Box 1012, Flint, Mich. 48501; *Publishers' Weekly* "Calendar," appearing each issue, and *Library Journal's* "Calendar" feature, appearing each semimonthly issue. See also the following article, "Library Association Meetings."

January: Newbery and Caldecott Awards Announcement. Sponsored by the Awards Committee of the Children's Services Div., ALA, 50 E. Huron St., Chicago, Ill. 60611.

January 1: New Year's Day.

January 16–22: Printing Week. Sponsored by International Association of Printing House Craftsmen, 7599 Kenwood Rd., Cincinnati, Ohio 45236.

January 22–February 5: World Book Fair. New Delhi, India.

January 27–February 6: International Book Fair. Cairo, Egypt.

February: American Music Month. Sponsored by Natl. Fed. of Music Clubs, 600 S. Michigan Ave., Chicago, Ill. 60605.

February: Boy Scout Month. Sponsored by the National Council Boy Scouts of America, New Brunswick, N.J. 08903.

February 4: Book-Bike Day. Sponsored by Book-Bike, Inc., P.O. Box 6, Doylestown, Pa. 18901.

February 12: Lincoln's Birthday.

February 14: Valentine's Day.

February 20–26: Brotherhood Week. Sponsored by the National Conference of Christians & Jews, 43 W. 57th St., New York, N.Y. 10019.

February 20–26: Catholic Book Week. Sponsored by the Catholic Library Assn., 461 W. Lancaster Ave., Haverford, Pa. 19041.

February 21: Washington's Birthday.

February 27–March 1: American Toy Fair. Sponsored by Toy Manufacturers of America, 200 Fifth Ave., New York, N.Y. 10010.

March (tentative): Boys' Club Week. Sponsored by Boys' Club of America, 771 First Ave., New York, N.Y. 10017.

March: National Book Awards. Sponsored by Association of American Publishers; Amer. Booksellers Assn.; Assn. of Amer. Univ. Presses; Book Manufacturers' Institute; Children's Book Council; Natl. Assn. of College Stores, through the National Book Committee, Inc., 1 Park Ave., New York, N.Y. 10016.

March 3: World Day of Prayer. Sponsored by Church Women United, 475 Riverside Dr., New York, N.Y. 10027.

March 11–19: International Book Fair. Brussels, Belgium.

March 12–18: Girl Scout Week. Sponsored by Girl Scouts of the U.S.A., 830 Third Ave., New York, N.Y. 10022.

March 12–21: International Book Fair. Leipzig, East Germany.

March 14–18: European Educational Materials Fair. Hanover, W. Germany.

March 17: Camp Fire Girls Founders Day. Sponsored by Camp Fire Girls, Inc., 65 Worth St., New York, N.Y. 10013.

March 19–25: National Wildlife Week. Sponsored by the National Wildlife Federation, 1412 16th St., N.W., Washington, D.C. 20036.

March 21–22: International Community of Booksellers Associations. Paris, France.

March 30–April 6: Passover.

April: International Book Fair for Children and Youth. Sponsored by the Bologna Trade Fair Agency, Ciamician 4, 40127, Bologna, Italy.

April 2: Easter Sunday.

April 2: International Children's Book Day. Sponsored by International Board on Books for Young People, U.S. Contact: Children's Book Council, 175 Fifth Ave., New York, N.Y. 10010.

April 2: Mildred L. Batchelder Award Announcement. Sponsored by Award Committee, Children's Services Div., ALA, 50 E. Huron St., Chicago, Ill. 60611.

April 9–15: National Assn. of College Stores Convention. Houston, Tex. Sponsored by Natl. Assn. of College Stores, Oberlin, Ohio 44074.

April 14: Pan American Day. Sponsored by the Pan American Union, Washington, D.C. 20006.

April 16–22: National Library Week. Sponsored by National Book Committee, in cooperation with ALA, 1 Park Ave., New York, N.Y. 10016.

May: Assn. of American Publishers. Sponsored by Assn. of Amer. Pubs., 1 Park Ave., New York, N.Y. 10016.

May: Pulitzer Prize Announcement. Sponsored by Columbia University, New York, N.Y. 10027.

May 5: May Fellowship Day. Sponsored by Church Women United, 475 Riverside Dr., New York, N.Y. 10027.

May 7: Children's Spring Book Festival. Sponsored by Book World, 342 Madison Ave., New York, N.Y. 10017.

May 7–12: Church Press Convention. Banff, Alberta. Sponsored by Associated Church Press, Alfred P. Klausler, Exec. Secy., 875 Dearborn St., Chicago, Ill. 60610.

May 7–14: National Music Week. Sponsored by National Federation of Music Clubs, 600 S. Michigan Ave., Chicago, Ill. 60605.

May 14: Mother's Day.

May 15–21: International Publishers Assn. UNESCO, Paris, France.

May 15–May 22: International Book Fair. Warsaw, Poland.

May 22–27: American Merchant Marine Book Week. Sponsored by American Merchant Marine Library Association, U.S. Customs House, 1 Bowling Green, New York, N.Y. 10004.

May 22–27: International Book Festival. Nice, France.

May 26–June 8: DRUPA 6th International Fair, Printing and Paper. Sponsored by Dusseldorfer Messegesellschaft, m6H-NOWEA, 4 Dusseldorf 10, Box 10203, West Germany.

May 29: Memorial Day.

June: Assn. of American Univ. Presses. Sponsored by Assn. of American Univ. Presses, 1 Park Ave., New York, N.Y. 10016.

June: International Exhibition of Scientific and Technical Books and Journals. Paris, France.

June: National Recreation Month. Sponsored by National Recreation & Park Association, 1700 Pennsylvania Ave., N.W., Washington, D.C. 20006.

June 4–7: American Booksellers Assn. Convention. Shoreham Hotel, Washington, D.C. Sponsored by Amer. Booksellers Assn., 175 Fifth Ave., New York, N.Y. 10010.

June 18: Father's Day.

June 18–25: International Book Biennial. Sao Paulo, Brazil.

June 25–July 1: ALA Annual Conference. Chicago, Ill. Sponsored by American Library Assn., 50 E. Huron St., Chicago, Ill. 60611.

July: Ghana International Book Fair. Accra, Ghana.

July 4: Independence Day.

July 30:–August 3: Christian Booksellers Assn. Convention Hall, Denver, Colo.

Sponsored by Christian Booksellers Assn., John T. Bass, 2031 W. Cheyenne Blvd., Colorado Springs, Colo. 80906.

August 6–10: International Convention. Cleveland, Ohio. Sponsored by Intl. Assn. of Printing House Craftsmen, John Davies, Exec. Secy., 7599 Kenwood Rd., Cincinnati, Ohio 45236.

September 3–10: International Book Fair. Leipzig, East Germany.

September 4: Labor Day.

September 9: Jewish New Year.

September 28–October 3: Frankfurt Book Fair. Frankfurt-am-Main, West Germany.

October 1–7: National 4-H Week. Sponsored by Federal Extension Service, E. Dean Vaughan, Dir. 4-H Youth Development, U.S. Dept. of Agriculture, Washington, D.C. 20250.

October 22–28: American Education Week. Sponsored by National Education Assn., 1201 16th St., N.W., Washington, D.C. 20036; American Legion; National Congress of Parents and Teachers; U.S.O.E.

October 24: United Nations Day. Sponsored by United Nations Assn. of the United States of America, Inc., 345 E. 46 St., New York, N.Y. 10017.

October 27–November 26: Jewish Book Month. Sponsored by Jewish Book Council of America, 15 E. 26 St., New York, N.Y. 10010.

November 5–11: American Art Week. Sponsored by American Artists' Professional League, Frank C. Wright, President, 112 E. 19th St., New York, N.Y. 10003.

November 10–26: International Book Exhibition. Berlin, Germany.

November 13–19: Children's Book Week. Sponsored by Children's Book Council, 175 Fifth Ave., New York, N.Y. 10010.

November 18–25: Festival of Literature. Cheltenham, Gloucestershire, England.

November 19–26: Bible Week. Sponsored by the American Bible Society, 1865 Broadway, New York, N.Y. 10023.

November 23: Thanksgiving Day.

November 23–December 25: Worldwide Bible Reading Month. Sponsored by American Bible Society, 1865 Broadway, New York, N.Y. 10023.

November 29–December 18: 23rd Annual International Children's and Youth Book Exhibition. Bavarian State Library, Ludwigstrasse, Munich, Germany.

December 2: World Community Day. Sponsored by Society for a World Service Federation, Kurt Dreifuss, Pres., Box 545, Wilmette, Ill. 60091.

December 11: Nobel Prize. Sponsored by Swedish Academy, Stockholm, Sweden.

December 25: Christmas Day.

LIBRARY ASSOCIATION MEETINGS
1972

January 8: Lutheran Church Library Association. St. Paul, Minn.

January 21: Bibliographical Society of America. New York, N.Y.

January 21–23: Association of American Library Schools. Chicago, Ill.

January 22: Association of Research Libraries. Mid-winter Conference. Chicago, Ill.

January 23–29: American Library Association. Midwinter. Chicago, Ill.

February 3–5: Music Library Association. Tucson, Ariz.

February 12–16: American Association of School Administrators. Atlantic City, N.J.

February 24–26: Colorado Association of School Librarians; Colorado AV Asso-

ciation (Joint Meeting). Colorado Springs, Colo.

March 8–11: California Association of School Librarians; AV Education Association of California (Joint Meeting). San Diego, Calif.

March 10–11: Utah Library Association. Salt Lake City, Utah.

March 17–18: Washington State Association of School Librarians. (Place not set).

March 17–21: National Association of Secondary School Principals; National Association of State Supervisors and Directors of Secondary Education; Professors of Secondary School Administration and Supervision (Joint Meeting). Anaheim, Calif.

March 22–25: Alaska Library Association. Whitehorse, Yukon Territory, Canada.

March 23–25: Louisiana Library Association. Baton Rouge, La.

March 25–28: Association of California School Administrators. Anaheim, Calif.

April 2–7: Association for Childhood Education International. Denver, Colo.

April 3–6: Catholic Library Association. Chicago, Ill.

April 3–6: National Catholic Educational Association. Philadelphia, Pa.

April 5–8: Texas Library Association. Galveston, Tex.

April 8–13: National Association of Elementary School Principals. Miami Beach, Fla.

April 10: Inter-American Association of Agricultural Librarians and Documentalists. General Assembly. Buenos Aires, Argentina.

April 13–15: Alabama Library Association. Anniston, Ala.

April 13–15: Arizona Library Association. Tucson, Ariz.

April 13–15: Oklahoma Library Association. Stillwater, Okla.

April 14–15: Hawaii Library Association. Honolulu, Hawaii.

April 15–20: Council of Planning Librarians. Detroit, Mich.

April 16–21: Association of Educational Communications and Technology. Minneapolis, Minn.

April 19–23: New Jersey Library Association; New Jersey School Media Association (Joint Meeting). Atlantic City, N.J.

April 20–21: Indiana School Librarians Association. Bloomington, Ind.

April 20–22: Alpha Beta Alpha. Murray State University, Murray, Ky.

April 21: St. Croix Library Association. Christiansted, St. Croix, V.I.

April 21–22: Vermont Library Association. (Place not set).

April 26–29: New Mexico Library Association. Albuquerque, N.M.

April 27: Tennessee Library Association. Memphis, Tenn.

April 27–28: Maryland Library Association. Ocean City, Md.

April 27–29: Connecticut Library Association; Connecticut School Library Association (Joint Meeting). Meriden, Conn.

April 27–29: Florida Library Association. Miami Beach, Fla.

April 27–29: Idaho Library Association. McCall, Idaho.

April 27–29: Illinois Association of School Librarians; Illinois AV Association; Illinois Curriculum Association (Joint Meeting). Chicago, Ill.

April 27–29: Oregon Library Association. Roseburg, Ore.

April 28–29: Pennsylvania School Librarians Association. Shippensburg, Pa.

May 4–6: Wyoming Library Association. Cheyenne, Wyo.

May 5–6: Washington Library Association. Spokane, Wash.

May 6–8: New England School Library Association. Portsmouth, N.H.

May 9–10: Kansas Library Association. Wichita, Kans.

May 9–10: Maine Library Association; Maine School Library Association (Joint Meeting). Kennebunkport, Maine.

May 9–12: National Microfilm Association. New York, N.Y.

May 9–13: Educational Film Library Assn. (EFLA). New York, N.Y.

May 11: Film Library Information Council. New York, N.Y.

May 11–12: New Hampshire Library Council; New Hampshire School Media Association (Joint Meeting). Place not set).
May 11–13: Montana Library Association. Helena, Mont.
May 11–14: Ontario Library Association. Queen's University, Kingston, Ont.
May 12–13: Association of Research Libraries. Spring Conference. Atlanta, Ga.
May 12–14: Alberta Library Association. Edmonton, Alta.
May 14–24: International Association of Metropolitan City Libraries. Annual General Meeting. Milan, Italy.
May 25: American Merchant Marine Library Association. New York, N.Y.
June: Association of Jewish Libraries. Toronto, Ont.
June 4–8: Special Library Association. Boston, Mass.
June 10–16: Canadian Library Association. Regina, Sask.
June 11–15: Medical Library Association. San Diego, Calif.
June 17–19: Church and Synagogue Library Association. University of Maryland, Catonsville, Md.
June 19–23: American Theological Library Association. Waterloo Lutheran Univ., Waterloo, Ont.
June 24–30: National Educational Association. Atlantic City, N.J.
June 25: Beta Phi Mu. Chicago, Ill.
June 25–July 1: American Library Association. Chicago, Ill.
June 25–July 1: Theatre Library Association. Chicago, Ill.
June 27–29: Music Library Association. Chicago, Ill.
July 2–6: American Association of Law Libraries. Chicago, Ill.
July 15–18: National Audio-Visual Association. Convention & Exhibit. Kansas City, Mo.
August: Association of International Libraries. General Assembly. Budapest, Hungary.
August: International Institute for Children's Juvenile and Popular Literature. Tyrol, Austria.

August 28–September 2: International Federation of Library Associations. Budapest, Hungary.
September: International Association of Music Libraries. Bologna, Italy.
September: International Association of Sound Archives. Congress. Bologna, Italy.
September: International Federation for Documentation. Biennial Congress. Budapest, Hungary.
September 21–22: South Dakota Library Association. Aberdeen, S.D.
October: Florida Association of School Librarians; Florida AV Association; Florida Association of Educational TV (Joint Meeting). Palm Beach Shores, Fla.
Mid-October: Iowa Library Association. Waterloo, Iowa.
October 4–6: American Council on Education. Miami Beach, Fla.
October 4–7: Pennsylvania Library Association. Pittsburgh, Pa.
October 5–7: West Virginia Library Association. Convention. Clarksburg, W.Va.
October 8–14: California Library Assn. Anaheim, Calif.
October 11–13: Wisconsin Library Association. Milwaukee, Wis.
October 12–13: Minnesota Library Association. Brainerd, Minn.
October 12–14: Illinois Library Association. Chicago, Ill.
October 12–14: Nevada Library Association. Las Vegas, Nev.
October 18–20: Mississippi Library Association. Biloxi, Miss.
October 18–20: Missouri Library Association. Kansas City, Mo.
October 19–21: Ohio Library Association. Cincinnati, Ohio.
October 23–27: American Society for Information Science. Washington, D.C.
October 25–27: Michigan Library Association. Grand Rapids, Mich.
October 26–28: Indiana Library Association. Indianapolis, Ind.
October 26–28: Ohio Association of School Librarians. Columbus, Ohio.
October 27–28: Nebraska Library Association. Kearney, Nebr.

October 31–November 3: Society of American Archivists. Columbus, Ohio.
November 1–4: Southeastern Library Association; Southwestern Library Association (Joint Meeting). New Orleans, La.
November 8–11: New York Library Association. Rochester, N.Y.
November 30–December 3: Virginia Library Association. Norfolk, Va.
December 14–19: Association of Visual Science Librarians. New York, N.Y.

1973

January 20–23: National Audio-Visual Association. Houston, Tex,
January 28–February 3: American Library Association. Midwinter. Washington, D.C.
February 1–3: Music Library Association. Bloomington, Ind.
February 24–28: American Association of School Administrators. Atlantic City, N.J.
March 29–31: Louisiana Library Association. Shreveport, La.
April 4–8: Texas Library Association. Fort Worth, Tex.
April 5–7: Oklahoma Library Association. Tulsa, Okla.
April 14–19: Association for Educational Communications & Technology (AECT). Las Vegas, Nev.
April 14–19: National Association of Elementary School Principals. Detroit, Mich.
April 23–26: Catholic Library Association. Denver, Colo.
May 3–5: Florida Library Association. St. Petersburg, Fla.
May 10–11: New Hampshire Library Council; New Hampshire School Media Association (Joint Meeting). (Place not set).
June 10–14: Special Libraries Association. Pittsburgh, Pa.
June 16–22: Canadian Library Association. Sackville, N.B.
June 24–29: Theatre Library Association. Las Vegas, Nev.
June 24–30: American Library Association. Las Vegas, Nev.
June 28–30: Music Library Association. Las Vegas, Nev.
June 30–July 5: American Association of Law Libraries. Olympia, Wash.
July 1–6: National Education Assn. Portland, Ore.
August: International Association of Music Libraries. London, England.
August: International Federation of Library Associations. Grenoble, France.
September 20–21: South Dakota Library Association. Sioux Falls, S.D.
September 25–28: Society of American Archivists. St. Louis, Mo.
September 26–29: Missouri Library Association. St. Louis, Mo.
October 7–9: South Carolina Library Association. Columbia, S.C.
October: North Carolina Library Association. Winston-Salem, N.C.
October 9–12: Michigan Library Association. Detroit, Mich.
October 11–13: Nevada Library Association. Carson City, Nev.
October 22–26: American Society for Information Science. Los Angeles, Calif.
October 25–27: Virginia Library Association. Richmond, Va.
December 6–11: Association of Visual Science Librarians. San Francisco, Calif.

1974

January 20–26: American Library Association. Midwinter. Chicago, Ill.
July 7–13: American Library Association. New York, N.Y.
August: International Federation of Library Associations. Washington, D.C.
October 15–20: Southeastern Library Association. Richmond, Va.
October 16–19: Southwestern Library Association. Galveston, Tex.
October 23–25: Michigan Library Association. Lansing, Mich.
November 14–16: Virginia Library Association. Hot Springs, Va.

LITERARY AND LIBRARY PRIZES AND AWARDS, 1971

For a complete list of library and literary prizes, see the 1970 edition of *Literary and Library Prizes* (Bowker). See also *Library Journal's* year-end index. For a list of literary prize winners of 1971, see the annual summary issue of *Publishers' Weekly;* for a complete listing of library prize winners through 1958, see the 1959 edition of the *Bowker Annual.* See also *Children's Books: Awards and Prizes,* published by the Children's Book Council. For ALA scholarship and fellowship awards, see "Library Scholarships and Fellowships," this volume.

ABINGDON AWARD — $5,000. *Offered by:* Abingdon Press. *Winner:* Dr. Roger L. Shinn for *Wars and Rumors of Wars.*

ACADEMY OF AMERICAN POETS FELLOWSHIP — $10,000. For "distinguished poetic achievement." *Winner:* Howard Nemerov.

AIR FORCE ORGANIZATIONAL EXCELLENCE AWARD. *Winner:* The Air University Library, Maxwell Air Force Base, Alabama.

ARMED FORCES LIBRARIANS ACHIEVEMENT CITATION—Citation. To members of the Armed Forces Librarians Section for a significant contribution to the development of Armed Forces Library Service and to organizations encouraging an interest in libraries and reading. *Offered by:* ALA. *Winner:* Dorothy Fayne.

ATLANTIC GRANT AWARD. To provide a young author with time in which to write and a contract for publication of the finished work. *Offered jointly by:* Atlantic Monthly magazine, Atlantic Monthly Press, and Little, Brown and Company. *Winner:* Sharon R. Curtin for *Nobody Ever Died of Old Age.*

BANCROFT PRIZES — $4,000 each. For "books of exceptional merit and distinction in American history." *Offered by:* Columbia University. *Winners:* Erik Barnouw for *The Image Empire* (Oxford); David M. Kennedy for *Birth Control in America: The Career of Margaret Sanger* (Yale); Joseph Frazier Wall for *Andrew Carnegie* (Oxford).

MILDRED L. BATCHELDER AWARD CITATION. For the best children's book originally published in a foreign language and country and then published in the United States. *Donor:* ALA. *Winner:* Pantheon Books for Hans Baumann's *In the Land of Ur: The Discovery of Ancient Mesopotamia.* Stella Humphries is the translator.

BETA PHI MU AWARD—$50 & Citation. For distinguished service to the education of librarians. *Offered by:* ALA Library Education Division. *Donor:* Beta Phi Mu Fraternity. *Winner:* Leon Carnovsky.

BLACK ACADEMY OF ARTS AND LETTERS AWARD. *Winner:* George Jackson for *Soledad Brother: The Prison Letters of George Jackson* (Coward-McCann).

NANCY BLOCH MEMORIAL AWARD. *Winners:* June Jordan and Terri Bush for *The Voice of the Children* (Holt).

B'NAI B'RITH BOOK AWARD — $500. For "a single work of distinction on Judaism or Jewish life." *Winner:* Rabbi Herbert Wiener for *9½ Mystics* (Holt).

BOLLINGEN PRIZE IN POETRY—$5,000. *Offered by:* Yale Univ. Library. *Winners (1969–1970):* Richard P. Wilbur for *Walking to Sleep* (Harcourt); Mona Van Duyn for *To See, To Take* (Atheneum).

BOOK-OF-THE-YEAR MEDAL. *Offered by:* Canadian Association of Children's Librarians. *Winner:* William Toye for *Cartier Discovers the St. Lawrence* (Walck).

BOOKER PRIZE — $12,000. *Offered by:* the (British) Publishers Association and Booker McConnell, Ltd. *Winner:* V. S. Naipaul for *In a Free State* (Knopf).

BOSTON GLOBE–HORN BOOK CHILDREN'S BOOK AWARDS. *Winners:* John Rowe Townsend (for text) for *The Intruder* (Lippincott); Ezra Jack Keats (for illustration) for *Hi, Cat!* (Macmillan).

JOHN BURROUGHS MEDAL. *Offered by:* The John Burroughs Memorial Association, Inc., and the American Museum of Natural History. For distinguished nature writing. *Winner:* John K. Terres for *From Laurel Hill to Siler's Bog* (Knopf).

EDITH BUSBY AWARD — $2,500 advance against royalties. For an unpublished original work for boys and girls, ages 6-16. *Offered by:* Dodd, Mead & Company. *Winner:* Jack Ishmole for *Walk in the Sky.*

CALDECOTT MEDAL—Medal. For illustrator of best picture book of the year. *Donor:* ALA Children's Services Division. Medal contributed by Daniel Melcher. *Winner:* Gail E. Haley for *A Story, A Story* (Atheneum). (For a list of previous winners, see the 1970 *Bowker Annual,* pp. 318-319.)

FRANCIS JOSEPH CAMPBELL CITATION — Citation. For outstanding contributions to the achievement of library service to the blind. *Donor:* ALA's Round Table on Library Services to the Blind. *Winner:* Mrs. Ranald H. Macdonald.

CAREY-THOMAS AWARD. For a distinguished project of creative publishing. *Offered by:* R. R. Bowker Company. *Winner:* Random House for *Picasso 347.*

THE LEWIS CARROLL SHELF AWARDS. *Offered by:* Univ. of Wisconsin Communications for Children Conference. *Winners:* Esther Hautzig for *The Endless Steppe* (Crowell); Ida Chittum for *Farmer Hoo and the Baboons* (Delacorte); Margery Williams for *The Velveteen Rabbit* (Doubleday); Duncan Emrich for *Nonsense Books* (Four Winds); Reginald Ottley for *Boy Alone* (Harcourt); James Weldon and J. Rosamond Johnson for *Lift Every Voice and Sing* (Hawthorn Bks.); Sheila Burnford for *The Incredible Journey* (Little, Brown); Ellis Credle for *Down, Down the Mountain* (Nelson); Kristin Hunter for *The Soul Brothers and Sister Lou* (Scribners); Friedrich de la Motte Fouqué for *Undine* (Simon & Schuster); Mary Q. Steele for *Journey Outside* (Viking); and Rosemary Sutcliff for *The Witch's Brat* (Walck).

ANNUAL CHILDREN'S BOOK AWARD of the Child Study Association of America. *Winners:* James Lincoln Collier for *Rock Star* (Four Winds); Carli Laklan for *Migrant Girl* (McGraw-Hill).

CHILDREN'S SCIENCE BOOK AWARD of the New York Academy of Science. *Winner:* Roberts Richardson for *The Stars and Serendipity* (Pantheon).

COLUMBIA UNIVERSITY PRIZE IN AMERICAN ECONOMIC HISTORY—$1,000 and publication. *Winner:* William G. Whitney for *The Structure of the American Economy in the Late Nineteenth Century.*

SILVER MEDAL OF THE COMMONWEALTH CLUB OF CALIFORNIA. For the best book of poetry. *Winner:* Kay Boyle for *Testament for My Students* (Doubleday).

JOHN COTTON DANA PUBLICITY AWARDS — Certificate. For outstanding library publicity work. *Offered by:* Wilson Library Bulletin and the Public Relations Section of the ALA Library Administration Division. *Winners: Public Ls. with Population Up to 25,000:* Madison P.L., N.J.; *Public Ls. with Population between 25,000 and 100,000:* Fair Lawn Free P.L., N.J.; *Public Ls. with Population between 100,000 and 200,000:* Glendale P.L., Calif.; *Coll. and Univ. Ls.:* Univ. of Houston Ls., Tex.; *School Ls.:* Greenwich H. S. L., Conn.; *Cooperating Ls.:* Appalachia Improved Reference Services, Ohio; *Service Ls.:* Randolph Air Force Base, Tex.

COUNCIL ON INTERRACIAL BOOKS FOR CHILDREN AWARD — $500. To seek out writing talent among ethnic minorities. *Winners:* Virginia Driving Hawk Sineve for *Jimmy Yellow Hawk;* Juan Valenzuela for *I Am Magic;* Ray Anthony Shepard for *Warball.*

CLARENCE DAY AWARD. For any distinctive production, such as a book, essay, or series of lectures or programs, which has promoted the love of books and reading. *Winner:* Dee Alexander Brown, Agriculture Librarian, Univ. of Illinois, Urbana, for his books on the history of the American West.

JEFFERSON DAVIS AWARD. See FLETCHER PRATT AWARD.

DELTA KAPPA GAMMA SOCIETY EDUCATOR'S AWARD — $1,500. *Winner:* Muriel Beadle for *A Child's Mind* (Doubleday).

DEVINS AWARD — $500. *Offered by:* Kansas City Poetry Contests. *Winner:* Henry Carlisle for *The Rough-Hewn Table* (Univ. of Missouri Press).

MELVIL DEWEY AWARD—Medal. For creative professional achievement of high order. *Offered by:* ALA. *Donor:* Forest Press, Inc. *Winner:* William J. Welsh.

DISTINGUISHED LIBRARY SERVICE AWARD. For contributions toward furthering the role of the library in elementary and secondary education. *Donor:* American Association of School Librarians. *Winner:* Paul Douglas West.

ROBERT B. DOWNS INTELLECTUAL FREEDOM AWARD. *Offered by:* Univ. of Illinois Graduate School of Library Science. *Winner:* The President's Commission on Obscenity and Pornography.

ENCYCLOPAEDIA BRITANNICA SCHOOL LIBRARY AWARDS — $5,000. For significant improvements in elementary library media services. *Winners:* first place — Leflore County Schools, Greenwood, Miss.; second place — Cedar Rapids, Iowa, Community Schools; third place — Oakland, Calif., Unified School District.

M. EVANS FICTION AWARD. *Winner:* Amos Kollek for *Don't Ask Me If I Love* (M. Evans).

EXCEPTIONAL SERVICE AWARD. *Offered by:* ALA's Association of Hospital and Institution Libraries Division. *Winner:* Margaret C. Hannigan.

FREE ENTERPRISE WRITER OF THE YEAR AWARD. To a writer who has made a major contribution to the understanding of the American free enterprise system through the printed word. *Offered by:* National Management Association. *Winner:* William F. Buckley, Jr.

GEORGE FREEDLEY MEMORIAL AWARD. *Offered by:* Theatre Library Association. *Winner:* Brooks Atkinson for *Broadway* (Macmillan).

FRIENDS OF AMERICAN WRITERS AWARD — $1,000. To a "native or resident author of the Middle West, or a book with a Mid-Western locale." *Winner:* Edward Robb Ellis for *A Nation in Torment: The Great American Depression, 1929-1939* (Coward, McCann).

J. MORRIS JONES–WORLD BOOK ENCYCLOPEDIA–ALA GOALS AWARD—$25,000. *Offered by:* Field Enterprises Educational Corp. *Winner:* The project "Total Community Library Service: A Conference and Follow-Up Activities."

GOLDEN ANNIVERSARY PRIZE AWARD — $1,000. For books and articles on an aspect of speech or the theater. *Offered by:* Speech Communications Association. *Winner:* Loren Reid for *Charles James Fox: A Man for the People* (Univ. of Missouri Press).

GOLDEN EAGLE AWARD of the International Book Festival at Nice. *Winner:* Edmund Wilson.

GRAPHIC PRIZE AWARD of the 1971 Children's Book Fair at Bologna, Italy. *Winner:* Parents' Magazine Press for *Arm in Arm* by Remy Charlip.

GROLIER AWARD—$1,000. To salaried librarian for outstanding contribution to the reading of young people. *Offered by:* ALA. *Donor:* Grolier Society. *Winner:* Sara L. Siebert.

C. S. HAMMOND AND COMPANY AWARD. For effectively encouraging the use of maps and atlases or promoting an interest in cartography. *Winner:* University of Chicago Laboratory School's High School Library.

AMELIA FRANCES HOWARD-GIBBON AWARD. To a Canadian artist for the best illustrated children's book. *Offered by:* Canadian Association of Children's Librarians. *Winner:* Elizabeth Cleaver for *The Wind Has Wings* (Walck).

ANNUAL IOWA SCHOOL OF LETTERS AWARD — $1,000. To an original book-length collection of short stories by a single author. *Offered by:* Univ. of Iowa. *Winner:* Philip O'Connor for *Old Morals, Small Continents, Darker Times* (Univ. of Iowa Press).

JOSEPH HENRY JACKSON AWARD — $2,000. *Offered by:* The San Francisco Foundation. *Winner:* Richard Lourie for *Sagittarius in Warsaw*.

JOURNAL OF LIBRARY HISTORY AWARD. For the best historical research manuscript to appear in *JLH*. *Winner:* Dr. Joseph A. Boromé for *The Origin and Growth of the Public Libraries of Dominica*.

KIKUCHI KAN PRIZE — $1,000. For "distinguished service in introducing Japanese literature to America and to Europe." *Offered by:* Japanese literary magazine *Bungeishunju*. *Winner:* Harold Strauss, senior editor at Knopf.

CORETTA SCOTT KING AWARD. *Winner:* Charlemae Rollins for *Black Troubadour: Langston Hughes* (Rand McNally).

ROGER KLEIN AWARD. For editing. *Winner:* Frances McCullough of Harper & Row.

FLORENCE AND HARRY KOVNER MEMORIAL AWARD. For English-Jewish poetry. *Winner:* Ruth Finer Mintz for *Traveler Through Time* (Jonathan David).

LAMONT POETRY SELECTION. *Offered by:* Academy of American Poets. *Winner:* Stephens Dobyns for *Concurring Beasts* (Atheneum).

LAYMEN'S NATIONAL BIBLE COMMITTEE AWARDS. *Winners:* Pearl S. Buck for *The Story Bible* (Bartholomew House); Kenneth N. Taylor for *The Living Bible* (Tyndale House Publishers).

LIBRARY PUBLIC RELATIONS COUNCIL AWARD. For the best library publicity materials. *Winners:* Enoch Pratt Free L., Baltimore, Md.; New York P.L., New York City, N.Y.; Gloucester P.L., N.J.; Nassau L. System, N.Y.; Chicago P.L., Ill.; Milwaukee P.L., Wis.; Dayton and Montgomery County P.L., Ohio.

JOSEPH WHARTON LIPPINCOTT AWARD —$1,000, Medal & Citation. For distinguished service in the profession of librarianship. *Offered by:* ALA. *Donor:* Joseph W. Lippincott. *Winner:* William S. Dix.

LOUISIANA LIBRARY ASSOCIATION'S LITERARY MEDALLION. For the "best book on a Louisiana subject published in 1970." *Winner:* Sister Dorothea McCants for *They Came to Louisiana* (Louisiana State Univ. Press).

JAMES RUSSELL LOWELL PRIZE. For an outstanding literary or linguistic study by a member of the Modern Language Association of America. *Winner:* Dr. Bruce A. Rosenberg for *The Art of the American Folk Preacher* (Oxford).

MADGA DONATO PRIZE — $2,000. For "the best book published in Mexico in 1970." *Winner:* Augusto Monterroso for *The Black Sheep and Other Fables* (Doubleday).

MARGARET MANN CITATION—Citation. For distinguished contribution to librarianship through cataloging and classification. *Donor:* Cataloging & Classification Section, ALA Resources & Technical Services Division. *Winner:* Henriette D. Avram.

MEDICAL LIBRARY ASSOCIATION REGENTS AWARD. For scholarship or technical achievement. *Winner:* Dr. Jaroslav Nemec for *International Bibliography of Medicolegal Serials*.

FREDERIC G. MELCHER BOOK AWARD — $1,000, Medallion, and Citation. For a work published in America "judged to be the most significant contribution to religious liberalism." *Winner:* Father Daniel Berrigan for *No Bars to Manhood* (Doubleday), *The Trial of the Catonsville Nine* (Beacon), and *Trial Poems* (Beacon).

THOMAS MORE MEDAL. For the most distinguished contribution to Catholic literature in 1970. *Winner:* Daniel Callahan for *Abortion: Law, Choice and Morality* (Macmillan).

ISADORE GILBERT MUDGE CITATION. For distinguished contributions to reference librarianship. *Donor:* ALA. *Winner:* James B. Childs.

NATIONAL BOOK AWARDS — $1,000 each. *Winners:* for arts and letters: Francis Steegmuller for *Cocteau* (Atlantic–Little, Brown); for children's books: Lloyd Alexander for *The Marvelous Misadventures of Sebastian* (Dutton); for fiction: Saul Bellow for *Mr. Sammler's Planet* (Viking); for history and biography: James McGregor Burns for *Roosevelt: The Soldier of Freedom* (Harcourt); for poetry: Mona Van Duyn for *To See, To Take* (Atheneum); for the sciences: Raymond Phineas Stearns for *Science in the British Colonies of America* (Univ. of Illinois Press); for translation: Frank Jones for *Saint Joan of the Stockyards* by Bertolt Brecht (Indiana Univ. Press), and Edward G. Seidensticker for *The*

Sound of the Mountain by Yasunari Kawabata (Knopf).

NATIONAL MEDAL FOR LITERATURE — $5,000 and Bronze Medal. To a living American writer for the excellence of his or her total contribution to the world of letters. *Offered by:* National Book Committee. *Winner:* E. B. White.

NATIONAL MEDIA AWARD. In recognition of outstanding reporting which increases public knowledge and understanding of psychology. *Offered by:* American Psychological Association. *Winner:* Emily Hahn for *On the Side of the Apes* (Crowell).

NEBULA AWARDS. *Offered by:* Science Fiction Writers of America. *Winners:* for novel: Larry Niven for *Ringworld* (Ballantine Books); for novella: Fritz Leiber for *Ill Met at Lankhmar;* for novelette: Theodore Sturgeon for *Slow Sculpture.*

NENE AWARD. *Offered by:* Hawaii Association of School Librarians and Children's Section of the Hawaii Library Association. For the book receiving the most votes cast by Hawaiian school children in grades 4–8. *Winner:* Beverly Cleary for *Ramona the Pest* (Morrow) and *Mitch and Amy* (Morrow).

FREDERICK NIVEN AWARD. For the best book — novel, poetry, biography — written either in Scotland or by a Scot anywhere else in the world. *Winner:* Mary Stewart for *The Crystal Cave* and other works (Morrow).

JOHN NEWBERY MEDAL—Medal. For most distinguished work of literature for children of the year. *Donor:* ALA Children's Services Division. Medal contributed by Daniel Melcher. *Winner:* Betsy Byars for *Summer of the Swans* (Viking). (For a list of previous winners see the 1970 Bowker Annual, pp. 317-318.)

NEW ZEALAND BUCKLAND LITERARY AWARD. *Winner:* Joy Cowley for *Man of Straw* (Doubleday).

NOBEL PRIZE FOR LITERATURE. *Administered by:* Swedish Academy in Stockholm. *Winner:* Pablo Neruda.

EUNICE ROCKWELL OBERLY MEMORIAL AWARD. For the best bibliography on agriculture or related sciences. *Offered by:* ALA, Reference Services Division. *Winner:* John T. Schlebecker for *Bibliography of Books and Pamphlets on the History of Agriculture in the United States, 1607–1967* (ABC-CLIO Press).

OHIOANA BOOK AWARDS *Offered by:* the Martha Kinney Cooper Ohioana Library Association. *Winners:* Dr. Foy Kohler for *Understanding the Russians: A Citizen's Primer* (Harper); John Unterecker for *Voyager: A Life of Hart Crane* (Farrar, Strauss); William Manners for *T. R. and Will* (Harcourt); Jesse Owens for *Blackthink: My Life as Black Man and White Man* (Morrow); Marion Renick for *Ohio* (Coward, McCann); Robert McKay for *Dave's Song* (Hawthorn Bks.); Alberta Pierson Hannum for *Look Back with Love* (Vanguard).

OKLAHOMA LIBRARY ASSOCIATION DISTINGUISHED SERVICE AWARD. To a librarian who has demonstrated a "valid, thorough, and imaginative concept of librarianship and library service." *Winner:* Esther Mae Henke.

ONTARIO LIBRARY TRUSTEES' LIBRARIAN AWARD. *Winner:* June Munro.

P.E.N. TRANSLATION PRIZE. *Winner:* Max Hayward for his translation of Nadezhda Mandelstam's *Hope Against Hope* (Atheneum).

ESTHER J. PIERCY AWARD. For contributions to librarianship in the field of the technical services by younger members of the profession. *Offered by:* ALA. *Winner:* John Phillip Immroth.

FLETCHER PRATT AWARD. *Offered by:* New York Civil War Round Table. *Winner:* Dr. Frank E. Vandiver for *Their Tattered Flags* (Harper's Magazine Press), which also received the first annual JEFFERSON DAVIS AWARD from the Confederate Memorial Literary Society.

PUTNAM AWARD. *Winner:* Henry Carlisle for *Voyage to the First of December.*

PULITZER PRIZES. *Winners:* for drama: Paul Zindel for *The Effects of Gamma Rays on Man-in-the-Moon Marigolds;* for history: James MacGregor Burns for *Roosevelt: The Soldier of Freedom* (Harcourt); for biography: Lawrence Thompson for *Robert Frost: The Years of Triumph, 1915–1938* (Holt); for poetry:

William S. Merwin for *The Carrier of Ladders* (Atheneum); for general nonfiction: John Toland for *The Rising Sun* (Random).

SIR WALTER RALEIGH AWARD. *Offered by:* the Historical Book Club of North Carolina. *Winner:* John Ehle for *Time of Drums* (Harper).

REGINA MEDAL AWARD. For continued distinguished contribution to the field of children's literature. *Offered by:* Catholic Library Association. *Winner:* Tasha Tudor.

ROBINSON MEDAL. *Offered by:* (British) Library Association. *Winner:* Frank Gurney, for developing an automated circulation system.

RUTGERS UNIVERSITY AWARD. For outstanding service to education and to librarianship. *Winner:* Ethel Marion Fair.

SCARECROW PRESS AWARD FOR LIBRARY LITERATURE. *Winner:* Irene B. Hoadley for *The Undergraduate Library* (American Library Association).

CHARLES SCRIBNER'S SONS AWARDS. For librarians working with children. *Winners:* Meredith Bishop; Sheila R. Furer; Mary Ann McIntire; Elizabeth M. Thompson.

CONSTANCE LINDSAY SKINNER AWARD. For "having given to humanity and to books something over and beyond the duty owed to her alloted tasks." *Offered by:* Women's National Book Association. *Winner:* Augusta Baker.

CHARLIE MAY SIMON CHILDREN'S BOOK AWARD. *Offered by:* Elementary Council of the Arkansas State Dept. of Education. *Winner:* Joan Lexau for *Striped Ice Cream* (Lippincott).

TRUSTEE CITATION OF MERIT — Certificates. For distinguished service to library development. *Offered by:* American Library Trustee Association of the ALA. *Winners:* Jean Smith and Jacqueline Enochs.

UNIVERSITY OF MICHIGAN PRESS BOOK AWARD. *Winner:* Sidney Fine for *Sit-Down: The General Motors Strike of 1936–1937* (Univ. of Michigan Press).

WILLIAM ALLEN WHITE CHILDREN'S BOOK AWARD. For the book receiving the most votes cast by Kansas children in grades 4–8. *Winner:* Walt Morey for *Kavik the Wolf Dog* (Dutton).

H. W. WILSON COMPANY LIBRARY PERIODICAL AWARD — Certificate. To a periodical published by a local, state, or regional library, library group, or library association in the U.S. or Canada for "outstanding contribution to the library profession." *Offered by:* ALA. *Donor:* H. W. Wilson Co. *Winner: Texas Library Journal.*

HALSEY W. WILSON LIBRARY RECRUITMENT AWARD — $1,000. To any local, state or regional library association, or other appropriate group concerned with recruitment to the profession for the development of a sustained program of recruitment for librarianship. *Donor:* ALA. *Winner:* Library Careers of Syracuse, N.Y.

WRANGLER AWARDS. For outstanding Western literary works. *Offered by:* National Cowboy Hall of Fame and Western Heritage Center. *Winners:* juvenile: Betty Baker for *And One Was a Wooden Indian* (Macmillan); novel: A. B. Guthrie Jr. for *Arfive* (Houghton); nonfiction: Harry Sinclair Drago for *The Great Range Wars* (Dodd, Mead); art book: Robert F. Karolevitz for *Where Your Heart Is: The Story of Harvey Dunn, Artist* (North Plains Press).

BASIC BOOKS AND PERIODICALS FOR LIBRARIANS

Compiled by

Flora D. Colton*

IN-PRINT BOOKS, 1971
General Works

AMERICAN LIBRARY DIRECTORY 1970–71. Revised biennially. 27th ed. New York: R. R. Bowker, 1970. $33.00.

ASH, Lee, ed. A Biographical Directory of Librarians in the United States and Canada. 5th ed. Chicago: American Library Association, 1970. $45.00.

BENTON, Mildred, and Signe Ottersen. Roster of Federal Libraries. Washington: George Washington University, Department of Medical and Public Affairs, 1970. Free from Federal Library Committee, Room 310, Library of Congress, Washington, D.C. 20540.

BOWKER ANNUAL OF LIBRARY AND BOOK TRADE INFORMATION. New York: R. R. Bowker, 1972. $18.50.

ENCYCLOPEDIA OF LIBRARY AND INFORMATION SCIENCE. Ed. by Allen Kent and Harold Lancour. New York: Marcel Dekker, 1968– 18 vols. in prep. Vols. 1-5 (1968 to 1971). $45.00 per vol. (nonsubscribers); $35.00 per vol. (subscribers).

GARVEY, Mona. Library Displays: Their Purpose, Construction and Use. New York: H. W. Wilson, 1969. $7.50.

HARROD, L. M., comp. The Librarians' Glossary. 3rd ed. rev. Dist. by British Book Centre. $25.00.

HICKS, Warren B., and Alma M. Tillin. Developing Multi-Media Libraries. New York: R. R. Bowker, 1970. $9.95.

JENNISON, Peter S., and Robert N. Sheridan, eds. The Future of General Adult Books and Reading in America. Chicago: American Library Association, 1970. $8.75.

KNIGHT, Douglas M., and E. Shepley Nourse, eds. Libraries at Large: Tradition, Innovation, and the National Interest. New York: R. R. Bowker, 1969. $16.50.

WORLD GUIDE TO LIBRARIES. 3rd ed. New York: R. R. Bowker, 1970. 4 vols. $44.00.

Administration

AMERICAN LIBRARY ASSOCIATION. Library Administration Division. Personnel Organization and Procedure; a Manual Suggested for Use in College and University Libraries. 2nd ed. Chicago: American Library Association, 1968. $2.50.

———. Personnel Organization and Procedure; a Manual Suggested for Use in Public Libraries. 2nd ed. Chicago: American Library Association, 1968. $2.50.

CORRIGAN, Dorothy D. Workbook for a Successful Workshop. Chicago: American Library Association, American Library Trustee Association, 1967. (ALTA Publication, No. 1). $1.00.

DOUGHERTY, Richard M., and Fred J. Heinritz. Scientific Management of Library Operations. Metuchen, N.J.: Scarecrow Press, 1966. $7.00.

GREGORY, Ruth W., and Lester L. Stoffel. Public Libraries in Cooperative Systems; Administrative Patterns for Service. Chicago: American Library Association, 1971. $9.95.

HARTMAN, W. H. Matthes, and A. Proeme. Management Information Systems Handbook. New York: McGraw-Hill, c1968. $29.50.

LANGMEAD, Stephen, and Margaret Beckman. New Library Design: Guide Lines to Planning Academic Library Buildings. New York: Wiley, 1971. $12.25.

THE LIBRARY BUILDING CONSULTANT; Role and Responsibility. Ed. by Ernest R. DeProspo, Jr. New Brunswick, N.J.: Rutgers University Press, 1969. $4.50.

LIBRARY SURVEYS AND DEVELOPMENT PLANS; an Annotated Bibliography. Min-

---

*Headquarters Librarian, American Library Association.

neapolis, Minn.: ERIC Clearinghouse for Library and Information Sciences, 1969. (ERIC/CLIS Bibliography Series, No. 3). Microfiche $.65; hard copy $3.29. Available from ERIC Document Reproduction Service.

MURDICK, Robert G., and Joel E. Ross. Information Systems for Modern Management. Englewood Cliffs, N.J.: Prentice-Hall, 1971. $11.95.

PENNA, C. V. The Planning of Library and Documentation Services, 2nd ed. Paris, UNESCO, 1970. (UNESCO Manuals for Libraries, No. 17). $4.00. Dist. by UNIPUB, Box 433, N.Y.C.

PLATE, Kenneth H. Management Personnel in Libraries; a Theoretical Model for Analysis. Rockaway, N.J.: American Faculty Press, 1970. $7.95.

PROBLEMS IN UNIVERSITY LIBRARY MANAGEMENT; A Study Conducted by Booz, Allen and Hamilton, Inc. Washington: Association of Research Libraries, 1970. $2.00.

RAFFEL, Jeffrey A., and Robert Shisko. Systematic Analysis of University Libraries: An Application of Cost Benefit Analysis to the M.I.T. Libraries. Cambridge, Mass.: M.I.T. Press, 1969. $6.95.

ROGERS, Rutherford D., and David C. Weber. University Library Administration. New York: H. W. Wilson, 1971. $24.00.

SINCLAIR, Dorothy. Administration of the Small Public Library. Chicago: American Library Association, 1965. $5.00.

STEBBINS, Kathleen B. Personnel Administration in Libraries. Second edition revised and largely rewritten by Foster E. Mohrhardt. Metuchen, N.J.: Scarecrow Press, 1966. $9.00.

STONE, Elizabeth. Training for the Improvement of Library Administration. Urbana, Ill.: University of Illinois, Graduate School of Library Science, 1967. (Monograph Series, No. 2). $3.00, pap. $2.00.

STUDY OF CIRCULATION CONTROL SYSTEMS. Chicago: American Library Association, 1961. (LTP Publication No. 1). $3.50.

YOUNG, Virginia G., ed. The Library Trustee; a Practical Guidebook. 2nd ed. New York: R. R. Bowker, 1969. $9.00.

Automation and Information Retrieval

ANNUAL REVIEW OF INFORMATION SCIENCE AND TECHNOLOGY. Vol. 6. Chicago: Encyclopaedia Britannica, 1971. $17.50.

C.A.C.U.L. Workshop on Library Automation, 4th ed. Hamilton, Ont., 1970. Automation in Libraries; Papers. Ottawa, Canadian Association of College and University Libraries, 1970.

DOLBY, J. L., V. J. Forsyth, and H. L. Resnikoff. Computerized Library Catalogs; Their Growth, Cost, and Utility. Cambridge, Mass.: M.I.T. Press, 1969. $10.00.

HAYES, Robert M., and Joseph Becker. Handbook of Data Processing for Libraries. New York: Wiley, 1970. $19.95.

MORSE, Philip M. Library Effectiveness; a Systems Approach. Cambridge, Mass.: M.I.T. Press, 1968. $10.00.

SARACEVIC, Tefko, comp. Introduction to Information Science. New York: R. R. Bowker, 1970. $25.00.

VICKERY, Brian Campbell. Techniques of Information Retrieval. Hamden, Conn.: Archon Books, 1970. $11.00.

Buildings, Furniture, and Equipment

BERKELEY, Bernard. Floors; Selection and Maintenance. Chicago: American Library Association, 1968. (LTP Publication, No. 13). $12.50.

CLINCHY, Evans. Joint Occupancy: Profiles of Significant Schools. New York: Educational Facilities Laboratories, 1970. Free.

EDUCATIONAL CHANGE AND ARCHITECTURAL CONSEQUENCES; a Report on Facilities for Individualized Instruction. New York: Educational Facilities Laboratories, 1968. $2.00.

ELLSWORTH, Ralph E. Planning the College and University Library Building; a Book for Campus Planners and Architects. Boulder, Colo.: Pruett Press, 1968. $8.00.

GAWRECKI, Drahoslav. Compact Library Shelving. Chicago: American Library Association, 1968. (LTP Publication, No. 14). $7.00.

GRIFFIN, C. W., Jr. Systems: an Approach to School Construction. New York: Educational Facilities Laboratories, 1971. $2.00.

GUIDE TO MICROREPRODUCTION EQUIPMENT. 4th ed. Annapolis, Maryland: National Microfilm Association, 1968. $12.50. Supplement 1970. $8.50.

HAWKEN, William R. Copying Methods Manual. Chicago: American Library Association, 1966. (LTP Publication, No. 11). $15.00.

LIBRARIES: BUILDING FOR THE FUTURE. Proceedings of the Library Buildings Institute and the ALTA Workshop, 1965. Chicago: American Library Association, 1967. $4.50.

LIBRARY ENVIRONMENT: ASPECTS OF INTERIOR PLANNING. Proceedings of the Library Equipment Institute, 1964. Chicago: American Library Association, 1965. $2.00.

MEASUREMENT AND COMPARISON OF PHYSICAL FACILITIES FOR LIBRARIES. Chicago: American Library Association, 1970. $1.50.

METCALF, Keyes D. Planning Academic and Research Library Buildings. New York: McGraw-Hill, 1965. $16.00.

MYLLER, Rolf. The Design of the Small Public Library. New York: R. R. Bowker, 1966. $12.75.

PROCUREMENT OF LIBRARY FURNISHINGS...Proceedings of the Library Equipment Institute, 1966. Chicago: American Library Association, 1969. $3.75.

PROTECTING THE LIBRARY AND ITS RESOURCES. Chicago: American Library Association, 1963. (LTP Publication No. 7). $8.50.

WHEELER, Joseph L. A Reconsideration of the Strategic Location for Public Library Buildings. Urbana, Ill.: University of Illinois, Graduate School of Library Science, 1967. (Occasional Papers, No. 85). $1.00.

Children's and Young Adults' Services and Materials

AFRICA; an Annotated List of Printed Materials Suitable for Children. New York: Information Center on Children's Cultures. U.S. Committee for UNICEF, 1968. $1.00.

BAKER, Augusta. The Black Experience in Children's Books. New York: New York Public Library, 1971. $.50.

BOOKS FOR CHILDREN 1960–1965; as Selected and Reviewed by the *Booklist and Subscription Books Bulletin*. Chicago: American Library Association, 1966. $10.00; 1965–1966, $2.00; 1966–1967, $2.25; 1967–1968, $3.00; 1968–1969, $3.50; 1969–1970, $3.50.

BRODERICK, Dorothy M. An Introduction to Children's Work in Public Libraries. New York: H. W. Wilson, 1965. $5.00.

CHILDREN'S BOOKS IN PRINT, 1971. New York: R. R. Bowker, 1971. $15.95.

CHILDREN'S CATALOG. 12th ed. New York: H. W. Wilson, 1971. $25.00. Includes four annual supplements.

COLBERT, Margaret, comp. Children's Books: Awards and Prizes. 1971 ed. New York: Children's Book Council, 1971. $2.95.

EGOFF, Sheila, G. T. Stubbs, and L. F. Ashley, eds. Only Connect; Readings on Children's Literature. New York: Oxford University Press, 1969. Paper $4.95.

FIELD, Carolyn W., ed. Subject Collections in Children's Literature. New York, R. R. Bowker, 1969. $7.95.

FOR STORYTELLERS AND STORYTELLING: Bibliographies, Materials and Resource Aids. Chicago: American Library Association, 1968. $1.50.

HAVILAND, Virginia, comp. Children and Poetry; a Selective, Annotated Bibliography. Washington: Government Printing Office, 1969. $.75.

HAVILAND, Virginia. Children's Literature; a Guide to Reference Sources. Washington, D.C.: Library of Congress, 1966. $2.50.

I READ, YOU READ, WE READ . . . Chicago: American Library Association, 1971. $2.00.

KARL, Jean. From Childhood to Childhood. New York: John Day, 1970. $6.50.

LATIN AMERICA; an Annotated List of Materials for Children. New York: Information Center on Children's Cultures.

U.S. Committee for UNICEF, 1969. $1.00.

LEPMAN, Jella. A Bridge of Children's Books. Chicago: American Library Association, 1969. $5.00.

LET'S READ TOGETHER; Books for Family Enjoyment. 3rd ed. Chicago: American Library Association, 1969. Paper. $1.50.

MEIGS, Cornelia Lynde. A Critical History of Children's Literature . . . Rev. ed. New York: Macmillan, 1969. $12.95.

THE NEAR EAST AND NORTH AFRICA; an Annotated List of Materials for Children. New York: Information Center on Children's Cultures. U.S. Committee for UNICEF, 1970. $1.00.

PELLOWSKI, Anne. The World of Children's Literature. New York: R. R. Bowker, 1968. $21.50.

SMITH, Lillian H. The Unreluctant Years; a Critical Approach to Children's Literature. New York: Viking Press, 1967. $1.50. Paperback reprint of 1953 A.L.A. imprint.

SUBJECT GUIDE TO CHILDREN'S BOOKS IN PRINT, 1971. New York: R. R. Bowker, 1971. $15.95.

TOWNSEND, John Rowe. A Sense of Story; Essays on Contemporary Writers for Children. London: Longman, 1971. £1.75 net.

College and University Libraries

AMERICAN LIBRARY ASSOCIATION. Association of College and Research Libraries. A Selected Bibliography on Library Development and Management for Junior College Libraries. Chicago: American Library Association, 1968. $1.25.

BERTALAN, Frank J. The Junior College Library Collection. Newark, N.J.: Bro-Dart Foundation, 1968. $34.75.

BOOKS FOR COLLEGE LIBRARIES: a Selected List of Approximately 53,400 Titles. Prepared under the direction of Melvin J. Voigt and Joseph H. Treyz. Chicago: American Library Association, 1967. $45.00.

BRADEN, Irene Andrea. The Undergraduate Library. Chicago: American Library Association, 1969. (ACRL Monograph, No. 31). $8.50.

GELFAND, Morris A. University Libraries for Developing Countries. Paris: UNESCO, 1968. (UNESCO Manuals for Libraries, No. 14). $3.00.

PIRIE, James W., comp. Books for Junior College Libraries. Chicago: American Library Association, 1969. $35.00.

REYNOLDS, Michael M., comp. Reader in the Academic Library. Washington: NCR Microcard Editions, [1970] $11.95.

Education for Librarianship

BONE, Larry Earl, ed. Library Education; an International Survey. Urbana, Ill.: University of Illinois, Graduate School of Library Science, 1968. $6.00.

———. Library School Teaching Methods: Courses in the Selection of Adult Materials. Urbana, Ill.: University of Illinois, Graduate School of Library Science, 1969. $3.50.

CARROLL, C. Edward. The Professionalization of Education for Librarianship with Special Reference to the Years 1940–1960. Metuchen, N.J.: Scarecrow Press, 1970. $10.00.

DANTON, J. Periam. Between M.L.S. and Ph.D.; a Study of Sixth Year Specialist Programs in Library School. Chicago: American Library Association, 1970. $3.75.

FINANCIAL ASSISTANCE FOR LIBRARY EDUCATION; Academic Year 1972–1973. Chicago: American Library Association, 1971. Single copy free.

GOLDHOR, Herbert, ed. Education for Librarianship: The Design of the Curriculum of Library Schools. Urbana, Illinois: University of Illinois, Graduate School of Library Science, 1971. (Monograph No. 11). $4.00.

GREAT BRITAIN. Library Advisory Council (England). A Report on the Supply and Training of Librarians. London: H.M.S.O., 1968. 6s.6d. (32½ p.)

KORTENDICK, James J., and Elizabeth W. Stone. Job Dimensions and Educational Needs in Librarianship. Chicago: American Library Association, 1971. $14.00.

LIBRARY EDUCATION AND MANPOWER; a Statement of Policy Adopted by the Council of the American Library Association, June 30, 1970. Chicago: American Library Association, 1970. Free.

LIEBERMAN, Irving. A Working Bibliography of Commercially Available Audio-Visual Materials for the Teaching of Library Science. Urbana, Ill.: University of Illinois, Graduate School of Library Science, 1968. (Occasional Papers, No. 94). Free.

Handicapped, Library Services for

ACCREDITATION COUNCIL FOR FACILITIES FOR THE MENTALLY RETARDED. Standards for Residential Facilities for the Mentally Retarded. Chicago: Joint Commission on Accreditation of Hospitals, 1971. $1.00. For library services see pages 59-63. Section 3.5.

BIBLIOTHERAPY: METHODS AND MATERIALS. Chicago: American Library Association, 1971. $5.95.

BOELKE, Joanne, comp. Library Service to the Visually and Physically Handicapped. Washington: ERIC Clearinghouse for Library and Information Sciences, 1970. (Bibliography Series. No. 4). Microfiche $0.25; hard copy $1.00.

DESIGN FOR ALL AMERICANS. Report of National Commission on Architectural Barriers to Rehabilitation of the Handicapped. Washington, D.C.: U.S. Government Printing Office, 1968. $.50.

LANDAU, Robert A., and Judith S. Nyren. Large Type Books in Print. New York: R. R. Bowker, 1970. $11.95.

STANDARDS FOR LIBRARY SERVICES FOR THE BLIND AND VISUALLY HANDICAPPED. Chicago: American Library Association, 1967. $1.67.

Intellectual Freedom

AMERICAN LIBRARY ASSOCIATION. Office for Intellectual Freedom. What to Do before the Censor Comes — and After. Rev. ed. Chicago: American Library Association, 1965. 4p. $.10.

DE GRAZIA, Edward. Censorship Landmarks. New York: R. R. Bowker, 1969. $21.95.

DOWNS, Robert B., ed. First Freedom; Liberty and Justice in the World of Books and Reading. Chicago: American Library Association, 1960. $8.50.

FISKE, Marjorie. Book Selection and Censorship: a Study of School and Public Libraries in California. Berkeley: University of California Press, 1968. (California Library Reprint, Series No. 1). $8.00.

FREEDOM TO READ STATEMENT. Revised. Chicago: American Library Association, 1953. Single copy free.

HARVEY, James A. Librarians, Censorship and Intellectual Freedom; an Annotated Bibliography 1968–69. Chicago: American Library Association, 1970. $1.25.

INTELLECTUAL FREEDOM STATEMENT; an Interpretation of the Library Bill of Rights. Chicago: American Library Association, Office for Intellectual Freedom, 1971. $.10.

LIBRARY BILL OF RIGHTS. Chicago: American Library Association, 1967. Single copy free.

MERRITT, LeRoy Charles. Book Selection and Intellectual Freedom. New York: H. W. Wilson, 1970. $6.00.

MOON, Eric, ed. Book Selection and Censorship. New York: R. R. Bowker, 1969. $11.95.

POLICY ON CONFIDENTIALITY OF LIBRARY RECORDS. Chicago: American Library Association, Office for Intellectual Freedom, 1971. Free.

RESOLUTION ON CHALLENGED MATERIALS. Chicago: American Library Association, Office for Intellectual Freedom, 1971. Free.

THE STUDENTS' RIGHT TO READ. Champaign, Ill.: National Council of Teachers of English, 1962. $.25.

Interlibrary Loan

THOMSON, Sarah K. Interlibrary Loan Involving Academic Libraries. Chicago: American Library Association, 1970. (ACRL Monograph, No. 32). $5.00.

———. Interlibrary Loan Procedure Manual. Chicago: American Library Association, 1970. $4.50.

Library History

WYNAR, Bohdan S. Research Methods in Library Science; a Bibliographic Guide with Topical Outlines. Littleton, Colo.: Libraries Unlimited, 1971. (Research

Studies in Library Science, No. 4). $8.50. See entries 199-209, 224-309.

Library Legislation

AMERICAN LIBRARY LAWS. 3rd ed. Chicago: American Library Association, 1964. $15.00. 1st Supp., 1965, $5.50; 2nd Supp., 1967, $6.00; 3rd Supp., 1969, $6.50; 4th Supp., 1971, $6.50.

Materials Selection

AUDIOVISUAL MARKET PLACE; a Multimedia Guide. 1972/73 ed. New York: R. R. Bowker, 1972. $17.50.

COURTNEY, Winifred F., ed. The Reader's Adviser; a Guide to the Best in Literature. 11th ed. New York: R. R. Bowker, 1968-1969. 2 vols. Vol. 1, $22.50; Vol. 2, $19.95. (Also available is *The Reader's Adviser: English Literature*. New York: Barnes & Noble. paper $3.50.)

EDUCATIONAL FILM LIBRARY ASSOCIATION. Film Evaluation Guide, Supplement 1965-1967. New York: The Association, 1968. $10.00.

FICTION CATALOG. 8th ed. New York: H. W. Wilson, 1971. $25.00. Includes four annual supplements.

GAVER, Mary Virginia, ed. Background Readings in Building Library Collections. Metuchen, N.J.: Scarecrow Press, 1969. 2 vols. $30.00.

JACKSON, Ellen. Subject Guide to Major United States Government Publications. Chicago: American Library Association, 1968. $5.50.

LEIDY, W. Philip. A Popular Guide to Government Publications. 3rd ed. New York: Columbia University Press, 1968. $12.00.

Periodicals and Serials

INTERNATIONAL SUBSCRIPTION AGENTS; an Annotated Directory. 2nd ed. Chicago: American Library Association, 1969. $3.50.

IRREGULAR SERIALS AND ANNUALS; an International Directory. 2nd ed. New York: R. R. Bowker, 1972. Price not set.

KATZ, Bill, and Berry Gargal. Magazines for Libraries; for the General Reader and Public, School, Junior College, and College Libraries. New York: R. R. Bowker, 1969. $18.95.

LIBRARY AND DOCUMENTATION JOURNALS. 3rd ed. The Hague: International Federation for Documentation. 20 Dutch guilders.

NEVERMAN, F. John. International Directory of Back Issue Periodical Vendors: Periodicals, Newspapers, Newspaper Indexes, Documents. 2nd enl. ed. New York: Special Libraries Association, 1968. $2.25.

NEW SERIAL TITLES 1950-1960. Washington, D.C.: Library of Congress, 1961. $56.25. 1966-1969 Cumulation. 2 vols. $115.00. Eight monthly and four quarterly issues and annual cumulation, 1970–. $150.00 a year.

———. 1961-1965 Cumulation. New York: R. R. Bowker, 1966. 3 vols. $49.50.

PAN, Elizabeth. Library Serials Control Systems: a Literature Review and Bibliography. Washington: ERIC Clearinghouse on Library and Information Sciences, 1970. Microfiche $0.25. Hard copy $2.25.

ULRICH'S INTERNATIONAL PERIODICALS DIRECTORY. 14th ed. New York: R. R. Bowker, 1971. 2 vols. $42.50.

UNION LIST OF SERIALS IN THE LIBRARIES OF THE UNITED STATES AND CANADA. 3rd ed. New York: H. W. Wilson, 1965. 5 vols. $120.00.

WINCKLER, Paul A. Library Periodicals Directory. Greenvale, L.I., N.Y.: Long Island University, Graduate Library School, 1967. $5.00.

Public Libraries

BOOKS FOR PUBLIC LIBRARIES: Selected Titles for Small Libraries and New Branches. New York: R. R. Bowker, 1970. $9.95.

BROWN, Eleanor F. Bookmobiles and Bookmobile Service. Metuchen, N.J.: Scarecrow Press, 1967. $11.50.

GUIDELINES FOR AUDIOVISUAL MATERIALS AND SERVICES FOR PUBLIC LIBRARIES. Chicago: American Library Association, 1970. $1.00.

GUTHMAN, Judith Dommu. Metropolitan Libraries; the Challenge and the Promise. Chicago: American Library Association, 1969. (Public Library Reporter, No. 15). $1.75.

MARTIN, Lowell A. Library Response to Urban Change; a Study of the Chicago Public Library. Chicago: American Library Association, 1969. $8.50.
MINIMUM STANDARDS FOR PUBLIC LIBRARY SYSTEMS, 1966. Chicago: American Library Association, 1967. $1.75.
NELSON ASSOCIATES, INC. Public Library Systems in the United States: a Survey of Multijurisdictional Systems. Chicago: American Library Association, 1969. $10.00.
NYREN, Dorothy, comp. Community Service: Innovations in Outreach at the Brooklyn Public Library. Chicago: American Library Association, 1970. (Public Library Reporter, No. 16). $1.75.
PENNELL, Lois G., ed. The Bookmobile — a New Look. Chicago: American Library Association, 1969. (Public Library Reporter, No. 14). $1.75.
PUBLIC LIBRARY CATALOG. 5th ed. New York: H. W. Wilson, 1968. Includes four annual supplements, 1969–1972. $50.00.
SMALL PUBLIC LIBRARY; a Series of Guides for Community Librarians and Trustees. Chicago: American Library Association, 1962–1970. $10.00. Includes 19 guides plus 16 supplements.
STANDARDS FOR LIBRARY FUNCTIONS AT THE STATE LEVEL. Revision of the 1963 edition. Chicago: American Library Association, 1970. $2.00.
STENSTROM, Ralph H. Cooperation between Types of Libraries 1940–1968; an Annotated Bibliography. Chicago: American Library Association, 1970. $4.00.

Reference Aids and Services

AMERICAN REFERENCE BOOKS ANNUAL. Littleton, Colo.: Libraries Unlimited, 1970–71. 1970 (2 vols.); 1971 (1 vol.) $19.75 a year.
ASH, Lee, and Denis Lorenz, comps. Subject Collections; a Guide to Special Book Collections in Libraries. 3rd ed. rev. and enl. New York: R. R. Bowker, 1967. $23.50.
CHENEY, Frances Neal. Fundamental Reference Sources. Chicago: American Library Association, 1971. $8.50.

DOWNS, Robert B., and Frances B. Jenkins, eds. Bibliography; Current State and Future Trends. Urbana, Ill.: University of Illinois Press, 1967. (Illinois Contributions to Librarianship, No. 8). $8.95. Appeared orig. in *Library Trends*, Jan. and Apr. 1967.
GROGAN, Denis. Case Studies in Reference Work. Hamden, Connecticut: Archon Books, 1967. $6.00.
KATZ, William A. Introduction to Reference Work. New York: McGraw-Hill, 1969. 2 vols. Vol. 1 $8.50; Vol. 2 $6.95.
LEARNING DIRECTORY 1970–71; Users' Guide, Source Index, Instructional Materials Index. New York: Westinghouse Learning Corporation, 1970. 7 vols. $90.00.
NICEM. Index to 8mm Motion Cartridges. New York: R. R. Bowker, 1969. $19.50.
———. Index to Overhead Transparencies. New York: R. R. Bowker, 1969. $22.50.
———. Index to 35mm Educational Filmstrips. 2nd ed. New York: R. R. Bowker, 1970. $34.00.
REFERENCE AND SUBSCRIPTION BOOKS REVIEWS 1968–70. Chicago: American Library Association, Dec. 1970. $2.75.
REFERENCE BOOKS FOR SMALL AND MEDIUM-SIZED PUBLIC LIBRARIES. Chicago: American Library Association, 1969. $4.50.
SHEEHY, Eugene P. Guide to Reference Books. 8th ed. First Supplement, 1965–1966. Chicago: American Library Association, 1968. $3.50. Second Supplement, 1967–1968. 1970. $4.00.
WALFORD, Albert John, ed. Guide to Reference Material. 2nd ed. London: Library Association, 1966–1970. 3 vols. $13.95 ea. Available from R. R. Bowker.
WALSH, S. Padraig. General Encyclopedias in Print, 1971–1972. New York: R. R. Bowker, 1971. $9.95.
———. Home Reference Books in Print; a Comparative Analysis. New York: R. R. Bowker, 1969. $10.95.
WINCHELL, Constance M. Guide to Reference Books. 8th ed. Chicago: American Library Association, 1967. $15.00.

School Libraries

AMERICAN LIBRARY ASSOCIATION. American Association of School Librarians. School Library Manpower Project. Occupational Definitions for School Library Media Personnel. Chicago: American Library Association, 1971. $2.00.

———. School Library Personnel; Task Analysis Survey. Chicago: American Library Association, 1969. $2.00.

———. Task Analysis Survey Instrument. Chicago: American Library Association, 1969. $1.00.

BREWER, Margaret L., and Sharon O. Willis. The Elementary School Library. Hamden, Conn.: Shoe String Press, 1970. $5.00.

DAVIES, Ruth Ann. The School Library; a Force for Educational Excellence. New York: R. R. Bowker, 1969. $10.95.

EAKIN, Mary K. Subject Index to Books for Primary Grades. 3rd ed. Chicago: American Library Association, 1967. $4.00.

GAVER, Mary V., ed. The Elementary School Library Collection. 6th ed. Newark, N.J.: Bro-Dart Foundation, 1971. $19.50.

GILLESPIE, John, and Diana Lembo. Introducing Books, a Guide for the Middle Grades. New York: R. R. Bowker, 1971. $10.50.

HODGES, Elizabeth D., comp. and ed. Books for Elementary School Libraries; an Initial Collection. Chicago: American Library Association, 1969. $7.50.

JUNIOR HIGH SCHOOL LIBRARY CATALOG. 2nd ed. New York: H. W. Wilson, 1970. Includes four annual supplements. $30.00.

LOWRIE, Jean E. Elementary School Libraries. 2nd ed. Metuchen, N.J.: Scarecrow Press, 1970. $5.00.

NATIONAL ASSOCIATION OF INDEPENDENT SCHOOLS. Library Committee. Books for Secondary School Libraries; a Basic List. 4th ed. New York: R. R. Bowker, 1971. $8.95.

RUFSVOLD, Margaret I., and Carolyn Guss. Guides to Educational Media. Chicago: American Library Association, 1971. $4.50.

SCHOOL LIBRARY SUPERVISORS' DIRECTORY. 3rd ed. New York: R. R. Bowker, 1968. $12.85.

SCOTT, Marion H., comp. and ed. Periodicals for School Libraries; a Guide to Magazines, Newspapers, and Periodical Indexes. Chicago: American Library Association, 1969. $3.50.

SELECTING MATERIALS FOR SCHOOL LIBRARIES: Guidelines and Selection Sources to Insure Quality Collections. Chicago: American Library Association, American Association of School Libraries, 1971. Single copy free.

SENIOR HIGH SCHOOL LIBRARY CATALOG. 9th ed. New York: H. W. Wilson Co., 1967. Includes five annual supplements. $20.00.

STANDARDS FOR SCHOOL MEDIA PROGRAMS; Prepared by the American Association of School Librarians and the Department of Audiovisual Instruction of the National Education Association. Chicago: American Library Association, 1969. $2.00.

THE TEACHERS' LIBRARY; How to Organize It and What to Include. Revised ed. Washington, D.C.: National Education Association, 1968. $1.50.

UNIVERSITY PRESS BOOKS FOR SECONDARY SCHOOL LIBRARIES. New York: American University Press Services, 1971. Free.

Special Libraries

COUNCIL OF NATIONAL LIBRARY ASSOCIATIONS. Joint Committee on Library Service in Hospitals. Basic List of Guides and Information Sources for Professional and Patients' Libraries in Hospitals. 6th rev. ed. Chicago: American Library Association, Association of Hospital and Institution Libraries, 1969. Single copy free.

CUPRALL, Henry F. J., ed. Phonograph Record Libraries . . . 2nd ed. Hamden, Conn.: Archon Books, 1970. $9.50.

FISHER, Eva Lou. A Checklist for the Organization, Operation and Evaluation of a Company Library. 2nd ed. New York: Special Libraries Association, 1966. $3.00.

MATERIALS SELECTION FOR HOSPITAL AND INSTITUTION LIBRARIES. Chicago:

American Library Association, Association of Hospital and Institution Libraries, 1967. Single copy free.
STANDARDS FOR LIBRARY SERVICES IN HEALTH CARE INSTITUTIONS. Chicago: American Library Association, 1970. $1.75.
STRABLE, Edward G., ed. Special Libraries; a Guide for Management. New York: Special Libraries Association, 1966. $4.00.

Statistics

See article entitled "Statistics of Libraries for the 1970s" by Dorothy Gilford and Frank L. Schick, this volume.

Technical Services

AMERICAN LIBRARY ASSOCIATION. Library Technology Program. Development of Performance Standards for Binding Used in Libraries, Phase 2. Chicago: American Library Association, 1966. (LTP Publication, No. 10). $3.00.
ARCHER, Horace Richard, ed. Rare Book Collections. Chicago: American Library Association, 1965. (ACRL Monograph, No. 27). $3.50.
BLOOMBERG, Marty, and G. Edward Evans. Introduction to Technical Services for Library Technicians. Littleton, Col.: Libraries Unlimited, 1971. $7.50.
COLLISION, Robert L. W. Indexes and Indexing. 3rd rev. ed. New York: DeGraff, 1969. $6.95.
DOUGHERTY, Richard M., and Lawrence E. Leonard. Management and Costs of Technical Processes: a Bibliographical Review 1876–1969. Metuchen, N.J.: Scarecrow Press, 1970. $5.00.
HORTON, Carolyn. Cleaning and Preserving Bindings and Related Materials. 2nd ed. Chicago: American Library Association, 1969. (LTP Publication, No. 16). $4.50.
LEONARD, Lawrence E., Joan M. Maier, and Richard M. Dougherty. Centralized Book Processing; a Feasibility Study Based on Colorado Academic Libraries. Metuchen, N.J.: Scarecrow Press, 1969. $10.00.
MILLER, Shirley. The Vertical File and Its Satellites. Littleton, Col.: Libraries Unlimited, 1971. $8.50.

RIDDLE, Jean, Shirley Lewis, and Janet MacDonald. Non-book Materials; the Organization of Integrated Collections. Ottawa: Canadian Library Association, 1970. $3.50. Distributed in the U.S. by the American Library Association.
SCHELLENBERG, Theodore R. The Management of Archives. New York: Columbia University Press, 1965. $13.50.
SEELY, Pauline A., ed. A.L.A. Rules for Filing Catalog Cards. 2nd ed. Chicago: American Library Association, 1968. $6.75.
———. A.L.A. Rules for Filing Catalog Cards. 2nd ed., abridged. Chicago: American Library Association, 1968. $2.00.
THOMAS, Pauline Ann, and H. East. The Use of Bibliographic Records in Libraries. London: Aslib, 1969. (Aslib, Occasional Publication, No. 3). 26s. (£1.30).
WESTBY, Barbara M. Commercial Processing Firms; a Directory. In *Library Resources and Technical Services.* Vol. 13, No. 2, pp. 209–286. Spring 1969. $2.50.
VEANER, Allen B. Evaluation of Micropublications . . . Chicago: American Library Association, 1971. (LTP Publication No. 17). $3.25.

Technical Services: Acquisitions

HENSEL, Evelyn, and Peter D. Veillete. Purchasing Library Materials in Public and School Libraries. Chicago: American Library Association, 1969. $3.00.
INTERNATIONAL SEMINAR ON APPROVAL AND GATHERING PLANS IN LARGE AND MEDIUM SIZE ACADEMIC LIBRARIES. 2nd ed. Advances in Understanding Approval and Gathering Plans in Academic Libraries. Kalamazoo: Western Michigan University Press, 1970. $11.95.

Technical Services: Cataloging and Classification

AKERS, Susan Grey. Simple Library Cataloging. 5th ed. Metuchen, N.J.: Scarecrow Press, 1969. $7.50.
AMERICAN LIBRARY ASSOCIATION. Library Technology Project. Catalog Card Reproduction. Chicago: American Li-

brary Association, 1965. (LTP Publication, No. 9). $8.50.

ANGLO-AMERICAN CATALOGING RULES ... North American Text. rev. ed. Chicago: American Library Association, 1970. $9.50, pap. $4.75.

BOLL, John J. Introduction to Cataloging. Vol. I: Descriptive Cataloging. New York: McGraw-Hill, 1970. $6.95.

DENISON, Barbara, comp. Selected Materials in Classification; a Bibliography. New York: Special Libraries Association, 1968. 142pp. $10.75.

DEWEY, Melvil. Dewey Decimal Classification and Relative Index. 17th ed. Lake Placid Club, N.Y.: Forest Press, 1965. 2 vols. $30.00; 9th abr. ed., 1965. $10.00.

DUNKIN, Paul S. Cataloging U.S.A. Chicago: American Library Association, 1969. $4.00.

MATTHIS, Raimund, and Desmond Taylor. Adopting the Library of Congress Classification System: A Manual of Methods and Techniques for Application or Conversion. New York: R. R. Bowker, 1971. $13.95.

SCHIMMELPFENG, Richard H., and E. Donald Cook, eds. The Use of the Library of Congress Classification; Proceedings of the Institute, July 7–9, 1966. Chicago: American Library Association, 1968. $6.50.

STANDARDS FOR CATALOGING NONPRINT MATERIALS. Washington, D.C.: Association for Educational Communications and Technology, 1971. $3.50.

U.S. LIBRARY OF CONGRESS. Subject Cataloging Division. Subject Headings, 7th ed. Washington, D.C.: Library of Congress, Card Division, 1966. $15.00; Supplement, July 1964–Dec. 1965, $2.50; Annual Supplements 1966–1969, $5.00 a year. 1970. $15.00 a year.

WESTBY, Barbara M., ed. Sears List of Subject Headings. 9th ed. New York: H. W. Wilson, 1965. $10.00.

PERIODICALS

(For bibliographic details, see *Ulrich's International Periodicals Directory*, R. R. Bowker.)

American Libraries
College and Research Libraries
Journal of Education for Librarianship
Journal of Library Automation
Journal of Library History
Library and Information Science Abstracts
Library Journal
Library Literature
Library of Congress Information Bulletin
Library Quarterly
Library Resources and Technical Services
Library Technology Reports
Library Trends
Libri
Newsletter on Intellectual Freedom
RQ
School Libraries
School Library Journal
Special Libraries
Top of the News
Wilson Library Bulletin

BASIC BOOKS FOR THE PUBLISHER AND THE BOOK TRADE

Compiled by
Jean R. Peters*

GENERAL WORKS

Bibliographies of Books About Books and The Book Trade

These four books contain extensive bibliographies.

THE BOOK IN AMERICA. by Hellmut Lehmann-Haupt, Lawrence B. Wroth, and Rollo Silver. New York: R. R. Bowker Co. 2nd ed., 1951; 4th printing 1967. $15.95. Bibliography covers cultural history, bibliography, printing and bookmaking, book illustration, bookselling and publishing.

BOOKMAKING: THE ILLUSTRATED GUIDE TO DESIGN AND PRODUCTION. by Marshall Lee. New York: R. R. Bowker Co., 1965. $14.00. Bibliography is divided into three parts: Part 1 covers books, and includes a general bibliography as well as extensive coverage of books on all technical aspects of bookmaking; Part 2 lists periodicals; Part 3 lists other sources, including associations, libraries, and films.

PRINTING AND PROMOTION HANDBOOK. by Daniel Melcher and Nancy Larrick. New York: McGraw-Hill Book Co. 3rd ed., 1966. $15.95. Bibliography covers general reference, advertising, art work, book publishing, color, copyright, copywriting, direct mail, displays, editing and proofreading, layout and design, lettering, magazine publishing, newspaper publishing, packaging, paper, photography, printing, publicity, radio and TV, shipping, typography, visual aids.

THE READER'S ADVISER. Edited by Winifred F. Courtney. New York: R. R. Bowker Co. 11th ed. 1968. Vol. 1. $22.50. A Guide to the Best in Literature. Chapters on "Books about Books" and "Bibliography" cover history of publishing and bookselling, practice of publishing, bookmaking, rare book collecting, trade & specialized bibliographies, directories, book selection tools, best books, etc. Vol. 2 covers Religion, Science, Philosophy, the Social Sciences, History. 1969. $19.95.

International

A GUIDE TO BOOK-PUBLISHING. See under "Book Publishing."

LA EMPRESA DEL LIBRO EN AMERICA LATINA. Edited by Mary C. Turner. A "Literary Market Place" for Latin America. Buenos Aires: Bowker Editores. 1968. $7.00. New edition coming in 1972.

INTERNATIONAL LITERARY MARKET PLACE. European Edition. New York: R. R. Bowker Co. Biennially. $13.50.

PUBLISHERS' INTERNATIONAL DIRECTORY. New York: R. R. Bowker Co. 4th ed. 1970. $30.00.

UNESCO STATISTICAL YEARBOOK. Covering 1970. New York: UNIPUB. 1971. $35.00.

WRITERS AND ARTISTS YEARBOOK. Covering British book world. Boston: The Writer, Inc. 1971. $6.95.

BOOK FINDING TOOLS

AMERICAN BOOK PUBLISHING RECORD CUMULATIVES. New York: R. R. Bowker Co. 1960–1964 Cumulative. 4 vols. $98.95. 1965–1969 Cumulative. 5 vols. $122.00. Annual vols. $35.00 each.

BOOKS IN PRINT. 2 vols. New York: R. R. Bowker Co. Annually. $42.50 the set.

BRITISH BOOKS IN PRINT: THE REFERENCE CATALOG OF CURRENT LITERATURE. New York: R. R. Bowker Co. 1970. $38.00 (plus duty where applicable).

EL-HI TEXTBOOKS IN PRINT 1971. New York: R. R. Bowker Co. $13.50.

CATALOG OF REPRINTS IN SERIES. Edited by Robert M. Orton. Metuchen, N.J.: Scarecrow Press. 21st ed. 1972. Price not set.

CUMULATIVE BOOK INDEX. New York: H. W. Wilson Co. Monthly with bound semi-annual and larger cumulations. Service basis.

---

*Librarian, R. R. Bowker Company.

FORTHCOMING BOOKS. New York: R. R. Bowker Co. $24.00 a year, $6.00 single copy. Bi-monthly supplement to "Books in Print."

SUBJECT GUIDE TO FORTHCOMING BOOKS. Bi-monthly supplement to Subject Guide to Books in Print. $11.00 a year. $32.00 in combination with "Forthcoming Books."

LIBROS EN VENTA. A Spanish language "Books in Print—Subject Guide." Edited by Mary C. Turner. New York: R. R. Bowker Co. 1964. $27.50. Supplement 1. 1968. o.p. Supplement 2. 1969. $20.00. Supplement 3. 1971. $20.00.

PAPERBOUND BOOKS IN PRINT. New York, R. R. Bowker Co. Two cumulative volumes per year, in March and October. $32.50. Single copies, $18.95.

PUBLISHERS' TRADE LIST ANNUAL. New York: R. R. Bowker Co. Annually. 6 vols. $29.50.

SUBJECT GUIDE TO BOOKS IN PRINT. 2 vols. New York: R. R. Bowker Co. Annually. $37.50 the set.

SUBJECT GUIDE TO FORTHCOMING BOOKS. See under FORTHCOMING BOOKS. See also THE READER'S ADVISER.

BOOK PUBLISHING

AMERICAN NATIONAL STANDARD FOR COMPILING BOOK STATISTICS. by ANSI Standards Committee Z-39. New York: American National Standards Institute. 1968. $2.25.

THE AMERICAN READING PUBLIC: A Symposium. Edited by Roger H. Smith from Winter 1962 issue of *Daedalus*. New York: R. R. Bowker Co. 1964. $8.95.

THE ART AND SCIENCE OF BOOK PUBLISHING. by Herbert S. Bailey, Jr. New York: Harper & Row. 1970. $7.95.

THE BOOK IN AMERICA. by Hellmut Lehmann-Haupt. New York: R. R. Bowker Co. 2nd ed. 1951. 4th printing 1967. $15.95.

BOOK PUBLISHING IN AMERICA. by Charles A. Madison. New York: McGraw-Hill Book Co. 1966. $12.50.

BOOK PUBLISHING: Inside Views. by Jean Spealman Kujoth. Metuchen, N.J.: Scarecrow Press. 1971. $12.50.

BOOKMAN'S GLOSSARY. by Mary C. Turner. New York: R. R. Bowker Co. 4th ed. 1961. $8.50.

BOWKER ANNUAL OF LIBRARY AND BOOK TRADE INFORMATION. New York: R. R. Bowker Co. Annually. 1972. $18.50.

BOWKER LECTURES ON BOOK PUBLISHING. New York: R. R. Bowker Co. 1957. $8.50.

ECONOMIC SURVEY OF THE BOOK INDUSTRY, 1930–31. (The Cheney Report). by O. H. Cheney. New York: R. R. Bowker Co. 1932. Reprinted 1960, with introduction by Robert Frase. $10.95.

A GUIDE TO BOOK-PUBLISHING. by Datus C. Smith, Jr. New York: R. R. Bowker Co. 1966. $7.95.

GUINNESS BOOK OF WORLD RECORDS. Section on Literature and Books. by Norris & Ross McWhirter. New York: Sterling Publishing Co. $5.95; Bantam pap. $1.50.

NOW, BARABBAS. by William Jovanovich. New York: Harcourt. pap. $1.65.

THE PUBLISHING EXPERIENCE. by Cass Canfield. Philadelphia: Univ. of Penna. Press. 1969. $5.00.

SO YOU WANT TO GET INTO BOOK PUBLISHING. by Daniel Melcher. New York: R. R. Bowker Co. revised 1969. $.25.

TRUTH ABOUT PUBLISHING. by Sir Stanley Unwin. New York: R. R. Bowker Co. 7th rev. ed. 1960. $3.00.

WHAT HAPPENS IN BOOK PUBLISHING. Edited by Chandler B. Grannis. New York: Columbia Univ. Press. 2nd ed. 1967. $10.00.

Special Fields of Publishing Interest

AMERICAN UNIVERSITY AS PUBLISHER. A Digest of a Report on American University Presses. by Chester Kerr. Norman: Univ. of Okla. Press. pap. $.50.

BIBLIOPOLA: PICTURES AND TEXTS ABOUT THE BOOK TRADE. by Sigfred Taubert. 2 vols. New York: R. R. Bowker Co. 1966. $65.00 the set.

GOLDEN MULTITUDES. A Study of Best Sellers 1662–1945. by Frank Luther Mott. New York: R. R. Bowker Co. 1960. Reprint Edition. $9.95.

LITERARY AND LIBRARY PRIZES. Edited by Olga S. Weber. New York: R. R. Bowker Co. 7th ed. 1970. $10.95.

PAPERBOUND BOOK IN AMERICA: The History of Paperbacks and Their European Background. by Frank L. Schick. New York: R. R. Bowker Co. 1958. o.p.

SEVENTY YEARS OF BEST SELLERS: 1895–1965. by Alice Payne Hackett. New York: R. R. Bowker Co. 1967. $9.25.

Special Houses

For biographies of individual publishing houses, see THE READER'S ADVISER, Vol. 1.

BOOKSELLING

BETTER BOOKSELLING SERIES. Edited by Gerald Bartlett. 6 booklets. New York: R. R. Bowker Co. 1966. Each $2.00.

DUKEDOM LARGE ENOUGH: Reminiscences of a Rare Book Dealer, 1929–1956. by David A. Randall. New York: Random House. 1969. $12.95.

HOW TO RUN A PAPERBACK BOOKSHOP. Edited by Sidney Gross and Phyllis B. Steckler. New York: R. R. Bowker Co. 4th printing 1971. $7.95.

MANUAL ON BOOKSELLING. Edited by Charles B. Anderson, Joseph A. Duffy, Jocelyn D. Kahn. New York: American Booksellers Assn. 1969. Distributed by R. R. Bowker Co. $9.95.

CENSORSHIP

BANNED BOOKS. by Anne Lyon Haight. New York: R. R. Bowker Co. 3rd ed. 1970. $8.95.

BOOK SELECTION AND CENSORSHIP IN THE SIXTIES. Edited by Eric Moon. New York: R. R. Bowker Co. 1969. $11.95.

CENSORSHIP. by Morris L. Ernst and Alan U. Schwartz. New York: Macmillan. 1964. $6.95.

CENSORSHIP LANDMARKS. Compiled by Edward de Grazia. New York: R. R. Bowker Co. 1969. $21.95.

FIRST FREEDOM: Liberty and Justice in the World of Books and Reading. by Robert B. Downs, ed. Chicago: American Library Assn. 1960. $8.50.

COPYRIGHT

A COPYRIGHT GUIDE. by Harriet F. Pilpel & Morton D. Goldberg. New York: R. R. Bowker Co. 4th ed. 1969. $5.50.

THE LAW OF COPYRIGHT UNDER THE UNIVERSAL CONVENTION. by Arpad Bogsch. New York: R. R. Bowker Co. 3rd ed. 1969. $26.50.

PROTECTION OF LITERARY PROPERTY. by Philip Wittenberg. Boston: The Writer, Inc. 1968. $7.95.

U.S. NATIONAL BIBLIOGRAPHY AND THE COPYRIGHT LAW: An Historical Study. by Joseph W. Rogers. New York: R. R. Bowker Co. 1960. $5.00.

DIRECTORIES

Book Trade

AB BOOKMAN'S YEARBOOK. Edited by Sol M. Malkin. Newark, N.J.: AB Bookman's Weekly. Annually. 2 vols. $5.00. Free with AB subscription.

AMERICAN BOOK TRADE DIRECTORY. 1971–72. Edited by Helaine MacKeigan. New York: Biennially. R. R. Bowker Co. 20th ed. 1971. $38.50.

LITERARY MARKET PLACE 1971–72: The Business Directory of American Book Publishing. New York: R. R. Bowker Co. Annually. $14.95.

ABD UPDATING SERVICE. 25 bi-weekly bulletins. $49.50 per year.

NAMES AND NUMBERS 1971–72. New York: R. R. Bowker Co. Annually. $15.00.

Newspapers & Periodicals

DIRECTORY OF NEWSPAPERS AND PERIODICALS. Philadelphia: N. W. Ayer. Annually. $42.00.

EDITOR AND PUBLISHER INTERNATIONAL YEAR BOOK. New York: Editor and Publisher. Annually. $12.00.

IRREGULAR SERIALS AND ANNUALS: An International Directory. Edited by Emery Koltay. New York: R. R. Bowker Co. New ed. 1972. Price not set.

NEW SERIAL TITLES 1950–70. New York: R. R. Bowker Co. 1972. Price not set.

THE PRESS IN LATIN AMERICA. THE PRESS IN AFRICA. THE PRESS IN ASIA. New York: R. R. Bowker Co. 3 vols. 2nd ed. 1972. Price not set.

ULRICH'S INTERNATIONAL PERIODICALS DIRECTORY. New York: R. R. Bowker Co. 2 vols. 14th ed. 1971. $42.50 the set.
WORKING PRESS OF THE NATION. Newspapers, Magazines, and Radio & TV. Chicago, Ill.: National Research Bureau. Annually. 4 vols. $30.00 each volume.

EDITING

THE CAREFUL WRITER. by Theodore Bernstein. New York: Atheneum. 1965. $10.00.
DICTIONARY OF MODERN ENGLISH USAGE. by H. W. Fowler. New York: Oxford Univ. Press. 1926. 2nd ed. 1965. rev. by E. Gowers. $6.75.
EDITORS ON EDITING. Compiled by Gerald Gross. New York: Grosset & Dunlap. 1962. $2.65.
ELEMENTS OF STYLE. by William Strunk, Jr. and E. B. White. New York: Macmillan. rev. ed. 1959. $2.95; pap. $.95; text ed. pap. $1.00.
MANUAL OF STYLE. Chicago: Univ. of Chicago Press. 1969. 12th rev. ed. $10.00.
WORDS INTO TYPE. by Marjorie E. Skillin and Robert M. Gay. New York: Meredith (Appleton). rev. ed. 1964. $7.50.
WATCH YOUR LANGUAGE. by Theodore Bernstein. New York: Atheneum. 3rd ed. 1965. $4.50. Also MORE LANGUAGE THAT NEEDS WATCHING. by Theodore Bernstein. New York: Atheneum. 2nd ed. 1964. $2.50.
WRITING, ILLUSTRATING AND EDITING CHILDREN'S BOOKS. by Jean P. Colby. New York: Hastings House. 1966. $7.95.

PERIODICALS

AB BOOKMAN'S WEEKLY. (weekly inc. Yearbook). Newark, N.J.: AB Bookman's Weekly. $13.50.
AMERICAN BOOK PUBLISHING RECORD. (monthly). New York: R. R. Bowker Co. $19.00.
PUBLISHERS' WEEKLY. New York: R. R. Bowker Co. $18.50.
For a list of periodicals reviewing books, see LITERARY MARKET PLACE.

PRINTING & BOOKMAKING

BOOKBINDING IN AMERICA. by Hellmut Lehmann-Haupt, Hannah D. French and Joseph Rogers. New York: R. R. Bowker Co. Reprint with supplementary material. 1967. $12.00.
BOOKMAKING: The Illustrated Guide to Design and Production. by Marshall Lee. New York: R. R. Bowker Co. 1965. $14.00.
BOOKS AND PRINTING: A Treasury for Typophiles. Edited by Paul A. Bennett. Gloucester, Mass.: Peter Smith. $4.25.
FIVE HUNDRED YEARS OF PRINTING. by S. H. Steinberg. New York: Penguin. pap. $2.45.
THE HERITAGE OF THE GRAPHIC ARTS. Edited by Chandler B. Grannis. New York: R. R. Bowker Co. 1972. $17.50.
PAPERMAKING: ART AND CRAFT. Washington, D.C.: Information Office, Library of Congress. 1968. $3.00.
PRINTING AND PROMOTION HANDBOOK. by Daniel Melcher and Nancy Larrick. New York: McGraw-Hill. 3rd ed., 1966. $15.95.
THE PRINTING INDUSTRY: An Introduction to Its Many Branches, Processes and Products. by Victor Strauss. New York: Printing Industries of America, Inc. in association with R. R. Bowker Co. 1967. $27.50.

BEST SELLERS, 1971

Compiled by
Alice Payne Hackett*

Fiction
1. WHEELS, by Arthur Hailey. Doubleday.
2. THE EXORCIST, by William P. Blatty. Harper & Row.
3. THE PASSIONS OF THE MIND, by Irving Stone. Doubleday.
4. THE DAY OF THE JACKAL, by Frederick Forsyth. Viking.
5. THE BETSY, by Harold Robbins. Trident.
6. MESSAGE FROM MALAGA, by Helen MacInnes. Harcourt Brace Jovanovich.
7. THE WINDS OF WAR, by Herman Wouk. Little, Brown.
8. THE DRIFTERS, by James Michener. Random House.
9. THE OTHER, by Thomas Tryon. Knopf.
10. RABBIT REDUX, by John Updike. Knopf.

Nonfiction
1. THE SENSUOUS MAN, by "M." Lyle Stuart.
2. BURY MY HEART AT WOUNDED KNEE, by Dee Brown. Holt, Rinehart & Winston.
3. BETTER HOMES & GARDENS BLENDER COOK BOOK. Meredith.
4. I'M OK, YOU'RE OK, by Thomas Harris. Harper & Row.
5. ANY WOMAN CAN! by David Reuben. McKay.
6. INSIDE THE THIRD REICH, by Albert Speer. Macmillan.
7. ELEANOR AND FRANKLIN, by Joseph P. Lash. Norton.
8. WUNNERFUL, WUNNERFUL, by Lawrence Welk. Prentice-Hall.
9. HONOR THY FATHER, by Gay Talese. World.
10. FIELDS OF WONDER, by Rod McKuen. Random.

*Author of *Seventy Years of Best Sellers* (Bowker), and contributing editor to *Publishers' Weekly*.

BEST CHILDREN'S AND YOUNG ADULTS' BOOKS OF 1971*

Reprints of the following list, including annotations, are available at $.25 each (self-addressed, stamped envelope with order) or at the following quantity rates: 25 copies for $2.45; 50 copies for $3.50; 100 copies for $5.25; 500 copies for $21; 1000 copies for $35. Payment must accompany orders under $5. Write: R. R. Bowker Company, Att: June Shapiro, 1180 Avenue of the Americas, New York, N.Y. 10036.

Key to symbols: C—cloth-bound; G—"perfect" bound with glue; P—paper over boards; Pf—paper with specially treated fibers, high tensile strength, water resistant; PLB—publisher's library binding; S—Saddle stitched; Sm—Smyth sewn; SS—side sewn.

BOOKS FOR CHILDREN
ADOFF, ARNOLD. MA nDA LA. color illus. by Emily McCully. Harper. 1971. PSm $3.95; PLB $4.43. PreS.
ALEXANDER, LLOYD. The King's Fountain. color illus. by Ezra Jack Keats. Dutton. 1971. PS $5.95. K-Gr 4.
BROOKS, LESTER. Great Civilizations of

*Selected by the Editors of *School Library Journal's* Book Review and compiled from the December 1971 issue.

Ancient Africa. maps. photogs. reprods. bibliog. chron. index. Four Winds: Scholastic. 1971. CSm $6.95; PLB $6.11. Gr 8-12.

BURNINGHAM, JOHN. Mr. Gumpy's Outing. color illus. by author. Holt. 1971. PSm $4.95; PLB $4.59. PreS.

BYARS, BETSY. Go and Hush the Baby. illus., some color, by Emily A. McCully. Viking. 1971. CSm $3.50; PLB $3.37. PreS-Gr 3.

CALLAHAN, PHILIP S. Insects and How They Function. diags., illus. & photogs. by author. glossary. index. Holiday. 1971. CSm $4.95. Gr 7-9.

CHWAST, SEYMOUR, and MARTIN STEPHEN MOSKOF. Still Another Number Book. color illus. by authors. McGraw. 1971. CSm $4.95; PLB $4.72. K-Gr 2.

CONFORD, ELLEN. Impossible, Possum. color illus. by Rosemary Wells. Little. 1971. CSm $3.95; PLB $3.95. K-Gr 3.

COOLIDGE, OLIVIA. Gandhi. photogs. Houghton. 1971. CSm $5.95. Gr 8-12.

DANIELS, GUY, tr. The Peasant's Pea Patch: a Russian Folktale. color illus. by Robert Quackenbush. Delacorte. 1971. CSm $5.95; PLB $5.47. K-Gr 3.

DAREFF, HAL. From Vietnam to Cambodia: a Background Book About the Struggle in Southeast Asia. maps. bibliog. index. notes. Parents Magazine Pr. 1971. CSm $4.95; PLB $4.28. Gr 6 Up.

DI VALENTIN, MARIA, and others, comps. Practical Encyclopedia of Crafts. illus. by Louis Di Valentin and others. photogs., some color. Sterling. 1971. CSm $20; PLB $16.79. Gr 7 Up.

DOMANSKA, JANINA, retel. If All the Seas Were One Sea. color illus. by retel. Macmillan. 1971. CS $4.95. K-Gr 2.

DONOVAN, JOHN. Wild in the World. Harper. 1971. CSm $3.50; PLB $3.27. Gr 6 Up.

FEELINGS, MURIEL. Moja Means One: Swahili Counting Book. illus. by Tom Feelings. Dial. 1971. CSm $4.50; PLB $4.17. PreS-Gr 2.

FUJA, ABAYOMI, coll. Fourteen Hundred Cowries & Other African Tales. illus. by Ademola Olugebefola. Lothrop. 1971. CSm $4.95; PLB $4.95. Gr 4-8.

GAINES, ERNEST J. A Long Day in November. illus. by Don Bolognese. Dial. 1971. CSm $4.95; PLB $4.58. Gr 5-8.

GARFIELD, LEON. The Strange Affair of Adelaide Harris. illus. by Fritz Wegner. Pantheon. 1971. CSm $4.95; PLB $5.39. Gr 7-12.

GOODALL, JOHN S. Shrewbettina's Birthday. color illus. by author. Harcourt. 1971. CSm $3.50. PreS-Gr 2.

HAMILTON, VIRGINIA. The Planet of Junior Brown. Macmillan. 1971. CSm $4.95. Gr 8 Up.

HAUGAARD, ERIK CHRISTIAN. The Untold Tale. illus. by Leo and Diane Dillon. Houghton. 1971. CSm $3.75. Gr 6-9.

HOBAN, RUSSELL. Emmet Otter's Jug-Band Christmas. color illus. by Lillian Hoban. Parents' Magazine Pr. 1971. PSm $3.95; PLB $3.78. K-Gr 2.

JONES, HETTIE, sel. The Trees Stand Shining: Poetry of the North American Indians. color illus. by Robert Andrew Parker. Dial. 1971. CSm $4.95; PLB $4.58. Gr 4 Up.

JORDAN, JUNE. His Own Where. Crowell. 1971. CSm $3.95. Gr 7 Up.

KEATS, EZRA JACK. Apt. 3. color illus. by author. Macmillan. 1971. PS $5.95. PreS-Gr 3.

KELLOGG, STEVEN. Can I Keep Him? illus., some color, by author. Dial. 1971. PSm $4.50; PLB $4.17. K-Gr 2.

KLASS, MORTON, and HAL HELLMAN. The Kinds of Mankind: an Introduction to Race and Racism. illus. Lippincott. 1971. CSm $5.95. Gr 9 Up.

KONIGSBURG, E. L. Altogether, One at a Time. illus. by Gail E. Haley and others. Atheneum. 1971. PLB $4.50. Gr 4-6.

MELTZER, MILTON. Slavery: From the Rise of Western Civilization to the Renaissance. maps. photogs. reprods. bibliog. index. Cowles. 1971. CSm $6.95. Gr 6 Up.

MORDILLO, GUILLERMO. The Damp and Daffy Doings of a Daring Pirate Ship. color illus. by author. Harlin Quist, dist. by Watts. 1971. PSm $3.95; PLB $3.84. PreS-Gr 2.

MOTHER GOOSE: the Classic Volland Edition. re-arranged & ed. by Eulalie Osgood Grover. color illus. by Frederick Richardson. Hubbard Pr. 1971. PLB $5.95; deluxe ed. $9.95. PreS-Gr 3.

NIC LEODHAS, SORCHE, retel. Twelve Great Black Cats and Other Eerie Scottish Tales. illus. by Vera Bock. Dutton. 1971. CSm $5.95. Gr 5-8.

O'BRIEN, ROBERT C. Mrs. Frisby and the Rats of NIMH. illus. by Zena Bernstein. Atheneum. 1971. CSm $5.95. Gr 5-7.

RANDALL, FLORENCE ENGEL. The Almost Year. Atheneum. 1971. PLB $5.95. Gr 8 Up.

RASKIN, ELLEN. The Mysterious Disappearance of Leon (I Mean Noel). illus. by author. Dutton. 1971. PLB $4.95. Gr 4-6.

RICE, EDWARD. Mother India's Children: Meeting Today's Generation in India. photogs. by author. Pantheon. 1971. CSm $4.95; PLB $5.59. Gr 7 Up.

SACHS, MARILYN. The Bear's House. illus. by Louis Glanzman. Doubleday. 1971. CSm $3.95; PLB 75¢ extra. Gr 4-6.

SULLY, FRANÇOIS, ed. with assist. of Marjorie Weiner Normand. We the Vietnamese: Voices from Vietnam. photogs. bibliog. index. Praeger, 1971. CSm $7.50; pap. $2.95. Gr 8 Up.

TRELEASE, ALLEN W. Reconstruction: the Great Experiment. photogs. reprods. bibliog. index. Harper. 1971. CSm $4.95; PLB $4.79. Gr 7 Up.

WATSON, CLYDE. Father Fox's Pennyrhymes. color illus. by Wendy Watson. Crowell. 1971. CSm $4.50; PLB 75¢ extra. K-Gr 3.

ZEMACH, HARVE. A Penny a Look. illus. by Margot Zemach. Farrar. 1971. CSm $4.95. Gr 1-3.

ZIMNIK, REINER. The Bear and the People. tr. from German by Nina Ignatowicz. illus. by author. Harper. 1971. PSm $3.95; PLB $3.79. Gr 3-7.

BOOKS FOR YOUNG ADULTS

ADAMS, HAZARD. The Truth About Dragons: An Anti-Romance. Harcourt. 1971. $6.50.

ANGELOU, MAYA. Just Give Me a Cool Drink of Water 'fore I Die. Random. 1971. $4.95.

ASINOF, ELIOT. Craig and Joan: Two Lives for Peace. Viking. 1971. $6.95.

BRENT, MADELINE. Tregaron's Daughter. Doubleday. 1971. $5.95.

DAVIS, CHRISTOPHER. A Peep Into the Twentieth Century. Harper. 1971. $5.95.

DU MAURIER, DAPHNE. Don't Look Now. Doubleday. 1971. $6.95.

FLOOD, CURT, and RICHARD CARTER. The Way It Is. Trident Pr. 1971. $5.95.

GAINES, ERNEST J. The Autobiography of Miss Jane Pittman. Dial. 1971. $6.95.

GOULART, RON. What's Become of Screwloose? and Other Inquiries. Scribners. 1971. $4.95.

GREGORY, RICHARD CLAXTON. No More Lies. ed. by James R. McGraw. Harper. 1971. $6.95.

KNOWLES, JOHN. The Paragon. Random. 1971. $5.95.

KOSINSKI, JERZY. Being There. Harcourt. 1971. $4.95.

LANGFORD, CAMERON. Winter of the Fisher. Norton. 1971. $5.95.

THE LAST WHOLE EARTH CATALOG. diags. illus. maps. photogs. index. Random. 1971. $5.

MATTHIESSEN, PETER. Blue Meridian: the Search for the Great White Shark. Random. 1971. $8.95.

NATHAN, ROBERT. The Elixir. Knopf. 1971. $5.95.

PARKS, GORDON. Born Black. Lippincott. 1971. $7.95.

POSTMAN, NEIL, and CHARLES WEINGARTNER. The Soft Revolution: a Student Handbook for Turning Schools Around. Delacorte. 1971. $4.95; pap. $1.95.

POWERS, THOMAS. Diana. Houghton. 1971. $5.95.

RAUCHER, HERMAN. The Summer of '42. Putnam. 1971. $5.95.

ROSENBERG, SHARON, and JOAN WIENER. Illustrated Hassle-Free Make Your Own Clothes Book. Straight Arrow Pr. 1971. $7.95.

SCHOLLANDER, DON, and DUKE SAVAGE. Deep Water. Crown. 1971. $5.95.
SHORRIS, EARL. The Death of the Great Spirit: an Elegy for the American Indian. S. & S. 1971. $6.95.

STEIN, SOL. The Magician. Delacorte. 1971. $6.95.
TRUDEAU, G. B. Doonesbury. illus. by author. American Heritage Pr. 1971. $2.95.

NOTABLE BOOKS OF 1970 AND 1971

Chosen by the Notable Books Council of the Adult Services Division, American Library Association.

1970

ANGELOU, MAYA. I Know Why the Caged Bird Sings. Random.
ARLEN, MICHAEL J. Exiles. Farrar.
BARTHELME, DONALD. City Life. Farrar.
BELLOW, SAUL. Mr. Sammler's Planet. Viking.
BOWEN, CATHERINE DRINKER. Family Portrait. Atlantic.
BUECHNER, THOMAS S. Norman Rockwell, Artist and Illustrator. Abrams.
BURNS, JAMES MCGREGOR. Roosevelt: The Soldier of Freedom. Harcourt.
CLARK, RAMSEY. Crime in America: Simon & Schuster.
DANIELS, JONATHAN. Ordeal of Ambition: Jefferson, Hamilton, Burr. Doubleday.
DICKEY, JAMES. Deliverance. Houghton.
DIDION, JOAN. Play It As It Lays. Farrar.
GAYLIN, WILLARD. In the Service of Their Country; War Resisters in Prison. Viking.
HERSH, SEYMOUR M. My Lai 4. Random.
HUXTABLE, ADA LOUISE. Will They Ever Finish Bruckner Boulevard? Macmillan.
JACKSON, GEORGE. Soledad Brother: The Prison Letters of George Jackson. Coward.

MANDELSTAM, NADEZHDA. Hope Against Hope. Atheneum.
MARQUEZ, GABRIEL GARCIA. One Hundred Years of Solitude. Harper.
MARTIN, MALACHI. The Encounter. Farrar.
MEHTA, VED. Portrait of India. Farrar.
MERIWETHER, LOUISE. Daddy Was a Number Runner. Prentice.
MILFORD, NANCY. Zelda. Harper.
MILLET, KATE. Sexual Politics. Doubleday.
OSTROW, JOANNA. . . . In the Highlands Since Time Immemorial. Knopf.
SILBERMAN, CHARLES E. Crisis in the Classroom. Random.
SPEER, ALBERT. Inside the Third Reich. Macmillan.
STEEGMULLER, FRANCIS. Cocteau: A Biography. Atlantic.
TERKEL, STUDS. Hard Times: An Oral History of the Great Depression. Pantheon.
WELTY, EUDORA. Losing Battles. Random.
WEST, PAUL. Words for a Deaf Daughter. Harper.
WIESEL, ELIE. A Beggar in Jerusalem. Random.

1971

AMADO, JORGE. Tent of Miracles. Knopf.
BLUNT, WILFRID. The Compleat Naturalist; A Life of Linnaeus. Viking.
BROWN, CHARLES H. William Cullen Bryant. Scribners.
BROWN, DEE. Bury My Heart at Wounded Knee: An Indian History of the American West. Holt, Rinehart & Winston.
CLARK, RONALD W. Einstein; The Life and Times. World.
CORNELISON, ANN. Vendetta of Silence. Little.
DOCTOROW, E. L. The Book of Daniel; A Novel. Random House. Random House.
ELON, AMOS. The Israelis: Founders and Sons. Holt, Rinehart & Winston.
FLANNER, JANET. Paris Journal, 1965–1971. Atheneum.
GAINES, ERNEST J. The Autobiography of Miss Jane Pittman. Dial.
GARDNER, JOHN. Grendel. Knopf.
GARRETT, GEORGE. Death of the Fox. Doubleday.
GLASSER, RONALD J. 365 Days. Braziller.
GREER, GERMAINE. The Female Eunuch. McGraw-Hill.
GRUNBERGER, RICHARD. The 12-Year Reich. Holt, Rinehart & Winston.
HOUSTON, JAMES. The White Dawn, Harcourt Brace Jovanovich.
HUGHES, TED. Crow: From the Life and Songs of the Crow. Harper & Row.
ILLICH, IVAN. Deschooling Society. Harper & Row.
LANDOLFI, TOMMASO. Cancerqueen and Other Stories. Dial.
LARTIGUE, JACQUES-HENRI. Diary of a Century. Viking.
LASH, JOSEPH P. Eleanor and Franklin. Norton.
LIDDELL-HART, SIR B. H. History of the Second World War. Putnams.
MCHALE, TOM. Farragan's Retreat. Viking.

MCPHEE, JOHN. Encounters with the Archdruid. Farrar, Straus & Giroux.
MAXWELL, NEVILLE. India's China War. Pantheon.
MEYER, MICHAEL. Ibsen: A Biography. Doubleday.
MORISON, SAMUEL ELIOT. The European Discovery of America: The Northern Voyages; A.D. 500–1600. Oxford.
MORRIS, WRIGHT. Fire Sermon. Harper & Row.
NAVASKY, VICTOR. Kennedy Justice. Atheneum.
OUOLOGUEM, YAMBO. Bound to Violence. Harcourt Brace Jovanovich.
PANTER-DOWNES, MOLLIE. London War Notes, 1939–1945. Farrar, Straus & Giroux.
THE PENTAGON PAPERS. Bantam.
PERCY, WALKER. Love in the Ruins. Farrar, Straus & Giroux.
PIRO, RICHARD. Black Fiddler. Morrow.
PIVEN, FRANCES FOX, and RICHARD CLOWARD. Regulating the Poor: The Functions of Public Welfare. Pantheon.
PLATH, SYLVIA. Crossing the Water. Harper & Row.
PUIG, MANUEL. Betrayed by Rita Hayworth. Dutton.
SAJER, GUY. The Forgotten Soldier. Harper & Row.
SKINNER, B. F. Beyond Freedom and Dignity. Knopf.
THOMAS, HUGH. Cuba: The Pursuit of Freedom. Harper & Row.
TUCHMAN, BARBARA. Stilwell and the American Experience in China, 1911–1945. Macmillan.
VAN LAWICK-GOODALL, JANE. In the Shadow of Man. Houghton Mifflin.
WILSON, EDMUND. Upstate: Records and Recollections of Northern New York. Farrar, Straus & Giroux.
WRIGHT, JAMES. Collected Poems. Wesleyan.
ZINDEL, PAUL. The Effect of Gamma Rays on Man-in-the-Moon Marigolds. Harper & Row.

PART 2 NATIONAL LIBRARY AND BOOK TRADE DEVELOPMENTS

Library and Book Trade Statistics

STATISTICS OF LIBRARIES FOR THE 1970s*

by

Dorothy M. Gilford** and Frank L. Schick***

From the 1870s until the 1930s, statistics on public, school, and society libraries were published with some regularity. From 1938 to 1958 nationwide surveys on public, school, and academic libraries were conducted on a five- to seven-year cycle. From 1958 to the present, the scope and frequency of library surveys were considerably increased.

The National Center for Educational Statistics was established in 1965, and the responsibility for libraries, along with Frank L. Schick, Assistant Director, Library Services Branch, was transferred to NCES. After Dr. Schick left NCES in 1966, first Morris Ullman, and from 1968 to 1970, Joel Williams were in charge of this operation. In February 1971, Frank Schick returned to NCES to head the Library Surveys Branch, which presently has a staff of six.

Today, as one of the major statistical centers of the federal government, NCES gathers, stores, analyzes, and disseminates educational information, including data on all types of libraries.

The major functions of NCES are:

To design and direct general statistical programs of the Office of Education and conduct special analytical studies on critical issues in education.

To coordinate educational statistical programs among federal agencies and with local, state, national, and international organizations.

To assist OE program administrators by providing consultative services about procedures for obtaining and interpreting educational data, and by preparing allotment tables for apportionments for forming grants among the states.

To provide basic statistical information to the federal, state, local, and nongovernmental community about many aspects of the general condition and trends of education in the United States.

To review plans for data collection by OE units and other federal agencies, providing a clearance function for the Bureau of the Budget pursuant to the Federal Reports Act of 1942.

---

*This article was originally a speech presented at the American Library Association's 90th Annual Conference, June 1971, and published in the July 1971 issue of the Federal Library Committee's *FLC Newsletter;* it has been revised for publication in the 1972 *Bowker Annual.*

**Assistant Commissioner for Educational Statistics, National Center for Educational Statistics, U.S. Office of Education.

***Chief, Library Surveys Branch, National Center for Educational Statistics, U.S. Office of Education.

133

To coordinate the development of standardized terminology and definitions for compatible recording and reporting of educational data at all levels of organization.

The function of the Library Surveys Branch is to relate these activities to library programs.

SURVEYS AND PUBLICATIONS

The Center now issues 55 series (reports published periodically) and many other studies that provide data to assist decision-makers in forming sound educational policies.

Between 1960 and 1970 the Office of Education (since 1965, through NCES) provided the following statistical publications for libraries:

Reports Published	Surveys In Process (survey year)
Colleges and universities 14	1 (for 1971)
Public 7	1 (for 1971)
School 3	2 (for 1970)
Special 2	1 (for 1972)
Library education 3	1 (for 1969–71)
General 1	1 (for 1971)

At present the schedule for library surveys is as follows:

Colleges and universities......every 2 years
Public ....every 3 years
School ....every 4 years
Special ....not on regular schedule
Library education..not on regular schedule

Starting in 1966 the Center decided to discontinue separate overlapping surveys and began to combine related statistical surveys in two data systems, HEGIS, the Higher Educational General Information Survey, and ELSEGIS, the Elementary and Secondary General Information Survey. We are presently completing work on HEGIS VI (for 1971–1972), which was mailed in June 1971 to academic institutions, and ELSEGIS V.

The College and University Library Survey for 1971 is a component of HEGIS VI. Work is now being completed on ELSEGIS III (1970), which presents data for public elementary and secondary school libraries and media centers.

Public, special, and library education surveys did not fit into the two existing programs. For this reason we started to work during the past year on the development of a national library statistics program which we are calling LIBGIS (Library General Information System).

LIBGIS

The purpose of LIBGIS will be to develop a national library statistics data system which will be primarily based on the cooperation between state library agencies and NCES. It is our plan to have all surveys about libraries and library programs included in one survey package.

The concept of LIBGIS is based on the close cooperation of the Office of Education with state library or other state agencies. What we hope to accomplish is that our forms will be sent to the state agencies, which will be asked to distribute the forms to the public, academic, school, and other types of libraries. If some state agencies can't cooperate with us, we will continue to contact individual libraries in these states. If in some states separate state agencies are responsible for academic or public or school libraries, we will be in touch with several state agencies. If these state agencies, in their responsibilities and for their purposes want to collect additional data, we will ask them to mail their state forms jointly with ours.

We hope that a majority of state agencies will undertake the following functions: (1) Distribute NCES library forms; (2) collect NCES library forms; (3) edit NCES library forms; (4) forward the completed forms for their state to NCES-OE.

At the same time the collecting state agencies will be encouraged to publish and disseminate the results of our combined survey activities. We believe that this procedure will work effectively because we have positive results from our other system-type surveys. We know that this approach lessens the burden on

PLANS FOR A NATIONWIDE SYSTEM OF LIBRARY STATISTICS

by

Ruth R. Frame*

The publication *Planning for a Nationwide System of Library Statistics*[1] identifies the major steps to be taken in establishing an adequate system of collecting and making available library statistics of the United States; it presents guidelines for the development and implementation of a library statistics program; and is also a compilation of considerable background information about library statistics publications, planning, needs, priorities, and problems.

This 117-page report was prepared (under contract with the National Center for Educational Statistics) by the Statistics Coordinating Committee, Library Organization and Management Section of the Library Administration Division, American Library Association. The committee's report to the NCES was revised slightly in format and published by the NCES in late 1970.

During the preparation of this report, the committee conferred frequently with the representatives of the NCES regarding statistical planning and techniques, but the viewpoints expressed and the recommendations made in this work are not necessarily those of the NCES, and the viewpoints and recommendations do not necessarily express an official opinion of the U.S. Office of Education.

Planning for a Nationwide System of Library Statistics is the distillation of several decades of work by many persons; it was developed by 13 contributors whose chapters were discussed (while in process) with pertinent library organization units.

A brief summary of the nine major recommendations is given below:

"1. Planning for standardized, meaningful, and even minimal library statistics must continue — indefinitely. Other research efforts, especially in the areas of management systems, data bank development, user data, and impact of library services are needed and should be coordinated with these guidelines.

"2. Efforts to standardize terminology must be continued and intensified. Definitions found in *Library Statistics: A Handbook of Concepts, Definitions, and Terminology* should be reviewed, refined, and expanded. While this is primarily the obligation of the profession at large, the terminology should be promulgated by the U.S. Government and revised as needed. Continued recognition by the United States of America Standards Institute [American National Standards Institute], and its cooperation, will contribute to the widest acceptance of this standardized terminology.

"3. The National Center for Educational Statistics (NCES) should be assisted by an advisory committee which represents fairly the numerous governmental, professional, and commercial interests in library statistics. This advisory input into planning and operating a national library statistics system should be augmented and supplemented by the National Commission on Libraries and Information Science and by state advisory committees. The Statistics Coordinating Committee of the American Library Association should continue its strong advisory and promotional roles.

"4. A program of shared responsibility between NCES and the states in nationwide (as well as state) library statistical coverage is essential and should be highly defined, coordinated, and regularized. NCES will have to take a close look at the library functions at the state level to determine which agencies are responsible for which functions.

---

*Executive Secretary, Library Administration Division, American Library Association.

[1]*Planning for a Nationwide System of Library Statistics*. Ed. by David C. Palmer. Available from the Superintendent of Documents. Government Printing Office, Washington, D.C. 20402. $1.25. Catalog No. HE 5.215:15070. U.S.

lic Libraries Serving Populations of 35,000 and Above: Institutional Data (OE-15051). 1965, 47 pp.

1962 The 1962 data for public libraries serving populations of less than 35,000 was published by the University of Illinois Graduate School of Library Science in 1966 under the title *1962 Statistics of Public Libraries Serving Populations of Less Than 35,000.*

*1965 *Statistics of Public Libraries Serving Communities with at Least 25,000 Inhabitants, 1965* (OE-15068). 1968, 65 pp.

*1968 *Statistics of Public Libraries Serving Areas With at Least 25,000 Inhabitants, 1968* (OE-15068). 1970, 144 pp.

*1971 A survey of public libraries serving areas with at least 25,000 inhabitants, fiscal year 1971, will be conducted by NCES early in 1972.

School Library Statistics 1960–1970

1960 *Statistics of Public School Libraries, 1960–61:* Part I, Basic Tables (OE-15049). 1964, 90 pp.

1960 *Statistics of Public School Libraries, 1960–61:* Part II, Analysis and Interpretation (OE-15056). 1965, 13 pp.

1962 *Public School Library Statistics, 1962–63* (OE-15020-63). 1964, 21 pp.

*1970 Surveys of school media centers (public and private schools), fall 1970. In preparation.

Special Library Statistics 1960–1970

1963–64 *Special Libraries Serving State Governments, 1963–64.* Available as ERIC document ED 013 374 from ERIC Document Reproduction Service, P.O. Drawer 0, Bethesda, Maryland 20014.

*1965 *Special Libraries Serving the Federal Government (1965)* (OE-15067). 1968, 108 pp.

*1971 A 1971 survey of federal libraries is under consideration.

Library Education Statistics 1960–1970

1964–65 *Library Education Directory, 1964–65* (OE-15046). 1965, 32 pp.

1964 "Survey of Library Education Programs, Fall 1964." Mimeographed OE release, issued in December 1965.

1966–68 *North American Library Education Directory and Statistics, 1966–68.* Survey conducted under Office of Education contract with the University of Wisconsin–Milwaukee and the American Library Association. Chicago: American Library Association, 1968. 106 pp.

1969–71 *North American Library Education Directory and Statistics, 1969–71.* Survey conducted under Office of Education contract with the University of Wisconsin–Milwaukee and the American Library Association. To be published by the American Library Association during spring 1972.

General Statistical Publications

1966 *Library Statistics: A Handbook of Concepts, Definitions, and Terminology.* Prepared by the staff of the ALA Statistics Coordinating Project. Chicago: American Library Association, 1966, 169 pp.

*1966 *National Conference on Library Statistics.* Proceedings of a conference cosponsored by the Library Administration Division of the American Library Association and the National Center for Educational Statistics of the Office of Education, June 6–8, 1966. Chicago: American Library Association, 1967, 100 pp.

*1970 *Planning for a Nationwide System of Library Statistics* (OE-15070). Report of a project of the Library Administration Division of the American Library Association prepared under contract with the National Center for Educational Statistics of the Office of Education. 1970, 117 pp.

occasional studies such as those relating to physical facilities, manpower, and nonprint media.

This description omits the infinite details, considerable expense, and time which are necessary to put a national data system into operation. However, when our library data system goes operational in the mid-seventies, it is very likely that the U.S. Library Data System will be the first one anywhere — and we would be very pleased to have other countries share in our experience which is based on the concepts of shared information, shared expenses, and close cooperation on all levels of administration.

A DECADE OF OE LIBRARY STATISTICS PUBLICATIONS

Publications of or funded by OE-NCES are indicated by an asterisk (*). (Editor's note: To the extent that supplies are available, requests for single copies can be sent to NCES; orders for more than one copy should be addressed to the Superintendent of Documents, U.S. Government Printing Office, Washington, D.C. 20402.)

College and University Library Statistics 1960–1970

1960 *Library Statistics of Colleges and Universities, 1959–60:* Institutional Data (OE-15023). 1961, 79 pp.

1960 *Library Statistics of Colleges and Universities, 1959–60:* Analytic Report (OE-15031-60). 1962, 45 pp.

1961 *Library Statistics of Colleges and Universities, 1960–61:* Institutional Data (OE-15023-61). 1962, 89 pp.

1962 *Library Statistics of Colleges and Universities, 1961–62:* Institutional Data (OE-15023-62). 1963, 172 pp.

1962 *Library Statistics of Colleges and Universities, 1961–62:* Analytic Report (OE-15031-62). 1964, 70 pp.

1963 *Library Statistics of Colleges and Universities, 1962–63:* Institutional Data (OE-15023-63). 1964, 120 pp.

1964 *Library Statistics of Colleges and Universities, 1963–64:* Institutional Data (OE-15023-64). 1965, 162 pp.

*1964 *Library Statistics of Colleges and Universities, 1963–64:* Analytic Report (OE-15031-64). 1968, 48 pp.

*1966 The American Library Association, with a grant from the Office of Education, published an institutional report, *Library Statistics of Colleges and Universities, 1965–66.*

*1967 *Library Statistics, 1966–67: Preliminary Report on Academic Libraries* (OE-15065). 1967, 38 pp.

*1967 *Library Statistics of Colleges and Universities: Data for Individual Institutions, Fall 1967* (OE-15023-67). 1969, 346 pp.

*1968 *Library Statistics of Colleges and Universities: Data for Individual Institutions, Fall 1968* (OE-15023-68). 1969, 172 pp.

*1968 *Library Statistics of Colleges and Universities: Analytic Report, Fall 1968* (OE-15031-68). 1970, 82 pp.

*1969 *Library Statistics of Colleges and Universities: Data for Individual Institutions, Fall 1969* (OE-15023-69). 1970, 158 pp.

*1969 *Library Statistics of Colleges and Universities: Analytic Report, Fall 1969* (OE-15031-69). 1971, 82 pp.

*1971 A survey of college and university libraries is being conducted (fall 1971). Publications will consist of institutional and analytic reports.

Public Library Statistics 1960–1970

1960 *Statistics of Public Library Systems Serving Populations of 100,000 or More: Fiscal Year 1960* (OE-15033). 1961, 24 pp.

1960 *Statistics of Public Library Systems Serving Populations of 50,000 to 99,999: Fiscal Year 1960* (OE-15034). 1962, 23 pp.

1960 *Statistics of Public Library Systems Serving Populations of 35,000 to 49,999: Fiscal Year 1960:* (OE-15035). 1962, 23 pp.

1962 *Statistics of Public Libraries, 1962. Part 1, Selected Statistics of Pub-

the respondents because the same information which they are asked to supply will be shared on the state and national levels and every three years on the international level with UNESCO.

Just as the data collection responsibility is shared, we hope to be able to share the costs for surveys. Shared data collection will reduce the time lag between data collection and publication, will reduce costs, and will result in cost-sharing arrangements which will strengthen the statistical operations in the various state agencies.

To be workable and economical this program requires some preliminary planning. With this task we received the support of the American Library Association and the library community. We contracted in 1967 with this association's Library Administration Division, for the design of a national library statistics plan. This work was effectively handled by Ruth Frame, Executive Secretary, the Library Administration Division of ALA. David Palmer, as principal investigator, assembled a group of 12 distinguished colleagues who completed this assignment last year. The resulting publication, entitled *Planning for a Nationwide System of Library Statistics,* was released by the Government Printing Office in May 1971.

In order to adjust our survey system to federal, state, regional, and local data requirements, it was essential to ascertain which agencies and organizations collect on a recurring basis what kind of library-related data. With this aim in mind, Joel Williams and Ruth Boaz designed a research project. A contract for this project was awarded on a competitive basis to Herner and Company, Washington, D.C. The basic contract will be completed in early 1972. Current local library data practices, the second phase of this project, is to be completed in June of 1972. The results of the Herner study will indicate library data overlaps as well as gaps.

The next phase of the LIBGIS development was to design core and model forms. The core forms as we now visualize them will consist of the following parts: the common core which will be identical for all types of libraries, the unique core which will contain the elements for each type of library, the infrequent core which will only be required every three or four years, and the state requirements which will differ with the needs of the states.

Model forms, a combination of the various core items, will always consist of the common and unique core forms and depending on needs also of the infrequent and state requirements.

The data items to be covered in these forms will deal with (1) library resources (i.e., books, periodicals, etc.), (2) library staff (i.e., professional, paraprofessional, etc.), (3) expenditures (dollars), (4) service population (i.e., borrowers, registered students, etc.), (5) physical facilities (i.e., floor space, seating facilities, etc.), and (6) library activities.

DATA SYSTEM PROGRESSION

Concurrently with the Herner and Company study, core forms are being designed under a personal services contract by David Palmer, Assistant New Jersey State Librarian. During the first part of 1972, the core forms will be reviewed at state-level meetings to ascertain user comments in the system's operation. During 1972–1973, demonstrations will be conducted with core forms in states that volunteer for this effort. The next phase will deal with the development of model forms and their experimental use on the state level.

The LIBGIS development will conclude with the drafting of a library statistics manual that will contain a glossary of terms, samples of the core and model forms, instructions for administering surveys, and specifications for national editing of forms and illustrative output tables.

After these tasks are accomplished the current library surveys will be phased out (1) by transferring the library components of HEGIS and ELSEGIS to LIBGIS, and (2) by incorporating into LIBGIS the public, special, and eventually library education surveys and other

"5. Federal financial assistance to the states to enable them to carry out their responsibilities in the foregoing system is mandatory. This assistance should be designed to both stimulate state investment in this area and to be used as a tool for regularization and compliance.

"6. Determination of library universes should take place at the state level according to definitions supplied by NCES.

"7. Training programs, with appropriate instructors, manuals, meetings, etc., are essential to the national statistics program, both at the state and local levels, for general understanding, accuracy of returns, and compliance.

"8. States should be encouraged to collect data beyond federal and national needs and should distribute these data widely. They should serve as true information centers on libraries and library conditions in the respective states.

"9. Continued national planning should incorporate appropriate steps toward the formation of a national data bank system for library statistics. Such a system should allow for retrieval of specialized library data at cost."

Table 1 (from page 16 of the publication) indicates in very general terms the minimum data recommended for collection. The report includes considerable discussion about needed frequency of collection, but it emphasizes the desirability of annual data. Some items, such as fringe benefits and physical facilities, may be collected less often — perhaps every five years.

Some of the basic concepts of the work which may not be apparent in the brief summary recommendations are: basic or core library data should be collected from all kinds of libraries in such a way as to make possible meaningful, combined inventories of holdings, funding, personnel use, and other related items; agencies with the primary and shared responsibilities for gathering and disseminating library data are the federal and state governments; state and local governmental units and nongovernmental

TABLE 1

Basic data required	Public	School	College and university	Library education	State	Special	Federal
Income by source	X	X		X	X		
Expenditure by type of program	X	X	X	X	X	X	X
Salaries	X	X	X	X	X	X	X
Fringe benefits[1]	X	X	X	X	X	X	X
Staff	X	X	X	X	X	X	X
Book stock	X	X	X		X	X	X
Periodicals	X	X	X		X	X	X
Microform	X	X	X		X	X	X
Nonbook materials	X	X	X		X	X	X
Reference	X				X		
Circulation	X	X	X		X		X
Interlibrary loans	X	X	X		X	X	X
Physical facilities[1]	X	X	X	X	X	X	X
Hours open	X	X	X				
Number of outlets		X	X		X		X
Population or clientele served	X	X	X		X	X	X

[1] To be reported approximately every 5 years.

agencies will wish to collect information beyond the core data required by NCES.

For a full understanding of the planning, development, and implementation of a nationwide system of library statistics as envisioned by the report, the entire Chapter III, Conclusions and Recommendations (pp. 7-21), must be read.

Chapter III presents information about needs and trends such as shared responsibilities for library statistical programs, emphasis on accountability, evaluation of the use of stratified and sampling techniques, and special problems requiring new kinds of statistics or data.

The chart entitled "A Nationwide System of Library Statistics" (from pp. 13-14) indicates the interrelationship of the many governmental and nongovernmental agencies which are concerned in this long-range program.

Six overview papers provide concerns and roles of the profession, the federal government, legislative bodies, state library agencies, library systems and networks, and research.

The overview papers are followed by the presentations of specific statistical concerns of public libraries, school libraries, college and university libraries, library education and manpower, state libraries, special libraries, and federal libraries.

All the specific statistical concerns chapters discuss aspects of needed data items; the library education and school libraries chapters are relatively detailed in their listing of data requirements. The public libraries chapter also points out the relation between statistics and program budgeting, and discusses the use of total inventory type data and the use of selected or sample data. The college and university chapter takes special cognizance of the problems of statistics of two-year colleges and of professional schools within universities, such as law and medical school libraries. The college and university chapter also emphasizes the need for utilization of adequate data in the preparation of library standards. The special libraries chapter emphasizes the need for more complete definitions and recognition of special libraries. The federal libraries chapter identifies eleven kinds of federal libraries and information centers, three types of management data required, and lists the principal users of such data.

Appendix C, pages 101-116, includes three background papers of special interest. These are "Needed Library Statistics," as reported to the ALA Executive Board by the divisions, a summary and appraisal by G. Flint Purdy, October 3, 1960; "A Proposal for a Survey of Library Statistics," by G. Flint Purdy, ALA, Midwinter 1962; and "Status of Library Statistics Publications 1970," by Frank L. Schick.

Some of the recommendations of this publication are suggestions for major improvements and expansions of those library statistical programs which have been conducted for some time but which have not been adequate. Many of the recommendations are for new approaches or procedures or goals.

The concept that the federal government will provide some financial assistance to states to enable the states to participate with shared responsibility is a new approach which requires new agreements, new funding patterns, and some new assumptions of responsibilities.

The concept of the collection of core data to be provided from all types of libraries on a nationwide basis (augmented by locally needed data) is not a new idea. But the collection of data in such a pattern requires the structuring of new forms, definitions, and schedules, and will provide a new range of uses of statistical data. The receipt of core data from all types of libraries for approximately the same time period is a new pattern for the federal government.

The establishment of a library data bank with the provision for retrieval of specialized information is strongly recommended throughout the report. This, of course, is a method of recording and preserving data which has not yet been used for nationwide library statistics. The use of a data bank would obviously make possible far greater collection and

LIBRARY AND BOOK TRADE STATISTICS / 141

A NATIONWIDE SYSTEM OF LIBRARY STATISTICS

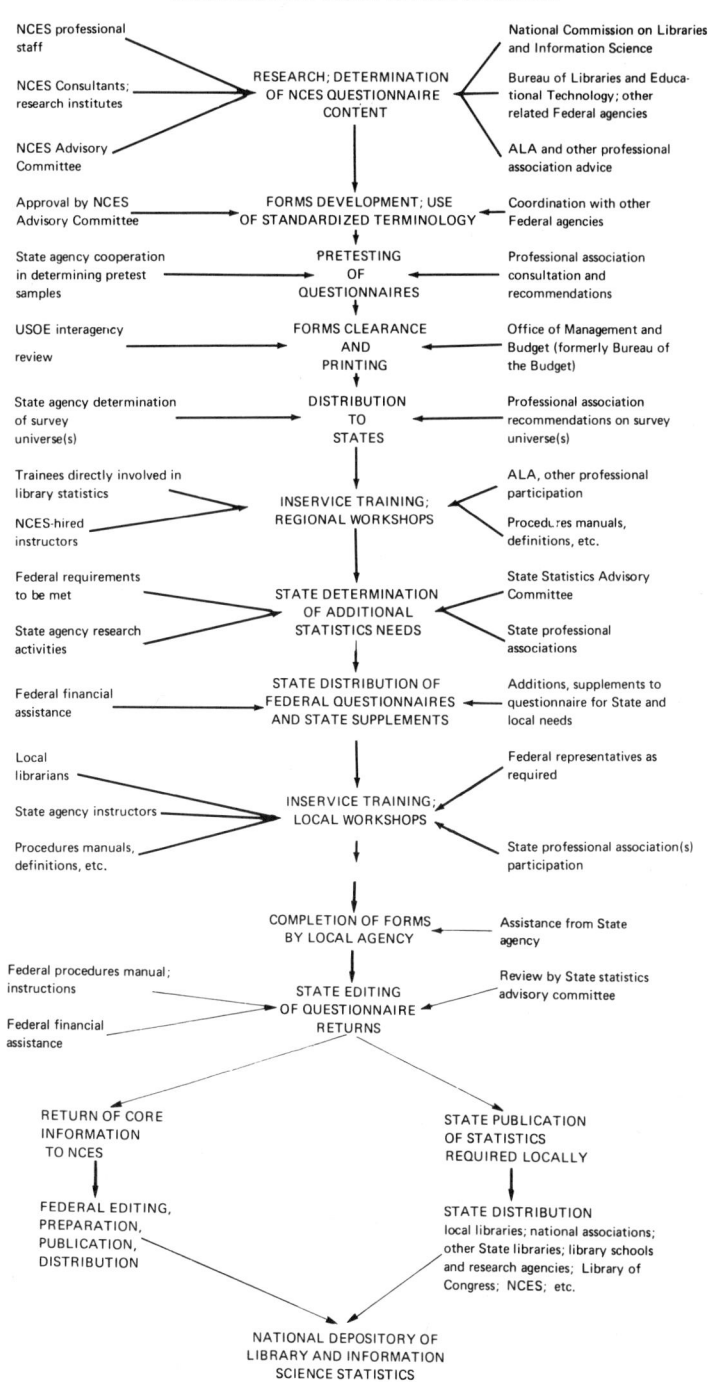

RESEARCH; DETERMINATION OF NCES QUESTIONNAIRE CONTENT
- NCES professional staff
- NCES Consultants; research institutes
- NCES Advisory Committee
- National Commission on Libraries and Information Science
- Bureau of Libraries and Educational Technology; other related Federal agencies
- ALA and other professional association advice

↓

FORMS DEVELOPMENT; USE OF STANDARDIZED TERMINOLOGY
- Approval by NCES Advisory Committee
- Coordination with other Federal agencies

↓

PRETESTING OF QUESTIONNAIRES
- State agency cooperation in determining pretest samples
- Professional association consultation and recommendations

↓

FORMS CLEARANCE AND PRINTING
- USOE interagency review
- Office of Management and Budget (formerly Bureau of the Budget)

↓

DISTRIBUTION TO STATES
- State agency determination of survey universe(s)
- Professional association recommendations on survey universe(s)

↓

INSERVICE TRAINING; REGIONAL WORKSHOPS
- Trainees directly involved in library statistics
- NCES-hired instructors
- ALA, other professional participation
- Procedures manuals, definitions, etc.

↓

STATE DETERMINATION OF ADDITIONAL STATISTICS NEEDS
- Federal requirements to be met
- State agency research activities
- State Statistics Advisory Committee
- State professional associations

↓

STATE DISTRIBUTION OF FEDERAL QUESTIONNAIRES AND STATE SUPPLEMENTS
- Federal financial assistance
- Additions, supplements to questionnaire for State and local needs

↓

INSERVICE TRAINING; LOCAL WORKSHOPS
- Local librarians
- State agency instructors
- Procedures manuals, definitions, etc.
- Federal representatives as required
- State professional association(s) participation

↓

COMPLETION OF FORMS BY LOCAL AGENCY
- Assistance from State agency

↓

STATE EDITING OF QUESTIONNAIRE RETURNS
- Federal procedures manual; instructions
- Federal financial assistance
- Review by State statistics advisory committee

↓

- **RETURN OF CORE INFORMATION TO NCES**
- **STATE PUBLICATION OF STATISTICS REQUIRED LOCALLY**

↓

- **FEDERAL EDITING, PREPARATION, PUBLICATION, DISTRIBUTION**
- **STATE DISTRIBUTION** local libraries; national associations; other State libraries; library schools and research agencies; Library of Congress; NCES; etc.

↓

NATIONAL DEPOSITORY OF LIBRARY AND INFORMATION SCIENCE STATISTICS

grouping of data and analysis of data than has ever been possible in the past.

There is also emphasis on the necessity for expansion in the use of sample and special statistical studies, which have seldom been made on a nationwide library basis. Previous emphasis has usually been on the acquisition of data of a total universe for one type of library.

The other major emphasis in this work is on the development of statistical data which can be used for the planning of services and in the measurement of effectiveness or accountability.

One of the areas which is perhaps not adequately emphasized in this work is the need for greater analysis of statistics. It may be understood or assumed that if all the necessary data were collected and disseminated that information would be fully analyzed and could be used by library administrators, legislators, boards, and commercial firms. But this assumption may be too simplistic. Library statistical data gathered in the past has tended to be reported with little analysis. More detailed and quicker analytical reporting of statistics by all levels of government, libraries, library agencies, and library associations would improve the benefits of all library statistical programs.

Some of the recommendations of this work have been initiated. The NCES is developing a core questionnaire and testing it with state library agencies; a study is being made (under the sponsorship of NCES) of the library data now being gathered by states and by national associations; representatives of ALA and other national groups have conferred regarding the standardization of nonprint terminology; the Library Administration Division, ALA, is planning for an expansion of the definitions in *Library Statistics: A Handbook of Concepts, Definitions, and Terminology*. The National Commission on Libraries and Information Science has been appointed, and the commission members have been briefed about the plans which are set forth in this publication.

Planning for a Nationwide System of Library Statistics does not answer all the questions of the profession regarding what is to be done about library statistics. Neither does it specify all the procedures to be used in gathering, recording, and reporting statistics. It does clarify the present status of library statistics; identifies many needs; recommends some basic and specific actions; and points the way toward a sound, nationwide system.

U.S. OFFICE OF EDUCATION PLANS FOR A SURVEY OF PUBLIC LIBRARIES

by

Ruth L. Boaz*

The survey of public libraries serving areas with at least 25,000 inhabitants in fiscal year 1971, to be conducted by the U.S. Office of Education in January 1972, continues a survey that has been conducted triennially since 1962.

Prior to the 1968 survey, both public libraries and nonconsolidated public library systems (i.e., systems composed of two or more locally autonomous public libraries) were included in the surveys as reporting units, but no distinction was made between libraries and nonconsolidated systems. The 1968 survey recognized the distinction, but libraries alone were surveyed; nonconsolidated systems were not accepted as reporting units.

The 1971 survey differs significantly

---

*Education Program Specialist, Library Surveys Branch, National Center for Educational Statistics, U.S. Office of Education, Washington, D.C. 20202.

from its predecessors in that it collects data for both public libraries and nonconsolidated public library systems that serve areas with at least 25,000 inhabitants; it also makes a sharp distinction between the two types of reporting units.

For the 1971 survey, as for earlier surveys, the Library Surveys Branch of the National Center for Educational Statistics has requested the assistance of state library agencies in providing lists of the public libraries and nonconsolidated public library systems serving areas with at least 25,000 inhabitants, in distributing the survey forms, and in collecting, pre-editing, and returning the reports to LSB. Most of the states are actively participating in the administration of the survey. Several states have elected to use the OE questionnaire for surveying their smaller libraries, as well as those serving areas with 25,000 or more inhabitants.

Although, in its general format, the 1971 survey form is similar to the 1968 survey, there are several new features. Items have been added for the reporting of the titles of book stock, motion pictures, and sound recordings added during the fiscal year and held at the end of the fiscal year, and for the number of magazine and newspaper titles, excluding duplicates, currently received. These categories of materials have been selected for title counts because they represent the major expenditures for library materials. A count of volumes is also requested in a separate item.

Every effort has been made to state the questions in terms of the record-keeping procedures that are ordinarily used in public libraries. Volumes and titles are to be reported by the collections into which they are organized, since this is the manner in which shelf lists and checklists are set up. Therefore, book stock is to be reported separately from periodicals collections.

An item has been added for the reporting of cash transmitted to other libraries or library agencies. This is to prevent these moneys from being counted as operating receipts and expenditures in one or more libraries and/or system headquarters.

Earlier public library surveys collected data on filled and vacant professional and nonprofessional library staff (excluding maintenance) positions. Because of the vast salary range for "professional" positions in public libraries, the 1968 survey of public libraries concluded that the data obtained for "professional" and "nonprofessional" positions were invalid. The two categories were combined as "library staff" in the 1968 report.

An important feature in the 1971 survey is an item that provides for the reporting of filled positions by the salary range and the educational qualifications of the incumbents, and for the reporting of vacant positions by salary range. This item should provide the public library community with valuable insights into its staffing patterns.

COLLEGE AND UNIVERSITY LIBRARY STATISTICS

by

Theodore Samore*

Two recent publications by the National Center for Educational Statistics of the U.S. Office of Education will prove highly useful to academic librarians, administrators, and funding agencies. Even though neither publication contains up-to-the-minute data, the information is still valuable because it is both comprehensive and specific. The two reports are *Library Statistics of Colleges & Universities; Data for Individual Institutions, Fall, 1969* (June 1970) and *Library Statistics of Colleges & Universities, Analytic Report, Fall, 1969* (1971). Both reports were written by Bronson Price of the Library Surveys Branch of the National Center for Educational Statistics (Dr. Price is now retired).

The first publication is the latest in a series that the Office of Education has been issuing since 1961. Future reports in the series will be issued biennially; for example, the Fall 1970 report (i.e., July 1970–June 1971) will be published in early 1972.

As in previous reports, data on collections, operating expenditures, and staff are for 1968–1969 while data for specific salaries and terms of employment are given for the fall of 1969. An impressive total of 2,122 individual college and university libraries is included.

Several observations are in order. First, in a number of states, having a particular public system of higher education (such as the University of California, University of Wisconsin, etc.) data for all the campuses in the system are lumped together. Hence it is impossible, for example, to separate the holdings of the University of California at Berkeley library from the holdings of the University of California at Los Angeles library.

Second, too many institutions still restrict the publication of individual salary data, particularly of the chief librarian. It appears that more private institutions than public ones restrict these data.

Last, the game of finding discrepancies in figures between the previous year's report and the present one is still amusing albeit trivial. For example, a library in Alaska reported holdings of around 40,000 volumes in 1967–1968. In 1968–1969 the number of volumes added was shown to be approximately 6,500, yet the net total of volumes reported for 1968–1969 was over 60,000. Where did those extra volumes come from?

All in all, however, the academic community will find the statistics reliable, valid and useful. For those who wish the most current figures it is a simple matter to update the 1968–1969 statistics by increasing them by about 4 to 8 percent per year.

The *Analytic Report, Fall 1969* is valuable in providing information on growth rates, trends, and comparative data among various types of academic libraries. There is a table on page 4 of the *Report* which indicates the percent of increase for various categories. For example, it shows that there was a 2 percent increase in the number of volumes added between fall 1968, and fall 1969. Some highlights are:

1. Some 328.6 million physical (unreduced) volumes were held at the end of 1968–1969, up 8 percent from the previous year's count. Periodical titles increased 4 percent, to 2.6 million titles. Microfilm reels rose 20 percent to a total of 6.3 million, while microtext other than microfilm reels increased 30 percent to 58.3 million units.

2. Nonbudgeted support services, or services not charged to the libraries' accounts (and not included in the above figures), totaled $16.0 million. Of that sum, 70 percent or $11.0 million was for

---

*Acting Director, School of Library and Information Science, University of Wisconsin — Milwaukee.

hourly assistance to the libraries by students paid under the federal College Work-Study Program.

3. From fall 1968 to fall 1969, regular (nonhourly) staff rose 4 percent, to 45,150 full-time-equivalent personnel. Of that total, 17,695 were librarians, 2,454 were professional staff other than librarians, and 25,001 were nonprofessional staff. The increases in those staff categories over the previous year were 2, 15, and 4 percent, respectively. Hours of student and other hourly assistance rose 9 percent, to 34.4 million hours. This was roughly equivalent to the service of 17,200 nonprofessional staff members working full time.

4. In relation to total positions authorized for the fall 1969 term, vacancies amounted to 4.5 percent.

5. Library expenditures per student rose 3 percent to $91.00, while expenditures per institutional staff member in instruction and research rose 24 percent to $1,212. The ratio of professional library staff to institutional staff in instruction and research rose 11 percent, to 4.2 (based on information given on the verso of the front cover of the *Analytic Report*).

Table 1 presents a national resume of college and university library statistics for the ten-year period 1962–1963 through 1971–1972.

146 / NATIONAL LIBRARY AND BOOK TRADE DEVELOPMENTS

TABLE 1 SUMMARY OF COLLEGE AND UNIVERSITY LIBRARY STATISTICS FOR ACADEMIC YEARS 1962–72: AGGREGATE UNITED STATES*

Item	1962–63	1963–64	1964–65	1965–66[1]	1966–67[1]	1967–68[1]	1968–69	1969–70	1970–71[1]	1971–72[1]
1. Number of libraries	2,075	2,140	2,175	2,207	2,252	2,300	2,370	2,400	2,450	2,500
2. Number of students served (enrollment)	4,345,000	4,800,000	5,300,000	5,900,000	6,400,000	7,000,000	7,300,000	7,600,000	8,200,000	8,800,000
Collections										
3. Number of volumes at end of year	215,000,000	227,000,000	240,000,000	265,000,000[2]	283,000,000[2]	295,000,000	305,000,000	329,000,000	355,000,000	383,000,000
4. Number of volumes per student	49.4	47.3	45.3	45.8	44.2	42.1	41.8	42.8	43.3	43.5
5. Number of volumes added during year	12,300,000	13,600,000	15,000,000	18,000,000	20,000,000	22,000,000	25,000,000	26,000,000	28,000,000	30,000,000
6. Number of volumes added per student	2.8	2.8	2.8	3.0	3.1	3.1	3.4	3.4	3.3	3.4
7. Number of periodicals received	1,600,000	1,760,000	2,000,000	2,700,000[3]	3,000,000[3]	3,400,000[3]	2,500,000[4]	2,600,000[4]	2,700,000[4]	2,800,000[4]
8. Number of periodicals per student	0.4	0.4	0.4	0.4	0.4	0.4[5]	Footnote[5]	Footnote[5]	Footnote[5]	Footnote[5]
Personnel										
9. Total (in full-time equivalents)	23,300	25,200	27,000	29,000	31,000	33,000	43,500	45,000	47,000	49,000
10. Professional personnel	11,200	11,900	12,500	13,000	14,000	15,000	17,400	17,700	18,700	19,700
11. Professional staff as percentage of total staff	48.0	47.0	46.0	45.0	45.0	45.0	42.3	39.3	39.8	40.2
12. Ratio of professional staff to students	1:388	1:401	1:402	1:454	1:457	1:466	1:419	1:430	1:440	1:450
13. Nonprofessional staff	12,100	13,300	14,500	16,000	17,000	18,000	26,100	27,000	28,000	29,000
14. Number of hours of student assistance	14,519,000	16,000,000	16,500,000	19,000,000	21,500,000	25,000,000	31,700,000	34,400,000	37,400,000	40,400,000

LIBRARY AND BOOK TRADE STATISTICS / 147

TABLE 1, Continued

	Operating Expenditures									
15.	Total (excludes capital outlay)	$213,000,000	$246,000,000	$276,000,000	$320,000,000	$366,000,000	$416,000,000	$510,000,000	$584,800,000	$660,000,000	$730,000,000
16.	Expenditures per student	$50.95	$51.25	$52.75	$54.23	$57.03	$59.29	$69.86	$76.95	$80.50	$82.95
17.	Expenditures as percentage of total education and general expenditures	3.2	3.3	3.3	3.3	3.6	3.7	3.7	4.3[6]	4.2[6]	4.2[6]
18.	Salaries (personnel not on hourly rate)	$113,000,000	$126,000,000	$141,000,000	$155,000,000	$172,000,000	$193,000,000	$235,000,000	$273,200,000	$315,000,000	$355,000,000
19.	Salaries as percentage of operating expenditures	53.1	51.2	51.0	49.0	47.0	46.4	46.0	46.6	47.5	48.7
20.	Wages (at hourly rates of pay)	$17,000,000	$19,000,000	$21,000,000	$23,500,000	$26,000,000	$29,000,000	$41,000,000	$44,300,000	$50,000,000	$54,000,000
21.	Wages as percentage of operating expenditures	8.0	7.7	7.6	7.3	7.1	7.0	8.0	8.0	8.0	7.1
22.	Books and other library materials expenditures	$65,000,000	$79,000,000	$90,000,000	$111,000,000	$134,000,000	$156,000,000	$189,000,000	$212,900,000	$235,000,000	$255,000,000
23.	Such expenditures percentage of operating expenditures	30.5	32.1	32.6	34.2	36.6	37.5	37.1	36.2	35.5	35.0
24.	Binding expenditures	$7,000,000	$9,000,000	$10,000,000	$11,500,000	$13,000,000	$14,000,000	$15,000,000	$17,500,000	$20,000,000	$22,000,000
25.	Such expenditures percentage of operating expenditures	3.3	3.7	3.8	3.5	3.5	3.3	2.9	3.0	3.0	3.1
26.	Other operating expenditures	$11,000,000	$13,000,000	$14,000,000	$19,000,000	$21,000,000	$24,000,000	$31,000,000	$36,900,000	$40,000,000	$44,000,000
27.	Such expenditures percentage of operating expenditures	4.2	5.3	5.0	6.0	5.8	5.8	6.0	6.2	6.0	6.1

Source: U.S. Office of Education: Library Statistics of Colleges and Universities, 1961/62–1968/69 Institutional Data; *Library Statistics of Colleges and Universities; Data for Individual Institutions, Fall, 1969* (June 1970); and *Library Statistics of Colleges and Universities, Analytic Report, Fall 1969* (1971).

*For statistics for years prior to 1962–63, see the 1971 edition and previous editions of *The Bowker Annual*.
[1]Estimated.
[2]The figures include microtext since some reporting institutions did not separate them from printed volumes.
[3]For 1965/66 through 1967/68 the figure is for *serials* which includes **periodicals, annuals, proceedings, transactions,** etc.
[4]Periodicals only.
[5]Since this figure remains constant, it will be omitted.
[6]The method of computing the library expenditure index was changed significantly in 1968–69. In that year, an institution's Educational and General Expenditure figure was redefined in accordance with recommendations of the National Association of College and University Business Officers. Of the changes made, the one of most importance was the deletion of federally sponsored organized research from the Educational and General expenditures category. Hence, the mean library expenditure index is appreciably higher than in the past.

HEALTH SCIENCES LIBRARIES IN THE UNITED STATES: SURVEY AND STATISTICAL PROFILE*

by

Susan Crawford**

During the past two decades the health care industry has experienced great growth. National expenditures for health care services increased from $12.9 billion in 1950 to $67.2 billion in 1970.[1] Over the same period of time the percentage of the gross national product expended on health care increased from 4.5 percent to 7.0 percent. Projected expenditures for 1980 are between 155.7 and $189.2 billion or 9.8 percent of the gross national product, an increase from 1950 by over a factor of two.[2]

Health care manpower, the users of library services, have also greatly increased over the past 20 years. In 1950, personnel in the health professions totalled around 1,682,000; by 1967, they numbered around 3,515,000. The number of allied health workers showed the greatest rate of growth: within the past decade they increased by factors between two and three. Concurrently, public demand for health, education, and welfare services heightened. Great challenges were consequently made upon health sciences libraries in the effort to train more health personnel, to reach toward the research front, and to apply new knowledge.

At the beginning of the 1960s, health sciences libraries were relatively independent units which were developed for local or special audiences. Cooperation existed among school, hospital, and society libraries, but relationships depended more upon the operation of natural forces than conscious design. The library community was slow to respond to the new challenges at first. It was not until 1965, when the Medical Library Assistance Act was passed, that a planned effort was made to improve biomedical communication on a national scale. The role of the National Library of Medicine (NLM) and the programs resulting from the Act have been well documented by Cummings and Corning.[3] The Act authorized funds for programs to improve biomedical communication through the construction of facilities, manpower training, research, provision of library resources, and establishment of regional medical libraries.

NLM's concept of a network of health science libraries in the United States divided the country into 11 geographic regions, each with a Regional Medical Library (RML) which would serve as a node or center to which inquiries not fulfilled by local libraries could be channelled. The network was decentralized and hierarchical, with three levels of nodes. The first-order nodes were the local libraries which communicated vertically upward with the regional libraries; the RMLs were the second-order nodes, in direct contact with the National Library of Medicine, which was at the apex of the system.

These and other developments underscored the necessity for developing a system for providing reliable, descriptive, and nationwide statistics on health sci-

---

*Research supported by grant no. 5 RO1 LM 00641 from the National Library of Medicine.
**Director, Archive-Library Department, American Medical Association.
[1]D. P. Rice and B. S. Cooper. National health expenditures, 1929–70. *Social Security Bulletin,* 34: 3-18, Jan. 1971.
[2]U.S. Dept. of Health, Education and Welfare. Social Security Administration. Projections of national health expenditures, 1975 and 1980. *Research and Statistics Notes,* No. 18, Oct. 30, 1970.
[3]M. M. Cummings and M. E. Corning. "The Medical Library Assistance Act: An Analysis of the NLM Extramural Programs, 1965–70." *Bulletin of the Medical Library Association,* 59: 375-391, July 1971.

ences libraries in the United States. Recognizing this need, the National Library of Medicine awarded to the American Medical Association a four-year grant to initiate a continuing data collection and analysis program with the objective of developing a national data bank for health sciences libraries. The methodology of the program is outlined in the first publication generated from the survey, the *Directory of Health Sciences Libraries, 1969*, issued under the auspices of the American Medical Association and the Medical Library Association.[4] This article analyzes the data generated from the 1969 survey.

THE SURVEY POPULATION

In the 1969 survey, health sciences libraries are defined as collections of published materials which are health related, serve health sciences personnel, and satisfy at least two of the following three criteria: a minimum of 500 bound volumes, a minimum of 25 current serial subscriptions, or some designated staff to administer the collection. The basic units identified and measured are defined according to administrative structure. In general, health sciences libraries are administratively organized according to one of three models:

1. Combined health sciences library whose collections include more than one subject specialty of the health sciences, and serve more than one professional group. An example is the large university medical center library which provides services for faculty and students in medicine, pharmacy, dentistry, and nursing.

2. Single user group library whose collection focuses on one specialty area. Examples are nursing school libraries and libraries of psychoanalytic training institutes.

3. General or multidisciplinary library which includes a health sciences collection interfiled and administered with the general collection. Examples are Los Angeles Public Library and John Crerar Library.

The survey, therefore, is a census of separately administered library units. These units are by no means equal, as they range from small hospital libraries to great national libraries such as the National Library of Medicine. The *Directory* is a listing of these separate administrative units.

A total of 3,155 health sciences libraries were identified in the 1969 survey and listed in the *Directory*. In the statistical analysis of this article, however, data for all libraries within each hospital was combined and the hospital was counted as a single unit in order that it could be related to the data on its total bed-size. Therefore, data for all libraries within each hospital (i.e., physician, nursing, etc.) were combined as a single library unit. As a result, the number of libraries analyzed in this article total 2,880 health sciences libraries.

QUESTIONNAIRE RESPONSE RATES

There was extensive variation in response rates among the various types of libraries and data items. Only actual and presumably valid responses to the AHA (American Hospital Association) or AMA questionnaires were used. Health sciences libraries with considerable holdings which failed to respond to the questionnaire were listed in the *Directory*, but considered nonrespondents in the statistical analysis. Among nonhospital libraries, the response rates for resources (bound volumes and current subscriptions)[5] varied from a high of 98 percent for medical school libraries

---

[4]F. Schick and S. Crawford. *Directory of Health Sciences Libraries, 1969*. Chicago, American Medical Association, 1971. 197 pp.

[5]A bound volume is defined as a physical unit of any printed, typewritten, handwritten, mimeographed, or processed work contained in one binding or portfolio, hardbound or paperbound, which has been classified, cataloged, or otherwise prepared for use. These include bound periodical volumes and all nonperiodical government documents.

Serials include periodicals, newspapers, annual reports, yearbooks, memoirs, proceedings, transactions of societies, and may include mimeographic and publishers' series.

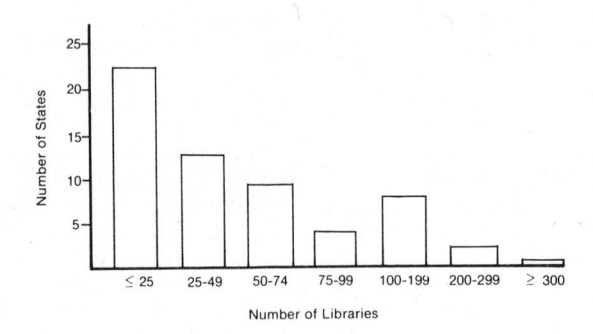

FIGURE 1. Geographic distribution of health sciences libraries: number of states and U.S. possessions by number of libraries.

to a low of 72 percent for health sciences collections in two-year academic institutions. Response rates were lower for personnel and for expenditures. Especially among collections within general libraries, respondents were not able to report separately identifiable budgets. Approximately two-thirds of the respondents provided data on total floor space.

The response rate among hospital health sciences libraries was lower, ranging from 75 percent for hospitals of bed-size 300 or over to 35 percent in those of bed-size below 25. Since the probability of having a library in a hospital of less than 25 beds is extremely low, we believe that small returns from this group do not significantly affect derivation of the true population.

GEOGRAPHIC DISTRIBUTION

The distribution of library resources has been found to be highly correlated with the distribution of the general population ($r = .90$, Rothenberg et al.).[6] It is therefore not surprising that health sciences libraries are unequally distributed over the states. In Figure 1, we have collapsed the data of Table 1 in the *Directory of Health Sciences Libraries* to show the distribution by states of the number of health sciences libraries.

Twenty-two states or U.S. possessions have 25 health sciences libraries or less, with Canal Zone and Guam having one library each. There are 12 states with 25 to 49 libraries; eight states with 50 to 74 libraries; and three states with 75 to 99 libraries. The nine states with the greatest number of libraries are Michigan (106), New Jersey (109), Texas (119), Massachusetts (143), Ohio (158), Illinois (197), Pennsylvania (246), California (255), and New York (378). This distribution of resources by state is an important consideration in the development of a nationwide network of health sciences libraries.

TYPES OF LIBRARIES BY INSTITUTIONAL CONTEXT

Table 1 indicates the great variety of health sciences libraries, classified by type of sponsoring organization. Hospital libraries are the most numerous, comprising 60 percent of all health sciences libraries. Following in order of frequency are allied health educational programs in academic institutions (508), business and industrial organizations (139), medical schools (103), and professional organizations (87). These five types of organizations account for 89 percent of all health sciences libraries.

---

[6] L. Rothenberg, A. Rees and D. Kronick. "An Investigation of the Educational Needs of Health Sciences Library Manpower. Part II: Health-related Institutions and their Library Resources." *Bulletin of the Medical Library Association*, 58: 510-520, Oct. 1970.

TABLE 1 HEALTH SCIENCES LIBRARIES: AVERAGE RESOURCES BY TYPE OF SPONSORING ORGANIZATION

Organizational Category	Number of Libraries	Percentage of Libraries	Average Number of Bound Volumes	Average Number of Serials
Hospitals[1]	1,727	60.0	3,730	115
Allied health educational programs in academic institutions	508	17.6	1,047	254
Business and industrial organizations	139	4.8	7,249	234
Medical schools	103	3.6	95,357	1,882
Professional societies	87	3.0	28,892	215
Foundations	62	2.1	9,729	205
Federal libraries[2]	50	1.7	NC[3]	NC
State or local public health department libraries	49	1.7	12,653	264
Group practice clinics	38	1.3	3,900	94
Voluntary health organizations	19	.7	2,944	185
Psychoanalytic societies and training institutions	18	.6	3,165	111
Municipal public libraries	8	.3	NC	NC
Miscellaneous[4]	72	2.6	NC	NC
TOTAL	2,880	100.0	—	—

[1]For this analysis, data for all libraries within each hospital (i.e., medicine, nursing, etc.) were combined and counted as a single unit. As 275 libraries were amalgamated, the result is a total of 2,880 libraries, in contrast with 3,155 libraries listed in the *Directory*.

[2]Libraries of federal, state, and local hospitals are included in statistics for hospital libraries.

[3]NC = Not computed.

[4]These include infrequently recurring classes of libraries or those which provided insufficient data and are not analyzed in this report.

SIZE OF HEALTH SCIENCES LIBRARIES

There are only 103 medical school libraries, but they are clearly the largest of health sciences libraries as measured by the average number of bound volumes and average number of serials. Figure 2 compares health sciences libraries by number of bound volumes. The average medical school library has over 95,000 bound volumes and almost 1,900 current serial subscriptions. Their bound volume collections are over three times the size of the average professional society library (29,000 bound volumes) and over 25 times that of the average hospital library (3,700 bound volumes). On the average, they exceed professional society libraries by a factor of eight in number of current serials, and hospital libraries by a factor of 15.

MANPOWER OF HEALTH SCIENCES LIBRARIES

An extensive analysis of manpower in health sciences libraries has been published in the Manpower Study papers of Kronick, Rees, and Rothenberg.[7] Based upon a 75 percent response rate, a total

[7]D. Kronick, A. Rees, and L. Rothenberg. "An Investigation of the Educational Needs of Health Sciences Library Manpower," *Bulletin of the Medical Library Association*, 58: 7-17. Jan. 1970; 58: 510-520, Oct. 1970; 59: 21-30, Jan. 1971; 59: 392-403, July 1971.

TABLE 2 PERSONNEL IN HEALTH SCIENCES LIBRARIES

| | Personnel Category | $N = 9390$ | |
Status	Professional	Nonprofessional	Student Assistant
Full-time	2,747	2,384	—
Part-time	1,079	1,760	1,420
TOTAL	3,826	4,144	1,420

of 9,390 professional and nonprofessional personnel[8] were identified, working part- or full-time in health sciences libraries (Table 2). Of the full-time personnel, 2,747 were rated as professional by the respondents and 2,384 were rated as nonprofessional. Of the part-time personnel, 1,079 were rated as professional and 1,760 as nonprofessional. There was a total of 1,420 student assistants.

Although medical school libraries constitute only 3.6 percent of all health sciences libraries, they accounted for 21 percent of all full-time professionals (566 professionals) and 38 percent of full-time nonprofessionals (905 nonprofessionals). Hospital libraries, which constitute 60 percent of all health sciences libraries, accounted for 40 percent of all full-time professionals (1,197 professionals) and 18 percent of all full-time nonprofessionals (434 nonprofessionals). Hospital libraries rely heavily upon voluntary help; indeed, the number of part-time nonprofessionals employed in hospitals (1,207) exceeds the total number of full-time professionals (1,197).

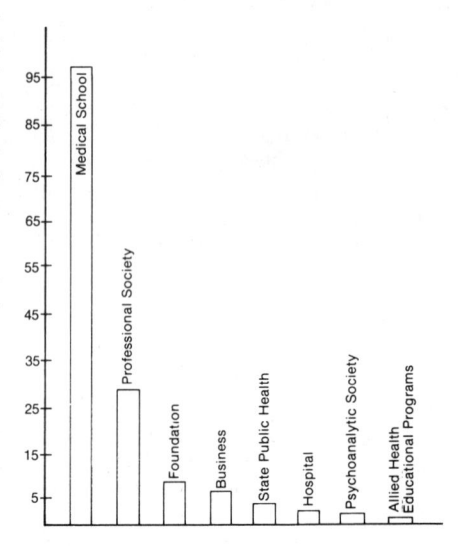

FIGURE 2. Health sciences libraries: average number of bound volumes by type of library (in thousands of volumes).

USER GROUPS

As a unit of analysis the separately administered library does not indicate the number of libraries which serve each user group. The "combined library" or library in which there is a co-occurrence of user groups is common among health sciences libraries. To derive data on the number of libraries which provide some type of service to the various user groups, we asked all libraries to check categories of occupation or area of training which were most representative of their users.

As shown in Table 3, 2,051 (71 percent) of the libraries serve physicians or medical students; 1,817 (63 percent) serve nurses or nursing students; and 1,168 (40 percent) serve health profes-

---

[8]*Library professionals* are defined as staff members occupying positions in the library which require training and skill in theoretical or scientific aspects of the library's work, as distinct from the mechanical aspects.

Nonprofessionals exclude maintenance personnel, but include clerical and similar personnel, who perform under supervision, duties requiring special skills and experience, but not the knowledge and theory of library work.

TABLE 3 OCCUPATIONAL GROUPS SERVED BY HEALTH SCIENCES LIBRARIES*

User Category	Number of Libraries Serving N = 2880	Percentage of Libraries Serving
Medicine or osteopathy	2,051	71.38
Nursing	1,817	63.17
Other health professions	1,168	40.06
Biomedical research	711	24.75
Nonhealth professions	253	8.87
Dentistry	243	8.44
Pharmacy	169	5.27
Veterinary medicine	105	3.65

*Based upon response rate of 99.7 percent.

sions other than medicine (nursing, dentistry, pharmacy, veterinary medicine, and biomedical research). Two hundred and fifty-three libraries (9 percent) indicated that they also served the nonhealth professions or the public at large.

SUMMARY

The *1969 Survey of Health Sciences Libraries* was conceived over an era of unprecedented growth of the health care industry. Within this dynamic context it attempted to identify all the components of the health sciences library community, and to find out something about their characteristics and their functions. This article analyzes the data of 1969 Survey — the types of libraries, their geographic distribution, their resources, manpower and user groups. It summarizes the content of *Health Sciences Libraries: a Statistical Profile*,[9] an eight-chapter monograph which analyzes in depth each subset of health sciences libraries by institutional context.

With completion of the *Statistical Profile* and the *Directory of Health Sciences Libraries, 1969,* the third phase of AMA-MLA Continuing Program for Statistical Surveys of Health Sciences Libraries is completed.

[9] S. Crawford, ed. *Health Sciences Libraries in the United States: A Statistical Profile* (to be published as supplement to the *Bulletin of the Medical Library Association,* April 1972).

CHARACTERISTICS OF THE U.S. POPULATION SERVED BY LIBRARIES

by

George Lind*

	Number	Percent
Total U.S. and outlying areas population	210,040,000	100.0
Resident population of 50 States and D.C.	206,187,000[1]	98.2
Armed forces overseas	819,000[1]	0.4
Civilian resident population of U.S. outlying areas	3,034,000[2]	1.4
Resident population by age[3]		
Under 18 years	70,730,000	34.1
Ages 18–20 years	11,169,000	5.4
Ages 21–64 years	105,573,000	50.8
Ages 65 and over	20,127,000	9.7
Public and nonpublic school enrollment[4]	60,240,000	100.0
Kindergarten through grade 8	36,700,000	60.9
Grades 9–12	15,150,000	25.2
Higher education	8,390,000	13.9
Nonpublic school enrollment[4]	7,830,000	13.0[5]
Kindergarten through grade 8	4,230,000	7.0
Grades 9–12	1,440,000	2.4
Higher education	2,160,000	3.6
Educational status of population aged 25 and over[6] (March 1970)		
Total aged 25 and over	109,310,000	100.0
With 4 or more years of college	12,063,000	11.0
With 4 years of high school and 0–3 years of college	48,298,000	44.2
With 8 years of grade school and 0–3 years of high school	33,277,000	30.5
With 0–7 years of grade school	15,671,000	14.3

*Mr. Lind is with the Division of Statistical Information and Studies; Reference, Estimates, and Projections Branch; the National Center for Educational Statistics; U.S. Office of Education.

[1] As of July 1, 1971, estimates of the Bureau of the Census, U.S. Department of Commerce, *Current Population Reports,* P-25, No. 464, August 19, 1971.

[2] As of April 1, 1970, preliminary estimates of the population of Puerto Rico, American Samoa, Guam, Virgin Islands, and Trust Territories. Data are the unpublished estimates of the Bureau of the Census, U.S. Department of Commerce. The Canal Zone data included in totals are as of April 1, 1960.

[3] As of July 1, 1971, age data are projections by the Bureau of the Census, U.S. Department of Commerce, *Current Population Reports,* P-25, No. 448, August 6, 1970.

[4] Estimates as of Fall 1971, U.S. Office of Education, Department of Health, Education, and Welfare, *Digest of Educational Statistics,* 1971, Table 1.

[5] Percentages for nonpublic school enrollment are based on the figure for total public and nonpublic school enrollment.

[6] As of March 1970, Bureau of the Census, U.S. Department of Commerce, *Current Population Reports,* P-20, No. 207, November 30, 1970. Data exclude armed forces overseas.

U.S. POPULATION SERVED BY LIBRARIES, Continued

	Number	Percent
Residence in and outside metropolitan areas[7]		
Total resident population (April 1970)	203,184,000	100.0
Nonmetropolitan areas	63,798,000	31.4
Metropolitan areas	139,387,000	68.6
In central cities	63,816,000	31.4
Outside central cities	75,570,000	37.2
Employment status[8]		
Total civilian noninstitutional population 16 years old and over (April 1971)	139,206,000	
Civilian labor force, total	82,898,000	100.0
Employed	78,204,000	94.3
Male	48,734,000	58.8
Female	29,470,000	35.5
Unemployed	4,694,000	5.7
Not in labor force	56,308,000	100.0
Keeping house	35,405,000	62.9
In school	9,165,000	16.3
Other	11,738,000	20.8
Occupational groups[9]		
Total employed civilian labor force persons 16 years old and over	78,204,000	100.0
Professional and technical	11,134,000	14.2
Managers, officials, and proprietors	8,590,000	11.0
Clerical	13,236,000	16.9
Sales	5,028,000	6.4
Craftsmen and foremen	9,899,000	12.7
Operatives	12,707,000	16.3
Service	10,595,000	13.5
Farm and nonfarm laborers	7,014,000	9.0
Total faculty and students served by college and universities libraries [10]	9,007,000	
Faculty	617,000	
Students	8,390,000	

[7] As of April 1970, Bureau of the Census, *Statistical Abstract of the United States,* 1971 edition, page 16.

[8] As of April 1971, Bureau of the Census, *Statistical Abstract of the United States,* 1971 edition, page 210.

[9] As of April 1971, Bureau of the Census, *Statistical Abstract of the United States,* 1971 edition, page 222.

[10] Estimates as of Fall 1971, U.S. Office of Education, Department of Health, Education, and Welfare, *Digest of Educational Statistics,* 1971, Tables 1 and 8.

STATISTICS ON LIBRARIES

Statistics from the *American Library Directory 1970–1971* (Bowker, 1970). Data are exclusive of school libraries.

LIBRARIES IN THE UNITED STATES

Public libraries	7190
Branch libraries of city, county, and regional systems, maintained by 1289 public libraries	4855
University and college libraries	1896
Junior college libraries	1072
Special libraries	4277
Special libraries part of university and college systems	1216
Special libraries within public library systems or part of armed forces installations	274
Law libraries[1]	477
Law libraries part of university and college systems	115
Medical libraries[2]	1315
Medical libraries part of university and college systems	181
Religious libraries	600
Religious libraries part of university and college systems	49
Public libraries of armed forces installations including veterans' hospitals	481

LIBRARIES IN REGIONS ADMINISTERED BY THE U.S.

Public libraries	16
Branch libraries	3
University, college, and junior college libraries	30
Special libraries including armed forces, law, medical, and religious	21

Special libraries part of university and public library systems	32

LIBRARIES IN CANADA

Public libraries	444
Branch libraries in cities and provinces maintained by 47 public library systems	313
University, college, and junior college libraries	262
Special libraries including law, medical, and religious	791
Special libraries part of university and public library systems	173

SUMMARY

Total of public, college, special, armed forces, law, medical, and religious libraries listed:	
United States	23,998
Regions administered by the U.S.	102
Canada	1983
Grand total of libraries listed	26,083
Total of libraries *not* listed in this directory but on Bowker stencil lists:	
Public libraries in the U.S. with annual incomes of less than $2000 or book funds of less than $500 approx.	2700
Law libraries in the U.S. of less than 10,000 volumes	380
Grand total of libraries in the U.S. and Canada	29,163

[1] See also Roy Mersky's article, "Law Library Statistics," 1971 *Bowker Annual*, pp. 27-48.

[2] See also Susan Crawford's article, "The AMA-MLA Program for Continuing Statistical Surveys of Health Sciences Libraries," and Frank L. Schick's article "Health Sciences Library Statistics, 1969," both in the 1971 *Bowker Annual*, pp. 22-26 and 18-22, respectively; and Crawford's article, "Health Sciences Libraries in the United States: Survey and Statistical Profile," this volume.

DATA ON PUBLIC LIBRARY BUDGETS AND EXPENDITURES FOR LIBRARY MATERIALS

Figures derive from the *American Library Directory 1970–1971* (Bowker, 1970) and include data from 7190 public libraries, 4855 branch libraries, and 481 public libraries of armed forces installations, including veterans' hospitals, reporting financial information.

	1 Income[1]	2 Expenditure[2]	3 Income[3]	4 Expenditure[4]
Alabama	$ 5,160,151	$ 934,330	$	$
Alaska	758,363	114,523		
Arizona	4,234,723	708,991	1,028,352	1,546
Arkansas	3,565,750	920,379		
California	98,514,147	14,549,469	2,087,654	324,469
Colorado	5,906,561	1,119,963	1,174,593	
Connecticut	15,357,996	2,278,886		6,269
Delaware	1,588,658	389,547	42,025	
District of Columbia	5,194,620	688,989	57,837,741[5]	
Florida	12,575,330	2,141,824	859,801	228,321
Georgia	17,643,245	1,507,283	236,076	57,248
Hawaii	4,736,561	1,007,994		
Idaho	1,814,540	282,383		
Illinois	46,378,481	5,802,372	555,816	246,120
Indiana	22,978,696	3,172,775	250,193	21,100
Iowa	8,901,622	1,263,006	294,823	200
Kansas	6,081,281	1,062,204	137,176	24,715
Kentucky	5,481,846	1,264,625	1,981,031	500
Louisiana	9,050,756	1,581,527	67,449	4,050
Maine	2,087,176	458,839		13,646
Maryland	19,365,988	3,473,905	792,528	10,600
Massachusetts	34,969,248	6,134,543	78,413	101,219

Note: For special library statistics see the following articles in the 1971 *Bowker Annual*: "Health Sciences Library Statistics, 1969" by Frank L. Schick, pp. 18-22; "Law Library Statistics" by Roy M. Mersky, pp. 27-48; "The AMA-MLA Program for Continuing Statistical Surveys of Health Sciences Libraries" by Susan Crawford, pp. 22-26. See also Crawford's article "Health Sciences Libraries in the United States: Survey and Statistical Profile," this volume.

See also Herbert Goldhor's article "Public Library Statistics, 1968," 1971 *Bowker Annual*, pp. 11-18. For further information on library book budgets for years 1959–1968, see 1970 *Bowker Annual*, pp. 21-22.

[1]Column 1 lists total income (expenditure or budget) for libraries reporting total income and a corresponding library materials expenditure figure, listed in column 2.

[2]Column 2 lists library expenditures for library materials (including books, periodicals, audiovisual materials, film, records, binding, microform, etc.) for those libraries reporting a corresponding income (expenditure or budget) figure, listed in column 1.

[3]Column 3 lists income for libraries reporting no corresponding figure for library materials expenditure.

[4]Column 4 lists expenditure for library materials for libraries reporting no corresponding income (budget or expenditure) figure.

[5]Inclusion of Library of Congress income accounts for high sum here.

DATA ON PUBLIC LIBRARY BUDGETS AND EXPENDITURES FOR LIBRARY MATERIALS, Continued

	1 Income[1]	2 Expenditure[2]	3 Income[3]	4 Expenditure[4]
Michigan	34,089,563	4,492,046	61,981	14,157
Minnesota	13,283,637	2,488,491	452,662	1,750
Mississippi	4,847,165	854,747		65,006
Missouri	15,277,511	2,464,842	692,498	12,255
Montana	1,064,829	213,889	596,740	163,646
Nebraska	1,892,254	363,526	1,385,976	
Nevada	1,720,508	353,640		
New Hampshire	2,835,551	577,741		800
New Jersey	30,225,712	5,893,838	459,222	33,535
New Mexico	2,014,549	207,041	386,696	25,100
New York	101,084,807	15,451,209	1,414,063	191,817
North Carolina	11,437,266	1,556,273	374,202	6,108
North Dakota	1,257,284	236,784	17,367	
Ohio	49,887,553	7,884,367	82,125	83,507
Oklahoma	5,681,960	967,221	27,902	10,176
Oregon	8,583,937	1,117,620		1,700
Pennsylvania	35,098,227	5,743,380	556,738	4,540
Rhode Island	2,662,122	408,011	3,746,216	
South Carolina	3,848,753	801,047		3,946
South Dakota	1,249,323	180,027	139,297	2,075
Tennessee	6,163,720	1,271,121		
Texas	20,392,751	3,828,083	34,809	961
Utah	3,535,707	621,896		
Vermont	1,394,491	194,732	7,150	7,769
Virginia	12,574,570	2,237,043	258,994	34,275
Washington	19,042,243	2,581,861		2,586
West Virginia	2,434,747	428,157	268,676	
Wisconsin	16,081,264	2,610,357	6,958	18,950
Wyoming	1,219,384	274,014	263,068	
Total[6]	$743,227,127	$117,161,361	$78,657,011	$1,724,662

[6]Total library income for the fifty states is $832,827,426. (This total is derived from the sum of the total of column 1 and a percentage of the totals of columns 3 and 4.) Total library expenditure for library materials is $131,282,368 (derived from the sum of the total of column 2 and a percentage of the totals of columns 3 and 4.)

DATA ON COLLEGE AND UNIVERSITY LIBRARY BUDGETS AND EXPENDITURES FOR LIBRARY MATERIALS

Figures derive from the *American Library Directory 1970–1971* (Bowker, 1970) and include data from 1896 university and college libraries; 1072 junior college libraries; 1216 special, 115 law, 181 medical, and 49 religious libraries — all part of university and college systems. Also included are theological seminaries, technical institutes, etc., where federal book funds were made available.

	1 Income[1]	2 Expenditure[2]	3 Income[3]	4 Expenditure[4]
Alabama	$ 7,255,674	$ 2,301,981	$ 269,418	$ 231,374
Alaska	853,889	400,881		2,250
Arizona	4,443,748	1,974,797	118,844	245,306
Arkansas	2,505,048	1,282,589		167,590
California	64,697,513	23,355,950	363,248	4,960,096
Colorado	7,844,218	3,139,159		59,396
Connecticut	6,814,413	3,148,447	6,000	2,546,263
Delaware	1,608,514	34,917		472,925
District of Columbia	5,375,155	2,583,234		520,704
Florida	14,707,610	5,401,659		1,120,261
Georgia	10,055,981	4,680,446	295,810	392,273
Hawaii	2,673,458	1,061,677		15,300
Idaho	1,454,070	567,759		140,300
Illinois	30,634,358	9,954,781	243,500	3,454,169
Indiana	8,447,970	3,252,483	147,868	1,805,233
Iowa	7,623,624	3,040,669	2,990,718	276,734
Kansas	9,231,588	2,788,809	39,800	211,093
Kentucky	9,427,408	2,927,655	56,000	74,468
Louisiana	10,760,559	2,715,874	99,540	195,308
Maine	2,012,385	729,429	6,150	135,233
Maryland	13,008,626	3,441,826	65,000	718,206
Massachusetts	13,995,064	5,376,531	417,008	4,346,528
Michigan	17,555,172	6,118,934	359,972	1,981,189
Minnesota	8,261,985	3,155,284	304,703	416,778
Mississippi	2,465,266	1,074,742		299,260
Missouri	6,579,569	3,032,891	138,556	3,178,866
Montana	1,003,616	418,114	56,507	341,947
Nebraska	3,861,818	1,719,994		224,554
Nevada	1,520,901	758,564		6,100
New Hampshire	3,248,175	1,236,857		84,332

See also "College and University Library Statistics," by Theodore Samore, this volume, and "Library Book Budgets," 1970 *Bowker Annual*, pp. 21-22.

[1]Column 1 lists total income (expenditure or budget) for libraries reporting total income and a corresponding library materials expenditure figure, listed in column 2.

[2]Column 2 lists library expenditures for library materials (including books, periodicals, audiovisual materials, film, records, binding, microform, etc.) for those libraries reporting a corresponding income (expenditure or budget) figure, listed in column 1.

[3]Column 3 lists income for libraries reporting no corresponding figure for library materials expenditure.

[4]Column 4 lists expenditure for library materials for libraries reporting no corresponding income (budget or expenditure) figure.

DATA ON COLLEGE AND UNIVERSITY LIBRARY BUDGETS AND EXPENDITURES FOR LIBRARY MATERIALS, Continued

	1 Income[1]	2 Expenditure[2]	3 Income[3]	4 Expenditure[4]
New Jersey	14,006,097	5,770,448	82,800	912,613
New Mexico	2,018,485	855,391		45,016
New York	54,984,598	19,846,987	1,694,634	3,574,813
North Carolina	13,394,574	5,398,698	104,204	603,097
North Dakota	1,556,231	638,116		35,228
Ohio	23,561,893	9,097,848	175,918	766,568
Oklahoma	3,817,119	1,422,951	16,500	794,027
Oregon	7,186,979	2,730,257		29,497
Pennsylvania	25,167,200	10,660,941	296,540	3,900,465
Rhode Island	3,329,775	1,394,719		180,548
South Carolina	4,186,598	1,970,640	50,283	229,487
South Dakota	1,436,536	587,360		60,800
Tennessee	10,773,927	4,156,306	227,156	167,334
Texas	24,846,610	10,503,892	145,350	1,069,140
Utah	2,905,440	1,016,477		880,000
Vermont	1,695,457	664,812		240,495
Virginia	9,518,673	4,312,271	384,530	245,560
Washington	10,013,121	3,228,073	122,890	547,446
West Virginia	2,656,164	1,084,255		323,012
Wisconsin	11,699,868	5,215,337	759,812	587,017
Wyoming	820,582	445,111		20,600
Total[5]	$509,503,302	$192,677,823	$10,039,259	$43,836,799

[5]Total income for college and university libraries was $635,451,601; total expenditures for library materials, $240,311,470. For explanation of how these sums were derived, see page 158, footnote 6, this volume.

PUBLIC LIBRARY DATA ON AUDIOVISUAL AND MICROFORM EXPENDITURES*

415 public libraries (representing 40 states and the District of Columbia) giving specific information on audiovisual expenditure had a total income of $193,023,091; a total audiovisual expenditure of $1,880,635. Of those 415 reporting, .974% of income was spent for audiovisual materials.

185 public libraries (representing 41 states and the District of Columbia) giving specific information on microform expenditure had a total income of $92,149,615; a total microform expenditure of $431,481. Of those 185 reporting, .468% of income was spent for microforms.

	Audiovisual		Microform	
State	Budget or Income	AV Exp.	Budget or Income	Micro Exp.
Alabama	$ 1,073,732	$ 9,168	$1,438,753	$ 6,595
Arizona	1,374,881	13,350	3,112,301	8,536
California	38,618,049	314,553	8,816,281	44,268
Colorado	2,832,530	24,916	293,321	1,029
Connecticut	2,134,784	25,627	2,336,395	17,115
District of Columbia	5,194,620	54,171	5,194,620	15,809
Florida	1,719,933	9,180	4,060,349	35,089
Georgia	2,791,383	30,992	2,330,844	4,891
Hawaii	4,736,561	47,868	4,736,561	14,750
Idaho			304,383	275
Illinois	11,397,897	95,229	2,499,973	22,069
Indiana	2,904,640	33,979	2,047,287	10,244
Iowa	359,153	2,715	830,325	5,904
Kansas	340,954	6,816	621,063	2,508
Kentucky	245,091	1,696		
Louisiana	1,768,853	22,209	108,100	42
Maine			382,486	2,200
Maryland	9,711,852	103,234	6,859,938	20,570
Massachusetts	8,938,265	44,350	2,586,051	13,134
Michigan	4,643,038	79,121	10,091,965	14,369
Minnesota	7,254,365	109,584		
Mississippi	350,717	1,434	185,332	407
Missouri	8,539,144	97,566	538,210	1,351
Montana	313,776	6,387		
Nebraska	137,663	9,370	26,735	2,100
Nevada	375,408	2,400	538,254	2,603
New Hampshire	346,702	4,816	931,822	5,000
New Jersey	6,313,217	70,776	4,936,831	32,951
New York	7,986,151	105,115	4,918,972	38,681
North Carolina	2,035,602	19,597	409,374	2,840
Ohio	32,115,742	294,439	3,007,169	28,826
Oklahoma			183,647	600
Oregon	2,615,719	13,000	369,899	1,200
Pennsylvania	2,125,427	39,498	1,574,055	17,830
Rhode Island	411,416	3,612	1,642,604	3,255
South Carolina	270,900	1,156	91,976	116
South Dakota	116,131	1,773	289,577	465
Tennessee	2,297,229	23,622	1,867,600	3,670
Texas	4,611,486	39,413	2,094,978	8,890
Utah	2,030,621	33,948		
Vermont			58,966	550
Virginia	2,469,288	27,790	3,253,463	13,738
Washington	8,149,370	41,704	4,654,652	12,093
Wisconsin	1,190,445	13,961	1,628,191	5,418
Wyoming	180,356	500	296,312	9,500

*Data derived from the *American Library Directory 1970–1971* (Bowker, 1970).

COLLEGE AND UNIVERSITY LIBRARY DATA ON AUDIOVISUAL AND MICROFORM EXPENDITURES*

508 college and university libraries (representing 48 states and the District of Columbia) giving specific information on audiovisual expenditure had a total income of $68,933,814; a total audiovisual expenditure of $2,593,899. Of those 508 reporting, 3.763% of income was spent for audiovisual materials.

564 college and university libraries (representing 48 states and the District of Columbia) giving specific information on microform expenditure had a total income of $96,448,988; a total microform expenditure of $1,940,359. Of those 564 reporting, 2.012% of the income was spent for microforms.

	Audiovisual		Microform	
State	Budget or Income	AV Exp.	Budget or Income	Micro Exp.
Alabama	$ 1,890,083	$27,360	$1,995,438	$22,925
Alaska	49,988	750	125,380	1,500
Arizona	541,055	123,870	487,876	6,995
Arkansas	360,702	8,304	294,538	11,744
California	12,832,709	413,102	19,119,193	361,278
Colorado	574,047	18,881	484,582	9,380
Connecticut	448,984	24,618	2,002,732	58,039
District of Columbia	287,499	9,353	168,995	1,830
Florida	2,821,568	226,420	2,034,493	45,768
Georgia	1,204,457	30,558	1,215,702	33,584
Hawaii	139,120	7,500	221,972	12,150
Idaho	10,800	3,000	467,607	9,800
Illinois	4,843,492	262,693	5,284,546	138,908
Indiana	354,094	3,783	500,182	8,970
Iowa	351,548	8,966	844,585	22,782
Kansas	2,956,408	32,220	2,446,263	23,781
Kentucky	2,797,368	21,143	3,531,661	33,797
Louisiana	258,462	3,464	1,326,269	27,663
Maine	99,071	700	1,023,411	26,574
Maryland	3,247,903	21,120	3,627,141	26,864
Massachusetts	1,598,272	49,163	3,152,338	63,100
Michigan	4,225,241	257,449	2,675,453	39,020
Minnesota	1,071,347	38,785	1,160,414	21,619
Mississippi	232,845	10,694	337,216	5,933
Missouri	1,526,790	92,469	1,230,001	47,017
Montana	133,755	7,000	82,211	1,643
Nebraska	556,874	9,132	714,150	7,703
New Hampshire	136,312	3,100	1,159,971	19,150
New Jersey	1,739,427	78,918	3,355,420	88,416
New Mexico	219,857	3,451	111,137	3,931
New York	2,888,207	74,739	9,159,349	183,043
North Carolina	800,240	36,009	1,151,080	39,741
North Dakota	343,526	13,708	230,146	2,133
Ohio	1,929,180	43,620	1,765,621	31,224
Oklahoma	738,915	20,561	2,246,140	43,044
Oregon	2,547,313	75,935	3,582,288	41,390
Pennsylvania	1,614,747	42,540	3,632,624	94,100
Rhode Island	536,583	10,600	1,112,613	19,325
South Carolina	296,877	7,211	356,793	6,253
South Dakota	51,518	753	169,867	1,799
Tennessee	453,777	8,216	584,153	7,729
Texas	3,528,704	248,395	4,499,113	137,506
Utah	141,238	4,400	84,696	1,451
Vermont	211,660	1,810	379,823	12,579
Virginia	1,968,771	54,444	2,552,904	34,716
Washington	2,179,242	132,602	1,073,369	29,503
West Virginia	108,697	204	206,244	11,882
Wisconsin	1,036,994	19,064	2,414,640	60,092
Wyoming	47,547	1,122	66,648	985

*Data derived from the *American Library Directory 1970–1971* (Bowker, 1970).

GROWTH OF THE BOOKSTORE INDUSTRY IN THE UNITED STATES*

by

William S. Lofquist**

Retail bookstores made rapid economic advances this past decade, reflecting the U.S. public's mounting interest in and purchase of books. The most recent data on retail trade, taken from the 1967 Census of Business, showed close to 3,000 U.S. bookstores operating the year round in 1967 with annual sales of all products and services totaling $428 million. Combined book and periodical sales in these stores was $326 million, accounting for just over three-fourths of total sales of all items. These 3,000 stores had slightly over 18,000 paid employees and an annual payroll of $62 million. Between 1958 and 1967, bookstores that were large enough to operate the year around, and meet a payroll, were increasing at the rate of more than 141 stores per year.

ANALYZING BOOKSTORE DATA

There are six principal retail outlets for the sale of U.S. books: book, department, and stationery stores, news dealers or newsstands, mail order houses, and direct selling (house-to-house) organizations. The 1963 and 1967 Census of Business publications analyze merchandise line sales through these retail outlets by broad product categories. The task of obtaining detailed statistics on the more than 1.2 million retail establishments in the United States is enormous, and this results in the Census selection of merchandise lines by individual store *department* rather than on an individual *product* basis. Thus, there is no pure category called "books," but rather a broader category termed "books and periodicals." Of the five retail outlets mentioned above, only bookstores and stationery stores provide data on the category "books and periodicals." Department store sales of books are reported on the merchandise line "books, stationery and photographic equipment" while news dealers or newsstands, mail order houses, and direct selling organizations report book sales under the line "all other merchandise."

Specifically excluded from this analysis of U.S. bookstores are the many college bookstores located throughout the United States. Because these organizations generally are nonprofit, nontaxpaying firms closely associated with their respective educational institutions, data on U.S. college bookstores are not included in the retail trade statistics published by the U.S. Commerce Department's Bureau of the Census.

LARGE BOOKSTORES INCREASE MARKET SHARE

For the purpose of this analysis, U.S. bookstores are categorized as either small-, medium-, or large-size. Small bookstores are establishments with annual sales under $50,000; medium-size bookstores are those with annual sales between $50,000 and $500,000; and large bookstores are credited with annual sales of $500,000 or more.

Table 1 provides statistics on U.S. bookstores according to annual sales of the store for the years 1958, 1963, and 1967. The 12 sales categories listed in this table include only stores in operation throughout the entire year.

The large retail bookstores are clearly making their presence felt in the retail marketplace. In the period 1958–1967, the number of bookstores with annual sales of $500,000 or more increased from 41 to 142. These 142 stores, constituting less than 5 percent of all bookstores, accounted for 40 percent of total book-

---

*Adapted from two articles appearing in the January 1971 and April 1971 issues of *Printing and Publishing* magazine: "Growth of U.S. Bookstores Spurs Publishers' Sales," pp. 8-11 (January issue); "The Growth of Regional Book Markets," pp. 4-7 (April issue).

**Book Publishing Specialist, U.S. Department of Commerce.

TABLE 1 U.S. BOOKSTORES, GENERAL STATISTICS BY SALES SIZE: 1958, 1963, 1967
(Data for 1958 do not include Alaska and Hawaii)

Sales size of bookstore	1967 Number of estab- lishments	1967 Annual sales ($1,000)	1967 Payroll, entire year ($1,000)	1967 Number of paid employees	1963 Number of estab- lishments	1963 Annual sales ($1,000)	1963 Payroll, entire year ($1,000)	1963 Number of paid employees	1958 Number of estab- lishments	1958 Annual sales ($1,000)	1958 Payroll, entire year ($1,000)	1958 Number of paid employees
All establishments, Total[1]	2,960	$427,590	$61,706	18,010	3,154	$279,484	$36,252	12,439	2,885	$196,283	$24,367	10,168
Establishments operated entire year, total	2,886	$417,065	$60,124	17,572	2,845	$266,906	$34,792	11,667	2,733	$187,979	$23,424	9,636
With annual sales of:												
$5 million or more	2	(d)	(d)	(d)	...	...	...	...	...	...	...	...
$2 million to $4,999 million	17	(d)	(d)	(d)	7	(d)	(d)	(d)	2	(d)	(d)	(d)
$1 million to $1,999 million	32	$46,547	$7,409	1,816	22	(d)	(d)	(d)	12	(d)	(d)	(d)
$500,000 to $999,000	91	61,294	8,378	2,228	46	$30,084	$3,996	1,075	27	$18,472	$2,626	935
$300,000 to $499,000	142	54,355	7,515	1,943	79	30,095	4,224	1,242	58	21,943	2,993	1,100
$100,000 to $299,000	649	110,339	14,877	4,557	520	84,922	11,650	3,867	363	59,349	8,139	3,247
$50,000 to $99,000	739	51,384	6,727	2,240	547	38,530	4,377	1,638	443	31,215	3,510	1,684
$30,000 to $49,000	412	16,149	2,190	776	454	17,548	1,786	831	395	15,365	1,265	729
$20,000 to $29,000	512	12,881	2,152	764	302	7,230	602	321	324	7,860	535	418
$10,000 to $19,000	181	2,649	577	198	400	5,617	362	239	501	7,285	286	228
$5,000 to $9,000	99	671	162	56	310	2,215	104	76	366	2,442	66	52
Less than $5,000	10	26	8	1	158	519	28	25	242	818	27	21
Establishments not operated entire year, total	(2)	$10,525	$1,582	438	(2)	$12,578	$1,460	772	(2)	$8,304	$943	532
in business at end of year	74	3,535	461	35	309	6,489	683	447	152	4,314	452	283

Note: (d)—Withheld to avoid disclosure.   ... Represents zero.
[1]Data provided only for establishments with payroll.
[2]Data on this line are for all part-year enterprises. Data for those part-year enterprises which were in business at the end of the Census year (which are the only part-year enterprises included in the count of establishments in Census tabulations) are shown on the following line.

Source: U. S. Department of Commerce, Bureau of the Census.

store sales, 40 percent of total employment, and 43 percent of total payroll. The nation's continued movement toward urbanization, coupled with increased demands for books, suggests this trend to larger retail bookstore establishments will continue.

While medium-size bookstores increased in number between 1958 and 1967, their proportion of total bookstore sales, employment, and payroll declined. There were 1,530 medium-size bookstores in 1967, up from 864 in 1958. However, 1967 sales volume of $216 million through these stores accounted for just 52 percent of total bookstore sales. In 1958 medium-size bookstore sales represented 60 percent of total bookstore volume. Exactly half of the 17,572 paid employees worked in the medium-size bookstores in 1967. In 1958 these stores employed 63 percent of all paid employees. Although these medium-size stores grew and prospered during 1958–1967, their economic influence on the total retail bookstore business appears to have lost ground to the larger stores.

The small bookstore, with annual sales volume of under $50,000, witnessed a sharp decline over the nine-year period 1958–1967. With over 1,800 establishments accounting for 18 percent of total bookstore sales in 1958, the small bookstores fell in both numbers and total sales volume by 1967. Two out of three U.S. bookstores had a sales volume of under $50,000 in 1958. A drop to 1,200 stores in 1967 provided the small units with just 42 percent of the total number of all bookstores in that year. Small bookstores total sales volume reached $34 million in 1958 but fell to $32 million in 1967, representing a decline in total shares from 18 percent to 8 percent. These data indicate that the small bookstore, which continues to be a permanent fixture of the retail scene, faces strong competition from medium- and large-size bookstores.

VARIATIONS IN STATES BOOK TRADE

The considerable expansion of retail bookstores, both in number of stores and their retail sales, has not been shared equally by all geographic sections of the United States. Tables 2 and 3 show retail bookstore growth by regions, divisions, and states, and by selected Standard Metropolitan Statistical Areas (SMSAs).

Total U.S. bookstore sales moved to $428 million in 1967 from $179 million in 1958, a growth of 139 percent. This may also be expressed as averaging 10.1 percent growth per year and used as one measure in examining variations in bookstore activity in the several states.

Most of the 50 states and the District of Columbia saw appreciable gains in both the number of bookstores and bookstore sales over the period 1958–1967. The more populous states made the largest additions to their total of retail bookstore establishments, as shown in the following table:

State	Number of bookstores added, 1958–1967
California	214
New York	107
Texas	69
Florida	67
Massachusetts	64
Pennsylvania	55
Illinois	53
Virginia	47
Michigan	40

These gains, however, were not always accompanied by strong increases in sales or in total bookstore employment. For example, bookstores in Massachusetts virtually doubled in number between 1958 and 1967, yet this nine-year period saw a decline in the state's total paid bookstore employees to 668 in 1967 from 694 in 1958. Of the nine states listed, only California, Florida, and Texas showed bookstore sales increases greater than the 139 percent U.S. average established in the 1958–1967 span.

In general, bookstores located in either the South or West of the United States experienced larger percentage gains in total sales than the increases noted by bookstores in either the northeastern

TABLE 2 SELECTED DATA ON U.S. BOOKSTORES, BY REGIONS, DIVISIONS, AND STATES: 1958–1967

Regions, division and States	1967[1] Number of estab-lishments	1967[1] Sales ($1,000)	1967[1] Annual payroll ($1,000)	1967[1] Paid employees	1963[1] Number of estab-lishments	1963[1] Sales ($1,000)	1963[1] Annual payroll ($1,000)	1963[1] Paid employees	1958[1],[2] Number of estab-lishments	1958[1],[2] Sales ($1,000)	1958[1],[2] Annual payroll ($1,000)	1958[1],[2] Paid employees
U.S., total	2,960	$427,590	$61,706	18,010	2,164	$264,586	$36,252	12,439	1,689	$179,175	$24,454	10,205
The Northeastern States	832	124,860	18,389	4,866	672	84,429	11,913	3,805	526	57,853	8,362	3,267
New England	240	32,076	4,616	1,265	185	21,970	3,229	1,133	126	16,628	2,394	1,065
Maine	16	773	95	35	12	820	89	39	9	836	96	70
New Hampshire	17	2,230	319	104	11	1,333	172	62	7	691	95	42
Vermont	7	513	84	29	8	531	94	41	5	220	20	14
Massachusetts	129	16,345	2,477	668	96	12,086	1,966	656	65	10,233	1,605	694
Rhode Island	13	883	138	40	6	186	43	15	3	128	26	12
Connecticut	58	11,332	1,503	389	52	7,014	865	320	37	4,520	552	233
Middle Atlantic	592	92,784	13,773	3,601	487	62,459	8,684	2,672	400	41,225	5,968	2,202
New York	376	61,192	9,300	2,334	333	44,228	6,245	1,761	269	30,642	4,698	1,610
New Jersey	70	14,317	2,002	543	53	7,601	921	362	40	2,689	294	141
Pennsylvania	146	17,275	2,471	724	101	10,630	1,518	549	91	7,894	976	451
The North Central States	697	105,160	14,075	4,436	515	(D)	(D)	(D)	452	(D)	(D)	(D)
East North Central	482	80,805	10,895	3,377	370	51,344	6,968	2,358	326	39,793	5,567	2,282
Ohio	99	16,690	2,373	770	77	8,732	1,215	415	74	8,806	1,334	523
Indiana	54	7,534	954	295	41	4,959	576	230	41	4,240	488	213
Illinois	172	30,560	4,004	1,365	138	21,018	3,021	991	119	15,319	2,171	954
Michigan	105	16,523	2,252	590	77	10,420	1,356	433	65	8,188	1,065	398
Wisconsin	52	9,498	1,312	357	37	6,215	800	289	27	3,240	509	194
West North Central	215	24,335	3,180	1,059	145	(D)	(D)	(D)	126	(D)	(D)	(D)
Minnesota	42	4,928	618	189	24	3,242	372	139	18	2,105	228	79
Iowa	33	6,050	883	242	24	3,943	517	168	18	2,993	422	142
Missouri	69	7,240	957	293	48	4,408	505	230	48	3,506	404	205
North Dakota	4	190	28	11	2	(D)	(D)	(D)	1	(D)	(D)	(D)
South Dakota	6	168	23	7	7	455	45	41	4	330	30	30
Nebraska	26	1,993	223	118	14	968	94	44	12	589	83	45
Kansas	35	3,786	448	199	26	2,959	468	167	25	1,927	227	114

LIBRARY AND BOOK TRADE STATISTICS / 167

The South	790	(D)	(D)	(D)	519	(D)	(D)	(D)	376	32,707	4,152	1,898
South Atlantic	399	(D)	(D)	(D)	261	(D)	(D)	(D)	178	16,320	2,337	970
Delaware	7	760	116	35	3	3,143	433	163	3	404	74	25
Maryland	41	5,265	782	195	37	3,957	565	175	32	1,839	189	120
District of Columbia	39	6,295	1,002	239	31	3,177	379	154	26	3,452	523	159
Virginia	70	(D)	(D)	(D)	40	664	73	35	23	2,042	268	118
West Virginia	15	1,281	186	54	11	664	73	35	12	1,750	311	119
North Carolina	50	4,643	622	238	31	2,129	300	124	27	2,388	328	158
South Carolina	21	1,607	206	73	9	2,355	511	156	5	367	31	15
Georgia	56	6,746	923	234	27	2,402	366	121	17	1,841	344	132
Florida	100	7,931	1,003	327	64	4,671	516	212	33	2,237	269	124
East South Central	148	20,132	4,776	1,326	90	12,748	1,763	672	64	5,730	636	281
Kentucky	32	4,546	637	229	12	1,628	268	89	13	1,320	158	65
Tennessee	57	9,432	3,369	867	33	6,590	943	391	20	1,222	135	77
Alabama	42	5,343	635	183	35	3,971	500	160	24	2,194	297	117
Mississippi	17	811	135	47	10	559	52	32	7	274	46	22
West South Central	243	25,231	3,338	1,096	168	16,288	1,975	766	134	10,657	1,179	647
Arkansas	20	1,103	151	61	11	679	75	32	13	730	77	48
Louisiana	38	3,284	407	160	24	2,195	211	81	18	1,291	102	64
Oklahoma	42	3,274	414	149	24	1,865	184	83	29	1,903	194	139
Texas	143	17,570	2,366	726	109	11,549	1,505	570	74	6,733	806	396
The West	641	(D)	(D)	(D)	458	(D)	(D)	(D)	335	(D)	(D)	(D)
Mountain	137	(D)	(D)	(D)	105	(D)	(D)	(D)	76	(D)	(D)	(D)
Montana	10	1,411	193	46	8	915	100	35	5	555	65	25
Idaho	9	866	106	39	7	432	40	16	10	570	78	29
Wyoming	4	203	14	8	5	171	13	9	4	165	23	11
Colorado	45	4,508	531	177	36	2,991	363	143	26	2,230	261	125
New Mexico	14	1,037	121	39	14	584	65	29	13	460	62	36
Arizona	35	2,673	412	118	20	(D)	(D)	(D)	9	970	119	44
Utah	17	5,026	703	181	11	1,078	119	48	8	852	84	25
Nevada	3	(D)	(D)	(D)	4	(D)	(D)	(D)	1	(D)	(D)	(D)
Pacific	504	94,540	13,274	3,982	353	52,204	7,394	2,516	259	31,411	4,278	1,837
Washington	41	10,703	1,518	494	29	7,066	989	319	21	4,223	625	259
Oregon	26	7,322	832	300	17	2,904	338	145	18	2,521	266	147
California	420	74,636	10,646	3,104	293	41,112	5,894	1,987	206	23,891	3,300	1,394
Alaska	3	211	15	4	3	195	19	3	3	197	8	4
Hawaii	14	1,668	263	80	11	927	154	62	11	579	79	33

(D).–Withheld to avoid disclosure.
[1] Data provided only for bookstores with payroll.
[2] Includes Alaska and Hawaii.

Source: U.S. Department of Commerce, Bureau of the Census.

TABLE 3 RANKING OF 46 PRINCIPAL BOOK MARKETS, BY RETAIL BOOKSTORE VOLUME: 1958–1967

Standard Metropolitan Statistical Area (SMSA)	1967[1] Number of establishments	1967[1] Sales ($1,000)	1963[1] Number of establishments	1963[1] Sales ($1,000)	1958[1,2] Number of establishments	1958[1,2] Sales ($1,000)
U.S., total	2,960	$427,590	2,164	$264,586	1,689	$179,175
New York, N.Y.	294	49,522	271	35,582	216	24,997
Los Angeles-Long Beach, Calif.	160	29,511	119	18,294	97	11,171
Chicago, Ill.	109	23,222	95	16,985	85	12,182
San Francisco-Oakland, Calif.	83	16,920	61	8,867	52	7,518
Boston, Mass.	71	10,989	62	9,412	48	7,406
Washington, D.C.-Md.-Va.	60	10,647	44	6,217	36	4,522
Philadelphia, Pa.-N.J.	78	8,954	52	6,136	46	4,033
San Jose, Calif.	29	8,207	20	5,223	14	1,739
Seattle-Everett, Wash.	16	6,720	15	5,278	5	2,781
Detroit, Mich.	45	4,811	30	2,064	24	1,996
Salt Lake City, Utah	10	4,594	5	808	5	(D)
San Diego, Calif.	31	4,341	15	1,827	11	1,117
Sacramento, Calif.	14	4,304	11	849	2	(D)
Anaheim-Santa Ana-Garden Grove, Calif.	25	3,598	15	1,412	n.a.	n.a.
Atlanta, Ga.	20	3,378	13	1,472	8	1,500
Newark, N.J.	21	3,338	20	1,809	11	695
Minneapolis-St. Paul, Minn.	22	3,273	14	2,306	9	1,579
Cleveland, Ohio	19	3,234	18	1,271	14	3,170
Dallas, Tex.	15	3,145	14	1,792	10	1,362
Denver, Colo.	27	2,892	21	1,828	16	1,537
Houston, Tex.	26	2,714	18	1,662	10	877
Portland, Ore.-Wash.	13	2,580	10	1,233	9	732
Columbus, Ohio	9	2,552	9	1,063	8	904
St. Louis, Mo.	28	2,525	11	928	8	405
Baltimore, Md.	28	2,212	27	1,569	22	1,374
Milwaukee, Wis.	20	1,998	12	1,239	8	476
Knoxville, Tenn.	9	1,935	5	(D)	2	(D)

Pittsburgh, Pa.	18	1,833	12	1,340	6	502
San Bernardino-Riverside-Ontario, Calif.	14	1,685	8	659	3	245
Miami, Fla.	22	1,631	14	908	4	312
Albany-Schenectady-Troy, N.Y.	15	1,607	8	664	7	445
Syracuse, N.Y.	11	1,589	5	1,171	5	685
Patterson-Clifton-Passaic, N.J.	14	1,519	7	787	5	195
New Orleans, La.	11	1,515	6	657	7	580
Phoenix, Ariz.	20	1,453	14	1,038	4	380
Buffalo, N.Y.	9	1,432	17	2,025	6	430
Nashville, Tenn.	15	1,303	10	1,118	5	509
Cincinnati, Ohio-Ky.-Ind.	10	1,303	6	986	8	764
Akron, Ohio	6	1,268	5	650	2	(D)
Dayton, Ohio	10	1,249	5	558	2	(D)
Louisville, Ky.	11	1,242	3	(D)	4	487
Memphis, Tenn.-Ark.	14	1,217	3	(D)	4	210
Toledo, Ohio-Mich.	8	1,165	3	296	3	(D)
Hartford, Conn.	8	1,129	7	529	7	714
Springfield-Chicopee-Holyoke, Mass.-Conn.	9	1,125	5	(D)	2	(D)
Kansas City, Mo.-Kans.	14	1,078	16	1,149	14	1,183

n.a.—Not available.
(D).—Withheld to avoid disclosure.
[1] Data provided only for bookstores with payroll.
[2] Includes Alaska and Hawaii.

Source: U.S. Department of Commerce, Bureau of the Census.

states or the north central states. The extensive data in Table 2 portray the economic condition of U.S. bookstores on a state-by-state basis.

Perhaps most striking is the impact California has on the U.S. bookstore business. In 1967, bookstores in California represented 17.5 percent of total U.S. bookstore sales, 17.2 percent of total employment, and 14.2 percent of total number of establishments. This state's rate of bookstore business growth between 1958 and 1967 was particularly impressive when contrasted with the retail book business in the state of New York. These two states together accounted for just under one-third of total U.S. retail bookstore sales in the 1958–1967 span. However, New York's percentage of the total U.S. market slipped to 14.3 percent in 1967 from 17.1 percent in 1958. During this period, California's share of retail bookstore sales jumped to 17.5 percent in 1967 from 13.3 percent in 1958. California's total bookstore sales alone were greater than sales in the combined state groupings of six of the nine U.S. geographic regions.

Despite overall industry prosperity, Table 2 reveals a number of states that failed to keep pace with U.S. bookstore growth. Idaho, Maine, Massachusetts, North Dakota, South Dakota, West Virginia, and Wyoming all experienced declines in at least one of the categories of sales, number of establishments, employment, or payroll in the nine-year 1958–1967 period.

RANKING OF SMSAs NOTES BOOKSTORE GROWTH

Table 3 contains a ranking of 46 SMSAs according to their retail bookstore volume. Data are provided for the Census years 1958, 1963, and 1967.

Comparisons of data among individual SMSAs, and for selected years of a given SMSA, must be tempered by the knowledge that the SMSA concept does not imply a static geographic area. As the nation's economy expands, and concentrated urban activity spreads to coextensive areas, the boundaries of a given SMSA may expand over time to include additional towns and/or counties. For example, a comparison of bookstore statistics for Washington, D.C.–Maryland–Virginia SMSA over the period 1958–1967 must consider the effect of adding two Virginia counties to this SMSA in 1967.

Although the 46 SMSAs shown in Table 3 had total bookstore sales of over $1 million in 1967, certain SMSAs with sales in this range are missing from the list due to problems of disclosure of individual establishment data. An example is the New Haven, Connecticut SMSA.

The influence of California's bookstore activity, so noticeable in Table 2, also is apparent in the Table 3 ranking of SMSAs. Six of the top 15 SMSAs are located in this state. New York City continues to maintain its dominance as the nation's principal center of the retail book trade, with sales of $50 million distributed through approximately 300 bookstores. In terms of sales per individual bookstore, New York City averaged $168,400 per establishment — somewhat above the U.S. average of $144,456 per bookstore establishment.

Three west coast SMSAs experienced average bookstore sales per establishment in excess of $300,000 per year. These SMSAs were:

SMSA	Average sales per establishment
Salt Lake City, Utah	$459,400
Seattle-Everett, Wash.	420,000
Sacramento, Calif.	307,400

These high averages may reflect unusual local conditions, not the least of which could be the presence of substantial institutional sales.

The largest SMSAs account for much of the nation's total bookstore sales and hold a majority of the country's bookstores. The 46 SMSAs shown in Table 3 had aggregate sales of $247 million, or 58 percent of total U.S. sales in 1967. These same SMSAs had 1,521 retail bookstore establishments, numbering just over 51 percent of all U.S. bookstores. In 1967, the ten largest SMSAs contained

32 percent of all bookstores in the United States and represented 40 percent of total bookstore sales.

CONCLUSION

By all the economic factors of sales, employment, payroll, and number of establishments, the U.S. retail bookstore business is undergoing rapid expansion. Sales in the period 1958–1967 advanced at the rate of 10.1 percent per year, reaching $428 million by the end of 1967. This strong growth in sales has coincided with an increase in bookstore establishments that provides a wider selection of printed materials to more U.S. communities than ever before. While some areas have witnessed greater bookstore growth than others, the overall expansion in the post-World War II period is clearly a trend that should continue in the years ahead.

BOOK PUBLISHING SALES STATISTICS*

Book sales in 1970 totaled about $2,924,340,000, an increase of 5.8 percent, or $161 million over 1969 sales, according to the annual survey of book publishers' sales receipts estimated by the Association of American Publishers and released early in December 1971. The AAP report is given in the form of five tables: 1, dollar volume of publishers' sales by categories; 2, publishers' sales of textbooks and standardized tests; 3, sales of subscription reference books; 4, percentage trends and index figures showing net sales of books, 1964–1970, as indicated in the reports of cooperating publishers; and 5, percentage changes in book prices compared with those in the U.S. Government's Price Index.

In commenting on the price comparisons, the AAP notes that "general" book prices increased 5 percent over 1969 (measured in the average per copy return to publishers). College textbook prices, measured in the same terms, increased even less, 3.7 percent; and elementary and high school textbook prices actually dropped slightly.

The AAP notes also that the 5.8 percent overall sales volume increase reflects the slowdown in the national economy and the continuing cutbacks in education and library budgets, since for ten years the average increase had been 8 percent.

Adult hardcover trade book sales showed a dollar increase of $15 million, or 7.5 percent from the 1969 total. The sales of adult trade paperbacks rose by $6 million, or 14.6 percent.

The largest single dollar increase in the general book categories was in book club sales, which rose by $28 million (12.7 percent), followed by sales in the mass market ("wholesaled") paperbacks category, which rose $26 million (15 percent).

Sales of Bibles, hymnals, and prayer books, which had dropped to $47 million in 1969, bounced up to $56 million in 1970, a 19 percent rise. Sales of "other" religious books, however, dropped back from $61 million in 1969 to $57 million in 1970, the same as in 1967.

Sales of children's books rose by about $8 million, or 5.7 percent; university press books, $2 million, or 5.4 percent; scientific, technical and vocational books, $3 million, or 2.4 percent.

In the textbook and subscription reference book areas, the sales increases, 1969 to 1970, are shown as: elementary and secondary textbooks, $29 million, or 6 percent; college textbooks, $14 million, or 4 percent; standardized tests, $1.4 million, or 6 percent; subscription reference books, $7 million, or 1.1 percent.

The AAP's Table 4 provides, among other interesting indications, a series of

*Reprinted from *Publishers' Weekly*, December 20, 1971.

TABLE 1 DOLLAR VOLUME OF BOOK SALES, 1963, 1967, 1969, and 1970
Receipts of Publishers (In thousands of dollars; add three zeroes)

Categories of Books	1963[1]	1967[1]	1969	1970
Adult Trade				
Hardbound	$ 108,515	$ 156,000	$ 199,000	$ 214,000
Paperbound	17,029	32,000	41,000	47,000
Subtotal	125,544	188,000	240,000	261,000
Juvenile Books				
Under $1 retail	31,257	35,000	36,000	38,000
$1 and over retail	72,678	130,000	104,000	110,000
Subtotal	103,935	165,000	140,000	148,000
Bibles, Testaments, Hymnals,				
and Prayer Books	34,622	51,000	47,000	56,000
Other religious	46,498	57,000	61,000	57,000
Subtotal	81,120	108,000	108,000	113,000
Professional Books				
Law	57,384	74,000	91,000	90,000
Medicine	24,148	38,000	50,000	57,000
Business Books	14,800	20,000	23,000	25,000
Technical, Scientific, and				
Vocational	69,218	105,000	122,000	125,000
Subtotal	165,550	237,000	286,000	297,000
Book Clubs	143,418	180,000	220,000	248,000
Wholesaled (mass-market)				
paperbound	87,380	130,000	173,000	199,000
University Press	18,274	31,000	37,000	39,000
Subtotal: General Books	725,221	1,039,000	1,204,000	1,305,000
Elementary and Secondary				
Textbooks	304,700	421,110	454,680	483,990
College Textbooks	160,200	286,670	346,370	360,450
Standardized Tests	12,660	21,570	21,690	23,100
Subtotal: Educational Books	477,560	729,350	822,740	867,540
Subscription Reference Books	380,900	500,750	605,450	612,800
Other books	102,056	110,000	131,000	139,000
Total	$1,685,737	$2,379,100	$2,763,190	$2,924,340

[1]The 1963 and 1967 figures are from the U.S. Census of Manufactures, except for the following categories for which data collected for the industry association are more complete for one year or both: elementary and secondary textbooks, college textbooks, subscription reference books, standardized tests, adult trade books, business books, university press books, book club books, and other books. The figures for 1969 and 1970 are based entirely on industry surveys for elementary and secondary textbooks, college textbooks, standardized tests, and subscription reference books. For the remaining categories in 1969 and 1970 the data are projections based on industry survey information from the base census year of 1967.

TABLE 2 PUBLISHERS' TOTAL TEXTBOOK AND STANDARDIZED TEST SALES

YEAR	HOMES & OFFICES $	%	SCHOOLS & LIBRARIES $	%	YEAR BOOKS $	%	MAIL ORDER OTHER $	%	TOTAL $	%	TOTAL DOMESTIC $	%	FOREIGN $	TOTAL SALES $
1960	260,700	87.0	10,300	3.4			30,550	9.4	28,700	9.6	299,700	100	28,950	328,650
1961	240,000	82.0	10,400	3.6	23,350	7.2	24,400	7.9	42,100	14.4	292,500	100	41,450	333,950
1962	258,500	79.6	12,250	3.8	27,400	8.9	28,350	8.5	53,900	16.6	324,650	100	53,400	378,050
1963	244,050	79.0	12,850	4.2	29,500	8.8	38,500	10.6	51,800	16.8	308,700	100	72,200	380,900
1964	256,500	76.8	19,850	5.9	32,150	8.8	38,650	10.3	57,850	17.3	334,200	100	79,750	413,950
1965	279,150	76.6	14,700	4.0	36,050	9.7	39,700	10.7	70,650	19.4	364,500	100	83,650	448,150
1966	273,550	73.2	25,500	6.8	38,200	10.3	47,400	11.7	74,700	20.0	373,750	100	99,800	473,550
1967	266,200	71.8	26,450	7.2	42,050	10.3	54,050	12.7	77,900	21.0	370,550	100	130,200	500,750
1968	297,150	73.0	20,250	5.0	48,700	11.5	62,300	15.7	89,450	22.0	406,850	100	150,450	557,300
1969	299,700	70.7	21,650	5.1	50,350	12.7			102,750	24.2	424,100	100	181,350	605,450
1970	264,750	66.7	19,650	4.9					112,650	28.4	397,050	100	215,750	612,800

TABLE 3 NET RETAIL SALES OF SUBSCRIPTION REFERENCE BOOKS
(By thousands of dollars and percent of domestic sales)

	THOUSANDS OF DOLLARS							PERCENT OF TOTAL TEXTBOOK SALES					INDEX NUMBERS 1960-1963 = 100			
	TEXTBOOKS				Stand.	Total Texts							Elhi	College	Stand. Tests
Year	Elementary	High School	Elhi	College	Total	Tests	& Tests	Elem	H S	Elhi	Coll	Total	Indus	Indus	Indus	Indus
1960	148,400	82,500	230,900	106,900	337,800	11,600	349,400	44.0	24.4	68.4	31.6	100	87	81	97
1961	158,050	93,800	251,800	121,650	373,450	11,490	384,940	42.3	25.1	67.4	32.6	100	95	92	96
1962	165,950	105,350	271,300	138,400	409,700	12,080	421,780	40.5	25.7	66.2	33.8	100	103	105	101
1963	183,950	120,750	304,700	160,200	464,900	12,660	477,560	39.6	26.0	65.6	34.4	100	115	122	106
1964	201,100	124,950	326,050	188,800	514,850	13,960	528,810	39.0	24.3	63.3	36.7	100	123	143	117
1965	225,950	138,050	364,000	223,300	587,300	16,420	603,720	38.5	23.5	62.0	38.0	100	138	169	137
1966	279,900	161,300	441,200	270,300	711,500	21,870	733,370	39.3	22.7	62.0	38.0	100	167	205	183
1967	265,610	155,500	421,110	286,670	707,780	21,570	729,350	37.5	22.0	59.5	40.5	100	159	218	180
1968	281,820	163,500	445,320	323,510	768,830	21,250	790,080	36.7	21.2	57.9	42.1	100	168	245	178
1969	283,420	171,260	454,680	346,370	801,050	21,690	822,740	35.4	21.4	56.8	43.2	100	172	263	181
1970	304,320	179,670	483,990	360,450	844,440	23,100	867,540	36.0	21.3	57.3	42.7	100	183	274	193

TABLE 4 TRENDS IN NET SALES OF BOOKS 1964–1970

Book Classification	Net Sales — Annual Indexes[1]							% Change[2] Dollar Volume	Copies Annual Indexes[3]		% Change[2] Copies	% of Total Net Sales		% of Total Copies		Average $ Per Book	
	1964	1965	1966	1967	1968	1969	1970		1969	1970		1969	1970	1969	1970	1969	1970
ADULT TRADE BOOKS																	
Hardbound	109.0	116.4	137.1	146.1	167.9	186.5	200.9	+7.7	144.9	149.2	+3.0	19.0	18.6	7.4	7.2	2.97	3.11
Paperbound[4]	118.9	132.0	154.6	198.1	238.5	260.0	303.7	+16.8	194.0	211.7	+9.1	4.1	4.3	5.3	5.5	0.89	0.95
Total Adult Trade Books	110.4	118.5	139.5	153.4	177.6	196.6	214.9	+9.3	162.4	171.4	+5.5	23.1	22.9	12.7	12.7	2.10	2.18
JUVENILE BOOKS																	
Under $1 retail	109.5	126.7	116.7	119.6	122.6	123.0	130.7	+6.3	165.4	172.7	+4.4	2.0	2.0	13.0	12.9	0.18	0.18
$1 & over retail	102.4	113.0	164.9	180.8	161.3	144.8	152.7	+5.5	106.8	113.0	+5.8	11.7	11.1	8.1	8.1	1.67	1.66
Total Juvenile Books	104.5	117.0	150.7	162.7	149.8	138.4	146.1	+5.6	148.4	155.8	+5.0	13.7	13.1	21.1	21.0	0.75	0.75
RELIGIOUS BOOKS																	
Bibles, testaments, hymnals & prayer books	93.1	99.1	107.5	97.8	104.8	88.9	107.0	+20.3	66.0	76.8	+16.4	1.8	1.9	0.7	0.7	3.01	3.11
Other religious	110.9	124.6	144.9	147.2	142.3	156.9	146.3	−6.8	126.7	108.8	−14.1	1.7	1.5	1.5	1.2	1.35	1.46
Total Religious Books	100.4	109.6	122.9	118.1	120.8	115.9	123.8	+6.9	102.9	98.2	−4.6	3.5	3.4	2.2	1.9	1.86	2.09
PROFESSIONAL BOOKS																	
Law books			Insufficiently Reported					−8.7			+10.1	0.3	0.2	—	—	8.35	6.93
Medical books	116.1	125.1	148.5	156.0	175.5	204.8	234.9	+14.7	194.7	210.9	+8.3	3.1	3.2	0.6	0.6	6.10	6.46
Business books	118.2	133.5	165.5	198.8	216.3	227.5	248.2	+9.1	152.3	148.9	−2.2	2.2	2.2	0.3	0.3	8.82	9.84
Technical & scientific books	102.6	106.7	126.1	141.3	151.8	164.7	167.9	+1.9	144.1	130.3	−9.6	2.9	2.7	0.3	0.3	10.29	11.60
Total Professional Books	109.0	116.6	139.4	156.3	171.0	189.6	205.0	+8.1	161.5	163.3	+1.1	8.5	8.3	1.2	1.2	7.92	8.48
OTHER BOOKS																	
Book club books[5]	112.4	129.8	152.3	170.5	193.7	208.6	235.3	+12.8	155.9	176.9	+13.5	23.0	23.5	11.1	12.0	3.09	3.11
Wholesaled paperbound	112.7	121.0	135.8	153.7	177.7	204.9	235.4	+14.9	140.7	147.5	+4.8	20.2	21.1	48.1	47.7	0.485	0.532
University press hardbound				170.4	184.5	195.4	208.1	+6.5	149.4	153.4	+2.7	0.5	0.4	0.4	0.3	4.22	4.56
University press paperbound				176.2	196.6	234.0	257.2	+9.9	154.0	151.7	−1.5	3.0	2.9	0.8	0.8	1.50	1.60
Total university press books	110.0	128.0	151.1	171.2	186.3	201.0	215.1	+7.0	151.4	151.1	−0.2	3.5	3.3	1.2	1.1	3.41	3.65
Other books	118.8	114.0	122.7	161.2	193.3	202.2	215.4	+6.5	213.7	224.6	+5.1	4.5	4.4	2.4	2.4	1.84	2.19
Total Other Books	112.7	125.3	144.1	163.6	186.8	206.6	235.8	+14.1	145.2	153.4	+5.7	51.2	52.3	62.8	63.2	0.97	1.04
TOTAL SALES OF THIS SURVEY	109.5	120.4	142.7	157.8	171.8	183.3	202.2	+10.3	146.4	154.6	+5.6	100.0	100.0	100.0	100.0	1.18	1.24
NUMBER OF PUBLISHERS REPORTING	184	145	152	182	159	157	138										
FOREIGN SALES[6] AS % OF TOTAL SALES IN EACH CLASSIFICATION	5.3%	5.4%	5.7%	6.1%	6.4%	7.2%	7.0%										
Book club books	11.8	11.7	12.3	12.1	11.9	12.1	11.0	−2.8									
Wholesaled paperbound books	13.0	13.0	13.4	13.1	12.5	12.6	13.7	−9.1									
University press books	7.6	7.3	7.4	7.4	8.1	4.0	4.7	+8.7									
All other books	8.1	7.8	8.0	8.1	8.6	7.3	7.3	+17.5									
Total Sales of This Survey								0.0									

[1]1963 Net Sales = 100.0.
[2]Percent Change from 1969 to 1970.
[3]1963 Copies = 100.0.
[4]Adult Paperbound does not include University Press Paperbound Books.
[5]Book Clubs Net Sales are at "Retail" prices. Book Club Number of Copies includes both those sold and distributed. Book Club Average $ per Book covers Books Sold only.
[6]Foreign Sales include U.S. Territories.

TABLE 5 PERCENTAGE CHANGES IN CONSUMER PRICE INDEX (CPI) AND BOOK PRICES — 1968–1970

(Percentage increases or decreases as compared with previous year)

	1968	1969	1970
CPI ALL ITEMS	+4.2%	+5.4%	+5.7%
CPI ALL COMMODITIES	+3.7%	+4.5%	+4.5%
CPI ALL COMMODITIES, LESS FOOD	+3.7%	+4.2%	+3.9%
CPI FOOD	+3.6%	+5.1%	+5.5%
CPI ALL SERVICES	+5.2%	+6.9%	+7.8%
ELEMENTARY TEXTBOOKS	+0.5%	+1.5%	−1.0%
HIGH SCHOOL TEXTBOOKS	+1.3%	+2.1%	−0.6%
COLLEGE TEXTBOOKS	+3.9%	+0.8%	+3.7%
GENERAL BOOKS	+3.0%	+3.0%	+5.0%

figures showing the percentage changes in numbers of copies sold. (The figures in Table 4, it should be kept in mind, are not derived from those in Table 1, but show the trends that are suggested by a strong sampling of all publishers — a sampling made up of those that coopererated in providing figures for the Table 4 report). Changes in sales of numbers of copies suggest that the biggest *percentage* increases were in Bibles, etc. (16.4 percent), book club books (13.5 percent), and adult trade paperbacks (9.1 percent). In several other categories, however, copies sold showed a decline — notably in "other" religious books (14.1 percent) and technical and scientific books (9.6 percent).

Table 4 also shows, for nontext volumes, average dollars received — the figures used to indicate average prices. Here, a little computation indicates the following percentage increases in average prices in certain categories, 1969 to 1970: adult trade hardcover, 4.7 percent; adult trade paperbacks, 6.8 percent; Bibles, etc., 3.3 percent; other religious books, 8.1 percent; mass market paperbacks, 9.6 percent; university press books, 7 percent; scientific and technical books, 12.7 percent; law books, down 17 percent. These average figures should be read only in the light of the preceding columns in the same table, showing the percentage of total sales which each category represents.

Of interest in view of some complaints about the pricing of children's books is the fact that price averages in the two juvenile categories remain virtually unchanged.

The information is derived from annual statistical surveys made for the AAP by two independent statistical agents, Stanley B. Hunt Associates and Ernst & Ernst.

AMERICAN BOOK TITLE OUTPUT — 1971

The data for the American Book Title Output tables are generated from the listing of books in the Weekly Record section of *Publishers' Weekly* (see Weekly Record heading for details). The following tables are compiled from *Publishers' Weekly*, February 7, 1972. For complete data on American book production for the years 1880–1969, see the article, "American Book Title Output — A Ninety-Year Overview," by Dorothy B. Hokkanen, pp. 65-69, 1971 *Bowker Annual*.

TABLE 1 TITLE OUTPUT BY DEWEY CLASSIFICATION

Classification with Dewey Decimal Numbers	1970 New Books	1970 New Editions	1970 Totals	1971 New Books	1971 New Editions	1971 Totals
Agriculture [630-639; 712-719]	200	65	265	241	83	324
Art [700-711; 720-779]	852	317	1,169	932	314	1,246
Biography [920-929]	735	801	1,536[1]	853	944	1,797[1]
Business [650-659]	658	139	797	550	150	700
Education [370-379]	842	336	1,178	1,020	230	1,250
Fiction	1,998	1,139	3,137	2,066	1,364	3,430
General Works [000-099]	568	278	846	715	297	1,012
History [900-909; 930-999]	1,010	985	1,995	949	1,029	1,978
Home Economics [640-649]	235	86	321	381	96	477
Juveniles	2,472	168	2,640	1,991	232	2,223
Language [400-499]	339	133	472	400	136	536
Law [340-349]	355	249	604	415	246	661
Literature [800-810; 813-820; 823-899]	1,349	1,736	3,085	1,383	1,603	2,986
Medicine [610-619]	1,144	332	1,476	1,252	403	1,655
Music [780-789]	217	187	404	214	188	402
Philosophy, Psychology [100-199]	843	437	1,280	947	407	1,354
Poetry, Drama [811; 812; 821; 822]	973	501	1,474	932	562	1,494
Religion [200-299]	1,315	473	1,788	1,140	427	1,567
Science [500-599]	1,955	403	2,358	2,225	472	2,697
Sociology, Economics [300-339; 350-369; 380-399]	3,867	2,045	5,912	4,268	1,827	6,095
Sports, Recreation [790-799]	583	216	799	645	245	890
Technology [600-609; 620-629; 660-699]	930	211	1,141	1,057	252	1,309
Travel [910-919]	848	546	1,394	950	659	1,609
TOTALS	24,288	11,783	36,071	25,526	12,166	37,692

[1] This figure includes biographies placed in other classes by the Library of Congress.

TABLE 2 TITLE OUTPUT BY CATEGORY

	1970			1971		
Category	New Books	New Editions	Totals	New Books	New Editions	Totals
	\multicolumn{6}{c}{1. Both Paperback and Hardbound Titles}					
Mysteries	300	289	589	358	320	678
Westerns	116	93	209	110	119	229
Science Fiction	175	94	269	195	109	304
Cookbooks	173	58	231	284	63	347
	\multicolumn{6}{c}{2. Paperback Titles at All Price Levels}					
Fiction	660	1,065	1,725	780	1,283	2,063
Nonfiction	5,412	2,142	7,554	5,934	2,279	8,213
Totals	6,072	3,207	9,279	6,714	3,562	10,276
Included in the above totals are the following:						
General Fiction	404	604	1,008	493	758	1,251
Mysteries	87	278	365	105	303	408
Westerns	74	90	164	66	115	181
Science Fiction	95	93	188	116	107	223
Cookbooks	47	39	86	75	40	115
Religious Books	460	157	617	442	122	564
	\multicolumn{6}{c}{3. Mass Market Paperbacks}					
Fiction	600	1,011	1,611	729	1,241	1,970
Nonfiction	296	486	782	419	596	1,015
Totals	896	1,497	2,393	1,148	1,837	2,985
Included in the above totals are the following:						
General Fiction	346	560	906	449	727	1,176
Mysteries	86	274	360	102	302	404
Westerns	74	86	160	65	111	176
Science Fiction	94	91	185	113	101	214
Cookbooks	16	24	40	22	17	39
Religious Books	2	25	27	7	12	19
	\multicolumn{6}{c}{4. Paperbacks other than Mass Market}					
Fiction	60	54	114	51	42	93
Nonfiction	5,116	1,656	6,772	5,515	1,683	7,198
Totals	5,176	1,710	6,886	5,566	1,725	7,291
Included in the above totals are the following:						
General Fiction	58	44	102	44	31	75
Mysteries	1	4	5	3	1	4
Westerns	0	4	4	1	4	5
Science Fiction	1	2	3	3	6	9
Cookbooks	31	15	46	53	23	76
Religious Books	458	132	590	435	110	545

TABLE 3 HARDBOUND TEXTBOOKS

Level	1971 New Books	New Editions	Totals
Elementary	189	12	201
High School	239	36	275
College	712	191	903
TOTALS	1,140	239	1,379

TABLE 4 TRANSLATIONS INTO ENGLISH
(Including both paperback and hardbound books)

Language	1970 Totals	1971 Totals
French	305	280
German	278	295
Italian	35	16
Oriental	61	48
Russian	139	126
Scandinavian	55	40
Spanish	39	47
Other languages	320	274
TOTALS	1,232	1,126

TABLE 5 BOOK IMPORTS

Category	1970 New Books	New Editions	Totals	1971 New Books	New Editions	Totals
Agriculture	55	9	64	56	13	69
Art	287	40	327	260	20	280
Biography	131	26	157*	89	11	100*
Business	102	7	109	62	9	71
Education	130	5	135	85	9	94
Fiction	49	3	52	29	3	32
General Works	86	13	99	71	18	89
History	197	48	245	125	26	151
Home Economics	28	8	36	34	2	36
Juveniles	111	6	117*	93	11	104
Language	66	9	75	110	8	118
Law	55	10	65	62	9	71
Literature	215	35	250	183	40	223
Medicine	232	32	264	179	48	227
Music	42	11	53	17	9	26
Philosophy, Psychology	134	23	157	122	11	133
Poetry, Drama	135	30	165	124	21	145
Religion	112	13	125	85	12	97
Science	452	57	509	406	51	457
Sociology, Economics	789	92	881	728	66	794
Sports, Recreation	85	7	92	70	13	83
Technology	188	24	212	169	29	198
Travel	221	49	270	249	35	284
TOTALS	3,902	557	4,459	3,408	474	3,882

*This figure includes biographies placed in other classes by the Library of Congress.

BOOKS IN THE MAILS

by

Robert W. Frase*

The following table gives the statistical picture for book mailings for the years 1948–1970.

Fiscal year ending June 30	Packages sent at special 4th class rate	Pounds sent at special 4th class rate	Packages sent at library materials rate	Pounds sent at library materials rate
1948	43,180,836	188,088,571	1,059,942	5,746,751
1949	39,665,933	200,123,842	1,112,246	6,366,279
1950	38,592,643	182,105,838	1,059,619	5,568,052
1951	49,451,182	211,962,372	911,639	4,582,016
1952	60,173,880	260,872,556	1,065,151	5,799,953
1953	66,461,328	292,762,106	1,140,998	7,133,881
1954	74,498,518[1]	351,617,822[1]	5,143,521[2]	31,033,343[2]
1955	77,207,083	363,348,642	5,828,387	34,821,494
1956	83,358,132	369,899,099	7,040,569	40,407,444
1957	83,883,698	402,941,469	7,722,275	42,726,783
1958	84,910,064	400,366,302	8,337,519	45,586,019
1959	92,744,699[3]	413,953,325[3]	11,196,483[3]	59,697,171[3]
1960	94,116,468	447,621,702	10,250,257	51,750,805
1961	94,879,848	447,235,496	12,078,283	59,891,083
1962	141,062,872	572,997,912	12,360,391	62,596,950
1963	193,146,880	698,557,999	13,696,898	69,327,734
1964	191,266,841	707,906,555	15,452,665	74,340,751
1965	193,209,000	740,403,000	17,463,000	89,970,000
1966	202,784,000	744,690,000	16,104,000	80,762,000
1967	222,425,000	850,493,000	16,822,000	78,328,000
1968	243,464,000	1,039,355,000	21,832,000	101,240,000
1969	256,380,000	1,049,540,000	26,401,000	114,590,000
1970	274,574,000	1,063,810,000	25,275,000	104,842,000

*Vice-President and Economist, Association of American Publishers, Inc.

[1]After July 20, 1953, includes also 16 millimeter films except when sent to commercial theaters. (Public Law 141)

[2]After July 20, 1953, includes also "sixteen-millimeter films, filmstrips, projected transparencies and slides, microfilms, sound recordings, and catalogs of such materials when sent to or from (A) schools, colleges, universities, or public libraries, and (B) religious, educational, scientific, philanthropic, agricultural, labor, veterans', or fraternal organizations or associations, not organized for profit and none of the net income of which inures to the benefit of any private stockholder or individual." (Public Law 141)

[3]After July 31, 1958, the book rate is known as the special 4th class rate and the library book rate as the library materials rate and several other classes of materials were made eligible under both rates.

Source: *Cost Ascertainment Reports,* 1949–1968, U.S. Post Office Department; *Revenue and Cost Analysis,* Fiscal Year 1969, U.S. Post Office Department; *Revenue and Cost Analysis,* Fiscal Year 1970, U.S. Postal Service.

BOOK REVIEW MEDIA*

Publications	Adult 1970	Adult 1971	Juvenile 1970	Juvenile 1971	Young Adult 1970	Young Adult 1971	Total 1970	Total 1971
ALA Booklist	2,729	2,635	683	670	246	252	3,658	3,557
Book World	1,250	600	200	200			1,450	800
Bulletin of the Center for Children's Books[1]			755	775			755	775
Choice	6,751	6,130					6,751	6,130
Horn Book			405	397[2]	45	47	450	444
Kirkus Service	2,591		1,484		212		4,287	4,500[3]
Library Journal — School Library Journal	6,003	5,422	2,367	2,088	456	445	8,826	7,955
N.Y. Times Book Review[1]	2,000	2,000	500	500			2,500	2,500
Publishers' Weekly[4]	3,596	3,020	593	518			4,189	3,538
Saturday Review	827	687	234	223			1,061	910

*Total number of books reviewed for calendar year 1970 and 1971.
[1]Estimated figures for 1970 and 1971.
[2]90 of which are paperbacks, 24 of which are new editions.
[3]Estimated; total for 1971 not broken down into separate groups.
[4]*Publishers' Weekly* totals include paperbacks: of the 1971 totals, 578 were paperbacks; of the 1970 totals, 854 were paperbacks. The temporary drop in number of paperbacks reviewed for 1971 is due to reorganization in *Publishers' Weekly* paperback coverage; the drop does not reflect the number of paperbacks actually published.

BOOK PUBLISHING STOCK PRICES, 1971*

STOCKS	PRICE RANGE 1936–69		PRICE RANGE 1970		PRICE RANGE 1971		P-E Ratio	DIVIDENDS			Year Ending	$ Per Shr — EARNINGS — $ Per Shr (Years)					Last 12 Mos.	INTERIM EARNINGS OR REMARKS		
Name of Issue	High	Low	High	Low	High	Low		—$— So Far 1971	Total Ind. Rate	—$— Paid 1970		1967	1968	1969	1970	1971		Period	$–Per Share–$ 1970	1971
Addison-Wesley Pub. Co.	34¾	[e]3⅛	17¾	8½	18⅛	13	14	0.20	0.20	0.15	November[1]	[ac]0.41	[a]0.40	[a]0.57	[ab]0.89	....	1.01	9 Mo Aug	[ab]0.63	[a]0.75
Allyn & Bacon, Inc.	44½	[e]2¼	18½	7½	17	8	87	....	Nil	0.40	April	[f]0.96	0.86	0.59	0.48	0.13	0.13			
American Book-Stratford Press	27½	[e]3⅝	9¼	4⅜	8¼	2½	g	4% Stk	Stk	4% Stk	December[2]	[e]0.57	[e]0.31	[e]0.40	[b]0.003	....	[g]0.56	9 Mo Sep	0.12	[g]0.44
Bartell Media Corp.	23½	[e]⅛	14	3⅝	8	2⅞	73	....	Nil	....	December	0.19	[c]0.26	0.19	[c]0.05	....	0.06	9 Mo Sep	[c]0.16	[b]0.17
Book-of-the-Month Club	37½	[e]4½	25	13⅝	28¼	19½	11	1.28	1.28	1.28	June[3]	[bi]1.59	[bi]2.15	1.45	1.90	2.22	2.24	3 Mo Sep	0.07	0.09
Bro-Dart Industries	[e]40	[e]7¼	19⅝	5	8⅝	2½	g	....	Nil	....	June[4]	[e]0.53	[e]0.73	0.61	0.24	[g]0.43	[g]0.46	3 Mo Sep	0.05	0.02
Cowles Communications	21¼	8	10⅞	3¼	13½	8	g	....	Nil	....	December	[bg]1.04	[bg]0.33	[c]0.07	[bg]0.58		[g]0.11	9 Mo Sep	[bg]0.50	[bg]0.03
Crowell-Collier & Macmillan	44	[e]1⅞	27⅜	8⅜	16¾	8¼	20	4% Stk	Stk	4% Stk	December[5]	[bj]0.93	[bj]1.12	[bj]1.31	[e]0.53	[h]0.60	0.51	9 Mo Sep	0.43	0.41
Grolier Inc.	[e]38	[e]1¾	32¼	17	35	16⅞	12	0.90	0.90	0.90	December[6]	[ace]1.87	[ae]1.79	[a]2.26	[a]2.41	[h]2.00	2.09	9 Mo Sep	1.85	1.53
Harcourt Brace Jovanovich	121	20¼	62¾	23¼	48	35½	17	1.00	1.00	1.00	December	[c]2.43	2.01	2.31	2.20	[h]2.35	2.31	9 Mo Sep	1.80	1.91
Harper & Row, Publishers	[e]40¼	[e]6	18¾	7¼	17½	11⅜	16	0.40	0.40	0.40	April[7]	[b]1.02	[bk]0.88	1.00	0.42	[c]0.76	0.86	6 Mo Oct	0.97	1.07
Houghton Mifflin Co.	41¼	17¾	25⅜	12¾	23	13	19	0.40	0.40	0.40	December	0.96	0.84	0.92	[c]1.08	[h]1.20	1.35	9 Mo Sep	[c]1.09	1.34
International Text-book Co.	40½	[e]0.04	13	6	11⅝	4½	g	4% Stk	Stk	4% Stk	December[8]	[e]1.23	[e]0.70	[ce]0.29	[c]0.73	....	[g]0.17	9 Mo Sep	0.51	[cg]0.39
Richard D. Irwin, Inc.	32	[e]2¾	28	15	24	14¼	20	0.32	0.40	0.32	February[9]	0.65	0.81	1.01	0.93	....	1.02	9 Mo Nov	0.63	0.72
McGraw-Hill, Inc.	56½	[e]⅛	29	10¼	24⅛	15½	24	0.60	0.60	0.60	December[10]	[b]1.15	1.13	1.02	0.82	....	0.79	9 Mo Sep	0.55	[b]0.52
Meredith Corp.	59¾	[e]4¾	44⅝	18	29⅛	19¾	19	0.70	0.70	1.30	June	[b]2.45	2.28	[bl]3.05	2.32	1.13	1.23	3 Mo Sep	0.37	0.47
Plenum Publishing Corp.	36	[e]⅝	12½	3¾	13½	4½	8	....	Nil	....	December	0.81	1.02	[g]0.82	[c]0.59	....	[m]0.71	9 Mo Sep	....	0.60
Prentice-Hall, Inc.	51	[e]⅜	52	27⅛	50¼	36⅞	29	0.74	0.76	0.68	December[11]	[e]1.19	1.30	1.48	1.50	[h]1.60	1.56	9 Mo Sep	1.07	[b]1.13
G. P. Putman's Sons	26½	10½	15¼	6¾	14⅞	8½	9	0.34	0.35	0.32½	January	1.00	1.15	1.16	1.14	....	1.19	9 Mo Oct	1.00	1.05

BOOK PUBLISHING STOCK PRICES, 1971, Continued

STOCKS	PRICE RANGE						P-E Ratio	DIVIDENDS			Year Ending	$ Per Shr — EARNINGS — $ Per Shr						INTERIM EARNINGS OR REMARKS		
	1936–69		1970		1971			—$—	Total	—$—		Years					Last		$–Per Share–$	
Name of Issue	High	Low	High	Low	High	Low		So Far 1971	Ind. Rate	Paid 1970		1967	1968	1969	1970	1971	12 Mos.	Period	1970	1971
Scott, Foresman & Co.	48	[e]7½	22½	10¼	25	14½	17	0.60	0.60	0.60	April	1.55	1.10	1.17	1.11	1.11	1.13	6 Mo Oct	1.56	1.58
Simon & Schuster, Inc.	41	3⅜	5¾	2⅛	5¾	2½	19	....	0.10	....	December	[a]0.16	[ab]0.21	[a]0.31	[a]0.15	....	0.20	9 Mo Sep	[a]0.12	[a]0.17
Time, Incorporated	115	[e]2¾	44½	25½	62¾	40⅝	18	1.90	1.90	1.90	December	4.36	[b]3.76	[b]2.81	[b]2.76	[h]3.15	2.94	9 Mo Sep	1.71	1.89
Universal Publishing & Distributing	16½	[e]2 3/16	12	3¾	6¾	2½	[g]	....	Nil	....	March[12]	[e]0.60	[bg]0.16	[bd]0.65	[g]1.27	....	[g]1.20	3 Mo Jun	[g]0.02	[b]0.05
Wadsworth Publishing Co.	26½	[e]2¼	27	11	25	12	20	....	Nil	....	December[13]	[e]0.51	[e]0.61	0.86	1.03	....	0.80	9 Mo Sep	0.79	[c]0.56
Western Publishing Co.	83½	13½	14½	6½	24⅝	13	17	‡0.36	0.36	0.36	December[14]	[ae]1.00	[ae]1.45	[ae]0.55	[ac]0.95	....	1.49	9 Mo Sep	[e]0.52	1.06
John Wiley & Sons	51½	8¾	40½	20	37	25½	17	0.33	0.36	0.15	April	[e]1.01	[e]1.41	1.59	[gn]0.33	1.65	1.74	6 Mo Oct	1.18	1.27

*Data are based on Standard & Poor's "Stock Guide," January 1972, and are included by permission of Standard & Poor's Corporation.

EARNINGS

[a]Combined various classes.
[b]Excluding extra-ordinary income.
[c]Excluding extra-ordinary charges.
[d]Before tax loss carryforward.
[e]Adjusted.
[f]Company only.
[g]Deficit.
[h]Standard & Poor's estimate.

DIVIDENDS

‡Also stock.

STOCK SPLITS & DIVIDENDS

[1]Adjusted to 5%, 1969.
[2]10%, 1967; to 4%, 1971.
[3]3-for-2, 1968.
[4]2-for-1, 1968.
[5]To 4%, 1971; 2-for-1, 1968.
[6]2-for-1, 1969.
[7]2-for-1, 1969.
[8]Adjusted to 4%, 1971.
[9]2-for-1, 1967.
[10]2-for-1, 1967.
[11]2-for-1, 1967; to 2%, 1969.
[12]3-for-2, 1969.
[13]2-for-1, 1969.
[14]Adjusted to 3%, 1971.

OTHER

[i]$0.06[b], 1967; $5.36[b], 1968.
[j]$0.37[be], 1967; $1.12[b], 1968.
[k]$0.09[c], 1969.
[j]$0.62[b], 1969.
[m]12 Mo Jun, 1971.
[n]4 Mos Apr 1970; prior fiscal Dec; 12 Mo Apr 1970, $1.50.

PRICES OF U.S. AND FOREIGN PUBLISHED MATERIALS*

compiled by

Hugh C. Atkinson**

TABLE 1 U.S. PERIODICALS: AVERAGE PRICES AND PRICE INDEXES FOR 1967–1969, 1970, AND 1971[1]

(Index of 100.0 equivalent to average price for 1967–1969)

Subject Area	1967–1969 Average Price	Index	1970 Average Price	Index	1971 Average Price	Index
U.S. Periodicals (Based on total group of 2,372 titles included in the indexes which follow)	$ 8.66	100	$10.41	120.2	$11.66	134.6
Agriculture	4.68	100	5.17	110.5	5.74	122.6
Business & Economics	7.54	100	9.03	119.8	9.72	128.9
Chemistry & Physics	24.48	100	33.45	136.6	38.31	156.5
Children's Periodicals	2.60	100	2.65	101.9	2.94	113.1
Education	6.34	100	7.09	111.8	8.25	130.1
Engineering	10.03	100	12.07	120.3	13.28	132.4
Fine & Applied Arts	6.71	100	7.50	111.8	8.17	121.8
General Interest Periodicals	7.28	100	8.47	116.3	9.32	128.0
History	6.04	100	6.90	114.2	7.40	122.5
Home Economics	6.45	100	7.56	117.2	7.94	123.1
Industrial Arts	6.87	100	7.59	110.5	8.14	118.5
Journalism & Communications	5.72	100	6.36	111.2	6.91	120.8
Labor & Industrial Relations	3.01	100	3.59	119.3	3.88	128.9
Law	8.71	100	9.84	113.0	10.19	117.0
Library Science	6.27	100	7.88	125.7	8.65	138.0
Literature & Language	5.38	100	6.15	114.3	6.88	127.9
Math., Botany, Geology, & General Sci.	15.30	100	18.11	118.4	20.06	131.1
Medicine	19.38	100	23.44	120.9	27.00	139.3
Philosophy & Religion	5.27	100	5.84	110.8	6.71	127.3
Physical Education & Recreation	4.89	100	5.34	109.2	5.72	117.0
Political Science	6.18	100	6.72	108.7	7.23	117.0
Psychology	14.55	100	17.12	117.7	18.70	128.5
Sociology & Anthopology	6.11	100	7.31	119.6	7.92	129.6
Zoology	13.39	100	16.86	125.9	19.29	144.1

[1]For comment on U.S. periodicals price indexes, see *Library Journal*, July 1971 issue, "Price Indexes for 1971: U.S. Periodicals and Serial Services," Periodicals, 1971, by Helen W. Tuttle, pp. 2271-2274. For average prices for years prior to 1970, see previous editions of the *Bowker Annual*.

*For background material on U.S. price indexes, see 1971 *Bowker Annual*, pp. 79-80. For prices for German books, 1966–1968, and index of U.S. library microfilm rates, 1959, 1962, 1966, and 1969, see Tables 5 and 6 in the 1971 *Bowker Annual*, pp. 84-85.

**Associate Professor, Library Administration, and Director of Libraries, Ohio State University, Columbus, Ohio.

TABLE 2 BRITISH PERIODICALS: AVERAGE PRICE AND PRICE INDEX, 1971[1]

(Index base, 1970 = 100)

Subject	No. of Titles	% Increase on 1970	Index 1970 = 100	Average Price 1971 £ : p
Humanities and Social Sciences	648	11.2	111.2	6 01
Medicine	193	15.1	115.1	12 32
Science and Technology	848	16.7	116.7	18 78
TOTAL	1,689	15.6	115.6	13 14

[1]Compiled by J. B. Merriman, Director, Periodicals Division, B. H. Blackwell Ltd., Oxford, England, in the *Library Association Record,* Vol. 73, No. 8, August 1971. See Tables 7 and 8 for British book average prices and price indexes.

TABLE 3 U.S. SERIAL SERVICE: AVERAGE PRICES AND PRICE INDEXES FOR 1967–1969, 1970, AND 1971[1]

(Index base 1967–1969 = 100)

	1967–1969 Average Price	Index	1970 Average Price	Index	1971 Average Price	Index
Business	$119.76	100	$131.14	109.5	$140.04	117.0
Law	60.87	100	72.78	119.6	75.87	124.6
Science & Technology	65.23	100	88.32	135.4	90.23	138.3
Miscellaneous	45.84	100	55.33	120.7	69.50	151.6
U.S. Documents	18.37	100	26.04	141.8	26.84	146.1
Soviet Translations	90.82	100	106.77	117.6	111.66	122.9
"Wilson Index"	253.33	100	276.73	109.2	289.00	114.1
Combined[2]	$ 72.42	100	$ 85.44	118.0	$ 90.05	124.3

[1]"The definition of a serial service has been revised this year and combines the elements of terms (serial, serial service, loose-leaf service, card service, and service) found in three sources: the *ALA Glossary of Library Terms* (Chicago, ALA, 1943); *Library Statistics: a Handbook of Concepts, Definitions, and Terminology* (Chicago, ALA, 1966); and *U.S.A. Standard for Library Statistics*, Z39.7–1968." For further comments see *Library Journal,* July 1971 issue, "Price Indexes for 1971: U.S. Periodicals and Serial Services," Serials Service, 1971, by William H. Huff and Norman B. Brown, pp. 2274-2275. For average prices for years prior to 1970, see previous editions of the *Bowker Annual,*

[2]Excludes "Wilson Index."

TABLE 4 U.S. HARDCOVER TRADE-TECHNICAL BOOKS: AVERAGE PRICES AND PRICE INDEXES FOR 1967–1969, 1970, AND 1971[1]

(Index of 100.0 is equal to the average price 1967 through 1969)

Category	1967–1969 Average Price	1967–69 Index	1970 Average Price	1970 Index	1971[4] Number of Books	1971[4] Total Price	1971[4] Average Price	1971[4] Index
Agriculture	$ 9.71	100.0	$10.42	107.3	273	$ 3,724.97	$13.64	141.5
Art	12.44	100.0	16.16	129.9	989	16,231.24	16.41	131.9
Biography[2]	9.71	100.0	11.49	118.3	1,674	19,479.67	11.64	119.8
Business	10.41	100.0	12.45	119.6	520	6,549.92	12.60	121.0
Education	6.58	100.0	10.75	163.4	910	7,105.15	7.81	108.6
Fiction	4.96	100.0	5.51	111.1	1,355	8,109.27	5.98	120.5
General Works[3]	15.28	100.0	24.96	163.3	1,065	27,443.23	25.77	141.9
History	9.95	100.0	14.75	148.2	1,704	22,097.07	12.97	130.3
Home Economics[3]	6.55	100.0	7.30	111.4	301	2,206.02	7.33	111.9
Juveniles	3.53	100.0	4.05	114.7	2,561	10,834.25	4.23	119.8
Language[3]	10.13	100.0	19.56	193.1	334	3,389.60	10.15	100.1
Law	13.22	100.0	16.41	124.1	603	11,075.57	18.37	138.9
Literature	8.04	100.0	11.05	137.4	2,463	28,151.80	11.43	142.1
Medicine	13.41	100.0	18.05	134.6	1,349	23,721.62	17.58	133.0
Music	9.08	100.0	11.44	126.0	303	3,554.10	11.73	129.1
Philosophy, Psychology[3]	8.41	100.0	10.72	127.5	925	9,957.74	10.77	128.0
Poetry, Drama	6.69	100.0	9.35	139.8	1,140	10,427.43	9.15	136.7
Religion	6.29	100.0	8.51	135.3	1,056	8,947.83	8.48	134.8
Science	12.67	100.0	14.95	118.0	2,311	36,834.44	15.94	125.8
Sociology, Economics[3]	9.35	100.0	12.38	132.4	4,901	85,630.51	17.47	186.8
Sports, Recreation	7.91	100.0	9.96	125.9	606	6,180.51	10.20	128.9
Technology	13.03	100.0	14.91	114.4	1,027	15,690.74	15.28	117.2
Travel[3]	9.34	100.0	12.39	132.6	1,466	28,066.95	19.15	205.0
TOTALS	$ 8.77	100.0	$11.66	132.9	29,836	$395,411.63	$13.25	151.0

[1] Index of prices. Based on the tabulation of the books recorded in the "Weekly Record" section of *Publishers' Weekly* for the years indicated. Not included are "mass market paperbacks," government documents, and certain multivolume encyclopedias. Compiled by Hugh C. Atkinson. For average prices of hardcover books for years prior to 1970, see the 1970 *Bowker Annual* and previous editions.

[2] These figures include biographies placed in other classes by the Library of Congress.

[3] A new category. Index base is 1967 and 1969 rather than 1967 through 1969.

[4] *Publishers' Weekly* figures for 1971 are reported per volume rather than per title as they had been in previous years. Thus care should be exercised when interpreting the figures. It is important to keep in mind that *Publishers' Weekly* (February 7, 1972) uses a one-year base, 1967, in computing its indexes, rather than the three-year base preferred by the Library Materials Price Index Committee of the American Library Association.

TABLE 5 U.S. MASS MARKET PAPERBACK BOOKS: AVERAGE PRICES AND PRICE INDEXES FOR 1962, 1969, 1970, AND 1971[1]

(Index base, 1962 = 100)

Category	1962 Average Price	1962 Index	1969 Average Price	1969 Index	1970 Average Price	1970 Index	1971 Number of Books	1971 Total Price	1971 Average Price	1971 Index
Agriculture	$.75	100.0	$.87	116.0	$1.04	138.7	8	$ 8.30	$1.04	138.7
Art	.64	100.0	1.03	160.9	.96	150.0	53	54.60	1.03	160.9
Biography	.68	100.0	.98	144.1	1.12	164.7	73	86.20	1.18	173.5
Business	.48	100.0	1.03	214.6	1.04	216.7	10	12.35	1.24	258.3
Education	.64	100.0	1.65	257.8	2.52	393.7	15	26.95	1.80	281.2
Fiction	.48	100.0	.85	177.1	.90	187.5	1,979	1,850.35	.93	193.7
General Works[2]			1.25		.97		16	17.15	1.07	
History	.69	100.0	1.11	160.9	1.20	173.9	89	104.50	1.17	169.6
Home Economics[2]			.76		.94		55	52.10	.95	
Juveniles	.60	100.0	.76	126.7	.73	121.7	58	44.30	.76	126.7
Language[2]			1.11		1.01		4	3.75	.94	
Law	.60	100.0	.87	145.0	.92	153.3	10	10.50	1.05	175.0
Literature	.70	100.0	1.18	168.6	.96	137.1	87	98.55	1.13	160.0
Medicine	.59	100.0	.91	154.2	1.00	169.5	69	81.10	1.18	200.0
Music	.50	100.0	.97	198.0	.91	182.0	11	11.55	1.05	210.0
Philosophy, Psychology[2]			.82		.92		140	125.30	.90	
Poetry, Drama	.48	100.0	.90	187.5	1.68	350.0	15	24.85	1.66	345.8
Religion	.67	100.0	.86	128.4	1.10	164.2	16	18.84	1.18	176.1
Science	.69	100.0	1.08	156.5	1.28	185.5	30	37.75	1.26	182.6
Sociology, Economics[2]			1.36		1.08		185	246.90	1.33	
Sports, Recreation	.52	100.0	.94	180.0	.87	167.3	79	85.20	1.08	207.7
Technology	.72	100.0	1.27	176.4	1.10	152.8	19	28.40	1.49	206.9
Travel[2]			1.10		1.43		23	30.65	1.33	
TOTALS	$ .53	100.0	$ .91	171.7	$ .95	179.2	3,044	$3,060.14	$1.01	190.6

[1] Data based on that contained in the "Weekly Record" section of *Publishers' Weekly*. Table compiled by Hugh C. Atkinson. 1969 data compiled by Florence DeHart. Not included are government documents and encyclopedias. For average prices and price indexes for years prior to 1969, see previous editions of the *Bowker Annual*.

[2] New category. No base for calculation of index has been established. Average prices reported only for 1969, 1970 and 1971.

TABLE 6 U.S. TRADE AND HIGHER PRICED PAPERBACK BOOKS: AVERAGE PRICES AND PRICE INDEXES FOR 1962, 1969, 1970, AND 1971[1]

(Index base, 1962 = 100)

Category	1962 Average Price	1962 Index	1969 Average Price	1969 Index	1970 Average Price	1970 Index	1971 Number of Books	1971 Total Price	1971 Average Price	1971 Index
Agriculture	$2.68	100.0	$3.55	132.5	$4.48	167.2	54	$ 304.07	$5.63	210.0
Art	2.23	100.0	3.71	166.4	4.34	194.6	259	1,298.18	5.01	224.7
Biography	1.55	100.0	2.07	133.5	2.74	176.8	110	279.60	2.54	163.9
Business	4.01	100.0	4.06	101.2	5.23	130.4	188	1,207.51	6.42	160.1
Education	1.75	100.0	3.76	214.9	6.33	361.7	444	1,643.41	3.70	211.4
Fiction	1.38	100.0	1.63	118.1	2.04	147.8	98	183.05	1.87	135.5
General Works[2]			4.52		5.08		194	913.10	4.71	
History	2.08	100.0	3.62	174.0	5.12	246.1	330	1,420.43	4.30	206.7
Home Economics[2]			2.70		2.70		118	371.71	3.15	
Juveniles	1.18	100.0	1.36	115.3	1.56	132.2	173	235.20	1.36	115.2
Language[2]			3.98		9.13		218	973.49	4.47	
Law	2.03	100.0	5.17	254.7	6.73	331.5	186	1,520.37	8.17	402.5
Literature	2.08	100.0	2.51	120.7	3.94	189.4	675	3,582.28	5.31	255.3
Medicine	3.17	100.0	5.02	158.4	6.91	218.0	278	1,446.66	5.20	164.0
Music	2.67	100.0	3.05	114.2	3.65	136.7	117	637.00	5.44	203.7
Philosophy, Psychology[2]			2.91		3.54		372	2,313.35	6.22	
Poetry, Drama	1.74	100.0	2.03	116.6	2.25	129.3	404	981.57	2.43	139.6
Religion	1.43	100.0	2.31	161.5	3.02	211.2	530	1,584.12	2.99	209.1
Science	2.82	100.0	4.09	145.0	4.95	175.5	697	6,456.29	9.26	328.4
Sociology, Economics[2]			3.91		5.35		1,648	8,647.63	5.25	
Sports, Recreation	1.46	100.0	2.20	150.7	2.55	174.7	227	638.20	2.81	192.5
Technology	3.21	100.0	9.19	286.3	9.92	309.0	283	2,405.37	8.50	264.8
Travel[2]			3.38		3.10		354	1,472.45	4.16	
TOTALS	$2.12	100.0	$3.58	168.9	$4.81	226.9	7,957	$40,515.04	$5.09	240.1

[1]Compiled by Hugh C. Atkinson from data contained in the "Weekly Record" section of *Publishers' Weekly* and supplied by the staff. 1969 data compiled by Florence DeHart. Not included are government documents and encyclopedias. For average prices and price indexes for years prior to 1969, see previous editions of the *Bowker Annual*. Average prices reported only for 1969, 1970 and 1971.

[2]New category. No base for calculation of index has been established.

TABLE 7[1] BRITISH BOOKS BY MAJOR CATEGORIES: AVERAGE PRICES AND PRICE INDEXES FOR 1969/70–1970/71[2]

Category	Mean Average Price 1969/70 £ p	Mean Average Price 1970/71 £ p	% Increase or Decrease	No. of Volumes 1970/71 (1969/70 in brackets)	Index (1964/65 = 100) 1969/70	1970/71
Adult Fiction	89	97	+9.0	3,664 (3,562)	127.1	138.6
Adult Nonfiction[3]	3 43	3 73	+8.7	19,354 (17,207)	205.4	224.4
Reference Books[4]	2 90	3 13½	+8.1	1,617 (1,536)	149.5	161.6
Children's Fiction	65	68½	+5.4	1,089 (951)	130.0	137.0
Children's Nonfiction	76	76	—	384 (352)	128.8	128.8
All Categories Combined	2 84	3 13	+8.5	25,140 (22,234)	193.2[5]	212.2

[1]Compiled by the British National Bibliography in association with the Library Association and the Department of Education and Sciences. Decimal coinage from the halfpenny table. For average prices and price indexes for years prior to 1969/70, see the previous editions of the *Bowker Annual*. Please note that in these previous editions, the following corrections have been made for the category, "All Categories Combined": for 1965/66, 114.3; 1966/67, 128.1; 1967/68, 149.8; 1968/69, 159.3. For British periodicals average price and price index for 1971, see Table 2.
[2]August 1969, August 1970, and August 1971 issues of *Library Association Record*.
[3]See Table 8 for classified breakdown by Dewey classes.
[4]Reference books are also included in the total for Adult Nonfiction.
[5]Corrected figure.

TABLE 8 BRITISH ADULT NONFICTION BOOKS: AVERAGE PRICES AND PRICE INDEXES FOR 1969/70–1970/71[1]

Dewey Main Classes	Average Price 1969/70[2] £ p	Average Price 1970/71[2] £ p	Percent Increase or Decrease 1970/71 over 1969/70	(Index 1966–67 Figures = 100) 1969/70	1970/71
000	4 40	5 27	+24.8	84.5	101.2
100	3 67	2 62	−3.2	197.3	142.4
200	2 65	4 12	+55.5	203.8	316.9
300	4 71	5 26	+22.9	320.4	357.7
400	2 40	2 21	−8.8	363.6	334.8
500	4 14	4 54	+11.3	138.5	151.8
600	3 50	3 77	+12.7	141.7	152.6
700	2 50	3 03	+18.0	105.0	127.3
800	1 68	1 98	+17.5	163.1	192.2
900	2 54	2 75	+10.9	150.3	162.7

[1]Compiled by the British National Bibliography in association with the Library Association and the Department of Education and Sciences. Decimal coinage from the halfpenny table. For average prices and price indexes for years prior to 1969/70, see previous editions of the *Bowker Annual*.
[2]For breakdown into subdivisions see August 1970 and August 1971 issues of *Library Association Record*.

TABLE 9 MEXICAN BOOK PRICES: AVERAGE PRICES AND PRICE INDEXES FOR 1947/49, 1960, 1965, 1968, AND 1970[1]

(Index base, 1947–49 = 100)

Subject Division	1947–49 Average Price U.S. $	Index	1960 Average Price U.S. $	Index	1965 Average Price U.S. $	Index	1968 Average Price U.S. $	Index	Total Items	1970 Average Price U.S. $	Index
Philosophy and Religion	$1.93	100	$1.67	86.6	$2.52	130.5	$2.80	145.1	30	$3.21	166.3
Fine Arts	2.82	100	1.82	64.6	4.90	173.7	5.13	181.9	22	4.47	158.5
Social Sciences	1.82	100	1.90	104.3	1.99	109.3	2.42	133.0	132	3.26	179.1
History	2.13	100	3.53	165.7	2.47	115.9	2.40	112.7	85	4.14	194.3
Law	1.97	100	3.76	190.8	5.00	253.8	3.11	157.9	89	4.30	218.2
Economics	1.62	100	3.04	187.6	3.46	213.5	4.97	306.8	62	4.72	291.3
Language & Literature	1.18	100	1.71	144.9	1.72	157.7	1.95	165.2	262	2.04	172.8
Science and Technology	1.84	100	4.87	264.6	2.87	155.9	2.80	152.2	58	4.02	218.4
Medicine	2.98	100	6.00	201.3	7.23	242.6	6.62	222.1	24	10.55	354.0
Agriculture	1.20	100	2.02	168.3	6.93	577.5	6.39	532.5	2	5.72	476.6
Total	$1.69	100	$2.57	153.7	$2.74	162.1	$3.12	184.6	766	$3.51	207.6

[1]Compiled by David Zubatsky, Bibliographer for Latin America and the Iberian Peninsula, and William H. Kurth, at the Washington University Libraries, St. Louis, Mo.

GROWTH OF U.S. TRADE IN BOOK EXPORTS AND IMPORTS

by

William S. Lofquist*

In the past decade the United States has become the world's major power in international book trade. By 1971 U.S. foreign trade in books reached $277.7 million, a value exceeded by no other country. Exports of U.S. books totaled $176.7 million in 1971, while U.S. book imports were $101.0 million. It is estimated that the annual value of U.S. exports is greater by approximately one third than that of its nearest competitor, the United Kingdom. The import situation is even more striking, with annual U.S. purchases of foreign books exceeding the combined book imports of France and the United Kingdom. U.S. exports and imports of books for 1965, 1967, and 1969–1971 are shown in Tables 1 and 2.

Exports of U.S. books grew at the annual rate of 10.1 percent between 1965 and 1971, but much of this growth took place in the 1965–1969 span. As noted in Table 1, 1971 U.S. book exports rose by only 1 percent from 1970's peak of $174.9 million. This low rate of growth was due primarily to reduced exports of encyclopedias to Japan ($23.1 million in 1970; $8.1 million in 1971). In both Tables 1 and 2, the totals shown at the top of the tables represent total U.S. exports to or imports from *all countries;* these totals are not the summation of U.S. book trade with the selected 30 countries listed on the two tables. U.S. exports of books to these principal countries accounted for 96 percent of total U.S. exports in 1971. (For U.S. export and import data for individual countries not listed in the tables, contact U.S. Department of Commerce, Bureau of the Census.)

Canada, the United Kingdom, Japan, and Australia are the primary markets for U.S. books. Exports to these four countries totaled $126.0 million in 1971, or about 71 percent of U.S. exports to all countries. Canada's purchases alone totaled $79.7 million, or 45 percent of all U.S. exports.

Despite the impressive U.S. export record displayed by the statistics of Table 1, there is general concurrence that the values shown considerably understate the U.S. publishing industry's commitment to foreign trade. Since October 1969, the federal government has excluded from statistical reporting all U.S. exports whose individual shipments are valued at less than $250. (Prior to this time, individual shipments valued at under $100 were excluded.) The purpose of this act was to reduce the paper work involved in the export of U.S. products, but the impact on U.S. book export data has been severe: the true value of U.S. exports may be as much as double the figures shown in Table 1. The export data may be as misleading in yet another manner. A drop in exports to a specific country may indicate that a sufficient market has been established such that U.S. publishers' works are now manufactured overseas to serve that market (e.g., the decline in U.S. exports of encyclopedias to Japan).

While U.S. exports have tended to level off in recent years, the data in Table 2 indicate that U.S. book imports have climbed rapidly. Total U.S. book imports from all countries were over $100 million in 1971, a gain of 10 percent above 1970. Imports grew at an annual average rate of 12.9 percent in the period 1965–1971 and currently represent over 3 percent of total U.S. consumption of books. The United Kingdom is the principal supplier of books to the United States, accounting for 38 percent of total shipments in 1971. The Netherlands, Japan, West Germany, Italy, and Canada had combined 1971 book sales to the United States of $42.4 million, or 42 percent

---

*Book Publishing Specialist, U.S. Department of Commerce.

of total U.S. book imports from all countries. This growth is a reflection of both U.S. interest in the works of foreign authors and the considerable quantity of art, gift, and other books manufactured abroad and imported by U.S. publishers.

TABLE 1   U.S. EXPORTS OF BOOKS TO SELECTED COUNTRIES, 1965, 1967, 1969–1971

Country of Destination	1965	1967	1969	1970	1971
Total U.S. exports to all countries[1]	$99,322,588	$143,193,226	$166,141,099	$174,936,928	$176,662,158
Canada	$43,479,981	$ 60,672,865	$ 72,325,007	$ 73,205,325	$79,682,482
Mexico	1,416,175	2,588,684	2,346,653	3,085,375	3,358,612
Panama	435,571	756,637	583,746	652,976	603,201
Colombia	296,628	166,487	624,840	1,082,098	318,432
Venezuela	585,470	551,487	1,006,716	1,177,866	1,181,617
Chile	1,007,954	913,514	741,782	568,400	755,358
Peru	374,355	571,111	645,436	441,271	803,653
Brazil	1,814,158	2,804,283	2,802,025	3,083,465	3,161,742
Argentina	698,537	659,011	1,445,855	1,598,991	1,811,201
Norway	249,310	224,222	142,538	1,703,480	210,104
Sweden	1,219,834	551,396	480,696	419,164	326,389
United Kingdom	11,928,896	17,460,023	16,835,890	16,723,866	20,658,298
Netherlands	1,836,889	2,990,179	2,833,038	2,971,143	3,283,822
Belgium-Luxembourg	468,758	730,122	769,463	456,075	542,377
France	581,997	683,367	595,733	884,177	660,051
West Germany	849,066	1,685,913	2,461,897	2,749,245	3,374,562
Switzerland	281,901	486,758	624,009	523,131	715,432
Spain	331,246	648,855	619,667	431,842	670,710
Italy	1,398,990	5,602,381	5,922,547	3,420,021	2,761,302
Israel	168,878	185,534	714,198	468,490	513,778
India	1,088,216	1,042,128	1,709,775	2,095,162	2,047,559
Thailand	251,958	450,710	906,709	618,429	626,101
Singapore	458,181[2]	505,436	314,274	1,335,895	3,024,770
Indonesia	1,487,750	66,089	386,019	402,607	1,092,426
Philippines Republic	2,398,600	2,490,905	3,918,124	2,531,833	3,814,410
Republic of Korea	112,301	218,252	744,456	1,384,340	1,380,961
Japan	8,574,508	17,165,889	23,152,784	28,324,936	12,314,700
Australia	7,243,446	8,444,132	8,696,581	10,356,797	13,388,183
New Zealand	1,128,528	1,984,334	833,377	1,055,588	1,531,908
Republic of South Africa	2,305,858	2,699,887	3,530,103	3,310,590	4,366,556

[1]Total values represent approximately 125 countries.
[2]Includes Malaysia.
Source: U.S. Department of Commerce, Bureau of the Census.

TABLE 2 U.S. IMPORTS OF BOOKS FROM SELECTED COUNTRIES, 1965, 1967, 1969–1971

Country of Origin	1965	1967	1969	1970	1971
Total U.S. imports from all countries[1]	$48,787,486	$69,241,912	$78,352,540	$92,022,837	$100,993,571
Canada	$ 1,397,819	$ 3,057,167	$ 3,400,294	$ 5,355,159	$10,615,863
Mexico	1,553,061	2,575,829	1,229,732	1,537,761	1,548,956
Panama	318,792	35,369	259,402	432,830	396,574
Colombia	3,447	100,534	37,263	244,689	359,257
Argentina	160,010	626,539	396,046	461,895	368,147
Sweden	236,663	620,193	494,876	531,929	898,439
Finland	4,834	25,606	565,024	426,802	236,335
Denmark	401,377	293,213	578,838	526,514	333,853
United Kingdom	24,375,096	27,837,150	30,360,697	33,919,226	38,599,427
Ireland	62,105	93,599	153,497	513,861	347,519
Netherlands	3,277,667	6,404,291	8,166,465	8,871,190	8,814,526
Belgium-Luxembourg	632,184	1,096,749	922,029	876,753	1,205,725
France	2,017,462	2,612,471	3,396,271	4,120,552	2,581,355
West Germany	3,740,450	5,763,354	6,670,563	7,242,679	6,329,774
Austria	256,017	329,895	390,715	259,083	193,273
Hungary	47,625	177,480	160,008	13,806	44,738
Czechoslovakia	743,773	924,152	430,182	327,841	365,654
Switzerland	2,893,466	3,219,065	3,609,576	4,102,388	2,867,459
Spain	962,707	1,866,627	1,717,248	3,598,730	2,871,040
Portugal	1,916	5,007	109,640	12,534	42,054
Italy	2,427,802	5,084,585	6,660,852	6,690,372	6,491,107
Yugoslavia	8,055	320,532	190,780	320,278	828,281
Israel	134,072	396,535	1,004,807	956,924	1,476,605
India	151,177	138,247	174,156	274,148	205,065
Singapore	2,808[2]	5,546	78,786	659,779	759,269
Hong Kong	60,228	104,698	350,264	516,489	663,814
Republic of China (Taiwan)	4,915	52,146	69,619	263,851	325,136
Japan	2,055,766	4,048,046	5,745,803	7,883,459	10,121,699
Australia	145,408	284,276	298,929	326,635	311,391
New Zealand	5,822	15,908	154,158	23,226	27,153

[1]Total values represent approximately 125 countries.
[2]Includes Malaysia.
Source: U.S. Department of Commerce, Bureau of the Census.

Library and Book Trade Standards

INTERNATIONAL LIBRARY STATISTICS STANDARDIZATION DEVELOPMENTS DURING 1971

by

Frank L. Schick*

During the past twelve months, the international standardization of library statistics made more significant advances than during the preceding 30 years when in 1932 the International Federation of Library Associations (IFLA) established a separate committee on Library Statistics and worked for the adoption of an international library statistics standard. The close cooperation between UNESCO, IFLA, and the International Organization for Standardization/Technical Committee 46 (ISO/TC 46) and various national library associations and national agencies laid the foundation for the adoption of this standard, which occurred in November 1970 when the General Conference of UNESCO unanimously approved the Recommendation Concerning the International Standardization of Library Statistics.[1]

Two months after the Conference, Mr. M. Babic, Chief, Division of Statistics on Culture and Communication, Office of Statistics of UNESCO, sent the following letter to the national libraries and statistics offices of the UNESCO Member States, indicating that his office will conduct in 1972 a library survey for the year 1971:

"In pursuance of Article 6 of the Recommendation according to which library statistics should be drawn up by Member States at regular intervals of three years in conformity with the recommended standards, UNESCO is planning to undertake the next statistical survey on libraries during the year 1972, the previous one having taken place in 1969. A new questionnaire prepared according to these standards will thus be distributed to Member States at the beginning of next year to collect the most recent national data on this subject. In case you should be called on to collaborate in such a survey we should like you to take the necessary steps to apply the standards and principles of this Recommendation as soon as possible in order to improve the international comparability of these statistics."

In April of 1971, ISO/TC 46 adopted this UNESCO Recommendation.

---

*Chief, Library Surveys Branch, National Center for Educational Statistics, U.S. Office of Education, Washington, D.C.

[1]See the 1971 *Bowker Annual,* pp. 97-102. For the text of the Recommendation see *American Libraries,* July/August 1971, pp. 729-731.

ADDITIONS TO THE UNESCO RECOMMENDATION

The 75 representatives of 47 countries (11 in Asia, 7 in Africa, 1 in Australia, 17 in Europe, 4 in North and Central America, 7 in South America), 4 international organizations (IFLA; ISO; International Federation for Documentation, FID; International Statistics Institute, ISI), observers of the Holy See World Health Organization (WHO), and League of Arab States (LAS), who had drafted the UNESCO Recommendation, were aware of omissions in the UNESCO standard, which were not previously covered in national surveys and had not been explored in the preparatory joint meetings of the Statistics Committees of IFLA, ISO and the East European Socialist Countries. For instance, the standard lacked commonly understood definitions, concepts, or measures of counting. It was agreed by the members of the three international statistics committees that some members of the committees would prepare working papers for a joint conference to discuss these omissions in detail and to adopt resolutions which would be possible amendments to the UNESCO Recommendation and be additional topics to be included in national library surveys.

PRAGUE INTERNATIONAL LIBRARY STATISTICS CONFERENCE, Sept. 6–10, 1971

The meeting, cosponsored by the Statistics Committees of the International Federation of Library Association (IFLA), the International Organization for Standardization, and the Statistics Commission of the East European Socialist Countries, elected Dr. Frank L. Schick (USA) as Chairman, Dr. E. A. Fenelonov (USSR, Ministery of Culture) and Dr. M. Velinsky (Charles University, Prague, Czechoslovakia) as Vice Chairmen, and Mr. Kenneth A. Mallaber (Board of Trade, UK) as Rapporteur. The conference hosts were the Czechoslovak Ministery of Culture and the National Library. The 22 participants included UNESCO's Bureau of Statistics, the ISO/TC 46 Secretariat, the Chairman (John G. Lorenz, Deputy Librarian of Congress), the Secretary of IFLA's Commission on Statistics and Standards (Mr. F. William Torrington, UK), and representatives of the following countries: Bulgaria, Czechoslovakia, Denmark, Finland, United Kingdom, German Federal Republic, Germany Democratic Republic, Hungary, Poland, Switzerland, USA, USSR. Representatives from Egypt and France were unable to attend.

Working papers implementing the 1970 UNESCO Library Statistics were submitted for the following topics:

1. Audiovisual Materials (United Kingdom)
2. Manuscripts (German Federal Republic)
3. Library Building Statistics (USA — F. L. Schick)
4. Statistical Analysis of Library Reports Using Group Departmental Indices (Poland)
5. Statistics of Library Services (Czechoslovakia)
6. Library Use Statistics (United Kingdom)

After discussion of these papers, resolutions were adopted either concluding the topic (2 and 3) or requiring further work by individuals (1 and 4) or by several participants (5 and 6). The following resolutions were adopted:

Audiovisual Materials

"The Conference, after a full discussion of the many difficulties created by the rapid technical developments in the field of audiovisual materials, requested Mr. Torrington and Mr. Mallaber [both from the United Kingdom] to prepare a paper for further discussion at the 1972 IFLA meeting at Budapest. This paper should summarize the discussion and should propose alternative methods of classification, definition and counting. The first draft of the paper should be circulated to all Conference members, who should send their comments to Mr. Torrington by 28th February 1972 so that a definitive paper can be circulated before the Budapest meeting."

Manuscripts

"This Conference agrees that the present methods of counting MSS [manuscripts] recommended by UNESCO are the best methods that can be formulated for national totals within international statistics. In view of the fundamental differences in the way in which MSS collections are housed and organized in different countries, it is recommended that each country should explore further the question of more detailed statistics for their own countries.

"As it would be difficult to report statistically on large manuscripts holdings of all libraries in a more detailed form, it is suggested to record in the national statistics only the yearly accessions of manuscripts in the following manner:
1. occidental manuscripts
   (a) to 1500
   (b) after 1500
2. oriental, east-asian and other non-occidental manuscripts
3. music manuscripts

"In these three categories it is proposed to record the number of the bibliographic items cataloged.
4. private archives (Nachlässe)
   (a) total number of collections (Nachlässe)
   (b) number of collections (Nachlässe) cataloged
   (c) number of cataloged items

"Statistics of this kind contribute to get an insight, on a national level, into the structure of manuscripts accessions. Moreover, the sum of items 1, 2, 3, 4c provides the information about manuscripts accessions, which is required by UNESCO. If the suggested approach would prove its feasibility, it would be possible to use it in many cases retrospectively for the total manuscripts holdings."

Library Building Statistics

"It is recommended that the UNESCO library statistics be supplemented by including a section on library buildings as follows:
1. Count in square metres the net area of buildings assigned at the time of reporting for library purposes, excluding custodial, mechanical and general access areas.
2. Count the number of seats made available for all users by the library at the time of reporting whether or not they are making use of the materials of the library, but excluding auditoriums, lecture rooms and cafeterias.
3. Count in metres the total length of shelving available for library materials."

Library Activities

"The Conference agrees with the proposal of Mr. Ernestus [from West Germany] and Dr. Velinsky [from Czechoslovakia] to establish a complete list of all library activities. This would make it possible to choose library activities to be included in international library statistics upon a solid basis and thus to ensure that no important element is omitted by chance.

"As, however, Mr. Mallaber's paper contains elements which in any case should be included in the statistical considerations, the actual lack of the proposed list should not prevent the Conference from dealing with them in its further discussions.

"The Conference thanks Dr. Velinsky for his willingness to elaborate the final list which should be supplemented by an indication for those elements already counted in national statistics together with their existing definitions. The list could be included in Dr. Velinsky's paper for the 1972 IFLA Conference at Budapest."

Interpretation and Analysis of Library Statistics

"The Conference agreed that Dr. Velinsky and his colleagues should prepare a paper which lays down a detailed basis for the further discussion of the proposals in his conference paper. This paper which should be ready within 4 months, should be discussed at the meetings of the IFLA Statistics and Standardization Committee at Budapest in 1972."

Analysis of Library Statistics by Group Indices

"The Conference welcomed the work being carried out by Mr. Maj [from Poland] which was regarded as being of very great importance. Mr. Maj was urged to publish the results of his work as soon as possible and to have it translated into other languages so that further examination of his methods and experimentations with them could take place. It was thought that the initial consideration would be best carried out in relation to homogeneous groups of libraries inside single countries. It was also felt to be important that Mr. Maj's publication should include practical examples of the application of his methods."

OUTLOOK

The six resolutions aim to bring international statistics relating to libraries up to date. During the discussions, the conferees realized that the topics will have relevance either to the international library community or will provide guidelines for national data developments.

The resolutions regarding "manuscripts" and "building statistics" are ready for international and national acceptance and use. The resolutions relating to "audiovisual materials," "library activities," and "analysis of library statistics" require additional work and will be discussed at the 1972 IFLA Conference in Budapest, Hungary. It can be assumed that during this meeting, which will be cosponsored by FID, several subject areas will be completed and be ready for national use. If considered successful by UNESCO, these fields will be eventually included in UNESCO's international surveys.

The data currently collected by the National Center for Educational Statistics of the U.S. Office of Education in the areas of public, college, and university libraries and school media centers will be transmitted to UNESCO for their 1971 survey of libraries of Member States. It can be anticipated that this UNESCO survey will present more meaningful and comparable information than could be obtained previously.

INTERNATIONAL STANDARD SERIAL NUMBERING (ISSN)

by

Emery I. Koltay*

An important step in international bibliographic standardization has been taken with the implementation of international standard serial numbering.

BACKGROUND

The Standard Serial Numbering (SSN) plan was prepared by Subcommittee 20 of the American National Standards Institute Committee Z39 on standardization in the field of library work, documentation, and related publishing practices. Committee Z39, organized under the procedures of the American National Standards Institute (ANSI), is sponsored by the Council of National Library Associations.

SSN AND ISSN

At the 1970 Oslo meeting, the International Organization for Standardization Technical Committee 46 (ISO/TC 46), Working Group No. 1, approved the present Z39 SSN as the basis for an international standard serial numbering (ISSN). The ISO/TC 46 plenary meeting in Lisbon, May 1971, approved this recommendation.

Following this meeting, ISO/TC 46 assigned a block of ISSN numbers to the United States; the R. R. Bowker Company's Current Serials Bibliography file was selected as the starting point for the implementation of the ISSN.

The SSN was formally approved and published by ANSI as *Identification Number for Serial Publications,* (Z39.9–1971, $2.25 per copy). The ISSN, though approved, has not yet been published by ISO/TC 46. However, for practical purposes, in order to avoid later changes in the format (this occurred when the SBN became the ISBN), and in order to conform to the content of the Bowker Current Serials Bibliography, which is international, the abbreviation used from the beginning will be ISSN.

DESCRIPTION OF THE STANDARD

The definition for "serial" used in the serial standard is from the Anglo-American cataloging rule: "A publication issued in successive parts bearing numbered or chronological designations and intended to be published indefinitely."

The purpose of the standard is to define the structure of a concise, unique, and unambiguous code for serial publications. This code is solely for identification of serials. The assignment of the code numbers must be centrally administered. While International Standard Book Numbering is decentralized, a centralized system for serials numbering is required because of the large number of serials publishers throughout the world. Some 45,000 publishers are represented by the 70,000 publications now being numbered at Bowker.

The registration number of the ISSN is seven numerical digits plus an eighth, the check digit. (See procedure for calculating check digits at end of article.) An example of an ISSN is 1234–5679. All digits must be printed. The hyphen is a recognition aid.

A unique correspondence exists between each assigned ISSN and the serial to which it is assigned. For each serial there is only one code number and for each code number there is only one serial.

The central authority in charge of the ISSN assignment is responsible for interpreting the cataloging rules, definitions, and distinctions between serial entities involved in splits, mergers, title changes, and other problems.

ASSIGNMENT OF ISSN

In assigning the ISSNs, bibliographic centers and some libraries requested a purely sequential numbering; subscription agencies wanted assignment by

---

*Director, Serials Bibliography, Standards and Services.

blocks of numbers so they could identify titles by country. A solution was worked out in which every entry would be coded with a two-digit country code. The country code in use by the Library of Congress for MARC II is applied for this purpose. Every title has the country code printed before the ISSN, in the following format: US ISSN 0000-0019. The country code is not part of the standard. When the ISO approves an international country code standard, the country code will be modified accordingly.

PUBLICATION OF THE ISSN

The first publication that will be assigned the ISSNs will be the Bowker Current Serials Bibliography, which is published in three segments: Volumes I and II, entitled *Ulrich's International Periodicals Directory,* issued in a new 14th edition in 1971; and Volume III, entitled *Irregular Serials and Annuals: An International Directory,* due to be published in its 2nd edition May 1972. Volume III contains a combined alphabetical index with ISSNs for every entry in Volumes I, II, and III.

Every effort has been made to include all serials that are subscribed to by major libraries and are currently abstracted and indexed. At the request of libraries, subscription agencies, abstracting and indexing services, and others using the ISSN system, Bowker will assign numbers to titles not represented in its database. Listings of newly assigned ISSNs will be published periodically.

The ISSN for each publication listed in this database will be sent by computer mailing on a specially designed form to the publisher with the request that the number be printed on the cover of each issue.

The New Serial Titles (NST) cumulative for 1950–1970, currently being developed, is the next large data base to which ISSNs will be assigned. It is scheduled to be published in 1972. The NST cumulative file together with the Bowker Current Serials Bibliography file will represent the largest computerized data base for serial users.

USES OF ISSN

ISSNs will do for serials what the International Standard Book Number (ISBN) is doing for books — that is, they will provide the serials publisher, the subscription agency, and the librarian with a tool for communicating basic information with a minimum of error. The advantages of such standardization are many. In the United States, the major subscription agencies handle approximately 85 percent of all periodical subscriptions and 60 percent of all irregular serials orders from libraries. By using ISSNs, no publication will be mistaken for another; the ISSN will aid in ordering, shipping, issue claiming, and billing. Cataloging will be facilitated, and circulation and interlibrary loan systems can become more efficient. It will open the possibility of creating regional holding lists for improved interlibrary cooperation; and, since the Standard Numbering Agency at Bowker is responsible for both book and serials numbering, the task of defining overlap of serials and monographs can be undertaken and resolved, providing the librarian with concise bibliographic information.

Specifically, the ISSN can be used by abstracting and indexing services as a unique code and a means to bridge the gap between the ALA entry (as set forth in the Anglo-American cataloging rules) and the title as it appears on the piece and the title citation; by subscription agencies who will use it for communication, billing, inventory, claims, announcements, etc.; by authors for copyright; by publishers for inventory, ordering, billing, and announcements; and by users for location of the item in the library — linking the citation to the title. It will be used in library processing for identification (ID) control on acquisitions, claiming, binding, accessioning, shelving, monitor-in process control, cooperative cataloging, circulation, inventory, updating holdings, developing local and regional holdings; in library reference for retrieval/request-identification, linkage-item with citation, interlibrary loan, etc. In machine use the ISSN will fulfill the need for file update and linkage, retrieval and transmittal of data.

CODEN CONVERSION TO ISSN

Before arriving at this ISSN code, Subcommittee 20 gave consideration to two alternate codes proposed, the Coden and the Ruly code, but they decided on ISSN. At the ISO Oslo meeting ISSN was again chosen in preference to the Coden code. Since serial titles are in all languages and alphabets, only a universally accepted set of symbols such as a numeric system with arabic numerals, common to all alphabets as well as to all computing machinery, could fulfill a serial standard code requirement. To solve the problem of converting the Coden to ISSN, there is a project under study to develop a translation table for the titles presently abstracted and indexed, indicating the corresponding ISSN for the presently used Coden.

INTERNATIONAL SERIAL DATA SYSTEM

At the ISO plenary meeting in Lisbon, May 1971, when the U.S./SSN standard was in the final stage of becoming an international standard, UNESCO/UNISIST requested and made a formal proposal to the ISO that they become the administering center for the ISSN, under the name of ISDS (International Serials Data System). This proposal was backed by financial commitments from UNESCO and the French government.

In October 1971 an agreement for cooperation and coordination had been reached among the International Serials Data System, the International Organization for Standardization, the Library of Congress, and the R. R. Bowker Company. The United States will go ahead with the implementation of the ISSN system with an international content until UNISIST/ISDS efforts to create ISDS materialize, and ISDS becomes capable of taking over and handling the task of assigning ISSNs.

Years of hard work and effort are behind the ISSN accomplishment. Besides the members of ANSI Z39 Subcommittee 20, many people from the publishing and library and information science world have contributed at the national and international levels to the development of this standard. Special thanks must go to Dr. Jerrold Orne, Chairman of the ANSI Committee Z39, who chaired the ISO plenary meeting in Stockholm; Fred Croxton of the Library of Congress, Chairman of Subcommittee 20 for Standard Serial Numbering; Lawrence Livingston at the Council of Library Resources; Samuel Lazerow, Chief, Serials Division, Library of Congress; and Dr. Hans-Jurgen Ehlers of Germany, who chaired the work of the ISO/TC 46 Working Group No. 1 on ISSN.

PROCEDURE FOR CALCULATING CHECK DIGITS

The use of a check digit helps guard against errors resulting from improper data transcription. The check digit, which is calculated on a Modulus 11 basis as indicated in the example below, is particularly effective in detecting transposition errors.

1. Write the digits of the basic number.

$$1\ 2\ 3\ 4\ 5\ 6\ 7$$

2. Write the constant weighting factors associated with each position of the basic number.

$$8\ 7\ 6\ 5\ 4\ 3\ 2$$

3. Multiply each digit by its associated weighting factor.

$$8\ 14\ 18\ 20\ 18\ 14$$

4. Sum the products of the multiplications.

$$8+14+18+20+20+18+14=112$$

5. Divide the sum by the Modulus 11 to find the remainder.

$$112 \div 11 = 10 \text{ plus a remainder of } 2$$

6. Subtract the remainder from Modulus 11 to generate the required check digit. If the check digit[1] is 10 generate

---

[1] Use of Modulus 11 can sometimes result in a check digit of 10. If this were used, the Standard Serial Number would not always be the required eight digits in length. Therefore, the X is used to represent the check digit 10, thus maintaining the uniform length of eight digits.

a check digit of X. If there is no remainder, generate a check digit of zero.

$$11 - 2 = 9$$

7. Append the check digit to create the standard eight-digit SSN.

$$1\ 2\ 3\ 4 - 5\ 6\ 7\ \underline{9}$$

STANDARD FOR TITLE LEAVES OF A BOOK*

The American National Standards Institute issued late in 1971 an American National Standard Z39.15–1971, of interest to publishers, covering Title Leaves of a Book. International and national standards covering the format of the contents of the title leaves, enabling publishers and editors to produce title pages in a form that will facilitate their use by bibliographers, librarians, and researchers around the world, are included.

This standard was prepared by Subcommittee 21 of Standards Committee Z39, whose responsibility is to promulgate standards for the field of library work, documentation, and related publishing practices.

Members of the subcommittee representing publishers were James A. McNeish, John Wiley & Co.; Emmert W. Bates, Litton Educational Publishing; James H. Silberman, Random House; and William A. Bayless, Rockefeller University Press. The library field was represented by James W. Henderson, chief of the research libraries at the New York Public Library; S. K. Cabeen, Engineering Societies Library; and Anne J. Richter, formerly editor-in-chief of the book department of R. R. Bowker Company. Mrs. Richter served as chairman of the committee.

The standard prepared by Subcommittee 21 was based on the International Organization for Standardization Recommendation, R1086 Title-Leaves of a Book, and took into consideration the Draft British Standard Specifications for Title Leaves of a Book. It also used the same terminology as that of other ANSI standards related to book publishing, such as Compiling Book Publishing Statistics, Z39.8–1968.

The essential information, according to the standard, that should appear on the initial printed leaves of a book is as follows: The title page should have the full title which may be amplified by a subtitle and the series title if the book forms part of a series, and the number of the book in that series. If the book is a translation, the title of the book in the original language should appear on the title page (unless the translated title is familiar to a wide audience and the book is designed for the popular market). The name of the author, or, in a composite or collective work, of the responsible editor or compiler, the name of the publisher, and place of publication should appear on the title page. Date of publication for every new book should be included. Also, translations of scientific and technical books should have the date of publication of the translation itself, and the date of the edition from which the translation has been made.

If the title is different from that of other editions of the same work, the alternative or earlier title should appear. This need not be on the title page, but on the verso or in a bibliographic note.

*Reprinted from *Publishers' Weekly,* June 14, 1971.

If the book has been published abroad under a variant title, this information should be clearly stated on the verso or in a bibliographic note.

ANSI recommends that if the book is a facsimile reprint, a facsimile of the original title page as well as the reprint publisher's title page should be given.

Other information that should appear on the initial printed leaves are the dates of all editions and printings (preferably on the verso). Each edition should show clearly its relationship with other editions. If there is a distributing publisher of a book originally published in a foreign country, the distributing publisher shall not obliterate or cover any bibliographic information furnished by the original publisher.

Copyright, ISBN, and Library of Congress Catalog Card Number should appear on the verso of the title leaf. The name of the printer and/or binder may be included. Abstracts should appear on the verso of the title page or on the right-hand page following it; separate abstracts of chapters should appear on or preceding their first pages.

It is also recommended by ANSI that when the Cataloging in Publication program is agreed upon, the basic cataloging information should appear on the verso of the title leaf.

Copies of the official ANSI standard are available from the American National Standards Institute, 1430 Broadway, New York 10018, (212) 868-1220. It is priced at $2.50 per single copy.

STANDARD FOR ADVERTISING OF BOOKS*

The American National Standards Institute, Inc., the official agency for certifying industry-wide standards in the United States, has approved a national standard for bibliographic data to be included in different marketing media.

A publication known as American National Standard Z39.13-1971 (issued in December 1971) includes a detailed table, listing the bibliographic elements recommended for inclusion in ten different media (catalogs, advertising, jackets, display material, etc.), aimed at the trade, institutional, educational, and consumer markets. The standard also elaborates on all the points shown in the table, which is reprinted here with permission from ANSI.

A committee of three publishers and two librarians worked on this publication for over two years, having consulted with many of their colleagues so as to make recommendations that were valid and appropriate. The committee consisted of Fon Boardman, Oxford University Press; Edward Matthews, McGraw-Hill; David Replogle, G. & C. Merriam; Mrs. Avis Zebker, Brooklyn Public Library; and Ellis Mount, Chairman, Columbia Libraries.

Single copy price of the publication is $3.00, available from the American National Standards Institute, 1430 Broadway, New York 10018.

---

*Reprinted from *Publishers' Weekly,* August 2, 1971 and August 20, 1971 issues.

RECOMMENDED BIBLIOGRAPHIC ELEMENTS

MEDIA	TRADE	INSTITUTIONAL	EDUCATIONAL	CONSUMER
Annual General Catalogs	1, 2, 3, 4, 5, 7, 8, 9, 10 12, 13, 14, 15, 16, 18, 20	Same as for Trade	Same as for Trade	Same as for Trade
Seasonal Catalogs	1, 2, 3, 4, 6, 7, 8, 9, 10 11, 12, 13, 14, 15, 16, 17 18, 20	Same as for Trade	Same as for Trade	Same as for Trade
Subject Catalogs	1, 2, 3, 4, 5, 7, 8, 9, 10, 12 13, 14, 15, 16, 17, 18, 20	Same as for Trade except add 19	Same as for Trade	Same as for Trade
Checklists	1, 2, 3, 4, 5, 8, 9, 10, 13	Same as for Trade	Same as for Trade	Same as for Trade
List Advertising	1, 2, 3, 4, 6, 8, 9, 10, 11	Same as for Trade except add 19	Same as for Trade except add 19	Same as for Trade except add 19
Display Advertising	1, 2, 3, 4, 6, 7, 8, 9, 10, 11 12, 13, 15, 16, 17, 18, 20	Same as for Trade except add 14 & 19	Same as for Trade	Same as for Trade except omit 10 & 20
Direct Mail	1, 2, 3, 4, 6, 7, 8, 9, 10, 11 12, 13, 14, 15, 16, 17, 18, 20	Same as for Trade except add 5 as an alternative to 6 and add 19	Same as for Trade	Same as for Trade except add 5 as an alternative to 6
Jackets	1, 2, 3, 4, 8, 9, 10, 12, 13 14, 15, 16, 17, 18	Same as for Trade	Same as for Trade	Same as for Trade
Display Material	1, 2, 4, 6, 8, 9, 11, 18	Same as for Trade except add 12	Same as for Trade	1, 2, 4, 6, 11
News/Publicity	1, 2, 3, 4, 6, 8, 9, 11, 12 13, 14, 15, 16, 17, 18, 20	Same as for Trade	Same as for Trade	Same as for Trade

KEY

1. Author(s)
2. Title
3. Subtitle
4. List price
5. Copyright date
6. Publication date
7. Paging
8. Edition number
9. Publisher's identification
10. Standard book number
11. Pre-publication price schedule
12. Special physical features (Large print, etc.)
13. Series name and number
14. Translation information
15. Contents description
16. Conference data (for proceedings)
17. Author's background
18. Graphic features, size
19. Library of Congress card number
20. Prior publication record

STANDARDS FOR THE BIBLIOGRAPHIC CONTROL OF NONPRINT MEDIA

by

Pearce S. Grove*

The culmination of professional activity in 1971 reveals several significant breakthroughs in the long and arduous task of acquiring some semblance of bibliographic control for the utilization of nonprint media by potential users.

In 1951 the first international conference[1] on the cataloging of films was convened by John Flory of Eastman Kodak Company in Rochester, New York. As is true with more recent accomplishments, this first major gathering of some 25 interested persons from Canada and the United States was the result of efforts by individuals and groups in preceding years. Mrs. John Flory, the first executive secretary of the Educational Film Library Association and a school librarian, was instrumental in capturing the interest of company executives, librarians, and audiovisual specialists.

Two years later a second conference was sponsored by UNESCO under the joint directorship of Irene Wright and Wilbert H. Pierson. Three active innovators at the Library of Congress, Lucille Morsch, Richard Angell, and Alpheus Walter, made numerous trips throughout North America discussing the need for bibliographic control of films. Their immediate goals were to provide 3" x 5" catalog cards utilizing standard Library of Congress cataloging rules for common usage of reference sources and catalogs. Richard Angell credits Alpheus Walter, head of the card division at the Library of Congress, with the determination necessary to succeed in this venture long before it was recognized as essential data by the profession. Angell says, "Walter risked his career and succeeded."

Active interest by Library of Congress personnel during the mid-1950s was particularly timely in view of the development of the *Anglo-American Cataloging Rules* which were an outgrowth of activity in the codification of cataloging rules for American and British libraries. The practical application in the Library of Congress of these systematic procedures that prior to mid-century were developed almost solely for print material began to be adapted for nonprint media control. Chapters devoted to music, photographic materials, maps, atlases, motion pictures, filmstrips, and phonorecords were included. The 1967 edition of the *Anglo-American Cataloging Rules* devoted an entire section (Part III) to nonbook materials. This has led to virtually all standardization for the bibliographic control of nonprint media now enjoyed by media specialists and consumers.

In 1966 the Department of Audiovisual Instruction (now AECT) organized a Task Force on Computerized Cataloging and Booking Educational Media for the purpose of developing "(1) standards for cataloging educational media and (2) coding standards for computerized cataloging and scheduling."[2] The results of this Task Force, composed largely of audiovisual administrators, were virtually ignored by those in positions of responsibility for the cataloging, classification, storage, and retrieval of nonprint media. It was not until 1971 that the

---

*Library Director, Eastern New Mexico University, Portales, N.M.

[1]"Proceedings of the First International Film Cataloging Conference (1951) convened under the auspices of the Film Council of America at George Eastman House, Rochester, New York, U.S.A., September 29 and 30, 1951." Ed. by Norman B. Moore and John Flory. Issued by the Conference Committee on behalf of The Film Council of America, Inc., 600 Davis Street, Evanston, Ill., June 1952.

[2]*Standards for Cataloging, Coding and Scheduling Educational Media.* Washington, D.C.: Department of Audiovisual Instruction, National Education Association, 1968.

Cataloging Committee of the Association for Educational Communications and Technology (AECT) recognized the shortcomings of their Association's initial effort and published a revised edition entitled *Standards for Cataloging Nonprint Media*.[3] Unlike the previous effort, Cataloging Committee Chairman William J. Quinly devoted considerable time to the coordination of his committee's work with corresponding activities in the American Library Association and the Canadian Library Association. Joint meetings in Canada and the United States led to mutually beneficial compromise and agreement in many areas which were previously unresolved.

During the previous two years, projects in Great Britain and Canada resulted in publications and the exchange of ideas between representatives in these three countries who control the *Anglo-American Cataloging Rules*. Bernard Chibnall completed "A Feasibility Study of a Multi Media Catalogue," a project financed by a grant from The Office for Scientific and Technical Information in Great Britain.[4] Mr. Chibnall's research fellow, Antony Croghan, published "A Thesaurus-Classification for the Physical Forms of Non-Book Media"[5] the following year.

Corresponding efforts in Canada by Jean Riddle (Weihs), Shirley Lewis, and Janet MacDonald resulted in a preliminary edition of the publication entitled *Non-book Materials; the Organization of Integrated Collections*.[6] The latter was completed in consultation with the Technical Services Committee of the Canadian School Library Association stressing the importance of standardized terminology, agreed-upon entry data, and integrated catalogs whereby all print and nonprint media receive equal consideration.

This same year, 1970, in the United States officials at the Library of Congress and members of several professional groups interested in the bibliographic control of nonprint media cooperated in the development of a MARC format for projected images. It is entitled *Films: A MARC Format Specifications for Magnetic Tapes Containing Catalog Records for Motion Pictures, Filmstrips, and Other Pictorial Media Intended for Projection*[7] and promises to become a basic source of agreed-upon standards for computerized bibliographic information required for access to existing nonprint media.

Activity continues in Great Britain under the chairmanship of Peter Lewis, who is considering a revision of the *Anglo-American Cataloging Rules* pertaining to nonprint media, while Jean Riddle Weihs and her associates in Canada work toward a second edition of their publication. Margaret Chisholm, Dean of Library and Information Science at the University of Maryland, is chairman of a North American group composed of representatives from the Canadian Library Association, American Library Association, and Association for Educational Communications and Technology that is striving to bring about agreement on rules for the organization of audio and visual information. Representatives of these respective associations and Katharine Clugston, Head, Descrip-

---

[3]Robert Steele, *The Cataloging and Classification of Cinema Literature*. Metuchen, N.J.: The Scarecrow Press, 1967.

[4]Bernard Chibnall and Antony Croghan. "A Feasibility Study of a Multi Media Catalogue." (Carried out under a grant from The Office for Scientific and Technical Information) University of Sussex, 1969.

[5]Antony Croghan, "A Thesaurus-Classification for the Physical Forms of Non-Book Media." London, 1970.

[6]Jean Riddle (Weihs), Shirley Lewis, and Janet MacDonald. *Non-book Materials; the Organization of Integrated Collections*. Ottawa: Canadian Library Association, 1970.

[7]*Films: A MARC Format*. MARC Development Office. Washington, D.C.: Library of Congress, 1970.

tive Cataloging for Nonprint Media at the Library of Congress, are instrumental in current cooperative efforts toward the standardization of procedures for the bibliographic control of nonprint media. Previous work by Mary D. Pearson,[8] Helen Roach,[9] Eunice Keen,[10] Caroline Saheb-Ettaba and Roger B. McFarland,[11] and Warren Hicks and Alma Tillin[12] has also been instrumental in the development of standards.

Public libraries were afforded *Guidelines for Audiovisual Materials and Services for Public Libraries*[13] by the Audiovisual Committee, Public Library Association of the American Library Association in 1970. Similar guidelines were issued two years previously by the Audiovisual Committee of the Association for College and Research Libraries.[14] The latter Committee has a manuscript[15] in preparation that treats the selection and organization of nonprint media in academic libraries. Also in preparation and scheduled for publication by the American Library Association in 1972 is a manuscript tentatively entitled "Systems and Standards for the Bibliographic Control of Nonprint Media" which evaluates the various needs and achievements toward the goal implied in the manuscript title.[16]

The Nonprint Media Statistics Committee of the American Library Association convened, in conjunction with the National Center for Educational Statistics, a National Planning Conference on Nonprint Media Statistics, March 26–27, 1971. Agreement among the 34 participants representing 20 professional organizations included six priority areas of concern:[17]

1. Identify types of data elements and unit designations of each for statistical measurement.

2. Identify organizations and institutions with whom the Task Force and Advisory Board should coordinate their work and request support.

3. Develop standard terminology for

---

[8] Mary D. Pearson, *Recordings in the Public Library*. Chicago: American Library Association, 1963.

[9] Helen Roach, *Spoken Records Second Edition*. New York and London: The Scarecrow Press, 1966.

[10] Eunice Keen, *Manual for Use in the Cataloging and Classification of Audio-Visual Materials for a High School Library*. Lakeland, Florida, 1955.

[11] Caroline Saheb-Ettaba and Roger B. McFarland. *ANSCR The Alpha-Numeric System for Classification of Recordings*. Williamsport, Pa.: Bro-Dart Publishing, 1969.

[12] Warren Hicks and Alma Tillin. *Developing Multi-Media Libraries*. New York: R. R. Bowker, 1970.

[13] Audiovisual Committee, Public Library Association, American Library Association. *Guidelines for Audiovisual Materials and Services for Public Libraries*. Chicago: American Library Association, 1970.

[14] American Library Association. Audio-Visual Committee. *Guidelines for Audio-Visual Services in Academic Libraries*. Prepared and published by the Audio-Visual Committee of the Association of College and Research Libraries and the ALA Audio-Visual Committee. (Chicago, 1968.)

[15] "Nonprint Media in Academic Libraries." (A manuscript in progress under the editorship of Pearce S. Grove.) Chicago: American Library Association, Association of College and Research Libraries, Audiovisual Committee, 1972.

[16] "Systems and Standards for the Bibliographical Control of Nonprint Media." (A manuscript in progress under the editorship of Pearce S. Grove with publication anticipated in the Spring of 1972). Chicago: American Library Association, 1972.

[17] A National Planning Conference on Nonprint Media Statistics, Minutes. Washington, D.C. March 26-27, 1971. Cosponsored by the American Library Association and National Center for Educational Statistics. Convened by Pearce S. Grove, Chairman ALA LAD Library Organization and Management Section Nonprint Media Statistics Committee. Mimeographed, 1971.

nonprint media essential to the statistics program.

4. Establish priorities for the data to be collected on a universal scale and that needed only on a representative sampling basis.

5. Plan for the systematic gathering of fiscal inventory information for nonprint media materials, personnel, equipment, facilities, and operational programs.

6. Include the identification of special nonprint media collections in a national plan for statistics.

Subsequent meetings of the Conference-appointed Task Force has led to coordinated efforts with the Council of Chief State School Officers' Committee on Educational Data Systems and a tentative proposal for the development of a "Library Statistics Handbook for Nonprint Media."[18]

The Hope Reports[19] offer some statistical data concerning the production and market trends of nonprint media in the United States and will have a continuing impact on the standardization of terminology and statistical concepts of measure.

According to an announcement of August 9, 1971 by Henriette D. Avram, "The Library of Congress is planning to convert the catalog records for motion pictures and filmstrips into machine-readable form beginning in 1972. It is also considering distributing these records on magnetic tapes on a subscription basis through the MARC Distribution Service. These records would be structured according to the specifications found in *Films: A MARC Format* (available from the Superintendent of Documents at $.65 a copy). Cataloging information would follow the guidelines provided in the *Anglo-American Cataloging Rules*. It is anticipated that approximately 8,000-9,000 records would be distributed in a year."[20]

Nonprint media have only recently begun to receive the attention necessary for their organization. Standard concepts, definitions, and terminology will increase the preciseness with which professionals and laymen may approach the development of procedures for the selection, acquisition, cataloging, classification, retention, and retrieval of nonprint media from libraries and other information centers throughout the United States and beyond.

Through the unprecedented display of cooperative endeavors in the 1970s, ready access by potential users to information in a variety of formats appears promising indeed. Continued progress is urgently needed in view of our society's rapidly increasing dependence on media in print and nonprint formats.

---

[18]Library Statistics Handbook for Nonprint Media, A Proposal. Prepared by the Joint Professional Association Task Force on Nonprint Media under the chairmanship of Pearce S. Grove. Mimeographed and distributed, 1971.

[19]*AV-USA, 1969.* (12th annual report.) Compiled by Thomas W. Hope, Hope Reports, Rochester, N.Y., 1970.

[20]Announcement by Henriette D. Avram, Chief, MARC Development Office, Library of Congress, dated August 9, 1971.

Legislation and Grants

FEDERAL LEGISLATION FOR LIBRARIES DURING 1971

by

Germaine Krettek* and Eileen D. Cooke**

This report covers 11 months of the first session of the 92nd Congress. Although the early months of the session were marked by frustrating pulling and hauling between the Congress and the Administration, the summer saw action on a number of bills of vital interest to librarians.

APPROPRIATIONS

For the first time in several years, the major appropriations bills affecting libraries were cleared by both House and Senate before the beginning of the new fiscal year. The $5.1 billion compromise version of HR 7016 providing appropriations for FY 1972 for the U.S. Office of Education was rushed through both Houses for final action on June 30, and was signed into law (PL 92-48) by the President on July 9. For a breakdown of the $164,459,000 provided for library programs, see Table 1. (For a complete list of U.S. Office of Education legislation for 1972, see "Guide to OE-Administered Programs Fiscal Year 1972" in the August-September 1971 issue of *American Education,* pp. 38-44, available at 50 cents a copy from the Superintendent of Documents, U.S. Government Printing Office, Washington, D.C. 20402.)

Also signed into law (PL 92-51) on July 9 was the Legislative Branch Appropriations Act for 1972. Included was the full $71,090,000 for the construction of the Library of Congress James Madison Memorial Building, even though House Speaker Carl Albert made a dramatic last-minute attempt to halt the construction of the building in order to hold the site for a future fourth House Office Building. In addition, $68,053,250 was appropriated to carry on the programs of the Library of Congress.

ONE-YEAR COPYRIGHT EXTENSION

S.J. Res. 132, a joint resolution extending the duration of copyrights until December 31, 1972, was introduced by Senator John McClellan on July 15, passed by the Senate and the House, and signed into law (PL 92-170) by the President on November 24, 1971. In his introductory remarks, the Senator, who is Chairman of the Senate Judiciary Subcommittee on Patents, Trademarks, and Copyrights, explained that this measure, similar to ones introduced and passed during the past several years, is meant to continue for another year the expiring second term copyrights, pending the enactment of a general revision of the copyright law, including a proposed increase in the term of copyright.

---

*Director, American Library Association, Washington D.C. Office.
**Deputy Director.

CABLE TELEVISION (CATV)

An issue of increasing concern to librarians and educators related to copyright revision is community antenna television (CATV) or cable television. According to the annual report of the Senate Subcommittee on Patents, Trademarks, and Copyrights (S.Rept. 92-74), the inability of the Senate to proceed with further consideration of copyright revision legislation in the 91st Congress can be attributed, in part, to the unresolved cable television issue. (Section 111 of S. 644, the copyright revision bill, relates to the copyright liability of secondary transmissions of cable television systems.)

Prior to drafting Section 111, the Subcommittee requested the Federal Communications Commission to advise it as to the Commission's recommendations. On February 17 Senator John Pastore, the Chairman of the Senate Commerce Committee, introduced, at the request of the FCC, S. 792, a bill to amend the Communications Act of 1934 to provide for the regulation of CATV systems.

Another bill to amend the Communications Act of 1934 was introduced on August 4 by Senator Harrison Williams, Chairman of the Labor and Public Welfare Committee, to provide for the regulation of community antenna television. S. 2427, the "National Community Antenna Television Act of 1971," would grant the FCC jurisdiction over CATV and would also establish national long-range policy to guide the FCC in exercising its authority. Furthermore, the bill would establish CATV as a public utility — a recognized monopoly — and would require establishment of a formula of channel allocation for communities of varying size. According to their current timetable, the FCC plans to promulgate their rules by the end of the year, with an effective date of March 1, 1972.

In the meantime, throughout the country, plans are being drafted, applications for CATV franchises are being made to governing bodies, and patterns for the development of CATV are being set. These patterns may endure indefinitely.

There is little reference to educational or other public service use of CATV channels in most of the 2,500 franchises already awarded. So far, only a few libraries are actually involved in cable negotiations.

PIRACY OF SOUND RECORDINGS

Also part of the whole copyright picture is a new law (PL 92-140), which provides for the creation of a limited copyright in sound recordings. Signed by the President on October 15, 1971, the bill makes the unauthorized reproduction and sale of copyrighted sound recordings unlawful. However, this copyright would be applicable only to sound recordings fixed, published, and copyrighted on or after the effective date of the legislation and before January 1, 1975.

Responding to the ALA's concern over language forbidding anyone but the copyright holder from distribution of recordings to the public by rental, leasing or lending, the House Judiciary Committee added a statement on "Library Uses" in their report on the bill. This states that it is not their intention that the limitation on lending or rental contained in the proposal reach out to apply to long-established practices by nonprofit libraries.

POSTAL RATES

Early in the year the shocking news came of rate increases being proposed by the U.S. Postal Service to the new Postal Rate Commission. The fourth-class special rate for books, records, films, and so forth, would be increased by 83 percent, from a base rate of $.12 to $.22 for the first pound. Rates for heavier pieces would be increased proportionately. The increase for this class of mail would be phased over five years, with the deferred amount provided by Congressional appropriations. The library rate (for books and other materials sent to and from libraries and schools) would also be increased substantially in order to meet the requirement that all classes of mail cover at least their handling costs. The increase proposed was from a base rate of $.05 per pound to a base rate of $.10 per pound, with further increases on matter weighing more than one pound. The average increase in this class would be 130 percent, but the increase would be phased over ten years, with Congress providing appropriations for the deferral for this period of time.

ALA presented testimony before both House and Senate Appropriations Subcommittees on Treasury–Post Office, urging that adequate funds be provided for the required general public service appropriations and to cover the phase-in transition period. Opposing the drastic rate changes proposed, ALA also, on February 22, filed a petition to intervene with the newly established Postal Rate Commission. On June 3, ALA filed testimony with the Commission, after previously responding to written interrogatories of the U.S. Postal Service, and on September 10, after responding to second interrogatories from both the Postal Service and Postal Rate Commission, testified as an intervenor before a hearing of the Commission. Hearings were concluded on September 24, and final briefs were filed by intervenors. The decision by the Hearing Examiner will be submitted to the five-man Postal Rate Commission, which will then make its own recommendation to the Governors of the U.S. Postal Service. The USPS is seeking Commission approval for permanent rate increases totaling $1.45 billion.

ALA SUPPORTS NLM

On April 29 the American Library Association filed a motion within the U.S. Court of Claims seeking leave to file a brief amicus curiae in the *Williams & Wilkins* case. In essence the brief supports the National Library of Medicine, which is being sued by publishers Williams & Wilkins for alleged violation of copyright in relation to NLM's photocopying their scientific publications.

In the statement of ALA's interest in this issue, the point is made that the case has potential ramifications transcending the interests of the actual litigants and vitally affecting all libraries which engage in photocopying practices which are similar to those of the National Institutes of Health and the National Library of Medicine.

TAX AMENDMENTS PROPOSED TO RESTORE CHARITABLE DEDUCTIONS

A resolution restoring charitable deductions to creative artists and authors was adopted by the ALA Council June 25, 1971. This action was taken at the recommendation of the ALA Legislation Committee, in anticipation of Congressional action on legislation designed to alleviate the unfortunate results of the Tax Reform Act of 1969, which eliminated the tax incentive for donors of manuscripts of their own creation.

The present law states that the donor of income property may deduct an amount which is equal to market value minus the amount of gain. This means that the collector of manuscripts may deduct the amount he paid for the materials, but the author or composer may deduct only the cost of the paper and ink, with no allowance for the value added by his creativity.

Prior to the Dallas 1971 conference, two bills had been introduced to rectify this situation: S. 1212, which would allow the donor of the income property to deduct the market value of the property minus "50 percent of the gain," and HR 9103, which would restore the full charitable deduction. On July 29, the cause was aided when Representative Wilbur Mills, Chairman of the House Ways and Means Committee, introduced a bill on the subject (HR 9505). This bill also provides for a 50 percent deduction, but is more likely to reach the floor because of its sponsorship.

OTHER LEGISLATIVE ACTION

A number of other measures, pending and enacted, have significant application to libraries:

The Emergency Employment Act of 1971, (PL 92-54), signed July 12 and funded at $1 billion for 1972, provides jobs in the field of public service, including libraries, whenever the national rate of unemployment is 4.5 percent (or that of a city is 6 percent) or above for three consecutive months. The primary goal is to place unemployed or underemployed persons in transitional jobs which will provide training and contribute to the occupational development of the participants. The Act is administered by the Manpower Administration of the Department of Labor.

The Small Community Development Act (in the form of several separate bills including HR 7843 and S. 2058) is currently in committee in both House and Senate. These bills provide grants, interest rate subsidies, and loan guarantees to small communities and regional units for the construction or rehabilitation of multipurpose community centers which may include library facilities. It is not known when action may be expected on these.

Comprehensive Child Development Act. Two separate bills with this title (S. 1512 and HR 6748) have been incorporated in broader bills extending for two years the programs authorized under the Economic Opportunity Act of 1964. Both of the comprehensive bills (S. 2007 and HR 10351) have been passed by their respective houses, sent to conference, and reported out on November 29, 1971 (H. Rept. 92-682). If the compromises reached in conference are approved by House and Senate, the measure would then await approval by the White House.[1] The basic program provides services of a medical, nutritional, educational, and social nature, through child development centers serving children through 14 years of age, with particular attention to the economically disadvantaged. Units of local government and public and private educational agencies and institutions are among those eligible to be prime sponsors of child development programs, and funds are provided for "preservice and inservice education and other training for professional and paraprofessional personnel."

HIGHER EDUCATION ACT

The Senate unanimously passed on August 6 an omnibus higher education bill (S. 659), and on November 5, the House passed its version of the legislation (HR 7248). The Senate measure extends Title II of the Higher Education Act of 1965 for four years, with FY 1972 at the level of 1971 and FY 1973-1975 at a new combined authorization of $130 million for college library resources and library training and research. In this consolidation, 70 percent of the funds appropriated are for resources (Part A) and 30 percent for research and training (Part B); of the latter, two-thirds are for training, and one-third for research and demonstration.

The House measure is a five-year extension and expansion of the Higher Education Act and other acts dealing with higher education, authorizing for college library resources and library training such sums as may be necessary for each of the five years. Specific amounts are authorized for library research and demonstration programs under Part B, increasing annually from $5 million in FY 1972 up to $40 million for FY 1976. Of funds appropriated for training programs, 50 percent must be used for fellowships and traineeships. Both House and Senate versions increase the maximum amount of supplemental grants up to $20 for each full-time student. The various changes in these two bills are analyzed in detail in the respective committee reports (H.Rept. 92-554 and S. Rept. 92-346).

In the final hours of debate on HR 7248, a revised version of the totally unrelated emergency school aid for desegregation bill (HR 2266) and a number of anti-busing amendments were attached to the higher education bill, and subsequently anti-busing amendments and other amendments were added to the Senate bill as well. As a result, on November 24, Senate Majority Leader Mike Mansfield announced that S. 659 was being sent back to committee and would likely not be reported out before late January 1972, bringing 1971 to a close without extension of the Higher Education Act.

---

[1]Although House and Senate subsequently agreed to a compromise version of the legislation, the President vetoed the Child Development Act on December 9, 1971.

LEGISLATION AND GRANTS / 211

TABLE 1 FUNDS FOR LIBRARY-RELATED PROGRAMS, FISCAL YEAR 1972

	Authorization	Budget Recommendation	Appropriation
Elementary and Secondary Education Act			
Title I Educationally Deprived Children	Unknown[1]	$1,500,000,000	$1,565,000,000
Title II School Library Resources, Textbooks, & Other Instructional Materials	$210,000,000	80,000,000	90,000,000
Title III Supplementary Education Centers, Guidance, Counseling & Testing	575,000,000	143,393,000	146,393,000
Title V-A Strengthening State Education Departments	85,000,000	33,000,000	33,000,000
Title VI-B Education of Handicapped Children	210,000,000	35,000,000	37,500,000
Title VII Bilingual Education Programs	100,000,000	25,000,000	35,000,000
Library Services and Construction Act	207,000,000	18,000,000	58,709,000
Title I Library Services	112,000,000	15,719,000	46,568,500
Title II Public Library Construction	80,000,000	0	9,500,000
Title III Interlibrary Cooperation	15,000,000	2,281,000	2,640,500
Title IV-A State Institutional Library Services		(Now under Title I)	
Title IV-B Library Services to the Physically Handicapped		(Now under Title I)	
National Defense Education Act			
Title III-A Instructional Assistance	—[2]	0	50,000,000
Title VI Language Development	—[2]	15,300,000	15,300,000
Higher Education Act			
Title I Community Service Program	—[2]	0	9,500,000
Title II College Library Assistance & Library Training & Research	—[2]	17,145,000	22,895,000[3]
Part A College Library Resources	—[2]	5,000,000	11,000,000
Part B Library Training	—[2]	2,000,000	2,000,000
Library Research		3,000,000	2,750,000
Part C LC Acquisition & Cataloging	—[2]	7,145,000	7,145,000[3]

TABLE 1 Continued

	Authorization	Budget Recommendation	Appropriation
Title III Developing Institutions	—[2]	38,850,000	51,850,000
Title V Education Professions Development	—[2]	135,800,000	135,800,000
Title VI-A Equipment & Materials for Higher Education	—[2]	0	12,500,000
Title VIII Networks for Knowledge	—[2]	0	0
Title IX Education for Public Service	—[2]	0	0
Title X Improvement of Graduate Programs	—[2]	0	0
International Education Act			
Higher Education Facilities Act, Construction, including Libraries:			
Title I Undergraduate	—[2]	0	43,000,000
Title II Graduate	—[2]	0	0
Title III Loans	—[2]	33,003,000	29,010,000
Medical Library Assistance Act and National Library of Medicine	25,500,000 (& Title 42 USC[4])	21,486,000	24,086,000
Older American Act	85,000,000	33,700,000	38,950,000[5]
Adult Education Act	225,000,000	25,850,000	61,300,000
ETV Facilities	15,000,000	4,000,000	13,000,000
National Agricultural Library	(Title V USC, Sec. 2204)	3,894,750	4,060,750
Library of Congress	(Title II USC, Sec. 131-167)	69,657,000	68,053,250
National Commission on Libraries & Information Science	750,000	200,000	200,000

[1] Based on formula.
[2] Education programs needing new authorizations. They were funded under the 1-year contingency authority provided in PL 91-230, Title IV.
[3] Included in the Legislative Branch Appropriations Act, PL 92-51.
[4] U.S. Code 275.
[5] Included in HEW Appropriations Act, PL 92-80.

LEGISLATION AND GRANTS / 213

TABLE 2 STATUS OF LEGISLATION OF INTEREST TO LIBRARIANS

The 92nd Congress, First Session, convened January 21, 1971. Table date, November 15, 1971.

Legislation	House Introduced	House Hearings	House Reported by Subcommittee	House Committee Report Number	House Floor Action	Senate Introduced	Senate Hearings	Senate Reported by Subcommittee	Senate Committee Report Number	Senate Floor Action	Conference Report	Final Passage	Public Law	ALA Division Concerned
Appalachian Regional Development	S. 2317				x	S. 2317	x	x	273	x		x	PL 92-65	ASLA, PLA
Community Antenna TV						S. 792								All Divisions
Natl. Community Antenna Act 1971						S. 2427								All Divisions
Copyright — 1 year Extension	SJRes 132			605	x	SJRes 132			277	x			PL 92-170	All Divisions
Copyright Revision	S. 646	x	x	487		S. 644	x							All Divisions
Copyright in Sound Recordings	HR 2356	x				S. 646	x		72	x			PL 92-140	All Divisions
Department of Educ.						S. 1485								All Divisions
Econ. Opportunity Amendments & Child Dev.	S. 2007	x		471	x	S. 2007	x	x	331	x	682			All Divisions
Educational Technology	HR 4916	x				S. 2011								AASL, ACRL
HEA Educ. Amendments of 1971	HR 7248	x	x	554	x	S. 659	x		346	x				All Divisions
HEA Higher Educ. Act of 1971	HR 5191	x				S. 1123	x							All Divisions
Higher Educ. Opportunity Act	HR 9155					S. 2581	x							All Divisions
Impoundment of Appropriations	HR 8937					S. 2482	x							AASL
Indian Educ. Act						S. 555			384	x				AASL
Older American Community Serv.						S. 643	x							ASD
Patent Revision	S. 31	x	x	176	x	S. 31	x	x	48	x	310	x	PL 92-54	ISAD
Public Serv. Employment	HR 6961					S. 1432	x							All Divisions
Reorganization, Executive Branch	HR 10947						x							All Divisions
Revenue Act of 1971	HR 4187	x	x	533	x				437					All Divisions
Revenue Sharing, General	HR 7796	x				S. 680	x							All Divisions
Revenue Sharing for Educ.	HR 1	x				S. 1669	x							AASL
Social Security Amendments	HR 1	x		231	x	HR 1	x							All Divisions
Tax Amendment on Manuscripts	HR 9505					S. 1212								All Divisions
APPROPRIATIONS														
Education, FY 1972	HR 7016	x		99	x		x	x	145	x	309	x	PL 92-48	All Divisions
Emergency Employment	HJRes 833			440	x				355	x		x	PL 92-72	All Divisions
Independent Offices and HUD	HR 9382	x	x	305	x		x	x	264	x	377	x	PL 92-78	All Divisions
Interior and Related Agencies	HR 9417	x	x	308	x		x	x	263	x	386	x	PL 92-76	All Divisions
Labor — HEW	HR 10061	x	x	374	x		x	x	316	x	461	x	PL 92-80	All Divisions
Legislative	HR 8825	x	x	236	x		x	x	224	x	317	x	PL 92-51	All Divisions
Public Works	HR 10090	x	x	381	x		x	x	327	x	479	x	PL 92-76	All Divisions
Treasury: Post Office & Genl. Govt.	HR 9271	x	x	290	x		x	x	243	x	326	x	PL 92-49	All Divisions

Note: For copies of bills and reports, write to House & Senate Documents Rooms, U.S. Capitol, Washington, D.C., 20515 & 20510, respectively.

THE LIBRARY SERVICES AND CONSTRUCTION ACT DURING FISCAL YEAR 1971

by

Elizabeth H. Hughey*

The Library Services and Construction Act — Amendments of 1970 extended the Act from fiscal year 1971 through fiscal year 1976 and consolidated former Titles I and IV[1] into Title I, Library Services. Title II, Public Library Construction, and Title III, Interlibrary Cooperation, remained as separate titles. The 1970 amendments allow the states greater flexibility in the administration of the program, add emphasis on services to the disadvantaged, provide for one advisory council in lieu of three separate councils, broaden the program with specific reference to metropolitan libraries serving as national or regional resource centers, and strengthen the capacity of the state library administrative agency for meeting the needs of the people of the state.

TITLE I — PUBLIC LIBRARY SERVICES

The federal allotment of $35 million, expanded by the required matching state and local allotments, brought first-time as well as improved library services to rural and urban users. State library agencies with their advisory councils continued to interpret and respond to the priority library development needs of their respective states.

Thus, library systems were established and strengthened, multiplying the resources available to enlarged clienteles. LSCA support enabled the cooperative buying and processing of media, as well as the creation and shared use of union catalogs. Increasingly sophisticated reference and interlibrary loan services plus growth in reciprocal borrowing arrangements were noticeable. State library agencies that recognized the immediate and long-range education needs of library personnel instituted recruiting, training and work-training programs, internships, and the development of new library careers to effect new library thrusts.

New library thrusts were experimental, as, for example, one which used "caseworkers" to interview 250 families within one ward of a Midwest city to determine their library interests and needs. The cost of eliciting and delivering these services was compared to the cost of on-site service, that is, traditional library service.

New strategy with new media was used to bring a formerly inaccessible group into the Right to Read library program. For instance, for children with identified learning disabilities, a media center was established in the public library; an array of learning aids was used in six-week series to effect learning breakthroughs.

Some LSCA projects, large and small, expressed new sensitivity to human needs. In Appalachia a library story hour regularly engaged the children whose parents wait in line next door for their food stamps.

Responsiveness to disadvantaged citizens who live in geographical, cultural, or linguistic isolation or blight was demonstrated. Bilingual centers were established in many parts of the country, with media and programs to build on the language, culture, and pride of Spanish-speaking people. Also, The "Biblioteca Ambulante" reached migrant families working in one fertile western valley.

Community responsibility in planning and operating LSCA supported services was exhibited. In a blighted area of New York, a citizen-planned library and cultural center continued to operate with

---

*Chief, Services and Facilities Branch, Division of Library Programs, Bureau of Libraries and Educational Technology, U.S. Office of Education, Washington, D.C.

[1] See article, "The Library Services and Construction Act, As Amended," 1971 *Bowker Annual*, p. 125.

maximum community direction and staffing, immediately responding to neighborhood information and education needs.

Projects were being designed with, rather than for, blacks, chicanos, Indian Americans, and other ethnic and racial groups, and being staffed with members of the group being served wherever possible. State recruitment programs and the composition of state advisory councils reflected the movement to include the participation of ethnic and racial minorities in state and local library development.

Reports attest to the growing number of programs supported by the Library Services and Construction Act, Title I, that are addressed to critical national priorities. These include the right to read effort to eliminate illiteracy and increase the ability and desire to read, drug abuse education, career development, early childhood education, and environmental and ecological education.

Although the percentage of federal support for library programs has not been high, it has generated a large percentage of the imaginative, user-related programs; it has helped extend the public library as a community learning and information center.

TITLE II — PUBLIC LIBRARY CONSTRUCTION

In fiscal year 1971, $8,570,604 from LSCA funds was obligated for 119 construction projects. These funds, including $4,337,133 in fiscal year 1970 carryover funds, were supplemented by $725,503 from the Appalachian Regional Development Act of 1965 plus $20,000 from Public Works and Economic Development Act, and matched with $34,435,353 from state and local funds, chiefly local. Total obligation for the 119 projects in fiscal year 1971 was $43,751,460.

During the seven-year period of public library construction funding under LSCA, 1,684 projects have been approved by the states for a total obligation of $147 million from LSCA, $8 million from Appalachian funds, and $378 million from state and local funds.

TITLE III — INTERLIBRARY COOPERATION

Of the 56 states and territories, 52 submitted annual programs for fiscal year 1971 under Title III, obligating $1,132,514 of $2,281,000 appropriated. Program activities included (1) identification and location of library resources available in a state or region; (2) establishment or expansion of interlibrary loan and reference networks to include all types of libraries and information centers and, in some states, regional medical libraries and technical information centers; (3) expansion or establishment of processing centers using modern technology and equipment; and (4) coordination of the acquisition of materials among types of libraries within a geographic area.

TITLE IV, PART A — STATE INSTITUTIONAL LIBRARY SERVICES

The regulations governing the Library Services and Construction Act state that "State Institutional Library Services . . . means the providing of books and other library materials, and of library services to (1) inmates, patients, or residents of penal institutions, reformatories, residential training schools, orphanages, or general or special institutions or hospitals operated or substantially supported by the state, and (2) students in residential schools for the handicapped (including mentally retarded, hard of hearing, deaf, speech impaired, visually handicapped, seriously emotionally disturbed, crippled or other health impaired persons, who by reason thereof require special education) operated or substantially supported by the state."

Under Title IV-A, 53 of the 56 states and territories submitted annual programs in fiscal year 1971, obligating $1,966,552 of the $2,094,000 available in federal funds for the purpose of establishing and improving library services for residents in state institutions. Funds were used to develop library services in institutions; demonstrate the benefits of good library service and the role of the library in the institution's total program; develop staff through in-service training and attendance at meetings, workshops, and institutes; add consultants to the state library; purchase library equipment and materials; improve and enlarge library quarters; contract with local public libraries; and develop cooperative networks among institutional and other libraries.

A list of services cannot convey the impact which Title IV-A is having on residents and staffs of institutions and on the library profession. Capable, enthusiastic, service-minded people are entering the field of institutional librarianship. Attractive libraries, well-stocked with multimedia materials, with a minimum of restrictive regulations and a maximum of accessibility, are becoming integral parts of their institutions and are making important contributions to educational, rehabilitative, treatment and training programs.

Noteworthy trends include marked improvement of library services to (1) inmates in prison and youth camps as well as in major correctional institutions; (2) prisoners needing legal reference materials; (3) residents in institutions for the mentally retarded and the mentally ill, and to (4) the physically handicapped in hospitals and homes for aged and chronically ill persons. An increasing number of institution libraries sponsor group bibliotherapy sessions, reading and discussion groups, creative writing clubs, storytelling and reading aloud activities, and field trips to public libraries and museums.

TITLE IV, PART B — LIBRARY SERVICES TO THE PHYSICALLY HANDICAPPED

Regulations governing the Library Services and Construction Act state that "Library Services to the Physically Handicapped means . . . provision of library services through public or other nonprofit libraries, agencies, or organizations, to physically handicapped persons, including the blind and visually handicapped, certified by competent authority as unable to read or to use conventional printed materials as a result of physical limitations."

Under Title IV-B, 51 of the 56 states and territories submitted annual programs obligating $1,233,550 of the $1,334,000 appropriated in fiscal year 1971 for the purpose of establishing and improving library services to the physically handicapped. Since many physically handicapped persons are limited socially and economically, Title IV-B programs are planned to help counteract these conditions. States continued to establish and strengthen libraries for the physically handicapped in cooperation with the Division for the Blind and Physically Handicapped, Library of Congress. They purchased specialized library equipment and materials; provided consultant services; conducted in-service training programs and enabled personnel to attend meetings, workshops, and institutes; established recording programs; encouraged local libraries to develop services for handicapped persons; and worked with state and local agencies and many volunteer groups on projects to reach the handicapped and publicize the services available to them.

Among the heartwarming results of Title IV-B are (1) the growing cooperation among individuals, agencies, and organizations in finding handicapped persons eligible for specialized library services, demonstrating talking books on tape, large-print books, and other materials and equipment to them, and helping them register for service; (2) the increased number of community libraries involved in finding and serving the handicapped; (3) the number of summer reading programs now expanded to include handicapped children; and (4) the development of educational and public relations techniques such as speakers' bureaus, slide-tape or film presentations of services for the handicapped, "traveling" exhibits, and a Talking Bookmobile, often manned by volunteers, which is scheduled throughout the state at fairs, festivals, schools and colleges, Indian reservations, hospitals, nursing homes, senior citizen centers, and shopping centers, and which, on occasion, serves as a lending library for the handicapped.

TABLE 1 STATE ALLOTMENTS AND MATCHING REQUIREMENTS FOR TITLES I AND II LIBRARY SERVICES AND CONSTRUCTION ACT, FY 1972

States and Outlying Areas	Title I Federal Allotment[1]	Title I State and Local Matching	Title II Federal Allotment[2]	Title II State and Local Matching
TOTALS	$46,568,500	$47,470,639	$ 9,500,000	$ 9,307,848
Alabama	801,520	424,233	170,495	90,241
Alaska	252,774	376,800	106,185	158,286
Arizona	509,562	410,723	136,279	109,845
Arkansas	535,902	276,070	139,366	71,794
California	3,684,797	5,160,131	508,399	711,953
Colorado	585,496	552,052	145,178	136,885
Connecticut	729,574	1,235,873	162,063	274,530
Delaware	295,726	376,378	111,219	141,552
District of Columbia	332,124	598,456	115,484	208,092
Florida	1,385,770	1,216,126	238,966	209,712
Georgia	1,001,565	697,443	193,939	135,050
Hawaii	334,465	366,132	115,159	126,719
Idaho	324,526	214,106	114,594	75,603
Illinois	2,141,046	3,010,653	327,480	460,489
Indiana	1,107,070	1,105,742	206,304	206,057
Iowa	693,391	646,754	157,823	147,208
Kansas	592,798	540,442	146,034	133,136
Kentucky	762,250	474,767	165,893	103,326
Louisiana	836,278	520,876	174,568	108,730
Maine	373,542	261,842	120,338	84,353
Maryland	885,043	1,078,229	180,283	219,635
Massachusetts	1,193,608	1,552,844	216,445	281,588
Michigan	1,750,025	2,051,897	281,654	330,239
Minnesota	864,552	829,983	177,882	170,770
Mississippi	587,182	302,487	145,376	74,891
Missouri	1,016,903	917,108	195,737	176,528
Montana	321,278	239,612	114,213	85,181
Nebraska	459,143	424,334	130,370	120,487
Nevada	285,358	405,582	110,003	156,348
New Hampshire	328,835	297,757	115,099	104,221
New Jersey	1,451,913	1,994,356	246,717	338,892
New Mexico	377,443	241,214	120,795	77,198
New York	3,376,997	5,137,871	472,327	718,613

Continued

[1] Distribution of $46,568,500 with a minimum allotment of $200,000 to the 50 states, District of Columbia, and Puerto Rico, and $40,000 to the other outlying areas; the remainder distributed on the basis of the total population, April 1, 1970. Matching funds computed on the basis of FY 1972–1973 "Federal Share" percentages.

Beginning with fiscal year 1972, funds for Title IV (Part A and Part B) are consolidated under Title I.

[2] Distribution of $9,500,000 with a minimum allotment of $100,000 to the 50 states, District of Columbia, and Puerto Rico, and $20,000 to the other outlying areas; the remainder distributed on the basis of the total population, April 1, 1970. Matching funds computed on the basis of FY 1972–1973 "Federal Share" percentage.

TABLE 1   Continued

States and Outlying Areas	Title I Federal Allotment[1]	Title I State and Local Matching	Title II Federal Allotment[2]	Title II State and Local Matching
North Carolina	1,087,577	690,963	204,019	129,618
North Dakota	307,891	204,748	112,644	74,908
Ohio	2,060,365	2,122,268	318,025	327,579
Oklahoma	646,971	458,773	152,383	108,056
Oregon	565,258	535,751	142,806	135,351
Pennsylvania	2,259,795	2,237,310	341,396	337,999
Rhode Island	365,868	405,517	119,439	132,383
South Carolina	652,431	350,692	153,022	82,252
South Dakota	316,361	220,208	113,637	79,099
Tennessee	885,352	536,900	180,319	109,351
Texas	2,155,499	1,692,919	329,174	258,532
Utah	385,001	266,549	121,681	84,243
Vermont	277,672	220,663	109,103	86,703
Virginia	1,011,855	817,901	195,145	157,739
Washington	795,408	905,272	169,779	193,229
West Virginia	504,629	281,030	135,701	75,572
Wisconsin	971,588	944,004	190,426	185,020
Wyoming	258,056	215,441	106,804	89,166
American Samoa	44,850	23,104	20,568	10,596
Guam	55,182	28,427	21,779	11,219
Puerto Rico	673,654	347,034	155,510	80,111
Virgin Islands	51,038	26,292	21,294	10,970
Trust Territory	57,743	—	22,079	—

TABLE 2 FEDERAL ALLOTMENTS FOR TITLE III LIBRARY SERVICES AND CONSTRUCTION ACT, FY 1972

States and Outlying Areas	Title III Federal Allotment[1]	States and Outlying Areas	Title III Federal Allotment[1]
TOTAL	$2,640,500		
Alabama	48,695	Nevada	41,234
Alaska	40,763	New Hampshire	41,862
Arizona	44,475	New Jersey	58,096
Arkansas	44,855	New Mexico	42,565
California	90,372	New York	85,923
Colorado	45,572	North Carolina	52,830
Connecticut	47,655	North Dakota	41,560
Delaware	41,384	Ohio	66,891
District of Columbia	41,910	Oklahoma	46,461
Florida	57,140	Oregon	45,280
Georgia	51,587	Pennsylvania	69,774
Hawaii	41,944	Rhode Island	42,398
Idaho	41,800	South Carolina	46,540
Illinois	68,058	South Dakota	41,682
Indiana	53,112	Tennessee	49,907
Iowa	47,132	Texas	68,266
Kansas	45,678	Utah	42,674
Kentucky	48,127	Vermont	41,123
Louisiana	49,197	Virginia	51,735
Maine	42,509	Washington	48,607
Maryland	49,902	West Virginia	44,403
Massachusetts	54,363	Wisconsin	51,153
Michigan	62,405	Wyoming	40,839
Minnesota	49,606	American Samoa	10,070
Mississippi	45,597	Guam	10,219
Missouri	51,808	Puerto Rico	46,847
Montana	41,753	Virgin Islands	10,160
Nebraska	43,746	Trust Territory	10,256

[1]Distribution of $2,640,500 with a minimum allotment of $40,000 to the 50 states, District of Columbia, and Puerto Rico, and $10,000 to the other outlying areas; the remainder distributed on the basis of total population, April 1, 1970. The Federal Share is "100" percent.

ESEA TITLE II PROGRAM ACCOMPLISHMENTS, 1966–1972

by

Harry L. Phillips*

The ESEA Title II program is concerned with printed and audiovisual materials for use in school libraries, classrooms, laboratories, and outside of school; it is also concerned with textbooks, but it is not a simple acquisitions program.

PARTICIPATION

ESEA Title II is to benefit children and teachers in public and private elementary and secondary schools and is to be administered in an equitable fashion. "Equitable" refers to the participation of the private school sector as compared with the public school, and the percentage of private school children and teachers benefiting from the use of the materials bought with Title II money compared with the number eligible regularly equals or surpasses the proportion of those participating in public schools. In each case, the number has been very high — above 90 percent.

Teachers, librarians, audiovisual coordinators, other support personnel, and administrators — almost the entire school staff, in fact — have benefited from the use of materials bought under Title II. With these media, teachers have been able to enrich and diversify their instruction with printed, and especially with audiovisual materials. Besides that, many have used review collections in district and regional centers and professional materials in those centers and in their own schools to good effect.

Working relationships among personnel representing public and private school interests both in state and local educational agencies have become much closer. In some cases, there had been few or no occasions prior to ESEA to work together; the consequences of cooperating on advisory committees and in workshops and other training sessions sponsored by states and school systems have been gratifying and profitable to both sectors.

QUANTITY AND QUALITY OF MATERIALS

A great deal of emphasis has been placed on the quality, appropriateness, and use of the materials bought. An evaluative survey of Title II showed that collections of both printed and audiovisual materials in schools have advanced from "poor" or "fair" to "good" or "excellent" in relevance to the children and the units of study or curricula, in currency, and in quality of format. Media centers formerly with few audiovisual materials have not only increased their holdings, but have also added new types of items. School libraries, especially those in elementary schools, with only printed materials began to integrate audiovisual media into their collections.

These advances have not been achieved automatically with the addition of the millions of items bought with Title II funds. Old notions and old standards are hard to dislodge. Yet many schools which had been forced to retain out-of-date, inappropriate, and worn-out materials in their libraries (including in some cases old textbooks) in order to meet quantitative state accreditation standards have been able to discard ancient reference books and periodicals, and other outmoded and unsuitable items. Regular weeding of collections has become a much more frequent practice, even for schools in districts with only average financial resources.

Title II coordinators in state and local education agencies can claim much of the credit for improving the ways school library and other instructional materials, especially print, are chosen. Mandating or encouraging the use of standard selection tools has helped in small isolated school districts which often have no pro-

---

*Director, Division of State Agency Cooperation, Bureau of Elementary and Secondary Education, U.S. Office of Education, Washington, D.C.

fessionally trained media personnel or whose staff do not have an opportunity to review titles before requesting them. Ordering by a school administrator with a publisher's representative sitting at his elbow or ordering sight unseen from a commercial catalog is now nearly a thing of the past. Use of state or school district lists from which school library books must be selected is also less common than in pre-ESEA days. The involvement of teachers in choosing materials is assured by means of the application form used in some states, and encouraged, along with other good selection practices, through in-service activities conducted by the states or local school systems.

ACCESSIBILITY

Title II staff in state departments of education and local education agencies have tried to make sure that the children for whom the materials were bought have the opportunity to use them freely. Almost all Title II programs are so operated that the items requested for use in an individual school are placed there and circulated from the media center or from classrooms. New media centers, especially in elementary schools, have been started with the materials bought with Title II funds forming the nucleus of their collections. Money for staff, equipment, and supplies comes, of course, from state and local sources; sometimes other federal sources are tapped, too. Lending audiovisual materials and equipment to children to use individually in school or at home is no longer rare, and having more titles and multiple copies of books has made it possible to liberalize loan policies. Service time in media centers during the noon hour and before and after school has been extended in many schools; some centers — still too few — remain open evenings and Saturdays. Certain kinds of audiovisual materials like films and some printed items that are seldom used in a single school but are needed in several buildings in the school system are often loaned from a district or regional media center, sometimes by a pickup and delivery service. These centers or special curriculum centers frequently house professional materials for teachers, administrators, and other school staff, along with selection tools, supplementary materials, and textbooks — all handy for review. Title II funds have been used to start and add to collections of materials like these.

OTHER SIGNIFICANT EFFECTS OF TITLE II
Changes in Teaching and Learning

ESEA Title II was the first federal program specifically designating funds for school library resources. As such, it was greeted with enthusiasm by state and local library supervisors, who immediately saw its potential for causing change in teaching and learning. School librarians, school administrators, and local school boards, always hard pressed to stretch available funds for library books and audiovisual materials, saw at once how much difference could be made by having materials to supplement those bought by the district or school.

Before 1965, many administrators and teachers, especially in districts with limited financial resources, could not modify organizational and teaching patterns because they simply did not have enough instructional materials in the schools. Ungraded classrooms, flexible scheduling, or team teaching cannot work without lots of materials. Some shifts away from the self-contained classroom and traditional teaching methods are credited to the additional printed and audiovisual materials made available by Title II. Even where teaching approaches have not changed much, learning in several subject areas has increased, and interest is higher because the larger amounts and greater variety of media allow in-depth exploration; less reliance on textbooks alone is now the pattern. Courses new for some schools have been started, again because of the availability of enough materials, in such areas as ecology, career, drug, and environmental education; the Pacific rim; studies about the cultural heritage of minority and ethnic groups; and special provisions for the gifted.

Introduction of New Kinds of Materials

The effects of putting into schools kinds of materials they have never before had is dramatic, and Title II is directly responsible. Paperbacks are often mentioned, as are transparencies, picture sets, art prints, microfilm, and professional journals. Surprising as it may seem, some schools, elementary and small rural ones in particular, now have periodicals, filmstrips, maps and globes, disc recordings, and even trade books for the first time. Changes brought about by differences in quantity, use, and lending policies of audiovisual media are equally outstanding.

Increase in State and Local Effort

During the first years of Title II, before the cutbacks in local financial support to schools, state and local efforts for acquiring instructional materials were not only being maintained, but were increasing. This increase was due, in part, to the stimulation of Title II. Parents observed their children bringing home for the first time bright new attractive books that absorbed their interest. In parts of the United States and the outlying areas, children are in small schools and are geographically or culturally isolated. The materials bought under Title II and loaned to these children were sometimes the first ones that had ever been in the home. Teachers, too, were motivated and able to try new teaching techniques, for example, through the use of multimedia materials.

Attitude Changes

Since the early 1940s, school libraries have been referred to as "the heart of the school." Many times school librarians and teachers have felt that the heart needed a transplant. Title II has served, if not as a transplant, at least as a pacemaker. Not only has it benefited instruction, but it has also increased the prestige of media personnel and school library programs and raised the morale of school librarians and teachers. The old image of school libraries as places to store books and of librarians as the guardians of such places has been replaced by the media center as the instructional hub of the school.

In addition, children have changed their feelings about the school library; they are using it differently and more extensively. They are really excited about the new materials, and their attitudes toward reading have improved significantly in a substantial number of cases. Numbers of state and local education agencies have increased their financial support for instructional materials because they are now more aware of the central role of media as an agent for educational change. That number would be greater if there were more money for education and less competition for the limited funds available.

PROGRAM MANAGEMENT
Office of Education

During the first years of the Office of Education's administration of the national ESEA Title II program, most of the time had to be spent on developing regulations, guidelines, state plans (and reviewing and negotiating them), and disseminating information about Title II. Policy questions about services to private school pupils and other matters had to be settled, and basic program development took a great deal of staff time. Much of the groundwork was done through national, regional, and individual conferences, by telephone, and during onsite program reviews which included school visits.

Since fiscal year 1967, there have been no substantive amendments to Title II legislation, and since most operational problems have been ironed out, it has become possible for the Office of Education Title II staff to spend more time on activities to help the states increase the effectiveness of their programs and make them genuine agents for educational change. Instead of a general approach, the greater concentration of funds on fewer projects and the spread of special projects have made the most difference.

Beginning with regional conferences in fiscal year 1970, OE staff have spent a great deal of time and effort working with the states on a systems approach to management, using management by objective (MBO) as a vehicle. The *ESEA Title II Guide for a Description of Program and Operational Procedures* (POP Document) is one means of helping states make better assessments of need and planning. The *Guide* and the MBO method of operation are both, in part, outcomes of State Management Reviews (SMRs). The SMRs (coordinated reviews of state department of education administration of federal programs) are now in their fourth year; team members include Title II program officers. Another purpose of the *Guide* is to assure that OE and state priorities, especially those on the Right to Read, are given the required attention.

State Department of Education

Administration of Title II in the states is not a simple matter, but it is being done with a minimum of paper work and a maximum of good will and diligence.

States which have used Title II directly as a means of improving their services in curriculum and instruction have obtained the most value from the program. They have done this in many ways. Revision, or even initial development in some cases, of school media center standards for materials, facilities, staff, and services is a major one. Another is the development and use of an application form showing a close relationship among the materials to be purchased to the curriculum or subject area they support, and to the way materials will be used in teaching and learning. In-service training sessions directed by state and local education agency personnel have focused on wise selection and use of materials in newer ways, as in the individual use of audiovisual media by pupils. State staff are generous with their time and help to individuals; generally they make visits to both public and private schools to work with librarians, teachers, and administrators. Their telephones ring constantly, and they are pleased that they do, because these requests for their services show that exciting things are happening in instruction.

Shifts in emphasis in the Title II program are coming about, with stress on reading and other high-priority concerns. There is also more time now to spend working on the problems of evaluation — and very difficult they are, too — and on disseminating information on good practices and successful Title II projects. Both OE and state departments of education are stressing the improvement of dissemination practices.

Due to initiative from the Title II coordinator, formulas for distributing materials are becoming more sophisticated and reflect true relative need more accurately. Combining Title II funds with those from more than one other federal, state, and local program in order to make best use of all possible resources is a thing of the past.

SPECIAL PURPOSE PROJECTS

A great deal of attention is paid to developing special-purpose programs which serve as demonstrations of excellence in the use of good materials to visitors from other school districts and states. It is in these projects that a management-by-objectives approach is the furthest along and where dissemination of information about Title II impact has been easiest.

Concentration of funds in a limited number of projects rather than in a general distribution of smaller and smaller amounts resulted in greater measurable program impact. Money has been set aside in about 30 states for bigger money projects in school units; new courses of study, serving specific kinds of children; or demonstrating what difference an abundance of high quality materials makes. These projects are variously called special-purpose grants, Open-Door or Phase II projects, or demonstration school media centers. Good results in these projects have had tremendous spin-off in the school environment and in the community.

TITLE II AND THE RIGHT TO READ PROGRAM

Title II has always been a reading program — reading being broadly defined to include motivation as well as skills, reading in the content areas, for pleasure and information, and viewing and listening. Title II has stimulated interest in reading, particularly for nonreaders and those with reading difficulties. It has provided paperback books for reluctant readers, who are often not attracted to hardcover books. The program is also responsible for putting more high-interest, low-vocabulary materials in schools.

Since President Nixon's Message on Educational Reform on March 3, 1970, Office of Education staff and the state departments of education cooperatively have made special efforts to strengthen Title II's support of the Right to Read. Three conferences were held in 1970-1971 to further this objective. They have also cooperated in the collection and dissemination of information on reading projects over the nation supported by Title II funds.

Five issues of a bulletin, *ESEA Title II and the Right to Read: Notable Reading Projects,* have been published. They, and the issues which will follow, are based on reports from the states, describing exemplary projects and telling where more information may be had.

EVALUATION

The Office of Education, state departments of education, and local school districts have cooperated in evaluation of the Title II program by three approaches:

1. *The ESEA Title II Evaluative Survey.* This survey collected data from a nationwide sample of school districts on program participation, expenditures, impact, and a number of other factors. A preliminary report was issued in November 1970 (see the 1971 *Bowker Annual,* pp. 131-138). The full report is soon to be published.

2. Case studies of nine elementary school media centers in three inner cities which, prior to 1965, had no media centers.

3. Case studies of eight school media programs where Title II special-purpose grants, in combination with other factors, brought ideal, or nearly ideal, conditions in the provision of materials. These case studies measured results in optimum conditions, and found very significant changes brought about in teaching and learning.

Currently, the Office of Education is beginning a new thrust to assist state departments of education and local school districts in developing sophisticated methods of evaluation. Regional conferences held from October to November in 1971 dealt with this subject. Some training programs are in the planning stage.

CONTINUING PROBLEMS

Title II is a fairly complex program to operate. Two of the requirements built into the legislation continue to be troublesome: maintenance of effort, and distribution of school library resources, textbooks, and other printed and published instructional materials on the basis of relative need.

Maintenance of the level of state, local, and private school expenditures for materials has been a problem for two or three years. Recent defeats of special local school tax levies, budgets, and bond elections, coming on top of cutbacks in state aid to education, add up to a genuine economic squeeze on the schools. It is unfortunate but true that when cuts must be made, they are often made in the budget for printed and audiovisual materials.

It is not surprising that criteria and formulas for distributing materials in the three categories are still underdeveloped. Although states had had limited amounts of federal funds for education to administer before ESEA, the concept of relative need was a new one for state department of education administrators. The immediate solution for many officials was to spread money throughout all school systems of the state, using the state equalization formula or other economic factors plus a per-pupil amount as a base. Experience in operating Title II, and better data on what materials were already in schools, made more sophisticated state formulas possible, but local school districts still lag behind in assessing needs in individual schools and allocating materials accordingly. The recent California court decision outlawing school financing based on local property tax has brought a widespread reexamination of state aid to education. It may serve also as a catalyst for applying true relative need measurement in Title II.

Years of inadequate spending for school library resources have created a tremendous materials gap which Title II moneys alone have been unable to close. Many schools still do not meet 1960 ALA Standards, and the number of those meeting or surpassing ALA-DAVI 1969 Standards could be readily counted.

Nobody associated with the Title II program is happy with these problems, yet nobody is discouraged by them either. They see their job as finding new ways to solve them.

BIBLIOGRAPHY

Descriptive Case Studies of Nine Elementary School Media Centers in Three Inner Cities, Title II, Elementary and Secondary Education Act of 1965: School Library Resources, Textbooks, and Other Instructional Materials. Washington, D.C.: Department of Health, Education, and Welfare, Office of Education, 1969. 200 pp. (OE-30021)

Emphasis on Excellence in School Media Programs, Special-Purpose Grant Programs, Title II, Elementary and Secondary Education Act of 1965: School Library Resources, Textbooks, and Other Instructional Materials. Washington, D.C.: U.S. Government Printing Office, 1969. 227 pp. (OE-20123)

ESEA Title II and The Right to Read: Notable Reading Projects. Washington, D.C.: U.S. Government Printing Office, March 1971, May 1971, July 1971, September 1971. 15 pp., 13 pp., 16 pp., 15 pp. (OE-30040, OE-30041, OE-72-15)

The ESEA Title II Evaluative Survey: A Preliminary Report. Washington, D.C.: Department of Health, Education, and Welfare, Office of Education, November 1970. 17 pp.

SUMMARY OF TITLE II-A GRANTS FOR ACADEMIC LIBRARY RESOURCES UNDER THE HIGHER EDUCATION ACT OF 1965

by

Frank A. Stevens[*]

In fiscal year 1971 (July 1, 1970–June 30, 1971), academic libraries serving a combined enrollment of 1,918,119 students on 548 campuses were awarded grants ranging from $3,520 to $94,061 for the acquisition of library resources. These grants were made from a total appropriation of $9,893,400 for Title II-A of the Higher Education Act of 1965 (P.L. 89-329), and must be expended or obligated by June 30, 1972.

There are three categories of grants: basic, supplemental, and special purpose.

Basic grants, which are limited to a maximum of $5,000, in fiscal year 1971 went to 548 institutions and totaled $2,698,383, which was matched dollar for dollar by the applicant institution from local funds.

Supplemental grants, which are related to enrollment, programs, and demonstrated need, were made to 531 institutions and totaled $5,574,730, which required no matching funds but did require eligibility for the receipt of a basic grant of at least $1,501. For the first time in the history of the program, supplemental grants were awarded up to $10

---

[*]Chief, Training and Resources Branch, Division of Library Programs, Bureau of Libraries and Educational Technology, U.S. Office of Education, Washington, D.C. 20202.

DISTRIBUTION ANALYSIS BY LEVEL OF HIGHER EDUCATION GRANTS MADE FOR TITLE II-A OF HEA – FISCAL YEAR 1971*

Prepared by Othello Jones, Grants Management Specialist, Division of Library Programs, Bureau of Libraries and Educational Technology

	1 Year Beyond 12	Junior College	4-Year	University	Total
Institutions Funded	0	303	131	172	606
No. of Grants	0	595	251	335	1,195[2]
Enrollment	0	609,417[1]	196,784[1]	1,111,918	1,918,119[1]
Percent	0	31.77	10.26	57.97	100.00
Basic	0	$1,379,043	$ 591,840	$ 727,500	$2,698,383
Supplemental	$0	$2,140,803	$ 819,740	$2,614,187	$5,574,730
Special Purpose					
A	$0	$ 295,910	$ 114,127	$ 254,250	$ 664,287
B	$0	$ 22,500	$ 15,000	$ 163,500	$ 201,000
C	0	0[2]	0[2]	0[2]	0[2]
Total	$0	$ 318,410[2]	$ 129,127[2]	$ 417,750[2]	$ 865,287[2]
TOTAL	$0	$3,838,256[2]	$1,540,707[2]	$3,759,437[2]	$9,893,400
Percent	0	42.00	16.86	41.14	100.00

*For distribution analysis for fiscal years 1967–1970, see the 1971 *Bowker Annual*, p. 140.
[1]Seventeen new institutions enrollment not shown.
[2]Fourteen combinations received $755,000 Special Purpose C grants undistributed.

per student, the maximum allowed by the statute.

The significant characteristic of the basic/supplemental grant program for fiscal year 1971 was the effort to concentrate funds on those institutions in greatest need. This was accomplished by limiting basic grants only to those institutions which qualified for a supplemental grant. The qualifying score for a supplemental grant was 21 points or more on a 60-point scale of need. This scale of need was based on five criteria: volume deficiency of the collection as contrasted with national standards, degree to which the student body was economically disadvantaged, age of the library, and participation in Title III and/or Title IV of the Higher Education Act of 1965 (Strengthening Developing Institutions and Special Services for Disadvantaged Students, respectively). By attaching a value of $.18 per point, the Office of Education was able to award a full $10 per student to institutions receiving a supplemental grant score of 60 points; institutions receiving a lesser score were awarded a proportionately lower per student allocation. The funds available for basic/supplemental grants were exhausted at the 21-point scoring level. Over 1,600 institutions received a supplemental grant score of 20 points or less, disqualifying them from both a basic and a supplemental grant award. The accompanying table summarizes the awards; it can be readily discerned how the funds were distributed by type of institution and type of grant.

The largest basic/supplemental grant award, of $94,061, went to Northeastern University, Boston, Massachusetts; the lowest basic/supplemental grant award, of $3,520, went to John H. Gupton College, Nashville, Tennessee.

In fiscal year 1971, special purpose grants were restored, having been dropped in fiscal year 1970 due to a reduced level of funding and due to the effort to support as many institutions as possible through the basic/supplemental grant program. Over 600 special purpose grant applications were received in fiscal year 1971 — 500 for Type A (special program needs), 50 for Type B (sharing of special institutional collections), and 60 for Type C (combinations of institutions of higher education). Seventy-six Type A grants were awarded, totaling $664,287 and averaging $10,000 apiece; 26 Type B grants were awarded, totaling $201,000 and averaging $20,000 apiece; and 14 Type C grants were awarded, totaling $755,000 but varying in size, with the Center for Research Libraries, Chicago, Illinois, receiving the largest grant of $125,000. It is significant to note that, with respect to Type A grants to individual institutions, the largest dollar share went to junior and community colleges situated in urban areas and characterized by socially and economically disadvantaged students.

For fiscal year 1972, present plans call for an even more concentrated approach to the distribution of Title II-A funds, with major revisions in the program criteria for supplemental and special purpose grants. The limitation of basic grants only to those institutions receiving a qualifying score on the supplemental grant criteria will continue. The appropriation for Title II-A in fiscal year 1972 is $11 million.

The accompanying table provides a distribution analysis for Title II-A for fiscal year 1971. Title II-A is administered in Washington, D.C., by the U.S. Office of Education, with the advice and counsel of a special Advisory Council appointed by the Commissioner of Education.

HIGHER EDUCATION ACT OF 1965, TITLE II-B: LIBRARY EDUCATION

by

Frank A. Stevens[*] and Frances Yvonne Hicks[**]

The Higher Education Act of 1965 authorizes a program of federal financial assistance to institutions of higher education to assist in training persons in librarianship. Grants may be used to assist institutions in covering the costs of courses of training or study, to upgrade or update the competencies of persons serving all types of libraries, information centers, or instructional material centers offering library type services, and those serving as educators. Grants are also made for fellowships at the master's, post-master's, and doctoral levels for training in librarianship and information science. The implementation of this legislation is carried out through the institute and the fellowship program.

FELLOWSHIP PROGRAM

For the academic year 1971–1972, a total of 122 fellowships have been awarded to 19 library and information science education programs under the Higher Education Act of 1965, as amended.

Table 1 represents a six-year review of the fellowship program.

Grants were awarded to provide continuing fellowships only at the doctoral and post-master's level. Twenty continuing traineeships were also awarded to the State University of New York at Albany at the undergraduate level, as part of an experimental program to recruit minority group/disadvantaged persons at the end of the sophomore year and support them in three phases through the graduate year. This experimental group will complete its program in June 1973. The reduction in the level of fellowship grant awards represents the next-to-last phasing-out period of the fellowship pro-

---

[*]Chief, Training and Resources Branch, Division of Library Programs, Bureau of Libraries and Educational Technology, U.S. Office of Education, Washington, D.C. 20202.
[**]Administrative Librarian, Training and Resources Branch.

TABLE 1 LIBRARY EDUCATION FELLOWSHIP PROGRAM

Acad. Year	Number of Institutions	D[1]	PM[2]	M[3]	Total	Fiscal Year
'66/67	24	52	25	62	139	'67
67/68	38	116	58	327	501	68
68/69	51	168	47	494	709	69
69/70	56	193	30	379	602	70
70/71	48	171	15	200	386	71
71/72	19	116	6	—	122	72

[1]Doctoral fellowships.
[2]Post-master's fellowships.
[3]Master's fellowships.

gram. Fiscal year 1972 will be the final year for the fellowship program, and grant awards will be made only for final renewals of continuing fellowships.

A continuing fellowship for a student at the doctoral or post-master's level provides a basic annual allowance of $5,000. If summer study is required, an additional stipend of $170 per week, not to exceed a total of $1,020, is made. In addition, $600 is granted for each dependent for the academic year; $120 for the summer session, if any; and travel expenses to and from the institution of attendance for the fellow only.

The selection of students as fellowship recipients was, and has been throughout the history of the program, entirely the responsibility of the institution receiving the grant award.

Fellowship grants were awarded to the following institutions:

California: University of California, Berkeley, doctoral, 13; total, 13. University of Southern California, University Park, doctoral, 7; total, 7.

Florida: Florida State University, Tallahassee, doctoral, 9; total, 9.

Illinois: University of Chicago, doctoral, 7; post-master's, 5; total, 12. University of Illinois, Urbana, doctoral, 5; total, 5.

Indiana: Indiana University, Bloomington, doctoral, 11; total, 11.

Maryland: University of Maryland, College Park, doctoral, 2; total, 2.

Michigan: University of Michigan, Ann Arbor, doctoral, 10; total, 10.

Minnesota: University of Minnesota, Minneapolis, doctoral, 3; total, 3.

New Jersey: Rutgers, The State University, New Brunswick, doctoral, 9; total, 9.

New York: Columbia University, New York City, doctoral, 9; total, 9. State University of New York at Albany, traineeships, 20. Syracuse University, doctoral, 2; total, 2.

North Carolina: University of North Carolina at Chapel Hill, doctoral, 1; post-master's, 1; total, 2.

Ohio: Case Western Reserve University, Cleveland, doctoral, 8; total, 8.

Oklahoma: University of Oklahoma, Norman, doctoral, 4; total, 4.

Pennsylvania: University of Pittsburgh, doctoral, 4; total, 4.

Texas: University of Texas at Austin, doctoral, 5; total, 5.

Washington: University of Washington, Seattle, doctoral, 2; total, 2.

Wisconsin: University of Wisconsin, Madison, doctoral, 5; total, 5.

Totals: Doctoral, 116; post-master's, 6; total, 122. This total does not include the 20 traineeships.

INSTITUTE PROGRAM

The institute program provides long- and short-term training and retraining opportunities for librarians and information scientists, and for persons desiring to enter the profession. Many institutes have given experienced librarians and information scientists the opportunity to update their skills and to advance themselves in a given problem or subject area. The institute program under the Higher Education Act reflects a legislative change which amended Section 1101 of the National Defense Education Act, formerly restricted to the training and retraining of school librarians. Section 225 of the Higher Education Act repealed Section 1101, and permitted the Office of Education to broaden the scope of library training to include all types of librarianship and information science activities.

In fiscal year 1971, the institute program was redirected dramatically to permit the Office of Education to focus on certain critical training needs and priority subject areas. Two key objectives were established.

The first objective is the training and retraining of a substantial number of the nation's librarians in the implementation of library, media, and information science programs in support of the following priorities: (a) training of minority and/or disadvantaged persons; (b) improvement of library service to minority and/or disadvantaged persons; (c) Right to Read; (d) early childhood; (e) drug abuse; (f) environmental/ecological education; (g) black and area studies librarianship; (h) training and retraining of junior and community college library educators; (i) training of paraprofessionals; (j) training of professionals in the effective utilization of paraprofessionals; (k) library education; (l) media programs.

The second objective is the support of several demonstration library training models designed to: (a) attract minority and low income group members into the library, media, and information science field as professionals and paraprofessionals; (b) train and retrain professionals to serve disadvantaged groups; (c) present alternatives for recruitment, training, and utilization of library personnel and manpower.

In fiscal year 1971, 98 proposals for institutes were received in support of the above objectives. From this total, 38 institutes were funded to train or retrain 1,557 participants. The length of the institutes varied from one day to 48 weeks; six of the institutes are multi-phased — that is, the programs are planned for two or more years of training activities. The average number of participants was 40.

For the first time since the inception of the institute program, grant funds were used for the recruitment and training of paraprofessionals. This thrust reflects the increasing complexity of tasks in information science and libraries, which requires the training of subprofessionals at a level of competence to relieve librarians, media specialists, and information scientists of subprofessional tasks, resulting in increased opportunity and economy in the utilization of human resources. Three such institutes were supported.

The recruitment of minority group persons and the disadvantaged also represented a dramatic new thrust in the institute program. The training models presented to the profession to implement the second objective built on the potential of libraries and media and information centers as employers of minority group disadvantaged persons and as primary social and educational agencies to improve service to the disadvantaged. They also provided the opportunity for library schools to innovate and experiment. Twelve institutes were supported in this area, resulting in the enrollment of 175 minority group disadvantaged persons who will enter the profession in 1972 and 1973. It is anticipated that this emphasis will have a marked influence on meeting the needs and problems of the disadvantaged using libraries and information centers, and will improve the capacity of the library profession to be responsive to such future needs. Contrasted with the past ten years, this represents a major shift in the use of Title II-B funds from that of general aid to library training institutions to categorical program support focusing on critical needs.

In the area of key priorities, three institutes were funded in support of the

TABLE 2   LIBRARY EDUCATION INSTITUTE PROGRAM

Academic Year	Participants	Institutions	Fiscal Year
'67/68	2,084	66	'68
68/69	3,101	91	69
69/70	1,347	46	70
70/71	1,557	38	71

Right to Read campaign, two in support of the improvement of library service related to environmental and ecological education, two in support of early childhood education, and one in support of drug abuse education.

Table 2 represents a four-year review of the institute program.

Institute participants are provided a weekly stipend of up to $75.00 in addition to an allowance of up to $15.00 per week for each dependent. In some instances, travel allowances were also made where severe economic deprivation justified it.

The following is the list of institutes for fiscal year 1971, conducted in the 1971–1972 academic year. The last line of each entry includes the beginning date and duration of the institute, the director, and the proposed number of participants.

ALABAMA
   Alabama Agricultural and Mechanical University, Huntsville
   Training in librarianship for drug education.
   June 7–July 23, 1971   Carl H. Marbury   30

   University of Alabama, University
   Right to Read: Alabama working in reading excellence.
   September 16–17, 1971   Ruth W. Waldrop   200

ARIZONA
   Arizona State University, Tempe
   Training for American Indians as school library media specialists.
   September 1, 1971–May 31, 1972   Vernon S. Gerlach   15

CALIFORNIA
   California State College at Long Beach
   Multimedia selection and production of environmental and ecological materials.
   August 1–August 14, 1971   Richard J. Johnson   30

   City College of San Francisco
   Training professionals in the effective use of paraprofessionals.
   July 19–30, 1971   Ethel S. Crockett   30

   United States International University, San Diego
   Leadership Training Institute — library institute program.
   May 11, 1971–June 30, 1972   Jack V. Edling   75

COLORADO
   Community College of Denver
   Retraining of middle managers in the utilization of paraprofessionals.
   October 2–16, 1971   Harry H. Robnett, Jr. 25

   University of Denver
   Utilization of library manpower.
   November 29–December 10, 1971   John Taylor Eastlick 20

GEORGIA
    Atlanta University, Atlanta
    Public library service to the urban disadvantaged.
    September 8, 1971–August 6, 1972   Virginia Lacy Jones   12

    Emory University, Atlanta
    Right to Read effort.
    December 3, 1971   A. Venable Lawson   75

HAWAII
    University of Hawaii, Honolulu
    The librarian in a pluralistic society.
    August 23, 1971–May 24, 1972   Joyce H. Haas   30

ILLINOIS
    University of Illinois, Urbana
    M.S. institute for members of minority groups.
    June 22, 1971–May 27, 1972   Terence Crowley   15

KENTUCKY
    University of Kentucky, Lexington
    Right to Read.
    Date to be announced.   Michael H. Harris   20

MARYLAND
    University of Maryland, College Park
    Improvement of library service to the disadvantaged.
    October 5, 1971–March 29, 1972   Robert L. Wright   50

MICHIGAN
    Wayne State University, Detroit
    Preparation for public library service to the disadvantaged.
    September 1971–August 1972   Genevieve M. Casey   20

    Western Michigan University, Kalamazoo
    Methods of disseminating environmental-ecological information.
    May 7–13, 1972   Hardy Carroll   25

MISSISSIPPI
    Rust College, Holly Springs
    Retraining of classroom teachers as school library media specialists.
    June 21–July 30, 1971   Johnny W. Jackson   30

NEW HAMPSHIRE
    University of New Hampshire, Durham
    The New England Network: Reaching the unreached.
    September 1, 1971–August 31, 1972   Barbara Conroy   180

    University of New Hampshire, Merrimack Valley Branch, Manchester
    Training in paraprofessional librarianship.
    September 1971–August 1972   Gordon O. Thayer   30

NEW JERSEY
    Rutgers University, New Brunswick
    Library education for educationally and economically disadvantaged
        students.
    September 13, 1971–August 8, 1972   Thomas Shaughnessy   15

NEW MEXICO
    University of New Mexico, Albuquerque
    Improvement of library services to Spanish-speaking Americans.
    September 13–24, 1971   Donald A. Riechmann   30

NEW YORK
  Columbia University, New York
  Library leadership development for inner city services.
  October 4, 1971–January 29, 1972   Miriam Braverman   20

  Queens College of the City University of New York, Flushing
  Library materials for minority groups.
  July 3–28, 1972   David Cohen   30

NORTH CAROLINA
  North Carolina Central University, Durham
  Public librarianship in service to young children.
  September 1971–August 1972   Annette Phinazee   15

OHIO
  Case Western Reserve University, Cleveland
  Model curriculum for library services to the disadvantaged.
  September 1, 1971–May 31, 1972   Alvin J. Goldwyn   20

  Ohio State University, Columbus
  Program for statewide library planning and evaluation.
  July 1, 1971–June 30, 1972   Daniel L. Stufflebeam 280

PENNSYLVANIA
  University of Pittsburgh, Pittsburgh
  Library service to inner city communities.
  July 13–30, 1971   Patrick R. Penland   25

SOUTH CAROLINA
  University of South Carolina, Columbia
  Information needs and library education; a curriculum model
    for the 1970s.
  September 1, 1971–August 31, 1972   Wayne Stewart Yenawine 11

  Voorhees College, Denmark
  Institute for paraprofessional library workers.
  June 14–August 6, 1971   Claude W. Green   30

SOUTH DAKOTA
  University of South Dakota, Vermillion
  Graduate study in library media.
  September 1, 1971–August 11, 1972   Dell M. Colwell   10

TENNESSEE
  East Tennessee State University, Johnson City
  School media program for rural disadvantaged youth.
  September 8, 1971–August 15, 1972   Elise D. Barrette   18

  Fisk University, Nashville
  Developing collections of black literature.
  June 21–July 30, 1971   Jessie Carney Smith   25
  Changing concepts and the school librarian.
  July 7–August 13, 1971   Eurydice W. Smith   25

  Tennessee Technological University, Cooksville
  Improved use of the media center in reading instruction.
  July 21, 1971–July 18, 1972   Jerry B. Ayers   19

WASHINGTON
  Highline Community College, Midway
  Training minority persons as paraprofessionals.
  September 27, 1971–June 8, 1972   Junius H. Morris   12

University of Washington, Seattle
Right to Read.
April 9–14, 1972   Spencer G. Shaw   30

WISCONSIN
University of Wisconsin, Madison
Library social action programs.
September 20, 1971–August 19, 1972   Margaret E. Monroe   14

University of Wisconsin, Milwaukee
Professional training for inner-city library services.
September 7, 1971–August 12, 1972   Laurence L. Sherrill   16

HIGHER EDUCATION ACT, TITLE II-B: LIBRARY AND INFORMATION SCIENCE RESEARCH

by

Paul C. Janaske*

Eighteen projects for research and demonstration in library and information science were funded by the Office of Education during fiscal year 1971 (July 1, 1970–June 30, 1971). The funds for this program are authorized by the Higher Education Act of 1965, Title II-B (PL 89-329) and the Cooperative Research Act, Title IV (PL 89-10). The program is administered within the Office of Education by the Division of Library Programs in the Bureau of Libraries and Educational Technology.

The major subject areas emphasized in the projects for fiscal year 1971 are: (1) Planning and Development; including such concepts as a survey of library services to the aging, a study of the informational needs of inner city citizens, and a system analysis of the library and information science statistical data system. (2) Disadvantaged; studies which include an analysis of the southwestern Spanish-speaking users and nonusers of library and information services, identification of the informational needs of the American Indian community, and a demonstration of the joint planning and implementation of library service between public and private schools and the public library in a large metropolitan setting. (3) Automated Data Processing; including projects such as the development of a computerized regional shared cataloging system and the development of an automated instructional materials handling program.

The Cooperative Research Act and the Higher Education Act authorize the Commissioner of Education to award grants to school districts, colleges and universities (including junior and community colleges and post-secondary vocational schools), state governments, and other public or private agencies and organizations for research and demonstration projects relating to the improvement of libraries or the improvement of training in librarianship. Table 2 lists all projects funded in 1971.

---

*Chief, Research and Program Development Branch, Division of Library Programs, Bureau of Libraries and Educational Technology, U.S. Office of Education, Washington, D.C. 20202.

TABLE 1 FACT SHEET*

	Fiscal Year 1971	Total (Fiscal Years 1967–1971)
Appropriation	$2,171,000	$14,442,000
Obligation	2,170,274	12,727,154
Projects	18	146
Subject Emphasis		
ADP: Information Retrieval	0	10
ADP: Operations	3	16
Education and Training	0	23
Microform Technology	0	12
Planning and Development	10	36
Readers Services	0	20
Technical Services	0	15
Networking	0	5
Disadvantaged	5	9
Sponsoring Organizations		
Universities and Colleges	7	76
Nonprofit Organizations	3	56
Profit Organizations	0	14
Public Libraries	1	2
Government Agencies	3	7
School Related	2	5
State and Municipal Governments	2	5

*For data for fiscal years 1967-1970, see the 1971 *Bowker Annual*, p. 149.

TABLE 2   TITLE II-B – LIBRARY RESEARCH PROJECTS SUPPORTED, FISCAL YEAR 1971 – SUBJECT LIST

Project Number	Institution	Title	Amount
AUTOMATED DATA PROCESSING: OPERATIONS			
9-0225C	Los Angeles Unified School District, Los Angeles, Calif. 90012	Study and Development of Automated Instructional Materials Handling Program	$234,102
9-0554C	Ohio College Library Center, Columbus, Ohio 43212	Development of a Computerized Regional Shared-Cataloging System	125,000
Transfer	Library of Congress, Washington, D.C. 20540	Retrospective Conversion Pilot Project	96,700
PLANNING AND DEVELOPMENT			
8-0802C	University of Pennsylvania, Philadelphia, Pa. 19104	A System Analysis of the Library and Information Science Statistical Data System	10,000
Transfer	Housing and Urban Development, Washington, D.C.	Urban Information Interagency Committee	150,000
1-0676	Baltimore Regional Planning Council, Baltimore, Md. 20202	Development and Testing of Methodology for Planning Urban Information Services	194,000
1-0677	Cleveland Public Library, Cleveland, Ohio 44114	National Survey of Library Services to the Aging	71,189
1-0715	North Carolina Central University, Durham, N.C. 27707	Identification and Coordination of African-American Materials in Six States	53,265
1-J-050	Washington State Library, Olympia, Wash. 98501	Operations Research Study of the Pacific Northwest Bibliographic Center	9,970
1-0733	United States International University, San Diego, Calif. 92112	Technological Applications Project (TAP)	100,000

TABLE 2, Continued

Project Number	Institution	Title	Amount
PLANNING AND DEVELOPMENT, Cont'd.			
1-8024	United States International University San Diego, Calif. 92112	Establishment of Center for Advanced Study of Technologies and Information Centers	$200,000
0-4026	Columbia University New York, N.Y. 10027	Commissioned Papers Project	124,848
0-4016	University of Maryland College Park, Md. 20742	Graduate Institute Program Curriculum Technology for Experienced Leadership Personnel	7,000
DISADVANTAGED			
0-0662C	National Educational Research Institute Washington, D.C. 20005	A Systems Analysis of Southwestern Spanish-Speaking Users and Nonusers of Library and Information Services	104,200
0-0519C	School District of Philadelphia Philadelphia, Pa. 19103	Demonstration to Test and Establish Effective Mechanisms for Joint Planning by School and Public Library Systems of Philadelphia along with Local Residence around an Inner City Innovative Library Program	$400,000
Transfer	Akron Public School District	Project TREND	32,000
1-0744	University of New Mexico Albuquerque, N.M. 87106	Evaluation of Impact, Costs, and Benefits of the Albuquerque Model Cities Library Materials and Cultural Centers	60,000
1-0622	National Indian Education Association Stillwater, Minn. 55082	Identification of Informational Needs of American Indian Community That Can Be Met by Library Science	198,000

TITLE II-C — NATIONAL ACQUISITIONS AND CATALOGING PROGRAM

In article about Library of Congress.

FOUNDATION GRANTS TO LIBRARIES OR FOR LIBRARY PURPOSES, 1971

Compiled from *Foundation News,* published bimonthly by The Foundation Center, Mt. Royal and Guilford Avenues, Baltimore, Md. 21202. The grants to libraries, etc., cited below, were given by the following foundations.

AEM Foundation, N.Y.
Abrams (Talbert and Leota) Foundation, Mich.
Allegheny Foundation, Pa.
American Group Charitable Trust, Mass.
Anderson (M. D.) Foundation, Texas
Arkell Hall Foundation, N.Y.
Atherton (F. C.) Trust, Hawaii
Atherton (Juliette M.) Trust, Hawaii
Babcock (Mary Reynolds) Foundation, N.C.
Beinecke Foundation, N.Y.
Biddle (Mary Duke) Foundation, N.Y.
Boeing Company Charitable Trust, Wash.
Boettcher Foundation, Colo.
Bridwell (J. S.) Foundation, Texas
Brush (Thomas S.) Foundation, N.Y.
Bush Foundation, Minn.
Cafritz (Morris and Gwendolyn) Foundation, Washington, D.C.
Calder (Louis) Foundation, N.Y.
Caridad Gift Trust, Minn.
Carlson Foundation, Conn.
Carnegie Corporation of New York
Carthage Foundation, Pa.
Cary (Mary Flagler) Charitable Trust, N.Y.
Casper Foundation, Texas
Chicago Community Trust, Ill.
Clark Foundation, N.Y.
Cleveland Foundation, Ohio
Commonwealth Fund, N.Y.
Copeland Andelot Foundation, Del.
Council on Library Resources, Washington, D.C.
Cowell (S. H.) Foundation, Calif.
Cullen Foundation, Texas
D and R Fund, Ill.

Dana (Charles A.) Foundation, Conn.
Davis (Arthur Vining) Foundations, Fla.
Demos (N.) Foundation, Ill.
Dillon Fund, N.Y.
Duke Endowment, N.Y.
Dula (Caleb C. and Julia W.) Educational and Charitable Foundation, N.Y.
Earhart Foundation, Mich.
Fels (Samuel S.) Fund, Pa.
Field Foundation of Illinois
Finch, Pruyn Foundation, N.Y.
Foot (S. B.) Tanning Company Foundation, Minn.
Ford Foundation, N.Y.
Franklin (John and Mary) Foundation, Ga.
Fruehauf (Andrew F.) Foundation, Mich.
Gannett (Frank E.) Newspaper Foundation, N.Y.
Gebbie Foundation, N.Y.
Gifford (Rosamond) Charitable Corporation, N.Y.
Given (Irene Heinz) and John LaPorta Given Foundation, N.Y.
Glosser (David A.) Foundation, Pa.
Goldwyn (Samuel) Foundation, Calif.
Green (Allen P. and Josephine B.) Foundation, Mo.
Haas (Phoebe W.) Charitable Trust, Pa.
Hamilton Foundation, Ind.
Harrington (Francis A.) Foundation, Mass.
Hartford Foundation for Public Giving, Conn.
Hayden (Charles) Foundation, N.Y.
Hill (Louis W. and Maud) Family Foundation, Minn.

Hillman Foundation, Pa.
Hoover Foundation, Ohio
Houston Endowment, Texas
Humble Companies Charitable Trust, Texas
Humphreys Foundation, Texas
Hunt Foundation, Pa.
Hyde (Lillia Babbitt) Foundation, N.J.
J.N.M. Gift Trust, Minn.
Jones (Eugenie and Joseph) Family Foundation, La.
Kellogg (W. K.) Foundation, Mich.
Kenan (William R.), Jr. Charitable Trust, N.Y.
Knapp Foundation, Conn.
Kresge Foundation, Mich.
Kress (Samuel H.) Foundation, N.Y.
Kulas Foundation, Ohio
Lakeview Fund, N.Y.
Lilly Endowment, Ind.
Lindsley (John) Fund, N.Y.
Longwood Foundation, Del.
Mack (J. S.) Foundation, Pa.
Markle (John and Mary R.) Foundation, N.Y.
Mayer (Louis B.) Foundation, Calif.
McCormick (Chauncey and Marion Deering) Foundation, Ill.
McCormick (Robert R.) Charitable Trust, Ill.
McDonald (J. M.) Foundation, Neb.
McGregor Fund, Mich.
McLean (Marrs and Verna) Foundation, Texas
Mellon (Andrew W.) Foundation, N.Y.
Mellon (Richard King) Charitable Trusts, Pa.
Memorial Foundation for Jewish Culture, N.Y.
Merrill (Charles E.) Trust, N.Y.
Mobil Foundation, N.Y.
Monell (Ambrose) Foundation, N.Y.
Moody Foundation, Texas
Mudd (Seeley G.) Fund, Calif.
New York Community Trust, N.Y.
Noble (Vivian Bilby) Foundation, Okla.
Norfolk Foundation, Va.
Permanent Charity Fund, Mass.
Pew Memorial Trust, Pa.
Pforzheimer (Carl and Lily) Foundation, N.Y.
Post (Marjorie Merriweather) Foundation, N.Y.

RAHR Foundation, Wis.
Raskob Foundation for Catholic Activities, Del.
Red Wing Shoe Company Foundation, Minn.
Rennebohm (Oscar) Foundation, Wis.
Reynolds (Z. Smith) Foundation, N.C.
Rhode Island Foundation
Rockefeller Brothers Fund, N.Y.
Rockefeller Foundation, N.Y.
Rockwell Foundation, Pa.
Rosenblatt Memorial Foundation, Utah
Ross (Arthur) Foundation, N.Y.
Rubicon Foundation, N.Y.
Rutledge (Edward) Charity, Wis.
Sage (Russell) Foundation, N.Y.
Scaife (Sarah Mellon) Foundation, Pa.
Shiffman Foundation, Mich.
Silberman (Lois and Samuel) Fund, N.Y.
Skerryvore Foundation, N.Y.
Slemp Foundation, Va.
Smith, Kline & French Foundation, Pa.
Southland Paper Mills Foundation, Texas
Spencer Foundation, Ill.
Surdna Foundation, N.Y.
Symmes (F. W.) Foundation, S.C.
Tinker Foundation, N.Y.
Trebor Foundation, Ga.
Turrell Fund, N.J.
van Ameringen Foundation, N.Y.
Van Nuys (I. N. and Susanna H.) Foundation, Calif.
Wallace-Eljabar Fund, N.J.
Wallace Genetic Foundation, N.Y.
Ward (A. Montgomery) Foundation, Ill.
Watson (John Jay and Eliza Jane) Foundation, N.J.
Welfare Foundation, Del.
Williams Family Foundation, Colo.
Wilson (H. W.) Foundation, N.Y.
Wood (Samuel J. and Evelyn L.) Foundation, N.Y.
Zale Foundation, Texas

EDUCATION
Buildings and Equipment

ALLEGHENY FOUNDATION, Pa., $50,000 to Robert Morris College, Pa., for library/learning center

ANDERSON (M. D.) FOUNDATION, Texas, $250,000 to University of St. Thomas, Texas, for library building

ATHERTON (F. C.) TRUST, Hawaii, $50,000 to Hawaii Loa College, for library classroom building

ATHERTON (JULIETTE M.) TRUST, Hawaii, $60,000 to Hawaiian Foundation Trust, for library classroom building at Hawaii Loa College

BOETTCHER FOUNDATION, Colo., $40,000 to United States International University, Colo., for library-academic complex

CALDER (LOUIS) FOUNDATION, N.Y., $20,000 to Massachusetts Institute of Technology, to rehabilitate facilities for library automation; $500,000 to University of Miami, Fla., for medical library

GANNETT (FRANK E.) NEWSPAPER FOUNDATION, N.Y., $50,000 to Eisenhower College, N.Y., for library

HAYDEN (CHARLES) FOUNDATION, N.Y., $25,000 to Curry College, Mass., to construct and equip library

HILLMAN FOUNDATION, Pa., $10,000 to Robert Morris College, Pa., for library/learning center

KRESGE FOUNDATION, Mich., $25,000 to Bethune-Cookman College, Fla., for library; $100,000 to Concordia College, Minn., for addition to library; $25,000 to Jamestown College, N.D., for library building; $100,000 to University of Pennsylvania, for research library in chemistry building; $25,000 to Wheeling College, W.Va., for library addition

MELLON (ANDREW W.) FOUNDATION, N.Y., $200,000 to Bank Street College of Education, N.Y., for library expansion; $250,000 to Connecticut College, for library addition; $500,000 to Duke University, N.C., for medical library and communications center; $300,000 to Washington and Lee University, Va., for undergraduate library

MERRILL (CHARLES E.) TRUST, N.Y., $30,000 to Bates College, Me., for library; $25,000 to University of Bridgeport, Conn., for library

MOODY FOUNDATION, Texas, $275,000 to Lubbock Christian College, Texas, to expand library facilities and construct education, arts, and communications center

MUDD (SEELEY G.) FUND, Calif., $2,750,000 to Oberlin College, Ohio, for library center

SCAIFE (SARAH MELLON) FOUNDATION, Pa., $200,000 to Robert Morris College, Pa., for library/learning center

SURDNA FOUNDATION, N.Y., $100,000 to University of Bridgeport, Conn., for library-learning resources center

Elementary and Secondary Education

BOETTCHER FOUNDATION, Colo., $51,145 to Associated Schools, Colo., for construction of library

HYDE (LILLIA BABBITT) FOUNDATION, N.J., $10,000 to Vail-Deane School, N.J., for Library and Science Wing

RHODE ISLAND FOUNDATION, $15,000 to Lincoln School, R.I., to enlarge library

Higher Education

Special Projects

BUSH FOUNDATION, Mich., $1,200,000 to Hamline University, Minn., for library, building program, alumni fund, and scholarships

DAVIS (ARTHUR VINING) FOUNDATIONS, Fla., $25,000 to Rensselaer Polytechnic Institute, N.Y., for costs of library planning

DUKE ENDOWMENT, N.Y., $220,000 to Davidson College, N.C., for faculty and staff salaries, library operations, Honors College program, and Career-Service program; $745,000 to Duke University, N.C., for anniversary fund, library fund, computer systems, and other projects

FORD FOUNDATION, N.Y., $250,000 to Talladega College, Ala., to improve faculty, course offerings, and library holdings in the social sciences

MELLON (ANDREW W.) FOUNDATION, N.Y., $1,000,000 to Carnegie-Mellon University College of Humanities and Social Sciences, Pa., for faculty support and library acquisitions

MERRILL (CHARLES E.) TRUST, N.Y., $25,000 to University of Massachusetts Library at Amherst for the purchase of books and other research materials

REYNOLDS (Z. SMITH) FOUNDATION, N.C., $75,000 to Sacred Heart College, N.C., for library support

SILBERMAN (LOIS AND SAMUEL) FUND, N.Y., $29,844 to Hunter College School of Social Work, N.Y., for library acquisitions and scholarships

WALLACE-ELJABAR FUND, N.J., $29,000 to Rochester Institute of Technology, N.Y., for operations of Wallace Library and for scholarships

Libraries

AMERICAN GROUP CHARITABLE TRUST, Mass., $20,000 to Clark University, Mass., for Goddard Library

ARKELL HALL FOUNDATION, N.Y., $25,000 to Canajoharie Library and Art Gallery, N.Y.

ATHERTON (JULIETTE M.) TRUST, Hawaii, $40,000 to Hawaii Medical Library, for capital funds

BABCOCK (MARY REYNOLDS) FOUNDATION, N.C., $10,000 to Appalachian State University, N.C., for special library collections; $15,000 to Stanford University, Hoover Institution, for Yearbook on International Communist Affairs

BEINECKE FOUNDATION, N.Y., $275,000 to Yale University, Conn., for general purposes of University library system and for acquisitions of Beinecke Rare Book and Manuscript Library

BIDDLE (MARY DUKE) FOUNDATION, N.Y., $15,000 to Campbell College, N.C., for library books

BOEING COMPANY CHARITABLE TRUST, Wash., $20,000 to Clark University, Mass., for Goddard Memorial Library (1969)

BRIDWELL (J. S.) FOUNDATION, Texas, $650,000 to Southern Methodist University, Texas, for Bridwell Library

BRUSH (THOMAS S.) FOUNDATION, N.Y., $526,696 to Mt. Union College, Ohio, to establish Library Endowment

CAFRITZ (MORRIS AND GWENDOLYN) FOUNDATION, Washington, D.C., $48,875 to Library of Congress, Washington, D.C., for symposia and publication of works relating to American Revolution; $20,000 to Folger Library, Washington, D.C., to evaluate the library's long-term space requirements

CARIDAD GIFT TRUST, Minn., $15,000 to Duluth Library Building Fund, Minn. (1969)

CARLSON FOUNDATION, Conn., $25,000 to Fairfield University, Conn., for library support

CARNEGIE CORPORATION OF NEW YORK, $65,000 to University of Illinois Graduate School of Library Science, for program for disadvantaged students

CARTHAGE FOUNDATION, Pa., $50,000 to Stanford University Hoover Institution, Calif.

CARY (MARY FLAGLER) CHARITABLE TRUST, N.Y., $111,865 to Pierpont Morgan Library, N.Y.

CASPER FOUNDATION, Texas, $11,070 to McLennan County Public Library of Waco, Texas

CHICAGO COMMUNITY TRUST, Ill., $45,000 to Newberry Library, Ill.

CLARK FOUNDATION, N.Y., $15,000 to Hartwick College, N.Y., for purchase of library books

CLEVELAND FOUNDATION, Ohio, $102,137 to Cleveland Public Library, to improve basic management procedures, and for services to shut-ins

COPELAND ANDELOT FOUNDATION, Del., $25,000 to Wilmington Institute Free Library, Del.

COUNCIL ON LIBRARY RESOURCES, Washington, D.C., $34,604 to American Association for State and Local History, Washington, D.C., for preparation of manual on collection of local history materials in libraries; $10,000 to American Council of Learned Societies, N.Y., for automated biographical control program; $200,959 to Library of Congress, Washington, D.C., for conversion of retrospective cataloging records to machine-readable form; $95,000 to Library of Congress for equipment for preservation research office; $25,000 to Mathematica, Inc., Washington, D.C., to study economics of university library operations; $50,920 to National Academy of Sciences, Washington, D.C., for appraisal of library and information system involving computers; $10,000 to New York Public Library, to experiment in microfilming card catalogue; $75,000 to Ohio College Library

Center, for research on computerized regional library system; $48,450 to United States Book Exchange, for employment of additional personnel; $34,249 to University of California, to prepare and publish handbook on data processing for libraries; $400,000 to University of Chicago Library, for investigation and development of computerized library data systems. (See also Grove's article, "The Council on Library Resources, Inc.," this volume.)

COWELL (S. H.) FOUNDATION, Calif., $50,000 to Stanford University Hoover Institution, Calif., for acquisitions

CULLEN FOUNDATION, Texas, $10,000 to City of Smithville Public Library

D AND R FUND, Ill., $12,317 to Newberry Library, Ill.

DAVIS (ARTHUR VINING) FOUNDATIONS, Fla., $50,000 to Marymount College, Fla., for library support

DEMOS (N.) FOUNDATION, Ill., $10,000 to Gennadius Library

DILLON FUND, N.Y., $50,000 to Library of Congress, Washington, D.C.

DULA (CALEB C. AND JULIA W.) EDUCATIONAL AND CHARITABLE FOUNDATION, N.Y., $12,500 to New York Public Library; $15,000 to Pierpont Morgan Library, N.Y.

EARHART FOUNDATION, Mich., $55,000 to Stanford University Hoover Institution, Calif., for Yearbook on International Communist Affairs and fellowship in military affairs

FIELD FOUNDATION OF ILLINOIS, $37,740 to Newberry Library, Ill., for research and cartography for atlas of American Revolution

FINCH, PRUYN FOUNDATION, N.Y., $20,000 to Crandall Library, N.Y.

FOOT (S. B.) TANNING COMPANY FOUNDATION, Minn., $25,000 to Red Wing Library, Minn., for building fund

FORD FOUNDATION, N.Y., $247,500 to Center for Research Libraries, to make available 1970 census summary tapes to research institutions

FRANKLIN (JOHN AND MARY) FOUNDATION, Ga., $10,000 to Reinhardt College, Ga., for library

FRUEHAUF (ANDREW F.) FOUNDATION, Mich., $10,000 to Wayne State University, Mich., for library (1969)

GEBBIE FOUNDATION, N.Y., $15,000 to Lakewood Memorial Library, N.Y.; $10,000 to James Prendergast Free Library, N.Y.

GIFFORD (ROSAMOND) CHARITABLE CORPORATION, N.Y., $10,000 to Jordan Free Library Association, N.Y., to defray costs entailed in construction

GIVEN (IRENE HEINZ) AND JOHN LAPORTE GIVEN FOUNDATION, N.Y., $100,000 to Given Memorial Library, N.C., for endowment fund; $100,000 to Middlebury College, Vt., for library endowment fund; $25,000 to New York Public Library

GLOSSER (DAVID A.) FOUNDATION, Pa., $100,000 to Cambria Library Association, Pa.

GOLDWYN (SAMUEL) FOUNDATION, Calif., $10,000 to American Film Institute, Washington, D.C., for Charles K. Feldman Memorial Library

HAAS (PHOEBE W.) CHARITABLE TRUST, Pa., $25,000 to William Jeanes Memorial Library, Pa., for construction of new building

HAMILTON FOUNDATION, Ind., $50,000 to Bartholomew County Public Library, Ind. (1969)

HARRINGTON (FRANCIS A.) FOUNDATION, Mass., $10,000 to Clark University, Mass., for Goddard Library

HARTFORD FOUNDATION FOR PUBLIC GIVING, Conn., $15,000 to Canton Public Library Association, Conn., for new wing

HILLMAN FOUNDATION, Pa., $52,000 to University of Pittsburgh Library, for Afro-American collection

HOOVER FOUNDATION, Ohio, $125,000 to North Canton Public Library, Ohio

HOUSTON ENDOWMENT, Texas, $10,000 to Rosenberg Library, Texas, for building fund

HUMBLE COMPANIES CHARITABLE TRUST, Texas, $10,000 to New York Public Library

HUMPHREYS FOUNDATION, Texas, $100,000 to Rosenberg Library Association, Texas, for construction of wing

HUNT FOUNDATION, Pa., $50,000 to Carnegie-Mellon University, Pa., for botanical library

J. N. M. Gift Trust, Minn., $10,000 to Duluth Public Library, Minn. (1969)

Kenan (William R.), Jr. Charitable Trust, N.Y., $300,000 to North Carolina Foundation of Church-Related Colleges, for book purchase programs of members' libraries

Knapp Foundation, Conn., $470,933 to American Library Association, Ill.

Kresge Foundation, Mich., $15,000 to Detroit Library Commission, Mich., to underwrite budget of Detroit Book Fair; $10,000 to Harrisville Library, N.H., for restoration; $10,000 to Independence Township Library, Mich.; $25,000 to Pequot Library, Conn., for building addition

Kress (Samuel H.) Foundation, N.Y., $90,000 to Harvard Business School, Kress Library of Business and Economic History, Mass., for purchase of books, modification of card catalog, seminars, publications, and conservation

Lakeview Fund, N.Y., $10,000 to Katonah Village Library, N.Y.

Lilly Endowment, Ind., $15,000 to Indiana Academy of Science, for support of John Shepard Wright Memorial Library

Longwood Foundation, Del., $200,000 to Newark District Library Commission, Del.; $100,000 to Wilmington Institute Free Library, Del.

Mack (J. S.) Foundation, Pa., $15,000 to Blairsville Library Association, Pa.

Mayer (Louis B.) Foundation, Calif., $10,000 to Mount St. Mary's College, Calif., for special library

McCormick (Chauncey and Marion Deering) Foundation, Ill., $100,000 to Northwestern University, Ill., for Deering Library complex

McCormick (Robert R.) Charitable Trust, Ill., $20,000 to Newberry Library, Ill.

McDonald (J. M.) Foundation, Neb., $20,000 to Cortland Memorial Library, N.Y.

McGregor Fund, Mich., $30,000 to University of Virginia, for library accessions

McLean (Marrs and Verna) Foundation, Texas, $15,000 to St. Mary's Hall, Texas, for library

Mellon (Andrew W.) Foundation, N.Y., $50,000 to Newberry Library, Ill., for acquisitions for collection of historical maps and atlases; $100,000 to Pierpont Morgan Library, N.Y., to remodel and improve physical facilities; $1,000,000 to Princeton University Firestone Library, N.J., for proposed Social Science Center; $500,000 to Tulane University, La., for library development programs; $500,000 to University of Chicago, for renovation of library building to house undergraduate library and related facilities

Mellon (Richard King) Charitable Trusts, Pa., $50,000 to George C. Marshall Research Library, Va., for endowment fund

Mobil Foundation, N.Y., $10,000 to Harvard College Library, Mass.

Monell (Ambrose) Foundation, N.Y., $10,000 to New York Public Library

Moody Foundation, Texas, $250,000 to Rosenberg Library, Texas, for new wing

New York Community Trust, $10,000 to New York Public Library

Norfolk Foundation, Va., $10,000 to Old Dominion University, Va., for library fund

Permanent Charity Fund, Mass., $15,000 to New England Community Development Corporation, Mass., for Afro-American teaching resource library

Pew Memorial Trust, Pa., $80,000 to Herbert Hoover Presidential Library, Washington, D.C., for unrestricted use and to complete Hoover oral history program; $50,000 to Stanford University Hoover Institution, Calif.

Pforzheimer (Carl and Lily) Foundation, N.Y., $16,500 to New York Public Library

Post (Marjorie Merriweather) Foundation, N.Y., $10,000 to Library of Presidential Papers, N.Y.

Rahr Foundation, Wis., $40,000 to City of Shakopee Library Fund, Wis.

Raskob Foundation for Catholic Activities, Del., $10,000 to College of Santa Fe, N.Mex., for library

Red Wing Shoe Company Foundation, Minn., $20,000 to Carnegie Lawther Library, Minn.

Rennebohm (Oscar) Foundation, Wis., $12,124 to University of Wisconsin Jackson Law Library

Reynolds (Z. Smith) Foundation, N.C., $30,000 to Elon College, N.C., for purchase of library books; $10,000 to Richmond Technical Institute of Hamlet, N.C., for purchase of library books; $10,000 to Washington County Public Library

Rhode Island Foundation, $10,000 to Jamestown Philomenian Library, R.I., for building fund

Rockefeller Brothers Fund, N.Y., $21,250 to Library of Congress, Washington, D.C., to organize, index, and microfilm papers of Nelson W. Aldrich

Rockwell Foundation, Pa., $15,000 to Clark University, Mass., for Goddard Library

Ross (Arthur) Foundation, N.Y., $23,000 to Brooklyn Public Library, N.Y.; $30,000 to New York Public Library; $22,000 to Queens Borough Public Library, N.Y.

Rubicon Foundation, N.Y., $220,000 to New York Public Library

Rutledge (Edward) Charity, Wis., $10,116 to Chippewa Falls Public Library, Wis.

Sage (Russell) Foundation, N.Y., $10,000 to New York Public Library, for Resources in the Social Sciences

Scaife (Sarah Mellon) Foundation, Pa., $15,000 to Carnegie Free Library, Pa., for building repairs; $50,000 to George C. Marshall Research Library, Va., for studies of Marshall Plan.

Shaw (Arch W.) Foundation, Ill., $10,000 to Stanford University Hoover Institution, Calif.

Shiffman Foundation, Mich., $13,914 to Wayne State University, Mich., for medical library

Skerryvore Foundation, N.Y., $125,000 to Yale University, Conn., for acquisitions for Beinecke Rare Book and Manuscript Library

Slemp Foundation, Va., $20,000 to Lee County Library Building Committee, Va.

Southland Paper Mills Foundation, Texas, $25,000 to Kurth Memorial Library, Texas, for building fund

Spencer Foundation, Ill., $10,000 to Harvard Graduate School, Mass., for library

Symmes (F. W.) Foundation, S.C., $100,100 to Greenville County Library, S.C.

Trebor Foundation, Ga., $100,000 to Atlanta Public Library, Ga.

Turrell Fund, N.J., $25,000 to Free Public Library of East Orange, N.J., to furnish and equip children's reading room

Van Ameringen Foundation, N.Y., $30,000 to New York Public Library, for Research Libraries collection in psychology and psychiatry

Van Nuys (I. N. and Susanna H.) Foundation, Calif., $34,515 to H. E. Huntington Library and Art Gallery, Calif., for purchase of art and rare books; $30,069 to Wellesley College, Mass., for rare books and book arts

Wallace Genetic Foundation, N.Y., $20,000 to University of Iowa, for libraries

Ward (A. Montgomery) Foundation, Ill., $15,000 to Newberry Library, Ill.

Watson (John Jay and Eliza Jane) Foundation, N.J., $22,000 to Friends of the Jamestown Philomenian Library, R.I., for construction of new library

Welfare Foundation, Del., $100,000 to Wilmington Institute Free Library, Del.

Williams Family Foundation, Colo., $10,000 to City of Fort Morgan Library; $15,000 to Fort Morgan Heritage Foundation, Colo., for library-museum complex

Wilson (H. W.) Foundation, N.Y., $55,568 to American Library Association, Ill., for Office of Library Education

Wood (Samuel J. and Evelyn L.) Foundation, N.Y., $25,000 to Hiram Halle Memorial Library, Conn.

Zale Foundation, Texas, $50,000 to Bishop College, Texas, for library (1969)

Theological Education

FELS (SAMUEL S.) FUND, Pa., $12,000 to Dropsie University, Pa., for work on annotated catalog of microfilms of Guenzburg Collection of Hebraica

HEALTH
Hospitals

ANDERSON (M. D.) FOUNDATION, Texas, $443,000 to Texas Medical Center, for land purchase, operating expenses, and library

Medical Education

DANA (CHARLES A.) FOUNDATION, Conn., $600,000 to Dartmouth Medical School, N.H., for construction of fourth floor to biomedical library

KRESGE FOUNDATION, Mich., $750,000 to Meharry Medical College, Tenn., for construction of library center; $25,000 to Union University Albany Medical College, N.Y., for medical library

MARKLE (JOHN AND MARY R.) FOUNDATION, N.Y., $12,000 to West Virginia University School of Medicine, for audio-visual self-teaching program in fundamentals of pediatric cardiology

MELLON (ANDREW W.) FOUNDATION, N.Y., $500,000 to Duke University Medical Center, N.C., for medical library building

SMITH KLINE & FRENCH FOUNDATION, Pa., $45,000 to College of Physicians of Philadelphia, to enlarge and improve library program

HUMANITIES
Art and Architecture

KRESS (SAMUEL H.) FOUNDATION, N.Y., $25,000 to College Art Association, N.Y., for international congress to plan computerized bibliography of art historical periodical literature; $148,000 to National Gallery of Art, Washington, D.C., for photographic archive for Center for Advanced Study in the Visual Arts

MELLON (ANDREW W.) FOUNDATION, N.Y., $200,000 to National Gallery of Art, Washington, D.C., for library acquisition program in connection with proposed Center for Advanced Study in the Visual Arts

History

ABRAMS (TALBERT AND LEOTA) FOUNDATION, Mich., $12,000 to National Archives, U.S.A., Washington, D.C. (1969)

FORD FOUNDATION, N.Y., $500,000 to Library of Congress, Washington, D.C., for extensive revision and enlargement of Burnett's *Letters of Members of the Continental Congress;* $150,000 to National Archives Trust Fund Board, to prepare computerized index of papers of the Continental Congress

HILL (LOUIS W. AND MAUD) FAMILY FOUNDATION, Minn., $231,761 to St. John's University, Minn., to microfilm monastic manuscripts of European abbeys and other institutions

Language and Literature

MEMORIAL FOUNDATION FOR JEWISH CULTURE, N.Y., $11,900 to Congress for Jewish Culture, N.Y., to prepare and publish lexica and monographs linked to Yiddish culture

Music

KULAS FOUNDATION, Ohio, approx. $20,000 to Cleveland Public Library (1969); $25,000 to Library of Congress, Washington, D.C., for translation of music notation into braille

PERMANENT CHARITY FUND, Mass., $10,000 to Longy School of Music, Mass., for concert hall-library

INTERNATIONAL ACTIVITIES
Cultural Relations

COUNCIL ON LIBRARY RESOURCES, Washington, D.C., $100,000 to International Federation of Library Associations, to strengthen administrative and staff operations

TINKER FOUNDATION, N.Y., $10,000 to International Institute for Girls in Spain, N.Y., to catalog and process Latin American literature collection

Education

COUNCIL ON LIBRARY RESOURCES, Washington, D.C., $15,000 to National Central Library of London, England, for publication and distribution of American acquisitions lists

KRESGE FOUNDATION, Mich., $25,000 to Mt. Allison University, New Brunswick, for library; $15,000 to United Board of Christian Higher Education in Asia, for library expansion at Tunghai University, Taiwan

LINDSLEY (JOHN) FUND, N.Y., $100,000 to American Library in Paris, France; $225,000 to French Library in Boston, Mass., for International Institute and general support

Health and Welfare

COMMONWEALTH FUND, N.Y., $150,000 to Pan American Health Organization, Washington, D.C., for regional library of medicine for Latin America

KELLOGG (W. K.) FOUNDATION, Mich., $282,000 to Pan American Health and Education Foundation, to improve library and information facilities and services in Latin American hospital and health programs

International Studies

FORD FOUNDATION, N.Y., $110,000 to Center of Human Sciences, France, for research, library purchases and international conferences; $250,000 to Overseas Development Institute, England, for library and information program, conferences, and publications

MEMORIAL FOUNDATION FOR JEWISH CULTURE, N.Y., $10,714 to Academy of the Hebrew Language, Israel, for preparation of historical dictionary of Hebrew language; $10,928 to Institute for Hebrew Bibliography, Israel, for research and publication; $85,714 to Yad Washem Martyrs' and Heroes' Memorial Authority, Israel, for bibliographical series and annals of the Jewish communities

Peace and International Cooperation

MELLON (ANDREW W.) FOUNDATION, N.Y., $120,000 to Atlantic Council of the United States, Washington, D.C., for library and other programs of Atlantic Institute

Technical Assistance

ROCKEFELLER FOUNDATION, N.Y., $71,675 to Colombian Institute of Agriculture, for equipment, supplies, and books for library and English language laboratory

SCIENCE AND TECHNOLOGY
Life Sciences

KELLOGG (W. K.) FOUNDATION, Mich., $400,000 to Interuniversity Communications Council, Mich., to develop techniques of communications, and information storage and retrieval in the biological sciences

Botany

GREEN (ALLEN P. AND JOSEPHINE B.) FOUNDATION, Mo., $19,800 to Missouri Botanical Garden, for library

Physical Sciences
Astronomy and Space

ROSENBLATT MEMORIAL FOUNDATION, Utah, $20,000 to Public Library Planetarium (1969)

Chemistry

HILL (LOUIS W. AND MAUD) FAMILY FOUNDATION, Minn., $13,000 to College of St. Scholastica, Minn., to develop major in chemistry library science

Earth Sciences and Oceanography

MOODY FOUNDATION, Texas, $44,000 to Texas A & M University College of Geosciences, for graduate fellowships and library acquisitions at Marine Laboratory in Galveston

Social Sciences
Law

JONES (EUGENIE AND JOSEPH) FAMILY FOUNDATION, La., $20,000 to Tulane Law School, La., for library

WELFARE
General

AEM FOUNDATION, N.Y., $25,000 to Eleanor Roosevelt Memorial Foundation, N.Y., for library fund

Handicapped

KRESGE FOUNDATION, Mich., $10,000 to Recording for the Blind, N.Y., for conversion of recording library from discs to tape

Child Welfare

NOBLE (VIVIAN BILBY) FOUNDATION, Okla., $10,000 to Denver Children's Home, Colo., for library and classrooms

FEDERAL LEGISLATION AFFECTING BOOK PUBLISHING IN 1971

by

Robert W. Frase*

INTERNATIONAL BOOK YEAR

The President, on December 15, 1971, signed a Congressional joint resolution on International Book Year as Public Law 92-192.

"*Resolved by the Senate and House of Representatives of the United States of America in Congress assembled,* That in recognition of (1) the fact that the United States, during its entire history, has recognized importance of universal education in a free society and the commitment of the people and Government of the United States to the free flow of information, (2) the fact that books are basic to both universal education and the free flow of information, and (3) the designation by the United Nations Educational, Scientific, and Cultural Organization of the year 1972 as "International Book Year," the President is authorized and requested to issue a proclamation designating the year 1972 as "International Book Year," and calling upon executive departments and agencies, the people of the United States, and interested groups and organizations to observe such year with appropriate ceremonies and activities both within and without the United States."

It is expected that the President will issue his proclamation on International Book Year early in 1972.

INTERNATIONAL COPYRIGHT

The United States along with 26 other countries signed a revision of the Universal Copyright Convention negotiated at a diplomatic conference in Paris, France, in early July 1971. At the same time parallel revisions of the Berne international copyright convention were also negotiated and signed by the Berne Union countries attending the Paris conference. The U.S. delegation was headed by Bruce C. Ladd, Jr., Deputy Assistant Secretary of State, and Abraham Kaminstein, then Register of Copyrights, who has since been succeeded by George D. Cary.

The Paris meetings were designed to overcome the impasse resulting from the Berne copyright treaty revisions in Stockholm in 1967 which adopted concessions to the developing countries — concessions which proved unacceptable to the countries originating copyrighted material. There is almost universal agreement that the compromises arrived at in Paris in 1971 not only meet the legitimate needs of the developing countries, but also preserve and strengthen the structure of international copyright and encourage authors to continue their creative work. It is expected that the Administration will submit the revised Universal Copyright Convention to the Senate as a treaty in 1972 and that the Foreign Relations Committee will hold public hearings. The U.S. position on these revisions was developed in collaboration with the State Department's international copyright panel, consisting of representatives from various domestic organizations, including the Association of American Publishers, concerned with copyright.

ECONOMIC CONTROLS

Following the unexpected imposition of wage and price controls by the Administration on August 14, the Association of American Publishers (AAP) became concerned with the application of these controls during the initial 90-day freeze period and with attempts to shape the control system in the following period of Phase II. The freeze had its greatest impact on book publishers wanting to make identical reprints of out-of-print books. In many cases the original book had been published anywhere from two to ten years earlier, and, since the original printing, book manufacturers' prices and

---

*Vice President and Economist, Association of American Publishers, Inc.

publishers' expenses had increased considerably. Therefore, publishers would have to take losses in maintaining the old prices for reprints; in some cases the publisher decided not to reprint a book due to the resulting financial losses.

Price control was a new experience for book publishers — during World War II and the Korean War, basic enabling legislation exempted books, magazines, newspapers, and the electronic media. The AAP and some of the other communications associations first requested the Cost of Living Council to exempt the communications media in Phase II by administrative action. When the Cost of Living Council failed to take affirmative action on this request the AAP, along with the Magazine Publishers Association and the National Newspaper Publishers Association (small newspapers) appeared in hearings on the economic stabilization amendments bill (S. 2891) before the Senate Committee on Banking, Housing, and Urban Affairs, and requested a legislative exemption. Thomas B. Curtis, Vice President and General Counsel of Encyclopaedia Britannica, and Robert W. Frase appeared as witnesses in the Senate Committee hearings. Subsequently, Senator Alan Cranston, Democrat from California, proposed an amendment in committee which would have reinstated the World War II and Korean War exemptions. This amendment, however, was defeated in committee by a narrow margin. Afterwards, Senator Cranston and more than 25 other senators introduced the same amendment on the Senate floor. After an initial defeat of the amendment on the evening of November 30, the Senate voted for a somewhat modified Cranston amendment by 50 to 36 on the following day. The Administration had opposed all amendments to the bill in committee; it had, however, adopted a more neutral position by the time the conference committee met on the Cranston amendment on December 13. In the conference committee the Cranston amendment was withdrawn before the House conferees (who had not considered the matter in committee), had a chance to make their views known — one of the key Democratic senators who had voted for the Cranston amendment in committee and in six roll call votes on the Senate floor reversed his position. This result followed a concerted campaign by a large number of metropolitan area newspapers editorializing and lobbying against the exemption, hoping to have the wages of their employees controlled. Both before and after the Congressional action on the Cranston amendment, the Price Commission approved price increases for advertising for many of these same newspapers. The Pay Board has not yet been faced with the necessity of making any decision with respect to wage increases in the press and communications fields.

Following the completion of action on the Cranston amendment and the enactment of the Economic Stabilization Act Amendments of 1971, the AAP renewed its request for exemption from price ceilings for books and educational materials; this time it went to the Price Commission. As of mid-January 1972 no decision on this request had been announced by the Price Commission.

The original measures announced by the President on August 14 also affected imports and exports. Imports, except those on the "free list," were subject to a temporary 10 percent ad valorem tariff during the period August 16 to December 19, 1971 inclusive. U.S. exports, however, were not subject to the price freeze. Because the United States had not only ratified the Florence Agreement, effective in 1967, but had granted duty-free status to all imports of materials covered by the Agreement, imports of books in the United States were not subject to the 10 percent emergency surcharge. A similar protection against an emergency tariff had been afforded by the Florence Agreement several years earlier in Great Britain. Analyzing the impact of the emergency import charge for the printing and publishing industries, the Department of Commerce, in the October 1971 issue of *Printing and Publishing* magazine, summarized the situation as follows:

"The UNESCO Agreement on the Importation of Educational, Scientific and Cultural Materials (Florence Agreement), providing for the elimination of tariffs on books, maps, music, newspapers, periodicals and selected other printed matter, was signed by the U.S. and became effective February 1, 1967. The duty-free stipulations contained in this Agreement have effectively shielded the great bulk of U.S. imported printed materials from the 10 percent surcharge, and thus contribute to the agreement's purpose of international understanding through the freer exchange of ideas and knowledge across national boundaries."

FREEDOM OF THE PRESS ISSUES

The question of continuing the price ceiling exemption for the press and other communications media in the last two wars, which was discussed in the preceding section, involved both constitutional and economic issues. When the witnesses for the AAP, the National Newspaper Association, and the Magazine Publishers Association appeared in the Senate Banking Committee hearings, the AAP concentrated on economic arguments, and the magazine witness on the free press issues. Because of the previous legislative exemptions, no court cases had ever been squarely decided on the question of whether price controls affecting the press came within the constitutional prohibition that "Congress shall make no law . . . abridging the freedom of speech, or of the press. . . ." It seemed quite clear, however, that if price controls should result in taking older book titles off the market because publishers would have to take losses on reprints, such controls would run squarely afoul of the First Amendment. A more subtle violation of the spirit, if not the letter of the First Amendment, would be pressures on newspapers or news magazines to soften their political reporting in order to secure approval for price increases from an administrative body. Senator Cranston put this issue well in the following remarks in a letter to all his Senate colleagues on November 24, 1971:

"The present bill delegates to the President's Pay Board and Price Commission the enormous power of granting or denying price, rate, or wage increases in the publishing and broadcast industries. Through individual case by case rulings, these bodies may be in a position to favor an administration's supporters with competitive price and wage advantages or to punish an administration's critics with adverse decisions. The bill may create what amounts to economic censorship.

"The board of commission members may never exercise this power of censorship. Their decisions may be even-handed and benevolent. But no administrative board should be given such enormous power over the press, since even an implied threat of economic censorship may deter both the thorough objective pursuit of information and the dynamic criticism that is so vital to the democratic process.

"We must not endanger the principles of the First Amendment for the sake of well-intended but as yet unproven efforts to control inflation. We should recall the warnings of the Supreme Court that 'freedoms such as these are protected (by the Constitution) not only against heavy-handed frontal assault, but also from being stifled by more subtle governmental influence.'"

There were in 1971 two major issues decided in favor of a strict interpretation of the Constitutional protections for the press in which the AAP participated actively. These were the cases involving the publishing of the "Pentagon Papers" by the *New York Times* and other newspapers, and the attempt to have the House of Representatives hold Frank Stanton, president of CBS, in contempt for refusing to turn over to the House Committee on Interstate and Foreign Commerce certain materials not used in a documentary film, *The Selling of the Pentagon.* In the court case involving the "Pentagon Papers," the AAP came to the support of the *New York Times.* In the Stanton case, AAP witnesses testified in hearings before the Subcommittee on Foreign Operations and Government Information of the House Committee on Government Operations, and in the Subcommittee on

Constitutional Rights of the Senate Judiciary Committee. In addition, the AAP played a very active role, along with other organizations, in the legislative efforts which resulted in the 226 to 181 vote in the House of Representatives on July 13, refusing the request of its Committee on Interstate and Foreign Commerce to hold Frank Stanton in contempt.

The House of Representatives passed a bill (H.R. 8805) on July 7, 1971, which attempted to legislate two major changes in the standards of obscenity evolved by the Supreme Court. The first change was an effort to set up a special category of materials which, though not legally obscene, nonetheless could not be mailed to minors. The other change was to remove from the standard of obscenity evolved by the courts the requirement that matter to be judged obscene and excluded from the mails had to be "utterly without redeeming social value." The AAP and other organizations opposed these amendments in the committee hearings in the House. After passage of the bill in the House the AAP requested an opportunity to present witnesses on the bill if it were taken up by the Senate committee to which it was referred, the Committee on Post Office and Civil Service. However, no action was taken in the Senate committee during 1971 on H.R. 8805.

EXEMPTION OF OUTSIDE SALESMEN

When the Fair Labor Standards Act (Wage and Hour Act) was enacted in 1938, among the exemptions from the maximum hour, minimum wage, and record-keeping provisions were persons employed as "outside salesmen." Congress determined that they should be exempt since they worked at irregular hours and since the employer had no way to verify the number of hours they actually worked. The Department of Labor's Wage and Hour Division held hearings in February 1971 on proposed changes in the regulations under the Fair Labor Standards Act on a number of points, including a proposal to put a monetary limit on the definition of outside salesmen. The AAP appeared in these hearings before a hearing examiner on February 9. Testimony in opposition was given by Robert W. Frase, Vice President and Economist, who had been on the staff of the Wage and Hour Division in 1938 and had participated in the drafting of the original regulations under the statute. On December 2, 1971 the Wage and Hour Division published its revised regulations, which continued unchanged the exemption for outside salesmen.

FEDERAL TRADE COMMISSION — NEGATIVE OPTION AND DOOR-TO-DOOR SALES

In 1970 the Federal Trade Commission published a proposed trade regulation rule which would in effect have outlawed the so-called "negative option" method of operation used by book, record, and various other clubs. Under "negative option," the customer, after signing a contract, receives the next selection unless he returns a postcard saying that he does not want it. The FTC-proposed rule was in such a general form that it would also have outlawed the standing order plans which many libraries use as a convenient and economical method of book selection. Both the AAP and ALA opposed the proposed FTC rule in hearings in the fall of 1970. The AAP along with other organizations proposed an alternate or substitute trade regulation rule which would permit the continuation of the negative option method of operation but tighten up on and make uniform certain procedural protections for the consumer. As of mid-January 1972, the FTC had not acted on this matter.[1]

---

[1] On February 3, 1972 the Federal Trade Commission released a revision of its proposed trade regulation rule on negative option selling. The revised proposed rule did not outlaw the practice of negative option but proposed further protection for the consumer along the lines of the alternate rule which the AAP and other organizations had proposed in the hearings. Comments on the revised rule are due in the hands of the FTC by April 10, 1972.

A similar action was taken by the FTC in proposing a trade regulation rule with respect to "door-to-door" sales. Hearings were held on this proposed rule in February and March 1971 in Washington and Chicago. Here again the AAP testified and joined in presenting an alternate proposal accepting the principle of regulating door-to-door sales, giving the consumer three days in which to change his mind after signing the contract in his home. The AAP's alternate proposal suggested various changes in other parts of the proposed rule which would make it more workable from the point of view of both the businesses involved and the consumer. Also, the AAP strongly proposed that if the FTC promulgated such a rule, it be on a nationwide basis, superseding any conflicting or differing legislation on the part of the states or ordinances on the part of municipalities. Since many companies, including the major encyclopedia companies, operate on a nationwide basis, national uniformity in the application of this rule is important in order that a single contract may be used throughout the country. From the point of view of enforcing the consumer's rights, a single national standard is also preferable. As of mid-January 1972 the Federal Trade Commission had not yet acted on this question. (See note, end of article.)

COPYRIGHT REVISION AND THE ONE-YEAR EXTENSION ACT

Since progress on the general copyright revision bill (S. 644) was delayed again by the CATV issue, another one-year extension bill was originated in the Senate by Senator McClellan. The AAP took an active role in urging the passage of S.J.Res. 132, especially in the House of Representatives. Failure to extend these expiring second-term copyrights another year to December 31, 1972, pending enactment of a general revision bill, would have had an unfortunate impact on the inclusion of a revised term of life plus 50 years in the general copyright revision bills. This in turn would have clouded the prospect of the United States joining the Berne international copyright convention and the total coordination or even amalgamation of the two separate and differing international copyright conventions (Berne and UCC). In the debate on the House floor on S.J.Res. 132 on November 15, Congressman Emanuel Celler, Democrat from New York, Chairman of the Judiciary Committee, made no commitment as he had in the previous year that he would not present another extension bill before the House if this proved necessary in 1972, because the general revision bill had not yet been enacted.

POSTAL RATES

The AAP took the lead role in appearances before the Postal Rate Commission in regard to setting special fourth-class rates for books and other educational and cultural materials. The AAP presented a case both for itself and the Book Manufacturers Institute. The other major intervenors on special fourth-class mail were the American Library Association, the National Association of College Stores, and the Record Industry Association of America, all of whom took similar positions. In addition to supporting the arguments of the ALA and the NACS on the educational and cultural values of books and other special fourth-class mail, the AAP attack on the rates proposed by the Postal Service was directed largely against cost estimates. The principal technical witness on this point was Robert W. Frase, who was aided on the question of statistical sampling by Morris H. Hansen, former Assistant Director of the U.S. Bureau of the Census. As of mid-January 1972, the hearing examiner for the Postal Rate Commission, Mr. Seymour Wenner, had not handed down his initial decision on the rate case. However, after the hearing record was closed on November 1, Examiner Wenner called for further argument on the Postal Service's estimated annual costs for special fourth-class mail, which was in essence asking the Postal Service to show cause why the estimated costs should not be reduced by 17.5 percent ($20 million) with an equivalent reduction in the proposed rates for special fourth-class mail.[2]

WILLIAMS AND WILKINS CASE

Williams and Wilkins, which brought suit against the National Library of Medicine for photocopying their medical journals, is a Baltimore-based publisher and printer of medical journals and books (not a member of the Association of American Publishers). Spokesmen for the predecessor organizations of the AAP had endeavored to persuade Williams and Wilkins not to try to resolve the photocopying issue in the courts but to attempt to arrive at a solution mutually acceptable to the principal parties as part of the legislative process. These efforts were not successful, and Williams and Wilkins brought suit against the Library after NLM had refused its offer to permit unlimited photocopying for a small per-page fee. After the suit was filed, the Association of Research Libraries, joined by the Medical Library Association and the American Association of Law Libraries, requested permission on March 31, 1971 of the Court of Claims to file an amicus brief in support of the National Library of Medicine. Subsequently the American Library Association, on April 29, filed a request with the Court for permission to submit an amicus brief. It was only after this filing of briefs amicae by the library associations that the Association of American Publishers felt impelled to enter the case, and an AAP brief on the general problems presented by photocopying was filed on June 28, 1971. As of mid-January 1972, the Commissioner of the Court of Claims had not yet handed down his opinion, although the record had been closed several months before. AAP feels that this case is not the appropriate way to settle some of the important, substantive problems relating to photocopying, and still hopes that a mutually agreed-to solution can be arrived at among publishers, authors, and libraries. Although library spokesmen have placed emphasis on the need for access to copyrighted materials through photocopying, and the spokesmen for AAP and authors have emphasized the importance of maintaining the necessary economic incentives for the creation and publishing of materials, it is obvious that both groups must realize the other's point of view. Therefore, the AAP for its part will pursue every possibility in order to arrive at a solution which will protect the public interest both with respect to access and with respect to continuing the necessary incentives for the creation of materials.

(See Krettek and Cooke's article, "Federal Legislation for Libraries during 1971," this volume, for information on educational appropriations, cable television, piracy of sound recordings, tax amendments on charitable deductions, the comprehensive child development act, the higher education act, and other legislative measures of mutual interest to book publishers and librarians.)

---

[2] On February 3 the Chief Hearing Examiner for the Postal Rate Commission handed down his initial decision and recommendation to the Commission itself. By and large the Examiner approved the rates proposed by the Postal Service but adjusted a few rates upward and a few downward. Among the reductions was a 17.5 percent decrease in the special fourth-class rate for books and other educational materials. If sustained by the Rate Commission and the Board of Governors of the Postal Service, this reduction will save consumers of books upwards of $50 million in postage over the next four years.

Note added in proof: In the *Federal Register* of February 17, 1972 the FTC published a revision of its proposed trade regulation on door-to-door sales with opportunity for written comment by March 24. The revised rule restricted itself to a three-day period in which the consumer might change his mind, but it did not, as requested by AAP, make this FTC rule a nationwide standard eliminating federal and state regulations in this field.

On February 16, 1972 the Commissioner for the Court of Claims who had heard the Williams and Wilkins case handed down his recommendations, finding in favor of Williams and Wilkins. Several additional legal steps lie between this recommendation of the Commissioner and a decision by the Court of Claims itself.

Library Education, Manpower, and Salaries

PLACEMENTS OF LIBRARY SCHOOL GRADUATES FOR THE ACADEMIC YEARS 1967/68 – 1969/70

by

D. Kathryn Weintraub*

SOURCE OF DATA

The survey for the second edition of the *North American Library Education Directory and Statistics 1969–1971*[1] identified 463 different programs of library education in the United States and its territories. These programs are at different levels of academic endeavor. They include library technical assistant programs; bachelor's degrees with either a library school major or a minor; and programs of graduate library education leading to a master's degree and, sometimes, also to a certificate of advanced study or a Ph.D. in library science.

The questionnaires asked for data on the number of placements of degree candidates in the three academic years 1967/68–1969/70. In addition, the graduate programs were asked for information on the types of libraries in which their students were placed and the salary range.

RESPONSE TO QUESTIONNAIRE

The total response to the questionnaire for American library education programs was 412, or 89 percent. Although 46 of these programs were included in the *Directory*, they were excluded from all statistical analyses because their programs were either in the planning stage or so specialized that they did not fit well within the categories of the survey.

Placement data were reported by only about 50 percent of the responding institutions. When the response for placement data is broken down by type of program (Table 1), it is apparent that 71.5 percent of the library technical assistant programs and 83.7 percent of the accredited graduate programs were able to supply some placement data.

NUMBER OF PLACEMENTS

The total number of placements by type of program for the three academic years 1967/68–1969/70 is shown in Table 2. This number increased each year in all categories except that of the graduate accredited programs; the rate of increase between 1967/68–1968/69 and 1968/69–1969/70 also increased for

---

*Assistant Professor, School of Library and Information Science, University of Wisconsin–Milwaukee.

[1] Frank L. Schick and D. Kathryn Weintraub, eds. *North American Library Education Directory and Statistics, 1969–1971.* 2nd ed. Chicago: American Library Association, to be published spring 1972.

all categories except the graduate accredited programs.

The exception is important, though, because the graduate accredited programs reported by far the largest number of placements. The number of reporting programs varies from year to year and the number reporting in 1969/70 was higher for all categories of program.

Accordingly, Table 2 gives rise to two different questions. First, did the number of placements increase, in fact, for each year? Second, did all the graduates who sought jobs find them? It is not possible to answer either of these questions definitively, but the available data is suggestive.

In Table 3, the total placements are shown by type of program for those programs which reported placement data for all of the three years. From this it can be inferred that, overall, the rate of increase in number of placements remained level during the period; but it decreased somewhat in all categories except undergraduate programs. This could mean that libraries are distinguishing more clearly between beginning professional and subprofessional positions.

The only academic year for which both placements and degrees were reported was the academic year 1969/70. Placements were not differentiated according to type of degree, although some reporting programs awarded both bachelor's and graduate degrees. Sixty-six percent of the graduates of those programs which reported both placements and degrees awarded were known to have been placed (Table 4). This figure corresponds approximately with Carlyle Frarey's finding in an independent survey of the accredited library schools. (See Frarey and Donley's article, "Placement and Salaries, 1970: The Year That Was *Not* What It Seemed," this volume.) Many of the remaining 34 percent undoubtedly did not inform their school of their employment; others may have been already employed; and a few probably did not seek employment immediately. It would be interesting to learn more about this 34 percent.

The graduate accredited programs reported the largest number of degrees awarded, the largest number of placements, and the smallest percentage of known placements of graduates (63.8 percent). The smaller and newer library technical assistant programs reported the largest percentage of known placements of graduates (85 percent).

REGIONAL DISTRIBUTION OF PLACEMENTS

The number and percentage of reported placements by type of program for each region of the country are shown in Table 5. There is some distortion in this table because the regional classification is defined according to the location of the reporting institution rather than according to the location of the position filled. Still, it is reasonable to assume that most graduates seek employment within the region where they received their education.

The largest number of reported placements was in the middle western regions V and IV. This was true for all types of library education programs, but the overwhelmingly largest number of placements in these regions was reported by the graduate accredited programs. Moreover, the graduate accredited programs reported a larger number of placements than other types of programs in virtually every region of the country.

In regions other than V and IV the number of placements reported by the other types of programs was proportionately greater in those regions where the graduate accredited programs were proportionately fewer. Thus, the graduate nonaccredited programs were stronger in the western regions VII, VIII, and IX; the undergraduate programs were stronger in the southeastern and southern regions III and VI; and the library technical assistant programs were particularly strong in the far western region, IX.

DISTRIBUTION OF PLACEMENTS BY TYPE OF LIBRARY

Only the graduate programs reported either on salary ranges or on placements by type of library (Table 6). The distribution is somewhat different for accredited and nonaccredited programs. As has been mentioned, the accredited programs reported a far larger number of placements. The largest number of their graduates (approximately one-third) were placed in college and university libraries, while somewhat smaller numbers were placed in public libraries and school libraries. The majority of graduates from nonaccredited programs were placed in school libraries.

The data on salary ranges are difficult to interpret, primarily because the data are inadequate. The highest and, in all but one case, the lowest salaries were reported by the graduate accredited programs. The low salaries may have been for part-time positions. Of the six salaries tallied for the three years and two types of program in Table 6, four of the high salaries were reported in special libraries and four of the low salaries were reported in school libraries.

SUMMARY AND CONCLUSION

The information on library placements reported herein was derived from a questionnaire survey of library education programs. A majority of the library technical assistant programs and the graduate accredited programs supplied information on the placement of their graduates. The graduate accredited programs reported, by far, the largest number of placements.

The total number of placements continues to increase each year. However, there is some evidence that the rate of increase in number of placements is leveling off and that libraries are making more effective use of subprofessionally trained assistants.

The graduate accredited programs dominate the placement picture in all parts of the country, and most especially in the middle western region where the largest number of positions are available. All other types of library education programs also report their largest number of placements in this region, but their remaining strength appears to be distributed across the country in a supplementary pattern.

The largest numbers of positions are available in (1) college and university libraries, (2) public libraries, and (3) school libraries. Positions in special libraries also account for a small but significant number of placements.

The graduate programs train librarians for positions in all types of libraries. However, the nonaccredited programs place the major portion of their graduates in school libraries.

Perhaps the most interesting conclusions to be drawn from this survey in relation to placements are that (1) the number of positions continues to increase somewhat, and that (2) libraries are developing more satisfactory classifications for professional and subprofessional positions.

TABLE 1 TYPES OF LIBRARY EDUCATION PROGRAMS REPORTING PLACEMENTS

Type of Program	Total Response	Response to Question on Placement	
		Number	Percent
Library Technical Assistant	65	46	71.5
Undergraduate	182	65	36
Graduate	119	73	61.3
Accredited	49	41	83.7
Nonaccredited	70	32	45.7
TOTAL	366	184	50.3

TABLE 2   TOTAL PLACEMENTS OF GRADUATES BY TYPE OF PROGRAM FOR THE YEARS 1967/68 – 1969/70

Type of Program	1967/68	1968/69	1969/70
Library Technical Assistant[1]	88	152	251
Undergraduate[2]	433	445	515
Graduate	3,084	3,305	3,486
Accredited[3]	2,829	2,952	2,933
Nonaccredited[4]	255	353	553
TOTAL	3,605	3,902	4,252

[1]Thirteen technical assistant programs reported on placements for the 3 academic years; 8 reported for the academic years 1968/69–1969/70 only; 18 reported only for the academic year 1969/70; 2 reported for 1968/69; 1 reported only for 1967/68; 1 reported only for the academic years 1967/68–1968/69; and 3 reported for the academic years 1967/68 and 1969/70.

[2]Forty-three undergraduate programs reported placements for all 3 academic years; 11 reported for 1969/70 only; 4 reported for 1968/69–1969/70; 2 reported for the academic year 1968/69 only; 4 reported only for the academic year 1967/68; and 1 for the academic years 1967/68–1968/69.

[3]Thirty-two accredited programs reported for all 3 academic years; 1 reported only for the years 1968/69–1969/70; 2 reported for the year 1969/70; 1 for the year 1968/69; 3 for the years 1967/68–1968/69; and 1 for the academic years 1967/68 and 1969/70. An additional accredited program reported on salaries but not on number of placements.

[4]Eighteen of the nonaccredited programs reported placement data for all 3 years; 2 reported placement data for the academic years 1968/69–1969/70; 11 reported for the academic years 1969/70; and 1 institution reported only on salaries and not on placements.

TABLE 3 TOTAL PLACEMENTS OF GRADUATES BY TYPE OF PROGRAM
FOR THOSE PROGRAMS WHICH REPORTED ON PLACEMENTS
FOR EACH OF THE THREE ACADEMIC YEARS 1967/68 – 1969/70

Type of Program	Number of Placements			Rate of Change	
	1967/68	1968/69	1969/70	1967/68 to 1968/69	1968/69 to 1969/70
Library Technical Assistant	73	90	93	+17	+3
Undergraduate	404	384	417	−20	+33
Graduate	2,721	2,872	2,991	+151	+119
Accredited	2,466	2,551	2,641	+85	+90
Nonaccredited	255	321	350	+66	+29
TOTAL	3,198	3,346	3,491	+148	+155

TABLE 4 NUMBER OF PLACEMENTS AND DEGREES GRANTED
FOR THE ACADEMIC YEAR 1969/70 FOR PROGRAMS
WHICH REPORTED FIGURES BY TYPE OF PROGRAM

Type of Program	Placements	Technical Certificates (1 & 2 yr.)	Bachelor's Degrees (4 yr.)	Master's Degree & Higher	Grads Placed (%)
Library Technical Assistant[1]	206	242	—	—	85
Undergraduate[2]	281		353	—	79.6
Graduate	3,478		395	4,985	64.6
Accredited[3]	2,933		105	4,493	63.8
Nonaccredited[4]	545		290	492	69.6
TOTAL	3,965	242	748	4,985	66.4

[1]Thirty-six library technical assistant programs reporting.

[2]Twenty-two undergraduate programs reporting.

[3]Thirty-six accredited graduate library programs reporting. Four of these programs also awarded bachelor's degrees.

[4]Twenty-nine programs reporting. Fifteen of these programs also awarded bachelor's degrees.

TABLE 5 TOTAL PLACEMENTS FOR THE ACADEMIC YEARS 1967/68 – 1969/70 FOR EACH TYPE OF PROGRAM BY REGION OF THE UNITED STATES

In this table the numerals I–X refer to the ten regions defined for regional offices of the U.S. Office of Health, Education, and Welfare. The states included in each region are: Region I: Connecticut, Maine, Massachusetts, New Hampshire, Rhode Island, Vermont. Region II: New York, New Jersey, Puerto Rico, Virgin Islands. Region III: Delaware, Maryland, Pennsylvania, Virginia, West Virginia. Region IV: Alabama, Florida, Georgia, Kentucky, Mississippi, North Carolina, South Carolina, Tennessee. Region V: Illinois, Indiana, Michigan, Minnesota, Ohio, Wisconsin. Region VI: Arkansas, Louisiana, New Mexico, Oklahoma, Texas. Region VII: Iowa, Kansas, Missouri, Nebraska. Region VIII: Colorado, Montana, North Dakota, South Dakota, Utah, Wyoming. Region IX: Arizona, California, Hawaii, Nevada. Region X: Alaska, Idaho, Oregon, Washington.

Type of Program	I No. & (%)	II No. & (%)	III No. & (%)	IV No. & (%)	V No. & (%)	VI No. & (%)	VII No. & (%)	VIII No. & (%)	IX No. & (%)	X No. & (%)	Total No. & (%)
Library Technical Assistant											
1967/68	—	2 (2.3)	1 (1.1)	5 (5.7)	32 (36.4)	—	—	—	4 (46.6)	7 (7.9)	88 (100)
1968/69	—	6 (3.9)	—	—	64 (42.1)	—	—	1 (.6)	69 (45.4)	12 (7.9)	152 (99.9)
1969/70	—	6 (2.4)	8 (3.2)	9 (3.6)	72 (28.7)	6 (2.4)	3 (1.2)	7 (2.8)	122 (48.6)	18 (7.2)	251 (100.1)
Undergraduate											
1967/68	10 (2.3)	13 (3)	129 (29.7)	124 (28.6)	48 (11.1)	77 (17.8)	13 (3)	10 (2.3)	6 (1.4)	3 (.7)	433 (99.9)
1968/69	12 (2.7)	15 (3.4)	80 (18)	110 (24.7)	97 (21.8)	67 (15)	33 (7.4)	15 (3.4)	11 (2.5)	5 (1.1)	445 (100)
1969/70	12 (2.3)	9 (1.7)	101 (19.6)	148 (28.7)	117 (22.7)	71 (13.8)	34 (6.6)	12 (2.3)	11 (2.1)	—	515 (99.8)
Graduate											
1967/68	—	414 (13.4)	498 (16.1)	484 (15.6)	830 (26.9)	237 (7.8)	124 (4)	19 (.6)	306 (9.9)	172 (5.6)	3,084 (99.9)
1968/69	—	428 (13)	491 (14.9)	515 (15.6)	788 (23.8)	289 (8.7)	173 (5.2)	150 (4.5)	305 (9.8)	146 (4.4)	3,305 (99.9)
1969/70	—	455 (13.1)	348 (10)	576 (16.5)	1011 (29)	317 (9.1)	208 (5.9)	116 (3.3)	311 (8.9)	144 (4.1)	3,486 (99.9)
Accredited											
1967/68	—	414 (14.6)	498 (17.6)	396 (14)	800 (28.3)	212 (7.5)	85 (3)	8 (.3)	250 (8.8)	166 (5.9)	2,829 (100)
1968/69	—	428 (14.5)	491 (16.6)	388 (13.1)	721 (24.4)	257 (8.7)	112 (3.8)	141 (4.8)	281 (9.5)	133 (4.5)	2,952 (99.9)
1969/70	—	455 (15.5)	338 (11.5)	446 (15.2)	889 (30.3)	273 (9.3)	117 (4)	37 (1.3)	244 (8.3)	134 (4.6)	2,933 (100)
Nonaccredited											
1967/68	—	—	—	88 (34.5)	30 (11.8)	25 (9.8)	39 (15.3)	11 (4.3)	56 (22)	6 (2.4)	255 (100.1)
1968/69	—	—	—	127 (36)	67 (19)	32 (9.1)	61 (17.3)	9 (2.5)	44 (12.4)	13 (3.7)	353 (100)
1969/70	—	—	10 (1.8)	130 (23.5)	122 (22.1)	44 (8.0)	91 (16.5)	79 (14.3)	67 (12.1)	10 (1.8)	553 (100.1)

TABLE 6 NUMBER OF PLACEMENTS REPORTED BY GRADUATE PROGRAMS BY TYPE OF LIBRARY, WITH MONTHLY SALARY RANGE[1] FOR ACADEMIC YEARS 1967/68 – 1969/70

Type of Program & Academic Year	Public Libraries No. of Placements & (%)	Public Libraries Salary Range	State Libraries No. of Placements & (%)	State Libraries Salary Range	School Libraries No. of Placements & (%)	School Libraries Salary Range	College & University Libraries No. of Placements & (%)	College & University Libraries Salary Range	Special & Other Libraries No. of Placements & (%)	Special & Other Libraries Salary Range	Total No. of Placements & (%)	Total Salary Range
Accredited												
1967/68	769 (27.2)	$1,250 – 417	35 (1.2)	$ 680 – 500	678 (24)	$1,333 – 375	954 (33.7)	$1,105 – 433	393 (13.9)	$1,400 – 500	2,829 (100)	$1,400 – 375
1968/69	782 (26.5)	1,254 – 416	38 (1.3)	910 – 500	674 (22.8)	1,630 – 417	1,039 (35.2)	1,091 – 450	419 (14.2)	1,250 – 375	2,952 (100)	1,630 – 375
1969/70	798 (27.2)	1,375 – 492	70 (2.4)	1,443 – 510	753 (25.7)	1,547 – 358	960 (32.9)	1,250 – 438	352 (12)	1,900 – 425	2,933 (100.2)	1,900 – 352
Nonaccredited												
1967/68	42 (16.5)	666 – 560	1 (0.4)	—	160 (62.8)	800 – 200	36 (14.1)	700 – 585	16 (6.3)	800 – 625	255 (100.1)	800 – 200
1968/69	36 (10.2)	—		—	237 (67.1)	900 – 425	47 (13.3)	966 – 584	33 (9.5)	800 – 625	353 (100.1)	966 – 425
1969/70	53 (9.6)	840 – 500	5 (0.9)	—	407 (73.6)	1,200 – 483	65 (11.8)	1,200 – 450	23 (4.1)	1,500 – 625	553 (100)	1,500 – 450
Total												
1967/68	811 (26.3)	1,250 – 417	36 (1.2)	680 – 500	838 (27.2)	1,333 – 200	990 (32.1)	1,105 – 433	409 (13.6)	1,400 – 500	3,084 (100.4)	1,400 – 200
1968/69	818 (24.8)	1,254 – 416	38 (1.1)	910 – 500	911 (27.6)	1,630 – 417	1,086 (32.9)	1,091 – 450	452 (13.7)	1,250 – 375	3,305 (100.1)	1,630 – 375
1969/70	851 (24.4)	1,375 – 492	75 (2.3)	1,443 – 510	1,160 (33.3)	1,547 – 358	1,025 (29.4)	1,250 – 438	375 (10.8)	1,900 – 425	3,486 (100.2)	1,900 – 352

[1]For accredited programs, 23 reported on salary ranges for all 3 academic years; 3 reported on salaries for the academic years 1968/69–1969/70; 3 reported on salaries for the academic year 1969/70 only; and 4 reported on salaries for the academic years 1967/68–1968/69. For the nonaccredited programs, 5 reported on salaries for all 3 academic years and 6 reported on salaries only for the academic year 1969/70.

LIBRARY MANPOWER STATISTICS 1969–1972 AND THE OUTLOOK FOR THE FUTURE

by

Sarah R. Reed*

Based upon the various surveys conducted by the National Center, Dr. Frank L. Schick, Chief, Library Surveys Branch, National Center for Educational Statistics, U.S. Office of Education, has provided projections of the number of librarians in the labor force and the number of library science degrees awarded. This summary data as shown in Tables 1 and 2 provide important background information for the period 1960–1971.

To supplement Dr. Schick's data, double postals were sent to public libraries and to school media center directors in 30 large cities and to 21 large academic libraries to request estimates of the numbers of placements, applicants, and staff in the years 1969–1972. Letters were sent to F. E. McKenna, Executive Director, Special Libraries Association, and to F. Kurt Cylke, Executive Secretary, Federal Library Committee, seeking their reactions concerning the library employment situation.

PUBLIC LIBRARIES

Of the 30 questionnaires sent to public libraries which this year, according to a recent listing,[1] received appropriations for print and nonprint materials including binding of $500,000 or more,[2] 14 replies provided the statistics reported in Tables 3 and 4. Two additional respondents indicated that while there are very few vacancies currently, they are still experiencing difficulty in securing experienced children's librarians. A third such response indicated imminent budget cuts; a fourth characterized the present employment outlook as steady.

According to the statistics on which Table 4 is based, large public libraries experienced a recession in terms of number of placements in 1970, which grew worse in 1971. A drop of 10 percent in the number of professional staff employed between 1969 and 1970 was a prelude to a further decrease of 39 percent in the succeeding year. Together with 63 percent fewer placements of technical assistants and 81 percent fewer placements of clerks, this results in a discouraging employment outlook at the close of 1971.

SCHOOL LIBRARIES

As previously indicated, questionnaires were sent to the directors of the school libraries in those cities in which the public libraries were canvassed. Of the nine respondents, one indicated that his system has lost all school library positions and that the employment outlook is "very poor." Others noted "tight" budgets, the need to double staff but no possibility of doing so "until austerity ends," a "grim" financial outlook, "freezings and refreezings." Five of the respondents are hopeful of employing a total of 134 school media personnel in order to maintain present staffing levels in the coming year. Three indicated difficulty in securing qualified personnel. Of these, two noted a shortage of elementary school librarians. Of the latter, one specified that the shortage was for personnel for inner-city elementary schools.

Respondents reported no marked changes in school media center personnel estimates for the years 1969 to 1972. Their estimates for 1971 are shown in Table 5.

---

*Associate Dean, Graduate Library School, Indiana University, Bloomington, Ind.

[1]Beth E. Carpenter and Abla M. Shaheen, comps., *Selected Statistics of Public Libraries in the United States and Canada Serving 100,000 Population or More, 1971* (Public Library of Fort Wayne and Allen County).

[2]The range of materials appropriations was $2,146,080, or from $503,920 to $2,650,000. The median appropriation was $727,235. The range in per capita support was $4.36, or from $3.41 to $7.77, with a median per capita support of $5.68.

ACADEMIC LIBRARIES

Of 21 inquiries to academic libraries which, according to the 1970 *Bowker Annual,* pp. 16-17, had budgets of $1,000,000 or more in 1968–1969 for library materials excluding binding, 15 respondents supplied the statistics reported in Tables 6 and 7.

The academic library employment picture is clearly one of a shrinking employment market. Three respondents, however, noted difficulty in employing experienced catalogers; three others, in finding experienced administrative and supervisory personnel.

Academic library respondents anticipate a 35 percent decrease in number of placements in 1972, after experiencing an almost 16 percent decrease in 1971 and a 15 percent decrease in 1970. As is shown in Table 7, this results in an anticipated net loss in all categories of academic library staff in 1972.

SPECIAL LIBRARIES

F. E. McKenna, Executive Director, Special Libraries Association, has indicated that there are special librarians unemployed, but that most of these either do not wish to move to locations where job vacancies do exist, or, due to family considerations, are not free to do so.[3] He observed that the registration at SLA's Employment Clearinghouse at the San Francisco Conference in June 1971 showed 80 job openings in the United States and Canada as compared with 54 job seekers. He also commented on the cutbacks a year ago in special libraries located in industries involved with government and space contracts, particularly those in Southern California, the Boston area, and the state of Washington, with somewhat less effect on those in New Jersey, eastern Pennsylvania, and Maryland. He pointed out too that during the spring of 1971, the number of "Positions Open" ads in *Special Libraries* decreased, but that in recent issues the number of ads is building up again.

F. Kurt Cylke, Executive Secretary of the Federal Library Committee, is more pessimistic. He characterized the employment outlook for federal libraries as "bleak" and indicated that whereas it has been usual to have openings for 100 to 125 positions at the GS9 level each year, in 1971 he had listings for approximately 50.[4] In early November of 1971 he had 900 people listed on the GS9 Register. He also compared listings of positions in fall 1970 and fall 1971. In 1970 he had notices of 34 positions, GS7 to GS16, whereas a year later he had only 18 positions, GS5 to GS16. He did indicate some difficulty in finding competent people to fill upper positions and people with strong science backgrounds to fill vacancies requiring subject specialization.

CONCLUSION

After living with an expanding library labor force during the decade of the 1960s, about half of the nation's largest public and academic libraries have estimated either a very slight gain, no change, or a net loss in staffing levels for the years 1970, 1971, and 1972. The shrinking employment market enables the employer to select staff from among many qualified applicants, but it does mean that there are more applicants than positions. Not a single respondent saw any immediate relief from the budget squeezes that created this major reversal in number of placements of library staff.

The difficulties which some employers still find in filling vacancies result from shortages in applications submitted by experienced professional personnel. Catalogers, librarians to work with children, particularly in inner-city school and public libraries, managerial and supervisory personnel, black male librarians, and librarians with strong science backgrounds are still in demand in some areas, and would be even more so if more money were available to employ them. These facts have marked implications for every

---

[3]Letter, November 23, 1971.
[4]Conversation, November 12, 1971.

director of a library education program which exists primarily for the purpose of meeting the personnel needs of libraries.

TABLE 1 ESTIMATED NUMBER OF U.S. LIBRARIANS,[a] BY TYPE OF LIBRARY IN WHICH EMPLOYED

Type of Library	1960	1970[b]
All librarians	61,200	97,420
Public elementary and secondary school	19,700	34,520
Nonpublic elementary and secondary school	3,200	4,300
College and university	9,000[c]	20,200
Public library	19,500[d]	24,400
Special library	9,800	14,000

[a]Includes the full-time equivalents of part-time professional librarians. Excludes partly trained librarians. Public and nonpublic elementary and secondary school librarians included in table are those with 15 or more semester hours of library science.
[b]Estimate based on NCES surveys and projections.
[c]Actual data from Office of Education surveys.
[d]Estimate based on survey of libraries serving population of 35,000 or over.
Source: U.S. Office of Education, *Digest of Educational Statistics,* 1967 edition (Washington, D.C.: GPO, 1967), p. 118.

TABLE 2 U.S. BACHELOR'S AND HIGHER DEGREES IN ALL FIELDS AND IN LIBRARY SCIENCE, 1960–61 TO 1970–71

	Degrees in All Fields		Library Science Degrees		
Year	Number of Degrees	Percent Change from Previous Year	Number of Degrees	Percent Change from Previous Year	Percent of All Degrees
1960–61	490,628	5	2,384	5	.5
1961–62	514,323	5	2,573	8	.5
1962–63	551,810	7	2,842	10	.5
1963–64	614,194	11	3,240	14	.5
1964–65	663,622	8	3,846	19	.6
1965–66	709,832	7	4,577	19	.6
1966–67	768,871	8	5,206	14	.7
1967–68	866,548	13	6,056	16	.7
1968–69	984,129	14	6,949	15	.7
1969–70	1,012,400[a]	3	7,810[a]	12	.8
1970–71	1,076,100[a]	6	8,700[a]	12	.8

[a]Projected.
Source: U.S. Office of Education, *Digest of Educational Statistics,* 1970 edition (Washington, D.C.: GPO, 1970), p 89; *Projections of Educational Statistics to 1978–79,* 1969 edition (Washington, D.C.: GPO, 1970), pp. 41, 45, 47, 49.

TABLE 3 PUBLIC LIBRARY ESTIMATES OF PLACEMENTS, APPLICANTS, AND STAFF, BY CITY, 1969–1972

Library	No. of Placements			No. of Applicants			Total Staff			Comments on Employment Outlook
	Librarians	Tech. Assts.	Clerks	Librarians	Tech. Assts.	Clerks	Librarians	Tech. Assts.	Clerks	
Montgomery Co. Dept. of P.L., Bethesda										Supply exceeds demand.
1969	61	15	77	100	25	125	79	33	106	
1970	59	15	74	110	27	138	84	40	110	
1971	44	11	54	120	30	150	86	40	111	
1972	42	11	52	148	37	185	90	40	112	
Buffalo & Erie Co. P.L.										Not very bright.
1969	12	—	26	40	—	a	125	—	168	
1970	22	—	24	64	—	a	127	—	168	
1971	16	—	16	97	—	a	128	—	168	
1972	—	—	—	—	—	a	—	—	—	
Chicago P.L.										Favorable for libraries.
1969	53	90[b]	120	194	243[b]	—	229	125[b]	549	
1970	54	61[b]	178	210	300[b]	a	273	115[b]	564	
1971	24	16[b]	75	159	481[b]	a	278	103[b]	552	
1972	—	—	—	—	—	a	—	—	—	
P.L. of Cincinnati & Hamilton Co.										Poor. More applicants than positions.
1969	13	—	75	25	—	150	132	—	230	
1970	14	—	59	20	—	150	135	—	236	
1971	20	—	45	40	—	300	147	—	233	
1972	22	—	50	50	—	350	150	—	240	
Cleveland P.L.										—
1969	22	58	120	—	—	—	178	396	c	
1970	43	45	107	—	—	—	179	377	c	
1971	14	17	82	—	—	—	198	390	c	
1972	—	—	—	—	—	—	—	—	c	
Dallas P.L.										Need mid-management applicants.
1969	28[d]	—	—	—	—	—	113	—	223	
1970	—	—	—	—	—	—	—	—	—	
1971	16[d]	—	—	—	—	—	—	—	—	
1972	—	—	—	—	—	—	—	—	—	
Denver P.L.										Many qualified applicants. Few openings.
1969	18	17	54	57	142	280	112	53	150	
1970	16	11	70	96	292	557	112	53	150	
1971	13	3	79	55	424	614	112	53	150	
1972	13	3	83	56	445	644	112	53	150	
Detroit P.L.										Staff freeze for fiscal year 1971–1972. Only hiring will be through special federal funding. Need black male librarians at all levels.
1969	69	—	49	—	—	—	265	—	208	
1970	28	—	26	—	—	—	261	—	203	
1971	10	—	10	—	—	—	245	—	166	
1972	—	—	—	—	—	—	—	—	—	

TABLE 3, Continued

Library	No. of Placements Librarians	No. of Placements Tech. Asstts.	No. of Placements Clerks	No. of Applicants Librarians	No. of Applicants Tech. Asstts.	No. of Applicants Clerks	Total Staff Librarians	Total Staff Tech. Asstts.	Total Staff Clerks	Comments on Employment Outlook
Fairfax Co. P.L.[e]										Will probably be an employer's market for another year. Have difficulty filling beginning level of clerical positions.
1969	18	36	13	—	—	—	56	111	39	
1970	13	49	22	—	—	—	61	124	45	
1971	8	39	20	—	—	—	65	135	39	
1972	13	15	14	—	—	—	66	139	40	
Queens Borough P.L., Jamaica										Did not do recruiting in 1971. See no significant change through this fiscal year. However, we were recently able to negotiate hiring of 29 positions outside of 10%. If and when we will be able to do this again is unknown.
1969	50	—	49	85	—	190	345	—	345	
1970	65	—	37	110	—	140	364	—	354	
1971	16	—	29	65	—	150	361	—	354	
1972	—	—	—	—	—	—	—	—	—	
Los Angeles P.L.										—
1969	60	6	60	100	15	300	360	69	650	
1970	60	5	60	125	20	300	370	75	660	
1971	50	5	65	250	20	330	370	79	665	
1972	30	5	75	250	15	400	375	80	670	
Los Angeles Co. P.L. System										Fair. No difficulty in filling positions.
1969	55	30	—	374	38	—	142	180	—	
1970	43	45	—	498	57	—	152	194	—	
1971	15	11	—	326	75	—	157	144[f]	—	
1972	36	30	—	300	70	—	175	165	—	
Minneapolis P.L.										No difficulty in filling positions. Many more applicants than jobs.
1969	1	—	42	43	—	[a]	92	—	200	
1970	5	—	55	75	—	[a]	98	—	209	
1971	5	—	27	85	—	[a]	98	—	212	
1972	5	—	35	80	—	[a]	98	—	215	
Free P.L. of Philadelphia										—
1969	61	10	194	100	20[a]	388[a]	256[g]	—	692	
1970	20	5	83	125	10[a]	166[a]	269[g]	—	678	
1971	33	5	92	150	10[a]	184[a]	252[g]	—	614	
1972	—	—	—	—	—	—	—	—	—	

[a] Controlled by civil service.
[b] Have baccalaureate degree.
[c] Includes both technical assistant and clerical categories.
[d] Do not keep statistics of applicants according to professional-nonprofessional breakdown.
[e] In addition, the Fairfax County Public Library employees include 32 pages in 1972, 31 in 1971, 30 in 1970, and 25 in 1964.
[f] This library uses the category library assistant rather than library technical assistant. In 1971, 36 were reclassed as senior library assistants.
[g] Includes librarian and technical assistant categories. Clerical category includes all other positions.

TABLE 4 RATE CHANGE FROM PREVIOUS YEAR IN PUBLIC LIBRARIES SURVEYED FOR PLACEMENTS, APPLICANTS, AND STAFF, 1969–1972[a]

Year	Placements			Applicants			Total Staff		
	Librarians	Tech. Assts.	Clerks	Librarians	Tech. Assts.	Clerks	Librarians	Tech. Assts.	Clerks
1970	-10.3	-9.9	-9.5	28.1	46.1	1.2	.04	1.1	1.2
1971	-39.3	-63.2	-81.1	-6.0	47.3	19.1	1.3	-14.0	-3.3
1972	3.8	-7.2	6.5	.91	3.2	13.2	2.9	5.7	1.2

[a]Number of libraries included in respective computation varies according to available statistics.

TABLE 5 SCHOOL MEDIA CENTER PERSONNEL ESTIMATES BY CITY, 1971

City	Total No. of Staff		
	Librarians	Tech. Assts.	Clerks
Boston	26	—	—
Buffalo	45	0	6
Chicago	718	0	103
Cincinnati	50	2	—
Detroit	270	—	—
Minneapolis	87	0	115
Philadelphia	101	—	252

TABLE 6 ACADEMIC LIBRARY ESTIMATES OF PLACEMENTS, APPLICANTS, AND STAFF, BY INSTITUTION, 1969–1972

Library	No. of Placements			No. of Applicants				Total Staff				Comments on Employment Outlook
	Librarians	Tech. Assts.	Clerks	Librarians	Tech. Assts.	Clerks	Librarians	Tech. Assts.	Clerks	
Columbia University										
1969	18[a]	—	241	300[a]	—	950	180[a]	—	291	Anticipate fewer openings for both professionals and clericals.
1970	14[a]	—	150	300[a]	—	950	165[a]	—	310	
1971	12[a]	—	91	300[a]	—	895	159[a]	—	327	
1972	—	—	—	—	—	—	—	—	—	
Cornell University										
1969	11	—	79[b]	290	—	460[b]	136	—	252[b]	At the present time we have only one vacant academic position and are unable to fill this position due to the freeze on state funds.
1970	14	—	64[b]	300	—	503[b]	130	—	252[b]	
1971	9	—	22[b]	253	—	379[b]	125	—	241[b]	
1972	—	—	—	—	—	—	—	—	—	
Indiana University, Bloomington[c]										
1969	15	—	93	75	—	200	98	—	131	—
1970	18	—	98	100	—	200	103	—	129	
1971	16	—	71	80	—	200	103	—	129	
1972	15	—	80	80	—	200	103	—	129	
Ohio State University										
1969	25	—	44	35	—	100	88	—	200	Plenty of good applicants except for cataloging vacancies.
1970	14	—	54	40	—	100	90	—	202	
1971	10	—	69	100	—	150	92	—	218	
1972	8	—	70	—	—	200	94	—	225	
Southern Illinois University										
1969	—	20	24	—	38	72	62	20	45	Employer's market. Need catalogers with language ability.
1970	—	11	5	—	33	15	55	24	40	
1971	—	7	5	—	12	15	51	26	37	
1972	—	—	—	—	—	—	—	—	—	
Stanford University										
1969	13	80	15	—	—	—	130	215	43	Many applicants for each placement. The number of placements will decrease since we have to examine each vacancy for budget savings.
1970	5	75	10	—	—	—	140	228	38	
1971	5	50	5	—	—	—	135	225	35	
1972	4	40	4	—	—	—	133	220	30	
SUNY College, Buffalo										
1969	22	—	31	—	—	—	77	—	141	We have 41 vacancies and cannot get permission to spend appropriated funds to fill them.
1970	15	—	22	—	—	—	78	—	142	
1971	3	—	—	—	—	—	66	—	133	
1972	—	—	—	—	—	—	—	—	—	
University of California, Berkeley										
1969	16	150	300	60	227	398	141	304	481	Very slow for at least the rest of fiscal 1971–72. Applicants appear to be in great abundance for the few positions available.
1970	18	109	284	90	199	403	145	324	476	
1971	12	65	153	103	126	236	142	315	455	
1972	—	—	—	—	—	—	—	—	—	

TABLE 6, Continued

University of Chicago										
1969	11	—	134	—	—	—	86	—	209	Few professional openings. Need candidates for professional positions requiring previous administrative or supervisory experience.
1970	13	—	113	—	—	—	84	—	230	
1971	8	—	100	—	—	—	80	—	230	
1972	—	—	—	—	—	—	—	—	—	
University of Illinois										
1969	33	—	112[b]	—	—	—	164	—	184[b]	Grim. There are professionals in the area without jobs.
1970	42	—	152[b]	—	—	—	170	—	214[b]	
1971	45	—	131[b]	—	—	—	171	—	225[b]	
1972	21	—	100[b]	—	—	—	162	—	221[b]	
University of Michigan										
1969	32	267	—	350	1,335	—	147	306	—	The number of new positions expected to be created in the near future is small. Many highly qualified applicants for each entry level professional vacancy. Need applicants for cataloging positions requiring 3 or 4 years of relevant experience.
1970	32	188	—	410	752	—	140	320	—	
1971	33	357	—	500	1,071	—	128	298	—	
1972	—	—	—	—	—	—	—	—	—	
University of Minnesota										
1969	18	12	28	22	20	40	136	40	101	Grim! Forsee few technical assistants and clerk jobs — *no* librarian jobs.
1970	8	10	20	30	40	40	143	45	110	
1971	4	10	18	35	50	55	157	55	111	
1972	0	12	25	40	50	45	145	58	105	
University of Texas										
1969	26	67[d]	e	—	—	e	92	120[d]	e	No vacancies 11/1/71.
1970	11	108[d]	e	—	—	e	97	134[d]	e	
1971	4	35[d]	e	87	335[d]	e	97	134[d]	e	
1972	—	—	—	—	—	—	—	—	—	
University of Wisconsin, Madison										
1969	10	60	116	75	180	352	91	93	107	Few vacancies. Oversupply of applicants.
1970	9	70	142	120	210	426	91	93	107	
1971	5	30	52	150	90	156	97	98	113	
1972	7	35	60	150	105	180	97	98	113	
Yale University										
1969	—	—	—	—	—	—	—	—	—	—
1970	20	—	—	200	—	1,000[b]	170	—	330[b]	
1971	30	—	200[b]	200	—	1,000[b]	170	—	330[b]	
1972	—	—	—	—	—	—	—	—	—	

[a]Columbia's librarian category includes professionals other than librarians.
[b]Includes both technical assistant and clerical categories.
[c]Excludes Law Library.
[d]Instead of technical assistant category, Texas used classified budgeted personnel.
[e]Positions filled by student employees.

TABLE 7 RATE CHANGE FROM PREVIOUS YEAR IN ACADEMIC LIBRARIES SURVEYED FOR PLACEMENTS, APPLICANTS, AND STAFF, 1969–1972[a]

	Placements			Applicants			Total Staff		
Year	Librarians	Tech. Assts.	Clerks	Librarians	Tech. Assts.	Clerks	Librarians	Tech. Assts.	Clerks
1970	−14.8	−12.9	−8.4	15.1	−31.1	2.5	.1	6.3	2.9
1971	−15.8	−5.7	−34.4	8.2	9.3	−15.1	−6.9	−1.4	.1
1972	−35.2	−3.3	−2.0	1.8	10.7	11.4	−2.7	−.5	−1.0

[a]Number of libraries included in respective computation varies according to available statistics.

PLACEMENTS AND SALARIES 1970: THE YEAR THAT WAS *NOT* WHAT IT SEEMED*

by

Carlyle J. Frarey** and Mary R. Donley***

This twentieth annual report on placements and salaries for librarians who completed their formal studies for a professional career in 1970 describes a year of discontent. By late spring last year, prophets of doom were beginning to be heard; many believed that there were not enough positions for those who would enter the profession in the summer and fall of 1970, and the outlook for salaries and jobs was grim. The happy news is that the Cassandras were wrong. The extent and the patterns of employment and salaries in 1970 are remarkably similar to those of previous years, and while employment may have been a bit more difficult to find, it was not impossible to locate good positions at good salaries. The evidence of this report makes clear that 1970 was a pretty good year after all.

Readers of this series know that the summaries given here are based upon reports from the library schools accredited by the American Library Association, of which there were 53 in the spring of 1970. Forty-eight of these responded to the authors' request for salary and placement information on 1970 graduates in time to have their reports included in this summary.

To summarize: 1970 salaries improved by almost 6 percent over 1969, a slightly smaller gain than that observed last year. The most typical beginning salary was between $8,000 and $8,500; the average (mean) for all graduates was $8,611, and the median, $8,275. Graduates with previous experience received an average salary of $9,239; without such experience, their average salary was $8,119. As in other years, the proportion of new graduates who seek employment in various types of libraries remains substantially the same: 61 percent gravitated to college, university, or public libraries; 26 percent found positions in our school systems, an increase of 3 percent over 1969; and the remaining 13 percent were employed in other library agencies. The details of these placement and salary data are set forth in the tables accompanying this article.

PLACEMENTS

The 48 respondent schools awarded first professional degrees to 5,569 graduates in 1970, an increase of 599 over the 4,970 graduates reported by 45 schools in 1969. It is difficult to determine whether this represents any increase in the number of newly graduated librarians, however, for three schools have been added to the ALA-accredited list since February 1970, and five schools, including one of these three, have not supplied 1970 reports; thus truly comparable data are not available. It does not appear from the evidence that there has been any significant increase in the number of librarians entering the employment market in 1970. As is customary, not all graduates seek immediate library employment; 6 percent (369) did not in 1970. And, as was true last year, nearly one-quarter of all 1970 graduates (1,347 or 24 percent) did not inform their schools of their employment status and are not, therefore, represented in this report. All told, we have known placement information for 3,853 or 70 percent of the 1970 graduates of the 48 schools represented in this report, down somewhat from the 72 percent representation in 1969.

	U.S.	Canada	Total
Graduates	5150	419	5569
Not in library positions	330	39	369

---

*Reprinted from *Library Journal*, June 1, 1971.
**Senior Lecturer, Columbia University School of Library Service, New York, N.Y.
***Candidate for the D.L.S. degree at the School.

Not known   1339   8   1347
Known placements   3481   372   3853

The distribution of these placements by type of library is given in Table 2, and the comparative distribution since 1951 is shown in Table 3. The stability in this distribution over the past 20 years is remarkable, and it is again clear that we can predict with considerable accuracy in what type of library how many of each new crop of librarians will find employment. The greatest shift in 1970 is reflected in the proportion of new graduates who are employed in the elementary and secondary school systems and in our colleges and universities. We can hope that the gain in school library employment in 1970 reflects the efforts of more school systems to bring their services more nearly into line with the 1969 *Standards for School Media Programs.*

Demand and Supply: The schools are asked each year to report on the number of vacant library positions reported to them. While not all are able to do this, 34 of them did supply either a count or an estimate, aggregating for 1970 some 30,600 vacancies, a decline of 1,400 (4 percent) from the 32,000 positions reported by 34 schools in 1969. These figures are not absolute values, of course, for most libraries report their vacant positions to more than one school, and some libraries, especially in metropolitan areas, do not report theirs at all. But the figure is useful as a comparative measure of the need for librarians when it is observed on a year-to-year basis as has been done in this series.

Despite the generally held view that 1970 was a grim year for library employment, the modest reduction in demand between 1969 and 1970 is considerably less than the 30 percent reduction in the number of vacant positions reported in 1968 and 1969. Surprisingly, the actual reduction in the number of vacancies reported in 1970 is considerably less than the 28 percent reduction, on the average, reported by 27 of the 34 schools that commented on this matter. And, in contrast with the general picture, two schools reported significant increases in 1970 vacancies — 25 percent and 50 percent, respectively. The schools were not asked to indicate in what types of libraries they observed the increases or decreases that they reported for 1970, but the evidence suggests that the decreasing needs were observed generally in all sectors of library service. One thing is clear, however. There were library positions available in 1970 for all graduates who wanted them, although the choices open to these librarians were narrower than we have been accustomed to report in the 20 years that this series has been published. Clearly, we no longer have any serious shortage of librarians.

SALARIES

Readers will recall that in this series of reports, salary data are given for annual full-time salaries only, without regard to length of work weeks, vacation periods, sick leave, or other fringe benefits that affect the true rate of annual compensation. While it would be highly desirable to account for these benefits, the range of variability is too great to be manageable. In point of fact, these year-to-year comparisons of simple annual salaries do provide valid insights into the nature of employment opportunities in librarianship and do give an accurate picture of cash income expectations even if they do not provide a complete picture of the economic status of the profession.

For 1970, 47 of the 48 schools responding in this survey supplied salary data for their graduates, although not all schools were able to include all of their graduates in the salary reports, either because the salaries were unknown, or because they were asked to exclude atypical salary reports such as those from graduates from abroad who returned to their homelands, from graduates whose appointments were in religious orders where there is no salary, and from graduates whose compensation took the form of some combination of

TABLE 1 PLACEMENTS AND SALARIES OF 1970 GRADUATES

School	Place-ments	Salaries	Low Salary	High Salary	Avg. Salary	Median Salary
Albany	45	36	$7,000	$13,310	$8,677	$8,500
Alberta	38	38	7,000	14,000	8,135	7,650
Atlanta	86	82	5,352	11,700	8,504	8,400
Brigham Young	29	19	6,200	11,388	8,000	8,000
British Columbia	75	34	7,000	11,600	8,190	7,548
California	72	72	5,772	12,000	8,377	8,222
California at LA	50	29	7,000	11,000	8,967	9,000
Case Western Reserve	121	109	6,100	14,300	8,484	8,149
Catholic	62	45	7,200	18,353	10,823	10,470
Columbia	142	138	7,200	17,300	8,683	8,300
Denver	61	61	5,500	15,000	8,349	8,100
Drexel	146	119	6,000	13,500	8,615	8,400
Emory	75	60	6,000	10,500	8,007	8,000
Florida	105	93	6,535	15,000	8,539	8,300
Illinois	101	89	6,000	12,000	8,428	8,550
Indiana	86	84	5,800	15,000	8,428	8,093
Kansas	71	63	5,100	12,000	8,459	8,500
Kent	41	36	7,020	12,800	8,054	8,000
Kentucky*	10	10	7,200	9,310	8,481	8,500
Louisiana	85	55	5,700	10,500	7,829	8,000
McGill	36	7	7,200	8,200	.....	.....
Maryland	80	83	4,300	14,300	10,501	9,028
Michigan	206	156	7,130	18,816	9,472	8,900
Minnesota	80	68	7,000	16,615	9,003	8,600
Missouri	27	27	6,800	13,600	8,350	8,250
Montreal	51	51	6,800	13,945	7,608	7,250
North Carolina	72	52	4,602	14,000	8,705	8,200
Oklahoma	56	38	6,400	11,200	8,059	8,000
Oregon	69	37	6,750	11,850	8,487	8,400
Peabody	58	37	6,000	16,547	8,073	8,184
Pittsburgh	113	70	6,500	12,600	8,402	8,048
Post (Long Island U.)	97	82	6,040	13,000	8,188	8,500
Pratt	89	80	6,370	12,500	8,638	8,500
Rosary	148	94	7,000	15,000	9,050	9,065
Rutgers	129	101	6,400	16,000	8,850	8,500
San Jose	48	28	6,800	12,950	8,150	7,900
Simmons	141	74	7,000	20,000	8,469	8,200
Southern California	72	52	6,240	17,000	9,201	8,490
Syracuse	59	52	6,000	16,000	8,491	8,000
Texas	75	67	5,900	17,319	8,006	7,800
Texas Woman's	49	49	6,636	10,730	8,090	8,100
Toronto	172	161	6,200	16,000	8,464	7,600
Washington	95	87	6,654	15,000	8,966	8,500
Wayne	77	76	4,088	17,000	10,185	9,700
Western Michigan	75	64	6,640	16,000	9,193	8,900
School A	22	.....	.....	.....	.....	.....
School B	109	76	6,000	15,889	9,051	8,600
School C	47	43	6,600	10,268	8,406	8,050
Summary by Region						
Northeast schools	1103	880	4,300	20,000	8,940	8,500
Southeast schools	491	389	4,602	16,547	8,305	8,200
Midwest schools	1164	942	4,088	18,816	8,846	8,575
Southwest schools	227	197	5,900	17,319	8,140	8,025
Western schools	496	385	5,500	17,000	8,562	8,311
Canadian schools	372	291	6,200	16,000	8,099	7,574

Note: The figures for Kentucky in Tables 1 and 2, as reported in the September 1, 1971 *Library Journal*, are incomplete. The following corrections should be noted: In Table 1, the number of placements for Kentucky is 65; in Table 2, placements by type of library are public, 17; school, 11; college and university, 25; other libraries and library agencies, 12; total, 65.

TABLE 2 PLACEMENTS BY TYPE OF LIBRARY

School	Public	School	College & University	Other Libraries & Library Agencies	Total
Albany	13	12	13	7	45
Alberta	13	8	14	3	38
Atlanta	10	39	31	6	86
Brigham Young	15	2	9	3	29
British Columbia	25	13	29	8	75
California	24	4	37	7	72
California at LA	19	2	20	9	50
Case Western Reserve	60	23	23	15	121
Catholic	15	7	23	17	62
Columbia	51	17	52	22	142
Denver	19	19	16	7	61
Drexel	32	45	39	30	146
Emory	22	17	23	13	75
Florida	35	27	34	9	105
Illinois	18	14	62	7	101
Indiana	22	17	38	9	86
Kansas	12	32	22	5	71
Kent	15	11	14	1	41
Kentucky*	5	1	2	2	10
Louisiana	24	20	28	13	85
McGill	1	7	13	15	36
Maryland	18	21	16	25	80
Michigan	71	53	68	14	206
Minnesota	19	23	27	11	80
Missouri	6	5	12	4	27
Montreal	7	9	23	12	51
North Carolina	16	10	31	15	72
Oklahoma	8	14	27	7	56
Oregon	15	28	21	5	69
Peabody	6	16	28	8	58
Pittsburgh	30	30	41	12	113
Post (Long Island Univ.)	22	55	15	5	97
Pratt	46	20	7	16	89
Rosary	43	64	28	13	148
Rutgers	44	29	37	19	129
San Jose	12	20	10	6	48
Simmons	44	28	51	18	141
Southern California	28	16	26	2	72
Syracuse	14	16	21	8	59
Texas	19	5	39	12	75
Texas Woman's	9	19	19	2	49
Toronto	63	30	48	31	172
Washington	34	34	19	8	95
Wayne	19	41	8	9	77
Western Michigan	21	32	17	5	75
School A	4	8	8	2	22
School B	32	27	42	8	109
School C	14	14	17	2	47
TOTALS	1114	1004	1248	487	3853

*See footnote for Table 1.

living plus stipend. In 1970, salary data were available for 3,084, or for 80 percent of the known placements.

Known placements	3,853
Salaries unknown or not reported	769
Known salaries	3,084

Table 1 shows the salary data reported by each of the schools and the results may be summarized as follows:

Average salary	$8,611
Median salary	$8,275
Cluster range	$8,000–8,500
Individual salary range	$4,088–20,000

Average salary: The average salary for 1970 increased by $450 over that for 1969, a change of 5.5 percent, 1 percent less than the 6.5 percent gain observed between 1968 and 1969. The details of the annual change since 1961 are shown in Table 5. The beginning salary index may be compared with the cost of living index which, at the end of 1970, stood at 135.3 on the 1957–1959 base. Thus beginning library salaries have increased during this 11-year period at somewhat more than twice the rate of increase in the cost of living. It is evident, however, that the greatest real gains in salary occurred in the first half of the decade, for in January 1971, the Bureau of Labor Statistics changed the base year for determining the cost of living index to 1967. When this measure is used, the beginning salary index stands at 118 at the end of 1970 in comparison with a cost of living index of 116.3. Library beginning salaries are still a bit ahead of the cost of living, but the difference has narrowed very markedly in the last three years.

The range in reported averages for 1970 is quite wide, from $7,608 to $10,823, a difference of $3,215, and there is no substantial grouping around the norm. Only 16 schools report averages that are within $200 either side of the national average and only 22 schools show averages within $300, but this distribution is very close to that reported for 1969.

This year, for the first time, all schools were asked to differentiate salary data for the several types of libraries, and their reports are summarized in Table 6. From these data, it is readily apparent that the highest average salaries are to be found in the school systems, and the lowest in our public libraries. The reason is obvious, of course. Salaries in the schools are determined by the highest degree held and the number of years of teaching, including library experience. Since many of those who become school librarians have had previous experience as teachers, their beginning salaries as librarians tend to be higher.

Median Salaries: Forty-six schools reported median salary data ranging from a low median of $7,250 to a high of $10,470, with the national median at $8,275. The two highest medians at $9,700 and $10,470, as well as the lowest median of $7,250 are clearly atypical. Even so, only 14 schools reported medians that were within $200 of the national median, but 31 gave figures that were within a $300 range. If atypical medians were to be excluded, the national median would change by only $53, from $8,275 to $8,222. In either case, the median salary for 1970 is more than $300 higher than the 1969 median of $7,900.

Cluster Range: Each school is asked to report the cluster of salaries within which a majority of its placements fell

TABLE 3   PLACEMENTS BY TYPE OF LIBRARY, 1951–1970

Year	Public	School	College & University	Other Library Agencies*	Total
1951–1955**	2076 (33%)	1424 (23%)	1774 (28%)	1000 (16%)	6274
1956–1960**	2057 (33%)	1287 (20%)	1878 (30%)	1105 (17%)	6327
1961–1965**	2876 (30%)	1979 (20%)	3167 (33%)	1600 (17%)	9622
1966	830 (29%)	631 (22%)	927 (32%)	477 (17%)	2865
1967	904 (28%)	686 (21%)	1180 (37%)	456 (14%)	3226
1968	944 (26%)	838 (23%)	1254 (35%)	535 (16%)	3571
1969	981 (28%)	810 (23%)	1225 (35%)	501 (14%)	3517
1970	1114 (29%)	1004 (26%)	1248 (32%)	487 (13%)	3853

*From 1951 through 1966 these tabulations were for "special and other placements" in all kinds of libraries. Beginning with 1967, these figures include only placements in library agencies that do not clearly belong to one of the other three library groups.
**Figures for individual years are reported in preceding articles of this series.

in order to provide a measure of central tendency to check the validity of the mean and median as norms. The cluster ranges reported in 1970 varied from a low of $6,900–7,000 to a high of $10,470–10,500. The ranges reported by 36 of the 46 schools coincided in substantial measure with the $8,000–8,500 reported here.

Salary Range: The range in beginning salaries accepted by new graduates is always quite large. In 1970, the range was from a low of $4,088 to a high of $20,000, a whopping difference of $15,912 much larger than the $13,500 differential reported last year. The 1970 low was $912 lower than 1969's $5,000, either of them an unbelievably low salary for today.

High Salaries: The range in high salaries for 1970 was from $8,200 to $20,000, distributed by type of library as follows:

Salary	Pub.	Acad.	Sch.	Others
$ 8,000s		Not specified		
$ 9,000s	—	—	1	—
$10,000s	1	—	2	1
$11,000–$14,999	1	4	12	5
Over $15,000	—	4	8	6
TOTALS	2	8	23	12

In 35 of the 46 cases, previous experience accounted for the high beginning salary; in most of the others, the determining factor was special education and preparation above and beyond the master's degree in librarianship.

Low Salaries: The depressing range in low salaries in 1970, $4,088 to $7,200, is even sadder than the $5,000–7,250 reported in 1969. The distribution of these was as follows:

Salary	Pub.	Acad.	Sch.	Others
$4,000s	—	—	2	1
$5,000s	1	2	2	2
$6,000s	13	2	8	1
$7,000s	4	3	1	4
TOTALS	18	7	13	8

With few exceptions, the reason for low salaries remains the same each year. People who accept them prefer not to

TABLE 4 SPECIAL PLACEMENTS*

Governmental Jurisdictions	
National libraries	38
State & provincial libraries	58
Other government agencies (except VA hospitals)	48
Armed Services libraries (domestic)	14
Overseas agencies (including Armed Services libraries)	20
Total Governmental Jurisdictions	178
Medicine (including Nursing schools)	84
Science and technology	81
Library Science	
Teaching, adm. & research	23
Advanced study	47
Total Library Science	70
Business (bus. adm., finance, industry)	62
Law	48
Education	30
Communications industry (publishing, advertising)	25
Music	25
Art and museum	24
Hospitals (incl. VA hospitals)	24
Audiovisual & media centers	21
Social science	20
Religion (seminary, theology)	17
Historical agencies	14
Rare books & special collections	13
Children's specialist	11
International relations	10
International agencies	6
Bibliographer	4
Schools for handicapped	4
Union catalog	4
Library School library	3
Research	3
Theater & motion picture	2
Architecture	2
Black studies	2
Humanities	2
Systems analyst	2
Pharmacy	1
Archivist	1
Linguistics documentation	1
Bookmobile specialist	1
Adult service & extension	1
Cooperative college center	1
Documents	1
Total Special Placements	798

*Includes special placements in all types of libraries; not limited to the "Other libraries and library agencies" tabulation shown in Table 2.

LIBRARY EDUCATION, MANPOWER, AND SALARIES / 275

TABLE 5 AVERAGE SALARY INDEX FOR STARTING LIBRARY POSITIONS, 1957–59–1970

Year	Library Schools	Fifth-Year Graduates	Average Beginning Salary	Increase in Average	Beginning Salary Index
1957–1959*	29	1311	$4665	.....	100
1960	32	1710	5083	$418	109
1961	31	1715	5365	282	115
1962	32	1925	5661	296	121
1963	33	2188	5902	241	126
1964	35	2568	6145	243	132
1965	35	3115	6468	323	139
1966	34	3552	6765	297	145
1967	40	4030	7305	540	156
1968	42	4625	7660	355	164
1969	45	4970	8161	501	175
1970	48	5569	8611'	450	185

* The years 1957, 1958, and 1959 were used to obtain an average to be used as a base for the other years. The figures for each of these years are:

	1957	1958	1959
No. of Library Schools:	29	28	29
No. of Graduates:	1254	1136	1544
Salary:	$4450	$4683	$4862

TABLE 6 COMPARISON OF SALARIES BY TYPE OF LIBRARY

Type of Library	U. S. Schools	Canadian Schools	All Schools
Public libraries			
No. of schools	41	3	44
Salary range	$5722–14,500	$6200–8500	$5722–14,500
Mean salary	8136	7454	8088
Median salary	8000	7500	8000
School libraries			
No. of schools	40	3	43
Salary range	$4300–18,816	$6900–16,000	$4300–18,816
Mean salary	9028	10,312	9117
Median salary	8570	8,745	8640
College, University & Jr. College libraries			
No. of schools	41	3	44
Salary range	$5100–20,000	$6800–14,000	$5100–20,000
Mean salary	8719	7660	8647
Median salary	8400	7625	8325
Other libraries & lib. agencies			
No. of schools	40	3	43
Salary range	$4088–18,353	$6660–10,500	$4088–18,353
Mean salary	8854	7608	8767
Median salary	8510	7200	8500

TABLE 7 EFFECTS OF EXPERIENCE ON SALARIES

	Salaries Without Previous Experience (39 Schools)	Salaries With Previous Experience (38 Schools)
Number of Positions	1600	1013
Range of Low Salaries	$4088–7200	$5100–11,000
Median	6536	7202
Mean	6391	7449
Range of High Salaries	$7300–15,000	$9000–20,000
Median	9881	14,000
Mean	10,312	14,011
Range of Average (Mean) Salaries	$6339–9433	$8216–13,342
Median	8119	9239
Mean	8079	9707

be or cannot be mobile because of family or other personal considerations. The other most common reason is that some graduates each year are "indentured" to a library that provided them with financial assistance for their professional studies, and until they "work this off" in a year or two, they have no freedom of choice to reject a low salary offering for a better employment opportunity. There is, however, some slight and disturbing evidence that a few libraries are taking advantage of the greater availability of personnel to hold their salary levels lower than they ought to be.

Effects of Experience: In 1970, 39 of the reporting schools were able to differentiate between salaries offered to those who were thought to have previous experience relative to the employment offered and to those for whom previous experience was not a factor in their salaries. These reports are summarized in Table 7. It continues to be distressing that salaries below the national mean and median are offered to and accepted by some of those whose experience should net them more compensation than they receive. The explanation is the same as it has been in other years: when an experienced new graduate is unwilling or unable to go where the better opportunities are to be found, he may be forced to accept substandard compensation for his qualifications.

THE CANADIAN PICTURE

Table 1 summarizes the 1970 salaries for graduates of the Canadian library schools. This indicates a lower salary range (although the lowest Canadian salary is substantially better than the lowest U.S. salary), and a lower average and median salary than that of the United States schools. The Canadian average is quite close to that reported by the Southwestern library schools in this country, however. The Canadian high salary range was from $8,200 to $16,000, and the highest salary was equaled by three and surpassed by nine of the U.S. salaries. All of the high Canadian salaries were in school systems. The low salaries ranged from $6,200–7,200 and were found in every type of library except the schools.

The pattern of placements for Canadian graduates is markedly similar to that observed in the United States and may be compared as follows:

Type of library	U.S.	Canada
	\multicolumn{2}{c}{Percentage}
Public	29	29
School	26	18
College, University	32	34
Other	13	19

The greatest difference is observed in the number of Canadian graduates who are employed in the schools.

WHAT OF 1971?

Each director was asked to comment on the placement situation in the spring of 1971 as he observed this from his own experience. Their replies are remarkably similar and are summarized here.

Salaries (40 reports): The deans and directors divided on the question of whether salaries being offered in 1971 are better than those available to 1970 graduates. Of the 40 who commented, 25 believe that salaries are better by from $300 to $500, while 15 think that they observe no change. Unquestionably, many libraries are holding the line in this year of economic stringency for nonprofit institutions, yet it seems likely that many others are attempting to make cost of living adjustments. It will be a year before we have firm data, but in all likelihood the typical beginning salaries being offered this spring are between $8,800 and $9,000. The pressures for wage adjustment are strong throughout the economy and seem certain to continue. If this proves to be true, the salaries that will be offered in the spring of 1972 to beginning librarians should approximate $9,200.

Vacancies (36 reports): The overwhelming majority of the deans and directors (33) agree that there are fewer vacancies for new librarians in 1971 than there were in 1970 and suggest that this reduction is between 25 and 30 percent, yet three directors believe that there are more positions open this spring than last and attribute this to a greater demand for minority-group librarians, such as blacks and the Chicanos, as well as for media specialists. Among those who believe that there are fewer vacancies, there is no disagreement concerning the reason: a lack of funds generally, exacerbated by a decreasing level of federal aid. There is no substantial agreement among the directors concerning the types of libraries in which they note the decreases or the increases that they report. All types of libraries are represented in both lists.

Most of the deans and directors also responded to a specific question concerning any difficulties that they had encountered in placing their 1970 graduates and any that they expected in placing graduates for 1971. Surprisingly, there was substantial agreement among them all that their 1970 graduates were largely placed either before or within a few weeks after they received their degrees, although they did note that their graduates needed to be more aggressive in searching out their positions in 1970, and sometimes had to settle for a location or an assignment that was not their first choice. In general, however, despite the popular view that 1970 was a bad year for library employment, most graduates had no real problems in finding an appropriate appointment.

The deans, however, were a little more cautious in assessing the opportunities that would be open to their 1971 graduates. Many noted that very few libraries are scheduling recruiting visits this spring, and they also commented on the negative or nonresponses that many students are receiving in reply to letters of inquiry about openings. Even so, they were not pessimistic except concerning the opportunities likely to be open to those graduates who cannot relocate where the positions are to be found. The answer seems to be clear. Graduates in 1971 who can consider a relatively broad range of opportunities and locations can expect to find employment within a few weeks of graduation. Those who cannot will probably encounter more difficulty than in previous years.

No one, however, is suggesting that we should sharply reduce the number of new graduates, at least not yet. There is faith that our libraries are still growing institutions, and that a continuing supply of new manpower is requisite to their continued growth. We do know now that the estimates of new librarians needed which were widely circulated a few years ago were grossly overstated, and that our existing schools should be able to supply our manpower needs easily for the next several years. But it seems clear that these schools must give more careful attention to judicious recruiting and selection if they are to supply the dynamic, motivated librarian-specialists that are now in demand. It never was enough just to "love books," but it is clearer now than ever that librarianship is not, and cannot be, a refuge and a sanctuary any more for those who want a quiet and serene environment in which to pursue their varied interests and enthusiasms. The pressures for continued library expansion and development are great, especially in the public schools, community colleges, and public libraries. While it may be true that the librarian-generalist is no longer needed in as large numbers as before, and while it is certain that paraprofessionals and technicians will fill many openings in the future that hitherto have been filled by professionals, there seems to be no diminution of demand for librarian-specialists who can work knowledgeably with diverse media; in systems analysis and automation; with special groups such as children, the elderly, and the disadvantaged; or in special subject disciplines. Our expansion is temporarily slowed by economic conditions, but our future opportunities appear to be many and challenging. Even by next year the so-called crisis in library employment may be past. The report for 1971 should be interesting indeed.

In conclusion, the authors wish to thank the deans and directors of the several schools and their staffs for supplying the information upon which this summary is based. Without their willing and helpful assistance over the last two decades, we would know less about ourselves and the state of our profession than we do, and we would be unable to keep placements and salaries for beginning librarians in the perspective needed to guide us in recruitment, curricular planning, and in improving the economic status of the profession.

LIBRARY SALARIES AND VACANCIES AS REFLECTED IN ADS

by

Ruth R. Frame*

A survey of "Positions Open" classified ads in the September 1971 issues of *American Libraries, Library Journal, Wilson Library Bulletin,* and *College & Research Libraries* indicates that the median salary for such positions increased slightly from 1970 to 1971 (Table 1). The survey also shows a 31 percent decrease from September 1970 to September 1971 in the number of jobs advertised.

The steady decline from 1969 to 1971 in the number of advertised positions is indicated in Table 2. It is also interesting to note that the percentage of advertised positions requiring no experience rose steadily from 1967 to 1969 and has declined sharply since 1969.

In March 1967 — 31% required no experience.
In March 1968 — 33% required no experience.
In April 1969 — 37% required no experience.
In September 1969 — 39% required no experience.
In September 1970 — 24% required no experience.
In September 1971 — 21% required no experience.

In 1967 the Library Administration Division office of the American Library Association began making a brief study of library salaries and positions as reflected in library periodicals' classified ads. This study has been updated each year.

---

*Executive Secretary, Library Administration Division, American Library Association.

TABLE 1 HIGHEST, MEDIAN, LOWEST STARTING SALARIES[1]

	Mar. 1967	Mar. 1968	Apr. 1969	Sept. 1969	Sept. 1970	Sept. 1971
Positions requiring M.S. in L.S. with no experience						
Highest	$7758	$8500	$9350	$9200	$10,400	$9,000
Median	6000–6499	7000–7499	7500–7999	7500–7999	7,700	8,000
Lowest	5474	5400	6360	6420	6,000	4,800
Positions requiring M.S. in L.S. with experience						
Highest	$11,600	$12,000	$15,946	$13,000	$19,000	$18,252
Median	7500–7999	8500–8999	8000–8499	9000–9499	9,804	10,000
Lowest	5460	6200	7000	6400	7,000	7,200

[1] In 1967, 1968, and 1969 *College & Research Libraries* ads were not included.

TABLE 2 NUMBER OF POSITIONS ADVERTISED[1]

Types of Libraries	M.S. in L.S. Required with No Experience			M.S. in L.S. Required with Experience		
	Sept. 1969	Sept. 1970	Sept. 1971	Sept. 1969	Sept. 1970	Sept. 1971
Academic	23	8	7	30	34	17
Public	33	21	7	52	50	37
State	3	0	0	9	2	4
School	0	0	1	0	0	0
Other	5	1	3	8	8	9
TOTAL	64	30	18	99	94	67

[1] In 1969 C&RL ads were not included.

These surveys have been made in order to ascertain some of the "going rates" of vacancies and salary trends. Obviously, ads do not present a complete picture of salaries and vacancies or of library salaries in general.

Some types of libraries tend to advertise in other publications, many positions are not advertised in periodicals, and many of the lower-salaried positions are not advertised in national publications.

It is not always possible to tell from brief ads whether some of the positions are for one job or for multiple jobs; therefore, some of the positions counted as "1" may be for several positions. In this limited study, whenever it was possible to tell that a position had been advertised in two periodicals, that position was counted only once.

It is not always possible to ascertain from ads the position's exact educational requirement and whether or not experience is an absolute requirement; but the surveyor has interpreted the educational requirement and the experience or no experience qualification as clearly as possible. As experienced employees are often hired within the salary range or schedule rather than at the minimum step, it is not possible to ascertain the exact hiring rate. For the purpose of this brief survey, the minimum salary rate was assumed. Tables showing salary data omit those jobs for which no salary figure was indicated and those whose salary was quoted in foreign currency.

In addition to the study made of ads in *American Libraries, Library Journal, Wilson Library Bulletin,* and *College & Research Libraries,* a brief study was also made of library openings listed in eight (August and September 1971) issues of the Sunday *New York Times.* The data from the *New York Times* ads are not included in these tables because 55 percent of the *New York Times* ads indicate no salary figure.

Thirty-eight positions requiring an M.S. in library science with no experience, and 47 positions requiring an M.S. in library science with experience were advertised in the *New York Times.* The median salary range for positions requiring no experience was $8,000–$8,499; the median salary range for positions requiring experience was $10,500–$10,999. These medians were identical with those of a similar study of *New York Times* ads in 1970.

Of the 85 positions listed, 38 were in academic libraries, 25 in public libraries, 13 in school libraries, one in a state library, and seven in other libraries. In addition to these 85 jobs, there were six other related positions advertised in the Sunday *New York Times;* however, they either were not classified as "library openings" or they did not require a professional library education; they were located in various types of informational or educational services.

TABLE 3 ANNUAL MINIMUM STARTING SALARIES[1]

	% of Positions Advertised						
	Positions Requiring M.S. in L.S. with No Experience			Positions Requiring M.S. in L.S. with Experience		
Salary	Sept. 1969	Sept. 1970	Sept. 1971	Sept. 1969	Sept. 1970	Sept. 1971
Less than $6,000			8			
$ 6,000 – 6,499	2.4	3.3		3	0	0
6,500 – 6,999	7.1	3.3		0	0	0
7,000 – 7,499	33.3	23	8	3	3.2	1.8
7,500 – 7,999	26	26		12.1	3.2	1.8
8,000 – 8,499	21.4	16	50	18.1	16	9.2
8,500 – 8,999	7.1	10	16	12.1	7.4	5.5
9,000 – 9,499	2.4	0	16	10.6	10.6	11
9,500 – 9,999		6.6		9	13	9.2
10,000 – 10,499		10		15	9.5	16
10,500 – 10,999				3	2.1	7.4
11,000 – 11,499				1.5	7.4	1.8
11,500 – 11,999				3	4.2	3.7
12,000 – 12,499				4.5	9.5	7.4
12,500 – 12,999				4.5[2]	12.7[2]	3.7
13,000 – 13,999						1.8
14,000 – 14,999						1.8
15,000 – 15,999						7.4
16,000 – 16,999						3.7
17,000 – 17,999						0
18,000 - up						5.5

[1] In 1969 *C&RL* ads were not included.

[2] 1969–1970 table indicated salary range as $12,500–up. The 1971 information breakdown is more explicit.

TABLE 4 FOUR HIGHEST POTENTIAL SALARIES (TOP OF THE SCALE) LISTED IN ADS[1]

Date	Position	Salary
March 1967	Librarian, College Library	$13,820
	Associate Director, County Library	13,270
	Reference Librarian, Academic Library	11,946
	Assistant Director, Public Library	11,705
March 1968	Library Supervisor, State Library	14,657
	Fine Arts Coordinator, Public Library	14,178
	Head, Technical Services, Public Library	14,178
	Director, County Library	14,040
April 1969	Director, Public Library	24,690
	Director, Public Library	20,000
	Associate Director, Public Library	19,739
	Chief, Special Library	18,000
Sept. 1969	Reference Librarian, Academic Library	15,000
	Librarian, Public Library	15,000
	Coordinator, Audiovisual, Public Library	14,490
	Editor, Special Library	14,376
Sept. 1970	System Director, Public Library	25,032
	Deputy Chief Librarian, University Library	19,000
	Regional System Director, Public Library	18,000
	Supervisor, Librarian, Special Library	17,704
Sept. 1971	Administrator, Public Library	22,204
	Chief Librarian, Historical Society	21,000
	Assistant Director, Public Library	20,000
	Assistant Director, State Library	19,854

[1] In 1967, 1968, and 1969 C&RL ads were not included.

GRADUATE LIBRARY SCHOOLS ACCREDITED BY THE AMERICAN LIBRARY ASSOCIATION*

NORTHEAST

Catholic University of America, Department of Library Science, Washington, D. C. 20017. Rev. James J. Kortendick, Chairman.

Columbia University, School of Library Service, New York, N.Y. 10027. Richard L. Darling, Dean.

Drexel University, Graduate School of Library Science, Philadelphia, Pa. 19104. Guy Garrison, Dean.

Long Island University, C. W. Post Center, Palmer Graduate Library School, P.O., Greenvale, N.Y. 11548. John T. Gillespie, Dean.

University of Maryland, School of Library & Information Services, College Park, Md. 20742. Margaret Chisholm, Dean.

State University of New York, Albany, School of Library & Information Science, Albany, N.Y. 12203. John J. Farley, Dean.

State University of New York at Geneseo, School of Library & Information Science, Geneseo, N.Y. 14454. Ivan L. Kaldor, Dean.

University of Pittsburgh, Graduate College of Arts & Science, School of Library & Information Sciences, Pittsburgh, Pa. 15213. Frank B. Sessa, Acting Dean.

Pratt Institute, Graduate School of Library & Information Science, Brooklyn, N.Y. 11205. Nasser Sharify, Dean.

Queens College, City University of New York, Department of Library Science, Flushing, N.Y. 11367. Morris A. Gelfand, Chairman.

University of Rhode Island, Graduate Library School, Kingston, R.I. 02881. E. J. Humeston, Jr., Dean.

Rutgers University, Graduate School of Library Service, New Brunswick, N.J. 08903. Thomas H. Mott, Jr., Dean.

Simmons College, School of Library Science, Boston, Mass. 02115. Kenneth R. Shaffer, Director.

Syracuse University, School of Library Science, Syracuse, N.Y. 13210. Roger C. Greer, Dean.

SOUTHEAST

Atlanta University, School of Library Service, Atlanta, Ga. 30314. Mrs. Virginia Lacy Jones, Dean.

Emory University, Division of Librarianship, Atlanta, Ga. 30322. A. Venable Lawson, Director.

Florida State University, School of Library Science, Tallahassee, Fla. 32306. Harold Goldstein, Dean.

University of Kentucky, College of Library Science, Lexington, Ky. 40506. Lawrence A. Allen, Dean.

Louisiana State University, Library School, Baton Rouge, La. 70803. Donald D. Foos, Director.

University of North Carolina, School of Library Science, Chapel Hill, N.C. 27514. Ray L. Carpenter, Acting Dean.

George Peabody College for Teachers, School of Library Science, Nashville, Tenn. 37203. Edwin S. Gleaves, Director.

MIDWEST

Case Western Reserve University, School of Library Science, Cleveland, Ohio 44106. William Goffman, Dean.

University of Chicago, Graduate Library School, Chicago, Ill. 60637. Don R. Swanson, Dean.

University of Illinois, Graduate School of Library Science, Urbana, Ill. 61801. Herbert Goldhor, Director.

Indiana University, Graduate Library School, Bloomington, Ind. 47401. Bernard M. Fry, Dean.

University of Iowa, School of Library Science, Iowa City, Iowa 52240. Frederick Wezeman, Director.

---

*A complete list of institutions in the United States and Canada offering training in librarianship appears in the 1970-71 American Library Directory. These institutions total 395, including those accredited by the American Library Association.

Kansas State Teachers College, Department of Librarianship, Emporia, Kans. 66801. Norman Clarke, Head.

Kent State University, School of Library Science, Kent, Ohio 44240. Guy A. Marco, Dean.

University of *Michigan,* School of Library Science, Ann Arbor, Mich. 48104. Russell E. Bidlack, Dean.

University of *Minnesota,* Library School, Minneapolis, Minn. 55455. David K. Berninghausen, Director.

University of *Missouri, Columbia,* School of Library and Informational Science, Columbia, Mo. 65201. Ralph H. Parker, Dean.

Northern *Illinois* University, Department of Library Science, DeKalb, Ill. 60115. LaVern Walther, Head.

Rosary College, Graduate School of Library Science, River Forest, Ill. 60305. Sister M. Lauretta McCusker, O.P., Dean.

Wayne State University, Department of Library Science, Detroit, Mich. 48202. Robert E. Booth, Chairman.

Western Michigan University, School of Librarianship, Kalamazoo, Mich. 49001. Jean Lowrie, Director.

University of *Wisconsin,* Library School, Madison, Wis. 53706. Charles A. Bunge, Director.

SOUTHWEST

North *Texas* State University, School of Library & Information Sciences, Denton, Texas 76203. Sarah Law Kennerly, Acting Dean.

University of *Oklahoma,* School of Library Science, Norman, Okla. 73069. Frank J. Bertalan, Director.

University of *Texas,* Graduate School of Library Science, Austin, Texas 78712. Stanley McElderry, Dean.

Texas Woman's University, School of Library Science, Denton, Texas 76204. D. Genevieve Dixon, Director.

WEST

Brigham Young University, Graduate Department of Library & Information Sciences, Provo, Utah 84601. H. Thayne Johnson, Director.

San *Jose* State College, Department of Librarianship, San Jose, Calif. 95114. Leslie H. Janke, Chairman.

University of *California,* School of Librarianship, Berkeley, Calif. 94720. Patrick Wilson, Dean.

University of *California, Los Angeles,* Graduate School of Library Service, Los Angeles, Calif. 90024. Andrew H. Horn, Dean.

University of *Denver,* Graduate School of Librarianship, Denver, Colo. 80210. Mrs. Margaret Knox Goggin, Dean.

University of *Hawaii,* Graduate School of Library Studies, Honolulu, Hawaii 96822. Robert D. Stevens, Dean.

University of *Oregon,* School of Librarianship, Eugene, Ore. 97403. Perry D. Morrison, Dean.

University of *Southern California,* School of Library Science, University Park, Los Angeles, Calif. 90007. Martha Boaz, Dean.

University of *Washington,* School of Librarianship, Seattle, Wash. 98105. Irving Lieberman, Director.

CANADA

University of *Alberta,** School of Library Science, Edmonton 7, Alberta. Mary E. P. Henderson, Acting Director.

University of *British Columbia,** School of Librarianship, Vancouver 8, B.C. Roy B. Stokes, Director.

McGill University, Graduate School of Library Science, Montreal 112, Quebec. Violet L. Coughlin, Director.

University of *Montreal,* Ecole de Bibliotheconomie, Montreal 101, Quebec. Richard K. Gardner, Director.

University of *Toronto,* School of Library Science, Toronto 181, Ontario. R. Brian Land, Director.

University of *Western Ontario,* School of Library and Information Science, London 72, Ontario. William J. Cameron, Dean.

---

*Basic program at the fifth-year level leads to the professional Bachelor's degree. As of September 1971, the University of British Columbia will offer only a two-year program leading to the Master of Library Science degree.

LIBRARY SCHOLARSHIPS AND FELLOWSHIPS

OFFERED IN 1971-1972

For a more complete list of the scholarships and fellowships offered for library study, see *Financial Assistance for Library Education, Academic Year 1971-1972*, published annually by the American Library Association. (Copies available at 50 cents each [10 copies, $4.75; 25 copies, $11.25; 100 copies, $42.00] from: Order Department, ALA, 50 E. Huron St., Chicago, Ill. 60611.) See also list of "Trainee or Student Librarian Programs" and "Grants to Libraries or for Library Purposes, 1971," this volume.

The ALA SCHOLARSHIP PROGRAM provides scholarships in the amount of $2,500, given annually to worthy students to begin and/or further their library education at the graduate level. Recipients must enter a formal program of graduate study leading to a degree or advanced certificate at an ALA-accredited school. The program is administered by the ALA Awards Committee and the Library Education Division. Application and recommendation forms are available from the jury chairman, J. Phillip Immroth, Graduate School of Library and Information Science, University of Pittsburgh, Pittsburgh, Pa. 15213. 1971 award winner: Janice Elizabeth Sims.

The CARNEGIE CORPORATION of New York awarded the School of Library Science of North Carolina Central University a grant of $120,000 for the development of a new program for the training of early childhood library specialists. The grant provides for five fellowships in the amount of $2,000 each to be awarded in the academic years of 1971–1973. Applicants should express an interest in young children and should plan to assume positions in early childhood work upon completion of the curriculum. Students admitted to the program will undertake one academic year and one summer of basic library training courses with a specialization in early childhood. Successful completion of the program qualifies the student to receive the Master of Library Science degree. Application forms are available from the Office of the Dean, North Carolina Central University, Durham, N.C. 27707.

The CATHOLIC LIBRARY ASSOCIATION is soliciting applications for the 1972 Reverend Andrew L. Bouwhuis Scholarship of $1,000 for graduate study in librarianship. Promise of success based on collegiate record, evidence of need for financial help, and acceptance in a graduate library school program are the criteria being considered. For applications, contact the Scholarship Committee, Catholic Library Association, 461 W. Lancaster Ave., Haverford, Pa. 19041. Deadline for 1972 scholarship, February 1, 1972.

The COUNCIL ON LIBRARY RESOURCES offers fellowships to midcareer librarians who have demonstrated a strong potential for leadership in the profession. The purpose is to enable librarians to familiarize themselves with new developments in their fields. The awards will cover costs incident to a fellow's program during a period of continuous leave which may range in time from a minimum of an academic quarter up to nine months; the candidate's salary will be continued for the period of absence by his institution. Apply to: Fellowship Committee, Council on Library Resources, Inc., One Dupont Circle, Suite 620, Washington, D.C. 20036.

The E. P. DUTTON–JOHN MACRAE Award is an annual scholarship of $1,000 and a certificate given to a librarian working with children or young adults in a public, school, or institutional library for informal or formal advanced study (beyond master's degree) in the field of library work for children and young people. Applicants must be graduates of an ALA-accredited library school and must have had at least three years of successful experience in libraries serving children, young people, or young adults. Donated by the E. P. Dutton Company. Administered by ALA Awards Committee. Applications are available from the jury chairman, Winifred C. Ladley, Graduate School of Library Science, University of Illinois, Urbana, Ill. 61801. 1971 award winner: Judith K. Meyers.

The CAROLINE M. HEWINS Scholarship of $900 is awarded to students planning to specialize in library work with children. Applicants must have a college degree by June, and have applied to an ALA-accredited library school. The fund, established in 1926, gives preference to those planning to work in public library service. Applications and information may be obtained by writing to Caroline M. Hewins Scholarships, c/o Librarian, Hartford Public Library, 500 Main St., Hartford, Conn. 06103.

The LIBRARY BINDING INSTITUTE Scholarship awards $1,000 annually to a worthy student to further his library education. Donated by the Library Binding Institute. Administered by the ALA Library Education Division. Information and application forms are available from the jury chairman, Martin Cohen, School of Librarianship, Western Michigan University, Kalamazoo, Mich. 49001. 1971 award winner: Margaret Ann Botchie.

The MEDICAL LIBRARY ASSOCIATION is offering a 1972/73 medical librarianship fellowship to foreign students, which provides traveling expenses to the United States in addition to a monthly stipend and tuition costs. The six-month program, to be held at a U.S. medical library, will include observation, work, and a six-week course in medical librarianship. Applicants must be working or preparing to work in a medical library and should be prepared to work in their own country for a period of two years after completion of the fellowship. Proficiency in the English language is required. For applications and further information contact Dr. Carroll Reynolds, Chairman, MLA Committee on International Cooperation, Falk Library of the Health Professions, University of Pittsburgh, Pittsburgh, Pa. 15213.

MEDICAL LIBRARY ASSOCIATION: One $1,500 scholarship and the Paul Jolowicz scholarship of $1,000 are offered by the Medical Library Association to qualified students who entered library school in the summer or fall of 1971. Applications available from any ALA-accredited library school or from the MLA central office, Suite 2023, 919 N. Michigan Avenue, Chicago, Ill. 60611.

The FREDERIC G. MELCHER Scholarship is an annual $3,000 scholarship established by the Children's Services Division of ALA to encourage and assist young people who wish to enter the field of library service to children. It is awarded to a qualified candidate who has been accepted for admission to an ALA-accredited library school. Donated by Daniel Melcher, administered by the Children's Services Division, ALA. Applications and information are available from the jury chairman, Patricia Cianciolo, Michigan State University, 360 Erickson Place, East Lansing, Mich. 48823. 1971 award winner: E. Relleen Smith.

USOE FELLOWS PROGRAM: A one-year program which takes the fellow to Washington for a ten-month assignment in the Office of Education. The ten-month stint pays up to $13,000. Fellows are selected for their evidence of leadership abilities. Send for application forms to regional Commissioner of Education.

The following institutions sponsor scholarship programs; for information, apply directly to them.

California: Immaculate Heart College, Los Angeles; San Jose State College, San Jose; University of California, Berkeley; University of California, Los Angeles; and University of Southern California, Los Angeles.

Colorado: University of Denver.

District of Columbia: George Washington University.

Georgia: Atlanta University, Atlanta; Emory University, Atlanta.

Hawaii: University of Hawaii, Honolulu.

Illinois: University of Chicago; University of Illinois, Urbana; Rosary College, River Forest.
Indiana: De Pauw University, Greencastle; Indiana State University, Terre Haute; Indiana University, Bloomington.
Iowa: University of Iowa, Iowa City.
Kansas: Kansas State Teachers College, Emporia.
Kentucky: Catherine Spaulding College, Louisville; University of Kentucky, Lexington.
Maryland: University of Maryland, College Park.
Massachusetts: Radcliffe Institute, Cambridge; Simmons College, Boston.
Michigan: University of Michigan, Ann Arbor; Western Michigan University, Kalamazoo.
Minnesota: College of St. Catherine, St. Paul; University of Minnesota, Minneapolis.
Mississippi: University of Mississippi, University; University of Southern Mississippi, Hattiesburg.
Missouri: University of Missouri, Columbia; Washington University, St. Louis.
Nebraska: University of Nebraska, Lincoln.
New York: Columbia University, New York; Long Island University, Greenvale; Pratt Institute, Brooklyn; Syracuse University.
North Carolina: University of North Carolina, Chapel Hill.
Ohio: Case Western Reserve University, Cleveland.
Oklahoma: Oklahoma State University, Stillwater; University of Oklahoma, Norman.
Oregon: University of Oregon, Eugene; University of Portland, Portland.
Pennsylvania: University of Pittsburgh.
Tennessee: George Peabody College for Teachers, Nashville.
Texas: Our Lady of the Lake College, San Antonio; Texas Woman's University, Denton; University of Texas, Austin.
Washington: University of Washington, Seattle.
Wisconsin: University of Wisconsin, Madison.

Additional information may be obtained from the Bureau of Libraries and Educational Technology, Regional Office Bldg., 7th and D Sts. S.W., Washington, D.C. 20202.

LIBRARY FRATERNITIES

ALPHA BETA ALPHA

(National undergraduate library science fraternity)

OBJECT

"To further the professional knowledge of its members, to promote fellowship, and to serve as a recruiting agency for librarians." Founded May 3, 1950, Northwestern State College of Louisiana, Natchitoches, La. Memb. 650.

OFFICERS

Pres. Linda Ward, Beta Chapter, 251 Candler Road S.E., Apt. C-16, Atlanta, Ga. 30317; *V.P.* Sally Jane Sorrells, Beta Chapter, The Magnolia, Box 635, Columbus, Miss. 39701; *Treas.* (To be appointed) Upsilon Chapter.
Exec. Secy. Miss Jean A. Elliott, Shepherd College Library, Shepherdstown, W.Va. 25443.

COUNCIL

Composed of the officers and one Councilman from each of the five districts. *Councilmen:* Ann Ayer, Delta Chapter, Dist. 1; Ann Wyatt, Epsilon Chapter, Dist. 2; Cecille McMahon, Alpha Kappa Chapter, Dist. 3; Maurice J.

Heim, Rho Chapter, Dist. 4; Betty Jean Navratil, Eta Chapter, Dist. 5.

CHAPTERS

Northwestern State Coll., Natchitoches, La. 71457; Mississippi State Coll. for Women, Columbus, Miss. 39701; Indiana State Univ., Terre Haute, Ind. 47809; Univ. of Alabama, Tuscaloosa, Ala. 35486; Murray State Univ., Murray, Ky. 42071; Concord Coll., Athens, W. Va. 24712; Texas Woman's Univ., Denton, Tex. 76204; Arizona State Univ., Tempe, Ariz. 85281; San Jose State Coll., San Jose, Calif. 95100; Millersville State Teachers Coll., Millersville, Pa. 17551; Louisiana State Univ., Baton Rouge, La. 70800; Illinois State Univ., Normal, Ill. 61761; Marshall Univ., Huntington, W. Va. 25700; Univ. of Northern Iowa, Cedar Falls, Iowa 50613; Florida A. & M. Univ., Tallahassee, Fla. 32301; Our Lady of the Lake Coll., San Antonio, Tex. 78207; Kutztown State Teachers Coll., Kutztown, Pa. 19530; Western Michigan Univ., Kalamazoo, Mich. 49001; Shepherd Coll., Shepherdstown, W. Va. 25443; Central Michigan Univ., Mount Pleasant, Mich. 48858; North Texas State Univ., Denton, Tex. 76203; Southeast Missouri State Coll., Cape Girardeau, Mo. 63203; Univ. of Tennessee, Knoxville, Tenn. 39700; Madison Coll., Harrisonburg, Va. 22802; Francis T. Nicholls State Coll., Thibodaux, La. 70301; Morehead State College, Morehead, Ky. 40351; Oklahoma State Univ., Stillwater, Okla. 74074; Florence State Coll., Florence, Ala. 35630; Shippensburg State Coll., Shippensburg, Pa. 17257; East Carolina Univ., Greenville, N.C. 27834; Louisiana Polytechnical Institute, Ruston, La. 71271; Glassboro State Coll., N.J. 08028; Central State Coll., Edmond, Okla. 73034; Edinboro State Coll., Edinboro, Pa. 16412; Northwest Missouri State Coll., Maryville, Mo. 64468; Radford Coll., Radford, Va. 24141; Eastern Illinois Univ., Charleston, Ill. 61920; West Virginia Wesleyan Coll., Buckhannon, W. Va. 26201; Mansfield State Coll., Mansfield, Pa. 16933; Austin Peay State Univ., Clarksville, Tenn. 37040; Sam Houston State Univ., Huntsville, Tex. 77340; Slippery Rock State Coll., Slippery Rock, Pa. 16057; State Coll. of Arkansas, Conway, Ark. 72032; Jackson State College, Jackson, Miss. 39217.

ACTIVITIES

Alpha Beta Alpha celebrated its twenty-first birthday on May 3, 1971. One chapter was installed in the spring. Two new chapters will be installed this year, one at Wisconsin State University, Whitewater, and the other at Western Illinois University, Macomb. The tenth national convention will be held at Murray State University, Murray, Kentucky on April 20-22, 1972.

BETA PHI MU

(International library science honorary society)

OBJECT

"To recognize high scholarship in the study of librarianship, and to sponsor appropriate professional and scholarly projects." Founded at the University of Illinois in 1948. Memb. 10,000.

OFFICERS

Pres. Dr. Frank B. Sessa, Grad. S. of L. & Info. Scis., Univ. of Pittsburgh, Pittsburgh, Pa. 15213; *V.P. & Pres. Elect.* Sarah R. Reed, Assoc. Dean, Indiana Univ., Grad. L. S., Univ. L., Bloomington, Ind. 47401; *Past Pres.* Dr. Jesse H. Shera, S. of L. Sci., Case Western Reserve Univ., Cleveland, Ohio 44106; *Treas.* Mrs. Marilyn P. Whitmore, 125 Johnston Rd., Upper St. Clair, Pa. 15241; *Exec. Secy.* Dr. Harold Lancour, Grad. S. of L. & Info. Sci., Univ. of Pittsburgh, Pittsburgh, Pa. 15213; *Assoc. Exec. Secy.* Alice Appell, Long Beach P.L., Long Beach, Calif. 90802; *Admin. Secy.-Editor.* Mrs. Mary Y. Tomaino, 1615 Clark St., Pittsburgh, Pa. 15221. (Send all general correspondence to the Exec. Secy. at Natl. Headquarters Office, Beta Phi Mu, Grad. S. of L. & Info. Scis.,

Univ. of Pittsburgh, LIS Bldg., Pittsburgh, Pa. 15213.)

DIRECTORS

Mrs. Elizabeth Rodell, Asst. Libn. for Tech. Servs., The Fondren L., Rice Univ., Houston, Tex. 77001; Carlyle J. Frarey, Senior Lecturer, S. of L. Serv., Columbia Univ., New York, N.Y. 10027; C. Donald Cook, Res. & Plan. Officer, Ontario Univs. Bibliographic Centre Project, 4 Devonshire Pl., Toronto 181, Ontario, Can.; Miss Karen Kivi, P. Servs. Libn., Moorhead State Coll. L., Moorhead, Minn. 56560; J. Richard Blanchard, Univ. L., Univ. of Calif., Davis, Calif. 95616; H. Joanne Harrar, Assoc. Dir. of Ls., Univ. of Georgia, Athens, Ga. 30601.

CHAPTERS

Univ. of Ill., Grad. S. of L. Sci., Urbana, Ill. 61801; Univ. of S. Calif., S. of L. Sci., Los Angeles, Calif. 90007; Fla. State Univ., S. of L. Sci., Tallahassee, Fla. 32306; Loughborough Coll. of Further Educ., S. of Libnshp., Loughborough, Eng.; Univ. of N.C., S. of L. Sci., Chapel Hill, N.C. 27514; Atlanta Univ., S. of L. Serv., Atlanta, Ga. 30314; Pratt Institute, Grad. S. of L. & Info. Sci., Brooklyn, N.Y. 11205; Catholic Univ. of America, Dept. of L. Sci., Washington, D.C. 20017; Univ. of Md., S. of L. & Info. Servs., College Park, Md. 20742; Western Mich. Univ., S. of Libnshp., Kalamazoo, Mich. 49001; Univ. of Okla., S. of L. Sci., Norman, Okla. 73069; Univ. of Mich., S. of L. Sci., Ann Arbor, Mich. 48104; Columbia Univ., S. of L. Serv., New York, N.Y. 10027; Univ. of Hawaii, Grad. S. of L. Studies, Honolulu, Hawaii 96822; Rutgers Univ., Grad. S. of L. Serv., New Brunswick, N.J. 08903; Univ. of Pittsburgh, Grad. S. of L. & Info. Scis., Pittsburgh, Pa. 15213; Kent State Univ., S. of L. Sci., Kent, Ohio 44240; Drexel Univ., Grad. S. of L. Sci., Philadelphia, Pa. 19104; State Univ. of N.Y. at Geneseo, S. of L. & Info. Sci., Coll. of Arts and Scis., Geneseo, N.Y. 14454; Univ. of Ky., Coll. of L. Sci., Lexington, Ky. 40506; Univ. of Denver, Grad. S. of Libnshp., Denver, Colo. 80210; Syracuse Univ., S. of L. Sci., Syracuse, N.Y. 13210; Indiana Univ., Grad. L. S., Bloomington, Ind. 47401; Univ. of Mo., Columbia, S. of L. & Info. Sci., Columbia, Mo. 65201; San Jose State Coll., Dept. of Libnshp., San Jose, Calif. 95114; Queens Coll., City Univ. of N.Y., Dept. of L. Sci., Flushing, N.Y. 11367. Professional chapters at Cornell Univ., Ithaca, N.Y. 14850; Univ. of Utah, Salt Lake City, Utah 84112; Univ. of Wash., Seattle, Wash. 98101.

ACTIVITIES

The annual business meeting and initiation was held in Dallas, Texas in June 1971. The 1972 annual business meeting and initiation will be held in Chicago, on June 25. (For history of Beta Phi Mu, see the 1971 *Bowker Annual,* pp. 183-184.)

TRAINEE OR STUDENT LIBRARIAN PROGRAMS

The following survey of states having formal trainee or student librarian programs, and offering some special arrangements for library education is compiled annually by the Editor of the *Bowker Annual*. This report, the eighth thus far published, is based on the replies of state librarians to the following questions: (1) "Are there any libraries in your state that have a formal trainee or student librarian program in which persons with undergraduate degrees are accepted on the staff with the understanding that they will work on and complete a library degree within a given period of time?" and (2) "Are there any Library Technician Programs operative in your state, including (a) libraries that have initiated such a program, and (b) colleges and universities that offer Library Technician Programs?"

Alabama

The *Alabama Public Library Service* has a program of Library Education which provides grants for education in the field of Library Science, on the graduate and/or undergraduate level. Each recipient must work in a public library for one year after completion of training. There is also a summer trainee program of eight weeks for young people in high school and college who might become prospective librarians.

Two junior colleges are currently offering a library technician course:

Theodore Alfred Lawson Jr. College, Birmingham and S. D. Bishop State Jr. College, Mobile.

Arkansas

Arkansas Library Commission has a trainee program for young people with college education who wish to attend graduate library school. They work in county and regional libraries as well as in state library headquarters, during summer vacations.

California

The following libraries currently have a formal trainee program:

Buena Park Library District
Corona Public Library
Daly City Public Library
Fresno County Free Library
Fullerton Public Library
Glendale Public Library
Inglewood Public Library
Kern County Library
Long Beach Public Library
Los Angeles Public Library
Mountain View Public Library
Napa City-County Library
Newport Beach Public Library
Orange County Public Library
Palo Alto Public Library
Pasadena Public Library
Placentia District Library
Pomona Public Library
Redondo Beach Public Library
Richmond Public Library
Riverside City and County Public Library
San Bernardino County Library
San Diego Public Library
San Mateo County Library
Santa Fe Springs Public Library
Santa Paula U.H.S.P.L. District Library
South Pasadena Public Library
Stockton-San Joaquin County Library
Upland Public Library
Ventura City-County Library
Yorba Linda District Library

The following is a list of California community colleges (junior colleges) that offer library technician programs in 1971–1972.

American River College, Sacramento
Antelope Valley College, Lancaster
Bakersfield College, Bakersfield
Bakersfield College, Desert Campus, Ridgecrest
Cabrillo College, Aptos
Canada College, Redwood City
Chabot College, Hayward
Chaffey College, Alta Loma
Citrus College, Azusa
College of the Canyons, Valencia
College of the Desert, Palm Desert

Cuesta College, San Luis Obispo
Foothill College, Los Altos Hills
Fullerton Community College, Fullerton
Los Angeles Trade-Technical College, Los Angeles
Merced College, Merced
Moorpark College, Moorpark
Mt. San Antonio College, Walnut
Napa College, Napa
Palomar College, San Marcos
Pasadena City College, Pasadena
Porterville College, Porterville
Rio Hondo Community College, Whittier
Riverside City College, Riverside
Sacramento City College, Sacramento
San Bernardino Valley College, San Bernardino
San Diego City College, San Diego
City College of San Francisco, San Francisco
San Jose City College, San Jose
College of San Mateo, San Mateo
Santa Ana College, Santa Ana
Santa Barbara City College, Santa Barbara
College of the Siskiyous, Weed

Canal Zone

In the *Canal Zone Library-Museum* leave-without-pay is granted whenever possible to staff members holding undergraduate degrees who wish to do graduate work in library service in the United States.

The Library participates in the Panama Canal Company tuition-refund program. Subject to certain requirements, any employee of the Panama Canal Company-Canal Zone Government may apply for the refund of tuition and fees for courses taken. The terms stipulate that courses be "appropriately related to the present work of the employee involved, and of such a nature as to contribute to a more effective job performance on the part of the employee."

Colorado

Denver Public Library has a limited program of accepting persons with undergraduate degrees on the staff with the understanding that they will complete a library degree. It also has a tuition refund policy which refunds tuition costs expended by full-time staff members when approved by the Tuition Refund Committee.

The *Arapahoe Regional Library* has a policy of tuition reimbursement and released time with graduate students reimbursed for tuition paid to the University of Denver and undergraduates asked to consider the Library Technical Assistant Program being offered by the Community College of Denver.

In addition, the following libraries are among those that arrange work schedules to encourage staff members to obtain library training:

Aurora Public Library
Boulder Public Library
Colorado Springs Public Library
Colorado State Library
Jefferson County Public Library

Library Technician programs are offered in the following institutions of higher education.

Community College of Denver offers a one-year Technician Training program leading to a certificate of achievement as Library Assistant and a two-year Library Technician program leading to a degree of Associate in Arts in Library Technology.

Southern Colorado State College in Pueblo offers a two-year Library Technician program leading to an Associate in Arts degree.

Connecticut

The *Connecticut State Library* makes provisions whereby staff members may take additional courses leading to degree programs which would help them in their work. Professional leave and reimbursement of tuition costs are frequently given for the professional positions.

Northwestern Community College, Winsted, and Norwalk Community College, Norwalk, have Library Technician Programs. Northwestern Community College also offers extension courses in its Library Technical Assistants program off campus.

Delaware

Both branches of Delaware Technical and Community College offer some courses for library technicians, but no longer offer a complete program.

District of Columbia

The *District of Columbia Public Library* has a continuing program of on-the-job training for which college graduates are accepted with the understanding that they will attend a local graduate library school. The trainees are helped to arrange their working schedules to allow them to attend classes. The program includes around 30 trainees — 27 in the first quarter of fiscal year 1972. A program is underway to allow Library Technicians, as paraprofessionals to hold a number of positions in public service through reclassification of some positions previously held by professional librarians. Library technicians participate, along with professional librarians, in the sessions of the Institute for Retraining of Library Staff to Improve Library Service to the Disadvantaged at the University of Maryland, School of Library and Information Services (fall 1971, spring 1972) for which funds have been obtained under the Higher Education Act of 1965, Title II-B. This Institute gives particular emphasis to the use of non-print multimedia materials.

Florida

Florida State Library has a library training program through salary grants to public libraries. Members of the staff without professional training are eligible for a grant of $3,600 for one year's training at the graduate level. Each trainee must remain with the library for two years after graduation.

Libraries which have received grants under this program this year are:

Hialeah John F. Kennedy Library
Jacksonville Public Library
Manatee County Library System, Bradenton
Melbourne Public Library
Miami Public Library
North Miami Public Library
Tampa Public Library
West Palm Beach Public Library

Library technician programs are offered by the following colleges:

Hillsborough Community College, Tampa
Polk Junior College, Winter Haven

Georgia

The State Department of Education has a grant-in-aid program for graduate study. Both school and public librarians are eligible for these funds for a full year of graduate study or for summer study in an ALA-accredited graduate library school.

The following libraries currently have a formal trainee program:

Augusta Public Library, Augusta
Okefenokee Regional Library, Waycross

Most regional libraries will employ a college graduate with at least four basic undergraduate courses in library science. No person can direct a public library program without a fifth-year degree from an ALA accredited library school.

Guam

The University of Guam offers a two-year program under the School for Continuing Education for Library Technicians. These students receive an AA degree after completion of the two-year program. The *Public Library* has a Student Trainee Program for students attending high school and college.

Hawaii

A degree program for library technicians is offered by Leeward Community College, Pearl City, Honolulu. The East West Center of the University of Hawaii offers nondegree refresher courses in library techniques for practicing librarians and for technicians.

Idaho

The *Idaho State Library* has a flexible Trainee Program, providing preprofessional work experience to college graduates wanting to go on to library school, providing scholarships for graduate work, and/or allowing staff members leave with pay to complete their graduate library degrees.

Several public and institutional libraries in Idaho participate in these programs from time to time.

The College of Southern Idaho, Twin Falls, has a Library Technician Program, with students working in the College Library.

Illinois

The following public libraries have formalized trainee or student librarian programs:

Belleville Public Library pays tuition and allows class time with pay for staff members who wish to take Library Science courses at Washington University (St. Louis) or the University of Illinois Extension. Staff members are expected to remain on the staff for a reasonable length of time beyond completion of the course. The salary schedule provides an extra step in pay for those who have completed courses.

Chicago Public Library trainee program is a work-study program for college graduates who have been accepted for admission to an accredited Chicago-area graduate library school. Trainees work and attend classes on a concurrent, year-round basis. Working hours are arranged on a full-time or half-time basis adjusted to class schedules. Trainees must complete a minimum of three courses a year, and all course requirements for the Master's degree in Library Science must be completed within four years from the date of library employment.

Some scholarships are available through membership in the Chicago Public Library Staff Association.

East St. Louis Public Library pays tuition and allows class time off for staff members who wish to take extension courses in library science.

The *Illinois Valley Library System* pays tuition for extension courses in library science at Illinois State University for staff of member libraries. In addition, the *Peoria Public Library*, headquarters library of the system, has a practice of different kinds of on-the-job training and higher salaries for college student assistants who plan to go to library school.

The *Kaskaskia Library System* pays the tuition of staff members taking extension courses from accredited library schools.

Oak Park Public Library has a Junior Librarian position in three departments. These are in Reference, Reader's Services and Children's Work.

A combination work-study program and scholarship is possible for individuals in these three positions. Schedules may be arranged to provide for part-time attendance at a graduate library school. The scholarship is provided through an endowment and usually covers the cost of tuition.

Rockford Public Library has a personnel policy which encourages the continuing development of its staff. A personnel category for staff having college degrees but no library school training has been established as a recruitment device. Reappointments in this category are limited to three years unless the employee has started taking courses in library science, or, when appropriate, in a specialized subject area.

As employees accrue a minimum number of hours of library school training, they are moved into a new pay category which provides an additional incentive for continuing education.

One three week period of leave with pay is granted an employee who wishes to attend library school on campus either in summer or winter. Employees granted such leaves must have been on the payroll at least for one year.

Liberal allowance is made in schedule adjustments for those who are taking courses.

The *Shawnee Library System* pays tuition for library staff members taking library science courses.

The *Starved Rock System* allows class time off for staff members taking the Library Technicians course.

Library technicians programs are offered by the following colleges and universities:

City College of Chicago, Chicago
College of DuPage, Glen Ellyn
Morton College, Cicero
Prairie State College, Chicago Heights

Southern Illinois University, Carbondale

Thornton Community College, Harvey

Triton College, River Grove

Indiana

Indiana State Library has a federally funded scholarship project which provides scholarships for graduate library study to enable qualified persons to prepare themselves for professional library work in the public libraries in the state and for undergraduate library study to enable public library employees to meet certification requirements. Recipients of a full semester or full summer session scholarship must agree to work in an Indiana public library, or the Indiana State Library, for at least 24 consecutive months after completion of the specified program.

Evansville-Vanderburgh County Public Library builds into its pay scale incentives for preprofessionals with bachelor's degrees to acquire library science hours. As a part of the library's continuing education requirement, within a five-year period the professional must acquire six semester hours (or designated equivalents) at a graduate library school or other relevant department of a college or university and the preprofessional must acquire three semester hours of academic courses relevant to his duties.

Fort Wayne-Allen County Public Library hires persons with bachelor's and master's degrees in subject areas who indicate an interest in becoming professional librarians. They work in from one to three departments at any one time with or under the department head or a professional librarian with some years of experience. In this way they work throughout the system and may earn credit hours in summer school to complete their master's degrees.

Gary Public Library employs college graduates when library science graduates are not available. College graduates are placed in top clerical grades and must complete three hours of library science during the calendar year; they advance on the salary scale $150 per three hours completed to fifteen hours. When fifteen hours are acquired, they are placed in the Professional classification.

Indiana State University Library employs persons with undergraduate degrees which include a minor in library science. These persons must complete an MLS at an accredited library school, or at Indiana State University, within six years. Full salary is allowed to those attending summer school; however, during years of such attendance, they receive no further vacation allowances.

Indiana University Libraries have a library intern program wherein persons with bachelor's degrees are hired with the understanding they will complete their master's degrees in library science and stay in the University libraries at least two years.

Indianapolis-Marion County Public Library has a Preprofessional Service Grade for college graduates interested in studying library science. This preprofessional assistant may remain in this grade for a maximum of three years during which time he is expected to complete at least fifteen semester hours of approved library education.

Monroe County Public Library, Bloomington, hires persons with undergraduate degrees provided they complete their library science degree. There is no time limit for completion of the MLS, but they must take classes applying to their degree each semester until work is completed. The Library has instituted a library technician program.

Vigo County Public Library hires personnel with undergraduate degrees with the understanding that they will work toward either a master's degree in library science or complete 24 hours of library science classes. Leaves of absence, adjustments of working hours, or special assignments may be arranged in order for employees to meet these educational requirements.

The *Indiana Vocational Technical College,* Indianapolis, has started a Library Aide program. The aim of the program is to qualify men and women to function as members of the library staff in a school, college or university, special, or public library; specifically to perform clerical and nonclerical tasks under supervision. The curriculum is designed to provide a basic level of competency in clerical, communication, and mathematical skills, and to acquaint the student with library organization and operations through classroom instruction balanced with practical experience.

Iowa

North Iowa Library Extension, Mason City trains approximately 15 college girls yearly (through work-study program).

University of Iowa, Iowa City. The Veterans' Administration Hospital Library in Iowa City has a library trainee program. They employ two students on a half-time basis with enrollment in the University of Iowa Graduate Library Science Program as a condition of employment.

Iowa City Public Library participates with the Graduate School of the School of Library Science of the University of Iowa in a program for practicum students. Each semester the library works with three students.

Library technician programs are offered at Kirkwood Community College, Cedar Rapids, and at Marycrest College, Davenport.

Kansas

The *Central, South Central, and Northeast Kansas Library Systems* have a training-scholarship program. Eligible candidates have generally been employees of one of the systems' member libraries. The *Northeast Kansas Library System* offers full salary while attending graduate library school to a staff member who qualifies by examination and interview.

The *Kansas State Library* employs persons with the understanding that they will attend library school on a part-time basis. Work schedule is arranged to permit the employee to attend classes.

Kentucky

The *Kentucky State Department of Libraries* grants scholarships to residents of the Commonwealth of Kentucky for study in library science on the graduate level. The recipient agrees to work in a library program approved by the State Librarian for a period to be computed at the rate of one year for each one thousand dollars received.

Louisiana

Louisiana State University and *East Baton Rouge Parish Library* have a trainee or student librarian program in which persons with undergraduate degrees are accepted on the staff with the understanding that they will work on and complete a library degree within a given period.

Courses in library techniques are offered by Delgado College, New Orleans.

Massachusetts

The following libraries have a formal trainee or student librarian program:

Boston Public Library
Cary Memorial Library, Lexington
Fitchburg Public Library
Springfield City Library
Harvard College Libraries, Cambridge
Massachusetts Inst. of Technology, Cambridge
Worcester Public Library

Library technician programs are offered by the following colleges: Worcester Junior College, Worcester; Mount Ida Junior College, Newton; and Bristol Community College, Fall River.

Michigan

Many of the public libraries employ college graduates on a trainee basis. Salaries vary with local scales and with the number of graduate credits earned. The following libraries hire trainees regularly:

Benton Harbor	Madison Heights
Dearborn	Michigan State
Detroit	Monroe
Flint	Mt. Clemens
Grand Rapids	Roseville
Grosse Pointe	Royal Oak
Hamtramck	Saginaw
Highland Park	St. Clair Shores
Kalamazoo	Washtenaw County
Kent County	Wayne County
Livonia	Willard, Battle
Macomb	Creek

The following offer two-year programs leading to a library technician certificate: Alpena Community College, Alpena; Ferris State College, Big Rapids; Flint Community Jr. College, Flint; Lansing Community College, Lansing; Macomb County Community College, Mt. Clemens; Washtenaw Community College, Ypsilanti.

Mississippi

The *Mississippi Library Commission* offers summer internships for college students who are majoring in library science or planning to attend graduate library school. Interns are assigned to work in public libraries cooperating with the program or to the Library Commission. The program is designed to orient students to public library work.

Missouri

The *St. Louis Public Library* has scholarships of $2500, which they encourage members of its staff who have undergraduate degrees to apply for. It is my understanding that these are also open to people who are not members of their staff. There is a two-year work commitment in that library. The Library encourages its staff to take the undergraduate library science courses that are available in the community, and may arrange time off the job and pay part of the tuition for such courses.

There is a Librarian Technician Program at Florissant Valley Community College, St. Louis.

New Hampshire

A library technician program is offered by the Merrimack Valley Branch of the University of New Hampshire, Manchester.

New Jersey

The following New Jersey public libraries have trainee programs:

Belleville Public Library
Burlington County Library
Camden City Public Library
Camden County Public Library
Cherry Hill Public Library
East Brunswick Public Library
Fair Lawn Public Library
Fanwood Public Library
Gloucester City Public Library
Hillside Public Library
Johnson Free Public Library, Hackensack
Linden Public Library
Livingston Public Library
Madison Public Library
Montclair Public Library
Morris County Public Library, Morristown
Newark Public Library
North Bergen Public Library
Paterson Public Library
Plainfield Public Library
Roselle Public Library
Somerset County Library
Trenton Public Library
Woodbridge Public Library

Library technician programs are offered by the following colleges:

Alphonsus College, Woodcliff Lake
Brookdale Community College, Lincroft
Camden County Vocational Technical School, Camden
Cumberland County Community College, Vineland
Mercer County Community College, Trenton

New York

Through agreement between the New York Library Assn., The Division of Library Development, and the New York State Dept. of Civil Service, there is a trainee classification available to any library in the state that wants it. Under a parallel program, any State agency operating a library may appoint as student librarian college graduates who are admissible to a nearby library school.

Student librarian programs are conducted as part of the Civil Service Professional Career Testing Program.

The following colleges in New York State offering library technician degrees at the associate level are Maria Regina, Syracuse; Hilbert College, Buffalo; Borough of Manhattan Community College, New York City; Onondaga Community College, Syracuse.

North Carolina

Durham City-County Library Professional Trainee Program.

Subprofessional positions with a fixed salary of $5,000.00 per year for college graduates to gain experience before entering graduate library school with the possibility of continuing employment on a part-time basis while in graduate library school.

North Carolina State Library offers Staff Employee Study Grants of $1,200 per employee for a regular fall or spring semester or a grant of $600 for each summer session to county and regional library systems for employees who have been full-time staff members of the applying library for at least one year, who meet basic requirements for admission to an ALA-accredited library school, who are recommended for professional study by the director of the county or regional library and/or by the library boards, and who give assurance to the director or library board that he or she will return to the library for a reasonable time following each period of study.

Public Library of Charlotte and Mecklenburg County Professional Trainee Program.

A subprofessional position with a beginning pay of $343 per month increasing to $360 after six months is available for college graduates for up to one year to gain experience before attending graduate library school.

Library technician programs are offered by the following colleges and technical institutes:

Caldwell Technical Institute and Community College, Lenoir

Lenoir Community College, Kinston

W. W. Holding Technical Institute, Raleigh

James Sprunt Technical Institute, Kenansville

Technical Institute of Alamance, Burlington

Ohio

Many Ohio libraries have a certain type of in-service training for college graduates. The following libraries have preprofessional in-training positions:

Dayton and Montgomery County Library has a three year position set-up in which trainee receives merit raises for the three years. At the end of this time trainee must either go to library school or remain in that position with no further raises until going to library school.

Cuyahoga County Library has a trainee program in which trainee works part-time and goes to school part-time.

Cleveland Public Library, Toledo-Lucas County Public Library, and *Public Library of Youngstown and Mahoning County* have similar plans.

Library technican programs are offered by the following schools:

Cuyahoga Community College, Cleveland

Miami University, Middletown Campus, Middletown

Ohio University, Lancaster Campus, Lancaster

University of Toledo, Community & Technical College, Toledo

Oregon

The public libraries in Oregon that have a formal trainee program are:

Portland Public Library

Springfield Public Library

The public libraries that have a library technican program are:

Jackson County Library

Springfield Public Library

The colleges that offer Library Technician Programs are:

Portland Community College, Portland

Southern Oregon College, Ashland

Treasure Valley Community College, Ontario

Pacific Islands

The Trust Territory of the Pacific Islands has a preprofessional in-training program for library personnel who receive management intern type training at the Headquarters of the Trust Territory's Department of Education on Saipan, Mariana Islands.

Rhode Island

The following libraries and agencies have a formal trainee or student librarian program:
Providence Public Library
Rhode Island Department of State Library Services
Warwick Public Library
Westerly Public Library

The following libraries have initiated a library technician program:
Newport Public Library
Rhode Island Department of State Library Services
Warwick Public Library
Westerly Public Library

A library technician program is also offered by the University of Rhode Island, Extension Division.

South Carolina

Programs offered by the *South Carolina State Library* include (1) summer internship program for college juniors and seniors and recent college graduates which is designed to give the students an opportunity to discover through full-time employment for the three summer months what a public or institutional librarian is and does; (2) summer scholarships for preprofessional staff taking undergraduate courses in library science; and (3) continuing education for professional librarians.

Tennessee

In some instances Boards of Trustees authorize leaves of absence for staff members to take library training. On occasion, time with pay is given for staff members to take courses in library science. Work schedules are arranged to permit class attendance. These arrangements are made by local libraries on an individual basis.

Texas

Friends of the Amarillo Library have a scholarship loan program for graduate library school student staff members. If the student returns to a position with the Amarillo Public Library for a period of two years, half the amount of the scholarship loan of $1,000 is repaid during the two years. If he does not return for two years he repays the full amount.

Austin Public Library Staff Association has a variable scholarship grant for graduate and undergraduate library school student staff members.

The *Dallas Public Library* allows a staff member to take a leave of absence to work on his library science degree. The Library will also pay the tuition of one library science course per semester per student, pending satisfactory completion of the course.

The *Friends of the Dallas Public Library* grant $1,500 annually for a staff member (or members) to complete a Master's Degree in Library Science.

The *Emily Fowler Public Library* in Denton participates in the Youth Corps Training Program, serving as a training station for library technicians.

Houston Public Library allows staff members to take a leave of absence to take an advanced degree in library science. Time is granted to staff members to take extension courses in library science. Interest free loans are made to staff members for tuition to take extension courses or for school expenses. The *Friends of the Houston Public Library* offer two $2,000 scholarships to qualified staff members for the successful completion of an advanced degree in library science.

Friends of the Lubbock City-County Libraries offers a $500 scholarship loan option to a college student or graduate student preparing for librarianship. Preference is given to staff members wishing to go to library school. If the recipient returns to a position with the Lubbock City-County Libraries for as long as a year the amount is a grant. Otherwise, the amount is to be repaid without interest within two years after graduation.

The *Mesquite Public Library* allows a staff member to take a leave of absence to work on his library science degree. For full time employees, the library will also pay the tuition for two courses per semester to work toward a Bachelor's or Master's Degree in Library Science.

The *Nicholson Memorial Library* in Garland offers a tuition refund program which pays half of all expenses on successful completion of course work toward a Master's Degree in Library Science.

The *San Antonio Public Library* employs persons with a Bachelor's degree with the understanding that they will take at least one library science course per semester until they have completed their requirements for a Master's Degree in Library Science.

Friends of the San Antonio Public Library offers for the spring and winter semesters three 3-hour course scholarships. The cost of the program has been $120 per semester or $720 per year for the six scholarships.

There are library technology programs at Amarillo College, Amarillo; El Centro College, Dallas; and San Antonio College, San Antonio.

Vermont

Vermont's Department of Libraries offers scholarships for attendance at summer institutes and tuition payments for library extension courses to staff of public libraries without professional training. It also provides scholarship aid to qualified agency staff for training at the graduate level.

Green Mountain College, Poultney, and Vermont College, Montpelier, began Library Technician Programs in academic year 1970–1971. The College of St. Joseph the Provider, Rutland, initiated a four-year program in the fall of 1971–1972. Johnson State College, Johnson, is also offering courses for credit as is the Vermont Regional Community College Commission. The latter organization will offer the courses in several locations around the state.

Washington

The following colleges offer Library Technician Programs:

Clark Community College, Vancouver
Highline Community College, Midway

West Virginia

A trainee program under LSCA will allow library boards for service centers or regional libraries to apply to the State Agency for a trainee grant for a staff member who has been admitted to an accredited library school. The grant will be a monthly salary for a maximum of 18 months with the trainee returning to any West Virginia public library for a period of two years, or repay the grant.

Regional libraries:

Alpha Regional Library, Spencer
Miracle Valley Regional Library, Moundsville
Potomac Valley Regional Library, Keyser
Stonewall Jackson Regional Library, Buckhannon
Western Counties Regional Library, Huntington

Service center libraries:

Carnegie Library of Parkersburg and Wood County, Parkersburg
Kanawha County Public Library, Charleston
Martinsburg Public Library, Martinsburg
Mary H. Weir Public Library, Weirton
Morgantown Public Library, Morgantown
Ohio County Public Library, Wheeling
Raleigh County Public Library, Beckley

Wisconsin

Milwaukee Public Library has a Junior Librarian Program for college graduates who intend to enter an ALA-accredited library school within two years. They are expected to return to the Milwaukee Public Library for at least two years after they receive their Master's degree. A Librarian I Trainee Position for college graduates with a minimum of 14 credits in library science, an undergraduate grade point of 2.75 and two years at college level of a modern foreign language or a letter showing admissibility to an accredited graduate library school. The Master's degree must be obtained within 3 years.

The University of Wisconsin Library School in Madison has a flexible work study program available as student demand and public library ability may require such a program.

Wisconsin Division for Library Services offers three to six scholarships of from $1,000 to $3,000. Applicants must be United States citizens, willing to work two years in a Wisconsin public library after graduation from an ALA-accredited graduate library school. Scholarships are LSCA-I funded. Apply: Scholarship Program, Division for Library Services, Box 1437, Madison, Wis. 53701.

A library technicians program is offered by Kenosha Technical Institute, Kenosha.

Library Building

PUBLIC LIBRARY BUILDING IN 1971*
by
Hoyt Galvin** and Barbara Asbury***

The number of new public library buildings completed in fiscal year 1971 was 22 percent less than in the previous year; for enlarged and remodeled (ARR) buildings, the reduction was 30 percent. A total of 148 new buildings and 60 ARRs were completed during 1971.

Construction costs increased 4 percent over the 1970 costs, which is approximately the amount of the previous year's increase. Table 1 shows the average square foot costs for new public library buildings during the past four years.

The 3 percent reduction in the square foot cost of furnishings and equipment may reflect the recession. Equipment orders are usually placed several months after the construction contracts are awarded. The construction contracts for buildings completed in FY 1971 are for amounts bid and contracted for two or three years ago, whereas most of the equipment was purchased in late FY 1970 or early FY 1971. Equipment bidders may have reduced the profit margin in their bids, or libraries may have selected less expensive items.

The surprise in the data was the sharp 13 percent increase in "other costs."

Architects' fees are the principal "other cost," and this may mean that architects have been increasing fees to cover the higher salary, rent, and related costs for operation of their service.

For those libraries purchasing sites, the cost of the site per square foot of building erected on the site increased 21 percent over FY 1970. We do not know if this was an exceptional year for site costs or if the cost of land is increasing more rapidly than other building costs.

The use of air conditioning and carpeting in both new and remodeled libraries did not grow as consistently as during the past two years:

	Air Conditioned (%)		Carpeted (%)	
	New Bldgs.	ARRs	New Bldgs.	ARRs
FY 1969	80	64	80	66
FY 1970	86	60	86	68
FY 1971	92	81	86	63

The automobile parking data supplied was interesting as 86 percent of the new buildings provided some auto parking on the library property. For the 128 buildings with parking, the average amount of

---

*Reprinted from *Library Journal,* December 1, 1971.
**Library consultant, Charlotte, N.C.
***Assistant to Mr. Galvin.

TABLE 1   SQUARE FOOT COSTS FOR NEW BUILDINGS

	191 bldgs. FY 1968	214 bldgs. FY 1969	191 bldgs. FY 1970	148 bldgs. FY 1971	FY 1971 Change from FY 1970 (%)
Construction cost	$19.93	$21.95	$22.97	$23.87	+ 4
Equipment & furnishings	2.83	2.87	3.05	2.96	− 3
Other costs	2.31	2.87	2.52	2.86	+13
Sites (when purchased)	3.65	3.45	3.92	4.76	+21

space dedicated to parking was one square foot of parking space for each square foot of library building.

Book capacity and reader seats per gross square foot of new public library buildings were as follows:

	Per Sq. Ft. of New Building Book Capacity	Reader Seats
FY 1969	4.7	.0068
FY 1970	4.5	.0069
FY 1971	3.8	.0061

Compared with the previous year, the total expenditure for new, enlarged, and remodeled public library buildings was down 22 percent. The amount of federal funds expended was down 41 percent; state funds increased 1½ percent; local government funds were down 9 percent; and the gift total was down 51 percent. A single gift of $4,200,000 for one library building in FY 1970, however, distorted the general level of giving. The percentage of projects receiving gifts in FY 1971 was approximately the same as in FY 1970.

To collect the data for the tables which follow, building data forms were mailed to state library agencies on June 1, 1971 with the request that a copy be sent to each librarian who had a construction project completed during the fiscal year ending June 30, 1971. The completed data forms were due to be returned by August 1, 1971 to the compilers in Charlotte, where the returns are audited and tabulated.

Each form must be audited to be certain that the total of federal, state, local, and gift funds is equal to the amount shown for the project cost. Likewise, the construction, equipment, site, and other costs must equal the project cost. Many errors are caught in these audits. Corrections for most of the errors are obvious, but some data forms must be returned to the local librarian.

This annual tabulation would not be feasible without the continued cooperation of the 50 state library agencies. Some of the state agency LSCA Title II supervisors have the data forms first returned to their offices to be assured that all projects are being reported. As for FY 1968, FY 1969, FY 1970, and FY 1971, we have assurance that most if not all the public library construction projects are included. Without the state agencies, this would not be possible.

Any data forms received after August 23, 1971 will have been omitted, but will be included in the FY 1972 tabulations. Librarians representing any omitted buildings are invited to write: Hoyt Galvin, 2259 Vernon Drive, Charlotte, N.C. 28211.

TABLE 2 PUBLIC LIBRARY BUILDINGS — A COST SUMMARY BY FISCAL YEAR

	F1968	F1969	F1970	F1971
New Bldgs.	191	214	191	148
ARR's	68	84	85	60
Sq. ft., new bldgs.	2,851,669	2,883,024	2,368,577	2,032,252
Sq. ft., ARR's	581,807	1,142,609	867,057	462,240
New bldgs:				
Construction	$55,954,356	$63,283,824	$55,406,189	$48,501,338
Equipment	6,784,857	8,266,563	7,237,897	6,015,692
Site	6,407,162	7,190,302	6,660,804	4,867,338
Other	N.A.	7,073,605	5,963,013	5,809,078
Project cost		$85,814,294	$75,267,903	$65,193,446
ARR's—Project cost	N.A.	21,318,560	22,294,269	10,952,245
All Project costs	$90,586,978	$107,132,854	$97,562,172	$76,145,691
Fund Sources:				
Federal, new bldgs.	N.A.	$21,917,716	$18,328,725	$11,214,090
Federal, ARR's	N.A.	4,683,567	4,536,599	2,211,752
Federal total	$20,751,282	$26,601,283	$22,865,324	$13,425,842
State, new bldgs.	N.A.	769,004	2,990,272	2,507,715
State, ARR's	N.A.	287,228	116,758	648,397
State, total	$895,941	$1,056,232	$3,107,030	$3,156,112
Local, new bldgs.	N.A.	58,973,470	43,366,599	45,803,096
Local, ARR's	N.A.	15,152,621	14,897,530	7,249,611
Local, total	$68,939,755	$74,126,091	$58,264,129	$53,052,707
Gift, new bldgs.	N.A.	4,154,104	10,582,307	5,668,545
Gift, ARR's	N.A.	1,195,144	2,743,382	842,485
Gift, total	N.A.	$5,349,248	$13,325,689	$6,511,030
Total funds used	$90,586,978	$107,132,854	$97,562,172	$76,145,691

NEW PUBLIC LIBRARY BUILDINGS CONSTRUCTED FROM JULY 1, 1970 TO JUNE 30, 1971

In the following table, all new library buildings reported have been arranged by state, and within states by municipality. This is followed by a column number giving the population served in thousands, and a letter code to indicate the type of library building (main, branch, system, etc.) with the following code: B: branch; BL: branch in leased space; BS: branch and system headquarters; M: main; MS: main and system headquarters; S: system headquarters; NA: not available. Remodeling projects and building additions are reported in the table which follows the new building tabulations.

Community	Pop. in M	Code	Project Cost	Gross Sq. Ft.	Constr. Cost	Sq. Ft. Cost	Equip. Cost	Site Cost	Other Costs	Vols.	Reader Seats	Fed. Funds	State Funds	Local Gvt. Funds	Gift Funds	Architect's Key
ALABAMA																
Butler	17	M	$117,785	4,000	$103,029	$25.76	$8,002	gift	$6,754	20,000	40	$60,000			$57,785	1
Demopolis	10	M	42,068	2,604	35,568	13.66	6,500	gift		12,000	30		5,000	$36,068	1,000	2
ALASKA																
Cordova	2	M	130,000	3,680	77,000	20.92	20,000	25,000	8,000	30,000	28	37,000	58,000	35,000		3
ARIZONA																
Wickenburg	2	M	125,000	4,200	103,000	24.52	16,000	gift	6,000	25,000	40				125,000	4
ARKANSAS																
Mena	4	B	67,338	4,530	60,464	13.35	1,589	owned	5,285	20,000	25	35,038			32,300	5
CALIFORNIA																
Culver City	31	B	1,325,981	31,620	929,625	29.40	83,930	204,400	108,026	98,000	88	309,875		1,016,106		6
Cupertino	50	B	655,914	24,000	504,900	21.04	66,014	27,000	58,000	125,000	240	159,000		496,914		7
Fig Garden	46	BL	18,000	5,000			18,000			22,000	40			17,500	500	8
Hesperia	8	BL	1,700	2,000			1,700			17,000	21			1,700		9
Huntington	33	BS	1,032,227	33,480	809,695	24.18,	120,981	owned	101,551	120,000	250	300,629		731,598		10

LIBRARY BUILDING / 305

Huron	2	B	132,000	3,200	102,909	32.16	20,130	owned	8,961	12,000	60		132,000		11
La Canada	NA	B	866,220	16,204	512,000	31.60	59,688	231,940	62,592	45,500	128		866,220		12
La Mirada	30	B	635,955	16,463	481,554	29.25	57,983	46,974	49,444	70,000	108		635,955		13
Long Beach	26	B	308,293	8,160	218,000	26.71	43,830	owned	46,463	50,000	82		308,293		14
Mariposa	8	B	88,800	2,200	61,600	40.37	8,500	13,200	5,500	6,000	28		18,260	70,540	15
Viejo	14	B	308,181	10,000	218,181	21.82	40,000	30,000	20,000	54,000	66		278,181	30,000	16
Novato	29	B	572,587	10,600	299,848	28.28	49,390	135,200	88,149	60,000	88		571,087	1,500	17
Orland	10	M	91,631	5,760	71,206	12.36	13,672	owned	6,753	40,000	52		84,631	7,000	18
Palo Alto	12	B	621,285	9,010	345,884	38.01	31,675	203,249	40,472	18,000	90		621,285		19
Palos Verdes	10	B	357,681	7,000	242,797	34.68	4,423	45,000	65,461	35,000	30	74,771	262,910	20,000	20
San Diego	NA	B	135,000	5,000	111,698	22.84	9,000	owned	14,302	22,000	50		135,000		21
San Dimas	16	B	539,331	13,510	434,500	32.16	51,024	5,150	48,657	54,000	98		409,283		22
Santa Ana	25	B	282,650	8,000	200,772	25.10	30,000	30,487	31,391	50,000	80	130,048	282,650		23
Torrance	132	M	1,738,035	57,400	1,522,515	26.52	117,720	owned	97,800	207,000	352		1,738,035		24
Trona	9	B	64,334	2,290	56,400	24.63	4,590	gift	3,344	20,000	26		64,334		25
Vacaville	17	M	377,858	9,480	310,377	32.73	22,996	1	44,484	37,000	90	101,233	276,625		26
Vallejo	72	M	2,933,940	92,309	2,348,042	25.44	256,300	59,570	270,028	450,000	600	900,000	2,033,940		27
Walnut Grove	3	BL	4,609	1,691			4,609			6,000	22		4,609		28
Yuba City	41	MS	654,945	22,230	542,276	24.39	49,852	owned	62,817	80,000	200		654,945		29
COLORADO															
Golden	9	M	149,671	6,350	111,594	17.57	21,600	owned	16,477	30,000	50	64,779	84,892		30
Leadville	4	M	180,196	5,700	154,240	27.06	7,406	4,993	13,557	18,000	40	75,000	71,923	33,273	31
CONNECTICUT	(None reported)														
DELAWARE	(None reported)														
FLORIDA															
Blountstown	8	B	117,864	4,500	83,263	18.50	9,441	20,000	5,160	10,000	40	50,000	67,864		32
Lynn Haven	4	B	97,495	3,200	79,157	24.74	7,435	owned	10,903	10,000	40	47,800	29,195	20,500	33
Ocala	69	MS	497,323	29,000	403,880	13.93	44,146	gift	49,297	63,950	148	210,000	287,323		34
GEORGIA	(None reported)														
HAWAII															
Ewa Beach	17	B	1,017,059	23,150	803,127	34.69	155,183	owned	58,749	65,000	276	948,763	68,296		35
IDAHO	(None reported)														

NEW PUBLIC LIBRARY BUILDINGS CONSTRUCTED FROM JULY 1, 1970 TO JUNE 30, 1971, Continued

Community	Pop. in M	M Code	Project Cost	Gross Sq. Ft.	Constr. Cost	Sq. Ft. Cost	Equip. Cost	Site Cost	Other Costs	Vols.	Reader Seats	Fed. Funds	State Funds	Local Gvt. Funds	Gift Funds	Architect's Key
ILLINOIS																
Chicago	27	B	525,547	10,469	339,781	32.45	54,423	84,033	47,310	60,000	80	103,200	274,545	147,802		36
Cuba	2	M	102,000	2,400	81,000	33.75	4,000	8,000	9,000	10,000	18	23,000		78,000	1,000	37
Hinsdale	2	S	903,569	20,992	659,179	31.40	53,911	121,808	68,671	20,000	0	225,839	677,730			38
Roxana	10	M	162,102	6,064	121,000	19.95	17,462	10,000	13,640	16,250	30	45,000		115,102	2,000	39
INDIANA																
Bloomington	85	M	2,636,613	42,500	1,396,036	32.85	412,764	528,632	299,181	250,000	150	514,000		1,512,234	610,379	40
Crown Point	131	MS	716,849	30,000	634,377	21.14	23,181	17,734	41,557	55,000	108	306,688		410,161		41
Indianapolis	50	B	598,063	15,000	503,415	33.56	54,648	gift	40,000	70,000	144			598,063		42
Lowell	3	M	255,000	9,600	197,005	20.52	44,501	10	13,484	35,000	60	45,000		207,000	3,000	43
S. Whitley	3	M	178,148	7,700	153,355	19.92	9,897	owned	14,896	30,000	80				178,148	44
IOWA																
Bancroft	2	M	48,520	2,046	32,507	15.88	9,449	5,000	1,564	5,000	40	25,243			23,277	45
KANSAS																
Great Bend	31	MS	788,834	38,000	641,746	16.88	87,101	gift	59,987	100,000	120	201,413		581,434	5,987	46
KENTUCKY																
Eddyville	5	M	130,868	6,000	107,328	17.88	13,930		9,610	17,800	30		22,966	107,902		47
Edmonton	8	M	161,091	4,560	128,618	28.20	12,506		8,967	33,850	24		22,966	138,125		48
Hawesville	6	M	138,544	5,400	120,600	22.33	6,940	11,000	11,004	23,350	22		22,966	107,993	7,585	49
Hyden	10	M	161,265	5,112	127,414	24.92	5,515	18,000	10,336	21,600	16		23,644	137,621		50
Lebanon	17	M	182,467	6,580	126,152	19.17	14,994	30,000	11,321	24,850	32		29,183	153,284		51
Morehead	15	M	241,000	6,200	187,808	30.29	9,545	30,000	13,647	21,425	24		29,952	211,048		52
Mundford-ville	14	M	158,814	7,600	127,239	16.74	14,000		17,575	17,900	38		26,357	132,457		53
Murray	24	MS	213,783	8,000	146,139	18.26	24,411	32,500	10,733	36,000	60		36,119	177,664		54
Stanford	16	M	164,005	6,060	122,344	20.18	14,070	20,000	7,591	32,100	34		28,112	135,893		55

LIBRARY BUILDING / 307

LOUISIANA													
Harrisonburg	12	MS	133,802	4,900	95,106	19.41	18,300	9,000	11,396	16,000	32	55,000		78,802		56
Jonesville	3	B	105,353	4,200	77,937	18.56	12,411	6,000	9,005	10,000	37	45,000		60,353		57
Lutcher	20	M	216,035	6,950	160,988	23.16	25,000	17,000	13,047	25,000	45	120,000		96,035		58
Sicily Island	1	M	63,178	2,500	49,170	19.67	7,322	3,000	3,686	4,000	15			63,178		59
Vacherie	4	B	151,400	3,936	104,368	26.51	11,373	17,745	17,914	10,000	20			151,400		60
MAINE		(None reported)													
MARYLAND															
Baltimore	50	B	588,999	12,100	412,294	34.07	15,486	108,830	52,389	40,000	75	139,814		449,185		61
Baltimore	35	B	649,121	13,500	434,867	32.21	21,409	143,016	49,829	70,000	106			649,121		62
New Carroll-															
ton	110	M	1,340,023	58,500	1,127,990	19.28	121,933	gift	90,100	200,000	246		44,280	1,295,743		63
Parkville-															
Carney	35	B	447,664	14,400	350,000	24.31	47,664	owned	50,000	45,000	55			447,664		64
MASSACHUSETTS															
Boston		(See explanation following tabulation)													
Rutland	3	MS	107,566	2,520	97,803	38.81	6,343	owned	3,420	6,000	44			89,544	18,022	65
Sherborn		(See explanation following tabulation)													
Westport	10	M	319,461	8,329	254,836	30.60	25,000	no cost	39,625	30,000	57	70,000		249,461		66
MICHIGAN															
Cass City	8	B	89,578	3,144	56,100	17.84	13,943	12,037	7,498	18,000	28			26,849	62,729	67
Detroit	45	B	573,891	11,865	425,805	35.87	39,591	46,366	62,129	30,000	114	181,891		392,000		68
Fowlerville	8	B	61,800	2,400	50,000	25.74	3,800	4,000	4,000	10,000	30			58,800	3,000	69
Otsego	7	M	234,980	6,800	162,177	23.85	43,947		28,856	20,000	60	82,425		152,555		70
Romulus	29	M	423,000	11,141	304,000	27.28	19,000		100,000	35,000	94			423,000		71
Sodus	NA	M	40,000	2,160	36,916	17.00	1,000		2,084	16,000	26			34,000	6,000	72
Troy	39	M	545,320	17,926	394,372	22.00	66,383		84,565	65,000	125			545,320		73
MINNESOTA															
Fairmont	24	MS	461,500	27,500	394,958	14.36	35,116	owned	31,426	100,000	92	195,000		266,500		74
Fulda	1	M	39,726	1,642	34,262	20.86	1,964	800	2,700	6,000	22			39,726		75
Harmony	2	M	64,004	2,152	43,073	20.02	12,807	3,200	4,924	10,250	23			53,204	10,800	76
Minneapolis	30	B	533,432	13,426	399,729	29.77	39,314	54,950	39,439	35,000	83	95,500		437,932		77
Minneapolis	35	B	708,372	12,300	378,885	30.80	48,596	128,616	152,275	30,000	123	109,421		598,951		78

NEW PUBLIC LIBRARY BUILDINGS CONSTRUCTED FROM JULY 1, 1970 TO JUNE 30, 1971, Continued

Community	Pop. in M	Code	Project Cost	Gross Sq. Ft.	Constr. Cost	Sq. Ft. Cost	Equip. Cost	Site Cost	Other Costs	Vols.	Reader Seats	Fed. Funds	State Funds	Local Gvt. Funds	Gift Funds	Architect's Key
MISSISSIPPI			(See explanation following tabulation)													
Centreville	8	B	150,264	7,150	111,026	15.53	19,117	10,000	10,120	22,000	42	67,724		62,540	20,000	79
Clinton	3	B	39,937	2,700	35,300	13.57	4,637			10,000	22	3,000		36,037	900	80
Drew	3	B	63,835	2,522	47,000	18.63	4,015	10,000	2,820	8,500	26	3,500		59,335	1,000	81
Morton																
Ridgeland	2	B	82,133	3,952	71,538	18.10	6,202	owned	4,393	11,000	28	51,130		30,203	800	82
MISSOURI																
Columbia	48	MS	1,754,964	49,750	1,164,643	23.40	206,313	276,056	107,952	200,000	250	600,000		1,154,964		83
Springfield	38	B	450,000	11,000	287,550	26.14	50,500	85,000	26,950	65,000	100	180,000		270,000		84
MONTANA																
Forsyth	6	M	134,242	10,000	129,142	12.91	4,300	owned	800.	25,000	40	73,622		49,220	11,400	85
NEBRASKA			(None reported)													
NEVADA																
Carson City	16	M	660,031	13,600	399,510	29.37	99,355	95,000	66,166	60,000	112	100,000		95,000	465,931	86
Las Vegas	100	MS	1,380,000	55,000	1,038,272	18.88	142,702	gift	199,026	220,000	238				1,380,000	87
NEW HAMPSHIRE			(None reported)													
NEW JERSEY																
Glouchester City	15	M	260,699	10,180	220,737	29.67	19,700	owned	20,262	34,000	58	56,300	2,600	184,799	17,000	88
Middlesex	15	M	295,000	7,400	214,400	28.98	34,000	owned	46,600	32,000	86			295,000		89
Middletown	54	MS	810,621	26,416	662,888	25.09	65,757	34,409	47,567	130,000	166	106,873		703,748		90
Mt. Holly	233	MS	1,190,400	35,000	1,050,000	30.00	40,000	owned	100,400	223,000	150	150,000	200,000	840,400		91
Neptune	28	M	404,053	16,226	324,053	19.97	50,000	owned	30,000	40,000	140	69,494		334,559		92
Wyckoff	16	M	483,325	17,002	435,390	25.60	33,154	owned	14,781	85,000	125	54,075		420,250	9,000	93

NEW MEXICO (None reported)

NEW YORK

Albertson	30	M	995,785	22,263	695,000	31.22	97,000	114,000	89,785	108,000	169	306,250	646,535		94
Brooklyn	42	B	652,126	7,300	477,126	65.36	46,000	owned	129,000	25,300	58	113,000	539,126	43,000	95
Port Wash-															
ington	32	M	1,600,000	36,500	1,135,622	31.11	125,732	150,000	188,646	130,000	220	200,000	1,400,000		96
Queens	31	B	559,600	7,500	443,460	59.12	39,000	39,390	37,750	24,000	102	167,475	392,125		97
Queens	30	B	515,000	7,500	371,000	49.46	39,000	30,000	75,000	28,000	104		515,000		98
Rochester	21	B	486,523	11,306	400,823	35.45	54,652	none	31,050	22,250	94	148,068	338,457		99
Wantagh	20	M	575,013	19,000	385,580	20.29	52,000	81,491	55,942	68,000	121		572,013	3,000	100

NORTH CAROLINA

Bryson City	8	MB	200,000	10,360	151,830	14.66	16,557	20,000	11,613	40,000	84	160,000	11,000	29,000	101
Greensboro	150	B	181,255	7,200	155,800	21.64	13,985	gift	11,470	24,000	75	56,487	106,668	18,100	102
Jackson	1	B	113,992	5,686	85,850	15.10	15,018	10,000	3,124	40,000	44	63,800	48,592	1,600	103
Shelby	71	M	260,788	13,166	188,054	14.28	50,008	gift	22,726	65,000	105			260,788	104
Sylva	22	M	180,000	6,400	121,924	19.05	12,620	41,333	4,123	12,000	60	128,000	46,298	5,702	105

NORTH DAKOTA (None reported)

OHIO

Cuyahoga Falls	53	M	1,309,145	39,495	923,530	23.38	147,067	120,946	117,602	100,000	210	100,000	1,209,145	106

OKLAHOMA (None reported)

OREGON

Baker	9	M	401,625	11,590	358,202	30.91	17,562	gift	25,861	60,000	53	120,000	60,000	221,625	107

PENNSYLVANIA

Southampton	14	M	254,861	12,500	198,009	15.84	31,960	owned	24,892	40,000	84	108,250	146,611		108
Whitemarsh Twp.	16	M	435,986	10,900	335,907	31.73	37,100	25,000	37,979	37,000	82	163,000		272,986	109

LIBRARY BUILDING / 309

NEW PUBLIC LIBRARY BUILDINGS CONSTRUCTED FROM JULY 1, 1970 TO JUNE 30, 1971, Continued

Community	Pop. in M	M Code	Project Cost	Gross Sq. Ft.	Constr. Cost	Sq. Ft. Cost	Equip. Cost	Site Cost	Other Costs	Vols.	Reader Seats	Fed. Funds	State Funds	Local Gvt. Funds	Gift Funds	Architect's Key
RHODE ISLAND																
East Providence	10	B	108,670	4,000	94,475	23.62	2,385	owned	11,810	14,000	42	48,000	2,000	58,670		110
SOUTH CAROLINA																
Lancaster	43	MS	342,515	16,434	249,983	15.21	70,000	gift	22,532	75,000	75	75,000		142,515	125,000	111
Moncks Corner	56	NA	204,038	7,680	167,907	21.86	23,038	owned	13,093	30,000	40	75,000		129,038		112
SOUTH DAKOTA (None reported)																
TENNESSEE																
Goodlettsville	26	B	140,129	5,000	115,567	23.11	15,709		8,853	10,000	25	70,000		70,129		113
Knoxville	175	M	1,997,650	72,170	1,415,986	19.62	215,664	290,000	76,000	400,000	265	604,000		1,388,250	5,400	114
Lawrenceburg	30	M	187,511	7,000	117,048	16.72	17,689	45,000	7,774	20,000	42	80,972		106,539		115
Nashville	35	B	248,918	7,965	142,436	17.88	22,132	75,379	8,970	12,000	95	83,000		165,918		116
Winchester	25	M	150,197	4,500	116,076	25.79	9,204	16,006	8,911	20,000	75	85,000		65,197		117
TEXAS																
Arlington	90	B	179,974	5,000	125,144	25.02	20,000	24,000	10,830	24,000	40	75,000		104,974		118
Arlington	90	B	185,645	5,000	131,160	26.20	13,205	22,500	18,940	18,000	63	91,600		94,045		119
Arlington	90	B	195,000	5,000	136,992	27.39	18,000	24,000	16,008	18,000	80	75,000		120,000		120
Dallas	38	B	619,420	13,089	447,782	34.21	72,634	57,173	41,831	49,000	85			619,420		121
Dallas	20	B	586,753	10,984	409,369	37.27	67,301	75,406	34,677	40,000	70			586,753		122
Dallas	29	B	605,157	15,700	402,783	25.65	62,425	63,000	76,949	63,000	100			605,157		123
Falfurrias	6	M	222,264	10,000	190,100	19.01	8,387	gift	23,777	26,000	62	50,000		97,264	75,000	124
Friendswood	6	M	145,000	5,000	110,000	22.00	12,500	9,500	13,000	15,000	40	50,000		52,500	42,500	125
Garland	85	MS	811,214	20,000	456,598	22.83	61,479	228,192	64,945	79,370	190	150,000		661,214		126
Hillsboro	23	MS	105,670	5,000	80,331	16.06	15,927	gift	9,412	8,000	50		50,000		55,670	127
Houston	18	B	111,676	5,000	87,493	17.50	17,855	1,439	4,889	25,000	40	50,000		61,676		128
Lewisville	10	M	147,606	5,000	118,000	23.60	19,000	owned	10,606	20,605	44	50,000		97,606		129
Liberty	8	M	603,861	23,518	512,925	21.81	31,895	gift	59,041	35,000	60	150,000		3,500	450,361	130
Panhandle	2	M	144,783	6,000	113,278	18.8	22,438	owned	9,067	30,000	62	50,000		9,783	85,000	131
Richardson	50	M	1,982,051	81,640	1,687,343	20.67	104,116	owned	190,592	250,000	182			1,982,051		132

310 / NATIONAL LIBRARY AND BOOK TRADE DEVELOPMENTS

LIBRARY BUILDING / 311

UTAH			(None reported)									
VERMONT			(None reported)									
VIRGINIA												
Alexandria	103	B	250,000	9,600	195,000	20.31	25,000	18,000	12,000	45,000	85	250,000	133
Chesapeake	87	MS	308,143	18,432	267,042	14.49	14,728	owned	26,373	35,000	34	235,522	134
Manassas	111	MS	544,000	23,215	407,664	14.00	87,000	gift	49,336	100,000	125	444,000	10,000	135
Norfolk	25	B	285,249	6,750	231,216	34.25	30,000		24,033	25,000	60	222,588	100,000	136
Pennington Gap	20	B	229,474	9,981	176,598	17.69	24,967	18,500	9,409	43,000	73	62,621		137
Roanoke County	25	B	275,000	6,000	190,000	31.66	30,000	30,000	25,000	35,000	70	62,661	43,711	138
Vinton	15	B	320,000	7,500	252,000	33.60	33,000	10,000	25,000	45,000	57	160,763		139
WASHINGTON													
Bellevue	15	M	324,527	7,500	230,121	30.68	30,287	22,737	41,382	30,000	32	62,622		140
Lynnwood	16	B	401,869	8,062	204,172	25.33	21,239	111,400	65,058	30,000	64	121,747		141
Richland	26	M	1,190,000	33,350	901,934	27.04	121,240	U.S. surplus	166,826	105,000	225	142,000		142
Silverdale	5	B	8,446	1,024	6,435	6.28	1,083	gift	928	8,500	10	2,200 hrs. labor donated	8,446	143
Stanwood	2	B	38,519	3,800	33,748	8.88	2,693	owned	2,078	15,000	23	1,503	37,016 (plus labor)	144
WEST VIRGINIA													
Elkins	24	M	199,871	5,180	151,341	29.22	8,000	29,070	11,460	20,000	40	132,153	65,186	145
WISCONSIN													
Cedarburg	7	M	250,000	12,000	199,000	16.58	26,000	owned	25,000	60,000	70	200,000	50,000	146
Mequon	11	M	550,000	15,001	487,000	32.46	23,000	owned	40,000	60,000	59	127,000	423,000	147
Milwaukee	60	B	457,200	15,000	382,500	25.50	51,200	owned	23,500	60,000	80	457,200		148
TOTALS			$65,193,446	2,032,252	$48,501,338	$23.87	$6,015,692	$4,867,338	$5,809,078	7,701,350	12,490	$11,214,090	$2,507,715	$45,803,096	$5,668,545

New Buildings Omitted From Totaled Table Because Information Was Incomplete

Boston	28	B	not known by library	9,443	$567,300	$60.07	not known by library	none	not known by library	22,000	103	not known by library	148a
Sherborn	3	M	not disclosed	18,000				N.A.	N.A.	36,000	80		not disclosed	148b
Centreville	2	B	not disclosed	2,000	not disclosed		$4,940	N.A.	N.A.	6,500	24	$1,790	$3,000 not disclosed	148c

PUBLIC LIBRARY BUILDINGS ENLARGED AND REMODELED FROM JULY 1, 1970 TO JUNE 30, 1971

Code: BAR: branch addition and remodeling; BR: branch remodeled; BRL: branch remodeled in leased space; MA: main addition; MAR: main addition and remodeling; MR: main remodeled; MRL: main remodeled in leased space; MSA: main and system addition and remodeling; MSR: main system remodeling; SA: system addition; SAR: system headquarters addition and remodeling.

Community	Pop. in M	Code	Project Cost	Gross Sq. Ft.	Constr. Cost	Sq. Ft. Cost	Equip. Cost	Site Cost	Other Costs	Vols.	Reader Seats	Fed. Funds	State Funds	Local Gvt. Funds	Gift Funds	Architect's Key
ALASKA	(None reported)															
ALABAMA	(None reported)															
ARIZONA	(None reported)															
ARKANSAS																
Fayetteville	29	MSA	90,000	3,800	70,668	18.59	63	13,500	5,769	58,100	107	54,000		36,000		149
Hot Springs	35	MSA	134,000	10,176	115,234	11.32	11,002	owned	7,764	134,800	80	80,000			54,000	150
CALIFORNIA																
Carpinteria	10	BAR	12,350	1,000	8,000	8.00	3,600	owned	,750	6,500	12			9,850	2,500	151
El Centro	20	MA	126,379	2,550	87,321	34.24	11,529	owned	27,529	14,000	50			111,209	15,170	152
Los Angeles	168	BR	18,465	2,638	18,465	7.00								18,465		153
Orange	655	SAR	201,400	22,000	191,254	8.69	10,146	owned		70,000	100			201,400		154
Orinda	17	BA	249,207	4,277	187,618	43.86	41,589	owned	20,000	37,000	100	52,423		179,584	17,200	155
Sunnyvale	95	MA	700,000	24,000	575,000	23.96	75,000	owned	50,000	132,000	200			700,000		156
Yorba Linda	14	MAR	585,000	24,425	387,842	15.88	47,000	91,000	59,158	150,000	165			582,400	2,600	157
COLORADO																
Hotchkiss	1	MAR	6,320	919	4,855	5.28	1,465	owned		500	8	2,880		3,440		158
Westminster	19	MA	163,860	4,100	135,518	33.05	8,611	owned	19,731	15,000	30	75,000		88,860		159
CONNECTICUT	(None reported)															

LIBRARY BUILDING / 313

DELAWARE		(None reported)									
FLORIDA											
Plant City	41	MAR	206,900	6,446	137,701	21.36		60,000	9,199	40,000	62	102,000	2,900	160
GEORGIA		(None reported)									
HAWAII		(None reported)									
IDAHO		(None reported)									
ILLINOIS											
Decatur	90	MR	1,401,992	67,000	789,560	11.79	214,480	300,000	97,952	500,000	324	1,037,992		161
Minonk	4	MR	52,000	4,896	47,400	9.68	4,600	owned	16,679	14,500	54	34,800		162
Morton Grove	27	MR	237,259	10,301	178,597	17.31	41,983		5,400	92,200	178	177,179	6,700	163
Woodridge	1	MR	23,000	1,000	14,000	14.00	1,700	1,900		5,000	12	23,000		164
INDIANA											
Noblesville	13	MAR	314,626	16,894	233,410	13.81	44,767	15,000	21,449	55,000	90	94,989	10,000	165
IOWA											
Fayette	3	MAR	69,507	3,441	50,262	14.60	14,214	owned	5,031	14,000	52	36,574	32,933	166
KANSAS											
Cawker City	1.5	MR	16,000	2,000	15,000	7.50		owned	1,000	10,000	14	16,000		167
Olathe	18	MR	202,000	7,781			11,372	170,000	20,628	60,000	73	192,000	10,000	168
KENTUCKY											
Brownsville	8	MAR	122,088	4,259	101,255	23.77	9,255	3,178	8,400	26,000	22		22,966	169
London	26	MSAR	238,206	7,660	183,808	24.00	18,300	18,000	18,098	50,000	30	177,060		170
Prestonsburg	38	MSA	59,761	1,652	50,776	30.73	5,366		3,619		32		21,828	171
LOUISIANA		(None reported)									
MAINE											
Rumford	10	MA	75,000	3,000	61,000	20.33	9,000	owned	5,000	18,688	40	70,000	5,000	172

PUBLIC LIBRARY BUILDINGS ENLARGED AND REMODELED FROM JULY 1, 1970 TO JUNE 30, 1971, Continued

Community	Pop. in M	Code	Project Cost	Gross Sq. Ft.	Constr. Cost	Sq. Ft. Cost	Equip. Cost	Site Cost	Other Costs	Vols.	Reader Seats	Fed. Funds	State Funds	Local Gvt. Funds	Gift Funds	Architect's Key
MARYLAND	(None reported)															
MASSACHUSETTS	(None reported)															
MICHIGAN																
Baldwin	2	MR	33,618	2,250	12,990	5.80	6,028	14,000	600	10,000	12			10,618	23,000	173
Edmore	4	MAR	8,778	2,460	6,278	2.55	1,400	gift	1,100	9,000	36			8,678	100	174
Laingsburg	3	MR	8,800	1,200	3,800	3.17	500	4,500		3,500	30			6,000	2,800	175
Lakeview	4	BR	21,030	1,600	10,515	6.58	2,515	8,000		6,000	26			18,330	2,700	176
Romeo	8	MA	167,624	4,100	154,448	35.23			13,176	2,500	48	47,562		120,062		177
MINNESOTA	(None reported)															
MISSISSIPPI																
Clarksdale	39	MSA	350,607	10,000	243,548	24.35	40,000	50,000	17,059	202,000	45	10,000		339,107	1,500	178
Yazoo City	11	MSA	44,267	1,600	39,560	24.72	2,545	owned	2,162	11,340	20	2,500		41,437	330	179
MISSOURI	(None reported)															
MONTANA																
Chester	2	MR	51,835	4,356	17,165	3.93	9,270	24,600	800	15,000	20	25,000		26,835		180
Choteau	2	MR	40,000	7,000	9,000	1.28	10,000	20,000	1,000	25,000	30	20,000		4,750	15,250	181
NEBRASKA	(None reported)															
NEVADA	(None reported)															
NEW HAMPSHIRE	(None reported)															
NEW JERSEY																
Cherry Hill	65	MR	55,000	3,175	42,500	13.40	11,900	owned	600	6,000	37		44,000	11,000		182
Livingston	30	MR	45,000	1,296	18,973	14.64	20,338		5,689	25,000				45,000		183

LIBRARY BUILDING / 315

Matawan	28	MA	48,000	2,000	43,000	21.50	5,000		3,000	10,000	30			47,000	1,000	184
Northvale	5	MR	10,700	3,300	4,200	1.31	3,500		4,245	15,000	60			34,000	10,700	185
Paterson	18	BR	46,697	7,070	42,452	6.00		owned		19,000	72		12,697			186
West Long Branch	7	MR	82,993	2,920	44,399	15.20	5,726	29,000	3,868	12,000	45			82,993		187
NEW MEXICO																
Los Alamos	15	MA	88,300	3,330	76,000	22.82	6,600	owned	5,700	58,308	100	37,843		50,457		188
Tucumcari	7.5	MAR	179,738	9,600	103,640	18.73	35,369	39,562	1,167	50,000	70		1,320	178,418		189
NEW YORK																
Ballston Spa	5	MAR	57,684	3,335	48,024	14.40	4,296	owned	5,364	35,000	42	1,500			56,184	190
Bellport	1	SA	835,000	23,700	708,771	29.90	47,549	owned	78,680			291,931	543,069			191
Brookhaven	10	MA	39,000	1,000	26,000	26.00	3,000	4,600	5,400	10,000	24				39,000	192
Earlville	1	MA	98,504	3,268	78,955	24.15	10,081	1.00	9,468	20,000	32	34,476		64,028		193
Hannibal	1	MRL	4,800	900	3,800	4.22	1,000			5,000	12			3,200	1,600	194
Jordan	3	MR	87,638	6,000	46,000	7.67	12,092	25,000	4,546	10,000	28	4,152		8,500	74,986	195
Queens	90	BAR	427,700	17,100	349,000	20.41	12,290		66,410	70,000	154			427,700		196
Queens	33	BR	411,176	9,100	411,176					27,000	60			411,176		197
Victor	8	MR	12,62	1,000	12,445	11.31	197	owned		8,500	20			5,928	6,714	198
NORTH CAROLINA (None reported)																
NORTH DAKOTA																
Grafton	6	MR	42,515	2,500	37,500	15.00	5,015			13,000	22	25,075		17,440		199
OHIO (None reported)																
OKLAHOMA (None reported)																
OREGON (None reported)																
PENNSYLVANIA																
Meadville	27	MR	323,680	10,026	176,377	17.59	91,961	17,622	37,720	60,000	105	121,362			202,318	200
Oxford	15	MA	187,800	8,000	150,000	18.75	15,000	8,000	14,800	25,000	60				187,800	201
RHODE ISLAND																
East Providence	9	BAR	67,830	2,340	60,735	25.95	1,190	owned	5,905	9,000	36	29,000	1,000	37,830		202

PUBLIC LIBRARY BUILDINGS ENLARGED AND REMODELED FROM JULY 1, 1970 TO JUNE 30, 1971, Continued

Community	Pop. in M	M Code	Project Cost	Gross Sq. Ft.	Constr. Cost	Sq. Ft. Cost	Equip. Cost	Site Cost	Other Costs	Vols.	Reader Seats	Fed. Funds	State Funds	Local Gvt. Funds	Gift Funds	Architect's Key
SOUTH CAROLINA	(None reported)															
SOUTH DAKOTA	(None reported)															
TENNESSEE	(None reported)															
TEXAS																
Big Spring	37	MR	73,196	8,160	62,265	7.64	7,195	free	3,736	26,670	76			72,696	500	203
Pineland	5	MA	50,000	2,000	43,000	21.50	3,000	gift	4,000						50,000	204
UTAH	(None reported)															
VERMONT	(None reported)															
VIRGINIA	(None reported)															
WASHINGTON																
Castle Rock	1.6	MR	7,800	2,000	7,800	3.90	gift	owned		10,000	25			800	7,000	205
Harrington	1	MR	4,756	1,140	4,198	3.68	56	502		5,000	15		1,517	3,239		206
Tacoma	20	BRL	32,633	3,328	21,728	6.53	10,905	leased		15,00	34			32,633		207
WEST VIRGINIA	(None reported)															
WISCONSIN																
Milwaukee	1054	MSR	1,599,584	53,771	1,498,402	27.87		owned	101,182	50,000	100	451,845		1,147,739		208
WYOMING	(None reported)															
TOTALS			$10,952,245	462,240	$8,263,188		$970,560		$917,965	$800,532	2,382,106	3,261	$2,211,752	$648,397	$7,249,611	$842,485

LIBRARY BUILDING / 317

ARCHITECTS

1. Charles H. McCauley Associates, Birmingham, Ala.
2. None given
3. Bob Wright Co., Tacoma/Seattle.
4. Bennie Gonzales, Phoenix.
5. Clark Buchner Environmental Design, Inc., Little Rock, Ark.
6. Deasy & Bolling, Los Angeles.
7. Wilfred E. Blessing, San Jose, Calif.
8. N.A.
9. Unknown
10. Williamson & Morris, Long Beach, Calif.
11. Robert F. Stuhr, Bakersfield, Calif.
12. Kistner, Wright & Wright, Los Angeles.
13. Anthony & Langford, Whittier, Calif.
14. Palmer W. Power, Thomas J. Morrison, Long Beach, Calif.
15. Spencer, Lee & Busse, San Francisco.
16. Tom & Truskier, Huntington Beach, Calif.
17. Marquis & Stoller, San Francisco.
18. Lawrence G. Thomson, Chico, Calif.
19. Spencer, Lee & Busse, Palo Alto, Calif.
20. A. E. Nine, Long Beach, Calif.
21. Selden Kennedy, Jr., no address given
22. Maul - Pulver - Schweickert, Covina, Calif.
23. Grillias, Savage, Alves, Santa Ana, Calif.
24. Heitschmidt/Mounce/Associates, Los Angeles.
25. Grover Taylor, Fontana, Calif.
26. James G. Hanson, Hanson & Gurhtie, Vacaville, Calif.
27. Beland, Gianelli & Associates, Vallejo, Calif. and Marquis & Stoller, San Francisco.
28. Angello & Vitiello, Sacramento, Calif.
29. Wadley & Mackensen, Yuba City, Calif.
30. William L. Coppock, Denver.
31. Harold R. Carver, Arvada, Colo.
32. Look & Morrison, Pensacola, Fla.
33. Norman P. Gross, Panama City, Fla.
34. Hal T. Reid, Ocala, Fla.
35. Robert M. Matsushita & Associates, Honolulu.
36. Jerome Butler, Chicago.
37. Cletus R. Foley, Peoria, Ill.
38. Bartolomeo & Hansen, Chicago.
39. Wm. B. Ittner Inc. St. Louis.
40. Perkins & Will, Chicago, and R. L. Hartung, Bloomington, Ind.
41. Wildermuth & Bone, Portage, Ind.
42. James Associates, Indianapolis.
43. J. James Fugenides, Highland, Ind.
44. Strauss Associates, Inc.—Richard Shaoon & Larry Reeves, Fort Wayne, Ind.
45. The Griffith Co., Fort Dodge, Iowa.
46. Rondeau, Williams & Smith, Great Bend, Kan.
47. Max Bisson, Owensboro, Ky.
48. Paul J. Kissell, Lexington, Ky.
49. D. G. Crawley, Henderson, Ky.
50. William B. Moore, Louisville, Ky.
51. William B. Moore, Louisville, Ky.
52. Clark Associates, Lexington, Ky.
53. Peyton Davis, Louisville, Ky.
54. Peck Associates, Inc. Paducah, Ky.
55. Foster Phillips, Stanford, Ky.
56. H. H. Land, Monroe, La.
57. H. H. Land, Monroe, La.
58. Hamilton, Meyer & Associates, Opelousas, La.
59. H. H. Land, Monroe, La.
60. Hamilton, Meyer & Associates, Opelousas, La.
61. Morris H. Steinhorn, Baltimore.
62. Rogers and Vaeth, Baltimore.
63. Masiello and Associates, Lanham, Md.
64. Watkins & Magee, Baltimore.
65. O. E. Nault & Sons, Worcester, Mass.
66. Drummey Rosane Anderson, Newton Lower Falls, Mass.
67. Prine, Toshack & Spears, Saginaw, Mich.
68. Louis G. Redstone, Associates, Detroit.
69. Manson, Jackson and Kane, Lansing, Mich.
70. Robert Cain, Kalamazoo, Mich.
71. O'Dell, Hewlett & Luckenbach, Birmingham, Mich.
72. G. J. McGrath, St. Joseph, Mich.
73. Straub, Van Dine Associates, Troy, Mich.
74. Graffunder-Berreau and Associates, Minneapolis.
75. Graffunder-Berreau and Associates, Minneapolis.
76. W—Smith Architectural and Engineering Services, Winona, Minn.
77. Buetow & Associates, St. Paul, Minn.
78. Brooks Cavin, Minneapolis, Minn.
79. Cooke-Douglass-Farr, Jackson, Miss.
80. Roy Collins Construction Co., Cleveland, Miss.
81. Clemmer and Clark, Jackson, Miss.

ARCHITECTS, Continued

82. Charles P. McMullan & Associates, Jackson, Miss.
83. Frederick C. Sternberg, St. Louis.
84. Eugene F. Johnson, Springfield, Mo.
85. Albert J. Gasvoda, Helena, Mont.
86. Raymond Hellmann, Reno, Nev.
87. Edwards & Daniels, Salt Lake City, Utah.
88. Hayes and Hough, Philadelphia.
89. McDowell-Goldstein, Madison, N.J.
90. Kobayashi & Bostrom, Red Bank, N.J.
91. Alexander Ewing & Sidney Scott Smith, Moorestown, N.J.
92. Wm. Rbt. Huntington, Asbury Park, N.J.
93. John A. Osborne, Wyckoff, N.J.
94. Bentel & Bentel, Locust Valley, N.Y.
95. Daniel Laitin, New York.
96. Curtis & Davis, New York.
97. Joseph A. Daidone, New York.
98. Albert Barash, New York.
99. James H. Johnson, Penfield, N.Y.
100. Henry J. Stojowski, New York.
101. J. Bertram King, FAIA, Asheville, N.C.
102. Loewenstein, Atkinson & Wilson, Greensboro, N.C.
103. W. D. Boone, Jr., Charlotte, N.C.
104. Holland and Riviere, Shelby, N.C.
105. Foy & Lee Associates, Waynesville, N.C.
106. Trefon Sagadencky, Cuhahoga Falls, Ohio.
107. Blanchard & Lamen, Salem, Ore.
108. Robert W. Frey, Allentown, Pa.
109. Charles Treat Arnold, Philadelphia.
110. Robinson, Green & Beretta, Providence, R.I.
111. Joseph H. Croxton, Lancaster, S.C.
112. Lafaye, Lafaye & Associates, Columbia, S.C.
113. Taylor & Crabtree, Nashville, Tenn.
114. Bruce McCarty & Associates, Knoxville, Tenn.
115. Burkhalter, Hickerson & Associates, Nashville, Tenn.
116. Taylor & Crabtree, Nashville, Tenn.
117. Burkhalter-Hickerson & Associates, Nashville, Tenn.
118. Albert S. Komatsu, Fort Worth, Tex.
119. Parker and Crouch, Arlington, Tex.
120. Parker and Crouch, Arlington, Tex.
121. William H. Hidell, Dallas.
122. Forrest Upshaw, Jr., Dallas.
123. Braden & Jones, Dallas.
124. Christian, Bright & Pennington, Corpus Christi, Tex.
125. Matt E. Howard & Associates, Houston.
126. Stanely S. Smith, Dallas.
127. Rucker & Chamleg, Temple, Tex.
128. Ernest Cole, Houston.
129. George L. Dahl, Inc., Dallas.
130. William R. Jenkins, Houston.
131. Rittenberry & Associates, Amarillo, Tex.
132. Jarvis, Putty, Jarvis, Dallas.
133. Vosbeck, Vosbeck, Kendrick & Redinger, Alexandria, Va.
134. Yates, Boggs, Berkeley & Service, Portsmouth, Va.
135. Spector, Peake & Howell, Falls Church, Va.
136. Oliver & Smith, Norfolk, Va.
137. Anderson & Gilliam, Bristol, Tenn.
138. Guerrant & Mounfield, Roanoke, Va.
139. Kinsey, Motley & Shane, Salem, Va.
140. Fred Bassetti & Co., Seattle.
141. Ridenour, Cochran & Lewis, Bellevue, Wash.
142. Durham, Anderson Freed, Seattle.
143. Donald P. Setter, Bremerton, Wash.
144. Perry Holdsworth, Camano Island, Wash.
145. Michael P. DiBella, New York.
146. W. C. Weeks, Sheboygan, Wis.
147. Kloppenburg & Kloppenburg, Milwaukee.
148. Burroughs & Van Lanen, Milwaukee.
148a. Mitchell/Guirgola Associates, N.Y.
148b. James A. S. Walker, Boston.
148c. E. C. Latham, Mobile, Ala.
149. Warren D. Segraves, Fayetteville, Ark.
150. I. Granger McDaniel, Hot Springs, Ark.
151. Jack Dewey, Santa Barbara, Calif.
152. William Jehle, El Centro, Calif.
153. W. R. Blakely, Los Angeles.
154. Salmi, Hockenberry & Associates, Orange, Calif.
155. Aitken & Collins, Berkeley, Calif.
156. Goodwin Steinberg, San Jose, Calif.
157. Charles M. Wickett, Fullerton, Calif.
158. None given
159. Charles Gathers & Associates, Denver.
160. Donald McIntosh, Tampa, Fla.
161. Spangler, Beal, Salogga, Bradley & Albers, Decatur, Ill.
162. Harry E. Riddle, Jr., Bloomington, Ill.
163. Laurence Schwall, Northbrook, Ill.
164. None given
165. Pecsok, Jelliffe & Randall, Indianapolis.
166. Stenson & Warm, Inc., Waterloo, Iowa.
167. Coler S. Hissem, Wichita, Kans.
168. None

169. Dixon Rapp, Glasgow, Ky.
170. D. E. Perkins, Harlan, Ky.
171. George Lee Shannon, Prestonsburg, Ky.
172. Leasure Lee & Tuttle, Portland, Me.
173. Gordon Corwell, Traverse City, Mich.
174. Duane K. Cote, Birmingham, Mich.
175. Robert Stinson, Laingsburg, Mich.
176. None given
177. Merritt McCollum Associates, Farmington, Mich.
178. Brewer, Godbold & Associates, Clarksdale, Miss.
179. John E. DeCell, Yazoo City, Miss.
180. Albert J. Gasvoda, Helena, Mont.
181. Albert J. Gasvoda, Helena, Mont.
182. Malcolm Wells, Cherry Hill, N.J.
183. Arthur Haas, So. Orange, N.J.
184. None given
185. None
186. Tischler & Comerro, Leonard N. Freed, Paterson, N.J.
187. James F. Roper, Red Bank, N.J.
188. John B. Arrison, Santa Fe, N.M.
189. B. J. Stratton, Tucumcari, N.M.
190. William E. Cooper, Amsterdam, N.Y.
191. Siegmund Spiegel, East Meadow, N.Y.
192. Frederick Allardt, Jr., Brookhaven, N.Y.
193. Granger & Gillespie, Syracuse, N.Y.
194. None given
195. Albert Arnold—Ketcham, Miller & Arnold, Syracuse, N.Y.
196. Harry Silberman, New York.
197. Dept. of Pub. Works, City of N.Y.
198. Straight & Weigert, Victor, N.Y.
199. Harrie & Kennedy, Grand Forks, N.D.
200. Hunter, Heiges & Associates, Meadville, Pa.
201. None
202. Robinson, Green & Beretta, Providence, R.I.
203. Olen L. Puckett, Big Spring, Tex.
204. Desmond, Miremont & Assoc., Inc., Hammond, La.
205. None given
206. None given
207. Johnson/Austin, Berg, Tacoma, Wash.
208. Johnson-Wagner-Isley & Widen, Milwaukee.

ACADEMIC LIBRARY BUILDING 1967–1971*

by

Jerrold Orne**

A billion dollars in five years! How many academic librarians five years ago would have believed it possible that nearly a billion dollars would be spent on academic libraries in the next five years? Incredible as it may seem, we now know it, and the record is represented with complete documentation in our tables and text. Our returns indicate a grand total expenditure in library projects for the five years beginning January 1, 1967, of $984,919,814. This does include Canadian libraries to the extent of slightly more than $64,000,000. The gross area completed amounted to over 34,000,000 square feet, providing accommodations for 127,377,821 volumes. The seating capacity built during this period totaled 338,458. It seems apparent from this that our students for the next few years should not be crowded for space and that most academic libraries will not be too hard pressed to accommodate their near future book additions.

It should be possible to analyze the statistics in various areas of this report for many useful functions. Unfortunately, time and space do not permit us to do it now. Perhaps other authors will find material here for specific analysis and comment and other articles will grow from this start. This was our hope when we began the series. It remains our hope for the future. With no more than the once-over-lightly analysis we have given here, one can readily derive standards for comparison that should serve building planners for a long time to come. It is doubtful that there will ever again be as prolific a period in academic library building history. The record of the past five years should give considerable satisfaction to all those who had so large a part in making it happen.

ACADEMIC BUILDING RENAISSANCE, 1967–1971

Five years ago American academic libraries experienced the first flush of a great change in building experience. The primary impetus was the booming population expansion in colleges and universities, and the secondary, but directly related influence, was the infusion of generous federal funding specifically for construction. The net results have been recorded initially for each of the past four years as isolated annual statistical summaries. The brief notes accompanying these annual compilations served to compare year to year, and to signal short-term variations. Without these primitive efforts, it would be impossible to compile the reliable broad base we now have.

The five-year period recorded here represents the greatest flowering of academic library building experience this country has ever known or is likely to see. This experience is almost incredible not only for volume but for variety of architectural form and for the orientation of planning personnel. Detailed analysis of the data now available provides new and stable standard measures against which future work can be plotted. Careful study of building planning by type reveals trends by type and form of structure which may serve all planners for some years to come. In a few areas our data serves best to demonstrate some inadequacies of measuring or reporting. It sometimes reveals professional ineptness or disinterest which perhaps time and stronger young professionals will correct. We suspect that many cases of inadequate reporting were due simply to poor or nonexistent communication between librarian-administrative-architectural bodies, a sad but well-known characteristic of the academic community.

---

*Reprinted from *Library Journal*, December 1, 1971.
**University Librarian, The University of North Carolina Library, Chapel Hill.

Despite these disclaimers, we are pleased with the abundance of data we have been able to acquire and with the commendable eagerness of most of our respondents to answer our questions. Where our charts are deficient, it commonly results from inherent difficulties of determining precisely what measures can be reliably made. In only a few cases did we find no response at all.

Our five-year review covering all college and university libraries completed and occupied from January 1967 to December 1971 includes a total of over 400 library building projects. Of these, 257 are completely new general academic library buildings built in the United States. Under the heading of Additions and Renovations, 73 projects will be found. These constitute additions to existing general library structures, with some part of the original structure being renovated as a part of the project. Listed in the table entitled Additions are 38 projects. In this group the new structure was added with negligible change in the original. One special table is devoted to Undergraduate Libraries, including seven structures designed to serve particularly the younger population on a campus where another, usually larger, library of a broader service range already exists. Two professional school areas are recorded as special types in a separate table. These include seven medical libraries and nine law libraries. We have brought together a number of other subject and specialized types of libraries in a separate table, again because data concerning these are comparable within the group, but not with other groups. Their numbers also suggest some new directions for campus planning which may be useful. There are 15 libraries in this group. In exact numbers there are 415 projects represented in our tables covering libraries in the United States. Thirty-two other library buildings should be represented and would be if we had been able to obtain any reliable data. Although they are not represented in our tables or their analysis, these libraries should be counted in the total product of our five-year period; with them, we have no less than 445 academic library projects completed in the United States in five years.

Our neighboring counterparts to the north have also been enjoying a like period of growth. Our first compelling force, the expanding student population, was also felt in Canada. The second factor, federal funding, found its counterpart in provincial grants for educational facilities. These, plus other factors peculiar to the Canadian pattern of higher education, resulted in the construction of at least 15 new library buildings for which we have data. Some comparisons between U.S. and Canadian libraries will be possible, but our list of Canadian libraries is not nearly as extensive as what we now have for U.S. libraries. These 15 libraries, added to our previous total, bring our total number for the five-year period to 462 library projects. Never before in the history of academic library building has such a large volume of data been available or assembled. It is not likely that there will ever be another period as prolific as this. Now is the time to consolidate what we have, wring out of it the best experience we have obtained, and apply it to what inevitably will be a more limited future.

Of the 257 academic libraries built at costs ranging from $1 million or less to over $20 million, there were 27 which cost more than $5 million. Fifty-five were in the range from $2 to $5 million, 108 from $1 million to $2 million, and 67 under $1 million.

THE BIG ONES: OVER $5 MILLION

In the first group, with project costs of over $5 million, the largest project cost $20,742,399 and delivered 584,886 square feet. At the other end of this group was a $5 million project which yielded a gross area of 123,500 square feet. Building costs varied from $15,-991,556 or $27.34 per square foot to $3,679,038 and $17.94 per square foot. Equipment costs varied from $126,300 to $3,500,000, and book capacity from as low as 140,000 to 3,533,550 volumes. The seating range was from 600 to 5,544.

Building costs ran from $17.94 to $42.86 per square foot.

The total cost of these 27 large projects was $220,650,797. This gives an average project cost figure of $8,172,252. The table reveals, however, that only seven of the 27 projects exceeded this average cost. The total gross area achieved was 6,764,890 square feet or an average of 250,551. Only nine libraries exceeded this average. Five of these institutions did not report on assignable space. Of the 22 reporting, with total space of 4,318,154 and an average of 196,280 square feet, we can calculate an average 78.34 percent assignable space overall in these very large structures. The range of this ratio runs from 63.64 percent to a high of 89.55 percent and averages 75.37 percent. Building costs for the 27 libraries amounted to $179,694,639, for an average $6,655,357. This average is skewed by the relatively few (eight) libraries above the average figure. The square foot cost range varies from $17.94 to $42.86, with an average of $27.48. Our 1967 report developed an average square foot cost of $25.60 for the entire list of 75 libraries, and $28.31 for the 26 larger libraries costing over $2 million. It is interesting to note in our extended table of this year that the two libraries which cost more than $40 per square foot were completed in 1967 and 1969. Those completed in 1970 and 1971 averaged $26.30 per square foot. Since we have good reason to believe that building costs are increasing year by year, we must believe that the apparently lower costs of recent years in this field are derived from more austere and/or efficient design.

Equipment costs in this group totaled $25,438,561, for an average $942,169. One would naturally expect the more costly buildings to require proportionately high equipment costs, but the table shows some notable exceptions. It is difficult, if not impossible, to isolate equipment costs in a consistent manner, particularly since more or less equipment may be provided by the contractor as a part of the building. In a very large library the shelving alone, depending upon where it is funded, may thoroughly distort any statistical balance.

The total book capacity of these large libraries is 28,382,175 volumes. The average, 1,051,192, is attained by only ten of the 27. Seats for readers totaled 64,550, an average of 2,391. Only 11 of the 27 libraries provided more seats than the average.

The statistics for this group of 27 libraries are not basically consistent, probably because the span of cost is too great. The ten or 12 very big libraries form a fairly standard pattern. They have enormous capacities for books, readers, and size to go with their high cost. Thoughtful perusal of the table, especially the columns indicating building cost, equipment cost, book and seating capacity will usually reveal the basic character of each library. Some of them sought large book capacity, some maximum seating, and some have both. A library showing low book and seating capacity, but high in cost, such as Radcliffe College, must be planned for luxury above utility. Another library listing large capacities and low square foot cost will be clearly utilitarian, without luxury. The one imponderable, how effectively good design can deliver high capacity at low cost with elegance, may be suggested by a low percentage of nonassignable space or a somewhat higher equipment cost. Note, for example, the figures reported for Georgetown University, Washington, D.C.; they indicate a highly efficient design. Other examples are readily found.

THE $2 TO $5 MILLION CLASS

A majority (30) of the group of libraries costing from $2 to $5 million lie in the area between $2 and $3 million. Libraries in the broad range are consistent enough to make a group of 55 fit well together.

Total project cost for the 55 is $166,014,170, making an average cost of $3,018,439. The gross area for 54 libraries reporting was 7,067,478 square feet, for an average of 130,879. Forty-five libraries reported assignable space totalling 3,733,536 square feet, giving an average figure of 82,967. This is not especially noteworthy, but the average 79.27 percent assignable space is significantly better than the 75.37 percent reported for the group of larger libraries. The assignable space ratio in this group runs from a low of 55.69 percent to a high of 97.49 percent. We begin to see evolving a new rule of thumb which says simply that it is much easier to attain high ratios of assignable space in medium or small libraries than in very large structures.

With 53 reporting building costs, a total of $133,478,758 leads to an average of $2,518,467. Of the 53, 21 were above the average level. Square foot cost ranged from $16.55 to $54.48, with the average at $27.41. There are wide and numerous variations between highs and lows in this entire group, more than in the very large libraries, but the average is more consistent. Specific checking of annual figures reveals, however, a distinctly higher square foot average cost of $30.14 for 1970 and 1971.

Equipment costs amounting to $16,123,742 were reported by 52 institutions for an average of $310,072. There are extreme variations, running from $32,518 to $661,065. Here again, cost figures cannot be depended upon; there are a number of imponderables or unknown factors which may affect these figures.

Book capacities are more reliable, and the extremes, from a low of 20,000 to a high of 800,000, more readily interpreted. The book capacity of 54 libraries reporting came to a total of 19,678,850 for an average of 364,423.

Seating was provided for 58,068 readers, averaging 1,075 per library. These figures ranged from 233 to 2,500.

THE $1 TO $2 MILLION CLASS

Our next and largest group includes 108 libraries having project costs from $1 million to $2 million. These libraries comprise 52 percent of the 257 libraries included in the general list. They are probably closer to the average or typical library of an academic institution than any of the other groups we present here. They have supplied enough data to assure statistical reliability, and offer us excellent measures of good practice.

The high in project cost is $1,992,073, giving a gross area of 71,030 square feet. The lowest, $1 million, provided a gross area of 18,560 square feet. The gross area range is from 18,053 to 122,631 square feet. The total gross area for all libraries was 5,943,916, leading to an average 55,036 square feet. The total project cost amounted to $153,208,265, giving an average figure of $1,418,595.

With only 92 libraries reporting assignable space, a total of 4,198,662 square feet averages to 45,376, with data ranging from 13,387 to a high of 92,619. The ratio of assignable area to gross area varies from 64.64 percent to 98.61 percent, with an average of 80.34 percent. This speaks for highly efficient design in buildings of this size, even better than the very good figure calculated for the next larger group, which came to 79.27 percent, and far better than the largest buildings, where the average percentage was 75.37.

Building costs reported by 104 libraries of this group were $124,830,356, giving an average cost of $1,200,292. The low was $644,763, the highest, $1,819,273. The square foot cost figures ran from $9.85 to a high of $49.25. The average square foot cost was $23.72. Obviously these cost figures are unusually low. Eight of the libraries reported costs below $15 per square foot, and as one might expect, six of the eight were completed in 1967 and 1968. The average costs for libraries in the group completed in 1970 and 1971 were $26.08; this compares favorably with the $23.72 average found when the whole five-year period is calculated.

Equipment costs for 104 libraries amounted to $16,243,802, averaging $156,190. The book capacities of 108 libraries were 19,488,148 volumes, or 180,446 per library as the average. This appears to be a high average, when many if not most of these are college libraries.

This may reflect the recent trend to seek university status and higher academic degree programs found in many erstwhile colleges. Seating was provided for 63,177 readers in 107 institutions, an average of 590.

Summing up the data analysis of this particular group, we note that at least 81 of the 108 institutions in this group are called colleges. Can we not assume that our averages, reported here, represent the typical college library of our time? The average project cost for a library in this group was $1,418,595, yielding a gross area of 55,036 square feet. The building cost was $1,200,292, resulting in a square foot cost of $23.72. The equipment average cost was $156,190, and 45,376 square feet of assignable space gave a ratio of 80.23 percent of the gross area. This space typically would accommodate 180,446 volumes and 590 readers. If this is not taken as typical, at least it will be readily granted that figures such as these represent an unmistakably well-designed, effective, and relatively inexpensive library structure.

The final group of 67 libraries includes those having a project cost under $1 million. Total costs of these projects reached $47,573,980. The average cost, $710,059, results from a range varying from $185,000 to $984,600. The total gross area achieved was 1,982,870 square feet, averaging 29,595 per library. The total assignable space, using only 48 libraries reporting, came to 1,275,505 square feet, yielding an average of 26,573. With the ratio of assignable to nonassignable space varying from 55.56 percent to 99.51 percent, the average attained was 84.12 percent. This final ratio calculation, representing the fourth step in the progression of higher ratios inversely by size, confirms our new rule of thumb: it is eminently possible to achieve the highest ratio of assignable to nonassignable space in small academic libraries.

Of this group of libraries, 66 reported total building costs of $39,465,754, an average of $597,966. The square foot cost varied from $10.12 to $37.65, and averaged $21.69. The average for buildings completed in 1970–1971 was $22.41. Of this group, 64 libraries reported equipment costs of $4,942,190, for an average of $77,222. Sixty-five reported book capacities from 13,125 volumes to 500,000 volumes, a total of 7,701,340 volumes and an average of 118,482 volumes. The same 65 reported a total seating for 22,776, an average of 350.

The typical library of this group would have a building cost of $597,966 and equipment costing $72,222. Dividing the sum of these by our average gross area suggests an average cost of $22.65 per square foot, including equipment. This is an extremely economical building cost for an academic library. From the number of seats reported by 65 of these libraries — 22,776 — you could expect an average seating capacity of 350. The average book capacity would be 118,482 volumes, based upon a total of 7,701,340 reported by 65 libraries.

The 257 libraries recorded in the first and most comprehensive table are all entirely new libraries completed in the five-year period 1967 through 1971. They are all general libraries; this list does not include professional, specialized subject or divisional libraries, undergraduate libraries, or the academic libraries of Canada. Each of these will be considered in separate tables and text. Although there are enormous variations of size or cost, these are a homogeneous type so far as function is concerned. Our tables are not absolutely complete, but there are relatively few gaps. We have complete figures for project costs, amounting to $587,447,212. With only one omission we have recorded gross area of 21,759,154 square feet. Two hundred and seven libraries reported total assignable space of 13,525,857 square feet. The average ratio of assignable to nonassignable space for all institutions reporting, calculated by extrapolation, would be 71.68 percent. New book capacity of 72,250,513 volumes was reported by 254 libraries, and 253 libraries reported a total of 211,009 seats for readers.

UNDERGRADUATE LIBRARIES

The seven undergraduate libraries reported total project costs of $21,083,792. Their combined gross area was 589,346 square feet, of which 436,119 is reported assignable space. Total building costs run to $15,655,978, with square foot costs averaging $30.17 in a range from $20.81 to $41.40. Equipment costs totaled $2,356,463, accounting for 858,139 volumes and 9,938 readers.

The data for these libraries clearly identify their special character. They have very large seating capacity and relatively smaller book capacities. Their equipment costs run high; this can be attributed to higher costs for reader service as compared with book accommodations. One unexpected average, the low-level assignable space ratio (74.05 percent), is surprising in view of the limited range of functions and activities in this type of library. The relatively high average square foot building cost ($30.17) is also curious. No doubt there are sound reasons for these averages, but we believe they lie in individual structures rather than in the group as a whole.

The average project cost of libraries in this group is $3,011,970. The gross area averaged 84,192 square feet, of which 62,303 is assignable space. The average building cost was $2,236,570, equipment cost $336,638, and the capacities amounted to 119,734 volumes and 1,420 readers.

PROFESSIONAL LIBRARIES: MEDICAL AND LAW

Seven new medical libraries were built during the past five years. These are commonly separate buildings, very consistent in cost and capacity data. The average project cost was $1,622,778 and the overall total $11,359,447. Gross area varied from 22,000 to 71,346, with an average of 47,886 square feet. Five of the seven reported a total of 164,502 square feet of assignable space, an average of 32,900, which gives an assignable ratio of 74.22 percent. This average seems low, since one reported 98.19 percent and another 83.58 percent. The remaining libraries thus do not make very good ratios. Building costs totaled $10,160,715 for the seven buildings, giving an average cost of $1,451,531. The square foot cost runs from $20 to $40, with an average of $30.96. Average equipment cost was $173,169, making a total of $1,212,181. Reader spaces total 2,793, allowing 399 seats on the average. The total book capacity provided was 1,219,125, an average 174,161 for each library.

The law libraries are not quite as consistent as the preceding group, the picture being grossly distorted by the inclusion of the L. B. Johnson complex in Texas. The total project cost, if we include the Texas entry, amounts to $34,721,324, giving an average of $3,857,924. Excluding the extremely high cost of the Johnson complex brings the average project cost to a more realistic $2,003,547. Even then, the project cost figures must be used with caution, since some of these libraries are also part of a structure serving the entire law school function, and it is not always clear how much of the project cost is in fact a library cost.

The gross area reported at 809,872 square feet is again distorted by the Texas figure, which accounts for more than half of the total. Excluding Texas again would bring our average figure for the law libraries to 48,793 square feet. In the same manner, we can report total assignable space at 495,739 for an average of 38,905 square feet. The assignable ratio works out at 72.02 percent for the whole list, but if Texas at 43.97 percent were excluded, the average ratio is 80.25 percent. The square foot cost for the eight libraries, excluding Texas, varies from $15.88 to $38.72 for an average $26.37. With eight libraries reporting, equipment costs ran from $57,572 to $1,626,545, totaling $2,900,352. Without Texas the average for the seven more typical law libraries was $181,972 for equipment. Provision was made for a total 2,733,200 volumes and seating for 4,121. The average volume capacity, excluding Texas, would be 226,915 and average seating 411.

Perhaps 20 years hence there will be a place for a table of Presidential libraries (perish the thought), but for the present there is no way rationally to consider such libraries in our academic collection.

SUBJECT AND DIVISION LIBRARIES

We have gathered a small group of libraries in one table by type, since they do not fit our usual pattern of general libraries. There is one special collections library, a fine arts library, nine science libraries, two theological libraries, an architecture and allied arts library, and one business administration library. We can hardly do more than present the data they have supplied and urge those who want specific data to write to the source, for, in fact, these data cannot be compared with anything else we have. A special collections building is one of a kind, and standard patterns do not apply. The science libraries are usually only part of a larger science structure, and project cost, building cost, and most of the other figures are not related to the library alone. The book capacity and seating capacity obviously are reliable measures and may be useful. The two theological libraries are indeed library buildings, but the specialized character of their collections and service loads affects their data. The architecture and business administration libraries are also parts of larger enterprises and cannot be considered with other complete library buildings.

These listings should be considered only as examples of types of libraries which our early planning did not include. We have avoided, in general, listing the many subject, branch, or departmental library units simply because they are not usually library buildings, and our efforts are designed to help us plan better *library buildings,* not parts of buildings made available for library use.

ADDITIONS

We have attempted to bring together in separate tables the five-year record of additions to existing buildings and also additions which were accompanied by renovation of an existing building. Any addition naturally involves some minor renovation, even if it is no more than the attachment or access, but these costs are negligible. The data for pure additions can indeed be analyzed and made to yield useful conclusions. The various costs are consistent within the group, and the yield in terms of space for books and people is significant.

There are 38 projects in our list of additions. The range of project cost varies from $121,600 to $5,521,335. The total project cost is $63,057,999. The gross area varies from 6300 to 170,736, giving a total of 2,283,489 square feet. Assignable space figures were not uniformly available, but the ratio for those reporting varied from 61.63 percent to 100 percent. The average is 84.20 percent, not such an unusual level, considering the commonly utilitarian character of library additions. It is a little difficult to visualize a library addition consisting of 100 percent assignable space, but perhaps it can happen. Building cost was reported by 36 of these libraries, in a range from $83,800 to $5,044,000, totaling $48,136,744. The square foot cost ran from $13.30 to $45.94, averaging $22.92. Equipment cost varied from $6,300 to $1,026,000, amounting in total to $6,141,677. The total book capacity for 38 libraries was 11,372,753 volumes, varying between 0 and 1,000,000. For this group, 29,058 seats were reported, including anything from 50 to 2,597. As one might expect, additions in this group are oriented more to book space than seating capacity.

ADDITIONS PLUS RENOVATION

We have included one table for library projects representing additions to existing buildings, together with notable renovations being made of old space. This table can only be presented with the variable data we have received, and it does not lend itself to detailed analysis as a group. Each project has its own individual goals and character, and the resulting cost and capacity data are not necessarily consistent with any other apparently similar project. The renovation part of a project may be minimal or a very large percentage. The cost of such alterations is proportionately low or high, and can vary for a multitude of reasons. We have tried to separate out new and renovation costs overall, but even if we had full reporting, there could be no assured consistency. Lacking full reporting, we have scrutinized and faithfully reported as much data as we could obtain for such useful purposes as it may serve. Those wanting other specific details may explore the reporting sources.

The total project cost for this group as we now have it cannot be interpreted as new space alone, and is, therefore, not recorded as such. Neither building cost nor square foot costs are consistent with other groups, since one cannot know how much belongs to the new or how much to the old. Insofar as it has been reported, we must include a total for gross area in the additions, and book and seating capacities. This is about as far as we can usefully go with this group. It is our hope that the individual reports will be helpful to others planning for this kind of building program. The project cost total for this group is $140,869,318. A grand total of 5,055,110 square feet of new space was provided, housing 24,821,978 volumes and 33,571 seats.

MULTIPURPOSE BUILDINGS

In the course of our data collection, a number of libraries were reported as parts of large multipurpose complexes or buildings. There has been a considerable volume of writing on the ideal form of combined teaching-library conglomerate, but actual conversion of theory into concrete and steel has been rather limited, at least at the college and university level. There are many multipurpose structures in community colleges and in local branches of some larger universities. Such structures are not usually comparable to those we have included in our survey. There is, indeed, a legitimate question of their being library buildings in any sense we know. We believe it may be useful, in any case, to include the small number we have encountered, as examples of the directions taken in some of the larger institutions. Each one of those listed is unique in function and form. Additional specific data may be readily obtained from the institution. Our table follows our usual pattern, but it must be remembered that all data may not be comparable, and much of it is not included in our overall totals.

CANADIAN LIBRARIES

We have tried to collect a reliable list of Canadian libraries completed or occupied in the same five-year period as our U.S. compilation, for comparative use and possibly to help establish a similar Canadian base. Because of distance and fewer sources of information, our data are somewhat less complete than we might wish. However, they may serve as a point of departure, and what we have been able to obtain is consistent with our U.S. data.

Ten university libraries are represented in a general new library list. Six of them report project costs of over $4 million, ranging from $4,056,250 to $8,692,000. The total investment is $42,414,680, for an average of $7,069,113. The gross area runs from 121,579 to 424,000 square feet, with the average being 251,971. The total gross area of these six libraries is 1,511,823 square feet. A total of 1,074,484 square feet of this is assignable space. The ratio of assignable to nonassignable space varies from 63.70 percent to 85.55 percent, and averages 71.32 percent. This average is slightly lower than the average for comparable new libraries of this size in the United States.

Total building costs of $34,848,769 represent a range of $2,982,720 to $7,844,000, averaging $5,808,128. The square foot cost range runs from $18.50 to $26.93, averaging $23.72. This is a very reasonable figure for buildings of this size. Equipment cost varies from $715,000 to $1,570,000, averaging $1,020,967 and totaling $6,125,800. Book capacity is in the range from 383,000 to 2,100,000 volumes, averaging 988,833 volumes and making a total of

5,933,000. A total of 9,688 seats was reported, making the average seating for this group 1,615.

Four smaller university libraries and one addition are considered in the next group. The data for the single addition are quite consistent with total building data; the inclusion of this one addition does not materially affect statistical analysis of the group. Their total project cost was $9,273,861, for an average of $1,854,772. The gross combined area of 289,039 square feet gives an average of 57,808. Assignable space was reported by four of the five, totaling 163,910 square feet, with an average of 40,977. The ratio of assignable space, from 69.02 percent to 87.22 percent, results in an average of 78.15 percent. This is consistent with the U.S. pattern of more productive use of available space in the smaller buildings. Total building costs for this group, $7,515,866, represents square foot costs from $19.59 to $29.03, averaging $25.71.

Equipment costs show a wide range, from 73,583 to $553,600, and average $242,227. The total equipment cost is $1,211,183. Book capacity varies from 68,000 to 400,000 volumes. The total book capacity designed was 1,318,000 volumes. Seating varies only from 335 to 800, averaging 480 and totaling 2,321.

The third group of four Canadian libraries includes two social science libraries and two law libraries; they form a comparable and reasonably consistent grouping. The total project cost of the four is $12,895,000, an average of $3,233,750. Total gross area is 298,416 square feet, an average of 74,604 square feet. Assignable areas total 272,565 square feet, an average of 68,141 square feet. The ratio of assignable to gross area varies from 76.82 percent to 95.45 percent and averages 90.31 percent. Building costs for the four average $1,988,675 and total $7,954,700. The cost per square foot ranges from $17.58 to $27.50 and averages only $23.60. These are four very efficient buildings, constructed at modest cost. The assignable gross area ratio exceeds by far the averages for comparable U.S. libraries.

Total equipment cost was 1,023,000. Equipment costs varied from $90,000 to $490,000 and averaged $255,750. Book capacity totaled 1,678,113 volumes, varying only from 200,000 to 628,313 volumes. The average was 419,528 volumes. Seating varied from 450 to 1,352, an average of 801 and a total of 3,202.

To summarize the Canadian libraries, our reports document 15 clearly well-designed, economical buildings. As a group they tend to be large buildings, providing adequate book capacity and seating. Total figures for all 15 libraries are: project cost: $64,583,541; gross area: 2,099,278 square feet; assignable space: 1,510,959 square feet; building costs: $50,319,355; equipment costs: $8,359,983; book capacity: 8,929,113 volumes; and seating for 15,211 readers. The overall averages can readily be worked out by anyone who may need them.

GENERAL ACADEMIC LIBRARIES

Institution	Project Cost	Gross Area	Net Assignable	Non-Assignable	Percent Assignable	Sq. Ft. Cost	Building Cost	Equipment Cost	Book Capacity	Seating Capacity	Architects	Year
Univ. of Chicago	$20,742,399	584,886	446,952	137,935	76.42	$27.34	$15,991,556	$2,301,361	3,533,550	3,150	Skidmore, Owings Merrill	1970
New York Univ. N.Y.	20,000,000	471,144				35.00	16,500,000	3,500,000	2,000,000	4,800	Johnson & Foster	1970
Univ. of Indiana Bloomington	14,871,000	582,185	378,420	203,765	65.00	23.40	13,621,000	1,250,000	2,600,000	5,544	Eggers & Higgins	1969
Univ. of Pittsburgh Pa.	13,411,870	255,289	177,477	77,842	69.51	38.71	9,881,989	885,815	1,200,000	2,067	Celli-Flynn	1967
Northwestern Univ. Evanston, Ill.	12,321,906	398,000	329,941	68,059	82.90	25.54	10,168,244	1,946,265	2,500,000	3,336	Skidmore, Owings Merrill	1970
Univ. of Minnesota Minneapolis	9,980,463	382,313	245,116	137,197	64.11	23.19	8,868,045	1,112,418	1,500,000	2,239	Cerney Assoc.	1968
Kent State Univ. Ohio	9,444,067	330,000	292,000	38,000	88.48	24.15	7,968,186	988,486	1,400,000	4,000	Stickle & Assoc.	1970
San Diego State Coll.	8,096,662	309,461	231,700	77,761	74.87	21.06	6,529,586	669,168	1,000,000	5,000	State Office of Arch. & Const.	1971
California State Coll. Hayward	7,855,900	247,900	174,323	73,577	70.32	27.56	6,830,900	1,300,000	750,000	3,000	State Office of Arch. & Const.	1971
Emory Univ. Atlanta	7,011,072	239,267	180,315	58,952	75.36	26.54	6,351,072	660,000	1,015,000	1,456	Warner, Burns, Toan, Lunde	1969
Univ. of Utah Salt Lake City	6,763,000	300,000	227,000	73,000	75.67	18.25	5,475,000	985,000	1,500,000	3,115	Lorenzo, Young & Partners	1968
Penn. State Univ. University Park	6,727,548	133,000				35.73	4,752,414	1,499,892	450,000	1,510	Eshbach, Pullinger & Sterens	1971
Tulane Univ. New Orleans	6,216,607	220,000	197,000	23,000	89.55	24.82	5,461,682	456,925	1,256,625	1,385	Nolan, Norman & Nolan	1968
Georgetown Univ. Washington, D.C.	6,165,306	205,000	181,576	23,424	88.57	17.94	3,679,038	774,972	1,000,000	1,450	John Carl Warnecke & Assoc.	1970
Bridgewater State Coll. Bridgewater, Mass.	6,125,000	172,000	135,357	36,643	78.70	23.88	4,038,000	750,000	425,000	2,500	Hoyle, Doran & Berry	1971
State Univ. Coll. at Oswego, N.Y.	5,862,639	173,050	119,110	53,940	68.83	25.50	4,962,639	126,300	600,000	2,200	Skidmore, Owings & Merrill	1968
Ohio Univ. Athens	5,660,245	241,467	176,792	64,675	73.22	20.98	5,067,008	593,237	600,000	3,268	Dalton, Dalton & Little	1969

GENERAL ACADEMIC LIBRARIES, Continued

Institution	Project Cost	Gross Area	Net Assignable	Non-Assignable	Percent Assignable	Sq. Ft. Cost	Building Cost	Equipment Cost	Book Capacity	Seating Capacity	Architects	Year
Univ. of Alaska College	5,550,989	113,356	83,051	30,305	73.27	41.40	4,323,989	837,000	400,000	1,300	Manley & Mayer	1969
State Univ. of N. Y. Fulton	5,494,050	173,050				28.67	4,962,639	532,000	600,000	2,200	Skidmore, Owings & Merrill	1968
Calif. State Coll. San Bernardino	5,448,000	166,287	110,969	55,318	66.73	24.62	4,095,000	620,000	317,000	1,300	William F. Cody & Assoc.	1971
Stanford Univ. Palo Alto	5,429,648	135,350	97,400	37,950	71.96	30.21	4,090,000	731,400	140,000	1,943	J. C. Warnecke & Assoc.	1967
Univ. of Calif. San Diego	5,400,000	176,000	112,000	64,000	63.64	25.00	4,400,000	580,000	750,000	1,244	William L. Pereira & Assoc.	1970
Long Island Univ. Greenvale, N. Y.	5,359,464	168,538	130,785	37,753	77.60	27.26	4,594,024	343,322	1,200,000	1,000	Alfred Shaknis	1969
Univ. of Northern Colorado, Greeley	5,341,620	221,847	188,570	33,277	85.01	20.71	4,594,901	750,000	525,000	2,500	Brelsford, Childress, Paulin	1971
Clark Univ. Worchester, Mass.	5,271,342	137,000				28.21	3,864,727	425,000	600,000	943	J. M. Johanson & Assoc.	1969
Radcliffe Coll. Cambridge, Mass.	5,100,000	105,000				42.86	4,500,000	400,000	170,000	600	Harrison & Abramovitz	1967
Salem State Coll. Salem, Mass.	5,000,000	123,500	102,300	21,200	82.83	33.38	4,123,000	420,000	350,000	1,500	Desmond & Lord, Inc.	1971
Univ. of Dayton Ohio	4,711,188	176,220	134,224	41,996	76.17	22.84	4,024,554	441,510	800,000	2,500	Pretzinger & Pretzinger	1971
Bowling Green State Univ., Ohio	4,660,260	193,865	157,813	36,052	81.40	20.63	3,999,195	661,065	640,000	2,100	Carl Bentz, State Architect	1967
Mundelein Coll. Chicago	4,590,339	131,648	89,144	42,504	67.71	23.40	3,080,339	600,000	250,000	800	Bartolomeo & Hansen	1969
Towson State Coll. Baltimore	4,361,000	180,000	145,000	35,000	80.56	21.20	3,824,000	325,000	600,000	1,700	Bacharach & Bacharach	1969
Univ. of N. Carolina Charlotte	4,320,062	139,596	119,260	20,336	85.43	28.78	4,015,117	314,000	391,125	1,140	J. N. Pease Assoc.	1971
Hofstra Univ. Hempstead, N. Y.	4,310,000	127,000	86,360	40,640	68.00	30.70	3,900,000	410,000	600,000	1,200	Warner, Burns, Toan, Lunde	1967
Calif. State Polytechnic Coll., Pomona	4,170,000	144,311	99,361	44,950	68.85	23.01	3,320,850	370,000	266,000	1,662	Kistner, Wright & Wright	1968

Institution										Architect	Year
Central Michigan Univ. Mt. Pleasant	4,113,816	179,996	136,999	42,997	76.11	18.18	3,272,400	641,745	515,000	2,285	Roger Allen & Assoc.	1966
Bryn Mawr Coll. Bryn Mawr, Pa.	4,100,000	102,000				30.19	3,090,000	250,000	655,000	700	Kilham, Beder & Chu	1970
Mankato State Coll. Mankato, Minn.	3,829,457	167,408	101,954	65,454	60.90	20.31	3,400,000	399,457	550,000	2,100	Ellerbe Archs.	1968
Univ. of Wisconsin Milwaukee	3,680,000	149,000	127,000	22,000	85.23	19.40	2,890,000	300,000	600,000	2,050	Fitzhugh Scott	1967
Univ. of Arkansas Fayetteville	3,620,481	149,859	122,769	27,090	81.92	19.19	2,875,797	523,085	655,000	1,730	Wittenberg, Deloney & Davidson	1968
Sam Houston State Univ. Huntsville, Tex.	3,524,015	132,948	106,737	26,211	80.28	24.07	3,200,000	284,015	600,000	2,000	Calhoun, Tungate & Jackson	1969
Rutgers Univ. Livingston, N.J.	3,514,000	57,000				35.00	1,995,000	272,315	95,000	900	Gregory Blauth	1971
North Texas State Univ. Denton	3,459,113	171,592	137,274	34,318	80.00	16.81	2,885,259	610,154	657,625	1,850	Caudill, Rowlett & Scott	1971
Providence Coll. Providence, R.I.	3,472,432	95,344	79,000	16,344	82.86	30.72	2,929,097	140,718	500,000	1,200	Sasaki, Dawson & DeMay	1968
Worcester State Coll. Worcester, Mass.	3,470,000	110,000				23.63	2,600,000	655,000	200,000	1,075	Munson & Mallis	1970
Univ. of Hawaii Honolulu	3,451,000	106,908	85,125	21,783	79.62	24.96	2,668,000	360,000	711,475	950	A. Quincy Jones, Frederick E. Emmons	1968
Elmira Coll. Elmira, N.Y.	3,300,000	72,000	63,000	9,000	87.50	32.54	2,343,250	319,456	250,000	555	Haskell & Conner	1969
Hawaii Loa Coll. Keneoke	3,285,303	52,184	36,212	15,972	69.39	54.48	2,843,282	69,783	167,000	500	William J. Pereira	1970
Carlow Coll. Pittsburgh	3,207,853	42,969	37,744	5,225	87.84	39.50	2,848,589	105,659	150,000	500	Alfred D. Reid & Assoc.	1969
S.W. Texas State Univ. San Marcos	3,201,867	134,584	120,206	14,378	89.32	21.24	2,858,855	343,012	363,750	2,355	Harvey P. Smith & Assoc.	1968
Pa. Military Coll. Chester	3,104,793	71,453	45,706	25,747	63.97	34.21	2,444,695	304,065	245,000	810	Vincent G. Kling & Assoc.	1970
Univ. of Hartford Conn.	3,032,000	50,000				50.00	2,500,000	132,000	215,000	500	Warner, Burns, Toan, Lund	1970
University of Missouri Kansas City	3,000,000	104,257	87,784	16,473	84.20	20.26	2,112,951	451,546	360,000	1,227	Marshall & Brown	1969
Bowling Green State Univ. Firelands, Ohio	2,978,580	11,900	11,600	300	97.49	19.30	2,296,290	47,637	20,000	233	Visnapuu & Gaede	1968
Millersville State Coll. Millersville, Pa.	2,950,000	97,404	54,244	43,160	55.69	20.53	2,000,000	950,000	350,000	1,500	Bernard Roney	1967

LIBRARY BUILDING / 331

GENERAL ACADEMIC LIBRARIES, Continued

Institution	Project Cost	Gross Area	Net Assignable	Non-Assignable	Percent Assignable	Sq. Ft. Cost	Building Cost	Equipment Cost	Book Capacity	Seating Capacity	Architects	Year
Western Ky. Univ. Bowling Green	2,947,480	103,478	75,197	28,281	72.67	23.40	2,418,000	240,000	375,000	781	Frank Cain, Jr.	1971
Portland State Univ. Portland, Ore.	2,934,880	103,520	82,230	21,290	79.43	20.47	2,119,490	299,298	423,000	1,167	Skidmore, Owings & Merrill	1968
Swarthmore Coll. Swarthmore, Pa.	2,812,925	101,000	90,000	11,000	89.11	25.07	2,532,385	280,540	415,000	600	Vincent G. Kling & Assoc.	1967
Rosary Coll. River Forest, Ill.	2,717,637	76,656	55,425	21,231	72.30	31.50	2,414,800	213,973	260,000	580	Perkins & Will Corp.	1971
Wisconsin State University Platteville	2,712,000	105,540	72,300	33,240	68.50	20.71	2,186,246	135,680	252,000	1,093	Frederick E. Wegener, Arch.	1969
Eastern Michigan Univ. Ypsilanti	2,680,000	145,400	135,792	9,608	93.39	18.43	2,280,000	400,000	360,000	1,700	Swanson Assoc.	1967
Marywood College Scranton, Pa.	2,608,000	67,796				33.55	2,274,814	106,000	150,000	500	Valverde & Franco	1967
Worcester Polytech. Worcester, Mass.	2,575,633	70,000	63,907	6,093	91.30	29.33	2,053,133	200,000	200,000	600	O. E. Nault & Sons	1967
Univ. of Redlands Redlands, Calif.	2,563,968	78,756	73,168	5,588	92.90	32.58	2,384,235		500,000	627	Powell, Morgridge, Richards & Coghlan	1969
Univ. of S. Alabama Mobile	2,517,000	70,880	56,050	14,830	79.08	34.72	2,325,000	159,000	350,000	1,100	Burmeister, Johnstone & Faddis	1968
Lock Haven State Coll Lock Haven, Pa.	2,358,259	80,224	67,351	12,873	83.95	25.61	2,054,259	304,000	350,000	1,000	Price & Dickey	1970
Dickinson Coll. Carlisle, Pa.	2,297,923	70,706				25.57	1,807,650	337,565	315,000	800	Howell Lewis Shay Assoc.	1967
Newark State Coll. Union, N. J.	2,290,000	59,375	47,225	12,150	79.54	24.25	1,440,000	450,000	180,000	700	Scrimenti, Swackhamer, Perantoni	1968
Memphis State Univ. Tenn.	2,277,682	130,500	98,212	32,288	75.26	16.55	2,159,438	279,882	734,000	663	Walk, Jones, Mah & Jones	1968
Univ. of Missouri St. Louis	2,250,000	106,944				18.49	1,977,460	114,936	240,000	1,000	Murphey & Mackey, Inc.	1968
Univ. of Mo. at Rolla, Sch. of Mines & Technology	2,250,000	79,303	64,826	14,341	81.74	24.28	1,920,000	330,000	350,000	700	Murphey & Mackey, Inc.	1968
Univ. of Florida Gainesville	2,237,442	115,480	84,851	30,629	73.48	18.09	2,089,154	148,288	465,625	590	Arthur L. Campbell	1967

LIBRARY BUILDING / 333

Institution									Architect	
Shippensburg State Coll. Shippensburg, Pa.	2,232,434	72,416	63,209	9,207	87.29	26.41	1,912,434	320,000	250,000	1,200	McLellan & Smith	1968
Ohio Dominican Coll. Columbus	2,204,061	65,580	48,017	17,563	73.22	23.97	1,571,920	372,000	147,500	583	Richardson, Severns, Scheeler	1971
Capital Univ. Columbus, Ohio	2,186,607	84,376	72,803	11,573	86.28	23.58	1,989,732	196,875	300,000	840	Richardson, Severns, Scheeler	1970
Va. Commonwealth Univ. Richmond	2,170,888	84,798	49,568	35,230	58.45	21.34	1,809,893	193,187	225,000	775	Lee, King & Poole	1970
Grand Valley State Coll. Allendale, Mich.	2,168,930	69,138	53,237	15,901	77.00	28.47	1,968,530	200,400	211,000	840	William Kessler & Assoc.	1969
Jersey City State Coll. Jersey City, N. J.	2,168,338	78,287				27.04	2,117,271	51,067	300,000	800	Frank Grad & Sons	1968
Luther Coll. Decorah, Iowa	2,163,083	99,504	94,547	4,957	95.02	18.49	1,840,266	322,817	300,000	977	Olson, Gray, Thompson & Lynnes	1969
Slippery Rock State Coll. Slippery Rock, Pa.	2,126,400										Murovich & Heitzewrater	1971
Ursinus Coll. Collegeville, Pa.	2,078,648	57,200	47,865	9,335	83.68	33.65	1,924,154	154,494	292,500	477	Bond & Miller	1970
Sonoma State Coll. Rohnert Park, Calif.	2,066,393	64,775	53,240	11,535	82.19	26.11	1,690,974	32,518	171,250	673	Germano Milono	1969
Otterbein Coll. Westerville, Ohio	2,000,000	54,400							155,000	580	Charles Edward Stade & Assoc.	1971
Lycoming Coll. Williamsport, Pa.	1,992,073	71,030	70,030	1,000	98.59	25.61	1,819,273	169,800	250,000	750	Wagner & Hartman Assoc.	1968
Rochester Inst. of Tech. Rochester, N. Y.	1,974,255	68,110				29.00	1,526,129	261,000	200,000	770	Harry Weese Assoc.	1967
Northeastern State Coll. Tahlequah, Okla.	1,967,219	120,731	92,619	28,112	76.72	13.91	1,679,053	135,000	300,000	2,000	Hudgins, Thompson & Ball	1968
Wells Coll. Aurora, N. Y.	1,958,000	55,000	41,569	13,431	75.58	29.12	1,601,768	174,608	250,000	415	Skidmore, Owings & Merrill	1968
Tougaloo Coll. Tougaloo, Miss.	1,949,125	57,995				27.12	1,573,000	228,600	165,000	530	Gunnar Birkerts & Assoc.	1971
Green Mountain Coll. Poultney, Vt.	1,940,000	34,900	26,850	8,050	76.93	49.25	1,721,000	219,000	100,000	350	Crandall Assoc.	1970
Barry Coll. Miami Shores, Fla.	1,901,500	85,461	68,612	16,849	80.28	17.90	1,529,500	372,000	135,000	800	Barry & Kay Inc.	1968
Merrimack Coll. Andover, Mass.	1,900,000	69,329	48,837	20,492	70.44	23.78	1,640,453	259,547	255,000	650	Shepley, Bulfinch Richardson & Abbott	1967

GENERAL ACADEMIC LIBRARIES, Continued

Institution	Project Cost	Gross Area	Net Assignable	Non-Assignable	Percent Assign-able	Sq. Ft. Cost	Building Cost	Equipment Cost	Book Capacity	Seating Capacity	Architects	Year
Thomas More Coll. Covington, Ky.	1,895,052	68,115	63,000	5,115	92.49	24.44	1,665,000	82,294	120,000	486	Perkins & Will Partnership	1968
Eastern Montana Coll. Billings	1,866,499	76,870	51,370	25,500	66.83	19.80	1,522,242	223,000	142,000	1,000	Cushing, Ferrell Assoc.	1968
Fla. Technological Univ. Orlando	1,865,000	122,631	80,112	42,519	65.33	14.63	1,794,203	203,520	111,125	549	Forest M. Kelley, Jr.	1968
Marian Coll. Indianapolis	1,843,024	54,364	41,605	12,759	76.53	27.52	1,496,315	149,198	200,000	464	Woolen Assoc.	1970
Wisconsin State Univ. La Crosse	1,826,000	92,348	78,948	13,400	85.49	16.28	1,503,795	262,000	350,000	1,600	Carl Schubert	1969
Winthrop Coll. Rock Hill, S. C.	1,818,366	88,895	76,236	12,659	85.76	15.35	1,365,000	299,793	400,000	765	Lyles, Bissett Carlisle & Wolff	1969
Wisconsin State Univ. Superior	1,809,521	70,046	50,146	19,900	71.59	19.97	1,398,879	91,987	200,000	600	Dobberman & Helske	1968
Appalachian State Univ. Boone, N. C.	1,800,000	84,000	79,275	4,725	94.38	17.93	1,506,284	190,000	310,000	890	Clemmer, Horton Bush Assoc.	1968
St. Peter's Coll. Jersey City	1,800,000	54,040	41,393	12,647	72.57	30.02	1,622,300	177,700	250,000	500	Dagit Assoc.	1967
Western Conn. State Coll. Danbury	1,792,224	49,718	34,786	14,932	69.97	31.68	1,575,224	217,000	225,000	584	William W. Sunderland	1969
Valdosta State Coll. Valdosta, Ga.	1,787,466	86,580	73,310	13,270	84.67	18.65	1,614,793	172,553	275,000	1,119	Ellis Ingram & Assoc.	1971
Baptist Coll. Charleston, S. C.	1,759,919	52,000	40,700	11,300	78.27	16.50	858,000	72,000	97,900	456	Simons, Lapham, Mitchell & Small	1970
Eastern Conn. State Coll. Willimantic	1,757,469	45,029	37,825	7,204	84.00	33.53	1,510,176	114,000	185,000	535	Olson & Miller	1970
Coll. of St. Elizabeth Convent Station, N. J.	1,738,000	59,432	45,796	13,636	77.06	25.70	1,531,786	90,000	250,000	500	Fulmer & Bowers	1969
De Anza Coll. Cupertino, Calif.	1,717,170	60,032	49,014	11,018	81.65	23.59	1,416,569	300,601	100,000	866	Kump, Masten & Hur	1967
King's Coll. Wilkes-Barre, Pa.	1,702,273	51,431	47,445	3,986	92.25	29.21	1,502,273	200,000	157,000	385	Burns & Loewe	1970

LIBRARY BUILDING / 335

Institution									Architect	Year
Virginia Wesleyan Coll. Norfolk	1,700,000	49,797						210,000	460 Perkins & Will	1969
Pacific Lutheran Univ. Tacoma, Wash.	1,697,158	66,947	44,294	22,653	66.16	20.61	115,213	225,000	700 Bindo, Wright & Partners	1967
St. Mary's Univ. San Antonio, Tex.	1,694,520	103,362	77,348	26,014	74.83	12.57	225,000	250,000	1,108 Brooks Martin	1967
Wilkes Coll. Wilkes-Barre, Pa.	1,691,000	59,002	50,344	8,658	85.33	24.00	120,000	350,000	600 Lacy, Atherton & Davis	1968
North Adams State Coll. North Adams, Mass.	1,680,000	34,352				43.66	100,000	100,000	450 James E. Lawrence	1969
Ohio Northern Univ. Ada, Ohio	1,675,481	53,610	48,289	5,321	90.07	28.31	157,566	147,480	625 Hellmuth, Obata, Kassabaum, Inc.	1968
Fairfield Univ. Fairfield, Conn.	1,662,000	61,194	48,343	12,851	79.00	24.65	153,905	265,000	625 Eggers & Higgins	1968
Abilene Christian Coll. Abilene, Tex.	1,661,002	74,051	62,650	11,401	84.60	14.89	193,972	300,000	950 James D. Tittle	1970
Southern Oregon Coll. Ashland	1,614,884	60,713	44,687	16,026	73.60	23.47	190,000	155,000	963 Vincent Oredson	1967
Monmouth Coll. Monmouth, Ill.	1,605,384	68,076	44,006	24,070	64.64	20.91	181,859	350,000	600 Stade, Dolan, Emrick & Assoc.	1970
Lewis & Clark Coll. Portland, Ore.	1,590,870	49,000	38,200	10,800	77.96	27.67	93,374	160,000	545 Paul Thiry	1967
Francis Marion Coll. Florence, S. C.	1,550,398	54,000	35,444	11,313	65.64	23.12	178,536	150,000	500 Lyles, Bissett, Carlisle, & Wolff	1971
William Paterson Coll. Wayne, N. J.	1,537,000	61,115	47,000	14,115	76.90	23.20	243,000	175,000	825 Gilbert Seltzer	1967
Univ. of W. Fla. Pensacola	1,534,127	94,604	70,311	24,293	74.32	13.25	189,243	270,000	850 Look & Morrison	1967
Wofford Coll. Spartanburg, S. C.	1,525,711	40,308	29,690	10,618	73.66	33.57	141,708	150,000	382 Lyles, Bissett, Carlisle & Wolff	1969
Fisk Univ. Nashville	1,519,285	74,610	60,411	14,199	80.97	16.52	190,953	350,000	400 Godwin & Beckett	1969
Angelo State Univ. San Angelo, Tex.	1,500,000	72,935	62,669	10,266	85.92	17.14	165,561	211,200	954 Lovett, Sellars & Assoc.	1967
Washington Coll. Chestertown, Md.	1,499,091	43,798	35,599	8,199	81.29	31.54	113,208	165,000	364 Bailey & Gardner	1970
Univ. of S. Dakota Vermillion	1,498,068	68,614	58,652	9,962	85.48	18.31	241,984	300,000	750 Harold Spitznagel & Assoc.	1967
Oklahoma City Univ. Okla.	1,491,228	60,921	52,385	8,536	85.99	22.29	133,055	218,000	635 Turnbill & Mills	1971

GENERAL ACADEMIC LIBRARIES, Continued

Institution	Project Cost	Gross Area	Net Assignable	Non-Assignable	Percent Assignable	Sq. Ft. Cost	Building Cost	Equipment Cost	Book Capacity	Seating Capacity	Architects	Year
Malone Coll. Canton, Ohio	1,486,586	51,910	37,401	14,509	72.05	26.02	1,350,724	135,862	157,125	458	Lawrence, Dykes, Goodenberger & Bower	1971
Kalamazoo Coll. Kalamazoo, Mich.	1,481,351	72,393	52,900	19,493	73.07	23.40	1,237,640	142,335	250,000	500	Edward Cole Embury	1967
Marymount Coll. Tarrytown, N.Y.	1,475,000	45,420	43,414	2,106	95.36	25.62	1,163,810	100,773	150,000	503	Robert A. Green	1967
Mt. Angel Abbey St. Benedict, Ore.	1,471,000	44,000				28.90	1,271,780		300,000	201	Alvar Aalto	1969
Susquehanna Univ. Selinsgrove, Pa.	1,445,000	40,000				30.00	1,200,000	120,000	150,000	400	Wagner & Hartman	1971
Spalding Coll. Louisville, Ky.	1,434,829	58,250	41,160	12,006	70.69	20.25	1,179,332	160,534	200,000	728	Thomas J. Nolan & Sons	1967
SUNY Coll. of Forestry Syracuse, N.Y.	1,406,000	38,236	31,514	6,722	82.42	27.17	1,039,000	200,000	132,400	575	Max O. Urbahn	1968
Eastern Mennonite Coll. Harrisonburg, Va.	1,401,788	47,250	43,182	4,068	91.39	23.34	1,107,333	161,404	175,000	455	Rancorn, Wildman, Krause, Architects	1971
Bemidji State Coll. Bemidji, Minn.	1,400,000	68,000	48,414	19,586	71.20	18.38	1,250,000	150,000	125,000	850	Syring & Whiteman	1967
The Western Coll. Oxford, Ohio	1,400,000	57,000	37,500	19,500	65.79	22.80	1,300,000	100,000	150,000	375	Keppel O. Small & Willis W. Wertz	1971
Mary Baldwin Coll. Staunton, Va.	1,399,529	48,400	46,000	2,400	95.04	23.00	1,094,978	99,297	200,000	300	Clark, Nexsen & Owen	1967
Austin Peay State Univ. Clarksville, Tenn.	1,390,320	76,500	68,429	8,071	89.45	15.48	1,189,482	138,023	150,000	740	Donald Crown Assoc.	1967
St. Michael's Coll. Winooski, Vt.	1,364,231	43,000	36,550	6,450	85.00	27.76	1,193,731	170,500	78,306	610	Freeman, French & Freeman	1968
Ferris State Coll. Big Rapids, Mich.	1,350,000	60,984	46,734	14,250	76.63	18.83	1,135,000	96,000	100,000	850	Roger Allen & Assoc.	1967
Roger Williams Coll. Bristoe, R.I.	1,321,499	30,000				35.63	1,068,956	83,633	96,000	250	Kent Cruise & Assoc.	1969
Univ. of N. Carolina Wilmington	1,305,000	66,608	45,514	21,094	68.33	18.15	1,218,950	48,754	200,000	600	Leslie N. Boney, Jr.	1969

LIBRARY BUILDING / 337

Institution											
Ill. Wesleyan Univ. Bloomington	1,300,000	49,918	45,000	4,918	90.15	21.72	1,084,104	115,000	250,000	780	Evans Assoc.	1968
Miami Univ. Hamilton, Ohio	1,300,000	43,200	42,600	600	98.61	23.61	1,020,000	190,000	75,000	700	Seigel, Steed & Hammond	1969
Heidelberg Coll. Tiffin, Ohio	1,300,000	36,900	29,520	7,380	80.00	27.00	990,000	400,000	126,000	526	Richards, Bauer & Moorshead	1967
Moravian Coll. Bethlehem, Pa.	1,300,000	36,000	32,000	4,000	88.89	28.25	1,017,000	130,000	200,000	420	Trautwein & Howard	1967
Pasadena Coll. Pasadena, Calif.	1,283,942	37,011	30,487	6,542	82.37	25.67	949,895	227,914	180,000	428	George Stoops & Glen Lareau	1971
Wesley Coll. Dover, Del.	1,280,281	29,658	20,506	9,152	69.14	32.95	978,631	196,419	108,000	428	Larson & Larson	1970
Hendrix Coll. Conway, Ark.	1,266,144	30,682	29,000	1,682	94.52	30.34	930,892	111,000	110,000	400	Philip Johnson	1971
West Georgia Coll. Carrollton	1,255,000	62,800	54,572	8,228	86.90	18.04	1,132,700	117,300	300,000	1,000	Robert & Company	1968
Texas A & I Univ. Kingsville	1,252,258	90,582	78,832	11,750	87.02	11.35	1,028,545	162,000	300,000	1,200	Smyth & Smyth	1968
Franklin Pierce Coll. Cambridge, Mass.	1,251,660	39,051	34,984	4,067	89.59	26.66	1,045,086	88,000	100,000	—	Whitman & Howard	1970
Nebraska Wesleyan Univ. Lincoln	1,245,295	60,628	40,189	18,683	66.29	17.17	1,040,909	121,824	200,000	421	Joseph Vaccaro-Leo Daly Co.	1970
Quincy Coll. Quincy, Ill.	1,239,185	46,453	43,353	3,100	93.33	23.56	1,094,334	138,673	250,000	600	Gaul & Voosen	1967
St. Mary's Coll. St. Mary's, Calif.	1,234,725	40,000	28,000	12,000	70.00	26.95	1,078,194	60,498	105,000	266	Wolff, Zimmer, Gunsul, Frasca & Assoc.	1967
Nazareth Coll. Kalamazoo, Mich.	1,233,717	44,748	36,601	8,147	81.79	22.04	986,124	167,572	120,000	486	Gaul & Voosen	1968
Jamestown Coll. Jamestown, N.D.	1,230,000	47,352	33,760	13,592	71.30	21.56	1,021,232	125,000	74,250	300	The Cerny Assoc.	1971
Fontbonne Coll. St. Louis, Mo.	1,225,700	39,000	25,518	13,482	65.43	28.45	1,109,700	116,000	104,000	447	Pistrui & Conrad	1967
George Mason Coll. Fairfax, Va.	1,223,554	31,460	22,122	9,338	70.32	38.20	1,235,500	56,754	60,000	285	Vosbeck, Vosbeck & Assoc.	1967
University of Conn. Waterbury	1,220,280	22,761	19,507	3,254	85.70	41.84	952,320	104,294	35,000	360	Alexander & Nichols	1971
Emory & Henry Coll. Emory, Va.	1,220,139	41,932	34,219	7,713	81.61	25.08	1,051,833	85,425	200,000	480	J. Russell Bailey	1968

GENERAL ACADEMIC LIBRARIES, Continued

Institution	Project Cost	Gross Area	Net Assignable	Non-Assignable	Percent Assignable	Sq. Ft. Cost	Building Cost	Equipment Cost	Book Capacity	Seating Capacity	Architects	Year
Alabama A. & M. Coll. Normal	1,200,000	60,000	56,000	4,000	93.33	16.16	1,000,000	200,000	300,000	1,000	Sherlock, Emith & Adams	1967
Salem Coll. Salem, W. Va.	1,200,000	28,349	21,608	6,741	76.22	30.51	865,000	28,250	145,000	300	W. H. Grant	1970
Fort Hays Kansas State Coll., Hays, Kans.	1,192,312	105,404	91,204	14,200	86.53	9.85	1,038,627	153,685	300,895	1,022	State Architect of Kansas	1967
Fort Lewis Coll. College Heights, Col.	1,191,561	64,914	42,703	22,211	65.78	16.10	1,045,561	146,000	84,380	328	James Hunter & Assoc.	1967
Univ. of Tampa Fla.	1,182,000	49,200	44,000	5,200	89.43	22.93	1,128,000	147,000	150,000	700	Fletcher-Valenti	1969
Goddard Coll. Plainfield, Vt.	1,179,210	30,525	25,625	4,900	83.95	32.44	990,099	70,598	75,000	250	Hill, Miller, Frielaender, Hollander	1969
Louisiana State Univ. Shreveport	1,178,316	63,716	48,765	14,951	76.53	13.72	644,763	325,536	100,000	300	Aubrey A. McKelvy	1967
Bloomsburg State Coll. Bloomsburg, Pa.	1,150,140	60,892	44,195	16,697	72.58	17.51	1,066,352	83,788	200,000	700	Dickey, Weissman Chandler & Holt	1967
Southwestern State Coll. Weatherford, Okla.	1,144,919	56,000	44,800	11,200	80.00	16.06	899,121	162,946	200,000	1,025	Locke, Smith & Wright	1968
Iowa Wesleyan Coll. Mt. Pleasant, Iowa	1,133,355	43,038	35,780	7,258	83.14	20.34	875,186	188,991	150,000	400	Stanley Consultants	1968
Westmont Coll. Santa Barbara, Calif.	1,131,488	37,195	29,312	3,850		27.28	1,014,982	115,000	125,000	425	Neill, Smith & Assoc.	1968
Holy Family Coll. Philadelphia	1,124,996	33,162	29,312	3,850	88.39	26.68	884,980	123,096	157,875	350	Henry D. Dagit & Sons	1968
Sacred Heart Univ. Bridgeport, Conn.	1,124,000	40,750	31,475	9,275	77.24	25.23	1,028,000	96,000	142,000	544	Val Carson	1968
Findlay Coll. Findlay, Ohio	1,117,000	54,938	45,000	9,928	81.93	16.36	900,000	111,000	98,300	330	Symns, Carlson, Engelhorn & Assoc.	1968
So. Utah State Coll. Cedar City	1,113,783	54,882	44,882	10,000	81.78	16.29	893,735	98,724	136,000	600	L. Robert Gardner	1969
Notre Dame Coll. Staten Island, N. Y.	1,095,000	23,000				32.47	747,000	137,000	65,000	232	Castro-Blanco, Piscioneri & Feder	1969
McPherson Coll. McPherson, Kans.	1,073,000	40,300	28,400	11,900	70.47	20.98	846,000	128,000	125,000	325	Robert Husmann	1970

St. Benedict's Coll. Atchison, Kans.	1,062,245	37,847	30,891	6,956	81.62	23.84	902,442	159,803	220,000	395	Hellmuth, Obata & Kassabaum	1968
Florida Southern Coll. Lakeland, Fla.	1,045,000	44,225				19.90	881,000	164,000	158,200	460	Schweizer Assoc.	1968
The Coll. of Idaho Caldwell	1,040,000	33,456	32,661	795	97.62	26.21	876,835	163,165	175,000	450	John W. Graham Co.	1967
Miss. St. Coll. for Women Columbus	1,033,823	45,495	42,113	3,382	92.57	16.59	754,862	212,824	223,450	707	William I. Rosamond	1969
Scarritt Coll. Nashville	1,022,363	38,733				21.37	827,731	136,170	100,000	160	J. A. Jones Constr.	1968
Delta State Coll. Cleveland, Miss	1,019,158	54,800				16.32	894,158	125,000	200,000	474	Brewer, Skewes, Godbold Archs.	1968
Voorhees Coll. Denmark, S. C.	1,010,000	40,673							115,000	485	Woodhurst & O'Brien	1971
Coll. of St. Francis Joliet, Ill.	1,009,606	48,426	36,579	11,847	75.54	15.94	772,000	220,000	200,000	600	Semitckol, Larson Stromsland, Inc.	1967
Alcorn A. & M. Coll. Lorman, Miss.	1,003,000	54,000						127,500	178,262	916	Mallett & Assoc.	1970
Coll. of Virgin Is. St. Thomas	1,001,615	18,053	13,387	4,666	74.15	47.80	863,860	80,000	35,000	257	Ernest J. Kump	1968
National Coll. of Education Evanston, Ill.	1,000,000	18,560							108,000	270	Perkins & Will	1967
S. Dakota Schl. of Mines & Techn., Rapid City	1,000,000	56,200				13.66	768,000	125,500	180,000	400	Craig Assoc.	1970
Agric., Mech. Normal Coll. Pine Bluff, Ark.	984,600	38,015	30,377	7,638	79.91	17.86	683,200	184,600	109,000	550	Paul Young, Jr.	1967
Texas Lutheran Coll. Seguin	983,534	47,258	45,039	2,219	95.30	16.38	774,377	162,599	158,000	480	Fehr, Granger & Emerson	1970
Rockhurst Coll. Kansas City, Mo.	970,723	40,840	38,196	2,644	93.53	19.57	799,168	122,203	135,000	675	Angus McCallus & Assoc.	1967
Graceland Coll. Lamoni, Iowa	970,564	39,099	37,545	1,554	96.03	22.26	870,564	100,000	120,000	550	Dane D. Morgan & Assoc.	1967
Dana Coll. Blair, Neb.	960,000	41,985	40,650	1,335	96.82	20.84	875,100	82,500	250,000	500	Helleberg & Helleberg	1969
Notre Dame Coll. Cleveland, Ohio	956,698	30,045	19,410	10,635	64.60	29.59	888,890	25,000	100,000	200	Rowley, Payer, Huffman & Caldwell	1971
S. Carolina State Coll. Orangeburg, S. C.	955,508	41,247	39,867	1,380	96.65	19.96	823,797	131,711	168,000	500	Lyles, Bissett, Carlisle & Wolff	1969
Pfeiffer Coll. Misenheimer, N. C.	954,930	36,527	25,740	10,787	70.47	24.71	902,930	52,000	144,750	505	Larson & Larson	1967

GENERAL ACADEMIC LIBRARIES, Continued

Institution	Project Cost	Gross Area	Net Assignable	Non-Assignable	Percent Assignable	Sq. Ft. Cost	Building Cost	Equipment Cost	Book Capacity	Seating Capacity	Architects	Year
Northrop Inst. of Tech. Englewood, Calif.	951,449	26,600	23,028	3,572	86.57	32.40	861,881	89,568	126,630	400	Neptune & Thomas Assoc.	1970
Westminster Choir Coll. Princeton, N. J.	933,364	25,000	19,500	5,500	78.00	34.00	861,359	60,000	40,000	135	Perkins & Will Assoc.	1969
Chadron State Coll. Chadron, Neb.	932,646	45,499	43,000	2,499	94.51	16.00	727,946	128,329	205,000	630	Kirkham Michaels	1967
Smith Univ. Charlotte, N. C.	927,000	34,000				23.53	800,000	85,000	200,000	400	A. G. O'Dell & Assoc.	1967
Univ. of Montevallo Montevallo, Ala.	922,099	52,430	43,716	8,714	83.38	15.09	791,155	130,944			Evan Terry	1967
Covenant Coll. Lookout Mt., Tenn.	918,900	20,400				37.65	768,100	78,900	37,000	151	Stade, Dolan Emrick & Assoc.	1971
Marylhurst Coll. Marylhurst, Ore.	908,906	29,118	22,083	7,035	75.84	28.19	820,626	36,005	150,000	350	Gordon & Hinchliff	1968
Univ. of Alabama Huntsville	874,000	41,000	37,711	3,289	91.98	18.90	775,000	89,000	123,000	303	Northington, Smith, Kranert	1969
Southern Univ.—A. & M. Shreveport, La.	865,000	45,400	32,400	13,000	71.37	12.22	550,000	215,000	50,000	350	Wilson, Sandifer, & Assoc.	1971
Louisiana State Univ. Unica	858,923	40,000							50,000	250	Tolsom & Hamilton	1967
Meredith Coll. Raleigh, N. C.	856,600	31,446	25,226	6,220	80.22	23.02	724,000	82,000	125,000	360	J. Russell Bailey	1969
Dakota State Coll. Madison, S. D.	855,000	40,984	26,560	14,424	64.81	16.92	693,423	104,547	120,000	600	Koch, Hazard Assoc.	1968
Murray State Coll. Murray, Ky.	850,000	26,800				27.24	730,000	10,000	50,000	945	Lee, Potter, Smith & Assoc.	1967
Wesleyan Coll. Macon, Ga.	849,074	43,000	41,000	2,000	95.35	16.38	704,314	89,143	150,000	327	J. Russell Bailey	1968
Dunbarton Coll. Washington, D. C.	841,500	26,244	19,170	7,074	73.05	32.06	841,500	50,000	100,000	200	Chatelain, Gauger & Nolan	1967
Arkansas Coll. Batesville, Ark.	803,959	26,249	22,547	3,702	85.90	28.21	740,633	63,326	100,000	300	Wittenberg, Delong & Davidson	1968

LIBRARY BUILDING / 341

Mount St. Mary Coll. Hooksett, N. H.	791,830	25,075	22,516	2,559	89.79	24.80	621,847	86,871	100,000	247 Andrew C. Issac	1969
General Beadle State Coll. Madison, S. D.	770,227	41,007				16.50	676,801	93,426	125,000	550 Ralph R. Koch	1969
Pacific Univ. Forest Grove, Ore.	767,000	41,067	39,670	1,367	96.60	16.59	681,260	85,740	235,375	358 Dukehart & Kinnie	1967
St. Mary's Dominican Coll. New Orleans	762,000	31,333	29,151	2,182	93.04	19.56	613,916	64,049	150,000	250 Lawrence & Saunders	1967
Bethany Coll. Lindsborg, Kans.	745,948	28,893	19,483	9,410	67.43	22.87	660,889	82,649	75,000	354 Shaver & Co.	1970
Sul Ross State Univ. Alpine, Tex.	745,598	44,000	41,700	2,300	94.77	15.26	671,847	72,751	500,000	800 J. W. Cooper Const. Co.	1969
US International Univ. San Diego	739,835	31,000				21.08	653,635	83,700		Richard John Lareau & Assoc.	1969
New Mexico Inst. of Mining & Technology, Socorro	735,000	25,250	22,000	3,250	87.13	22.18	560,000	123,000	100,000	300 John Reed	1970
Sacred Heart Coll. Wichita, Kans.	728,392	30,463	28,697	1,766	94.20	19.13	582,874	101,832	131,000	400 Hanney-Sanders & Assoc.	1971
Ricker Coll. Houlton, Me.	698,665	36,381	33,954	2,427	93.33	17.63	641,519	57,146	175,000	360 Deane M. Woodward	1969
Shaw Univ. Raleigh, N. C.	690,772	30,375	24,793	5,582	81.62	22.74	488,658		170,000	680 McGee & Scovil	1967
Rust Coll. Holly Springs, Miss.	672,171	29,600	25,500	4,100	86.15	19.00	543,000	106,000	125,000	350 Gassner, Nathan, & Brown	1970
Penn State Univ. University Park, Pa.	669,910	20,852	14,780	6,072	70.88	32.12	534,974	55,430	15,000	325 Harbeson, Hough Livingston & Larson	1967
Louisiana State Univ. Alexandria	661,400	39,000				16.96	661,400		150,000	650 Barron, Heinberg & Brocato	1968
Chapman Coll. Orange, Calif.	657,505	32,000	26,500	5,500	82.81	15.91	509,047	97,113	118,000	350 Powell, Margridge Richards, & Coghlan	1967
Clinch Valley Coll., Univ. of Va., Wise	654,420	20,722				27.45	568,920	85,500	70,000	331 Oliver & Smith	1968
Yankton Coll. Yankton, S. D.	653,018	28,326	22,744	5,582	80.29	19.25	545,296	100,514	100,000	250 Leo A. Daly	1970
Elon Coll. Elon, N. C.	643,665	33,669	29,072	4,597	86.35	14.21	478,348	108,815	110,000	610 Guy E. Crampton Assoc.	1968
St. Francis Coll. Biddeford, Me.	639,000	16,770				32.55	545,922	81,273	66,125	100 Bro. Cajetan Baumann	1970

GENERAL ACADEMIC LIBRARIES, Continued

Institution	Project Cost	Gross Area	Net Assignable	Non-Assignable	Percent Assignable	Sq. Ft. Cost	Building Cost	Equipment Cost	Book Capacity	Seating Capacity	Architects	Year
Coll. of Emporia Emporia, Kans.	630,000	32,069	27,710	4,359	86.41	15.52	497,818	132,182	250,000	200	Neil Pettit	1968
Pembroke State Univ. Pembroke, N. C.	625,000	34,502	32,590	1,912	94.46	15.92	550,000	75,000	209,435	321	W. E. Matthews Co.	1968
Southwest State Coll. Marshall, Minn.	617,000	17,000				31.00	527,000	90,000	50,000	450	Walter Butler Co.	1967
Northland Coll. Ashland, Wis.	604,378	25,764	23,990	1,774	93.11	19.09	491,869	78,299	75,500	348	Carl Schubert	1970
Lees-McRae Coll. Banner Elk, N. C.	600,000	31,125	25,840	5,285	83.02	17.28	537,998	62,002	100,000	216	Holland & Reviere Inc.	1969
McKendree Coll. Lebanon, Ill.	600,000	22,198	16,010	6,188	72.12	25.67	570,000	30,000	65,000	283	Wilson, Hodge & Groh	1969
Princeton Univ. Princeton, N. J.	590,578	18,100				25.46	461,000	2,500	400,000	12	Warner, Burns, Toan, Lunde	1968
New England Coll. Henniker, N. H.	570,000	18,000	10,000	8,000	55.56	27.06	487,000	33,000	65,000	214	Stephen Tracy	1967
Winston-Salem State Univ. Winston-Salem, N. C.	555,000	20,700	18,923	1,777	91.42	18.33	379,505	75,000	80,000	400	Lashmit, Brown & Pollock	1967
Christian Brothers Coll. Memphis	553,000	33,130				14.36	476,000	32,000	100,000	300	Mel O'Brien	1969
Western Montana Coll. Dillon	540,000	33,085	25,474	7,611	77.00	14.87	492,000	30,000	100,000	213	Drake, Gustafson & Assoc.	19—
Vermont Technical Inst. Randolph Center	534,410	13,830	11,263	2,569	81.44	26.88	371,826	54,954	30,000	200	Calcogni, Frazier & Zoichowski	1967
Claflin Coll. Orangeburg, S. C.	524,000	20,459	15,286	5,173	74.72	20.43	418,108	52,550	100,000	300	Godwin & Beckett Inc.	1967
Thomas Coll. Waterville, Me.	520,000	24,000				18.75	450,000	70,000	40,000	150	Alonzo Harriman Assoc.	1970
Univ. of Arkansas Little Rock	520,000	19,683	16,577	3,106	84.22	22.40	440,000	80,000	100,000	340	Ginocchio, Cromwell Carter & Weyland	1967
Wiley Coll. Marshall, Tex.	485,000	22,466	17,141	5,325	76.30	18.92	425,000	60,000	61,400	289	Edward Mattingly & Assoc.	1967
Milton Coll. Milton, Wis.	482,000	22,500				19.82	446,000	78,865	100,000	250	Frelich-Angus Assoc.	1967

Institution	Project Cost	Gross Area	Net Assignable	Non-Assignable	Percent Assignable	Sq. Ft. Cost	Building Cost	Equipment Cost	Book Capacity	Seating Capacity	Architects	Year
Windham Coll. Putney, Vt.	480,000	19,500				21.10	411,500	23,400	55,000	264	Edward Durrell Stone	1967
N. Carolina Wesleyan Coll. Rocky Mount	475,800	15,260				26.92	410,800	48,500	60,000	150	Lashmit, Brown & Pollock	1967
Blackburn Coll. Carlinville, Ill.	440,574	34,442				10.12	348,402	62,885	150,000	300	Mittelbusher & Tourtelot	1970
Urbana Coll. Urbana, Ohio	409,332	11,960	10,740	1,220	89.80	28.64	342,536	56,259	45,000	200	Sullivan, Issacs, Sullivan	1968
Alabama Christian Coll. Montgomery	375,000	14,940				25.00	252,158	30,000	100,000	250	Pearson, Humphries & Jones	1970
Calif. Coll. of Arts & Crafts, Oakland	346,575	10,688	10,636	52	99.51	24.43	261,118	15,610	13,125	100	DeMars & Wells	1967
Coll. of the Southwest Hobbs, N. M.	185,000	12,500				14.80	170,000	11,000	25,000	100	J. M. Murray III	1967

UNDERGRADUATE LIBRARIES

Institution	Project Cost	Gross Area	Net Assignable	Non-Assignable	Percent Assignable	Sq. Ft. Cost	Building Cost	Equipment Cost	Book Capacity	Seating Capacity	Architects	Year
Univ. of Calif. Berkeley	$5,346,600	136,100	88,727	47,373	65.19	$31.70	$4,315,000	$450,000	160,375	1,784	John Carl Wernecke & Assoc.	1970
Univ. of Ill. Urbana-Champaign	4,240,125	98,689	67,121	31,568	68.01	31.91	3,150,000	400,000	150,000	1,899	Richardson, Severns, Scheller	1969
Rutgers Univ. New Brunswick, N. J.	2,775,829	54,650	41,796	12,854	76.48	37.60	2,054,645	293,000	100,000	631	Uniplan	1971
Ohio State Univ. Columbus	2,714,163	80,556	63,190	17,366	78.44	26.32	2,120,000	584,163	50,000	1,605	Kellam & Foley	1971
Univ. of Tenn. Knoxville	2,577,900	110,706	90,000	20,706	81.30	20.81	2,303,000	274,300	289,000	1,886	Yeates & Gaskill	1969
Univ. of N. Carolina Chapel Hill	1,954,340	79,809	66,300	13,509	83.07	21.47	1,713,333	255,000	148,764	1,758	Little, Lee & Assoc.	1968
Claremont Colleges Claremont, Calif.	1,474,835	28,836	18,985	9,851	65.84	41.40	1,214,141	100,000	60,000	375	Flewelling & Moody	1970

PROFESSIONAL LIBRARIES

Institution	Project Cost	Gross Area	Net Assignable	Non-Assignable	Percent Assignable	Sq. Ft. Cost	Building Cost	Equipment Cost	Book Capacity	Seating Capacity	Architects	Year
MEDICAL LIBRARIES												
Univ. of Nebraska Omaha	2,450,455	71,346	59,629	11,717	83.58	$29.22	$2,085,081	$356,487	296,876	445	Leo A. Daly	1971
Wayne State Univ. Detroit	2,200,000	65,700				29.63	1,947,000	85,000	160,000	750	Ralph Calder	1970
Med. Univ. of S. C. Charleston	1,600,000	38,855	22,120	16,735	56.93	37.54	1,458,616	105,265	140,000	273	Lyles, Carlisle, Bissett, & Wolff	1971
Univ. of So. Calif. Los Angeles	1,513,282	47,201	32,073	15,128	67.95	32.04	1,512,480	176,429	233,250	225	Albert C. Martin & Assoc.	1968
Univ. of N. C. Chapel Hill	1,452,538	45,100	29,078	16,022	64.47	28.32	1,277,538	175,000	144,000	560	J. N. Pease Assoc.	1970
Univ. of Wisconsin Madison	1,143,172	45,000				20.00	900,000	150,000	145,000	370	Graven, Kinney & Iverson	1967
Loyola Univ. Chicago	1,000,000	22,000	21,602	400	98.19	40.00	880,000	175,000	100,000	230	Schmidt, Garden & Erikson	1968
LAW LIBRARIES												
Univ. of Texas Austin	18,692,950	419,525	184,500	235,025	43.97	33.12	13,897,430	1,626,545	917,875	837	Skidmore, Owings & Merrill	1971
Univ. of So. Calif. Los Angeles	3,400,000	38,988	26,611	12,377	68.25	38.72	1,509,600	145,815	250,000	284	Albert C. Martin & Assoc.	1970
Southern Methodist Univ. Dallas	3,220,758	100,000	76,000	24,000	76.00	26.66	2,665,870	259,500	400,000	800	Thomas, Booziotis & Assoc.	1969
Univ. of Oregon Eugene	2,291,116	30,002	26,815	3,187	89.38	30.14	914,378	80,920	172,250	304	Wilmsen, Endicott & Unthank	1970
University of New Mexico Albuquerque	2,000,000	22,000	19,488	2,512	88.51	27.25	1,720,000	57,572	108,075	173	George Wright	1971
Univ. of Houston Texas	1,462,500	65,800	62,800	3,000	95.44	15.58	1,102,500	360,000	350,000	600	VanNess & Mower	1969
Univ. of N. Carolina Chapel Hill	1,454,000	44,656	39,978	4,678	89.52				300,000	459	Wheatley, Whisnat & Assoc.	1969

Institution	Project Cost	Gross Area	Net Assignable	Non-Assignable	Percent Assignable	Sq. Ft. Cost	Building Cost	Equipment Cost	Book Capacity	Seating Capacity	Architects	Year
George Washington Univ. Washington, D. C.	1,250,000	50,000	35,000	15,000	70.00	20.00	1,000,000	250,000	175,000	430	Mills, Petticord & Mills	1967
St. Mary's Univ. San Antonio, Tex.	950,000	38,901	24,547	14,354	63.10	19.49	758,500	120,000	60,000	234	Brooks Martin	1967

SUBJECT OR DIVISIONAL LIBRARIES

Institution	Project Cost	Gross Area	Net Assignable	Non-Assignable	Percent Assignable	Sq. Ft. Cost	Building Cost	Equipment Cost	Book Capacity	Seating Capacity	Architects	Year
SPECIAL COLLECTIONS												
Univ. of Kansas Lawrence	$2,342,819	107,929	99,470	8,459	92.16	$18.13	$1,956,710	$386,109	670,000	185	Linscott, McArthur & Assoc.	1968
FINE ARTS LIBRARY												
Univ. of Virginia Charlottesville	672,803	19,635	13,129	6,236	66.87	30.77	604,169	16,558	56,000	170	Rawlings, Wilson, Richmond, Belluschi	1968
SCIENCE LIBRARIES												
Univ. of Oregon Eugene	4,763,021	21,591	21,313	278	98.71	32.20	695,401	83,506	130,500	252	Skidmore, Owings & Merrill	1967
Univ. of So. Calif. Los Angeles	4,442,822	36,521	26,661	9,860	73.00	36.54	1,334,651	139,826	137,250	225	William L. Pereira & Assoc.	1970
Brown Univ. Providence	4,205,000	122,000	77,250	44,750	63.32	29.60	3,611,500	327,350	400,000	600	Warner, Burns, Toan, Lunde	1971
Rutgers Univ. New Brunswick, N. J.	3,078,125	87,737	85,737	2,000	97.72	30.00	2,628,323	279,202	200,000	470	Warner, Burns, Toan, Lunde	1970
Wayne State Univ. Detroit	2,562,610	104,141	80,643	23,498	77.44	21.73	2,262,997	195,861	279,375	1,434	Ralph Calder & Assoc.	1968
Univ. of Georgia Athens	2,000,000	84,300	66,330	18,000	78.68	20.17	1,700,000	300,000	350,000	1,200	Aeck Assoc.	1968
Lehigh Univ. Bethlehem, Pa.	1,605,240	41,000	26,650	14,350	65.00	29.36	1,204,000	215,000	162,250	350	Walker O. Cain & Assoc.	1969
Harvey Mudd Coll. Claremont, Calif.	819,000	30,133	24,753	5,380	82.15	27.18	819,000	40,000	75,000	200	Stone, Heitschmidt, Mounce & Assoc.	1970
Univ. of Wyoming Laramie	767,590	27,800	27,800		100.00	24.16	671,648	95,942	180,000	403	Hutchings, Helzinger, Kellogg	1970

SUBJECT OR DIVISIONAL LIBRARIES, Continued

Institution	Project Cost	Gross Area	Net Assignable	Non-Assignable	Percent Assignable	Sq. Ft. Cost	Building Cost	Equipment Cost	Book Capacity	Seating Capacity	Architects	Year
THEOLOGICAL LIBRARIES												
St. John's Seminary Boston	$1,540,866	56,000	52,000	4,000	92.86	$24.02	$1,345,497	$101,175	250,000	300	Carroll & Greenfield	1967
Eden Theological Seminary Webster Groves, Mo.	1,195,850	37,000	25,000	12,000	67.57	26.68	987,250	105,000	160,000	168	William P. Wenzler	1968
ARCHITECTURE AND ALLIED ARTS												
Univ. of Oregon Eugene	1,362,000	6,517	6,335	182	97.21	30.30	197,490	11,500	13,500	110	Campbell, Yost & Partners	1971
BUSINESS ADMINISTRATION												
Univ. of So. Calif. Los Angeles	3,261,843	15,633	8,847	6,786	56.69	39.22	613,218	46,203	37,250	152	I. M. Pei & Partners	1967

ADDITIONS

Institution	Project Cost	Gross Area	Net Assignable	Non-Assignable	Percent Assignable	Sq. Ft. Cost	Building Cost	Equipment Cost	Book Capacity	Seating Capacity	Architects	Year
Univ. of Michigan Ann Arbor	$5,521,335	132,866	87,812	45,054	66.09	$37.21	$5,044,000	$321,000	900,000	674	Albert Kahn	1970
Univ. of Calif.	4,530,040	106,800	82,575	24,225	77.32	27.47	2,933,656	1,026,000	648,000	715	Jones & Emmons	1971
Marquette Univ. Milwaukee, Wis.	3,707,049	111,324							650,000	2,597	Grellinger-Rose Assoc.	1971

Univ. of New Hampshire Durham	2,841,011	84,483				2,198,739	427,463	325,000	410	Irving W. Hersey Assoc.	1960
Univ. of Calif. Davis	2,692,536	94,865	79,332	15,533	83.63	26.03	2,410,259	259,477	750,000	2,550	Kitchen & Hunt	1967
Villanova Univ. Villanova, Pa.	2,590,369	102,309	84,792			25.41	2,099,121		600,000	2,090	Albert F. Dagit Assoc.	1968
Iowa St. Univ. of Science & Technology, Ames	2,585,198	115,128	103,055	12,073	89.51	20.52	1,908,013	400,000	670,250	1,561	Brooks, Borg & Skiles	1969
Western Michigan Univ. Kalamazoo	2,564,000	170,736	152,726	18,010	89.45	16.58	2,414,000	150,000	700,000	2,000	Ralph R. Calder	1967
Ohio Univ. Athens	2,300,000	79,256	71,420	7,836	90.11	14.13	2,000,000	300,000	600,000	300	Dalton, Dalton & Little	1971
Kansas State Univ. Manhattan	2,250,000	100,000	98,000	2,000	98.00	25.23	2,000,000	250,000	250,000	2,000	State Architect of Kansas	1970
Eastern Illinois Univ. Charleston	2,199,907	92,000	56,699		61.63	20.00	1,927,953	191,954	350,000	807	Johnson, Kile, Seehausen	1968
Univ. of So. Calif Los Angeles	2,090,657	52,235	43,182	9,053	82.67	20.90	2,090,656	111,341	400,822	50	Lunden & Johnson Architects	1967
Florida State Univ. Tallahassee	2,012,812	107,530	91,530	16,000	85.12	25.00	1,705,000	110,000	1,000,000	500	Myrl Hanes Assoc, Forrest M. Kelley, Jr.	1967
Wisconsin State Univ. Whitewater	1,980,825	71,500	50,000	21,500	69.93	15.86	1,681,330	87,330	117,500	585	Plunkett, Keymar Reginato & Assoc.	1969
Oregon State Univ. Corvallis	1,865,000	59,736	53,923	5,813	90.27	27.70	1,398,250	240,000	300,000	1,100	Hamlin, Martin, & Schultz	1971
Loyola Univ. Chicago	1,845,110	50,000	42,789	7,211	85.56	23.37	1,507,351	256,752	130,000	750	Barry & Kay, Inc.	1968
Nevada Southern Univ. Las Vegas	1,577,978	52,280	48,152			30.10	1,333,442	146,871	300,000	1,000	James, Brooks, McDaniel	1967
Clarion State Coll. Clarion, Pa.	1,535,221	42,052	33,413	8,639	79.45	25.51	1,155,221	380,000	200,000	700	W. G. Eckles Co.	1970
Wheeling Coll. Wheeling, W. Va.	1,500,000	58,800				27.47			200,000	400	Rowley, Payer, Huffman, Leithold	1970
Southern Methodist Univ. Dallas	1,496,689	54,065	42,608	11,997	78.81	18.12	979,950	177,400	175,000	500	Harper & Kemp	1969
Univ. of Nevada Las Vegas	1,457,051	61,050	54,940	6,110	89.99	21.38	1,305,051	152,000	300,000	1,000	James B. McDaniel	1967
Winona State Coll. Winona, Minn.	1,269,996	55,774	44,619	11,155	80.00	21.00	1,187,008	82,988	75,000	744	Carl Graffunder & Assoc.	1967
Mercyhurst Coll. Erie, Pa.	1,242,424	37,250	32,720	4,530	87.84	28.01	1,043,500	113,116	130,000	400		1971

LIBRARY BUILDING / 347

ADDITIONS, Continued

Institution	Project Cost	Gross Area	Net Assignable	Non-Assignable	Percent Assignable	Sq. Ft. Cost	Building Cost	Equipment Cost	Book Capacity	Seating Capacity	Architects	Year
Univ. of Tulsa, Tulsa, Okla.	982,777	35,070	33,950	1,120	96.81	28.02	805,117	159,660	304,950	639	H. G. Bernard, Jr.	1967
Univ. of Southern Miss. Hattiesburg	978,000	50,000	38,000	12,000	76.00	14.73	736,500	200,000	200,000	793	Briggs, Neal, Weir & Chastain	1968
S. F. Coll. for Women San Francisco	944,754	18,034	14,581			45.94	828,490		160,000	115	Ohmura, Teague & Assoc.	1967
Oklahoma State Univ. Stillwater	906,816	50,544	33,882	16,662	67.03	15.79	798,379	60,528	90,000	490	Sorey, Hill & Binnicker	1967
St. Francis Coll. Loretto, Pa.	869,083	33,180	29,066	4,114	87.60	23.69	786,083	83,000	175,000	300	Hunter, Campbell & Rea	1967
Southwest Mo. State Coll. Springfield, Mo.	666,667	30,000	29,000	1,000	96.67	19.00	573,072	47,254	95,250	426	A. C. Esterly	1967
Wayne State Coll. Wayne, Neb.	600,000	29,217	23,260	5,957	79.61	17.84	521,513	78,487	76,681	800	Leo A. Daly	1970
Western Carolina Coll. Cullowhee, N. C.	584,694	28,059				20.84	467,650	40,000	62,300	114	Six Assoc. of Asheville	1967
Univ. of Minnesota Duluth	582,115	26,121				17.47	456,385	60,000	50,000	400	Melander-Fugelso Assoc.	1967
Prairie View A & M Coll. Prairie View, Tex.	502,250	29,500				15.12	446,250	56,000	100,000	400	Edward Mattingly Assoc.	1968
Point Park Coll. Pittsburgh	485,000	8,700				35.28	308,000	6,300	95,000	131	Nathan Cantor	1970
Kentucky State Coll. Frankfort	470,000	15,885	15,525	3,360	97.73	22.00	374,970	47,956	100,000	160	Berry, Burris & Thompson	1970
Panhandle State Coll. Goodwell, Okla.	371,000	18,550	14,225	4,325	76.68	18.87	350,000	21,000	55,000	466	Sorey, Hill & Bennicker	1970
Winston-Salem State Univ. Winston-Salem, N. C.	338,035	12,290	10,733	1,557	87.33	19.70	278,035	60,000	40,000	306	Lashmit, Brown & Pollock	1971
Univ. of North Dakota Grand Forks	121,600	6,300	6,300		100.00	13.30	83,800	37,800		85	Foss, Englestad, & Foss	1970

ADDITION-RENOVATION PROJECTS

Institution	Area	Project Cost	Gross Area	Net Assignable	Non-Assignable	Percent Assign-able	Sq. Ft. Cost	Building Cost	Equipment Cost	Book Capacity	Seating Capacity	Architects	Year
Duke Univ. Durham, N.C.	Total	$8,923,775	348,609	246,288	102,321	70.65	20.63	$7,194,114	$755,623	2,100,000	2,040	Perry, Dean & Stewart	1969
	New	7,417,780	242,152	170,783	71,369	70.53	24.65	5,969,114	678,258	1,250,000	1,424		
	Renovated	1,505,995	106,457	75,505	30,952	70.93	11.50	1,225,000	77,365	850,000	616		
California St. Coll., Los Angeles	Total	8,371,506	322,098	248,382	73,716	77.11	19.92	5,588,000	836,506	826,000	4,200	Honnold, Reib samen & Rex	1970
	New	7,739,944	235,098	189,974	54,124	76.98	21.98	5,168,000	519,006	640,000	2,660		
	Renovated	631,562	87,000	67,508	19,492	77.60	4.72	420,000	217,500	186,000	1,540		
Univ. of Rochester N.Y.	Total	6,939,000	351,544				15.33	5,389,000	805,000	1,200,000	1,500	Murphy & Mackey	1969
	New	6,339,000	193,113										
	Renovated	600,000	158,431										
California St. Coll., Long Beach	Total	5,403,000	292,184	208,033	84,151	71.20	15.62	4,565,000	917,471	800,000	4,000	A.A. Froelich & Assoc.	1970
	New	5,203,000	200,184	140,873	59,311	70.37	21.59	4,322,400	578,580	525,000	2,250		
	Renovated	200,000	92,000	67,160	24,840	73.00	17.39	160,000	338,891	275,000	1,750		
Yale Univ. New Haven	Total	5,250,000						4,598,000	140,000			Edward Larabee	1970
	New	4,336,000	62,000	51,800	10,200	83.55	61.03	3,784,000	115,000	225,000	712		
	Renovated	920,000						814,000	25,000				
Univ. of P. R., Rio Piedras	Total	5,041,900	250,000				16.98	4,245,000	271,900	651,264		Henry Klumb	1969
Michigan State Univ., Lansing	Total	4,293,305	430,000	310,000	120,000	72.09	9.15	3,933,108	360,197	2,000,000	4,000	Ralph R. Calder Assoc.	1968
	New	3,693,305	150,000	120,000	30,000			3,433,108	260,197				
	Renovated	600,000	280,000	190,000	90,000			500,000	100,000				
Univ. of California, Santa Barbara	New	4,072,257	123,559	78,679	44,880	63.68	30.69	3,334,696	280,300	371,422	1,487	Arendt, Mosher Grant	1968
	Renovated		12,000	4,000	8,000	33.33					200		
Texas A. & M. Univ., College Station	Total	3,690,194	269,043				11.68	3,141,570	548,624	1,000,000	2,000	Jarvis, Putty & Jarvis	1968
	New	3,608,624	181,418				16.92	3,060,000	548,624	750,000	1,900		
	Renovated	81,570	87,625				.93	81,570		250,000	100		
Univ. of Texas Arlington	Total	3,511,487	191,362				28.89	3,029,664	481,823	750,000	2,500	George L. Dahl, Inc.	1967
	New	2,118,000	109,350				16.36	1,790,000	328,000	440,000	1,565		
N. Carolina State Univ. Raleigh	Total	3,381,474	224,716	176,642	48,074	78.61	13.98	3,141,474	240,000	1,100,000	2,400	A. G. O'Dell, Jr. & Assoc.	1971
	New	3,014,170	110,216	77,456	32,760	70.28	26.62	2,934,170	80,000	900,000	900		
	Renovated	367,304	114,500	99,186	15,314	15.44	1.40	207,004	160,000	200,000	1,500		
Ga. Inst. of Tech, Atlanta	New	3,374,335	138,307	87,526	52,781	63.28	23.01	3,182,201	186,551	670,000	800	Robert & Co.	1968

ADDITION-RENOVATION PROJECTS, Continued

Institution	Area	Project Cost	Gross Area	Net Assignable	Non-Assignable	Percent Assignable	Sq. Ft. Cost	Building Cost	Equipment Cost	Book Capacity	Seating Capacity	Architects	Year
Univ. of Houston, Houston Tex.	Total	3,355,316	131,397				19.46	2,556,928	194,813	1,000,000	2,000	Staub, Rather, & Howze	1967
	New	3,302,661	128,897				19.00	2,531,928	167,158		500		
	Renovated	52,655	2,500				10.00	25,000	27,655		1,500		
Rice Univ. Houston	Total	3,106,794	221,100	180,700	40,400	81.73	10.31	2,281,000	500,000	902,000	1,033	Staub, Rather, & Howze	1963
	New		95,000	82,900	12,100	87.26				674,000	502		
	Renovated		126,100	47,800	28,300	37.91				228,000	531		
Southeast Mo. State Coll.	Total	3,009,024	152,480	118,333	34,147	77.61	17.73	2,702,896	306,128	350,000	1,425	Pearce & Pearce Inc.	1963
	New		131,696	104,447	27,249	79.31	20.52	940,293		315,000	1,300		
Cape Guardian	Renovated		20,784	13,886	6,898	66.81				35,000	125		
Western Wash. State Coll.	Total	3,000,000	147,300	117,840	29,460	80.00	14.75	2,172,305	357,759	315,000	1,910	Fred Massetti & Co	1971
	New	2,700,000	83,300	66,640	16,660	80.00	23.50	1,962,305	321,984	115,000	1,110		
Bellingham	Renovated	300,000	64,000	51,200	12,800	80.00	3.28	210,000	35,775	200,000	800		
Loyola Univ. Chicago	Total	2,915,627	121,000	101,600	19,400	83.97	18.77	2,270,958	434,642	540,000	1,385	Barry & Kay, Inc.	1968
	New		86,500	72,500	14,000	83.82				380,000	914		
	Renovated		34,500	29,100	5,400	84.35				160,000	471		
Eastern Kentucky Univ. Richmond	Total	2,801,910	147,780	137,780	10,000	92.48	13.62	2,012,070	400,000	260,000	1,871	Louis & Henry & Assoc.	1967
	New		109,780	106,080	2,700	97.45				259,000	1,800		
	Renovated		38,000	31,700	7,300	83.42				133,000	401		
Boise State Coll. Boise, Ida.	Total	2,546,443	144,000				12.57	1,820,000	526,443	400,000	1,750	Hummell, Hummell, Jones & Shawver	1971
Joint Univ. Nashville, Tenn.	Total	2,533,913	93,000	67,000	26,000	72.04	25.38	2,361,000	90,000	350,000	677	Shepley, Bulfinch, Richards & Abbott	1969
	New	2,291,918	76,000	53,600	22,400	70.53	26.00	2,000,000	80,000	350,000	677		
	Renovated	241,995	17,000	13,400	3,600	78.82	21.00	361,000	10,000				
Wisconsin State Univ., Oshkosh, Wis.	Total	2,405,000	119,180	85,700	33,480	71.91	17.20	1,953,000	140,000	600,000	2,500	Irion, Reinke & Assoc., Inc.	1969
	New	2,365,000	113,440	82,000	31,440	72.28	17.20	1,913,000	140,000	240,000	950		
	Renovated	40,000	5,740	3,700	2,040	64.46	7.00	40,000					
Haverford Coll. Haverford, Pa.	New	2,300,000	44,775				39.57	1,771,000	228,000	500,000	500	Harbeson, Hough, Livingston, Larson	1968
	Renovated	148,886	35,210				4.23	148,886					
Univ. of Ala. Tuscaloosa	Total	2,300,000	104,427				20.60	2,150,903	170,000	2,000,000	800	Davis-Speaks	1970
Calvin Coll. Grand Rapids, Mich.	Total	2,260,642	90,000	80,000	10,000	88.88	22.50	2,026,000	235,000	326,400	1,064	Perkins & Will	1970

LIBRARY BUILDING / 351

Univ. of Calif. Irvine	Total	2,185,200	152,542					2,026,200	159,000	525,000	725	A. Quincy Jones, Frederick E. Emmons	1969
	New		69,042	58,900		24.36		1,682,000				
Central Mo. State Coll. Warrensburg	New	2,157,122	84,000	62,264	21,736	74.12	19.48	1,636,500	429,100	270,000	800	Mantel & Steele	1969
	Renovated		76,200	39,759	35,441	89.14				240,000	500		
Trenton State Coll., N.J.	Total	2,018,661	101,000	76,376	24,624	75.62	16.32	1,648,482	238,829	330,000	1,500	Kramer, Hirseh & Carchidi	1970
Georgia State Univ., Atlanta	Total	1,911,742	93,048	81,201	11,847	87.27	16.17	1,512,721	296,570	512,250	1,566	Aeck Assoc.	1968
	New	1,891,413	90,504	78,657	11,847	86.91	16.44	1,446,696	239,276				
	Renovated	20,329	2,544	2,544		100.00	6.29	16,025	57,294				
Univ. of Arizona Tucson	Total	1,720,809	73,459	62,453	11,006	85.02	19.30	1,418,257	166,000	370,000	500	Place & Place	1971
	New		66,870	57,520	9,350	86.02							
	Renovated		6,589	4,933	1,656	74.87							
Miss. State Univ, State Coll.	Total	1,612,500	127,000				9.75	1,238,177	247,869	225,000	1,000	Thomas S. Jones & Assoc.	1969
	New	1,467,500	68,000										
	Renovated	145,000	59,000										
Univ. of S.W. La, Lafayette	Total	1,600,000	135,663	88,951	46,712	65.57	18.28	2,481,000	227,526	445,500	2,000	Lagrove & Perkins	1967
Wisconsin State Univ., River Falls	Total	1,594,400	70,702	53,331	17,371	75.43	21.50	1,520,000	74,400	271,375	773	Foster, Shavie & Murray	1968
Univ. of Texas El Paso	Total	1,500,000	82,000	56,158	25,842	68.49	16.74	1,372,935	127,065	400,000	1,000	Brooks, Barr, Graeber & White	1968
	New	1,307,935	52,000	36,976	15,024	71.11	23.23	1,207,935	100,000	250,000	800		
	Renovated	192,065	30,000	19,182	10,818	63.94	5.50	165,000	27,065	150,000	200		
Univ. of Illinois Urbana-Champaign	Total	1,449,103	44,995	41,138	3,857	91.43	27.86	1,253,745	40,000	600,000	85	Lankton, Ziegle, Terry & Assoc.	1970
	New	1,409,103	44,995	41,138	3,857	91.43	27.86	1,253,745	40,000	600,000	85		
	Renovated	40,000											
Jacksonville Univ., Fla.	Total	1,426,000	53,200	40,407	12,789	75.95	20.95	1,114,921	170,000	210,000	850	Reynolds, Smith & Hills	1970
Univ. of Virginia Charlottesville	Total	1,423,493	108,600				9.21	1,000,000	250,000	1,000,000	178	J. Russell Bailey	1967
Moorhead State Coll., Moorhead, Minn.	Total	1,420,000	56,200	50,860	5,340	90.50	22.27	1,251,750	96,150	100,000	600	Foss, Englestead & Foss	1971
	New		45,300	40,250	5,050	88.85	25.00	1,132,280					
	Renovated		10,900	10,610	290	97.34	10.96	119,470					
Rutgers Univ. Camden, N.J.	New	1,300,000	37,113					925,000	125,000	136,280	422	Holt & Morgan	1969
Middle Tenn. State Univ., Murfreesboro	Total	1,269,730	107,496	90,551	16,954	84.24	10.39	1,034,730	175,000	266,013	1,375	John Charles Wheeler & Assoc.	1970

ADDITION-RENOVATION PROJECTS, Continued

Institution	Area	Project Cost	Gross Area	Net Assignable	Non-Assignable	Percent Assignable	Sq. Ft. Cost	Building Cost	Equipment Cost	Book Capacity	Seating Capacity	Architects	Year
Randolph Macon	Total	1,247,422	57,588	40,800	6,599	70.85	15.90	915,755	116,667	185,000	622	J. Russell Bailey	1967
Women's Coll.	New	1,115,735	33,760	24,760	5,103	73.34	23.92	807,403	93,332	106,750	388		
Lynchburg, Va.	Renovated	131,687	23,828	16,040	1,496	67.32	4.55	108,352	23,335	78,250	234		
Stout State	Total	1,226,820	80,373	62,974	17,399	78.35	14.54	1,168,089	58,730	172,800	960	Tilleman Assoc.	1968
Univ., Meno-	New	770,220	50,459	39,346	11,113	77.98	14.54	733,326	36,870	100,308	709	Inc.	
monie, Wis.	Renovated	456,600	29,914	23,628	6,286	78.99	14.54	434,763	21,860	72,492	251		
Kansas State Teachers Coll. Emporia	Total New	1,200,000	53,800					895,242	100,000	300,000	640	Eicholtz & Groth	1970
Northeast Mo.	Total	1,196,500	55,000	49,700	5,800	90.36	19.78	1,098,000	98,500	175,000	600	Hammond, Burnes	1971
State Coll.	New	800,000	31,400	18,400	3,000	58.60	23.18	728,000	72,000	115,000	425	Charlie (add.)	
Vicksville, Mo.	Renovated	396,500	24,100	21,300	2,800	87.97	15.35	370,000	26,500	60,000	175	Pearce & Pearce (renov.)	
Goucher Coll. Towson, Md.	Total	1,055,650	21,336				41.97	895,650	85,000	90,000	175	Moore & Hutchins Partnership	1969
Texas Southern	Total	1,046,032	85,500				10.10	863,806	277,402	350,000	1,100	Wilson, Morris,	1967
Univ.	New	816,032	37,550				16.87	633,806		200,000	650	Crain & Anderson	
Houston	Renovated	230,000	47,950				4.79	230,000		150,000	450		
East Texas State Univ. Commerce	Total	907,898	31,048	21,399	10,649	68.92	27.29	847,158	60,740	97,000	130	George Dahl & Assoc.	1970
Millsaps Coll.	Total	893,400	33,000	30,000	3,000	90.91	22.22	743,400	150,000	140,000	425	Biggs, Weir, Neal,	1971
Jackson, Miss.	New		20,000	20,000		100.00			150,000	70,000	200	Chastain	
	Renovated		13,000	10,000	3,000	79.62				70,000	225		
Eastern N. M.	Total	880,000	60,000	48,000	12,000	80.00	13.50	810,000	70,000	400,000	600	Chambers &	1971
Univ.	New	750,000	28,000	24,000	6,000	85.71	25.00	700,000	50,000	150,000	200	Campbell	
Portales	Renovated	180,000	32,000	24,000	6,000	75.00	3.44	110,000	20,000	250,000	400		
Upper Iowa	Total	850,585	41,542	37,129	3,852	89.38	18.54	770,000	80,585	124,875	500	Toenjes, Stenson,	1967
Coll, Fayette,	New	691,832	25,000	23,000	2,850	92.00	24.72	603,000	55,000			& Warm	
Iowa	Renovated	158,753	16,542	14,129	1,002	85.41	10.10	167,000	25,585				
Univ. of	Total	840,757	32,805	27,024	5,781	82.38	19.10	627,786	136,709	136,000	366	Ginocchio, Cromwell	1969
Arkansas	New	320,757	13,122	10,477	2,675	79.84	14.30	187,768	56,709	36,000		Carter & Neyland	
Little Rock	Renovated	520,000	19,683	16,577	3,106	84.22	22.40	440,000	80,000	100,000	340		

LIBRARY BUILDING / 353

Institution										Architect	Year
Georgia College Milledgeville	Total New Renovated	836,000 587,136 248,864	44,442 26,666 17,776	27,925 17,950 9,975	11,600 5,561 6,039	62.83 67.31 56.11	14.83 14.83 14.83	659,000 395,400 263,600	135,000 81,000 54,000	633 422 211	Dennis & Dennis	1967
Pan American Coll., Edinburg, Tex.	Total	827,756	32,476				19.97	648,800	71,500	520	Kenneth Bentsen	1970
Augustana Coll. Rock Island, Ill.	Total	789,247	41,356	35,236	6,120		18.46	650,417	43,000	525	Lundeen & Toline	1968
Lenoir Rhyne Coll. Hickory, N.C.	Total	685,000	29,972						53,000	375	Clemmer, Horton, Bush, Assoc.	1967
Lindenwood Coll. Mo.	Total	609,794						549,119	60,675	300	Kenneth E. Wischmeyer & Partner	1968
St. John's Coll. Annapolis, Md.	Total	605,388	12,335	10,705	1,630	86.79	47.53	585,092	19,286	100	Rogers, Taliaferro, Kostritsky & Lamb	1969
Bethany Nazarene Coll.	Total New	537,200 375,000	41,450 27,126	38,890 25,348	2,560 1,778	93.82 93.45	21.77 11.79	462,900 320,000	74,300 55,000	544 292	Nowman, Nicek, & Assoc.	1970
Bethany, Okla. Madison Coll. Harrisonburg, Va.	Renovated Renovated	162,200 556,245	14,324 18,092	13,542	782	94.54	9.98 29.02	142,900 525,000	19,300 50,000	252 250	Wright, Jones & Wilkerson	1969
Delaware Coll. of Sci. & Agric., Doylestown	Total	536,000	13,771	9,577	4,194	69.54	33.43	460,468	10,644	154	Gamer & White Assoc.	1970
Univ. of Hawaii Hilo	Total New Renovated	530,000 520,000 10,000	19,830 12,330 7,500				18.30 29.03 .66	363,000 358,000 5,000	84,375 76,375 8,000	252 108 144	Park Assoc.	1970
Westmar Coll. Le Mars, Iowa	Total New Renovated	457,521 366,248 91,273	35,098 14,694 20,404	25,731 13,703 12,028	9,367 1,750 7,617	73.31 93.26 58.95	9.92 21.65 1.62	348,098 318,098 33,000	150,000 85,000 65,000	325 195 130	Johnson, Jamerson Assoc. Inc.	1971
Sweet Briar Coll. Sweet Briar, Va.	Total New Renovated	417,250 350,830 16,420	15,053 13,635 1,418	12,918 11,500 1,418	2,135 2,135	85.82 84.34 100.00	21.18 22.00 11.58	318,865 302,445 16,420	68,000 68,000	92 68 24	J. Russell Bailey	1967
Farmington State Coll. Farmington, Me.	Total	404,842	15,150				20.22	303,468	70,000	200	Alonzo J. Harriman & Assoc.	1969
Univ. of Me. Farmington, Me.	Total New Renovated	384,842	20,447 12,500 7,947	16,447 11,000 5,447	4,000 1,500 2,500	80.44 88.00 68.54	14.84	303,468	85,000 50,000 35,000	200 125 75	Alonzo J. Harriman & Assoc.	1969

ADDITION-RENOVATION PROJECTS, Continued

Institution		Project Cost	Gross Area	Net Assignable	Non-Assignable	Percent Assignable	Sq. Ft. Cost	Building Cost	Equipment Cost	Book Capacity	Seating Capacity	Architects	Year
Greenville Coll. Greenville, Ill.	Total	375,139	18,182				16.33	296,994	56,495	105,000	274	Wilson, Hodge & Groh	1970
Western New Mexico Univ. Silver City	Total	349,549	11,889	7,569	4,320	63.66	24.18	287,482	35,989	21,875	163	Chambers & Campbell Inc.	1971
St. Augustine Coll., Raleigh, N. C.	Total	325,000	12,586							66,840	300	McGee & Scovil	1967
Univ. of S. Calif., Los Angeles	Total	257,837	10,561	8,242	2,319	78.09	24.76	261,555	44,524	52,500	78	Edward Durell Stone	1968
East Carolina Univ., Greenville, N. C.	Total	247,627	16,074	15,048	1,026	93.84	14.91	239,686	7,941	20,000	200	McGee & Scovil	1967
Carthage Coll. Kenosha, Wis.	Renovated	135,000	12,000				7.91	95,000	40,000	50,000	75	Lawrence Malmberg & Assoc.	1967
Ogelthorpe Coll. Atlanta	Renovated	100,500	10,963	7,457	2,202	62.51	8.44	92,500		60,000	84	Thompson & Hancock	1969
Univ. of N. Carolina Asheville	Renovated	90,658	6,400	6,226	174	97.28	10.15	65,000	25,658	15,951	57		
Maryville Coll. St. Louis, Mo.	Total New Renovated	90,197	3,612 3,180 432				20.43	73,802	6,170	12,000	84	Hellmuth, Obata & Kassabaum	1967

MULTIPURPOSE BUILDINGS

Institution	Project Cost	Gross Area	Net Assignable	Non-Assignable	Percent Assignable	Sq. Ft. Cost	Building Cost	Equipment Cost	Book Capacity	Seating Capacity	Architects	Year
Northern Michigan Univ. Marquette	5,400,000	191,311	84,101	107,210	43.96	25.71	4,478,000	799,000	300,000	2,438	Dow Assoc.	1969
Lewis Coll. Lockport, Ill.	3,700,000	92,000				29.34	2,700,000	500,000	205,000	510	Barry & Kay	1970
Westfield State Coll. Westfield, Mass.	3,312,000	88,342				22.42	2,950,000	362,000	200,000	600	Associated Architects	1970
Utica Coll. Syracuse, N. Y.	3,147,138	91,362	66,711	24,651	73.02	28.83	2,633,608	124,826	325,000	521	Perkins & Will	1969
Hampshire Coll. Amherst, Mass.	2,690,000	60,997	44,000	17,000	72.13	36.48	2,225,000	264,000	210,000	335	Hugh Stubbins & Assoc.	1971
Purdue Univ. Hammond, Ind.	2,605,680	63,440	45,668	18,254	71.98	36.53	2,317,980	168,557	201,875	624	Walter Scholler & Assoc.	1971
Lake Superior State Coll. Sault Ste. Marie, Mich.	2,500,000	31,280	22,280	9,000	71.23	30.50	2,069,700	130,000	100,000	400	Ralph Calder & Assoc.	1971
Hartwick Coll. Oneonta, N. Y.	2,051,774	98,000	53,000	45,000	54.08	20.93	2,051,774		300,000	300	Bice & Baird	1967
Pace Coll. New York	1,775,000	42,000				35.71	1,500,000	275,000	250,000	750	Eggers & Higgins	1970

CANADIAN LIBRARIES

Institution	Project Cost	Gross Area	Net Assignable	Non-Assignable	Percent Assignable	Sq. Ft. Cost	Building Cost	Equipment Cost	Book Capacity	Seating Capacity	Architects	Year
GENERAL ACADEMIC												
Univ. Laval Quebec	8,692,000	424,000	300,000	124,000	70.70	18.50	7,844,000	848,000	2,100,000	2,000	St. Gelais, Tremblay, Labbe, Ste. Foy	1968
York Univ. Toronto	8,620,000	265,000	177,000	88,000	66.79	24.87	6,590,000	1,570,000	800,000	1,750	Shore, Moffat & Partners	1970

CANADIAN LIBRARIES, Continued

Institution	Project Cost	Gross Area	Net Assignable	Non-Assignable	Percent Assignable	Sq. Ft. Cost	Building Cost	Equipment Cost	Book Capacity	Seating Capacity	Architects	Year
Univ. of Guelph Guelph, Ont.	8,175,000	258,077	220,790	28,258	85.55	25.25	6,515,500	1,268,500	650,000	2,116	Hancock, Little Calvert Assoc.	1968
Dalhousie Univ. Halifax	7,178,400	240,000	152,874	87,126	63.70	26.93	6,463,000	715,400	1,000,000	1,450	Leslie R. Fairn & Assoc.	1971
Brock Univ. St. Catherine's Ont.	5,693,030	203,219	130,304	72,915	64.12	22.20	4,453,549	950,000	1,000,000	1,500	Parkin, Searle Wilbee, Rowland	1967
Trent Univ. Peterborough, Ont.	4,056,250	121,527	93,516	28,011	76.95	24.54	2,982,720	773,900	383,000	872	Thompson, Berwick & Pratt	1969
Lakehead Univ. Thunder Bay, Ont.	2,937,025	85,480	59,000	26,480	69.02	26.57	2,271,053	533,600	400,000	800	Fraser-Brown	1971
Mount Allison Univ. Sackville, N. B.	2,425,000	71,800				27.78	1,995,000	300,000	400,000	500	Brown-Brisley & Brown	1970
Laurentian Univ. Sudbury, Ont.	1,850,600	55,546	39,116	16,430	70.43	29.03	1,613,000	129,000	200,000	350	Adamson & Assoc.	1969
Univ. of New Brunswick Saint John, N. B.	778,583	24,115	21,034	3,081	87.22	25.55	616,000	73,583	68,000	335	Mott, Myles & Chatwin	1969
ADDITIONS												
Univ. of Alberta Edmonton	1,282,653	52,098	44,760	7,338	85.92	19.59	1,020,833	175,000	250,000	336	D. Jenkins	1969
SOCIAL SCIENCES LIBRARIES												
Univ. de Montréal Quebec	3,210,000	65,000	61,000	4,000	93.85	27.50	1,788,000	120,000	550,000	800	Beauvoir & Lusignan	1958
Univ. of New Brunswick Fredericton	2,800,000	131,400	125,000	6,400	95.13	17.58	2,310,000	490,000	628,113	1,352	Larson & Larson	1967
LAW LIBRARIES												
Univ. of Alberta Edmonton	3,675,000	58,016	44,565	13,451	76.82	21.81	2,644,700	323,000	200,000	450	D. C. Bittorf	1971
Univ. de Montréal Quebec	3,210,000	44,000	42,000	22,000	95.45	27.50	1,212,000	90,000	300,000	600	Beauvoir & Lusignan	1968

TWO-YEAR ACADEMIC LIBRARY BUILDINGS*

by

Joleen Bock**

From a library to a learning resource center, to an instructional media center, to a learning skills center, it all adds up to hundreds of thousands of yards of stone, brick, and mortar being converted into library-type buildings on two-year college campuses. A recent survey of all private and public two-year colleges in the country (1,091 in number) showed that 9 percent of the two-year colleges built edifices concerned with learning resources in the past six years. In addition, many more campuses constructed temporary facilities as new colleges were begun or as older colleges expanded their services and increased in number of students.

The number of two-year colleges has increased from 678 to 1,091 in the past ten years. Not only have states recognized the economic benefits of local commuting colleges in systems of higher education, but a major emphasis on occupational programs related to local needs, community service, and adult education is a vital factor in the rapid development of these colleges. This uniquely American form of education has come of age in this century to fulfill a seemingly never-ending need for more education of both youth and adults.

Although libraries in all segments of education are often spoken of as the "hub" and "center of learning," the two-year community (public) and private junior colleges are finding a way to make this statement come true in a way never dreamed of in the first half of this century, when they were only a few struggling institutions. The two-year college libraries are making contact at the basic level with instructional programs to combat a part of the problem of the "lost self" as described in Reich's *The Greening of America*. Two-year college librarians, media specialists, and names *ad infinitum* which may be given to this breed of educator, are sometimes leading and sometimes being led into the area of individualizing instruction. Two important elements of individualized instruction are (1) the fact that students do not bring the same background to a subject which they undertake to study and (2) the fact that they do not learn at the same rate of speed.

Element 1: It behooves the institution to discover the level of understanding which a student has at the beginning of his study, and allow him to begin at this point. In order to do this, the study of a subject needs to be broken into small units to allow entrance (after testing) at any point, and there must be a way to test the student so that he may proceed from unit to unit with some sense of security, knowing that he has the necessary knowledge to succeed. This is neither the time nor the place to discuss the revolution in writing specific objectives and designing learning activities and testing tools to accompany them. Let it suffice to say that specialists in learning centers are being called upon as resource faculty members to work with classroom instructors in developing just such materials. It does not mean that we need to learn everything we can about all subject areas, but it is important that we understand the psychology of learning and know how to organize programmed materials, and that we staff our centers with professional personnel to produce a variety of materials.

Element 2: What role does the resource center play in the time variable which Benjamin Bloom and many others feel is so important a factor in learning? The resource center is the facility on most two-year college campuses which is open the greatest number of hours; thus, while everyone who wishes to study air-

---

*Reprinted from *Library Journal,* December 1, 1971.
**Director, Instructional Resources, College of the Canyons, Valencia, Calif.

conditioning systems in auto technology may not be able to attend a lecture class at 2 P.M. MWF, they may be able to schedule their lab sessions and learn the backup lecture-type material at *any* hour in the resource center. Likewise, if a student has missed a class or wishes to review the material presented in a lecture, he can do so on his own time, utilizing any number of materials such as slides, filmstrip/tape presentations, or video or audio tapes. This means longer daily and weekend hours of operation for our centers. It also provides a means for more adequately handling the thousands of students as enrollments increase.

What does this bit of instructional philosophy have to do with the topic at hand, which is supposed to be two-year college library buildings? The returns from 35 states and 121 campuses showed one thing in common — from the smallest campus of 150 students to the largest of 11,000, whether it be called a library or a resource center, a total concept of learning resources is being considered. The learning resource centers now include, in varying degrees, language laboratories, reading and study skill centers, audio and video laboratories and listening stations, production facilities for graphics, photographic, audio, and video materials, closed circuit television and recording studios, printing facilities, business machines practice rooms, data processing facilities, mobile television units, and, lest we forget, many thousands of square feet of book stacks. The buildings reported ranged in cost from $220,000 to $4,000,000 and in square footage from 12,000 to 89,000 square feet. California led in number with 15 buildings, followed closely by North Carolina (14) and Texas (11).

These buildings also reflect the current trends in personnel utilization. They are built for widespread use of paraprofessionals in all areas. As the individualization of instruction takes form, instructors, resource librarians, and media specialists can go only so far. The heart of this approach is local production of materials, which requires graphic artists, photographers, audio and video technicians, printing specialists, etc. In addition, as librarians and media specialists have become in greater demand as resource consultants, they have had to examine their work closely to see what could be handled by library/media technical assistants and library associates for more effective use of everyone's time.

The whole point of this brief discourse, as I dare to take a second look, seems to be that the past six years of library building on two-year college campuses reflect the changes in instructional techniques — and that, after all, is the way it should be. Can it be that the "lady-in-tennis-shoes" image is being replaced by a jet-propelled campus leader type? The building programs would so indicate.

JUNIOR COLLEGE LIBRARY CONSTRUCTION, 1965–1971

Institution	Project Cost	Total Area	Sq. Ft. Cost	Building Cost	Equipment Cost	Book Capacity	Seats	Architects
ALABAMA								
Gadsden State J. C.	$450,000	25,258	$16.00	$400,000	$50,000	125,000	350	Hofferbert & Ellis
Mobile State J. C.	756,799	28,837	20.63	594,874	97,192	75,000	425	Prolsdorfer & Smith
Theodore Alfred Lawson State J. C.	245,700	16,000	15.35	245,700	19,028	50,000	250	Chas. H. McCauley
Walker College	195,000	10,000	18.00	150,000	30,000	25,000	200	Henry Sprott Long
Northeast State J. C.	247,000	12,350	20.00	N.A.	55,700	26,000	190	Chas. H. McCauley
ARIZONA								
Glendale C. C.	3,500,000	38,000	21.00	800,000	150,000	75,000	800	Varney, Sexton, Sydnor
Phoenix Coll.	647,689	33,354	18.29	610,009	62,000	85,000	447	Haver, Nunn & Jensen
ARKANSAS								
Southern Baptist Coll.	291,000	16,000	18.00	249,000	42,000	40,000	235	Erhart, Eichenbaum, Rauch & Blass
CALIFORNIA								
Fullerton J. C.		50,000				100,000	800	
College of the Desert	1,055,000	33,500	28.73	1,005,000	50,000	76,000	250	John Carl Warnecke Assoc.
Cypress Coll.	1,730,700	68,431	22.50	1,560,000	112,149	100,000	500	Wm. Blurock & Partners
College of the Redwoods		19,246	28.00	850,000	100,000	75,000	375	Falk & Booth
De Anza Coll.	1,626,521	60,039	23.59	1,416,569	209,962	100,000	866	Kump, Maxten & Hurd
Diablo Valley Coll.	1,854,928	55,914	30.14	1,685,298	373,376	95,500	820	Cometta & Cianfichi
Feather River Coll.		3,400			25,000	8,500	48	Skidmore, Owings, Merrill
Golden West Coll.	784,300	22,000	31.00	682,000	102,300	60,000	335	Wm. Pereira Assoc.
Los Angeles Valley Coll.	790,000	39,272	40.00	690,000	100,000	102,650	684	
Moorpark Coll.	1,135,829	40,079	25.80	1,034,000	101,829	48,180	526	Daniel, Mann, Johnson & Mendenhall
Orange Coast Coll.	1,500,000	40,444	37.00	1,278,740	128,000	80,000	1,000	Wm. Blurock, & Partners
Palo Verde Coll.	220,400	4,578				15,000	65	Bryant, Jehle & Assoc.
Rio Hondo Coll.	1,026,640	48,000	17.33	831,600	195,040	79,000	400	Powell, Morgridge, Richards & Coghlin
Riverside City Coll.	872,240	38,729	22.52	744,758	120,135	89,238	650	Neptune & Thomas; Moise & Harbach
Shasta Coll.		37,800	19.20	852,625	90,000	50,000	400	Johnson, Storm & Poole
Mesa Coll.	866,000	25,375	21.00	685,848	100,459	75,000	500	Robert A. Van Deusen
FLORIDA								
Edison J. C.		54,642				76,000	600	McBride & Parker, W. R. Frizzell
Florida Coll.	240,953	13,680	12.50	170,858	59,296	30,000	148	Paul B. Henderson
Polk Community Coll.	3,000,000	89,837	29.00	2,600,000	400,000	45,000	334	Bright & Straughn
Tallahassee C. C.	661,892	26,800	22.14	593,352	56,430	60,000	355	Barrett, Daffin & Figg
GEORGIA								
Oxford College (Emory Univ.)	515,000	19,168	24.19	463,715	20,166	60,000	350	Abreu & Robeson
HAWAII								
Maui C. C.	890,751	25,485	33.84	862,550	126,000	50,000		Shoso Kagawa
IOWA								
Indian Hills C. C.	495,000	4,240	13.00	65,000	35,000	200	75	Shaver & Co.
Grand View Coll.	943,216	27,390	25.00	776,216	110,000	58,000	400	Architects Associated
Iowa Western C. C.	73,300	5,841	9.76	57,000	12,000	25,000	120	I. T. Carruthers

JUNIOR COLLEGE LIBRARY CONSTRUCTION, 1965–1971, Continued

Institution	Project Cost	Total Area	Sq. Ft. Cost	Building Cost	Equipment Cost	Book Capacity	Seats	Architects
ILLINOIS								
Black Hawk Coll.	1,400,000	33,000	30.00			70,000	850	Bernbrook Assoc.
Elgin C. C.	5,500,000	17,000	30.00	4,925,000	75,000	60,000	333	Perkins & Will
Forest Park C. C.	1,777,555	64,330	20.03	1,289,115	488,400	70,000	600	Harry Weese & Assoc.
Waubonsee C. C.	4,000,000	71,300	32.00	2,300,000	141,000	100,000	550	Caudill, Rowlett, Scott
Wm Rainey Harper Coll.	12,200,000	105,000	23.28	2,500,000	892,000	100,000	700	Caudill, Rowlett, Scott
KANSAS								
Coffeyville J. C.	874,690	41,982	18.36	770,607	104,082	35,000	325	Shaver & Co.
Colby C. C.		15,000				35,000	150	Kiene & Bradley
Highland C. J. C.	288,884	19,312	14.96	112,908	18,198	20,000	106	Knight, Remele, Eaton
Independence C. J. C.	2,289,000	8,263	19.25	159,063	32,879	25,000	225	Kiene & Bradley
Neosho County C. J. C.	320,000	17,580	18.20	320,000	40,000	20,000	100	Kiene & Bradley
KENTUCKY								
Paducah C. C. (U.Ky.)	1,200,000	41,000	23.17	949,948	96,278	50,000	385	Lee, Potter, Smith
MASSACHUSETTS								
Cape Cod C. C.		40,450	36.00	1,900,000	90,000	55,000	450	Desmond & Lord
MICHIGAN								
Gogebic C. C.	2,211,134		33.75	2,153,184	57,950	17,000	225	Warren Holmes
Grand Rapids J. C.		20,000	22.50	4,500,000	60,000	50,000	400	Perkins & Will
Kalamazoo Valley C. C.	2,925,000	31,000		2,667,847	257,153	50,000	1,400	Alden B. Dow
Lake Michigan Coll.		36,030	33.00	4,871,899	113,290	80,000	500	Henry Weese & Assoc.
Macomb County C. C.	2,890,465	89,176	25.65	2,288,080	467,385	120,000	1,000	Harley Ellington Assoc., E. Walfred Erikson
Meramee C. C.		47,625	30.83	1,447,000	756,156	50,000	750	Smith & Enzeroth
Southwestern Mich. Coll.	295,009	10,000	29.50	259,911	35,098	15,000	150	Warren Holmes
Suomi Coll.	121,400	4,856	25.00			30,000	125	Warren Holmes
MISSISSIPPI								
East Mississippi J. C.		9,670	13.08	105,800		20,000+	100	Wakeman & Martin
MINNESOTA								
Bethany Lutheran Coll.	275,000	12,268	21.50	260,000	15,000	30,000+	130	Ernest H. Schmidt Co.
NEBRASKA								
York Coll.	314,839	15,699	16.52	259,340	37,678	50,000	200	Carmichael-Wheatcroft
NEW HAMPSHIRE								
New Hampshire Tech. Inst.	368,000	9,434	31.60	298,729	20,000	20,000	160	Andrew C. Isaak Assoc.
NEW JERSEY								
Cumberland County Coll.	331,900	12,100	27.43	248,292	35,456	48,000	158	Fulmer & Bowers
NEW YORK								
Auburn C. C.	700,000	12,820	28.00	628,735	97,000	50,000	200	Beardsley & Beardsley
Mater Dei Coll.	405,000	19,183	21.00	374,000	31,000	100,000	250	Finnegan, Lyon & Colburn
Genesee C. C.								
Monroe C. C.	22,000,000	670,000	25.00	2,295,000	215,000	100,000	900	Caudill, Rowlett & Scott
SUNY Agric. & Tech. Coll.		22,373			76,000	36,000	250	Carson, Lundin & Shaw

JUNIOR COLLEGE LIBRARY CONSTRUCTION, 1965–1971, Continued

Institution	Project Cost	Total Area	Sq. Ft. Cost	Building Cost	Equipment Cost	Book Capacity	Seats	Architects
NORTH CAROLINA								
Beaufort Co. Tech. Inst.	465,000	26,000	18.00	465,000	100,000		500	Guy Wilson & Assoc.
Brevard Coll.	516,703	22,837	22.63	490,264	38,878	100,000	195	McDonald & Brewton Assoc.
Caldwell C. C. & Tech. Inst.	1,400,000	4,084	30.00	700,000	40,000	12,000	100	Leslie N. Boney
Central Carolina T. I.	210,000	9,216	22.80	175,000	35,000	20,000	200	Hayes & Howell Assoc.
Chowan Coll.	849,667	43,000	17.00	735,667	114,000	100,000	450	W. D. Boone
Fayetteville T. I.	680,000	28,500	23.00	630,000	50,000	20,000	215	MacMillan & MacMillan
Forsyth T. I.	1,333,333	49,364	23.72	1,333,333	124,257	20,000	175	Fred W. Butner Jr.
Mount Olive Coll.	389,476	12,400	31.40	344,122	45,354	35,000	194	G. Milton Small & Assoc.
Peace Coll.	357,000	14,000	25.00	315,000	35,000	56,400	230	Arthur McKimmon & Assoc.
Rockingham C. C.	522,000	28,348	18.41	483,186	38,814	50,000	300	Leslie N. Boney
Rowan Technical Inst.	399,000	27,000	19.00	391,000	14,922	15,000	75	Robert F. Stone
St. Mary's J. C.	326,490	16,500	18.40	303,535	22,955	50,000	185	Holloway-Reeves
Southwood Coll.	50,000	5,000	7.00	35,000	10,000	25,000	60	J. L. Holland & Sons Inc.
Wilkes C. C.	2,100,000	93,000	21.50	1,500,000	417,570	930,000	1,400	J. Hyatt Hammond Assoc.
NORTH DAKOTA								
Bismark J. C.	548,892	25,000	18.80	471,608	16,536	30,000	200	Leonhard & Askew
N. D. State Sch. of Science	820,000	40,000	18.90	700,000	120,000	95,000	575	Bernard Hillyer
OHIO								
Columbus Tech. Inst.	474,000	3,030	22.00	474,000	24,000	12,000	100	MacDonald, Cassell, Basset
OKLAHOMA								
Ellen Cushing J. C.	500,000		31.12	470,000	30,000	75,000	200	Vim Piland
Okla. City Southwestern Coll.	160,000	3,800		135,000	25,000	33,520	170	Bowman-Nicek & Assoc.
OREGON								
Clatsop C. C.	418,500	12,750	25.00	374,295	44,286	60,000	200	Brown, Brown & Grider
Mt. Hood C. C.	1,967,990	68,271	23.00	1,585,748	155,000	75,000	492	Lutest Amundson
S. W. Oregon C. C.	1,411,645	53,503	23.91	1,279,379	300,000	250,000		Skidmore, Owens
Umpqua C. C.	1,200,000	14,840	22.00	332,718	36,000	80,000	250	Hewlitt & Jamison
PENNSYLVANIA								
C. C. of Beaver Co.	1,282,000	38,300	34.00	1,055,000	227,000	28,000	150	Joseph Bontempo
Keystone J. C.	988,082	32,193	27.18	874,980	47,029	50,000	663	Joseph H. Young
Manor J. C.	829,236	27,200	30.00	745,784	83,452	60,000	150	Henry Dagit & Sons
SOUTH CAROLINA								
Sumter Area Tech. Ed. Ctr.	230,000	9,697	21.87	212,000	18,000	20,000	125	Demosthenes-Riley
Greenville Tech. Ed. Ctr.		24,000		2,500,000	100,000	50,000	320	Architects Engineers
TENNESSEE								
Cleveland State C. C.	313,800	18,178	17.26	313,800	50,000	25,000	220	Harrison Gill & Assoc.
State Tech. Inst. Memphis	4,262,679	8,192	20.00	163,840	20,000	12,000	190	Wadlington & Marshall
TEXAS								
Del Mar Coll.		37,200	24.00	800,000	82,180	100,000	500	Page, Southerland, Page & Whittet
Eastfield Coll.		23,000	32.59			50,000	274	Harwood K. Smith
Coll. of the Mainland	1,474,000	56,000	20.61	1,154,254	200,000	60,000	300	Hoover & Morgan, Reed & Clements

JUNIOR COLLEGE LIBRARY CONSTRUCTION, 1965–1971, Continued

Institution	Project Cost	Total Area	Sq. Ft. Cost	Building Cost	Equipment Cost	Book Capacity	Seats	Architects
McLennan C. C.	657,739	33,708	19.51	569,364	88,375	65,000	352	
Kilgore Coll.	702,639	40,500	15.66	634,387	68,252	78,000	500	Allen & Guinn
Mountain View Coll.	15,405,700	13,600	31.03			40,000	270	Harrell & Hamilton
Frank Phillips Coll.	540,000	35,000	14.80	518,000	22,000	100,000	266	Cantrell & Co.
Dodge City C. C.	666,814	20,513	3.03	621,421	45,393	40,000	225	Caudill, Rowlett Scott
Blinn College J. C.	406,349	18,640	18.81	350,619	35,730	40,000	425	Edward F. Hildebrandt
Navarro J. C.	591,716	29,803	18.37	547,716	44,000	70,000	344	Bush and Witt
San Jacinto Coll.	1,236,322	58,392	17.44	967,691	210,569	125,000	1,130	James A. Burleson & Assoc.
Southwest Texas J. C.	490,000	24,442	17.00	440,000	50,000	50,000	200	Harvey P. Smith & Assoc.
Tarrant Co. J. C., NE Campus	1,115,338	44,934	19.20	862,750	252,588	65,000	300	Albert S. Komatsu
Tarrant Co. J. C., So. Camp.	1,037,264	45,463	17.05	775,309	261,955	65,000	750	Parker & Croston

UTAH

Institution	Project Cost	Total Area	Sq. Ft. Cost	Building Cost	Equipment Cost	Book Capacity	Seats	Architects
Snow Coll.	576,720	26,054	22.14	508,518	68,202	50,000	220	Willard Nelson

VERMONT

Institution	Project Cost	Total Area	Sq. Ft. Cost	Building Cost	Equipment Cost	Book Capacity	Seats	Architects
Vermont Tech. Coll.	534,410	13,830	26.88	371,826	54,954	30,000	200	Calcagni, Frazier, Zajchowski

VIRGINIA

Institution	Project Cost	Total Area	Sq. Ft. Cost	Building Cost	Equipment Cost	Book Capacity	Seats	Architects
Ferrum J. C.	1,175,952	36,071	23.75	867,200	62,820	60,255	390	Wright, Jones & Wilkerson
New River C. C.	975,000	6,500	30.00	250,000	29,000	20,000	125	Hayes, Mattern & Mattern
Northern Va. C. C.	1,527,000	33,800	16.08	1,319,000	208,000	78,988	503	LBC & W Assoc.

WISCONSIN

Institution	Project Cost	Total Area	Sq. Ft. Cost	Building Cost	Equipment Cost	Book Capacity	Seats	Architects
Stout State U.	500,000	15,452	32.00			62,000	150	Hirsch, Stevens & Samuelson
Univ. of Wis., Washington Co. Campus	224,498	8,702	25.79	190,633	32,863	28,000	131	Lawrence E. Bray
Waukesha Co. Campus	296,711	12,680	23.39	266,657	30,054	36,000	266	Lefebvre, Wiggins-Lublin, McGaughy & Assoc.
Sheboygan Co. Campus	285,917	8,806	32.46	238,850	47,067	28,000	175	Lawrence E. Bray Assoc.
Rock Co. Campus	181,710	7,840	23.17	157,945	23,765	28,000	157	Knodle-Rose & Assoc.
Marshfield-Wood Co.	313,540	9,750	32.15	273,588	39,952	28,000	169	Weiler, Strang, McMullin
Baraboo-Sauk Co. Campus	381,000	11,000	34.63	318,000	73,000	28,000	192	Graven, Kenny & Iverson
Waukesha County T. I.		10,000				30,000	250	Flad & Assoc.

WYOMING

Institution	Project Cost	Total Area	Sq. Ft. Cost	Building Cost	Equipment Cost	Book Capacity	Seats	Architects
Casper Coll.	645,906	35,700	18.09	645,906	50,000	50,000	500	Gerald Deines

PART 3 LIBRARY AND BOOK TRADE ASSOCIATIONS AND AGENCIES

Library and Book Trade Associations and Agencies

NATIONAL ASSOCIATIONS*

AMERICAN ASSOCIATION OF LAW LIBRARIES
53 West Jackson Blvd., Chicago, Ill. 60604
312-939-4764

OBJECT

"To promote librarianship, to develop and increase the usefulness of law libraries, to cultivate the science of law librarianship and to foster a spirit of cooperation among members of the profession." Established 1906. Memb. 1,475. Dues. (Inst.) $60–300; (Indiv.) $30. Year. June 1, 1971–May 31, 1972.

MEMBERSHIP

Persons officially connected with a law library or with a law section of a state or general library, separately maintained; and institutions. Associate membership available for others.

OFFICERS (June 1971–June 1972)

Pres. Mrs. Viola A. Bird, Univ. of Washington Law L., 205 Condon Hall DO-10, Seattle, Wash. 98105; *Treas.* Eugene M. Wypyski, Hofstra Univ. S. of Law L., Hempstead, N.Y. 11550; *Secy.* Mrs. Marian Boner, Tarleton Law L., Univ. of Texas, 2500 Red River, Austin, Tex. 78705; *Pres. Elect.* Mary W. Oliver, Univ. of North Carolina Law L., Chapel Hill, N.C. 27514.

Admin. Secy. Antonette Russo.

EXECUTIVE BOARD

The officers and Morris L. Cohen, Harvard Law S. L., Langdell Hall, Cambridge, Mass. 02138; Connie E. Bolden, Washington State Law L., Temple of Justice, Olympia, Wash. 98504; Mrs. Meira G. Pimsleur, Columbia Univ., S. of Law L., 435 W. 116 St., New York, N.Y. 10027; Betty V. LeBus, Indiana Univ. Law L., Bloomington, Ind. 47401.

PUBLICATIONS

Law Library Journal (q.; $10); *Index to Legal Periodicals* (mo. and cum.) in cooperation with H. W. Wilson Co. (price on request); *Index to Foreign Legal Periodicals* (q.; 4th q. cum. $50); *Current Legal Publications* (9 times per year; $10); *Law Libraries in the U.S. and Canada* (bi-enn.; $10); *AALL Publication Series* (prices vary).

COMMITTEE CHAIRMEN *(Please direct correspondence c/o national headquarters)*

1972 Annual Meeting. Robert Q. Kelly (local arrangements); William D. Murphy (program).

Audiovisual. Patrick E. Kehoe.

---

*For dates and places of annual conventions, see "Library Association Meetings," this volume.

Automation & Scientific Development. David Badertscher.
Cataloging & Classification. Nancy F. Miller.
Certification Board. Lawrence L. Kiefer.
Chapters. Mathew F. Dee.
Conference of Newer Law Librarians. Anita K. Head; Mildred Mason.
Constitution & By-laws. Roger F. Jacobs.
Directories. Lorraine A. Kulpa; Margaret S. Andrews.
Education. Iris J. Wildman.
Education: Institute — 1972, Subcommittee of. Edward F. Hess, Jr. (local arrangements); Shirley R. Bysiewicz, Leah F. Chanin (program).
Elections. Frank DiCanio.
Ethics of Law Librarians. Ervin H. Pollack.
Exchange of Duplicates. Laura M. Pershing; Joseph Ciesielski.
Financial Development & Growth. Betty Virginia LeBus.
Foreign & International Law. Adolf Sprudzs; Igor I. Kavass.
Foreign Law Indexing. William D. Murphy; Frank Lukes.
Headquarters. William D. Murphy.
Index to Legal Periodicals. Jane L. Hammond.
Job Security, Remuneration & Employment Practices. George S. Grossman; Charlie R. Harvey.
Joseph Andrews Bibliographic Award. Kate Wallach.
LC Liaison. Morris L. Cohen.
Law Library Journal. Jack S. Ellenberger.
Legislation & Legal Developments. John Harrison Boyles.
Membership. Irwin G. Manley; William C. Younger.
Memorials. Jean Ashman.
Nominations. Marian G. Gallagher.
Placement. Edwin G. Schuck; Stanley Pearce.
Private Law Libraries. Beatrice McDermott.
Publications. Betty Wilkins.
Recruitment. Simon Goren; Magda Boehm.
Relations with Publishers & Dealers. Julius Marke; Raymond M. Taylor.
Scholarship. Jacquelyn J. Jurkins; Pat B. Piper.
Standards. Edwin M. Schroeder.
Statistics. Alfred J. Lewis; Marlene C. McGuirl.

SPECIAL COMMITTEES

Elections, Officers & Executive Board. Mary Sanders.
Finance Comm. of Executive Board. Mary Oliver.
Library Services to Prisoners. Elizabeth Poe.
Minorities. Connie E. Bolden.

AMERICAN LIBRARY ASSOCIATION
50 East Huron Street, Chicago, Ill. 60611
312-944-6780

OBJECT

"To extend and improve library service and librarianship in the United States and throughout the world." Founded 1876. Memb. 30,314. For specific information on dues for ALA and its divisions, see the ALA Constitution and Bylaws, available in the November 1971 *American Libraries,* pp. 1093–1101. Year. Jan. 1, 1972–Dec. 31, 1972.

MEMBERSHIP

Any person, library or other organization interested in library service and librarianship.

OFFICERS (June 1971–June 1972)

Pres. Keith Doms, Dir., Free L. of Philadelphia, Logan Sq., Philadelphia, Pa. 19103; *1st V.P. & Pres. Elect.* Katherine Laich, S. of L. Scis., Univ. of

Southern California, Los Angeles, Calif. 90007; *2nd V.P.* A. P. Marshall, Eastern Michigan Univ. L., Ypsilanti, Mich. 48197; *Treas.* Robert R. McClarren, Exec. Dir., N. Suburban L. Syst., 5814 Dempster St., Morton Grove, Ill. 60053; *Past Pres.* Mrs. Lillian M. Bradshaw, Dir., Dallas P.L., 1954 Commerce, Dallas, Tex. 75201. *Exec. Dir.* David H. Clift.

EXECUTIVE BOARD

The officers, past president, and Mrs. Augusta Baker, N.Y.P.L., New York, N.Y. 10019; Mrs. Marietta Daniels Shepard, L. Devel. Program, Organization of American States, Washington, D.C. 20006; Jean E. Lowrie, Dept. of Libnshp., Western Michigan Univ., Kalamazoo, Mich. 49001 (1973); Marion A. Milczewski, Univ. of Washington Ls., Seattle, Wash. 98195 (1973); David W. Heron, Univ. of Kansas Ls., Lawrence, Kans. 66044 (1974); Evelyn Levy, Enoch Pratt Free L. Community Action Program, 606 S. Ann St., Baltimore, Md. 21231 (1974); John G. Lorenz, L. of Congress, Washngton, D.C. 20540 (1975); Mrs. Virginia Lacy Jones, S. of L. Sci., Atlanta Univ., Atlanta, Ga. 30314 (1975).

PUBLICATIONS

American Libraries (11 issues; memb.)
ALA Membership Directory (a.; $10)
Proceedings (a.; memb.)

DIVISIONS

See the separate entries[1] — Adult Services Division, American Association of School Librarians, American Library Trustee Association, Association of College and Research Libraries, Association of Hospital and Institution Libraries, Association of State Library Agencies, Children's Services Division, Information Science and Automation Division, Library Administration Division, Library Education Division, Public Library Association, Reference Services Division, Resources and Technical Services Division, Young Adult Services Division.

ROUND TABLE CHAIRMEN

American Library History. N. Orwin Rush, Strozier L., Florida State Univ., Tallahassee, Fla. 32306.
Exhibits. John E. Wall, Demco Educ. Corp., P.O. Box 1488, Madison, Wis. 53701.
International Relations. Frank M. McGowan, L. of Congress, Washington, D.C. 20540.
Junior Members. Mrs. Shirley Olofson, Capitol Bldg., Frankfort, Ky. 40601.
Library Research. Roger C. Greer, S. of L. Sci., Syracuse Univ., Syracuse, N.Y. 13210.
Library Service to the Blind. Alfred D. Hagle, 2608 Ridge Rd. Dr., Alexandria, Va. 22302.
Social Responsibilities. Mrs. Jaqualyn Eubanks, Brooklyn Coll. L., Brooklyn, N.Y. 11210.
Staff Organization. Jerome K. Corrigan, Oxon Hill Br. L., Oxon Hill, Md. 20021.

COMMITTEE CHAIRMEN

Accreditation. F. William Summers, Grad. L. S., Univ. of South Carolina, Columbia, S.C. 29208 (1973). Agnes Reagan, Staff Liaison.
Appointments. Katherine Laich, Univ. of Southern California, Los Angeles, Calif. 90007. David H. Clift, Staff Liaison.
Audiovisual. Richard L. Ducote, Coll. of DuPage, Glen Ellyn, Ill. 60137. To be appointed, Staff Liaison.
Awards. Robert F. Delzell, Univ. of Illinois L., Urbana, Ill. 61801. Mrs. Judith F. Krug, Staff Liaison.
Centennial 1976 Action. Frank B. Sessa, Grad. S. of L. & Info. Scis., Univ. of Pittsburgh, Pittsburgh, Pa. 15213. David H. Clift, Staff Liaison.
Chapter Relationships, Coordinating on. John F. Anderson, P.L., San Francisco, Calif. 94102. Ruth Warncke, Staff Liaison.
Conference Format. Mrs. Elizabeth E. Hamer, L. of Congress, Washington, D.C. 20540. David H. Clift, Staff Liaison.

---

[1] ALA divisions are listed alphabetically following this entry.

Conference Program. Keith Doms, Free L. of Philadelphia, Logan Sq., Philadelphia, Pa. 19103. Ruth Warncke, Staff Liaison.

Constitution and Bylaws. William D. Murphy; Kirkland, Ellis, Hodson, Chaffetz and Masters, 2900 Prudential Plaza, Chicago, Ill. 60601. Mrs. Miriam L. Hornback, Staff Liaison.

Disadvantaged, Coordinating Committee on Library Service to the. Vincent Aceto, S. of L. Sci., State Univ. of New York, Albany, N.Y. 12226. Ira Phillips, Staff Liaison.

Editorial. Donald E. Wright, P.L., Evanston, Ill. 60201. Pauline A. Cianciolo, Secy.

Elections. To be appointed from nominations from following divisions: Adult Services Division, American Association of School Librarians, American Library Trustee Association, Association of College and Research Libraries, Children's Services Division, Information Science and Automation Division, and Reference Services Division. Ernest J. Martin, Staff Liaison.

Ethics. Margaret Monroe, Univ. of Wisconsin, Madison, Wis. 53706. Ruth R. Frame, Staff Liaison.

Instruction in the Use of Libraries. Mrs. Jean A. Coleman, L. Servs., Hammond Public Ss., Hammond, Ind. 46320. Delores K. Vaughan, Staff Liaison.

Intellectual Freedom. Richard L. Darling, Grad. S. of L. Serv., Columbia Univ., New York, N.Y. 10027. Mrs. Judith F. Krug, Staff Liaison.

Internal Revenue Service, Advisory Committee to. Alexander Wainwright, Princeton Univ. L., Princeton, N.J. 08540. David H. Clift, Staff Liaison.

International Relations. Emerson Greenaway, 97 E. Bell's Mill Rd., Philadelphia, Pa. 19118. David G. Donovan, Staff Liaison.

Legislation. Joseph F. Shubert, State L. of Ohio, Columbus, Ohio 43215. Germaine Krettek, Staff Liaison.

Library Education, Office for. Wesley Simonton, L. S., Univ. of Minnesota, Minneapolis, Minn. 55455. Agnes L. Reagan, Staff Liaison.

Library Technology Program. Russell Shank, Smithsonian Inst. L., Washington, D.C. 20560. Forrest F. Carhart, Jr., Staff Liaison.

Mediation, Arbitration and Inquiry, Staff Committee on. David H. Clift, ALA Headquarters, 50 E. Huron St., Chicago, Ill. 60611.

Membership. Mrs. Allie Beth Martin, Tulsa City-County L. Syst., Tulsa, Okla. 74103. David W. Salan, Staff Liaison.

National Library Week. Walter Curley, P. L., Cleveland, Ohio 41144. David H. Clift, Ruth Warncke, Staff Liaison.

National Library Week Evaluation. To be appointed. David H. Clift, Ruth Warncke, Staff Liaison.

Nominating. Mrs. Susanna Alexander, Missouri State L., Jefferson City, Mo. 65101. David H. Clift, Staff Liaison.

Nominating, Council. James F. Holly, Evergreen State Coll. L., Olympia, Wash. 98501. David H. Clift, Staff Liaison.

Organization. Mrs. Helen W. Tuttle, Princeton Univ. L., Princeton, N.J. 08540. Ruth Warncke, Staff Liaison.

Planning. To be appointed. David H. Clift, Staff Liaison.

Policy Implementation. Keith Doms, Free L. of Philadelphia, Logan Sq., Philadelphia, Pa. 19103. David H. Clift, Staff Liaison.

Program Evaluation and Support. Helen M. Brown, Wellesley Coll. L., Wellesley, Mass. 92181. LeRoy J. Gaertner, Staff Liaison.

Recruitment, Office for. Donald Hunt, Free L. of Philadelphia, Logan Sq., Philadelphia, Pa. 19103. Margaret E. Barber, Staff Liaison.

Reference and Subscription Books Review. Mrs. Jeanette Swickard, Central Elem. S. L., Evanston, Ill. 60202. Mrs. Helen K. Wright, Staff Liaison.

Research. Raynard Swank, Univ. of California S. of Libnshp., Berkeley, Calif. 94720. Forrest F. Carhart, Jr., Staff Liaison.

Resolutions. To be appointed by President Doms.

Standards. Phyllis Hochstettler, S. of Educ., Portland State Univ., Portland, Ore. 97207. Ruth Warncke, Staff Liaison.

JOINT COMMITTEES

Canadian Library Association—ALA. Mrs. Helen Howard, Sir George Williams Univ., Montreal. David H. Clift, Staff Liaison.

Catholic Library Association—ALA. Sister Helen Sheehan, Trinity Coll. L., Washington, D.C. 20017. Mrs. Helen K. Wright, Staff Liaison.

Children's Book Council—ALA. Mary V. Gaver, L. Cons. Servs., Bro-Dart, 29 Baldwin St., New Brunswick, N.J. 08900. Ruth W. Tarbox, Staff Liaison.

National Education Association—ALA. James Igoe, Vermont State L., Montpelier, Vt. 05602; Philip A. Gonyar, 23 Harrison Ave., Orono, Me. 04473. Ruth Warncke, Staff Liaison.

Society of American Archivists—ALA. Mrs. Elizabeth E. Hamer, L. of Congress, Washington, D.C. 20540. David H. Clift, Staff Liaison.

ADULT SERVICES DIVISION
50 East Huron Street, Chicago, Ill. 60611
312-944-6780

OBJECT

"The Adult Services Division has the responsibility for those library services designed to provide continuing educational, recreational, and cultural development for adults in all types of libraries. This responsibility includes identification and evaluation of those materials (book and non-book) which are useful in adult services (except reference); stimulation of the production and use of such materials; the identification of the principles involved in their selection and use for these purposes; and the responsibility for activities related to the bibliography, compilation, publication, study, and review of professional literature related to adult services." Organized 1957. Memb. 2,983. (For dues and membership year, see ALA entry.)

OFFICERS (June 1971–June 1972)

Pres. John A. McCrossan, Bureau of L. Devel., Pennsylvania State L., Harrisburg, Pa. 17126; *1st V.P. & Pres. Elect.* Walter Allen, Grad. S. of L. Sci., Univ. of Illinois, Urbana, Ill. 61801; *2nd V.P.* Dr. Lawrence A. Allen, S. of L. Sci., Univ. of Kentucky, Lexington, Ky. 40500; *Secy.* Mary Adele Springman, Adult Educ. Dept., Cleveland Public L., Cleveland, Ohio 44146; *Past Pres.* Peter Hiatt, Western Interstate Commission for Higher Educ., Boulder, Colo. 80302.

Exec. Secy. Andrew M. Hansen, Adult Serv. Div., ALA, 50 E. Huron St., Chicago, Ill. 60611.

DIRECTORS

The officers and Kathryn J. Gesterfield, Illinois State L., Centennial Bldg., Springfield, Ill. 62706; Norman Finkler, Montgomery County Dept. of P.L.'s, Bethesda, Md. 20034; Marilee Fogelsong, Free L. of Philadelphia, Philadelphia, Pa. 19103; Dorothy Nyren, Brooklyn P.L., Brooklyn, N.Y. 11238; Lelia B. Saunders, Arlington County Dept. of Ls., Arlington, Va. 22201.

PUBLICATIONS

Adult Services (3 issues per yr.; memb.)

COMMITTEE CHAIRMEN

Adult Library Materials. Mrs. Peggy Glover, Free L. of Philadelphia, Logan Sq., Philadelphia, Pa. 19103.

Materials for American Indians, Subcommittee. Mrs. June S. Smith, Coll. of St. Catherine, St. Paul, Minn. 55116.

Materials for the Spanish-Speaking, Subcommittee. Mrs. Victoria Wallace, P.L., Northport, N.Y. 11768.

AFL/CIO-ALA (ASD) Joint Committee on Library Service to Labor Groups. Mrs. Pearl Frankenfield, Montgomery County-Norristown P.L., Norristown, Pa. 19401.

Archives. Robert Baumruk, P.L., Chicago, Ill. 60602.

Association of American Publishers–ALA (ASD) Joint Committee. Bernice MacDonald, N.Y.P.L., New York, N.Y. 10016.

Bylaws. Robert N. Sheridan, P.L., Levittown, N.Y. 11756.
Common Concerns, RSD/ASD. To be appointed.
Conference Program (Chicago). To be appointed.
Cooperation, ASD/YASD. Muriel L. Fuller, Univ. of Wisconsin, Madison, Wis. 53706.
Library Rights of Adults—A Call for Action, Special Committee for Promotion of. Marion L. Simmons, METRO, 11 W. 40 St., New York, N.Y. 10018.
Library Service to an Aging Population. Miss Leslyn Schmidt, Tippecanoe L., Milwaukee, Wis. 53207.
Nominating. Marie A. Davis, Free L. of Philadelphia, Logan Sq., Philadelphia, Pa. 19103.
Notable Books Council. Raymond Agler, P.L., Boston, Mass. 02117.
Notable Books, Subcommittee for Promotion of. Kate Kolish, Carnegie L., Pittsburgh, Pa. 15213.
Committee on Orientation, ASD/RSD. To be appointed.
Program and Budget. Walter Allen, Univ. of Illinois, Urbana, Ill. 61801.
Program Policy. Mrs. Marilyn Simon, Free L. of Philadelphia, Philadelphia, Pa. 19118.
Publications Advisory Committee. Mrs. Helen H. Lyman, Univ. of Wisconsin Research Project "Library Materials," Madison, Wis. 53706.
Relations with State and Regional Library Associations. Emily Reed, Enoch Pratt Free L., Baltimore, Md. 21201.

AMERICAN ASSOCIATION OF SCHOOL LIBRARIANS
(A Division of the American Library Association and an Associated Organization of the National Education Association)
50 East Huron Street, Chicago, Ill. 60611
312-944-6780

OBJECT

"The general improvement and extension of library services for children and young people. AASL has specific responsibility for: planning of programs of study and service for the improvement and extension of library services in elementary and secondary schools as a means of strengthening the educational program; evaluation, selection, and interpretation of books and nonbook materials as they are used in the context of the school program; stimulation of continuous study and research to the library field and to establish criteria of evaluation; synthesis of the activities of all units within the American Library Association in areas of mutual concern; representation and interpretation of the need for and function of school libraries to other educational and lay groups; stimulation of professional growth, improvement of the status of school librarians, and encouragement of participation by members in appropriate type-of-activity divisions; conduct of activities and projects for improvement and extension of service in the school library when such projects are beyond the scope of type-of-activity divisions, after specific approval by the ALA Council. The American Association of School Librarians became a department of the National Education Association in June, 1960. In 1969 the American Association of School Librarians changed its status to Associated Organization of the National Education Association." Established in 1951 as a separate Division of ALA. Memb. 10,000. (For dues and membership year, see ALA entry.)

MEMBERSHIP

Open to all libraries, librarians, interested individuals and business firms with requisite membership in the ALA.

OFFICERS (June 1971–June 1972)

Pres. Frances Hatfield, Coordinator of Instructional Materials, The S. Bd., Broward County, P.O. Box 8369, Fort Lauderdale, Fla. 33310; *V.P. & Pres. Elect.* Mrs. Elnora Portteus, Directing

Supv., S. Ls., Cleveland Public Ss., Woodhill-Quincy Center, 10600 Quincy, Cleveland, Ohio 44106; *Recording Secy.* F. Luree Jaquith, Libn., Bowman Elem. S., Lexington, Mass. 02173; *Past Pres.* Mrs. Roberta Young, Dir., L. Devel., Office of L. Servs., Colorado Dept. of Educ., 1362 Lincoln St., Denver, Colo. 80203; *Ed. of "School Libraries" (ex officio)* Mrs. Mary Frances K. Johnson, Assoc. Prof., S. of Educ., Univ. of North Carolina at Greensboro, N.C. 27412; *Supv. Section Chmn.* Mrs. Elizabeth P. Hoffman, Coord., Div. of S. Ls. & ESEA Title II, Pa. Dept. of Public Instruction, P.O. Box 911, Harrisburg, Pa. 17126.

Exec. Secy. Lu Ouida Vinson, AASL, 50 E. Huron St., Chicago, Ill. 60611.

Asst. Exec. Secy. Mrs. Joe Ann Stenstrom, NEA Hq., Washington, D.C. 20036.

DIRECTORS

Region I: Mrs. Judy Powell; *Region II:* Teresa Doherty; *Region III:* Dr. Miriam E. Peterson; *Region IV:* Michael Printz; *Region V:* Margaret Sue Copenhaver; *Region VI:* Mrs. Louie Reifel; *Region VII:* John G. Wright; *Region VIII:* Mrs. Mary Chambers Jones.

COUNCILORS (nonvoting)

Mrs. May Chun, Leila Doyle, Grace Hightower, Eileen Noonan, Mrs. Carrie Robinson, Kenneth Taylor, Mary Ann Swanson, Mrs. Jane Vance.

PUBLICATION

School Libraries. (q.; memb.)

COMMITTEE CHAIRMEN

American Association of University Presses (Advisory). Alice E. Johnson, Evanston Township H.S., 1600 Dodge Ave., Evanston, Ill. 60201.

American School Counselor Association — AASL (joint). Rebecca Bingham, 3608 Dumesnil St., Louisville, Ky. 40211.

Archives. Rev. Edward T. LaMorte, Tolentine Coll., P.O. Box 747, Olympia Fields, Ill. 60461.

Award for School Administrators, Distinguished Library Service. Dr. Ruth W. White, Dept. of L. Educ., Coll. of Educ., Univ. of Georgia, Athens, Ga. 30601.

Awards, Encyclopaedia Britannica School Library. D. Philip Baker, Dir. of Ls., Darien Bd. of Educ., P.O. Box 1167, Darien, Conn. 06820. (Mailing address: 30 Glenbrook Rd., Apt. 9A, Stamford, Conn. 06902.)

Bureau of Independent Publishers & Distributors (BIPAD). Members serve with representatives from NEA and NCTE.

Bylaws. Robert Graham, 5 Hayes C, S. of Info. & L. Studies, State Univ., Buffalo, N.Y. 14214.

Centennial. To be appointed.

Conference Program Planning, Chicago, 1972. Frances Hatfield, Coord. of Instructional Materials, The S. Bd., Broward County, P.O. Box 8369, Fort Lauderdale, Fla. 33310.

Conference Program Planning, NEA, 1972. Mrs. Elnora Portteus, Directing Supv., S. Ls., Cleveland P. Ss., Woodhill-Quincy Center, 10600 Quincy, Cleveland, Ohio 44106.

Editorial, School Libraries. Mrs. Mary Frances K. Johnson, Assoc. Prof., S. of Educ., Univ. of North Carolina at Greensboro, N.C. 27412. (Mailing address: 109 Falkener Dr., Greensboro, N.C. 27410.)

Election. Winifred Duncan, Supv., Cataloging Sect., Div. of Ls., Chicago Public Ss., 228 N. LaSalle St., Chicago, Ill. 60601.

Elementary–Kindergarten–Nursery Education Service Bulletin Revision. Marian Capozzi, 6802 Dunhill Rd., Baltimore, Md. 21222.

Grolier Grant. Mrs. Jean E. Wichers, Assoc. Prof., Dept. of Libnshp., San Jose State Coll., San Jose, Calif. 95114.

Guidelines for Personnel Working with Children & Young People in Special Situations, AHIL/AASL/CSD/YASD. Margaret Cheeseman, Institutional Servs. Supv., Pennsylvania State L., P.O. Box 1601, Harrisburg, Pa. 17126.

History, Oral. To be appointed.

Improvement of School Library Programs. Mrs. Barbara Koplein Elleman, 2260 N. Summit Ave., No. 208, Milwaukee, Wis. 53202.

Instructional Media. Evelyn Geller, Editor, *School Library Journal*, R. R. Bowker Co., 1180 Avenue of the Americas, New York, N.Y. 10036.

International Relations. Phyllis Hochstettler, S. of Educ., Portland State Coll., Portland, Ore. 97201.

Legislation. Mrs. Mary B. Boyvey, Media Program Dir., Texas Educ. Agency, Austin, Tex. 78711.

Local Arrangements, Chicago, 1972. Dr. Miriam E. Peterson, Div. of Ls., Bd. of Educ., 228 N. LaSalle St., Chicago, Ill. 60601.

Manpower Project Advisory, School Library. Dr. Leslie H. Janke, Head, Dept. of Libnshp., San Jose State Coll., San Jose, Calif. 95114.

Minority Groups in Library Books & Other Instructional Materials, Treatment of. David Cohen, Libn., Plainview-Old Bethpage H.S., Plainview, N.Y. 11803. (Mailing address: 68-71 Bell Blvd., Bayside, N.Y. 11364.)

National Library Week. James L. Smith, Coord. of L. Servs., Instructional Materials Center, Monongalia County Ss., 300 McLane Ave., Morgantown, W. Va. 26505.

Nominating 1971/1972. Mrs. Dorothy Heald, P.O. Box 1074, Tallahassee, Fla. 32302.

Professional Relations. Dr. Miriam E. Peterson, Div. of Ls., Bd. of Educ., 228 N. LaSalle St., Chicago, Ill. 60601.

Professional Status & Growth. Mrs. Rachael W. DeAngelo, Grad. S. of L. Studies, Univ. of Hawaii, Sinclair L. B-15, 2425 Campus Rd., Honolulu, Hawaii 96822.

Publications. Mrs. Mary Joan Egan, L. Dept., Burnt Hills-Ballston Lake Central Ss., Admin. Bldg., 491 Saratoga Rd., Scotia, N.Y. 12302.

Research. Vincent J. Aceto, Prof., S. of L. Sci., State Univ. of New York at Albany, N.Y. 12203.

Right to Read Task Force. Mrs. Elnora Portteus, Directing Supv., S. Ls., Cleveland Public Ss., Woodhill-Quincy Center, 10600 Quincy, Cleveland, Ohio 44106.

Self-Study. James Liesener, Assoc. Prof., S. of L. & Info. Servs., Univ. of Maryland, College Park, Md. 20742.

Social Studies in World Affairs. Wylma C. Woolard, S. & L. Consultant, World Book Encyclopedia, 6230 Fairview Rd., Suite 317, Charlotte, N.C. 28210.

Standards Development. To be appointed.

Standards Implementation. Bernard Franckowiak, State S. L. Supv., Wis. Dept. of Public Instruction, Madison, Wis. 53702; Mrs. Judy W. Powell, Rte. 1, Fairfield, Me. 04937.

State Assembly Planning. Mrs. Louie Reifel, 12118 Queensbury, Houston, Tex. 77024.

Student Library Assistants. Mrs. Estelle B. Williamson, Supv. of S. Ls., Div. of L. Devel., Maryland Dept. of Educ., 600 Wyndhurst Ave., Baltimore, Md. 21201.

Urban School Libraries. Dr. Lillian Batchelor, Asst. Dir., Div. of Ls., Bd. of Educ., Parkway at 21 St., Philadelphia, Pa. 19103.

REPRESENTATIVES

ALA Membership Committee. Mrs. Betty J. Buckingham, L. Consultant, Iowa Dept. of Pub. Instruction, Grimes State Office Bldg., Des Moines, Iowa 50319.

ALA-NCTE Committee. Sara Innis Fenwick, Assoc. Prof., Grad. L. S., Univ. of Chicago, 1116 E. 59 St., Chicago, Ill. 60637.

ALA-SRRT — The American Indian. Mrs. Helen E. Saunders, 264 Winrock Village, N.E., Albuquerque, N.M. 87110.

Associated Organizations for Teacher Education (AOTE). Mrs. Catheryne S. Franklin, Assoc. Prof., Grad. S. of L. Sci., Univ. of Tex., P.O. Box 7576, University Station, Austin, Tex. 78712. (Mailing address: 505 W. 7 St., Apt. 212, Austin, Tex. 78701.)

Cataloging of Children's Materials (RTSD:CCS). Mrs. Priscilla Moulton, Dir., Brookline L. Servs., Brookline H.S., 115 Greenough St., Brookline, Mass. 02146.

Conference on Interlibrary Communications and Information Networks

(ISAD-all other divisions). Dr. Alvin J. Goldwyn, Dir., Communication Center, Case Western Reserve Univ., 10831 Magnolia Dr., Cleveland, Ohio 44106.

Education USA Advisory Board. Dr. Lillian Batchelor, Asst. Dir., Div. of Ls., Bd. of Educ., Parkway at 21 St., Philadelphia, Pa. 19103.

AMERICAN LIBRARY TRUSTEE ASSOCIATION
(A Division of the American Library Association)
50 East Huron Street, Chicago, Ill. 60611
312-944-6780

OBJECT

"The development of effective library service for all people in all types of communities and in all types of libraries; it follows that its members are concerned as policymakers with organizational patterns of service, with the development of competent personnel, the provision of adequate financing, the passage of suitable legislation, and the encouragement of citizen support for libraries." Open to all interested persons and organizations. Organized 1890. Became an ALA division 1961. Memb. 3,479. (For dues and membership year, see ALA entry.)

OFFICERS (June 1971–June 1972)

Pres. Chester B. Ostrander, 149 Main St., Glens Falls, N.Y. 12801; *1st V.P. & Pres. Elect.* Mrs. Ann Woodward, 834 Oakdale Rd. NE, Atlanta, Ga. 30307; *2nd V.P.* Daniel W. Casey, 202 Scarboro Dr., Solvay, N.Y. 13209; *Libn. V.P.* Denny R. Stephens, DHEW, Office of Educ., 601 E. 12 St., Kansas City, Mo. 64106; *Secy.* Mrs. Jean M. Coleman, 2101 University Pl., Dayton, Ohio 45406. *Exec. Secy.* Don S. Culbertson.

DIRECTORS

The officers and Joseph W. Lippincott, Jr., 307 Laurel Lane, Haverford, Pa. 19041; George W. Coen, 311 Equitable Bldg., Lancaster, Ohio 43130; Mrs. Evelyn Kennedy, Barret Rd., New London, N.H. 03257; James A. Hess, 91 Farms Rd. Circle, East Brunswick, N.J. 08816; Jerome M. Levy, Box 340, Demopolis, Ala. 36732; Mrs. Jean M. Coleman, 2101 University Pl., Dayton, Ohio 45406; Mrs. Jeanne Davies, Deer Trail, Colo. 80105; Alan Patteson, Jr., P.O. Box 400, Jonesboro, Ark. 72401; Mrs. Leontyne King, 1251 Redondo Blvd., Los Angeles, Calif. 90019; W. W. Esseks, 108 E. Main St., Riverhead, N.Y. 11901; Mrs. Virginia Young, 10 E. Parkway Dr., Columbia, Mo. 65201; Martin Phelan, Eastin-Phelan Corp., 1235 W. Fifth St., Davenport, Iowa 52808; John T. Short, P.O. Box E, Avon, Conn. 06001; Mrs. Alice Ihrig, 9322 S. 53 Ave., Oak Lawn, Ill. 60453; Andrew Geddes, Nassau L. Syst., Roosevelt Field, Garden City, N.Y. 11530.

COUNCILS

Council for Action. W. W. Esseks, 108 E. Main St., Riverhead, N.Y. 11901.
Council for State Liaison. Mrs. Virginia Young, 10 E. Parkway Dr., Columbia, Mo. 65201.
Council for Communications. Martin Phelan, Eastin-Phelan Corp., 1235 W. Fifth St., Davenport, Iowa 52808.
Council for Conferences. John T. Short, P.O. Box E, Avon, Conn. 06001.

PUBLICATION

Public Library Trustee (q.; memb.)

COMMITTEE CHAIRMEN

Action Development. Donald Earnshaw, 226 S. Douglas St., Lee's Summit, Mo. 64063.
Conference Program. John T. Short, P.O. Box E, Avon, Conn. 06001.
Endowment Fund. W. M. Usher, 837 Highland, Salina, Kans. 67401.
Governors' Conferences. Mrs. Ella Pretty, P.O. Box 28, Harrison Mills, B.C., Canada.
Intellectual Freedom. Mrs. Florence McMullin, 14302 23 St., Seattle, Wash. 98166.
Jury on Citation of Trustees. Eloise Ebert, State Libn., Oregon State L., Salem, Ore. 97310.

Legislative. John S. Robling, V.P., Encyclopaedia Britannica, 425 N. Michigan Ave., Chicago, Ill. 60611.
Library Service to the Unserved. Dr. Irving Lieberman, S. of Libnshp., 133 Library, Univ. of Washington, Seattle, Wash. 98105.
Membership. Mrs. Nancy Steigemeyer, 125 Camellia Dr., Cape Girardeau, Mo. 63701.
Nominating. Mrs. Rachael C. Gross, 387 Tomlinson, Huntingdon Valley, Pa. 19006.
Publications. Douglas W. Downey, 2236 Maple Ave., Northbrook, Ill. 60062.
State Associations. Daniel W. Casey, 202 Scarboro Dr., Syracuse, N.Y. 13209.

ASSOCIATION OF COLLEGE AND RESEARCH LIBRARIES
(A Division of the American Library Association)
50 East Huron Street, Chicago, Ill. 60611
312-944-6780

OBJECT
"Representation and promotion of the libraries of higher education, independent research libraries, and specialized libraries." Founded 1889. Memb. 11,763. (For dues and membership year, see ALA entry.)

OFFICERS (June 1971–June 1972)
Pres. Joseph H. Reason, 1242 Girard St. N.E., Washington, D.C. 20017; *V.P. & Pres. Elect.* Russell Shank, Dir. of Ls., Museum of Natural History, Rm. 22, Smithsonian Institution, Washington, D.C. 20560; *Past Pres.* Anne C. Edmonds, Libn., Mount Holyoke Coll., South Hadley, Mass. 01075.
Exec. Secy. J. Donald Thomas.

DIRECTORS
Page Ackerman, Assoc. Libn., Univ. of California, Los Angeles, 401 Hilgard Ave., Los Angeles, Calif. 90024; Evan Ira Farber, Libn., Earlham Coll., Richmond, Ind. 47374; James F. Govan, Libn., Swarthmore Coll., Swarthmore, Pa. 19081; Warren J. Haas, Dir. of Ls., Columbia Univ. Ls., 535 W. 114 St., New York, N.Y. 10027; James F. Holly, Dean of L. Serv., Evergreen State Coll., Olympia, Wash. 98501; Andrew Horn, Dean, S. of L. Sci., Univ. of California, 401 Hilgard Ave., Los Angeles, Calif. 90024; Robert K. Johnson, Univ. Libn., Univ. of Arizona, Tucson, Ariz. 85721; Richard L. O'Keeffe, Libn., Rice Univ., Fondren L., Houston, Tex. 77001; Roscoe Rouse, Univ. Libn., Oklahoma State Univ., Stillwater, Okla. 74075.
Directors-at-Large: Herbert A. Cahoon, Dir. of L. Servs., The Pierpont Morgan L., 33 E. 36 St., New York, N.Y. 10016; Mark M. Gormley, Dir. of Ls., Univ. of Missouri, Thomas Jefferson L., St. Louis, Mo. 63121; Norman E. Tanis, Dir. of Ls., San Fernando Valley State Coll., Northridge, Calif. 91324; David C. Weber, Assoc. Dir., Stanford Univ. Ls., Stanford, Calif. 94305.

PUBLICATIONS
College & Research Libraries (17 times a yr.; memb. or $10)
Choice: Books for College Libraries (mo.; $20)
ACRL Publications in Librarianship (Occ.)

SECTION CHAIRMEN
College Libraries. Carl R. Cox, Chief Libn., Herbert H. Lehman Coll., Bedford Park Blvd. W., Bronx, N.Y. 10468.
Junior College Libraries. Hal C. Stone, Coordinator, L. & Learning Resources Center, Los Angeles City Coll., 855 N. Vermont Ave., Los Angeles, Calif. 90029.
Rare Books and Manuscripts. Lee Ash, L. Consultant, 31 Alden Rd., New Haven, Conn. 06515.
Subject Specialists. Wolfgang M. Freitag, Lecturer on the Fine Arts & Libn. for the Fine Arts L., Fogg Art Museum, Harvard Univ., Cambridge, Mass. 02138.
University Libraries. Ralph H. Hopp, Dir. of Ls., Univ. of Minnesota, Wilson L., Minneapolis, Minn. 55455.

COMMITTEE CHAIRMEN

Academic Status. Roy L. Kidman, Univ. Libn., Univ. of Southern California, Los Angeles, Calif. 90007.

Appointments (1972) and Nominations (1973). Donald Anthony, Assoc. Dir. of Ls., Columbia Univ., New York, N.Y. 10027.

Audiovisual. Herman L. Totten, Apt. 1, 175 Malabu Dr., Lexington, Ky. 40503.

Bibliographic Instruction (Ad Hoc). Thomas G. Kirk, Box E-72, Earlham Coll., Richmond, Ind. 47374.

Chicago Conference Planning — 1972. Ellsworth G. Mason, Dir. of L. Servs., Hofstra Univ., Hempstead, N.Y. 11550.

Community Use of Academic Libraries. Miss Yen-Tsai Feng, Asst. Dir. for Research L. Servs., Boston P.L., Copley Sq., Boston, Mass. 02117.

Constitution and Bylaws. William R. Pullen, Libn., Georgia State Coll., 104 Decatur St. S.E., Atlanta, Ga. 30303.

Cooperation with Educational & Professional Organizations. James F. Govan, Libn., Swarthmore Coll., Swarthmore, Pa. 19081.

Internship. Mrs. Virginia Lacy Jones, Dean, S. of L. Serv., Atlanta Univ., Atlanta, Ga. 30314.

Legislation. Philip J. McNiff, Dir., Boston P.L., Copley Sq., Boston, Mass. 02117.

Library Surveys. Stephen Ford, Libn., Grand Valley State Coll., Allendale, Mich. 49401.

Local Arrangements. Theodore F. Welch, Asst. Univ. Libn. for Public Servs., Northwestern Univ., Evanston, Ill. 60201.

Planning. Russell Shank, Dir. of Ls., Museum of Natural History, Rm. 22, Smithsonian Institution, Washington, D.C. 20560.

Publication of a Book Catalog for Core Collections, Advisory Committee for the. Philip J. McNiff, Dir., Boston P.L., Copley Sq., Boston, Mass. 02117.

Publications. Robert M. Pierson, Dir. of Ls. for Admin., Univ. of Maryland, McKeldin L., College Park, Md. 20742.

Standards and Accreditations. H. William Axford, Univ. Libn., Arizona State Univ., Tempe, Ariz. 85281.

ASSOCIATION OF HOSPITAL AND INSTITUTION LIBRARIES
(A Division of the American Library Association)
50 East Huron Street, Chicago, Ill. 60611
312-944-6780

OBJECT

"Represents libraries and librarians serving residents, patients, and inmates under treatment and care in all types of institutions, and all levels of personnel and students at these institutions. These libraries are an integral part of the care program provided by hospitals and institutions." Memb. 1,628. (For dues and membership year, see ALA entry.)

OFFICERS (June 1971–June 1972)

Pres. Earl C. Graham, 2023 W. Ogden Ave., Chicago, Ill. 60612; *V.P. & Pres. Elect.* Mrs. Phyllis I. Dalton, Calif. State L., Library-Courts Bldg., Sacramento, Calif. 95809; *Secy.* Mrs. Agnes Griffen, King County L. Syst., 1100 E. Union, Seattle, Wash. 98122.

Exec. Secy. Ira Phillips.

DIRECTORS

The officers and William T. Henderson, Institution L. Unit, Bureau of L. Servs., 735 E. Michigan Ave., Lansing, Mich. 48913; Margaret M. Kinney, Chief Libn., U.S. Veterans Admin. Hosp., Bronx, N.Y. 10468; Dorothy Fleak, Hospitals & Institutions Dept., Cleveland P.L., 325 Superior St., Cleveland, Ohio 44114; Mrs. Eileen Kraus, Chief Libn., V.A. Hosp., Montrose, N.Y. 10548; Mrs. Marion G. Patmon, S.L., Resources Branch, Oklahoma City, Okla. 73111.

PUBLICATION

AHIL Quarterly (q.; memb.)

COMMITTEE CHAIRMEN

ACA-ALA (AHIL) Joint Committee on Institution Libraries. Mrs. Andree F. Bailey, Consultant, Institution Ls., State L., Tallahassee, Fla. 32303.

Archives. M. Jean Paige, Chief Libn., V.A. Hosp., Iowa City, Iowa 52240.

Audiovisual Advisory. Mrs. Theda A. Kellner, Coordinator, L. Servs. to Institions & the Handicapped, Colorado State L., 1362 Lincoln St., Denver, Colo. 80203.

Awards. Adelia P. Mustain, 3603 29 St., San Diego, Calif. 92104.

Bibliotherapy. To be appointed.

Bylaws. To be appointed.

Conference Program (Chicago 1972). Earl C. Graham, 2023 W. Ogden Ave., Chicago, Ill. 60612.

Guidelines AHIL/AASL/CSD/YASD. Margaret Cheeseman, Pa. State L., Box 1601, Harrisburg, Pa. 17126.

International Relations: Subcommittee of International Relations — ALA. Elizabeth Lindsey, Consultant, Michigan State L., Bureau of L. Servs., 735 E. Michigan Ave., Lansing, Mich. 48913.

Nominating. Adelia P. Mustain, 3603 29 St., San Diego, Calif. 92104.

Organization. Mrs. Phyllis I. Dalton, Asst. State Libn., California State L., Library-Courts Bldg., Sacramento, Calif. 95809.

Patient Education (Ad Hoc). Ruth Tews, Hosp. Libn., Mayo Clinic, Rochester, Minn. 55901.

Publications Advisory. Jackie Rustigian, L. Consultant, L. of the Coll. of Physicians of Philadelphia, Mid-Eastern Regional Medical L., 19 So. 22 St., Philadelphia, Pa. 19103.

Research. John A. Timour, L. Servs. Dir., Connecticut Regional Medical Program, 272 George St., New Haven, Conn. 06510.

Special Projects. Stefan B. Moses, Exec. Dir., California L. Assn., 717 K St., Suite 300, Sacramento, Calif. 95814.

Standards. U. M. (Lee) Steele, Div. of Ls., P.O. Box 635, Dover, Del. 19901.

ASSOCIATION OF STATE LIBRARY AGENCIES
(A Division of the American Library Association)
50 East Huron Street, Chicago, Ill. 60611
312-944-6780

OBJECT

"The Association of State Library Agencies is interested in the development and coordination of library resources and services of all types of libraries. Its responsibility covers those functions and services relating to statewide library development and those pertaining to library services performed at the state level, including specialized book and information resources and services in support of the work of state government." Established 1957. Memb. 1,914. (For dues and membership year, see ALA entry.)

MEMBERSHIP

Open to ALA members interested in any aspect of library service provided by states and provinces.

OFFICERS (June 1971–June 1972)

Pres. Ernest E. Doerschuk, Jr., State L., Harrisburg, Pa. 17126; *V.P. & Pres. Elect.* James R. Hunt, P.L., Cincinnati, Ohio 45202; *Past Pres.* Philip S. Ogilvie, State L., Raleigh, N.C. 27601.

Exec. Secy. Gerald M. Born.

DIRECTORS

The officers and members-at-large, Vivian Cazayoux, L. Devel., Baton Rouge, La. 70808; Rose Vainstein, S. of L. Sci., Univ. of Michigan, Ann Arbor, Mich. 48104; Margaret Willis, State L., Dept. of Ls., Frankfort, Ky. 40601; Joseph F. Shubert, State L., Columbus, Ohio 43215; Nathan Einhorn, L. of Congress, Washington, D.C. 20540; Herschel V. Anderson, State L. & Archives, Nashville, Tenn. 37219; Denny R. Stephens, L. Serv. Program Officer, USOE, Kansas City, Mo. 64106; Ray M. Fry, Bureau of Ls. & Educ. Technology, USOE, Washington, D.C. 20202; Mrs. Brooke Sheldon, State L., P.O. Box 1629, Santa Fe, N. Mex. 87501; James G. Igoe, State L., Dept. of Ls., Montpelier, Vt. 05602; John A. Humphry, Univ. of New York, Albany, N.Y. 12224.

PUBLICATIONS

ASLA President's Newsletter (2 times a yr.; memb.)

DISCUSSION GROUP

Mary Ann Wentroth, P.L. Consultant for Children's Serv., Oklahoma City, Okla. 73105.

COMMITTEE CHAIRMEN

Legislation Liaison. James G. Igoe, State L., Montpelier, Vt. 05602.

Nominating. Jack M. Tyler, Div. of Ls., Dover, Del. 19901.

Planning. John A. Humphry, Univ. of New York, State Educ. Dept., Albany, N.Y. 12224.

Bylaws. Vivian Cazayoux, L. Devel., Baton Rouge, La. 70808.

CHILDREN'S SERVICES DIVISION
50 East Huron Street, Chicago, Ill. 60611
312-944-6780

OBJECT

"Interested in the improvement and extension of library services to children in all types of libraries. Responsible for the evaluation and selection of book and nonbook materials for, and the improvement of techniques of, library services to children from pre-school through the eighth grade or junior high school age, when such materials or techniques are intended for use in more than one type of library." Founded 1957. Memb. 6,324. (For dues and membership year, see ALA entry.)

MEMBERSHIP

Open to anyone interested in library services to children.

OFFICERS (June 1971–June 1972)

Pres. Sara I. Fenwick, Assoc. Prof., Grad. L. S., Univ. of Chicago, Chicago, Ill. 60637; *V.P. & Pres. Elect.* Anne R. Izard, Children's Serv. Consultant, Westchester L. Syst., 285 Central Ave., White Plains, N.Y. 10606; *2nd V.P.* Frances A. Sullivan, Head, Children's Dept., P.L., 223 S. Main, Wichita, Kans. 67202; *Past Pres.* Mary Elizabeth Ledlie, Coordinator of Youth Servs., P.L., 814 W. Wisconsin Ave., Milwaukee, Wis. 53233.

Exec. Secy. Ruth W. Tarbox.

DIRECTORS

The officers and Martha C. Bentley, Consultant, Children's & Young Adult Servs., N. Bay Cooperative L. Syst., 725 Third St., Santa Rosa, Calif. 95404; Virginia Chase, Head, Boys & Girls Dept., Carnegie L., 4400 Forbes Ave., Pittsburgh, Pa. 15213; Jane McGregor, Supv., Work with Children, P.L. of Cincinnati & Hamilton County, 8th & Vine, Cincinnati, Ohio 45202 (ALA Councilor); Nina Greig, Children's Libn., Central Children's Room, L. Assn. of Portland, 801 S.W. 10th Ave., Portland, Ore. 97205; Jane Botham, Children's Servs. Consultant, New York St. L., Albany, N.Y. 12224; Beverly A. Hall, Coordinator, Children's Serv., Baltimore County, P.L., 25 Chesapeake Ave., Towson, Md. 21204; Anne Pellowski, Dir.-Libn., Info. Ctr. on Children's Cultures, UNICEF, 331 E. 38 St., New York, N.Y. 10016 (ALA Councilor); Margaret E. Poarch, Coordinator, Children's & Young People's Serv., Memphis P.L. & Info. Ctr., 1850 Peabody Ave., Memphis, Tenn. 38104 (ALA Councilor); Jean Karl, Ed., Children's Books, Atheneum Publishers, 122 E. 42 St., New York, N.Y. 10017; Peggy Sullivan, Asst. Prof., Univ. of Pittsburgh, Grad. S. of L. & Info. Sci., Pittsburgh, Pa. 15219; Mrs. Yolanda D. Federici, Supv., Work with Children, Central Dist., Chicago P L., 78 E. Washington, Chicago, Ill. 60602 (ALA Councilor).

PUBLICATION

Top of the News (q.; memb.)

COMMITTEE CHAIRMEN

Arbuthnot Honor Lecture. Mrs. Diane Chrisman, Coordinator, Work with Children, Buffalo & Erie County P.L., Lafayette Sq., Buffalo, N.Y. 14203.

Audiovisual: Subcommittee of Audiovisual-ALA. Mrs. Marilyn Berg Iarusso, Asst. Storytelling & Group Work Specialist, N.Y.P.L., 8 E. 40 St., New York, N.Y. 10016.

Mildred L. Batchelder Award Selection 1972. Rosemary Weber, Asst. Prof., Grad. S. of L. Sci., Drexel Univ., 33 & Lancaster Aves., Philadelphia, Pa. 19104.

Mildred L. Batchelder Award Selection 1973. Mrs. Clara Hulton, formerly Asst. Coordinator of Children's Servs., N.Y.P.L., 8 E. 40 St., New York, N.Y. 10016. (Mailing address: P.O. Box 461, Anthony, Fla. 32617.)

Book Evaluation. Mrs. Barbara Rollock, Children's Specialist, Bronx Borough Office, N.Y.P.L., 2555 Marion Ave., Bronx, N.Y. 10458.

Bookstores and Book Distributors, Liaison with. Anne C. Santangelo, Head, Children's Dept., White Plains P.L., 115 Grand Ave., White Plains, N.Y. 10601. (Mailing address: Amberlands 12-K, Albany Post Road, Croton-on-Hudson, N.Y. 10520.)

Boy Scouts of America Advisory. Herbert L. Leet, Dir., Southern Tier L. Syst., 114 Chestnut St., Corning, N.Y. 14830.

Children's Books in Relation to Radio and Television. Mrs. Augusta Baker, Coordinator, Children's Servs., N.Y.P.L., 8 E. 40 St., New York, N.Y. 10016.

Children's Books in Relation to Radio and Television: Bibliography Subcommittee. Naomi Noyes, Children's Specialist, N.Y.P.L., Manhattan Borough Office, 20 W. 53 St., New York, N.Y. 10019.

Collections, Special, National Planning of. Marian C. Young, Coordinator, Work with Children, Detroit P.L., 5201 Woodward Ave., Detroit, Mich. 48202.

Disadvantaged Child, Library Service to the. Mrs. Brooke E. Sheldon, Head, P.L. Devel., New Mexico State L., Box 1629, Santa Fe, N. Mex. 87501.

Exceptional Children, Library Service to. Harris C. McClaskey, Asst. Prof. of L. Sci., L.S., Coll. of Liberal Arts, Univ. of Minnesota, 3 Walter L., Minneapolis, Minn. 55455.

Film Award Proposal (Ad Hoc). Anne Pellowski, Dir., Info. Ctr. on Children's Cultures, U.S. Comm. for UNICEF, 331 E. 38 St., New York, N.Y. 10016.

Foreign Children's Books, Acquisition of (Ad Hoc). Anne Izard, Children's Servs. Consultant, Westchester L. Syst., 285 Central Ave., White Plains, N.Y. 10606.

Foreign Children's Books, Selection of. Angeline Moscatt, Supervising Libn., Donnell Regional L. Center, 20 W. 53 St., New York, N.Y. 10019.

International Relations: Subcommittee of International Relations — ALA. Mrs. Della Thomas, 217 N. Stallard, Stillwater, Okla. 74074.

Local Arrangements, Chicago, 1972. Florence Burmeister, Head, Young People's & Children's Dept., Skokie P.L., 5215 Oakton St., Skokie, Ill. 60076.

Magazine Evaluation. Mrs. Bertha P. Phillips, Coordinator of Children's Servs., Atlanta P.L., 126 Carnegie Way N.W., Atlanta, Ga. 30303.

Melcher Scholarship. Dr. Patricia J. Cianciolo, Prof., Michigan State Univ., 360 Erickson, East Lansing, Mich. 48823.

Newbery-Caldecott Awards. Anne R. Izard, Children's Servs. Consultant, Westchester L. Syst., 295 Central Ave., White Plains, N.Y. 10606.

Nominating Committee 1972 Election. Dr. Alice Brooks McGuire, Assoc. Prof., Grad. S. of L. Sci., Univ. of Texas, Austin, Tex. 78712.

Organization. Harriet B. Quimby, Asst. Prof., St. John's Univ., Grad. S., Dept. of L. Sci., Jamaica, N.Y. 11432.

Organizations Serving the Child, Liaison with. Mrs. Carolyn W. Field, Coord. of Work with Children, Free L. of Philadelphia, Logan Square, Philadelphia, Pa. 19103.

Patterns in Library Service to Children (Ad Hoc). Jane Botham, Children's

Servs. Consultant, Div. of L. Devel., New York State L., 99 Washington Ave., Albany, N.Y. 12210. (Mailing address: 105 Beverwyck Dr., Apt. 5, Guilderland, N.Y. 12084.)
Program Evaluation and Support. Anne R. Izard, Children's Servs. Consultant, Westchester L. Syst., 285 Central Ave., White Plains, N.Y. 10606.
Research and Development. Mrs. Priscilla L. Moulton, Dir. of S. L. Servs., Brookline P. Ss., Brookline, Mass. 02146. (Mailing address: 10 Pinecliff Dr., Marblehead, Mass. 01945.)
Right to Read (Ad Hoc). Bonnie Beth Mitchell, L. Devel. Consultant, Children's Servs., State L. of Ohio, 65 Front St., Columbus, Ohio 43215.
Charles Scribner's Sons Award 1972 (Ad Hoc). Florence Burmeister, Head, Young People's & Children's Dept., Skokie P.L., Skokie, Ill. 60076.

INFORMATION SCIENCE AND AUTOMATION DIVISION
50 East Huron Street, Chicago, Ill. 60611
312-944-6780

OBJECT

"Development and application of electronic data processing techniques and the use of automated systems in all areas of library work, and within this field fosters research, promotes the development of appropriate standards, disseminates information, and provides a forum for the discussion of common problems." Organized 1966. Memb. 4,731. (For dues and membership year, see ALA entry.)

OFFICERS (June 1971–June 1972)

Pres. Dr. Jesse H. Shera, S. of L. Sci., Case Western Reserve Univ., Cleveland, Ohio 44106; *V.P.* Ralph M. Shoffner, Head, Operations Task Force, Inst. of L. Research, Berkeley, Calif. 97420.
Exec. Secy. Don S. Culbertson.

DIRECTORS

The officers and Richard DeGennaro, Dir., Van Pelt L., Univ. of Pennsylvania, Philadelphia, Pa. 19104; Donald P. Hammer, Head, L. Systems Devel., Purdue Univ. Ls., Lafayette, Ind. 47909; Charles H. Stevens, Asst. Dir. for L. Devel., MIT, Cambridge, Mass. 02139; Richard S. Angell, Chief, Technical Processes, Research Office, L. of Congress, Washington, D.C. 20450; Paul Fasana, Preparations Servs., N.Y.P.L., New York, N.Y. 10019; Frederick G. Kilgour, Dir., OCLC, 1314 Kinnear Rd., Columbus, Ohio 43212.

PUBLICATIONS

Journal of Library Automation (q.; $15 per yr.; single copies, $3.50; back issues $10 per vol. Also sent as a prerequisite of membership in Information Science and Automation Division of ALA.)
Jola Technical Communications; newsletter (bi-mo.; $15 per yr.)

COMMITTEE CHAIRMEN

Character Set Escape Sequence Code. Paul Fasana, Preparations Servs., N.Y. P.L., New York, N.Y. 10019.
COLA Discussion Group. Don L. Bosseau, L. Syst. Analyst, Univ. of California L. at San Diego, La Jolla, Calif. 92037.
Conference Planning. Dr. Russell Shank, Dir. of Ls., Smithsonian Inst., Washington, D.C. 20560.
Editorial Board. A. J. Goldwyn, Prof., S. of L. Sci., Case Western Reserve Univ., Cleveland, Ohio 44106.
LED/ISAD Interdivisional Comm. on Education for Library Automation and Information Science. Mrs. Pauline Atherton, Assoc. Prof., S. of L. Sci., Syracuse Univ., Syracuse, N.Y. 13210.
Nominating. Dr. Wesley Simonton, L. S., Univ. of Minn., Minneapolis, Minn. 55455.
Telecommunications. Brigitte L. Kenney, Asst. Prof., Grad. S. of L. Sci., Drexel Univ., Philadelphia, Pa. 19104.
MARC Users Discussion Group. Frederick G. Kilgour, Dir., OCLC, 1314 Kinnear Rd., Columbus, Ohio 43212.

LIBRARY ADMINISTRATION DIVISION
50 East Huron Street, Chicago, Ill. 60611
312-944-6780

OBJECT

"To guide and to conduct the activities of the ALA which pertain to library administration in general." Established 1957. Memb. 5,095. (For dues and membership year, see ALA entry.)

OFFICERS (June 1971–June 1972)

Pres. Lester L. Stoffel, Exec. Dir., Suburban L. Syst., Hinsdale, Ill. 60521; *V.P. & Pres. Elect.* Grace P. Slocum, Asst. Dir., Enoch Pratt Free L., Baltimore, Md. 21201; *Past Pres.* James H. Richards, Jr., Dir., Univ. of Wyoming Ls., Laramie, Wyo. 82070.

Exec. Secy. Mrs. Ruth R. Frame.

DIRECTORS

The officers, section chairmen, section vice-chairmen, and Robert F. Delzell, Dir. of Personnel, Univ. of Illinois L., Urbana, Ill. 61801; Lawrence J. Downey, Personnel Coord., Indianapolis-Marion County P.L., Indianapolis, Ind. 46204; David R. Smith, Dir., Hennepin County L., Minneapolis, Minn. 55401.

SECTION CHAIRMEN

Buildings and Equipment. John H. Rebenack, Libn., Akron P.L., Akron, Ohio 44308; *Vice-Chairman.* M. Joan Woodruff, Dir., Learning Resources, Monroe County Community Coll., Monroe, Mich. 48161.

Circulations Services (Acting). Edward B. Hayward, Dir., Hammond P.L., Hammond, Ind. 46320.

Library Organization and Management. Henry G. Shearouse, Jr., Libn., Denver P.L., Denver, Colo. 80203; *Vice-Chairman.* Luella R. Pollock, Libn., Reed Coll., Portland, Ore. 97202.

Personnel Administration. Peter Spyers-Duran, Dir., Florida Atlantic Univ. Ls., Boca Raton, Fla. 33432; *Vice-Chairman.* Mrs. Frances Henselman, City Libn., Long Beach P.L., Long Beach, Calif. 90802.

Public Relations. Mrs. Betty P. Rice, P.R. Consultant, 2 Middle Lane, Westbury, N.Y. 11590; *Vice-Chairman.* Verna R. Nistendirk, Dir., L. Syst., Leon County P.L., Tallahassee, Fla. 32302.

COMMITTEE CHAIRMEN

Local Public Library Administration, Adv. Comm. for Rev. of (Ad Hoc). Gary E. Strong, Dir., Lake Oswego P.L., Lake Oswego, Ore. 97034.

Nominating. Mary Frances Borden, Asst. Dir., Tacoma P.L., Tacoma, Wash. 98402.

Organization. Julius R. Chitwood, Dir., Rockford P.L., Rockford, Ill. 61101.

Small Libraries Publications. Helen M. Miller, Libn., Idaho State L., Boise, Idaho 83706.

LIBRARY EDUCATION DIVISION
50 East Huron Street, Chicago, Ill. 60611
312-944-6780

OBJECT

"Specific responsibility for continuous study and review of changing needs for library education, development of educational programs, and continuing education of library personnel; conduct of activities and projects within its areas of responsibility; synthesis of the consideration by library educators and practicing librarians of education for librarianship; representation and interpretation of library education in contact with other educational groups; stimulation of the development of librarians engaged in its type of activity, and stimulation of participation by members in appropriate type-of-library divisions; planning and development of programs of study and research which will improve and extend library education for the total profession; identifying materials needed in library education and promoting their preparation, publication, evaluation, dissemination and use." Established 1946. Memb. 2,650. (For dues and membership year, see ALA entry.)

MEMBERSHIP

Any member of the ALA interested in the object of this Division may become a member.

OFFICERS (June 1971–June 1972)

Pres. Genevieve M. Casey, Dept. of L.S., Wayne State Univ., Detroit, Mich. 48202; Recording Secy. Jean L. Connor, Div. of L. Devel., New York State L., Albany, N.Y. 12224.
Exec. Secy. Delores K. Vaughan.

DIRECTORS

The officers and Martha T. Boaz, S. of L. Sci., Univ. of Southern California, Los Angeles, Calif. 90007; Cora Paul Bomar, S. of Educ., Univ. of North Carolina, Greensboro, N.C. 27412; Mrs. Hallie B. Brooks, S. of L. Serv., Atlanta Univ., Atlanta, Ga. 30314; Robert M. Pierson, McKeldin L., Univ., of Maryland, College Park, Md. 20742; Thomas P. Slavens, S. of L. Sci., Univ. of Michigan, Ann Arbor, Mich., 48104. Melvin J. Voigt, Univ. of California, San Diego, La Jolla, Calif. 92037; Frank B. Sessa, Grad. S. of L. & Info. Scis., Univ. of Pittsburgh, Pittsburgh, Pa. 15213.

PUBLICATION

LED Newsletter (q.; memb.)

SECTION CHAIRMEN

Teachers. Nicholas G. Stevens, Dept. of L.S., Kutztown State Coll., Kutztown, Pa. 19530.

DISCUSSION GROUP CHAIRMAN

Discussion Group for Librarians of Library Science Collections. Mrs. Doris H. Asher, S. of L. Sci., Univ. of Michigan, Ann Arbor, Mich. 48104.

COMMITTEE CHAIRMEN

Beta Phi Mu Awards. Mrs. Clara O. Jackson, S. of L. Sci., Kent State Univ., Kent, Ohio 44240.
Education for Library Associates. Dorothy E. Ryan, Grad. S. of L. & Info. Sci., Univ. of Tennessee, Knoxville, Tenn. 37915.
Equivalencies & Reciprocity. Norman Horrocks, S. of L. Serv., Dalhousie Univ., Halifax, N.S., Canada.
Financial Assistance for Library Education. Revision. Miss Cosette Kies, The Ferguson L., Stamford, Conn. 06901.
International Library School. Guy A. Marco, S. of L. Sci., Kent State Univ., Kent, Ohio 44240.
LED/AHIL Interdivisional Committee on Education for Hospital and Institution Librarianship. Harris C. McClaskey, L.S., Univ. of Minnesota, Minneapolis, Minn. 55455.
Nominating. Sister Lauretta McCusker, S. of L. Sci., Rosary Coll., River Forest, Ill. 60305.
Organization & Activities. Cora Paul Bomar, S. of Educ., Univ. of North Carolina, Greensboro, N.C. 27412.
Publications. Eileen Noonan, Grad. S. of L. Sci., Rosary Coll., River Forest, Ill. 60305.
Research. Ray L. Carpenter, S. of L. Sci., Univ. of North Carolina, Chapel Hill, N.C. 27514.
Role of ALA in Library Education (Ad Hoc). Martha T. Boaz, S. of L. Sci., Univ. of Southern California, Los Angeles, Calif. 90007.
Scholarship & Awards. Martin Cohen, S. of Libnshp., Western Michigan Univ., Kalamazoo, Mich. 49001.
Training Programs for Supportive Library Staff. Miss Dorothy F. Deininger, Grad. S. of L. Sci., Rutgers Univ., New Brunswick, N.J. 08903.

PUBLIC LIBRARY ASSOCIATION
(A Division of the American Library Association)
50 East Huron Street, Chicago, Ill. 60611
312-944-6780

OBJECT

"To provide for the exchange of ideas and experience, and to stimulate continued professional growth, to improve and extend public library services, to raise library standards, to secure adequate support for libraries and to cooperate in the promotion of library service generally." Organized 1951. Memb. 10,727. (For dues and membership year, see ALA entry.)

MEMBERSHIP

Open to all ALA members interested in the improvement and expansion of public library services to all ages in various types of communities.

OFFICERS (June 1971–June 1972)

Pres. Effie Lee Morris, P.L., San Francisco, Calif. 94102; *V.P. & Pres. Elect.* David Henington, P.L., Houston, Tex. 77002; *Past Pres.* Andrew Geddes, Nassau L. Syst., Garden City, N.Y. 11530. *Exec. Secy.* Gerald M. Born.

DIRECTORS

The officers, past president, section president, and R. Paul Bartolini, Lake Co. P.L., Crown Point, Ind. 46307; William S. Geller, Los Angeles Co. P.L., Los Angeles, Calif. 90053; Jane S. McClure, Free P.L., Summit, N.J. 07901; Orin M. Moyer, Edwards AFB, Calif. 93523; Richard Parsons, Baltimore P.L., Towson, Md. 21204; Mary E. Phillips, L. Assn. of Portland, Ore. 97205; Donald E. Wright, Evanston P.L., Evanston, Ill. 60201; M. Eugene Wright, Jr., P.L., New Orleans, La. 70053; Josephine N. Neil, Hq. 6th Naval Dist., U.S. Naval Base, Charleston, S.C. 29408; Mrs. Alice Ihrig, Oak Lawn, Ill. 60453; Howard R. Downey, P.L., Bellingham, Wash. 98225.

PUBLICATIONS

PLA Newsletter; newsletter to members (2 times a yr.)

SECTION PRESIDENT

Robert W. Severance, Air Univ. L., Maxwell AFB, Ala. 36112.

COMMITTEE CHAIRMEN

Audiovisual. Mrs. B. Penny Northern, Film Dept., P.L., Kansas City, Mo. 64106.
Bylaws. Ruth Gregory, P.L., Waukegan, Ill. 60085.
Costs of Public Library Services. Christopher B. Devan, Cuyahoga County P.L., Cleveland, Ohio 44144.
Editorial. Marvin M. Scilken, P.L., Orange, N.J. 07050.
Interim Standards Revision. Mrs. Barbara O. Slanker, Illinois State L., Springfield, Ill. 62706.
Interlibrary Cooperation. Gilbert McNamee, P.L., San Francisco, Calif. 94102.
Legislation. Arthur Curley, P.L., Montclair, N.J. 07042.
Metropolitan Area Library Service. Alex Ladenson, P.L., Chicago, Ill. 60602.
Nominating. William S. Geller, Los Angeles County P.L., Los Angeles, Calif. 90053.
Public Library Activities. Hank J. Blasick, State L., Supreme Court Bldg., Tallahassee, Fla. 32304.
Public Libraries Study. Milton S. Byam, St. John's Univ., Dept. of L. Sci., Jamaica, N.Y. 11432.
Registration of Libraries. James H. Pickering, Warder P.L., Springfield, Ohio 45502.
Service to Children. Spencer Shaw, S. of Libnshp., Univ. of Washington, Seattle, Wash. 98105.
Standards. Miss Rose Vainstein, S. of L. Sci., Univ. of Michigan, Ann Arbor, Mich. 48104.
Starter List of New Branch Library. Nolan Lushington, Greenwich L., Greenwich, Conn. 06830.

REFERENCE SERVICES DIVISION
50 East Huron Street, Chicago, Ill. 60611
312-944-6780

OBJECT

"The improvement and extension of the informational, bibliographical, and research activities in all types of libraries, at all levels and in every subject field; reference materials—their production, listing, and evaluation; inquiries and inquirers—their identification, classification, and appraisal; indexes and indexing—their extension and improvement; bibliographies and bibliographic method—their place and development in scholarly investigations." Organized 1956. Memb. 6,966. (For dues and membership year, see ALA entry.)

OFFICERS (June 1971–June 1972)

Pres. Donald A. Riechmann, Albuquerque P.L., Albuquerque, N.Mex. 87101; *V.P. & Pres. Elect.* Mrs. Thelma K. Freides, S. of L. Sci., Atlanta Univ., Atlanta, Ga. 30314; *2nd V.P.* James B. Woy, Free L. of Philadelphia, Philadelphia, Pa. 19107.

Exec. Secy. Andrew M. Hansen.

DIRECTORS

The officers and Mary Jo Lynch, S. of L. Sci., Univ. of Michigan, Ann Arbor, Mich. 48104; Roger C. Greer, S. of L. Sci., Syracuse Univ., Syracuse, N.Y. 13210; Thomas P. Slavens, S. of L. Sci., Univ. of Michigan, Ann Arbor, Mich. 48104; John Fall, Public Affairs Information Service, Inc., New York, N.Y. 10018; Irene Christopher, 790 Boylston St., Apt. 9A, Boston, Mass. 02199; Gary R. Purcell, S. of L. & Info. Sci., Univ. of Tennessee, Knoxville, Tenn. 37916; Shirley M. Shisler, Des Moines P.L., Des Moines, Iowa 50309; Robert J. Adelsperger, Univ. of Illinois, Chicago Circle, Chicago, Ill. 60680; William A. Katz, L. S., State Univ. of New York, Albany, N.Y. 12203.

PUBLICATION

R.Q. (q.; memb.). Single copies, $3.

SECTION CHAIRMAN

History. Robert J. Adelsperger, Univ. of Illinois, Chicago Circle, Chicago, Ill. 60680.

COMMITTEE CHAIRMEN

Affiliates, Division. Richard L. Waters, Dallas P.L., Dallas, Tex. 75201.

Archives. Elizabeth Jane Highfield, North Park Coll. L., Chicago, Ill. 60625.

Bibliography. Roger C. Greer, S. of L. Sci., Syracuse Univ., Syracuse, N.Y. 13210.

Business Reference Services. James B. Woy, Free L. of Philadelphia, Philadelphia, Pa. 19107.

Catalog Use. Concetta Sacco, P.L., West Haven, Conn. 06516.

Census Bureau Advisory Subcommittee. Clifford Crowers, Free L. of Philadelphia, Philadelphia, Pa. 19103.

Common Concerns, RSD/ASD. To be appointed.

Conference Services (Chicago). Mrs. Yuri Nakata, Univ. of Illinois, Circle Campus L., Chicago, Ill. 60680.

Cooperative Reference Services. George Bailey, Claremont Coll. L., Claremont, Calif. 91711.

Information Retrieval. John M. Morgan, Univ. of Toledo L., Toledo, Ohio 43606.

Interlibrary Loan. Sarah K. Thomson, Bergen Community Coll., Paramus, N.J. 07652.

Library Journal List of Reference Books. Gary R. Purcell, Univ. of Tennessee, Grad. S. of L. & Info. Sci., Knoxville, Tenn. 37916.

Isadore Gilbert Mudge Citation. Walter Allen, Grad. S. of L. Sci., Univ. of Illinois, Urbana, Ill. 61801.

New Reference Tools. Hobart Berolzheimer, Free L. of Philadelphia, Philadelphia, Pa. 19103.

Nominating. Phoebe Hayes, Bibliographic Center for Research, Denver, Colo. 80203.

Organization and Activities. James B. Woy, Free L. of Philadelphia, Philadelphia, Pa. 19103.

Orientation, ASD/RSD. To be appointed.

Public Documents, RSD/RTSD. Mrs. Joyce Ball, Univ. of Nevada L., Reno, Nev. 89507.

Publications. Charles R. Andrews, Case Western Reserve Univ. L., Cleveland, Ohio 44106.

Reference Books for Small- and Medium-Sized Public Libraries, Review (Ad Hoc). Charles Andrews, Case Western Reserve Univ. L., Cleveland, Ohio 44106.

Science and Technology Reference Services. Cynthia Steinke, Univ. of Illinois, Chicago, Ill. 60680.

Standards. Robert Klassen, Bureau of Ls. & Educational Tech. Research & Program Devel. Branch, USOE, Washington, D.C. 20202.

Users Needs (ad hoc). Thomas W. Shaughnessy, Grad. S. of L. Sci., Rutgers Univ., New Brunswick, N.J. 08900.

Wilson Indexes. Ruth Grotheer, Nassau L. Syst., Garden City, N.Y. 11530.

RESOURCES AND TECHNICAL SERVICES DIVISION
50 East Huron Street, Chicago, Ill. 60611
312-944-6780

OBJECT

"Responsible for the following activities: acquisition, identification, cataloging, classification, reproduction, and preservation of library materials; and the development and coordination of the country's library resources. Any member of the American Library Association may elect membership in this Division according to the provisions of the Bylaws." Established 1957. Memb. 8,723. (For dues and membership year, see ALA entry.)

OFFICERS (June 1971–June 1972)

Pres. Barbara M. Westby, Catalog Management Div., L. of Congress, Washington, D.C. 20540; *V.P. & Pres. Elect.* Mrs. Connie R. Dunlap, 820 Hatcher, Grad. L., Univ. of Michigan, Ann Arbor, Mich. 48104; *Chairman, Council of Regional Groups.* Carol F. Ishimoto, Harvard Coll. L., Cambridge, Mass. 02138; *Past Pres.* C. Donald Cook, Dir., Office of L. Coordination, Council of Ontario Univs., 102 Bloor St. W., Toronto 181, Ontario, Canada.

Exec. Secy. Mrs. Carol Raney Kelm.

DIRECTORS

The officers, section chairmen and Ashby J. Fristoe, Grad. Research L., Univ. of Hawaii, 2550 The Mall, Honolulu, Hawaii 96822; Maurice E. Lapierre, 2649 E. 111 St., Cleveland, Ohio 44104; Joseph A. Rosenthal, Assoc. Libn., General L. 248, Univ. of California, Berkeley, Calif. 94720; Mrs. Luella B. Higley, City Independent S. Dist., Fort Worth Public Ss., Fort Worth, Tex. 76107; Robert Wedgeworth, Grad. S. of L. Serv., Rutgers State Univ., 189 College Ave., New Brunswick, N.J. 08903; Marietta Chicorel, Chicorel Library Publishing Co., 330 W. 58 St., New York, N.Y. 10019; Paul J. Fasana, Preparations Services, New York Public Library, New York, N.Y. 10027; Richard Loreck, Univ. of Wisconsin-Milwaukee L., 2311 E. Hartford Ave., Milwaukee, Wis. 53201; C. Sumner Spalding, Processing Dept., L. of Congress, Washington, D.C. 20540; Joseph Treyz, Memorial L., Univ. of Wisconsin, Madison, Wis. 53706; Allen B. Veaner, Stanford Univ., Main L., Stanford, Calif. 94305.

PUBLICATION

Library Resources and Technical Services. (q.; memb. or $8.00)

SECTION CHAIRMEN

Acquisitions. Norman H. Dudley, Univ. Research L., Univ. of California, Los Angeles, Calif. 90024.

Cataloging & Classification. Barbara A. Gates, Oberlin Coll. L., Oberlin, Ohio 44074.

ASSOCIATIONS AND AGENCIES / 385

Reproduction of Library Materials. Howard Cordell, Florida International Univ., Tamiami Trail, Miami, Fla. 33144.
Serials. Edmund G. Hamann, Catalog Maintenance Dept., Cornell Univ. Ls., Ithaca, N.Y. 19850.

COMMITTEE CHAIRMEN

Association of American Publishers/ RTSD Joint Committee. Warren B. Kuhn, Dir. of the L., Iowa State Univ., Ames, Iowa 50010; Carl B. Hansen, Asst. Dir., Columbia Univ. Press, 562 W. 113 St., New York, N.Y. 10025.
Book Catalogs Committee. Joseph A. Rosenthal, Assoc. Libn., General L. 248, Univ. of California, Berkeley, Calif. 94720.
Bylaws Committee. William C. Roselle, Dir. of the L., Univ. of Wisconsin-Milwaukee, Milwaukee, Wis. 53201.
Commercial Processing Services Committee. Mrs. Abigail Dahl-Hansen, Asst. Univ. Libn., Univ. of California, Riverside, Calif. 92507.
Conference Program Committee. Barbara M. Westby, Catalog Management Div., L. of Congress, Washington, D.C. 20540.
International Relations. George M. Jenks, Ellen Clarke Bertrand L., Bucknell Univ., Lewisburg, Pa. 17837.
Legislation Committee. Mrs. Elizabeth G. Ellis, W106 Pattee L., Pennsylvania State Univ., University Park, Pa. 16802.
New Directions for RTSD (AHONDA) (Ad Hoc). Glen A. Zimmerman, L. of Congress, Descriptive Cataloging Div., Washington, D.C. 20540.
Nominating. Mrs. Annette L. Phinazee, S. of L. Sci., North Carolina Central Univ., Durham, N.C. 27707.
Organization. C. Donald Cook, Dir., Office of L. Coordination, Council of Ontario Univs., 102 Bloor St. W., Toronto 181, Ont., Canada.
Piercy Award Jury. Mrs. Roma S. Gregory, Univ. of Rochester, Rochester, N.Y. 14627.
Planning. Richard L. Darling, S. of L. Serv., Columbia Univ., 516 Butler, New York, N.Y. 10027.
Preservation of Library Materials. Matt T. Roberts, Binding Officer, L. of Congress, Washington, D.C. 20540.
Program Evaluation and Support. Barbara M. Westby, Catalog Management Div., L. of Congress, Washington, D.C. 20540.
Public Documents (RSD/RTSD). Mrs. Joyce Ball, Reference Dept., Univ. of Nevada L., Reno, Nev. 89507.
Public Documents; Census Bureau Advisory Subcommittee. Clifford P. Crowers, Free L. of Philadelphia, Philadelphia, Pa. 19103.
Resources. James W. Henderson, N.Y. P.L., Fifth Ave. & 42 St., New York, N.Y. 10018.
Resources; Micropublishing Projects Subcommittee. Hendrik Edelman, Asst. Dir. for Devel. of the Collections, Cornell Univ., Ithaca, N.Y. 14850.
Resources; National Union Catalog Subcommittee. Gordon R. Williams, Center for Research Ls., 5721 Cottage Grove Ave., Chicago, Ill. 60637.
Technical Services Costs. George Shipman, Univ. of Tennessee L., Knoxville, Tenn. 37916.

YOUNG ADULT SERVICES DIVISION
50 East Huron Street, Chicago, Ill. 60611
312-944-6780

OBJECT

"Interested in the improvement and extension of services to young people in all types of libraries; has specific responsibility for the evaluation, selection, interpretation and use of books and non-book materials for young adults except when such materials are intended for only one type of library." Established 1957. Memb. 6,716. (For dues and membership year, see ALA entry.)

MEMBERSHIP

Open to anyone interested in library services to young adults.

OFFICERS (June 1971–June 1972)

Pres. Jane Manthorne, Coord., Young Adult Serv., Boston P.L., Copley Sq., Boston, Mass. 02117; *V.P. & Pres. Elect.* Thomas Alford, L. Dir., Benton Harbor P.L., 213 E. Wall St., Benton Harbor, Mich. 49022; *2nd V.P.* Reed Coats, Young Adult Coord., Camino Real L. Syst., 180 W. San Carlos St., San Jose, Calif. 95113; *Past Pres.* Mrs. Mary Ann Hanna, Head S. L. Consultant, Michigan Dept. of Educ., Bureau of L. Serv., Lansing, Mich. 48913.
Exec. Secy. Ruth W. Tarbox.

DIRECTORS

The officers and Mrs. Mary L. Pickett, Libn.-in-Charge, Atkinson L., 1960 W. Atkinson Ave., Milwaukee, Wis. 53209; Anne Kincaid, Coord. of Adult Serv., San Francisco Civic Center L., San Francisco, Calif. 94102 (ALA Councilor); Jane D. Strebel, Consultant, L. Serv., Minneapolis P. Ss., S. Admin. Bldg., 807 N.E. Broadway, Minneapolis, Minn. 55413; Mrs. Patricia Pond, Asst. Prof., S. of Libnshp., Univ. of Oregon, Eugene, Ore. 97405 (ALA Councilor); Mrs. Mary M. Spradling, Head, Young Adult Dept., P.L., Kalamazoo, Mich. 49001 (ALA Councilor); Linda F. Lapides, Asst. Coord., Work with Young Adults, Enoch Pratt Free L., 400 Cathedral St., Baltimore, Md. 21201; Mrs. Helen W. Cyr, Dir. of Instructional Media, Oakland Public Ss., 1025 Second Ave., Oakland, Calif. 94606 (ALA Councilor).

PUBLICATION

Top of the News (q.; memb.)

COMMITTEES

Activities. Thomas Alford, L. Dir., Benton Harbor P.L., 213 E. Wall St., Benton Harbor, Mich. 49022.
Audiovisual: Subcommittee of Audiovisual—ALA. Robert E. Barron, S.-P.L. Liaison, Div. of L. Devel., New York State L., Albany, N.Y. (Mailing address: 142 Stonington Hill Rd., Voorheesville, N.Y. 12186.)
Best Books for Young Adults. Eileen E. Burgess, Asst. Coord., Young Adult Servs., Prince George's County Memorial L., 6532 Adelphi Rd., Hyattsville, Md. 20782.
Bylaws. Freddy Schader, Administrative Asst. & Elem. S. L. Consultant, Arkansas L. Comm., 506½ Center St., Little Rock, Ark. 72201.
Drug Information, Exploratory YASD Task Force on (Ad Hoc). Donald L. Roberts, Asst. Prof., S. of Info. & L. Studies, State Univ. of New York at Buffalo, Hayes C, Rm. 5, Buffalo, N.Y. 14223.
Local Arrangements, Chicago, 1972. Blanche Janecek, Head Libn., H.S. Laboratory Ss., Univ. of Chicago, Chicago, Ill. 60637. (Mailing address: 1150 Lake Shore Dr., Chicago, Ill. 60611.)
Magazine Evaluation. Raymond W. Barber, Coord., Educational Media, Asst. Prof., Kent State Univ., Kent, Ohio 44242. (Mailing address: 819 Saxon Ave., Akron, Ohio 44314.)
Nominating—1972 Election. A. Michael Deller, Head of Programming, Bloomfield Township P.L., 1099 Lone Pine Rd., Bloomfield Hills, Mich. 48013.
Organization. Julia Losinski, Young Adult Servs. Coord., Prince George's County Memorial L., 6532 Adelphi Rd., Hyattsville, Md. 20782.
Outreach Programs for Young Adults (Ad Hoc). Reed Coats, Young Adult Coord., Camino Real Regional L. Syst., 180 W. San Carlos St., San Jose, Calif. 95113.
Program and Budget Development. Thomas Alford, L. Dir., Benton Harbor P.L., 213 E. Wall St., Benton Harbor, Mich. 49022.
Publishers' Relations. Mrs. Jacqueline A Rollins, Young Adult Servs. Consultant, Westchester L. Syst., 285 Central Ave., White Plains, N.Y. 10606. (Mailing address: 224 Coach Light Square-on-Hudson, Montrose, N.Y. 10548.)
Research. James W. Liesener, Assoc. Prof., S. of L. & Info. Servs., Univ. of Maryland, College Park, Md. 20742. (Mailing address: 1906 Dana Dr., Adelphi, Md. 20783.)
Selection of Books and Other Materials. Mrs. Elizabeth Morse O'Donnell, Young Adult Specialist, Contra Costa

County L., 1750 Oak Park Blvd., Pleasant Hill, Calif. 94523.
Television. Mrs. Penelope Stiffler Jeffrey, Group Work Specialist, Office of Young Adult Servs., N.Y.P.L., 8 E. 40 St., New York, N.Y. 10016. (Mailing address: 2025 Continental Ave., 7-E, Bronx, N.Y. 10461.)

AMERICAN MERCHANT MARINE LIBRARY ASSOCIATION
1 Bowling Green, New York, N. Y. 10004
212-269-0220

OBJECT

"To maintain a library service for the free use of the officers and crews of American merchant vessels." Founded 1921. Memb. 4,560. Annual membership dues $5. Year. Jan.–Dec.

OFFICERS

Chairman of the Board. Mrs. George Emlen Roosevelt; *Chairman of the Exec. Comm. & V.P.* George M. Paduano; *Pres.* W. T. Moore; *V.P.* Robert Stone, Jr.; *Treas.* Hon. James C. Kellogg, III; *Asst. Treas.* Raymond V. O'Brien, David T. McGarry, Edward J. Burke.
Exec. Secy. Charles S. Francis.

PUBLICATION

Annual Report.

TRUSTEES

Joseph Andreae, Sherman, Conn.; Ralph R. Bagley, Boston Port & Seaman's Aid Society, New York; Capt. Hewlett R. Bishop, Exec. V.P., National Cargo Bureau, Inc., New York, N.Y.; Ralph E. Casey, Chief Counsel, Comm. on Merchant Marine & Fisheries, U.S. House of Representatives, Washington, D.C.; Charles M. Clark, Jr., Dir., Dun & Bradstreet, New York, N.Y.; Worth B. Fowler, Chairman of the Board, American Mail Lines, Ltd., Seattle, Wash.; Hon. Andrew B. Gibson, Asst. Secy. of Commerce for Maritime Affairs, Washington, D.C.; Rear Adm. John Harllee, USN (Rct.), Front Royal, Va.; Hon. James C. Kellogg, III, Chairman, Port of New York Authority, New York, N.Y.; Charles Kurz, Pres., Keystone Shipping Co., Philadelphia, Pa.; Jack Mace, Exec. Secy., Hampton Roads Maritime Assn., Norfolk, Va.; Carl E. McDowell, Chairman, Seamen's Service Comm., New York, N.Y.; Mrs. Henry D. Mercer, New York, N.Y.; W. T. Moore, Chairman, Exec. Comm., Moore & McCormack Co., Inc., New York, N.Y.; Clarence G. Morse, Proctor in Admiralty, San Francisco, Calif.; Raymond V. O'Brien, Jr., V.P., Chase Manhattan Bank, New York, N.Y.; George M. Paduano, Regional Dir., Public Buildings Serv., General Servs. Admin., New York, N.Y.; Mrs. George Emlen Roosevelt, New York, N.Y.; H. G. Schad, Jenkintown, Pa.; Philip Steinberg, Regional V.P., American Institute of Merchant Shipping, San Francisco, Calif.; Robert G. Stone, Jr., Pres., States Marine-International, Stamford, Conn.; Vice Adm. Paul E. Trimble, USCG (Rct.), Pres., Lake Carriers Assn., Cleveland, Ohio; Solon B. Turman, Chairman of the Exec. Comm., Lykes Bros. Steamship Co., New Orleans, La.

AMERICAN SOCIETY FOR INFORMATION SCIENCE
1140 Connecticut Avenue, N.W., Suite 804, Washington, D.C. 20036
202-659-3644

OBJECT

"The American Society for Information Science is a nonprofit professional association organized for scientific, literary, and educational purposes, and dedicated to the creation, organization, dissemination, and application of knowledge concerning information and its transfer." Founded 1937 as the American Documentation Institute. Memb. (Indiv.) 3,300; (Student) 385; (Inst.) 51. Dues. (Indiv.) $25; (Student) $10;

(Inst.) Nonprofit $200, Profit $300. Year. Jan. 1972–Dec. 1972.

OFFICERS (Nov. 1971–Oct. 1972)

Pres. Robert J. Kyle, Emory Univ., Atlanta, Ga. 30322; *Pres. Elect.* John Sherrod, National Agricultural L., Beltsville, Md. 20250; *Past Pres.* Mrs. Pauline Atherton, Syracuse Univ., Syracuse, N.Y. 13210; *Secy.* Mrs. Lois F. Lunin, Johns Hopkins Medical Institutions, Baltimore, Md.; *Treas.* Oliver H. Buchanan, Pratt Institute, Brooklyn, N.Y. 11205; *Editor.* Arthur W. Elias, 3I/Information Interscience, Inc., Philadelphia, Pa.
Exec. Dir. Herbert R. Koller.

COUNCIL

The officers and Dale B. Baker, Chemical Abstracts Serv.; F. Kennett Broome, Abbott Labs., Chicago, Ill.; Paul J. Fasana, N.Y.P.L.; Mrs. Margaret T. Fischer, Time, Inc.; Edward M. Housman, General Telephone & Electronics Labs., New York, N.Y.; Ben-Ami Lipetz, Yale Univ., New Haven, Conn.; Tefco Saracevic, Case Western Reserve Univ., Cleveland, Ohio; Martha E. Williams, Illinois Institute of Technology.

PUBLICATIONS

Annual Review of Information Science & Technology (Vol. 1, 1966, Vol. 2, 1967, Vol. 3, 1968: $15.00 each, memb. $12.75; Vol. 4, 1969: $16.00, memb. $13.60; Vol. 5, 1970: $17.50, memb. $14.87; Vol. 6, 1971: $17.50, memb. $14.87).
Handbook & Directory (annual; memb. or $25)
Information Science Abstracts; formerly *Documentation Abstracts* (bi-mo.; $40; memb. of sponsoring society $25)
Journal of the American Society for Information Science; formerly *American Documentation* (bi-mo.; memb. or $35 domestic, $40 foreign)
Newsletter (bi-mo.; memb.)
Proceedings of the ASIS Annual Meetings (prices upon request)
Directory of Educational Programs in Information Science (1971–1972: $5.00, memb. $4.50.)

COMMITTEE CHAIRMEN

Budget & Finance. Oliver H. Buchanan, Pratt Institute, Brooklyn, N.Y.
Conferences & Meetings. Gerard O. Platau, Chemical Abstracts Serv., Columbus, Ohio.
Constitution & Bylaws. William N. Locke, MIT, Cambridge, Mass.
Education. Victor Rosenberg, Univ. of California, Berkeley, Calif.
Executive. Robert J. Kyle, Emory Univ., Atlanta, Ga.
Liaison. Lois F. Lunin, Johns Hopkins Medical Institutions, Baltimore, Md.
Membership. Stella Keenan, National Fed. of Science Abstracting & Indexing Servs., Philadelphia, Pa.
Nominations. John Sherrod, National Agricultural L., Beltsville, Md.
Proprietary Use/Rights. Ben H. Weil, Esso Research & Engineering Co., Linden, N.J.
Publications. Joseph H. Kuney, American Chemical Society, Washington, D.C.
Standards. Charles P. Bourne, Charles Bourne & Associates, Menlo Park, Calif.

AMERICAN SOCIETY OF INDEXERS

OBJECTIVES

"To improve the quality of indexing and to secure useful standards for the field; to act as an advisory body on the qualification and remuneration of indexers to which authors, editors, publishers and others may apply for guidance; to issue from time to time books, articles, and other material on the subject of indexing and to cooperate with other societies and organizations in such publication; to defend and safeguard the professional interests of indexers; to cooperate with other societies and organizations in the fields of indexing and information science and especially with The Society of Indexers (Great Britain)." Dues. (Indiv.) $10; (Inst.) $100.

OFFICERS (April 1971–April 1972)

Pres. John Fall, Public Affairs Information Service, 11 W. 40 St., New York, N.Y. 10018; *V.P.* Mrs. Barbara M.

Preschel, 400 E. 56 St., New York, N.Y. 10022; *Secy.* Mrs. Marlene Hurst, University Microfilms, 300 N. Zeeb Rd., Ann Arbor, Mich. 48106; *Corres. Secy.* Alan R. Greengrass, The New York Times Index, Rm. 1285, 229 W. 43 St., New York, N.Y. 10036; *Treas.* Philip Deemer, Jarrow Press, Inc., 1556 Third Ave., New York, N.Y. 10028; *Past Pres.* Mrs. Eleanor Steiner-Prag, 125 Christopher St., New York, N.Y. 10014.

(Note: Address all general correspondence to Mrs. Marlene Hurst, Secretary.)

DIRECTORS

Robert Palmer, 15 W. 11 St., New York, N.Y. 10011; Dr. Maurice F. Tauber, S. of L. Serv., Columbia Univ., New York, N.Y. 10027; Dr. Theodore Hines, 54 North Dr., East Brunswick, N.J. 08816; Dr. Charles L. Bernier, 1088 Delaware Ave., Buffalo, N.Y. 14209; Mrs. Anne J. Richter, 222 Valley Rd., Montclair, N.J. 07042.

PUBLICATIONS

The Indexer; journal of the Society of Indexers, London, Eng. (2 issues, free to memb.)

ASI Newsletter (2 issues, free to memb.)

Membership List (free to memb.)

Guidelines (as issued, free to memb.)

COMMITTEE CHAIRMEN

American Contributions to The Indexer. Prof. Jessica L. Harris, S. of L. Serv., Columbia Univ., New York, N.Y. 10027.

Chapters and Regional Meetings. Mrs. Eleanor Steiner-Prag, 125 Christopher St., New York, N.Y. 10014.

Constitution and Bylaws. Harold L. Roth, Nassau County Reference L., Firehouse Lane, Garden City, N.Y. 11530.

Council of National Library Associations. Mrs. Eleanor Steiner-Prag, representative, 125 Christopher St., New York, N.Y. 10014.

Ethics, Standards & Specifications. Prof. Jessica L. Harris, S. of L. Serv., Columbia Univ., New York, N.Y. 10027.

Honors. Jane Stevens, The H. W. Wilson Co., 950 University Ave., Bronx, N.Y. 10452.

Index Users. Mrs. Barbara S. Marks, Educ. L., New York Univ., 4 Washington Place, New York, N.Y. 10003.

Indexer Finances. Alan R. Greengrass, The New York Times Index, Rm. 1285, 229 W. 43 St., New York, N.Y. 10036.

Indexer Qualifications for the Register. Mrs. Barbara M. Preschel, 400 E. 56 St., New York, N.Y. 10022.

Membership. Mrs. Marlene Hurst, University Microfilms, 300 N. Zeeb Rd., Ann Arbor, Mich. 48106.

Nominating. George F. Heise, The H. W. Wilson Co., 950 University Ave., Bronx, N.Y. 10452.

Organization, Affiliations & Correspondents. Raymond Hamilton, Ray Editorial Servs., 205 W. 95 St., New York, N.Y. 10025.

Program. Mrs. Barbara M. Preschel, 400 E. 56 St., New York, N.Y. 10022.

Publications. Alan Greengrass, New York Times Index, Rm. 1285, 229 W. 43 St., New York, N.Y. 10036.

ASI Liaison with The Society of Indexers. Robert L. Palmer, 15 W. 11 St., New York, N.Y. 10011.

ASI Representative to ANSI Z-39. Dr. John Rothman, The New York Times, 3P53, 229 W. 43 St., New York, N.Y. 10036.

AMERICAN THEOLOGICAL LIBRARY ASSOCIATION

OBJECT

"To bring its members into closer working relations with each other, to support theological and religious librarianship, to improve theological libraries, and to interpret the role of such libraries in theological education. In order to accomplish these objectives, the Association shall develop and implement standards of library service, promote research and experimental projects, encourage cooperative programs that make resources more available, publish and disseminate literature, and cooperate with organizations having similar aims." Founded 1947. Memb. (Inst.) 124; (Indiv.) 423. Dues. (Inst.) $25–$60, based on total library expenditure; (Indiv.) $6–$25, based on salary scale. Year. May 1–Apr. 30.

MEMBERSHIP

Persons engaged in professional library or bibliographical work in theological or religious fields and others who are interested in the work of theological librarianship.

OFFICERS (June 1971–June 1972)

Pres. Dr. Genevieve Kelly, California Baptist Theological Seminary, Seminary Knolls, Covina, Calif. 91722; *V.P. & Pres. Elect.* Peter VandenBerge, Colgate Rochester/Bexley Hall/Crozer Seminary, 1100 S. Goodman St., Rochester, N.Y. 14620; *Treas.* The Rev. Warren R. Mehl, Eden Theological Seminary, 275 E. Lockwood Ave., Webster Groves, Mo. 63119.

Exec. Secy. The Rev. David J. Wartluft, Lutheran Theological Seminary, 7301 Germantown Ave., Philadelphia, Pa. 19119.

Newsletter Editor. Mr. Donn Michael Farris, Divinity S. L., Duke Univ., Durham, N.C. 27706.

EXECUTIVE COMMITTEE

The officers and members-at-large: Oscar Burdick, Pacific S. of Religion, 1798 Scenic Ave., Berkeley, Calif. 94709; Dorothy J. Gilliam, Union Theological Seminary, 3401 Brook Rd., Richmond, Va. 23227; The Rev. David E. Green, Grad. Theological Union L., 2451 Ridge Rd., Berkeley, Calif. 94709; Erich R. W. Schultz, Waterloo Lutheran Univ., 235 Erb St. E., Waterloo, Ont., Canada; Past Pres. Dr. Henry Scherer, Lutheran Theological Seminary, 7301 Germantown Ave., Philadelphia, Pa. 19119; AATS Representative, Dr. Marvin Taylor, 609 W. 46 St., Kansas City, Mo. 64112.

PUBLICATIONS

Proceedings (a.; memb. or $3.00)
Newsletter (q.; memb. or $2.00)
Index to Religious Periodical Literature, 1949-date.

COMMITTEE CHAIRMEN

ATLA Newsletter. Donn Michael Farris, Editor, Divinity S. L., Duke Univ., Durham, N.C. 27706.

ATLA Representative on the ALA Council. Arthur E. Jones, Jr., Rose Mem. L., Drew Univ., Madison, N.J. 07940.

ATLA Representative to United States Book Exchange. Roland E. Kircher, Wesley Theol. Sem., 4400 Mass. Ave., N.W., Wash., D.C. 20016.

Archives. Gerald W. Gillette, Presbyterian Historical Society, 425 Lombard St., Philadelphia, Pa. 19147.

Bureau of Personnel & Placement. Elmer J. O'Brien, Head, United Theol. Sem., 1810 Harvard Blvd., Dayton, Ohio 45406.

Cataloging & Classification. Mrs. Margaret Whitelock, Princeton Theological Seminary, Princeton, N.J. 08540.

Coordinator of Consultant Services. Dr. Keith C. Wills, Southwestern Baptist Theological Seminary, P.O. Box 22000-2E, Fort Worth, Tex. 76122.

Financial Assistance from Foundations. Raymond P. Morris, Chairman, Yale Div. S. L., 409 Prospect St., New Haven, Conn. 06510.

Membership. Dr. William Sparks, St. Paul S. of Theology Methodist, 5123 Truman Rd., Kansas City, Mo. 64127.

Microtext Reproduction Board. Raymond P. Morris, Chairman, Yale Div. S. L., 409 Prospect St., New Haven, Conn. 06510.

Nominating. The Rev. Joel W. Lundeen, Lutheran S. of Theology, 1100 E. 55 St., Chicago, Ill. 60615.

Periodical Exchange. Wilson N. Flemister, Chairman, Interdenom. Theol. Center, 671 Beckwith St., S.W., Atlanta, Ga. 30314.

Periodical Indexing Board. Calvin H. Schmitt, Chairman, McCormick Theol. Sem., 800 W. Belden Ave., Chicago, Ill. 60614.

Statistical Records. Arthur Kuschke, Jr., Westminster Theological Seminary, Chestnut Hill, Philadelphia, Pa. 19118.

ASSOCIATION OF AMERICAN LIBRARY SCHOOLS

OBJECT

"To advance education for librarianship." Founded 1915. Memb. 546. Dues. (Inst.) $100; (Assoc. Inst.) $50; (Personal) $10; (Assoc. Personal) $8. Year. Sept. 1971–Aug. 1972.

MEMBERSHIP

Any library school with a program accredited by the ALA Committee on Accreditation may become an institutional member; any educator who is employed full-time for a full academic year in a library school with an accredited program may become a personal member.

Any school that offers a graduate degree in librarianship or a cognate field, but whose program is not accredited by the ALA Committee on Accreditation, may become an associate institutional member; any part-time faculty member or doctoral student of a library school with an accredited program, or any full-time faculty member employed for a full academic year at other schools which offer graduate degrees in librarianship or cognate fields, may become an associate personal member.

OFFICERS (Feb. 1971–Jan. 1972)

Pres. Margaret E. Monroe, Prof., L. S., Univ. of Wisconsin, Madison, Wis. 53706; *V.P. & Pres. Elect.* Thomas Slavens, Assoc. Prof., S. of L. Sci., Univ. of Michigan, Ann Arbor, Mich. 48104; *Secy.-Treas.* Violet L. Coughlin, Dir. & Prof., Grad. S. of L. Sci., McGill Univ., 3459 McTavish St., Montreal 112, Quebec, Canada.

Exec. Secy. Mrs. Janet Phillips, 471 Park Lane, State College, Pa. 16801.

DIRECTORS

The officers and Patricia B. Knapp, Assoc. Prof., S. of L. Sci., Wayne State Univ., Detroit, Mich. 48202; Charles Bunge, Dir., L. S., Univ. of Wisconsin, Madison, Wis. 53706; Guy Garrison, Dean & Prof., Grad. S. of L. Sci., Drexel Univ., Philadelphia, Pa. 19104; Cora E. Thomassen, Assoc. Prof., Grad. S. of L. Sci., Univ. of Ill., Urbana, Ill. 61801.

PUBLICATION

Journal of Education for Librarianship (q.)

COMMITTEE CHAIRMEN

AALS/LED Links and Roles. Thomas Slavens, Assoc. Prof., S. of L. Sci., Univ. of Mich., Ann Arbor, Mich. 48104.

Accreditation. Harold Goldstein, Dean & Prof., L. S., Florida State Univ., Tallahassee, Fla. 32306.

Archives. Howard Winger, Prof., Grad. L. S., Univ. of Chicago, Chicago, Ill. 60637.

Directory. Dorothy E. Cole, Assoc. Prof., S. of L. Sci., State Univ. of New York at Albany, Albany, N.Y. 12203.

Journal of Education for Librarianship: Editorial Board. Norman Horrocks, Asst. Dir., S. of L. Serv., Dalhousie Univ., Halifax, N.S., Canada.

Legislation. Guy Garrison, Dean, Grad. S. of L. Sci., Drexel Univ., Philadelphia, Pa. 19104.

Newsletter. Nasser Sharify, Dean, L. S., Pratt Institute, Brooklyn, N.Y. 11205.

Nominations. Thomas Galvin, Asst. Dir. & Assoc. Prof., S. of L. Sci., Simmons Coll., Boston, Mass. 02115.

Regional Cooperation Among Library Schools. Herbert Goldhor, Dir., Grad. S. of L. Sci., Univ. of Ill., Urbana, Ill. 61801.

Research. Guy A. Marco, Dean & Prof., S. of L. Sci., Kent State Univ., Kent, Ohio 44240.

Role of AALS in Continuing Education. Elizabeth Stone, Assoc. Prof., Dept. of L. Sci., Catholic Univ. of America, Washington, D.C. 20017.

REPRESENTATIVES

ALA Council. John Larsen, Asst. Prof., Coll. of L. Sci., Univ. of Kentucky, Lexington, Ky. 40506.

ALA Library Education Board. Thomas Slavens, Assoc. Prof., S. of L. Sci., Univ. of Michigan, Ann Arbor, Mich. 48104.

United States Book Exchange. Mathilde Verner Rovelstad, Assoc. Prof.,

Catholic Univ. of America, Dept. of L. Sci., Washington, D.C. 20017.
CNLA. Father James J. Kortendick, Chairman & Assoc. Prof., Dept. of L. Sci., Catholic Univ. of America, Washington, D.C. 20017.

ASSOCIATION OF JEWISH LIBRARIES
2 Thornton Road, Waltham, Mass. 02154
617-891-8110

OBJECT

"To promote and improve library services and professional standards in all Jewish libraries and collections of Judaica; to serve as a center of dissemination of Jewish library information and guidance; to encourage the establishment of Jewish libraries and collections of Judaica; to promote publication of literature which will be of assistance to Jewish librarianship; to encourage people to enter the field of librarianship." Organized 1966 from the merger of the Jewish Librarians Association and the Jewish Library Association. Memb. 289. Dues. (Inst.) $10; (Indiv.) $5. Year. Jan. 1972–Dec. 1972.

OFFICERS (June 1970–June 1972)

Pres. Dr. Nathan M. Kaganoff, American Jewish Hist. Society, 2 Thornton Rd., Waltham, Mass. 02154; *V.P. & Pres. Elect.* Mrs. Anne Kirshenbaum, Temple Beth El, 165 Mayflower Dr., Rochester, N.Y. 14618; *V.P.* Theodore Wiener, 1701 N. Kent St., Arlington, Va. 22209; *Rec. Secy.* Mrs. Rose Miskin, 2121 Bathurst St., Toronto 10, Ont., Can.; *Treas.* Mrs. Mildred Kurland, 808 69 Ave., Philadelphia, Pa. 19126.
Corres. Secy. Mrs. Maryland Estes, Temple Beth El, 226 Freeborn Ave., E. Providence, R.I. 02914. (Send all general correspondence to Corres. Secy. at Rhode Island address.)

PUBLICATIONS

Bulletin (4 issues)
Membership Kit
Proceedings
Standards for Jewish Libraries in Synagogues, Schools and Centers

DIVISIONS

Research & Special Libraries. Theodore Wiener, 1701 N. Kent St., Arlington, Va. 22209.
Synagogue School & Center Libraries. Mrs. Rose Miskin, Beth Tzedec Sisterhood L., 1700 Bathurst St., Toronto 10, Ont., Canada.

ASSOCIATION OF RESEARCH LIBRARIES
1527 New Hampshire Ave., N.W., Washington, D.C. 20036
202-232-2466

OBJECT

"To initiate and develop plans for the strengthening of research library resources and services in support of higher education and research." Established in 1932 by the chief librarians of 43 research libraries. Memb. (Inst.) 89. Dues. (ann.) $1,500. Year. Jan. 1972–Dec. 1972.

MEMBERSHIP

Membership is institutional, by invitation only.

OFFICERS (Jan. 1972–Jan. 1973)

Pres. John McDonald, Dir., Univ. of Connecticut L., Storrs, Conn. 06268; *Past Pres.* Warren Haas, Dir., Columbia Univ. Ls., New York, N.Y. 10027. *V.P.* To be appointed.
Exec. Dir. Stephen A. McCarthy.
Assoc. Exec. Dir. Louis E. Martin.

DIRECTORS

Robert Blackburn, Dir., Univ. of Toronto L., Toronto, Ont., Canada; Ben Bowman, Dir., Univ. of Rochester L., Rochester, N.Y. 14627; William Budington, Dir., John Crerar L., Chicago, Ill. 60616; David Kaser, Dir., Cornell Univ. Ls., Ithaca, N.Y. 14850; Arthur McAnally, Libn., Univ. of Oklahoma L., Norman, Okla. 73609; Basil Stuart-Stubbs, Libn., Univ. of British Columbia L., Vancouver, B.C., Canada; Robert Vosper, Libn., Univ. of California L., Los Angeles, Calif. 90024; David Weber, Dir., Stanford Univ. L., Stanford, Calif. 94305.

PUBLICATIONS

ARL Minutes (semi-a.; $5 per issue)
Foreign Acquisitions Newsletter (semi-a.; May & Oct.; $2.50 per issue)
ARL Academic Library Statistics (annual; $1 to nonacademic inst.)

COMMITTEE CHAIRMEN

Availability of Resources. Richard Chapin.
Copying Manuscripts & Unpublished Materials. James Henderson.
Copyright. Verner Clapp.
Federal Relations. Robert Vosper.
Foreign Acquisitions. Philip McNiff.
Foreign Acquisitions Area Subcommittees. Louis Jacob (South Asia); Robert Johnson (Latin America); David Kaser (Southeast Asia); Marion Milczewski (Eastern Europe); Hans Panofsky (Africa); David Partington (Middle East); Howard Sullivan (Western Europe); Warren Tsuneishi (Far East).
Library Security. Ben Bowman.
Membership. William Locke.
Microfilming Dissertations. Gustave Harrer.
Negro Academic Libraries. Frank Grisham.
Nominating. John McDonald.
Periodicals Resources Center Study. Joseph Jeffs.
Preservation. Warren Haas.
Recommendations of Federal Information Resources Conference. W. Carl Jackson.
Shared Cataloging. David Kaser.
Standards. Jerrold Orne.
Training for Research Librarianship. David Kaser.
Joint ACRL-ARL Committee on University Library Standards. Robert B. Downs.
Joint ARL-ACE University Library Management Study. Warren Haas.

PROJECTS

Center for Chinese Research Libraries. Philip McNiff.
Foreign Newspaper Microfilm. John Lorenz.
Interlibrary Loan Study. Arthur McAnally.
Microform. Task I: Bibliographic Control. Felix Reichman, Principal Investigator. Task II: National Microform Agency. Edward Miller, Principal Investigator.
Slavic Bibliographic & Documentation Center. Marion Milczewski.

ASSOCIATION OF VISUAL SCIENCE LIBRARIANS

OBJECT

"To foster collective and individual acquisition and dissemination of visual science information, to improve services for all persons seeking such information, and to develop standards for libraries to which members are attached." Founded 1968. Memb. (U.S.) 22; (foreign) 11. Annual meetings held in December, in connection with the American Academy of Optometry, in Toronto, Can. (1971), New York, N.Y. (1972), San Francisco, Calif. (1973), Birmingham, Ala. (1974), Columbus, Ohio (1975), London, Eng. (1976).

OFFICERS

Chairmen. Thomas Lange (1970–72), Libn., Southern Coll. of Optometry, 1245 Union Ave., Memphis, Tenn. 38104; Elizabeth Egan (1972–74), Libn., Div. of Optometry, Indiana Univ., Bloomington, Ind. 47401.

(Note: Address general correspondence to the chairman.)

PUBLICATIONS

Visual Union List of Serials (irreg.)
PhD Theses in Physiological Optics (irreg.)

BIBLIOGRAPHICAL SOCIETY OF AMERICA

P. O. Box 397, Grand Central Station, New York, N. Y. 10017

OBJECT

"To promote bibliographical research and to issue bibliographical publications." Organized 1904. Memb. 1,550. Dues. $10. Year. Jan.–Dec.

OFFICERS (Jan. 1971–Dec. 1972)

Pres. Robert H. Taylor, 511 Lake Dr., Princeton, N.J. 08540; *1st V.P.* James J. Heslin, N.Y. Hist. Soc., 170 Central Park West, New York, N.Y. 10024; *2nd V.P.* William H. Bond, Houghton L., Harvard Univ., Cambridge, Mass. 02138; *Secy.* Thomas R. Adams, John Carter Brown L., Brown Univ., Providence, R.I. 02192; *Treas.* Stuart B. Schimmel, 516 Fifth Ave., New York, N.Y. 10036.

(Note: Address general correspondence to headquarters address.)

COUNCIL

The officers and Frances Hamill, 230 N. Michigan Ave., Chicago, Ill.; Herman W. Liebert, 210 St. Ronan St., New Haven, Conn.; Thomas R. Adams, John Carter Brown L., Brown Univ., Providence, R.I.; Lawrence S. Thompson, Univ. of Kentucky, Lexington, Ky.; Robert M. Metzdorf, Route 183 North, Colebrook, Conn.; Dorothy M. Schullian, Cornell Univ., Ithaca, N.Y.; G. Thomas Tarselle, 410 W. Washington St., Lebanon, Ind.; Frederick R. Goff, L. of Congress, Washington, D.C. 20540; Edwin Wolf 2nd, L. Co. of Philadelphia, 1314 Locust St., Philadelphia, Pa. 19107.

PUBLICATION

Papers (q.; memb.)

COMMITTEE CHAIRMEN

Publication. Gabriel Austin, Parke-Bernet Galleries, 980 Madison Ave., New York, N.Y. 10022.

CANADIAN LIBRARY ASSOCIATION

151 Sparks Street, Ottawa, Ont.

613-232-9625

OBJECT

"To promote education, science and culture within the nation through library service; to promote high standards of librarianship and the welfare of librarians; to co-operate with library associations both within and outside of Canada and with other organizations interested in the promotion of education, science and culture." Founded 1946. Memb. (Indiv.) 3,100; (Inst.) 900. Dues. (Indiv.) $10 and up, sliding scale; (Inst.) $15 and up, sliding scale. Year. Sept. 1, 1971–Aug. 31, 1972.

MEMBERSHIP

Open to anyone interested in library service.

OFFICERS (Sept. 1, 1971–Aug. 31, 1972)

Pres. Dean W. Halliwell, Univ. Libn., Univ. of Victoria, Victoria, B.C.; *Pres. Elect.* H. H. Easton, City Libn., Winnipeg P.L., 380 William Ave., Winnipeg 2, Man.; *2nd V.P.* Harry E. Newsom, Assoc. Prof., S. of L. Sci., Univ. of Alberta, Edmonton 7, Alta.; *Treas.* Stanley E. Beacock, Dir., Midwestern Regional L. Syst., 637 Victoria St. N., Kitchener, Ont.; *Past Pres.* Martha Shepard, Head, Ref. Div., National L., Ottawa, Ont.

Acting Exec. Dir. Mrs. Isabel Pitfield.

COUNCIL

The officers, section chairmen, and Mr. John E. Dutton, North York P.L., Willowdale, Ont.; Mr. T. Garth Graham, Yukon Regional L., Whitehorse, Yukon; Miss Barbara Hann, Memorial Univ. of Newfoundland, St. John's, Nfld.; Diane MacQuarrie, Supv. of P.L., Nova Scotia Prov. L., Halifax, N.S.; Robert Shanks, Asst. Libn. Tech. Servs., National Science L., Ottawa, Can.; Frederick White, Reg. L., Vancouver Is. Reg. L., Nanaimo, B.C.; Mrs. Lois Bewley, Asst. Prof., S. of Libnshp., Univ. of British Columbia, Vancouver, B.C.; Brian L. Cahill, Chief

Libn., Sources P.L., 110 Cartier St., Roxboro, P.Q.; Margaret Scott, Assoc. Prof., Coll. of Educ., Univ. of Toronto, 371 Bloor St. W., Toronto, Ont.

PUBLICATIONS

Canadian Periodical Index. (11 issues monthly; annual cumulation. Price on request.)

Canadian Library Journal (6 issues; memb. or $10.)

Feliciter (irreg.; memb.)

Other miscellaneous publications of interest are available to librarians (catalog on request).

SECTION CHAIRMEN

Adult Services. Brian Dale, Kitchener P.L., 85 Queen St. N., Kitchener, Ont.

Canadian Association of Children's Librarians. Mrs. Margaret Vatcher, Head, Children's Servs., Vancouver P.L., Vancouver, B.C.

Canadian Association of College and University Libraries. Rev. Daniel Croteau, Université de Sherbrooke, Sherbrooke, P.Q.

Canadian Association of Special Libraries and Information Services. Eileen B. Morash, National Film Board, Ref. L., P.O. Box 6100, Montreal, P.Q.

Canadian Library Trustees' Association. A. R. Pile, 63 Bowerbank Dr., Willowdale, Ont.

Canadian School Library Association. Mrs. Florence Willson, S. Dist. No. 57, Prince George, B.C.

Information Services. Mrs. Lorraine Garry, Asst. to the Head of Science & Medicine Dept., Univ. of Toronto L., Toronto 181 (Mailing address: 44 Jackes Ave., #811, Toronto 290).

Technical Services. Gurdial Pannu, S. of L. Sci., Univ. of Alberta, Edmonton 7, Alta.

Young People's. Maureen Allen, Ottawa P.L., 237 Queen St., Ottawa, Ont.

COMMITTEE CHAIRMEN

ACBLF/CLA Canadian Committee for Liaison with IFLA Committee on Cataloguing. Dr. Jean Lunn, Dir., Cataloguing Br., National L. of Canada, 395 Wellington St., Ottawa, Ont.

ACBLF/CLA Liaison. M. Gilles M. Bergevin, Bibliotheque Central, Univ. d'Ottawa, 165 Waller St., Ottawa, Ont.

ALA/CLA (Joint Comm.) Mrs. Helen Howard, Chief Libn., Sir George Williams Univ., 1435 Drummond St., Montreal, Que.

Accreditation (Subcomm.) Katharine Ball, 60 Highland Lane, Richmond Hill, Ont.

Administrators of Large Public Libraries. Morton P. Jordan, Dir., Vancouver P.L., 750 Burrard St., Vancouver, B.C.

Advisability of CLA's Assuming Responsibility for Conference Exhibits, Committee to Study the (Ad Hoc). Robin W. MacDonald, Univ. of British Columbia L., Vancouver 8, B.C.

CLA/Information Canada (Joint Comm.) Mr. C. Deane Kent, London P.L. & Art Museum, 305 Queens Ave., London, Ont.

Canadian Books in Print. Betty Hardie, Chief Libn., Etobicoke P.L., Box 501, Etobicoke, Ont.

Constitution. Appointment deferred pending final report of Structural Committee.

Copyright. Allen H. Soroka, Law L., Univ. of British Columbia, Vancouver 8, B.C.

Education for Library Manpower. Dr. Olga B. Bishop, S. of L. Sci., Univ. of Toronto, 140 St. George St., Toronto, Ont.

Editorial & Publications Policy. Dr. Hugh L. Smith, Chief Libn., Erindale Coll. L., Univ. of Toronto, Mississauga Rd. N., Clarkson, Ont.

Elections. Miss Jean Higginson, Chief, General Acquisitions Div., National L. of Canada, 395 Wellington St., Ottawa, Ont.

Ephemeral Materials (Ad Hoc). Leonard J. Gottselig, Glenbow Alberta Institute, 902 11 Ave. S.W., Calgary, Alta.

Government Publications. Clementine Combaz, Legislative Libn., 257 Legislative Bldg., Winnipeg, Man.

Grants-in-Aid. Ex-officio Chmn. Stanley Beacock, Midwestern Regional L. Syst., 637 Victoria St. N., Kitchener, Ont.

Intellectual Freedom. Martha Shepard, Head, Ref. Div., National L. of Canada, 395 Wellington St., Ottawa, Ont.

Legislation. Steven A. Horn, Carleton Univ. L., Colonel By Drive, Ottawa, Ont.

Membership. Mrs. Carin A. Somers, Chief Libn., Halifax County Regional L., Box 300, Armdale P.O., Halifax, N.S.

Nominating. Robert M. A. Park, Planning Assoc. (Ls.), Government of Manitoba, Winnipeg, Man.

Non-Book Materials, Joint Advisory Committee on. Dr. Margaret Chisholm, Assoc. Prof. of Libnshp., 456 McKeldin, S. of L. & Info. Servs., Univ. of Maryland, College Park, Md. 27040.

Possible Equivalence of the Fellowship (with thesis) of the Library Association to CLA's Established Standards of Professional Qualification, to Consider the (Ad Hoc). Mary E. P. Henderson, S. of L. Sci., Univ. of Alberta, Edmonton, Alta.

Resolutions. Mr. A. R. Pile, 63 Bower Bank Dr., Willowdale, Ont.

Rural Regional Libraries (subcomm). Fred White, Vancouver Island Regional L., 10 Strickland St., Nanaimo, B.C.

Salaries (subcomm). Joe Carver, Chief Libn., Medicine Hat P.L., 414 First St. S.E., Medicine Hat, Alta.

Statistical Research. Mrs. Sheila J. Bertram, S. of L. Sci., Univ. of Alberta, Edmonton, Alta.

Structural. Douglas N. McInnes, Univ. of British Columbia L., Vancouver 8, B.C.

Training of Library Technicians (subcomm). John Marshall, S. of L. Sci., Univ. of Toronto, 140 St. George St., Toronto 181, Ont.

Union List of Serials, Joint Committee on. Flora E. Patterson, Chief, Serials Div., National L. of Canada, 395 Wellington St., Ottawa, Ont.

Use of Professional Staff (subcomm). Joseph Princz, Acting Chief, Georges P. Vanier L., Loyola Coll., 7141 Sherbrooke St. W., Montreal 28, Que.

CATHOLIC LIBRARY ASSOCIATION
461 West Lancaster Ave., Haverford, Pa. 19041
215-Midway 9-5250-1

OBJECT

"The promotion and encouragement of Catholic literature and library work through cooperation, publications, education and information." Founded 1921. Memb. 3,431. Dues. $10-$500. Year. July 1971–June 1972.

OFFICERS (April 1971–April 1973)

Pres. Rev. Joseph P. Browne, C.S.C., Univ. of Portland, Portland, Ore. 97203; *V.P.* Dr. Mary Jo DiMuccio, Immaculate Heart Coll. L., 2070 E. Live Oak Dr., Los Angeles, Calif. 90028; *Past Pres.* Sister Helen Sheehan, S.N.D., Trinity Coll., Washington, D.C. 20017.

Exec. Dir. Matthew R. Wilt.

EXECUTIVE BOARD

The officers and James C. Cox, 1221 W. Catalpa, Chicago, Ill. 60640; Marilyn D. Lamsey, 2600 N. Nordica Ave., Chicago, Ill. 60635; Sister Marie Inez Johnson, C.S.J., Coll. of St. Catherine, St. Paul, Minn. 55116; Joanne M. Klene, 1321 Balmoral, Westchester, Ill. 60153; Brother John Corrigan, C.F.X., Spalding Coll., Louisville, Ky. 40203; Sister Jane Marie Barbour, C.D.P., Our Lady of the Lake Coll., San Antonio, Tex. 78207.

PUBLICATIONS

Catholic Library World (10 issues; memb. or $10)

Catholic Periodical and Literature Index (subscrip.)

Network Concepts ($2.50)

SECTION CHAIRMEN

Children's Libraries. Sister M. Julanne Good, O.P., 1354 Tamm Ave., St. Louis, Mo. 63139.

College and University Libraries. Eugene P. Kennedy, New York Univ. L., 10 Washington Pl., Rm. 403, New York, N.Y. 10003.

High School Libraries. Sister Carol Louise Hiller, St. Thomas H.S., 2700 S.W. Tenth St., Ft. Lauderdale, Fla. 33312.

Library Education. Dr. Jo Ann McCreedy, Our Lady of the Lake Coll., San Antonio, Tex. 78207.

Parish & Community Libraries. Miriam F. Cummings, 5344 Penn Ave. S., Minneapolis, Minn. 55419.

School Library Supervisors. Brother John Corrigan, C.F.X., Spalding Coll., 851 S. Fourth St., Louisville, Ky. 40203.

COMMITTEE AND BOARD CHAIRMEN

Advisory Council. Dr. Mary Jo DiMuccio, Immaculate Heart Coll. L., 2070 E. Live Oak Dr., Los Angeles, Calif. 90028.

Book Fair. Sister Martinez Holloran, R.S.M., St. Bernard H.S., Bernard Ave. at 24 St., Nashville, Tenn. 37212.

Catholic Library World Editorial. Sister Chrysantha Rudnik, C.S.S.F., Felician Coll. L., 3800 Peterson Ave., Chicago, Ill. 60645.

Catholic Periodical and Literature Index. Arnold Rzepecki, Sacred Heart Seminary, 2701 W. Chicago Blvd., Detroit, Mich. 48206.

Constitution and Bylaws. Robert Q. Kelly, DePaul Univ. Law L., Chicago, Ill. 60604.

Elections. Sister Eulema Lyvers, S.S.N.D., St. Joseph H.S. L., 375 Harkrider St., Conway, Ark. 72032.

Finance. Rev. Robert Cawley, C.M., St. John's Univ., Jamaica, N.Y. 11432.

Legislative. Mary K. Feldman, Trinity Coll. L., Washington, D.C. 20017.

Membership. Joanne M. Klene, 1321 Balmoral, Westchester, Ill. 60153.

Nominations. Sister M. Agnes Sullivan, O.P., St. Catherine Coll., St. Catherine, Ky. 40061.

Parliamentarian. Robert Q. Kelly, De Paul Univ. Law L., Chicago, Ill. 60604.

Program Coordinator. Sally Ann Quinn, 160 Stratford St., West Roxbury, Mass. 02132.

Public Relations. Donald H. Hunt, Deputy Dir., Free L. of Philadelphia, Philadelphia, Pa. 19103.

Publications. Margaret Mary Henrich, 1709 Pasadena Dr., Dunedin, Fla. 33528.

Regina Medal. Catherine J. Butler, 221 Kennedy Ave., Munhall, Pa. 15120.

Scholarship. Dr. Jo Ann McCreedy, Our Lady of the Lake Coll., 411 S.W. 24 St., San Antonio, Tex. 78207.

Unit Coordinator. Sister Franz Lang, O.P., Barry Coll. L., Miami Shores, Fla. 33116.

CHURCH AND SYNAGOGUE LIBRARY ASSOCIATION
P.O. Box 530, Bryn Mawr, Pa. 19010

OBJECT

"To act as a unifying core for the many existing church and synagogue libraries; to provide the opportunity for a mutual sharing of practices and problems; to inspire and encourage a sense of purpose and mission among church and synagogue librarians; to study and guide the development of church and synagogue librarianship toward recognition as a formal branch of the library profession. Founded 1967. Members 410. Dues (Contributing) $100; (Institutional) $50; (Affiliated) $25; (Active church or synagogue) $10; (Active individual) $5. Year. Sept. 1, 1971–Aug. 31, 1972.

MEMBERSHIP

Any person or institution interested in church and synagogue libraries may become a member.

OFFICERS (Sept. 1, 1971–Aug. 31, 1972)

Pres. Mrs. Wilma Jensen, Lutheran Church L. Assn., 122 W. Franklin Ave., Minneapolis, Minn. 55404; *1st V.P. & Pres. Elect.* Betty Lou Hammargren, Catalog Div., Minneapolis P.L., 300 Nicollet Mall, Minneapolis, Minn. 55401; *2nd V.P.* Maurice Tuchman, 16 Duffield Rd., Auburndale, Mass. 02166; *3rd V.P.* Rev. William Gentz, Editorial Consultant Servs., P.O. Box 613, Cherry Hill, N.J.

08034; *Secy.* Mrs. Marilyn Applebaum, 438 Robinson Court, Pittsburgh, Pa. 15213; *Treas.* Rev. Donald L. Leonard, Exec. Ed., Board of Christian Educ., United Presbyterian Church U.S.A., 1115 Witherspoon Bldg., Philadelphia, Pa. 19107; *Past Pres.* Rev. Arthur W. Swarthout, Libn., Pickett L., Alderson-Broaddus Coll., Philippi, W.Va. 26416.
Exec. Secy. Joyce L. White, Libn., Penniman L., Univ. of Pennsylvania, 36th & Walnut Sts., Philadelphia, Pa. 19104. ((Note: Send general correspondence to Miss Joyce L. White, at headquarters address.)
Editor, "Church and Synagogue Libraries." Mrs. Claudia Hannaford, 5350 Gardner Dr., Erie, Pa. 16509.

EXECUTIVE BOARD

The officers named above.

PUBLICATIONS

Church & Synagogue Libraries (bimo.; memb.)

Bibliography of Church & Synagogue Library Resources.

COMMITTEE CHAIRMEN

Awards. Ruth Winters.
Bylaws. Jacqulyn Anderson.
Conference Arrangements. Ralph Wilbur.
Conference Exhibits. Mrs. John P. Toomey.
Conference Sites. Ruth C. Roth.
Finance. The Rev. Donald Leonard.
Historian. Jane F. Hindman.
Library World Liaison. The Rev. Anthony Lachner.
Membership. Helen Geer.
Nominations and Elections. Mrs. Gordon Rodda.
Public Relations. Mrs. Shirley G. Brown.
Publications. Mrs. Ruth Smith.
Publishers' Liaison. Mrs. Elizabeth S. Halbrooks.

COUNCIL OF NATIONAL LIBRARY ASSOCIATIONS

OBJECT

"To promote a closer relationship among the national library associations of the United States and Canada." Organized 1942. Memb. 14. Year. July 1971–June 1972.

MEMBERSHIP

Open to national associations of the U.S. or Canada as well as those in related fields.
Amer. Assn. of Law Ls.; ALA; Amer. Society of Indexers; Assn. of Amer. L. Schs.; Assn. of Jewish Ls.; Amer. Theological L. Assn.; Catholic L. Assn.; Church and Synagogue Library Assn.; Council of Planning Libns.; L. Public Relations Council; Medical L. Assn.; Music L. Assn.; Special Ls. Assn.; Theatre L. Assn.

OFFICERS (July 1971–June 1972)

Chairman. Robert W. Gibson, Jr., General Motors Corp. Research Labs., 12 Mile & Mound Rds., Warren, Mich. 48090; *Secy.-Treas.* Jane L. Hammond, Law L., Garey Hall, Villanova Univ., Villanova, Pa. 19085.
(Note: Send general correspondence to Secy.-Treas.)

DIRECTORS

Rev. James J. Kortendick, Dept. of L. Sci., Catholic Univ. of America, Washington, D.C. 20017; Rabbi Theodore Wiener, Hebraic Language Unit, Descriptive Cat. Div., L.C., Washington, D.C. 20540; Richard Wilt, Catholic L. Assn., 461 W. Lancaster Ave., Haverford, Pa. 19041; Mrs. Beatrice M. James, Bergenfield P.L., Bergenfield, N.J. 07621.

PUBLICATIONS

Library Placement Services. (Available from the Catholic L. Assn., 461 W. Lancaster Ave., Haverford, Pa. 19041. Price $.10.)

COMMITTEE CHAIRMAN

Bylaws and New Members. Helen Brown Schmidt.

COUNCIL OF PLANNING LIBRARIANS

OBJECT

"To exchange information about professional practices in libraries with particular concern for those practices peculiar to planning libraries; to provide fellowship among its members and an opportunity for librarians to meet with other librarians, faculty, professional planners, public officials, and vice versa; to formulate and to administer projects which the Council decides are of service to the planning profession and librarianship; to act in an advisory capacity on library organization for new planning programs in institutions and agencies; to aid and support administrators, faculty, and librarians in their efforts to educate the public and their appointed or elected representatives to the necessity for strong library programs in support for planning." Founded 1960. Memb. 200. Dues. (Inst.) $35; (Indiv.) $6. Year. Calendar.

MEMBERSHIP

Open to any individual or institution which supports the purposes of the Council, upon written application and payment of dues.

OFFICERS

Pres. Melva J. Dwyer, Libn., Fine Arts L., Univ. of British Columbia, Vancouver 8, British Columbia, Canada (Apr. 1970–Apr. 1972); *V.P. & Pres. Elect.* Peter Anthony, Libn., Arch. & Fine Arts L., Univ. of Manitoba, Winnipeg, Man., Canada (Oct. 1971–Apr. 1972); *Secy.* Elizabeth K. Miller, Libn., The Urban Institute, 2100 M St. N.W., Washington, D.C. 20037 (Apr. 1971–Apr. 1973); *Treas.* Barbara Williams, Libn., Kentucky Program Devel. Office, The Capitol, Frankfort, Ky. 40601 (Apr. 1971–Apr. 1973); *Member-at-Large.* Thomas Haggerty, 3212 Wellington Rd., Alexandria, Va. 22302 (Apr. 1970–Apr. 1972).

(Note: Address all general correspondence to the president.)

PUBLICATIONS

CPL Exchange Bibliographies (irreg.)
CPL Newsletter (3–4 times a yr.)
Directory of Planning Libraries (irreg.)
Planning Agency Library Manual (irreg.)

COMMITTEE CHAIRMEN

Membership. Barbara Williams, Libn., Kentucky Program Devel. Office, The Capitol, Frankfort, Ky. 40601.

Development Advisory. Dorothy Whiteman, Asst. Dir., Research Center for Urban & Environmental Planning, Princeton Univ., Princeton, N.J. 08540.

Interagency. Elizabeth K. Miller, Libn., The Urban Institute, 2100 M St. N.W., Washington, D.C. 20037.

Library Advisor. Johan Ronningen, Planner, City & County of Honolulu, P.O. Box 4413, Honolulu, Hawaii 96813.

EDUCATIONAL FILM LIBRARY ASSOCIATION
17 West 60 Street, New York, N. Y. 10023
212-246-4533

OBJECT

"To promote the production, distribution and utilization of educational films and other audio-visual materials." Incorporated 1943. Memb. 18,000. Dues. (Inst.) $25–$50; (Indiv.) $10. Year. Sept. 1971–Aug. 1972.

OFFICERS (Sept. 1971–Aug. 1972)

Pres. Abraham Cohen, White Plains Bd. of Educ., White Plains, N.Y. 10605; *V.P.* Dr. Robert Wagner, Ohio State Univ., Columbus, Ohio 43210; *Secy.* Lewis Saks, East Detroit P.S., East Detroit, Mich. 48021.

Admin. Dir. Mrs. Esmé J. Dick.

COMMITTEE CHAIRMEN

Festival. Mrs. Esmé J. Dick, 17 W. 60 St., New York, N.Y. 10023.

Membership. Lewis Saks, East Detroit P.S., East Detroit, Mich. 48021.

Nominations. James L. Limbacher, Henry Ford Centennial L., 16301 Michigan Ave., Dearborn, Mich. 48126.

PUBLICATIONS

EFLA Evaluations (10 issues; a.; memb.)

Sightlines (bi-mo.)
Film Evaluation Guide (supplemented every 3 years)
Films for Young Adults ($2)
99 + Films on Drugs ($3)
Contact Admin. Dir. for list of other publications.

FEDERAL LIBRARY COMMITTEE
Library of Congress, Washington, D.C. 20540
202-426-6055

OBJECT

"For the purpose of concentrating the intellectual resources present in the federal library and library related information community: To achieve better utilization of library resources and facilities; to provide more effective planning, development, and operation of federal libraries; to promote an optimum exchange of experience, skill, and resources. Secretariat efforts and the work groups are organized to: Consider policies and problems relating to federal libraries; evaluate existing federal library programs and resources; determine priorities among library issues requiring attention; examine the organization and policies for acquiring, preserving, and making information available; study the need for a potential of technological innovation in library practices; and study library budgeting and staffing problems, including the recruiting, education, training, and remuneration of librarians." Founded 1965. Memb. (Federal Ls.) 2,600, (Federal Libns.) 4,001. Year. July 1–June 30.

MEMBERSHIP

Permanent Membership. L. of Congress, National Agricultural L., National L. of Medicine, Dept. of State, Dept. of the Treasury, Dept. of Defense, Dept. of Justice, Post Office Dept., Dept. of the Interior, Dept. of Commerce, Dept. of Labor, Dept. of Health, Education, & Welfare, Dept. of Housing & Urban Devel., and Dept. of Transportation.

Rotating Membership, 1971–1973. Federal Communications Commission, General Services Administration, National Aeronautics & Space Administration, National Science Foundation, Supreme Court of the United States, Veterans Administration.

Observers. Office of Management & Budget and Office of Science & Tech. of the Exec. Office of the President; L. of Congress; Bureau of Ls. & Educ. Tech., USOE.

Guest Observers. American Library Association, American Society for Information Science, Association of Research Libraries, Association of State Libraries, Council on Library Resources, Information Industry Association, Special Libraries Association.

OFFICERS

Chairman. L. Quincy Mumford, Libn. of Congress, L. of Congress, Washington, D.C. 20540.
Exec. Secy. Frank Kurt Cylke.

EXECUTIVE ADVISORY COMMITTEE

Chairman (July 1, 1971– June 30, 1972). John Sherrod, Dir., National Agricultural L.

1971–1972. Dr. Martin Cummings, Dir. of National L. of Medicine; Lillian Hamrick, Libn. of U.S. Dept. of Labor; Dr. Russell Shank, Dir., Smithsonian Institution Ls.

1970–1972. Erik Bromberg, Dir., Office of L. Servs., Dept. of the Interior; William K. Brussat, Management Analyst, Office of Management & Budget; Dr. Stanley J. Bougas, Dir., Dept. of Commerce L.

Ex Officio. L. Quincy Mumford, Chairman, Federal L. Comm; Frank Kurt Cylke, Exec. Secy., Federal L. Comm.; Mrs. Marlene D. Morrisey.

Exec. Asst. to the Libn. of Congress, L. of Congress.

PUBLICATIONS

FLC Newsletter (mo.)
Library Vacancy Roster (mo.)
Roster of Prospective Federal Librarians (mo.)
Advanced Technology/Libraries (mo.)
Annual Report.

TASK FORCE CHAIRMEN

Acquisition of Library Materials & Correlation of Federal Library Resources. Mrs. Elsa S. Freeman, Dir. of the L., Dept. of Housing & Urban Devel.
Automation of Library Operations. Mrs. Madeline Henderson, Computer Systems Analyst, Center for Computer Sciences & Tech., National Bureau of Standards.
Interlibrary Loan Arrangements for Federal Libraries. Dr. Elizabeth L. Tate, Chief, L. Div., National Bureau of Standards.
Library Education. Dr. Russell Shank, Dir. of Ls., Smithsonian Inst.
Mission of Federal Libraries & Standards for Federal Library Service. Ruth Fine, Libn., Office of Management & Budget.
Physical Facilities of Federal Libraries. Henry J. Gartland, Dir. of L. Serv. 11A3, Veterans Admin.
Procurement Procedures in Federal Libraries. Katherine Magraw, Field L. Servs. Administrator, L. Servs. Dept., Naval Training Support Command.
Public Relations. Mrs. Lois Fern, Ref. Libn., U.S. Info. Agency.
Recruiting of Personnel in Federal Libraries. Mrs. Elaine Woodruff, Libn., U.S. Civil Service Commission.
Role of Libraries in Information Systems. Herbert H. Fockler, Senior Program Officer, Office of Voluntary Action.

WORK GROUP CHAIRMEN

Census. Dorothy W. Kaufman, Libn., Bureau of the Census.
FLC/COSATI Ad Hoc Group to Work with the President's Proposed Restructuring of the Executive Branch. John Sherrod, Dir., National Agricultural L.
Map. David K. Carrington, Coordinator MARC Map Project, Geography & Map Div., L. of Congress.
Procurement. Katherine Magraw, Field L. Servs. Administrator, L. Servs. Dept., Naval Training Support Command.
Statistics. Frank Kurt Cylke, Exec. Secy., Federal L. Comm.

LIBRARY PUBLIC RELATIONS COUNCIL

OBJECT

"To investigate, discuss, and promote every phase of library public relations." Established 1939. Memb. 250. Dues. $5. Year. June 1971–May 1972.

MEMBERSHIP

Any person engaged in or actively interested in library public relations shall be eligible for membership.

OFFICERS (June 1971–May 1972)

Pres. Ruth Kimball Baum, Dir. of Public Relations, N.Y.P.L., Fifth Ave. & 42 St., New York, N.Y. 10018; *V.P. & Pres. Elect.* John Ryan, Dir., North Bellmore P.L., North Bellmore, N.Y. 11710; *Secy.* Constance A. Blandy, Asst. Dir., Mt. Vernon P.L., Mt. Vernon, N.Y. 10550; *Treas.* Marvin Scilken, Dir., Orange P.L., Orange, N.J. 07050; *Past Pres.* Harold Roth, Dir., Nassau County Reference L., Firehouse Lane, Garden City, N.Y. 11530.

(Note: Address all general correspondence to the Secy.)

EXECUTIVE BOARD

Gloria Glaser, Public Relations Dir., Nassau L. Syst., Roosevelt Field, Garden City, N.Y. 11530; Louise Liebold, Public Relations Dir., East Meadow P.L., Front St., East Meadow, N.Y. 11554; Edward Montana, Jr., Asst. to Regional Administrator, Boston P.L., Copley Square, Boston, Mass. 02117; Irene Moran, Dir. of Public Relations, Brooklyn P.L., Grand Army Plaza, Brooklyn, N.Y. 11238; Arthur Plotnik, Asst. Ed., *Wilson Library Bulletin,* 950 University Ave., Bronx, N.Y. 10452.

COMMITTEE CHAIRMEN

Awards. Edward Montana, Jr., Asst. to Regional Administrator, Boston P.L., Copley Square, Boston, Mass. 02117.

Hospitality. Marion Lawrence, Press & Comm. Off., N.Y.P.L., New York, N.Y. 10018.

Membership. Walter Haber, Dir., Baldwin P.L., 2385 Grand Ave., Baldwin, N.Y. 11510.

Packets. Louise Liebold, Public Relations Dir., East Meadow P.L., Front St., East Meadow, N.Y. 11554.

Program. John Ryan, Dir., North Bellmore P.L., North Bellmore, N.Y. 11710.

LUTHERAN CHURCH LIBRARY ASSOCIATION
122 West Franklin Ave., Minneapolis, Minnesota 55404
612-333-3814

OBJECT

"To promote the growth of church libraries by publishing a quarterly journal, *Lutheran Libraries;* furnishing booklists; assisting member libraries with technical problems; providing meetings for mutual encouragement, assistance and exchange of ideas among members." Founded 1958. Memb. 1,250. Dues. $5, $10, $25, $100. Year. Jan. 1972–Jan. 1973.

OFFICERS (Jan. 1972–Jan. 1973)

Pres. Rose Mary Ulland, Dir. of Christian Educ., First Lutheran Church, 1005 Oxford Ave., Eau Claire, Wis. 54701; *V.P. & Pres. Elect.* To be appointed; *Secy.* Mrs. John Kendall, R. D. 2, St. Peter, Minn. 56082; *Treas.* Arthur Ellisen, 3428 Elmwood Place, Minnetonka, Minn. 55343; *Past Pres.* Rev. Carl L. Manfred, Minnesota Synod, LCA, 122 W. Franklin Ave., Minneapolis, Minn. 55404.

Exec. Secy. Mrs. E. T. Jensen.

Editor, Lutheran Libraries. Mr. Erwin E. John, 6148 Morgan Court, Minneapolis, Minn. 55419.

ADVISORY BOARD

Chairman. Rev. Malvin H. Lundeen, 122 W. Franklin, Minneapolis, Minn. 55404; Rev. Wallace J. Asper, California Lutheran Coll., Mountclef Village, Thousand Oaks, Calif. 91360; Dean Dammann, Asst. Exec. Secy., Board of Youth Ministry, Lutheran Church-Missouri Synod, 210 N. Broadway, St. Louis, Mo. 63102; Herb W. David, Secy. of Pub., Div. of Public Relations, Lutheran Council U.S.A., St. Mark's Center, 1101 O'Farrell St., San Francisco, Calif. 94109; Rev. William Gentz, Editorial Consultant Servs., P.O. Box 613, Cherry Hill, N.J. 08034; Mrs. Harold Groff, Libn., 1505 Mahan, Richland, Wash. 99352; Rev. James E. Gunther, Transfiguration Lutheran Church, 70-74 W. 126 St., New York, N.Y. 10027; Rev. Anders Hanson, Lutheran Literature Society, 50A Waterloo Rd., Hong Kong; Walter Hartkopf, Exec. Secy. Educ. & Youth, California-Nevada Dist. LCMS, 465 Woolsey St., San Francisco, Calif. 94134; Rev. Rodney D. Hokenson, Gloria Dei Lutheran Church, 505 Resurrection St., Hancock, Mich. 49930; James H. Robinson, Peace Lutheran Church, 5675 Field St., Arvada, Colo. 80002; William Wright, Capitol Univ., Columbus, Ohio 43209.

PUBLICATION

Lutheran Libraries (q.; members free; nonmembers $5.00)

COMMITTEE CHAIRMEN

Budget. Rev. Rolf Aaseng, Assoc. Ed., *Lutheran Standard,* 426 S. Fifth St., Minneapolis, Minn. 55415.

Library Services Board. Mrs. Forrest Carpenter, 6211 Logan Ave. S., Minneapolis, Minn. 55423.

Membership. Rev. A. Curtis Paul, Libn., Northwestern Lutheran Theological Seminary, 1501 Fulham St., St. Paul, Minn. 55108.

Publications Board. Rev. Carl Weller, Augsburg Publishing House, 426 S. Fifth St., Minneapolis, Minn. 55415.

MEDICAL LIBRARY ASSOCIATION
919 North Michigan Avenue, Chicago, Ill. 60611
312-642-3724

OBJECT

"(a) The fostering of medical and allied scientific libraries and the exchange of medical literature among its members. (b) To organize efforts and resources for the furtherance of the purposes and objects of the Association." Founded 1898. Memb. (Inst.) 900; (Indiv.) 1,700. Dues (Inst.) $75; (Indiv.) $30. Year. Jan.–Dec.

MEMBERSHIP

Open to those working in or interested in medical libraries.

OFFICERS (June 1971–June 1972)

Pres. Mrs. Bernice M. Hetzner, Coll. of Medicine L., Univ. of Nebraska, 42 St. & Dewey Ave., Omaha, Nebr. 68105; *V.P. & Pres. Elect.* Helen Crawford, Univ. of Wisconsin Medical S. L., 1305 Linden Dr., Madison, Wis. 53706; *Secy.* Marie Harvin, Univ. of Texas, M. D. Anderson Hospital & Tumor Institute at Houston, Houston, Tex. 77025; *Treas.* Richard A. Davis, Rosary Coll., Grad. S. of L. Sci., River Forest, Ill. 60305; *Past Pres.* Donald Washburn, D.D.S., Bureau of L. & Indexing Serv., American Dental Assn., 211 E. Chicago Ave., Chicago, Ill. 60611. *Exec. Secy.* Mrs. Helen Brown Schmidt.

DIRECTORS

Joan Titley, Health Scis. L., Univ. of Louisville, 101 W. Chestnut St., Louisville, Ky. 40202; David Bishop, McGill Univ. Medical L., 3655 Drummond St., Montreal 109, P.Q., Canada; Martin M. Cummings, M.D., National L. of Medicine, 8600 Rockville Pike, Bethesda, Md. 20014; Mrs. Helen Kovacs, State Univ. of New York, Downstate Medical Center L., 450 Clarkson Ave., Brooklyn, N.Y. 11203; Sam W. Hitt, Lyman Maynard Stowe L., Univ. of Connecticut Health Center, 1000 Asylum Ave., Hartford, Conn. 06105.

PUBLICATION

Bulletin (q.; $20)
Vital Notes (issued 3 times a year; $7.50)

STATUTORY COMMITTEE CHAIRMEN

Central Office, Subcommittee. Dr. Donald Washburn, American Dental Assn., Bureau of L. & Indexing Serv., 211 E. Chicago Ave., Chicago, Ill. 60611.

Certification. Robert T. Lentz, Jefferson Medical Coll. L., 1025 Walnut St., Philadelphia, Pa. 19107.

Committee Recruitment. Mrs. Jacqueline L. Picciano, Academy of Medicine of New Jersey L., 307-17 Belleville Ave., Bloomfield, N.J. 07003.

Convention. Robert Lewis, Biomedical L., Univ. of California at San Diego, La Jolla, Calif. 92037.

Curriculum. Mrs. Beatrice F. Davis, L. of Coll. of Physicians of Philadelphia, 19 S. 22 St., Philadelphia, Pa. 19103.

Exchange. Miss Minnie Orfanos, Dental S. L., Northwestern Univ., 311 E. Chicago Ave., Chicago, Ill. 60611.

Finance. Richard A. Davis, The John Crerar L., 35 W. 33 St., Chicago, Ill. 60616.

International Cooperation. Carroll F. Reynolds, Ph.D., Univ. of Pittsburgh, Falk L. of the Health Professions, DeSota & Terrace Sts., Pittsburgh, Pa. 15213.

Internships. Mrs. Nancy E. Zinn, History of the Health Sciences L., Univ. of Calif., San Francisco, Calif. 94122.

Membership. Gilbert J. Clausman, New York Univ., Medical Center L., 550 First Ave., New York, N.Y. 10016.

Nominating. Helen Crawford (ex officio), Univ. of Wisconsin Medical S. L., 1305 Linden Dr., Madison, Wis. 53706.

Publication. Mrs. Doris Bolef, Washington Univ. S. of Medicine, 4580 Scott Ave., St. Louis, Mo. 63110.

Scholarships. Eleanor Pasmik, New York Univ., Medical Center L., 550 First Ave., New York, N.Y. 10016.

ADDITIONAL COMMITTEE CHAIRMEN

Advice on Medical Library Problems. Mrs. Charlotte Lindner, Albert Einstein Coll. of Medicine L., Morris Park Ave. & Eastchester Rd., Bronx, N.Y. 10461.

Bibliographical Projects & Problems. Miss Joan Staats, The Jackson Lab., Res. L., Bar Harbor, Me. 04609.

Bylaws. Emilie V. Wiggins, Head, Cataloging Sec., Technical Servs. Div., National L. of Medicine, 8600 Rockville Pike, Bethesda, Md. 20014.

Committees of the Board of Directors. Helen Crawford, Univ. of Wisconsin, Medical S. L., 1305 Linden Dr., Madison, Wis. 53706.

Continuing Education. Raymond A. Palmer, Francis A. Countway L. of Medicine, 10 Shattuck St., Boston, Mass. 02115.

Continuing Education, Ad Hoc Advisory Council on. Dr. David A. Kronick, Med. S. at San Antonio L., 7703 Floyd Curl Dr., Univ. of Texas, San Antonio, Tex. 78229.

Develop a New Certification Code (Ad Hoc). Mrs. Martha Jane Zachert, L. S., Florida State Univ., Tallahassee, Fla. 32306.

Editorial Comm. on the "Handbook of Medical Library Practice." Stanley D. Truelson, Jr., Yale Medical L., 333 Cedar St., New Haven, Conn. 06510.

Editorial Comm. on Supplements to "Medical Reference Works, 1679–1966." Mrs. Edith D. Blair, Reference Sec., National L. of Medicine, 8600 Rockville Pike, Bethesda, Md. 20014.

Editorial Comm., "Vital Notes." William K. Beatty, Editor, The Archibald Church Med. L., Northwestern Univ., 303 E. Chicago Ave., Chicago, Ill. 60611.

Education Grant (Ad Hoc). Robert T. Lentz, Jefferson Medical Coll. L., 1025 Walnut St., Philadelphia, Pa. 19107.

Honors & Awards. Dr. Frank B. Rogers, Univ. of Colorado Medical Center, Charles Denison Memorial L., 4200 E. Ninth Ave., Denver, Colo. 80220.

Ida & George Eliot Prize Essay, Subcommittee. Nancy M. Lorenzi, Univ. of Louisville, Health Scis. L., 520 S. Preston St., Louisville, Ky. 40202.

Janet Doe Lecture, Subcommittee. Dr. Frank B. Rogers, Univ. of Colorado Medical Center, Charles Denison Memorial L., 4200 E. Ninth Ave., Denver, Colo. 80220.

Legislation. Mrs. Jacqueline W. Felter, Medical L. Center of New York, 17 E. 102 St., New York, N.Y. 10029.

MLA/NLM Liaison. William Beatty, Northwestern Univ. Medical S., Archibald Church L., 303 E. Chicago Ave., Chicago, Ill. 60611.

Medical Library Technician Training. Richard A. Miller, Virginia Commonwealth Univ., Tompkins-McCaw L., Box 667, Richmond, Va. 23219.

Murray Gottlieb Essay, Subcommittee. Dr. Peter D. Olch, Deputy Chief, History of Medicine Div., National L. of Medicine, 8600 Rockville Pike, Bethesda, Md. 20014.

Past Presidents' Council. Elliott H. Morse, Coll. of Physicians of Philadelphia L., 19 S. 22 St., Philadelphia, Pa. 19103.

Program & Convention. Elliott H. Morse, Coll. of Physicians of Philadelphia L., 19 S. 22 St., Philadelphia, Pa. 19103.

Publication of "Current Catalog" Proof Sheets. Sheldon Kotzin, Technical Servs. Div., National L. of Medicine, 8600 Rockville Pike, Bethesda, Md. 20014.

Regional Medical Library Programs. Dr. Andrew Lasslo, Univ. of Tennessee Medical Units, Coll. of Pharmacy, Dept. of Medicinal Chemistry, Memphis, Tenn. 38103.

Review the Goals & Structure of the Medical Library Association, Ad Hoc Comm. to. Erich Meyerhoff, Health Sciences L., State Univ. of New York, Buffalo, 141 Capen Hall, 15 The Circle, Buffalo, N.Y. 14214.

Rittenhouse Award, Subcommittee. Alice C. Joyce, Washington Univ., School of Medicine L., 4580 Scott Ave., St. Louis, Mo. 63110.

Selection Comm. for Director of Medical Library Education (Ad Hoc). Richard A. Davis, John Crerar L., 35 W. 33 St., Chicago, Ill. 60616.

Surveys & Statistics. Susan Crawford, Ph.D., Archive-L. Dept., American Medical Assn., 535 North Dearborn St., Chicago, Ill. 60610.

MUSIC LIBRARY ASSOCIATION

OBJECT
"To promote the development of music libraries; to encourage studies in the organization and administration of music libraries and music in libraries." Founded 1931. Memb. 1,650. Dues. (Inst.) $15; (Indiv.) $12; (Students) $6.50. Year. September 1, 1971–August 31, 1972.

MEMBERSHIP
All persons or institutions actively engaged in library work, or who have an interest in the stated purposes of the Association.

OFFICERS (term staggered)
Pres. William McClellan, Music L., Univ. of Illinois, Urbana, Ill. 61801; *V.P.* Donald Seibert, Music L., Syracuse Univ., Syracuse, N.Y. 13210; *Recording Secy.* Beverly Proctor, Catalog Dept., Univ. of Toronto, Toronto 5, Ont., Canada; *Treas.* Mrs. Ruth Hilton, Music L., New York Univ., New York, N.Y. 10003; *Ed. of "Notes."* Frank C. Campbell, Music Div., L. of the Performing Arts, Lincoln Center, New York, N.Y. 10023.
Exec. Secy. William J. Weichlein, 104 W. Huron St., Rm. 329, Ann Arbor, Mich. 48108.

BOARD OF DIRECTORS (term staggered)
The officers and Walter Gerboth, Music L., Brooklyn Coll., Brooklyn, N.Y. 11210; Mrs. Dena Epstein, Music L., Univ. of Chicago, Chicago, Ill. 60637; Marion Korda, Music L., Univ. of Louisville, Louisville, Ky. 40222; Richard Colvig, Oakland P.L., Oakland, Calif. 94610; James Pruett, Music L., Univ. of North Carolina, Chapel Hill, N.C. 27514; Mary Wallace, Music L., Wellesley Coll., Wellesley, Mass. 02181; William J. Weichlein, 104 W. Huron St., Rm. 329, Ann Arbor, Mich. 48108.

PUBLICATIONS
Notes (q.; institutional memb. or subscrip., $15.00; personal memb., $12.00; personal subscription, $10.00)

MLA Cataloging Bulletin (mo.; $5.00 per year to U.S. and Canada)

MLA Index Series (irreg.; price varies according to size)

MLA Newsletter (irreg.; free to memb.)

COMMITTEE CHAIRMEN
Automation. Carol Bradley, Music Dept. SUNY, Buffalo, N.Y. 14214.

Buildings & Equipment. Mary Wallace, Music L., Wellesley Coll., Wellesley, Mass. 02181.

Cataloging & Classification. Donald Seibert, Music L., Syracuse Univ., Syracuse, N.Y. 13210.

Continuing Education. Lenore Coral, Univ. of California, Irvine, Calif. 92664.

Library Personnel & Placement. Shirley Piper, Music L., Northwestern Univ., Evanston, Ill. 60201.

Phonorecord Analytics. Olga Buth, Music L., Ohio State Univ., Coumbus, Ohio 43210.

Professional Training. Donald W. Krummel, S. of L. Sci., Univ. of Illinois, Urbana, Ill. 61801.

Publications. James Pruett, Music L., Univ. of North Carolina, Chapel Hill, N.C. 27514.

Standards. Jean Bowen, Music Div., L. & Museum of the Performing Arts, Lincoln Ctr., New York, N.Y. 10023.

NATIONAL MICROFILM ASSOCIATION
8728 Colesville Road, Silver Spring, Md. 20910
301-587-8444

OBJECT

"The promotion of lawful interests of the microreproduction industry in the direction of good business ethics; the liberal discussion of subjects pertaining to the industry; technological improvement and research; standardization; the methods of manufacturing and marketing; the education of the consumer in the use of microreproduction systems." Founded 1943. Memb. 6,000. Dues. $30. Year. July 1, 1971–June 30, 1972.

OFFICERS (May 1971–May 1972)

Pres. John R. Robertson, Eastman Kodak Co., 343 State St., Rochester, N.Y. 14650; *V.P. & Treas.* Milton Mandel, Microfilming Corp. of America, 21 Harristown Rd., Glen Rock, N.J. 07452; *Exec. V.P.* Frederick L. Williford, National Microfilm Assn., 8728 Colesville Rd., Silver Spring, Md. 20910.

(Note: Address all general correspondence to Frederick L. Williford, Exec. V.P., NMA at headquarters address.)

PUBLICATIONS

The Journal of Micrographics (bi-mo.; memb.)
  Micro-News Bulletin (bi-mo.; memb.)
  Proceedings of the Annual Convention (a.; memb.)
  Other publications available.

CHAPTERS

Capitol. Harry Fegan, 3M Co., BPSI, 5570 Port Royal Rd., Springfield, Va. 22151.
Chicago. John A. Neuzil, Spiegel, Inc., 1040 W. 35 St., Chicago, Ill. 60609.
Connecticut Valley. Joseph J. Forgione, Travelers Insurance Co., 1 Tower Sq., Hartford, Conn. 06115.
Garden State. A. J. Seele (acting pres.), Eastman Kodak, BSMD, 240 Sheffield St., Mountainside, N.J. 07092.
Golden Gate. Edward Cox, Fireman's Fund Insurance Co., 3333 California St., San Francisco, Calif. 94120.
Long Island. Robert T. McGrath, P.O. Box 712, Melville, N.Y. 11746.
Maryland. John P. Sheffield, 1504 Kirkwood Rd., Baltimore, Md. 21207.
Metropolitan New York. Cy Brownstein, Microfiche Systems Corp., 305 E. 46 St., New York, N.Y. 10017.
Michigan. Arthur H. Droman, Jr., North American Rockwell, Technical Center, 2445 W. Maple Rd., Troy, Mich. 48084.
Midwest. David D. Amren, Charles Bruning Co., 3127 Brady St., Davenport, Iowa 52808.
Minnesota. Henry Whitbeck, Investors Diversified Service, Investors Bldg., Minneapolis, Minn. 55402.
New England. Chester I. Jackman, Foxboro Co., Dept. 322, Foxboro, Mass. 02035.
North Texas. Joseph E. Grimsley, LTV-Vought Aero Co., 1713 Briardale Court, Arlington, Tex. 76013.
Northwest. Paul Chasey, Eastman Kodak Co., 9675 Sunset Hwy., Mercer Island, Wash. 98040.
Ohio. Dwight J. Snyder, Marathon Oil Co., 539 S. Main St., Rm. 3645, Findlay, Ohio 45840.
Rocky Mountain. Ron Sundstrom, Eastman Kodak Co., P.O. Box 1587, Denver, Colo. 80210.
San Diego. Gerald H. Todd, Bell & Howell Co., 1024 Monterey Court, Chula Vista, Calif. 92011.
Southeastern. Pierce Lowrey, Jr., Atlanta Blue Print Co., 1055 Spring St. N.W., Atlanta, Ga. 30309.
Southwest. Norris Majors, County Clerk's Office, Harris County, P.O. Box 1525, Houston, Tex. 77001.
St. Louis. Burton Granat, Microtek/ Microfilm Techniques, Inc., 820 Hanley Industrial Court, St. Louis, Mo. 63144.
William Penn. James E. Crow, E. I. duPont de Nemours & Co., Secretary's Dept., 708 Farmer's Bank Bldg., Wilmington, Del. 19898.
Wisconsin. Charlesworth L. Dickerson, S. C. Johnson & Son, Inc., 1525 Howe St., Racine, Wis. 53403.

SOCIETY OF AMERICAN ARCHIVISTS

OBJECT

"To promote sound principles of archival economy and to facilitate cooperation among archivists and archival agencies." Founded 1936. Memb. 1,600. Dues. (Indiv.) $15; (Contributing) $25; (Life) $300; (Inst.) $25; (Sustaining) $100.

OFFICERS (Oct. 1971–Nov. 1972)

Pres. Charles E. Lee, South Carolina Dept. of Archives & History, 1430 Senate St., Columbia, S.C. 29201; *V.P. & Pres. Elect.* Wilfred I. Smith, Public Archives of Canada, 295 Wellington St., Ottawa, Ont., Canada; *Secy.* Robert M. Warner, Michigan Historical Collections, Rackham Bldg., Ann Arbor, Mich. 48104; *Treas.* Mr. A. K. Johnson, Jr., Society of American Archivists, P.O. Box 7993, Atlanta, Ga. 30309; *Ed.* Edward Weldon, *The American Archivist*, The National Archives, Washington, D.C. 20408.

(Note: Address all general correspondence to the Secy.)

COUNCIL

Dr. Frank B. Evans, 3102 Belair Dr., Bowie, Md. 20715; Dr. C. Herbert Finch, 904 Coddington Rd., Ithaca, N.Y. 14850; Barbara G. Fisher, Univ. Archivist, Univ. of Oregon, Eugene, Ore. 97403; Mrs. Elizabeth E. Hamer, 6620 River Rd., Bethesda, Md. 20034; Edward N. Johnson, Bureau of Archives & Records Management, The Capitol, Tallahassee, Fla. 32304; Harold T. Pinkett, National Archives & Records Serv., Washington, D.C. 20408; James B. Rhoads, Archivist of the United States, National Archives & Records Serv., Washington, D.C. 20408; Walter Rundell, Jr., Dept. of History, Iowa State Univ., Ames, Iowa 50010.

PUBLICATIONS

The American Archivist (q.; $15)

SAA Placement Newsletter (bi-mo.; upon request)

COMMITTEE CHAIRMEN

Archives-Library Relationships (Ad Hoc). Mrs. Elizabeth E. Hamer, 6620 River Rd., Bethesda, Md. 20034.

Archives of Science. Murphy D. Smith, American Philosophical Society, 105 S. Fifth St., Philadelphia, Pa. 19106.

Audiovisual Records. John B. Kuiper, 6305 Stoneham Rd., Bethesda, Md. 20034.

Auditing. Robert Williams, 401 E. Gaines St., Tallahassee, Fla. 32301.

Buildings & Technical Services. Frank B. Evans, 3102 Belair Dr., Bowie, Md. 20715.

Church Archives. August R. Suelflow, Concordia Historical Inst., 801 DeMun Ave., St. Louis, Mo. 63105.

Collecting of Personal Papers & Manuscripts. John E. Wickman, Dwight D. Eisenhower L., Abilene, Kans. 67410.

College & University Archives. Mrs. Ruth W. Helmuth, 19200 Genesee Rd., Euclid, Ohio 44117.

Data Archives & Machine-readable Records. Meyer H. Fishbein, National Archives & Records Serv., Rm. 2W, Washington, D.C. 20408.

Education & Training. David C. Duniway, State Archivist, Oregon State L., Salem, Ore. 97310.

Federal & State Governmental Relations. Robert Williams, 401 E. Gaines St., Tallahassee, Fla. 32301.

International Archival Affairs. Wilfred I. Smith, Public Archives of Canada, Ottawa 2, Ont., Can.

Local Arrangements—1972. David R. Larson, Ohio Historical Society, 17 Ave. & Rte. 71, Columbus, Ohio 43211.

1970s, Comm. of the. Philip P. Mason, 144 General L., Wayne State Univ. Archives, Detroit, Mich. 48202.

Oral History. John F. Stewart, John F. Kennedy L., 380 Trapelo Rd., Waltham, Mass. 02154.

Paper Research (Ad Hoc). Gordon L. Williams, The Center for Research Ls., 5721 Cottage Grove Ave., Chicago, Ill. 60637.

Preservation Methods. Clark W. Nelson, 930 Seventh Ave. S.W., Rochester, Minn. 55901.

Professional Standards. Philip P. Mason, 144 General L., Wayne State Univ. Archives, Detroit, Mich. 48202.
Program. Herman Viola, National Archives & Records Serv., Washington, D.C. 20408.
Publications. Howard L. Applegate, Balch Institute, 1627 Fidelity Bldg., 123 S. Broad St., Philadelphia, Pa. 19109.
Records Management. Ivan Eyler, 4301 Winding Way, Fort Worth, Tex. 76126.
Reference, Access & Photoduplication Policies. Mary Lynn McCree, Jane Addams' Hull-House, Univ. of Illinois-Chicago Circle, Box 4348, Chicago, Ill. 60680.
State & Local Records. Edward N. Johnson, 1106 Sandhurst Dr., Tallahassee, Fla. 32303.
Symposia & Regional Activities, Coordinating Comm. for. Paul A. Kohl, National Archives & Records Serv., 6125 Sand Point Way N.E., Seattle, Wash. 98115.
Techniques for the Control & Description of Archives & Manuscripts. Frank G. Burke, National Archives & Records Serv., Washington, D.C. 20408.
Terminology (Ad Hoc). William L. Rofes, IBM Corp., Armonk, N.Y. 10504.
Urban & Industrial Archives. Dennis East, 5802 Harvard, Detroit, Mich. 48224.

SPECIAL LIBRARIES ASSOCIATION
235 Park Avenue South, New York, N. Y. 10003
212-777-8136

OBJECT

"To encourage and promote the utilization of knowledge through the collection, organization and dissemination of information, to develop the usefulness and efficiency of special libraries or information centers to stimulate research in the field of information services, to promote high professional standards, to facilitate communications among its members, and to cooperate with organizations that have similar or allied interests." Organized 1909. Memb. 6,800. Dues. (Sustaining) $100; (Indiv.) $30; (Student) $5. Year. Jan.–Dec.

OFFICERS (June 1971–June 1972)

Pres. Efren W. Gonzalez, Bristol-Myers Products, Science Information Servs., 1350 Liberty Ave., Hillside, N.J. 07207; *Pres. Elect.* Edward G. Strable, J. Walter Thompson Co., Information Servs., 875 N. Michigan Ave., Chicago, Ill. 60611; *Advisory Council Chairman.* Forrest H. Alter, Flint P.L., Art, Music & Drama Dept., Flint, Mich. 48502; *Advisory Council Chmn.-Elect.* Mrs. Zoe L. Cosgrove, 3M Co., Tape Technical L., 3M Center, Bldg. 230-1S, St. Paul, Minn. 55010; *Treas.* Janet M. Rigney, Foreign Relations L., 58 E. 68 St., New York, N.Y. 10021; *Past Pres.* Florine Oltman, Air Univ. L., Maxwell AFB, Ala. 36112.
Exec. Dir. F. E. McKenna.

DIRECTORS

Edythe Moore, Aerospace Corp., Charles C. Lauritsen L. (A4/108), P.O. Box 95085, Los Angeles, Calif. 90045; Loyd R. Rathbun, Massachusetts Institute of Technology, Lincoln Laboratory L., Lexington, Mass. 02173; John P. Binnington, Brookhaven National Laboratory, Research L., Upton, N.Y. 11973; Miriam H. Tees, Royal Bank of Canada, P.O. Box 6001, Montreal 3, P.Q.; Mark H. Baer, Hewlett-Packard Co. Ls., 1501 Page Mill Rd., Palo Alto, Calif. 94304; Molete Morelock, Purdue Univ. Ls., Inter-Institutional L. Servs., West Lafayette, Ind. 47907.

PUBLICATIONS

Scientific Meetings (4 issues; $17.50; other than U.S. & Canada, add $1.00 postage)
Special Libraries (10 issues; $22.50; other than U.S. & Canada, add $2.00 postage)

Technical Book Review Index (10 issues; $16; other than U.S. & Canada, add $1.50 postage)

COMMITTEE CHAIRMEN

Bylaws. Edward P. Miller, Tulsa City-County L., Tulsa, Okla. 74103.

Chapter Liaison Officer. Joseph M. Dagnese, Rm. 14E-210, M. I. T. Ls., Cambridge, Mass. 02139.

Committee on Committees. Rosemary R. Demarest, Price Waterhouse Co., 60 Broad St., New York, N.Y. 10004.

Conference. Loyd Rathbun, M. I. T., Lincoln Lab., Lexington, Mass. 02173.

Conference Advisory. Mark H. Baer, Hewlett-Packard County Ls., 1501 Page Mill Rd., Palo Alto, Calif. 94304.

Consultation Service. Mrs. Audrey N. Grosch, 3314 Kyle Ave. N., Minneapolis, Minn. 55422.

Division Liaison Officer. Bess P. Walford, Philip Morris USA, Research Center L., P.O. Box 26583, Richmond, Va. 23261.

Education. Harold R. Malinowsky, 2214 Hillcourt, Lawrence, Kans. 66044.

Finance. Janet M. Rigney, Foreign Relations L., 58 E. 68 St., New York, N.Y. 10021.

Government Information Services. Mrs. Ruth Smith, Inst. for Defense Analyses, 400 Army Navy Dr., Arlington, Va. 22202.

Governmental Relations Project. Mrs. Mary A. Huffer, Smithsonian Institution Ls., Washington, D.C. 20560.

Headquarters Operations. Efren W. Gonzalez, Bristol-Myers Products, Science Information Servs., 1350 Liberty Ave., Hillside, N.J. 07207.

International Relations. Mrs. Herta D. Fischer, California State Coll. at Fullerton L., Fullerton, Calif. 92631.

Membership. Alberta D. Berton, Medical Documentation Serv., Coll. of Physicians of Philadelphia, 19 S. 22 St., Philadelphia, Pa. 19103.

Nominating. James Humphry, H. W. Wilson Co., 950 University Ave., Bronx, N.Y. 10452.

Placement Policy. Florence M. McKenna, 4517 Parade St., Pittsburgh, Pa. 15207.

Planning. Alleen Thompson, General Electric Co., Atomic Power Equipment Dept., 175 Curtner Ave., San Jose, Calif. 95125.

Public Relations Officer. Appointment pending.

Publisher Relations. Robert G. Krupp, 1 Dewitt Rd., Apt. 103, Elizabeth, N.J. 07208.

Recruitment. Mrs. Joan M. Toeppe, 28784 Johnson Dr., Wickliffe, Ohio 44092.

Research. Dr. Martha Jane K. Zachert, S. of L. Sci., Florida State Univ., Tallahassee, Fla. 32306.

Resolutions. Sally C. Birch, Main St., Bolton, Mass. 01740.

SLA Professional Award & SLA Hall of Fame. Robert W. Gibson, Jr., General Motors Corp., Research Labs. L., 12 Mile & Mound Rds., Warren, Mich. 48090.

SLA Scholarship. Clement G. Vitek, The Baltimore Sunpapers, Calvert & Centre Sts., Baltimore, Md. 21203.

Standards. Logan O. Cowgill, 26 Sixth St. S.E., Washington, D.C. 20003.

Student Relations Officer. Dr. Lucille Whalen, S. of L. Sci., State Univ. of New York at Albany, Albany, N.Y. 12203.

Tellers. Barbara Thompson, American Iron and Steel Institute, 150 E. 42 St., New York, N.Y. 10017.

THEATRE LIBRARY ASSOCIATION

OBJECT

"To further the interests of collecting, preserving, and using theatre, cinema, and performing arts materials in libraries, museums, and private collections." Founded 1937. Memb. 500. Dues (Indiv.) $5; (Inst.) $8. Year. Sept. 1971–Aug. 1972.

OFFICERS (Sept. 1970–Aug. 1972)

Pres. Louis A. Rachow, Libn., Walter Hampden Mem. L., The Players, 16 Gramercy Park, New York, N.Y. 10003; *V.P.* Robert M. Henderson, L.-Museum of the Performing Arts, New York, N.Y. 10023; *Secy.-Treas.* Richard M. Buck,

Research L. of the Performing Arts, New York, N.Y. 10023; *Recording Secy.* Miss Mary Grahn, 420 Whitney Ave., New Haven, Conn. 06511; *Chairman of Board.* Mrs. Marguerite McAneny, 67 Grover Ave., Princeton, N.J. 08540.

(Note: All general correspondence is to be sent to Mr. Richard M. Buck, Secretary-Treasurer, Theatre Library Assn., 111 Amsterdam Ave., New York, N.Y. 10023.)

EXECUTIVE BOARD

The officers and Hobart Berolzheimer, Mark Wilson Collection of Lit. Dept., Free L. of Philadelphia, Logan Sq., Philadelphia, Pa. 19103; William S. Forshaw, Humanities Dept., Enoch Pratt Free L., Baltimore, Md. 21201; Mrs. Sarah Chokla Gross, Editor, *Broadside,* 11 Newkirk Ave., E. Rockaway, N.Y. 11518; Fredric M. Litto, Editor, *Theatre Documentation,* International Theatre Studies Center, Univ. of Kans., Lawrence, Kans. 66045; Robert M. MacGregor, Dir., Theatre Arts Books, 333 Sixth Ave., New York, N.Y. 10014; Brooks McNamara, Dept. of Drama & Cinema, N.Y. Univ., Washington Sq., New York, N.Y. 10003; Miss Helen D. Willard, Curator, Theatre Collection, Harvard Coll. L., Cambridge, Mass. 02138.

COMMITTEE CHAIRMEN

Constitution & Bylaws. Robert M. MacGregor.

George Freedley Award. Robert H. Ball, Dept. of Eng., Queens Coll., Flushing, N.Y. 11367.

Program & Special Events. Robert M. Henderson.

PUBLICATION

Broadside (irreg.; memb.)

Theatre Documentation (bi-a; memb.)

UNITED STATES BOOK EXCHANGE, INC.

3335 V Street, N.E., Washington, D.C. 20018

202-LAwrence 9-2555

OBJECT

"To promote the distribution and interchange of books, periodicals, and other scholarly materials among libraries and other educational and scientific institutions of the United States, and between them and libraries and institutions of other countries." Organized 1948. Membership in USBE is open to any library which serves a constituency and which is an institution or part of an institution or organization. The USBE corporation includes a representative from each member library and from each of a group of sponsoring organizations listed below.

OFFICERS

Chmn. of Board & Pres. Dr. David Kaser, Dir. of Ls., Cornell Univ., Ithaca, N.Y. 14850; *V.P. & Pres. Elect.* Mrs. Avis Zebker, Book Order Coord., Brooklyn P.L., Brooklyn, N.Y. 11225; *Secy.* (1972–1973) F. Kurt Cylke, Exec. Secy., Federal Library Committee, L. of Congress, Washington, D.C. 20540; *Treas.* (1972) Havard Rovelstad, Dir. of Ls., Univ. of Maryland, College Park, Md. 20742.

Exec. Dir. Alice D. Ball, U.S. Book Exchange.

Assoc. Exec. Dir. Mrs. Elaine A. Kurtz.

Immediate Past Pres. W. Porter Kellam, Dir. of Ls., Univ. of Georgia, Athens, Ga. 30601.

BOARD OF DIRECTORS

Mrs. Lillian M. Bradshaw, Dir., Dallas P.L., Dallas, Tex. 75201; Myrl Ebert, Chief Libn., Health Scis. L., Univ. of North Carolina, Chapel Hill, N.C. 27514; Mrs. Helen Howard, Univ. Libn., Sir George Williams Univ., Montreal 25, Quebec, Canada; John H. Rebenack, Chief Libn., Akron Public Library, 55 So. Main St., Akron, Ohio 44308; Mrs. Elizabeth B. Roth, Chief Libn., Standard Oil Co. of California, 225 Bush St., San Francisco, Calif. 94120; David S. Zubatsky, Chief, Acquisitions Dept., Washington

Univ., Skinker & Lindell Blvd., St. Louis, Mo. 63130.

SPONSORING MEMBERS

American Association of Law Libraries, American Council of Learned Societies, American Council on Education, American Society for Information Science, American Library Association, American Theological Library Association, Association American Library Schools, Association of Jewish Libraries, Association Research Libraries, Catholic Library Association, Engineers Joint Council, Federal Library Committee, Library of Congress, Medical Library Association, Music Library Association, National Academy of Sciences, National Agricultural Library, National Library of Medicine, Smithsonian Institution, Social Science Research Council, Special Libraries Association, Theatre Library Association.

412 / LIBRARY AND BOOK TRADE ASSOCIATIONS AND AGENCIES

CHART OF NATIONAL LIBRARY ASSOCIATIONS

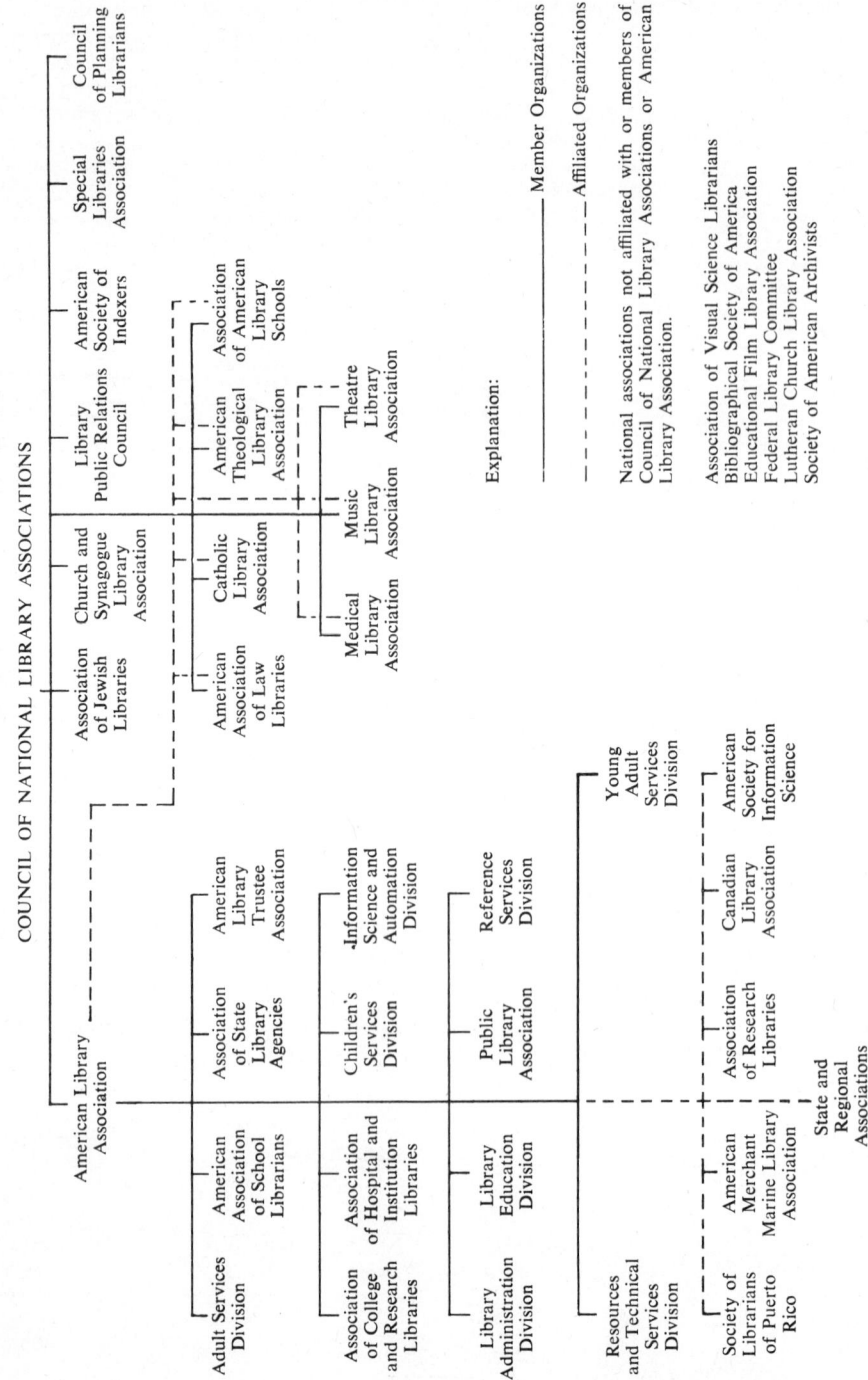

COUNCIL OF NATIONAL LIBRARY ASSOCIATIONS

American Library Association
- Adult Services Division
- American Association of School Librarians
- Association of State Library Agencies
- Association of College and Research Libraries
- Association of Hospital and Institution Libraries
- American Library Trustee Association
- Children's Services Division
- Information Science and Automation Division
- Library Administration Division
- Library Education Division
- Public Library Association
- Reference Services Division
- Resources and Technical Services Division
- Young Adult Services Division

Association of Jewish Libraries
Church and Synagogue Library Association
Library Public Relations Council
American Society of Indexers
Special Libraries Association
Council of Planning Librarians

American Association of Law Libraries
Catholic Library Association
American Theological Library Association
Association of American Library Schools

Medical Library Association
Music Library Association
Theatre Library Association

Society of Librarians of Puerto Rico
American Merchant Marine Library Association
Association of Research Libraries
Canadian Library Association
American Society for Information Science

State and Regional Associations

Explanation:
———— Member Organizations
– – – – Affiliated Organizations

National associations not affiliated with or members of Council of National Library Associations or American Library Association:

Association of Visual Science Librarians
Bibliographical Society of America
Educational Film Library Association
Federal Library Committee
Lutheran Church Library Association
Society of American Archivists

STATE, REGIONAL, AND PROVINCIAL ASSOCIATIONS

For dates and places of annual conventions, see "Library Association Meetings," this volume.

Alabama

Pres. Nancy R. Agnew,* Dir., Wheeler Basin Regional L., Decatur 35601; *V.P. & Pres. Elect.* George Johnson, Dir., Cross Trails Regional L., 111 E. Hart Ave., Opp 36467; *2nd V.P.* Mrs. Jimmie McWhorter, Mobile P.L., Mobile 36608; *Secy.* Mrs. Arloene B. Becklund, 5900 Woodvale Dr., Mobile 36608; *Treas.* Robert D. Schalau, Dir., Anniston-Calhoun County, P.O. Box 308, Anniston 36201. Memb. 991. Term of Office. Apr. '71–Apr. '72. Publication. *The Alabama Librarian* (3 issues).

Alberta

Pres. John G. Wright, Assoc. Prof., S. of L.Sci., Univ. of Alberta, Edmonton 7; *1st V.P.* Joseph Carver, Chief Libn., Medicine Hat P.L., Medicine Hat; *2nd V.P.* Joseph Siqueira, Dir., Curriculum Materials Centre, Faculty of Educ., Univ. of Calgary, Calgary 44; *Secy.* Mrs. Elizabeth Schwob, Ref. Libn., Cameron L., Univ. of Alberta, Edmonton 7; *Treas.* Mrs. Flora Reed, Off. Mgr., Parkland Regional L., Lacombe. *Past Pres.* David Emery, Univ. of Alberta L., Edmonton 7. Memb. (Indiv.) 304; (Inst.) 136; (Trustees) 39. Term of Office. June '71–June '72. Publication. *The Bulletin* (q.). (Address correspondence to: Mrs. Flora Reed, Library Association of Alberta, Box 1000, Lacombe, Alberta.)

Arizona

Pres. Mrs. Betty Thomas,* Dir., Yuma City-County L.; *Pres. Elect.* Frank VanZanten, Dir., Tucson P.Ls.; *V.P.* Betty Burson, Phoenix P.L.; *Secy.* Mrs. Elizabeth Puckett, Saguaro H.S.; *Treas.* Gertrude James, Consultant, Phoenix Elem. Ss.; *Immediate Past Pres.* Marguerite Pasquale, Rincon H.S. Memb. 876. Term of Office. Apr. '71–Apr. '72. Publication. *ASLA Newsletter*. Ed. Mrs. Coralee Parsil, Valencia L., Tucson.

Arkansas

Pres. J. William Hansard, Arkansas State Univ., Jonesboro; *V.P. & Pres. Elect.* Mrs. Mary Gale Ownbey, Woodland Jr. H.S., Fayetteville; *2nd V.P.* Larry Larson, Conway; *Secy.* Mrs. Mary B. Parker, Pine Bluff; *Treas.* George A. Severson, Peel. Term of Office. 1971–1972. Publication. *Arkansas Libraries* (q.).

Atlantic Provinces

(New Brunswick, Newfoundland, Nova Scotia, Prince Edward Island) *Pres.* Don Ryan, St. John's, Newfoundland; *Immediate Past Pres.* Eleanor Magee, Sackville; *V.P. for Newfoundland.* Sally Davis, St. John's; *V.P. for N.S.* Beverly True, Amherst; *V.P. for N.B.* Ian Wilson, St. John's; *V.P. for P.E.I. & Pres. Elect.* Don Scott, Charlottetown; *Secy.* Harriett Pearce, St. John's; *Treas.* Bill Partridge, Halifax. Memb. (Indiv.) 175; (Inst.) 207. Term of Office. Sept. '71–Sept. '72.

Connecticut

Pres. Dr. Evelyn R. Robinson,* Southern Connecticut State Coll., New Haven 06515; *V.P. & Pres. Elect.* Mrs. Grace M. Birch, Trumbull P.L., Trumbull 06611; *2nd V.P.* William Clayton Massey, South Windsor P.L., South Windsor 06074; *Treas.* Denis M. Lorenz, Bridgeport P.L., 925 Broad St., Bridgeport 06603. Memb. (Indiv.) 1,147. Term of Office. July '71–June '72. Publication. *Connecticut Libraries* (q.).

Florida

Pres. Leo Meirose, Ft. Lauderdale P.L., 1300 E. Sunrise Blvd., Ft. Lauderdale 33304; *V.P. & Pres. Elect.* David Kantor, Volusia County Ls., Daytona Beach 32014; *Secy.* Mrs. Janis Coker,* Tampa P.L., 900 Ashley, Tampa 33602; *Treas.* Paul Donovan, Florida Atlantic

---

*Indicates to whom all general correspondence should be addressed.

Univ. L., Boca Raton 33432. Memb. (Indiv.) 1,137; (Inst.) 78. Term of Office. May '71–May '72.

Georgia

Pres. Mrs. Margaret Kerr, City of Decatur Ss., Decatur 30030; *1st V.P.* Mary Louise Rheay, Atlanta P.L., Atlanta 30303; *2nd V.P.* Ray Rowland, Augusta College, Augusta 30904; *Exec. Secy.* Mrs. Ann W. Morton,* P.O. Box 176, Decatur 30301; *Treas.* Leroy Childs, West Georgia Regional L., Carrollton 30117. Memb. 1,300. Term of Office. Oct. '71–Oct. '73. Publication. *Georgia Librarian* (q.).

Hawaii

Pres. Br. Richard Roesch, S.M., St. Anthony's S., Wailuku, Maui 96793; *V.P.* Gloria Miyashiro, Hawaii State L., 478 S. King St., Honolulu, Hawaii 96813; *Secy.* Mrs. Maile Williams, Hawaiian Sugar Planters' Assn., 1527 Keeaumoku St., Honolulu, Hawaii 96822; *Treas.* William Lindstrom, Gifts and Exchanges, Hamilton L., Univ. of Hawaii, Honolulu, Hawaii 96822. Memb. 436. Term of Office. Apr. '71–Apr. '72. Publications. *Hawaii Library Association Journal* (s-a); *Hawaii Library Association Newsletter* (q.).

(Address correspondence to: Hawaii Library Association, P.O. Box 4441, Honolulu, Hawaii 96812.)

Idaho

Pres. Rex A. White,* Idaho State Univ. L., Pocatello 83201 ; *V.P. & Pres. Elect.* Mrs. Mabelle Wallan, 801 E. Jefferson, Boise 83702; *Secy.* Mrs. Sandra Roberts, Idaho State Univ., Pocatello 83201; *Treas.* Mrs. Helen C. Smith, 1121 S. Fourth Ave., Pocatello 83201. Memb. (Indiv.) 417; (Inst.) 47. Term of Office. May '71–May '72. Publication. *The Idaho Librarian* (q.).

Illinois

Pres. Donald E. Wright,* Evanston P.L., Evanston 60201; *1st V.P. & Pres. Elect.* Peter Bury, Glenview P.L., Glenview 60025; *2nd V.P.* Richard Brandelino, Joliet Township H.S. & Jr. Coll., Joliet 60431; *Secy.* Beth Mueller, Suburban L. System, Burr Ridge 60521; *Treas.* Sidney Matthews, Southern Illinois Univ., Carbondale 62901. Memb. 4,187. Term of Office. Oct. '71–Oct. '72. Publication. *ILA Reporter.*

Indiana

Pres. Edward A. Howard,* Evansville P.L., 22 S.E. 5 St., Evansville 47708; *V.P. & Pres. Elect.* Ruth E. Kellogg, Elkhart P.L., 300 S. Indiana St., Elkhart 46514; *Secy.* Mrs. Mary M. McMillan, Plainfield P.L., Plainfield 46168; *Treas.* Mrs. Phyllis Manago, The Peabody L., Columbia City 46725; *Dir.-at-Large.* Molete Morelock, Purdue Univ. Ls., West Lafayette 47906. Memb. (Life) 81; (Indiv.) 941; (Inst.) 115. Term of Office. Oct. '71–Oct. '72. Publication. *Focus on Indiana Libraries* (q.).

Iowa

Pres. Marjorie Humby, Libn., P.L., Waverly 50677; *V.P. & Pres. Elect.* H. Wendell Alford, Asst. Dir. L. Servs., Univ. of Northern Iowa, Cedar Falls 50613; *Exec. Assts.* Don H. Allen and Mildred K. Allen,* P.O. Box 771, Des Moines 50303. Memb. 1,450. Term of Office. Nov. '71–Oct. '72. Publication. *The Catalyst* (bi-m.), Ed. Don H. Allen, P.O. Box 771, Des Moines 50303.

Kansas

Pres. William M. Usher, Natl. Bank of America, 100 S. Santa Fe, Salina 67401; *V.P. & Pres. Elect.* Mrs. Margaret Meyer,* Topeka P.L., 1515 W. 10 St., Topeka 66604; *Secy.* Joyce Davis, Southwest Kansas L. System, Dodge City 67801; *Treas.* Raymond Willson, Southeast Kansas L. System, 218 E. Madison, Iola 66749. Memb. 685. Term of Office. July '71–June '72. Publication. *KLA Newsletter* (q.).

Kentucky

Pres. Mrs. Madge C. Davis,* Info. Referral Center, Univ. of Louisville, Louisville 40208; *V.P. & Pres. Elect.* Ernest E. Weyrauch, Dir. of Ls., Eastern Kentucky Univ., Richmond 40475; *Secy.* Mary E. Quin, Govt. Documents Libn., Louisville Free P.L., Louisville 40203; *Treas.* Mrs. Lucile Callis, Regional Libn., Green River Regional L., 450 Griffith Ave., Owensboro 42301; *ALA Councilor.* Nella Bailey, Supervisor of S. Ls., Kentucky Dept. of Ls., Frankfort 40601. Memb. 800. Term of Office. Pres. & V.P./Pres. Elect — Jan. '72–Dec. '72; Secy. & Treas. — Jan. '72–Dec. '73. Publication. *Kentucky Library Association Bulletin* (q.).

Louisiana

Pres. Mrs. Reva Chesson, 1040 Holly St., Lake Charles 70601; *1st V.P. & Pres. Elect.* John Ische, Libn., La. State Univ. Medical Center L., 1542 Tulane Ave., New Orleans 70112; *2nd V.P.* Mrs. Mabel Hemphill, Catalog Dept., La. Tech. Univ., Ruston 71270; *Secy.* Mrs. Ferne Tucker, 3737 Eddy Place, Shreveport 71107; *Treas.* Doris Lessel, Libn., Webster Parish L., 521 East & West St., Minden 71055; *Parliamentarian.* Alex Allain, Trustee, St. Mary Parish L. Board, P.O. Box 329, Jeannerette 70544. Memb. (Indiv.) 1,127; (Inst.) 81. Term of Office. July '71–June '72. Publication. *L.L.A. Bulletin* (q.).

(Address correspondence to: Mrs. Chris Thomas, Exec. Secy., P.O. Box 131, Baton Rouge, La. 70821.)

Manitoba

Pres. John S. Russell, Chief Libn., St. James-Assiniboia P.L., 1910 Portage Ave., Winnipeg 12; *V.P.* J. A. Burgess, Chmn., Russell and District Regional L. Board, Main St. N., Russell; *Recording Secy.* Mrs. Mary Jane Gordon, Educ. L., Univ. of Manitoba, Winnipeg 19; *Corr. Secy.* Sharon Tully,* Elizabeth Dafoe L., Univ. of Manitoba, Winnipeg 19; *Treas.* Mrs. Florence MacKenzie, Winnipeg P.L., West End Branch, 823 Ellice Ave., Winnipeg 10. Memb. (Indiv.) 160; (Inst.) 17. Term of Office. Sept. '71–Sept. '72. Publication. *Manitoba Library Association Bulletin* (q.).

Maryland

Pres. Virginia Phillips, McKeldin L., Univ. of Md., College Park 20740; *V.P. & Pres. Elect.* Louis C. Wilson, Div. of Library Devel. & Servs., Md. State Dept. of Educ., 600 Wyndhurst Ave., Baltimore 21210; *2nd V.P.* Kenna Forsyth, Baltimore County P.L., 25 W. Chesapeake Ave., Towson 21204; *Recording Secy.* Marjorie Crammer, New Carrollton Branch, PGCML, 7414 Riverdale Rd., New Carrollton 20784; *Treas.* William Kirwan, Dir., Jenkins Memorial L., Loyola Coll., 4501 N. Charles St., Baltimore 21210. Memb. 700. Term of Office. Pres., V.P. & Pres. Elect — May 1, '71–Apr. 30, '72; Secy. & Treas. — May 1, '71–Apr. 30, '73. Publication. *The Crab* (bi-m.).

(Address correspondence to: Maryland Library Association, 115 W. Franklin St., Baltimore 21201.)

Massachusetts

Pres. Warren E. Watson, Thomas Crane P.L., Quincy 02169; *V.P.* Mrs. Sigrid R. Reddy, Watertown P.L., Watertown 02172; *Recording Secy.* Mrs. Joyce K. Miller, Reading P.L., Reading 01867; *Treas.* Thomas C. Higgins, Middlesex Community Coll., Bedford 01730; *Exec. Secy.* Mrs. Melvin E. Demit, Jr.,* Mass. Library Assn., P.O. Box 7, Nahant 01908. Memb. (Indiv.) 1,550; (Inst.) 165. Term of Office. July '71–June '72. Publication. *Bay State Librarian* (q.), Ed. Robert E. Cain, Cary Memorial L., Lexington 02173.

Michigan

Pres. Bernard C. Rink, Libn., Northwestern Michigan Coll., Traverse City 49684; *1st V.P. & Pres. Elect.* Mrs. Mary Daume, Dir., Monroe County L., 3700 S. Custer, Monroe 48161; *2nd V.P.* Elizabeth Hayden, Lansing P.L., 401 S. Capitol, Lansing 48914; *Exec. Secy.* Mrs. H. F. Pletz,* 226 W. Washtenaw, Lansing 48933; *Treas.* William S. Stoddard, Mich. State Univ. L., East Lansing 48823. Memb. (Indiv.) 1,511; (Inst.) 55. Term of Office. Nov. '71–Oct. '72. Publication. *Michigan Librarian* (q.).

Middle Atlantic

(Delaware, Maryland, New Jersey, New York, Pennsylvania, West Virginia) *Pres., Bd. of Dirs.* John Zimmerman,* MARLF, Inc., Jerome Frampton L.,

Frostburg State Coll., Frostburg, Md. 21532; *V.P.* William Rohrenbeck, Jersey City P.L.; *Secy.-Treas.* Marie Davis, Free L. of Philadelphia. Term of Office. Calendar year.

Minnesota

Pres. David R. Smith, Dir., Community L. Servs., Hennepin County L., 300 Nicollet Mall, Minneapolis 55401; *V.P. & Pres. Elect.* Edward Swanson, Head of Tech. Servs., Minnesota Historical Society L., St. Paul 55101; *Secy.* Mrs. Beatrice R. Bailey,* St. Paul P.L., 90 W. 4 St., St. Paul 55102; *Treas.* Margaret Bosshardt, Dir., Marshall-Lyon County L., Marshall 56258; *Past Pres.* Gil Johnsson, Dir., Nobles County L., Worthington 56187. Memb. 985. Term of Office. Pres. & V.P. — Oct. '71–Oct. '72; Secy. & Treas. — Oct. '71–Oct. '74. Publication. *M.L.A. Bulletin* (q.).

Mississippi

Pres. Mrs. Iola Magee, Lincoln-Lawrence-Franklin Regional L., P.O. Box 157, Monticello 39674; *V.P. & Pres. Elect.* Eleanor Drake, Peoples Jr. H.S., 276 Rosalyn Ave., Jackson 39209; *Secy.* Mrs. Jane Bryan, Pike-Amite L. System, 114 State St., McComb 39648; *Treas.* Mrs. Ernestine Lipscomb, Jackson State Coll., 1316 Florence Ave., Jackson 39204. Memb. 966. Term of Office. Jan. '72–Dec. '72. Publication. *Mississippi Library News* (q.).

Montana

Pres. Douglas Mills,* Univ. of Montana L., Missoula 59801; *V.P. & Pres. Elect.* Mrs. Frances Wells, Dir., L. Servs., S. Dist. 2, Billings 59102; *Secy.* Minnie Paugh, Montana State Univ. L., Bozeman 59715; *Treas.* Mrs. Helen Anderson, Great Falls P.L., Great Falls 59401; *Past Pres.* Mrs. Mabel M. Brewer, Libn., Flathead County L., 247 1st Ave. N.E., Kalispell 59901. Memb. 688. Term of Office. June '71–June '72. Publication. *MLA Newsletter* (irreg.).

Mountain Plains

(Colorado, Kansas, Nebraska, Nevada, North Dakota, South Dakota, Utah, Wyoming) *Pres.* Harold G. Morehouse, Dir., Univ. of Nevada Ls., Reno, Nev. 89507; *Pres. Elect.* Kilbourn L. Janecek, Libn., North Dakota State Univ., Fargo, N.D. 58103; *Recording Secy.* Kate Flanagan, AV Libn., Univ. of Utah, Salt Lake City, Utah 84112; *Exec. Secy.* Daniel A. Seager, Dir. of Ls., Univ. of Northern Colorado, Greeley, Colo. 80631. Term of Office. 1971–1972. Publication. *Mountain-Plains Library Quarterly,* Ed. Ford A. Rockwell, Wichita P.L., Wichita, Kans. 67202.

Nebraska

Pres. R. W. Brown, Libn., Sidney P.L., Sidney 69192; *V.P. & Pres. Elect.* Vivian Peterson, Midland Coll. L., Fremont 68025; *Secy.* Mrs. Margaret Masters, Syracuse-Dunbar-Avoca Ss., Syracuse 69446; *Treas.* William McDermott, Fremont P.L., Fremont 68025; *Exec. Secy.* Mrs. Louise B. Shelledy,* 3420 S. 37th St., Lincoln 68506. Memb. 672. Term of Office. Oct. '71–Oct. '72. Publication. *Nebraska Library Association Quarterly.*

Nevada

Pres. Billie Mae Polson, Univ. of Nevada, Las Vegas 89109; *1st V.P. & Pres. Elect.* Jack I. Gardner, Nevada State L., Carson City 89701; *2nd V.P.* Mrs. Hazel Potter, Sparks H.S., Sparks 89431; *Secy.* Barbara J. Mauseth,* Nevada State L., Carson City 89701; *Treas.* William E. Andrews, Washoe County L., Reno 89505; *Dir. I.* Mrs. Mary Noyes, Washoe County L., Reno 89505; *Dir. II.* Mrs. Alice Brown, Univ. of Nevada, Las Vegas 89109. Memb. (Indiv.) 278; (Inst.) 7. Term of Office. Oct. '71–Oct. '73. Publication. *Nevada Libraries* (5 issues).

New England

(Connecticut, Maine, Massachusetts, New Hampshire, Rhode Island, Vermont) *Pres.* F. Charles Taylor, Providence P.L., Providence, R.I.; *V.P. & Pres. Elect.* Mrs. Mary McKenzie, Conn. Coll. L., New London, Conn.; *Secy.* Jeanne Menard, Middle S., South Burlington, Vt.; *Treas.* Joseph Komidar, Tufts Univ. L., Medford, Mass.; *Dir. I.* Alice M.

Cahill, Bureau of L. Extension, 648 Beacon St., Boston, Mass.; *Dir. II.* Mrs. Marianna Rowe, Portland P.L., Portland, Me.; *Exec. Secy.* Mrs. Nan Berg,* P.O. Box 413, Mattapoisett, Mass. 02739. Memb. 1,050. Term of Office. Oct. '71–Oct. '72. Publication. *NELA Newsletter* (4 issues), Ed. Mr. Lee Ash, 31 Alden Rd., New Haven, Conn. 06515.

New Jersey

Pres. Schuyler L. Mott, Ocean County L., 15 Hooper Ave., Tom's River 08753; *Pres. Elect.* Mrs. Elizabeth Budell, Madison P.L., Main St., Madison 07940; *2nd V.P.* Kenneth F. McPherson, Morris County L., 30 E. Hanover Ave., Whippany 07981; *Treas.* Thomas W. Schear, Passaic P.L., Passaic 07055; *Recording Secy.* Mrs. June Adams, Westwood P.L., Westwood 07675; *Corr. Secy.* Mrs. Janet Burness,* Bergenfield P.L., Bergenfield 07621. Memb. 1,473. Term of Office. May '71–May '72. Publication. *New Jersey Libraries* (bi-m.), Ed. Arthur Curley, Dir., Montclair P.L., Montclair.

New Mexico

Pres. Peggy M. Tozer,* Eastern New Mexico Univ. L., Portales 88130; *V.P.* Mrs. Mildred Neal, Carlsbad Sr. H.S. L., Carlsbad 88220; *Secy.* Mrs. Deiores Lanier, 10320 Betts Dr. N.E., Albuquerque 87112; *Treas.* Mrs. Alma Daniels, Sierra Middle S. L., Roswell 88201. Memb. (Indiv.) 361; (Inst.) 33. Term of Office. Apr. '71–Apr. '72. Publication. *New Mexico Libraries* (q.), Ed. Christine L. Buder, P.O. Box 4141, University Park 88001.

New York

Pres. Mrs. Jean H. Porter, Dir., Edcom Center, Orleans-Niagara BOCES, 4124 Saunders Settlement Rd., Sanborn 14132; *1st V.P. & Pres. Elect.* Stanley A. Ransom, Dir., Huntington P.L., 338 Main St., Huntington 11743; *2nd V.P.* Leon Karpel, Dir., Mid-Hudson Ls., 103 Market St., Poughkeepsie 12601; *Exec. Secy.* Margaret E. Martignoni,* NYLA, 230 W. 41st St., Suite 1800, New York City 10036. Memb. 4,000. Term of Office. Oct. '71–Nov. '72. Publication. *NYLA Bulletin* (m., Sept.–June).

North Carolina

Pres. Elizabeth H. Copeland, Libn., Sheppard Memorial L., Greenville 27834; *1st V.P. & Pres. Elect.* Gene Lanier, Chmn., Dept. of L.Sci., East Carolina Univ., Greenville 27834; *2nd V.P.* Mrs. Marion J. Phillips, Libn., First Ward S., Charlotte 28208; *Secy.* Gary Barefoot, Libn., Mt. Olive Jr. Coll., Mt. Olive 28365; *Treas.* Richard T. Barker, Libn., Appalachian State Univ., Boone 28607; *Dir. I.* Kenneth Brown, Dir., Buncombe County Ls., Asheville 28801; *Dir. II.* Catherine Weir, Libn., Smith H.S., Greensboro 27408; *A.L.A. Dir.* Neal F. Austin, Libn., High Point P.L., High Point 27260. Memb. 1,500. Term of Office. Nov. '71–Oct. '73. Publication. *North Carolina Libraries* (q.), Ed. Mell Busbin.

(Address correspondence to: Mrs. Virginia Roesler, Exec. Secy., P.O. Box 212, Appalachian State Univ., Boone 28607.)

North Dakota

Pres. Everett Foster,* Minot P.L., Minot 58701; *V.P. & Pres. Elect.* Paul Nyquist, Mary Coll., Bismarck 58501; *Secy.* James Dertien, Veterans Memorial P.L., Bismarck 58501; *Treas.* Ruth Ralph, Divide County L., Crosby 58730. Memb. (Indiv.) 172; (Inst.) 42. Term of Office. Oct. '71–Oct. '73. Publication. *The Good Stuff* (q.), Ed. James Dertien.

Ohio

Pres. Sarah I. Cody, Dir., Cleveland Heights, University Heights P.L., Cleveland Heights 44118; *V.P. & Pres. Elect.* Dr. Irene Braden Hoadley, Libn. for Gen. Admin. & Research, The Ohio State Univ., Columbus 43210; *Secy.* Mrs. Frances A. Krieger, Clerk-Treas., Akron P.L., Akron 44308; *Exec. Dir. & Treas.* A. Chapman Parsons,* 40 S. Third St., Suite 409, Columbus 43215. Memb. 2,205. Term of Office. Oct. '71–Oct. '72. Publications. *Ohio Library Association Bulletin* (q.); *Ohio Libraries Newsletter* of the Ohio Library Association (8 issues).

Oklahoma

Pres. Dr. Roscoe Rouse, Dir., Oklahoma State Univ. L., Quail Ridge, Route 4, Stillwater 74074; *1st V.P. & Pres. Elect.* Dee Ann Ray, Dist. Libn., Western Plains L. System, P.O. Box 627, Clinton 73601; *2nd V.P.* Carl E. Reubin, 106 Ohio, Tishomingo 73460; *Past Pres.* Mrs. Thelma H. Jones, Coord., S. Media Servs., Oklahoma City P. Ss., 900 North Klein, Oklahoma City 73106; *Secy.* Mrs. Mary Beth Ozmun, Eastern Oklahoma Dist. L., 401 E. Broadway, Muskogee 74401; *Treas.* Leonard M. Eddy, Libn., P.O. Box 346, Moore 73060; *Past Secy.* John E. Hinkle, Acting Dir., Oklahoma Dept. of Ls., 109 State Capitol, Oklahoma City 73105. Memb. (Indiv.) 719; (Inst.) 21. Term of Office. May '71–May '72. Publication. *The Oklahoma Librarian* (q.), Ed. Mrs. Mary Lee DeVilbiss, Libn., 509 Coronado, Norman 73069.

Ontario

Pres. Mr. F. C. Israel,* Windsor P.L., 434 Victoria Ave., Windsor; *V.P.* Peter P. Hallsworth, Sudbury P.L., 74 Mackenzie St., Sudbury; *Secy.* Mrs. Patricia Wilcox, Ontario L. Assn., 2487 Bloor St. W., Toronto 9; *Treas.* Alan G. Pepper, Northwestern Regional L. System, 910 Victoria Ave., Thunder Bay; *Past Pres.* Mrs. Irma McDonough, Provincial L. Serv., 14th floor, Mowat Block, Queens Park, Toronto 5. Memb. 1,800. Term of Office. July 1, '71–June 30, '72. Publication. *OLA Newsletter* (q.), Ed. Mr. Bernard Katz, Guelph Univ. L., Guelph.

Oregon

Pres. Mrs. Edna Karczag, L. Dir., Klamath County L., 126 S. Third St., Klamath Falls 97601; *V.P. & Pres. Elect.* Mrs. Mary Bates, Libn., Blue Mountain Community Coll., Pendleton 97801; *Secy.* Mr. Kay H. Salmon,* L. Dir., Corvallis P.L., Corvallis 97330; *Treas.* Mrs. Louise P. Gerity, Ref. Libn., Lewis & Clark Coll., 0615 S.W. Palatine Hill Rd., Portland 97219. Memb. (Indiv.) 614; (Inst.) 20. Term of Office. Apr. '71–Apr. '72. Publication. *Oregon Library News* (bi-m.).

Pacific Northwest

(Alaska, Idaho, Montana, Oregon, Washington, British Columbia). *Pres.* Marion A. Milczewski,* Dir. of Ls., Univ. of Washington, Seattle, Wash. 98195; *1st V.P. & Pres. Elect.* Warren S. Owens, Dir. of Ls., Univ. of Idaho, Moscow, Idaho 83843; *2nd V.P.* H. Theodore Ryberg, Dir. of Ls., Univ. of Alaska, College, Alaska 99701; *Secy.* Phoebe Harris, Seattle P.L., Seattle, Wash. 98104; *Treas.* Richard E. Moore, Southern Oregon Coll., Ashland, Ore. Memb. (Indiv.) 921; (Inst.) 146. Term of Office. Oct. '71–Sept. '73 (biennial term). Publication. *PNLA Quarterly,* Ed. Perry D. Morrison, S. of Libnshp., Univ. of Oregon, Eugene, Ore. 97403.

Pennsylvania

Pres. Mrs. Carolyn W. Field, Free L. of Philadelphia, Logan Square, Philadelphia 19103; *1st V.P. & Pres. Elect.* Joseph F. Falgione, Carnegie L. of Pittsburgh, Pittsburgh 15213; *2nd V.P.* Mrs. Mary Ivy Bayard, Tyler S. of Art, Temple Univ., Philadelphia 19126; *Treas.* Rosemary Weber, Grad. S. of L.Sci., Drexel Univ., Philadelphia 19104; *Exec. Secy.* Mrs. Nancy L. Blundon,* Pennsylvania L. Assoc., 200 S. Craig St., Pittsburgh 15213. Memb. 2,959. Term of Office. Oct. '71–Oct. '72. Publication. *PLA Bulletin* (bi-m.).

Puerto Rico

Pres. Mrs. Oneida R. Ortiz; *V.P.* Mrs. Carmencita H. Leon; *Recording Secy.* Mrs. Rosa Monclova; *Corr. Secy.* Dr. Frederick E. Kidder,* P.O. Box 22898, University Station, San Juan 00931. Memb. 250. Term of Office. Apr. '71–Apr. '72. Publications. *Boletín* (s-a); *Informa* (m.).

Quebec

Pres. Mme. Anna Rovira, Lasalle P.L., 414 Lafleur, Lasalle 650; *Treas.* Bernard McNamee, Dawson Coll., 535 Viger, Montreal 132; *Eng. Secy.* Mrs. Norah Bryant,* Westmount P.L., 4574 Sherbrooke West, Montreal 215; *Fr. Secy.* Mme. Ginette Boyer-Caya, Bibliothèque médicale, Hotel-Dieu de Montreal 131.

Memb. (Indiv.) 231; (Inst.) 69. Term of Office. May '71–Apr. '72. Publication. *Revue* (s-a).

Rhode Island

Pres. William D. Alexander IV,* Westerly P.L., Broad St., Westerly 02891; *V.P.* Dolores McKeough, Robert H. Champlin Memorial L., West Warwick; *Recording Secy.* Sally Wilson, R.I. Coll., James P. Adams L., Mt. Pleasant Ave., Providence 02903; *Corr. Secy.* Barbara Wilson, D.S.L.S., 95 Davis St., Providence 02903; *Treas.* Walter F. Whitney, Providence P.L., 150 Empire St., Providence 02903. Memb. 775. Term of Office. May '71–May '72. Publication. *Bulletin of the Rhode Island Library Association* (m.).

South Carolina

Pres. J. Frank Nolen, P.O. Box 406, Florence 29501; *V.P. & Pres. Elect.* Estellene P. Walker, South Carolina State L., P.O. Box 11469, Columbia 29211; *Secy.* Mrs. Libby Patton Law,* 525-9D Country Club Apts., Florence 29501; *Treas.* Col. James M. Hillard, Libn., The Citadel, Charleston 29409. Memb. 795. Term of Office. Jan. '72–Dec. '73. Publication. *The South Carolina Librarian* (s-a).

South Dakota

Pres. Keith W. Warne,* Libn., Northern State Coll., Aberdeen 57401; *Pres. Elect.* Paul W. Wittkopf, Libn., South Dakota State Univ., Brookings 57006; *Secy.* Mrs. Caryl Ellis, S. Libn., 458 W. 8, Winner 57580; *Treas.* Mrs. Mona Swanson, Libn., Brookings P.L., Brookings 57006. Memb. (Indiv.) 284; (Inst.) 40. Term of Office. Sept. '71–Sept. '72.

Southeastern

(Alabama, Florida, Georgia, Kentucky, Mississippi, North Carolina, South Carolina, Tennessee, Virginia) *Pres.* Porter Kellam,* Dir., Univ. of Georgia Ls., Athens, Ga. 30601; *V.P.* Dorothy Ryan, S. of L. Servs., Univ. of Tenn., Knoxville, Tenn. 37916; *Treas.* Cecil Beach, Dir., Tampa P.L., Tampa, Fla. 33602; *Exec. Secy.* Mrs. Ann W. Morton, 2133 Aldah Dr., Tucker, Ga. 30084. Memb. 2,000. Term of Office. Nov. '70–Nov. '72. Publication. *The Southeastern Librarian* (q.).

Southwestern

(Arizona, Arkansas, Louisiana, New Mexico, Oklahoma, Texas) *Pres.* Lee Brawner, Exec. Dir., Oklahoma County Ls., 131 N.W. 3 St., Oklahoma City, Okla. 73102; *1st V.P. & Pres. Elect.* Pearce Grove, Libn., Eastern New Mexico Univ. L., Portales, N.M. 88130; *2nd V.P.* Dr. Shirley Stephenson, Prof. L. S., Louisiana State Univ., Baton Rouge, La. 70803; *Secy.* Mrs. Pat Woodrum, Chief of P. Servs., Tulsa City-County L. System, 400 Civic Center, Tulsa, Okla. 74103; *Treas.* Mrs. Katharine Keathley, Libn., Arkansas River Valley Regional L., Dardanelle, Ark. 72834; *Past Pres.* Mrs. Allie Beth Martin, Dir., Tulsa City-County L. System, 400 Civic Center, Tulsa, Okla. 74103; *Exec. Secy.* Mrs. Della Thomas,* Oklahoma State Univ. L., Stillwater, Okla. 74074. Memb. (Indiv.) 6,000; (Inst.) 315. Term of Office. Jan. '71–Dec. '72. Publications. *SWLA Bulletin* (s-a); *Biennial Proceedings;* occasional papers.

St. Croix

Pres. Robert V. Vaughn,* P.O. Box 1122, Christiansted 00820; *V.P. & Treas.* Charles A. Emanuel, P.O. Box 265, Christiansted 00820; *Secy.* Mrs. Ena G. Henderson, P.O. Box 701, Christiansted 08820; *Board Members.* Mrs. Marjorie Masters, P.O. Box 2199, Frederiksted 00840; Eva Lawaetz, P.O. Box 3001, Christiansted 00820. Memb. 26. Term of Office. May '71–Apr. '72. Publications. *SCLA Newsletter* (q.); *Studies in Virgin Islands Librarianship* (irreg.).

Tennessee

Pres. Dr. Edwin S. Gleaves, Dir., Peabody L. S., George Peabody Coll. for Teachers, Nashville 37203; *V.P. & Pres. Elect.* Mrs. Anne Marie Falsone, Asst. Head, History Dept., Memphis P.L. & Info. Center, 1850 Peabody Ave., Memphis 38104; *Secy.* Mrs. Lois N. Clark,* Head Libn., Knoxville Coll., Knoxville

37921; *Treas.* Mrs. Jane Webb, Assoc. Libn., Crisman Memorial L., David Lipscomb Coll., Nashville 37203. Memb. 1,363. Term of Office. Apr. '71–Apr. '72. Publication. *Tennessee Librarian* (q.).

Utah

Pres. Arlene H. Grover, Utah State L. Commission, 2150 S. 2 W., Salt Lake City 84115; *1st V.P.* Richard Rademacher,* Salt Lake City P.L., 209 E. 5 S., Salt Lake City 84111; *2nd V.P.* Phyllis Shaw, Horace Mann S., 1300 9 St., Ogden 84401. Memb. 550. Term of Office. Mar. '71–Mar. '72. Publication. *Utah Libraries* (s-a).

Vermont

Pres. Mr. Leslie Smith, Libn., St. Johnsbury Regional L., St. Johnsbury 05819. Memb. (Indiv.) 206; (Inst.) 19. Term of Office. Jan. '72–Dec. '72. Publication. *Vermont Libraries,* published by Vt. Dept. of Ls. and VLA.

Virginia

Pres. Ray W. Frantz, Jr.,* Univ. Libn., Alderman L., Univ. of Virginia, Charlottesville 22904; *1st V.P. & Pres. Elect.* Mary Stuart Mason, Supervisor of S. Ls. & Textbooks, Virginia State Board of Educ., 1322 E. Grace St., Richmond 23216; *2nd V.P.* Mrs. Verdelle V. Bradley, Libn., William T. Clark L., Virginia Union Univ., Richmond 23220; *Secy.* Mrs. Jane L. Black, Dir., Lynchburg P.L., 914 Main St., Lynchburg 24504; *Treas.* Mrs. Antje L. Smith, Asst. City Libn., Richmond P.L., Richmond 23219. Memb. 950. Term of Office. Dec. '71–Nov. '72.

Washington

Pres. Dr. Junius Morris,* 23147 20 Ave. S., Des Moines 98188; *1st V.P. & Pres. Elect.* Mrs. Shirley Tucker, Mid-Columbia Regional L., Kennewick 99336; *2nd V.P.* Michael Lynch, North Central Regional L., Wenatchee 98801; *Secy.* Howard R. Downey, Bellingham P.L., Bellingham 98225; *Treas.* Mary Frances Borden, Tacoma P. L., Tacoma 98402. Memb. (Indiv.) 1,127; (Inst.) 44. Term of Office. Aug. '71–July '73.

West Virginia

Pres. Robert Murphy, Medical Center L., W. Va. Univ., Morgantown 26506; *1st V.P. & Pres. Elect.* Josephine Fidler, Acquisitions Libn., Marshall Univ., Huntington 25701; *2nd V.P.* Elliott Horton, Libn., Morgantown P.L., Morgantown 26506; *Secy.* Judy K. Rule,* Cabell County P.L., 900 Fifth Ave., Huntington 25701; *Treas.* James L. Smith, Monongalia County IMC, 300 McLane Ave., Morgantown 26505. Memb. (Indiv.) 338; (Inst.) 42. Term of Office. Dec. '71–Nov. '72. Publication. *West Virginia Libraries* (q.).

Wyoming

Pres. Mrs. Ruth E. Wilson, P.O. Box 147, Pinedale 82941; *V.P. & Pres. Elect.* Mrs. Wilmot C. McFadden, 300 Blair Ave., Rock Springs 82901; *Exec. Secy.* Irene Nakako,* P.O. Box 1104, Rock Springs 82901; *Recording Secy.* Mrs. Georgia Shovlain, P.O. Box 1039, Sheridan 82801. Memb. (Indiv.) 269; (Inst.) 29. Term of Office. May '71–May '72. Publication. *Wyoming Library Roundup* (q.).

STATE SCHOOL LIBRARY ASSOCIATIONS

The following states have reported state school library associations.

Alabama
Children and School Librarians Division, Alabama Library Association. *Chmn.* Mrs. Mary Ella Terrill, 3109 Freemont Dr., Tuscaloosa 35401

Alabama Instructional Media Association. *Pres.* Mrs. Geraldine Bell, 3061 Wenonah Park Rd., Birmingham 35211

California
California Association of School Libraries (CASL), P.O. Box 1277, Burlingame 94010

Colorado
The Colorado Association of School Libraries. *Pres.* Sandy Patton, Irving Jr. H.S., N. Murray Blvd., Colorado Springs 80915.

Delaware
Delaware School Library Association. *Pres.* Mrs. Trudy Kemlein, 1109 Piper Rd., Graylyn Crest, Wilmington 19803

Florida
Florida Association of School Librarians. *Pres.* Mrs. Elizabeth B. Bias, Supervisor, Media Utilization, P.O. Box 2469, West Palm Beach 33401

Georgia
School and Children's Library Section of the Georgia Library Association. *Chmn.* Mrs. Dorothea Goodloe, Library Supervisor, Clarke County School District, Athens 30601

Hawaii
Hawaii Association of School Librarians. *Pres.* Mrs. Nona A. Minami, c/o School Library Services Office, 4211 Waialae Ave., Honolulu, Hawaii 96816

Idaho
School Libraries Division of the Idaho Library Association, c/o School Library Consultant, Idaho Dept. of Educ., Statehouse, Boise 83707. *Pres.* Mrs. Irene Tolmie, Vallivue School, Route 4, Caldwell 83605

Illinois
Illinois Association of School Libraries. Headquarters: ILA, Office of the Secretarial Asst., Mrs. Dorothy Salchenberger, 6725 N. Rockwell St., Chicago 60645. *Pres.* Donald Adcock, 363 Windsor Ave., Glenn Ellyn 60137

Indiana
Indiana School Librarians Association. *Pres.* Mrs. Ferne Johnson, School Admin. Bldg., 1230 South Clinton, Ft. Wayne 46802

Iowa
Iowa School Library Media Association. *Pres.* Marie Haley, Sioux City Schools, 1221 Pierce St., Sioux City 51105

Kansas
Kansas Association of School Libraries. *Pres.* Myrna Wagner, Topeka Public Schools, 16 and Van Buren, Topeka 66612

Louisiana
Louisiana Association of School Librarians. c/o Louisiana Library Association, P.O. Box 131, Baton Rouge 70821

Massachusetts
Massachusetts School Library Association. *Pres.* Arthur C. Gillis, Quincy Public Schools, 44 Coddington St., Quincy 02169

Massachusetts Audio-Visual Association. *Pres.* Bruce Oldershaw, Amherst Regional High School, Amherst 01002

Michigan
Michigan School Library Association, Bureau of School Services, Univ. of Michigan, 401 S. Fourth, Ann Arbor 48103. *Exec. Secy.* Mrs. Maxine Larson

Mississippi
Mississippi School Library Association. *Pres.* Sue Strub, Aberdeen High School, Aberdeen 39730

Missouri

Missouri Association of School Librarians. c/o MLA Executive Office, 403 South 6 St., Columbia 65201.

Montana

School Library Division of the Montana Library Association. *Chmn.* Mrs. Edna Berg, Bozeman Senior High School Librarian, Bozeman 59715

Nevada

Nevada Association of School Librarians. *Chmn.* Mrs. Virginia Lee, P.O. Box 162, Fernley 89408

New Hampshire

New Hampshire School Media Association. c/o Mrs. Winona F. Brown, 32 Rolfe St., Penacook 03301

New Jersey

New Jersey School Media Association. *Pres.* Elizabeth Morse, Washington School, 427 Darrow Ave., Plainfield 07060

New York

School Libraries Section, New York Library Association, 230 W. 41st St., Suite 1800, New York City 10036. *Pres.* Mrs. Evelyn Rice, Greece School District, Rochester

North Carolina

North Carolina Association of School Librarians. *Pres.* Mr. B. M. Sheffield, Library Supervisor, High Point City Schools, High Point 27260

North Dakota

Instructional Media Dept. of the North Dakota Education Association, Bismarck 58501

Ohio

Ohio Association of School Libraries. *Pres.* Mrs. Margaret Mantz, Library Coordinator, Beachwood Schools, 24601 Fairmount Blvd., Cleveland 44124

Oregon

Oregon Educational Media Association, 1111 Court St., Roseburg 97470

South Carolina

South Carolina Association of School Librarians. *Pres.* Mrs. Helen Callison, Airport High School, West Columbia 29169

Tennessee

Tennessee School Library Association. c/o Tennessee Education Association, 598 James Robertson Parkway, Nashville 37219

Texas

Texas Association of School Librarians. *Chmn.* Mrs. Jo Ann Bell, Richardson ISD, 801 Carney, Garland 75040

Washington

Washington State Association of School Librarians. *Pres.* Mrs. Jean Thompson, 2006 Turner, Richland 99352.

Wyoming

Wyoming Association of School Librarians. *Pres.* Violet Lowe, Midwest 82643

DIRECTORY OF FEDERAL LIBRARY PROGRAMS

Compiled by

Frank Kurt Cylke*

For addresses and telephone numbers for HEW Regional Offices, see Burton Lamkin's article, "The Bureau of Libraries and Educational Technology in 1971," this volume. See also "Library Addresses and Telephone Numbers."

BUREAU OF LIBRARIES AND EDUCATIONAL TECHNOLOGY
(Area Code 202)

Office of the Associate Commissioner, BLET

Burton E. Lamkin, Assoc. Comm., 963-6381; William J. Barefoot, Exec. Officer, 962-8046; Patricia Smith, Asst., 963-7492; Robert L. Waters, Asst. Exec. Officer, 963-5166.

Planning and Evaluation Staff

R. Kathleen Molz, Chief, 962-8816; Robert L. Klassen, Program Officer, 962-8816; Nathan Cohen, Program Officer, 962-8038.

Division of Library Programs

Ray M. Fry, Dir., 963-6271; Herbert A. Carl, Special Asst. to the Dir., 963-6271; Michelle R. Vale, Evaluation Specialist, 963-6271.

Mrs. Elizabeth Hughey, Chief, Services & Facilities Br., 962-1403; Dorothy Kittel, Program Coord., Interlibrary Cooperation, 963-6023; Margaret C. Hannigan, Program Coord., Lib. Serv. for State Inst. and the Handicapped, 963-6060; Pauline Winnick, Program Coord., Public Library Serv., 963-4384.

Paul Janaske, Chief, Res. & Program Devel. Br., 963-7759; Henry T. Drennan, Program Officer, 962-7908; Lawrence Papier, Program Officer, 962-7909.

Frank A. Stevens, Chief, Training and Resources Br., 963-7496; Katharine M. Stokes, College and Univ. Lib. Specialist, 963-4384; Yvonne Hicks, Program Officer, 963-4384.

LIBRARY-RELATED PROGRAMS
(Area Code 202)

Adult Education

Paul Delker, 963-7445.

Arts and Humanities

Harold Arberg, 963-7843.

Committee on Scientific and Technical Information (COSATI)

Melvin S. Day, 632-5824.

Education Professions Development Act

Charles E. Grady, 962-2734.

Elementary and Secondary Education Act

Title I, Richard Fairley, Director of Compensatory Education, 962-8831.

Title II (All by region: administer ESEA II & NDEA III, V, & V-A), Northeast: D'Alan E. Huff, 962-4601; Western: Mary Helen Mahar, 962-4141; Upper Midwest: Charles Fitzwater, 962-4662; Southeast: Louis Sutherland, 962-5211; Mid-Continent: Verl W. Snyder, 962-5224.

Title III, Ray Warner, 755-7644.

Federal Library Committee

Frank Kurt Cylke, 426-6055.

Handicapped

Elizabeth M. Goodman, 962-7683.

Higher Education Act

Title III, Developing Institutions, Dr. James M. Holley, 962-3859.

Title II-C, Library of Congress, Edmond Applebaum, 426-5330.

Higher Education Facilities Act

Thomas F. McAnallen, 963-7760; Royall Webster, Model Cities, 963-7774.

International Librarianship

Jean Allaway, Library of Congress, 426-5218.

Junior Colleges

(Division of College Support, BHE) John Orcutt, 962-1954.

---

*Executive Secretary, Federal Library Committee.

Legislative Materials
Joseph Moore, 962-4416.

Model Cities
Neal Shedd, 963-7432.

National Center for Educational Statistics
Dr. Frank L. Schick, Chief, Library Surveys Branch, 963-4587; Ruth Boaz, 963-4587; Ann Deitrick, 962-7443.

National Defense Education Act, Title III
See ESEA II.

Networks for Knowledge, HEA Title VIII
Harriet Bramble, 962-1954.

Office of Program Planning & Evaluation
Authur Kirschenbaum, 962-1114.

Office of Science Information Service, National Science Foundation
Melvin S. Day, 632-5824.

Right to Read
Louis G. Mendez, Jr., Dir., 963-3456; Julia Hamblet, 963-3456.

Spanish-speaking American Affairs
Armando Rodriguez, 962-7736.

Vocational and Technical Education
Michael Russo, 963-7641.

STATE LIBRARY AGENCIES

The state library extension agencies in each of the states have the latest information on their state plans for public library services and public library construction. The names and addresses of these state agencies with their directors are listed below. For telephone numbers see section "Library Addresses and Telephone Numbers," this volume.

Alabama
Mrs. Elizabeth P. Beamguard, Director, Alabama Public Library Service, 155 Administrative Building, Montgomery, Ala. 36105.

Alaska
Richard Engen, Director of Libraries, Department of Education, Pouch G, Juneau, Alaska 99801.

American Samoa
Mrs. Betty S. Lunnon, Supervisor of Libraries, Department of Education, Pago Pago, American Samoa 96920.

Arizona
Mrs. Marguerite B. Cooley, Director, Arizona State Department of Library and Archives, Phoenix, Ariz. 85007.

Arkansas
Mrs. Karl Neal, Executive Secretary, Arkansas Library Commission, 506½ Center Street, Little Rock, Ark. 72201.

California
Mrs. Carma R. Leigh, State Librarian, California State Library, P.O. Box 2037, Sacramento, Calif. 95809.

Colorado
James D. Meeks, Assistant Commissioner, Colorado State Library, 1362 Lincoln Street, Denver, Colo. 80203.

Connecticut
Walter Brahm, State Librarian, Connecticut State Library, 231 Capitol Avenue, Hartford, Conn. 06115.

Delaware
Jack Tyler, Director, Division of Libraries, P.O. Box 635, W. Loockerman Street, Dover, Del. 19901.

District of Columbia
Joe Lee, Acting Director, D.C. Public Library, 499 Pennsylvania Avenue N.W., Washington, D.C. 20001.

Florida
Director (to be appointed), Division of Library Services, Department of State, Tallahassee, Fla. 32304.

Georgia
Carlton Thaxton, Administrator, Public Library Service, Georgia State Department of Education, 156 Trinity Ave. S.W., Atlanta, Ga. 30303.

Guam

Mrs. Magdalena S. Taitano, Librarian, Nieves M. Flores Memorial Library, P.O. Box 652, Agana, Guam 96910.

Hawaii

Norman P. Horne, Acting State Librarian, Department of Education, Division of Library Services, P.O. Box 2360, Honolulu, Hawaii 96804.

Idaho

Miss Helen M. Miller, State Librarian, Idaho State Library, 325 W. State Street, Boise, Idaho 83702.

Illinois

Alphonse F. Trezza, Director, Illinois State Library, Centennial Memorial Building, Springfield, Ill. 62706.

Indiana

Miss Marcelle Foote, Director, Indiana State Library, 140 North Senate Avenue, Indianapolis, Ind. 46204.

Iowa

Maurice Travillian, Director, State Traveling Library, Historical Building, Des Moines, Iowa 50319.

Kansas

Dean R. Gross, State Librarian, Kansas State Library, Topeka, Kans. 66601.

Kentucky

Miss Margaret Willis, State Librarian, Department of Libraries, P.O. Box 537, Frankfort, Ky. 40601.

Louisiana

Miss Sallie J. Farrell, State Librarian, Louisiana State Library, P.O. Box 131, Baton Rouge, La. 70800.

Maine

Miss Ruth A. Hazelton, State Librarian, State Library, Augusta, Me. 04330.

Maryland

Miss Nettie B. Taylor, Asst. State Superintendent for Libraries, Division of Library Development and Services, State Department of Education, 600 Wyndhurst Avenue, Baltimore, Md. 21210.

Massachusetts

Mrs. V. Genevieve Galick, Director, Massachusetts Bureau of Library Extension, Department of Education, 648 Beacon Street, Boston, Mass. 02215.

Michigan

Francis X. Scannell, State Librarian, Michigan State Library, 735 E. Michigan Avenue, Lansing, Mich. 48913.

Minnesota

Hannis S. Smith, Director, Library Division, Department of Education, 117 University Avenue, St. Paul, Minn. 55101.

Mississippi

Miss Mary Love, Director, Mississippi Library Commission, 405 State Office Building, Jackson, Miss. 39201.

Missouri

Charles O'Halloran, State Librarian, Missouri State Library, State Office Building, Jefferson City, Mo. 65102.

Montana

David R. Hoffman, State Librarian, Montana State Library, 930 East Lyndale Avenue, Helena, Mont. 59601.

Nebraska

Robert Kemper, Executive Secretary, Nebraska Public Library Commission, Lincoln, Neb. 68509.

Nevada

Joseph J. Anderson, State Librarian, Nevada State Library, Carson City, Nev. 89701.

New Hampshire

Emil W. Allen, Jr., State Librarian, New Hampshire State Library, 20 Park Street, Concord, N.H. 03302.

New Jersey

Roger H. McDonough, Director, Division of State Library Archives and History, State Department of Education, 185 West State Street, Trenton, N.J. 08625.

New Mexico

C. Edwin Dowlin, State Librarian, New Mexico State Library, 300 Don Gasper Street, Santa Fe, N. Mex. 87501.

New York

Miss Jean L. Connor, Director, Division of Library Development, New York State Library, State Department of Education, Albany, N.Y. 12201.

North Carolina

Philip S. Ogilvie, State Librarian, North Carolina State Library, P.O. Box 27727, Raleigh, N.C. 27601.

North Dakota

Richard Wolfert, Director, North Dakota State Library Commission, Bismarck, N.D. 58501.

Ohio

Joseph F. Shubert, State Librarian, Ohio State Library, State Office Building, Columbus, Ohio 43215.

Oklahoma

Ralph H. Funk, Director, Oklahoma State Department of Libraries, 109 State Capitol, Oklahoma City, Okla. 73105.

Oregon

Miss Eloise Ebert, State Librarian, Oregon State Library, Salem, Ore. 97310.

Pennsylvania

Ernest E. Doerschuk, Jr., State Librarian, Pennsylvania State Library, Education Building, Harrisburg, Pa. 17126.

Puerto Rico

Gonzalo Velazquez, Director, Department of Education, Library Division, P.O. Box 3127, San Juan, Puerto Rico 00936.

Rhode Island

Miss Elizabeth G. Myer, Director, Department of State Library Services, 95 Davis Street, Providence, R.I. 02908.

South Carolina

Miss Estellene P. Walker, Director, The South Carolina State Library, 1500 Senate Street, P.O. Box 11469, Columbia, S.C. 29201.

South Dakota

Miss Mercedes B. MacKay, Director and Secretary, South Dakota State Library Commission, 322 South Fort Street, Pierre, S.D. 57501.

Tennessee

Herschel V. Anderson, Acting State Librarian and Archivist, Tennessee State Library and Archives, Nashville, Tenn. 37219.

Texas

Dr. Dorman H. Winfrey, Director-Librarian, Texas State Library, P.O. Box 12927, Capitol Station, Austin, Tex. 78711.

Trust Territory of the Pacific Islands

Daniel J. Peacock, Supervisor of Library Services, Department of Education, Trust Territory of the Pacific Islands, Saipan, Mariana Islands 96950.

Utah

Russell L. Davis, Director, Utah State Library, Suite 16, 2150 South 2nd West, Salt Lake City, Utah 84115.

Vermont

James Igoe, Commissioner, State of Vermont, Department of Libraries, Montpelier, Vt. 05602.

Virgin Islands

Miss Enid M. Baa, Director, Libraries and Museums, Department of Conservation & Cultural Affairs, P.O. Box 390, Charlotte Amalie, St. Thomas, V.I. 00801.

Virginia

Randolph W. Church, State Librarian, Virginia State Library, Richmond, Va. 23219.

Washington

Miss Maryan E. Reynolds, State Librarian, Washington State Library, Olympia, Wash. 98501.

West Virginia

Miss Dora Ruth Parks, Executive Secretary, Library Commission, 2004 Quarrier Street, Charleston, W. Va. 25300.

Wisconsin

W. Lyle Eberhart, Director, Division of Library Services, Department of Public Instruction, Wisconsin Hall, 126 Langdon Street, Madison, Wis. 53703.

Wyoming

William H. Williams, State Librarian, Wyoming State Library, Supreme Court Building, Cheyenne, Wyo. 82001.

STATE SCHOOL LIBRARY SUPERVISORS

Alabama
Mrs. Carrie Robinson, School Libraries Consultant, State Office Building, Montgomery 36104. Tel: 205-269-6535

Alaska
Library and Media Consultant, State Department of Education, Pouch F, Juneau 99801. Tel: 903-586-5231

Arizona
Miss Mary Choncoff, Director, Library, Title II, ESEA, State Department of Education, 1626 W. Washington Avenue, Suite 108, Phoenix 85007. Tel: 602-271-5271

Arkansas
Mrs. Anne L. Jackson, Director, ESEA Title II, State Department of Education, Arch Ford Education Building, Little Rock 72201. Tel: 501-371-1041

California
Dr. Harry J. Skelly, Chief, Audiovisual Education and School Library Education, State Department of Education, Bureau of Audio-Visual and School Library Education, 721 Capitol Mall, Sacramento 95814. Tel: 916-445-2622

Colorado
Mrs. Roberta E. Young, Director, Library Development, Colorado State Dept. of Education, 1362 Lincoln Street, Denver 80203. Tel: 303-892-2133

Connecticut
Miss Rheta A. Clark, School Library Consultant, Connecticut State Dept. of Education, Bureau of Elementary and Secondary Schools, P.O. Box 2219, Hartford 06115. Tel: 203-566-3873

Delaware
Richard L. Krueger, Supervisor of Audiovisual Education, State Department of Public Education, Box 697, Dover 19901. Tel: 302-734-5711, ext. 235

District of Columbia
Miss Olive De Bruler, Director, Department of Library Science, Public Schools of the District of Columbia, 415–12th Street, N.W., Room 609, Washington, D.C. 20004. Tel: 202-629-2988

Florida
Mrs. Eloise T. Groover, Director, Educational Media, State Department of Education, Tallahassee 32304. Tel: 904-599-5155

Georgia
Miss Grace Hightower, Coordinator, School Library Services Unit, Georgia State Department of Education, 156 Trinity Avenue, S.W., Atlanta 30303. Tel: 404-656-2418

Hawaii
Mrs. Mae C. Chun, Director, School Libraries and Instructional Materials Branch, State Department of Education, Kahala Office Center, Room 203, 4211 Waialae Avenue, Honolulu 96816. Tel: 808-732-1402

Idaho
Mrs. Ruth Seydel, Consultant, Library and Audiovisual Services, Idaho State Department of Education, State House, Boise 83702. Tel: 208-384-2187

Illinois
Miss Valerie J. Downes, Consultant, Instructional Materials and Director, ESEA Title II, Office of Superintendent of Public Instruction, 316 S. Second Street, Springfield 63706. Tel: 217-525-2927

Indiana
Dale Hartzler, Director, Division of Instructional Media and ESEA II Supervisor, State Department of Public Instruction, Indianapolis 46204. Tel: 317-633-4790

Iowa
Miss Betty Jo Buckingham, Library Consultant, Educational Media Section, Iowa State Department of Public Instruction, Grimes State Office Building, Des Moines 50319. Tel: 515-281-3475

Kansas
Mrs. Mona Alexander, Library Media Coordinator, ESEA Title II, State De-

partment of Public Instruction, 120 E. Tenth Street, Topeka 66612. Tel: 913-296-3433

Kentucky

Miss Nella Bailey, Library Consultant, State Department of Education, Commonwealth of Kentucky, Frankfort 40601. Tel: 502-564-4507

Louisiana

James S. Cookston, State Supervisor of School Libraries, Division of Curriculum and Instruction, State Department of Education, Room 602 Education Building, P.O. Box 44064, Baton Rouge 70804. Tel: 504-389-5760

Maine

Clyde Swett, Coordinator, Instructional Media, Maine State Department of Education, Education Building, Augusta 04330. Tel: 207-289-2475

Maryland

Miss Mae Graham, Assistant Director, Division of Library Development and Services, Maryland State Department of Education, 600 Wyndhurst Avenue, Baltimore 21210. Tel: 301-383-3424

Massachusetts

Miss Suzanne R. Noonan, Supervisor of School Libraries, Massachusetts State Department of Education, Bureau of Library Extension, 648 Beacon Street, Boston 02215. Tel: 617-536-4030

Michigan

Mrs. Mary Ann Hanna, Head School Library Consultant and Coordinator of Title II, ESEA, Michigan State Department of Education, 735 E. Michigan, Lansing 48913. Tel: 517-373-1557

Minnesota

Miss Ruth Ersted, Supervisor, School Libraries, Minnesota State Department of Education, Centennial Office Building, St. Paul 55101. Tel: 612-221-2091

Mississippi

John L. Barlow, Audio-Visual Consultant and Coordinator, Library Services, State Department of Education, P.O. Box 771, Jackson 39205. Tel: 601-354-6864

Missouri

Carl F. Sitze, State School Library Supervisor, Missouri State Department of Education, Division of Public Schools, P.O. Box 480, Jefferson City 65101. Tel: 314-635-8125

Montana

John W. Koetter, Director, General Support for Schools' Educational Programs, State Department of Public Instruction, Helena 59601. Tel: 406-449-2052

Nebraska

Mrs. Esther Bronson, ESEA Title II Coordinator, State Department of Education, Lincoln 68509. Tel: 402-471-2448

Nevada

Thomas E. Ogg, Consultant, Federal Programs, ESEA Title II & III, State Department of Education, Carson City 89701. Tel: 702-882-7161

New Hampshire

Mrs. Harriet A. Adams, Supervisor of School Libraries, State Department of Education, State House Annex, Concord 03301. Tel: 603-271-2401

New Jersey

Miss Ann Voss, Coordinator of School Libraries, State Department of Education, Trenton 08625. Tel: 609-292-6256

New Mexico

George K. McBane, Director, ESEA Title II, Library Media Specialist, New Mexico State Department of Education, Capitol Building, Santa Fe 87501. Tel: 505-827-2684

New York

Mrs. Lore Howard, Chief, Bureau of School Libraries and Coordinator of ESEA Title II, Bureau of School Libraries, State Department of Education, Albany 12201. Tel: 518-474-6420 or 4972

North Carolina

James W. Carruth, Director, Division of Instructional Media, State Department of Public Instruction, Raleigh 27602. Tel: 919-829-3193

ASSOCIATIONS AND AGENCIES / 429

North Dakota

Miss Genevieve L. Buresh, State School Library Supervisor, State Department of Public Instruction, State Capitol, Bismarck 58501. Tel: 701-224-2281

Ohio

Miss Mirjam A. Saukkonen, Consultant, School Library Services, Division of Elementary and Secondary Education, 65 S. Front Street, Columbus 43215. Tel: 614-469-2761

Oklahoma

Mrs. Elizabeth Geis, Consultant, Library Resources Division, State Department of Education, Oklahoma City 73105. Tel: 405-521-3482

Oregon

Lyle Wirtanen, Specialist, Library Services, State Board of Education, Salem 97310. Tel: 503-378-3778

Pennsylvania

Mrs. Elizabeth P. Hoffman, Division of School Libraries and Coordinator of ESEA Title II, State Department of Education, 13 N. Fourth Street, Harrisburg 17101. Tel: 717-787-6704

Rhode Island

Mrs. Ruth Wade Cerjanec, Consultant, Media Centers and Title II, ESEA, State Department of Education, Roger Williams Building, Providence 02908. Tel: 401-277-2701

South Carolina

Mrs. Margaret W. Ehrhardt, Consultant, Library Services, State Department of Education, 810 Rutledge Building, Columbia 29201. Tel: 803-758-3287, ext. 28

South Dakota

Delezin Carter, School Library Consultant and Media Specialist, Box 853, Northern State College, Aberdeen 57401. Tel: 605-224-3243

Tennessee

Miss Louise Meredith, Director, School Library Services, State Department of Education, Division of Instruction, 132-A Cordell Hull Building, Nashville 37219. Tel: 615-741-3116

Texas

Dr. Mary R. Boyvey, Library Program Director, Instructional Media Division, Texas Education Agency, Austin 78711. Tel: 512-475-3236

Utah

Dr. LeRoy R. Lindeman, Administrator, Instructional Media Division, State Department of Public Instruction, Suite 1400 University Club Building, 136 E. South Temple, Salt Lake City 84111. Tel: 801-328-5571

Vermont

Mrs. Eleonora P. Harman, School Library Consultant and ESEA, Title II, State Department of Education, State Office Building, Montpelier 05602. Tel: 802-223-2311, ext. 416

Virginia

Miss Mary Stuart Mason, Supervisor, School Libraries and Textbooks, State Department of Education, Richmond 23216. Tel: 703-770-2680

Washington

Mrs. Jean Badten Wieman, Supervisor of Learning Resources (Library), State Department of Public Instruction, Olympia 98501. Tel: 206-753-7395

West Virginia

Miss Nancy Jo Canterbury, Program Specialist, Library Services, Department of Education, 4500 MacCorkle Avenue, Charleston 25304. Tel: 304-348-2489

Wisconsin

Bernard Franckowiak, State School Library Supervisor, State Department of Public Instruction, Madison 53702. Tel: 608-266-1965

Wyoming

Mrs. Alice Hild Farris, Library and Media Consultant, State Department of Education, State Capitol Building, Cheyenne 82001. Tel: 307-777-7533

American Samoa

Mrs. Betty S. Lunnon, Supervisor of Libraries, Library of American Samoa, Department of Education, Pago Pago 96920

Bureau of Indian Affairs

Ray Reese, Librarian, Servicewide Library, Field Technical Service, Bureau of Indian Affairs, P.O. Box 66, Brigham City, Utah 84302. Tel: 801-723-4230

Guam

Miss Corazón P. Salazar, Coordinator of Library Services and Curriculum Materials Center, Department of Education, Agana 96910

Puerto Rico

Miss Alice Iglesias, Director, School Libraries and Coordinator, ESEA Title II, Avenue Teniente Cesar Gonzalez, Hato Rey 00919. Tel: 307-765-3432, ext. 230

Trust Territory of the Pacific Islands

Daniel J. Peacock, Director, Library Services and Instructional Materials, Department of Education, Saipan, Mariana Islands 96950

Virgin Islands

James Oliver, Director, Library Services, Department of Education, P.O. Box 1505 Frederiksted, St. Croix 00840. Tel: 809-773-1025 (Mon. & Thurs.); 809-774-0100, ext. 252, (Tues., Wed., Fri.)

BOOK TRADE ASSOCIATIONS

For a more complete listing of book trade associations see the annual issues of the *Literary Market Place* (Bowker).

Advertising Typographers Assn. of America, Inc.
461 Eighth Ave., New York 10001
212-LO4-3500
Exec. Sec. Walter A. Dew, Jr.

American Book Publishers Council, Inc.
See Association of American Publishers, Inc.

American Booksellers Assn.
175 Fifth Ave., New York 10010
212-AL4-5520
Pres. Howard Klein, Burrows, 419 Euclid Ave., Cleveland, Ohio 44144. 216-861-1400

American Educational Publishers Institute
See Association of American Publishers, Inc.

American Institute of Graphic Arts
1059 Third Ave., New York 10021
212-PL2-0813
Pres. Henry Wolf
Workshop Dir. Max Stein
Exec. Dir. Edward Gottschall

American Society of Magazine Photographers
60 E. 42 St., New York 10017
212-661-6450
Dir. John Gilman

American Society of Picture Professionals, Inc.
Box 5283, Grand Central Sta., New York 10017
Pres. Wesley Day
Sec. Margaret Skaggs

American Translators Association
Box 129, Croton-on-Hudson, N.Y. 10520. 914-271-3260
Pres. William I. Bertsche
Sec. Sheema Z. Buehne

Antiquarian Booksellers Assn. of America
Shop 2 Concourse, 630 Fifth Ave., New York 10020. 212-CI6-2564
Pres. William Salloch
Exec. Sec. Mrs. Anne Spiegler

Assn. of American Medical Book Publishers
Pres. Frederick A. Rogers, Year Book Medical Publishers, 35 E. Wacker Dr., Chicago, Ill. 60601. 312-726-9733
Sec.-Treas. Kenneth Bussy, Lea & Febiger, 600 S. Washington Sq., Philadelphia, Pa. 19106. 215-WA5-5342

ASSOCIATIONS AND AGENCIES / 431

Association of American Publishers, Inc.
1 Park Ave., New York 10016
212-689-8920
Pres. Sanford Cobb
V.P. Austin J. McCaffrey
V.P. Robert W. Frase, Suite 101, 1826 Jefferson Place, N.W., Washington, D.C. 20036. 202-293-2585

Assn. of American University Presses
1 Park Ave., New York 10016
212-889-6040
Pres. William B. Harvey, Univ. of Florida Press, Gainesville, Fla. 32601
904-392-1351
Exec. Dir. John B. Putnam

Assn. of Jewish Book Publishers
House of Living Judaism, 838 Fifth Ave., New York 10021
212-249-0100
Pres. Ralph Davis
Sec. George L. Levine

Bibliographical Society of America
See section on National Associations, this volume

Book Manufacturers Institute
904 Ethan Allen Hwy., Ridgefield, Conn. 06877. 203-438-0478
Pres. Robert A. Wunsch, Becktold Co., 1600 Macklind Ave., St. Louis, Mo. 63110. 314-771-9900
Exec. Dir. Robert M. Peck

Book Week Headquarters
See Children's Book Council.

The Bookbuilders of Boston
Pres. Douglas B. Rhodes, Federated Lithographers, 353 Prairie Ave., Providence, R.I. 02905. 401-941-1200
Sec. Janet S. Levine, Nat'l Education Assn., 20 Ashburton Place, Boston, Mass. 02139. 617-227-4044

Booksellers League of New York
Pres. Theodore Wilentz, Gotham Book Mart, 41 W. 47 St., New York 10036
212-757-0367
Treas. A. C. Frasca, Jr., Freshet Press, Inc., 90 Hamilton Rd., Rockville Centre, N.Y. 11570. 516-766-3011

Brotherhood of Book Travelers
Pres. William P. Adams, Cowles Book Co., 14 Langdon Rd., Carle Place, N.Y. 11514. 516-766-3011

Bureau of Independent Publishers & Distributors
122 E. 42 St., New York 10017
212-MU7-8790
Chmn. George Epstein
Sec. Dwight Yellen
Exec. Dir. Alan P. Fort

Canadian Book Publishers' Council
Suite 701, 45 Charles St. E., Toronto 5, Ontario. 416-964-7231
Pres. Campbell B. Hughes, Van Nostrand Reinhold (Canada) Ltd.
Exec. Sec. Mrs. Ruth A. Cole

Canadian Booksellers Assn.
Royal Bank Bldg., 2 Bloor St. E., Suite 31, Toronto 5, Ont.
416-922-4158
Pres. George A. Ramsey
Sec. Mrs. Barbara Burt

Chicago Book Clinic
Pres. Alfred E. Fisher, John F. Cuneo Co., 2085 N. Cornell Ave., Melrose Pk., Ill. 60160. 312-345-7000
Treas. Brooks Crum, Laidlaw Bros., Inc., Madison St. at Thatcher Ave., River Forest, Ill. 60305. 312-369-5320

Chicago Educational Publishers Assn.
Pres. Dr. William Nault, Field Enterprises Educ. Corp., Chicago, Ill. 60654
312-341-8781
Exec. Sec. Frederic R. Sherwood, 75 E. Wacker Dr., Chicago, Ill. 60601
312-341-4232

The Children's Book Council, Inc.
175 Fifth Ave., New York 10010
212-AL4-2666
Pres. Miss Ann Durrell, E. P. Dutton & Co., 201 Park Ave. S., New York 10003. 212-674-5900
Exec. Dir. John Donovan
Assoc. Dir. Miss Paula Quint
Chmn. of Book Fair Comm. Mrs. Judith Whipple, Four Winds Press, 50 W. 44 St., New York 10036
212-867-7700

Christian Booksellers Assn.
2031 West Cheyenne Rd., Colorado Springs, Colo. 80906. 303-632-2655
Pres. William Long
Exec. V.P. John T. Bass

College Stores Assn. of New York State
Pres. Ernest Baker, Bee-Hive Campus

Store, N.Y.C. Community Coll., 300 Jay St., Brooklyn, N.Y. 11201 212-855-8671
Sec.-Treas. Stan Clark, State Univ. College at Cortland Bookstore, Neubig Hall, New Paltz, N.Y. 13045 607-753-4621

College Stores Assn. of North Carolina
Pres. Richard T. Clay, College Book Store, Wake Forest Univ., Box 7717, Winston-Salem, N.C. 27109 919-752-9711
Sec.-Treas. Lloyd D. Myers, Student Stores Staff, Univ. of North Carolina, Chapel Hill, N.C. 27514 919-933-5066

Connecticut Book Publishers Assn.
Pres. John Snow, Long House Publishers, Box 3, New Canaan, Conn. 06840 203-966-3808
Treas. Lewis M. Wiggin, Shoe String Press, 995 Sherman Ave., Hamden, Conn. 06514. 203-248-6307

Copyright Society of the U.S.A.
New York Univ. Law Center, Washington Sq., New York 10003. 212-598-2580
Pres. Leonard Zissu
Exec. Dir. Walter J. Derenberg, 60 E. 42 St., New York 10017. 212-MO1-1400

Council for Periodical Distributors Assns., Inc.
527 Madison Ave., New York 10022 212-PL3-5044
Exec. Dir. George Wright

Edition Bookbinders of New York, Inc.
421 Seventh Ave., New York 10001. 212-LA4-5619
Pres. Martin Blumberg, American Book-Stratford Press
Sec. William F. Fortney, Russell-Rutter Co., Inc.

Fourth Avenue Booksellers
Perm. Sec. Stanley Gilman, 237 E. Ninth St., New York 10003

Information Industry Assn.
Exec. Dir. Paul G. Zurkowski, 1025 15 St., N.W., Suite 700, Washington, D.C. 20005. 202-659-3928

International Assn. of Book Publishing Consultants
20/24 Uxbridge St., Kensington, London W. 8. 7TA England
Chmn. M. Hughes Miller, Book Publishers Projects, Inc., Rockefeller Center, 1270 Ave. of the Americas, Suite 2830, New York 10020. 212-JU2-1300, Ext. 42
Pres. John Grant
Sec. Miss Janet Macbain

International Assn. of Printing House Craftsmen, Inc.
7599 Kenwood Rd., Cincinnati, Ohio 45236. 513-891-0611
Pres. Bert Hagg
Exec. Sec. John A. Davies

International Community of Booksellers Assns.
Lindelaan 12, Delft, Holland. Tel: 33111
Gen. Sec. Nic. Hesseler

International Copyrights Information Center
Franklin Book Programs, Inc., 801 Second Ave., New York 10017. 212-683-2500
Cable Address. FRANBOOK NEWYORK
Dir. John H. Kyle

International League of Antiquarian Booksellers
Pres. Fernand De Nobele, 35 rue Bonaparte, Paris VIe, France
Treas. Glen Dawson, 535 N. Larchmont Blvd., Los Angeles, Calif. 90004 213-469-2186

International Standard Book Numbering Agency
1180 Ave. of the Americas, New York 10036. 212-581-8800
Exec. Dir. Emery I. Koltay

Jewish Book Council of America
15 E. 26 St., New York 10010 212-532-4949
Pres. Judah Nadich
Exec. Sec. Philip Goodman

Metropolitan Lithographers Association
250 W. 57 St., New York 10019 212-246-2044
Pres. Alan Enos, III

ASSOCIATIONS AND AGENCIES / 433

Midland Booksellers Assn.
550 11 St., Des Moines, Iowa 50309
515-282-0221
Pres. Robert Sutherlin

Midwest Book Travelers Assn.
c/o The Publishers Center, 64 E. Randolph St., Chicago, Ill. 60602
312-782-0710
Pres. Russell Kingsland, Follett Pub. Co., 1010 W. Washington Blvd., Chicago, Ill. 60607. 312-666-5858
Treas. Henry Fujii, Fujii Associates, 501 Whittier Ave., Glen Ellyn, Ill. 60137. 312-469-3799
Sec. Schuyler Huntoon, Houghton Mifflin Co., 30 N. Michigan Ave., Chicago, Ill. 60602. 312-FR2-1802

National Assn. of Book Editors
80 Fourth Ave., New York 10003
212-AL4-2550
Corres. Sec. Arnold Andersen

National Assn. of College Stores
55 E. College St., Oberlin, Ohio 44074
216-775-1561
Pres. J. C. Underwood, Baylor Univ. Bookstore, Waco, Tex. 76706
817-755-2161
Gen. Mgr. Russell Reynolds

National Assn. of Publishers
Chmn. & Sec. Saul Weiss, c/o Bantam Books, Inc., 666 Fifth Ave., New York 10019. 212-765-6500
Vice-Chmn. Sidney B. Kramer, c/o New American Library, 1301 Ave. of the Americas, New York 10019. 212-956-3838

National Book Committee
1 Park Ave., New York 10016
212-689-8620
Exec. Chmn. John C. Frantz

National Council of Churches of Christ in America — Publishers' Associated Section
Sec. Arthur A. Wahmann, The Westminster Press, Witherspoon Bldg., Philadelphia, Pa. 19107. 215-735-6722

National Library Week Program
1 Park Ave., New York 10016
212-689-8620
Staff Dir. Miss Virginia H. Mathews

Northern California Booksellers Assn.
Pres. Herbert W. Beckman, The Tides Book Co., Inc., 749 Bridgeway, Sausalito, Calif. 94965. 415-332-1188

Ohio Assn. of College Stores
Pres. Don Noll, College Bookstore, College of Wooster, Wooster, Ohio 44691. 216-264-1234
Sec. Mrs. Glenda Copeland, Ashland Comm. Bookstore, Ashland, Ohio 44805. 419-324-4561

Overseas Bookmen's Assn.
Box 42-202, Mexico 4, D.F., Mexico
Pres. Robert F. Molitor, Prentice-Hall Int'l., Inc.
Sec.-Treas. Luis Nistal, Crowell Collier & Macmillan, Inc.

Pacific Coast Independent Magazine Wholesalers Association (PACIMWA)
Pres. Arthur Jacobs, San Diego Periodical Dist., 5260 Anna Ave., San Diego, Calif. 92110. 714-297-4945
Sec. Roger Oates, Santa Barbara News Agency, 879 S. Kellogg Ave., Goleta, Calif. 93017. 805-967-2367

Periodical & Book Assn. of America, Inc.
215 Park Ave. S., New York 10003.
212-228-3900
Pres. Michael Morse

Philadelphia Book Clinic
Chmn. Phila. Book Show. Henry Baust, Jr., F. A. Davis Co., 1915 Arch St., Philadelphia, Pa. 19103
215-LO8-2270

Philadelphia Booksellers Assn.
Pres. Herbert Shugar, How-To-Do-It Bookstore, 1526 Sansome St., Philadelphia, Pa. 19102. 215-LO3-1516

Printing Industries of America, Inc.
Graphic Communications Center, 1730 N. Lynn St., Arlington, Va. 22209.
703-527-6000
Pres. Rodney L. Borum
Sec. James J. Woods, Sorg Printing Co., 424 E. 15 St., Los Angeles, Calif. 90015. 213-747-7373

Professional Bookmen of America, Inc.
Box 1571, Indianapolis, Ind. 46026
Pres. Glenn C. Steiner
Exec. Sec. C. B. Ulery

Proofreaders Club of New York
Pres. Allan Treshan, 38-15 149 St., Flushing, N.Y. 11354. 212-IN1-8509

Protestant Church-Owned Pubs. Assn.
10 S. Bryn Mawr Ave., Bryn Mawr, Pa. 19010
215-527-3332
Pres. Charles Colman III, Westminster Press, Witherspoon Bldg., Philadelphia, Pa. 19107. 215-PE5-6722
Exec. Sec. James H. Cooper

Publishers' Adclub
Pres. Richard F. X. O'Connor, Doubleday & Co., Inc., Garden City, N.Y. 11530. 516-747-1700
Sec. Mrs. Linda Exman, John Day Co., Inc., 257 Park Ave. S., New York 10010. 212-533-9000

Publishers' Library Promotion Group
Pres. Miss Lorrie Lewis, Delacorte Press, 750 Third Ave., New York 10017. 212-YU6-6300
Sec. Miss Vicki Brooks, World Publishing Co., 110 E. 59 St., New York 10022. 212-759-9500

Publishers' Publicity Assn., Inc.
Pres. Nicholas Benton, Time-Life Books, Time-Life Bldg., Rockefeller Ctr., New York 10022. 212-556-4506
Sec. Mrs. Letty C. Pogrebin, 33 W. 67 St., New York 10023
212-873-1460

Religious Book Publishing
Div. of the Assn. of American Publishers Council, 1 Park Ave., New York 10016. 212-689-8920
Mgr. W. L. Smith

Research & Engineering Council of the Graphic Arts Industry, Inc.
1515 Wilson Blvd., Arlington, Va. 22209. 703-522-8300
Pres. Dr. Albert R. Materazzi, Lith Kemp Corp., Div. of Rogers Corp., 46 Harriet Place, Lynbrook, N.Y. 11563. 516-536-4242
Mgr. Dir. Robert E. Rossell

Society of Authors' Representatives, Inc.
101 Park Ave., New York 10017
212-MU3-5890
Pres. Paul R. Reynolds
Sec.-Treas. Sterling Lord

Society of Photographer & Artist Representatives, Inc. (SPAR)
210 E. 58 St., New York 10022. 212-PL2-7174
Pres. Miss Jane Lander
Sec. Jay Grayson

Southern California, Book Publishers Assn. of
410 N. La Cienega Blvd., Los Angeles, Calif. 90048. 213-657-6100
Pres. Sol J. Grossman, Western Periodicals Co., 13000 Raymar, North Hollywood, Calif. 91605. 213-875-0555

Southern California Booksellers Assn.
Pres. Miss Roberta Whitehead, Doubleday Book Shop, 18451 Nordhoff St., Northridge, Calif. 91324
213-DI9-5484
Sec. Frances Freedman, Martindales, 9477 Santa Monica, Beverly Hills, Calif. 90210. 213-BR2-9746

TAPPI-Technical Assn. of the Pulp & Paper Industry
360 Lexington Ave., New York 10017. 212-MU2-8313
Pres. Lyle J. Gordon
Exec. Sec. & Treas. Philip E. Nethercut

Technical, Scientific & Medical Book Publishers Group (Div. of The Assn. of American Book Publishers Council)
1 Park Ave., New York 10016.
212-689-8920
Chmn. James Munford, Appleton-Century-Crofts
Sec.-Treas. Richard P. Zeldin, R. R. Bowker Co., 1180 Ave. of the Americas, New York 10036. 212-581-8800

Washington Booksellers Assn.
Pres. Lynwood Giacomini, Harper & Row, Pubs., 7004 W. Greenvale Pkwy., Chevy Chase, Md. 20015. 202-652-4709
Sec. Miss Norma Blazer, Kann's, Pennsylvania Ave. & Eighth St., N.W., Washington, D.C. 20004
202-DI7-7200

West Coast Bookmen's Assn.
Pres. William McKay, 9931 Garden Grove, Northridge, Calif. 91324
213-349-6483
Sec. Frank G. Goddall, 27 McNear Dr., San Rafael, Calif. 94901
415-454-7090

Western Book Publishers Assn.
Pres. Richard B. Paulsen, Pacific Coast Publishers, 4080 Campbell Ave., Menlo Park, Calif. 94025. 415-365-5256
Sec. A. E. Hansen, Wadsworth Pub. Co., 10 Davis Dr., Belmont, Calif. 94002. 415-592-1300

Western College Bookstore Assn.
Pres. Jeff Wanee, Student Bookstore, Chico State College, Chico, Calif. 95929. 916-345-5222
Sec.-Treas. Dean Haslem, Utah State Univ. Bookstore, Union Bldg., Logan, Utah 84321. 801-752-4100

Wisconsin Booksellers Assn.
Box 1812, Milwaukee, Wis. 53201.
Pres. Harry W. Schwartz, Harry W. Schwartz Book Store, Inc., 440 W. Wisconsin Ave., Milwaukee, Wis. 53203. 414-272-2700
Sec.-Treas. Miss Margery Hart, Des Forges, Inc., 427 E. Wisconsin Ave., Milwaukee, Wis. 53202. 414-BR1-3061

Women's National Book Assn.
Nat'l. Pres. Miss Virginia H. Mathews, Nat'l. Book Committee, 1 Park Ave., New York 10016. 212-689-8920
Nat'l. Sec. Miss Jeannette Clark, 54 St. John Ave., Binghamton, N.Y. 13905. 607-723-7981
Nat'l. Treas. Mrs. Anne J. Richter, 222 Valley Rd., Montclair, N.J. 07042. 201-746-5166

PART 4 INTERNATIONAL LIBRARY AND BOOK TRADE DEVELOPMENTS

International Library and Book Trade Developments

INTERNATIONAL BOOK YEAR – 1972

by

Edward Wegman*

International Book Year – 1972 entered its operational phase with an early and notable plus sign. In country after country, and on the international scene as well, the representatives of the book professions reported to UNESCO on how they had joined together in this common enterprise. That cooperation, which seemed likely to extend far beyond December 31, 1972, is best symbolized by the major international nongovernmental organizations' approval of the text of a Charter of the Book, which sets forth in ten articles guiding principles for the free flow of books, for the promotion of readership, the encouragement of authorship and translation, wider production and distribution, the use of books for education, and their role in promoting international understanding.

In addition to the organizations' approval is the approval of the Support Committee for IBY which met at Brussels in October 1971 and gave its benediction to the text of the Charter. The meeting was attended by representatives of the publishers, authors, booksellers, librarians, and documentalists drawn from a wide range of countries: Austria, Belgium, Colombia, France, Federal Republic of Germany, Ghana, Hungary, India, Japan, Netherlands, United Arab Republic, United Kingdom, United States of America, and USSR. The Charter of the Book thus becomes the first international declaration of its kind bringing together the differing regions of the world as well as the book professions.

Members of the United States Committee for International Book Year consider the approval of the Charter such a major step that it is now envisaged to send a copy to the moon with Apollo XVI! On a more mundane level, the international organizations of the book world are expected to adopt the text formally at each of their international congresses scheduled in 1972 under the aegis of International Book Year. Furthermore, all nongovernmental organizations, international, regional, or national, are being invited to associate themselves with this declaration, the text of which will figure importantly in the report on International Book Year to be submitted to UNESCO's General Conference, October 1972.

Plans for regional and national cooperation among book professionals are

---

*Head, International Book Year Unit, UNESCO, Paris, France.

being drawn up for the Year in various parts of the world. In developing countries, this cooperation is found in the organization or strengthening of national book development councils where authors, publishers, booksellers, educators, librarians, and government officials are brought together to draft joint plans for the production and use of books. In developed nations, there is a growing sense of solidarity with colleagues in less advanced regions; professional organizations have widened their efforts to include more members from developing countries.

A substantial amount of aid is being given to book development in national planning for the Year. Training courses, gifts of paper and machinery, library twinning, and other ways of providing material and moral assistance occupy an important role. At the same time, the importance of associating economic planners with the programs for book development has been recognized. For instance, the United States Committee has decided to convene an international seminar which will bring to the same discussion table economists, educators, and the producers of books and other audiovisual products.

A sidelight to this concept of mutual efforts among the book professions is the Japanese proposal for joint production of children's books among the 18 countries (Member States) in the Asian region. Preliminary meetings have already selected five titles to be published simultaneously in 1972 in editions of 500 to 1,000 copies for each language (if the project proves viable, edition sizes will be enlarged). The scheme depends upon the agreement among participating Asian countries on what children's book titles to publish from the region. Then each country will make its own translation of the selected book(s), and paste the type-set copy into the original book which will already contain the illustrations. These are then returned to the country where the book originated, which undertakes the printing of the book. For the initial round, the Tokyo Book Development Center is paying translation and editorial expenses and will handle copyright arrangements. It is hoped that all of the 18 countries of the region will participate, with the Center coordinating efforts. In addition, an African country has already made inquiries about the possibility of participating in the plan.

To further these international efforts, UNESCO presented a report entitled "Book Development in the Service of Education," dealing with International Book Year's purposes, to the Economic and Social Council (ECOSOC) of the United Nations, at the latter's request. The discussion of the report at the Council's fiftieth session proved to be a wide-ranging one. Spokesmen for the developing countries welcomed International Book Year, particularly as a means of promoting book development and of increasing the supply of textbooks. They also expressed the hope that International Book Year, in conjunction with UNESCO's newly established International Copyright Information Center, would ease the pressing problem of access to copyrighted works. The more advanced countries saw International Book Year as a unique occasion for enhancing the role of books in international cooperation and greater mutual understanding of cultures.

At the conclusion of its discussion, ECOSOC unanimously adopted a resolution supporting International Book Year and calling on all institutions and organs of the United Nations, as well as other interested intergovernmental organizations, to assist in attaining IBY's objectives. The resolution also recommended the provision of "international assistance for low-cost local reprint and translation or adaptation into national languages of developing countries of books" for higher education, and urged financial and technical assistance "to create the infrastructure in the developing countries for the promotion of domestic book production."

UNESCO also presented a report to the United Nations Conference on Trade and Development (UNCTAD) suggesting steps that might be taken to overcome foreign currency obstacles to the importation of books and of the raw materials necessary for their manufacture. UNCTAD's Trade and Development Board asked UNESCO to continue to study such proposals and present at a future meeting a possible program of action.

Following UNESCO's suggestions, other intergovernmental organizations also are assisting International Book Year. The Universal Postal Union, for example, proposed that its Member States issue special International Book Year stamps. The Council of Europe planned a symposium on how public libraries can identify and meet the educational and cultural needs of individuals and groups; multimedia systems in public libraries were also to be examined.

These efforts on the international scene are being supplemented by often extensive national programs to stimulate among people an awareness of the value of books and related materials in promoting economic and social progress, in acquiring a broader understanding of other nations, and in adding to the personal well-being of the reader. The creation of an effective demand for books goes hand in hand with efforts to increase the availability of the printed word.

International Book Year is thus lending added impetus to campaigns to encourage more reading. These range from book and library weeks — traditional in some countries but new initiatives in many others — to special book fairs for the general public, rather than the trade, at which books are often being made available at special discounts.

Considerable ingenuity is displayed in many of the plans. The Canadians, for example, are planning a contest among schoolchildren to produce their own books. The winning class will see their creation actually printed and distributed. Internally, Haiti is promoting books as gifts under the slogan, "A book given, twenty hearts won." India is using the Year to launch an extensive training program for editors and booksellers in order to "reduce and progressively eliminate the grave shortage of qualified personnel from which the book industry now suffers." Almost a dozen Member States are planning to make readership and market surveys in their countries. Iraq will erect a giant statue of the book in a public square. Belgium is financing part of its extensive Book Year program by issuing surcharge postage stamps. Special issues of periodicals dealing with books are under consideration in half a dozen countries. These countries, as well as others, are planning radio and television programs and special films during the Year. The general press is also playing a major role in promoting public acceptance of IBY's objectives.

To advise UNESCO in the coordination and stimulation of these IBY activities, an International Planning Committee met in April 1971 at UNESCO House, where experts established the Support Committee for the Year (mentioned previously) which approved the text of the Charter of the Book. A further meeting of this Committee was planned for May 1972 in Vienna.

One of the obligations the Support Committee assumed was to help in the search for outside sources of financing for International Book Year projects. UNESCO itself had been able to provide only a limited budget to assist Member States to initiate activities; also, it began to receive proposals of considerable long-term merit which exceeded its financial capacities, such as one for stimulating the production of books for the blind and another for the establishment of regional training centers for book development in Africa. Members of the Support Committee undertook to explore in their respective countries the possibility of securing bilateral or private assistance for those projects which met the requirements of contributing to the more effective use of books, which were carefully costed, had a definite timetable, and whose results could be quantified.

Beyond these immediate tasks, it was considered that the Support Committee in itself constituted a nucleus for continuing professional advice to UNESCO on its book programs. The possibility is being studied that the group might continue its operations beyond 1972, thus strengthening the cooperation between the Organization and the professionals of the book world.

Within UNESCO, broad efforts were made to integrate ongoing programs with the objectives of International Book Year. A special IBY unit was established with liaison officers for each of UNESCO's major sectors of activity. In addition, a number of publications were foreseen for International Book Year. A study entitled "The Book Hunger" was prepared for publication. Drawing upon UNESCO's regional meetings on book development, it describes the pattern of world book production and distribution and suggests measures to promote wider access to books. A popular brochure on International Book Year and UNESCO's involvement with books was issued in English and French under the title of *Books for All*, the slogan for the Year. Finally, the pamphlet on the Program of Action approved by the General Conference of the Organization was published in English, French, Spanish, Russian, and Arabic.

A multilingual newsletter containing information on International Book Year activities began publication in mid-1971 and will continue during 1972. Through the newsletter, reports received from Member States and international organizations are widely disseminated.

UNESCO's own periodicals are reporting extensively on International Book Year. The popular magazine, the *Unesco Courier*, published in 12 languages in identical editions, devoted its January 1972 issue to International Book Year, with lead articles by Marshal McLuhan and Alberto Moravia. A further issue on books was planned for later in the Year. Other periodicals such as *Unesco Features*, the *Chronicle, Bulletin for Libraries, International Social Science Journal, Journal of World History, Prospects in Education,* and the *Copyright Bulletin* prepared articles or issues on IBY in their respective spheres of competence. All periodicals, as well as UNESCO books published in 1972, are featuring the International Book Year symbol.

International Book Year was similarly featured by UNESCO's audiovisual services, symbolizing the marriage between the printed word and the other mass media in the world today. Television and radio programs were issued. A 20-minute color documentary on books was prepared for distribution early in 1972. Posters were printed and distributed; photographs and press kits were made available.

Finally, UNESCO pressed its plans for an international symposium on books, scheduled to be held in September. The four themes of the Year, authorship and translation, production and distribution, the reading habit, and books in the service of education and peaceful cooperation, are to be discussed by distinguished experts from various parts of the world.

With all of these activities, the Year was launched on 1 January with a message from the Director-General of UNESCO and similar proclamations and messages from chiefs of state in various countries. Recognizing the difficulty of maintaining momentum throughout the twelve-month period, UNESCO had advised Member States to try to concentrate their principal activities, insofar as possible, in two peak periods, May and September. In March and in May, for example, both the International Community of Booksellers Associations and the International Publishers Association scheduled their congresses at UNESCO House, with IBY and the Charter of the Book major items on the agenda. In September, among other events, the international symposium entitled "Books for All," is scheduled. Many national plans also took note of these periods, although it was evident that previously scheduled national book weeks or book fairs could not be changed just for 1972.

It is apparent that International Book Year has stirred widespread enthusiasm which ranges far beyond the perhaps parochial interests of the book professions. While few have set quantitative targets for increases in book production or reading during the Year, most concerned with its preparation are convinced that the long-term effect of the Year will be a steady rise in the production and consumption of printed matter in all parts of the world.

INTERNATIONAL RELATIONS ACTIVITIES OF THE AMERICAN LIBRARY ASSOCIATION IN 1971

by

David G. Donovan*

INTERNATIONAL RELATIONS OFFICE

During 1971 the International Relations Office (IRO) of ALA continued to offer assistance to foundations, government agencies, and institutions to develop, administer, and evaluate projects involving libraries abroad and the international aspects of library programs in the United States; encourage the exchange of librarians; promote library education and training programs abroad, and the training of librarians from overseas in the United States; and disseminate information about the international activities of ALA to interested individuals in the United States and abroad.

During 1971, the IRO administered major projects in such countries as Colombia, Ethiopia, Ghana, Indonesia, Thailand, and Venezuela. During the year the Office also completed the administration of Ford Foundation grants for assistance in rehabilitating the library of the University of Algiers, developing the library collection of Haile Selassie I University in Addis Ababa, and developing the central, science, and educational libraries at the University of Brasilia. Also completed was a Rockefeller Foundation grant to assist the University of Delhi to expand and develop its programs of library education.

IRO, through a contract with the U.S. Agency for International Development (AID), provided the Agency and its overseas Missions with advice and technical assistance on library development, monitored book procurement programs for Ghana and Thailand, and provided Colombia with university and school library consultants, a textbook specialist, and audiovisual experts to assist in the development of learning resource centers. IRO also continued to publish its monthly newsletter, *Libraries in International Development*, with AID support.

INTERNATIONAL RELATIONS SUBCOMMITTEES

The International Relations Subcommittee for Liaison with Japanese Librarians is presently engaged in the follow-up program of a conference held in Japan in 1969 on the role of libraries in higher education and research. A second international meeting of U.S. and Japanese librarians is planned for 1972 and will be held in the United States.

The International Relations Subcommittee of the Children's Services Division (CSD) annually selects repositories abroad for collections of children's books of international importance. The books for each repository are selected in accord with the needs and stated interests of the recipient country. The books serve as a reference collection for local writers, illustrators, publishers, educators, and librarians. The collections are a project of the United States Section of the International Board of Books for Young Peo-

---

*Director, International Relations Office, American Library Association, 1420 N Street N.W., Washington, D.C. 20005.

ple. The books are presented by the publishers and the Children's Book Council, Inc. and honor the late Margaret Scoggin, Coordinator of Young Adult Services of the New York Public Library from 1952 to 1967. During 1971 five additional repositories were selected for the Scoggin Memorial Collections, making a total of 11 such repositories to date. The International Relations Committee of the Children's Services Division is also compiling a list of "Children's Books of International Interest" for publication during International Book Year in 1972. The 1970 "Children's Books of International Interest" list was prepared for distribution to the Children's Sub-Section, Public Library Section of the International Federation of Library Associations' Liverpool Conference in 1971.

The American Association of School Librarians Subcommittee of IRC developed guidelines for persons from other countries planning visits to school library media centers in the United States. The guidelines outline the typical school year, noting holidays and other factors to be considered in planning the itinerary. The Subcommittee also updated "The Good School Library," developed by the School Library Development Project. It was translated into French and Spanish with the cooperation of the International Relations Office.

All units of ALA were involved in planning Association activities for International Book Year. The Association's program will be formally initiated during a special program at the ALA Midwinter Meeting in January 1972.

ACTIVITIES OF OTHER ALA UNITS

Membership in the International Relations Round Table is available to all members of ALA and is one of the major opportunities for the membership to become involved directly in the Association's international activities. The Round Table has area committees for individuals wishing to be associated with colleagues concerned with libraries and librarianship in the major geographic areas of the world. The Round Table conducts a program on aspects of international librarianship at ALA Annual Conferences, and hosts a reception to honor conference registrants from other countries. During 1971 the Africa Area Committee of the Round Table has explored, as a special project, ways of assisting in the restoration of the war-devastated libraries of Nigeria. The Round Table publishes a newsletter entitled *Leads* as part of its effort to keep its members aware of significant developments in international librarianship.

Ten Asian students studying in U.S. library schools were awarded travel grants to attend meetings of state library associations during the 1970–1971 academic year, and 55 complimentary 1971 ALA membership were granted to librarians, libraries, and library associations in ten Asian countries. These travel grants and memberships were made possible by a grant from the Asia Foundation to ALA and were administered by the Library Education Division Grants Committee.

The Equivalencies and Reciprocity Committee of the Library Education Division continued to identify individuals who could provide information to library educators and administrators needing evaluations of the academic and professional qualifications of individuals educated abroad and seeking admission to graduate schools of library science or employment in a library in the United States or Canada.

Librarians from abroad requesting information accounted for 15 percent of the written inquiries received by the Library Technology Program (LTP) of ALA. The information most frequently requested concerned microtext equipment. Other areas in which librarians demonstrated particular interest were circulation systems, binding, library furniture, and audiovisual equipment.

LTP was named a runner-up for the 1970 Robinson Medal for development of the SE-LIN book labeling system. A commemorative scroll was accepted on behalf of LTP by Sir Frank Francis, former Director of the British Museum, at a reception given in London in June. The award is made biannually by The Library Association, England, recognizing the "originality and inventive ability of librarians and interested persons or firms in connection with devising new and improved methods of library technology."

The fourth Mildred L. Batchelder Award was presented in 1971 to a representative of Pantheon Books for *In the Land of Ur,* by Hans Baumann, translated from the German by Stella Humphries. Nominations for the 1972 Award are: *The Crane,* by Reiner Zemnik (Harper and Row); *Escape,* by Ota Hofman (Knopf); *Friedrich,* by Hans Peter Richter (Holt); *The Little Chalk Man,* by Václav Ctvrtek (Knopf); and *Marius,* by Rolf Docker (Harcourt). Announcement of the result of the vote of the CSD members will be made on April 2, 1972, International Children's Book Day.

The 1972 Hans Christian Andersen Awards Nominations Ad Hoc Committee of CSD selected the U.S. nominations for the 1972 Hans Christian Andersen Awards: author, Scott O'Dell; illustrator, Evaline Ness; honor book, *The Trumpet of the Swan,* by E. B. White.

(For background material on the International Relations Office, see the 1971 *Bowker Annual,* pp. 454-456.)

THE INTERNATIONAL FEDERATION OF LIBRARY ASSOCIATIONS, ACTIVITIES FOR 1971*

by

Herman Liebaers**

UNIVERSALITY OF IFLA

Thanks to UNESCO, the Commonwealth Foundation, and the British Council, IFLA has been able to organize for the first time in its history a presession seminar for developing countries, on the theme, "the latest developments in advanced librarianship." Thus the number of participants from Asia and Africa in the IFLA General Council has considerably increased and the geographic impact of IFLA has practically doubled.

IFLA has no reason to export western solutions to the Third World. That part of the world should take its own initiatives and should know that we are ready to respond to any request for assistance — assistance being merely an accurate and critical description of the manner in which we have tried to solve our own technical problems. It is useful for librarians in South East Asia to know how we try to unify cataloging principles within western languages, but the same work has to be carried out by colleagues in Bangkok, Singapore, or Manila for eastern languages. The experience of technical experts from our committee on cataloging may be a precious asset to accelerate the right solution.

Similarly, IFLA must give attention to regional groups, and they should tell us what they expect from us. During the last year a meeting of Oriental librarians in Canberra, a meeting of CONSAL (Conference of Southeast Asian Librarians) in Singapore, a meeting of eastern librarians from SCAUL (Southeast African University Libraries) in Addis Ababa, and the good will of the FID/CLA (Committee for Latin America) in Buenos Aires and Rio de Janeiro were opportunities for contacts between local librarians and IFLA representatives,

---

*Adapted from Dr. Liebaers' Presidential Address, given at the IFLA conference, Liverpool, England, October 1971.
**President, International Federation of Library Associations (IFLA).

which may lead in the near future to closer links between IFLA and local libraries. The IFLA Board is certainly eager to expand cooperation in all directions.

UNIVERSAL BIBLIOGRAPHICAL CONTROL (UBC)

In recent times IFLA has taken a series of initiatives or has cooperated with initiatives taken elsewhere concerning UBC: the meeting on Cataloguing Principles in Paris in 1961 and its sequel in Copenhagen in 1969, the various meetings on international standards for library statistics, culminating last year in the intergovernmental conference at UNESCO which led to an international recommendation for the standardization of library statistics, the seminar organized last year in Regensburg and this year in Berlin on the problems related to the international use of magnetic tapes with bibliographic information, the bold initiative of the American Congress to initiate a National Program of Acquisitions and Cataloging, better known as Shared Cataloging.

IFLA's Board thought that the time was ripe to try to link all these initiatives in a rather ambitious program of Universal Bibliographical Control, which should be concerned with a series of problems which involved all our sections and committees whose members would find food for thought and action through the definition of these problems.

The program for UBC has been published in the *Unesco Bulletin for Libraries* (Vol. XXV, No. 5, pp. 252-259); the following are the headlines: problems related to the recording of bibliographic data, such as size and content of national bibliographies, the legal grounds on which descriptions are recorded in national bibliographies, the demand for the most complete possible listing of literature in existing national bibliographies, the reduction of time lag in recording in national bibliographies, the creation of national bibliographies in developing countries, prepublication cataloging; problems of standardization and compatibility in bibliographic information, such as technical standardization including library requirements on hardware and software, the format of bibliographic data on tape, standardization of cataloging rules, the standard bibliographic description, lists of standard titles, ISBN and ISSN from a librarian's point of view, uniformity in the treatment of book contents; and finally a series of organizational questions, such as the spreading of machine-readable catalogs, regional centers for distribution of machine-readable data originating in foreign countries, and databanks of older titles.

INTERNATIONAL BOOK YEAR

The avowed aim of IBY is to bring books to countries, or in a given country to those population groups which have not yet fully discovered them. This means promotion of books among children and young people, and among underprivileged groups who are either minorities in rich countries or majorities in poor countries.

These terms of reference indicate quite clearly that organizations of school, children's, and public libraries have to bear the main responsibility for implementing IBY. In some countries we have gathered the technical expertise to deal with underprivileged groups, that is to say, all kinds of handicapped readers.

The Public Library Section of IFLA has accepted to revise the UNESCO Public Library Manifesto of 1949 and to distribute it early in 1972 in as many languages as possible in order to convince public opinion and the authorities alike of the beneficial role of public libraries in individual self-fulfillment and in collective advancement.

Other types of libraries besides public also have a role to play. There is a long list of topics of research in reading which can best be carried out by librarians, either individually or in cooperation with other representatives of the book industry or the educational system. This long list extends from the relapse of illiteracy to the history of reading.

One positive advantage of IBY, both at the international and the national levels, is that it brings together the various professional groups concerned with the book. Librarians discover that authors and publishers are not just obstacles to the use of books, as when they insist on lending rights or limit reproduction; publishers in turn realize that librarians are not exactly hiring the books which they try to buy at a discount. Besides deep involvement with the reading habit, librarians may also give their own view on "books," and may help publishers to prove that books are indeed different from other articles of commerce. Mallarmé said that all that exists in the world ends in a book, but it does not need a poet to add that what exists in the world also starts with a book.

The mass media are also inextricably tied to books. Television, newspapers, radios, records, are all by-products of books. The area with the largest concentration of televisions, newspapers, etc., will also have the largest concentration of books. The more books, the more libraries. The place with the largest concentration of libraries has also the largest concentration of bookshops. Libraries often pave the way for bookshops, and sometimes it is the other way around.

Besides systematic research in reading and the sociology of the book, the library community can make specific contributions to IBY. At random, one may cite the tremendous impact of the reprint business — that tycoon of modern publishing — which is clearly aimed at a nearly exclusive library "clientele," stressing the importance of noncommercial book circulation through interlibrary loan and international exchange of library materials. Librarians, representing the nonprofit part of the book business, are also well equipped to make all kinds of selections, from the best children's books to a worldwide circulation of that outstanding British initiative known under the excellent title, "Printing and Mind of Man."

THE ORGANIZATION OF THE PROFESSION

IFLA is an "international organization," but an international organization does not exist in a vacuum; it has ties — simple and sophisticated ones — with national, regional, and local organizations, and cannot ignore other international organizations with related interests.

IFLA is much concerned with the disparity between the ideal situation and the reality of international librarianship. Excessive nationalism is of course a problem. On the one hand it is needed for our international work; on the other hand it is a constant obstacle to cooperation beyond political borders. Yet one must be realistic and accept it as being with us for years to come.

All we may expect to achieve at the international level requires us to transcend nationalism. This does not mean that IFLA should not remain the most suitable forum for the exchange of valuable national experiences. We have done it successfully in the past and we shall go on doing it in the future. For instance, the recent history of American librarianship has been strongly influenced by the various programs which the Council on Library Resources, Inc. has financed. Most of these projects were limited to the United States, while it was felt outside the United States that the problems for which new solutions were sought existed everywhere with more or less the same urgency. IFLA is the right place to interpret this impact of the CLR on American librarianship in terms which are understandable in countries with a less sophisticated development, which are poorer, which are different from the United States in many ways. To do this, however, IFLA needed a much stronger secretarial and organizational structure, or, in other words, needed more financial resources. While working on a fair scheme of dues, IFLA received a generous grant from the Council on Library Resources, Inc., which enables it to match immediately the expectations of the international library community. Expectations are growing steadily in size and in complexity. This is quite normal in our present time when all aspects of human life are getting more and more international. The time is gone when IFLA could live from ridiculously low dues paid by some rich countries, a nice handshake by old friends who meet once a year, and the isolated initiatives of an active committee chairman. We have tried to explain this to all members. Thanks to the CLR grant we can now live up to this new commitment. But it was agreed with the CLR that their assistance would only be a bridge between the good old past and the challenging future, and that in two years' time we should be able to maintain the same level of operation with our own means.

Let us consider our relations with other international organizations, with FID and UNESCO. With FID we are now definitely beyond the stage of the exchange of courtesies. We have achieved efficient cooperation in a certain number of fields. The relations between UNESCO, our main international governmental organization, and the body of nongovernmental international organizations are presently under strain. UNESCO is a huge bureaucratic machine where political conflicts often have a paralyzing effect. One way out for UNESCO — and most of its highest officers consider this to be the only way out — is to gain the cooperation of nongovernmental organizations. The last sexennial report about the contribution of the nongovernmental organizations, IFLA included, to the implementation of the UNESCO program, is an impressive record. But to maintain this position the nongovernmental organizations in general, and IFLA in particular, should by all means keep politics out and remain in the strictest sense professional organizations. This does not mean that we close our eyes to what is going on in the world, this does not mean that we ignore the ethical implications of our work or that we do not abide by the Universal Declaration of the Human Rights, but this does mean that we bring together people with different political opinions and respect these differences with the sole purpose of the advancement of the profession everywhere.

Furthermore, in regard to the whole profession, IFLA must deliberately try to open itself up to international groups of librarians — important ones like the medical and musical librarians — who are organized outside IFLA, and well organized, indeed. We hope that the image of IFLA will prove attractive enough to bring all groups in our midst and that we can truly speak for the whole profession, a profession which still requires that a lot of talking be done about it to the outside world.

DEVELOPMENTS IN LIBRARIANSHIP IN CANADA

by

Katherine H. Packer*

In 1971 the Canadian National Library continued to fulfill the role it had defined for itself of "prime mover": its goal being the creation and implementation of a library network at the governmental, national, and international level. The Systems Development Division of the Research and Planning Branch of the National Library began to lay the foundations for such a development by establishing two task groups, one on cataloging standards, which began its work in the early part of 1971, and a second, the Task Group on a Canadian MARC format, which met to consider standards for automation and for machine-readable formats. Under consideration are not only the Library of Congress MARC

---

*Assistant Professor, School of Library Science, University of Toronto.

TABLE 1   CANADIAN UNION CATALOGUE

	Staff	Reporting Libraries	Union Catalogue Accessions	Location Requests
1969/70	35	300	1,212,000	87,400
1970/71	39	317	1,406,000	100,770

format and the British MARC format, but also variations introduced or suggested by other countries. Of special importance in the Canadian bilingual situation is the possibility of classed searching. Both of these task groups are to have made their reports by the end of 1971.

Another section of this Branch, the Resources Development Division, has carried on the work of surveying and making an inventory of Canadian research library collections. To date 33 of the 42 university libraries to be covered have been surveyed, and work on seven others is in progress. Information gathered includes statistics on books and serials, reports on collection strengths and weaknesses — particularly with respect to special collections — and capacity to support graduate studies. Publication of the results of these surveys is expected in the near future.

In 1967 the Canadian National Science Library began a computerized selective dissemination of information service on a trial basis. Operated for the past year under the name of CAN/SDI, this project now has 700 subscribers. There are six scientific data bases available for searching. The format adopted for CAN/SDI data bases is the Library of Congress MARC format. A study of user reaction to the service was published in the *Canadian Library Journal,* Vol. 28, No. 1, January-February 1971. The hope has been expressed that the National Library will find it possible to provide publications and services for the humanities and social sciences comparable to the National Science Library's *Union List of Serials in Science and Technology* and CAN/SDI by adapting the programs that have been tested and proven by the National Science Library.

The National Library reported the statistics found in Table 1 for the Canadian Union Catalogue, which was started just over 20 years ago.

The Catalogue now contains approximately 12,000,000 cards. Automating the Union Catalogue has been given a high priority by the National Library, in accord with the recommendations in the two-volume systems study *An Integrated Information System for the National Library.* A task group to consider the problems of a national bibliographic data bank is to be organized this year.

Looking to the future, the National Library is to establish a multicultural language and literature center. This project was recommended by the Canadian Library Association, and its approval reflects the concern of the Canadian government for the support and preservation of the so-called nonofficial languages of Canada. The center will administer a program designed to deposit books in languages other than English and French in local libraries.

Finally, the Canadian National Library is becoming increasingly involved in international library organizations. Members of its staff played an active role at the Paris meeting of representatives of OECD (Organization for Economic Cooperation and Development) countries, and more recently at the UNISIST conference called by UNESCO and ISCU (International Council of Scientific Unions).

While continuing to survey library services in Canada, the Dominion Bureau of Statistics has undertaken to reorganize this important information service in 1971. As a result, the cumulations for 1969 and 1970 which are found in the tables in this report had to be ob-

TABLE 2 TOTALS FOR CANADA, STATISTICS FOR ALL PUBLIC LIBRARIES

Year	Population	Population Served	Libraries Reporting (Number)	Stock	Circulation	Current Operating Payments ($)	Full-time Staff (No.)
1962	18,570,000	12,996,051	874	15,580,359	65,143,573	21,931,095	2,962
1963	18,872,000	13,236,808	884	16,609,264	70,418,478	24,187,650	3,116
1964	19,237,000	13,394,453	889	18,981,077	76,177,759	27,012,250	3,204
1965	19,546,000	14,102,520	910	20,192,135	78,288,557	30,023,404	3,464
1966	19,986,142	15,592,074	890	20,572,981	80,823,699	34,858,834	3,538
1967	20,405,000	16,100,496	855	21,634,868	81,788,829	41,153,985	3,838
1968	20,744,000	15,653,713	716	23,008,802	88,586,493	46,844,260	4,348
1969	21,061,000	—	723	24,374,244	92,910,068	51,867,000	4,573
1970	21,377,000	—	732	26,159,632	96,324,476	65,100,000	4,519

TABLE 3 TOTALS FOR CANADA, CURRENT OPERATING RECEIPTS FOR URBAN PUBLIC LIBRARIES

	Local Taxes	Provincial Grants (dollars)	Other Sources	Total
1963				19,199,383
1964	17,770,799	2,317,852	1,404,826	21,493,477
1965	19,329,272	2,872,644	1,611,543	23,813,459
1966	22,009,876	3,679,292	3,197,981	28,887,149
1967	25,260,238	4,549,244	3,943,208	33,752,690
1968	29,104,277	5,118,981	2,150,017	36,373,275
1969	32,190,639	5,446,525	2,621,000	40,258,000
1970	37,057,774	5,336,247	3,927,934	46,321,955

TABLE 4 TOTALS FOR CANADA, CURRENT OPERATING PAYMENTS OF URBAN PUBLIC LIBRARIES

	Personnel Costs	Library Materials (dollars)	Binding and Repair	Other	Total
1963					19,062,906
1964					21,348,373
1965					23,615,106
1966	16,463,335	5,047,046	643,302	5,146,048	27,299,731
1967	19,358,452	5,055,106	637,916	6,300,350	31,351,824
1968	22,673,014	6,032,350	620,986	6,817,471	36,143,821
1969	25,003,167	6,715,292	724,861	7,532,425	39,975,745
1970	28,496,894	7,201,546	671,922	8,617,062	44,987,424

TABLE 5   TOTALS FOR CANADA, CURRENT OPERATING RECEIPTS FOR REGIONAL PUBLIC LIBRARIES

	Local Taxes	Provincial Grants (dollars)	Other Sources	Total
1963				2,177,689
1964	1,337,081	1,159,449	230,100	2,726,630
1965	1,552,878	1,368,609	198,138	3,119,625
1966	1,808,753	1,957,035	219,667	3,985,455
1967	2,384,918	2,459,595	325,326	5,169,839
1968	2,924,198	3,033,517	304,783	6,262,498
1969	3,621,143	3,619,331	1,134,187	8,374,661
1970	6,292,040	5,499,227	1,814,127	13,605,394

TABLE 6   TOTALS FOR CANADA, CURRENT OPERATING PAYMENTS OF REGIONAL PUBLIC LIBRARIES

	Personnel Costs	Library Materials (dollars)	Binding and Repair	Other	Total
1963					2,198,826
1964	1,308,859	791,648	39,023	536,116	2,675,646
1965	1,527,897	881,137	43,498	629,125	3,081,657
1966	1,912,804	1,035,003	63,403	765,298	3,776,508
1967	2,487,944	1,345,089	72,618	1,184,148	5,089,799
1968	3,158,509	1,614,268	75,831	1,279,932	6,128,540
1969	3,887,322	2,229,611	79,907	1,670,972	7,817,812
1970	6,461,364	2,551,157	148,554	3,360,305	12,521,380

tained in advance of publication from Mr. J. E. Wicks, Chief, Cultural Information, Statistics Canada.

PUBLIC LIBRARIES

Public libraries are reported in two categories, Urban Public Libraries and Regional Public Libraries. For information on the distinction between these two categories, see the 1971 *Bowker Annual*, pp. 461-462.

The most important development affecting public libraries in Canada in 1970–1971 was the establishment of a new government agency known as Information Canada to expand Canadians' access to government information. The distribution function of the Queen's Printer was transferred to this agency. The intent was to provide a two-way channel for communication, and as a means to this end Information Canada was authorized to establish 11 centers across Canada. A joint committee of the Canadian Library Association and Information Canada was set up to explore avenues for cooperation between the two organizations and to study the possibility of having Information Canada booths in public libraries, especially in centers not having government bookstores or other offices. One center has already been set up in the public library in St. Johns, Newfoundland, and others are being planned. The library will act as an agent for Information Canada by selling government publications and will receive support for an expanded reference facility with backup in the form of a communications link with Ottawa. Other centers scheduled to open in the near future will not necessarily be modeled on the center in Newfoundland, but will be tailored to the particular locale and its requirements.

In an attempt to provide public libraries and public librarians across the country with current information regarding starting salaries for the current year, the *1971 Canadian Library Association Public Library Salary Survey* was carried out. The national average for professional librarians was found to be $7,460, and for library technicians $4,520.

SCHOOL LIBRARIES

Due to changes being made by the Dominion Bureau of Statistics in collecting and reporting data for school libraries, no figures for library growth are available beyond 1967–1968. (For this data, see table, "All Schools and Centralized Libraries," 1971 *Bowker Annual*, p. 464.) Figures for schools and enrollment, however, reflect a continued trend toward larger school units.

TABLE 7 SCHOOLS AND ENROLLMENT

	Canada Totals Publicly Operated Schools	Enrollment of Publicly Operated Schools
1961–62	24,717	4,181,515
1962–63	23,706	4,359,044
1963–64	22,554	4,520,961
1964–65	21,521	4,721,294
1965–66	19,987	4,882,397
1966–67	18,365	5,046,272
1967–68	17,091	5,218,898
1968–69	17,787	5,572,824
1969–70	17,029	5,751,064
1970–71	16,485	5,822,243

COLLEGE AND UNIVERSITY LIBRARIES

Expansion and growth have taken place very recently in technical institutes and community colleges in some parts of Canada, notably in Ontario. In Quebec the post-secondary education system has undergone a complete change with

TABLE 8 LIBRARIES OF NONUNIVERSITY POST-SECONDARY INSTITUTIONS

	Full-time Enrollment	Book Stock	Expenditure per Full-time Student (dollars)
1965–66	57,312	254,728	11.35
1966–67	34,852	336,979	29.96
1967–68	27,524	1,047,808	71.06
1968–69	29,925	1,156,146	69.82
1969–70	—	2,020,885	—

TABLE 9 CURRENT OPERATING EXPENDITURES OF NONUNIVERSITY POST-SECONDARY INSTITUTIONS

	Personnel	Library Materials (dollars)	Total
1965–66	$ 212,119	$ 244,256	$ 481,065
1966–67	308,458	366,950	721,732
1967–68	817,183	831,641	1,753,973
1968–69	1,746,621	1,539,390	3,525,255
1969–70	3,229,969	2,667,906	6,247,133

the establishment of Collèges d'Enseignement Général et Professionel (CEGEP), which have incorporated the former specialized institutes. The official figures in Tables 8 and 9 do not include the teachers' colleges in Ontario or the normal schools in Quebec, nor do they reflect any appreciable growth in enrollment, possibly due to incomplete returns.

Preliminary figures for 1970–1971 indicate that there was then a total of 418 post-secondary institutions in Canada, of which approximately 134 were community colleges and CEGEPs, and 127 universities or colleges. In 1962 the first of several surveys of the resources of Canadian academic libraries was published. Since that date academic libraries have enjoyed a period of phenomenal growth, to which the statistical summaries in Table 10 will attest.

The Canadian Association of College and University Libraries has provided leadership for academic librarians during this period, and has worked closely with the Association of Universities and Colleges of Canada (AUCC). While the first concern of university librarians has been the national planning of resources, cooperation has taken other forms as well. A consulting service has been established to assist college libraries. In January of 1971 a Commission of the AUCC was set up "to study, report, and make recommendations on the mechanisms, structures and processes required to ensure that research undertakings in the universities of Canada can

TABLE 10 TOTALS FOR CANADIAN UNIVERSITY AND COLLEGE LIBRARIES

	Staff	Students Full-time Equivalent	Book Stock	Library Expenditure Per Student (dollars)	Library Expenditure (% of Total Univ. Exp.)	Full-time Positions
1961–62	12,927	130,026	8,130,841	67.18	5.12	
1962–63	12,443	144,513	9,085,088	69.83	4.71	
1963–64	12,426	160,072	10,206,880	90.08	5.7	1,245
1964–65	16,555	192,614	11,103,527	98.89	6.7	1,620
1965–66	18,531	204,679	12,071,671	126.85	7.0	2,295
1966–67	21,156	230,640	13,857,933	160.09	7.2	3,102
1967–68	25,725	276,411	16,173,024	180.39	7.3	3,494
1968–69	26,414	314,766	18,778,177	184.63	7.4	—
1969–70	—	—	20,583,285	—	—	—
1970–71	—	—	23,860,278	—	—	—

	Income (dollars)	Expenditures (dollars) Personnel Costs	Total
1962–63	10,176,176	5,623,761	10,514,654
1963–64	14,338,797	7,248,032	14,316,680
1964–65	18,975,810	9,490,894	18,907,572
1965–66	26,632,989	12,742,564	26,974,783
1966–67	37,842,897	17,916,901	37,806,459
1967–68	50,590,096	24,804,625	50,832,990
1968–69	60,641,476	30,522,970	59,998,616
1969–70	70,270,063	37,422,469	68,293,096
1970–71	—	—	78,774,716

TABLE 11   SHARED CATALOGING STATISTICS, JULY–DECEMBER 1970

	Simon Fraser Univ.	Univ. of B.C.	Univ. of Victoria	Univ. of Waterloo	Univ. of Windsor	Univ. of York	Total
Received from:	283	1,440	830	322	151	497	3,523
Used by:	203	322	315	470	146	267	1,723

be planned to serve, without undue duplication, both the advancement of knowledge, and provincial, regional and national development." The AUCC Committee on Library Rationalization is to meet with regional groups of library administrators to discuss alternatives in the development of library collections. It will also exchange information regularly with the Commission. This program represents the most recent attempt on the part of university libraries to work out a viable procedure for interlibrary cooperation in all areas, especially in regard to collection policies.

Since 1969 a program of Shared Cataloguing has been under way in Canada. Beginning with the three British Columbia university libraries, the program was expanded in 1970 to include three eastern universities: the University of Windsor, York University, and the University of Waterloo. This project supplements, for the participating libraries, the Library of Congress cataloging services. Shared Cataloguing copy is interfiled in the proofslip file. Each participant is responsible for a section of the alphabet, which is worked out to distribute the cataloging load as evenly as possible. Variations in volume of purchasing result, however, in considerable range in the number of titles cataloged.

Five new participants joined the program this year. With these additions to the group some specialization of contributions was introduced; for example, the University of Ottawa will supply all its cataloging of French language materials.

SPECIAL LIBRARIES

In the past the Dominion Bureau of Statistics has not surveyed special libraries. The data published in its 1967 *Survey* were based on the statistical summaries in Anthony T. Kruza's *Directory of Special Libraries and Information Centers* (Detroit: Gale Research Co., 1963). The gap has been partially filled by *Special Libraries in Canada; a Directory,* compiled by Beryl L. Anderson and first published in 1969. The 1970 edition of this work, entitled *Special Libraries and Information Centres in Canada; a Directory,* also compiled by Beryl L. Anderson, was sponsored by the Canadian Association of Special Libraries and Information Services (CASLIS), a section of the Canadian Library Association. Approximately 1,500 questionnaires were sent out, including 200 to laboratory libraries. While only 800 were returned, the information obtained was supplemented with data from other tools. In all, 1,075 centers are listed. Only 670 special libraries were listed in the 1969 edition, although the estimated total at that time was 900. The increase in the figure for 1970 is partially explained by the inclusion for the first time of subject departments in public and university libraries.

LIBRARY EDUCATION

Library education in Canada has changed rapidly since 1964, when there were five library schools in Canada, all offering the B.L.S. degree. At present, there are eight library schools, the majority of which offer the M.L.S. as the first professional degree. Other changes include the shift from a one-year to a two-year program. The major event in library education in 1971, however, was the authorization of the Graduate Department of Library Science by the

TABLE 12 PROFESSIONAL GRADUATES OF CANADIAN LIBRARY SCHOOLS

	M.L.S.	B.L.S.	Total
1964	4	286	270
1965	10	318	328
1966	17	319	336
1967	64	313	377
1968	61	385	446
1969	113	482	595
1970	297	470	767

TABLE 13 MEDIAN SALARIES OF LIBRARY SCHOOL GRADUATES BY TYPE OF LIBRARY

	Public	University	School	Govt.	Special
1965	$5365	$5529	$6808	$5588	$5500
1966	5680	6020	7450		5970
1967	6150	6650	9500	6366	6370
1968	6755	7055	7500	6840	6838
1969	7187	7470	9214	7205	7050

Board of Governors of the University of Toronto to begin offering its Ph.D. program in Library Science with the 1971–1972 session. The objectives of this first doctoral program in library science in Canada have been stated as follows: "To develop research capabilities in qualified candidates in order to prepare them for careers in teaching and research at the university level or for careers in research in the library profession." Two candidates were admitted in the fall of 1971.

Another important related development was the decision of the Canada Council to accept applications from Ph.D. students in library science for doctoral fellowships. Heretofore, library science has not been considered an eligible discipline for purposes of Canada Council fellowships. The Canada Council also announced that research projects in library science would be deemed eligible for support under its Research Grants Project.

Growth in this field is also reflected by the statistics of library school graduates and salaries quoted in Tables 12 and 13.

Interest in programs for the training of library technicians continued to occupy members of the library profession in Canada. Training programs for library technicians are now being conducted in 19 post-secondary institutions, four of which are in central and western Canada, nine in Ontario (seven at colleges of applied arts and technology), and six in colleges of general and vocational education (CEGEP) in Quebec.

The latest statistical data available comes from a summary of a survey of library technician training programs covering Ontario and western Canada only. A supplement is planned to cover the six Quebec programs. Figures were lacking also for three of the seven programs in Ontario. In 1970 there were 46 graduates from one-year programs and 116 graduates from two-year programs. The projected figure for 1971 for two-year programs is 128, but since not all institutions provided this information, the figure may be regarded as a minimum.

PROFESSIONAL ASSOCIATIONS

In Canada there are two national library associations, the Canadian Library Association and the Association Canadienne des Bibliothécaires de Langue Française, linked by the CLA-ACBLF Liaison Committee. A "Directory of Canadian Library Associations and Associations with Mutual Interest" was published in *Feliciter,* Vol. 17, Nos. 11-12, November-December 1971, Pt. II.

The Canadian Association for Information Science announced its incorporation in 1971. Its avowed purpose is to organize meetings and seminars, encourage research, and publish papers and bulletins with a view to facilitating the exchange of information on technical subjects relating to the processing, storage, and dissemination of information.

One new national organization, the Canadian Council of Library Schools, was formed in 1971. Membership consists of the eight graduate library schools in Canada. The orientation of this organization is toward problems of administration of library schools rather than toward education for librarianship, which is the focus of the Canadian Association of Library Schools.

One of the important activities of library associations in Canada has been the development of standards for various types of libraries and library services. These include:

Guide to Canadian University Library Standards, prepared by the Canadian Association of College and University Libraries, 1965. (Under revision 1971.)

Public Library Standards, prepared by a Project Committee of the Canadian Library Association, 1967.

Standards for Work with Young People in Canadian Public Libraries, prepared by the Young People's Section of the Canadian Library Association, 1966.

Standards of Library Service for Canadian Schools, recommended by the Canadian School Library Association, 1967. (Revision planned for 1972.)

LIBRARY DEVELOPMENTS IN THE UNITED KINGDOM IN 1971

by

N. B. W. Thompson*

Even if 1971 has not been the "annus mirabilis" for all libraries in the United Kingdom, it will undoubtedly long be remembered as such for the national institutions. January saw the publication of the eagerly awaited White Paper on the British Library, the statement of government policy on the 1968 recommendations of the Dainton Committee on the national libraries. This announced that a new organization for the national libraries — to be called the British Library — was to be established, thus accepting the main recommendations of the Dainton Report.

The British Library will be formed by bringing together the library departments of the British Museum Library (including the National Reference Library of Science and Invention), the National Lending Library for Science and Technology, the National Central Library, and the British National Bibliography. It will be an independent body, enjoying the maximum freedom over its own affairs; it will employ its own staff, and it will be governed by a board with a substantial proportion of full-time members.

Because legislation will be needed to establish the new administration, it will be 1973 before the British Library can come into being, but for the interim period, an Organising Committee under the Chairmanship of Viscount Eccles, the Minister with responsibilities for the arts and libraries, will plan the new organiza-

---

*Mr. Thompson is with the Arts and Libraries Branch, Department of Education and Science, London, England.

tion and develop and coordinate policy. Already this interim body is working at high pressure, with four planning groups currently considering the problems of reference and bibliographic facilities, lending services, buildings, and manpower, respectively.

Apart from providing the impetus for the creation of the new British Library, the White Paper announced the government's decision to spend $93 million on new accommodation — as part of the British Library — for the British Museum Library and for the National Reference Library of Science and Invention, which in the future will be known as the Science Reference Library. The new buildings, to be designed by architect Colin St. John Wilson, will be in Bloomsbury, on a site immediately adjacent to the existing British Museum. It is expected that the new Science Reference Library building will be completed by the late 1970s, but it will be 1984 before the whole project is realized.

Other new buildings for the British Library are under construction at Boston Spa, Yorkshire, partly to provide urgently needed extensions to the rapidly growing National Lending Library for Science and Technology, and also to make possible the transfer to there in 1973 of the National Central Library to form a single interlending unit covering all disciplines and all types of literature.

In November, the report was received of the feasibility study into the application of ADP to the national libraries. This project, costing about $200,000 of government funds, was initiated at the recommendation of the Dainton Committee. It has been carried out in less than two years by a team led by Maurice B. Line, who has subsequently been appointed Librarian of the National Central Library. The report of the study is now under consideration by the Organising Committee, and it is expected to have a profound influence on the future shape of library services of many kinds in the United Kingdom, as well as on the organization and management of the British Library itself.

An important new computer-based bibliographic service was inaugurated by the British National Bibliography in November after the successful completion of extensive field trials. "Books in English" combines details of books in the English language cataloged either by the Library of Congress or by the British National Bibliography. Produced from computerized data in MARC format onto 6" x 4" ultramicrofiches by the COM and PCMI processes, "Books in English" is being cumulatively updated every two months; in a typical year 100,000 entries will be recorded.

Not all the developments of library ADP have been associated primarily with the national library institutions, however. The introduction of computers for circulation control extended considerably during the year, particularly in public libraries. Moreover, a most fruitful experiment by the London and South Eastern Library Region working with the British National Bibliography has led to the successful introduction of a COM union catalog for the region, based on ISBN records of holdings; this is now being produced cheaply enough for each library in the region to receive an updated version every eight weeks.

Another White Paper published in 1971, announcing the government's proposals for the reorganization of local government in England, also promises to have profound and far-reaching effects on library services. This, with the consultative document on local government in Wales, was the precursor of the new Local Government Bill published in November, whose proposals, if implemented as planned, will by 1974 lead to the first comprehensive restructuring of local government administration outside London for almost a century.

As far as public library service is concerned, the implementation of the bill's proposals would result in the disappearance of small- and medium-sized local library authorities; the 315 existing library authorities in England (outside London) being replaced by 72 new ones serving populations ranging from about

200,000 to nearly 1½ million. Moreover, under the new system, both education and libraries would for the first time be administered everywhere by authorities serving the same areas, thus opening up new opportunities to extend substantially the cooperation between these two complementary social services. Also of considerable importance was the publication of the government's consultative document on the future of the National Health Service, which pointed to the likelihood that this service also will be reorganized, probably on the basis of the same administrative areas as library and education services. If this comes about, additional potential will be created for public libraries to contribute to library services for hospitals, post-graduate medical centers, and other units of the health service. As this report is being written, the Local Government Bill is being considered by Parliament.

The year has also seen new proposals for the administration of local government in both Scotland and Northern Ireland. The government of Northern Ireland proposed to introduce a system under which centrally determined policies will be regionally administered. Although different from the two-tier type structure for England and Wales, this arrangement will lead to much the same results for the public libraries — large, strong units administered coterminously with the education service. In Scotland, however, which is to have a two-tier structure based on regions and districts, education and libraries are to be in the same (upper) tier only in the least densely populated regions, if the proposals contained in the White Paper on the Reform of Local Government in Scotland are implemented. Elsewhere library powers will be exercised by the 31 districts, half of which will have populations of under 100,000. Unlike the generally favorable response of the professional associations to the proposals for the reorganization of public library administration in other parts of the United Kingdom, this aspect of the government's proposals for public libraries in Scotland has met with considerable criticism in professional circles, on the grounds that the resources of large authorities offer the only possibility of developing the new and sophisticated services which will be increasingly required in the future.

The year has also seen a glimmer of hope for authors and publishers who have long been campaigning for additional payments in respect to library lending—that is, a Public Lending Right. In February a Ministerial statement indicated that the government would be prepared to consider amending the copyright legislation to make this possible. It was, however, made clear that the government would not countenance a scheme of the type operated in some Scandinavian countries on the basis of grants from central funds. Such a scheme would in the government's view be an arbitrary subsidy, not a genuine lending right. A decision on this issue now depends on whether solutions can be found to the manifold practical problems of operating and administering an acceptable scheme. A Working Party consisting of representatives of authors, publishers, booksellers, the Arts Council, the local authorities, and central government has been examining these problems and is expected to report to the Minister in the near future. There is, therefore, every likelihood that by next year this important issue will be resolved, one way or the other.

Reference was made in the 1971 *Bowker Annual* to the possibility that the new Conservative Administration might introduce charges for borrowing books from public libraries. It has now been made clear, however, that the basic library services provided by the national and public libraries are to remain available to all without direct charge.

If these are the most significant developments of 1971 in the United Kingdom, there are others of considerable importance. One of our cities, Liverpool, was host to IFLA early in September, and it gave great satisfaction to British librarians to welcome a record number of colleagues from overseas representing more countries at the IFLA General Council than ever before.

Library research in the United Kingdom continues to expand, mainly under the stimulus of government support and encouragement. The Office for Scientific and Technical Information remains the principal channel for government funding of library, information, and documentation research. During the year, this agency has been supporting 80 projects costing about $1.8 million, mainly in the sciences and the social sciences. A new development, however, has been the funding by the Department of Education and Science of applied research related to specific issues of departmental policy. So far, the areas of research include design criteria for public library buildings, the scope for cooperation between different types of libraries at local level, the requirement for and utilization of staff in public libraries, and the provision and use of serial literature. The two Library Advisory Councils — statutory bodies for England and for Wales advising the Secretary of State for Education and Science — have played an important part in these developments, as indeed they have in many other matters affecting government policy toward libraries. One further manifestation of the Councils' work, a report on Public Library Service Points, is likely to be published by the end of the year.

A further source of professional advice to the government in library matters are the Library Advisers, who are librarians of wide experience employed by the Department of Education and Science. As part of their duties, they undertake inspections of public and other libraries at the Minister's instigation or at the invitation of local authorities or central government agencies. Their current program includes studies of certain aspects of library services to schools — including the potentialities of providing public and school or college library services from the same buildings, and of library services in penal institutions. Their most important assignment in 1971, however, has been in connection with local government reorganization, in examining how some of the most important practical problems of transition for the library service can be overcome, and how the potentialities of the reorganized local government structure can most effectively be realized.

Following the pubication in 1970 of the Library Association's recommendations for standards for school library resource centers, progress in this and related fields has been significant, if unspectacular. During the year the Association published policy statements relating to resource centers in schools and in colleges of education. A welcome trend has been the increase in the numbers of schools employing professionally qualified library staff. The Department of Education and Science for its part has produced new standards of accommodation for polytechnics and for colleges of further education, and considerable progress has been made toward the collection of library statistics in conformity with the new UNESCO international standard.

These then are the landmarks of library development in the United Kingdom this year. If much has been achieved, much remains to be done.

LIBRARY DEVELOPMENTS IN THE SOVIET UNION IN 1971

by

L. I. Vladimirov*

The activities of Soviet libraries in 1971 were directed toward carrying into effect the resolutions of the 24th Congress of the Communist Party of the Soviet Union as well as the objectives of the new Five-Year Plan, envisaging the development of national economy and cultural construction in the Soviet Union for the period of 1971–1975. At the Congress much attention was devoted to the problems and objectives of the truly gigantic scientific-technological revolution going on in this country at the present time.

Naturally Soviet libraries must occupy and do occupy a significant position in the revolution — raising the cultural standard of the nation to a higher level, disseminating scientific and technological knowledge, assisting the nation in solving scientific and practical problems.

The role of the Soviet library in the solution of the problems raised by the 24th Congress of the Communist Party was the principal topic of the 18th plenary session of the USSR Ministry of Culture Council on Library Work, which was held May 11–12, 1971 in the Lenin State Library, Moscow. The main speaker on this occasion was V. V. Serov, head of the Chief Library Inspection of the Ministry of Culture. His report dealt with the results of library development during the past five years and the objectives of the new Five-Year Plan.

The achievements of library development in the Soviet Union are obvious and impressive, but still do not come up to our expectations. The first concern is the development of the mass libraries (i.e., public libraries) which play the leading role in the dissemination of books throughout the country. During the past Five-Year Plans the process of formation of networks of this type of library was more or less completed. In the year 1965, reaching the impressive quantity of 127,000, the number of the mass libraries reached its zenith, and the statistical data for the following years do not display any further considerable enlargement of the library network, such as was characteristic of the first ten post-war years. Actually, there was no need for any greater enlargement.

At the present time the network of libraries evenly covers the whole territory of the Soviet Union, from Brest-Litovsk in the west to Vladivostok on the Pacific Ocean. In all the Soviet Union there is not to be found a single city district, rural community, industrial or agricultural enterprise without a mass library or at least a temporary mobile library. Of course library development continues. The Five-Year Plan for 1971–1975 envisages the opening of another 3,000 new state mass libraries and about a thousand new trade union mass libraries. Yet in this Five-Year Plan the chief financial resources will be allotted not so much to a further development of the library network as to a rational distribution of libraries within separate geographic regions, in accordance with the demographic changes in the country that occur with the construction of new industrial regions and centers, enlargement of agricultural enterprises, and similar phenomena. The chief objectives of 1971 as well as of the following years will concern the qualitative contents of library work more than the growth of libraries.

A most eloquent result of library work is the growth of library collections. In the past years these collections were considerably enriched. In January 1967 all mass libraries of the Soviet Union comprised 1 billion, 51 million books and magazines, whereas at the beginning of 1971 all these libraries already possessed 1 billion, 258 million units. This shows

---

*Dean, Chair for Librarianship and Information Science, Vilnius State University, Vilnius, Lithuanian SSR, USSR.

that the annual growth of library collections exceeds 40 million units. Preliminary data for 1971 suggest that this annual growth rate of library collections will be greatly exceeded in this and the following years. It should be borne in mind that the rate of the growth of collections exceeds the rate of the growth of population. So in 1966 there were on the average 453 books for every hundred people; in 1970 the average had reached 521.

The striking thing about this is that the growth particularly concerned rural regions. Here, in 1965, there were 449 books for every hundred people, and in 1970 as many as 535. That is more than the average rate of all-Union libraries taken together. Thus we face a most striking fact: for the first time in the history of mass libraries, rural mass libraries surpass the urban ones in providing the population with books. This in no way indicates that the urban population is not as well-supplied with books. The intellectual needs of the urbanites are largely satisfied by the network of scientific and special libraries, of which there are few in the countryside. Yet the fact that the per capita number of mass library books in rural regions is greater than that in the cities speaks in favor of significant achievements in the country's cultural development.

A no less imposing achievement of the past five years is the growth of the number of library readers by 20 million. The mass, research, and technological libraries alone were used by 130 million registered readers (excluding school libraries, used by about 40 million children). Book lending has greatly increased, achieving 3 billion volumes annually. Judging by the preliminary data for 1971 it will, for the first time, exceed this number. All these data are, doubtless, impressive, particularly in comparison with analogous data of other countries in the world. Yet we do not regard these results as optimal; they simply do not satisfy us. We cannot be satisfied with the number of 3 billion volumes lent, whereas the general book collection comprises 2.7 billion volumes; this speaks of an insufficient circulation of books. We are equally unsatisfied by the figure of 170 million library readers, because it shows that great numbers of the population still do not make use of libraries. The average number of units lent per person in the past year alone surpassed the number of 20.0, thus showing an insignificant growth in comparison with 1965 (19.0). This indicates an insufficient use of mass library collections. Also, the book supply and circulation in different Soviet republics are not equally developed. For example, circulation data differed from 29 to 14 books and magazines lent on an average to one reader. Thus, we may presume that in some Soviet republics library collections are made better use of than in others. Soviet libraries intend to do away with these shortcomings in the course of the next five years.

A most effective measure in this direction should be the implementation of centralization of state mass libraries. To determine the optimal variables of this new organizational structure of the library network, a special research commission has been founded at the USSR Ministry of Culture to deal with the centralization of state mass libraries. The fact that the duties of the scientific supervisor of this Commission were assumed by the head of the Chief Library Inspection of the USSR Ministry of Culture, V. V. Serov, speaks of the significance with which this reform is regarded by the Soviet government. The recent session of the Research Commission for centralization concluded that the experiments in the implementation of centralization, carried on in different parts of the Soviet Union, are yielding positive results. Noteworthy in this respect are the results of this experiment carried on in Sebastopol, which has a population of 229,000. The centralized network includes the city's 24 mass libraries. Gradually this centralized library system will come to embrace over 20 rural libraries of the Sebastopol zone, situated within a radius of 80 kilometers (50 miles).

Thus, large-scale centralization will for the first time be put to trial. Also, it will be tried without increasing the number of personnel, by making more efficient use of the existing library staff.

Similar centralization is being carried on in the capital of Latvia, Riga, and the capital of Georgia, Tbilisi. However, it is the city of Kutaisi which is the pioneer of this movement. Here centralization will unite 21 city and nine children's libraries with the central public library, which will play the central role in the unified system. Experiments within one administrative district are being carried out in Lithuania as well. This cardinal reform will greatly improve the work of mass libraries in their effort to satisfy the growing intellectual needs of the population.

In the course of the current year the broad network of research and technological libraries and documentation services had to deal with tasks of no smaller scope. At the beginning of 1971, all in all, the number of such libraries exceeded 50,000, while their book collections achieved the imposing quantity of 1.2 billion.

Apart from these huge primary sources of information, libraries of this type concentrate a wealth of secondary information sources, which are an aid in the solution of problems of science and national economy. For the rest, Soviet research and special libraries have to deal with the same difficulties as do other libraries in other countries of the world in this age of information explosion and huge proliferation of scientific knowledge and printing. Bearing in mind the disassociation of different systems of research and special libraries and information services (e.g., the system of the USSR Academy of Sciences, the system of the Ministry of Higher and Special Education, the systems of other ministries and establishments) that lead to duplication and a waste of means and energy, measures have been taken to carry into effect coordination and collaboration in the sphere of bibliography and documentation development. All-Union coordination centers for different branches of science also expand their work. So, in 1969 on the basis of the fundamental library of the Academy of Social Sciences in Moscow, the Institute of Scientific Information in Social Sciences was founded. In 1970–1971 corresponding centers of scientific information in social sciences were organized at the Academies of Sciences in Soviet republics. The All-Union Institute of Scientific-Technological Information (VINITI) and institutes of scientific-technological information in separate republics are playing an ever-growing role in the coordination of bibliographic and documentation work in the sphere of technological and precise sciences. We are studying the most efficient methods for application of computers and other technological means which would help to fully satisfy the growing needs for scientific and technological information in the country.

Libraries of different types and systems are striving to determine their concrete role in the sphere of documentation.

In 1971 materials of the research commission Library and Documentation, which worked at the M. E. Saltykov-Shchedrin State Public Library in Leningrad, were published. The book, based on the materials of this commission and entitled *Specialist — Library — Bibliography* (Moscow: Kniga, 1971), widely reflects for the first time the results of an investigation into the needs of Soviet specialists for information and better library-bibliographic services. On the basis of comprehensive statistical data and in collaboration with sociologists and mathematicians, the Library and Documentation Commission revealed the weak points and shortcomings in the process of supplying the huge army of Soviet specialists with their professional information. One of the main conclusions of the finished investigation is the need for coordination between bibliographic and documentation work, which in its turn requires the establishment of specialized territorial centers of coordination. The chief national library of the Soviet Union, the V. I. Lenin State Library, serves as the basis for the creation of a new all-Union information and coordination center, the building of which has already begun. This center will possess data concerning the sources of information on all sciences (with special emphasis on the humanities).

Some Soviet republics are trying to create a model system to supply themselves with scientific-technological information. For example, in Lithuania such a model is being developed by the local Institute of Scientific-Technological Information in collaboration with the Chair of Librarianship and Scientific Information of the Vilnius State University. Organization of a unified system of scientific and technological documentation is successfully carried on in the Ukraine and Armenia.

The complex problems which the libraries and documentation institutions have to deal with in the era of scientific-technological revolution and information explosion call for a further improvement in research activities in the field of librarianship, bibliography, and documentation. With this end in mind, in 1971 the USSR Ministry of Culture created several new research councils as, for example, the Research Council on Theory and History of Librarianship. The first session of this council was held December 16–17, 1971 at the Lenin Library in Moscow.

In this writer's estimation, the foregoing have been the most significant of the manifold activities carried on by the libraries of the Soviet Union in 1971.

LIBRARY DEVELOPMENTS IN FINLAND IN 1971

by
Ritva Sievanen-Allen*

Lately, the primary issues in Finnish librarianship have been library education, national and international library cooperation, library automation, library problems in new institutions of higher education, and the role of public libraries.

LIBRARY EDUCATION

The most recent significant event in Finnish librarianship was the founding of the first professorship of library and information science. This professorship was not only the first in Finland, but also the first in Scandinavia as well. This event changed the entire picture of Finnish library education, for instead of being a kind of vocational training merely supplementing academic studies, library education became part of the academic studies themselves. Now it will be possible to acquire formal academic training in librarianship, including advanced degrees in library and information science. Hopefully, this event will encourage librarians to acquire advanced degrees in their field, for many high library positions, which require these advanced degrees, have remained vacant for years due to the lack of qualified personnel. Also, many Finnish libraries require their directors to have a doctor's degree or a licentiate examination, and since salaries have been rather low, very few people have been willing to acquire the competence in two fields which this requirement implies.

Along with the formal academic studies in library and information science, basic library education continues. For instance, library examinations are given at Tampere University and the Swedish School of Social Sciences, a research library examination is given at the Council of Research Libraries, and an informa-

---

*Librarian, Central Medical Library, Helsinki, Finland.

tion science examination is arranged by the Finnish Association for Documentation. In addition to this basic library education, library assistants who up to now have not had any formal education for their posts have begun to take courses in librarianship and to plan for formal training as library technicians.

NATIONAL AND INTERNATIONAL COOPERATION

Interlibrary cooperation is facilitated by the work committees, the two main ones being the Council of Research Libraries, founded in 1954, and the Finnish Council for Scientific and Technical Information (TINFO), founded in 1969. Both councils are coordinating organs which advise, plan, and support cooperation between libraries and information centers. The former's main emphasis is on libraries, the latter's on information services and their problems. Other Scandinavian countries have lacked committees such as these until only recently. In late 1972 these two committees will combine; the result of this combination will be most interesting.

The very first tasks of this new organ will be to continue the "Scandia Plan," a joint acquisition plan for the Scandinavian research libraries. This plan, which went into effect as early as the 1950s, has been sponsored by the Nordic library associations, who unfortunately have been hampered in the full realization of this idea due to their limited resources. The Scandia Plan includes other forms of cooperation such as interlibrary lending, which is the most significant and visible form of library cooperation on both a national and an international level. In Finland, the Interlibrary Lending Section of the Council of Research Libraries has arranged special meetings on interlibrary lending in the country, with participants from both research and public libraries. These meetings, along with the new interlibrary lending forms and the IFLA forms, special rules for interlibrary lending (including telex), and wider training in lending techniques, have already brought noticeable progress in day-to-day library work.

LIBRARY AUTOMATION

In 1971, as in previous years, library automation was one of the most debated topics. In early 1971 the Council of Research Libraries arranged an exhibition of the Swedish library automation system project LIBRIS (Library Information System). This project covers almost every aspect of library work: cataloging, lending (including interlibrary lending), and information services. Whether Finland will participate in this project is not yet certain; however, the Committee on the Objectives of Automation in Research Libraries, established in May 1971, will consider this possibility.

Smaller automated projects such as those in periodical cataloging and information services have been realized in Finland; more advanced automation will, however, involve being part of a larger system, such as MARC.

The Finnish Council for Scientific and Technical Information has been active in planning information services in all fields. Its main emphasis in 1971 was in establishing a technical information network. The planning of biomedical and pedagogical information networks is still going on in the Council's respective sections. In many ways this planning merely supports already existing forms of information service and emphasizes cooperation within the country. Automated information systems like MEDLARS, BIOSIS, CASC, ASCA, etc. are already being used in Finland, since they are available in neighboring countries or elsewhere in Europe.

A significant and unique progressive step in international information service cooperation was the bilateral agreement made between the Central Medical Library in Finland and the biomedical information system VNIIMI in the Soviet Union; this enables Finland to receive biomedical information from the eastern countries more freely than before.

COLLEGE AND UNIVERSITY LIBRARIES

New institutions of higher education were created in Finland in the 1960s on a very large scale, and the expansion of universities and colleges has been remarkable. This expansion, however, created many new problems for libraries in new institutions and for those in older institutions which had to support the new ones in their first years. In 1970–1971 new institutions of technology started in Tampere and Lappeenranta, and a new university college was begun in Joensuu. Their libraries are operative but have very limited resources and only a few trained librarians on their staff. New libraries, however, can be a challenge, and in the middle of everyday difficulties the librarian can become more free from the bonds of his traditional thinking and take a more innovative approach to solving library problems.

The fact that Finnish college and university libraries are lacking a solid organization and, above all, a national comprehensive program, including rules for cooperation and division of labor between Finnish research libraries, is perhaps the biggest barrier to future development. For instance, the establishment of central libraries has been postponed from year to year. A committee called the Organizational Committee for Reserve Libraries has undertaken the study of the organizational problems of university and college libraries as a whole; the last proposals made by the Committee have, however, not been published. The staff problems of college and university libraries have been a subject for discussion in the Information Service Section of the Council of Finnish Colleges and Universities, which issues recommendations concerning the establishment of new posts for university and college libraries.

PUBLIC LIBRARIES

The foregoing has been mainly a discussion of research libraries. The state of public libraries has not been a matter of such intense interest. The most discussed topic, however, has been the role of the public library and its future. What kind of an institution will it be in the society of tomorrow — a center for cultural activities, an information center like the research libraries, a place where audiovisual material plays a more significant part than the traditional printed book? Furthermore, how much should the political life of the country influence library work? Such has been the concern maintained in *Kirjastolehti* (Library Journal), the organ of the Finnish Library Association, and at the 1971 Library Conference which took place in Joensuu in mid-June. These conferences are arranged semiannually and are attended by all the library associations in Finland. The school reform scheduled to take place in Finland before long will also affect the role of the public library.

In talking about Finnish public libraries, one must keep in mind that although the Finns read a great deal, they take less interest in their libraries than one might expect. In one year, approximately one million books are bought by the public libraries, but only one-quarter of the population uses the services of the libraries. The bookmobiles, however, seem to make library nonusers more active. There are approximately 75 bookmobiles in the country now, and their number is rising.

Finland is proud of its modern architecture, and a few library buildings are included among the best-known products of the architects. In 1971 some new library buildings were erected. Two deserve mention since they have been the subject of lively interest: Töölö branch library in Helsinki, and Kouvola public library. Töölö represents the more traditional library, with special sections for children, young adults, and adults, and for various activities such as music. On the other hand, Kouvola is an example of a more free use of library space.

There has been no library research in Finland in the real sense of the word, but in 1971 an extensive research project on librarianship as a profession was completed. A unique profile of the librarian emerged. According to this, the typical Finnish librarian is a hard-working and modest person who is intellectually alert and enjoys his profession in spite of its poor status and even poorer working conditions. As Sven Hirn, Director of Helsinki Public Library, says in *Kirjastolehti,* No. 9, 1971, "A professional librarian turns out to be a rather interesting being, in whom there is a bit of prosaic heroism." Let's hope that in future years the job of librarian will be both more cheerful and materially more rewarding.

LIBRARY DEVELOPMENTS IN THE CZECHOSLOVAK SOCIALIST REPUBLIC DURING 1971

by

Mirko Velinsky*

The year 1971 was an important and extraordinary one for the whole Czechoslovak Socialist Republic. It was the year of the 50th anniversary of the founding of the Communist Party of Czechoslovakia, the year of the 14th congress of the Communist Party, a year of general elections, and a year in which the whole country gave thought and attention to the future development of the entire nation.

Naturally, Czechoslovak librarianship could not stand aloof from this nationwide movement. It, too, on the basis of an analysis of the past, had to give much thought to its future, and coordinate its current activities with its long-range plans.

A UNIFIED LIBRARY SYSTEM

Such activities included preparing the new laws concerning libraries, especially in connection with the formulation of new principles and guidelines for developing a unified system of libraries.

At the present time, along with the rapid development of science and technology, the function and role of libraries in society are rapidly changing. Ever more urgent is the necessity of discarding the old theory that the primary function of libraries is simply to accumulate and preserve literature. Modern society requires that libraries become active mediators in the circulation of scientific literature and other library materials; in addition to their traditional functions, libraries must act to an ever-increasing degree as bibliographic and information centers. In connection with this trend, libraries cannot remain autonomous units with their own individual, complex service systems. Each library, large or small, universal or specialized, scientific or public, must inevitably become an integral part of a unified library-information system.

Functional and effective integration of the library in this system is a vital issue facing any library. For this reason, interlibrary cooperation, both on the national and international levels, is of foremost importance. Only through the establishment of a centrally controlled and administered unified system can all the inhabitants of communities both large and small be assured access to the holdings of all libraries and information institutions in the country.

In addition to Czechoslovakia's already well-developed interlibrary loan service, it will also be necessary to establish interlibrary information and bibliographic service, and to establish bibliographic-information systems within the individual libraries.

DISTRICT LIBRARIES

An important event in Czechoslovak librarianship in 1971 was the "Conference on District Libraries," held in Poprad (Slovak Socialist Republic) on June 15-16. This conference, organized by the Czech and Slovak Ministries of Culture, the National Library of the Czech Socialist Republic, and Matica Slovenská,

---

*Head, Department of Public Libraries, Chair of Library and Information Science, Faculty of Social Sciences and Journalism, Charles University, Prague, Czechoslovak Socialist Republic.

was attended by more than 300 Czech and Slovak librarians.

The main objective of the conference, organized on the occasion of the 20th anniversary of the establishment of district libraries in Czechoslovakia, was the formulation of a new concept of the district library, which represents the fundamental link in the country's unified library-information system. The conference participants agreed that these libraries must be restructured in such a manner that their activities and services are placed on a qualitatively higher level in order to satisfy the ever more differentiated cultural, literary, and scientific information demands of their district. District libraries will also have to be restructured as central libraries, linking their districts with other libraries in the unified information system.

LIBRARY EDUCATION

The Chair of Librarianship and Scientific Information at Charles University organized on November 18, 1971, a conference on "The Education of Librarians and Information Workers in Socialist Society," which introduced the library world to a new concept of the academic study of library science and information communication. This concept is the result of several years of theoretical and scientific research conducted by the staff of the Chair. The papers read at this conference were concerned with the curricula of new study programs, and it is expected that education based on this new study program prepared for librarians and information workers will start in the school year 1973–74. A characteristic feature of this new program is that it is oriented toward two different subjects: scientific information on the one hand and culture and education on the other. Students of both these branches will study Marxism-Leninism as a fundamental world outlook, and also general information communication. (Information communication, as seen by the Prague Chair of Librarianship and Scientific Information, must be understood as a theoretical discipline concerned with the problems of the social communication process and the communication of documentation information as a whole. Thus, it is a theoretical basis from which a theory of scientific information and the theory of library science begins.)

Other concerns involving library education were the importance of the libraries' impact on the education of adults and their responsibility to society as a whole in helping each individual to become an actively contributing member of society. An extensive research program on the social function of libraries, organized by the National Library of the Czech Socialist Republic, the Central Scientific and Methodical Cabinet of Library Science, and Matica Slovenská, which had lasted several years, was concluded; the results of the program will be published in the near future.

The city library in Bratislava and the Chair of Librarianship and Scientific Information of Komensky University in Bratislava organized an international seminar on the work of libraries with children and youth, stressing the importance of reading, the study of literature, and the role of libraries in the education of the young.

LIBRARY STATISTICS

In connection with UNESCO's adopted recommendation on the international standardization of library statistics, a plan was prepared in 1971 for a new system for collecting statistical data in Czechoslovak libraries. Under this new plan, such data will be collected at regular intervals. Now it is possible — by using the most up-to-date statistical methods — to obtain an analytical picture of the state and activities of Czechoslovak libraries and library science in general.

Czechoslovak library science benefited greatly by the international conference on library statistics held in Prague in September 1971, and attended by members of the IFLA Committee on Statistics and Standards as well as specialists from socialist and other countries working in the field of library statistics. (See also

Schick's article, "International Library Statistics Standardization Developments during 1971," this volume.) The fact that the conference was a success, not only as a working session for specialists, but also as a social event, proves that Czechoslovak librarians are determined to contribute to the best of their abilities to the successful cooperation in library work on the international level, to the better understanding among the nations, and to all of mankind's continued quest for a peaceful, good, and creative life.

LIBRARY DEVELOPMENTS IN THE FEDERAL REPUBLIC OF GERMANY IN 1971

by

Otto Löhmann*

UNIVERSITY LIBRARIES

During the past few years and in 1971 the development of new universities and university libraries in the Federal Republic of Germany has been extensive. This is a result of the extremely expansive tendency in German education. After the war new universities were founded in Saarbrücken, Mainz, and West Berlin. Their library systems were conventional, that is, there was a central library along with independent institute libraries. With the beginning of the sixties the need for a drastic increase in institutions of higher education became obvious. In the course of this decade new universities were founded in Augsburg, Bielefeld, Bochum, Bremen, Dortmund, Konstanz, Regensburg, and Ulm; medical academies were instituted in Lübeck and Hanover. The medical academy of Düsseldorf was transformed into a university, as were the institutes of technology in Aachen and Hanover and the economic academy in Mannheim. In 1971 the universities of Trier–Kaiserslautern, Kassel, and Oldenburg were established; a university in Osnabrück is in the stage of preparation.

In all these institutions of higher education new libraries have been developed, are developing, or are in the planning stage. Trier–Kaiserslautern will have two separate libraries, one in Trier for the humanities, the other in Kaiserslautern for science and technology.

Since the university at Bochum was founded in 1963, new methods have been introduced into libraries, such as electronic data processing; and new structures in libraries are evolving as a consequence of the explosion of student numbers and the reform of universities. The general trend in the new university libraries is to create a single comprehensive library system for the whole university under one direction. The director of the university library is becoming the librarian of the university: acquisition, accession, and cataloging of all books are done under his responsibility by trained personnel. This integration of the library into the university system will certainly affect the position of librarians. Hopefully, the position of the subject specialist, a typical achievement of German libraries, will be strengthened and not weakened.

Interesting models in university libraries have been developed at the universities of Bremen, Konstanz, Bielefeld, Dortmund, Regensburg, and Augsburg. The trend is toward having single libraries serve whole groups of related fields (Fachbereichsbibliotheken) rather than having individual institute libraries serve specialized needs. These new tendencies will, of course, affect the old traditional university libraries; they will become more closely integrated into the university system. The German Research Association has developed recommendations

---

*Director of the Marburg branch of the Staatsbibliothek Preussischer Kulturbesitz Berlin–Marburg.

for these libraries, to regulate a close cooperation between the central university libraries and the institute libraries.

PUBLIC LIBRARIES

In former times there was in Germany a rather severe separation between scholarly (academic or research) libraries and the so-called "popular" (public) libraries (Volksbüchereien). Because of this separation, the popular libraries could not meet the needs of a growing, better-educated population that wanted access not only to "popular" literature, but to scholarly and educational materials as well. These libraries are now developing into public libraries in the Anglo-American sense, so that they can begin to provide their users access to materials of a more sophisticated and scholarly nature. The new trend in the concept of a public library is indicated by the transformation of the organ of the German Association of Public Libraries, which in 1971 changed its title from *Bücherei und Bildung* to *Buch und Bibliothek*. Now there is a growing cooperation between the two types of libraries. In order to find a system of interlibrary cooperation to facilitate the supply of books to public libraries and to the whole country, the German Association of Public Libraries has initiated Library Plan I (Bibliotheksplan I), which was in turn modified by proposals of the Association of German librarians in order that academic libraries be better integrated into the system. This system will have four levels: (1) small-sized public libraries in little communities; (2) medium- and large-sized public libraries in towns and cities; (3) regional and academic libraries; and (4) the large central and supraregional libraries — Deutsche Bibliothek (Frankfurt), Staatsbibliothek Preussischer Kulturbesitz (West Berlin and Marburg), Bayerische Staatsbibliothek (Munich) — and the four central special libraries for technology (Hanover), medicine (Cologne), economics (Kiel), and agriculture (Bonn). By a connection and cooperation of these four levels with all their resources (catalogs, union catalogs, information centers, etc.) a complete supply of literature will be made available to the whole country. The ideal "every book to every man at every place," formulated first by Danish librarians, is beginning to be realized in Germany with the establishment of this system. A revised Library Plan II is under discussion.

GERMAN LIBRARIANSHIP

Though there is a *Handbuch der Bibliothekswissenschaft,* library science in Germany has not had a systematic base. Aside from works on the history of libraries, books, and manuscripts, library science had consisted only of a knowledge of practical administration. Since 1970 new efforts have been made to establish a systematic foundation of library science. In October 1969, at the library school of Cologne (Bibliothekar-Lehrinstitut Köln), a colloquium on library science was convened to discuss new concepts for academic libraries. The discussion quickly extended to public libraries, which long had felt the need for new concepts in organization and orientation. The results of the discussion concluded that library science is possible within the framework of information and communication science and as a part of operations research; the next aim should be to introduce this new concept of library science into the research and teaching programs of the universities.

USER STUDY

One part of this new concept of library science must be emphasized. In Germany many efforts have been concentrated in creating a cooperative system of interlibrary loan, but the user himself, his needs and his behaviour, have not been as fully investigated as they have in some other countries. For this reason a project on user research was begun with the support of the German Research Association. The behavior and the needs of users will be explored by the distribution of questionnaires. In this writer's opinion, data from these questionnaires should give an exact statistical analysis of the books used, broken up into the different fields of knowledge, and also give an analysis of the user demands not fulfilled (i.e., books and materials not provided), broken up into these same fields of knowledge. This survey should cover the whole country, and the results could have an important impact on library operations and the improvement of library services.

EDUCATION FOR LIBRARIANSHIP

New trends in library education are developing in academic libraries as well as public libraries. There is a growing trend to incorporate the education of all librarians — both academic as well as certified librarians[1] of the upper medium level (Diplombibliothekare, gehobener Dienst) for scholarly as well as public libraries — into the university curriculum. The library schools of West Berlin and Hamburg have, more or less, already been integrated into the university system. Surely, more highly qualified certified librarians will be useful to ease the work load of the academic librarians in some respects. However, if the certified librarian becomes better trained, who will be left to do the routine work, especially cataloging, which must be done at a constant high quality? In any event, the role of the academic subject specialists (Fachreferenten), a characteristic achievement of German librarianship, an achievement acknowledged by other countries, should remain unchanged. Otherwise, a general disqualification of the librarian in the university system could be the consequence. On the other hand, gifted certified librarians should be given the chance to enter the career of their academic colleagues in a regulated and easier way. In public libraries this problem does not present itself in such acuteness. However, in any case, the reform of library education is under full discussion.

SPECIAL DEVELOPMENTS

The German Library Conference plays an important part in coordinating the work of the different categories of libraries. It has formed four working groups: (1) library education; (2) library science; (3) classification; and (4) Library Plan II. A lively discussion arose within the Conference against the plans of the federal government to impose a tax in favor of the authors on the lending of books by libraries. The rights of authors can only be ensured by a special social law or a public foundation. The library office for foreign relations (Bibliothekarische Auslandsstelle) in 1971 mediated numerous visits of foreign librarians to Germany and of German librarians to foreign countries.

In charge of the German Library Conference and in cooperation with the Working Office for Public Libraries (Arbeitsstelle für das Büchereiwesen), an editorial committee for German library statistics was founded in connection with the Staatsbibliothek Preussischer Kulturbesitz in West Berlin. Representatives of all library associations belong to the editorial committee. The aim of this committee is to compile for the first time in a comprehensive form the German national library statistics on the basis of the UNESCO recommendations. These statistics will cover about 25,000 libraries. A by-product of this work will be a complete library directory, to be done with the help of automatic data processing. A national standard of library statistics

---

[1] Editor's note: A certified librarian is equivalent to a library school graduate who has not received an advanced degree. He has received a certificate or diploma and is used in all branches of library work. For a long time he was considered to be the right-hand man of the academic librarian. Since World War II, however, the certified librarian's education has been expanded by the inclusion of documentation courses and modern technical procedures and his duties made more complex. The academic librarian serves as a specialist, responsible for selection of acquisitions and for their entry in the subject catalogs; he has also been trained as a top-level administrator. For further clarification of these concepts, see *West German Library Developments since 1945*, by Gisela von Busse (Washington, D.C.: Library of Congress, 1962) pp. 56-58.

is being developed by the German Standards Association following the principles of the UNESCO recommendation, certain points of which will be adapted to meet German conditions. The permanent secretariat of the International Organization for Standardization, Technical Committee 46, is in the hands of the German Standards Committee for books, librarianship, and documentation. This important international organization guarantees the close cooperation of German libraries and documentation institutions.

International Standard Book Numbering has been introduced into the Federal Republic of Germany; this system will bring advantages to publishers and libraries, especially in regard to electronic data processing. The national agency for the German Book Numbers was taken over by the Deutsche Bibliothek in Frankfurt. The international agency for Standard Book Numbering was offered to the Staatsbibliothek Preussischer Kulturbesitz in West Berlin, and will probably be installed there in 1972.

The Deutsche Bibliothek is now receiving deposit copies of all German publications by law (since 1971). Formerly this activity took place on the basis of a free-will agreement with the publishers.

Academic libraries are trying to establish their own association. Previously the development of academic libraries was promoted essentially by the Association of German Librarians, which employed a large part of the personal fees of its members for this cause. This will not be possible in the future; public funds will be necessary for this aim. One must earnestly regret that these endeavors have elicited only little understanding from the Conference of Cultural Ministries, one more indication of how little effective this institution has been. However, new attempts will continue. For decades the German Research Association, in cooperation with the Association of German Librarians, played an important role in the advancement of the system of academic libraries; this is evidenced in its annual reports. No less than 6.5 million DM were spent in 1971 for library projects, mostly of supraregional scope. In addition to the already existing four central special libraries, a central collection of comparative foreign law was founded at the Staatsbibliothek Preussischer Kulturbesitz in West Berlin; the cost of this was divided between the German Research Association and the library.

A further concern of the German Research Association is the improvement and acceleration of the supply of literature to all scientific institutions and users of this material. The sometimes slow lending system of the seven regional union catalogs must be reformed, and direct access to selected special collections will be instituted. The special libraries, of course, will also have an important part in supplying special literature by allowing more access to their information retrieval system and to their holdings.

Electronic data processing is slowly but steadily spreading in German academic and public libraries. The Working Office for Library Technology (Arbeitsstelle für Bibliothekstechnik), which was instituted in connection with the Staatsbibliothek Preussischer Kulturbesitz in West Berlin, is playing a special role in this field. After taking an important part in the UNESCO Seminar on electronic data processing in Regensburg in 1970, it convoked an international conference on machine-readable cataloging in Berlin in 1971. The results of this conference are an important step forward in this field and will be published.

In the Staatsbibliothek Preussischer Kulturbesitz Berlin–Marburg a new union catalog of German periodicals and serials is in the making. It will comprise all German periodicals and serials since the seventeenth century and, together with the union catalog of foreign periodicals, will result in a union catalog including all periodicals in German libraries on the basis of automatic processing (Gesamtzeitschriftenverzeichnis — GZS). As a result of the investigations of a consultants' bureau, an experiment is being made in the Staatsbibliothek Preussischer

Kulturbesitz to integrate accession and cataloging in order to accelerate these operations and to prepare for electronic data processing. The introduction of automatic processing into the library system of the state of Hessen will, after some years, accomplish this same aim.

The construction of the library building of the Staatsbibliothek Preussischer Kulturbesitz in West Berlin (architect Prof. Scharoun) continues to make visible progress. It is the largest new library building in Europe now in process of construction.

The development of the public libraries is characterized by efforts for needed library legislation. The German Library Association has published principles and standards for library laws in the German Federal States (Bundesländer). In the States of Hessen and Nordrhein-Westfalen laws are being discussed. The public libraries hope that laws will be created in the Federal States according to the developed principles and standards. The integration of all libraries into one system with the aim of having a good supply of literature and information available to all citizens was already mentioned. Here the public libraries have a special task. They are supplemented by workers' libraries of industrial plants (Werkbüchereien) and libraries supported by the Catholic and Protestant churches (Kirchliche Büchereien). The number of these libraries is surprisingly high: 326 workers' libraries, 9,500 church libraries. These libraries form an important extension of the public library system, because they perform a service to readers who otherwise are scarcely reached by libraries.

School libraries are still underdeveloped, but there are efforts to improve the situation, especially in connection with the new comprehensive schools (Gesamtschulen), which are offering education of the elementary and secondary level in one school unit organism.

Finally, mention must be made of the increase in audiovisual materials in libraries of all types. The use of nonbook media will also lead to new forms of university studies, which will affect libraries. Telestudies (Fernstudium) will gain more and more importance in Germany as in other countries, and will be comparable to the "open university" in Great Britain.

In general, the library system in Germany is one of movement after a period of relative stagnation. The mind of the librarian is changing; he is beginning to realize his tasks and possibilities in a rapidly changing society of the modern industrial world. It is a period of transition, and without doubt one of the most interesting periods of German library history. (Dr. Löhmann has provided an extensive bibliography, which due to limitations of space was unable to be included along with his article. The editor will, however, provide copies of this bibliography upon request.)

INTERNATIONAL BOOK PRODUCTION STATISTICS, 1968–1970

The statistical figures below were submitted by the individual countries to UNESCO for publication in the UNESCO Statistical Yearbook.

Despite the UNESCO Standards, adopted in 1964, as a basis for reporting and counting the national title output, the interpretation of these instructions is still so different from country to country that a comparison based on these figures can be drawn only by knowing the country's individual approach to the compilation of these statistics.

First edition totals are also provided for those countries reporting this data.

Country	1968 Total	1968 First Eds.	1969 Total	1969 First Eds.	1970 Total	1970 First Eds.
Afghanistan			83			
Albania	635		645			
Algeria	289					
Angola	8	8				
Argentina			4,395[1]		4,627[2]	
Australia[3]	3,430		3,939	3,634	4,935	4,246
Austria	5,164	3,972	5,204	4,089	4,781	3,836
Belgium	4,843	4,059	5,089	4,119	4,414	3,524
Bhutan					19[4]	19
Bolivia					104	77
Botswana			57	57	20	20
Brazil			6,392[5]	5,302		
Bulgaria	3,579	3,048	3,548	3,022	3,799	3,293
Burma	1,926				2,127[6]	1,823
Cambodia	185	184				
Cameroon					41	40
Canada[7]	3,527	3,006	3,659	3,066	3,457	3,042
Ceylon	1,570	1,276	1,586	1,256	1,566	1,257
Chile	1,546	1,421	1,100	1,052	1,370	1,366
China (Taiwan)	3,858		3,616			
Costa Rica	294	7	284	9		
Cuba	955	870	995	839		
Cyprus			341	341	205	194
Czechoslovakia	8,103	6,459	8,210	6,496	9,041	
Denmark	4,972	3,974	4,978	3,979	5,052	4,000
El Salvador			39	32		
Finland	5,835	4,348	5,876	4,219	5,595	4,080
France	18,646		21,958		22,935[5]	

Source: Office of Statistics, UNESCO, Paris, France.

[1] Including 392 titles in which the UDC classification is unknown.

[2] Including 313 titles in which the UDC classification is unknown.

[3] Number of publications received by the National Library of Australia during the year under review, including titles published in earlier years.

[4] School textbooks included in the total are not identified in the 10-subject breakdown of the UDC.

[5] Children's books and school textbooks are included in the total but are not identified in the 10-subject breakdown of the UDC.

[6] Children's books are included in the total but are not identified in the 10-subject breakdown of the UDC.

[7] Not including official publications.

INTERNATIONAL BOOK PRODUCTION STATISTICS, Continued

Country	1968 Total	1968 First Eds.	1969 Total	1969 First Eds.	1970 Total	1970 First Eds.
Germany, Democratic Republic	5,568[5]		5,169[5]		5,234[5]	
Germany, Federal Republic	30,223	25,382	33,454	28,110	45,369	37,150
Ghana	374[8]	163	446[8]	85	104	27
Greece			1,822	96		
Guatemala	70	70	50	50		
Guyana			51	40		
Hong Kong	399	286			723	470
Hungary	5,030	3,907	4,831	3,664	5,238	4,007
Iceland	687	656	683	634		
India	11,413	10,456	13,733	12,660	14,145	13,327
Iran					1,381	
Iraq	473	452	569	543	515	478
Ireland	342	225	467	219	615	251
Israel[9]	1,878	1,678	2,038	1,870	2,072[5]	1,979
Italy	8,868	7,348	8,440	7,246	8,615	7,332
Ivory Coast			38	37		
Jamaica	136	132	175	170	159[4]	159
Japan	31,086	22,387	31,009	17,836	31,249	19,591
Jordan	154		224	134	114	114
Kenya	177	165	193	165	164	147
Korea, Republic of			2,501	2,146	4,207	3,794
Kuwait	132		80		104	
Laos	30		57			
Lebanon	543	512	685	469		464
Luxembourg	214				232	
Madagascar	188	174	156	118	158	129
Malaysia			1,184	949	874	732
Mali			20	20		
Malta			51		93	86
Mauritius	42	42	42	41	68	68
Mexico	2,646	2,180	2,983	2,628	4,812[5]	3,433
Monaco			188	188	167	167
Mongolia	509					
Mozambique	122	121				
Netherlands	11,174	6,432	11,204	6,377	11,159	6,594
New Zealand	1,403[10]		1,275	1,065	1,580	1,314
Niger					23	23
Nigeria	1,004		1,099			
Norway	3,982	2,865	3,935	3,782		
Panama			195		132	
Peru	783	691	535	498		
Philippines	335					
Poland	9,361	7,521	9,413	7,570	10,038	8,144
Portugal	5,760	5,511	5,340	5,317		
Qatar	51	51			99	80

[8]Including newspapers and periodicals.

[9]Twelve months ending March 31 of the year stated.

[10]These figures include yearbooks and serial publications issued at intervals of one year or more as well as bills and parliamentary papers.

INTERNATIONAL BOOK PRODUCTION STATISTICS, Continued

Country	1968 Total	1968 First Eds.	1969 Total	1969 First Eds.	1970 Total	1970 First Eds.
Romania	7,032	6,908	7,440	7,284	7,681	7,523
Sierra Leone	75	72				
Singapore	414	367	533	499	520	490
South Africa	1,833		2,190	1,966		
Spain	20,008	18,525	20,031	18,868	19,717	18,486
Sweden	7,482	5,738	7,404	5,630	7,709	5,893
Switzerland[11]	6,228	6,153	7,505	7,387	8,321[15]	8,212
Thailand	1,364	1,364	2,457	2,228	2,085	1,935
Tunisia			134	104		
Turkey	5,492		5,669		5,854	
U.S.S.R.	75,723	68,661	74,611	67,697	78,899	72,215
United Arab Republic[12]	1,695	1,636	1,872	1,782		
United Kingdom[13]	31,372	22,624	32,321	23,235	33,441	23,468
United Republic of Tanzania	18	18	30	21	20	14
United States of America[14]	59,247[15]	52,470	62,083[15]	60,238	79,530[15]	67,609
Viet-Nam, Republic of	398	348	497	460	503	426
Yugoslavia	9,586	8,620	8,708	7,553	8,119	7,076

[11] Including works published abroad by Swiss nationals.

[12] Twelve months ending June 30 of the year stated.

[13] Including books published in Ireland. Books and pamphlets priced at less than 6 d. (2½p.) are omitted.

[14] The statistics concern only the production of book trade (namely, the industry engaged in the publishing of books for sale to the general public) and omit a large part of total book production (publications of the state governments, local authorities, universities, churches and other organizations, most reports and accounts of proceedings, laboratory manuals, workbooks). However, they include publications of the federal government and university theses.

[15] Including 12,449 federal government publications (4,487 books and 7,962 pamphlets) and 20,414 university theses in 1968; 11,862 federal government publications (4,805 books and 7,057 pamphlets) and 26,813 university theses in 1969; and 13,182 federal government publications (5,075 books and 8,107 pamphlets) and 30,933 university theses in 1970 for which a subject breakdown was not available.

BRITISH BOOK PRODUCTION*

In 1971 British publishers issued 32,538 titles, 23,563 of which were new books and 8,975 reprints and new editions.

	1970	1971	(+ or −)
Total	33,489	32,538	(− 951)
New Editions	9,977	8,975	(− 1,002)
Art	967	967	—
Biography	940	979	(+39)
Chemistry and Physics	803	1,001	(+198)
Children's Books	2,406	2,001	(− 405)
Commerce	759	841	(+82)
Education	973	941	(− 32)
Engineering	1,015	1,132	(+117)
Fiction	4,449	3,759	(− 690)
History	1,556	1,453	(− 103)
Industry	481	502	(+21)
Law and Public Administration	960	1,026	(+66)
Literature	1,320	1,100	(− 220)
Medical Science	1,285	1,439	(+154)
Natural Sciences	928	982	(+54)
Political Science	2,575	2,541	(− 34)
Religion and Theology	1,245	1,132	(− 113)
School Textbooks	1,875	2,040	(+165)
Sociology	699	747	(+48)
Travel and Guidebooks	637	589	(− 48)

This total was 951 less than the 1970 figure, and for the first time since 1959 there has been a reduction in total titles published. A drop of over a thousand in the number of reprints and new editions accounts for the reduction, and the rise in the number of new titles published, only 51, could not make up for the decrease in reprints and new editions.

Comparisons in specific categories were of particular interest in 1971. Fiction, typically the largest category but always unpredictable, was down by 690 titles, while children's books, which are generally considered a steady market, were down by 405 — a decline of 17 percent. Religious books were down by 113. School textbooks were up 165 to a total of 2,040 to become the third largest category, the position held in 1970 by children's books. (See also Whitaker's article, "Book Publishing in the United Kingdom, 1971: A Cautious Year.")

Year	Total	Reprints and New Editions
1947	13,046	2,441
1948	14,686	3,924
1949	17,034	5,110
1950	17,072	5,334
1951	18,066	4,938
1952	18,741	5,428
1953	18,257	5,523
1954	18,188	4,846
1955	19,962	5,770
1956	19,107	5,302
1957	20,719	5,921
1958	22,143	5,971
1959	20,690	5,522
1960	23,783	4,989
1961	24,893	6,406
1962	25,079	6,104
1963	26,023	5,656
1964	26,154	5,260
1965	26,358	5,313
1966	28,883	5,919
1967	29,619	7,060
1968	31,420	8,778
1969	32,393	9,106
1970	33,489	9,977
1971	32,538	8,975

*Figures taken from the January 1, 1972 issue of *The Bookseller*, 13 Bedford Square, London, England.

THE STATE OF CANADIAN PUBLISHING*

by

Patricia A. Farrell**

Pierre Berton is a name known throughout English-speaking Canada. At least one of his books (*The Comfortable Pew*, Lippincott) has had a modest success in the United States. His latest book, *The Last Spike* (McClelland & Stewart), the second volume of a two-part series (the first was *The National Dream*, also McClelland & Stewart) has sold over 70,000 copies. Best sellers in Canada usually sell around 2,800 copies.

Berton is one of the handful of Canadian authors with whom the Canadian man on the street is acquainted. For the most part, the average Canadian knows more about American writers than he does about those who have grown up in his country. In the past, writers who wanted fame and fortune left Canada and melted into the American or the English creative scene, content to return home in triumph for visits.

Ninety percent of the Canadian population of 21 million people lives within 200 miles of the U.S. border. The great majority of them are situated in the major cities near the border. Six million Canadians are French-speaking citizens living in Quebec.

The great size of the country has created difficulties. Canada is about 1,000 miles wider than the United States and has two more time zones. Its great cities are far from each other, making it difficult to service them via salesmen's visits or saturation advertising campaigns.

Quebec has become so accustomed to its isolation of thought from the rest of Canada that it has begun to consider itself a country apart. French language and culture have become increasingly emphasized and Quebecois are beginning to refer to the "foreign" power that controls their mails and taxes their people. Their embitterment over the abuses they think they have suffered at the hands of other Canadians is finding expression in provincial laws now taking effect.

In addition to its size, the country is split into two major ethnic industries (one for English- and one for French-speaking Canadians). This removes six million readers from the market of the English-language publishers and creates a linguistic roadblock for the French-language publisher who might like to increase his books' sales. Little has been accomplished in securing translation rights for French-language Canadian books.

These are some of the inherent problems the people of Canada face today. The special problems of book publishing in Canada can best be understood after a brief summation of the history and events which shaped the industry as it is today.

BACKGROUND

Publishing of books in Canada began as an ancillary function of newspaper and government printing in Nova Scotia and moved westward from there. The industry never really flourished until after World War II.

By 1850 Montreal was an important center for directories, almanacs, religious publications, and legal pamphlets. Specializing as they did, many of the firms, nevertheless, occasionally ventured into the area of general literature, with limited success.

Booksellers began in the country as peddlers of cheap American pirated editions of British books, imported British and American school books for the home market, and wallpaper and fancy goods.

Egerton Ryerson founded the Methodist Book and Publishing House in 1829 to publish the *Christian Guardian* and a number of other religious publications.

---

*This article originally appeared in the September 13, 1971 and September 20, 1971 issues of *Publishers' Weekly*, and has been revised for publication in the *Bowker Annual*.

**Formerly Associate Editor, *Publishers' Weekly*.

He was to be one of the important founders of the industry in Canada. The name would later change to the Ryerson Press, and out of it would come a textbook empire that would be a training ground for the next generation of Canadian publishers. Ryerson was to show a decided bent away from what he considered the eroding influence on national pride and the fostered misconceptions of Canada as well as the decidedly anti-British attitudes of the American textbooks of the time. He was instrumental in swinging the English publishing industry from Montreal to Toronto, where many of the printer-publishers already had branches.

The first move he made in bringing order and uniformity to curriculum and textbooks was to arrange for the publication of the Irish National Schoolbooks under contract by Canadian printer-publishers.

The indigenous publishing industry received a blow with passage of the 1847 Colonial Copyright Act, which permitted cheap colonial editions to flood the market from Britain. Canadian authors received little protection under this act, also known as the Foreign Reprints Act, if they were published in Canada and many of them, who felt they had a strong British or American audience, emigrated or offered their manuscripts to publishing houses in London or New York. Canada took on the aspects of a "cultural dumping ground."

An archaic textbook system, which was to continue for about 100 years, nurtured printing and bookselling, but not creative publishing. Under this system, texts were commissioned and printing contracts were negotiated for seven or ten years.

Bookseller-publishers sprang up, however. Among them were James Campbell, Mercer Adam, Maclear and Chewett, and Samuel Thompson. They helped develop Toronto into the book and magazine center of English Canada.

Before the turn of the century, printer-publishers began to act as agents for British and American publishers. This system was largely instrumental in the economic growth and development of Canadian publishing and still dominates the market, in which a good sale is somewhere around 2,000 copies of a trade book.

Bankruptcies began to leave empty spots as James Campbell and Mercer Adam, Stevenson & Company folded. The firm of Maclear and Chewett was to become Copp Clark under the leadership of three young men who had trained there. William Gage acquired the firm of his mentor, Adam Miller, and founded W. J. Gage Co., a textbook and stationery house.

The move of the people to the west, the eagerness of young men to found their own companies, and the rapid growth of the public library system in Canada all contributed to the new-found health of publishing. Under the stimulus of the Carnegie Foundation, 125 Carnegie libraries were built between 1901 and 1917. A powerful customer for books was thus created and would continue to grow, commanding considerable sums of money for book acquisition. It would also create a major problem for the industry.

The appearance of two more "names" among a rich crop of new houses in Canadian publishing occurred with the founding of McClelland and Goodchild (which would later become McClelland & Stewart) and the Musson Book Company. They started out, as so many others had, as agents for British and American houses, and assumed publishing responsibility and its associated risk after they had gained sufficient capital from their primary roles.

Textbook publishing in Canada promised rewards which drew several foreign houses to establish branch offices. Companies or divisions were set up by Oxford University Press, Macmillan & Company, J. M. Dent, and Thomas Nelson. They operated primarily as sales outlets for the parent and also undertook some production of Canadian textbooks already in use. In 1901 the University of Toronto Press was founded; its imprint was to become one of the most respected for its contribution to Canadian publishing and its authors.

Changes in the educational area eliminated choice of books and limited most subjects to one text; contracts were written to insure a favorable return and a long life for the texts. Often, these contracts had catastrophic effects for the children being instructed. In 1935, children were using books which ignored the existence of the airplane, automobile and radio, having been written much earlier.

Merchants came into publishing when the T. Eaton Company published the Ontario school readers from 1908 to 1935. Eaton's competition, the Robert Simpson Company, was the "publisher" of the arithmetic text.

Distribution of texts was handled by local booksellers, which led to a thriving trade across the country. Most of them carried the Ontario texts because limited markets in other areas precluded the publication of special texts for individual provinces.

Canadian publisher-agents were the sole means of supply for libraries and bookstores because, at that time, United States wholesalers had not attempted to tap the market.

The period after World War II brought floods of immigrants to Canada's shores and the country experienced a rising birth rate. Several publishers banded together and formed the Cooperative Book Centre to service the many libraries and to help hang on to the Canadian dollars that were beginning to trickle across the border.

Americans began to evaluate the market north of them and a number of Canadian companies were set up by U.S. publishing firms. The Ontario government tended to support Canadian-written and produced books for its schools, but imported books began nibbling out a larger market in the post-secondary school area.

Many of the American subsidiaries went after textbook adoptions. They too, however, encountered difficulties occasioned by changes in the philosophy of education and revamping of teaching methods. Ontario greatly expanded its Circular 14, the list of approved texts, as more and more courses were offered and an ever-increasing number of titles became possibilities for adoption. Individual school boards and teachers were responsible for the final selections, and standing orders for 25,000 or more copies became increasingly rare. The circular no longer was an assured sale.

Individual provinces began to see inadequacies in texts and requested books tailored to their needs. Most of them had populations below one million in 1969 and here, as in the more populous Ontario, individual boards picked and chose the texts they wanted. Decentralization compounded the publishers' difficulties.

American subsidiaries found a Canadian market for texts developed in the States in the areas of mathematics, physics, and chemistry. In other areas, where the board liked a text but felt it needed a little work in some aspects, texts were "Canadianized." Some changes were superficial, such as the changing of spellings; others incorporated new sections on Canadian life and its culture.

The majority of Canadian publishing houses had developed their expertise in trade, college and professional books, and school texts and references. There still remained, according to an Ernst & Ernst study of the Canadian publishing industry, "some 'publishers' [who] used that designation only to maintain a degree of respectability in the market place and provide them the opportunity to have their name included on a Canadian edition of foreign works where such would help Canadian sales."

This same study pointed out that Canadian book publishing's "contribution to the national economy of 0.06 percent is significantly lower than the United States." This comparison seems unfair, and Ernst & Ernst amplified the plight of Canadian publishing by relating it to "statistics in other countries who have a well-developed book industry," which show that in these countries, the book industry contributes "from 0.21 percent to 0.24 of G.N.P." The potential market is, therefore, estimated at three to four times the 1969 sales level of Canadian-made books. The 1969 demand for books was estimated by Ernst & Ernst at $222 million. Of this 90 percent was derived from the sales of books in English and 10 percent from books in French. Sales of books in other than English or French, which amounted to $3 million, were included in the English totals for purposes of analysis.

Indigenously printed and published books sold by Canadian publishers amounted to $54.8 million, or 24.7 percent of 1969 sales. Canadian-printed, adapted books sold by Canadian publishers accounted for $22.4 million, or 10 percent, while books not printed in Canada which were imported and sold by Canadian publishers amounted to $83.7 million, or 37.8 percent of the total sales.

CHARGES "BRAINWASHING" OF CHILDREN BY BOOKS

Canadians' concern for their national identity has cropped up several times over the past few years. Copper, oil, and gas were being tapped from the Canadian soil by foreign companies financed wholly or in part by Canadian banks with Canadian money that would eventually pour into foreign corporations.

The steady tapping of other resources, less tangible than minerals, also began to trouble the man on the street. His children, he was told, were being educated with "foreign" textbooks which presented a non-Canadian point of view. They were, some zealous nationalists charged, being brainwashed to protect foreign publishing interests in Canada.

In schools, books neglected Canadian folk heroes and pioneers in favor of more international figures. Slips on the part of local school boards brought a particularly questionable text entitled *How People Live in Canada* into the schools; on the cover was a picture of Abraham Lincoln.

On the higher level in post-secondary schools, the administration of many colleges attempted to bridge the gap of ignorance about Canada among young Canadians by providing "Canadian readers" to supplement those texts which were imported. The Department of Industry, Trade and Commerce, in a study prepared in 1970, showed that only 13 percent of college textbooks were of Canadian origin. Textbook sales represent 50 percent of the total publishers' sales in Canada. In terms of value of books sold and the number of titles, over 70 percent of the books sold in Canada do not have significant editorial alterations.

Standard reading in some Canadian schools is *Scholastic Magazine,* which informs students about "our troops in Vietnam" or "our President."

Whether they were acting out of a true spirit of altruism or for their own personal gain, as some Canadians claim, particularly incensed citizens began to grab newspaper headlines with their charges of "American takeovers" in Canada. The flurry of publicity aimed at the many "branch plant" operations of American firms began to be directed at publishing when two venerable old houses were sold to American publishing houses. The Ryerson Press was sold to McGraw-Hill (*PW,* November 16, 1970) and W. J. Gage (*PW,* October 12, 1970) was acquired by Scott, Foresman and Company — the company for which it had served as Canadian agent.

Since both of the above are textbook operations, the nationalists were especially sensitive to the possibilities of further foreign influence in Canada's schools and of the desiccation of indigenous edutional publishing. Canadian resources were insufficient to keep the ownership of the firms within the country.

GOVERNMENT LOAN ALMOST ONE MILLION

The lingering financial troubles of one of Canada's most creative houses, McClelland & Stewart, under the acknowledged editorial genius of Jack McClelland, again made news as McClelland announced that he could not continue without financial aid. He might, this energetic nationalist hinted, even have to consider offers from American houses for his firm. That, however, was to be his last refuge.

Fellow publishers in Canada have mixed feelings about the dramatic announcement of McClelland & Stewart's money troubles. "He has published an awful lot that is good in Canadian literature," one executive said, "but he has also published a lot that is bad and he certainly isn't a businessman in the true sense of the word." Another suggested that it was McClelland's way of forcing the government to act in this crisis situation. An organization which McClelland helped get off the ground, the Committee for an Independent Canada, was instrumental in creating demands for government intervention, a position strangely alien to McClelland's previous stand against the government's entry in any way into the field of publishing.

Reacting promptly in view of the impending collapse of McClelland & Stewart, the Ontario Royal Commission on Book Publishing, which had been formed by an anxious Ontario government attempting to assuage the fears of Canadians, drafted its first interim report since its creation in December 1970. The Commission stated that "a situation has arisen recently and that is of such importance and urgency that it requires special consideration at this early stage in the work of the Commission." The situation was the proposed sale of McClelland & Stewart.

Following an accounting firm's analysis of the financial records of the floundering firm, the Commission recommended a low-interest government loan of approximately $1 million to preserve the publishing house from bankruptcy, and recommended that McClelland & Stewart "should not be permitted to be transferred to foreign ownership." This latter concern has led to charges of xenophobia.

SAFEGUARDS TAGGED
TO McCLELLAND & STEWART LOAN

It was the opinion of the Commission members that McClelland & Stewart "represents an accumulated creative momentum in original Canadian publishing which could not quickly be replaced by other Canadian publishing enterprises should its program terminate or be sharply curtailed." The investigators, however, were not unmindful of the charges of lack of business acumen, and stated that the McClelland & Stewart program which "is itself a national asset worthy of all reasonable public encouragement and support" would have to incorporate "prudent safeguards" to preserve the firm from bankruptcy.

Accordingly, the government was to acquire "from McClelland and Stewart Limited ten-year term convertible debentures issued by the company in an amount not to exceed $961,645, which is the rounded equivalent of one-third of its reported current assets ($2,884,930)."

The debentures bear no interest during the first five years and low, although unstated, interest thereafter. At the option of the government, they would be convertible into common shares "in sufficient number to provide at the minimum control of the company (i.e., more than 50 percent)." The conversion option would be in effect during the entire ten-year term.

Representation on the board of directors was also mandated. Mr. McClelland and the government would each appoint an equal number of directors, with the directors then selecting a chairman who was not a director.

How has this action by the government of Ontario affected book publishing? It is the opinion of a source close to the Commission that it has not set a precedent for further loans to firms in financial trouble. He feels that it was an isolated instance of the government stepping in just before the collapse of what it feels is a valuable Canadian asset. A third interim report from the Royal Commission has suggested, however, that the government of Ontario should make loans available to publishing companies in financial distress.

The clamor for assistance has risen from many quarters of the Canadian publishing scene and, in view of the actions for McClelland & Stewart, small publishers are asking what they can expect. A majority of them express a certain ambivalence regarding loans. Wallace Matheson, President of Prentice-Hall Ltd. of Canada, is an outspoken critic, not of loans per se, but of the conditions of the loan to McClelland & Stewart. Interviewed by *PW,* he expressed the belief that the convertible aspects of the debenture into a majority of stock to control the company, should the government's interest be in jeopardy, would not be in the public interest. "I oppose that principle very strongly."

In lieu of a loan program he would favor certain subsidies by private groups or by the government to encourage various aspects of Canadian publishing. Two examples he gave were the areas of children's literature and textbook development.

SUBSIDIZING LIBRARIES
TO AID BOOK SALES

Owing to the limited market for Canadian children's books, he said, there are very few good ones available. Public libraries, he said, would seem to be the major purchasers of these books. This market he estimated at around 2,000 to 2,500 copies the first year; this unattractive sales projection was not conducive either to interesting new authorship or to encouraging Canadian publishers in this area. Subsidizing library purchases of Canadian children's books might encourage librarians to spend the monies in this area. This would also have the added benefit of putting the money to public rather than private use. For libraries to purchase five copies of a book rather than a single copy would then enable the publisher to print and sell 10,000 copies, and would create a viable publishing venture.

One Canadian publishing house, W. J. Gage Ltd., began a program known as "Writing for Young Canada" in 1960. It was designed to encourage Canadian authors to create literature for children from six to twelve years of age. The program solicited manuscripts for short stories, essays, biographies, one-act plays, and poems. Payment for accepted prose was $150, and all accepted works were to be published as anthologies. An additional award of $300 was offered annually for the most distinguished manuscript in each anthology.

Most authors could expect a payment of only $25 for a children's story previously published, and recognition centered around an occasional medal given out by one of the library groups. Gage was deluged with 8,000 manuscripts in its first year of the program. Ninety percent of the material was unusable and few established authors came forward with anything. Disappointing sales failed to justify the substantial sums of money invested by Gage and the project was abandoned in 1966.

LIBRARIES SEEN AS
ANGELS AND CULPRITS

Libraries, many Canadian citizens and publishers feel, can play a more decisive role in the future growth and development of the whole Canadian publishing scene in terms of books and authors and benefits to the public. The practice of Canadian librarians of purchasing their books from American wholesalers rather than the Canadian agent representing the various houses has been viewed as detrimental to Canada's publishing industry. University libraries spend an estimated $24 million yearly for books and periodicals.

Restrictions have been suggested by some nationalists who would like to prohibit the libraries from purchasing outside Canada with the Canadian taxpayer's money. Plowing the money back into the Canadian economy, they argue, is only right. Publisher-agents indicate that this money is needed to support their publishing ventures and that without it they cannot engage in speculative publishing.

The firm of Burns & MacEachern Ltd. produces general trade, educational, college books and paperbacks as well as serving as agent for a number of American companies. The list of companies represented was recently pruned by B. D.

Sandwell, chairman of the board and president of the company, and now includes only those which produce the most income. Mr. Sandwell is not in favor of restricting librarians. "In all my thinking, I've tried to avoid recommending actual prohibition or government legislation because, once you've got it on the books, it can work in a variety of ways that were not originally anticipated and it's very often difficult to get legislation repealed when you find it isn't working satisfactorily."

Librarians should be free to obtain material not available in Canada from specialist jobbers out of the country when necessary. Convenience and lower prices, however, have led many university librarians to order all their books in the United States.

**AGENCY BUSINESS IS
SLOWLY GROWING WEAKER**

Canadian agents who are cataloging and promoting books are placed in a situation where they do not benefit from their labors. Librarians use these catalogs to order from the wholesalers, and overhead of agents becomes unnaturally high because of the limited return. Librarians argue that they are saving the taxpayer money by buying at the lower American prices. Technically, too, if they buy from agents or Canadian wholesalers, they are paying duty on their books, which they are exempted from by law.

When contractual agreements prevent American publishers from selling to Canada except via the approved agent, how can wholesalers, who buy from these American publishers, sell to Canadian booksellers and libraries? The answer is simply that the American publisher cannot determine which books are being sold to Canada or if any, in fact, are to be sold to Canadian buyers.

The agency business may be on the wane in Canada. Firms being represented recognize a strong enough market and invariably discontinue agency representation and open up a Canadian subsidiary. For this reason, many agents are going increasingly into their own publishing programs if they envision a future existence.

Nationalists are calling for more restrictions on American subsidiaries opening up or of sales of Canadian companies to foreign firms. Some call for restrictions, such as duty, on all foreign books coming into Canada. The government is weighing these viewpoints. Most Canadian publishers see it as a step backward.

The Canada Council has made grants to select Canadian publishing ventures and, in some cases, this has made possible a book that otherwise would have proved too costly for the publisher to produce. The grants are small, sometimes as little as $150.

**SOLIDLY AGAINST ANY
GOVERNMENT SUBSIDIES**

Subsidies are one thing against which the majority of Canadian publishers, both large and extremely small, are united. They view them as a potential form of censorship, in that books which may not view the government favorably or which are produced by an author in some official disfavor would not receive funds. The refusal would not necessarily be a "no" to the project, but an indication that no more funds were available for book projects of this nature.

The marketing aspect has been initiated by the federal government which is sending a display of Canadian books to various conventions and book fairs around the world. This exhibit was at the 1971 ALA meeting in Dallas, Texas, and the Frankfurt Book Fair. A list of Canadian publishers, which caused some disagreement, has been compiled, and it is hoped that this will familiarize potential buyers with the various publishing houses in Canada.

**U.S. COPYRIGHT CLAUSE
BLOCKS SOME AUTHORSHIP**

Many Canadian publishers are misinformed on the manufacturing clause in the U.S. copyright law and how it affects their sales to buyers in the United States.

They see this as a block to their selling more than 1,500 copies of a book; sales above that figure would result in loss of their copyright. This is true only for American citizens who author books published in Canada and offered for sale in the United States. The restriction is not placed on Canadian authorship. American citizens, however, who have applied for citizenship in Canada and who are classified as "landed immigrants" still come under the provisions of the law.

The one aspect of Canadian publishing which is affected most is the scholarly or textbook field, because a large number of American university professors have signed contracts to teach in Canadian schools and their authorship would be valuable to indigenous publishers. Without the potential U.S. sale, Canadian publishers cannot compete for these authors.

A tacit agreement has been reached, according to some sources within the industry, whereby the Canadian government will effect the necessary legislation to remove duty from American books entering Canada if this manufacturing clause is removed from the new legislation before the United States Congress. Canada is not a signer of the Florence Agreement.

A president of a large Canadian publishing firm, who requested that he remain anonymous, indicated that book reviewers in Canada could be instrumental in opening up the Canadian market to more Canadian publishers. Too many of them, he contended, stick to the *Time* magazine list of best sellers for their review guidelines. They tend to discount Canadian books and Canadian authors. The reviewers counter that too many Canadian books are centered around subjects such as totem poles, national monuments, or fish and flora of the country.

Dennis Lee, poet and president of House of Anansi, takes a pragmatic view of the present state of Canadian authorship, and stated in an interview that he would welcome "outright trash" if it sold and helped support an author who would then go on to writing literature. He and others are calling for a Canadian counterpart of Jacqueline Susann.

FOREIGN COMPANIES "URGED" TO SELL STOCK TO CANADIANS

Ownership, specifically foreign ownership, has been singled out as one of the deterrents to furthering Canadian authorship and Canadian publishing. Canadian presidents of American- and British-owned firms protest that they are not prevented from formulating their own programs, but the nationalists charge the controls are not in Toronto. The nationalists call for outright Canadian ownership even if this means that firms presently operating in Canada must be sold to Canadians or that part of their stock must be offered to the Canadian public to give them a voice.

One firm, McGraw-Hill, has already stated its intention of offering between 25 and 50 percent of its stock to the Canadian public. Another large firm is considering taking similar action at some time in the future. The president of this firm was not as sanguine as the nationalists regarding the outcome of these sales. "You know you can hold only 10 percent of the stock and still maintain control if all the other shares are so distributed that no one holds that much themselves. Fifty percent," he said, "isn't the magic number."

One critical observer of the Canadian publishing scene, Mel Hurtig, a bookseller and publisher from Alberta who is also active in the Committee for an Independent Canada, agrees on this point. He is calling for majority Canadian ownership *and* control of these companies. Traveling around the country, he has attacked foreign ownership. In a recent speech he said, "Some naive people have suggested foreign ownership of publishing is not worrisome because the curriculum people can demand and control. This is simply not true. Most curriculum committees meet and choose from among what is available." During the same speech, Mr. Hurtig called for legislation "encouraging" foreign-owned publishers such as Oxford and Macmillan "to make an even greater contribution (to Canadian publishing) by selling majority ownership and control to Canadian citizens." Replying to this, a chief executive of a foreign-owned publishing firm said, "There won't be lines of people waiting to buy our stock" when it is offered, and he indicated some doubt that an offering could be successfully sold to the public.

A confidential Canadian government report on foreign ownership, the Gray Report, which was leaked to the Canadian press, recommended that a screening agency be set up to oversee proposed foreign takeovers of Canadian corporations. Release of the report, which was not to have been made public, has led to an official government probe of the entire cabinet.

PUBLISHERS' COUNCIL
ATTACKED ON ITS MEMBERSHIP

The Canadian Book Publishers' Council has come under attack by the nationalists. Out of 43 members, only 14 are Canadian-owned publishing houses, and the officers of the CBPC are all from American-owned firms. Charges have been made that while booksellers and the interested citizens of Canada have been trying vainly to get the duty removed from books coming into Canada, the Council has been operating for its retention in order to protect its agency system and the real estate and warehouse investment its members have in Canada. Most of the members, the nationalists charge, have been able to open subsidiaries in Canada by borrowing money from Canadian banks — money that is not available to the Canadian publisher because of his lack of collateral and often nebulous future. They have also been given tax advantages back home for their foreign investments, which make Canadian operations more attractive to them.

Council President Campbell Hughes, who is president of Van Nostrand Reinhold Ltd., is of the opinion that "the people who really support the agency business are the booksellers. They have no desire, except in a very few instances, to go to the country of origin to buy books. They haven't got the mechanism, the jobber won't give them the discounts so that our most enthusiastic backers for a continuing agency system are the established booksellers in this country — more particularly the smaller booksellers."

In this climate of concern, the Committee for an Independent Canada is predicting gains. Attendance at their meetings across the country, they claim, has been growing, and many American branch plant executives have been contributing to their fund.

(For further data on Canadian publishing, see the article "The Book Industry of Canada" by Charles R. Cook, pp. 7-10, in the July 1971 issue of *Printing and Publishing* magazine, available from the Superintendent of Documents, U.S. Government Printing Office, Washington, D.C. 20402, at $.25 per copy. Also, a limited number of copies of the full report, *The Book Publishing and Manufacturing Industry in Canada: A Statistical and Economic Analysis,* are available from the Government of Canada, Department of Industry, Trade and Commerce, Printing, Publishing and Allied Industries, Ottawa, Canada.)

BOOK PUBLISHING IN THE UNITED KINGDOM, 1971: A CAUTIOUS YEAR

by

David Whitaker*

During 1971 British publishers issued a total of 32,538 titles, of which 23,563 were new books and 8,975, reprints and new editions.[1] This is a reduction of 951 from the 1970 grand total of 33,489. The decline was entirely in reprints and new editions, down 1,002 from last year's total; the rise in new titles published (in itself so small, 51 only) was equally startling. The last time there was a decline in the overall number of titles published was in 1959, over a decade ago, and that was due to a long printing strike in the summer of that year. Apart from 1959, there has been no such tiny increase in new titles published as last year's 51 since the Hitler war.

One swallow flying south does not mean autumn, and unusual statistics for one year do not establish a trend. Taken with other indications, however, the figures may be allowed at the very least to suggest that there is a slight chill in the air and that some of the publishing birds are a bit ruffled: hawks are less hawkish and high-flying; ostriches have had their heads dug out of the sands by accountants; and some of the conglomerates are looking a bit dodoish in parts. (Translator's note: Dodo — an extinct species of bird, which lost its wings because of a lack of problems for too long a period of time; neither was it fast on its feet.)

The Bookseller's Frankfurt Book Fair correspondent wrote of this year's fair that: "From a bookseller's point of view one of the few cheerful aspects of the current scene must be confirmation of what he has always held to be true: that while he and his brethren live where life is hardest it is, nonetheless, only a short while after they feel the draft that the publisher starts sneezing and sometimes choking." He went on to quote the manager of a large university press: "Books that would once have sold out their edition haven't done so. Generally publishers are having to be more careful. Educational publishers are finding that the institutions are cutting back; a lot of schools are going back to the old textbooks which are cheaper. Booksellers are more interested than ever in terms, and they are paying more slowly." The report continued, "The 1971 Frankfurt Book Fair was, in consequence, a more than usually professional affair." The same phrase might be used to describe the publishing year as a whole. The professional publishers were busy watching costs and margins, ruthlessly chopping those books which might once have sold out their edition and so contributed to overheads if not to profit, but which would now no longer do any more than make a dull loss. What everyone wanted was good books, of all kinds, which would earn their own and their publisher's living. It is surprising what a downturn in the economy can do for quality.

FINANCES

It was not a year of very many mergers. The First National Industrial Trust bought Ward Lock for a cash payment of £328,000; Howard & Wyndham bought W. H. Allen & Company from Walter Reade Organization, Inc., of New York for about £500,000 in cash and shares. This was the fourth sale of that company in recent years. E. S. Pearson bought in the remaining outside share holdings in Penguin, and later added Wills & Hepworth, publishers of "Ladybird" children's books. Mills & Boon merged with Harlequin Enterprises of Canada, which meant another house

---

*Mr. Whitaker is with J. Whitaker & Sons, Ltd., 13 Bedford Square, London, W.C. 1, England.

[1]See "British Book Production," this volume.

tied to the American continent, but that it should be the Canadian part made a change.

Financial results announced during the year were interesting. The news and book chain of W. H. Smith & Son with some 400 shops announced increased profits of £4,689,000 in 1970 before tax on a turnover of over £117,000,000. Before 1971 ended this increasingly tightly run multiple was forecasting even better results for the current year. Collins, headed by Sir William Collins, had a record profit before tax of £1,836,000. Collins has printing interests and is one of the few publisher-printers to be successful in both fields. Associated Book Publishers' profit was £684,936, and forecasts for the current financial year are for a substantial increase. British Printing Corporation, a group which takes in Purnell, Macdonald, Jane's and other publishing imprints, magazines and part works, encyclopedias, and printing, had a loss of £2,686,000. Hutchinson, a sizable group, had profits reduced from £340,173 to £97,414 but anticipates doing better this year. The Hamlyn Group turned in another large loss.

The United Kingdom turnover figures are now produced by the Department of Trade & Industry and appear later than ever. The most recent figures available are for 1969, when home turnover was £77,170,000 and export £68,523,000. In that year exports increased more sharply than home trade. Indications in 1970 were that the trend would be reversed; for 1971 it is probably safe to say that there will be no temptation to use the word "sharply" about any of the figures. In 1967 the total turnover was £145,693,000; it should be around £170,000,000 for 1971 if price inflation alone has been kept pace with. If that figure is only slightly exceeded, it will give real pleasure.

INFLATION

Why have times been harder? Galloping inflation; savage printing price increases that steadily erode the price advantage of United Kingdom books over U.S. productions; a general depression in world trade of all kinds; and, of course, cut-backs in institutional expenditure. Library funds have been frozen, or increased by amounts that scarcely keep pace with the ever upward climb of prices; schools' expenditure, which has never been good, has been cut back.

At a recent talk, Mr. Ben Winter Goodwin, Managing Director of Book Centre, produced these figures from *Whitaker's Almanack 1972*. "Between the years 1960 to 1970 public expenditure on recreational goods as a whole rose by 102 percent. Expenditure on newspapers increased by 100 percent, on magazines by 82 percent, and on books by 75 percent. Taking 1970 sales at 1963 prices, the increases are: recreational goods 55 percent, books 17 per cent, magazines 9 percent and newspapers 6 percent.

"From this one can gather that although we have increased the number of books sold, price increase has been considerably less in the case of books as compared with other goods, and that the profits of bookselling must therefore be on a downward trend."

The situation with educational books can be regarded as almost desperate. The increase of turnover in the period 1969-70 over 1968-69 was 7 percent. "Taking into account cost inflation of 10 percent and growth of the school population we have a definite downward trend."

It makes a gloomy picture. On the other hand, why were things not worse? Why did some publishing houses do notably well? There is a belief in the book trade that during recessions, or when money is even temporarily tight, books are affected less than other commodities; books even profit. Certainly *The Bookseller* roundup of Christmas trade in the bookshops saw plenty of seasonal glee. Austick's of Leeds reported trade over 25 percent up on last year at the same time; Lear's of Cardiff said that trade was making their enlarged premises seem inadequate; High Hill Bookshop in Hampstead reported trade at least 20 percent up again; even Over's of Rugby — in the redundancy- and unemployment-hit Midlands — reported that "unless the public have been shopping early [subsequently the papers reported a last-minute further splurge of spending] we should end up in a good position."

It is pleasant to believe that with consumer frenzy abated by the economic climate, the reflective pleasure of books comes into its own; that round the winter fire the readers sit engrossed in *The Guinness Book of Records, And Miss Carter Wore Pink, Bury My Heart at Wounded Knee, Fillets of Plaice, Impossible Voyage,* or *Monty Python's Big Red Book,* which were a few of the titles among the year-end best sellers. George's of Bristol reported that "due to the lack of an outstanding best seller . . . customers were choosing from a wide range in which hobbies (cookery and gardening especially) and crafts are very much to the fore." Perhaps the smaller pleasures and the less expensive pastimes are having a quiet boom.

There was a certain amount of price resistance reported during the year, but "if the book is right the price is right" (Blackwell's of Oxford). Those books that "once would do to fill out a list" have had a thin time of it, but the good ones have sold well, as ever. But to make sure that the books *are* good means careful buying on the part of the bookseller, and escalating costs mean even more careful buying. Consequently, those publishers' lists that cannot stand up to really close inspection must inevitably suffer. If their overheads are too high the suffering can be very acute. There was more redundancy in the publishing trade during 1971 than there has been since the Second World War.

Taking a subjective glance around the general publishing houses, it seems that success attended those where good editors were backed by good sales managers. It may be a truism, but it does seem to have been overlooked here and there over recent years that editorial excellence is the prime function of publishing, and this is not something that can merely be paid polite lip service by accountants or sales managers who think that they are really the most important people.

ODDMENTS

Pornography exercised the trade but fleetingly during the year. The Arts Council set up a committee to study the working of the obscenity laws. The committee produced what Lord Goodman, Chairman of the Arts Council, called a "very cogent and splendidly written report." Its conclusion was that the laws serve no useful purpose and are positively vicious. With an eye to political reality Lord Goodman and the Council decided not to adopt their own committee's report, but to forward it to the Home Secretary for him to peruse. The Danish *Little Red School Book,* published in translated and edited form, ran afoul of the obscenity laws and was successfully prosecuted with enormous publicity. Sales for the next edition, which had a red sticker over the offending passage, were substantial. Sex education in schools occupied the papers for weeks as a result. Overall, however, general publishers found little to concern them — underground newspapers and imported magazines were the main areas of concern. The traditional book trade has probably pushed back the limits of what is permissible as far as it needs or cares to do.

Distribution — the nuts and bolts of the trade — was of much more pressing concern. The United Kingdom is a tiny area, and it is possible to dream of supplying any book from any publisher in ten working days at the most. Some publishers can have special orders back to booksellers in three working days. Others take, at worst, over 30. The poor performers lose trade for themselves, and, much worse, for everyone else. In regard to service, customers equally form attitudes not from the best, or even the middle standard of performance, but from the worst, and booksellers' customers are therefore frequently disenchanted people. Booksellers complain bitterly because they lose sales and bear the brunt of customer complaints over bad service, over which they have no control whatever. There are no jobbers in the United Kingdom to speak of. Publishers Parcels Delivery Service (PPDS) was set up last year by Book Centre to rationalize the carrier situation, and its yellow vans are already welcome callers at bookshops as its service steadily improves and expands.

The ISBN system (International Standard Book Numbering) also progressed well. Every book published in the United Kingdom has an ISBN allocated to it, and the backlists of all major publishers are numbered. During 1972 virtually every book available will have been numbered. Now that allocation of ISBNs to books is so far advanced the advantages of the system begin to show. W. H. Smith have a computer system at their vast Swindon warehouse, and the systems for handling books are built around the ISBN scheme. The London and South Eastern Region interlibrary lending system is also computer controlled and equally dependent upon ISBNs. Also ISBN-oriented are the educational purchasing systems of the Greater London Council, which buys over £1 million worth of books a year for the schools within the area. The educational authorities of West Riding of Yorkshire and Kent are expected to adopt similar systems this year. A new service available for computer users is ready-made book files and weekly updating information (new books, price changes, details of books no longer available, etc.) in magnetic tape form. Without the ISBN system it would have been years before this could have come into being. This purchasing-orientated file comes from Whitakers, publishers of *British Books in Print* and the other trade book lists. A cataloging-orientated file and update service, the MARC tapes, is available from the British National Bibliography.

LITERATURE

There is more to publishing than just its concern with literature, but some of its finest moments involve that small part of its product. It seems suitable, therefore, to end with a look at what won the literary prizes. The £5,000 Booker Prize for fiction was presented to V. S. Naipaul for *In a Free State* (Andre Deutsch). Other novels on the short list were *The Big Chapel* by Thomas Kilroy, *Briefing for a Descent into Hell* by Doris Lessing, *St. Urbain's Horseman* by Mordecai Richler, *Goshawk Squadron* by Derek Robinson, and *Mrs. Palfrey at the Claremont* by Elizabeth Taylor. Three Whitbread literary awards, worth £1,000 each, were presented for the first time this year. The biography award went to Michael Meyer for his three-volume study of Ibsen (Hart-Davis), the fiction award to Gerda Charles for *The Destiny Waltz,* and the poetry award to Geoffrey Hill for his *Mercian Hymns.* The judges were J. B. Priestley, Margaret Drabble, and Anthony Thwaite. The W. H. Smith £1,000 literary award for 1971 proved a uniquely sad occasion as the winner, Nan Fairbrother (Mrs. William Mackenzie) author of *New Lives, New Landscapes* (Architectural Press) died on November 24 in the knowledge that she had won the award but a few days before the formal presentation.

The year was (looking back on it from a rather close perspective) pretty mixed. Because of this limited perspective it is difficult to draw viable conclusions on which to base predictions about the near future. But having been asked to do so, I must try. Money is tight. Publishing, and the communications industries generally, have temporarily lost their glamor for big business. Some of the biggest problems are in the biggest groups. The old professionals are doing best — perhaps because they have seen recessions before. Some of the small companies being set up by editors are making a good living; their owners say that they have found the true economy of scale: when you are small so are your overheads. So-so books flop; good books of all kinds can still have big sales.

About the only safe prediction is that money will not be much easier this year. The houses that were "exploiting assets to the full" (a euphemism for doing it all on borrowed money) will continue to be hard-pressed. The slowing-down process will go on in some of the groups, but there will still be a good market for the right book.

INTERNATIONAL BOOK PROGRAMS

FRANKLIN BOOK PROGRAMS

Franklin Book Programs is a unique development institution, providing technical assistance to the less developed countries requiring educational materials. Founded in 1952, Franklin began by translating desired books from languages of the developed world into local languages; and to date 4,435 titles have been translated into one or more of the following languages: Arabic, Bengali, Hausa, Igbo, Indonesian, Malay, Peshtu, Portuguese, Persian, Spanish, Swahili, Urdu, and Yoruba. From translation, Franklin moved into training: teachers and artists were trained to write textbooks, editors and marketing managers were trained in publishing, compositors and pressmen were trained as printers. Next, printing plants were upgraded or built. Now, Franklin provides a full range of contract services: educational materials planning, training in the creation of a wide range of formal and informal education materials, and active development programs in printing and production, in marketing and distribution, and in publishing.

Governed by a board of publishers, printers, businessmen, development economists, and educators (both American and non-American), Franklin maintains offices in New York, Cairo, Tehran, Lahore, Dacca, Kabul, and Djakarta.

Members of the board are: Abdolreza Ansari, Lucius D. Battle, Edward W. Barrett, Simon Michael Bessie, Harrison Brown, Adam Curle, Jack Dalton, Charles M. Frankel, Edward K. Hamilton, Michael Harris, Raymond C. Harwood (Chairman), Harold H. Helm, Mrs. Aziza Hussein, Jeremiah Kaplan, Chester B. Kerr, Martin P. Levin, Harry R. Most, Alfred C. Neal, Mrs. Harvey Picker, Datus C. Smith, Jr., Davidson Sommers, Mead Stone, Gordon Tweedy, and Theodore Waller (Vice-Chairman).

The officers are: John H. Kyle (President), Anders Richter (Vice-President), P. Lynn Mayer (Secretary), and Norman Poinsett (Treasurer).

Resident managers are: Ahmed Riad Abaza (Cairo), Ali Asghar Mohajer (Tehran), Hamid Ali Khan (Lahore), Mannan Chowdhury (Dacca), Atiqullah Pazhwak (Kabul), and Hassan Shadily (Djakarta).

Highlights of past and present Franklin activities include:

1. Translating and, through private publishers in Cairo, publishing over 130 college, university, and teacher-training texts in virtually all undergraduate subject areas;

2. Training teachers and artists to create all elementary school textbooks for Iran and to manage their production by a printing press built and originally managed by Franklin;

3. Increasing the productivity of the Afghanistan Ministry of Education's printing plant — the Educational Press — from 200,000 textbooks per year to nearly 4,000,000 units per year;

4. Launching a new scientific, technical, and vocational textbook program in English and other national languages in cooperation with the U.S. Agency for International Development and Pakistan Ministry of Education;

5. Adapting a basic reference work, the *Columbia-Viking Desk Encyclopedia*, into local editions in Indonesian, Arabic, Persian, Bengali, and Urdu;

6. Translating virtually all required medical textbooks into Spanish and Portuguese (to be used in Brazil) for Latin American medical instruction.

Franklin, a private, nonprofit educational corporation chartered in the State of New York, has no endowment but operates on funds donated, granted, or contracted for performing its projects. Its past and present support comes from the governments of Afghanistan, Iran, Kuwait, and the United States; foundations and corporations such as Commonwealth, Ford, Kellogg, Charles E. Merrill Trust, Rockefeller, Weyerhaeuser, and Xerox Fund; and research or development agencies such as the Population Council, Asia Foundation, Twentieth Century Fund. Its major current support is from business communities, private foundations, and from concerned individuals the world over.

An annual report covering its program, past projects, and detailing its past and present support can be obtained by writing Franklin Book Programs, Inc., 801 Second Avenue, New York, New York 10017.

FREEDOM HOUSE/BOOKS USA

Freedom House/Books USA is a nonprofit, educational program of Freedom House created to distribute American books to potential leaders of the developing nations in Asia, Africa, and Latin America. Some schools, libraries, and other institutions, particularly those not supported by a government, are also sent book collections.

The titles are selected by a committee of 54 prominent authors. Overseas representatives of some sixty American voluntary agencies select the recipients. Volunteers with the Peace Corps overseas also assist in the distribution.

The books are selected to share the American cultural heritage and provide a picture of the United States that will counteract misconceptions about it abroad.

Support for Freedom House/Books USA comes exclusively from the American public on a voluntary basis.

The president of Freedom House/Books USA is Dr. Harry D. Gideonse, Chancellor of the New School for Social Research; treasurer is Mrs. Andrew Jackson, Consultant, *Harper's Magazine;* secretary is Philip Van Slyck. Other Board members include: George Backer, former publisher; Leo Cherne, Executive Director of the Research Institute of America; Roscoe Drummond, columnist; Mrs. Helen Meyer, President, Dell Publishing Co.; Dr. Dwayne Orton; Steuart L. Pittman, attorney; Hon. Francis E. Rivers, retired judge and labor arbitrator; Whitney North Seymour, attorney, past President, American Bar Association; John T. Sargent, President, Doubleday and Co.; Rex Stout, author; Frank E. Taylor, book publisher; and Mrs. George C. Vietheer, Director, League of Women Voters of New York City.

Leonard R. Sussman, Executive Director of Freedom House, is also the supervisor of the book distribution program.

The present operation is the result of a merger in 1967 of the Freedom House Bookshelf and Books, USA, Inc. The Bookshelf is in its thirteenth year while Books, USA was created nine years ago by Edward R. Murrow when he headed the U.S. Information Agency.

There is currently a backlog of thousands of unfilled requests for book packets with additional requests arriving daily. As Mr. Murrow stated, "The hunger of people abroad for books" is "insatiable."

Requests for further information should be addressed to Freedom House/Books USA, 20 West 40th Street, New York, N.Y. 10018.

GOVERNMENT ADVISORY COMMITTEE ON INTERNATIONAL BOOK AND LIBRARY PROGRAMS

The Government Advisory Committee on International Book and Library Programs was established in October 1962 by the Secretary of State, under the authority of the Fulbright-Hays Act (PL 87-256), to advise the Government on the policies and operations of its overseas book and library programs and to achieve closer coordination between public and private book and library activities overseas.

The Committee consists of twelve members appointed by the Secretary of State to serve for three-year terms. Appointments are staggered so that four new members start their terms each year. Nine of the members represent various branches of the publishing industry, including all aspects of educational materials; two are librarians and one an educator.

In addition to the twelve regular members, there are three exofficio members: the chairman of the Board of Directors of the Association of American Publishers, Inc.; the President of the American Booksellers Association; and the chairman of the AAI International Trade Committee. All members serve without compensation.

The present chairman is Ross D. Sackett, President, CBS/Education & Publishing Group.

Nine official observers from the private sector also attend Committee meetings as representatives of: the Association of American Publishers, Inc., the Association of American University Presses, the American Booksellers Association, the Book Manufacturers Institute, the Printing Industries of America, and the American Library Association.

There are three official Government representatives to the Committee: the Assistant Secretary of State for Educational and Cultural Affairs, the Assistant Director (Information Centers) of the U.S. Information Agency, and the Director, Office of Education and Human Resources, Bureau for Technical Assistance, Agency for International Development. In his capacity as coordinator of all the Government's international educational and cultural activities, the Assistant Secretary is the senior representative. Other Government agencies concerned with international book and library programs send observers to Committee meetings. These include: the Department of Commerce; the Office of Education in the Department of Health, Education, and Welfare; Library of Congress; Peace Corps; Smithsonian Institution; Atomic Energy Commission; and the National Archives and Records Service.

In October 1966 a member of the U.S. Advisory Commission on International Educational and Cultural Affairs was appointed to the Committee to provide a means of direct liaison between the two groups. The Commission member serves as the educator on the Book Committee.

The Committee meets quarterly in Washington, D.C. By definition its sole function is to advise. It has no operational responsibilities nor has it the authority to allocate funds.

During its eight years of existence the Committee has reviewed all the major book programs conducted by Government agencies overseas, giving advice which has resulted in improved coordination and efficiency. At the Government's request it has established *ad hoc* panels of private experts to study such matters as: the USIA and AID book programs in Latin America; means for increasing overseas distribution of American scientific and technical books; textbook needs and marketing problems in the UAR; book selection criteria of the former IMG program; the effect of the rupee devaluation on the availability of American books in India; what the legal status and proper role of the East-West Center Press should be; what the nature and goals of the American library presence overseas should be; and what the Government's policy on overseas textbook programs should be. Other problems discussed by the Committee include: the implications for U.S. publishing and overseas book programs of the 1967 Stockholm Protocol to the Berne Copyright Convention; the effect of the demise of IMG on the distribution of American books abroad; the difficulty American scholars teaching overseas have in obtaining course books for their students; the nontariff barriers impeding the flow of U.S. books overseas; and the potential for international book and library programs of ultramicrofiche libraries.

One of the Committee's most significant contributions thus far is the part it played in the formulation of the National Policy Statement on International Book and Library Activities, and implementing Directive, which were approved by President Lyndon B. Johnson in January 1967. Since that time the Committee has devoted a great deal of its attention to carrying out the National Book and Library Policy by developing regional policies tailored to local needs in Latin America, East Asia and the Pacific, the Near East and South Asia, and Africa.

Possibly the Committee's greatest value, in the long term, lies in what it has done to improve coordination, not only among U.S. public and private book and library programs, but also between those of the U.S. Government and the multilateral organizations—notably UNESCO and the OAS—and among the different Government agencies. The chairman of the Committee headed the U.S. observer delegation to two UNESCO-sponsored meetings of experts on book development in Asia and in Africa held respectively at Tokyo in May 1966 and at Accra in February 1968. A member of the Committee also attended a similar meeting on book development in Latin America in Bogota, in September 1969; the then chairman participated in a UNESCO consultation in March 1970 for International Book Year (1972).

The Committee secretariat is located in the office of the U.S. Advisory Commission on International Educational and Cultural Affairs, Department of State (CU/ACS) and serves as a central point for information about Government book and library activities abroad. The Executive Secretary, Miss Carol M. Owens, is a Government official whose address is: Government Advisory Committee on International Book and Library Programs, CU/ACS, Department of State, Washington, D.C. 20520; telephone 202-632-2841.

Shortly after the 1970 UNESCO General Conference declared 1972 International Book Year, the Government Advisory Committee established an ad hoc Committee for IBY. Broadly representative of the American book and library community, the IBY Committee is encouraging Government agencies at the federal, state and local levels, organizations, educational institutions, and companies in the world of books to develop IBY programs and to help them emphasize and expand their international activities. The U.S. effort is both domestic and international — an attempt to initiate long-range programs that will promote the reading habit, increase the availability of books and strengthen library development at home, and cooperate with other countries and UNESCO in achieving these goals everywhere. The IBY Committee has agreed to undertake a number of projects itself, including publication of a guidebook for librarians, teachers and community leaders to help them plan IBY programs; publication of special bibliographies, a newsletter and a poster; convening of an international conference on books, education and economic development; and support of several international seminars. Additional information on IBY may be obtained from Miss Esther Walls, Director, IBY Secretariat, National Book Committee, One Park Avenue, New York, N.Y. 10016; telephone 212-689-8620. (For further information on IBY programs, see Frantz's article, "National Book Committee, Inc." and Wegman's article, "International Book Year — 1972," this volume.)

AGENCY FOR INTERNATIONAL DEVELOPMENT

The Agency for International Development is continuing to carry out a variety of book activities in conformance with the guidance embodied in the U.S. National Book and Library Development policy statement issued in January 1967.

A new and expanded statement of A.I.D.'s policy relating to the use of books in overseas development programs was issued in Manual Order form, identified as M.O. 1612.69.3, "The Use of Books in the A.I.D. Program." This order emphasizes the responsibility for the Agency, on a long-term basis, to facilitate the development of appropriate and needed indigenous book industry capability. It also emphasizes the importance of the development of indigenous textbook programs, framed in the context of bilateral programs for educational improvement.

A highlight of the Agency's book-related activities during the past few years has been the initiation of large-scale bilateral textbook development programs, based on long-term, low-interest loans to the governments of Brazil, Chile and India. Under the Brazil program, through which A.I.D. supports efforts of the Brazilian Ministry of Education, efforts are underway to produce a total of about 51,000,000 Portuguese-language textbooks, targeting the needs of the school system from the elementary to the college level. Under the Chile program, the need of Chilean students for elementary school textbooks may be met for the first time.

The Latin American Bureau's program for regional book activity under the Alliance for Progress has, for several years, emphasized the sponsorship of commercial publication of Spanish versions of U.S. technical and professional books.

The provision of books needed to start university textbook rental libraries in sixteen countries, on a demonstration basis, is also an activity under the Alliance program.

A.I.D. has placed increased emphasis on collaborating with other agencies and private organizations on sponsored research relating to the applicability of new educational media in overseas situations. In El Salvador, for example, a cooperative instructional television program is underway which is directly related to curriculum modernization and educational reform initiated by the ministry of education. Many experts are convinced that the new media holds the key to overcoming the developing countries' apparently insoluble dilemma of expanding educational demands and aspirations with grossly inadequate resources.

FRANKFURT BOOK FAIR, 1971

A cautious crowd seemed to outnumber the books at the Frankfurt Book Fair in 1971. The 3,581 publishers present, 2,150 of which had individual stands, represented an increase of almost 200 over the 1970 attendance. However, the big deals which have characterized the fair in the past were lacking. Many of the "good books" — the Gehlen memoirs, Solzhenitsyn's *1914*, and the Nasser-Heikel memoirs — had previously been sold.

Although German students briefly occupied the Brazilian stand and German and Iranian students held a teach-in in the fair restaurant, demonstrations were at a minimum. Some of the credit could be given to a special stand which had been set up to show books suppressed in nations which had official stands at the fair.

Time-Life Books and the Soviet publisher Mir made news with the announcement of an agreement for Russian translations of two volumes of the Life Nature Library. One will be published this year in an edition of 100,000 copies, the second next year. This represents the first official co-publication project between the two countries.

The Fair's Peace Prize was awarded to a native of East Germany, Marion Gräfin Dönhoff, editor of *Die Zeit*, one of Germany's major weeklies, and an advocate of East-West detente.

INTERNATIONAL ASSOCIATIONS*
ASSOCIATION OF INTERNATIONAL LIBRARIES

OBJECT

"To increase cooperation among international libraries." Founded 1964. Memb. (Indiv.) 120; (Inst.) 30. Dues. (Inst.) $10; (Indiv.) $3.

OFFICERS

Pres. Mr. J. Leymarie, Ministère du Développement Industriel et Scientifique, 101, rue de Grenelle, F-75 Paris 7e, France; V. Presidents. Miss N. E. S. Coops, UNESCO L., Paris, France; Mr. T. Dimitrov, United Nations L., Geneva, Switzerland; Mr. M. Loftus, World Bank IMO Joint L., Washington, D.C. Secy. Miss R. Cormier, Bibliothèque de l'OCDE, Château de la Muette, 2, rue André-Pascal, F-75 Paris 16e, France; Treas. Mr. O. Cerny, Case Postale 500, Ch-1211 Geneva 22, Switzerland; Members. Mr. E. Johnson, ILO L., Geneva, Switzerland; Miss E. Poprawski, Council of Europe Library, Strasbourg, France; Mrs. Elisabeth H. Nebehay, United Nations L., New York, N.Y.

(Note: Address correspondence to either Pres. or Secy.)

PUBLICATION

Newsletter (irreg.; memb.)

INTER-AMERICAN ASSOCIATION OF AGRICULTURAL LIBRARIANS AND DOCUMENTALISTS

OBJECT

"To serve as liaison among the agricultural librarians and documentalists of the Americas and other parts of the world; to promote the exchange of information and experiences through technical publications and meetings; to promote the improvement of library services in the field of agriculture and related sciences; to encourage the improvement of the professional level of the librarians and documentalists in the field of agriculture in Latin America."

OFFICERS

Pres. María Dolores Malugani, Instituto Interamericano de Ciencias Agricolas (IICA), Turrialba, Costa Rica; V.P. Pablo Velásquez, National Agricultural Library, México D.F.; Exec. Secy. Ana María Paz de Erickson, IICA, Turrialba, Costa Rica.

MEMBERS

Amalia Cavero de Cornejo, National Agricultural Library, Lima, Perú; Angel Fernández, Library, School of Agric. & Vet. Sci., Buenos Aires Univ., Buenos Aires, Argentina; Alejandro MacLean, Zona Sur IICA, Montevideo, Uruguay.

PUBLICATIONS

Boletín Informativo (bi-mo.)
Bibliografía Agrícola Latinoamericana (q.)
Boletín Tecnico (irreg.)
Boletín Especial (irreg.)

INTER-AMERICAN BIBLIOGRAPHICAL AND LIBRARY ASSOCIATION
P.O. Box 583, N. Miami Beach, Fla. 33160

OBJECT

"To furnish investigators, research workers, students, writers, etc., with information on bibliographical sources; to act as a clearing house for requests about organizations, libraries, or individuals known to possess, have access to, or know of particular bibliographical sources; to undertake bibliographical, library, and archival work, in cooperation with other related agencies in all countries of the Americas; and to publish from time to time bibliographical and library aids." Founded 1930. Dues $4.

---

*For dates and sites of associations' annual conferences, see "Library Association Meetings," this volume.

OFFICERS

Pres. A. Curtis Wilgus, P.O. Box 583, N. Miami Beach, Fla. 33160; *Secy.-Treas.* Magdalen M. Pando; *Hon. V. Presidents.* Ricardo J. Alfaro (Panama), Rafael Arévalo Martínez (Guatemala), Jorge Basadre (Peru), Guillermo Feliú Cruz (Chile), Hector García Chuecos (Venezuela), Agustín Nieto Caballero (Colombia), Victoria Ocampo (Argentina), Richard Pattee (Canada), Elena Vérez De Peraza (Cuba).

COUNCIL

Enid Baa, Nettie Lee Benson, James B. Childs, Gilberto V. Fort, Arthur Gropp, Sturgis E. Leavitt, Janeiro Brooks Schmid, Marietta Daniels Shepard, Karna S. Wilgus, Edith Wise, Irene Zimmerman.

PUBLICATION

Doors to Latin America (q.; memb.)

INTERNATIONAL ASSOCIATION OF AGRICULTURAL LIBRARIANS AND DOCUMENTALISTS
Tropical Products Institute, 56/62 Gray's Inn Road, London WCIX/8Lu, England

OBJECT

"The Association shall, internationally and nationally, promote agricultural library science and documentation as well as the professional interest of agricultural librarians and documentalists." Founded 1955. Memb. 650. Dues. (Inst.) $13.50; (Indiv.) $6.

OFFICERS

Pres. P. Aries (France), *V.P.* K. Harada (Italy), *Secy.-Treas.* H. E. Thrupp (United Kingdom), *Editor.* G. de Bruyn (Netherlands).

EXECUTIVE COMMITTEE

A. M. Bochever (U.S.S.R.), Miss S. Contour (France), Miss J. Edwardes (Nigeria), Mrs. A. M. P. de Erikson (Costa Rica), A. L. Geisendorf (Switzerland), H. Haendler (Germany), F. C. Hirst (United Kingdom), T. Sasaki (Japan), P. G. Velasquez (Mexico), V. Vitins (U.S.A.).

PUBLICATION

Quarterly Bulletin of the IAALD (memb.)

AMERICAN MEMBERSHIP

By individuals or institutions.

INTERNATIONAL ASSOCIATION OF LAW LIBRARIES
c/o Prof. Dr. H. G. Leser, Institut für Rechtsvergleichung, Savignyhaus-Universitätsstr. 6, D-355 Marburg, W. Germany

OBJECT

"To promote on a cooperative, non-profit, and fraternal basis the work of individuals, libraries, and other institutions and agencies concerned with the acquisition and bibliographic processing of legal materials collected on a multinational basis, and to facilitate the research and other uses of such materials on a worldwide basis." Founded 1959. Memb. 300.

OFFICERS

Pres. Prof. Dr. H. G. Leser, Institut für Rechtsvergleichung, Savignyhaus-Universitätsstr. 6, D-355 Marburg, W. Germany; *1st V.P.* Prof. Leon M. Liddell, Law Libn., Univ. of Chicago, Chicago, Ill.; *2nd V.P.* Prof. Maurizio Lupoi, Via A. Bertoloni, 55, 00197 Roma, Italy; *Secy.-Treas.* Dr. Gerhard J. Dahlmanns, Institute für Rechtsvergleichung, Savignyhaus-Universitätsstr. 6, D-355 Marburg, W. Germany; *Ed. of the Bulletin,* Ivan Sipkov, Law Library, L. of Congress, Washington, D.C. 20540, U.S.A.

EXECUTIVE BOARD

The Officers and Miss Muriel Anderson, Institute of Advanced Legal Studies, 25 Russell Square, London, W.C. 1, England; Mr. Lewis C. Coffin, Law Libn., L. of Congress, Washington, D.C. 20540; Mlle. Paulette Guillitte, Bibliothèque de la Faculté de droit de l'Université de Liège, 7, Place du XX Aout, Liège, Belgium; Mrs. Frances Jill McIvor, The Queen's University of Belfort, Law Faculty Library, Belfast, 7, N. Ireland; Dr. J. D. Korevaar, 20 Chemin Colladon, App. 041, Petit Saconnex, Geneva, Switzerland; Dr.

Karl Kreuzer, Akad. Rat, Juristisches Seminar der Universität Freiburg, Belfortstr. 11, Germany; Miss Lotte Kunz, Bibl.-Leiterin, Juristische Seminarbibliothek der Universität Bern, Bern, Switzerland; Mlle. Elisabeth Traissac, Bibliothèque Juridique Universitaire de Bordeaux, Allée Maine de Biran, Domaine Universitaire 33, Pessac, France.

PUBLICATION

Bulletin (3 times a yr.)

INTERNATIONAL ASSOCIATION OF METROPOLITAN CITY LIBRARIES

OBJECT

"The Association was founded to assist the worldwide flow of information and knowledge by promoting practical collaboration in the exchange of books, exhibitions, staff, and information." Memb. 77.

PROGRAM

A research team and correspondents have been appointed and for the next three years will be engaged in drawing up a practical code of recommended practice in international city library cooperation and in formulating objectives, standards, and performance measures for metropolitan city libraries.

OFFICERS (April 1971–April 1974)

Pres. H. C. Campbell, Toronto P.L., 40 St. Clair Ave. E., Toronto 290, Ont., Canada; *Hon. Treas. & Hon. Secy.* K. C. Harrison, City Librarian, Westminster City Ls., Marylebone P.L., Marylebone Rd., London N.W.1, England; *Past Pres.* Dr. G. Chandler, Liverpool City Ls., William Brown St., Liverpool 3, England.

(Note: Address general correspondence to K. C. Harrison.)

PUBLICATION

Review of the Three Year Research and Exchange Programme 1968–1971

INTERNATIONAL ASSOCIATION OF MUSIC LIBRARIES

OBJECT

"To constitute a representative international organization charged with stimulating and coordinating all the activities, national and international, of music libraries, and to study and facilitate the realization of all projects dealing with music bibliography and music library science." Memb. 1,500.

OFFICERS (Aug. 1971–Aug. 1974)

Hon. Pres. Vladimir Fédorov, Département de la Musique, Bibliothèque Nationale, 2 rue Louvois, Paris 2e, France; *Pres.* John H. Davies, BBC, Yalding House, 152 Gt. Portland St., London W1, England; *V. Presidents.* Mercedes de Moura Reis Pequeno, rua Gustavo Sampaio 344, Rio de Janeiro, Brazil; Thor E. Wood, Res. L. of the Performing Arts, 111 Amsterdam Ave., New York, N.Y. 10023; *Secy.* Harald Heckmann, Deutsches Rundfunkarchiv, Bertramstrasse 8, D-6 Frankfurt/Main, W. Germany; *Treas.* Wolfgang Rehm, Heinrich-Schütz-Allee 29, 35, Kassel-Wilhelmshöhe, W. Germany.

(Note: Address general correspondence to Secy.)

COMMISSION CHAIRMEN

Cataloging Code. Kurt Dorfmüller, Musiksammlung, Bayerische Staatsbibliothek, 8 München 34, W. Germany.

International Repertory of Music Literature. Barry S. Brook, RILM Center, City Univ. of N.Y., 33 W. 42 St., New York, N.Y. 10036, U.S.A.

International Inventory of Musical Sources. Friedrich Blume, Postfach 182, 649 Schlüchtern, W. Germany

Libraries of Music Schools. Karol Musiol, Państwowa Wyzsza Szkola Muzyczna, ul. Stycznia 33, Katowice, Poland

Music Information Centers. André Jurres, Stichting Donemus, Jacob Obrecht Straat 51, Amsterdam, Netherlands

Music Libraries in Public Libraries. Alfons Ott, Staedtische Musikbibl., Salvatorplatz, Munich 2, W. Germany

Music Libraries in Radio Stations. John Howard Davies, British Broadcasting Corp., Yalding House, London W. 1, England

Dating of Music. François Lesure, Départ. de la Musique, Bibliothèque Nationale, 2 Rue de Louvois, Paris 2e, France

Sound Archives. Harold Spivacke, Music Div., L. of Congress, Washington, D.C. 20540, U.S.A.

University & Research Music Libraries. Mrs. Rita Benton, Music L., Iowa State Univ., Iowa City, Iowa 52240, U.S.A.

U. S. BRANCH

Acting Pres. & Delegate. Thor E. Wood, Research Library of the Performing Arts, 111 Amsterdam Ave., New York, N.Y. 10023; *Secy.-Treas.* Mrs. Harriet Nicewonger, Music L., Univ. of Calif., Berkeley, Calif. 94720.

PUBLICATION

Fontes Artis Musicae (3 per yr.; memb.)

INTERNATIONAL ASSOCIATION OF SOUND ARCHIVES

OBJECT

"To increase international cooperation, including the exchange of information, techniques, and materials, between institutions which collect sound recordings of all types, both musical and nonmusical."

MEMBERSHIP

Open to all interested in the problems of the preservation and service of recorded sound materials for research.

OFFICERS

Pres. Donald L. Leavitt, Head, Recorded Sound Section, L. of Congress, Music Div., Washington, D.C. 20540, U.S.A.; *V.P.s.* Patrick Saul, Dir., British Institute of Recorded Sound, 29 Exhibition Rd., London, S.W. 7, England; Claudie Marcel-Dubois, Musée National des Arts et Traditions Populaires, Route de Madrid 75, Paris XVI, France; *Secy.* R. L. Schuursma, Stichting Film en Wetenschap, Afdeling Documentatie, Hengeveldstraat 29, Utrecht, The Netherlands; *Treas.* Claes M. Cnattingius, Sveriges Radio, 105 10, Stockholm, Sweden.

(Note: Address correspondence to Secy.)

PUBLICATION

Phonographic Bulletin (irreg.; memb.)

INTERNATIONAL FEDERATION FOR DOCUMENTATION

OBJECTS

To group internationally organizations and individuals interested in the problems of documentation and to coordinate their efforts; to promote the study, organization, and practice of documentation in all its forms, and to contribute to the creation of an international network of information systems.

PROGRAM

The program of the Federation includes activities for which the following Study Committees have been established: Central Classification Committee (for UDC); Research on the Theoretical Basis of Information; Linguistics in Documentation; Information for Industry; Education Training and Classification Research; Theory of Machine Techniques and Systems; Operational Machine Techniques and Systems; Developing Countries. It also includes Working Groups on Business Archives and Data Documentation.

OFFICERS

Pres. R. E. McBurney, Tech. Info. Serv., Natl. Research Council of Canada, Sussex Dr., Ottawa K1A. OS3; *V. Presidents.* Prof. Dr. H. Arntz, Deutsches Komitee für Dokumentation, Burg Arntz, 534 Bad Honnef/Rhein, Germany; Prof. A. I. Mikhailov, Institut Naucnoj Informacii Akademii Nauk SSRR (VINITI), Bahijskala ul. 14, Moscow A-219, USSR; *Treas.* A. van der Laan, NIDER, The Hague, Netherlands; *Councillors.* Dr. J. E. Brown, Ottawa, Canada; R. A. Gietz, Buenos Aires, Argentina; Dr. R. A. Harte, Bethesda, Md., U.S.A.; L. Janszky, Budapest, Hungary; F. Liebesny, United Kingdom; Dr. R. Lopes de Sousa, Lisbon, Portugal; Dr. H. Ootuka, Tokyo, Japan; S. Parthasarathy, New Delhi, India; W.

Pirog, Warsaw, Poland; P. Poindron, Paris, France; Prof. C. Ribeiro Zaher, Rio de Janeiro, Brazil; K. Stenstadvold, Trondheim, Norway; *Belgian Member.* J. de Keersmaecker; *Ex-Officio Deputy Secy. Gen.* W. van der Brugghen, The Hague, Netherlands; *Pres. of FID/CLA.* Prof. C. Ribeiro Zaher, Rio de Janeiro, Brazil; *Pres. of FID/CAO.* Dr. S. Hamada, Tokyo, Japan.

PUBLICATIONS

FID News Bulletin (m.) with supplements on Document Reproduction (q.); *FID Yearbook* (a.); *Report of the Secretary General* (a); Universal Decimal Classification editions; manuals; directories.

AMERICAN MEMBERSHIP

National Academy of Sciences—National Research Council.

MEMBERSHIP

Approval by the FID Council; ratification by the FID General Assembly.

INTERNATIONAL FEDERATION OF FILM ARCHIVES

Secretariat, 74 Galerie Ravenstein, Brussels 1000, Belgium

OBJECT

"To facilitate communication and cooperation between its members, and to promote the exchange of films and information; to maintain a code of archive practice calculated to satisfy all national film industries, and to encourage industries to assist in the work of the Federation's members; to advise its members on all matters of interest to them, especially the preservation and study of films; to give every possible assistance and encouragement to new film archives and to those interested in creating them. Founded in Paris 1938. Members in 36 countries."

EXECUTIVE COMMITTEE

Pres. Jerzy Toeplitz, Poland; *V. Presidents.* John Kuiper, U.S.A.; Vladimir Pogacic, Yugoslavia; Victor Privato, USSR; *Secy.-General.* Jacques Ledoux, Belgium; *Deputy Secy. Gen.* Wolfgang Klaue, E. Germany; *Treas.* Peter Konlechner, Austria; *Deputy Treas.* John Stenklev, Norway.

MEMBERS

Raymond Borde, France; Dimitri Fernoaga, Romania; Françoise Jaubert, Canada. *Reserve Members:* Eileen Bowser, U.S.A.; Ernest Lindgren, Great Britain; Ib Monty, Denmark.

PUBLICATIONS

FIAF Constitution & Internal Rules
Film Preservation (report)
Books 1914 (Union catalogue of books & periodicals published before 1914)
Why Preserve Films (pamphlet)
Proposals for an Archive Building (booklet)

INTERNATIONAL FEDERATION OF LIBRARY ASSOCIATIONS (IFLA/FIAB)

OBJECT

"To promote cooperation in the field of librarianship and bibliography and particularly to carry out investigations and make propositions concerning the international relations between libraries, library associations, bibliographers, and other organized groups." Founded 1927.

OFFICERS

Pres. H. Liebaers, Dir., Royal L., Brussels, Belgium (1969–1972); *V. Presidents.* Mrs. M. I. Rudominó, Dir., State L. of For. Literature, Moscow, USSR (1970–1973); E. Allerslev Jensen, L. Inspectorate, Copenhagen, Denmark (1970–1973); J. Wieder, L., Technische Hochschule, Munich, W. Germany (1970–1973); R. Málek, Dir., Central L., Prague, Czech. (1969–1972); P. Havard Williams, Dir., L. Sch., Ottawa, Canada (1970–1973); R. Vosper, Univ. L., University of Calif. at Los Angeles; *Treas.* P. Kirkegaard, Danmarks Biblioteksskole, Copenhagen, Denmark; *Secy.* Miss M. Wijnstroom, Headquarters, Hufweg 7, The Hague, Netherlands

PUBLICATIONS

IFLA Annual
IFLA News/Nouvelles de la FIAB (q.)
IFLA Directory (a.)

AMERICAN MEMBERSHIP

American Association of Law Libraries; American Library Association; Medical Library Association; Special Libraries Association; Association of Research Libraries.

Associate Members: There are 55 libraries and related institutions that are associate members of IFLA in the U.S.A. (out of a total of 300).

INTERNATIONAL INSTITUTE FOR CHILDREN'S JUVENILE AND POPULAR LITERATURE
Fuhrmannsgasse 18a, 1080 Vienna, Austria

OBJECT

"To create an international centre of work and coordination; to take over the tasks of a documentations centre of juvenile literature; to mediate between the individual countries and circles dealing with children's books." Established April 7, 1965. Dues. $5.50 (with a subscription to *Bookbird*); $8 (with a subscription to *Bookbird* and *Jugend und Buch*).

OFFICERS

Pres. Dr. Josef Stummvoll; *V.P.* Dr. Rudolf Müller; *Dir.* Dr. Richard Bamberger; *V.-Dir.* Dr. Otwald Kropatsch.

(Note: address all inquires to Director.)

PROGRAM

Promotion of international research in field and collection and evaluation of results of such research; international bibliography of technical literature on juvenile reading; meetings and exhibitions; compilation and publication of recommendation lists; advisory service; concrete studies on juvenile literature; collaboration with publishers; reading research.

PUBLICATIONS

Bookbird (q.; memb. or $5)
Jugend und Buch (memb. or Austrian shilling 56 [approx. $2])
Schriften zur *Jugendlektüre* (series of books and brochures dealing with questions on juvenile literature and literary education in German)

INTERNATIONAL ORGANIZATION FOR STANDARDIZATION
ISO Central Secretariat
1, rue de Varembé, 1211 Geneva 20, Switzerland

OBJECT

To promote the development of standards in the world in order to facilitate the international exchange of goods and services and to develop mutual cooperation in the spheres of intellectual, scientific, technological, and economic activity.

OFFICERS

Pres. Dr. Francis L. LaQue, U.S.A.; *V.P.* Dr. R. Shayegan, Iran; *Secy.-General.* Mr. Olle Sturen, Sweden.

TECHNICAL WORK

The technical work of ISO is carried out by some 150 Technical Committees. These include:

TC 46 — Documentation. (Secretariat, Deutscher Normenausschuss DNA, 4-7, Burggrafenstrasse, 1 Berlin 30, Germany.) Scope: Standardization in the field of documentation, libraries and related information handling, including information systems and interchange networks as applied to documentation. Liaison shall be maintained with ISO/TC 37, TC 42, TC 95, TC 97, and TC 130 and with relevant documentation sections or committees of international organizations and professional groups.

TC 37 — Terminology (Principles & Coordination). (Secretariat, Osterreichisches Normungsinstitut, Leopoldgasse 4, A-1020 Vienna, Austria.) Scope: Standardization of methods of setting up and coordinating national and international standardized terminologies.

TC 97 — Computers & Information Processing. (Secretariat, American National Standards Institute ANSI, 1430 Broadway, New York, N.Y. 10018, U.S.A.) Scope: Standardization of the terminology, problem description, programming languages, communication/characteristics, input-output, and physical (nonelectrical) characteristics of computers and data processing devices, equipment, and systems.

PUBLICATIONS
ISO Catalogue of Recommendations (annual; 24 Sw. fr.)
ISO Memento (annual; 18 Sw. fr.)
ISO Bulletin (mo.)

INTERNATIONAL YOUTH LIBRARY
Kaulbachstrasse 11a, 8 Munich 22, Germany

OBJECT
To maintain and develop an international reference library and clearinghouse for children's literature both primary and secondary; to organize exhibitions of children's books in Munich, and for travel throughout the world; to maintain a lending library for children in 5 languages (English, French, German, Italian, Spanish), and to promote activities in this; to promote international cooperation and understanding by the development of exchange in this field among the various countries; to provide opportunity for study for leaders in the field from other countries by providing a three months' scholarship (8 per year) to work in the library for study and to develop their country's collection at the IYL. To cooperate closely with the subsection for children's libraries of IFLA and with UNESCO (IYL is an associated project). Founded 1949 by Mrs. Jella Lepman.

OFFICERS
Dir. Walter Scherf

Pres. of Library Board. Carl Mayer-Amery

PUBLICATIONS
Children's Prize Books: A Catalog from the International Youth Library Concerning 67 Prizes (the leading national children's book awards from various countries). Editor, Walter Scherf, Verlag Dokumentation, München-Pullach, Germany; R. R. Bowker, New York, N.Y.
Catalogs from the Internationale Jugendbibliothek (18 vols.) G. K. Hall & Co., Boston, Mass.; comprising 5 catalogs: alphabetical, by language, classified, title, illustrator.
Quarterly Program; announcement of activities (International Youth Library, Munich, Germany)
The Best of the Best: Picture, children's and youth books from 57 countries or languages. Ed. Walter Scherf, Verlag Dokumentation, München-Pullach, Germany; R. R. Bowker, New York, N.Y.

FOREIGN LIBRARY ASSOCIATIONS

Africa (Regional)
Association Internationale pour le Développement des Bibliothèques en Afrique, Boite Postale 375 Dakar, Sénégal
East African Library Assn., Box 5894, Kampala, Uganda

Argentina
Asociación Argentina de Bibliotecas y Centros de Informacion Cientificos y Tecnicos, Santa Fe, 1145, Buenos Aires
Asociación de Bibliotecarios de Cordoba, Antonio del Viso 571 (E) 337, Cordoba
Asociación de Bibliotecarios Graduados de la República Argentina, Avenida Corrientes 1723, Buenos Aires
Asociación de Bibliotecarios de Paraná, Buenos Aires 256, Paraná, Entre Ríos
Asociación de Bibliotecarios Profesionales, 9 de Julio 1247, Rosario
Asociación de Bibliotecarios de la Provincia de Tucumán, 9 de Julio 162, Tucumán

Asociación de Bibliotecarios de Santa Fé, San Jeronimo 2833, Santa Fe
Asociación de Ex-Alumnos de la Escuela, Nacional de Bibliotecarios, Mexico 564, Buenos Aires
Colegio de Bibliotecarios de la Provincia de Buenos Aires, Casilla de Correo 309, La Plata
Federación de Bibliotecas Populares de la Capital Federal y Alrededores, Australia 1835, Buenos Aires
Junta de Bibliotecas Universitarias Nacionales Argentinas, Biblioteca Central, Universidad Nacional de Tucumán, Casilla de Correo 167, San Miguel de Tucumán.

Australia

Association of Special Libraries & Information Services, Box 9A, GPO, Melbourne, C.I.
Library Assn. of Australia, 32 Belvoir St., Surry Hills, N.S.W. 2010
School Library Association of New South Wales, 72 Balaclava Rd., Eastwood, N.S.W., 2122
School Library Association of Victoria, 15 Spensley St., Clifton Hill, 3068

Austria

Verband Osterreichischer Volksbüchereien, Skodagasse 20, A1080 Wien
Vereinigung Osterreichischer Bibliothekare, Osterreichische Nationalbibliothek, Josefsplatz 1, A-1014 Wien

Belgium

Association des Archivistes et Bibliothécaires de Belgique, 4 boulevard de l'Empereur, 1000 Bruxelles
Association des Bibliothécaires Flamands, 39, rue Dagobert, Louvain
Association des Bibliothécaires et du Personnel des Bibliothèques des Ministères de Belgique, 22, rue des Petits Carmes, Bruxelles
Association Nationale des Bibliothécaires d'Expression Française, 56 rue de la Station, Havelange (Namur)
Conseil National des Bibliothèques d'Hôpitaux de la Croix-Rouge de Belgique, 98 CH de Vleurgat, Bruxelles 1050
Fédération Nationale des Bibliothèques Catholiques, (ASBL), 21, rue du Marais, Bruxelles 1

Union des Bibliothécaires Auxiliaires Sociaux, 49 rue des Atrébates, Brussels 4
Vlaamse Vereniging van Bibliotheeken Archiefpersoneel, Blindestraat 19, Antwerpen 1

Bolivia

Asociación de Bibliotecarios de Cochabamba "A.B.C.," Casilla 658, Cochabamba
Asociación de Bibliotecarios de La Paz, Edificio IBEAS, Av. Arce No. 2147, La Paz

Brazil

Federação Brasileira de Associações de Bibliotecários, Rua Avanhandava, 40, conj. 110, São Paulo
Associação Bahiana de Bibliotecários, Biblioteca Central do Estado da Bahia, Av. Gal. Labatut, s/n, Salvador, Bahia
Associação Baiana de Bibliotecários, Av. Sete de Setembro, 81, 2°, sala 95, São Paulo
Associação Bibliotecária do Paraná, Rua Cândido Lopes, Curitiba, Paraná
Associação Brasileira de Bibliotecários, Av. Rio Branco, 219, Biblioteca Nacional, Rio de Janeiro, Guanabara
Associação Brasileira de Documentação, Documentalistas e Técnicas de Informação, Rua Teodoro Sampaio 417, conj. 11, São Paulo, SP.
Associação Brasileira de Escolas de Biblioteconomia e Documentação, C.P. 1906, Belo Horizonte, MG.
Associação Campineira de Bibliotecários, Caixa Postal, 317, Campinas, Estado de São Paulo
Associação dos Bibliotecários de Minas Gerais, Caixa Postal, 1277, Belo Horizonte, Minas Gerais
Associaãço dos Bibliotecários do Ceará, Rua 24 de Maio, 893, Fortaleza, Ceará
Associação dos Bibliotecários do Distrito Federal, Caixa Postal, 15-2833, Brasília, Distrito Federal
Associação dos Bibliotecários Municipais de São Paulo, Biblioteca Infantil, Rua General Jardim, 485, São Paulo
Associação Paraense de Bibliotecários, Travessa Padre Eutíquio, 1370, Belém, Pará
Associação Paulista de Bibliotecários, Av. Ipiranga, 877, 9°, sala 93, São Paulo

Associação Profissional de Bibliotecários de Pernambuco, Rua do Hospício 299, sala 4, Recife, Pernambuco

Associação Riograndense de Bibliotecários, Caixa Postal, 2344, Pôrto Alegre, Rio Grande do Sul

Associação Sãocarlense de Bibliotecários, Caixa Postal, 378, São Carlos, Estado de São Paulo

Burma

Burma Library Assn., c/o International Institute of Advanced Buddhistic Studies, Kaba Aya, Rangoon

Jubilee Library Assn., Steel Rd., Toungoo

Canada

Association Canadienne des Bibliothécaires de Langue Française, 8515 Blvd. St. Laurent, Montréal 351, Que.

British Columbia Library Association, McPherson Library, University of Victoria, Victoria, B.C.

Canadian Library Assn., 151 Sparks St., Ottawa 4, Ontario

Medical Library Assn., Academy of Medicine, 288, Blott St. West, Toronto 5, Ontario

(See also "State, Regional, and Provincial Associations" and "National Association," this volume.)

Ceylon

Ceylon Library Assn., 490, Havelock Rd., Colombo 6

Chile

Asociación de Bibliotecarios Profesionales de Chile, Biblioteca Central de la Universidad de Chile, Casilla 10-d, Santiago

China (Formosa)

Library Assn. of China, c/o National Central Library, 43 Nan-hai Road, Taipei, Taiwan

Colombia

Asociación Colombiana de Bibliotecarios (ASCOLBI), Carrera 5 # 16-73, Oficina 405, Apartado Nacional 3654, Bogotá

Asociación Colombiana de Bibliotecarios Seccional de Caldas, c/o Corporación Financiera de Caldas, Manizales

Asociación Colombiana de Bibliotecarios Seccional del Valle, Departamento de Bibliotecas, Cali

Asociación de Bibliotecarios de Antioquía, Biblioteca Publica Piloto, Autopista Nortex, Avenida Columbia N° 50-5, Medellin

Asociación de Egresados de la Escuela Interamericana de Bibliotecologia (ASEIB), Apartado Aereo 1307, Medellin

Biblioteca Instituto Colombiano Agropecuario, Tibaitá, Cund., Apartado aéreo No. 7984, Nal. 3413, Bogotá D.E.

Costa Rica

Asociación Costarricense de Bibliotecarios, Apartado Postal 3308, San José

Asociación Interamericana de Bibliotecarios y Domentalistas Agrícolas, AIBDA, Instituto Interamericano de Ciencias Agrícolas, Turrialba

Cyprus, see Greece

Czechoslovakia

Sväz Ceskych Knihovniku, 190, Klementinum, Praha 1

Svaz slovenskych knihovnikov, bibliografov a informacnych pra covnikov, Klemensova ul. 27, Bratislava

Slovenska kniznicna rada, Suvorovova 16, Bratislava

Svaz ceskych knihovniku a informacnich pracovniku, Liliova 5, Praha 1

Denmark

Danmarks Biblioteksforening, Mosedalvej 11, 2500 Copenhagen Valby

Danmarks Videnskabelige og Faglige Bibliotekers Sammenslutning, c/o Rigsbibliotekarembedet, Christians Brygge 8, DK 1219 Copenhagen K

Ecuador

Asociación Ecuatoriana de Bibliotecarios, Apartado A 87, Quito

El Salvador

Asociación General de Archivistas de El Salvador, Apartado Postal N° 664, San Salvador

Asociación Salvadoreña de Bibliotecarios y Amigos de la Biblioteca, a/c Biblioteca Nacional, Calle Delgado y 8a, avenida Norte, San Salvador

Ethiopia
Ethiopian Library Assn., c/o University Library, P.O. Box 1176, Addis Ababa

Finland
Suomen Kirjastoseura (Finnish Library Association), Museokatu 18 A8, Helsinki 10

Suomen tieteellinen kirjastoseura (Finnish Research Library Assn.), c/o Library of the Finnish Meteorological Institute, Box 10503, Helsinki 10

France
Association des Archivistes Français, 60, rue des Francs-Bourgeois, Paris 3e

Association des Bibliothécaires Français 4, rue Louvois, Paris, 2e

Association des Documentalistes et Bibliothécaires Spécialisés (ADBS), B.P. 96, 75, Paris 5e

German Democratic Republic
Deutscher Bibliotheksverband, Luisenstrasse 57, 104 Berlin

German Federal Republic
Arbeitsgemeinschaft der Parlaments und Behordenbibliotheken, 45a Herrenstrasse, Karlsruhe, Bibliothek des Bundesgerichtshofs

Arbeitsgemeinschaft der Spezialbibliotheken e.V., c/o Adolf-von-Baeyer, Bibliothek, Postfach 11 90 75, 6 Frankfurt

Arbeitsgemeinschaft für das Archiv und Bibliothekswesen in der evangelischen Kirche, Sektion Bibliothekswesen, 2000, Grindelallee 7, Hamburg 13

Arbeitsgemeinschaft Katholisch-Theologischer Bibliotheken, D 5303 Bornheim-Walberberg, Albertus- Magnus-Akademie, Postfach 20

Arbeitsgemeinschaft kommunaler wissenschaftlicher Bibliotheken im Verein Deutscher Bibliothekare, Hansaplatz, Stadt und Landes-bibliothek, 46 00 Dortmund

Deutscher Buchereiverband e.V., Gitschinerstrasse 97/103, 1 Berlin 61

Deutsche Gosellschaft für Dokumentation e.V., Westendstrasse 19, 6 Frankfurt am Main 1

Verband der Bibliotheken des Landes Nordrhein-Westfalen, 463 Bochum-Querenburg, Universitatsbibliothek, Postfach 2148

Verein der Bibliothekare an Offentlichen Büchereien e.V., Roonstrasse 57, 28 Postfach 1288, Bremen 1

Verein der Diplom-Bibliothekare an wissenschaftlichen Bibliotheken e.V., Bayerische Staatsbibliothck, Ludingstr. 16, Abholtach, 8000 München 34

Verein Deutscher Bibliothekare e. V., Westring Olshausenstrasse, Universitatsbibliothek, 23 Kiel

Ghana
Ghana Library Association, P.O. Box 4105, Accra

Great Britain
Assn. of Assistant Librarians, County Branch Library, Church St., Mansfield Woodhouse, Mansfield, Notts.

Assn. of British Library Schools (ABLS), College of Librarianship, Aberystwyth, Cardiganshire, Wales

Association of Libraries of Judaica and Hebraica in Europe, c/o Librarian, Jews' College, 11 Montagu Place, Montagu Square, W. 1

Assn. of Special Libraries and Information Bureaus (ASLIB), 3 Belgrave Square, London, S.W. 1

The Library Assn., 7 Ridgmount Street, Store Street, London, W.C. 1

Library Assn., Brynmor Jones Library, The University, Hull

Private Libraries Assn., 41 Cuckoo Hill Rd., Pinner, Middlesex, England

School Library Assn., Premier House, 150 Southampton Row, London, W.C. 1

Scottish Library Assn., Department of Librarianship, University of Strathclyde, Livingstone Tower, Richmond St., Glasgow C.1

Standing Conference of National and University Libraries, The Library, University College, P.O. Box 78, Cardiff

Greece and Cyprus
Association des Bibliothécaires Grecs, Bibliothèque Nationale, Athens

Greek Library Assn. of Cyprus, Box 1039, Nicosia, Cyprus

Guatemala
Asociación Bibliotecológica Guatemalteca, Biblioteca Central, Universidad de San Carlos de Guatemala, Ciudad Universitaria, Zona 12

Honduras
Asociación de Bibliotecarios y Archiveros, c/o Dirección de Bibliotecas Públicas, Apartado Postal 982, Tegucigalpa

Hong Kong
Hong Kong Library Assn., c/o The Library, University of Hong Kong, Pokfulam

Hungary
Magyar Könyvtárosok Egyesülete (Assn. of the Hungarian Librarians), Szentkirályi ut 21, Budapest 8
Tajekoztatási Tudományos Társaság, Szabadság Ter 17, Budapest V

Iceland
Bókavardafélag Islands (Assn. of Icelandic Librarians), c/o The National Library, Reykjavík

India
Andhra Pradesh Library Assn., Sri Sarvottama Bhavanam, Patamata P.O. Vijayawada–6, Andhra Pradesh
Assam Library Assn., High Court Library of Assam and Nagaland, Gauhati
Bengal Library Assn., P-134, C.I.T. Scheml II, Calcutta 14
Bihar Library Assn., Sinha Library Rd., Patna–1, Bihar
Delhi Library Assn., c/o Hardinge Public Library, P.O. Box 1270, Queen's Garden, Delhi 6
Federation of Indian Library Associations, Misri Bazar, Patiala, Punjab
Haryana Library Assn., c/o State Central Library, Ambala Cantt
Hooghly District Library Assn., Prasad Das Sen Rd., P.O. Chinsura, Hooghly, West Bengal
Indian Assn. of Special Libraries and Information Centres, Albert Hall, 15, Bankim, Chatterjee St., Calcutta 12
Indian Assn. of Teachers of Library Science, Department of Library Science, Banaras Hindu University, Varanasi–5
Indian Library Assn., Delhi Public Library, S.P. Mukerji Marg, Delhi 6
Jammu and Kashmir Library Assn., S P Public Library, Srinagar, Kashmir
Kerala Granthalaya Sangham, c/o Kerala University Library, Trivandrum
Mysore Library Assn., c/o DRTC, 112 Cross Rd. 11, Malleswaram, Bangalore–3
Punjab Library Assn., 233 Model Town, Jullundur City–3
Rajasthan Library Assn., c/o Rajasthan University Library, Jaipur
U P Library Assn., c/o Amin-ud-Daulah Public Library, Kaiser Bagh, Lucknow (U P)
Vidarbha Granthalaya Sangh, c/o Rajaram Sitaram Dixit Library, Sitabuldi, Nagpur-1, Maharashtra State

Indonesia
Asosiasi Perpustakaan Arsip Dan Dokumentasi Indonesia (A.P.A.D.I.), Djl. Medan Merdeka Selatan 11 (Perpustakaan Sedjarah Politik dan Sosial), Djakarta
Himpunan Pustakawan Chusus Indonesia (Indonesia Special Library Assn.), Djl. Raden Saleh 43, Djakarta

Iran
Iranian Library Association, P.O. Box 11–1391, Tehran

Iraq
Iraq Library Assn., c/o Central Library, Univ. of Baghdad, P.O. Box 12, Baghdad

Ireland
Library Assn. of Ireland, 46 Grafton St., Dublin 2

Israel
Israel Library Assn., c/o Jewish National and University Library, Box 7067, Jerusalem
Israel Society of Special Libraries and Information Centers, P.O. Box 20125, Tel Aviv

Italy
Associazione Italiana Biblioteche, Piazza dei SS. Apostoli 49, c/o Soprintendenza bibliografica, Rome 00187

Jamaica
The Jamaica Library Assn., c/o 2 Tom Redcam Ave., Kingston 5

Japan
Japan Documentation Society (NIPDOK), Sasaki Bldg., 5–7 Koisikawa 2-Tyome, Bunkyo-ku, Tokyo
Japan Library Assn., 12-51 Ueno Park, Taito-ku, Tokyo

Nippon Igaku Tosyokan Kyôkai (Japan Medical Libraries Assn.), Central Office, Medical Library, University of Tokyo, Hongô, Tokyo

Nippon Kokumentêsyon Kyôkai, Kikai Shinkokaikan, 1–5 Siba-koen-21, Minato-ku, Tokyo

Nippon Nogaku Tosyokan Kyôgikai (Japan Assn. of Agricultural Librarians and Documentalists), c/o Library, Faculty of Agriculture, Tokyo University, Hongô 7, Bunkyô-ku, Tokyo

Nippon Yakugaku Tosyokan Dyogikai (Japan Pharmaceutical Libraries Assn.), c/o Library, Institute of Pharmaceutical Sciences, Tokyo University, Hongô 7, Bunkyô-ku, Tokyo

Senmon Tosyokan Kyogikai (Special Libraries Association), c/o National Diet Library, Nagata-cho 1-10-1, Chiyoda-ku, Tokyo

Korea

Korean Library Assn., Sokong-Dong 6, Chung-Ku, Seoul

Lebanon

Lebanese Library Assn., c/o National Library, Place de l'Etoile, Beirut

Liberia

Monrovia Library Assn., c/o USIS Library, Monrovia

Luxembourg

Bibliotheque nationale du Grand-Duche de Luxembourg, 9, rue Notre-Dame, Luxembourg-Ville

Malaysia

Library Assn. of Malaysia, c/o University of Malaya Library, Kuala Lumpur, P.O. Box 2072, Kuala Lumpur

Malta

Malta Library Assn., c/o Students' Union, 220 St. Paul St., Valetta

Mexico

Asociación de Bibliotecarios de Instituciones de Enseñanza Superior y de Investigación, Dirreccion de la Presidencia, Playa Tecolutla 512, Mexico 13, D.F.

Asociación Mexicana de Bibliotecarios, A.C., Apartado Postal 27–L32, Mexico 18, D.F.

Monaco

Bibliothèque de Monaco, Rue de la Poste

Nepal

Nepal Library Assn., Box 207, GPO, Asan Tok., Katmandu

Netherlands

Centrale Vereniging voor Openbare Bibliotheken, Bezuidenhoutseweg 239, The Hague

Nederlandse Vereniging van Bibliothecarissen, att.: Heer P. Verboom, Burg. Elsenlaan 136, Rijswijk, Z.H.

Rijkscommissie van Advies inzake het Bibliotheekwezen (State Advisory Committee on Library Affairs), Koninklijke Bibliotheek, Lange Voorhout 34, The Hague

Vereniging van Seminarie-en Kloosterbibliothecarissen (V.S.K.B.), (Assn. de Bibliothècaires de Seminaires et de Couvents), Biest 43, Weert, Limburg

New Zealand

New Zealand Library Assn., 10 Park Street, Wellington 1

Nicaragua

Asociación de Bibliotecas Universitarias y Especializadas de Nicaragua, c/o Escuela Nacional de Agricultura y Ganadería, Apartado 453, Managua, D.N.

Asociación Nicaraguense de Bibliotecarios, Apartado 101, Managua

Asociación Nicaraguense de Bibliotecarios, Biblioteca Central U.N.A.N., Leon

Nigeria

Eastern Nigeria School Libraries Assn., c/o British Council, Box 330, Enugu

Nigerian Library Assn., c/o Mrs. Dorothy S. Obi, Secretary, University of Nigeria, Enugu Campus Library, P.M.B. 1080, Enugu

Nigerian Library Assn., c/o Sam O. Oderinde (Hon. Secy.), Ibadan University Library, Ibadan

West African Library Assn., North Regional Library, Kaduna

Norway

Norsk Bibliotekarlag, Deichmanske Bibliotek, Henrik Ibsen St. 1, Oslo 1

Norsk Bibliotekforening, Maurstien 6, Oslo 8

Norske Forskningsbibliotekarers Forening, c/o Bjorg Löken, Secretary, Maurstien 6, Oslo 8

Pakistan
East Pakistan Library Assn., c/o Central Public Library, Shahbagh, Ramna, Dacca 2, East Pakistan
Karachi Library Assn., Ministry of Education, S.M. Law College Building, Karachi
Pakistan Assn. of Special Libraries, P.O.B. 534, Karachi 1
Pakistan Library Association, c/o Punjab University Library, University of the Punjab, Lahore
Pakistan Special Library Assn., Bengali Academy, Dacca 2
West Pakistan Library Assn., c/o Hailey College of Commerce, Lahore, West Pakistan

Panama
Asociación de Bibliotecarios Agrícolas Corresponsal, Apartado 3277, Panama 3
Asociación Panameña de Bibliotecarios, att.: Biblioteca, Universidad Nacional, Apartado 3277, Panama 3

Paraguay
Asociación de Bibliotecarios del Paraguay, c/o Sra. Mafalda Cabrera, Cerro Cora 402, San Lorenzo

Peru
Asociación Peruana de Bibliotecarios, Secretaría de Correspondencia, General La Fuente 592, Apartado 3760, Lima

Philippines
Assn. of Special Libraries of the Philippines, College of Public Administration, University of the Philippines, Padre Faura St., P.O. Box 474, Manila
Philippine Library Assn., c/o The National Library, Teodoro M. Kalaw St., Manila

Poland
Stowarzyszenie Bibliotekarzy Polskich, Ul. Konopczynskiego 5/7, Warsaw

Portugal
Inspeccao Superior das Bibliotecas e Arquivos de Portugal, Ministerio de Educacao Nacional, (Direccao-Geral do Ensino Superior e das Belas-Artes), Lisboa

Rhodesia
Rhodesia Library Assn., P.O. Box MP45, Mt. Pleasant, Salisbury

Romania
Asociatia Bibliotecarilor din Republica Socialistà România, Strada Ion Ghica 4, Sector 4, Bucuresti

Scandinavia
Nordiska Vetenskapliga Bibliotekarieforbundet Statsbiblioteket, DK-8000 Aarhus C, Denmark
The Scandinavian Assn. of Scientific Librarians, c/o Kst. overbibliotekar Karl V. Thomsen, Statsbiblioteket, DK-8000 Aarhus C, Denmark

Singapore
Persatuan Perpustakaan Singapura (Library Assn. of Singapore), c/o National Library, Stamford Rd., Singapore 6

South Africa (Republic of)
South African Library Assn., c/o Ferdinand Postma Library, Potchefstroom University, Potchefstroom

Spain
Asociación Nacional de Bibliotecarios, Archiveros y Arqueólogos, Paseo de Calvo Sotelo 22, Madrid 1

Sweden
De vetenskapliga bibliotekens tjänstemann-aförening, c/o 1:e bibliotekarie Marie-Louise Bachman, Kungl. biblioteket, Box 5039, 102 41 Stockholm 5
Svenska Bibliotekariesamfundet, University Library, Uppsala
Svenska Folkbibliotekarieförbundet c/o SACO:s kanslikartell, Nybrogatan 28, 114 39 Stockholm
Sveriges Allmänna Biblioteksförening (The Swedish Library Assn.), Bibliotekstjänst, Fack, S 221 01 Lund 1
Sveriges Vetenskapliga Specialbiblioteks Förening, Skogsbiblioteket, 104 05 Stockholm 50

Switzerland
Association des Bibliothécaires Suisses, Universitatsbibliothek, Schöbeinstrasse 20, 4056 Basel
Assn. Suisse des Bibliothèques d'Hopitaux, Eleonorenstr. 26, Zurich 32

Schweizerische Vereinigung für Dokumentation SVD, Postfach 2303, 3001 Bern

Vereinigung Schweizerischer Krankenhausbibliotheken, Neumarkt 4, 800 Zurich

Tanzania

Tanzania Library Assn., P.O. Box 2645, Dar-es-Salaam

Thailand

Thai Library Assn., 241 Prasumaeru Rd., Bangkok 2

Togo

Association Internationale pour le Développement de la Documentation, des Bibliothèques et des Archives en Afrique-Section Togolaise, B.P. 67, Lome (Togo), West Africa

Trinidad

Library Assn. of Trinidad & Tobago, 20 Queens Park East, Port of Spain

Tunisia

Association des Bibliothécaires Tunisiens, B.P. 88, Tunis

Association Tunisienne des Documentalistes, Bibliothécaires et Archivistes, B.P. 575, Tunis

Turkey

Turk Kutuphanceciler Dernegi (Turkish Librarians' Association), Posta Kutusu: 175, Yenisehir, Ankara

United Arab Republic

Alexandria Library Assn., Alexandria

The Egyptian Association for Archives & Librarianship, Strand Building, Apt. 201, Bab-El-Loug, P.O. Box 1309, Cairo

Egyptian School Library Assn., 35, Galaa St., Ramsis Square, Cairo

USSR

USSR Library Council, Main Library Inspectorate, Ministry of Culture of the USSR, 10 Kujbishev St., Moscow, Centre

Uruguay

Agrapación Bibliotecológica del Uruguay, Calle Cerro Largo 1666, Montevideo

Asociación de Bibliotecarios del Uruguay, Casilla de Correo 1415, Montevideo

Vatican

Vatican Library Assn., Bibliothèque Apostolique Vaticane, Cité du Vatican

Venezuela

Asociación Bibliotecaria Venezolana, Apartado 6283, Caracas

Viet-Nam

Viet-Nam Library Assn., 8, Le-Quy-Don, Saigon

Yugoslavia

Drustvo Bibliotekara Srbije, Knez Mihailova 56, Beograd

Drustvo Bibliotekara Crne Gore, Njegoseva 100, Cetinje

Drustvo Bibliotekarjev Slovenije Turjaska 1, Ljubljana

Drustvo Bibliotekara Bosne i Hercegovine, Obala 42, Sarajevo

Drustvo Bibliotekara Hrvatske, Marulicev trg 21, Zagreb

Savez Drustava Bibliotekara Jugoslavije, Lenjinov trg. 2/1, Zagreb

Society of Librarians of Macedonia, Narodna i univerzitetska biblioteka "Kliment Chridski," P.O. Box 566, Skopje

Zambia

Zambia Library Association, P.O. Box 802, Lusaka

FOREIGN ANTIQUARIAN, BOOKSELLERS, AND PUBLISHERS ASSOCIATIONS

This list of associations is keyed to areas of interest as follows: (1) Antiquarian; (2) Booksellers; (3) Publishers.

International Associations

European Association of International Booksellers, 11, rue Lavoisier, Paris 8, France

International Community of Booksellers Associations (2), A-1010 Wein 1, Grunangergasse 4, Austria

International League of Antiquarian Booksellers (1), c/o Fernand De Nobele, 35, rue Bonaparte, Paris 6e, France

International Publishers Association (3), Avenue Miremont 3, Geneva, Switzerland

Algeria

Syndicat des Libraires d'Algerie (2), 18 Avenue de la Marne, Algiers

Argentina

Cámara Argentina de Editores de Libros (3), Maipu 359, Buenos Aires

Cámara Argentina de Publicaciones, Florida 259, 2° piso, Oficina 224, Buenos Aires

Cámara Argentina del Libro (3), Paraguay 610, Buenos Aires

Federación Argentina de Librerías, Papelerías y Actividades Afines (3), Sarmiento 580, 3er. piso, Buenos Aires

Australia

Australian Book Publishers' Association (3), 163 Clarence Street, Sydney, N.S.W.

Australian Booksellers Association (2), Box 1386, GPO, Sydney, N.S.W.

Wholesale Booksellers Association of Australia (2), 55 York Street, Sydney, N.S.W.

Austria

Hauptverband der Graphischen Unternehmungen Osterreichs, Gruenangergasse 4, A-1010 Vienna 1

Hauptverband des Osterreichischen Buchhandels (1,2,3), Gruenangergasse 4, A-1010 Vienna 1

Verband der Antiquare Oesterreichs (1), Gruenangergasse 4, Vienna 1

Belgium

Cercle Belge de la Librairie (2), 111 Avenue du Parc, Brussels 1060

Syndicat Belge de la Librairie Ancienne et Moderne (1,2), 112 Rue de Trèves, Brussels

Syndicat de Editeurs Belges (3), 111 Avenue du Parc, Brussels 1060

Vereeniging ter Bevordering van Het Vlaamsche Boekwezen (Flemish Publishers & Booksellers Association) (2,3), Frankrijklei 93, Antwerp

Bolivia

Cámara Boliviana del Libro (2), Librería Selecciones, Casilla 972, La Paz

Brazil

Associação Brasileira de Livreiros Antiquarios (1), Rua Rosario 137, Rio de Janeiro

Associação Brasileira do Livro (2), Avenida 13 de Maio N-23, 16 andar, Rio de Janeiro

Cámara Brasileira do Livro (2,3), Avenida Ipiranga 1267-10 andar, São Paulo

Sindicato Nacional dos Editores de Livros (3), Avenue Rio Branco, 37-15 andar, Rio de Janeiro

Burma

Burmese Publishers' Union (3), 146 Bogyoke Market, Rangoon

Canada

Canadian Booksellers Association (2), Suite 31, 2 Bloor Street East, Toronto 285, Ontario

Canadian Book Publishers' Council (3), 45 Charles Street East, Suite 701, Toronto 285, Ontario

Member organizations at 45 Charles Street: The Book Publishers Association of Canada (3), Canadian Textbook Publishers' Institute (3)

Le Conseil Superieur du Livre (2,3), 3405 rue Saint-Denis, Montreal 130, Quebec

Member organizations at 3405, rue Saint-Denis, Montreal 130, Quebec: Association des Editeurs Canadiens (3) Société des Editeurs Canadiens de Manuels Scolaires (3), Société des Libraires Canadiens (2), Société des Libraires Grossistes Canadiens (2)

Ceylon
All Ceylon Publishers Association (3), 185 Olcott Mawatha, Colombo 11
Booksellers Association of Ceylon (2), P.O. Box 244, 100 Sir Chittampalam Gardiner Mawatha, Colombo 2

Chile
Cámara Chilena del Libro (2,3), Ahumada 312, 8° piso, Santiago

Columbia
Cámara Colombiana del Libro (2,3), Calle 15 No. 9-30, Oficinas 205-206, Apartado Aereo 8998, Bogotá

Czechoslokavia
Ministry of Culture Department for Publishing & Booktrade, Perstyn 1, Prague 1
Slovak Center for Publishing & Booktrade, nam. SNP 11, Bratislava

Denmark
Dansk Boghandleres Importorforening (2), Nørregade 6, 1165 Copenhagen K
Den Danske Antikvarboghandlerforening (1), Kron-Prinsens-Gade 3, 1114 Copenhagen
Den Danske Boghandlerforening (2), Boghandleres Hus, Siljangade 6, 2300 Copenhagen S
Den Danske Forlaeggerforening (3), Vesterbrogade 41B, 1620 Copenhagen V

Ecuador
Sociedad de Libreros del Ecuador (2), Calle Mejía 44, Quito

Finland
Kirja-ja Paperikauppojen Liitto (2), Kalevankatu 16, Helsinki 10
Suomen Antikvariaattiyhdistys (1), P. Makasiininkatu 6, Helsinki
Suomen Kustannusyhdistys (3), Kalevankatu 16, Helsinki 10

France
Cercle de la Librairie (2), 117 boulevard St.-Germain, Paris 6e
Comité Permanent des Expositions du Livre et des Arts Graphiques Français, 15 rue de Buci, Paris 6e
Fédération Française des Syndicats de Libraires (2), 117 boulevard St.-Germain, Paris 6e
Import & Export National French Booksellers Association (1,2,3), 117 boulevard St.-Germain, Paris 6e
Ligue Internationale de la Librairie Ancienne, Président F. De Nobele, 35, rue Bonaparte, Paris 6e
Syndicat de la Librairie Ancienne et Moderne (1,2), 117 boulevard St.-Germain, Paris 6e
Syndicat National des Editeurs (3), 117 boulevard St.-Germain, Paris 6e
Union Nationale des Editeurs—Exportateurs de Publications Françaises (3), 55 Avenue des Champs Elysées, Paris 8e

German Democratic Republic
Boersenverein der Deutschen Buchhaendler zu Leipzig (2,3), P.O. Box 146 Gerichtsweg 26, 701 Leipzig

German Federal Republic
Arbeitsgemeinschaft der Buchhandlungen e.V., Bleichstrasse 38a, D-6000 Frankfurt am Main
Arbeitsgemeinschaft von Jugendbuchverlegern in der Bundesrepublik Deutschland, Talavera 7-11, 8700 Wurzburg
Arbeitsgemeinschaft Wissenschaftlicher Sortimenter (Europaische Organisation) Geschaftsstelle, Gerhofstrasse 25, D-2000 Hamburg 36
Bayerischer Verleger & Buchhaendlerverband (2,3), Thierschstrasse 17, Munich 22
Borsenverein des Deutschen Buchhandels (2,3), Grosser Hirschgraben 17-21, Postfach 3914, D-6000 Frankfurt am Main 1
Bundesverband der Deutschen Versandbuchhaendler e.V. (2), Burchardstr. 14, 2 Hamburg 1
Gruppe Sozialistischer Verleger, Buchhaendler und Bibliothekare und ILA Internationale Literarische Arbeitsgemeinschaft, Odeonstrasse 12, Postfach 149, 3 Hannover
Hessicher Verleger und Buchhaendler Verband (2,3), Grosser Hirschgraben 17/19, 6 Frankfurt am Main

Landesverband der Buchhaendler und Verleger in Niedersachsen e.V. (2,3), Nordmannpassage 6, 3 Hannover

Landesverband der Verleger & Buchhaendler Bremen-Unterweser (2,3), Contrescarpe 17, Bremen

Norddeutscher Verleger & Buchhaendlerverband (2,3), Brahmsallee 24, Hamburg 13

Rheinisch-Westfaelischer Verleger und Buchhaendler-Verband e.V. (2,3), Marienstrasse 41, 4000 Dusseldorf

Verband der Schulbuchverlage (3), Zeppelinallee 33, 6000 Frankfurt am Main 1

Verband der Verlage & Buchhandlungen in Baden-Wuerttemberg (2,3), Leonhandsplatz 28, 7000 Stuttgart-1

Verband Deutscher Antiquare e.V., Poseldorfer Weg 1, 2 Hamburg 13

Verband Deutscher Bahnhofsbuchhaendler (2), Grosser Hirschgraben 15, 6000 Frankfurt am Main

Verband Deutscher Buch-, Zeitungs- & Zeitschriften-Grossisten (2), Theodor-Heuss-Ring 32, 5 Koln

Vereinigung des Katholischen Buchhandels e.V. (2), Mendelssohnstrasse 42, 6000 Frankfurt am Main

Vereinigung Evangelischer Buchhaendler (2), Silberburgstrasse 58, Postfach 721, Stuttgart-W

Ghana

Ghana Booksellers Association (2), P.O. Box 899, Accra

Great Britain

Antiquarian Booksellers' Association (1), 9 Stanton Road, London S.W. 20

Booksellers Association of Great Britain & Ireland (2), 152 Buckingham Palace Road, London S.W. 1

National Book League, 7 Albemarle Street, London W. 1

National Federation of Retail Newsagents (2), 2 Bridewell Place, London E.C. 4

Publishers Association (3), 19 Bedford Square, London W.C. 1

Union of Welsh Publishers & Booksellers (2,3), Gomerian Press, Llandysul, Cards., Wales

Greece

Sylogos Ekdoton & Vivliopolon Athinon (2,3), Stadiou 40, Athens

Hong Kong

Hong Kong Booksellers & Stationers Association (2), 48 Graham Street, Kowloon

Hong Kong Publishers & Distributors Association (3), National Building, 240-246 Nathan Road, Kowloon

Iceland

Booksellers Association of Iceland (2), Skólavordustíg 2, Reykjavik

Icelandic Publishers' Association (3), Laugavegi 8, Reykjavik

India

Antiquarian Booksellers' Association of India (1), 115a Tarak Pramanick Road, Calcutta 6

Bombay Booksellers & Publishers Association (2,3), c/o India Book House, Rusi Mansion, 2nd floor, 29, Wode House Road, Bombay-1

Booksellers & Publishers Association of South India (2,3), c/o Higginbothams Pvt. Ltd., Mount Road, Madras 2

Delhi State Booksellers Association (2), c/o Atma Ram & Sons, Kashmere Gate, Delhi-6

Federation of Publishers' & Booksellers' Associations in India (2,3), 7-L Connaught Circus, New Delhi-1

Publishers Association of India (3), 14-18 Calicut Street, Ballard Estate, Bombay 1

Punjab Publishers Association (3), c/o O.P. Ghai, University Publishers, Jullundur City

Indonesia

Gabungan Importir Buku Indonesia (GIBI) (2), c/o Penerbit Swada, Djalan Nusantara 1/1, Djakarta

Ikatan Penerbit Indonesia Pusat (Indonesian Publishers Association) (3), Djalan Pengarengan 32, Djakarta

Ireland

Book Association of Ireland (2,3), 21 Shaw Street, Dublin

Booksellers Association of Great Britain & Ireland (2), 3 Home Lee, Ballsbridge, Dublin 4

Irish Publishers' Association (3), 179 Pearse Street, Dublin 2

Israel

Book Publishers' Association of Israel (3), P.O. Box 1317, 29 Carlebach Street, Tel Aviv

Israel Book & Printing Center, P.O. Box 29732, 47 Nahlat Benjamin Street, Tel Aviv

Italy

A.I.E., Associazione Italiana Editori (3), Foro Buonoparte, 24, 20120 Milano

Associazione Librai Italiani (2), Piazza G. G. Belli 2, 00153 Rome

Circolo dei Librai Antiquari (1), Via Accademia Albertina, N. 3 bis, 10123 Turin

Unione Editori Cattolici Italiani (3), Via Domenico Silveri 9, 00165 Rome

Jamaica

Booksellers Association of Jamaica (2), c/o Sangster's Book Store, 97 Harbour Street, Kingston, Jamaica W.I.

Collins & Sangsters Publishers Limited Publishers (3), Barclays Bank Building, 54 King Street, Kingston, Jamaica W.I.

Sangster's Book Stores Limited (2), 97 Harbour Street, Kingston, Jamaica W.I.

Japan

Books-on-Japan-in-English Club, (2, 3), 2-1 Sa-rugaku-cho 1-chome, Chiyoda-ku, Tokyo

Japan Book Importers Association (2), Room 302, Aizawa Building, 15-5 Nihonbashi Edobashi, 1-chome, Chuo-ku, Tokyo

Japan Book Publishers Association, 6 Fukuro-machi, Shinjuku-ku, Tokyo

The Research Institute for Publications, The Japan Magazine, Book Publishers and Editors Association, 53, Higashigoken-cho, Shinjuku-ku, Tokyo, 162

Textbook Publishers Association of Japan (Kyokasho Kyokai) (3), 4-13 Iida-bashi 4-chome, Chiyoda-ku, Tokyo

Korea

Korean Publishers Association (3), 3-1 Doyum-Dong, Chongno-ku, Seoul

Luxembourg

Fédération des Commerçants Groupe Papetiers-Libraires (2), 5, rue Jean-Origer, Luxembourg

Mexico

Cámara Nacional de la Industria Editorial (3), Vallarta 21, Mexico City 4

Centro Impulsor de la Industria y del Comercio del Libro Mexicano A. C. (3), c/o Sr. Francisco Trillas, Avenida 5 de Mayo 43, Desp. 105, Mexico City 1

Istituto Mexicano del Libro (3), Paseo de la Reforma 95, Desp. 202, Mexico City 4

Morocco

Syndicat des Libraires de Maroc (2), 10, Avenue Dar el Maghzen, Rabat

Netherlands

Koninklijke Nederlandsche Uitgeversbond (3), Herengracht 209, Amsterdam C

Nederlands Vereeninging van Antiquaren (1), 5 Delilaan, Hilversum 1304

Nederlandse Boekverkopersbond (2), Waalsdorperweg 119, The Hague

Vereeniging ter bevordering van de belangen des Boekhandels (2,3), Jan Tooropstraat 109, Amsterdam W

New Zealand

Auckland Booksellers Association (2), 13 Commerce Street, Auckland 1

Booksellers Association of New Zealand, Inc. (2), P.O. Box 1102, Wellington

British Publishers' Representatives Association in New Zealand (3), c/o J. R. Haines, P.O. Box 3437, Auckland 1

New Zealand Book Publishers' Association (3), P.O. Box 11005, Wellington

New Zealand Book Trade Organization, Inc., P.O. Box 1102, Wellington

Nigeria

Nigerian Publishers Association (3), Secretariat, c/o Thomas Nelson & Sons Limited, 12 Ibikunle Avenue, Bodija, Ibadan

Norway
Den Norske Bokhandlerforening (2), Øvre Vollgate 15, Oslo 1
Den Norske Forleggerforening (3), Øvre Vollgate 15, Oslo 1
Norsk Antikvarbokhandlerforening (1), Oygardveien 16C, 1340 Bekkestua
Norsk Bokhandler-Medhjelper-Forening (2), Arbeidersamfunnets Plass 1, Oslo 1

Pakistan (East)
Pakistan Publishers & Booksellers Association (2,3), 3/12 Liaquat Avenue, 3rd Floor, Victoria Park (South), Dacca 1

Paraguay
Cámara Paraguaya del Libro (2), Librería Internacional, Estrella 380, Asunción

Peru
Cámara Peruana del Libro (3), Minera 196, Oficina 422, Apartado 3744, Lima

Philippines
Philippine Book Dealers' Association (2), 1633 C. M. Recto Avenue, Manila

Poland
Polskie Towarzystwo Wydawców Ksiazek (3), Mazowiecka 2/4, Warsaw 1
Stowarzyszenie Ksiegarzy Polskich (2), Mokotowska 4/6, Warsaw

Portugal
Gremio Nacional dos Editores e Livreiros (2,3), Largo de Andaluz 16, 1° Lisbon 1

Rhodesia
Booksellers Association of Rhodesia (2), Chamber of Mines Building, 47 Gordon Avenue, Salisbury
Publishers Association of Central Africa (3), P.O. Box 396, Salisbury

Romania
Central Office of the Romanian Publishing Houses and Book Distribution, 5-7 Str. Biserica Amzei, Bucharest

South Africa (Republic of)
Associated Booksellers of South Africa (2), 1 Meerendal, Nightingale Way, Pinelands, Cape Province
Overseas Publishers Representatives Association (3), P.O. Box 8879, Johannesburg
South African Publishers' Association (3), P.O. Box 122, Parow

Spain
Gremio Sindical de Editores, Luisa Fernanda 16, Madrid 8
Gremio Sindical de Editores (3), Mallorca 274, Barcelona 9
Gremio Sindical de Libreros (2), Luisa Fernanda 16, Madrid 8
Gremio Sindical de Libreros (2), Mallorca 272-276, Barcelona 9
Istituto Nacional del Libro Español (3), Ferraz 11, Madrid 8 *and* Mallorca 274, Barcelona 9

Sweden
Svenska Antikvariatforeningen (1), c/o Thulins Antikvariat, Tysta Gatan 6, Box 27174, 102 52 Stockholm 27
Svenska Bokfoerlaeggareforeningen (3), Kungsholmstorg 13 A, 112 21 Stockholm
Svenska Bokhandlareforeningen (2), Skeppargatan 27, 114 52 Stockholm
Svenska Boktrycharefoereningen, Blasieholmstorg 4, 111 48 Stockholm

Switzerland
Schweizerischer Buchhändler-und-Verleger-Verein (2,3), Bellerivestrasse 3, 8008 Zurich
Société des Libraires et Editeurs de la Suisse Romande (2,3), 2 avenue Agassiz, 1000 Lausanne
Vereininqung der Buchantiquare der Schweiz (1), c/o Mme. Eugene Reymond, 14 Faubourg de l'Hôpital, 2000 Neuchâtel

Tunisia
Syndicat des Libraires de Tunisie (2), 10, avenue de France, Tunis

Turkey
Editörler Birligi (3), Ankara Caddesi 93, Istanbul

Uruguay
Asociación de Libreros del Uruguay (2), Avenida Uruguay 1325, Montevideo
Cámara Uruguaya del Libro (2,3), Calle Ibicuy 1276, Piso 1, Oficina 4, Montevideo

Venezuela

Cámara Venezolana del Libro, Edificio "Cine San Bernardino," Oficina 10, Avenida Andrés Bello, Caracas

Vietnam

Syndicat des Libraires (2), 185, rue Catinat, Saigon

Yugoslavia

Association of Yugoslav Publishers & Booksellers (2,3), Kneza Milosa Str. 25/I, P.O. Box 883, Belgrade

Zambia

Booksellers Association of Zambia (2), P.O. Box 139, Ndola

Appendix A

ACTIVITIES INDEX TO LIBRARY ASSOCIATIONS

This index lists by interest or activity the various committees, boards, sections, and specialized associations, with the names of the respective chairmen or other heads. It does not include the "housekeeping" committees, such as Budget, Committees, Conference, Constitution, Elections, Membership, Nominating, etc.; nor does it include committees which would fall under the same heading as the parent organization, e.g., Resources Committee of the ALA Resources and Technical Services Division. This index is compiled from the "National Associations" and "International Associations" sections, located in Part 3 and Part 4, respectively, this volume.

Accreditation

ALA Accreditation Comm. F. William Summers, Grad. L. S., Univ. of South Carolina, Columbia, S.C. 29208.

Assn. of American Library Schools. Accreditation Comm. Harold Goldstein, Dean & Prof., L. S., Florida State Univ., Tallahassee, Fla. 32306.

Assn. of College & Research Libraries. Standards & Accreditations Comm. H. William Axford, Univ. Libn., Arizona State Univ., Tempe, Ariz. 85281.

Canadian Library Assn. Accreditation Subcomm. Katharine Ball, 60 Highland Lane, Richmond Hill, Ont.

Acquisition

ALA Resources & Technical Services Div. Acquisitions Section. Norman H. Dudley, Univ. Research L., Univ. of California, Los Angeles, Calif. 90024.

Assn. of Research Libraries. Foreign Acquisitions Comm. Philip McNiff.

Federal Library Comm. Acquisition of Library Materials & Correlation of Federal Library Resources Task Force. Mrs. Elsa S. Freeman, Dir. of the L., Dept. of Housing & Urban Devel.

Society of American Archivists. Collecting of Personal Papers & Manuscripts Comm. John E. Wickman, Dwight D. Eisenhower L., Abilene, Kans. 67410.

Administration

ALA Library Administration Div. Advisory Comm. for Review of Local Public Library Administration (ad hoc). Gary E. Strong, Dir., Lake Oswego P.L., Lake Oswego, Ore. 97034.

ALA Library Administration Div. Library Organization & Management Section. Henry G. Shearhouse, Jr., Libn., Denver P.L., Denver, Colo. 80203.

ALA Library Administration Div. Lester L. Stoffel, Exec. Dir., Suburban L. Syst., Hinsdale, Ill. 60521.

Assn. of Research Libraries. ARL-ACE University Library Management, Study Joint Comm. Warren Haas.

Canadian Library Assn. Administrators of Large Public Libraries Comm. Morton P. Jordan, Dir., Vancouver P.L., 750 Burrard St., Vancouver, B.C.

515

Adult Services

ALA Adult Services Div. John A. McCrossan, Bureau of L. Devel., Pennsylvania State L., Harrisburg, Pa. 17126.
Canadian Library Assn. Adult Servs. Section. Brian Dale, Kitchener P.L., 85 Queen St. N., Kitchener, Ont.

Agricultural Libraries

Inter-American Assn. of Agricultural Librarians & Documentalists. María Dolores Malugani, Instituto Interamericano de Ciencias Agrícolas (IICA), Turrialba, Costa Rica.
International Assn. of Agricultural Librarians & Documentalists. H. E. Thrupp, Tropical Products Institute, 56/62 Gray's Inn Rd., London, England.

Architecture

ALA Library Administration Div. Buildings & Equipment Section. John H. Rebenack, Libn., Akron P.L., Akron, Ohio 44308.
Music Library Assn. Buildings & Equipment Comm. Mary Wallace, Music L., Wellesley Coll., Wellesley, Mass. 02181.
Society of American Archivists. Buildings & Technical Services Comm. Frank B. Evans, 3102 Belair Dr., Bowie, Md. 20715.

Archives

American Assn. of School Librarians. Archives Comm. Rev. Edward T. LaMorte, Tolentine Coll., P.O. Box 747, Olympia Fields, Ill. 60411.
ALA Adult Services Div. Archives Comm. Robert Baumruk, P.L., Chicago, Ill. 60602.
ALA Reference Services Div. Archives Comm. Elizabeth Jane Highfield, North Park Coll. L., Chicago, Ill. 60625.
American Theological Library Assn. Archives Comm. Gerald W. Gillette, Presbyterian Historical Society, 425 Lombard St., Philadelphia, Pa. 19147.
Assn. of American Library Schools. Archives Comm. Howard Winger, Prof., Grad. L. S., Univ. of Chicago, Chicago, Ill. 60637.
Assn. of Hospital & Institution Libraries. Archives Comm. M. Jean Paige, Chief Libn., V.A. Hospital, Iowa City, Iowa 52240.
International Assn. of Music Libraries. Sound Archives. Harold Spivacke, Music Div., L. of Congress, Washington, D.C. 20540.
International Assn. of Sound Archives. Donald L. Leavitt, Head, Recorded Sound Section, Music Div., L. of Congress, Washington, D.C. 20540.
International Federation of Film Archives. Jacques Ledoux, Secy.-General, 74 Galerie Ravenstein, Brussels 1000, Belgium.
Society of American Archivists. Charles E. Lee, South Carolina Dept. of Archives & History, 1430 Senate St., Columbia, S.C. 29201.
Society of American Archivists. Archives of Science Comm. Murphy D. Smith, American Philosophical Society, 105 S. Fifth St., Philadelphia, Pa. 19106.
Society of American Archivists. Data Archives & Machine-readable Records Comm. Meyer H. Fishbein, National Archives & Records Serv., Rm. 2W, Washington, D.C. 20408.
Society of American Archivists. International Archival Affairs Comm. Wilfred I. Smith, Public Archives of Canada, Ottawa 2, Ont., Canada.
Society of American Archivists. Techniques for the Control & Description of Archives & Manuscripts. Frank G. Burke, National Archives & Records Serv., Washington, D.C. 20408.
Society of American Archivists. Urban & Industrial Archives Comm. Dennis East, 5802 Harvard, Detroit, Mich. 48224.

Audiovisual Materials

ALA Audiovisual Comm. Richard L. Ducote, Coll. of DuPage, Glen Ellyn, Ill. 60137.
ALA Children's Services Div. Audiovisual–ALA Subcomm. Mrs. Marilyn Berg Iarusso, Asst. Storytelling & Group Work Specialist, N.Y.P.L., 8 E. 40 St., New York, N.Y. 10016.
American Assn. of Law Libraries. Audiovisual Comm. Patrick E. Kehoe.
Assn. of College & Research Libraries. Audiovisual Comm. Herman L. Totten,

Apt. 1, 175 Malabu Dr., Lexington, Ky. 40504.

Assn. of Hospital & Institution Libraries. Audiovisual Advisory Comm. Mrs. Theda A. Kellner, Coordinator, L. Servs. to Institutions & the Handicapped, Colorado State L., 1362 Lincoln St., Denver, Colo. 80203.

Music Library Assn. Phonorecord Analytics Comm. Olga Buth, Music L., Ohio State Univ., Columbus, Ohio 43210.

Public Library Assn. Audiovisual Comm. Mrs. B. Penny Northern, Film Dept., P.L., Kansas City, Mo. 64106.

Society of American Archivists. Audiovisual Records Comm. John B. Kuiper, 6305 Stoneham Rd., Bethesda, Md. 20034.

Automation

American Assn. of Law Libraries. Automation & Scientific Development Comm. David Badertscher.

ALA Information Science & Automation Div. Dr. Jesse H. Shera, S. of L. Sci., Case Western Reserve Univ., Cleveland, Ohio 44106.

ALA Information Science & Automation Div. Character Set Escape Sequence Code Comm. Paul Fasana, Preparations Servs., N.Y.P.L., New York, N.Y. 10019.

ALA Information Science & Automation Div. Telecommunications Comm. Brigitte L. Kenney, Asst. Prof., Grad. S. of L. Sci., Drexel Univ., Philadelphia, Pa. 19104.

Federal Library Committee. Automation of Library Operations Task Force. Mrs. Madeline Henderson, Computer Systs. Analyst, Center for Computer Sciences & Technology, National Bureau of Standards.

Music Library Assn. Automation Comm. Carol Bradley, Music Dept., State Univ. of New York, Buffalo, N.Y. 14214.

Awards

American Assn. of Law Libraries. Joseph Andrews Bibliographic Award Comm. Kate Wallach.

American Assn. of School Librarians. Distinguished Library Service Award for School Administrators Comm. Dr. Ruth W. White, Dept. of L. Educ., Coll. of Educ., Univ. of Georgia, Athens, Ga. 30601.

American Assn. of School Librarians. Encyclopaedia Britannica School Library Award Comm. D. Philip Baker, Dir. of Ls., Darien Board of Educ., P.O. Box 1167, Darien, Conn. 06820.

ALA Awards Comm. Robert F. Delzell, Univ. of Illinois L., Urbana, Ill. 61801.

ALA Children's Services Div. Arbuthnot Honor Lecture Comm. Mrs. Diane Chrisman, Coordinator, Work with Children, Buffalo & Erie County P.L., Lafayette Sq., Buffalo, N.Y. 14203.

ALA Children's Services Div. Charles Scribner's Sons Award 1972 Comm. (ad hoc). Florence Burmeister, Head, Young People & Children's Dept., Skokie P.L., Skokie, Ill. 60076.

ALA Children's Services Div. Film Award Proposal Comm. (ad hoc). Anne Pellowski, Dir., Information Center on Children's Cultures, U.S. Comm. for UNICEF, 331 E. 38 St., New York, N.Y. 10016.

ALA Children's Services Div. Mildred L. Batchelder Award Selection 1972 Comm. Rosemary Weber, Asst. Prof., Grad. S. of L. Sci., Drexel Univ., 33rd & Lancaster Aves., Philadelphia, Pa. 19104.

ALA Children's Services Div. Mildred L. Batchelder Award Selection 1973 Comm. Mrs. Clara Hulton, P.O. Box 461, Anthony, Fla. 32617.

ALA Children's Services Div. Newbery-Caldecott Awards Comm. Anne R. Izard, Children's Servs. Consultant, Westchester L. Syst., 295 Central Ave., White Plains, N.Y. 10606.

ALA Library Education Div. Beta Phi Mu Awards Comm. Mrs. Clara O. Jackson, S. of L. Sci., Kent State Univ., Kent, Ohio 44240.

ALA Library Education Div. Scholarship & Awards Comm. Martin Cohen, S. of Libnshp., Western Michigan Univ., Kalamazoo, Mich. 49001.

ALA Reference Services Div. Isadore Gilbert Mudge Citation. Walter Allen,

Grad. S. of L. Sci., Univ. of Illinois, Urbana, Ill. 61801.

ALA Resources & Technical Services Div. Piercy Award Jury. Mrs. Roma S. Gregory, Univ. of Rochester, Rochester, N.Y. 14627.

American Library Trustee Assn. Jury on Citation of Trustees Comm. Eloise Ebert, State Libn., Oregon State L., Salem, Ore. 97310.

American Society of Indexers. Honors Comm. Jane Stevens, H. W. Wilson Co., 950 University Ave., Bronx, N.Y. 10452.

Assn. of Hospital & Institution Libraries. Award Comm. Adelia P. Mustain, 3603 29th St., San Diego, Calif. 92104.

Catholic Library Assn. Regina Medal Comm. Catherine J. Butler, 221 Kennedy Ave., Munhall, Pa. 15120.

Church & Synagogue Library Assn. Awards Comm. Ruth Winters.

Library Public Relations Council. Awards Comm. Edward Montana, Jr., Asst. to the Regional Administrator, Boston P.L., Copley Sq., Boston, Mass. 02117.

Medical Library Assn. Honors & Awards Comm. Dr. Frank B. Rogers, Univ. of Colorado Medical Center, Charles Denison Memorial L., 4200 E. Ninth Ave., Denver, Colo. 80220.

Medical Library Assn. Ida & George Eliot Prize Essay Subcomm. Nancy M. Lorenzi, Univ. of Louisville, Health Sciences L., 520 S. Preston St., Louisville, Ky. 40202.

Medical Library Assn. Janet Doe Lecture Subcomm. Dr. Frank B. Rogers, Univ. of Colorado Medical Center, Charles Denison Memorial L., 4200 E. Ninth Ave., Denver, Colo. 80220.

Medical Library Assn. Murray Gottlieb Essay Subcomm. Dr. Peter D. Olch, Deputy Chief, History of Medicine Div., National L. of Medicine, 8600 Rockville Pike, Bethesda, Md. 20014.

Medical Library Assn. Rittenhouse Award, Subcomm. on. Alice C. Joyce, School of Medicine L., Washington Univ., 4580 Scott Ave., St. Louis, Mo. 63110.

SLA Professional Award & SLA Hall of Fame Comm. Robert W. Gibson, Jr., General Motors Corp., Research Laboratories L., 12 Mile & Mound Rds., Warren, Mich. 48090.

Theatre Library Assn. George Freedley Award Comm. Robert H. Ball, Dept. of English, Queens Coll., Flushing, N.Y. 11367.

Bibliography

ALA Reference Services Div. Bibliography Comm. Roger C. Greer, S. of L. Sci., Syracuse Univ., Syracuse, N.Y. 13210.

Assn. of College & Research Libraries. Bibliographic Instruction Comm. (ad hoc). Thomas G. Kirk, Box E-72, Earlham Coll., Richmond, Ind. 47374.

Assn. of Research Libraries. Slavic Bibliographic & Documentation Center Project Comm. Marion Milczewski.

Bibliographical Society of America. Robert H. Taylor, 511 Lake Dr., Princeton, N.J. 08540.

Inter-American Bibliographical & Library Assn. A. Curtis Wilgus, P.O. Box 583, N. Miami Beach, Fla. 33160.

Medical Library Assn. Bibliographical Projects & Problems Comm. Joan Staats, The Jackson Laboratory, Research L., Bar Harbor, Me. 05609.

Blind

ALA Library Service to the Blind Round Table. Alfred D. Hagle, 2608 Ridge Rd. Dr., Alexandria, Va. 22303.

Book and Instructional Materials Selection

American Assn. of School Librarians. Instructional Media Comm. Evelyn Geller, Ed., *School Library Journal*, R. R. Bowker Co., 1180 Avenue of the Americas, New York, N.Y. 10036.

American Assn. of School Librarians. Treatment of Minority Groups in Library Books & Other Instructional Materials. David Cohen, Libn., Plainview-Old Bethpage H.S., Plainview, N.Y. 11803.

ALA Adult Services Div. Adult Library Materials Comm. Mrs. Peggy Glover, Free L. of Philadelphia, Logan Sq., Philadelphia, Pa. 19103.

ALA Adult Services Div. Materials for American Indians Subcomm. Mrs. June S. Smith, Coll. of St. Catherine, St. Paul, Minn. 55116.

ALA Adult Services Div. Materials for the Spanish-speaking Subcomm. Mrs. Victoria Wallace, P.L., Northport, N.Y. 11768.

ALA Adult Services Div. Notable Books Council Comm. Raymond Agler, P.L., Boston, Mass. 02117.

ALA Children's Services Div. Acquisition of Foreign Children's Books Comm. (ad hoc). Anne Izard, Children's Servs. Consultant, Westchester L. Syst., 285 Central Ave., White Plains, N.Y. 10606.

ALA Children's Services Div. Book Evaluation Comm. Mrs. Barbara Rollock, Children's Specialist, Bronx Borough Office, N.Y.P.L., 2555 Marion Ave., Bronx, N.Y. 10458.

ALA Children's Services Div. Magazine Evaluation Comm. Mrs. Bertha P. Phillips, Coordinator of Children's Servs., Atlanta P.L., 126 Carnegie Way N.W., Atlanta, Ga. 30303.

ALA Children's Services Div. Selection of Foreign Children's Books Comm. Angeline Moscatt, Supervising Libn., Donnell Regional L. Center, 20 W. 53 St., New York, N.Y. 10019.

ALA Reference Services Div. New Reference Tools Comm. Hobart Berolzheimer, Free L. of Philadelphia, Logan Sq., Philadelphia, Pa. 19103.

ALA Reference Services Div. Reference Books for Small- & Medium-sized Public Libraries Review Comm. (ad hoc). Charles Andrews, Case Western Reserve Univ. L., Cleveland, Ohio 44106.

ALA Young Adult Services Div. Best Books for Young Adults Comm. Eileen E. Burgess, Asst. Coordinator, Young Adult Servs., Prince George's County Memorial L., 6532 Adelphi Rd., Hyattsville, Md. 20782.

ALA Young Adult Services Div. Magazine Evaluation Comm. Raymond W. Barber, Coordinator, Educational Media, Asst. Prof., Kent State Univ., Kent, Ohio 44242.

ALA Young Adult Services Div. Selection of Books & Other Materials Comm. Mrs. Elizabeth Morse O'Donnell, Young Adult Specialist, Contra Costa County L., 1750 Oak Park Blvd., Pleasant Hill, Calif. 94523.

Canadian Library Assn. Ephemeral Materials Comm. (ad hoc). Leonard J. Gottselig, Glenbow Alberta Institute, 902 11 Ave. S.W., Calgary, Alta.

Public Library Assn. Starter List of New Branch Library Comm. Nolan Lushington, Greenwich L., Greenwich, Conn. 06830.

Book and Library Weeks

American Assn. of School Librarians. National Library Week Comm. James L. Smith, Coordinator of L. Servs., Instructional Materials Center, Monongalia County Ss., 300 McLane Ave., Morgantown, W. Va. 26505.

ALA National Library Week Comm. Walter Curley, P.L., Cleveland, Ohio 41144.

Book Fair

Catholic Library Assn. Book Fair Comm. Sister Martinez Holloran, R.S.M., St. Bernard H.S., Bernard Ave. at 24 St., Nashville, Tenn. 37212.

Business Libraries

ALA Reference Services Div. Business Reference Servs. James B. Woy, Free L. of Philadelphia, Philadelphia, Pa. 19107.

Cataloging and Classification

American Assn. of Law Libraries. Cataloging & Classification Comm. Nancy F. Miller.

ALA Information Science & Automation Div. MARC Users Discussion Group. Frederick G. Kilgour, Dir. OCLC, 1314 Kinnear Rd., Columbus, Ohio 43212.

ALA Reference Services Div. Catalog Use Comm. Concetta Sacco, P.L., West Haven, Conn. 06516.

ALA Resources & Technical Services Div. Books Catalogs Comm. Joseph A. Rosenthal, Assoc. Libn., General L. 248, Univ. of California, Berkeley, Calif. 94720.

ALA Resources & Technical Services Div. Cataloging & Classification Section. Barbara A. Gates, Oberlin Coll. L., Oberlin, Ohio 44074.

American Theological Library Assn. Cataloging & Classification Comm. Mrs.

Margaret Whitelock, Princeton Theological Seminary, Princeton, N.J. 08540.
Assn. of Research Libraries. Shared Cataloging Comm. David Kaser.
International Association of Music Libraries. Cataloging Code Comm. Kurt Dorfmüller, Musiksammlung, Bayerische Staatsbibliothek, 8 München 34, W. Germany.
Music Library Assn. Cataloging & Classification Comm. Donald Seibert, Music L., Syracuse Univ., Syracuse, N.Y. 13210.

Catholic Libraries

Catholic Library Assn. Rev. Joseph P. Browne, C.S.C., Univ. of Portland, Portland, Ore. 97203.

Census

Federal Library Committee. Census Work Group. Dorothy W. Kaufman, Libn., Bureau of the Census.

Centennial 1976

ALA Centennial 1976 Action Comm. Frank B. Sessa, Grad. S. of L. & Info. Sci., Univ. of Pittsburgh, Pittsburgh, Pa. 15213.

Certification

American Assn. of Law Libraries Certification Board. Lawrence L. Kiefer.
Medical Library Assn. Certification Comm. Robert T. Lentz, Jefferson Medical Coll. L., 1025 Walnut St., Philadelphia, Pa. 19107.
Medical Library Assn. Comm. to Develop a New Certification Code (ad hoc). Mrs. Martha Jane Zachert, L. S., Florida State Univ., Tallahassee, Fla. 32306.

Children's Libraries

ALA Children's Services Div. Sara I. Fenwick, Assoc. Prof., Grad. L. S., Univ. of Chicago, Chicago, Ill. 60637.
Canadian Library Assn. Canadian Assn. of Children's Librarians Section. Mrs. Margaret Vatcher, Head, Children's Servs., Vancouver P.L., Vancouver, B.C.
Catholic Library Assn. Children's Libraries Section. Sister M. Julanne Good, O.P., 1354 Tamm Ave., St. Louis, Mo. 63139.

International Youth Library. Walter Scherf, Kaulbachstrasse 11a, 8 Munich 22, W. Germany.
Public Library Assn. Service to Children Comm. Spencer Shaw, S. of Libnshp., Univ. of Washington, Seattle, Wash. 98105.

Church and Synagogue Libraries

Assn. of Jewish Libraries. Synagogue, School & Center Libraries Div. Mrs. Rose Miskin, Beth Tzedec Sisterhood L., 1700 Bathurst St., Toronto 10, Ont., Canada.
Catholic Library Assn. Parish Community Libraries Section. Miriam F. Cummings, 5344 Penn Ave. S., Minneapolis, Minn. 55419.
Church and Synagogue Library Assn. Mrs. Wilma Jensen, Lutheran Church L. Assn., 122 W. Franklin Ave., Minneapolis, Minn. 55404.
Lutheran Church Library Assn. Rose Mary Ulland, Dir. of Christian Education, First Lutheran Church, 1005 Oxford Ave., Eau Claire, Wis. 54701.

Circulation

ALA Library Administration Div. Circulation Services Section. Edward B. Hayward, Acting Dir., Hammond P.L., Hammond, Ind. 46320.

College and University Libraries

Assn. of College & Research Libraries. Joseph H. Reason, 1242 Girard St. N.E., Washington, D.C. 20017.
Assn. of Research Libraries. Negro Academic Libraries Comm. Frank Grisham.
Canadian Library Assn. Canadian Assn. of College & University Libraries. Rev. Daniel Croteau, Université de Sherbrooke, Sherbrooke, P.Q.
Catholic Library Assn. College & University Libraries Section. Eugene P. Kennedy, New York Univ. L., 10 Washington Pl., Rm. 403, New York, N.Y. 10003.
International Assn. of Music Libraries. University & Research Libraries Comm. Mrs. Rita Benton, Music L., Iowa State Univ., Iowa City, Iowa 52240.

Copyright

Assn. of Research Libraries. Copyright Comm. Verner Clapp.

Canadian Library Assn. Copyright Comm. Allen H. Soroka, Law L., Univ. of British Columbia, Vancouver 8, B.C.

Dissertations

Assn. of Research Libraries. Microfilming Comm. Gustave Harrer.

Documentation

Assn. of Research Libraries. Slavic Bibliographic & Documentation Center Project Comm. Marion Milczewski.

International Federation for Documentation. R. E. McBurney, Tech. Info. Serv., Natl. Research Council of Canada, Sussex Dr., Ottawa K1A 053, Canada.

International Institute for Children's Juvenile & Popular Literature. Dr. Richard Bamberger, Fuhrmannsgasse 18a, 1080 Vienna, Austria.

International Organization for Standardization. Technical Comm.–46. Secretariat, Deutscher Normenausschuss DNA, 4-7, Burggrafenstrasse, 1 Berlin 30, Germany.

Editorial

American Assn. of Law Libraries. Directories Comm. Lorraine A. Kulpa, Margaret S. Andrews.

American Assn. of Law Libraries. *Law Library Journal.* Jack S. Ellenberger.

American Assn. of School Librarians. Elementary-Kindergarten-Nursery Education Service Bulletin Revision Comm. Marian Capozzi, 6802 Dunhill Rd., Baltimore, Md. 21222.

American Assn. of School Librarians. *School Libraries* Editorial Comm. Mrs. Mary Frances K. Johnson, Assoc. Prof., S. of Educ., Univ. of North Carolina at Greensboro, N.C. 27412.

ALA Editorial Comm. Donald E. Wright, P.L., Evanston, Ill. 60201.

ALA Children's Services Div. National Planning of Special Collections Comm. Marian C. Young, P.L., 5201 Woodward Ave., Detroit, Mich. 48202.

ALA Information Science & Automation Div. Editorial Bd. A. J. Goldwyn, Prof., S. of L. Sci., Case Western Reserve Univ., Cleveland, Ohio 44106.

ALA Reference Services Div. *Library Journal* List of Reference Books Comm. Gary R. Purcell, Univ. of Tennessee, Grad. S. of L. & Info. Scis., Knoxville, Tenn. 37916.

American Library Trustee Assn. Publications Comm. Douglas V. Downey, 2236 Maple Ave., Northbrook, Ill. 60062.

American Society of Indexers. American Contributions to *The Indexer* Comm. Prof. Jessica L. Harris, S. of L. Serv., Columbia Univ., New York, N.Y. 10027.

Assn. of American Library Schools. Directory Comm. Dorothy E. Cole, Assoc. Prof., S. of L. Sci., State Univ. of New York at Albany, N.Y. 12203.

Assn. of American Library Schools. Editorial Board of the *Journal of Education for Librarianship.* Norman Horrocks, Asst. Dir., S. of L. Serv., Dalhousie Univ., Halifax, N.S., Canada.

Assn. of American Library Schools. *Newsletter* Comm. Nasser Sharify, Dean, L. S., Pratt Institute, Brooklyn, N.Y. 11205.

Assn. of College & Research Libraries. Advisory Comm. for the Publication of a Book Catalog for Core Collections. Philip J. McNiff, Dir., Boston P.L., Copley Sq., Boston, Mass. 02117.

Canadian Library Assn. Canadian Books in Print Comm. Betty Hardie, Chief Libn., Etobicoke P.L., Box 501, Etobicoke, Ont.

Catholic Library Assn. *Catholic Library World* Editorial Comm. Sister Chrysantha Rudnik, C.S.S.F., Felician Coll. L., 3800 Peterson Ave., Chicago, Ill. 60645.

Catholic Library Assn. Catholic Periodical and Literature Index Comm. Arnold M. Rzepecki, Sacred Heart Seminary, 2701 W. Chicago Blvd., Detroit, Mich. 48206.

Medical Library Assn. Editorial Comm. on the *Handbook of Medical Library Practice.* Stanley D. Truelson, Jr., Yale Medical L., 333 Cedar St., New Haven, Conn. 06510.

Medical Library Assn. Editorial Comm. on Supplements to *Medical Reference Works, 1679–1966.* Mrs. Edith D. Blair, Reference Section, National L. of Medicine, 8600 Rockville Pike, Bethesda, Md. 20014.

Medical Library Assn. Editorial Comm. *Vital Notes.* William K. Beatty, Editor, Archibald Church Medical L., Northwestern Univ., 303 E. Chicago Ave., Chicago, Ill. 60611.

Public Library Assn. Editorial Comm. Marvin M. Scilken, P.L., Orange, N.J. 07050.

Education for Librarianship

American Assn. of Law Libraries. Education Comm. Iris J. Wildman.

ALA Instruction in the Use of Libraries Comm. Mrs. Jean A. Coleman, L. Servs., Hammond P. Ss., Hammond, Ind. 46320.

ALA Office for Library Education Comm. Wesley Simonton, L. S., Univ. of Minnesota, Minneapolis, Minn. 55455.

ALA Information Science & Automation Div. LED/ISAD Interdivisional Comm. on Education for Library Automation & Information Science. Mrs. Pauline Atherton, Assoc. Prof., S. of L. Sci., Syracuse Univ., Syracuse, N.Y. 13210.

ALA Library Education Div. Genevieve M. Casey, Dept. of L. Sci., Wayne State Univ., Detroit, Mich. 48202.

ALA Library Education Div. Discussion Group for Librarians of Library Science Collections. Mrs. Doris H. Asher, S. of L. Sci., Univ. of Michigan, Ann Arbor, Mich. 48104.

ALA Library Education Div. Education for Library Associates Comm. Dorothy E. Ryan, Grad. S. of L. & Info. Sci., Univ. of Tennessee, Knoxville, Tenn. 37915.

ALA Library Education Div. Financial Assistance for Library Education Revision Comm. Cosette Kies, Ferguson L., Stamford, Conn. 06901.

ALA Library Education Div. International Library School Comm. Guy A. Marco, S. of L. Sci., Kent State Univ., Kent, Ohio 44240.

ALA Library Education Div. LED/AHIL Interdivisional Comm. of Education for Hospital & Institutional Librarianship. Harris C. McClaskey, L. S., Univ. of Minnesota, Minneapolis, Minn. 55455.

ALA Library Education Div. Training Programs for Supportive Library Staff. Dorothy F. Deininger, Grad. S. of L. Sci., Rutgers Univ., New Brunswick, N.J. 08903.

American Society for Information Science. Education Comm. Victor Rosenberg, Univ. of California, Berkeley, Calif.

Assn. of American Library Schools. Margaret E. Monroe, Prof., L. S., Univ. of Wisconsin, Madison, Wis. 53706.

Assn. of American Library Schools. Role of AALS in Continuing Education Comm. Elizabeth Stone, Assoc. Prof., Dept. of L. Sci., Catholic Univ. of America, Washington, D.C. 20017.

Assn. of College & Research Libraries. Bibliographic Instruction Comm. (ad hoc). Thomas G. Kirk, Box E-72, Earlham Coll., Richmond, Ind. 47374.

Assn. of Research Libraries. Training for Research Librarianship. David Kaser.

Canadian Library Assn. Education for Library Manpower Comm. Dr. Olga B. Bishop, S. of L. Sci., Univ. of Toronto, 140 St. George St., Toronto 181, Ont.

Canadian Library Assn. Training of Library Technicians Subcomm. John Marshall, S. of L. Sci., Univ. of Toronto, 140 St. George St., Toronto 181, Ont.

Catholic Library Assn. Library Education Section. Dr. Jo Ann McCreedy, Our Lady of the Lake Coll., San Antonio, Tex. 78207.

Federal Library Committee. Library Education Task Force. Dr. Russell Shank, Dir. of Ls., Smithsonian Institution, Washington, D.C. 20560.

Medical Library Assn. Continuing Education Comm. Raymond A. Palmer, Francis A. Countway L. of Medicine, 10 Shattuck St., Boston, Mass. 02115.

Medical Library Assn. Curriculum Comm. Mrs. Beatrice F. Davis, L. of Coll. of Physicians of Philadelphia, 19 S. 22 St., Philadelphia, Pa. 19103.

Medical Library Assn. Medical Library Technician Training Comm. Richard A. Miller, Virginia Commonwealth Univ., Tompkins-McCaw L., Box 667, Richmond, Va. 23219.

Music Library Assn. Continuing Education Comm. Lenore Coral, Univ. of California, Irvine, Calif. 92664.

Music Library Assn. Professional Training Comm. Donald W. Krummel, S. of L. Sci., Univ. of Illinois, Urbana, Ill. 61801.

Society of American Archivists. Education & Training Comm. David C. Duniway, State Archivist, Oregon State L., Salem, Ore. 97310.

SLA Education Comm. Harold R. Malinowsky, 2214 Hillcourt, Lawrence, Kans. 66044.

Equipment

ALA Library Administration Div. Buildings & Equipment Section. John H. Rebenack, Libn., Akron P.L., Akron, Ohio 44308.

ALA Library Technology Program. Russell Shank, Smithsonian Institution L., Washington, D.C. 20560.

Federal Library Committee. Physical Facilities of Federal Libraries Task Force. Henry J. Gartland, Dir. of L. Serv., 11A3, Veterans Admin.

Music Library Assn. Buildings & Equipment Comm. Mary Wallace, Music L., Wellesley Coll., Wellesley, Mass. 02181.

Exchanges

American Assn. of Law Libraries. Exchange of Duplicates Comm. Laura M. Pershing; Joseph Ciesielski.

American Theological Library Assn. Periodical Exchange Comm. Wilson N. Flemister, Chmn., Interdenominational Theological Center, 671 Beckwith St. S.W., Atlanta, Ga. 30314.

Medical Library Assn. Exchange Comm. Minnie Orfanos, Dental S. L., Northwestern Univ., 311 E. Chicago Ave., Chicago, Ill. 60611.

Exhibits

ALA Exhibits Round Table. John E. Wall, Demco Educ. Corp., P.O. Box 1488, Madison, Wis. 53701.

Federal Libraries

Federal Library Committee. Frank Kurt Cylke, Exec. Secy., L. of Congress, Washington, D.C. 20540.

Federal Relations

Assn. of Research Libraries. Federal Relations Comm. Robert Vosper.

Society of American Archivists. Federal & State Governmental Relations Comm. Robert Williams, 401 E. Gaines St., Tallahassee, Fla. 32301.

SLA Government Information Services Comm. Mrs. Ruth Smith, Institute for Defense Analyses, 400 Army Navy Dr., Arlington, Va.

SLA Governmental Relations Project Comm. Mrs. Mary A. Huffer, Smithsonian Institution Ls., Washington, D.C. 20560.

Foreign Law

American Assn. of Law Libraries. Foreign & International Law Comm. Adolf Sprudzs; Igor I. Kavass.

American Assn. of Law Libraries. Foreign Law Indexing Comm. William D. Murphy; Frank Lukes.

Foreign Librarians

ALA Education Div. Equivalencies & Reciprocity Comm. Norman Horrocks, S. of L. Serv., Dalhousie Univ., Halifax, N.S., Canada.

Foundation Grants

American Assn. of School Librarians. Grolier, Inc., Grant Comm. Mrs. Jean E. Wichers, Assoc. Prof., Dept. of Libnshp., San Jose State Coll., San Jose, Calif. 95114.

American Library Trustee Assn. Endowment Fund Comm. W. M. Usher, 837 Highland, Salina, Kans. 67401.

American Theological Library Assn. Financial Assistance from Foundations Comm. Raymond P. Morris, Yale Divinity S. L., 409 Prospect St., New Haven, Conn. 06510.

Canadian Library Assn. Grants-in-Aid Comm. Stanley Beacock, Midwestern Regional L. Syst., 637 Victoria St. N., Kitchener, Ont.

Medical Library Assn. Education Grant Comm. (ad hoc). Robert T.

Lentz, Jefferson Medical Coll. L., 1025 Walnut St., Philadelphia, Pa. 19107.

Historical Libraries

ALA Reference Services Div. History Section. Robert L. Adelsperger, Univ. of Illinois, Chicago Circle, Chicago, Ill. 60680.

Society of American Archivists. Oral History Comm. John F. Stewart, John F. Kennedy L., 380 Trapelo Rd., Waltham, Mass. 02154.

Hospital and Institution Libraries

ALA Library Education Div. LED/AHIL Interdivisional Comm. on Education for Hospital & Institutional Librarianship. Harris C. McClaskey, L. S., Univ. of Minnesota, Minneapolis, Minn. 55455.

Assn. of Hospital & Institution Libraries. Earl C. Graham, 2023 W. Ogden Ave., Chicago, Ill. 60612.

Indexing

American Assn. of Law Libraries. Foreign Law Indexing Comm. William D. Murphy; Frank Lukes.

American Assn. of Law Libraries. Index to Legal Periodicals Comm. Jane L. Hammond.

ALA Reference Services Div. Wilson Indexes Comm. Ruth Grotheer, Nassau L. Syst., Garden City, N.Y. 11530.

American Society of Indexers. John Fall, Public Affairs Information Serv., 11 W. 40 St., New York, N.Y. 10018.

American Theological Library Assn. Periodical Indexing Bd. Calvin H. Schmitt, Chmn., McCormick Theological Seminary, 800 W. Belden Ave., Chicago, Ill. 60614.

Information Science

ALA Information Science & Automation Div. Dr. Jesse H. Shera, S. of L. Sci., Case Western Reserve Univ., Cleveland, Ohio 44106.

ALA Reference Services Div. Information Retrieval Comm. John M. Morgan, Univ. of Toledo L., Toledo, Ohio 43606.

American Society for Information Science. Robert J. Kyle, Emory Univ., Atlanta, Ga. 30322.

Canadian Library Assn. Information Servs. Section. Mrs. Lorraine Garry, Asst. to the Head of Science & Medicine Dept., Univ. of Toronto L., Toronto 181, Ont.

Federal Library Committee. Role of Libraries in Information Systems Task Force. Herbert H. Fockler, Senior Program Officer, Office of Voluntary Action.

Intellectual Freedom

ALA Intellectual Freedom Comm. Richard L. Darling, Grad. S. of L. Serv., Columbia Univ., New York, N.Y. 10027.

ALA Staff Committee of Mediation, Arbitration, & Inquiry. David H. Clift, ALA Headquarters, 50 E. Huron St., Chicago, Ill. 60611.

American Library Trustee Assn. Intellectual Freedom Comm. Mrs. Florence McMullin, 14302 23 St., Seattle, Wash. 98166.

Canadian Library Assn. Intellectual Freedom Comm. Martha Shepard, Head, Reference Div., National L. of Canada, 395 Wellington St., Ottawa, Ont.

Interlibrary Cooperation

ALA Reference Services Div. Cooperative Reference Servs. Comm. George Bailey, Claremont Coll. L., Claremont, Calif. 91711.

Public Library Assn. Interlibrary Cooperation Comm. Gilbert McNamee, P.L., San Francisco, Calif. 94102.

Interlibrary Loans

ALA Reference Services Div. Interlibrary Loan Comm. Sarah K. Thomson, Bergen Community Coll., Paramus, N.J. 07652.

Assn. of Research Libraries. Interlibrary Loan Study Project Comm. Arthur McAnally.

Federal Library Committee. Interlibrary Loan Arrangements for Federal Libraries Task Force. Dr. Elizabeth L. Tate, Chief, L. Div., National Bureau of Standards.

International Libraries

Assn. of International Libraries. Mr. J. Leymarie, Ministère du Développement Industriel et Scientifique, 101, rue de Grenelle, F-75 Paris 7e, France.

International Assn. of Metropolitan City Libraries. H. C. Campbell, Toronto P.L., 40 St. Clair Ave. E., Toronto 290, Ont., Canada.

International Federation of Library Assns. H. Liebaers, Dir., Royal L., Brussels 1000, Belgium.

International Relations

American Assn. of School Librarians. International Relations Comm. Phyllis Hochstettler, S. of Educ., Portland State Coll., Portland, Ore. 97201.

ALA Children's Services Div. International Relations–ALA Subcomm. Mrs. Della Thomas, 217 N. Stallard, Stillwater, Okla. 74074.

ALA Library Education Div. International Library School Comm. Guy A. Marco, S. of L. Sci., Kent State Univ., Kent, Ohio 44240.

ALA International Relations Comm. Emerson Greenaway, 97 E. Bell's Mill Rd., Philadelphia, Pa. 19118.

ALA International Relations Round Table. Frank M. McGowan, L. of Congress, Washington, D.C. 20540.

ALA Resources & Technical Services Div. International Relations Comm. George M. Jenks, Ellen Clarke Bertrand L., Bucknell Univ., Lewisburg, Pa. 17837.

Medical Library Assn. International Cooperation Comm. Carroll F. Reynolds, Univ. of Pittsburgh, Falk L. of the Health Professions, DeSota & Terrace Sts., Pittsburgh, Pa. 15213.

SLA International Relations Comm. Mrs. Herta D. Fischer, California State Coll. at Fullerton L., Fullerton, Calif. 92631.

Internships

Assn. of College & Research Libraries. Internship Comm. Mrs. Virginia Lacy Jones, Dean, S. of L. Serv., Atlanta Univ., Atlanta, Ga. 30314.

Medical Library Assn. Internships Comm. Mrs. Nancy E. Zinn, History of the Health Sciences L., Univ. of Calif., San Francisco, Calif. 94122.

Jewish Libraries

Assn. of Jewish Libraries. Dr. Nathan M. Kaganoff, American Jewish Historical Society, 2 Thornton Rd., Waltham, Mass. 02154.

Junior College Libraries

Assn. of College & Research Libraries. Junior College Libraries Section. Hal C. Stone, Coordinator, L. & Learning Resources Center, Los Angeles City Coll., 855 N. Vermont Ave., Los Angeles, Calif. 90029.

Junior Members

ALA Junior Members Round Table. Mrs. Shirley Olofson, Capitol Bldg., Frankfort, Ky. 40601.

Law Libraries

American Assn. of Law Libraries. Mrs. Viola A. Bird, Univ. of Washington Law L., 205 Condon Hall DO-10, Seattle, Wash. 98105.

American Assn. of Law Libraries. Conference of Newer Law Librarians. Anita K. Head; Mildred Mason.

American Assn. of Law Libraries. Private Law Libraries Comm. Beatrice McDermott.

International Association of Law Libraries. Dr. H. G. Leser, Institut für Rechtsvergleichung, Savignyhaus-Universitatsstr. 6, D-355 Marburg, W. Germany.

Legislation

American Assn. of Law Libraries. Legislation & Legal Developments Comm. John Harrison Boyles.

American Assn. of School Librarians. Legislation Comm. Mrs. Mary B. Boyvey, Media Program Dir., Texas Educ. Agency, Austin, Tex. 78711.

American Assn. of State Librarians. Legislation Liaison Comm. James G. Igoe, State L., Montpelier, Vt. 05602.

ALA Legislation Comm. Joseph F. Shubert, State L. of Ohio, Columbus, Ohio 43215.

ALA Resources & Technical Services Div. Legislation Comm. Mrs. Elizabeth G. Ellis, W106 Pattee L., Pennsylvania State Univ., University Park, Pa. 16802.

American Library Trustee Assn. Legislative Comm. John S. Robling, Encyclopaedia Britannica, 425 N. Michigan Ave., Chicago, Ill. 60611.

Assn. of American Library Schools. Legislation Comm. Guy Garrison, Dean, Grad. S. of L. Sci., Drexel Univ., Philadelphia, Pa. 19104.

Assn. of College & Research Libraries. Legislation Comm. Philip J. McNiff, Dir., Boston P.L., Copley Sq., Boston, Mass. 02117.

Canadian Library Assn. Legislation Comm. Steven A. Horn, Carleton Univ. L., Colonel By Dr., Ottawa, Ont.

Catholic Library Assn. Legislative Comm. Mary K. Feldman, Trinity Coll. L., Washington, D.C. 20017.

Medical Library Assn. Legislation Comm. Mrs. Jacqueline W. Felter, Medical L. Center of New York, 17 E. 102 St., New York, N.Y. 10029.

Public Library Assn. Legislation Comm. Arthur Curley, P.L., Montclair, N.J. 07042.

Library History

ALA American Library History Round Table. N. Orwin Rush, Strozier L., Florida State Univ., Tallahassee, Fla. 32306.

Library Services

ALA Adult Services Div. AFL/CIO-ALA/ASD Library Service to Labor Groups Joint Comm. Mrs. Pearl Frankenfield, Montgomery County-Norristown P.L., Norristown, Pa. 19401.

ALA Children's Services Div. Library Service to the Disadvantaged Child. Mrs. Brooke E. Sheldon, Head, P.L. Devel., New Mexico State L., Box 1629, Santa Fe, N. Mex. 87501.

ALA Children's Services Div. Library Service to Exceptional Children Comm. Harris C. McClaskey, Asst. Prof. of L. Sci., L. S., Coll. of Liberal Arts, Univ. of Minnesota, 3 Walter L., Minneapolis, Minn. 55455.

ALA Children's Services Div. Patterns in Library Service to Children Comm. (ad hoc). Jane Botham, Children's Servs. Consultant, Div. of L. Devel., New York State L., 99 Washington Ave., Albany, N.Y. 12210.

ALA Reference Services Div. Users Needs Comm. (ad hoc). Thomas W. Shaughnessy, Grad. S. of L. Sci., Rutgers Univ., New Brunswick, N.J. 08900.

American Library Trustee Assn. Library Service to the Unserved. Dr. Irving Lieberman, S. of Libnshp., 133 Library, Univ. of Washington, Seattle, Wash. 98105.

Lutheran Church Library Assn. Library Services Bd. Mrs. Forrest Carpenter, 6211 Logan Ave. S., Minneapolis, Minn. 55423.

Public Library Assn. Costs of Public Library Servs. Christopher B. Devan, Cuyahoga County P.L., Cleveland, Ohio 44144.

Public Library Assn. Metropolitan Area Library Serv. Comm. Alex Ladenson, P.L., Chicago, Ill. 60602.

Public Library Assn. Public Library Activities. Hank J. Blasick, State L., Supreme Court Bldg., Tallahassee, Fla. 32304.

Library Surveys

Assn. of College & Research Libraries. Library Surveys Comm. Stephen Ford, Libn., Grand Valley State Coll., Allendale, Mich. 49401.

Medical Library Assn. Surveys & Statistics Comm. Mrs. Susan Crawford, Archive-L. Dept., American Medical Assn., 535 N. Dearborn St., Chicago, Ill. 60610.

Manuscripts

Assn. of Research Libraries. Copying Manuscripts & Unpublished Materials Comm. James Henderson.

Maps

Federal Library Committee. Map Work Group. David K. Carrington, Coordinator MARC Map Project, Geography & Map Div., L. of Congress.

Medical Libraries

Medical Library Assn. Mrs. Bernice M. Hetzner, Coll. of Medicine L., Univ. of Nebraska, 42 St. & Dewey Ave., Omaha, Nebr. 68105.

Moving Pictures

Educational Film Library Assn. Abraham Cohen, White Plains Bd. of Educ., White Plains, N.Y. 10605.

Music Libraries

International Association of Music Libraries. John H. Davies, BBC, Yalding House, 152 Gt. Portland St., London W1, England.

International Assn. of Music Libraries. International Repertory of Music Literature Comm. Barry S. Brook, RILM Center, City Univ. of N.Y., 33 W. 42 St., New York, N.Y. 10036.

Music Library Assn. William McClellan, Music L., Univ. of Illinois, Urbana, Ill. 61801.

Newspapers

Assn. of Research Libraries. Foreign Newspaper Microfilm Project Comm. John Lorenz.

Nonbook Materials

Canadian Library Assn. Nonbook Materials Joint Advisory Comm. Dr. Margaret Chisholm, Assoc. Prof. of Libnshp., S. of L. & Info. Servs., 456 McKeldin, Univ. of Maryland, College Park, Md. 27040.

Personnel

American Assn. of Law Libraries. Job Security, Remuneration & Employment Practices Comm. George S. Grossman; Charlie R. Harvey.

American Assn. of School Librarians. Guidelines for Personnel Working with Children & Young People in Special Situations, AHIL/AASL/CSD/YASD. Margaret Cheeseman, Institutional Servs. Supv., Pennsylvania State L., P.O. Box 1601, Harrisburg, Pa. 17126.

American Assn. of School Librarians. Professional Status & Growth Comm. Mrs. Rachael W. DeAngelo, Grad. S. of L. Studies, Univ. of Hawaii, Sinclair L. B-15, 2425 Campus Rd., Honolulu, Hawaii 96822.

American Assn. of School Librarians. School Library Manpower Project Advisory Comm. Dr. Leslie H. Janke, Head, Dept. of Libnshp., San Jose State Coll., San Jose, Calif. 95114.

ALA Library Administration Div. Personnel Administration Section. Peter Spyers-Duran, Dir., Florida Atlantic Univ. Ls., Boca Raton, Fla. 33432.

American Theological Library Assn. Bureau of Personnel & Placement Comm. Elmer J. O'Brien, Head, United Theological Seminary, 1810 Harvard Blvd., Dayton, Ohio 45406.

Assn. of College & Research Libraries. Academic Status Comm. Roy L. Kidman, Univ. Libn., Univ. of Southern California, Los Angeles, Calif. 90007.

Canadian Library Assn. Salaries Subcomm. Joe Carver, Chief Libn., Medicine Hat P.L., 414 First St. S.E., Medicine Hat, Alta.

Canadian Library Assn. Use of Professional Staff Subcomm. Joseph Princz, Acting Chief, Georges P. Vanier L., Loyola Coll., 7141 Sherbrooke St. W., Montreal 28, P.Q.

Music Library Assn. Library Personnel & Placement Comm. Shirley Piper, Music L., Northwestern Univ., Evanston, Ill. 60201.

Photoduplication

ALA Resources & Technical Services Div. Reproduction of Library Materials Section. Howard Cordell, Florida International Univ., Tamiami Trail, Miami, Fla. 33144.

American Theological Library Assn. Microtext Reproduction Bd. Raymond P. Morris, Chmn., Yale Divinity S. L., 409 Prospect St., New Haven, Conn. 06510.

Assn. of Research Libraries. Foreign Newspaper Microfilm Project Comm. John Lorenz.

Assn. of Research Libraries. Microform Project Comm. Task I: Bibliographic Control. Felix Reichman, Principal Investigator.

Assn. of Research Libraries. Microfilm Project Comm. Task II: National Microform Agency. Edward Miller, Principal Investigator.

Assn. of Research Libraries. Microfilming Dissertations Comm. Gustave Harrer.

National Microfilm Assn. John R. Robertson, Eastman Kodak Co., 343 State St., Rochester, N.Y. 14650.

Society of American Archivists. Reference, Access & Photoduplication Policies Comm. Mary Lynn McCree, Jane Addams' Hull House, Univ. of Illinois–Chicago Circle, P.O. Box 4348, Chicago, Ill. 60680.

Placement Service

American Assn. of Law Libraries. Placement Comm. Edwin G. Schuck; Stanley Pearce.

American Theological Library Assn. Bureau of Personnel & Placement Comm. Elmer J. O'Brien, Head, United Theological Seminary, 1810 Harvard Blvd., Dayton, Ohio 45406.

Music Library Assn. Library Personnel & Placement Comm. Shirley Piper, Music L., Northwestern Univ., Evanston, Ill. 60201.

SLA Placement Policy Comm. Florence M. McKenna, 4517 Parade St., Pittsburgh, Pa. 15207.

Planning and Research

American Assn. of School Librarians. Research Comm. Vincent J. Aceto, Prof., S. of L. Sci., State Univ. of New York at Albany, N.Y. 12203.

American Assn. of State Libraries. Planning Comm. John A. Humphrey, State Univ. of New York, State Educ. Dept., Albany, N.Y. 12224.

ALA Children's Services Div. Research & Development Comm. Mrs. Priscilla L. Moulton, Dir. of S. L. Servs., Brookline P. Ss., Brookline, Mass. 02146.

ALA Library Education Div. Research Comm. Ray L. Carpenter, S. of L. Sci., Univ. of North Carolina, Chapel Hill, N.C. 27514.

ALA Library Research Round Table. Roger C. Greer, S. of L. Sci., Syracuse Univ., Syracuse, N.Y. 13210.

ALA Research Comm. Raynard Swank, Univ. of California S. of Libnshp., Berkeley, Calif. 94720.

ALA Resources & Technical Services Div. Planning Comm. Richard L. Darling, S. of L. Serv., Columbia Univ., 516 Butler, New York, N.Y. 10027.

ALA Young Adult Services Div. Research Comm. James W. Liesener, Assoc. Prof., S. of L. & Info. Servs., Univ. of Maryland, College Park, Md. 20742.

Assn. of American Library Schools. Research Comm. Guy A. Marco, Dean & Prof., S. of L. Sci., Kent State Univ., Kent, Ohio 44240.

Assn. of College & Research Libraries. Planning Comm. Russell Shank, Dir. of Ls., Smithsonian Institution, Washington, D.C. 20560.

Assn. of Hospital & Institution Libraries. Research Comm. John A. Timour, L. Servs. Dir., Connecticut Regional Medical Program, 272 George St., New Haven, Conn. 06510.

Assn. of Hospital & Institution Libraries. Special Projects Comm. Stefan B. Moses, Exec. Dir., California L. Assn., 717 K St., Suite 300, Sacramento, Calif. 95814.

Public Library Assn. Public Libraries Study Comm. Milton S. Byam, Dept. of L. Sci., St. John's Univ., Jamaica, N.Y. 11432.

Society of American Archivists. Paper Research Comm. (ad hoc). Gordon L. Williams, The Center for Research Ls., 5721 Cottage Grove Ave., Chicago, Ill. 60637.

SLA Planning Comm. Alleen Thompson, General Electric Co., Atomic Power Equipment Dept., 175 Curtner Ave., San Jose, Calif. 95125.

SLA Research Comm. Dr. Martha Jane K. Zachert, S. of L. Sci., Florida State Univ., Tallahassee, Fla. 32306.

Planning Libraries

Council of Planning Librarians. Melva J. Dwyer, Libn., Fine Arts L., Univ. of British Columbia, Vancouver 8, B.C., Canada.

Preservation of Books and Manuscripts

ALA Resources & Technical Services Div. Preservation of Library Materials Comm. Matt T. Roberts, Binding Officer, L. of Congress, Washington, D.C. 20540.

Assn. of Research Libraries. Preservation Comm. Warren Haas.

Society of American Archivists. Preservation Methods Comm. Clark W. Nelson, 930 Seventh Ave. S.W., Rochester, Minn. 55901.

Procurement

Federal Library Committee. Procurement Procedures in Federal Libraries Task Force. Katherine Magraw, Field L. Servs. Administrator, L. Servs. Dept., Naval Training Support Command.

Public Documents

ALA Reference Services Div. Public Documents, RSD/RTSD Comm. Mrs. Joyce Bell, Univ. of Nevada L., Reno, Nev. 89507.

ACTIVITIES INDEX / 529

ALA Resources & Technical Services Div. Public Documents: Census Bureau Advisory Subcomm. Clifford P. Crowers, Free L. of Philadelphia, Logan Sq., Philadelphia, Pa. 19103.

ALA Resources & Technical Services Div. Public Documents, RSD/RTSD Comm. Mrs. Joyce Ball, Reference Dept., Univ. of Nevada L., Reno, Nev. 89507.

Public Libraries

International Assn. of Music Libraries. Music Libraries in Public Libraries Comm. Alfons Ott, Staedtische Musikbibliothek, Salvatorplatz, Munich 2, W. Germany.

Public Library Assn. Ellie Lee Morris, P.L., San Francisco, Calif. 94102.

Public Library Assn. Costs of Public Library Servs. Comm. Christopher B. Devan, Cuyahoga County P.L., Cleveland, Ohio 44144.

Public Relations and Publicity

ALA Adult Services Div. Promotion of Notable Books Subcomm. Kate Kolish, Carnegie L., Pittsburgh, Pa. 15213.

ALA Library Administration Div. Public Relations Section. Mrs. Betty P. Rice, Public Relations Consultant, 2 Middle L., Westbury, N.Y. 11590.

Catholic Library Assn. Public Relations Comm. Donald H. Hunt, Deputy Dir., Free L. of Philadelphia, Logan Sq., Philadelphia, Pa. 19103.

Church & Synagogue Library Assn. Public Relations Comm. Mrs. Shirley G. Brown.

Federal Library Committee. Public Relations Task Force. Mrs. Lois Fern, Ref. Libn., U.S. Information Agency.

Library Public Relations Council. Ruth Kimball Baum, Dir. of Public Relations, N.Y.P.L., Fifth Ave. & 42 St., New York, N.Y. 10018.

Publications

American Assn. of Law Libraries. Publications Comm. Betty Wilkins.

American Assn. of School Librarians. Publications Comm. Mrs. Mary Joan Egan, L. Dept., Burnt Hills-Ballston Lake Central Ss., Admin. Bldg., 491 Saratoga Rd., Scotia, N.Y. 12302.

ALA Adult Services Div. Publications Advisory Comm. Mrs. Helen H. Lyman, Univ. of Wisconsin Research Project "Library Materials," Madison, Wis. 53706.

ALA Library Administration Div. Small Libraries Publications Comm. Helen M. Miller, Idaho State L., Boise, Idaho 83706.

ALA Library Education Div. Publications Comm. Eileen Noonan, Grad S. of L. Sci., Rosary Coll., River Forest, Ill. 60305.

ALA Reference Services Div. Publications Comm. Charles R. Andrews, Case Western Reserve Univ. L., Cleveland, Ohio 44106.

American Library Trustee Assn. Publications Comm. Douglas V. Downey, 2236 Maple Ave., Northbrook, Ill. 60062.

American Society for Information Science. Publications Comm. Joseph H. Kuney, American Chemical Society, Washington, D.C.

American Society of Indexers. Publications Comm. Alan Greengrass, New York Times Index, 229 W. 43 St., New York, N.Y. 10036.

Assn. of American Library Schools. Directory Comm. Dorothy E. Cole, Assoc. Prof., S. of L. Sci., State Univ. of New York at Albany, N.Y. 12203.

Assn. of American Library Schools. *Newsletter* Comm. Nasser Sharify, Dean, L. S., Pratt Institute, Brooklyn, N.Y. 11205.

Assn. of College & Research Libraries. Publications Comm. Robert M. Pierson, Dir. of Ls. for Admin., Univ. of Maryland, McKeldin L., College Park, Md. 20742.

Assn. of Hospital & Institution Libraries. Publications Advisory Comm. Jackie Rustigan, L. Consultant, L. of the Coll. of Physicians of Philadelphia, Mid-Eastern Regional Medical L., 19 S. 22 St., Philadelphia, Pa. 19103.

Bibliographical Society of America. Publication Comm. Gabriel Austin, Parke-Bernet Galleries, 980 Madison Ave., New York, N.Y. 10022.

Canadian Library Assn. Editorial & Publications Policy Comm. Dr. Hugh L. Smith, Chief Libn., Erindale Coll. L.,

530 / ACTIVITIES INDEX

Univ. of Toronto, Mississauga Rd. N., Clarkson, Ont.

Canadian Library Assn. Government Publications Comm. Clementine Combaz, Legislative Libn., 257 Legislative Bldg., Winnipeg, Man.

Catholic Library Assn. Publications Comm. Margaret Mary Henrich, 1709 Pasadena Dr., Dunedin, Fla. 33528.

Church & Synagogue Library Assn. Publications Comm. Mrs. Ruth Smith.

Lutheran Church Library Assn. Publications Bd. Rev. Carl Weller, Augsburg Publishing House, 426 S. Fifth St., Minneapolis, Minn. 55415.

Medical Library Assn. Publication Comm. Mrs. Doris Bolef, Washington Univ. S. of Medicine, 4580 Scott Ave., St. Louis, Mo. 63110.

Medical Library Assn. Publication of *Current Catalog* Proof Sheets Comm. Sheldon Kotzin, Technical Servs. Div., National L. of Medicine, 8600 Rockville Pike, Bethesda, Md. 20014.

Music Library Assn. Publications Comm. James Pruett, Music L., Univ. of North Carolina, Chapel Hill, N.C. 27514.

Society of American Archivists. Publications Comm. Howard L. Applegate, Balch Institute, 1627 Fidelity Bldg., 123 S. Broad St., Philadelphia, Pa. 19109.

Radio and Television

ALA Children's Services Div. Children's Books in Relation to Radio & Television Comm. Mrs. Augusta Baker, Coordinator of Children's Servs., N.Y.P.L., 8 E. 40 St., New York, N.Y. 10016.

ALA Children's Services Div. Children's Books in Relation to Radio & Television: Bibliography Subcomm. Naomi Noyes, Children's Specialist, N.Y.P.L., Manhattan Borough Office, 20 W. 53 St., New York, N.Y. 10019.

ALA Young Adult Services Div. Television Comm. Mrs. Penelope Stiffler Jeffrey, Group Work Specialist, Office of Young Adult Servs., N.Y.P.L., 8 E. 40 St., New York, N.Y. 10016.

International Assn. of Music Libraries. Music Libraries in Radio Stations Comm. John Howard Davies, British Broadcasting Corp., Yalding House, London W.1, England.

Rare Books

Assn. of College & Research Libraries. Rare Books & Manuscripts Section. Lee Ash, L. Consultant, 31 Alden Rd., New Haven, Conn. 06515.

Reading

American Assn. of School Librarians. Right to Read Task Force. Mrs. Elnora Portteus, Directing Supv., S. Ls., Cleveland P. Ss., Woodhill-Quincy Center, 10600 Quincy, Cleveland, Ohio 44106.

ALA Children's Services Div. Right to Read Comm. (ad hoc). Bonnie Beth Mitchell, L. Devel. Consultant, Children's Servs., State L. of Ohio, 65 Front St., Columbus, Ohio 43215.

Recruiting

American Assn. of Law Libraries. Recruitment Comm. Simon Goren; Magda Boehm.

ALA Office for Recruitment. Donald Hunt, Free L. of Philadelphia, Logan Sq., Philadelphia, Pa. 19103.

Federal Library Committee. Recruiting of Personnel in Federal Libraries Task Force. Mrs. Elaine Woodruff, Libn., U.S. Civil Service Commission.

SLA Recruitment Comm. Mrs. Joan M. Toeppe, 28784 Johnson Dr., Wickliffe, Ohio 44092.

Reference Work

ALA Reference Services Div. Donald A. Riechmann, Albuquerque P.L., Albuquerque, N.Mex. 87101.

Society of American Archivists. Reference, Access & Photoduplication Policies. Mary Lynn McCree, Jane Addams' Hull House, Univ. of Illinois–Chicago Circle, P.O. Box 4348, Chicago, Ill. 60680.

Regional Libraries

Medical Library Assn. Regional Medical Library Programs Comm. Andrew Lasslo, Univ. of Tennessee Medical Units, Coll. of Pharmacy, Dept. of Medicinal Chemistry, Memphis, Tenn. 38103.

Public Library Assn. Metropolitan Area Library Serv. Alex Ladenson, P.L., Chicago, Ill. 60602.

Relations with Publishers and Booksellers

American Assn. of Law Libraries. Relations with Publishers & Dealers Comm. Julius Marke; Raymond M. Taylor.

American Assn. of School Librarians.

American Assn. of University Presses Advisory Comm. Alice E. Johnson, Evanston Township H.S., 1600 Dodge Ave., Evanston, Ill. 60201.

ALA Adult Services Div. Assn. of American Publishers–ALA (ASD) Joint Comm. Bernice MacDonald, N.Y.P.L., New York, N.Y. 10016.

ALA–Children's Book Council Joint Comm. Mary V. Gaver, L. Consulting Servs., Bro-Dart, 29 Baldwin St., New Brunswick, N.J. 08900.

ALA Children's Services Div. Liaison with Bookstores & Book Distributors. Anne C. Santangelo, Head, Children's Dept., White Plains P.L., 116 Grand Ave., White Plains, N.Y. 10601.

ALA Resources & Technical Services Div. Assn. of American Publishers/RTSD Joint Comm. Warren B. Kuhn, Dir. of the L., Iowa State Univ., Ames, Iowa 50010.

ALA Young Adult Services Div. Publishers' Relations Comm. Mrs. Jacqueline A. Rollins, Young Adult Servs. Consultant, Westchester L. Syst., 285 Central Ave., White Plains, N.Y. 10606.

Church & Synagogue Library Assn. Publishers' Liaison Comm. Mrs. Elizabeth A. Halbrooks.

SLA Publisher Relations Comm. Robert G. Krupp, 1 Dewitt Rd., Apt. 103, Elizabeth, N.J. 07208.

Relations with Special Groups

American Assn. of Law Libraries. LC Liaison Comm. Morris L. Cohen.

American Assn. of School Librarians. AASL-American School Counselor Assn. Joint Comm. Rebecca Bingham, 3608 Dumesnil St., Louisville, Ky. 40211.

American Assn. of School Librarians. Professional Relations Comm. Dr. Miriam E. Peterson, Div. of Ls., Bd. of Educ., 228 N. LaSalle St., Chicago, Ill. 60601.

ALA Advisory Comm. to Internal Revenue Service. Alexander Wainwright, Princeton Univ. L., Princeton, N.J. 08540.

ALA Adult Services Div. Relations with State and Regional Library Assns. Comm. Emily Reed, Enoch Pratt Free L., Baltimore, Md. 21201.

ALA–Canadian Library Assn. Joint Comm. Mrs. Helen Howard, Sir George Williams Univ., Montreal, P.Q., Canada.

ALA–Catholic Library Assn. Joint Comm. Sister Helen Sheehan, Trinity Coll. L., Washington, D.C. 20017.

ALA–Children's Book Council. Mary V. Gaver, L. Cons. Servs., Bro-Dart, 29 Baldwin St., New Brunswick, N.J. 08900.

ALA Children's Services Div. Boy Scouts of America Advisory Comm. Herbert L. Leet, Dir., Southern Tier L. Syst., 114 Chestnut St., Corning, N.Y. 14830.

ALA Children's Services Div. Liaison with Organizations Serving the Child. Mrs. Carolyn W. Field, Coordinator of Work with Children, Free L. of Philadelphia, Logan Sq., Philadelphia, Pa. 19103.

ALA–National Education Association Joint Comm. James Igoe, Vermont State L., Montpelier, Vt. 05602.

ALA Reference Services Div. Census Bureau Advisory Subcomm. Clifford Crowers, Free L. of Philadelphia, Logan Sq., Philadelphia, Pa. 19103.

ALA–Society of American Archivists Joint Comm. Mrs. Elizabeth E. Hamer, L. of Congress, Washington, D.C. 20540.

American Library Trustee Assn. State Assns. Comm. Daniel W. Casey, 202 Scarboro Dr., Syracuse, N.Y. 13209.

American Society of Indexers. ASI Liaison with The Society of Indexers Comm. Robert L. Palmer, 15 W. 11 St., New York, N.Y. 10011.

Assn. of College & Research Libraries. Cooperation with Educational & Professional Organizations. James F. Govan, Libn., Swarthmore Coll., Swarthmore, Pa. 19081.

Church & Synagogue Library Assn. Library World Liaison Comm. Rev. Anthony Lachner.

Medical Library Assn. MLA/NLM Liaison Comm. William Beatty, Northwestern Univ. Medical S., Archibald Church L., 303 E. Chicago Ave., Chicago, Ill. 60611.

Society of American Archivists. Archives-Library Relationships (ad hoc). Mrs. Elizabeth E. Hamer, 6620 River Rd., Bethesda, Md. 20034.

Research Libraries

Assn. of College & Research Libraries. Joseph H. Reason, 1242 Girard St. N.E., Washington, D.C. 20017.

Assn. of Jewish Libraries. Research & Special Libraries Div. Theodore Wiener, 1701 N. Kent St., Arlington, Va. 22209.

Assn. of Research Libraries. John McDonald, Dir., Univ. of Connecticut L., Storrs, Conn. 06268.

Assn. of Research Libraries. Center for Chinese Research Libraries Project Comm. Philip McNiff.

International Assn. of Music Libraries. University & Research Music Libraries Comm. Mrs. Rita Benton, Music L., Iowa State Univ., Iowa City, Iowa 52240.

Resources

ALA Resources & Technical Services Div. Barbara M. Westby, Catalog Management Div., L. of Congress, Washington, D.C. 20540.

ALA Resources & Technical Services Div. Resources: Micropublishing Projects Subcomm. Hendrik Edelman, Asst. Dir. for Devel. of the Collections, Cornell Univ. Ls., Ithaca, N.Y. 14850.

ALA Resources & Technical Services Div. Resources: National Union Catalog Subcomm. Gordon R. Williams, Center for Research Ls., 5721 Cottage Grove Ave., Chicago, Ill. 60637.

Assn. of Research Libraries. Availability of Resources Comm. Richard Chapin.

Assn. of Research Libraries. Periodicals Resources Center Study. Joseph Jeffs.

Assn. of Research Libraries. Recommendations of Federal Information Resources Conference Comm. W. Carl Jackson.

International Assn. of Music Libraries. International Inventory of Musical Sources Comm. Friedrich Blume, Postfach 182, 659 Schlüchtern, W. Germany.

Scholarships

American Assn. of Law Libraries. Scholarship Comm. Jacquelyn J. Jurkins; Pat B. Piper.

ALA Children's Services Div. Melcher Scholarship Comm. Dr. Patricia J. Cianciolo, Prof., Michigan State Univ., 360 Erickson, East Lansing, Mich. 48823.

ALA Library Education Div. Scholarship & Awards Comm. Martin Cohen, S. of Libnshp., Western Michigan Univ., Kalamazoo, Mich. 49001.

Catholic Library Assn. Scholarship Comm. Dr. Jo Ann McCreedy, Our Lady of the Lake Coll., 411 S.W. 24 St., San Antonio, Tex. 78207.

Medical Library Assn. Scholarships Comm. Eleanor Pasmik, New York Univ., Medical Center L., 550 First Ave., New York, N.Y. 10016.

SLA Scholarship Comm. Clement G. Vitek, The Baltimore Sunpapers, Calvert & Centre Sts., Baltimore, Md. 21203.

School Libraries

American Assn. of School Librarians. Frances Hatfield, Coordinator of Instructional Materials, S. Bd., Broward County, P.O. Box 8369, Fort Lauderdale, Fla. 33310.

American Assn. of School Librarians. Urban School Libraries Comm. Dr. Lillian Batchelor, Asst. Dir., Div. of Ls., Bd. of Educ., Parkway at 21 St., Philadelphia, Pa. 19103.

Assn. of Jewish Libraries. Synagogue, School & Center Libraries Div. Mrs. Rose Miskin, Beth Tzedec Sisterhood L., 1700 Bathurst St., Toronto 10, Ont., Canada.

Canadian Library Assn. Canadian School Library Assn. Section. Mrs. Florence Willson, S. Dist. 57, Prince George, B.C.

Catholic Library Assn. High School Libraries Section. Sister Carol Louise Hiller, St. Thomas H.S., 2700 S.W. Tenth St., Ft. Lauderdale, Fla. 33312.

Catholic Library Assn. School Library Supervisors Section. Brother John Corrigan, C.F.X., Spalding Coll., 851 S. Fourth St., Louisville, Ky. 40203.

International Assn. of Music Libraries. Libraries of Music Schools Comm. Karol Musiol, Państwowa Wyzsza Szkola Muźyczna, 41. Stycznia 33, Katowice, Poland.

Science Technology Libraries

ALA Reference Services Div. Science & Technology Reference Services Comm. Cynthia Steinke, Univ. of Illinois, Chicago, Ill. 60680.

Assn. of Visual Science Librarians. Thomas Lange, Libn., Southern Coll. of Optometry, 1245 Union Ave., Memphis, Tenn. 38104.

Serials

ALA Resources & Technical Services Div. Serials Section. Edmund G. Hamann, Catalog Maintenance Dept., Cornell Univ. Ls., Ithaca, N.Y. 19850.

Canadian Library Assn. Union List of Serials Joint Comm. Flora E. Patterson, Chief, Serials Div., National L. of Canada, 395 Wellington St., Ottawa, Ont.

Ship Libraries

American Merchant Marine Library Assn. W. T. Moore, Pres.

Social Responsibilities

American Assn. of Law Libraries. Library Services to Prisoners Comm. Elizabeth Poe.

American Assn. of Law Libraries. Minorities Comm. Connie E. Bolden.

American Assn. of School Librarians. Treatment of Minority Groups in Library Books & Other Instructional Materials. David Cohen, Libn., Plainview-Old Bethpage H.S., Plainview, N.Y. 11803.

ALA Coordinating Comm. on Library Service to the Disadvantaged. Vincent Aceto, S. of L. Sci., State Univ. of New York, Albany, N.Y. 12226.

ALA Social Responsibilities Round Table. Mrs. Jaqualyn Eubanks, Brooklyn Coll. L., Brooklyn, N.Y. 11210.

ALA Adult Services Div. Library Service to an Aging Population Comm. Leslyn Schmidt, Tippecanoe L., Milwaukee, Wis. 53207.

ALA Adult Services Div. Promotion of Library Rights of Adults — A Call for Action, Special Comm. Marion L. Simmons, METRO, 11 W. 40 St., New York, N.Y. 10018.

ALA Children's Services Div. Library Service to the Disadvantaged Child. Mrs. Brooke E. Sheldon, Head, P.L. Devel., New Mexico State L., P.O. Box 1629, Santa Fe, N. Mex. 87501.

ALA Reference Services Div. Users' Needs Comm. (ad hoc). Thomas W. Shaughnessy, Grad. S. of L. Sci., Rutgers Univ., New Brunswick, N.J. 08900.

ALA Young Adult Services Div. Exploratory YASD Task Force on Drug Information (ad hoc). Donald L. Roberts, Asst. Prof., S. of Info. & L. Studies, Hayes C, Rm. 5, State Univ. of New York at Buffalo, N.Y. 14223.

ALA Young Adult Services Div. Outreach Programs for Young Adults Comm. (ad hoc). Reed Coats, Young Adult Coordinator, Camino Real Regional L. Syst., 180 W. San Carlos St., San Jose, Calif. 95113.

American Library Trustee Assn. Library Service to the Unserved. Dr. Irving Lieberman, S. of Libnshp., 133 Library, Univ. of Washington, Seattle, Wash. 98105.

Assn. of College & Research Libraries. Community Use of Academic Libraries Comm. Yen-Tsai Feng, Asst. Dir. for Research L. Servs., Boston P.L., Copley Sq., Boston, Mass. 02117.

Assn. of Hospital & Institution Libraries. Patient Education Comm. (ad hoc). Ruth Tews, Hospital Libn., Mayo Clinic, Rochester, Minn. 55901.

Assn. of Research Libraries. Negro Academic Libraries Comm. Frank Grisham.

Social Studies

American Assn. of School Librarians. Social Studies in World Affairs Comm. Wylma C. Woolard, S. & L. Consultant, *World Book Encyclopedia*, 6230 Fairview Rd., Suite 317, Charlotte, N.C. 28210.

534 / ACTIVITIES INDEX

Special Libraries

Assn. of College & Research Libraries. Subject Specialists Section. Wolfgang M. Freitag, Lecturer on the Fine Arts & Libn. for the Fine Arts L., Fogg Art Museum, Harvard Univ., Cambridge, Mass. 02138.

Assn. of Jewish Libraries. Research & Special Libraries Div. Theodore Wiener, 1701 N. Kent St., Arlington, Va. 22209.

Canadian Library Assn. Canadian Assn. of Special Libraries & Information Servs. Section. Eileen B. Morash, National Film Board, Ref. L., P.O. Box 6100, Montréal, P.Q.

Special Libraries Assn. Efren W. Gonzalez, Bristol-Myers Products, Science Information Servs., 1350 Liberty Ave., Hillside, N.J. 07207.

Staff Organizations

ALA Staff Organization Round Table. Jerome K. Corrigan, Oxon Hill Branch L., Oxon Hill, Md. 20021.

Standards

American Assn. of Law Libraries. Standards Comm. Edwin M. Schroeder.

American Assn. of School Librarians. Improvement of School Library Programs Comm. Mrs. Barbara Koplein Elleman, 2260 N. Summit Ave., No. 208, Milwaukee, Wis. 53202.

American Assn. of School Librarians. Standards Implementation Comm. Bernard Franckowiak, State S. L. Supv., Wis. Dept. of Public Instruction, Madison, Wis. 53702; Mrs. Judy W. Powell, Rte. 1, Fairfield, Me. 04937.

ALA Standards Comm. Phyllis Hochstettler, S. of Educ., Portland State Univ., Portland, Ore. 97207.

ALA Reference Services Div. Standards Comm. Robert Klassen, Bureau of Ls. & Educational Tech., USOE, Washington, D.C. 20202.

American Society for Information Science. Standards Comm. Charles P. Bourne, Charles Bourne & Associates, Menlo Park, Calif.

American Society of Indexers. Ethics, Standards & Specifications Comm. Prof. Jessica L. Harris, S. of L. Serv., Columbia Univ., New York, N.Y. 10027.

Assn. of College & Research Libraries. Standards & Accreditations Comm. H. William Axford, Univ. Libn., Arizona State Univ., Tempe, Ariz. 85281.

Assn. of Hospital & Institution Libraries. Standards Comm. U. M. (Lee) Steele, Div. of Ls., P.O. Box 635, Dover, Del. 19901.

Assn. of Research Libraries. ACRL-ARL Joint Comm. on University Library Standards. Robert B. Downs.

Assn. of Research Libraries. Standards Comm. Jerrold Orne.

Canadian Library Assn. To Consider Possible Equivalence of the Fellowship (with thesis) of the Library Association to CLA's Established Standards of Professional Qualification Comm. (ad hoc). Mary E. P. Henderson, S. of L. Sci., Univ. of Alberta, Edmonton, Alta.

Federal Library Committee. Mission of Federal Libraries & Standards for Federal Library Serv. Task Force. Ruth Fine, Libn., Office of Management & Budget.

International Organization for Standardization. ISO Central Secretariat, 1, rue de Varembé, 1211 Geneva 20, Switzerland.

International Organization for Standardization. Technical Comm.-46. Secretariat, Deutscher Normenausschuss DNA, 4-7, Burggrafenstrauss, 1 Berlin 30, Germany.

International Organization for Standardization. Technical Comm.-37. Secretariat Osterreichsches Normungsinstitut, Leopoldgasse 4, A-1020 Vienna, Austria.

International Organization for Standardization. Technical Comm.-97. Secretariat, American National Standards Institute, 1430 Broadway, New York, N.Y. 10018.

Music Library Assn. Standards Comm. Jean Bowen, Music Div., L. & Museum of the Performing Arts, Lincoln Center, New York, N.Y. 10023.

Public Library Assn. Interim Standards Revision Comm. Mrs. Barbara O.

Slanker, Illinois State L., Springfield, Ill. 62706.

Public Library Assn. Standards Comm. Rose Vainstein, S. of L. Sci., Univ. of Michigan, Ann Arbor, Mich. 48104.

Society of American Archivists. Professional Standards Comm. Philip P. Mason, 144 General L., Wayne State Univ. Archives, Detroit, Mich. 48202.

SLA Standards Comm. Logan O. Cowgill, 26 Sixth St. S.E., Washington, D.C. 20003.

State Libraries and Library Agencies

Assn. of State Library Agencies. Ernest E. Doerschuk, Jr., State L., Harrisburg, Pa. 17126.

Statistics

American Assn. of Law Libraries. Statistics Comm. Alfred J. Lewis; Marlene C. McGuirl.

American Theological Library Assn. Statistical Records Comm. Arthur Kuschke, Jr., Westminster Theological Seminary, Chestnut Hill, Philadelphia, Pa. 19147.

Canadian Library Assn. Statistical Research Comm. Mrs. Sheila J. Bertram, S. of L. Science, Univ. of Alberta, Edmonton, Alta.

Federal Library Committee. Statistics Work Group. Frank Kurt Cylke, Exec. Secy., Federal L. Comm.

Medical Library Assn. Surveys & Statistics Comm. Mrs. Susan Crawford, Archive-L. Dept., American Medical Assn., 535 N. Dearborn St., Chicago, Ill. 60610.

Student Assistants

American Assn. of School Librarians. Student Library Assistants Comm. Mrs. Estelle B. Williamson, Supv. of S. Ls., Div. of L. Devel., Md. Dept. of Educ., 600 Wyndhurst Ave., Baltimore, Md. 21201.

Subscription Books

ALA Reference & Subscription Books Review. Mrs. Jeanette Swickard, Central Elem. S. L., Evanston, Ill. 60202.

Technical Processes

ALA Resources and Technical Services Div. Barbara M. Westby, Catalog Management Div., L. of Congress, Washington, D.C. 20540.

ALA Resources & Technical Services Div. Commercial Processing Services Comm. Mrs. Abigail Dahl-Hansen, Asst. Univ. Libn., Univ. of California L., Riverside, Calif. 92507.

ALA Resources & Technical Services Div. Technical Services Costs Comm. George Shipman, Univ. of Tennessee L., Knoxville, Tenn. 37916.

Canadian Library Assn. Technical Servs. Section. Gurdial Pannu, S. of L. Sci., Univ. of Alberta, Edmonton 7, Alta.

Theater Libraries

Theatre Library Assn. Louis A. Rachow, Libn., Walter Hampden Memorial L., The Players, 16 Gramercy Park, New York, N.Y. 10003.

Theological Libraries

American Theological Library Assn. Dr. Genevieve Kelly, California Baptist Theological Seminary, Seminary Knolls, Covina, Calif. 91722.

Trustees

American Library Trustee Assn. Chester B. Ostrander, 149 Main St., Glens Falls, N.Y. 12801.

Canadian Library Assn. Canadian Library Trustees' Assn. Section. A. R. Pile, 63 Bowerbank Dr., Willowdale, Ont.

Young People's Libraries

ALA Young Adult Services Div. Jane Manthorne, Coordinator, Young Adult Serv., Boston P.L., Copley Sq., Boston, Mass. 02117.

Canadian Library Assn. Young People's Section. Maureen Allen, Ottawa P.L., 237 Queen St., Ottawa, Ont.

International Youth Library. Walter Scherf, Kaulbachstrasse, 11a, 8 Munich 22, Germany.

Appendix B

LIBRARY PURCHASING GUIDE 1972*

This year's revision of the purchasing guide has again been edited by Thomas W. McConkey, Chief, Administrative Services, Free Library of Philadelphia. It provides all the names and addresses he has been able to gather of firms offering products or services of particular interest to libraries. The list ranges all the way from suppliers of adhesives to publishers of micro-opaques, from poster supplies to foreign booksellers. The full names and addresses are listed in the Directory of Suppliers. Under products or services the name is abbreviated for quick identification. As in previous years, we have tried to indicate at least one source for items used only by libraries and also for such items of general use as are not always easy to procure locally. No attempt has been made to list items which are available in office supply stores. *LJ* will be pleased to have suggestions about areas not covered or unusual sources of supply.

ABSTRACTING
LEASCO, Thompson

ACCESSION BOOKS AND SHEETS
Am Library Line, Bro-Dart, Demco, Fordham, Gaylord, Highsmith

ACID-FREE MATERIALS (see Restoration & Preservation)

ADDING MACHINES
Victor Comptometer

ADDRESSING MACHINES
AM Corp, Dick, Elliott Addressing

ADDRESSING SERVICE
Cheshire

ADHESIVE
ACID-FREE (See Restoration & Preservation)
APPLICATORS: Fordham, Potdevin
BOOK LABEL: Am Library Line, Bro-Dart, Demco, Fordham, Gaylord, Highsmith
CALL NUMBER LABEL: Am Library Line, Bro-Dart, Demco, Fordham, Gaylord, Highsmith
DISPLAY: Crossley-VanDeusen, Demco, Fordham, Gaylord, Highsmith, Mutual Education
FILM SPLICING (see Films, Motion Picture, Equipment, etc.)
GLUE: Am Instructional, Am Library Line, Borden, Bro-Dart, Demco, Fordham, Gaylord, Higgins, Highsmith, RemRand, Sanford, Talas
MYLAR JACKET: Am Instructional, Am Library Line, Bro-Dart, Crossley-VanDeusen, Demco, Fordham, Gaylord, Highsmith
PASTE: Am Library Line, Borden, Bro-Dart, Crossley-VanDeusen, Demco, Fordham, Gaylord, Highsmith, Potdevin, Sanford
PLASTIC: Am Instructional, Am Library Line, Bro-Dart, Demco, Fordham, Gaylord, Highsmith, Mystic
PRESSURE SENSITIVE: Talas
RUBBER CEMENT: Am Library Line, Bro-Dart, Crossley-VanDeusen, Demco, Fordham, Highsmith, Sanford
VINYL: Am Library Line, Bro-Dart, Crossley-VanDeusen, Highsmith

ADHESIVE CLOTH
Am Library Line, Bro-Dart, Demco, Fordham, Gaylord, Highsmith

ADHESIVE DISPENSERS (see Dispensers)

---

*Reprinted from *Library Journal* April 1, 1972.

ADHESIVE TAPE (see Tape)

APPLICATION CARDS (see Cards, Circulation)

ART REPRODUCTIONS (see Prints and Reproductions)

ASH STANDS AND TRAYS (see Smoking Equipment)

ATLAS CASES (see Furniture, Library)

AUDIO TAPE EQUIPMENT, SERVICES & SUPPLIES
DUPLICATORS: Audiotronics, DuKane, Infonics, Rheem-Califone, Viewlex
PROCESSING KITS: Bro-Dart
RECORDERS & PLAYBACKS: Acoustifone, Ampex, Audio-Master, Audiotronics, Avid, Bell & Howell (AV Div), Capitol, Demco, DuKane, Fordham, Gaylord, Goody, McClurg, M P Audio, Newcomb, NORELCO, RCA AV Div, Radio-Matic, Rheem-Califone, 3M, Viewlex
STORAGE CABINETS: Am Instructional, Bro-Dart, Coffey, Crossley-VanDeusen, Demco, Fordham, Gaylord, Highsmith, Kersting, Neumade, Smith System, Wallach

AUDIO TAPES, PRE-RECORDED (see Recordings, Cassettes, Discs & Tapes)

AUDIOVISUAL
CARDS AND FORMS (see Cards, Audiovisual and Forms)
CONTROL SYSTEMS (see Cataloging Services, Audiovisual Materials)
EQUIPMENT (see article wanted, e.g., Projectors, Record Players, etc., or write to Nat'l Audio-Visual Assn., Inc., Fairfax, Va., for copy of latest edition of "Audio-Visual Equipment Directory"; see also "Audiovisual Market Place: a Multimedia Guide," Bowker)
EQUIPMENT CARTS: Demco, Ferno-Washington, Highsmith
MATERIALS (see latest Audiovisual Guide, "Library Journal" and "Audiovisual Market Place: a Multimedia Guide," Bowker)
MOBILE EQUIPMENT CENTERS: Advance Prod, Am Instructional, Am Library Line, Demco, Fordham, Highsmith, Monroe Ind, Wallach
PROCESSING KITS: Bro-Dart, Eye Gate, Stone Bridge, Xerox BiblioGraphics

AUTOMATED BOOK RETRIEVAL SYSTEM
Library Bureau, Supreme

AUTOMATION & SYSTEMS DESIGN
System Development, Thompson

AWARD PINS & RIBBONS
Am Instructional, Am Library Line, Demco, Fordham, Highsmith, Library Prod, Murphy

BADGES, CONFERENCE
Am Instructional, Fordham, Highsmith

BEST SELLER LIST HOLDER, LUCITE
Am Library Line, Fordham

BIBLIOGRAPHIC SERVICE
Bro-Dart, Documentation & Procurement, Thompson

BICYCLE RACKS (see Recreational Equipment)

BINDERS
BOOK JACKET: Am Instructional, Am Library Line, Bro-Dart, Crossley-VanDeusen, Demco, Fordham, Highsmith
CLEANER: Am Library Line, Crossley-VanDeusen, Highsmith, Marador
DECORATIVE INSERTS: Bro-Dart, Crossley-VanDeusen, Elliott (John), Fordham
MAGAZINE: Am Instructional, Am Library Line, Bowker (LJ & PW), Bro-Dart, Demco, EBSCO Subscription, Fordham, Gaylord, Highsmith, Marador
NEW BOOK LISTER: Fordham
NEWSPAPER: Bro-Dart, Fordham, Highsmith
PAMPHLET: Bro-Dart, Demco, Fordham, Gaylord, Highsmith, Marador
PERIODICALS: Ruzicka
PHONO DISCS: Emend
SHEET MUSIC: Bro-Dart, Demco, Gaylord
SINGLE AND DOUBLE STITCHED: Bro-Dart, Demco, Gaylord, Highsmith
TRANSPARENT: Am Instructional, Am Library Line, Bro-Dart, Crossley-VanDeusen, Demco, Fordham, Gaylord, Highsmith, Marador, Talas

BINDER STRIPS
U-File M

BINDING MATERIALS & EQUIPMENT
BINDER'S BOARD: Davey, Talas
CLOTH: Arkwright-Interlaken, Bro-Dart, Columbia Mills, Demco, Fordham, Gaylord, Highsmith, Holliston, Huntting, Picture Cover, Talas
EQUIPMENT: Bro-Dart, Demco, Fordham, Gaylord, Highsmith, Potdevin, Talas
GENERAL SUPPLIERS: Am Instructional, Am Library Line, Bro-Dart, Crossley-VanDeusen, Demco, Fordham, Gane, Gaylord, Highsmith, Liquick-Leather, Paper Corp, Picture Cover, Talas
LATEX FIBER: Latex Fiber
LEATHER: Talas
MACHINES: Bro-Dart, Devoke, Fordham, Gen Binding, Highsmith, Talas
PAPER: Paper Corp, Talas
PAPERBACK REINFORCING: Am Instructional, Bro-Dart, Demco, EBS, Emend, Hertzberg, Highsmith, Seaward Commerce, Vinabind
PERIODICAL REBINDING: Emend
PREBINDING SUPPLIES: Library Bind Serv, Picture Cover

PRESERVATIVE, LEATHER: Am Library Line, Fordham, Liquick-Leather, Talas
SLIDE-ON SPINES: Bro-Dart, Devoke ("Bac-Bones"), Highsmith, Talas
SPIRAL SPINES: Devoke, Gen Binding

BINDING SERVICES
CERTIFIED BINDERS (for addresses of nearest certified binders write to Library Binding Institute, 160 State Street, Boston, Mass. 02109).
PICTURE BINDINGS: Bound-To-Stay-Bound, Library Binding (Treasure Trove), Library Bind Serv, Picture Cover
PREBINDERS, HARDBACKS: Associated Libraries, Bound-To-Stay-Bound, Bro-Dart, Federal, Follett, Hertzberg, Huntting, Leibel, Library Binding (Treasure Trove), McClurg, Phillips, Regent, Ruzicka, Sapsis, Sutliff, Univ Bindery
PREBINDERS, MAGAZINE: Am Bindery, Subscribe-A-Bind
PREBINDERS, PAPERBACKS: A & A Distributors, Am Bindery, Associated Libraries, Bro-Dart, Heckman, Hertzberg, Huntting, LEC, Reynolds (Armor Books), Ruzicka, Smith (Peter), Vinabind

BLACKBOARDS (see also Chalkboards and Accessories)
ELECTRONIC: Bell System (AT & T)

BLIND, MATERIALS FOR (see Physically Handicapped, Reading Aids for)

BOOK BLOCKS, DECORATIVE
Fordham

BOOK CARDS (see Cards, Circulation)

BOOK CARRYING BAGS
CANVAS: Advertisers Mfg, Am Instructional, Am Library Line, Demco, Fordham, Gaylord, Owens
PAPER (SHOPPING): Equitable
PLASTIC: Am Library Line, Fordham, Highsmith

BOOK CARTS, FOLDING
Ferno-Washington

BOOK CASES (see Shelving)

BOOK CATALOG SERVICES
Am Library Line, Baker & Taylor, Bro-Dart, Demco, Greenwood, Hall, Huntting, IBM, Input Services, LEASCO, Princeton, Science Press, Sedgwick, Xerox BiblioGraphics

BOOK CHARGING SYSTEMS
AUTOMATIC: AM Corp, Bro-Dart (Dickman & Sysdac), Demco, Elliott, Gaylord, McBee
COMPUTER BASED: Automated Business, Bro-Dart, Colorado Instruments, IBM, Omni-Card, Standard Register, Supreme
ELECTROSTATIC: Xerox

MICROFILMING: Eastman, Filmdex, Regiscope
THERMOGRAPHIC: Bro-Dart (Brodac)
VISIBLE: Demco

BOOK CLEANERS
Am Library Line, Demco, Highsmith, Talas

BOOK COATING, PLASTIC
Am Instructional, Am Library Line (Book Spray), Bro-Dart (Plasti-lac), Crossley-VanDeusen (Krylon), Demco (Demcote), Fordham (Lackote & Lifekote), Gaylord (Spraylon), Highsmith, Liquick-Leather, Talas (Krylon)

BOOK CONVEYORS
Library Bureau, Mosler (Dropository), Selectamatic

BOOK COPYING SERVICE (see Book Reproduction)

BOOK COVER DISPENSER BOXES
Am Library Line, Bro-Dart, Demco, Fordham

BOOK COVER MEASURING BOARDS
Bro-Dart, Gaylord

BOOK COVERS
ACETATE: Bro-Dart, Highsmith
DECORATIVE: Am Library Line, Bro-Dart, Crossley-VanDeusen, Elliott (John), Fordham, Library Binding (Treasure Trove), Picture Cover
MYLAR: Am Instructional, Am Library Line (All-Fit), Bro-Dart (Plasti-Kleer), Crossley-VanDeusen, Demco (Crystaljacs), Fordham (Krack-A-Jack), Gaylord, Highsmith
PAPER: Am Library Line, Bro-Dart
VINYL: Am Library Line, Bro-Dart, Crossley-VanDeusen, Demco, Gaylord, Highsmith

BOOK EXHIBITS
Baker & Taylor, Books on Exhibit, Children's Book, Educational Reading, Scholastic

BOOK HANDLING EQUIPMENT (see item desired, e.g., Book Lifts, Book Conveyors, Shipping Cases, etc.)

BOOK HOLDERS AND DISPLAYERS
Am Instructional, Am Library Line, Bro-Dart, Buckstaff, Demco, Fordham, Gaylord, Highsmith, Library Prod, Selectamatic, Sjostrom, Slyd-In

BOOK IMPORTERS (see Booksellers, Importers)

BOOK JACKET BINDERS (see Binders)

BOOK JACKET COVERS (see Book Covers)

BOOK LIST DISPLAYERS (see Pamphlet Display Case, Lucite)

BOOK LISTS (see Publicity Services and Materials)

BOOK MAILING BAGS
Am Library Line, Demco, Fordham, Highsmith, Jiffy

BOOK MARKING EQUIPMENT & SUPPLIES (see Marking Equipment & Supplies)

BOOKMARKS
Antioch, Bowker, Bro-Dart, Children's Book, Fordham, Highsmith, Ivins, Library Prod, Murphy

BOOKMOBILES
NEW: Boyertown, Gerstenslager, Moroney
REBUILDING: Gerstenslager, Moroney
TRAILER LIBRARIES: Bro-Dart
TRAILERS: Gerstenslager
USED: Moroney

BOOK ORDER CARDS AND FORMS (see Cards, Book Order and Forms)

BOOKPLATES
Am Library Line, Antioch, Bro-Dart, Fordham, Gaylord, Highsmith, Library Prod, Murphy

BOOK POCKETS
GUMMED BACK: Am Instructional, Am Library Line, Bro-Dart, Crossley-VanDeusen, Demco, Fordham, Gaylord, Highsmith
PRESSURE SENSITIVE: Am Library Line
REGULAR: Am Library Line, Bro-Dart, Demco, Fordham, Gaylord, Highsmith

BOOK PROCESSING KITS (see also Cataloging Services)
Associated Libraries, Bound-To-Stay-Bound, Bro-Dart, Capital Library, Demco, Huntting, Midwest Library, Xerox BiblioGraphics

BOOK RACKS (see Display Racks)

BOOK-RECORDS (Combination sets; see also Multimedia Kits)
Am Instructional, Caedmon, Demco, Rosenberg

BOOK RENTAL (see Rental, Books)

BOOK REPAIRING
EQUIPMENT: Am Library Line, Bro-Dart, Crossley-VanDeusen, Demco, Fordham, Gane, Gaylord, Highsmith, Potdevin, Talas
KITS: Bro-Dart, Demco, Fordham, Gaylord, Talas
MATERIALS (see item desired, e.g., Book Cleaners; Binding Materials and Equipment; Tape; Lacquer, Book, etc.)

BOOK REPRODUCTION (incl. periodicals)
AMS Press, Arno Press, Bell & Howell (Micro Photo Div), Greenwood, Hall, Johnson Reprint, Kraus, Maxwell Reprint, Microcard Editions (NCR), Microfilm Co of Calif, Microfilming Corp, Smith (Peter), Univ Microfilms (Xerox), Zeitlin; (see also "Announced Reprints" and "Guide to Reprints" published by Microcard Editions (NCR)

BOOK RESTS (see Book Holders and Displayers)

BOOK RETURNS
BUILT-IN: Herring, Highsmith, Kingsley, Mosler
FINE ENVELOPES & DISPENSERS: Mosler
OUTDOOR: Am Library Line, Boardman, Highsmith, Kingsley, Nat'l Metal

BOOK REVIEW CARDS
ADULT: Library Journal
JUVENILE: Library Journal

BOOKSELLERS (for additional booksellers see "Literary Market Place" and "American Book Trade Directory," both published by Bowker)
FOREIGN: Ars Polona (Polish), Aux Amateurs de Livres (French), Brockhaus (German), Harrassowitz, Library Service Assn, Stevens & Brown, Swets & Zeitlinger
IMPORTERS: Abel, British Book Centre, Cass, Consolidated, De Gruyter, Documentation & Procurement, Emery-Pratt, Four Continents (Russian), French & European, Herder (German, French, Spanish), Int'l University, Japan Publications (Japanese & Asian), Johnson (Walter), Librairie de France, Maxwell Scientific, Phiebig, Rosenberg (French, German, & Juvenile), Stechert, Toggitt, Wittenborn (Art)
OUT-OF-PRINT BOOKS: Abel, Abrahams, Austin Book, Barnes, Book Land, Brainard, British Book Centre, Canner, Colonial, EBS, French & European (French & Spanish), Gaisser, Harrassowitz, Hoffman, Int'l Bookfinders, Int'l University, Johnson (Walter), Library Service Assn (French), Lincoln, Phiebig, Rosenberg (German & French), Smith (Peter), Stechert, Stevens & Brown, Univ Microfilms (Xerox), Wittenborn (Art)
REPRINTS: Reprint Distribution
REPRODUCED BOOKS (see Book Reproduction)
USED BOOKS: Tartan
WHOLESALE, HARDBACK & PAPERBACK: A & A Distributors, Abel, Acme Code, Alanar, ALESCO, Ancorp, Baker & Taylor, Barnes, Bookazine, Books on Exhibit, Bound-To-Stay-Bound, Bro-Dart Books, Campbell & Hall, Clark, Consolidated, Cosmo, Dame, Dimondstein, Documentation & Procurement, EBS, Educational Reading, Emery-Pratt, French & European, Gardner, Hennessey & Ingalls, Herder, Highsmith, Huntting, Inter-Pac, Int'l University, Interstate, Johnson (Walter), Leibel, McClurg, Maxwell Scientific, Midwest Library, Monarch Book, Purnell, Regent (Juvenile & Art), Ruzicka, St. Paul, Schirmer (Music), Scholastic, Sci-Tech, Silver-Burdett, Stacey, Stone

Bridge, Sutliff, University Microfilms (Xerox), West-State (West US), Western Publishing
WHOLESALE, PAPERBACK: Am Bindery, Bacon, BIPAD, Book Supply, CW Assoc, Demco, Hertzberg, Reynolds (Armor Books), Vinabind
WHOLESALE, REMAINDERS: Acme Code

BOOK SHELVING, STACKS AND ACCESSORIES (see Shelving)

"BOOKS I HAVE READ"—NOTEBOOK
Gaylord

BOOKS PROCESSED (see Cataloging Services, Books)

BOOK SUPPORTS
MAGNETIC: Weyll
METAL: Am Instructional, Am Library Line, Ames, Bro-Dart, Demco, Estey, Fordham, Gaylord, Hamilton, Highsmith, Va Metal
PLASTIC: Am Instructional, Bro-Dart, Crossley-VanDeusen, Demco, Estey, Fordham, Gaylord, Highsmith
SPRING TENSION: Bro-Dart, Crossley-VanDeusen, Highsmith
WALL ATTACHED: Merlin

BOOK TRUCKS
DEPRESSIBLE (see Furniture, Library)
LOCKING: Bro-Dart, Demco, Fordham, Highsmith
METAL: Aetna, Am Instructional, Am Library Line, Ames, Bretford, Bro-Dart, Crossley-VanDeusen, Demco, Equipto, Estey, Fordham, Gaylord, Hamilton, Highsmith, Reska, Royalmetal, Smith System, Va Metal
PORTABLE: Advance Prod, Highsmith
STEP STOOL: Am Library Line, Bro-Dart, Crossley-VanDeusen, Fordham
UPRIGHT: Book-Kart, Library Microfilms & Materials
WIRE: Am Instructional, Fordham, Gaylord, Highsmith, Metropolitan
WOOD: Am Instructional, Am Library Line, Bro-Dart, Buckstaff, Catskill, Croyden, EBSCO Subscription, Fetzer's, Fleetwood, Fordham, Gaylord, Heller, Highsmith, Library Bureau, Myrtle, Risom, Sjostrom, Southern Desk, Standard Wood, Weinberg, Worden

BOOK WEEK MATERIALS (see Publicity Services and Materials)

BORROWERS' REGISTER (see Register, Borrowers')

BOXES
BOOK, SHIPPING: Am Instructional, Demco
GENERAL (see specific type, i.e., Files, Microfilm, Shipping Cases, etc.)

BRAQUETTE (see Picture, Frames, Adjustable)

BULLETIN BOARDS
CHANGEABLE (see Signs, Movable Letters)
CORK: Am Instructional, Am Library Line, Beckley-Cardy, Crossley-VanDeusen, Croyden, Demco, Estey, Fordham, Gaylord, Highsmith, Sjostrom, Talas
HOOK 'N LOOP: Demco
PLASTIC: Demco, Fordham (Alpha-Peg)

BUSINESS MACHINES (see machine desired, Addressing, etc.)

CABINETS, STORAGE, STATIONERY (see also Files and Furniture, Office)
Art Metal, Bro-Dart, Crossley-VanDeusen, Demco, Fordham, Gen Fireproofing, Hamilton, Highsmith, Republic, Talas

CALL NUMBER LABEL PROTECTORS
Am Library Line, Bro-Dart, Crossley-VanDeusen, Fordham, Highsmith

CALL NUMBER LABELS (see Labels, Call Number)

CALL NUMBER STAMPING MACHINES (see Marking Equipment & Supplies)

CAMERAS, CATALOGING (see Cataloging Cameras)

CARD CATALOG FILES (see Furniture, Library)

CARDS
AUDIOVISUAL, ACQUISITION: Am Instructional, Am Library Line, Crossley-VanDeusen, Demco, Fordham, Gaylord, Highsmith
AUDIOVISUAL, FILM BOOKING: Am Instructional, Am Library Line, Demco, Fordham, Gaylord, Highsmith
AUDIOVISUAL, INSTRUCTIONAL MATERIALS: Am Instructional, Crossley-VanDeusen, Demco, Fordham, Gaylord
AUDIOVISUAL, LOCATOR: Demco, Fordham, Gaylord
AUDIOVISUAL, RECORDING BOOKING: Am Instructional, Am Library Line, Demco, Fordham, Gaylord
BOOK CARD PROTECTORS: Am Library Line, Bro-Dart, Crossley-VanDeusen, Demco, Fordham, Gaylord, Highsmith
BOOK COVER/SIGNALS: Bro-Dart, Demco, Gaylord
BOOK ORDER: Am Library Line, Bro-Dart, Crossley-VanDeusen, Demco, Fordham, Gaylord, Highsmith
CATALOG: Am Instructional, Am Library Line, Bro-Dart, Brown, Chiang, Crossley-VanDeusen, Demco, Fordham, Gaylord, Highsmith, Library Prod, Talas, Walker-Goulard
CATALOG, ACID-FREE: Standard Paper
CATALOG, COLOR BANDED: Am Instructional, Am Library Line, Bro-Dart, Crossley-VanDeusen, Demco, Fordham, Gaylord, Highsmith
CATALOG, CROSS REFERENCE: Demco, Woods Library

542 / LIBRARY PURCHASING GUIDE

CATALOG, DISPLAY: Fordham, Library Prod
CATALOG, DUPLICATED: Advance Reproductions, Atlantic Microfilm, Gen Microfilm, Midwest Library
CATALOG, FLAG: Am Library Line, Crossley-VanDeusen, Demco, Fordham, Highsmith
CATALOG, LIBRARY OF CONGRESS, INDEX TO: Bibliographic Data
CATALOG, LIBRARY OF CONGRESS, MACHINE READABLE ORDER FORMS: Bro-Dart, Demco, Gaylord
CATALOG, LIBRARY OF CONGRESS, ON MICROFICHE: Demco, Information Dynamics, Library Processing
CATALOG, PRINTED: Alanar, Am Library (ALESCO), Am Library Line, Associated Libraries, Baker & Taylor, Bro-Dart, Catalog Card Corp, Crossley-VanDeusen, Demco, Educational Reading, Follett (Juvenile), Huntting, Leibel, Library of Congress, McNaughton, Stone Bridge, Wilson, Xerox BiblioGraphics
CATALOG, PROTECTORS: Am Instructional, Am Library Line, Bro-Dart, Cel-U-Dex, Crossley-VanDeusen, Demco, Fordham, Gaylord, Highsmith
CATALOG, SHEET OR STRIP FORM: Am Library Line, Bro-Dart, Crossley-VanDeusen, Demco, Fordham, Gaylord, Highsmith, Walker-Goulard
CATALOG, TEMPLATES (Xerox): Am Library Line, Demco
CATALOG, XEROX COPYING: Am Library Line, Demco, Gaylord
CIRCULATION, APPLICATION OR REGISTRATION: Am Library Line, Bro-Dart, Crossley-VanDeusen, Demco, Fordham, Gaylord, Highsmith
CIRCULATION, BOOK: Am Instructional, Am Library Line, Bro-Dart, Crossley-VanDeusen, Demco, Fordham, Gaylord, Highsmith, Library Prod
CIRCULATION, BORROWERS: Am Instructional, Am Library Line, Bro-Dart, Crossley-VanDeusen, Demco, Fordham, Gaylord, Highsmith, Library Prod
CIRCULATION, DATE DUE: Am Instructional, Am Library Line, Bro-Dart, Crossley-VanDeusen, Demco, Fordham, Gaylord, Highsmith
CIRCULATION, IDENTIFICATION: Bro-Dart, Crossley-VanDeusen, Demco, Fordham, Gaylord, Highsmith, Omni-Card
CIRCULATION, MAGAZINE CHARGING: Am Library Line, Bro-Dart, Crossley-VanDeusen, Demco, Fordham, Gaylord
CIRCULATION, OVERDUE FINE: Am Library Line, Bro-Dart, Crossley-VanDeusen, Demco, Fordham, Gaylord
CIRCULATION, OVERDUE POST CARDS: Am Library Line, Bro-Dart, Crossley-VanDeusen, Demco, Fordham, Gaylord, Highsmith
COIN MAILING: Crossley-VanDeusen, Demco, Dennison
DOCUMENT RECORD: Demco
MAGAZINE RECORD: Am Library Line, Bro-Dart, Crossley-VanDeusen, Demco, Fordham, Gaylord, Highsmith
PRACTICE (INDEX): Am Instructional, Am Library Line, Bro-Dart, Crossley-VanDeusen, Demco, Fordham, Gaylord, Highsmith
RESERVE BOOK: Am Instructional, Am Library Line, Bro-Dart, Crossley-VanDeusen, Demco, Fordham, Gaylord, Highsmith
RESERVE POST: Am Library Line, Bro-Dart, Crossley-VanDeusen, Demco, Fordham, Gaylord
SHELF-LIST: Am Instructional, Am Library Line, Bro-Dart, Crossley-VanDeusen, Demco, Fordham, Gaylord, Walker-Goulard
SUBJECT HEADING CATALOG GUIDE: Bro-Dart, Gaylord

CARD SORTER (see Sorting Equipment)

CARRELS
ACOUSTICAL: MPC, Wenger
AUDIOVISUAL ("Wet") (see also Learning Laboratory Systems): Advance Prod, Am Instructional, Am Library Line, Am Seating, Audio-Tutorial, Audio-Visual Research, Bro-Dart, Directional, DuKane, Estey, Fordham, Gaylord, Highsmith, Howe, Library Bureau, Library Filmstrip, Monroe Ind, RCA AV Div, Rheem-Califone
BOOK TRUCK (see Book Trucks, Locking)
PORTABLE, FOUR STATION: Creative Environments
STANDARD ("Dry"): Advance Prod, Aetna, Am Desk, Am Instructional, Am Seating, Ames, Art Metal, Bro-Dart, Brown, Buckstaff, Crossley-VanDeusen, Croyden, Estey, Fordham, Gaylord, Gen Fireproofing, Heller, Highsmith, Howe, Inter-Royal, Library Concepts, Library Filmstrip, Miller, Monroe Ind, MPC, Myrtle, Reska, Risom, Sjostrom, Southern Desk, Standard Wood, Steelcase, Thonet, Va Metal, Weinberg, Worden

CARROUSELS, BOOK
Am Library Line, Demco, Highsmith

CARTON
SIZERS & CUTTING KNIVES: Pasch, Talas
STITCHING MACHINES: Bostitch

CASES EXHIBIT (see Exhibit Cases)

CASES, SHIPPING (see Shipping Cases)

CASH BOXES
Am Instructional, Crossley-VanDeusen, Fordham, Highsmith

CASH REGISTERS
Nat'l Cash

CASH SORTER
Evans Specialty, Fordham

CASSETTES
EQUIPMENT, SERVICES & SUPPLIES (see Recordings, Equipment, etc. or Audio Tape, Equipment, etc.)
RECORDINGS (see Recordings, Cassettes, etc.)

CATALOG CARD COPY HOLDER (for typewriters)
Demco

CATALOG CARDS (see Cards, Catalog)

CATALOG CARD SETS (see Book Processing Kits)

CATALOGING GUIDES (see Guides, Catalog)

CATALOGING CAMERAS
Am Library Line, Copy Cat, Polaroid

CATALOGING SERVICES
AUDIOVISUAL MATERIALS: Alanar, Automated Business, Bro-Dart, Demco, Instructo, Library of Congress, Stone Bridge, Xerox BiblioGraphics
BOOKS (see also Book Processing Kits): Abel, Alanar, ALESCO, Associated Libraries, Baker & Taylor, Bro-Dart, Capital Library, Catalog Card Corp, Cosmo, Demco, Follett (Juvenile), Gardner, Herner, Huntting, Inter-Pac, Interstate, Leibel, Library Processing, McClurg, McNaughton, Monarch Book, Stone Bridge, Thompson, Xerox BiblioGraphics

CEILING SYSTEMS
Armstrong Cork

CHAIRS (see Furniture: Library, Office, etc.)

CHALKBOARDS AND ACCESSORIES (see also Blackboards)
Advance Prod, Am Instructional, Arlington, Attwood, Crossley-VanDeusen, Demco, Fordham, Highsmith, Instructo, Judy, Oravisual, Talas

CHANGEMAKERS (see Coin Operated Equipment)

CHARGING DESKS (see Furniture, Library)

CHARGING SYSTEMS (see Book Charging Systems)

CHARGING TRAY GUIDES (see Guides, Charging Tray)

CHARGING TRAYS (see Trays, Charging)

CHART MATERIAL
Chart-Pak, Demco, Devoke, Fordham, Talas

CHILDREN'S MAGAZINES, INDEXED
Subject Index

CHILDREN'S READING PROGRAMS
Demco, Fordham, Library Prod, Murphy

CIRCULATION CONTROL SYSTEMS (see Book Charging Systems)

CLASSIFICATION GUIDES
Am Library Line, Bro-Dart, Crossley-VanDeusen, Demco, Fordham, Gaylord, Highsmith, Huntting

CLIPPING ENVELOPES (see Envelopes, Clipping)

CLOCKS, TIME RECORDING
Force, Highsmith, Simplex

COIN OPERATED EQUIPMENT
CHANGEMAKERS: Nat'l Rejectors, Standard Change
COPYING MACHINES: AM Corp, DASA, Dennison, Olivetti, Savin, SCM, Xerox
LAMINATING MACHINES: Selectra, U-Seal-It
LOCKERS: Sentinel Lockers
MICROFILM READER-PRINTERS: 3M, Xerox
STAMP MACHINES: Selectra
TYPEWRITERS, ELECTRIC: Type-A-Line, Type-Ur-Own

COIN SORTERS: Fordham

COLLATORS
AM Corp, Dick, Gen Binding

COMMEMORATIVE TABLETS (see Signs, Metal)

CONSULTING SERVICES, LIBRARY (see also "Directory of Library Consultants," Bowker)
Bro-Dart, Herner, LEASCO, Library Management, Library Processing, Nelson, System Development, Thompson

CONVEYORS, BOOK (see Book Conveyors)

COPYING MACHINES
COIN OPERATED (see Coin Operated Equipment)
DIAZO: Bruning
DUAL SPECTRUM: 3M
ELECTROSTATIC: AM Corp, DASA, Dennison, Dick, Friden, GAF Corp, IBM, Olivetti, Savin, SCM, Xerox
PHOTOCOPY: Itek

CORK BOARDS (see Display Panels)

CORNER GUARDS, BOOKS
Talas

CORNER GUARDS, BUILDING INDOOR
STAINLESS STEEL: Wilkinson Chutes
VINYL: AFCO Rubber

CORRECTION FLUID, CATALOG CARD MATCHING
Am Library Line, Highsmith

COVERS, PROTECTIVE
BOOK (see Book Covers)
BOOK CARD (see Cards, Book Card Protectors)
CATALOG CARD (see Cards, Catalog, Protectors)
DOCUMENT: Am Instructional, Bro-Dart, Crossley-VanDeusen, Demco, Fordham, Gaylord, Highsmith
ENCYCLOPEDIA: Bro-Dart, Fordham, Gaylord
PAGE: Am Instructional, . Bro-Dart, Crossley-VanDeusen, Demco, Fordham, Highsmith
PAPERBACKS (see Binding Materials, Paperback Reinforcing)
PERIODICAL: Am Instructional, Am Library Line, Bro-Dart, Crossley-VanDeusen, Demco, Fordham, Gaylord, Highsmith
PHONOGRAPH RECORD: Am Instructional, Am Library Line, Bro-Dart, Demco, Fordham, Gaylord, Highsmith
PICTURE: Am Instructional, Bro-Dart, Demco, Gaylord

CUMULATIVE BOOK INDEX (CBI) CABINET (see Furniture, Library)

CUTTER NUMBER TABLES
Huntting

DARKENING SHADES (for darkening projection rooms)
Beckley-Cardy

DATA PROCESSING, EQUIPMENT, SERVICES & SUPPLIES
CATALOG CARDS TO MAGNETIC TAPE: Input Services
COMPUTERS: Friden, IBM, RemRand Systems, 3M
DATA BINDING SUPPLIES: Fordham
DATA COLLECTING MACHINES: Standard Register
DATA TRANSMISSION: Spiras Systems
PRINTERS: IBM, Nat'l Cash, RemRand Systems, 3M

DATE CARD HOLDERS
Bro-Dart, Demco, Fordham, Gaylord

DATE DUE CARDS AND SLIPS (see Cards, Circulation)

DATE HOLDERS, PENCIL (see Pencil Date Holders)

DATE-POCKET (combination book pocket and date slip)
Am Instructional, Am Library Line, Bro-Dart, Demco, Fordham, Gaylord, Highsmith

DATERS
AUTOMATIC: Am Library Line, Bro-Dart, Crossley-VanDeusen, Demco, Force, Fordham, Highsmith
BAND: Am Instructional, Am Library Line, Bro-Dart, Demco, Fordham, Gaylord, Highsmith

SELF INKING: Am Instructional, Am Library Line, Crossley-VanDeusen, Demco, Gaylord, Highsmith

DECALCOMANIA
Ever Ready, 3M

DECORATIVE BOOK COVERS (INSERTS) (see Book Covers, Decorative)

DEHUMIDIFIERS (see Humidifiers)

DEPOSITORIES, BOOKS (see Book Returns)

DESKS (see Furniture: Library, Office)

DICTIONARY STANDS (see Stands, Dictionary)

DIRECTORY BOARDS (see Signs, Movable Letters)

DISPENSERS
ADHESIVES: Bro-Dart, Crossley-VanDeusen, Demco, Fordham, Sanford
PRESSURE SENSITIVE TAPE: Am Instructional, Am Library Line, Bro-Dart, Crossley-VanDeusen, Demco, Fordham, Gaylord, Highsmith, Talas, 3M

DISPLAY
ADHESIVES (see Adhesive, Display)
BOOK RACKS (see Furniture, Library)
CARD HOLDERS: Fordham, Lawrence
CASES (see Exhibit Cases)
CUTTING MACHINE: Cutawl
FASTENERS: Am Library Line (Plasti-Tak), Crossley-VanDeusen (Hold-it), Demco (Stik-tack), Fordham (Plasti-Tak), Gaylord (Plasti-Tak), Graffco (map tacks), Highsmith, Scovill (bank pins)
FIXTURES (see Display, Racks; Exhibit Cases, etc.)
LETTERS (see Letters, Display)
LIGHTING FIXTURES (see Lighting Fixtures)
MATERIALS, GENERAL SUPPLIERS: Am Crayon, Beckley-Cardy, Brewster, Chart-Pak, Demco, Fordham, Gaylord, Highsmith, Talas
OF-THE-MONTH: Library Prod
PANELS: Arlington, Attwood, Brewster, Demco, Fordham, Gaylord, Highsmith, Talas, Walker Systems
RACKS, LITERATURE: Am Instructional, Am Library Line, Arlington, Bro-Dart, Crossley-VanDeusen, Demco, EBSCO Subscription, Fordham, Gaylord, Highsmith, Safco, Talas
RACKS, METAL (book, magazine, newspaper): Acton, Am Instructional, Am Library Line, Ames, Art Metal, Backus, Bro-Dart, Butler, Crossley-VanDeusen, Demco, EBSCO Subscription, Estey, Fordham, Gaylord, Globe, Highsmith, Library Bureau, Smith System, Supreme, Talas, Weinberg

LIBRARY PURCHASING GUIDE / 545

RACKS, MOBILE: Am Instructional, Am Library Line, Bro-Dart, Catskill, Crossley-VanDeusen, Demco, Estey, Fordham, Gaylord, Highsmith
RACKS, PAPERBACKS: Am Instructional, Am Library Line, Bro-Dart, Butler, Crossley-VanDeusen, Demco, EBSCO Subscription, Fordham, Gaylord, Highsmith, Kersting, Reflector, Reynolds Enterprises, Selectamatic (automated), Talas
RACKS, RECORDINGS (see Recordings, Equipment, etc.)
RACKS, WOOD (book, magazine, newspaper): Am Instructional, Am Library Line, Backus, Bro-Dart, Buckstaff, Croyden, Demco, EBSCO Subscription, Estey, Fordham, Gaylord, Globe, Heller, Highsmith, Library Bureau, Sjostrom, Standard Wood, Talas, Weinberg
SUPPORTS, VERTICAL POLES: Brewster (Polecats)
TABLES: Slyd-In

DOCUMENT
BOXES, ACID-FREE (see Restoration & Preservation)
PROTECTORS (see Covers, Protective)
RECORD CARDS (see Cards, Document Record)

DOOR COUNTERS, ELECTRIC
Worner Electronic

DRILLS AND DRILL POINTS (see Magazine, Drills)

DRY MOUNTING EQUIPMENT & SUPPLIES (see Laminating)

DUPLICATE PERIODICALS AND BOOKS, EXCHANGE SERVICE (see Exchange Service, etc.)

DUPLICATING EQUIPMENT
ADHEROGRAPHY: 3M
MIMEOGRAPH: Chiang, Dick, Gaylord (Mini-Graph), Gestetner
MULTIGRAPH: AM Corp
OFFSET: AM Corp, Dick, Itek
OFFSET PLATE MAKING EQUIPMENT: AM Corp, Dick, Itek, Xerox
SMALL STENCIL: Am Library Line, Cardmaster, Chiang, Highsmith, Rudco
SPIRIT: Dick, Bell & Howell (Ditto Div), Fordham
STENCIL DUPLICATOR: Dick, Gestetner
XEROGRAPHY: Xerox

EASELS (see Chalkboards and Accessories)

EMBOSSING
MACHINES & TAPE (see Label Makers)
STAMP (see Stamps, Library Embossing)

EMPLOYMENT AGENCIES
Am Librarians, Burke (Theresa), Howard, Library Career

ENVELOPES
ACID-FREE: (see Restoration & Preservation)
CLIPPING: Am Library Line, Bro-Dart, Crossley-VanDeusen, Demco, Fordham, Gaylord, Highsmith
MICROFICHE (see Microfiche, Envelopes)
TRANSPARENT: Bro-Dart, Cel-U-Dex, Crossley-VanDeusen, Fordham, Gaylord, Talas
WINDOW, INTERLIBRARY LOAN: Demco, Gaylord

ERASERS
ELECTRIC: Am Instructional, Am Library Line, Bro-Dart, Bruning, Demco, Fordham, Gaylord, Highsmith, Keuffel, Sanford
STEEL: Am Library Line, Bro-Dart, Demco, Gaylord, Highsmith

EXCHANGE SERVICE FOR DUPLICATE PERIODICALS AND BOOKS
US Book Exchange

EXHIBIT CASES
INDOOR: Am Library Line, Art Metal, Attwood, Bro-Dart, Estey, Fordham, Gaylord, Gen Fireproofing, Highsmith, Kewanee, Michaels, Myrtle, Sjostrom, Weinberg
OUTDOOR: Fordham

EYELETTERS & EYELETS
Bates

FACSIMILE TRANSMITTERS
Dictaphone (Datafax), Xerox (LDX)

FIGURINES, CHINA (Beatrix Potter characters)
Elliott (John)

FILES
AUTOMATED ELECTRONIC: Supreme
CARD CATALOG (see Furniture, Library)
ENVELOPE: Am Instructional, Am Library Line, Bro-Dart, Crossley-VanDeusen, Demco, Fordham, Gaylord, Highsmith
FILM (see Films, Motion Picture)
FILMSTRIPS (see Filmstrip)
MAP: Art Metal, Bro-Dart, Crossley-VanDeusen, Demco, Fordham, Gen Fireproofing, Hamilton, Plan Hold, Stacor, Talas
MICROFICHE (see Microfiche)
MICROFILM (see Microfilm)
MICRO-OPAQUE (see Micro-Opaque)
NEWSPAPER: Am Instructional, Art Metal, Bro-Dart, Crossley-VanDeusen, Demco, Fordham, Gaylord, Globe, Highsmith, Library Bureau, Myrtle, Plan Hold
OPEN SHELF: Am Instructional, Ames, Art Metal, Bro-Dart, EQUIPTO, Estey, Fordham, Gaylord, InterRoyal, Library Bureau, Republic, Steelcase, Supreme, Talas, Yawman

PAMPHLET: Am Instructional, Am Library Line, Apex, Bro-Dart, Colbert, Crossley-VanDeusen, Demco, Fordham, Gaylord, Hamilton, Highsmith, Library Bureau, Magafile, Slyd-In, Steelcase, Talas
PERIODICAL: Am Bindery, Am Instructional, Am Library Line, Art Metal, Bro-Dart, Colbert, Crossley-VanDeusen, Demco, Estey, Fordham, Gaylord, Globe, Hamilton, Highsmith, Library Bureau, Magafile, Myrtle, Safco, Slyd-In, Steelcase, Talas, Weinberg
PERIODICAL (LIBRARY TECH PROG): Bro-Dart, Demco, Fordham
PRINCETON: Am Library Line, Bro-Dart, Crossley-VanDeusen, Demco, Estey, Fordham, Gaylord, Highsmith, Talas
PUNCHED CARD (see Tabulating Cards, Equipment & Supplies)
RECORDINGS (see Recordings, Equipment, etc.)
ROTARY: Am Instructional, Am Library Line, Bates, Bro-Dart, Crossley-VanDeusen, Diebold, Fordham, Globe, Highsmith, Stacor
SLIDES (see Slides, Equipment, etc.)
STEEL: Am Instructional, Am Library Line, Art Metal, Bro-Dart, Demco, Estey, Fordham, Gaylord, Gen Fireproofing, Globe, Hamilton, Highsmith, Neumade (AV), RemRand Systems, Sjostrom, Talas, Va Metal, Wallach, Yawman
STORAGE: Am Instructional, Art Metal, Bro-Dart, Crossley-VanDeusen, Demco, Fordham, Gaylord, Highsmith, RemRand Systems, Talas
VERTICAL: Am Instructional, Ames, Art Metal, Bro-Dart, Crossley-VanDeusen, EQUIPTO, Estey, Fordham, Gen Fireproofing, Globe, Hamilton, Myrtle, RemRand Systems, Sjostrom, Va Metal, Yawman
VISIBLE: Am Instructional, Art Metal, Crossley-VanDeusen, Demco, Fordham, Gaylord, Globe, Highsmith, RemRand Systems, Talas, Yawman
WOOD: Am Instructional, Bro-Dart, Buckstaff, Crossley-VanDeusen, Croyden, Estey, Fordham, Heller, Highsmith, Library Bureau, Myrtle, Sjostrom, Standard Wood, Weinberg

FILING
DRAWER DIVIDERS, STEEL: Cel-U-Dex, Crossley-VanDeusen
FLAGS, CARD CATALOG: Am Library Line, Cel-U-Dex, Crossley-VanDeusen, Demco, Fordham, Highsmith
SIGNALS (see Signal Tabs)
SUPPLIES: Am Instructional, Am Library Line, Bro-Dart, Cel-U-Dex, Crossley-VanDeusen, Demco, Fordham, Gaylord, Globe, Highsmith, Horders, Nat'l Stationers, Yawman

FILMS, MOTION PICTURE (see Motion Picture Films)

FILMS, MOTION PICTURE, EQUIPMENT, SERVICES & SUPPLIES
CEMENT: Bro-Dart, Demco, Eastman, Fordham, Harwald, Int'l Film, Neumade
CLEANERS, PRESERVATIVES & PRESERVATION SERVICES: Am Instructional, Demco, Documat, Eastman, Fordham, Harwald, Int'l Film, Neumade
8MM FILM LOOP PROJECTORS: Fairchild Industrial, Fordham, Jayark, Technicolor
8MM PROJECTORS: Am Instructional, DuKane, Eastman, Fairchild Industrial, Honeywell Photo, Viewlex
GENERAL SUPPLIERS: Am Instructional, Am Library Line, Beseler, Demco, Eastman, Fordham, Harwald, Int'l Film, Neumade, Wallach
RECORD CARDS (Acquisition, Booking, etc.) (see Cards, Audiovisual)
RETURN DEPOSITORIES: Mosler, Highsmith
REVIEWING SERVICES: Educational Film, Films in Review, Landers
REWINDERS: Eastman, Harwald, Int'l Film, Kodak, Library Microfilms & Materials, Neumade
SEPARATOR RACKS: Am Instructional, Bro-Dart, Demco, Fordham, Gaylord, Harwald, Neumade, Wallach
SHIPPING CASES: Am Library Line, Bal, Demco, Library Microfilms & Materials, Neumade, Talas
16MM PROJECTORS: Bell & Howell (AV Div), Eastman, Fordham, Graflex, Honeywell Photo, NORELCO, RCA AV Div, Viewlex
SPLICERS: Bro-Dart, Demco, Eastman, Harwald, Library Microfilms & Materials, Neumade
STORAGE CABINETS (FILES): Advance Prod, Am Instructional, Am Library Line, Bro-Dart, Crossley-VanDeusen, Demco, Fordham, Gaylord, Hamilton, Harwald, Highsmith, Library Filmstrip, Library Microfilms & Materials, Mosler, Neumade, Smith System, Talas, Wallach

FILMSTRIP
PREVIEWERS: Avid, Bell & Howell (AV Div), Bro-Dart, Demco, Fordham, Graflex, Hudson, Viewlex
PROJECTORS: Am Instructional, Audio-Masters, Avid, Bell & Howell (AV Div), Bro-Dart, Coffey, Demco, DuKane, Ealing Film, Eastman, Fordham, Graflex, Hudson, Library Filmstrip, Viewlex
SOUND PROJECTORS: Am Instructional, Audio-Master, Avid, Bell & Howell (AV Div), Beseler, DuKane, Fordham, Graflex, Library Filmstrip, Viewlex

STORAGE CASES & RACKS: Advance Prod, Am Instructional, Am Library Line, Bro-Dart, Demco, Estey, Fordham, Gaylord, Highsmith, Kersting, Library Filmstrip, Society for Visual Ed, Talas, Wallach

FILMSTRIPS, SILENT & SOUND (for additional listings see "Audiovisual Market Place," Bowker)
LIBRARY SKILLS: Am Instructional, Am Library Line, Bro-Dart, Encyclopaedia Britannica, Fordham, Highsmith, Library Filmstrip
VARIOUS SUBJECTS: Acoustifone, Am Instructional, Avid, Benefic Press, Bowmar Records, Bowmar (Stanley), Bro-Dart Caedmon, Clark, Collier-Macmillan, Coronet, CW Assoc, Demco, Denoyer-Geppert, Ealing Films, Educational Activities, EMC Corp, Encyclopaedia Britannica, Enrichment Materials, Eye Gate, Filmstrip House, Fordham, Graflex, Hammett Hudson, Imperial Film, Int'l Film, Learning Media, Library Filmstrip, Listening Library, Lyceum, McGraw-Hill, Olin, Potters, Popular Science, Q-ED Productions, Scholastic, Scott Education, Simon & Schuster (Ed Div), Spoken Arts, United Prod, Univ Ed, Univ Wash, Valiant, Viewlex, Western Publishing, Weston Woods, Westport

FINE CALCULATOR
Demco, Gaylord

FINGER TIP MOISTENERS
Am Library Line, Cel-U-Dex, Crossley-VanDeusen, Demco, Fordham, Highsmith

FIRE PROTECTION
ALARMS: Benedict, Honeywell Commercial, Norris, Simplex, Worner Electronic
EXTINGUISHERS: Norris

FLAGS (pennants, banners, etc.) Am Instructional, Fordham, Highsmith

FLANNEL BOARDS AND ACCESSORIES (see Chalkboards and Accessories)

FLOOR COVERINGS
CARPETING (indoor & outdoor: Armstrong Cork
RESILIENT TILE: Armstrong Cork
RUBBER RUNNERS: Crown Rubber

FLOOR MAINTENANCE SUPPLIES
Armstrong Cork, Johnson (SC)

FOLDING MACHINES
Dick, Pitney-Bowes

FOLIO SUPPORTS (see Book Supports)

FOREIGN BOOKSELLERS (see Booksellers, Foreign)

FORMS
AUDIOVISUAL: Am Instructional, Am Library Line, Bro-Dart, Coffey, Crossley-VanDeusen, Demco, Fordham, Gaylord, Highsmith
BOOK ORDER, NO CARBON REQUIRED: Am Instructional, Am Library Line, Bro-Dart, Crossley-Van Deusen, Demco, Fordham, Gaylord, Highsmith
BOOK ORDER, OPTICAL CHARACTER RECOGNITION: Am Library Line, Demco, Fordham, Gaylord
BOOK ORDER, REGULAR: Am Library Line, Baker & Taylor, Bro-Dart, Demco, Fordham, Gaylord, Highsmith
CIRCULATION: Am Library Line, Bro-Dart, Crossley-VanDeusen, Demco, Fordham, Gaylord, Highsmith
INTERLIBRARY LOAN: Am Instructional, Am Library Line, Bro-Dart, Demco, Gaylord, Highsmith
OVERNIGHT BOOK SLIPS: Am Library Line, Bro-Dart, Crossley-VanDeusen, Demco, Fordham, Gaylord, Highsmith
PHONOGRAPH RECORD ORDER: Bro-Dart, Demco, Fordham
PHOTODUPLICATION ORDER: Am Library Line, Bro-Dart, Demco, Gaylord
PRINTED TO ORDER: Am Instructional, Am Library Line, Bro-Dart, Crossley-VanDeusen, Demco, Fordham, Gaylord, Nat'l Stationers
SCHOOL LIBRARY: Am Instructional, Am Library Line, Baker & Taylor, Bro-Dart, Demco, Fordham, Gaylord, Highsmith
STATISTICAL REPORTS: Demco, Gaylord, Highsmith

FREE EDUCATIONAL MATERIALS, GUIDES TO
Educators Progress

FURNITURE
AUDITORIUM: Am Seating, Southern Desk, Thonet
IMPORTED: Langfeld Manex, Risom
LIBRARY: Am Desk, Am Instructional, Am Library Line, Am Seating, Art Metal, Backus, Bro-Dart, Brown, Buckstaff, Crossley-VanDeusen, Croyden, Decor Plastic, Demco, Directional, EBSCO Subscription, Estey, Fetzer's, Fixtures Mfg, Fleetwood Furniture, Fordham, Gaylord, Gen Fireproofing, Globe, Hammett, Heller, Highsmith, Inter-Royal, Knipp (custom), Knoll, Langfeld Manex, Library Bureau, Miller, Myrtle, Probber, Reflector, Reska, Risom, Sjostrom, Slyd-In, Smith System, Southern Desk, Stacor, Standard Wood, Steelcase, Talas, Vista Costa, Weinberg, Worden
LOUNGE: Am Desk, Bro-Dart, Buckstaff, Demco, Dux, Fordham, Knoll, Library

548 / LIBRARY PURCHASING GUIDE

Bureau, Miller, Myrtle, Risom, Sjostrom, Stacor, Steelcase, Thonet, Weinberg
METAL: Am Instructional, Am Seating, Art Metal, Beckley-Cardy, Bro-Dart, Brown, Demco, Estey, Fixtures Mfg, Fordham, Gaylord, Globe, Hamilton, Highsmith, InterRoyal, Knoll, Library Bureau, Miller, Steelcase, Weinberg, Wilson (Andrew), Yawman
OFFICE: Am Desk, Am Instructional, Art Metal, Bro-Dart, Buckstaff, Crossley-VanDeusen, Estey, Fordham, Gen Fireproofing, Globe, Hamilton, InterRoyal, Knoll, Library Bureau, Miller, Risom, Sjostrom, Stacor, Steelcase, Thonet, Tiffany, Vogel-Peterson (coat racks), Weinberg
SCHOOL: Am Instructional, Am Seating, Beckley-Cardy, Bro-Dart, Fordham, Highsmith, Reflector, Southern Desk, Thonet
WOOD: Am Desk, Am Instructional, Am Seating, Bro-Dart, Brown, Buckstaff, Croyden, Decor Plastic, Directional, Estey, Fetzer's Fordham, Gaylord, Heller, Highsmith, Knoll, Library Bureau, Miller, Myrtle, Probber, Risom, Sjostrom, Southern Desk, Stacor, Standard Wood, Subscription, Talas, Thonet, Vista Costa, Worden
WORKROOM: Bro-Dart, Fordham, Sjostrom

FURNITURE, FOLDING
CHAIRS: Am Seating, Crossley-VanDeusen, Fordham, Monroe
LECTERNS (see Lecterns, Folding)
TABLES: Am Instructional, Am Seating, Crossley-VanDeusen, Fordham, Howe, Monroe, Weinberg

FURNITURE PLANNING
LAYOUT SERVICE: Art Metal, Bro-Dart, Brown, Buckstaff, Croyden, Fetzer's, Gen Fireproofing, Interiors, Knoll, Library Bureau, Library Microfilms & Materials, Miller, Myrtle, Reflector, Reska, Sjostrom, Southern Desk, Standard Wood, Steelcase, Weinberg, Worden, Yawman
SCALE MODELS (library equipment): M&M Industries, Visual Industrial

FURNITURE POLISH
Crossley-VanDeusen, Johnson (SC)

GAMES
EDUCATIONAL: Educational Reading
FOREIGN LANGUAGE: French & European (French), Rosenberg
LIBRARY TRAINING: Fordham

GLOBES (see Maps and Globes)

GLUE (see Adhesive, Glue)

GLUING MACHINES
Am Library Line, Fordham, Potdevin, Talas

GOVERNMENT PUBLICATIONS
Bernan (US), Bliss, British Info (UK), Microcard Editions (NCR) (US, UK, Fr, Ger, OAS), Readex Microprint (US, UK, UN), Ward (US), US Book Exchange

GUIDES
CATALOG: Am Instructional, Am Library Line, Bro-Dart, Demco, Fordham, Gaylord, Highsmith
CATALOG, CATHOLIC: Demco
CATALOG, INSTRUCTION: Bro-Dart, Demco, Fordham, Gaylord, Highsmith
CATALOG, PLASTIC: Am Library Line, Crossley-VanDeusen, Demco, Fordham, Gaylord, Highsmith
CHARGING TRAY: Am Instructional, Am Library Line, Bro-Dart, Crossley-VanDeusen, Demco, Fordham, Gaylord, Highsmith
RESERVE BOOK CARDS: Am Library Line, Bro-Dart, Crossley-VanDeusen, Demco, Fordham, Gaylord, Highsmith
SHELF-LIST: Am Instructional, Am Library Line, Bro-Dart, Crossley-VanDeusen, Demco, Fordham, Gaylord, Highsmith

HEADPHONES
Audiotronics, Avedex, Avid, Bell & Howell, MPC, Newcomb, Perry, RCA AV Div, Rheem-Califone

HINGE TAPE (see Tape, Mending)

HOLIDAY CUT-OUTS
Dennison, Library Prod

HUMIDIFIERS & DEHUMIDIFIERS
Abbeon, Walton

IDENTIFICATION CARDS (see Cards, Circulation, Identification)

INDEX HOLDERS
Ames, Demco, Va Metal

INDEXING SERVICES
Herner, LEASCO, Talas, Thompson

INDEX TABLES (CBI) (see Furniture, Library)

INDEX TABS AND DIVIDERS
Cel-U-Dex, Crossley-VanDeusen, Demco, Dennison, Highsmith

INFORMATION RETRIEVAL SYSTEMS (see Retrieval Systems)

INK
DRAWING: Am Library Line, Crossley-VanDeusen, Higgins, Highsmith
DUPLICATING MACHINE: Demco, Dick, Fordham, Gaylord, Highsmith
ENGROSSING: Am Library Line, Bro-Dart, Crossley-VanDeusen, Demco, Gaylord, Higgins, Highsmith
INDELIBLE: Sanford
MARKING: Am Library Line, Bro-Dart, Crossley-VanDeusen, Demco, Gaylord, Highsmith

STAMP PAD: Am Instructional, Am Library Line, Bro-Dart, Crossley-VanDeusen, Demco, Fordham, Gaylord, Highsmith
WHITE (book or spine marking): Am Library Line, Bro-Dart, Crossley-VanDeusen, Demco, Gaylord, Highsmith, Sanford
WRITING: Higgins, Highsmith, Sanford

INSURANCE
Byrne (comprehensive), Hartford (fire)

INTERIOR DESIGNERS
Concept Designs, Interiors

INTERLIBRARY LOAN FORMS (see Forms, Interlibrary Loan)

JIFFY BOOK BAGS (see Book Mailing Bags)

JOBBERS (see Booksellers, Wholesale)

KEY FILING CABINETS (see Security Equipment)

KEYSORT (tabulating cards)
McBee

KITCHEN UNITS (compact stove, sink, etc.)
Dwyer

LABEL GUMMING MACHINES
Diagraph-Bradley, Fordham, Potdevin, Talas

LABEL HOLDERS (see Shelf Label Holders)

LABEL MAKERS AND TAPE
Am Instructional, Am Library Line, Bro-Dart, Crossley-VanDeusen, Demco, Dennison, Fordham, Gaylord, Highsmith

LABELS
CALL NUMBER: Am Instructional, Am Library Line, Bro-Dart, Crossley-VanDeusen, Demco, Fordham, Gaylord, Highsmith, Omni-Card
DATA PROCESSING: Ever Ready
FILM STRIP CAN: Am Library Line, Crossley-VanDeusen, Demco, Fordham, Gaylord, Highsmith
GUMMED: Am Library Line, Bro-Dart, Crossley-VanDeusen, Demco, Dennison, Fordham, Gaylord, Highsmith
MAILING: Crossley-VanDeusen, Demco, Dennison
PHONOGRAPH RECORD: Am Library Line, Crossley-VanDeusen, Demco, Highsmith
PRESSURE SENSITIVE: Am Instructional, Am Library Line, Bro-Dart, Chart-Pak, Crossley-VanDeusen, Demco, Dennison, Ever Ready, Fordham, Gaylord, Highsmith
PRESSURE SENSITIVE PRINTED & DECORATIVE: Am Library Line, Bro-Dart, Crossley-VanDeusen, Demco, Fordham, Gaylord, Highsmith
PRINTED ("7 day book," etc.): Am Library Line, Bro-Dart, Crossley-VanDeusen, Demco, Fordham, Gaylord, Highsmith
SHELF (ENGRAVED PLASTIC): Bro-Dart, Cel-U-Dex, Crossley-VanDeusen, Demco, Fordham, Gaylord, Highsmith, Library Prod
SHELF (MAGNETIC): Weyll

LACQUER, BOOK
Am Library Line, Bro-Dart, Crossley-VanDeusen, Demco, Fordham, Gaylord

LADDERS
Talas

LAMINATING
MATERIALS AND EQUIPMENT: Am Instructional, Am Library Line, Arbee, Barrow, Crossley-VanDeusen, Demco, DuPont, Fordham, Gaylord, Gen Binding, Highsmith, Seal, 3M
SERVICES: (see Restoration & Preservation)
VENDING-MACHINE (see Coin Operated Equipment)

LEARNING LABORATORY SYSTEMS (see also Audiovisual Mobile Equipment Centers; Carrels, Audiovisual)
FIXED INSTALLATIONS: Am Seating, Backus, Chester Electronics, DuKane, MP Audio, MPC, Perry, RCA AV Div, Radio-Matic, Rheem-Califone, Sjostrom
MOBILE-PORTABLE: Am Seating, Avid, Bell & Howell, (AV Div), Bro-Dart, Demco, DuKane, Electronic Futures, MPC, NORELCO, PH Electronics, Radio-Matic, Rheem-Califone, Wilson Corp

LEASED BOOKS AND EQUIPMENT (see Rental)

LEATHER BOOKBINDING (see Binding Materials & Equipment)

LEATHER PRESERVATIVE (see Binding Materials & Equipment)

LECTERNS
FOLDING: Am Instructional, Highsmith, Oravisual
MOBILE: Am Instructional, Crossley-VanDeusen, Demco, Highsmith
STANDARD (see Furniture, Library)
TABLE: Am Instructional, Demco, Fordham, Highsmith

LETTERING PENS (see Pens)

LETTERS, DISPLAY
CERAMIC: Demco, Highsmith, Mitten
MAGNETIC: Highsmith
PAPER AND CARDBOARD: Crossley-VanDeusen, Demco, Dennison, Highsmith, Judy, Mutual Education
PLASTIC: Am Instructional, Am Library Line, Attwood, Crossley-VanDeusen (Planotype), Demco (Profile & Hook 'N Loop), Fordham (Alpha Peg), Gaylord, Highsmith, Mutual Education
TRANSFER: Talas

550 / LIBRARY PURCHASING GUIDE

LIBRARY AIDE BUTTON (see also Award Pins)
Demco, Highsmith

LIBRARY INSTRUCTION CHARTS (see also Posters, Library Instruction)
Am Library Line, Fordham, Highsmith, Ideal School, Perfection

LIBRARY LISTENING CENTERS (see also Learning Laboratory Systems; Carrels, Audiovisual)
Acoustifone, Avedex, Bell & Howell AV Div, Electronic Futures

LIBRARY PUBLIC RELATIONS (see Publicity Services & Materials)

LIBRARY SUPPLIERS
(Firms listed offer extensive selections of library supplies and send catalogs free on request)
Am Instructional, Am Library Line, Bro-Dart, Demco, Fordham, Gaylord, Highsmith, Talas

LIGHTING CONTROLS
Honeywell Commercial, Tork

LIGHTING FIXTURES
DESK: Amplex, Crossley-VanDeusen, Fordham, Highsmith
DISPLAY: Amplex, Brewster
EMERGENCY: Tork
FLUORESCENT: Holophane
INCANDESCENT: Holophane
STACK: Holophane, Reflector

LISTENING CENTERS & TABLES (see Learning Laboratory Systems)

LOCKERS
EQUIPTO, Fordham, Sentinel Lockers

MAGAZINE
CHARGING CARDS (see Cards, Circulation, Magazine Charging)
DISPLAY RACKS (see Display, Racks)
DRILLS: Bro-Dart, Demco, Highsmith
PREBINDERS (see Binding Services)
PROTECTIVE COVERS (see Binders, Magazine)
RECORD CARDS (see Cards, Magazine Record)
RECORD SYSTEM: Highsmith
REPRINTS (see Book Reproduction)

MAGAZINE DEALERS
BACK NUMBERS: Abrahams, Back Issues, Bliss, British Book Centre, Four Continent (Russian), Harrassowitz, Hoffman, Int'l University, Johnson (Walter), Kraus, Maxwell Scientific, Midtown, Phiebig, Rosenberg (German & French), Smith (Don), Stechert, US Book Exchange, Zeitlin
DOMESTIC SUBSCRIPTIONS: Ancorp, BIPAD, EBSCO Subscription, Faxon, Franklin Sq, McGregor, Maxwell Scientific, Mayfair, Moore-Cottrell
FOREIGN SUBSCRIPTIONS: Ancorp, British Book Centre, Brockhaus (German), Four Continent (Russian), Franklin Sq, French & European, Harrassowitz, Int'l University, Japan Publications, Johnson (Walter), Librairie de France, McGregor, Maxwell Scientific, Mayfair, Moore-Cottrell, Phiebig, Rosenberg (German & French), Stechert, Stevens & Brown, Swets & Zeitlinger, Wittenborn (Art)

MAGNIFIERS
Am Library Line, Am Optical, Apex Specialties, Bausch & Lomb, Gaylord, Opaque Systems, Swift Instruments, Talas

MAILING BAGS, BOOKS (see Book Mailing Bags)

MAILING MACHINES
Pitney-Bowes

MAPS & GLOBES
Am Instructional, Am Map, Benefic Press, Cram, Demco, Denoyer-Geppert, Farquhar, Fordham, Hagstrom, Hammond, Highsmith, Hubbard, Nystrom, Rand McNally, Replogle

MAP TACKS
Fordham, Graffco, Highsmith, Talas

MARGIN GLUERS
Am Library Line, Fordham, Potdevin

MARKING EQUIPMENT & SUPPLIES
CALL NUMBER LABELS: Am Instructional, Am Library Line, Bro-Dart, Crossley-VanDeusen, Demco, Fordham, Gaylord (Se-Lin), Highsmith
CALL NUMBER LABEL SHEARS: Demco, Swift Cutter
CALL NUMBER STAMPING EQUIPMENT: Altair, Demco
COLD TRANSFER CALL NUMBERS: Bro-Dart, Demco, Fordham, Highsmith
ELECTRIC PENCILS (see Pencils, Electric)
ELECTRIC SEALING IRON: Am Library Line, Bro-Dart, Demco, Gaylord, Highsmith
FLAT STAMPING MACHINES: Altair
HOT STAMPING TYPE: Altair
LABEL PRINTING EQUIPMENT: Gaylord (Se-Lin), Scientific (Se-Lin)
MARKING INK (see Ink, Marking)
MARKING KITS: Am Instructional, Bro-Dart, Fordham, Highsmith
MARKING TAPE (see Tape, Marking)
PENS (see Pens, Marking)
PENS, FELT TIP (see Pens, Felt Tip Marking)
SUBJECT SYMBOLS: Bro-Dart, Demco, Fordham, Highsmith
TABLES AND HOLDERS: Altair, Bro-Dart, Demco, Fordham, Gaylord
TRANSFER PAPER (see Paper, Transfer)

MEMORIAL BOOKS, PROMOTIONAL MATERIAL
Antioch, Fordham, Highsmith

MEMORIAL PLAQUES (see Signs, Metal)

LIBRARY PURCHASING GUIDE / 551

MENDING
  TAPE (see Tape, Mending)
  TISSUE: Bro-Dart, Crossley-VanDeusen, Demco, Seal
MICRODATA CATALOGING SYSTEM (see Cards, Catalog, Library of Congress on Microfiche)
MICROFICHE (see also Ultrafiche)
  CAMERAS: Audio-Visual Research, Microcard Editions (NCR)
  COPYING SERVICE: Fordham
  DEVELOPERS: Atlantic Microfilm
  ENVELOPES: Highsmith, Microcard Editions (NCR)
  GUIDES: Am Instructional, Bro-Dart, Demco, Fordham, Highsmith
  PROJECTORS: Fordham
  PROTECTORS: Bro-Dart, Fordham, Highsmith, Microcard Editions (NCR)
  PUBLISHERS: AMS Press, Bay Microfilm, Bell & Howell (Micro Photo Div), CCM Information, Demco, Ecology Forum, EP Group, Godfrey, Greenwood, IM Press (3M), Jackson Reprint, LEASCO, Library Resources, Lost Cause, Maxwell Int'l, Microcard Editions (NCR), Microfilming Corp, NY Times, Pandex (Science Index), Paris Publications, Readex, Univ Microfilms (Xerox), Univ Music
  READER-PRINTERS: Readex Microprint, Univ Microfilms (Xerox)
  READERS: Am Instructional, Atlantic Microfilm, Audio Visual Research, Canon, DASA, Eastman, Fordham, Library Bureau, Library Microfilms & Materials, Library Resources, Microreader, Nat'l Cash (Ind Prod Div), Paris Publications, Readex Microprint, Univ Microfilms (Xerox)
  STORAGE CABINETS: Am Instructional, Am Library Line, Atlantic Microfilm, Bro-Dart, Crossley-VanDeusen, Demco, Estey, Fordham, Gaylord, Highsmith, Library Microfilm & Materials, Microcard Editions (NCR), Mosler, Univ Microfilms (Xerox)
MICROFILM
  BOXES: Library Microfilms and Materials
  COPYING SERVICES: Atlantic Microfilm, Bell & Howell (Micro Photo Div), Gen Microfilm, Hall, Herner, Microfilming Corp, Univ Microfilms (Xerox)
  MAGAZINES (ROLLS TO CARTRIDGES): Eastman
  MICROFILMERS: Bell & Howell (Micro Photo Div), Eastman, Itek, Regiscope
  PRESERVATIVE TREATMENT (see Films, Motion Picture, Equipment, etc.)
  PROCESSORS: Eastman
  PROJECTORS: Library Microfilms & Materials
  PUBLISHERS: AMS Press, Arcata, Atlantic Microfilm, Bay Microfilm, Bell & Howell (Micro Photo Div), CCC Information, Chemical Abstracts, Cowles Educ, EP Group, Eastman, Gen Microfilm, IM Press (3M), Library Micrographic, Library of Congress, Maxwell Int'l, Microcard Editions (NCR), Microfilming Corp, Nat'l Planning, NY Times, Princeton, Univ Microfilms (Xerox)
  READER-PRINTERS: Bell & Howell (Micro Photo Div), DASA, Eastman, Itek, Library Bureau, 3M, Xerox
  READER-PRINTERS, COIN OPERATED (see Coin Operated Equipment)
  READERS: Am Instructional, Audio Visual Research, Atlantic Microfilm, DASA, Eastman, Information Design, Itek, Library Bureau, Library Microfilms & Materials, Microreader, 3M, Univ Microfilms (Xerox)
  REPRODUCTIONS FROM: Bell & Howell (Micro Photo Div), Gen Microfilm, Microfilming Corp, Univ Microfilms (Xerox)
  REWINDERS: Library Microfilms & Materials
  SHIPPING CASES: Library Microfilms & Materials
  STORAGE CABINETS (FILES): Am Instructional, Am Library Line, Art Metal, Atlantic Microfilm, Bro-Dart, Demco, Estey, Fordham, Gaylord, Hamilton, Highsmith, Information Design, Library Microfilms & Materials, Microcard Editions (NCR) Mosler, Neumade, Steelcase, Talas, Univ Microfilms (Xerox), Wallach, Yawman
MICROFORMS (for listing see "Guide to Microforms in Print" and "Subject Guide to Microforms in Print," published by Microcard Editions (NCR)
MICRO-OPQAUE (MICROCARDS)
  PUBLISHERS: Canner, EP Group, Godfrey, Graphic, Lawyers (Microlex), Lost Cause, Maxwell Scientific, Microcard Editions (NCR), Readex Microprint, Stechert
  READER-PRINTERS: Readex Microprint
  READERS: Lawyers (Microlex), Microreader (Mini-Print), Nat'l Cash (Ind Prod Div), Readex Microprint (Microprint)
  STORAGE CABINETS: Library Microfilms & Materials, Microcard Editions (NCR)
MICROPHONES
  Ampex, Audiotronics, DuKane, Rheem-Califone
MICROPRINT (see Micro-Opaque, Publishers)
MICROTEXT (see Microfiche, Microfilm, or Micro-Opaque Publishers)
MOISTENER, BOOK POCKET
  Demco, Gaylord, Highsmith
MOTION PICTURES, Equipment, Services & Supplies (see Films, Motion Picture, Equipment, etc.)

MOTION PICTURE FILMS (for additional listings see "Audiovisual Market Place: A Multimedia Guide," Bowker)
  8MM (standard & super): Bell System (AT&T), Brandon, Coffey, Coronet, CRM Films, Crowell, CW Assoc, Demco, Dick, Doubleday, EMC Corp, Encyclopaedia Britannica, Eye Gate, Film Classic, Jayark, McGraw-Hill, Potters, Scott Education, Society for Visual Ed, Univ Ed, Univ Wash, Weston Woods
  8MM FILM LOOPS (standard & super): Am Instructional, Assoc Instr Mats, Bell System (AT&T), Bowmar (Stanley), Bro-Dart, Churchill, Clark, Coffey, Coronet, CW Assoc, Demco, Ealing Films, EMC Corp, Encyclopaedia Britannica, Eye Gate, Fordham, Graflex, Hubbard, Learning Media, McGraw-Hill, Popular Science, Potters, Q-ED Productions, Scott Education, Society for Visual Ed, Thorne, Univ Ed, Weston Woods
  LIBRARY SKILLS: Am Instructional, Demco, Encyclopaedia Britannica, Eye Gate, Fordham, Wing
  16MM: Am Instructional, Assoc Instr Mats, Bell System (AT&T), Bro-Dart, Carousel Films, CCM Films, Churchill, Coffey, Contemporary Films, Coronet, Counterpoint, Demco, Denoyer-Geppert, Doubleday, DuPont, Ealing Films, EMC Corp, Encyclopaedia Britannica, Film Classic, Films Inc, Fleetwood Films, Fordham, Greenwood, Int'l Film, King Screen, Kodak, McGraw-Hill, NY Times, Q-ED Productions, Scott Education, Stuart Reynolds, Teleketics, Thorne, Time-Life, Univ Ed, Univ Wash, Weston Woods, Wing, Xerox Films

MOUNTING PAPER (see Paper, Mounting)

MULTIMEDIA MATERIALS (see also Book, Records)
  Aevac, ALESCO, Am Instructional, Clark, Demco, EMC Corp, Fordham, IM Press (3M), Instructo, Learning Media, Lyceum, McGraw-Hill, Scholastic Audio Visual, Scott Education, Simon & Schuster, Spoken Arts, Weston Woods

MUSEUM CASES (see Exhibit Cases)

MUSIC, SHEET
  BINDERS (see Binders, Sheet Music)
  BROWSERS: Reynolds Enterprises
  FILES (see Files, Pamphlet)
  WHOLESALERS: Bro-Dart, Fischer, Goody, Schirmer

MYLAR (DuPont Polyester film—see also Book Covers, Mylar)
  Dupont

NAME PLATES
  Attwood, Bro-Dart, Cel-U-Dex, Crossley-VanDeusen, Demco, Embosograf, Ever Ready, Fordham, Gaylord, Highsmith

NEWSPAPERS
  CLIPPING KNIFE: Am Library Line, Crossley-VanDeusen, Fordham, Highsmith
  FILES (see Files, Newspaper)
  IN MICROFORM (see Microfilm, Microfiche & Micro-Opaque, Publishers)
  RACKS (see Furniture, Library)

NUMBERING MACHINES
  Am Instructional, Am Library Line, Bates, Bostitch, Bro-Dart, Crossley-VanDeusen, Demco, Force, Fordham, Gaylord, Highsmith, Simplex

OFFICE LANDSCAPE PARTITIONS
  Reflector, Steelcase

OFFICE SUPPLY STORES
  Horder's, Nat'l Stationers

ORDER FORMS, BOOK OR RECORDINGS (see Forms, Book Order or Phonograph Record Order)

OUT-OF-PRINT BOOKS (see Booksellers, Out-of-print Books)

OUT-OF-PRINT BOOKS REPRODUCED (see Book Reproduction)

OUT-OF-PRINT US GOV'T DOCUMENTS (see Government Publications)

OVERDUE
  NOTICES (see Forms, Circulation)
  POST CARDS (see Cards, Circulation, Overdue Post)

OVERNIGHT BOOK SLIPS (see Forms)

OVERHEAD TRANSPARENCIES
  LIBRARY SKILLS: Am Instructional, Am Library Line, Demco, Encyclopaedia Britannica, Fordham, Highsmith, Microcard Editions (NCR)
  VARIOUS SUBJECTS: Aevac, Am Instructional, Am Map, Benefic Press, Beseler, Bowmar (Stanley), Bro-Dart, Clark, Creative Visuals, Coffey, Demco, Encyclopaedia Britannica, Eye Gate, Fordham, GAF Corp, Hammett, Hammond, Hubbard, Ideal School, Instructo, Jayark, Keuffel, Learning Media, McGraw-Hill, Popular Science, Potters, Scholastic Audio-Visual, Scott Education, Technifax, 3M, Tweedy, Univ Ed, Valiant, Western Publishing (for additional listings see "Audiovisual Market Place: a Multimedia Guide,' Bowker)

OVERHEAD TRANSPARENCIES, EQUIPMENT, SERVICES, & SUPPLIES
  ENVELOPES: Am Instructional, Coffey, Crossley-VanDeusen, Demco, Fordham, Gaylord, Highsmith
  FILM: Am Instructional, Demco, Fordham, Highsmith, Talas

GENERAL SUPPLIERS: Am Instructional, Ampex, Beseler, Chart-Pak, Coffey, Creative Visuals, Crossley-VanDeusen, Demco, Dick, Fordham, Gaylord, Gestetner, Highsmith, Keuffel, Seal, Talas, Technifax, 3M, Viewlex
LETTERING SETS: Demco, Fordham, Talas, Woods-Regan
MAKING EQUIPMENT: Coffey, Demco, Eastman, Honeywell, Seal, Talas, Technifax, 3M, Viewlex
MARKING PENS (see Pens, Overhead Transparency Marking)
MOUNTS: Am Instructional, Demco, Fordham, Gaylord, Highsmith, Talas
PROJECTORS: Am Instructional, Am Optical, Beseler, Fordham, Highsmith, Technifax, 3M, Wilson Corp
STORAGE CABINETS: Am Instructional, Am Library Line, Bro-Dart, Coffey, Crossley-VanDeusen, Demco, Fordham, Gaylord, Highsmith, Library Filmstrip, Talas, Wallach

PACKAGE TYING MACHINE
Bunn

PAGE PROTECTORS (see Covers, Protective, Page)

PAMPHLET CASES (see Files, Pamphlet)

PAMPHLET DISPLAY CASE
CLOTH: Demco
LUCITE: Fordham

PAMPHLET JOBBERS
Bacon, William-Frederick

PAPER
ACID-FREE (see Restoration & Preservation)
BOOKBINDING (see Binding Materials & Equipment)
DISPLAY: Am Library Line, Demco, Nelson-Whitehead, Paper Corp
MARGIN: Demco
MOUNTING: Bro-Dart, Demco, Gaylord, Highsmith, Talas
TISSUE AND CREPE: Dennison
TRANSFER: Am Library Line, Bro-Dart, Demco, Fordham, Gaylord, Highsmith

PAPERBACKS (see Binding Materials & Equipment; Binding Services, Booksellers; Display, Racks, etc.)

PAPER BOXES (see Files, Pamphlet or Periodical)

PAPER CLIPS
PLASTIC: Crossley-VanDeusen, Talas
STAINLESS STEEL: (see Restoration & Preservation)

PAPER CUTTERS
Am Library Line, Bro-Dart, Crossley-VanDeusen, Demco, Fordham, Gaylord, Highsmith, Michael Business, Talas

PARTITIONS
MOVABLE: Brewster, Walker Systems
OFFICE: Art Metal, Fordham, Gen Fireproofing

PASTE (see Adhesive, Paste)

PEGBOARD (see Display, Panels)

PENCIL DATE HOLDERS
Bro-Dart, Demco, Fordham, Gaylord, Highsmith

PENCILS
CHAIN SECURED: Am Library Line, Crossley-VanDeusen, Demco, Fordham, Gaylord, Highsmith
ELECTRIC: Am Instructional, Am Library Line, Bro-Dart, Crossley-VanDeusen, Demco, Fordham, Gaylord, Highsmith
FILM MARKING: Am Instructional, Bro-Dart, Crossley-VanDeusen, Demco, Fordham, Staedtler

PENS
BALL POINT: Am Instructional, Crossley-VanDeusen, Fordham, Gaylord
BALL POINT, CHAIN SECURED: Am Instructional, Am Library Line, Bro-Dart, Crossley-VanDeusen, Demco, Fordham, Gaylord, Highsmith
BALL POINT, VENDING MACHINE (see Coin Operated Equipment)
FELT TIP MARKING: Am Instructional, Am Library Line, Bro-Dart, Crossley-VanDeusen, Demco, Diagraph-Bradley, Fordham, Gaylord, Highsmith, Sanford
LETTERING: Beckley-Cardy, Bro-Dart, Crossley-VanDeusen, Demco, Fordham, Gaylord, Highsmith, Keuffel, Staedtler
LIBRARY: Am Instructional, Am Library Line, Crossley-VanDeusen, Demco, Fordham, Gaylord, Highsmith
MARKING: Am Instructional, Bro-Dart, Crossley-VanDeusen, Demco, Fordham, Gaylord, Highsmith
OVERHEAD TRANSPARENCY MARKING: Am Instructional, Bro-Dart, Crossley-VanDeusen, Demco, Fordham, Highsmith, Sanford, Talas
PASTE: Bro-Dart, Crossley-VanDeusen, Fordham, Highsmith

PERIODICALS (see Magazine Dealers)

PETTY CASH RECORD
Demco, Highsmith

PHONOTAPES & PHONODISCS (see Recordings, etc)

PHYSICALLY HANDICAPPED, READING AIDS FOR (see also "Reading Aids for the Handicapped," Am Library Assn)
BRAILLE TYPEWRITERS (see Typewriters, Braille)
LARGE PRINT JOBBERS: (see "Large Type Books in Print," Bowker): Large Print

MAGNIFIERS (see Magnifiers)
PAGE TURNERS: Hagman, Preston
PRISMATIC GLASSES: Preston, Swift Instruments
PROJECTORS: 3M (desk-top)
READING STANDS & BOOK HOLDERS: Am Printing, Preston, Replogle
TALKING BOOKS (see Recordings, Talking Books)
TYPE ENLARGERS & DUPLICATORS: Bell & Howell (Micro Photo Div), Gaylord, Univ Microfilms (Xerox)

PICTURE BINDINGS (see Binding Services)

PICTURE
CARRYING CASES: Bro-Dart, EBSCO Subscription, Gaylord
COVERS, PROTECTIVE (see Covers, Protective)
FRAMES, ADJUSTABLE: Braquette, Bro-Dart, Crossley-VanDeusen, Gaylord
HANGERS & RODS: Crossley-VanDeusen, Dennison (gummed cloth), Walker Systems
MOUNTS: Bro-Dart, Gaylord

PICTURES (see Prints & Reproductions)

PLANETARIUMS
Coffey

PLASTIC
ADHESIVE (see Adhesive, Plastic)
BOOK COATING (see Book Coating, Plastic)
BOOK COVERS (see Book Covers, Acetate or Mylar)
CATALOG GUIDES (see Guides, Catalog)
DISPLAY LETTERS (see Letters, Display)
SIGNS (see Signs, Plastic)

POLECATS (display board supports)
Brewster

POSTERS
CHILDREN'S: Poster House
LIBRARY INSTRUCTION: Am Instructional, Am Library Line, Baker & Taylor, Bro-Dart, Demco, Fordham, Gaylord, Highsmith, Perfection
LIBRARY PROMOTION: Am Instructional, Beckley-Cardy, Children's Book, Demco, Fordham, Ivins, Library Prod, Library Publicity, Murphy, Regent
TRAVEL: Poster House

PRACTICE CARDS (see Cards, Practice, Index)

PREBINDERS (see Binding Services)

PRESENTATION BOARDS & ACCESSORIES (see Chalkboards, etc.)

PRESS, DRY MOUNTING/LAMINATING (see Laminating)

PRINCETON FILES (see Files, Princeton)

PRINTED LABELS (see Labels, Printed)

PRINTING SERVICE
Demco, Library Prod, Murphy

PRINTS & REPRODUCTIONS
ART REPRODUCTIONS: Abrams, Am Instructional, Bro-Dart, Connex, Encyclopaedia Britannica, Gaylord, NY Graphic, Oestreicher, Regent, Society for Visual Ed, University Prints
BROWSER UNITS: Am Instructional, Reynold Enterprises
CARRYING CASES: Advertisers Mfg, Am Instructional, Bro-Dart, EBSCO Subscription, Gaylord
CATALOGED AND PROCESSED: Bro-Dart
FRAMED: Abrams, Bro-Dart, Connex, Gaylord, NY Graphic, Oestreicher, Regent
LOANED: NY Graphic
STUDY PRINTS: Am Instructional, Benefic Press, Coronet, Demco, Eye Gate, Hubbard, Scholastic

PROCESSED BOOKS & A/V MATERIALS (see Cataloging Services)

PROCESSING KITS (see Book and/or Audiovisual Processing Kits)

PROGRAMMED LEARNING MATERIALS (see Multimedia Materials; Teaching Machines)

PROJECTION SCREENS
FRONT: Am Instructional, Bro-Dart, Brewster, Demco, Ealing Films, Eastman, Fordham, Library Filmstrip
REAR: Hudson, Library Filmstrip, Technicolor
SELF-CONTAINED REAR: Advance Prod, Audio Visual Research, Hudson, RCA AV Div

PROJECTION TABLES & STANDS (see Stands, Audiovisual)

PROJECTORS
FILMSTRIP: (see Filmstrips, Equipment, etc.)
MICROFILM (see Microfilm, Equipment, etc.)
MOTION PICTURE (see Films, Motion Picture Equipment, etc.)
OPAQUE: Am Optical, Beseler, Highsmith
OVERHEAD TRANSPARENCIES (see Overhead Transparencies, Equipment, etc.)
REAR SCREEN: Advance Prod, Bro-Dart, DuKane, Fordham, Graflex
SOUND-FILMSTRIP (see Filmstrips, Equipment, etc.)

PROTECTIVE COVERS (see Covers, Protective)

PROTECTORS, CALL NUMBER LABEL (see Call Number Label Protectors)

PUBLIC ADDRESS SYSTEMS
H-R Productions, MP Audio, Newcomb, Radio-Matic, RCA AV Div, Smith System

LIBRARY PURCHASING GUIDE / 555

PUBLICITY SERVICES AND MATERIALS (see also Bookmarks; Display, etc.)
Am Library Assn, Bowker, Children's Book, Ivins, Library Prod, Library Publicity, Murphy, Westport (radio-TV)

PUNCHED CARDS (see Tabulating Cards, Equipment & Supplies)

RADIO PROGRAMS (see Publicity Services & Materials)

RADIOS, CLASSROOM
Audiotronics, Goody, Newcomb, Rheem-Califone

RAILINGS
METAL: Art Metal, Gen Nucleonics, Lawrence Metal, Perey
ROPE: Fordham, Lawrence Metal

READERS (see type, Microfiche, Microfilm, Microform, Micro-Opaque)

REALIA
French & European, Judy, Learning Media, Regent

RECASING LEATHER
Bro-Dart, Gaylord

RECORD PLAYERS (see Recordings, Equipment, etc.)

RECORDERS (see Audio Tape, Equipment, etc.)

RECORDINGS, BINDERS, PHONO DISCS (see Binders, Phono Discs)

RECORDINGS, CASSETTES, DISCS, & TAPES (for additional listings see "Audiovisual Market Place: a Multimedia Guide," Bowker)
FOREIGN LANGUAGE: Am Instructional, Caedmon, Chesterfield, CMS Records, CW Assoc, Demco, Folkways, Four Continent (Russian), French & European, Gaylord, Japan Publications, Regent, Rosenberg (French & German), Spoken Arts
LANGUAGE COURSES: CW Assoc, Demco, Four Continent (Russian), French & European, Linguaphone Inst, RCA Records, Regent, Rosenberg, Univ Wash
LIBRARY SKILLS: Am Instructional, Am Library Line, Burke, Demco, Fordham, Highsmith
OUT-OF-PRINT: Rococo
SUBSCRIPTION SERVICE: Record Hunter
TALKING BOOKS: Am Printing, CW Assoc, Demco, Enrichment Records, Folkways, Gaylord, Goody, Nat'l Braille, Recordings for the Blind, Spoken Arts
VARIOUS SUBJECTS: Acoustifone, Am Instructional, Ampex, Avid, Bell & Howell AV Div, Benefic Press, Big Sur, Bowmar Records, Bowmar (Stanley), Broadside, Bro-Dart, Caedmon, Capitol, Center for Cassette Studies, Chambers, Chesterfield, Clark, CMS Records, Coffey, Collier-Macmillan, Creative Visuals, CW Assoc, Demco, Denoyer-Geppert, Educational Activities, Educational Reading, Electronic Futures, EMC Corp, Enrichment Materials, Enrichment Records, Eye Gate, Film Strip House, Fordham, Four Continents, Gaylord, Goody, Hudson, Ideal School, Imperial Films, Ingram Book, Japan Publications, Jayark, King Karol, Learning Media, Linguaphone, Listening Library, McGraw-Hill, Potters, RCA Records, Readers Digest, Regent, Rose, Ross, Scholastic Audio Visual, Society for Visual Ed, Simon and Schuster (Ed Div), Spoken Arts, SWF Assoc, Teaching Resources, Teleketics, Univ Wash, Valiant, Western Publishing, Weston Woods, Westport, Wilson Corp

RECORDINGS, EQUIPMENT SERVICES & SUPPLIES (includes Cassettes, Discs & Tapes)
BINDERS, PHONO DISCS (see Binders)
BROWSERS & DISPLAY UNITS: Am Instructional, Am Library Line, Bro-Dart, Demco, Estey, Fordham, Gaylord, Highsmith, Kersting, Reynolds Enterprises
CARRIERS: Advertisers Mfg, Am Library Line, Bro-Dart, Demco, Fordham, Gaylord, Owens (canvas bags)
CASSETTE DUPLICATION: Library Filmstrip
CASSETTE TAPE CLEANER: Ampex
CATALOGS, COMPREHENSIVE: Schwann
FORMS: (see Cards, Audiovisual)
GUIDES, BROWSERS: Demco, Fordham, Gaylord
LABELS (see Labels, Phonograph Record)
PLAYERS: Audtronics, Avid, Bro-Dart, Capitol, Center for Cassette Studies, Demco, Electronic Futures, Fordham, Goody, H-R Productions, M P Audio, Radio-Matic, RCA AV Div, Regent, Reynolds Enterprises, Rheem-Califone
PROTECTIVE COVERS: Am Instructional, Am Library Line, Bro-Dart, Demco, Fordham, Gaylord, Highsmith
RECORD CLEANING MACHINE: Anglo Int'l
REVIEW CARDS: Audio Cardalog (nonmusical)
SHIPPING CASES: Bal, Demco, Talas
STORAGE CABINETS: Advance Prod, Am Instructional, Am Library Line, Bro-Dart, Demco, Fordham, Gaylord, Hamilton, Highsmith, Kersting, Library Filmstrip, Mosler, Neumade, Reynolds Enterprises, Slyd-In, Talas, Wallach, Wilson Corp

RECREATIONAL EQUIPMENT
Am Playground, Recreation Equipment

REFERENCE TABLES (see Furniture, Library)

REGISTER, BORROWERS'
Bro-Dart, Crossley-VanDeusen, Demco, Fordham, Gaylord

REGISTRATION CARDS (see Cards, Circulation)

REGISTRATION SUPPLIES
Am Library Line, Bro-Dart, Crossley-VanDeusen, Demco, Fordham, Gaylord

REINFORCEMENTS, LOOSE LEAF NOTEBOOK
Bro-Dart, Crossley-VanDeusen, Dennison, Highsmith

REINFORCING TAPE (see Tape, Reinforcing)

RENTAL BOOKS
Am Lending, Am Library Line, ANCO Lease, Bro-Dart, McNaughton, Monarch Lease

REPRODUCED BOOKS (see Book Reproduction)

REPRODUCTIONS (see Prints & Reproductions)

RESERVE BOOK CARD GUIDES (see Guides, Reserve Book Cards)

RESERVE BOOK CARDS (see Cards, Reserve Book)

RESTORATION AND PRESERVATION, EQUIPMENT, ETC
  ADHESIVE, ACID-FREE: Talas
  CELLULOSE TAPE REMOVER (AEROSOL): Manuscripts Supply
  CLEANER (AEROSOL): Manuscripts
  DEACIDIFICATION SERVICE: Barrow, Manuscripts
  DOCUMENT BOXES, ACID-FREE: Cambridge Paper, Highsmith, Manuscript Supply, Talas
  ENVELOPES, ACID-FREE: Gaylord, Talas
  FILE FOLDERS, ACID-FREE: Talas
  FUMIGANT (AEROSOL): Manuscripts
  FUMIGATION SERVICE: Vacudyne
  LAMINATING SERVICE: Arbee, Barrow
  MOLDICIDE (AEROSOL): Manuscripts
  NEUTRALIZING FIXATIVE: Manuscript Supply
  PAPER, ACID-FREE: Brown Paper, Talas, Warren
  PAPER CLIPS, STAINLESS STEEL: Am Library Line, Demco, Highsmith, Manuscripts, Talas
  STAPLES, RUSTPROOF: Talas

RETRIEVAL SYSTEMS
Ampex, Harwald

RETRIEVAL SYSTEMS DESIGN
Chester Electronic, Herner, LEASCO, Library Micrographic, Nelson

REVIEWS (see Book Review Cards; Films, Motion Picture, Equipment, etc.)

RUBBER BANDS, FOUR WAY
Keener Rubber

RUBBER CEMENT (see Adhesive, Rubber Cement)

RULERS, CENTIMETER
Keuffel

SAFES AND STRONG BOXES (see Security Equipment)

SCALES, POSTAL
Am Library Line, Fordham, Highsmith

SCHOOL LIBRARY FORMS (see Forms, School Library)

SCOTCH TAPE (see Tape, Transparent Plastic)

SCREENS, PROJECTION (see Projection Screens)

SCULPTURE
  LOANED: NY Graphic
  REPRODUCTIONS: Alva, Am Instructional, Austin, Museum, NY Graphic, Regent

SEALS, HOLIDAY, GIFT, etc.
Dennison

SECTION LABELS (see Labels, Shelf)

SECURITY EQUIPMENT
  BURGLAR ALARMS: Benedict, Detex, Gen Nucleonics, Honeywell Commercial, Mosler, Worner Electronic
  CLOSED CIRCUIT TELEVISION: Filmdex, Graflex, Mosler, RCA AV Div
  COMMUNICATIONS EQUIPMENT: Filmdex
  COMPUTER PROTECTION DEVICES: Sentronic
  DETECTOR MIRRORS: Micro Die
  EXIT ALARM LOCKS: Detex
  IDENTIFICATION SYSTEMS: Gen Binding, Gen Nucleonics
  KEY FILING CABINETS: Fordham, Moore
  SAFES AND STRONG BOXES: Diebold, Herring, Mosler
  SURVEILLANCE CAMERAS: Filmdex
  THEFT DETECTION SYSTEMS: Checkpoint, Gaylord (Checkpoint), Gen Nucleonics (Sentronic), Library Bureau (Book Mark), Sensormatic, 3M (Tattle Tape)
  TURNSTILES: Alvarado, Gen Nucleonics, Lawrence Metal, Perey
  ULTRA-VIOLET INK & POWDER: Stroblite
  WATCHMEN'S CLOCKS SYSTEMS: Detex

SHELF LABEL HOLDERS (card frames, index holders, range indicators)
Am Instructional, Am Library Line, Ames, Art Metal, Bro-Dart, Cel-U-Dex, Crossley-VanDeusen, Demco, Estey, Fordham, Gaylord, Hamilton, Highsmith, Library Bureau, Va Metal, Weyll (magnetic)

SHELF LABELS (see Labels, Shelf)
SHELF-LIST CARDS (see Cards, Shelf-List)
SHELF-LIST GUIDES (see Guides, Shelf-List)
SHELF PARTITIONS
Cel-U-Dex, Sjostrom, Slyd-In
SHELLAC
Bro-Dart, Demco, Fordham, Gaylord
SHELVING
AUTOMATED: Estey, Library Bureau, Selectamatic
COMPACT (STORAGE): Am Instructional, Ames, Art Metal, Bro-Dart, Brown, Estey, Fordham, Hamilton, Highsmith, Library Bureau, Lundia, Supreme, Va Metal, Wilson Metal
IMPORTED: Reska (Swedish)
MAGAZINE: Aetna, Am Instructional, Am Library Line, Ames, Bro-Dart, Brown, Buckstaff, Croyden, Demco, Estey, Fetzer's, Fleetwood, Fordham, Gillotte, Heller, Highsmith, Library Bureau, Miller, Myrtle, Sjostrom, Slyd-In, Standard Wood, Steelcase, Supreme, Talas, Va Metal, Weinberg
MOVABLE: Ames, Aurora, Bro-Dart, Estey, Fordham, Highsmith, Kidde, Library Bureau, Selectamatic, Supreme
MULTI-TIER (STACK): Aetna, Am Instructional, Ames, Art Metal, Bro-Dart, Brown, Crossley-VanDeusen, Estey, Gen Fireproofing, Hamilton, InterRoyal, Library Bureau, Va Metal, Wilson Metal
NEWSPAPER: Am Instructional, Am Library Line, Ames, Art Metal, Bro-Dart, Brown, Buckstaff, Croyden, Estey, Fetzer's, Fordham, Gillotte, Hamilton, Highsmith, Library Bureau, Myrtle, Sjostrom, Standard Wood, Supreme, Talas, Va Metal, Weinberg
RECORD ALBUM & PICTURE BOOK: Am Library Line, Ames, Art Metal, Bro-Dart, Brown, Buckstaff, Crossley-VanDeusen, Croyden, Demco, Estey, Fetzer's, Fordham, Hamilton, Heller, Highsmith, Library Bureau, Miller, Myrtle, Sjostrom, Slyd-In, Standard Wood, Weinberg
STEEL: Aetna, Am Instructional, Ames, Art Metal, Aurora, Brown, Butler, Crossley-Van-Deusen, Estey, EQUIPTO, Fordham, Gen Fireproofing, Hamilton, Highsmith, InterRoyal, Library Bureau, Reflector, Republic, Reska, Smith System, Steelcase, Supreme, Va Metal, Wilson Metal
WALL HUNG: Ames, Bro-Dart, Estey, Highsmith, Library Bureau, Reska
WIRE: Am Instructional, Butler, Fordham, Metropolitan
WOOD: Am Instructional, Am Library Line, Backus, Bro-Dart, Brown, Buckstaff, Croyden, Estey, Fetzer's, Fleetwood, Fordham, Gaylord, Heller, Highsmith, Library Bureau, Lundia, Miller, Myrtle, Risom, Sjostrom, Southern Desk, Standard Wood, Weinberg, Worden
WORKROOM: Bro-Dart, EQUIPTO, Estey, Fordham, Highsmith, Sjostrom, Weinberg
SHIPPING CASES
FIBERBOARD: Am Library Line, Bal, Crossley-VanDeusen, Demco, Diagraph, Highsmith, Safco
PLASTIC: Am Library Line, Hollywood Plastics
SHOPPING CART, FOLDING
Lumex
SIGNAL TABS
Am Instructional, Am Library Line, Bro-Dart, Cel-U-Dex, Crossley-VanDeusen, Demco, Fordham, Graffco, Highsmith, Talas
SIGNATURE STAMPS
Am Library Line, Crossley-VanDeusen, Demco, Fordham, Murphy
SIGN MAKING
KITS: Attwood, Crossley-VanDeusen, Demco, Highsmith, Milex
MACHINES: Embosograf, Fordham, Milex, Showcard
SIGNS
MATERIAL FOR (see Display, Materials)
METAL: Fordham, Michaels
MOVABLE LETTERS (Building Directories): Am Instructional, Attwood, Crossley-VanDeusen, Demco, Fordham, Highsmith, Michaels
PLASTIC: Am Instructional, Attwood, Bro-Dart, Cel-U-Dex, Crossley-VanDeusen, Demco, Fordham, Gaylord, Highsmith
SLIDES
DUPLICATION SERVICE: Color Slide
PROJECTORS: Am Instructional, Am Optical, Beseler, Eastman, Fordham, Graflex, Harwald, Honeywell Photo, Hudson, 3M
STORAGE CABINETS (FILES): Advance Prod, Am Instructional, Am Library Line, Bro-Dart, Demco, Elden, Fordham, Gaylord, Highsmith, Neumade, Talas, Wallach
VARIOUS SUBJECTS: Am Instructional, Am Library Color Slide, Beaux Arts, Bro-Dart, Coffey, Color Slide, C W Assoc, Demco, Fairchild Visuals, Hubbard, Imperial Film, Popular Science, Scholastic Audio-Visual, Society for Visual Ed, Talas, 3M, Univ Color, Univ Ed, Univ Prints, Univ Wash (for additional listings see "Audiovisual Market Place: a Multimedia Guide," Bowker)
VIEWERS: Elden, Hudson

SLIPCASES
Am Instructional, Gaylord, Highsmith

SMOKING EQUIPMENT
Fordham, Jackson Co, McDonald

SORTING EQUIPMENT
MANUAL: Am Instructional, Am Library Line, Bro-Dart, Crossley-VanDeusen, Demco, Fordham, Gaylord, Highsmith, Yawman
TRAYS (see Trays, Sorting)

SOUND CONTROL ROOMS, MODULAR
Wenger

SPINE MARKING EQUIPMENT (see Marking Equipment & Supplies)

STAGES, FOLDING
Vecta

STAMPING MACHINES (see Marking Equipment & Supplies)

STAMPS
ELECTRIC TIME, DATE, NUMBER (see Numbering Machines)
LIBRARY EMBOSSING: Crossley-VanDeusen, Demco, Fordham, Gaylord
PADS & INKS: Am Instructional, Am Library Line, Bro-Dart, Crossley-VanDeusen, Demco, Fordham, Gaylord, Highsmith

STANDS
AUDIOVISUAL: Advance Prod, Am Instructional, Am Library Line, Audio-Visual Research, Bausch & Lomb, Beseler, Bro-Dart, Crossley-VanDeusen, Coffey, Demco, EBSCO Subscription, Estey, Fordham, Gaylord, Highsmith, Neumade, Smith System, Steelcase, Talas, Wallach, Wilson Corp
DICTIONARY (see Furniture, Library)
TYPEWRITER AND OFFICE MACHINE: Art Metal, Crossley-VanDeusen, EBSCO Subscription, Fordham, Steelcase, Tiffany

STAPLES, RUSTPROOF (see Restoration & Preservation)

STAPLING MACHINES
ELECTRIC: Bates, Bostitch, Crossley-VanDeusen, Demco, Fordham, Highsmith, Staplex
MANUAL: Am Instructional, Am Library Line, Bostitch, Bro-Dart, Crossley-VanDeusen, Demco, Fordham, Gaylord, Highsmith
SADDLE (ELECTRIC): Staplex
SADDLE (MANUAL): Crossley-VanDeusen, Fordham, Gaylord, Highsmith
STAPLESS: Fordham

STATIONERS (see Office Supply Stores)

STATISTICAL REPORTS (see Forms)

STEP STOOLS
MOBILE: Am Instructional, Am Library Line, Bro-Dart, Crossley-VanDeusen, Demco, Fordham, Gaylord, Highsmith
STANDARD (see Furniture, Library)

STIK-TACK (adhesive discs)
Am Library Line, Crossley-VanDeusen, Demco, Fordham, Highsmith

STORY HOUR LOUNGERS
Fordham

STUDY PRINTS (see Prints & Reproductions)

SYNCHRONIZER, SLIDE OR FILMSTRIP PROJECTORS
NORELCO

TABLES, ALL TYPES (see Furniture)

TABLETS, BRONZE (see Signs, Metal)

TABULATING CARDS, EQUIPMENT & SUPPLIES
IBM, Royal, SCM

TACKING GUNS
Bostitch, Crossley-VanDeusen, Fordham

TACKING IRONS (see Laminating)

TALKING BOOKS (see Recordings, Talking Books)

TAPE
ATTACHING (BOOK JACKET COVER): Am Instructional, Am Library Line, Bro-Dart, Crossley-VanDeusen, Demco, Fordham, Gaylord, Highsmith
BOOK DISPLAY: Bro-Dart
EDGING: Am Library Line, Bro-Dart, Crossley-VanDeusen
IMPRINTED CLASSIFICATION: Am Library Line, Bro-Dart, Chart-Pak, Crossley-VanDeusen, Highsmith
MARKING: Am Instructional, Am Library Line, Bro-Dart, Crossley-VanDeusen, Demco, Fordham, Highsmith
MENDING: Am Instructional, Am Library Line, Bro-Dart, Crossley-VanDeusen, Demco, Dennison, Fordham, Gaylord, Highsmith, Mystik, Seal, 3M
MOUNTING (PICTURES, POSTERS, ETC.): Am Instructional, Am Library Line, Bro-Dart, Crossley-VanDeusen, Demco, Fordham, Gaylord, Highsmith
NON-SKID (FOR BOOK SUPPORTS): Crossley-VanDeusen, Fordham, Highsmith
RED: Am Library Line, Bro-Dart, Crossley-VanDeusen, Demco, Fordham, Gaylord, Highsmith
REINFORCING: Am Instructional, Am Library Line, Bro-Dart, Crossley-VanDeusen, Demco, Dennison, Fordham, Gaylord, Highsmith, Mystik

LIBRARY PURCHASING GUIDE / 559

TRANSPARENT PLASTIC: Am Instructional, Am Library Line, Bro-Dart, Chart-Pak, Crossley-VanDeusen, Demco, Dennison, Fordham, Gaylord, Highsmith, Mystik, 3M

TAPE DISPENSERS (see Dispensers)

TAPE RECORDERS (see Audio Tape, Equipment, etc.)

TAPEWRITERS (see Label Makers)

TEACHING MACHINES
Bell & Howell AV Div, Beseler, Encyclopaedia Britannica, NORELCO, Viewlex

TELEPHONE DATA SERVICE
Bell (AT&T)

TELEVISION MATERIAL (see Publicity Service & Materials)

THEFT DETECTION DEVICES (see Security Equipment)

TIME
STAMPS (see Numbering Machines)
SWITCHES (see Lighting Controls)

TISSUE, DRY MOUNTING (see Laminating)

TOTE TRUCKS
Bal

TOYS
Schwartz

TRAFFIC CONTROL SYSTEMS (see Railings; also Security Equipment, Turnstiles)

TRANSFER PAPER (see Paper, Transfer)

TRANSPARENCIES (see Overhead Transparencies)

TRAYS
CHARGING: Am Instructional, Am Library Line, Bro-Dart, Crossley-VanDeusen, Demco, Fordham, Gaylord, Highsmith
SORTING: Am Instructional, Bro-Dart, Crossley-VanDeusen, Demco, Fordham, Gaylord, Highsmith

TURNSTILES (see Security Equipment)

TYPE CLEANERS
Crossley-VanDeusen, Demco, Gaylord

TYPE, HOT STAMPING (see Marking Equipment)

TYPEWRITERS
AUTOMATIC: Friden, Olivetti, RemRand (Machines), Royal
BRAILLE: IBM
CATALOGER'S: Highsmith, IBM, Olivetti
COIN OPERATED (see Coin Operated Equipment)
ELECTRIC: IBM, Olivetti, RemRand (Machines), Royal, SCM
JUSTIFYING: IBM, Olivetti, Varityper
STANDARD AND PORTABLE: Highsmith, Olivetti, RemRand (Machines), Royal, SCM
TELEGRAPHIC: SCM, Teletype

TYPEWRITER STANDS (see Stands, Typewriter)

ULTRAFICHE
PUBLISHER: Nat'l Cash (Ind Prod Div)
READER: Nat'l Cash (Ind Prod Div)
READER-PRINTER: Nat'l Cash (Ind Prod Div)

U.S. GOV'T PUBLICATIONS (see Government Publications)

VACATION READING CLUB MATERIALS (see Publicity Services & Materials)

VENDING MACHINES (see Coin Operated Equipment)

VIDEOTAPE, EQUIPMENT, SERVICES & SUPPLIES
RECORDERS: Ampex
STORAGE RACKS (FILES): Bro-Dart, Demco, Fordham, Gaylord, Talas
TAPE: Ampex, Talas

VIDEO TAPES, PRE-RECORDED
Bowmar (Stanley), Goody

VIEWERS (see type, Microform, Filmstrip, etc.)

WARDROBE RACKS
Fordham, InterRoyal, Vogel-Peterson

WHOLESALERS, BOOKS (see Booksellers, Wholesale)

DIRECTORY OF SUPPLIERS

A & A DISTRIBUTORS, INC
 Mear Rd, Holbrook, Mass 02343 (617) 963-8000

ABBEON, INC
 179-15 Jamaica Ave, Jamaica, NY 11432 (212) AX 7-5600

ABEL, RICHARD & CO
 Box 4245, Portland, Ore 97208 (503) 246-7786

ABRAHAMS MAGAZINE SERVICE, INC
 56 E 13th St, New York, NY 10008 (212) 777-4700

ABRAMS, HARRY N, INC
 110 E 59th St, New York, NY 10022 (212) 758-8600

ACME CODE CO, INC
 102 1st St, Hackensack, NJ 07601 (201) HU 7-3663

560 / DIRECTORY OF SUPPLIERS

ACOUSTIFONE CORP
  8954 Comanche Ave, Chatsworth, Calif 91311 (213) 882-1380
ADVANCE PRODUCTS CO, INC
  2300 E Douglas Ave, Wichita, Kan 67214 (316) 263-4231
ADVERTISERS MFG CO
  415 E Oshkosh St, Ripon, Wis 54971 (414) 748-5101
AETNA STEEL PRODUCTS CORP
  300 Peacock St, Pottsville, Pa 17901 (717) 622-4600
AEVAC, INC
  500 Fifth Ave, New York, NY 10036 (212) 594-8655
AFCO RUBBER CORP
  7505 Freedom St, N Canton, Ohio 44720 (216) 499-7850
ALANAR BOOK PROCESSING CENTER
  (Div, Bro-Dart, Inc)
  PO Box 921, Williamsport, Pa 17701 (717) 326-1935
ALESCO (AMERICAN LIBRARY & EDUCATIONAL SERVICE)
  404 Sette Dr, Paramus, NJ 07452 (201) 265-5730
ALTAIR MACHINERY CORP
  55 Vandam St, New York, NY 10013 (212) AL 5-4510
ALVA MUSEUM REPLICAS, INC
  30-30 Northern Blvd, Long Island City, NY 11101 (212) 392-6760
ALVARADO MFG CO, INC
  11204 Rush St, S El Monte, Calif 91733 (213) 444-9268
AM CORP
  (Addressograph-Multigraph)
  1200 Babbit Rd, Cleveland, Ohio 44117 (216) 731-8000
AMERICAN BINDERY, INC
  914 Jefferson St, Topeka, Kan 66607 (913) 233-4252
AMERICAN CRAYON CO
  (Div Jos Dixon Crucible Co)
  1706 Hayes Ave, Sandusky, Ohio 44870
AMERICAN DESK MFG CO
  Temple, Tex 76501
AMERICAN INSTRUCTIONAL MATERIALS, INC
  Box 22748, Texas Women's Univ Sta, Denton, Tex 76204 (817) 387-5591
AMERICAN LENDING LIBRARY, INC
  659 Ethel St NW, Atlanta, Ga 30318
AMERICAN LIBRARIANS' AGENCY
  535 Fifth Ave, New York, NY 10017 (212) MU 7-1787
AMERICAN LIBRARY ASSOCIATION
  50 E Huron St, Chicago, Ill 60611 (312) 944-6780
AMERICAN LIBRARY COLOR SLIDE CO, INC
  305 E 45th St, New York, NY 10017 (212) 684-6800
AMERICAN LIBRARY LINE (JOSTEN'S)
  4070 Shirley Dr, SW, Atlanta, Ga 30336 (404) 691-7200
AMERICAN MAP CO, INC
  3 W 61st St, New York, NY 10023 (212) 245-7840
AMERICAN NEWS CO
  (see Ancorp National Services, Inc)
AMERICAN OPTICAL CO
  Eggert Rd, Buffalo, NY 14215 (716) 895-4000
AMERICAN PAPERBACK SERVICES
  (see American Bindery, Inc)
AMERICAN PLAYGROUND DEVICE CO
  1801-31 S Jackson St, Anderson, Ind 46011 (317) 642-0288
AMERICAN PRINTING HOUSE FOR THE BLIND, INC
  Box 6085, Louisville, Ky 40206 (502) 895-2405
AMERICAN SEATING CO
  901 Broadway Ave, NW, Grand Rapids, Mich 49504 (616) 456-0600
AMES LIBRARY SYSTEMS
  (Div Harvard Interiors Mfg Co)
  4820 Durfee Ave, Pico-Rivera, Calif 90660 (213) 685-7053
AMPEX CORP
  2201 Estes Ave, Elk Grove Village, Ill 60007
AMPLEX CORP
  214 Glen Cove Rd, Carle Place, NY 11514
AMS PRESS, INC
  56 E 13th St, New York, NY 10003 (212) 777-4700
ANCO LEASE COLLECTION SERVICE, INC
  659 Ethel St, NW, Atlanta, Ga 30318 (404) 872-4319
ANCORP NATIONAL SERVICES, INC
  131 Varick St, New York, NY 10013 (212) 255-5100
ANGLO INT'L MARKETING CORP
  1100 W Newport Pk, Wilmington, Del 19804 (302) 998-4840
ANTIOCH PRESS
  Yellow Springs, Ohio 45387
APEX PAPER BOX CO
  311 W Superior St, Chicago, Ill 60610
APEX SPECIALTIES CO
  1115 Douglas Ave, Providence, RI 02904 (401) 274-6687
ARBEE CO, INC
  6 Claremont Rd, Bernardsville, NJ 07924 (201) 766-5534
ARCATA MICROFILM CORP
  700 S Main St, Spring Valley, NY 10977 (914) 356-2700
ARKWRIGHT-INTERLAKEN, INC
  Main St, Fiskeville, RI 02823 (401) 821-1000
ARLINGTON ALUMINUM CO
  19303 W Davison, Detroit, Mich 48223 (313) 837-1212
ARMOR BOOKS
  (see Reynolds Bindery)
ARMSTRONG CORK CO
  Liberty & Charlotte Sts, Lancaster, Pa 17604 (717) 397-0611
ARNO PRESS
  (Div NY Times)

DIRECTORY OF SUPPLIERS / 561

330 Madison Ave, New York, NY 10017 (212) 697-0044
ARS POLONA—RUCH
Box 1001, Krakowskie Przedmiescie, Warsaw, Poland 26-47-58
ART METAL—US CORP
1099 Jay St, Rochester, NY 14603 (716) 436-5160
ASSOCIATED LIBRARIES, INC
229-33 N 63rd St, Philadelphia, Pa 19139 (215) GR 6-3200
ASSOCIATION INSTRUCTIONAL MATERIALS (AIM)
600 Madison Ave, New York, NY 10022 (212) 421-3900
ATLANTIC MICROFILM CORP
700 S Main St, Spring Valley, NY 10977 (914) 356-2700
ATTWOOD PRODUCTS INC
525 Smith St, Farmingdale, NY 11735 (516) 694-1535
AUDIO CARDALOG
Box 989, Larchmont, NY 10538 (516) 735-4600
AUDIO-MASTER CORP
(see H-R Productions)
AUDIOTRONICS CORP
7428 Bellaire Ave, N Hollywood, Calif 91605 (213) 765-2645
AUDIO-TUTORIAL SYSTEMS
426 S Sixth St, Minneapolis, Minn 55415 (612) 333-4456
AUDIO-VISUAL RESEARCH
1509 8th St, SE, Waseca, Minn 56093 (507) 835-2250
AURORA STEEL PRODUCTS
153 3rd St, Aurora, Ill 60507 (312) 892-7696
AUSTIN BOOK SHOP
82-60A Austin St, Kew Gardens, NY 11415 (212) 441-1199
AUSTIN MUSEUM STUDIOS, INC
1637 62nd St, Brooklyn, NY 11204 (212) 256-9400
AUTOMATED BUSINESS SYSTEMS
(Div Litton Industries)
600 Washington Ave, Carlstadt, NJ 07072 (201) 935-2200
AUX AMATEURS DE LIVRES
62, Avenue de Suffren, 75 Paris XV, France
AVEDEX, INC
(Audio-Visual Div)
7326 Niles Center Rd, Skokie, Ill 60070
AVID CORP
10 Tripps Lane, E Providence, RI 02914 (401) 438-5400

BACK ISSUES CORP
16 E 46th St, New York, NY 10017
BACKUS BROS CO
212-218 E Third St, Cincinnati, Ohio 45202 (513) 421-1118
BACON PAMPHLET SERVICE, INC
East Chatham, NY 12060
BAKER & TAYLOR CO
Eastern Division: 50 Kirby Ave, Somerville, NJ 08876 (201) 722-8000 (NYC: 212-227-8470)
Midwest & Southern Division: Gladiola Ave, Momence, Ill 60954 (815) 472-2444 (Chicago: 312-641-3233)
Western Division: 380 Edison Ave, Reno, Nev 89502 (702) 786-6700
Interstate Library Service Co (Subs): 4600 N Cooper, Oklahoma City, Okla 73118 (405) 525-6561
BAL, WILLIAM CORP
947 Newark Ave, Elizabeth, NJ 07208 (201) 354-9625
BARNES & NOBLE, INC
105 Fifth Ave, New York, NY 10003 (212) 255-8100
BARROW, J W, RESTORATION SHOP, INC
State Library Bldg, Richmond, Va 23219 (703) 770-2310
BATES MFG CO
18 Central Ave, West Orange, NJ 07051 (201) 676-9200
BAUSCH & LOMB, INC
83962 Lomb Park, Rochester, NY 14602
BAY MICROFILM, INC
737 Loma Verde Ave, Palo Alto, Calif 94303 (415) 326-1812
BECKLEY-CARDY CO
10300 W Roosevelt Rd, Westchester, Ill 60153
BELL & HOWELL AV DIV
7100 McCormick Rd, Chicago, Ill 60645 (312) 262-1600
BELL & HOWELL CO
6800 McCormick Rd, Chicago, Ill 60645
BELL & HOWELL CO
(Micro Photo Div)
Old Mansfield Rd, Wooster, Ohio 44691 (216) 264-6666
BELL SYSTEM (AT&T)
Consult local Bell Telephone business office
BENEDICT ELECTRONICS TECHNOLOGY, INC
506 State St, Schenectady, NY 12305 (518) 374-8468
BENEFIC PRESS
10300 W Roosevelt Rd, Westchester, Ill 60153 (312) 287-7110
BERNAN ASSOCIATES
4701 Willard Ave, Suite 102, Washington, DC 20015
BESELER, CHARLES, CO
219 S 18th St, East Orange, NJ 07018 (201) 676-6500
BIBLIOGRAPHIC DATA CENTER
Box 146, Maynard, Mass 01754
BIG SUR RECORDINGS
117 Mitchell Blvd, San Rafael, Calif 94903 (415) 472-2070
BIPAD
(Bureau of Independent Publishers & Distributors)
122 E 42nd St, New York, NY 10017 (212) 687-6790
BLISS, P & H

562 / DIRECTORY OF SUPPLIERS

Middletown, Conn 06457 (203) 347-2255

BOARDMAN CO
Box 26088, Oklahoma City, Okla 73126 (405) 634-5434

BOOKAZINE CO, INC
303 W Tenth St, New York, NY 10014 (212) 675-8877

BOOK-KART CO
Box 22, Wooster, Ohio 44692

BOOK LAND
1615 Montana Ave, Santa Monica, Calif 90403 (213) 394-0726

BOOKS ON EXHIBIT
North Bedford Rd, Mt Kisco, NY 10549 (914) 666-7587

BORDEN CHEMICAL
(Div Borden, Inc)
350 Madison Ave, New York, NY 10017 (212) 573-4000

BOSTITCH DIV TEXTRON, INC
Briggs Dr, E Greenwich, RI 02818 (401) 884-2500

BOUND-TO-STAY-BOUND BOOKS, INC
W Morton Rd, Jacksonville, Ill 62650 (217) 245-5191

BOWKER, R R CO (Xerox)
1180 Ave of the Americas, New York, NY 10036 (212) 581-8800

BOWMAR RECORDS, INC
622 Rodier Dr, Glendale, Calif 91201 (213) 247-8995

BOWMAR, STANLEY, CO, INC
4 Broadway, Valhalla, NY 10595 (914) WH 6-2600

BOYERTOWN AUTO BODY WORKS
Third & Walnut St, Boyertown, Pa 19512 (215) 367-2146

BRAINARD BOOK CO
Box 444, La Grange, Ill 60525

BRANDON FILMS
221 W 57th St, New York, NY 10019 (212) CL 6-4867

BRAQUETTE, INC
Lenox, Mass 01240 (413) 637-0000

BRETFORD MFG, INC
3951 25th Ave, Schiller Park, Ill 60176 (312) 678-2545

BREWSTER CORP
Old Saybrook, Conn 06475 (203) 388-4441

BRITISH BOOK CENTRE, INC
966 Lexington Ave, New York, NY 10021 (914) 592-9141

BRITISH INFORMATION SERVICES
845 Third Ave, New York, NY 10022 (212) 752-8400

BROCKHAUS, F A
Raepplenstr 20, POB 1164, Stuttgart, Germany

BRO-DART BOOKS
(Div Bro-Dart, Inc)
Box 923, Williamsport, Pa 17701 (717) 326-2461

BRO-DART FOUNDATION
113 Frelinghuysen Ave, Newark, NJ 07114 (201) 242-7500

BRO-DART, INC
56 Earl St, Newark, NJ 07114 (201) 242-7500
Eastern Division: 1609 Memorial Ave, Williamsport, Pa 17701 (717) 242-7500
Western Division: 15255 E Don Julian Rd, City of Industry, Calif 91747 (213) 968-6411
Bro-Dart of Canada: 6 Edmondson St, Brantford, Ont (519) 759-4350

BROWN, C S & CO
N 76 W 22300 Cherry Hill Rd, Sussex, Wis 53089 (414) 255-1405

BROWN PAPER CO, L L
2 Commercial St, Adams, Mass 01220 (413) 743-3300

BRUNING, CHARLES, CO DIV (AM Corp)
1800 W Central Rd, Mt Prospect, Ill 60056

BUCKSTAFF CO
1127 S Main St, Oshkosh, Wis 54901 (414) 235-5890

BUNN, B. H. CO
12550 S Lombard Lane, Alsip, Ill 60658 (312) 568-3200

BURKE, CHARLES
Box 494, Westport, Conn 06880

BURKE, THERESA M, EMPLOYMENT AGENCY
8 W 40th St, New York, 10018 (212) LO 3-6075

BUTLER INDUSTRIES, INC
637 Central Ave, Newark, NJ 07107 (201) 484-1515

BYRNE, BYRNE & CO
120 S LaSalle St, Chicago, Ill 60603 (312) 346-2150

CAEDMON RECORDS, INC
505 8th Ave, New York, NY 10018 (212) 594-3122

CAMBRIDGE PAPER BOX, INC
196 Broadway, Cambridge, Mass

CAMPBELL & HALL
(Div Learning Resources, Inc)
1075 Commonwealth Ave, Boston, Mass 02117 (617) 254-4500

CANNER, J S & CO
49-65 Lansdowne St, Boston, Mass 02215 (617) 261-8000

CANON USA, INC
64-10 Queens Blvd, Woodside, NY 11377

CAPITAL LIBRARY SERVICE
133 Centerway, Greenbelt, Md 20770 (301) 345-3844

CAPITOL RECORDS
520 Fifth Ave, New York, NY 10036 (212) PL 7-7470

CARDMASTER CO
1920 W Sunnyside Ave, Chicago, Ill 60640 (312) SU 4-7300

CAROUSEL FILMS, INC
1501 Broadway, Suite 1503, New York, NY 10036 (212) 279-6734

CASS, FRANK & CO, LTD
c/o Int'l Scholarly Book Services, Box 4347, Portland, Ore 97208 (503) 645-3511

CATALOG CARD CORP OF AMERICA (JOSTEN'S)

DIRECTORY OF SUPPLIERS / 563

888 E 80th St, Minneapolis, Minn 55420 (612) 854-3113
CATSKILL CRAFTSMEN, INC
575 Lexington Ave, New York, NY 10022 (212) 751-3600
CCM INFORMATION CORP
(Subs of Crowell Collier & Macmillan, Inc)
866 Third Ave, New York, NY 10022 (212) 935-4292
CCM FILMS, INC
(see CCM Information Corp)
CEL-U-DEX CORP
23 McArthur Ave (PO Box 84), New Windsor, NY 12550 (914) 562-4510
CENTER FOR CASSETTE STUDIES
8110 Webb Ave, N Hollywood, Calif 91605
CHAMBERS RECORD CORP
97 Chambers St, New York, NY 10007 (212) 233-6280
CHART-PAK, INC
1 River Rd, Leeds, Mass 01053
CHECKPOINT SYSTEMS
Barrington, NJ 08007 (609) 547-1110
CHEMICAL ABSTRACTS SERVICE
Ohio State Univ, Columbus, Ohio 43210 (614) 422-7423
CHESHIRE, INC (XEROX)
2474 Dempster, Des Plaines, Ill 60016 (312) 297-2093
CHESTER ELECTRONIC LABORATORIES, INC
(GTE Information Systems, Inc)
957 Winthrop Rd, Chester, Conn 06412 (203) 526-5325
CHESTERFIELD MUSIC SHOPS, INC
12 Warren St, New York, NY 10007 (212) 964-3380
CHIANG SMALL DUPLICATORS
53100 Juniper Rd, South Bend, Ind 46637 (219) 272-2024
CHILDREN'S BOOK COUNCIL, INC
175 Fifth Ave, New York, NY 10010 (212) 254-2666
CHURCHILL FILMS
662 N Robertson Blvd, Los Angeles, Calif 90069 (213) 657-5110
CLARK, CHARLES W, CO, INC
564 Smith St, Farmingdale, NY 11735 (516) 694-4666
CMS RECORDS, INC
14 Warren St, New York, NY 10007 (212) 964-3381
COFFEY, JACK C CO
104 Lake View Ave, Waukegan, Ill 60085 (312) 244-1800
COLBERT PACKAGING CORP
(formerly Kroeck Paper Box Co)
1701 W Superior St, Chicago, Ill 60622
COLLIER-MACMILLAN INTERNATIONAL
866 Third Ave, New York, NY 10022 (212) 935-2000
COLONIAL "OUT OF PRINT" BOOK SERVICE
23 E 4th St, New York, NY 10003 (212) 769-1704
COLOR SLIDE ENTERPRISES
Box 150, Oxford, Ohio 45056

COLORADO INSTRUMENTS, INC
1 Park St, Broomfield, Colo 80020 (303) 466-1881
COLUMBIA MILLS, INC
Syracuse, NY 13201 (315) 422-0111
CONCEPT DESIGNS
Box 913, New Canaan, Conn 06840 (203) 966-3615
CONSOLIDATED BOOK SERVICE, INC
302 Fifth Ave, New York, NY 10001
CONTEMPORARY FILMS/McGRAW-HILL
330 W 42nd St, New York, NY 10036 (212) 971-6761
COPY CAT, INC
(SEE Midwest Library Service, Inc)
CORONET FILMS
65 E South Water St, Chicago, Ill 60601 (312) 332-7676
COSMO BOOK DISTRIBUTING CO
(Subs Wellington Book Co)
33-49 Whelan Rd, East Rutherford, NJ 07073 (201) 933-8300
COUNTERPOINT FILMS
5823 Santa Monica Blvd, Hollywood, Calif 90038 (213) 462-2243
COWLES EDUC CORP
488 Madison Ave, New York, NY 10022 (212) MU 8-0300
CRAM, GEORGE, F, CO, INC
301 S LaSalle St, Indianapolis, Ind 46206 (317) 635-5564
CREATIVE ENVIRONMENTS, INC
85 Hoffman La S, Hauppauge, NY 11787 (516) 582-4600
CREATIVE VISUALS DIV
(Gamco Industries)
Box 310, Big Spring, Tex 79720 (915) 367-8791
CRM FILMS
Del Mar, Calif 92014
CROSSLEY-VANDEUSEN CO, INC
(see American Library Line)
CROWN RUBBER CO
Fremont, Ohio 43420
CROYDEN DIV
(InterRoyal Corp)
201 S Washington St, Herkimer, NY 13350
CUTAWL CORP
Route 6, Bethel, Conn 06801 (203) 748-3521
CW ASSOCIATES
Box 34099, Washington, DC 20034 (301) 881-2120
DAME, NATHANIEL & CO
133 Walden St, Cambridge, Mass 02140 (617) 876-6846
DASA CORP
15 Stevens St, Andover, Mass 01810 (617) 475-4940
DAVEY CO
164 Laidlaw Ave, Jersey City, NJ 07306 (201) 653-0606
DECOR PLASTIC CORP
2600 Washington Blvd, Bellwood, Ill 60104
DE GRUYTER, INC, WALTER
162 Fifth Ave, New York, NY 10010 (212) 255-0808

DIRECTORY OF SUPPLIERS

DEMCO EDUCATIONAL CORP
 Box 1488, Madison, Wis (Hq) 53701 (608) 241-1201
 Box 7767, Fresno, Calif 93701 (209) 291-2576
DENNISON MFG CO
 300 Howard St, Framingham, Mass 01701
DENOYER-GEPPERT CO
 5235 Ravenswood Ave, Chicago, Ill 60640 (312) 561-9200
DETEX CORP
 53 Park Pl, New York, NY 10007 (212) 732-6450
DEVOKE CO
 1015 Corporation Way, Palo Alto, Calif 94303 (415) 964-3883
DIAGRAPH-BRADLEY IND, INC
 Box 520, Herrin, Ill 62948 (618) 997-3321
DICK, A B, CO
 5700 W Touhy Ave, Chicago, Ill 60631 (312) 763-1900
DICTAPHONE CORP
 120 Old Post Rd, Rye, NY 10580
DIEBOLD, INC
 818 Mulberry Rd, SE, Canton, Ohio 44709 (216) 453-4592
DIMONDSTEIN BOOK CO, INC
 38 Portman Rd, New Rochelle, NY 10801 (914) NE 6-6000
DIRECTIONAL CONTRACT FURNITURE CORP
 979 Third Ave, New York, NY 10022 (212) 751-3350
DOCUMAT
 (see Savin)
DOCUMENTATION AND PROCUREMENT CENTER
 (Div Maxwell Scientific Int'l, Inc)
 44-01 21st St, Long Island City, NY 11101
DOUBLEDAY & CO, INC
 277 Park Ave, New York, NY 10017 (212) 826-2000
DREXEL ENTERPRISES INC
 (Southern Desk Div)
 Hickory, NC 28601
DROPOSITORY
 (see Mosler Corp)
DUKANE CORP
 2900 DuKane Dr, St Charles, Ill 60174 (312) 584-2300
DUPONT CO
 Film Dept (Mylar)
 Wilmington, Del 19898
DWYER PRODUCTS CORP
 Calumet Ave, Michigan City, Ind 46360 (219) 874-5236

EALING FILMS
 2225 Massachusetts Ave, Cambridge, Mass 02140 (617) 491-5870
EASTMAN KODAK CO
 343 State St, Rochester, NY 14650 (716) 325-2000
EBS BOOK SERVICE INC
 290 Broadway, Lynbrook, NY 11563 (516) 593-1195

EBSCO SUBSCRIPTION SERVICE CO
 (Hq) 1230 First Ave, Birmingham, Ala 35201 (205) 323-6351; Branch Offices: EBSCO Bldg, Red Bank, NJ 07701 (201) 741-4300; EBSCO Bldg, 826 S Northwest Highway, Barrington, Ill 60010 (312) 381-2190-1; 2352 Utah Ave, El Segundo, Calif 90245 (213) 772-2831; 681 Market St, San Francisco, Calif 94105. (415) 391-3500; 5256 Port Royal Rd., Springfield, Va 22151 (703) 321-7630; 415 Douglas Plaza Bldg, Dallas, Tex 75225 (214) 369-7591; Continental Terrace Bldg, Denver, Colo 80211 (303) 433-3235; 512 Nicollet Bldg, Minneapolis, Minn 55402 (612) 233-5081; 540 Granite St, Braintree, Mass 02184 (617) 843-2383-4.
ECOLOGY FORUM, INC
 Suite 303E, 200 Park Ave, New York, NY 10017 (212) 972-0523
EDUCATIONAL ACTIVITIES, INC
 Box 392, Freeport, NY 11520 (516) 223-4666.
EDUCATIONAL FILM LIBRARY ASSOCIATION, INC
 17 W 60th St, New York, NY 10023 (212) 246-4533
EDUCATIONAL READING SERVICE, INC
 320 Rt 17, Mahwah, NJ 07430 (201) 529-4000
EDUCATORS PROGRESS SERVICE
 214 Center St, Randolph, Wis 53956 (414) 326-3126
ELDEN ENTERPRISES
 Box 3201, Charleston, W Va 25332 (304) 344-2335
ELECTRONIC FUTURES, INC (EFI)
 (Div KMS Industries, Inc)
 57 Dodge Ave, North Haven, Conn 06473 (203) 239-5341
ELLIOTT BUSINESS MACHINES, INC
 Randolph Industrial Park, Randolph, Mass 02368 (617) 963-8500
ELLIOTT LIBRARY SERVICE (JOHN M)
 607 W 2nd St, Pittsburg, Kan 66762 (913) 231-6074
EMBOSOGRAF CORP OF AMERICA
 38 W 21st St, New York, NY 10010 (212) 243-8663
EMC CORP
 180 E 6th St, St Paul, Minn 55101 (612) 227-7366
EMEND CO
 110-47 71st Ave, Forest Hills, NY 11375 (212) 263-4878
EMERY-PRATT CO
 1966 W Main St, Owosso, Mich 48867 (517) 723-5291
ENCYCLOPAEDIA BRITANNICA EDUCATIONAL CORP
 425 N Michigan Ave, Chicago, Ill 60611 (312) 321-6763
ENRICHMENT MATERIALS, INC
 (Div Scholastic Bk Services)
 906 Sylvan Ave, Englewood Cliffs, NJ 07632
ENRICHMENT RECORDS
 20 E 8th St, New York, NY 10003

DIRECTORY OF SUPPLIERS / 565

EP GROUP OF COMPANIES
(Microform Div)
E Ardsley nr Wakefield, Yorkshire, Eng Lofthouse Gate 3971
EQUIPTO
225 S Highland Ave, Aurora, Ill 60507 (312) 896-4641
EQUITABLE BAG CO. INC
45-50 Van Dam St, Long Island City, NY 11101 (212) ST 6-0620
ESTEY CORP
Drawer E, Red Bank, NJ 07701 (201) 542-5000
EVANS SPECIALTY CO, INC
14 E 15th St, Richmond, Va 23224 (703) 232-8946
EVER READY LABEL CORP
357 Cortlandt St. Belleville, NJ 07109 (201) PL 9-5500
EYE GATE HOUSE, INC
146-01 Archer Ave, Jamaica, NY 11435 (212) 291-9100

FAIRCHILD INDUSTRIAL PRODUCTS
75 Mall Dr, Commack, NY 11725 (516) 864-8500
FAIRCHILD VISUALS
(Div Fairchild Pubns, Inc)
7 E 12th St, New York, NY 10003 (212) AL 5-5252
FARQUHAR TRANSPARENT GLOBES
5007 Warrington Ave, Philadelphia, Pa 19143 (215) 747-5333
FAXON, F W, CO, INC
15 Southwest Park, Westwood, Mass 02090 (617) 329-3350
FERNO-WASHINGTON, INC
Greenfield, Ohio 45123 (513) 981-2148
FETZER'S SALT LAKE CABINET & FIXTURE CO
1436 SW Temple St, Salt Lake City, Utah 84110 (801) 484-6103
FILM CLASSIC EXCHANGE
1926 S Vermont Ave, Los Angeles, Calif 90007 (213) 731-3854
FILMDEX CORP
15500 Lee Hwy, Centerville, Va 22020 (703) 631-0600
FILMS INC
1144 Wilmette Ave, Wilmette, Ill 60091 (312) 256-4730
FILMS IN REVIEW
31 Union Sq, New York, NY 10003 (212) AL 5-6655
FILMSTRIP HOUSE, INC
432 Park Ave South, New York, NY 10016 (212) LE 2-4750
FISCHER, CARL, INC
62 Cooper Sq, New York, NY 10003 (212) 777-0900
FIXTURES MFG CORP
1642 Crystal St. Kansas City, Mo 64126 (816) 241-4500
FLEETWOOD FILMS, INC
(Subs Crowell Collier & Macmillan, Inc)
34 MacQuesten Pkwy S, Mt. Vernon, NY 10550 (914) MO 4-5051
FLEETWOOD FURNITURE CO
25 Washington St, Zeeland, Mich.

49464 (616) 772-4693
FLXIBLE CO
(see Sentinel Lockers)
FOLKWAYS/SCHOLASTIC
(see Scholastic Audio-Visual)
FOLLETT LIBRARY BOOK CO
1018 W Washington Blvd, Chicago, Ill 60607 (312) 666-5863
FORCE, WM A, AND CO, INC
216 Nichols Ave, Brooklyn, NY 11208 (212) 647-3800
FORDHAM EQUIPMENT & PUBLISHING CO (FECO)
2377 Hoffman St. Bronx, NY 10458 (212) SE 3-4131
FOUR CONTINENT BOOK CORP
156 Fifth Ave, New York, NY 10010 (212) CH 2-4500
FRANKLIN SQUARE/MAYFAIR SUBSCRIPTION AGENCY
545 Cedar Lane (Hq), Teaneck, NJ, 07666 (201) 863-8700 Regional Offices: Southeast Region, 8701 F Dunwoody Pl, NE, Atlanta, Ga 30338 (404) 993-4082; Midwest Region, 230 N Michigan Ave, Chicago, Ill 60601 (312) 782-7174; Central States Region, 2708 W Berry, Ft Worth, Tex 76109; Western Region, 418-C Glendale Ave, Glendale, Calif 91206 (213) 245-0016; Pacific Northwest Region, Box 2031, Olympia, Wash (206) 491-8309; Dawson Subscription Agency, 6 Thorncliffe Pk Dr, Toronto 17, Ont (416) 421-9000
FRENCH & EUROPEAN PUBLICATIONS, INC
610 Fifth Ave, New York, NY 10020 (212) 247-7475
FRIDEN DIV
(Singer Co)
2350 Washington Ave, San Leandro, Calif 94577 (415) 357-6800

GAF CORP
140 W 51st St, New York, NY 10020 (212) 582-7600
GAISSER, KENDALL G
1242 Broadway, Toledo, Ohio 43609 (419) 243-7631
GANE BROTHERS AND LANE, INC
1335 W Lake St, Chicago, Ill 60607 (312) 666-5840
GARDNER, CHARLES M, CO
(Div Learning Resources, Inc)
1047 Commonwealth Ave, Boston, Mass 02117 (617) 254-4500
GAYLORD BROS, INC
Box 61, Syracuse, NY 13201 (315) 457-5070; West Coast Office: Box 710, Stockton, Calif 95201 (209) 466-9456
GENERAL ANILINE & CHEMICAL CORP
(Photo & Repro Division)
140 W 51st St, New York, NY 10020
GENERAL BINDING CORP
1101 Skokie Blvd, Northbrook, Ill 60062 (312) 272-3700
GENERAL FIREPROOFING CO
E Dennick Ave, Youngstown, Ohio 44501 (216) 746-7271

GENERAL MICROFILM CO
  100 Inman St. Cambridge, Mass 02139
  (617) 864-2820
GENERAL NUCLEONICS, INC
  2104 Superior Ave, Cleveland, Ohio
  44114 (216) 621-2068
GERSTENSLAGER CO
  1425 E Bowman St, Wooster, Ohio
  44691 (216) 262-2015
GESTETNER DUPLICATOR CORP
  216 Lake Ave, Yonkers, NY 10702 (914)
  968-6666
GILLOTTE ROBERT P & CO
  2230 Commerce Dr, Columbia, SC
  29205 (803) 254-8452
GODFREY MEMORIAL LIBRARY
  134 Newfield St, Middletown, Conn
  06457 (203) 346-4375
GOODY, SAM, INC
  46-35 54th Rd, Maspeth, NY 11378
  (212) 361-7211
GRAFFCO DIV
  (Labelon Corp)
  226 Lowell St, Somerville, Mass 02144
GRAFLEX DIV
  (Singer Co)
  3750 Monroe Ave, Rochester,
  NY 14603 (716) 586-2020
GREENWOOD PRESS, INC
  51 Riverside Ave, Westport,
  Conn 06880 (203) 226-3571

HAGMAN ENTERPRISES
  2606 E Glenoaks Blvd, Glendale,
  Calif 91206
HAGSTROM CO
  311-315 B'way, New York, NY 10007
  (212) CO 7-8790
HALL, G K, & CO
  70 Lincoln St, Boston, Mass 02111
  (617) 426-8190
HAMILTON MFG CO
  1316 18th St, Two Rivers, Wis 54241
HAMMETT, J L CO
  Hammett Pl, Braintree, Mass 02184
  (617) 848-1000
HAMMOND, INC
  515 Valley St, Maplewood, NJ 07040
  (201) 763-6000
HARRASSOWITZ, OTTO
  Taunusstrasse 5, Wiesbaden, Germany
HARTFORD FIRE INSURANCE CO
  Hartford, Conn 06115
HARWALD CO
  1245 Chicago Ave, Evanston,
  Ill 60202 (312) 491-1000
HECKMAN BINDERY, INC
  1010 N Sycamore St, N Manchester,
  Ind 46962 (219) 982-2107
HELLER, W C & CO
  210 Wabash Ave, Montpelier,
  Ohio 43543 (419) 485-3176
HENNESSEY & INGALLS, INC
  8419 Lincoln Blvd, Los Angeles, Calif
  90045 (213) 670-7976
HERDER & HERDER, INC
  232 Madison Ave, New York, NY 10016
  (212) 679-8050

HERNER & CO
  2100 M St NW, Washington, DC 20037
  (202) 293-2600
HERRING HALL MARVIN SAFE CO
  1100 S Erie Blvd, Hamilton,
  Ohio 45010 (513) 863-5900
HERTZBERG-NEW METHOD, INC
  Vandalia Rd, Jacksonville, Ill 62650
  (217) 245-7131
HIGGINS INK CO, INC
  41 Dickerson St, Newark, NJ 07103
  (201) 484-4141
HIGHSMITH CO, INC
  Box 25, Ft Atkinson, Wis 53538
  (414) 563-6356
HOFFMAN RESEARCH SERVICES
  124 Whitmore Rd, Irwin, Pa 15642
  (412) 863-2367
HOLLISTON MILLS, INC
  111 Lenox St, Norwood, Mass 02062
  (617) 762-1490
HOLLYWOOD PLASTICS, INC
  4560 Worth St, Los Angeles, Calif
  90063 (213) 268-1181
HOLOPHANE CO, INC
  1120 Ave of the Americas, New York,
  NY 10036 (212) MU 2-5320
HONEYWELL INC, COMMERCIAL SALES
  DIV
  2701 Fourth Ave, Minneapolis,
  Minn 55408
HONEYWELL INC, PHOTOGRAPHIC
  PRODUCTS DIV
  5501 S Broadway, Littleton,
  Colo 80120
HORDER'S
  231 S Jefferson St, Chicago, Ill 60606
  (312) 372-6760
HOWARD, DON, PERSONNEL, INC
  290 Madison Ave, New York, NY 10017
  (212) LE 2-8300
HOWE FOLDING FURNITURE, INC
  360 Lexington Ave, New York,
  NY 10017 (212) 867-4460
H-R PRODUCTIONS, INC
  251 W 57th St, New York, NY 10019
  (212) 246-5133
HUBBARD SCIENTIFIC CO/ THE HUBBARD
  PRESS
  Box 105, Northbrook, Ill 60062
  (312) 272-7810
HUDSON PHOTOGRAPHIC INDUSTRIES,
  INC
  S Buckhout & Station Rds, Irvington-
  on-Hudson, New York, NY 10533
  (914) 591-8700
HUNTTING CO, INC, H R
  Burnett Rd and First Ave, Chicopee
  Falls, Mass 01020 (413) 594-4728-9

IBM OFFICE PRODUCTS DIV
  Armonk, NY 10504
IDEAL SCHOOL SUPPLY CO
  11010 S Lavergne Ave, Oak Lawn,
  Ill 60453 (312) 425-0800
IM (INTERNATIONAL MICROFILM) PRESS
  (3M)
  3M Center, St Paul, Minn 55101

DIRECTORY OF SUPPLIERS / 567

(612) 733-4791
IMPERIAL FILM CO, INC
4404 S Florida Ave, Lakeland, Fla 33803 (813) 646-5705
INFONICS, INC
1722 Cloverfield Blvd, Santa Monica, Calif 90404 (213) 828-6471
INFORMATION DESIGN, INC
3247 Middlefield Rd, Menlo Park, Calif 94025 (415) 369-2962
INFORMATION DYNAMICS CORP
80 Main St, Reading, Mass 01867 (617) 944-2224
INGRAM BOOK CO
Box 3712, Nashville, Tenn 37217
INPUT SERVICES
(Div Autographics, Inc.)
111 E Fourth St, Dayton, Ohio 45402 (513) 224-7386
INSTRUCTO PRODUCTS
(Subs McGraw-Hill)
Cedar Hollow & Matthews Rds, Paoli, Pa 19301 (215) 644-7700
INTERIORS FOR BUSINESS, INC
1705 Commerce Dr, Atlanta, Ga. 30318 (404) 355-7604
INTERLAKEN DIV
(see Arkwright-Interlaken, Inc)
INTERNATIONAL BOOKFINDERS INC
Box 1, Pacific Palisades, Calif 90272
INTERNATIONAL FILM BUREAU, INC
332 S Michigan Ave, Chicago, Ill 60604 (312) 427-4545
INTERNATIONAL UNIVERSITY BOOKSELLERS, INC
101 Fifth Ave, New York, NY 10003 (212) 691-5252
INTER-PAC INTERMOUNTAIN, INC
332 N Broadway, N Tarrytown, NY 10591 (914) 631-1776
INTERROYAL CORP
(Library Div)
One Park Ave, New York, NY 10016 (212) 686-3500
INTERSTATE LIBRARY SERVICE CO
(see Baker & Taylor Co)
ITEK BUSINESS PRODUCTS DIV
(Itek Corp)
1001 Jefferson Rd, Rochester, NY 14603
IVINS, HADDON WOOD
Box 304, Plainfield, NJ 07061 (201) 356-0484

JACKSON CO MANUFACTURERS
1879 Mt Vernon Ave, Pomona, Calif 91768 (714) 622-5440
JAM HANDY
(see Scott Education Div)
JAPAN PUBLICATIONS TRADING CO (USA), INC
1255 Howard St, San Francisco, Calif 94103 (415) 431-3384
JAYARK INSTRUMENTS CORP
10 E 49th St, New York, NY 10017 (212) 751-3232
JIFFY MANUFACTURING CO
360 Florence Ave, Hillside, NJ 07205

(201) 688-9200
JOHNSON REPRINT CORP
111 Fifth Ave, New York, NY 10003 (212) 677-6713
JOHNSON, S C & SON, INC
(Service Products Division)
1525 Howe St, Racine, Wis 53403
JOHNSON, WALTER J, INC
111 Fifth Ave, New York, NY 10003 (212) 677-6713
JORE & CO
33-04 Downing St, Flushing, NY 11354
JOSTEN'S
(see American Library Line or Catalog Corp of America)
JUDY CO
310 N Second St, Minneapolis, Minn 55401 (612) 333-6471

KEENER RUBBER, INC
Box 327, Alliance, Ohio 44601 (216) 821-1880
KERSTING MFG CO
504 S Date Ave, Alhambra, Calif 91803 (213) 283-6369
KEUFFEL & ESSER CO
20 Whippany Rd, Morristown, NJ 07960
KEWANEE SCIENTIFIC EQUIPMENT CO
4122 Logan St, Adrian, Mich 49221 (313) 263-5731
KIDDE MERCHANDISING EQUIP GROUP
100 Bidwell Rd, S Windsor, Conn 06074 (203) 289-8267
KING KAROL RECORDS
Box 629, Times Sq Sta, New York, NY 10036 (212) BR 9-2342
KING SCREEN PRODUCTIONS
320 Aurora Ave N, Seattle, Wash 89109 (206) MU 2-3555
KINGSLEY LIBRARY EQUIPMENT CO
(Subs Jackson Co Mfg)
1879 Mt Vernon Ave, Pomona, Calif 91766 (714) 622-5440
KNIPP & CO, INC
3401 S Hanover St, Baltimore, Md 21225 (301) 355-0440
KNOLL INTERNATIONAL
745 Fifth Ave, New York, NY 10022 (212) 688-7900
KRAUS PERIODICALS, CO
(Div Kraus-Thompson Organization, Ltd)
16 E 46 St, New York, NY 10017 (212) MU 7-4808

LANDERS ASSOCIATES
Box 69760, Los Angeles, Calif 90069 (213) 656-6802
LANGFELD MANEX CORP
350 Fifth Ave, Rm 8201, New York, NY 10001 (212) 594-4570
LARGE PRINT, LTD
505 Pearl St, Buffalo, NY 14202 (716) 856-4638
LATEX FIBER INDUSTRIES
Beaver Falls, NY 13305 (315) 346-8301
LAWRENCE METAL PRODUCTS, INC

568 / DIRECTORY OF SUPPLIERS

60 Prospect La, Lynbrook, NY 11563 (516) 593-9001
LAWYERS COOPERATIVE PUBLISHING CO
Aqueduct Bldg, Rochester, NY 14603 (716) 546-5530
LEARNING MEDIA CORP
231 N 63rd St, Philadelphia, Pa 19151 (215) 748-3333
LEASCO SYSTEMS & RESEARCH CORP
4833 Rugby Ave, Bethesda, Md 20014 (301) 656-9723
LEC BOOKBINDERS, INC
1091 Rockaway Ave, Valley Stream, NY 11581 (516) 593-1196
LIEBEL, CARL J, INC
(Div Bro-Dart, Inc)
1236 S Hatcher Ave, La Puente, Calif 91747 (213) 964-6591
LIBRARIE DE FRANCE
(see French & European Publications, Inc)
LIBRARY BINDING INSTITUTE
160 State St, Boston, Mass 02109 (617) 227-9614
LIBRARY BINDING SERVICE, INC
Box 1413, Des Moines, Iowa 50305 (515) 262-3191
LIBRARY BUREAU DIV
(of Remington Rand)
801 Park Ave, Herkimer, NY 13350 (315) 866-1330
LIBRARY CAREER CONSULTANTS
Suite 212, 915 Saxoonburg Blvd, Pittsburgh, Pa 15223 (412) 781-8712
LIBRARY CONCEPTS, INC
892 Broad St, Newark, NJ 07102 (201) 643-2645
LIBRARY FILMSTRIP CENTER
3033 Aloma, Wichita, Kan 67211 (316) 682-5925
LIBRARY AND INFORMATION SERVICES DIV
(see New York Times)
LIBRARY JOURNAL
1180 Ave of the Americas, New York, NY 10036 (212) 581-8800
LIBRARY MANAGEMENT AND BUILDING CONSULTANTS, INC
Suite 258, Willow Hill Executive Center, 540 Frontage Rd, Northfield, Ill 60093 (312) 446-8862
LIBRARY MICROFILMS
4009 Transport St, Palo Alto, Calif 94303
LIBRARY MICROFILMS AND MATERIALS CO
5709 Mesmer Ave, Culver City, Calif 90230 (213) 870-7355
LIBRARY MICROGRAPHIC SERVICES, INC
225 Park Ave S, New York, NY 10003 (212) 777-5600
LIBRARY OF CONGRESS
Washington, DC 20540 (202) ST 3-0400
LIBRARY PROCESSING SYSTEMS
404 Union Blvd, Allentown, Pa 18103 (215) 432-8516

LIBRARY PRODUCTS, INC (STURGIS)
Box 130, Sturgis, Mich 49091 (616) 651-5076
LIBRARY PUBLICITY SERVICE
Box 742, Santa Ana, Calif 92702
LIBRARY RESOURCES, INC
(An Encyclopaedia Britannica Co)
301 E Erie St, Chicago, Ill 60611 (312) 321-7444
LIBRARY SERVICE ASS'N
47-51 Rue Barrault, Paris 12, France 589.20-58
LINCOLN BOOK SHOPPE, INC
905 Westminster St, Providence, RI 02903 (401) 331-0932
LINGUAPHONE INSTITUTE OF AMERICA, INC
437 Madison Ave, New York, NY 10020 (212) 350-0343
LIQUICK-LEATHER
Sunset Island, Onset, Mass 02558 (617) 295-3002
LISTENING LIBRARY, INC
1 Park Ave, Old Greenwich, Conn 06870 (203) 637-3616
LOST CAUSE PRESS
750-56 Starks Bldg, Louisville, Ky 40202 (502) 584-8404
LUMEX, INC
100 Spence St, Bayshore, NY (516) 273-2200
LUNDIA MYERS INDUSTRIES, INC
Box 309, Decatur, Ill 62525
LYCEUM PRODUCTIONS, INC
Box 1226, Laguna Beach, Calif 92652 (714) 494-6253

McBEE SYSTEMS
(Div Litton Inds)
Port Chester, NY 10573
McCLURG, A C
(Div Bro-Dart, Inc)
2121 Landmeier Rd, Elk Grove Village, Ill 60007 (312) 625-0850
McDONALD PRODUCTS CORP
721 Seneca St, Buffalo, NY 14210 (716) 853-7200
McGRAW-HILL/EARLY LEARNING
(see Instructo Corp)
McGRAW-HILL FILMS
(Div McGraw-Hill Book Co)
330 W 42nd St, New York, NY 10036 (212) 971-6637
McGREGOR MAGAZINE AGENCY
Mount Morris, Ill 61054 (815) 734-4183
McNAUGHTON BOOK SERVICE
(Div Bro-Dart, Inc)
Box 914, Williamsport, Pa 17701
MAGAFILE CO
2800 Market St, St Louis, Mo 63103 (314) 652-2933
MANUSCRIPTS SUPPLY CO
100 Rodney Rd, Dover, Del 19901 (302) 734-2423
MARADOR DIVISION
(see EBSCO Subscription Services)

MAXWELL INT'L MICROFORMS CORP
(see Maxwell Scientific)
MAXWELL REPRINT CO
(see Maxwell Scientific)
MAXWELL SCIENTIFIC INT'L, INC
Fairview Pk, Elmsford, NY 10523
(914) 592-9141
MAYFAIR SUBSCRIPTION AGENCY
(see Franklin Sq Subn Agency)
MERLIN MFG CO
3545 N Clark St, Chicago, Ill 60657
(312) 348-2640
METALAB EQUIPMENT CO
(see Standard Wood Products Corp)
METROPOLITAN WIRE GOODS CORP
N Washington St & George Ave, Wilkes-Barre, Pa 18705
MICHAEL BUSINESS MACHINES CORP
145 W 45th St, New York, NY 10036
(212) 582-2900
MICHAELS ART BRONZE CO
Box 668, Covington, Ky 41012
(606) 341-5400
MICROCARD EDITIONS
(Div, Nat'l Cash Register Co)
901 26th St, NW, Washington, DC 20037 (202) 333-6393
MICRO DIE, INC
30 Ogden St, Newark, NJ 07104
(201) 483-0670
MICROFILM CO OF CALIFORNIA
(Library Reproduction Service)
1977 S Los Angeles St, Los Angeles, Calif 90011 (213) 749-2463
MICROFILMING CORP OF AMERICA
(Subs NY Times)
21 Harristown Rd, Glen Rock, NJ 07452 (201) 447-3000
MICROPUBLISHERS, THE
(see Bell & Howell Co)
MICROREADER MFG & SALES CORP
2217 N Summit Ave, Milwaukee, Wis 53202
MIDTOWN MAGAZINE SERVICE
Box 917, Maywood, NJ 07607
(212) 933-6579
MIDWEST LIBRARY SERVICE, INC
11400 Dorsett Rd, Maryland Heights, Mo 63043 (314) 739-3100
MILEX CO
821 Malcolm Rd, Burlingame, Calif 94010
MILLER, HERMAN, INC
140 W McKinley St, Zeeland, Mich 49464
MINNESOTA MINING & MFG CO
(see 3M Co)
MITTEN DESIGNER LETTERS
85 Fifth Ave, New York, NY 10003
(212) 757-6730 or Mitten Bldg, Redlands, Calif 92373
M & M INDUSTRIES
Box 188, S Milwaukee, Wis 53172
MONARCH BOOK CO
(see American Library Line)
MONARCH LEASE PLAN
(see American Library Line)

MONROE INDUSTRIES, INC
910 E Indianapolis, Wichita, Kan 67211
(316) 262-4448
MONROE TABLE CO
424 Church St, Colfax, Iowa 50054
(515) 674-3511
MOORE-COTTRELL SUBSCRIPTION AGENCIES, INC
North Cohocton, NY 14868 (716) 534-5221
MOORE, P O, INC
(Subs Sunroc Corp)
Glen Riddle, Pa 19037
MORONEY, THOS F & CO, INC
433 Boston Tpke, Shrewsbury, Mass 01545 (617) 842-8862
MOSLER SAFE CO
1561 Grand Blvd, Hamilton, Ohio 45012 (513) 867-4292
M P AUDIO CORP
Fairfield, Conn 06430 (203) 268-2385
MPC EDUCATIONAL SYSTEMS, INC
35 Fulton St, New Haven, Conn 06512
(203) 469-6481
MURPHY, MICHAEL M, LIBRARY & SCHOOL SPECIALTIES
Box 1108, St Cloud, Minn 56301
MUTUAL EDUCATION AIDS
1924 Hillhurst Ave, Los Angeles, Calif 90027 (213) 661-4503
MYRTLE DESK CO
Box 1750, High Point, NC 27261
(919) 885-4021
MYSTIC TAPE
(Div Borden, Inc)
LeVeque Lincoln Tower, 50 W Broad St, Columbus, Ohio 43215 (614) 461-8530

NATIONAL AUDIO-VISUAL ASSN
3150 Spring St, Fairfax, Va 22030
(703) 273-7200
NATIONAL CASH REGISTER CO (NCR)
(Industrial Products Division)
1000 Cox Plaza, 3131 S Dixie Dr, Kettering, Ohio 45439 (513) 449-8316
NATIONAL METAL SPECIALTIES, INC
10 Thompson Lane, Edgewater, NJ 07020 (201) 943-2121
NATIONAL PLANNING DATA CORP
65 Broad St, Rochester, NY 14614
(716) 454-6084
NATIONAL REJECTORS, INC
9516 Lakeland Rd, St Louis, Mo
(314) 429-6076
NATIONAL STATIONERS
NW Cor 11th & Filbert, Philadelphia, Pa 19107 (215) 922-1760
NCR (NAT'L CASH REGISTER) MICROCARD EDITIONS
(see Microcard Editions)
NELSON ASSOCIATES
815 Connecticut Ave, NW, Washington, DC 20006 (202) 298-8630
NEUMADE PRODUCTS CORP
720 White Plains Rd, Scarsdale, NY 10583 (914) 725-4900

570 / DIRECTORY OF SUPPLIERS

NEWCOMB AUDIO PRODUCTS CO
  12881 Bradley Ave, Sylmar, Calif
  91342 (213) 367-1921
NEW ENGLAND BINDERY, INC
  (see Huntting Co, Inc, HR)
NEW METHOD BOOK BINDERY, INC
  (see Bound to Stay Bound Books, Inc)
NEW YORK GRAPHIC SOCIETY
  (Div Time-Life Books)
  140 Greenwich Ave, Greenwich, Conn
  06830 (212) 933-1134 (NYC)
  (203) 869-3955 (Conn)
NEW YORK TIMES LIBRARY SERVICES DIV
  229 W 43 St, New York, NY 10036
  (212) 556-1001
NORELCO (NORTH AMERICAN PHILIPS CO, INC)
  100 E 42nd St, New York, NY 10017
  (212) 697-3600
NORRIS INDUSTRIES
  (Fire & Safety Equip Div)
  Box 2750, Newark, NJ 07114
  (201) 248-2200
NYSTROM & CO, A J
  (Div Field Enterprises Educ Corp)
  3333 Elston Ave, Chicago, Ill 60618
  (312) IN 3-1144

OESTREICHER'S PRINTS, INC
  43 W 46 St, New York, NY 10036
  (212) PL 7-1190
OLIN EDUCATIONAL SERVICES
  460 Park Ave, New York, NY 10022
OLIVETTI CORP OF AMERICA
  500 Park Ave, New York, NY 10022
  (212) 371-5500
OMNI-CARD SYSTEMS, INC
  37-06 61st St, Woodside, NY (212) 779-2000
OPAQUE SYSTEMS, LTD
  100 Taft Ave, Hempstead, NY 11550
  (516) 485-3322
ORAVISUAL CO, INC
  Box 11150, St Petersburg, Fla 33733
OWENS AWNING & SUPPLY CO
  123-25 N Second St, Springfield, Ill
  62701 (217) 522-9921

PANDEX, INC
  22 W 34th St, New York, NY
  (212) 736-5477
PAPER CORP OF US
  630 Fifth Ave, New York, NY 10020
  (212) CI 7-1637
PARIS PUBLICATIONS, INC
  14 Maple St, Port Washington, NY
  11050 (516) 767-0727
PASCH BROTHERS
  (Div Markay Products Co)
  2255 Howell Ave, Milwaukee, Wis
  53207
PEREY TURNSTILES
  101 Park Ave, New York, NY 10017
  (212) 679-6080
PERFECTION FORM CO
  214 W 8th St, Logan, Iowa 51546
PERRY CO

Box 7187, Waco, Tex 76710
  (817) 756-2137
P/H ELECTRONICS
  117 E Helena St, Dayton, Ohio 45404
  (513) 461-5898
PHIEBIG, ALBERT J, INC
  Box 352, White Plains, NY 10602
  (914) WH 8-0138
PHILLIPS, DON R, INC
  Box 68, Spring Grove, Ill 60081
  (815) 675-2383
PICTURE COVER BINDINGS
  430 Lincoln St, Easton, Pa 18042
  (215) 258-7231
PITNEY-BOWES, INC
  Pacific & Walnut Sts, Stamford, Conn
  06904
PLAN HOLD CORP
  21611 Perry St, Carson, Calif 90745
POLAROID CORP
  549 Technology Sq, Cambridge, Mass
  02139
POPULAR SCIENCE PUB CO, INC
  (AV Div, Subs of Times Mirror Co)
  355 Lexington Ave, New York, NY
  10017 (212) 687-3000
POSTER HOUSE, INC
  Box 366, Short Hills, NJ 07078
  (201) 376-3385
POTDEVIN MACHINE CO
  283 North St, Teterboro, NJ 07608
  (201) 288-1941
POTTER'S PHOTOGRAPHIC APPLICATIONS CO (PAC Films, Inc)
  160 Herricks Rd, Mineola, NY 11501
  (516) 248-7070
PRESTON, J A, CORP
  71 Fifth Ave, New York, NY 10003
  (212) AL 5-8484
PRINCETON MICROFILM CORP
  Alexander Rd, Princeton, NJ 08540
  (609) 452-2066
PROBBER, HENRY, INC
  44 Probber La, Fall River, Mass 02722
  (617) 674-3591
PROFESSIONAL LIBRARY SERVICE
  (see Xerox BiblioGraphics)
PURNELL LIBRARY SERVICE
  850 7th Ave, New York, NY 10019
  (212) 765-7530

Q-ED PRODUCTIONS
  (Div Cathedral Films, Inc)
  2921 W Alameda Ave, Burbank, Calif
  91505 (213) 848-6637

RADIO-MATIC OF AMERICA, INC
  760 Ramsey Ave, Hillside, NJ 07205
  (201) 687-0929
RAND McNALLY & CO
  Box 7600, Chicago, Ill 60680
  (312) OR 3-9100
RCA AUDIO VISUAL MARKETING DIV
  Front & Copper Sts, Camden, NJ 08102
  (609) 963-8000
RCA RECORDS
  (Educational Sales)
  1133 Ave of Americas, New York, NY

DIRECTORY OF SUPPLIERS / 571

10036 (212) JU 6-3000
READER'S DIGEST EDUCATIONAL DIV
 Pleasantville, NY 10570
READEX MICROPRINT CORP
 5 Union Sq, New York, NY 10003
 (212) 243-3822
RECORD HUNTER
 507 Fifth Ave, New York, NY 10017
 (212) 697-8970
RECORDINGS FOR THE BLIND
 215 E 58th St, New York, NY 10022
 (212) 751-0860
RECREATION EQUIPMENT CORP
 Box 2188, Anderson, Ind 46011
 (317) 643-5315
REFLECTOR HARDWARE CORP
 (Educational Prods Div)
 1400 N 25th Ave, Melrose Park, Ill
 60160 (312) 261-1800
REGENT BOOK CO, INC
 107 Prospect Pl, Hillsdale, NJ 07642
 (201) 664-8900
REGISCOPE CORP OF AMERICA
 7 East 43rd St, New York, NY 10017
 (212) 661-1730
REMINGTON RAND LIBRARY BUREAU DIV
 (see Library Bureau Div)
REMINGTON RAND OFFICE MACHINES DIV
 (Sperry Rand Corp)
 333 Wilson Ave, S Norwalk, Conn 06856
REMINGTON RAND
 (Sperry Rand Corp)
 Box 171, Marietta, Ohio 45750
REPLOGLE GLOBES
 1901 N Narragansett Ave, Chicago, Ill
 60639
REPRINT DISTRIBUTION SERVICE, INC
 Box 245, Kent, Conn 06757
 (203) 927-3521
REPUBLIC STEEL CORP MFG DIV
 1315 Albert St, Youngstown, Ohio
 44505 (216) 746-7211
RESKA, INC
 985 Jefferson Ave, Buffalo, NY 14204
REYNOLDS BINDERY, INC
 1701 Lister St, Kansas City, Mo 64127
 (201) 722-8000
REYNOLDS ENTERPRISES
 512 S Fair Oaks Ave, Pasadena, Calif
 91101 (213) MU 1-7059
RHEEM-CALIFONE CORP
 5922 Bowcroft St, Los Angeles, Calif
 90016 (213) 870-9631
RISOM, JENS, DESIGN, INC
 505 Park Ave, New York, NY 10022
 (212) 688-0030
ROCOCO RECORDS LTD
 3244 Yonge St, Toronto 12, Canada
 (416) 483-1636
ROSE DISCOUNT RECORDS, INC
 214 S Wabash Ave, Chicago, Ill 60604
 (312) 663-0660
ROSENBERG, MARY S, INC
 100 W 72nd St, New York, NY 10023
 (212) EN 2-4873
ROYAL TYPEWRITER CO

(Div Litton Industries)
 850 Third Ave, New York, NY 10022
 (212) 752-7900
RUDCO MANUFACTURING CO
 Box 13087, Houston, Tex 77019
 (713) 523-9440
RUZICKA, JOSEPH, INC
 911 Northridge St, Greensboro, NC
 27402 (919) 299-7534

ST PAUL BOOK & STATIONERY CO
 6th & Cedar Sts, St Paul, Minn 55101
 (612) 222-8421
SAN VAL INC
 (see Vinabind)
SANFORD INK CO
 2740 Washington Blvd, Bellwood, Ill
 60104
SAFCO PRODUCTS CO
 7425 Laurel Ave, S, Golden Valley, Minn
 55426 (612) 544-8471
SAPSIS, PERC B, BOOKS
 1795 Del Monte Blvd, Seaside, Calif
 93955 (408) 394-6715
SAVIN BUSINESS MACHINES CORP
 (Documat Div)
 Columbus Ave, Valhalla, NY 10595
 (914) 769-9500
SCHIRMER, G, INC
 609 Fifth Ave, New York, NY 10017
 (212) PL 2-3800
SCHOLASTIC AUDIO-VISUAL
 (see Scholastic Book Services)
SCHOLASTIC BOOK SERVICES
 50 W 44th St, New York, NY 10036
 (212) 867-7700
SCHWANN, INC, W
 137 Newbury St, Boston, Mass 02116
 (617) 261-3143
SCHWARTZ, F A O
 745 Fifth Ave, New York, NY 10022
 (212) 688-2200
SCIENCE PRESS, INC
 300 W Chestnut St, Ephrata, Pa 17522
 (717) 733-7981
SCIENTIFIC ADVANCES, INC
 4041 Roberts Rd, Columbus, Ohio
 43228 (614) 876-2461
SCI-TECH BOOK SERVICE, INC
 252 W 30th St, New York, NY 10001
 (212) 594-4747
SCM (Smith-Corona-Marchant)
 (Div SCM Corp)
 299 Park Ave, New York, NY 10017
 (212) 752-2700
SCOTT EDUCATION DIV
 (Scott Graphics, Inc)
 104 Lower Westfield Rd, Holyoke, Mass
 01040 (413) 536-8380
SCOVILL MFG CO
 Waterbury, Conn 06795
 (203) 757-6061
SEAL, INC
 215 Roosevelt Dr, Derby, Conn 06418
 (203) 734-1643
SEDGWICK PRINTOUT SYSTEMS
 410 E 62nd St, New York, NY 10021
 (212) 838-5304

SELECTAMATIC OF AMERICA CORP
310 E 44th St, New York, NY 10017
(212) 686-1450
SELECTRA, INC
28 W 005 Industrial Ave, Barrington, Ill
60010 (312) 381-7177
SENSORMATIC ELECTRONICS CORP
265 S Main St, Akron, Ohio 44308
(216) 762-2431
SENTINEL LOCKERS/THE FLXIBLE CO
326 N Water St, Loudonville, Ohio
44842
SHOWCARD MACHINE CO
320 W Ohio St, Chicago, Ill 60610
(312) 944-3829
SILVER BURDETT CO
(Div General Learning Corp)
250 James St, Morristown, NJ 07960
(201) 538-0400
SIMON & SCHUSTER, INC
(Educational Div)
1 W 39th St, New York, NY 10018
(212) CI 5-6400
SIMPLEX TIME RECORDER CO
26 S Lincoln St, Gardner, Mass 01440
(617) 632-2500
SJOSTROM USA, INC
1700 Market St, Philadelphia, Pa 19103
(215) 236-4600
SLYD-IN PRODUCTS
1507 Wilton Dr, Greensboro, NC 27408
(919) 288-8474
SMITH, DON
3930 Rankin St, Louisville, Ky 40214
(502) 366-1704
SMITH, PETER, PUBLISHERS, INC
6 Lexington Ave, Magnolia, Mass 01932
(617) 525-3562
SMITH SYSTEM MFG CO
1405 Silver Lake Rd, New Brighton,
Minn 55112 (612) 336-1784
SOCIETY FOR VISUAL EDUCATION, INC
(Subs Singer Co)
1345 Diversey Pkwy, Chicago, Ill 60614
(312) 525-1500
SOUTHERN DESK CO
(Div Drexel Enterprises, Inc)
Hickory NC 28601 (704) 345-7161
SPANISH BOOK CORP OF AMERICA
(see French & European Publications,
Inc)
SPIRAS SYSTEMS, INC
332 Second Ave, Waltham, Mass 02154
(617) 891-7300
SPOKEN ARTS, INC
301 North Ave, New Rochelle, NY
10801 (914) 636-7972
STACEY'S
(Subs Bro-Dart, Inc)
15255 E Don Julian Rd, City of Industry,
Calif 91747 (213) 968-6411
STACOR CORP
285 Emmet St, Newark, NJ 07114
STAEDTLER, J S, INC
Box 68, Boonton Ave, Montville, NJ
07045 (201) 235-1800
STANDARD CHANGE MAKERS, INC
422 E New York St, Indianapolis, Ind
46202 (317) 639-3423

STANDARD PAPER MFG CO
Richmond, Va
STANDARD REGISTER CO
Dayton, Ohio 45401 (513) 223-6181
STANDARD WOOD PRODUCTS CORP
270 Duffy Ave, Hicksville, NY 11801
STAPLEX CO
777 Fifth Ave, Brooklyn, NY 11232
(212) 768-2335
STECHERT-HAFNER, INC
31 E Tenth St, New York, NY 10003
(212) 674-6210
STEELCASE, INC
1120 36th St, SE, Grand Rapids, Mich
49501 (616) 241-2681
STEVENS & BROWN, B F, LTD
Ardon House, Godalming, Surrey, Eng
STONE BRIDGE PRESS
Gilsum, NH 03448 (603) 352-1026
STROBLITE CO, INC
29 W 15th St, New York, NY 10011
(212) 255-5450
STUART REYNOLDS PRODUCTIONS, INC
9465 Wilshire Blvd, Beverly Hills, Calif
90212 (213) 274-7863
STURGIS DISPLAYS
(see Library Products, Inc)
SUBJECT INDEX TO CHILDREN'S
MAGAZINES
2223 Chamberlain Ave, Madison, Wis
53705
SUBSCRIBE-A-BIND LTD
(Subs Demander Bookbindery, Inc)
840 Dixwell Ave, Hamden, Conn 06514
(203) 562-9495
SUPREME EQUIPMENT & SYSTEMS CORP
170 53rd St, Brooklyn, NY 11232
(212) 492-7777
SUTLIFF, GERALD F, CO, INC
Garden City, NY 11530
(516) 483-9533
SWETS & ZEITLINGER
Keizergracht 487, Amsterdam, Noord
Holland
SWF ASSOCIATES
2140 W Olympic Blvd, Los Angeles,
Calif 90006
SWIFT CUTTER CO
PO Box 496, Wooster, Ohio 44691
(216) 262-6546
SWIFT INSTRUMENTS, INC
952 Dorchester Ave, Boston, Mass
02125 (617) 436-2960
SYSTEM DEVELOPMENT CORP
2500 Colorado Ave, Santa Monica, Calif
90406

TALAS DIV
(Technical Library Services)
104 Fifth Ave, New York, NY 10011
(212) 675-0718
TARTAN BOOK SALES
(Div Bro-Dart)
Box 914, Williamsport, Pa 17701
(717) 326-1935
TEACHING RESOURCES CORP
100 Boylston St, Boston, Mass 02116
(617) 357-8446

TECHNICOLOR, INC
  (Commercial & Educational Div)
  1300 Frawley Dr, Costa Mesa, Calif
  92627 (714) 540-4330
TECHNIFAX EDUCATION DIV
  (Scott Graphics Inc)
  20 First Ave, Chicopee, Mass 01020
  (413) 592-7794
TELEKETICS
  (Div Franciscan Communications Center)
  1229 S Santee St, Los Angeles, Calif
  90015 (213) 748-2191
TELETYPE CORP
  5555 Touhy Ave, Skokie, Ill 60078
THOMPSON, JOHN I & CO
  1601 Research Blvd, Rockville, Md.
  20850 (202) 424-1310
THONET INDUSTRIES, INC
  One Park Ave, New York, NY 10016
  (212) 725-1100
THORNE FILMS, INC
  1229 University Ave, Boulder, Colo
  80302 (303) 443-4480
3M CO (MINN MINING & MFG CO)
  3M Center, St Paul, Minn 55101
  (612) 733-1110
3M IM (INT'L MICROFILM) PRESS
  (see IM Press)
TIFFANY STAND & FURNITURE CO
  100 Progress Pkw, Maryland Hts, Mo
  63043
TIME-LIFE FILMS
  43 W 16th St, New York, NY 10011
  (212) 691-2930
TOGGITT, JOAN, LTD
  1170 Broadway, Rm 406, New York, NY
  10001 (212) 684-0636
TORK TIME CONTROLS, INC
  1 Grove St, Mt Vernon, NY 10551
  (914) 664-3542
TREASURE TROVE COVERS
  (see Library Binding Service, Inc)
TWEEDY TRANSPARENCIES
  208 Hollywood Ave, E Orange, NJ
  07018 (201) 676-6500
TYPE-A-LINE BUSINESS MACH CO
  168 E Second St, Salt Lake City, Utah
  84111 (801) 322-1249
TYPE-UR-OWN CO
  6520 E Halbert Rd, Bethesda, Md
  20034 (301) 229-6599

U-FILE-M BINDER MFG CO, INC
  Box 206, Lafayette, NY 13084
UNITED PRODUCTS OF AMERICA
  600 Madison Ave, New York, NY 10022
  (212) 758-8400
UNITED STATES BOOK EXCHANGE, INC
  3335 V St NE, Washington, DC 20018
  (202) 529-2555
UNIVERSAL COLOR SLIDE CO
  136 W 32nd St, New York, NY 10001
  (212) 564-8880
UNIVERSAL EDUCATION & VISUAL ARTS
  221 Park Ave South, New York, NY
  10003 (212) 777-6600
UNIVERSITY BINDERY OF ST LOUIS
  1909 Locust St, St Louis, Mo 63103
UNIVERSITY MICROFILMS
  (Xerox Education Group)
  300 N Zeeb Rd, Ann Arbor, Mich 48106
  (313) 761-4700
UNIVERSITY MUSIC EDITIONS
  Box 192, Ft George Sta, New York, NY
  10040 (212) 569-5340
UNIVERSITY PRINTS
  15 Brattle St, Harvard Sq,
  (617) 864-6599
UNIVERSITY OF WASHINGTON PRESS
  Seattle, Wash 98195 (206) 543-4050
U-SEAL-IT, INC
  20th & Callowhill Sts, Philadelphia, Pa
  19130 (215) 561-6171

VACUDYNE CORP
  375 E Joe Orr Rd, Chicago Hts, Ill
  60411 (312) 757-5200
VALIANT INSTRUCTIONAL MATERIALS CORP
  237 Washington Ave, Hackensack, NJ
  07602 (201) 487-6340
VARITYPER CORP
  11 Mt Pleasant Ave, Hanover, NJ 07936
VECTA EDUCATIONAL CO
  2605 E Kilgore Rd, Kalamazoo, Mich
  49003
VICTOR COMPTOMETER CORP
  (Business Machine Group)
  3900 N Rockwell St, Chicago, Ill 60618
  (312) 539-8210
VIEWLEX, INC
  1 Broadway Ave, Holbrook, NY 11741
  (516) 589-6600
VINABIND
  (San Val, Inc)
  Box 340, Steelville, Mo 35565
VIRGINIA METAL PRODUCTS DIV
  (Div Gray Mfg Co)
  Orange, Va 22960 (703) 672-2800
VISTA COSTA MESA FURNITURE CO
  (Div Dictaphone Corp)
  411 E Julianna St, Anaheim, Calif
  92803
VISUAL INDUSTRIAL PRODS, INC
  Box 50, Indianola, Pa 15051
VOGEL-PETERSON CO
  Box 90, Elmhurst, Ill 60126
  (312) BR 9-7123

WALKER GOULARD PLEHN CO, INC
  109 Lafayette St, New York, NY 10013
  (212) 966-5700
WALKER SYSTEMS, INC
  520 S 1st Ave E, Duluth, Minn 55812
  (218) 728-4434
WALLACH & ASSOCIATES, INC
  5701 Euclid Ave, Cleveland, Ohio
  44103 (216) 361-7616
WALTON LABORATORIES DIV
  (Melnor Industries)
  Moonachie, NJ 07074
WARD, SAMUEL
  La Plata, Md 20646 (301) 934-8298
WARREN, SD CO
  (Div Scott Paper Co)
  225 Franklin St, Boston, Mass 02101
WEINBERG CORP

574 / DIRECTORY OF SUPPLIERS

145 W Columbia Ave, Philadelphia, Pa 19122 (215) GA 6-6364
WENGER CORP
Owatonna, Minn 55060 (507) 451-3010
WESTERN PUBLISHING CO, INC
850 Third Ave, New York, NY 10022 (212) 753-8500
WESTON WOODS STUDIOS, INC
Weston, Conn 06880 (203) 226-3355
WESTPORT COMMUNICATIONS GROUP, INC
155 E State St, Westport, Conn 06880 (203) 226-3525
WEST-STATE BOOKS
4047 Transport St, Palo Alto, Calif 94303 (415) 321-1897
WEYLL CORP
Box 62, Glen Cove, NY 11542 (516) 671-8783
WILKINSON CHUTES, INC
619 E Tallmadge Ave, Akron, Ohio 44310
WILLIAM-FREDERICK PRESS
Pamphlet Distributing Co Inc
55 E 86th St, New York, NY 10028 (212) SA 2-7272
WILSON, H CORP
555 W Taft Dr, S Holland, Ill 60473 (312) 339-5111
WILSON, H W CO
950 University Ave, Bronx, NY 10452 (212) 588-8300
WILSON METAL PRODUCTS
616 Essex St, Lawrence, Mass 01842 (617) 683-2403

WING PRODUCTIONS, INC
252 Great Road, Bedford, Mass 01730 (617) 275-6928
WITTENBORN & CO
1018 Madison Ave, New York, NY 10021 (212) BU 8-1558
WOODS LIBRARY PUBLISHING CO
12131 S Elizabeth St, Chicago, Ill 60643 (312) 468-3553
WORDEN CO
199 E 17th St, Holland, Mich 49423 (616) 392-1848
WORNER ELECTRONIC DEVICES, INC
121 N Main St, Rankin, Ill 60960 (217) 397-4555

XEROX BIBLIOGRAPHICS
2500 Schuster Dr, Cheverly, Md 20781 (301) 773-9750
XEROX BUSINESS PRODUCTS GROUP
Xerox Sq, Rochester, NY 14603 (716) 546-4500
XEROX FILMS
(Xerox Education Group)
1200 High Ridge Rd, Stamford, Conn 06903 (203) 329-0951

YAWMAN & ERBE DIV
(Tomar Industries)
1099 Jay St, Rochester, NY 14603 (716) 328-1010

ZEITLIN PERIODICALS CO
817 S La Brea Ave, Los Angeles, Calif 90036 (213) 933-7175

Index

A

AAP, *see* Association of American Publishers

AASL, *see* American Association of School Librarians

AAUP, *see* American Association of University Professors

AECT, *see* Association of Educational and Communications Technology

AID, *see* U.S. Agency for International Development

AIM, *see* Abridged Index Medicus

AIM-TWX
  bibliographic service, 31
  data base, 93

ALA, *see* American Library Association

ANS, *see* American National Standard

ANSI, *see* American National Standards Institute

ASIN, *see* Agricultural Sciences Information Network (proposed)

ASIS, *see* American Society for Information Science

AV Education Association of California, meeting, date of, 102

AV materials, *see* Nonprint media

Abingdon Award, 105

Abridged Index Medicus, 31
  data base of AIM-TWX, 93

Academic libraries, *see* College and university libraries, Junior college libraries, Law libraries, Medical libraries, Research libraries

Academy of America Poets Fellowship, 105

Acquisitions, *see* Library of Congress, National Program for Acquisitions and Cataloging; *also* Acquisitions under Libraries, Public libraries, College and university libraries; *also* under names of specific libraries

Adam, Mercer, Publisher, 478
  see also Copp Clark

Adult Education Act, appropriations (table), 212

Advertising of books, standard, 201-202

Agency for International Development, *see* U.S. Agency for International Development

Agents, publisher, *see* Publisher agents

Agricultural Sciences Information Network (proposed), 35-36, 93

Air-conditioning in libraries, *see* Public libraries, air-conditioning

Air Force Organizational Excellence Award, 105

Alabama Library Association, meeting, date of, 102

Alaska Library Association, meeting, date of, 102

Alberta Library Association, meeting, date of, 103

Albuquerque Model Cities Library Materials and Cultural Center, evaluation, 38

Allain, Alex P., statement on penal codes affecting acquisition of books, 69-70

Alliance for Progress Regional Book Program, 494

Allotments, state and federal, library services and construction (table), 217

Alpha Beta Alpha
  chapters (list), 287
  council (list), 286
  meeting, date of, 102
  officers (list), 286

Alternatives in Print, 20

American Art Week, date of, 10

American Association of Law Libraries
  committee chairmen, 365-366
  executive board, 365
  meeting, date of, 103, (1973) 104
  membership, 365

575

officers, 365
publications, 365
special committees, 366
American Association of School Administrators meeting, date of, 101, (1973) 104
American Association of School Librarians
committee chairmen (list), 371-372
councilors, 371
directors, 371
membership, 370
officers, 370-371
publication, 371
representatives, 372-373
role under ALA, 12
statement of purpose, 21
American Association of School Librarians IRC subcommittee, guidelines for foreigners, 444
American Association of School Librarians/National Education Association, standards for school media programs, 17
American Association of University Professors, librarian membership, 10
American Booksellers Association Convention, date of, 100
American Council on Education
meeting, date of, 100
see also Association of Research Libraries and American Council on Education
American Education Week, date of, 101
American Federation of Library Associations, Public Library Section, revises UNESCO Public Library Manifesto, 446
American Library Association, 51-54
Batchelder, Mildred L., Award, see Batchelder, Mildred L. Award
committee chairmen (list), 367-368
executive board, 367
firing of Peter Doiron, 11
intellectual freedom activities, 70
international relations activities, 443-445
international relations subcommittees, 443-444
joint committees, 368-369
Library Technology Program, see Library Technology Program
meeting, date of, 101, midwinter 103, (1973) 101, midwinter 104, (1974) 104, midwinter 104
membership, 366
officers, 366-367
overlapping jurisdictions, 71
priorities, 51-53
publications, 367
reorganization program, 53-54
resolution on obscenity, 67

round table chairmen (list), 367
scholarship program, 284
American Library Association, Adult Services Division
committee chairmen, 369-370
directors, 369
officers, 369
publications, 369
American Library Association Annual Conference, 1969
ALA priorities established, 53
date of, 100
American Library Association, Children's Services Division
committee chairmen, 378-379
directors, 377
international relations subcommittee repositories abroad, 443-444
membership, 377
officers, 377
publication, 378
American Library Association, Committee on Planning, functions, 53
American Library Association, Coordinating Committee on Library Services to the Disadvantaged, work for unified program in ALA, 52
American Library Association, Council, disbanded, 12, 54
American Library Association, Information Science and Automation Division
committee chairmen, 379
directors, 379
officers, 379
publications, 379
Television Communications Applications Seminars, 89
American Library Association, Intellectual Freedom Committee
Black Caucus resolution, 20, 70
policy on challenged materials, 67
purpose, 51
American Library Association, International Relations Committee
report in Dallas, 12
Subcommittee for Liaison with Japanese Librarians, 443
American Library Association, International Relations Office
ALA support, 12
assistance to AID, 443
international projects, 443
American Library Association, International Relations Round Table, 444
American Library Association, Library Administration Division
committee chairmen, 380
directors, 380

Library Organization and Management Section
  Statistics Coordinating Committee, 138
  national library statistics plan, 135
  Nonprint Media Statistics Committee formed, 89
  officers, 380
  section chairmen, 380
American Library Association, Library Education Division
  committee chairmen, 381
  directors, 381
  discussion group chairmen, 381
  Equivalencies and Reciprocity Committee, 444
  membership, 381
  officers, 381
  publication, 381
  section chairmen, 381
American Library Association, Office for Intellectual Freedom
  conflicting policies, 70
  goal, 51-52
  Memorandum on Citizens for Decent Literature, 67
  Memorandum on *Sylvester and the Magic Pebble*, 68-69
American Library Association, Office of Library Manpower (proposed), 52
American Library Association, Office for Library Service to the Disadvantaged (proposed), 52
American Library Association, Reference Services Division
  committee chairmen, 383-384
  directors, 383
  officers, 383
  publication, 383
  section chairman, 383
American Library Association, Resources and Technical Services Division
  committee chairmen, 385
  directors, 384
  officers, 384
  publication, 384
  section chairmen, 384-385
American Library Association, Social Responsibilities Round Table, 367
American Library Association, Social Responsibilities Round Table Task Force, plan for minority publishers' books, 20
American Library Association, Social Responsibilities Round Table Task Force on the Status of Women, alternative Newbery-Caldecott Award, 20

American Library Association, Staff Committee on Mediation, Arbitration and Inquiry
  established, 70-71
  functions, 52-53
  McConnell case, 70
American Library Association, Young Adult Services Division
  committees, 386-387
  directors, 386
  membership, 385
  officers, 386
  publication, 386
American Library Trustee Association
  committee chairmen, 373-374
  councils, 373
  directors, 373
  officers, 373
  publication, 373
American Merchant Marine Book Week, date of, 100
American Merchant Marine Library Association
  meeting, date of, 103
  officers, 387
  publication, 387
  trustees, 387
American Music Month, date of, 99
American National Standard for Bibliographic Information Interchange on Magnetic tape, published, 45
American National Standard for Directories of Libraries and Information Centers, published, 45
American National Standard for Identification Number for Serial Publications, published, 45
American National Standard for Proof Corrections, set in type, 46
American National Standard for Romanization of Arabic, approved, 46
American National Standard for Romanization of Japanese, approved, 46
American National Standard for Scientific and Technical Reports, submitted, 46
American National Standard for Specialized Vocabulary of Information Dissemination, circulated for comment, 46
American National Standard for Title Leaves of a Book, published, 45
American National Standard for the Advertising of Books, published, 45
American National Standard for the Preparation of Scientific Papers, submitted, 46
American National Standard for Transliteration of Slavic Cyrillic Characters, submitted, 46

American National Standard for Writing Abstracts, published, 45
American National Standard Guidelines for Thesaurus Structure, Construction and Use, drafts submitted, 46
American National Standard Identification Number for Serial Publications, accepted for international use, 47
American National Standards Institute
 American National Standard Z39.15-1971, 200
 Committee PH5 Photographic Reproduction of Documents, 96
 Committee PH7 Audiovisual Photographic Standards, 96
 Committee Z39, 14, 49
  meeting, Washington, D.C., 47
  member organizations (list), 47-8
  officers, 47
  publications (list), 49
  Subcommittee 21 (list), 200
  system for assigning Standard Serial Numbers, 44
  Subcommittee on Bibliographic Entries for Microfiche Headers and Roll Microfilm Containers, organized, 46
  Subcommittee on Bibliographic References, reorganized, 46
  Subcommittee on Interchange of Bibliographic information on magnetic tape, reactivation, 46
  Subcommittee on Music Industry Code, organized, 46
  Subcommittee on Periodical Title Arrangement, reactivated, 46
  Subcommittee on Publicity and Promotion, reorganized, 46
  Subcommittee on Technical Report Numbering, organized, 46
  subcommittees and their chairmen, 48-49
 Committee Z85: Library supplies and equipment, 96
American Society for Information Science
 committee chairmen, 388
 council, 388
 meeting, date of, 103, (1973) 104
 merger with ALA (proposed), 56-57
 merger with SLA (proposed), 12
 Nonprint Media Special Interest Group formed, 89
 officers, 388
 publications, 388
American Society of Indexers
 committee chairmen, 389
 directors, 389
 officers, 388-389
 publications, 389
American Student Media Association, 21

American subsidiary companies in Canada, see Publishing, Canadian, American subsidiaries
American Theological Library Association
 committee chairmen, 390
 executive committee, 390
 meeting, date of, 103
 membership, 390
 officers, 390
 publications, 390
American Toy Fair, date of, 99
Anderson, Beryl L., 454
Anglo-American Cataloging Rules, adapted for nonprint media, 203
Antiquarian bookmens associations (list), 430-435
Antiquarian bookmens associations, foreign (list), 509-514
Appropriations Act, 1972, 207
Architects (list by libraries designed), 317-319
Arizona Library Association, meeting, date of, 102
Armed Forces Librarians Achievement Citation, 105
Asbury, Barbara, 301
Associates of the National Agricultural Library, 36-37
Association for Childhood Education International, meeting, date of, 102
Association for Educational Communications, Cataloging Committee, 204
Association for Educational Communications and Technology, meeting, date of, 1973, 104
Association for Educational Communications and Technology, Information Systems Division, study of bibliographic control, 89
Association for Educational Communications and Technology, Telecommunications Division, position paper on CATV, 88
Association of American Library Schools
 committee chairmen, 391
 directors, 391
 meeting, date of, 101
 membership, 391
 officers, 391
 publication, 391
 representatives, 391-392
Association of American Publishers
 meeting, date of, 100
 report on sales, 171
Association of American University Presses, meeting, date of, 100
Association of California School Administrators, meeting, date of, 102

Association of College and Research Libraries
  committee chairmen, 375
  directors, 374
  officers, 374
  publications, 374
  role under ALA, 12
  section chairmen, 374
Association of Educational Communications and Technology, meeting, date of, 102
Association of Educational and Communications Technology Conference, 21
Association of Hospital and Institution Libraries
  committee chairmen, 376
  directors, 375
  officers, 375
  publication, 376
Association of International Libraries
  officers, 495
  publication, 495
Association of International Libraries, General Assembly, date of, 103
Association of Jewish Libraries
  divisions, 392
  meeting, date of, 103
  officers, 392
  publications, 392
Association of Research Libraries
  committee chairmen, 393
  directors, 392-393
  meeting, date of, 101, 103
  membership, 392
  officers, 392
  projects, 393
  publications, 393
Association of Research Libraries, Office of University Library Management Studies, established, 42
Association of Research Libraries and American Council on Education, study of academic library management, 42
Association of State Library Agencies
  committee chairmen, 377
  directors, 376-377
  discussion group, 377
  membership, 376
  officers, 376
  publications, 377
Association of Visual Science Librarians
  meeting, date of, 104, (1973) 104
  officers, 393
  publications, 393
Associations, Book trade, *see* Antiquarian associations, foreign; Book Trade associations; Booksellers associations; International associations; Library associations; Publishers associations

Atlanta University School of Library Service, 2-year institute for college graduates, 38
Atlantic Grant Award, 105
Audiovisual equipment
  pricing and availability, 87
  standardization, 87
Audiovisual materials, *see* Nonprint materials
Audiovisual Photographic Standards Committee PH7, *see* American National Standards Institute Committee PH7
Aurora Hills Library, Arlington, Va., elementary school annex, 18
Automation
  bibliography, 112
  see also Libraries, automated functions
Automation and the Federal Library Community, 24
Automobile parking, 301-302
Avram, Henriette D., 80
Awards, literary and library (list), 105-110
Awards, literary and library, Great Britain, 489

B

Bailey, Janet D., 57
Baillie, Stuart, 11
Bancroft Prizes, 105
Barrow (W. J.) Research Laboratory, grant from Council on Library Resources, 45
Batchelder, Mildred L., Award, 445
  announcement, date of, 100
  citation, 105
Berninghausen, David K., 66
Best sellers, bibliography, 125
Beta Phi Mu
  chapters, 288
  directors, 288
  meeting, date of, 103
  officers, 287-288
Beta Phi Mu Award, 105
Bible Week, date of, 101
Bibliographical Center for Research, Denver State Communications Center, 90
Bibliographical Society of America
  committee chairmen, 394
  council, 394
  meeting, date of, 101
  officers, 394
  publication, 394
Bibliography of Agriculture, 34
Black Academy of Arts and Letters Award, 105
Black Caucus Resolution, *see* American Library Association, Intellectual Freedom Committee, Black Caucus Resolution

Black Like Me, censorship, 68
Block, Nancy, Memorial Award, 105
Boaz, Ruth, L., 135, 142
B'nai B'rith Book Award, 105
Bock, Joleen, 357
Bollinger Prize in Poetry, 105
Book advertising, *see* Advertising of books
Book and library programs, coordination of, 493
Book-Bike Day, date of, 99
Book Development in the Service of Education, 440
Book exhibits, *see* Exhibits
Book exports, 190-191
  effect of wage and price freeze, 247-248
  U.S. (table), 191
Book Fair, International
  Brussels, date of, 99
  Cairo, date of, 99
  Ghana, date of, 100
  Leipzig, date of, 99, 100
  Warsaw, date of, 100
Book Fair, International, for Children and Youth, date of, 100
Book fairs, *see* names of specific book fairs
Book finding tools, bibliography, 121-122
Book Hunger, 442
Book imports, 190-191
  effect of wage and price freeze, 247-248
  statistics, *see* Publishing statistics, book imports
  U.S., 192
Book manufacture, *see* Bookmaking
Book numbering, *see* International Standard Book Numbering
Book-of-the-Year Medal, 105
Book papers, permanent/durable, specifications for, 45
Book production, *see* Bookmaking; Publishing
Book programs, international, 490-494
Book Publishers' Council, Canadian, *see* Canadian Book Publishers' Council
Book review media (table), 180
Book reviewers, *see* Reviewers
Book reviews, statistics (table), 180
Book sales
  statistics (table), 168-169
  see also Publishing statistics; Textbooks, sales
Book sales, Canadian, statistics, 480
Book sales, door to door, regulations, 250
Book sales, publishers
  adult hardcover increases, 171
  Bibles, hymnals, prayerbooks increase, 171
  book club sales, 171
  children's books, 171
  dollar volume (table), 172
  net sales (table), 174
  percentage changes in CPI, 175
  reference books (table), 173
  statistics, 171-175
  textbook and subscription reference books, 171
  textbooks (table), 173
Book title output (tables), 176-178
  see also Publishing statistics
Book trade
  bibliography, 121-124
  Calendar of Events 1972, 99-101
  directories, bibliography, 123
  mergers, 74, 468-487
  see also Publishing industry
Book trade associations (list), 430-435
Booker Prize, 105
Books
  advertising, *see* Advertising of books
  best books, 125, 129
  bibliography, 121
  censorship, *see* Censorship
  distribution, British, 488-489
  postal rates, *see* Postal rates
  prices
    Great Britain (tables), 188
    hardcover books (table), 185
    Mexico (table), 189
    paperbacks (table), 186, 187
  title leaves, standard for, 200-201
Books, mailing of, statistics (table), 179
Books and the Teen-Age Reader, 72
Books For All, 442
Books for children, *see* Children's books
Books for librarians, bibliography, 111-120
Books in English, MARC format data, 457
Books in the mails, 179
Books U.S.A., *see* Freedom House/Books U.S.A.
Bookmaking, bibliography, 124
Booksellers' associations (list), 430-435
  see also International Community of Booksellers Associations
Booksellers associations, foreign, (list), 509-514
Bookselling, bibliography, 123
Bookstores
  analyzing data, 163
  growth by geographic sections, 165-167, 170
  growth by SMSAs, 170-171
  rank by SMSAs (table), 168-169
  sales statistics, 163-165
  table, 164
  by volume (table), 168-169
  statistics, 163-171
  statistics by regions, divisions and states (table), 166-167

Boston Globe-Horn Book Children's Book Awards, 105
Bouwhuis, Rev. Andrew L., Scholarship, see Catholic Library Association, Rev. Andrew L. Bouwhuis Scholarship
Boy Scout Month, date of, 99
Boys' Club Week, date of, 99
Brecksville, Ohio, Branch Library, graffiti exhibit, 69
Brigham Young University, closed circuit television system, 87-88
British Library
  buildings, 457
  organization, 456-457
British Museum Library, new building, 457
Brooklyn Public Library
  cultural programs, 13
  union contract, 11
Brotherhood Week, date of, 99
Brown, Raymond R., 7
Buckley, William F., Jr., challenges requirement to pay dues to private organization for TV appearances, 67-68
Buffalo Public Library, Project RAM, 6
Bureau of Libraries and Educational Technology, 7, 37-39
  College Library Resources Program, 37
  grants, 37
  Library Research and Demonstration Program, branch activities, 38
  Library Training Program, 37-38
  organization and funding, 39
  program redirection, 37-38
Burkhardt, Frederick, 50
Burroughs, John, Medal, 105
Busby, Edith, Award, 106
Byam, Milton, 7

C

CAIN, see National Agricultural Library
CAN/SDI, see Canadian National Science Library, selective dissemination of information
CATV, see Television, community antenna
CBPC, see Canadian Book Publishers' Council
CCLD, see New York State Commissioner's Committee on Library Development
CDB, see Child Development Bill
CDL, see Citizens for Decent Literature
CIJE, see *Current Index to Journals in Education*
CIP, see Library of Congress Cataloging in Publication Program
CLEP, see College Level Examination Program
CLIC, see College Libraries in Consortium
CLIS, see ERIC Clearinghouse on Library and Information Sciences
COM, see Tulane University Library, computer-output-microfilm short title catalog
COSATI, see Committee on Scientific and Technical Information
COSATI Guidelines for Descriptive Cataloging, 64
COSATI Subject Category List, 64
CRS, see Library of Congress, Congressional Research Service
CSD, see American Library Association, Children's Services Division
Cable television, see Television, community antenna
Caldecott Medal Award, 106
  announcement, date of, 99
Calendar of Book Trade and Promotional Events, 99-101
California Association of School Librarians, meeting, date of, 102
California Library Association
  meeting, date of, 103
  reorganization, 12-13
Cameron, Donald F., study of economics of librarianship in university and college libraries, 42-43
Camp Fire Girls Founders Day, date of, 100
Campbell, Francis Joseph, citation, 106
Campbell, James, publisher, 478
Canada, Department of Industry, Trade and Commerce, study of college textbooks, 480
Canadian Association for Information Science, incorporated, 456
Canadian Association of College and University Libraries, 453
Canadian Book Publishers' Council
  grants, 483
  membership, attacks on, 485
Canadian book sales, see Book sales, Canadian
Canadian college and university libraries, see College and university libraries, Canadian
Canadian Council of Library Schools, formed, 456
Canadian librarians, see Librarians, Canadian
Canadian librarianship, see Librarianship, Canadian
Canadian Library Association
  committee chairmen, 395-396
  council, 394-395
  internal strains, 13
  meeting, date of, 103, (1973) 104
  membership, 394
  officers, 394

Public Library Salary Survey, 452
publications, 395
section chairmen, 395
Canadian MARC, 448-449
Canadian National Institute for the Blind, reading to children program, 18
Canadian National Library
multicultural language and literature center (proposed), 449
union catalog, automation of, 449
Canadian National Library, Research and Planning Branch, Systems Development Division, library network plans, 448-449
Canadian National Science Library, selective dissemination of information, 449
Canadian publisher–agents, *see* Publisher–agents, Canadian
Canadian textbooks, *see* Textbooks, Canadian
Canadian Union Catalog (table), 449
Card catalog cabinets, testing, 97
Cards, catalog, *see* Catalog cards
Carey-Thomas Award, 106
Carlsen, G. Robert, 72
Carnegie Corporation of New York, scholarships, 284
Carnegie libraries in Canada, 478
Carpet wear tester, patents for, 98
Carpeting in libraries, *see* Public libraries, carpeting
Carrels, study, testing, 97
Carroll, Lewis, Shelf Awards, 106
Cary, George, 12
Catalog cards, testing, 96-97
Catalog-indexing system, *see* National Agricultural Library, CAIN system
Cataloging, library, bibliography, 119-120
Cataloging, shared, Canadian, 454
Cataloging of technical reports, standard, 64
Cataloging in Publication Program, *see* Library of Congress Cataloging in Publication Program
Catholic Book Week, date of, 99
Catholic Library Association
committee and board chairmen, 397
executive board, 396
meeting, date of, 102, (1973) 104
officers, 396
publications, 396
Rev. Andrew L. Bouwhuis Scholarship, 284
section chairmen, 396-397
Censorship, 18-19
bibliography, 123
see also Censorship under titles of books, etc.

Center for Research Libraries, Chicago, special purpose grant under HEA Title II-A, 227
Chairs, evaluation, 97
Charter of the Book, 439
adoption, 72
Chicago Public Library
aid to Helen Robinson Library and Study Center, 18
extension service program, 18
Young Filmmakers' Festival, 18
Chicago Model Cities Program, *see* Model Cities Program, Chicago
Child Development Bill, 16
Children, library services for, *see* Library services for children and young adults
Children's Book Award of the Child Study Association of America, 106
Children's Book Week, date of, 101
Children's books
bibliography, 125-127
joint production in the Asian regions, 440
see also Young adults' books
Children's books, Canadian, subsidies to libraries for, 482
Children's Science Book Award, 106
Children's Spring Book Festival, date of, 100
Chinese Glossary of International Conference Terminology, 28
Christian Booksellers Association Convention, date of, 100-101
Church and Synagogue Library Association
committee chairmen, 398
executive board, 398
meeting, date of, 103
membership, 397
officers, 397-398
publications, 398
Church Press Conference, date of, 100
Citizens for Decent Literature, protested by ALA, 67
Civil rights, 67-68
Civil Service Commission, *see* U.S. Civil Service Commission
Clearinghouse on Library and Information Sciences, *see* ERIC Clearinghouse on Library and Information sciences
Cleaver, Eldridge, 19
Clemmer, Dan, 90
Clift, David, 11
Coden code, translation table (proposed), 199
College and university librarians
academic status, 10-11, 42-43
demand and supply (table by institution), 266-267
rate change (table), 268

College and university libraries
additions and renovations, costs, 326-327; tables, 346-354
bibliography, 114
budgets (table), 159-160
collections, size of, 144
construction
book capacity, 322, 323-324
costs, 320; multipurpose buildings (table), 355; tables by cost, 329-343
costs of equipment, 322, 323-324
costs of subject and division libraries, 326
costs of undergraduate libraries, 325; table
costs, $1-$2 million, 323-325
costs, $2-$5 million, 322-323
costs, under $1 million, 324-325
costs, over $5 million, 321-322
reader seats, 320, 323, 324
size of, 320, 322
statistics, 320-356
expenditures for library materials (table), 159-160
expenditures on AV and microform materials (table), 162
expenditures, per student, 145
management, *see* Association of Research Libraries, and American Council on Education, study of academic library management
personnel, 145
statistics, 261
vacancies, 145
statistics, 144-145
bibliography, 136
summary (table), 146-147
support services, non-budgeted, 144-145
see also Research libraries
College and university libraries, Canadian
construction, 321
book capacity, 328
costs, 327-328; table, 355-356
costs of equipment, 328
multipurpose buildings, 327
reader seats, 328
expenditures, nonuniversity (table), 452
statistics, 452-453
College and university libraries, Finnish 464-465
College and university libraries, German (Western), 468
College Level Examination Program, study guides, 43
College Library Program, *see* Council on Library Resources/National Endowment for the Humanities College Library Program, College Library Program

College Library Resources programs, *see* Bureau of Libraries and Educational Technology, College Library Resources programs
Colonial Copyright Act, 1847, 478
Colorado Association of School Librarians, meeting, date of, 101
Colorado AV Association, meeting, date of, 101-102
Colorado Statewide Reference Network, evaluation, 90
Colton, Flora D., 111
Columbia University Libraries, organization and staffing, study of, 42
Columbia University Prize in American Economic History, 106
Committee for an Independent Canada, demands for government aid to McClelland and Stewart, 481
Committee on Scientific and Technical Information, 62-65
achievements, 64-65
bibliography, 65
charter, 63
conferences, 64
international exchange of information, 64-65
microfiche standard, 64
organization, 63-64
origin, 62-63
panels and work groups, 63-64
plans for restructuring library/information systems, 22
review group organized, 65
Commonwealth Club of California, Silver Medal, 106
Communications Act of 1934, amendment, 208
Communications Technology for Urban Improvement, 94
Community antenna television, *see* Television, community antenna
Community library project, Philadelphia, 18
Comprehensive Child Development Act, 210
Conference on District Libraries, Poprad, 466-467
Conference on Legal Aspects of National and International Computerized Information Systems, 65
Connecticut, automated union catalog project, 14
Connecticut Library Association, meeting, date of, 102
Connecticut School Library Association, meeting, date of, 102
Contemporary Photographs from Sweden, exhibit, 27

Conversion of Retrospective Catalog Records to Machine Readable Form, 81
Cooke, Eileen D., 207
Cooperating Libraries in Consortium, 37
Cooperation, library
  Finland, 464
  Germany, Western, 469
  LSCA funds for, 215
  school and public libraries, 17-18
Cooperative Book Centre, 479
Cooperative Research Act, *see* Higher Education Act, Title II-B and Cooperative Research Act
Coordinating Meeting of International Organizations on the Representation and Coding of Country Names, 46-47
Copp Clark, 478
  see also Adam, Mercer, Publisher
Copyright
  bibliography, 123
  extension of duration, 207, 250
  international, 246
  revision legislation, 208
  sound recordings, 208
Copyright law, *see* Copyright Revision Bill
Copyright Revision Bill, 29
Core library data, collection, 139-140
Corporate Author Headings, 64
Council of National Library Associations, 42-45
  committee chairmen, 398
  directors, 398
  membership, 398
  officers, 398
  publications, 398
Council of Planning Librarians
  committee chairmen, 399
  meeting, date of, 102
  membership, 399
  officers, 399
  publications, 399
Council of Research Libraries (Finland), 464
Council on Interracial Books for Children, support minority publishers' fund, 20
Council on Interracial Books for Children Award, 106
Council on Library Resources, 42-45
  fellowship program, 45
  grant from Ford Foundation, 42
  grants
    library, 42-45
    publications resulting from, 45
    National Endowment for the Humanities, college library program, 43
  scholarships, 284
Cranston amendment, *see* Legislation, publishing, Cranston amendment
Crawford, Susan, 148, 153

Crisis in Educational Technology, 21
Crisis Information Center workshop, 18
Cultural programs, *see* Libraries, cultural programs
Cummings, Martin M., 31
Current Index to Journals in Education, 59
Cylke, Frank Kurt, 22, 423
Czechoslovak libraries, *see* Libraries, Czechoslovak

D

DAIRS, *see* Dial access information retrieval systems
DHEW, *see* U.S. Department of Health, Education, and Welfare
DRUPA 6th International Fair, Printing and Paper, date of, 100
Dallas Public Library, public library as center for independent study, study of, 43
Dana, John Cotton, Publicity Awards, 106
Danvers, Mass., Public Library, charged for unbalanced left-wing collection, 68
Dartmouth College Library, micropublishing rare scholarly material, 44
Dartmouth College Medical School, television link-closed circuit, 32
Day, Clarence, Award, 106
Day, Melvin S., 62
Delta Kappa Gamma Society Educator's Award, 106
Detroit Public Libraries, Funmobile, 18
Deutsche Bibliothek, deposit copies of books, 471
Devins Award, 106-107
Dewey, Melvil, Award, 107
Dewey Decimal Classification, 18th ed., 29
Dial access information retrieval systems, 87-88
Dictionary Catalog of the National Agricultural Library, 1862-1965, 34-35
Dictionary of Information Resources in Agriculture and Biology, 36
Directors of Large Public Libraries, formed, 12
Directory of Information Resources in the United States: Physical Sciences, Engineering, 25
Distinguished Library Service Award, 107
District of Columbia Public Library, cable information system, 94-95
Do It!, censorship of, 19
Doiron, Peter, 11
Doms, Keith, 51
Donley, Mary R., 269
Donovan, David G., 443
Down These Mean Streets, censorship of, 19, 68
Downs, Robert B., Intellectual Freedom Award, 107

Drug education films, evaluation, 19
Drury, Harold, 23
Duman, Robert, 11
Dutton, E.P.–John Macrae Award, 284-285

E

ECOSOC, see United Nations Economic and Social Council
ELSEGIS, see Elementary and Secondary General Information Survey
ERIC, see U.S. Office of Education, Educational Resources Information Center
ERIC/CLIS, see ERIC Clearinghouse on Library and Information Sciences
ERIC Clearinghouse on Adult Education, 60
ERIC Clearinghouse on Counseling and Personnel Services, 60
ERIC Clearinghouse on the Disadvantaged, 60
ERIC Clearinghouse on Early Childhood Education, 60
ERIC Clearinghouse on Educational Management, 60
ERIC Clearinghouse on Educational Media and Technology, 60-61
ERIC Clearinghouse on Exceptional Children, 61
ERIC Clearinghouse on Higher Education, 61
ERIC Clearinghouse on Junior Colleges, 61
ERIC Clearinghouse on Languages and Linguistics, 61
ERIC Clearinghouse on Library and Information Sciences, 6, 58-62
  functions, 59-60
  information analysis activities, 59-60
  titles included in National Technical Information System, 59
ERIC Clearinghouse on Reading, 61
ERIC Clearinghouse on Rural Education and Small Schools, 61
ERIC Clearinghouse on Science, Mathematics, and Environmental Education, 61-62
ERIC Clearinghouse on Social Studies/Social Science Education, 62
ERIC Clearinghouse on Teacher Education, 62
ERIC Clearinghouse on Teaching of English, 62
ERIC Clearinghouse on Tests, Measurements, and Evaluation, 62
ERIC Clearinghouse on Vocational and Technical Education, 62
ESEA, see Elementary and Secondary Education Act
Eaton, T., Company, 479
Editing, bibliography, 124

Education for librarianship
  bibliography, 114-115
  continuing education, 9
    see also Special Libraries Association, continuing education seminars
  Czechoslovakia, 467
  Finland, 463-464
  Germany, Western, 470
  grants for recruiting minority group persons, 229
  grants for training paraprofessionals, 229
  scholarships and fellowships, see Scholarships
  statistics, bibliography, 137
  see also Institutes for library education
Education of Librarians and Information Workers in Socialist Society, Conference, 1971, 467
Educational Film Library Association
  committee chairmen, 399-400
  meeting, date of, 102
  officers, 399
  publications, 400
Educational materials
  accessibility of ESEA Title II materials, 221
  minority group bases in, 19-21
  supplied under ESEA Title II program, 220-221
  see also Nonprint media
Educational Resources Information Center, see U.S. Office of Education, Educational Resources Information Center
Educational television facilities, appropriations (table), 212
Elementary and Secondary Education Act
  appropriations (table), 211
  Title I, educationally deprived children, 15
    funds, use of, 17
  Title II, library services and materials, 15-16
  Title II, school library resources, 17
  Title II program
    accomplishments, 220-225
    administration in states, 223
    bibliography, 225
    evaluation, 224
    management, 222-223
    problems, 224-225
    special projects, 223
  Title III (with NDEA title V-A), supplementary education centers, 16
Elementary and Secondary General Information Survey, 134
Emergency Employment Act, 10, 209-210
Encyclopaedia Britannica School Library Awards, 107

Equal Rights, Amendment, 20-21
Equipment, library
  bibliography, 112-113
  see also Library materials
Ernst & Ernst study of Canadian publishing, 479-480
European Educational Materials Fair, date of, 100
Evaluation of Micropublications, 97
Evaluation System for Administrative, Professional and Technological Positions, 23
Evans, M., Fiction Award, 107
Evergreen Review, censorship, 10, 19
Ewa-Beach Community School Library, 17
Exceptional Service Award, 107
Exhibits, Canadian books, 483
Expenditures, library, *see* Libraries, expenditures

F

FCC, *see* U.S. Federal Communications Commission
FIAB, *see* International Federation of Library Associations
FIAF, *see* International Federation of Film Archives
FID, *see* International Federation for Documentation
FLC, *see* Federal Library Committee
Facsimile transmission, 91
Farrell, Patricia A., 477
Federal Communications Commission, *see* U.S. Federal Communications Commission
Federal libraries, 22-24
  automated functions, 24, 75-80, (table), 79
  budgets, 76-77, (table), 77
  cooperative networks, 77
  Executive Advisory Committee, 400-401
    membership, 400
    officers, 400
    plans for restructuring library/information systems, 22
    publications, 401
    task force chairmen, 401
    vacancy roster, 9
    work group chairmen, 401
  geographical distribution, 76
  information networks, 24
  interlibrary activities, 77-78, (table), 78
  machine-readable data bases, 78
  reorganizational efforts, 22-23
  size, 76-77
  staff, size of, 77
  survey, 76-80
Federal Library Committee, ad hoc group, working with Civil Service Commission, 23

Federal Library Committee, Task Force on Automation and Other Cooperative Services
  coordination of automation, 43-44
  objectives, 75
  study of automated systems, 75-76
Federal Library Committee, Task Force on Role of Libraries in Information Systems, research findings, 24
Federal library legislation, *see* Legislation, library, federal
Federal library programs, directory, 423-424
Federal Republic of Germany: A Selected Bibliography of English-language Publications with Special Emphasis on the Social Sciences, The, 25
Federal Trade Commission, *see* U.S. Federal Trade Commission
Fellowships, *see* Scholarships
Feminists on Children's Media, report on recommended lists, 20
Festival of Chamber Music, 14th, 26
Festival of Literature, Cheltenham, date of, 101
Film Library Information Council, meeting, date of, 102
Films: A MARC Format, 206
Films Review Index, 89
Films, MARC format catalog, 88
Films, nitrate, reprinting on acetate film, 26
Finnish Council for Scientific and Technical Information, 464
Finnish librarians, *see* Librarians, Finnish
Finnish libraries, *see* Libraries, Finnish
Florence Agreement, *see* UNESCO Agreement on the Importation of Educational, Scientific and Cultural Materials
Florida AV Association, meeting, date of, 103
Florida Association of School Librarians, meeting, date of, 103
Florida Association of Educational TV, meeting, date of, 103
Florida Library Association, meeting, date of, 102, (1973) 104
Food and Nutrition Information and Educational Materials Center, *see* National Medical Library, Food and Nutrition Information and Educational Materials Center
Foreign antiquarian associations, *see* Antiquarian associations, foreign
Foreign library associations, *see* Library associations, foreign
Foreign Reprints Act, *see* Colonial Copyright Act, 1847
Foundation grants, *see* Grants, library

Frame, Ruth R., 135, 138, 278
Frankfurt Book Fair, 494
  date of, 101
  peace prize, 494
Franklin, Hardy R., study of Bedford-Stuyvesant area library users, 43
Franklin Book Programs
  activities, 490-491
  board members (list), 490
  officers, 490
  resident managers, 490
Frantz, John C., 71
Frantz Fanon Collection, see Harvard University, Countway Library of Medicine, Frantz Fanon Collection
Frarey, Carlyle J., 269
Frase, Robert W., 179, 246
Fraternities, library, 286-288
Free Enterprise Writer of the Year Award, 107
Freedley, George, Memorial Award, 107
Freedom, intellectual, see Intellectual freedom
Freedom of the press, legislation, 248-249
Freedom to Read Foundation
  grant to Rochester, Mich., Community Schools Appeal Fund, 69
  objectives, 52
Freedom House/Books, U.S.A., 491
  board members, 491
Friends of American Writers Award, 107
Fullerton, Calif. Junior College, digital access TV, 87
Furniture, library, see Equipment, library

G

GRTA, see National Technical System, Governmental Report Topical Announcements
Gage, W. J., Ltd., 478
  sold to Scott, Foresman and Co., 480
  Writing for Young Canada Program, 482
Galvin, Hoyt, 301
German Association of Public Libraries, Library Plan I, 469
German libraries, see Libraries, German
German Library Conference, working groups, 470
Gilford, Dorothy M., 133
Girl Scout Week, date of, 99
Golden Anniversary Prize Award, 107
Golden Eagle Award, 107
Government Advisory Committee on International Book and Library Programs, see U.S. Government Advisory Committee on International Book and Library Programs
Government publications, see Public documents

Grants, library
  art and archaeology
  astronomy and space, 245
  automation in libraries, 43-44
  buildings and equipment, 238-239
  child welfare, 245
  Council on Library Resources, from, 42-45
  education, elementary and secondary, 239
  education, higher, special projects, 239-240
  education, theological, 244
  foundation grants (list), 237-245
  HEA funded, 233-236
  handicapped, 245
  history, 244
  hospitals, 244
  information networks, 44
  international cultural relations, 244
  international education, 244-245
  international health and welfare, 245
  international studies, 245
  international technical assistance, 245
  languages and literature, 244
  law, 245
  libraries, 240-243
  library management, 42-43
  library services, 43
  life sciences, 245
  medical education, 244
  music, 244
  peace and international cooperation, 245
  under Title II-A, Higher Education Act, 225-227
  welfare, 245
Graphic Prize Award, 107
Great Britain Colonial Copyright Act, see Colonial Copyright Act, 1847
Great Britain, Department of Education and Science
  funding of applied research, 459
  library advisers, 459
Grolier Award, 107
Grove, Lee E., 42
Grove, Pearce S., 203
Guide for a Description of Program and Operational Procedures, 223
Guidelines for Audiovisual Materials and Services for Public Libraries, 205
Gurfein, Murray I., decision on Pentagon Papers, 66
Gwin, James M. Poultry Collection, see National Agricultural Library, James M. Gwin Poultry Collection

H

HEGIS, see Higher Educational General Information Survey
HEW, see U.S. Department of Health, Education, and Welfare

HUD, see U.S. Department of Housing and Development
Hackett, Alice Payne, 125
Hall of Fame Award, see Special Libraries Association, Hall of Fame Award
Hammond, C.S., and Co. Award, 107
Handbook on Federal Library Automation, 76
Handicapped, library services for, see Library services to the handicapped
Hans Christian Andersen Awards ad hoc Committee, selected U.S. nominations, 445
Harris, Charles W., 7
Harrison, Ind., Library, check-a-pet program, 18
Harvard University, Countway Library of Medicine, Frantz Fanon Collection, 8
Hawaii Library Association, meeting, date of, 102
Health care services
  manpower, 148
  national expenditures for, 148
Health science libraries
  average number of volumes (figure), 152
  geographic distribution, 150
  personnel, 151-152, (table), 152
  resources by types (table), 151
  size, 151
  statistics, 148-153
  survey, 148-153
  survey population, 149
  survey questionnaire response, 149-150
  types, 150
  user groups, 152-153, (table), 153
Heim, Peggy F., study of economics of librarianship in university and college libraries, 42-43
Helen Robinson Library and Study Center, 18
Henderson, Madeline M., 75
Hewins, Caroline M., Scholarship, 285
Hicks, Frances Yvonne, 227
Higher Education Act
  appropriations (table), 211
  Title II, 210
  Title II-A
    distribution analysis (table), 226
    grants, 225-227
  Title II-B, 210
    Institute Program, 228-233
    Library and Information Science Research, 233-236
    Library Education Fellowship program, 227-228
    Library Education grants, 227-233
  Title VIII, networks for knowledge, funding, 90

Higher Education Facilities Act, appropriations (table), 212
Higher Educational General Information Survey, 134
History, Library, see Library history
History of the Supreme Court of the United States, 27
Holloway, Ruth, 16
Hoover, Charles W., 58
Howard-Gibbon, Amelia Frances, Award, 107
Hughey, Elizabeth H., 214

I

IAALD, see International Association of Agricultural Librarians and Documentalists
IAC, see National Agricultural Library, Information Analysis Center
IBY, see International Book Year, 1972
IFC, see American Library Association Intellectual Freedom Committee
IFLA, see International Federation of Library Associations
INTREX, see Massachusetts Institute of Technology, Information Transfer Experiments
IRO, see American Library Association, International Relations Office
ISBN, see International Standard Book Numbering
ISO, see International Organization for Standardization, Library of Congress, Information Systems Office
ISO/TC 46, see International Organization for Standardization, Technical Committee 46
Idaho Library Association, meeting, date of, 102
Illinois AV Association, meeting, date of, 102
Illinois Association of School Librarians, meeting, date of, 102
Illinois Curriculum Association, meeting, date of, 102
Illinois Library Association, meeting, date of, 103
Illiteracy, see Literacy
Indian Historian Press, report on textbook treatment of American Indians, 20
Indiana Library Association, meeting, date of, 103
Indiana School Librarians Association, meeting, date of, 102
Indiana Union List of Serials, data base for Indiana Teletype Network, 91
Inflation, effect on British publishing, 487-488

Information Analysis Center, see National Agricultural Library, Information Analysis Center
Information Canada plan, 6, 407
Information centers, New York City libraries, 5
Information networks, 90-95
  Finland, 464
  performance evaluation, 91
  underuse of, 90-91
  see also Library networks; New England Library Information Network; Federal libraries, Information networks; National Agricultural Library, Agricultural Science Information Network
Information Science Abstracts, sponsorship, 57
Inner City Mother Goose, censorship, 19
Instructional materials, see Educational materials
Institute program, see Higher Education Act, Title II-B, institute program
Institutes for Library education (list), 230-233
Integrated Knowledge Services, see National Agricultural Library, Integrated Knowledge Services
Integration of schools, effect on black personnel, 20
Intellectual freedom, 66-71
  bibliography, 115
Intellectual Freedom Committee, see American Library Association, Intellectual Freedom Committee
Intellectual Freedom Statement, 70
Inter-American Association of Agricultural Librarians and Documentalists
  meeting, date of, 102
  members, 495
  officers, 495
  publications, 495
Inter-American Bibliographical and Library Association
  council, 496
  officers, 495-496
  publication, 496
Interface of Technical Libraries with Information System, 24
Interlibrary loans, bibliography, 115
International Association of Agricultural Librarians and Documentalists
  executive committee, 496
  officers, 496
  publication, 496
International Association of Law Libraries
  executive board, 496-497
  officers, 496
  publication, 496-497

International Association of Metropolitan City Libraries
  meeting, date of, 103
  program, 497
  publication, 497
International Association of Music Libraries
  commission chairmen, 497
  meeting, date of, 103, (1973) 104
  officers, 497
  publication, 498
International Association of Printing House Craftsmen, International Convention, date of, 101
International Association of Sound Archives
  meeting, date of, 103
  membership, 498
  officers, 498
  publication, 498
International Book Biennial, São Paulo, 100
International Book Exhibition, Berlin, date of, 101
International Book Festival, Nice, date of, 100
International book programs, see Book programs, international
International Book Year, 439-443
  AFLI activities, 446-447
  multilingual newsletter, 442
  objectives, 72
  Presidential proclamation, 246
  programs, 441
  theme "Books for All," 71, 72
International Book Year, Support committee, see Support Committee for International Book Year
International Book Year, U.S. Secretariat, 72
International Book Year, 1972: A Handbook for U.S. Participation, 72
International Children's and Youth Book Exhibition, 23rd, date of, 101
International Children's Book Day, date of, 100
International Community of Booksellers Associations Congress, 442
  date of, 100
International Education Act, appropriations (table), 212
International Exhibition of Scientific and Technical Books and Journals, Paris, date of, 100
International Federation for Documentation
  meeting, date of, 103
  officers, 498
  program, 498
  publications, 499
International Federation of Film Archives
  executive committee, 499
  members, 499
  publications, 499

International Federation of Library Associations
  activities, 445-448
  American membership, 500
  assistance to developing countries, 445
  Committee on Library Statistics, 193
  grant from CLR, 13, 447
  meeting, date of, 103, (1973) 104, (1974) 104
  officers, 499
  pre-session seminar for developing countries, 445
  publications, 499
  relations with other international organizations, 448
International Federation of Library Associations, General Council, Liverpool, 458-459
International Film Cataloging Conference, 1st, 203, 2nd, 203
International Institute for Children's Juvenile and Popular Literature
  meeting, date of, 103
  officers, 500
  program, 500
  publications, 500
International library statistics, standardization, 193-195
International Meeting of U.S. and Japanese Librarians, 2nd (proposed), 443
International Organization for Standardization
  officers, 500
  publications, 501
  technical work, 500
International Organization for Standardization, Technical Committee 46, 193
  approves SSN as basis for ISSN, 197
  Working Group 3, Vocabulary of Documentation
    ANS for Specialized Vocabulary of Information Dissemination, 46
International Organization for Standardization, Technical Committee 46. Documentation, Plenary session, 13th. ANSI comm. Z39 delegates, 46
International Press Institute, disqualifies U.S. as "free," 66
International Publishers Association Congress, 442
  date of, 100
International Standard Book Numbering
  British use of, 489
  German use of, 471
  Library of Congress work on, 14
International Standard Serial Numbering, 197-200
  assigned to R. R. Bowker, 47, 197
  check digits, 199-200
  Coden conversion, 199
  publications using, 198
  uses, 198-199
  see also Standard Serial Numbers
International Youth Library
  officers, 501
  publications, 501
Interpretations of the Library Bill of Rights, 70
Iowa Library Association, meeting, date of, 103
Iowa School of Letters Award, 107

J

Jackson, Joseph Henry, Award, 107
Janaske, Paul C., 233
James Madison Memorial Building, see Library of Congress, James Madison Memorial Building
Jewish Book Month, date of, 101
Job evaluation, in federal libraries, 22-23
Job Evaluation and Pay Review Task Force, see U.S. Civil Service Commission, Job Evaluation and Pay Review Task Force
John H. Gupton College, basic/supplemental grant under HEA Title II-A, 226
Jones, J. Morris–World Book Encyclopedia–ALA Goals Award, 107
Josey, E. J., 7
Journal of Library History Award, 107
Junior college libraries, 357-362
  construction (table), 359-362
  costs, 358-362

K

Kansas City Public Library, teen-age guides, 18
Kansas Library Association, meeting, date of, 102
Kikuchi Kan Prize, 107-108
King, Coretta Scott, Award, 108
Klein, Roger, Award, 108
Knapp School Library Manpower Project, phase II, 21
Koltay, Emery I., 197
Kovner, Florence and Henry, Memorial Award, 108
Krettek, Germaine, 207

L

LIBGIS, see Library General Information System
LIBRIS, see Library Information System (Sweden)
LIBSKED, see Library of Congress, machine filing program

LSB, *see* U.S. Office of Education, National Center for Educational Statistics, Library Surveys Branch
LSCA, *see* Library Services and Construction Act
LTP, *see* Library Technology Program
Lamkin, Burton E., 7, 37
Lamont Poetry Selection, 108
Larrick, Nancy, 72
Lasswell, Harold, 66
Latin American Bureau, *see* U.S. Agency for International Development, Latin American Bureau
Law libraries, construction costs, 325-326, (table) 344-345
Laymen's National Bible Committee Awards, 108
Legislation, library
 bibliography, 116
 federal, 207-213, (table), 213
 Germany (Western), 472
 new trends, 16-17
 see also Copyright
Legislation, publishing
 Cranston amendment, 247
 federal, 246-251
Legislative Reference Service, *see* Library of Congress, Congressional Research Service
Letters of Delegates to the Continental Congress, Ford Foundation grant for, 27
Librarians
 academic degrees (table), 262
 continuing education, *see* Education for librarianship; Special Libraries Association, continuing education
 criminal liability in purchase of books, 69-70
 demand and supply, 270, 277; advertised, 278-281, (table), 279
 education, *see* Education for librarianship
 estimated number by type of library (table), 262
 in small communities, 8
 placements, 9
 see also Library schools, placements
 role in IBY, 446-447
 salaries, 269-278, (table by location), 271, (table by type of library), 274-275
  average starting, 273, (table), 275
  cluster range, 273-274
  effects of experience on, 276
  high salaries, 274
  low salaries, 274
  median salary, 273
  salary range, 274
 salaries, advertised, 278-281
  highest potential (table), 281
  minimum salary (table), 280
  starting salary (table), 279
 salaries of women, 21
 tenure and due process, 11-12
 see also College and university librarians
Librarians, black, discrimination, 7-8
Librarians, Canadian
 placements, 276
 salaries, 276
  median (table), 455
Librarians, Finnish, status, 465-466
Librarianship, Canadian, 448-456
Librarianship, German (Western), 469
Libraries
 acquisitions, bibliography, 119
 administration, *see* Library management
 automated functions, 13-14, 43-44; grants from HEA Title II-B, 235
 automation and information retrieval, bibliography, 112
 construction, *see* College and university libraries; Public libraries
 contribution to IBY, 447
 cultural programs, 13
 effects of federal funds, 17
 expenditures, *see* College and university libraries; Public libraries
 guidelines for nonprint media, 205
 in educational process, 43
 management, *see* Library management
 number of (table), 156
 periodicals, *see* Periodicals for librarians
 standards, *see* Standards for library service
 statistics, *see* Library statistics
 surveys, *see* Library surveys; Public library surveys
 technical services, bibliography, 119-120
 trustees, *see* Library trustees
 user groups, characteristics of (table), 154-155
 see also Public libraries, user groups
 vacancies, *see* Librarians, demand and supply
 see also College and university libraries; Federal libraries; Law libraries; Medical libraries; Public libraries; School libraries
Libraries, British, 456-459
 automated functions, 457-458
 see also National libraries, British
Libraries, Canadian
 foreign purchasing, 482
 number of (table), 156
 see also Public libraries, Canadian
Libraries, Czechoslovak, 466-468
 district libraries, 466-467
Libraries, Finnish, 463-466
 automated functions, 464
Libraries, German (Western), 468-472
 automated functions, 471-472
 user group study, 469-470

Libraries, health sciences, *see* Health sciences libraries
Libraries, public *see* Public libraries
Libraries, Russian, 460-463
Libraries, school, *see* School libraries
Libraries, special, *see* Special libraries
Library Advisers, *see* Great Britain, Department of Education and Science, Library Advisers
Library agencies, state (list), 424-426
Library Association of the University of California, University recognition, 13
Library associations, 12-13
  meetings (list), 101-104
Library associations, Canadian, 456
Library associations, foreign (list), 501-508
Library associations, German (Western), formation of Academic Library Association (proposed), 471
Library associations, international, Canadian participation, 449
Library associations, national (chart), 412
Library associations, state, 12-13
Library associations, state, regional and provincial (list), 413-420
Library awards, *see* Awards, literary and library
Library Bill of Rights, see *Interpretations of the Library Bill of Rights*
Library Binding Institute Scholarship, 285
Library buildings, bibliography, 112-113
  see also Libraries, construction; Libraries, additions and renovations
Library cooperation, *see* Cooperation, library
Library data bank, 140-142
Library equipment, *see* Equipment, library
Library expenditures, *see* Expenditures; College and university libraries; Libraries; Library materials; Public libraries
Library fraternities, *see* Fraternities, library
Library furniture
  bibliography, 112-113
  see also Equipment, library
Library General Information System, 134-136
  core forms, 135-136
Library history, bibliography, 115-116
Library Information System (Sweden), 464
Library learning center, community controlled, Philadelphia, 38
Library legislation, *see* Legislation, library
Library management
  bibliography, 111
  economic aspects, 42
Library manpower, *see* Library personnel
Library materials
  conservation, 98
  expenditures for, 157-162
  selection, bibliography, 116
Library materials for blacks, 7
Library materials for children, bibliography, 113-114
Library networks, 8, 90-95
  Hawaii, 17
  see also National Agricultural Library, Agricultural Science Information Network
Library networks, Canadian, 448-449
Library networks, Czechoslovak, 466
Library networks, Russian, 462-463
Library of Congress, 25-30
  Administrative Department, 29-30
  American Law Division, 28
  appropriations, 30, (table), 212
  authority files, machine readable, 84-85
  automation in technical processing, 80-85
  book catalogs from MARC records, 85
  Cataloging in Publication Program, 14, 28; grants to, 44
  collections, 25
  Computer Service Center, *see* Library of Congress, Information Systems Office
  Congressional Research Service, 28; Government and General Research Division, 7
  Division for the Blind and Physically Handicapped, 27
  Federal Library Committee, *see* Federal Library Committee
  Geography and Map Division, acquisitions, 26
  guidelines for systematic automation, 83
  Information Systems Office, Computer Service Center, 30
  James Madison Memorial Building, 30, 207
  Law Library
    collections, 27
    indexing projects, 28
    U.S. Supreme Court Records and Briefs Project, 27
  Law Library microtext reading room, 27-28
  MARC Development Office, 80-81
  MARC Distribution Service, 81; expansion, 83
  MARC format
    for films, 206
    recognition, 82-83
    use in other libraries, 91-92
  MARC subsets, 82
  machine filing program, 85
  Manuscript Division
    acquisitions, 26
    Poetry Office, L. C. literary programs, 27

Multiple Use MARC System, 83-84; applied to PIF, 84
Music Division
  Festival of Chamber Music, 26
  Gabriela Mistral recording, 26-27
name reference list, machine readable, 85
National Program for Acquisitions and Cataloging, 28
Order Division Project, 84
Orientalia Division
  panel discussion at Assn. for Asian Studies meeting, 26
  Persian exhibit, 26
Photoduplication Service, 30
Preservation Office, 29-30
Preservation Research and Testing Laboratory, 29-30
Prints and Photographs Division, exhibitions, 26
Prints and Photographs Division, Motion Picture Section, technical advances, 26
Process Information File, automated, 84
Processing Department, 28-29
  catalog cards, 28-29
  cataloging of serials, 29
  monographs in series, 29
Public Law 480 Program, 28
RECON Pilot Project, 81-82
RECON Working Task Force, 82
racial discrimination in, 11-12
Rare Book Division, acquisitions, 25-26
Reference Department, 25-27; bibliographies, 25
Serial Division, microfilming of newspaper, 26
Subject Heading List, machine readable, 84
traveling exhibits, 27
Library of Congress Catalog: Motion Pictures and Filmstrips, from MARC data, 85
Library personnel
  ALA concerns in, 52-53
  cutbacks in special libraries, 57
  education, *see* Education, and Employees, *under* National Agricultural Library; Library technician programs; Library trainee programs
  statistics, 260-265
  volunteers, 9-10
  see also Personnel, *under* College and university libraries, etc.
Library programs, appropriations, federal (table), 211-212
  see also Bureau of Libraries and Educational Technology, Library programs; Library services to children and young adults, programs; U.S., appropriations bills affecting libraries
Library Public Relations Council
  committee chairman, 402
  executive board, 401
  membership, 401
  officers, 401
Library Public Relations Council Award, 108
Library reference aids, *see* Reference aids and services
Library research
  grants from HEA, 235
  United Kingdom, 459
Library Research and Demonstration Program, *see* Bureau of Libraries and Educational Technology, Library Research and Demonstration Program
Library salaries, *see* Librarians, salaries
Library school planning and direction, student participation, 9
Library schools
  curriculum changes, 8-9
  grants to, *see* Grants, library
  placements, 253-257, 269-278
  number of, 253-254
  special, 274
  placements by location (table), 271
  placements by region, 254, (table), 258
  placements by type of library, 254-255, (table), 272-273
  placements by type of program (tables), 255-257, 258
  scholarships and fellowships, *see* Scholarships
  see also Education for librarianship
Library schools, Canadian, statistics, 454-455
Library schools, graduate, ALA-accredited (list), 282-283
Library services
  developments in, 5-6
  use of, 43
  see also Public library services
Library Services and Construction Act, 214-219
  amendments, 38-39, 214
  appropriations (table), 211
  Title I: Public Library Services, 214-215
  Title II: Public Library Construction, 215
  Title III: Interlibrary Cooperation, 215
    allotments by state (table), 219
  5-year extension, 90
  Title IV-A: State Institutional Library Services, 215-216
  Title IV-B: Library Services to the Physically Handicapped, 216
  Titles I and II, allotments by state (table), 219

Library services for blacks, 8
Library services for children and young adults, 15-21
 bibliography, 113-114
 New York State plan, 11
 programs, 18
Library services for the handicapped, 6-7
 bibliography, 115
 see also Library Services and Construction Act, Title IV-B
Library services to the aged, 6-7
Library service to the disadvantaged, grants from HEA Title II-B, 236
Library Sort Key Edit, see Library of Congress, machine filing program
Library statistics, 133-137
 basic data for national data bank, 139-140
 bibliography, 136-137
 data collection by NCES, 134-135
 national data bank for health science libraries, 149
 national data bank system, 139
 nationwide system, 138-142
  see also Core library data
 nationwide system function chart, 141
 standardization, 138
 standardized terminology, 138
 tables, 154-162
 see also Placements, and statistics under College and university libraries; Education for librarianship; Library schools; Public libraries, Special libaries; also International library statistics
Library statistics, Czechoslovak, standardization, 467-468
Library statistics, German (Western), standardization, 470-471
Library Statistics of Colleges & Universities; Analytical Report, 144-145
Library Statistics of Colleges & Universities: Data for Individual Institutions, 144
Library Supplies and Equipment Committee Z85, see American National Standards Institute, Committee Z85
Library surveys, 134-136
 published, 134
 research project for NCES, 135
 schedules for, 134
 see also Elementary and Secondary General Information Survey; Higher Education General Information Survey; Public libraries, surveys
Library surveys, Canadian research libraries, 449
Library Surveys Branch, NCES, see U.S. Office of Education, National Center for Educational Statistics, Library Surveys Branch
Library technician programs (list), 289-299
 Canada, 455
Library Technology Program, 95-98
 book publishing, 97
 Conservation Project, 98
 evaluation programs, 96-97
 requests for information, 444
 Robinson Medal runner-up, 444-445
 Subcommittee on Technical Processing Standardized Times, 96
Library Technology Reports, 96
 subscriptions, 97
Library Training Institute, 38
Library Training Program, see under Bureau of Libraries and Educational Technology, Higher Education Act
Library trainee programs (list), 289-299
Library trustees, 10
Liebaers, Herman, 445
Lima, Ohio, Public Library, educational kits for the deaf, 18
Lind, George, 154
Lippincott, Joseph Wharton Award, 108
Lister Hill National Center for Biomedical Communications, see National Library of Medicine/Lister Hill National Center for Biomedical Communications
Literacy programs, 13
Literary awards, see Awards, literary and library
Literature, children's, see Children's books
Little Black Sambo, censorship, 19, 69
Little Miss Muffet Fights Back, 20
Loans, interlibrary, see Interlibrary loans
Lofquist, William S., 163, 190
Löhmann, Otto, 468
Los Angeles Free Press, censorship, 19
Los Angeles Public Library, Institute on Racism in Books for Children and Young People, 20
Los Angeles Unified School District, computerized access to all instructional materials stocked, 38
Louisiana Library Association, meeting, date of, 102, (1973) 104
Louisiana Library Association's Literary Medallion, 108
Louisiana Rapid Communication Network, underuse of, 90-91
Lowell, James Russell, Prize, 108
Lutheran Church Library Association, advisory board, 402
 committee chairmen, 402
 officers, 402
 publication, 402

M

MARC, *see* Canadian MARC; Library of Congress, MARC
MARC-O, *see* Oklahoma, Department of Libraries, MARC-O; Southwestern Interstate Cooperative Effort, use of MARC-O tapes
MEDLARS, *see* Medical Literature Analysis and Retrieval System
MEDLINE, *see* Medical Literature Analysis and Retrieval System On-Line
MIC, *see* American National Standards Institute, Committee Z39, Subcommittee on Music Industry Code
MMRI, *see* Multi-media Reviews Index
MUMS, *see* Library of Congress, Multiple Use MARC System
McClelland and Goodchild, 478
McClelland & Stewart, Ltd.
 board of directors, 481
 debentures, 481
 financial troubles, 480-481
McConnell, J. Michael, appointment refused, 70
Machine readable cataloging, *see* Canadian MARC; Library of Congress, MARC
Machine readable data bases, additions to MARC (proposed), 82
McKenna, F. E., 54
Maclear and Chewett, 478
Madga Donato Prize, 108
Maine Library Association, meeting, date of, 102
Maine School Library Association, meeting, date of, 102
Manchild in the Promised Land, censorship, 19
Mann, Margaret, Citation, 108
Manpower, library, *see* Library personnel
Many Splendored Thing, 7
Markuson, Barbara Evans, 75
Martin Luther King Library, Washington, D.C., 8
Maryland Interlibrary Loan Network, evaluation, 91
Maryland Library Association, meeting, date of, 102
Mason, Ellsworth, 14
Massachusetts Institute of Technology, Information Transfer Experiments, 44
Mathematica, Inc., Princeton, economic aspects of library management, study of, 42
May Fellowship Day, date of, 100
Medford, Mass., Public Library, instructional materials center for workers with handicapped youth, 18
Medical libraries, construction, costs, 325, (table) 344
Medical Library Association
 committee chairmen, 403-405
 directors, 403
 international activities, 12
 meeting, date of, 103
 membership, 403
 officers, 403
 publications, 403
 scholarships, 285
Medical Library Association Regents Award, 108
Medical Literature Analysis and Retrieval System, 31
Medical Literature Analysis and Retrieval System Centers, decentralization, 92
Medical Literature Analysis and Retrieval System On-Line, 32
 data base, 93
Melcher, Frederic G., Book Award, 108
Melcher, Frederic G., Scholarship, 285
Melton, Jewel, 18
Memphis Public Library and Information Center, 5-6
Mergers, *see* Book trade mergers
Merriam, Eve, 19
Methodist Book and Publishing House, 477
Michigan Library Association, meeting, date of, 103, (1973) 104, (1974) 104
Microform readers, evaluation, 97
Microwave links, approved by FCC, 95
Middleton, Bernard, 98
Minnesota Library Association, meeting, date of, 103
Mississippi Library Association, meeting, date of, 103
Missouri Library Association, meeting, date of, 103, (1973) 104
Mistral, Gabriela, recording, 26-27
Model Cities Program, Chicago, Co-Plus, 18
Montana Library Association, meeting, date of, 103
Montgomery Co., Md., Public Schools, ban *Little Black Sambo*, 19, 69
Moran, Leila P., 34
More, Thomas, Medal, 108
Motion picture production in libraries, 86
Mount Vernon, N.Y., Public Library, multimedia room, 18
Mudge, Isadore Gilbert, Citation, 108
Multi-Media Reviews Index, 88-89
Multiple Use MARC System, *see* Library of Congress, Multiple Use MARC System
Mumford, L. Quincy, sued by Barbara Ringer, 12

Music Library Association
  board of directors, 405
  committee chairmen, 405
  meeting, date of, 101, 103, (1973) 104
  membership, 405
  officers, 405
  publications, 405
Musson Book Company, 478

N

NAACP, see National Association for the Advancement of Colored People
NAL, see National Agricultural Library
NCES, see U.S. Office of Education, National Center for Educational Statistics
NCPTWA *Word Abbreviation List,* 46
NEA, see National Education Association
NELINET, see New England Library Information Network
NLM, see National Library of Medicine
NMAC, see National Library of Medicine, National Medical Audiovisual Center
NOW, see National Organization of Women
NPAC, see Library of Congress, National Program for Acquisition and Cataloging
NTS, see New Serial Titles
NTIS, see National Technical Information System
NYCLU, see New York Civil Liberties Union
NYSIL, see New York State Interlibrary Loan Network
National Agricultural Library, 34-37
  acquisitions program, 34
  appropriations (table), 212
  CAIN system, 35
  Code-A-Phone system, 35
  collection, 34
  coordinator for ASIN (proposed), 93
  education of agricultural librarians and technical specialists, 36
  employees, professional development of, 36
  Food and Nutrition Information and Educational Materials Center, 36
  Information Analysis Center, 36
  Information System, 34
  Integrated Knowledge Services, 36
  International Cooperation Programs, 36
  James M. Gwin Poultry Collection, 34
  library services (output function), 35-36
  publications, 34-35
  research and development programs, 36
  Resource Development (input functions), 34

National Agricultural Library, Associates of the, see Associates of the National Agricultural Library
National Agricultural Library, and University of Maryland, School of Library and Information Services, training in research methodology, 36
National Agricultural Library Catalog, 35
National Association for the Advancement of Colored People, Survey for Black Caucus, 20
National Association of College Stores, convention, date of, 100
National Association of Elementary School Principals, meeting, date of, 102, 104
National Association of Secondary School Principals, meeting, date of, 102
National Association of State Supervisors and Directors of Secondary Education, meeting, date of, 102
National Audio-Visual Association, meeting, date of, 103, (1973) 104
National Book and Library Policy, see U.S. National Book and Library Policy
National Book Awards, 108
  date of, 99
National Book Awards program, 72-73
National Book Committee, 71-73
  Educational Media Selection Centers Program, 73
  grants to establish U.S. Secretariat for IBY, 71
National Book Awards, see National Book Awards
National Medal for Literature, see National Medal for Literature
  publications (list), 72
National Catholic Educational Association, meeting, date of, 102
National Center for Educational Statistics, see U.S. Office of Education, National Center for Educational Statistics
National Clearinghouse for Periodical Title Word Abbreviations, 46
National Commission on Libraries and Information Science, 50-51
  appropriations (table), 212
  first meeting, 24
  functions, 50
  memberships (list), 50-51
National Community Antenna Television Act of 1971, 208
National Coordinating Council on Drug Abuse, Survey of drug education films, 19
National Council of Teachers of English, charge bias in educational materials, 19

National Defense Education Act, appropriations (table), 211
National Education Association, meeting, date of, 103, (1973) 104
National Education Association, Department of Audiovisual Instruction, Task Force on Computerized Cataloging and Booking Educational Media, 203
National Education Association and American Association of School Librarians, standards for school media programs, 17
National Educational Finance Project, survey of school finances, 15
National Exhibit of Prints, 22nd, 27
National 4-H Week, date of, 101
National Health Service (U.K.), reorganization, 458
National Institute of Education (proposed), 16-17
National Lending Library for Science and Technology, new building, 457
National Libraries, British
 automated functions, 457
 see also British Library, National Reference Library of Science
National library associations, see Library associations, national
National Library of Medicine, 31-33
 AIM-TWX service, see AIM-TWX
 appropriations (table), 212
 assistance programs, 33
 bibliographies, 31
 extramural programs, 33
 summary, 33
 foreign currency program, 33
 grants, 33
 health science libraries network, 92, 148
 Health Science Research Communications in Poland, 33
 highlights of NLM activities, 33
 interlibrary loans, 31
 international exchange of published biomedical information, 33
 library operations, 31-32
 MEDLARS, see Medical Literature Analysis and Retrieval System
 MEDLINE, see Medical Literature Analysis and Retrieval System On-Line
 multimedia resource area, 32
 network services, 92-93
 projects in Israel, 33
 Regional Medical Library Program, 33
 sued by Williams and Wilkins, 251
 Toxicology Information Program, 32
National Library of Medicine, Board of Regents, members, 31

National Library of Medicine, Lister Hill National Center for Biomedical Communications
 health care services in Alaska, 32
 satellite communications, 32
 television link, closed circuit, 32
National Library of Medicine, National Medical Audiovisual Center, 32-33
 computer-supported distribution system, 32-33
 instructional units, 32
National Library Week
 date of, 100
 program, 71, 72
National Medal for Literature, 73, 109
National Media Award, 109
National Medical Audiovisual Center, see National Library of Medicine, National Medical Audiovisual Center
National Microfilm Association
 chapters, 406
 Materials and Supplies Standards Comm., subcommittee on Storage Containers for Imaged Microfilm, 96
 meeting, date of, 102
 officers, 406
 publications, 406
National Music Week, date of, 100
National Organization of Women, Princeton chapter, report on recommended book lists, 20
National Planning Conference on Nonprint Media Statistics, 205-206
National policy statement on International Book and Library Activities, 492-493
National Program for Acquisitions and Cataloging, see Library of Congress, National Program for Acquisitions and Cataloging
National Reading Center, 72
National Recreation Month, date of, 100
National Reference Library of Science, new building, 457
National Science Foundation, Office of Science Information, Committee on Scientific and Technical Information, see Committee on Scientific and Technical Information
National Security and Individual Freedom, 66
National Standard Reference Data System, established, 64
National Technical Information System, 59, 64
 Government Report Topical Announcements, 59
National Union Catalog: Pre-1956 Imprints, 29

National Wildlife Week, date of, 100
Natrona County, Wyo., Public Library, use of CATV, 94
Nebraska Library Association, meeting, date of, 103
Nebula Awards, 109
Nene Award, 109
Networks, Information, *see* Information networks
Networks, Library, *see* Library networks
Nevada Library Association, meeting, date of, 103, (1973) 104
New England Library Association, meeting, date of, 102
New England Library Information Network grant from Council on Library Resources, 44
  use of MARC tapes, 92
New Hampshire Library Council, meeting, date of, 103, (1973) 104
New Hampshire School Media Association, meeting, date of, 103, (1973) 104
New Jersey Library Association
  defends membership, 13
  meeting, date of, 102
New Jersey School Media Association, meeting, date of, 102
New Mexico Library Association, meeting, date of, 102
New Serial Titles, ISSN assigned to, 198
New York City, library urban information network (proposed), 93-94
New York City, Washington Irving High School, students, 68
New York Civil Liberties Union, 19
  challenges banning of *Down These Mean Streets*, 68
New York Public Library
  catalogs on microfilm, grant for, 44
  union contract, 11
New York State Commissioner's Committee on Library Development, report, 17
New York State Department of Education, 7
New York State Interlibrary Loan Network, conversion to dataphone teletype, 91
New York State Library Association, defends membership, 13
New York Library Association, meeting, date of, 104
New Zealand Buckland Literary Award, 109
Newbery, John, Medal Award, 109
  announcement, date of, 99
News Report: 1971, 3-14
Newspapers, directories, bibliography, 123-124
Newspapers on microfilm, 26
Niven, Frederick, Award, 109

Nobel Prize for Literature, 109
  date of, 101
Nonprint media, 86-89
  bibliographic control
    standards, 203-206
      Great Britain and Canada, 204
  delivery systems, 87-88
  developments within professional associations, 89
  Germany (Western), 472
  indexes and review sources, bibliography, 88-89
  MARC format for projected images, 204
  performance standards development, 96
  technological developments, 86-87
  see also Educational materials
North American Library Education Directory and Statistics, 1969-71, questionnaire, 253
North Carolina Library Association, meeting, date of, 1973, 104
Northeastern University, Boston, basic/supplemental grant under HEA Title II-A, 226
Notable Books of 1970 and 1971, 129
Nyren, Karl, 3

O

OCLC, *see* Ohio College Library Center
OE, *see* U.S. Office of Education
Oak Ridge National Laboratory, Toxicology Information Response Center, 32
Oberly, Eunice Rockwell, Memorial Award, 109
Obscenity, 66-67
  see also Pornography
Office of University Library Management Studies, *see* Association of Research Libraries, Office of University Library Management Studies
Ohio Association of School Libraries, meeting, date of, 103
Ohio College Library Center
  computerized library cataloging service, 38
  grant from Council on Library Resources, 44
  use of MARC information, 91
Ohio Library Association, meeting, date of, 103
Ohio OPRIS project, 6
Ohio State Library Board, 7
Ohio State University Evaluation Center, Library Training Institute, 39
Ohioana Book Awards, 109
Oklahoma Department of Libraries, use of MARC tapes, 92
Oklahoma Library Association, meeting, date of, 102, (1973) 104
Oklahoma Library Association Distinguished Service Award, 109

Older American Act, appropriations (table), 212
Oliver, Philip M., 22-23
Ontario Royal Commission on Book Publishing, interim report on government aid to McClelland & Stewart, 481
Ontario Library Association, meeting, date of, 103
Ontario Library Trustees' Librarian Award, 109
Oregon Library Association, meeting, date of, 102
Organizational Committee for Reserve Libraries (Finland), study of college libraries, 465
Orne, Jerrold, 320
 honored by ASIS, 47
 represents ISO/TC 46 at UNISIST meeting, 47

P

PEN Translation Prize, 109
PH7 Committee, *see* American National Standards Institute, Committee PH7
PIF, *see* Library of Congress, Process Information File
PONY-U, *see* Parents of New York United
Packer, Katherine H., 448
Palmer, David, 135, 138
Pan American Day, date of, 100
Paraprofessionals in libraries, *see* Scholarships, library, grants for training paraprofessionals
Parent's Guide to Children's Reading, 72
Parents of New York United, 19
Pennsylvania Library Association, meeting, date of, 103
Pennsylvania School Librarians Association, meeting, date of, 102
Pentagon Papers, 66
Performing Arts in 19th Century America Exhibition, 26
Periodical Literature on the American Revolution, 25
Periodicals
 bibliography, 116, 120, 124
 directories, bibliography, 123-124
 prices (table), 183
Periodicals, British, prices (table), 184
Peters, Jean R., 121
Phillips, Harry L., 220
Photography in libraries, 86
Piercy, Esther J., Award, 109
Planning for a Nationwide System of Library Statistics, 135
 summary of recommendations, 138-142
Population, U.S., *see* U.S. population

Pornography
 in British book trade, 488
 legislation, 249
 see also Obscenity
Position Paper on Community Antenna Television, 88
Postal rates, *see* U.S. Postal Service
Prague International Library Statistics Conference, 1971, 194-196
 Resolution on Analysis of Library Statistics by Group Indices, 195-196
 Resolution on Audiovisual Materials, 194
 Resolution on Interpretation and Analysis of Library Statistics, 195
 Resolution on Library Activities, 195
 Resolution on Library Building Statistics, 195
 Resolution on Manuscripts, 194-195
Pratt, Fletcher, Award, 109
Prejudice in educational materials, 19-21
President's Commission on Obscenity and Pornography, *see* U.S. President's Commission on Obscenity and Pornography
Prince George's County, Md., School Board, decision in favor of *Sylvester and the Magic Pebble*, 68
Printing, bibliography, 124
Printing Week, date of, 99
Prizes, *see* Awards
Professors of Secondary School Administration and Supervision, meeting, date of, 102
Public documents, on microform, 96
Public Lending Right (U.K.), 458
Public librarians, demand and supply (table), 263-264
 rate change (table), 265
Public libraries
 additions and renovations (table by location), 312-316
 air-conditioning, 301
 bibliography, 116-117
 budgets (table), 157-158
 construction (table by location), 304-311
 book capacity, 302
 carpeting, 301
 costs, 301, (table), 302
 costs summary, 303
 government funds for, 302
 reader seats, 302
 LSCA funds for, 215
 statistics, 301-319
 see also Library Services and Construction Act, Title II
 expenditures for library materials (table), 157-158
 expenditures on AV and microform materials (table), 161
 personnel, statistics, 260

statistics, bibliography, 136-137
  use of, 43
Public libraries, British, charges for borrowing, 458
Public libraries, Canadian
  statistics (table), 450
    operating costs (table), 450
    operating costs, regional (table), 451
    operating receipts (table), 450, 451
  subsidized to aid book sales, 482
Public libraries, Finnish, 465
Public libraries, German (Western), 469
Public libraries, Russian
  centralization, 461-462
  circulation, statistics, 461
  growth, 460-461
Public Library Association
  committee chairmen, 382
  directors, 382
  goals and services of public libraries, study of, 43
  membership, 382
  officers, 382
  publications, 382
  section president, 382
Public library programs, effect of LSCA on, 214-215
Public library services
  evaluative study of, 43
  see also Library Services and Construction Act, Title I
Public library services, British, reorganization, 457-458
Public library surveys, 142-143
Publisher-agents, Canadian, 479, 482-483
Publishers, mergers, see Book trade, mergers
Publishers associations, 430-435
Publishers associations, foreign (list), 509-514
Publishing
  bibliography, 121-124
  economic controls, 246-248
  legislation, see Legislation, publishing
Publishing, British, 486-489
  finances, 486-488
  profits, 487
  turnover statistics 487
Publishing, Canadian, 477-485
  American subsidiaries, 483
  foreign ownership, 484-485
  government aid to 480-482, 483
  history, 477-480
  U.S. copyright law, effect of, 483-484
  see also Textbook publishing in Canada
Publishing statistics
  book imports, 178
  book title output by category, 177
  book title output by Dewey classification (table), 176
  hardcover textbooks (table), 178
  stock prices (table), 181-182
  translations into English (table), 178
  see also Book sales, statistics
Publishing statistics, British
  tables
    by subject, 476
    by year, 476
Publishing statistics, Canadian, 480
Publishing statistics, international (table by country), 473-475
Pulitzer Prize announcement, date of, 100
Pulitzer Prizes, 109
Putnam Award, 109

Q

Queen's University, Kingston, Ont., union contract, 11

R

RECON, see Library of Congress, RECON Pilot Project
RIE, see Research in Education
Raleigh, Sir Walter, Award, 110
Ralston, Anthony, 14
Recommendation Concerning the International Standardization of Library Statistics, UNESCO approval, 193-194
Recommended Practice of Library Lighting, 96
Reed, Sarah R., 260
Rees, Alan M., 24
Reference aids and services, bibliography, 117
Reference books, subscription sales (table), 173
Regina Medal Award, 110
Research, library, see Library research
Research in Education, 58
  micro-library of titles, 59
Research Libraries, Association of, see Association of Research Libraries
Restoration of Leather Bindings, 98
Retrospective Conversion of Bibliographic Materials, see Library of Congress, RECON Pilot Project
Revenue sharing plans, education, 16
Reviewers, Canadian, effect upon publishing industry, 484
Revised Guide to the Law and Legal Literature of Mexico, 28
Rhode Island State Library Association
  defends membership, 13
  defense of Richard Waters, 11
Ridgefield, Conn., Taxpayers League, removes books from schools and libraries, 67
Right to Read Program, 16
  ESEA Title II support, 224
  grants in support of, 229-230

Ringer, Barbara, 12
Robinson, Carrie, denied promotion, 20
Robinson Medal, 110
Roster of Authorities in Specialized Subtopics of Toxicology and Related Fields, 32
Roster of Federal Libraries, 76
Rubin, Jerry, 19
Rutgers University Award, 110
Ryerson, Egerton, 447-478

S

SCMAI, *see* American Library Association, Staff Committee on Mediation, Arbitration and Inquiry
SE-LIN book labelling system, 98
SIS, *see* National Library of Medicine, Specialized Information Services
SLA, *see* Special Libraries Association
SLICE, *see* Southwestern Library Interstate Cooperative Effort, use of MARC tapes
SRRT, *see* American Library Association, Social Responsibilities Round Table
SSN, *see* Standard Serial Numbering
SUNYLA, *see* State University of New York Library Association
SWRN, *see* Colorado Statewide Reference Network
St. Croix Library Association, meeting, date of, 102
St. John's University Library School, 7
Salaries, *see* Librarians, salaries
Salton, Gerard, 14
Samore, Theodore, 144
San Antonio Public Library, peer group storytelling workshop, 18
San Jose State College, tenure denied Robert Duman, 11
Scandia Plan, 464
Scarecrow Press Award for Library Literature, 110
Schick, Frank L., 133, 193
Schneider, Linda, 45
Scholarships, library (list), 284-286
  institutions sponsoring programs (list), 285-286
  under HEA Title II-B, 227-228; institutions (list), 228
  see also Council on Library Resources; Education for Librarianship; also names of specific scholarships
School districts
  budgets, 15-16
  property taxes, 15
School of Library and Information Services, University of Maryland, *see* National Agricultural Library; University of Maryland, School of Library and Information Services
School libraries
  bibliography, 118
  budgets, *see* School districts, budgets
  effect of ESEA Title II, 221
  personnel, statistics, 260
  statistics, bibliography, 137
School libraries, Canadian, statistics, 452
School libraries, German (Western), 472
School library associations, state (list), 421-422
School Library Journal, exposé of plight of black southern librarians, 7
School library supervisors, state (list), 427-430
School media centers, personnel (table), 265
Schools effect of ESEA Title II, 221-222
Schools, integration of, *see* Integration of schools
Schools, Canadian, statistics (table), 452
Schuman, Patricia, 15
Science and technology research centers, 6
Science information system, worldwide (proposed), 65
Scribner's, Charles, Sons, Awards, 110
Serial publications
  bibliography, 116
  prices (table), 184
Sesame Street, in library programs, 18
Shank, Russell, 90
Shared cataloging, Canadian, *see* Cataloging, shared, Canadian
Sievanen-Allen, Ritva, 463
Simon, Charlie May, Children's Book Award, 110
Simpson, Robert, Company, 479
Skinner, Constance Lindsay, Award, 110
Slaughterhouse Five, censorship, 19, 69
Sloan, Irving, 20
Small Community Development Act, 210
Smyth Cleat Sewing Machine, modification, 98
Snow Library, Orleans, Mass., school-public library union catalog, 18
Social Responsibilities Round Table, *see* American Library Association, Social Responsibilities Round Table
Society of American Archivists
  committee chairmen, 407-408
  council, 407
  meeting, date of, 104, (1973) 104
  officers, 407
  publications, 407
Soul on Ice, censorship, 19
South Carolina Library Association, meeting, date of, 1973, 104
South Dakota Library Association, meeting, date of, 103, (1973) 104

Southeastern Library Association, meeting, date of, 104, (1974) 104
Southwestern Library Association, meeting, date of, 104, (1974) 104
Southwestern Library Interstate Cooperative Effort, use of MARC-O services, 92
Special libraries
 bibliography, 118-119
 definition, 54-55
 development of, 55-56
 personnel cutbacks, 57
 personnel statistics, 261
 statistics, bibliography, 137
Special Libraries
 editorial policy, 57
 position open ads, 57
 position wanted ads, 9
Special libraries, Canadian, statistics, 454
Special Libraries and Information Centres in Canada; a Directory, 454
Special Libraries Association, 54-58
 book publication program (list), 58
 committee chairmen, 409
 committees discontinued, 56
 Continuing Education Seminars, 57
 cooperation with other organizations, 58
 directors, 408
 Employment Clearing House at San Francisco Conference, 57
 fiscal year changed, 56
 Hall of Fame Award, 58
 meeting, date of, 103, (1973) 104
 merger with ASIS (proposed), 12, 56-57
 officers, 408
 organizational changes, 56-57
 publications, 408-409
 student groups authorized, 56
Special Libraries Association, Ad Hoc Group, working with the Civil Service Commission, 23
Special Libraries Association Conference, San Francisco, 57
Standard Serial Numbering, 47
 Committee Z39 system approved, 44
 see also International Standard Serial Numbering
Standard times, 96
Standards for Cataloging, Coding and Scheduling Educational Media, 203
Standards for Cataloging Nonprint Materials, 88, 204
Standards for library service, Canadian, 456
Standards for School Media Programs, 17
State institutional library services, *see* Library Service and Construction Act, Title IV-A
State library agencies, *see* Library agencies, state
State library associations, *see* Library associations, state
State school library supervisors, *see* School library supervisors, state
State University of New York Library Association, member participation, 13
State institutions, library services in, 215-216
Statistics, book trade, *see* Book trade statistics
Statistics, library, *see* Library statistics
Steig, William, 18
Stereo recording, four-channel, 86-87
Stevens, Frank A., 225, 227
Stocks, publishers', prices (table), 181-182
Storage Containers for Imaged Microfilm, Subcommittee, *see* National Microfilm Association, Materials and Supplies Comm., Subcommittee on Storage Containers for Imaged Microfilm
Student librarian programs, *see* Library trainee programs
Student librarians, foreign, travel grants to, 444
Student participation in library school planning, *see* Library school planning and direction, student participation
Student publications, unauthorized distribution prohibited, 68
Student Rights Handbook for New York City, distribution at Washington Irving H.S., 68
Students, *see* Student librarians
Sub-Saharan Africa: A Guide to Serials, 1970, 25
Supervisors, state school library, *see* School library supervisors, state
Support Committee for International Book Year, 439
 nucleus for advice to UNESCO, 441-442
 search for sources of financing IBY projects, 441
Survey of Health Sciences Libraries, 1969, 153
Suyin, Han, 7
Sylvester and the Magic Pebble
 censorship, 18-19
 ruling in favor, 68-69
System Development Corporation, report on automation, 24

T

TFA, *see* Federal Library Committee, Task Force on Automation of Library Operations
TIP, *see* National Library of Medicine, Toxicology Information Program
Tape recorders, cassette, evaluation, 96

Task Force on Role of Libraries in Information Systems, *see* Federal Library Committee Task Force in Information Systems
Tax amendments, for charitable deductions, 209
Teachers, teacher and parent bonus plan, 17
Teaching, effects of ESEA Title II, 221
Technical Processing Standardized Times, subcommittee, *see* Library Technology Program, Subcommittee on Standardized Times
Technical services, library, *see* Libraries, technical services
Television, community antenna
 copyright legislation, 29
 in information services, 87-88
 in information networks, 94-95
 legislation, 208
 library use of, 94-95
 see also CATV *under* U.S. Department of Housing and Urban Development; U.S. Federal Communications Commission
Tennessee Library Association, meeting, date of, 102, (1973) 104
Textbook development programs, *see* U.S. Agency for International Development, textbook development programs
Textbook publishing in Canada, 478-479
Textbooks
 sales (table), 173
 statistics, *see* Publishing statistics, hardcover textbooks
Theater Library Association
 committee chairmen, 410
 executive board, 410
 meeting, date of, 103, (1973) 104
 officers, 409-410
 publication, 410
Thomas, Piri, 19
Thompson, Noel, 456
Thompson, Samuel, Publisher, 478
Thorpe, Fred, 7
Times, standard, *see* Standard times
Timpano, Doris, 21
Title leaves, book, *see* Books, title leaves
Tokyo Book Development Center, 440
Toronto Public Library, social science data study, 6
Toronto University Press, *see* University of Toronto Press
Toxicology Information Programs, *see* National Library of Medicine, Toxicology Information Program
Toxicology Information Response Center, *see* Oak Ridge National Laboratory, Toxicology Information Response Center
Trainee programs, *see* Library traineee programs
Translations, statistics, *see* Publishing statistics, translations
Translations Register-Index, transferred to National Translations Center, 57
Treatment of Black Americans in Current Encyclopedias, 20
Trustee Citation of Merit, 108
Tulane University Library, computer-output-microfilm short title catalog, testing, 44
Two-year colleges, *see* Junior colleges

U

UBC, *see* Universal Bibliographic Control
ULTC, *see* Urban Library Trustees' Council
UNESCO
 audiovisual services reporting on IBY, 442
 integration of programs with IBY, 442
 periodicals reporting on IBY, 442
 recommendation on library statistics, 193-194
 report on IBY purposes, 440
 report to UNCTAD on currency obstacles to importing books, 441
UNESCO Agreement on the Importation of Educational, Scientific and Cultural Materials, 247-248
UNESCO Courier, IBY Issue, 442
UNESCO Economic and Social Council, resolution to support IBY, 440
UNESCO General Conference, 193
UNESCO International Copyright Information Center, 440
UNESCO International Symposium on Books (proposed), 442
UNESCO Library Statistics, 1970, working papers, 194
UNISIST, *see* World Science Information System
Unions, library, 11
United Nations Day, date of, 101
United States
 appropriations bills affecting libraries, 207
 population served by libraries, characteristics of (table), 154-155
U.S. Agency for International Development
 book activities, 493-494
 Latin American Bureau, program for regional book activity, 494
 textbook development programs, 494
United States Book Exchange, Inc.
 board of directors, 410-411
 officers, 410
 sponsoring members, 411

U.S. Civil Service Commission, Job Evaluation and Pay Review Task Force, report on evaluation system, 22-23
U.S. Committee for International Book Year, 439, 440
U.S. Copyright Office, 29
U.S. Department of Health, Education, and Welfare, regional offices (list), 39-40
U.S. Department of Housing and Urban Development
  CATV networks, report on, 94
  information program, 6
U.S. Federal Communications Commission
  CATV rulings, 94
  recommendations on CATV, 208
U.S. Federal Trade Commission, negative option, 249
U.S. Government Advisory Committee on International Book and Library Programs
  activities, 492-493
  Ad Hoc Committee for IBY, 493
  members, 491-492
U.S. House Judiciary Committee, statement on library uses of sound recordings, 208
U.S. Library Data System (proposed), 136
U.S. Library of Congress, *see* Library of Congress
U.S. National Book and Library Development Policy, 493
U.S. Office of Education
  Bureau of Libraries and Educational Technology, *see* Bureau of Libraries and Educational Technology
  Educational Resources and Information Center, 6
  ERIC Clearinghouses (list), 60-62
  ERIC program, 58-59
  see also names of specific Clearinghouses, *under* ERIC
  educational Special Revenue Sharing proposal, 16
  Fellows Program, 285
  National Center for Educational Statistics, 133-139, 144
    advisory committee for, 138
    cooperation with states, 138
    functions, 133-134
    Library Surveys Branch, 133, 143
  Office of Renewal (proposed), 16
  organization chart, 41
  plans for a Survey of Public Libraries, 142-143
  Right to Read Program, *see* Right to Read Program
U.S. Postal Service
  rates, 208-209
  regulations, 250-251

U.S. President's Commission on Obscenity and Pornography, report, 66-67
U.S. Senate Judiciary Subcommittee on Patents, Trademarks, and Copyrights, 208
U.S. Supreme Court Records and Briefs, 27
Urban Information Specialist Program, *see* University of Maryland, Urban Information Specialist Program
Urban Information Systems, Inter-Agency Committee, information network program, 6
Urban Library Trustees Council, 10
  formed, 12
Use of Books in the A.I.D. Program, 493
Utah Library Association, meeting, date of, 102
Universal Bibliographic Control
  IFLA activities, 446
  program, 446
Universal Copyright Convention, revision signed, 246
Universal Postal Union, IBY special stamps, 441
University of Chicago Library, book circulation, automatic control of, 44
University of Colorado Library, automated circulation system, 14
University of Colorado Medical Center, Denison Memorial Library, TWX for interlibrary loan, 91
University of Florida Libraries at Gainesville, use of MARC tapes, 92
University of Lancaster, England, study on the use of library services, 43
University of Maryland
  Dean of Admissions, 7
  Urban Information Specialist Program, 7
University of Maryland, School of Library and Information Services, *see* National Agricultural Library and University of Maryland, School of Library and Information Services
University of Massachusetts Library, computerized acquisitions system, 14
University of Michigan Press Book Award, 110
University of Minnesota Library, McConnell case, 70
University of Toronto Press, 479

V

Vancouver Island Regional Library, Central buying and cataloging plan, 18
Veaner, Allen, 97
Velinsky, Mirko, 466
Vermont Library Association, meeting, date of, 102
Virginia Library Association, meeting, date of, 104, (1973) 104, (1974) 104

Vladimirov, L. I., 460
Volunteer library workers, *see* Library personnel, volunteers
Vonnegut, Kurt, 19

W

Wage and price freeze
 effect on federal libraries, 23
 effect on publishing, 246-248
Wage and Hour Act, exemption of outside salesmen, 249
Washington Library Association, meeting, date of, 102
Washington State Association of School Librarians, meeting, date of, 102
Waters, Richard, 11
Wegman, Edward, 439
Weintraub, D. Kathryn, 253
Weissman, Marjorie E., 95
West Virginia Library Association, meeting, date of, 103
Western Kentucky University Library, automated reclassification project, 14
Whitaker, David, 486
White, William Allen, Children's Book Award, 110
Williams, Joel, 135
Williams and Wilkins *vs.* NLM, ALA support of NLM, 209
Wilson, Halsey W., Library Recruitment Award, 110

Wisconsin Library Association, meeting, date of, 103
Woodbridge, N.J., Public Library, survey, 18
World Book Fair, date of, 99
World Community Day, date of, 101
World Day of Prayer, date of, 99
Worldwide Bible Reading Month, date of, 101
Wrangler Awards, 110
Wright, Robert, 7
Wyoming Library Association, meeting, date of, 102

Y

Young adults, library services for, *see* Library services for children and young adults
Young adults' books, bibliography, 127-128

Z

Z39, *see* American National Standards Institute, Committee Z39
Z39.13-1971, *see* American National Standards Institute, American National Standard Z39.13-1971
Z39.15-1971, *see* American National Standards Institute, American National Standard Z39.15
Z85, *see* American National Standards Institute, Committee Z85

Library Addresses and Telephone Numbers

The following list of selected addresses and telephone numbers, important in the library world, has been compiled at the suggestion of users of the *Bowker Annual*. For other library numbers, see individual entries in the *American Library Directory*, 27th edition (Bowker, 1970) and "Directory of Federal Library Programs," this volume.

AKRON P. L., 55 S. Main St., Akron, Ohio 44308. Tel: 216-762-7621

UNIV. OF ALABAMA, AMELIA GAYLE GORGAS L., Box S, Tuscaloosa, Ala. 35486. Tel: 205-348-6231

ALABAMA P.L. SERVICE, 155 Administrative Bldg., Montgomery, Ala. 36105. Tel: 205-269-6767

ALASKA P.L. AGENCY, DEPT. OF EDUCATION, Pouch G, Juneau, Alaska 99801. Tel: 907-586-5242

AMERICAN LIBRARY ASSN., 50 E. Huron St., Chicago, Ill. 60611. Tel: 312-944-6780. Teletype: 312-222-0914; 110 Maryland Ave. N.E., Suite 101, Washington, D.C. 20004. Tel: 202-547-4440. Teletype: 202-399-9366

UNIV. OF ARIZONA L., Tucson, Ariz. 85721. Tel: 602-884-2101. Telex: 910-952-1143

ARIZONA STATE DEPT. OF LIBRARY & ARCHIVES, Phoenix, Ariz. 85007. Tel: 602-271-5101. Teletype: Phoenix LES 910-951-1543

UNIV. OF ARKANSAS L., Fayetteville Campus, Fayetteville, Ark. 72701. Tel: 501-575-4101

ARKANSAS L. COMMISSION, 506½ Center St., Little Rock, Ark. 72201. Tel: 501-371-1524

ATLANTA P.L., 126 Carnegie Way, N.W. Atlanta, Ga. 30303. Tel: 404-522-9363

ATLANTA UNIV. SCHOOL OF L. SERVICE, 273 Chestnut St., Atlanta, Ga. 30314. Tel: 404-JA3-6431

AUBURN UNIV., RALPH BROWN DRAUGHON L., Auburn, Ala. 36830. Tel: 205-826-4500

AUSTIN P.L., 401 W. 9th St., Austin, Texas 78767. Tel: 512-472-5433. Telex: 77-6430

BAYLOR UNIV. L., Box 6307, Waco, Texas 76706. Tel: 817-755-2111. Telex: 910-894-5200

BIRMINGHAM P.L. & JEFFERSON COUNTY P.L., 2020 7th Ave. N., Birmingham, Ala. 35203. Tel: 205-252-5106

BOSTON ATHENAEUM, 10½ Beacon St., Boston, Mass. 02108. Tel: 617-227-0270

BOSTON COLLEGE LS., Chestnut Hill, Mass. 02167. Tel: 617-969-0100

BOSTON P.L., Copley Sq., Boston, Mass. 02117. Tel: 617-536-5400

BOSTON UNIV. L., 771 Commonwealth Ave., Boston, Mass. 02215. Tel: 617-353-3710

R. R. BOWKER CO., 1180 Avenue of the Americas, New York, N.Y. 10036. Tel: 212-581-8800. Telex: 12-7703

BRANDEIS UNIV. L., 415 South St., Waltham, Mass. 02154. Tel: 617-894-6000

UNIV. OF BRITISH COLUMBIA, SCHOOL OF LIBRARIANSHIP, Zone 8, Vancouver, B.C. Tel: 604-228-3871. Telex: 04-5979

BROOKLYN COLL. L., Bedford Ave. & Ave. H, Brooklyn, N.Y. 11210. Tel: 212-780-5342. Teletype: 212-763-1392

BROOKLYN P.L., Grand Army Plaza, Brooklyn, N.Y. 11238. Tel: 212-488-3529. TWX: 710-584-2253

BROWN UNIV., JOHN D. ROCKEFELLER, JR. L., Providence, Rhode Island 02912. Tel: 401-863-2167

BUFFALO & ERIE COUNTY P.L., Lafayette Sq., Buffalo, N.Y. 14203. Tel: 716-856-7525. Telex: 716-842-4501

UNIV. OF CALIFORNIA, GEN. L. & SCH. OF LIBNSHIP., Berkeley, Calif. 94720. Tel: 415-642-3773. Teletype: 910-336-7337; Davis L., Davis, Calif. 95616. Tel: 916-752-2110; Santa Barbara L., Goleta, Calif. 93106. Tel: 805-968-1511. Teletype: 805-449-7248; University L., Riverside, Calif. 92507. Tel: 714-787-3223

UNIV. OF CALIFORNIA AT LOS ANGELES, UNIV. L., 405 Hilgard Ave., Los Angeles, Calif. 90024. Tel: 213-825-1323. Teletype: 213-490-3978; SCHOOL OF L. SERVICE, Los Angeles, Calif. 90024. Tel: 213-272-8911; WILLIAM ANDREWS CLARK MEMORIAL L., 2205

W. Adams Blvd., Los Angeles, Calif. 90018. Tel: 213-731-8529

CALIFORNIA STATE L., Library & Courts Bldg., Box 2037, Sacramento, Calif. 95809. Tel: 916-445-2585, 4027. Teletype: 910-367-3553

CARNEGIE L. OF PITTSBURGH, 4400 Forbes St., Pittsburgh, Pa. 15213. Tel: 412-621-7300. TWX: 710-664-4280

CARNEGIE MELLON UNIV. L., Schenley Park, Pittsburgh, Pa. 15213. Tel: 412-621-4619

CASE WESTERN RESERVE UNIVERSITY LS., 11161 East Blvd., Cleveland, Ohio 44106. Tel: 216-368-3506. Telex: 810-421-8818

CATHOLIC UNIV. OF AMERICA L. & DEPARTMENT OF L. SCIENCE, Michigan Ave. betw. 4th & 7th Sts., N.E., Washington, D.C. 20017. Tel: 202-LA9-6000

CHARLOTTE & MECKLENBURG COUNTY P.L., 310 N. Tryon St., Charlotte, N.C. 28202. Tel: 704-376-6401

UNIV. OF CHICAGO L. & GRADUATE L. SCHOOL, 1100 E. 57 St., Chicago, Ill. 60637. Tel: 312-MI3-0800

CHICAGO P.L., Michigan Ave., Chicago, Ill. 60602. Tel: 312-CE6-8922

UNIV. OF CINCINNATI L., Cincinnati, Ohio 45221. Tel: 513-475-8000

P.L. OF CINCINNATI & HAMILTON COUNTY, 800 Vine St., Cincinnati, Ohio 45202. Tel: 513-241-2636

CITY COLL. OF NEW YORK L., 135 St. & Convent Ave., New York, N.Y. 10031. Tel: 212-621-2159. Telex: 640-5033

CLEVELAND P.L., 325 Superior Ave., Cleveland, Ohio 44114. Tel: 216-241-1020

UNIV. OF COLORADO L., Boulder, Colo. 80302. Tel: 303-443-2211. TWX: 910-940-5892

COLORADO STATE L., 1362 Lincoln St., Denver, Colo. 80203. Tel: 303-892-2174. Teletype: 303-292-1942 (Bibliographical Ctr. for Research, Denver)

COLUMBIA UNIV. L. & SCHOOL OF L. SERVICE, Broadway & 116 St., New York, N.Y. 10027. Tel: 212-280-1754

COLUMBUS P.L., 96 S. Grant Ave., Columbus, Ohio 43215. Tel: 614-228-6081

UNIV. OF CONNECTICUT, WILBUR L. CROSS L., Storrs, Conn. 06268. Tel: 203-429-3311

CONNECTICUT STATE L., DIVISION OF L. DEVELOPMENT, 231 Capitol Ave., Hartford, Conn. 06115. Tel: 203-566-4192. Telex: 710-425-0181

CORNELL UNIV., OLIN L., Ithaca, New York 14850. Tel: 607-AR 5-3689

COUNCIL ON LIBRARY RESOURCES INC., 1028 Connecticut Ave., N.W., Washington, D.C. 20036. Tel: 202-296-4757

CUYAHOGA COUNTY P.L., 4510 Memphis Ave., Cleveland, Ohio 44144. Tel: 216-398-1800

DALLAS P.L., 1954 Commerce St., Dallas, Texas 75201. Tel: 214-748-9071

DARTMOUTH COLL., BAKER L., Hanover N.H. 03755. Tel: 603-646-2236. Telex: 710-366-1829

DAYTON & MONTGOMERY COUNTY P.L., 215 E. 3rd St., Dayton, Ohio 45402. Tel: 513-224-1651

UNIV. OF DELAWARE, MEMORIAL L., Newark, Del. 19711. Tel: 302-738-2236

DELAWARE STATE L. COMMISSION, Box 635, W. Loockerman St., Dover, Del. 19901. Tel: 302-674-2240

UNIV. OF DENVER, GRADUATE SCHOOL OF LIBRARIANSHIP, Denver, Colo. 80210. Tel: 303-753-2557; MARY REED LIBRARY. Tel: 303-753-2006

DENVER P.L., 1357 Broadway, Denver, Colo. 80203. Tel: 303-266-0851

DE PAUL UNIV. L., 25 E. Jackson Blvd., Chicago, Ill. 60604. Tel: 312-931-3525

DES MOINES P.L., 100 Locust St., Des Moines, Iowa 50309. Tel: 515-283-4152. Telex: 910-520-2567

UNIV. OF DETROIT L., 4001 W. McNichols Rd., Detroit, Mich. 48221. Tel: 313-342-1000. Ext. 295

DETROIT P.L., 5201 Woodward Ave., Detroit, Mich. 48202. Tel: 313-321-1000

P.L. OF THE DISTRICT OF COLUMBIA, 499 Pennsylvania Ave., N.W., Washington, D.C. 20001. Tel: 202-NA8-6000. Ext. 4786

DRAKE UNIV., COWLES L., 28th St. & University Ave., Des Moines, Iowa 50311. Tel: 515-271-2198

DREXEL INSTITUTE OF TECHNOLOGY L. & GRADUATE SCHOOL OF L. SCIENCE, 32nd & Chestnut Sts., Philadelphia, Pa. 19104. Tel: 215-EV 7-2400

DUKE UNIV. L., Durham, N.C. 27706. Tel: 919-684-2034. TWX: 510-927-0916

EL PASO P.L., 501 N. Oregon St., El Paso, Texas 79901. Tel: 915-543-3804. Telex: 74-9463

EMORY UNIV., ASA GRIGGS CANDLER L. & DIVISION OF LIBRARIANSHIP, Atlanta, Ga. 30322. Tel: 404-377-2411

ENOCH PRATT FREE L., 400 Cathedral St., Baltimore, Md. 21201. Tel: 301-685-6700

UNIV. OF FLORIDA L., University Station, Gainesville, Fla. 32601. Tel: 904-392-0341. Telex: 810-825-6320

FLORIDA STATE L., DIV. OF L. SERVICES, Dept. of State, Tallahassee, Fla. 32304. Tel: 904-222-2315. TWX: 810-931-3689

FORDHAM UNIV., DUANE L., Bronx, N.Y. 10458. Tel: 212-FO7-5400

FORT WORTH P.L., 9th & Throckmorton Sts., Fort Worth, Texas 76102. Tel: 817-335-4781. Telex: 75-8221

FREE L. OF PHILADELPHIA, Logan Square, Philadelphia, Pa. 19103. Tel: 215-MU 6-3990. TWX: 710-670-9719

GARY P.L., 220 W. 5th Ave., Gary, Ind. 46402. Tel: 219-886-2484

GEORGE WASHINGTON UNIV. L., 2023 G St., N.W., Washington, D.C. 20006. Tel: 202-676-6840. TWX: 710-822-9278

GEORGETOWN UNIV., RIGGS MEMORIAL L., 37 & O Sts., N.W., Washington, D.C. 20007. Tel: 202-625-4095. TWX: 710-822-9284

UNIV. OF GEORGIA L., Athens, Ga. 30601. Tel: 404-542-2716

GEORGIA STATE DEPT. OF EDUC. P.L. SERV., 156 Trinity Ave., S.W., Atlanta, Ga. 30303. Tel. 404-656-2461

GRAND RAPIDS P.L., Library Plaza, N.E., Grand Rapids, Mich. 49502. Tel: 616-456-4400

GREENSBORO P.L., 201 Greene St., Greensboro, N. C. 27402. Tel: 919-378-1671

HARVARD UNIV. L., Cambridge, Mass. 02138. Tel: 617-495-1000. Ext. 2401; GRADUATE SCHOOL OF BUSINESS ADMIN., BAKER L., Boston, Mass. 02163. Tel: 617-547-9800. Ext. 361

HAWAII STATE L. SYSTEM, Dept. of Education, Div. of L. Services, P.O. Box 2360, Honolulu, Hawaii 96804. Tel: 533-6081. State Libr., Tel: 548-2811. Ext. 670

UNIV. OF HAWAII, GRADUATE SCHOOL OF L. STUDIES, Honolulu, Hawaii 96822. Tel: 944-8219

HONNOLD L., Claremont Colleges, 9th & Dartmouth Sts., Claremont, Calif. 91711. Tel: 714-626-8511. Ext. 3721

UNIV. OF HOUSTON, M.D. ANDERSON MEMORIAL L., Cullen Blvd., Houston, Texas 77004. Tel: 713-748-6600. TWX: 910-881-3754

HOUSTON P.L., Civic Center, 500 McKinney Ave., Houston, Texas 77002. Tel: 713-224-5441

HOWARD UNIV. L., Washington, D.C. 20001. Tel: 202-797-1420. Telex: 710-822-9798

IDAHO STATE L., 325 W. State St., Boise, Idaho 83702. Tel: 208-344-5811. Ext. 508. Telex: 910-970-5952

IDAHO STATE UNIV. L., Pocatello, Idaho 83201. Tel: 208-236-3480

UNIV. OF ILLINOIS L., Urbana, Ill. 61801. Tel: 217-333-0791; Graduate School of L. Science. Tel: 217-333-3281

ILLINOIS STATE L., Centennial Memorial Bldg., Springfield, Ill. 62706. Tel: 217-525-2994. Telex: 910-242-0575

INDIANA STATE L., 140 N. Senate Ave., Indianapolis, Ind. 46204. Tel: 317-633-5441

INDIANA UNIV., DIV. OF L.S., Bloomington, Ind. 47401. Tel: 812-332-0211

INDIANA UNIV. L., Bloomington, Ind. 47401. Tel: 812-337-3403. TWX: 810-351-1386

INDIANAPOLIS-MARION COUNTY L., 40 E. St. Clair St., Indianapolis, Ind. 46204. Tel: 317-638-4552

INSTITUTE FOR ADVANCED STUDY L., Princeton, N.J. 08540. Tel: 609-924-4400

IOWA STATE TRAVELING LIBRARY, Historical Bldg., Des Moines, Iowa 50319. Tel: 515-281-5237

IOWA STATE UNIV. OF SCIENCE & TECHNOLOGY L., Ames, Iowa 50010. Tel: 515-294-1442

UNIV. OF IOWA L., Iowa City, Iowa 52240 Tel: 319-353-4450

JOHN CRERAR L., 35 W. 33 St., Chicago, Ill. 60616. Tel: 312-225-2526. Teletype: 312-431-1758

JOHNS HOPKINS UNIV. L., Charles & 34 Sts., Baltimore, Md. 21218. Tel: 301-366-3300

JOINT UNIV. LIBRARIES, Nashville, Tenn. 37203. Tel: 615-254-1429

UNIV. OF KANSAS L., Lawrence, Kansas 66044. Tel: 913-UN4-3601. Teletype: 910-749-6571

KANSAS CITY P.L., 311 E. 12th St., Kansas City, Mo. 64106. Tel: 816-221-1717. Teletype: 816-556-0377

KANSAS STATE L., Topeka, Kans. 66601. Tel: 913-296-3259

KENT STATE UNIV., DEPARTMENT OF L. SCIENCE, Kent, Ohio 44240. Tel: 216-672-2121

UNIV. OF KENTUCKY, KING L. & DEPARTMENT OF L. SCIENCE, Lexington, Ky. 40506. Tel: 606-258-9000. Ext. 2821. Telex: 510-476-8816

KENTUCKY DEPARTMENT OF LIBRARIES, Box 537, Frankfort, Ky. 40601. Tel: 502-564-4346

P. L. OF KNOXVILLE & KNOX COUNTY, 217 Market St., Knoxville, Tenn. 37902. Tel: 615-523-0781

LEHIGH UNIV., LUCY PACKER LINDERMAN MEM. L., Bethlehem, Pa. 18015. Tel: 215-867-5071. Telex: 510-651-4740

LIBRARY OF CONGRESS, Washington, D.C. 20540. Tel: 202-426-5000

LITTLE ROCK P.L., 700 Louisiana St., Little Rock, Ark. 72201. Tel: 501-FR4-1677

LONG BEACH P.L., Ocean at Pacific Ave., Long Beach, Calif. 90802. Tel: 213-437-0141

LONG ISLAND UNIV. L., 385 Flatbush Ave. Ext., Brooklyn, N.Y. 11201. Tel: 212-UL2-9100

LOS ANGELES COUNTY P.L., 320 W. Temple St., Los Angeles, Calif. 90053. Tel: 213-628-9211

LOS ANGELES P.L., 630 W. 5th St., Los Angeles, Calif. 90017. Tel: 213-626-7461. TWX: 321-2422

LOUISIANA STATE L., Capitol Grounds, Box 131, Baton Rouge, La. 70800. Tel: 504-389-6651. TWX 510-993-3539

LOUISIANA STATE UNIV. L. & L. SCHOOL, University Station, Baton Rouge, La. 70803. Tel: 504-388-3969

UNIV. OF LOUISVILLE L., Belknap Campus, Louisville, Ky. 40208. Tel: 502-636-4621

LOUISVILLE FREE P.L., 4th & York St., Louisville, Ky. 40203. Tel: 502-584-4154

LOYOLA UNIV., ELIZABETH M. CUDAHY MEMORIAL L., 6525 N. Sheridan Rd., Chicago, Ill. 60626. Tel: 312-BR4-3000

MCGILL UNIV. L. SCH., 3459 McTavish St., Montreal, Que., Zone 110. Tel: 514-392-4948

UNIV. OF MAINE L., Orono, Maine 04473. Tel: 207-866-7328

MAINE STATE L., Augusta, Maine 04330. Tel: 207-289-3561

MARQUETTE UNIV. L., 1415 W. Wisconsin Ave., Milwaukee, Wis. 53233. Tel: 414-224-7214

UNIV. OF MARYLAND L., College Park, Md. 20742. Tel: 301-454-3011. TWX: 710-826-1128

MARYLAND STATE DEPT. OF EDUC., DIV. OF L. & DEVELOPMENT SERVICES, 600 Wyndhurst Ave., Baltimore, Md. 21210. Tel: 301-383-3010. Ext. 8247

UNIV. OF MASSACHUSETTS L., Amherst. Mass. 01002. Tel: 413-545-0284

MASSACHUSETTS INSTITUTE OF TECHNOLOGY L., Memorial Dr., Cambridge, Mass. 02139. Tel: 617-864-6900

MASSACHUSETTS BUREAU OF L. EXTENSION, 648 Beacon St., Boston, Mass. 02215. Tel: 617-536-4030

MEMPHIS P.L., 1850 Peabody Ave., Memphis, Tenn. 38104. Tel: 901-274-4593

UNIV. OF MIAMI L., Box 8214, Coral Gables, Fla. 33124. Tel: 305-284-3551. TWX: 810-848-7042

MIAMI UNIV. L., Oxford, Ohio 45056. Tel: 513-529-2161. Ext. 2351

UNIV. OF MICHIGAN, GENERAL L. & DEPARTMENT OF L. SCIENCE, Ann Arbor. Mich. 48104. Tel: 313-764-9356

MICHIGAN STATE L., 735 E. Michigan Ave., Lansing, Mich. 48913. Tel: 517-373-1580

MICHIGAN STATE UNIV. L., East Lansing, Mich. 48823. Tel: 517-355-2344

MID-YORK L. SYSTEM, 1602 Lincoln Ave., Utica, N.Y. 13502. Tel: 315-735-8328. Teletype: 510-242-0762

MILWAUKEE P.L., 814 W. Wisconsin Ave., Milwaukee, Wis. 53233. Tel: 414-276-7578. Teletype: 910-262-1120

MINNEAPOLIS P.L., 300 Nicollet Ave., Minneapolis, Minn. 55401. Tel: 612-372-6500

UNIV. OF MINNESOTA, WALTER L. & L.
SCHOOL, Minneapolis, Minn. 55455.
Tel: 612-373-3082. Telex: 910-576-3491
MINNESOTA STATE DEPT. OF EDUC., L. Div.
(State L. Agency), 117 University Ave.,
St. Paul, Minn. 55101. Tel: 612-221-2821. TWX: 910-563-3571
UNIV. OF MISSISSIPPI, GENERAL L., P. O.
University, Oxford, Miss. 38677. Tel:
601-232-6237. Telex: 510-980-2058
MISSISSIPPI L. COMMISSION, 405 State Office Bldg., Jackson, Miss. 39201. Tel:
601-354-6389. Ext. 559
UNIV. OF MISSOURI L., Columbia, Mo.
65201. Tel: 314-449-9241. Telex: 914-442-2440
MISSOURI STATE L., State Office Bldg.,
Jefferson City, Mo. 65102. Tel: 314-635-7985
MOBILE P.L., 701 Government St., Mobile, Ala. 36602. Tel: 205-433-0484
MONTANA STATE L. COMMISSION, 930 E.
Lyndale Ave., Helena, Mont. 59601.
Tel: 406-449-3004. Ext. 304
MONTANA STATE UNIV. L., Bozeman, Mont.
59715. Tel: 406-587-3121. Ext. 306
UNIV. OF MONTANA L., Missoula, Mont.
59801. Tel: 406-243-2053
UNIV. OF MONTREAL, ECOLE DE BIBLIO-
ECONOMIE, Montreal, Quebec. Tel:
514-343-6044
MT HOLYOKE COLL., WILLISTON ME-
MORIAL L., South Hadley, Mass. 01075.
Tel: 413-536-4000
MT VERNON P.L., 28 S. 1st Ave.,
Mount Vernon, N.Y. 10550. Tel: 914-668-1840

PUBLIC LIBRARY OF NASHVILLE & DAVID-
SON COUNTY, 222 8th Ave. N., Nashville, Tenn. 37203. Tel: 615-244-4700.
Telex: 810-371-1541
NAU LIBRARY SYSTEM, Lower Concourse, Roosevelt Field, Garden City,
N.Y. 11530. Tel: 516-741-0060
UNIV. OF NEBRASKA, DON L. LOVE ME-
MORIAL L., Lincoln, Nebr. 68508. Tel:
402-472-2511 & 2526
NEBRASKA P.L. COMM., 7th Floor, State
Capitol, Lincoln, Nebr. 68509. Tel:
402-473-1545. TWX: 910-621-8119
UNIV. OF NEVADA L., Reno, Nevada
89507. Tel: 702-784-6533
NEVADA STATE L., Carson City, Nevada

89701. Tel: 702-882-7373. Teletype:
702-863-0197
UNIV. OF NEW HAMPSHIRE L., Durham,
N.H. 03824. Tel: 603-862-1540
NEW HAMPSHIRE STATE L., 20 Park St.,
Concord, N.H. 03302. Tel: 603-271-2711
NEW JERSEY STATE L. DEPT. OF EDUC., 185
W. State St., Trenton, N.J. 08625. Tel:
609-292-6200. PUBLIC & SCHOOL LS.
SERVS. BUREAU. Tel: 609-292-6450
NEW MEXICO STATE L., 300 Don Gaspar,
Santa Fe, N. Mex. 87501. Tel: 505-827-2106
NEW ORLEANS P.L., 219 Loyola Ave., New
Orleans, La. 70140. Tel: 504-523-4602
NEW YORK P.L., 5th Ave. & 42nd St., New
York, N.Y. 10018. Tel: 212-790-6262;
DONNELL L. CENTER, 20 W. 53rd St.,
New York, N.Y. 10019. Tel: 212-790-6463
NEW YORK STATE EDUC. DEPT., L. Ext.
Div., Albany, N.Y. 12224. Tel: 518-474-5930
NEW YORK STATE L., Education Bldg., Albany, N.Y. 12201. Tel: 518-474-4969.
Dataphone: 518-474-5782
STATE UNIV. OF NEW YORK, ALBANY,
SCHOOL OF L. SCIENCE, Albany, N.Y.
12203. Tel: 518-457-8542
STATE UNIV. OF NEW YORK, Buffalo, Libraries, 14214. Tel: 716-837-2000
NEW YORK UNIV. L., Washington Sq., New
York, N.Y. 10003. Tel: 212-598-3601;
UNIVERSITY HEIGHTS L., Bronx, N.Y.
10453. Tel: 212-LU4-0700
NEWARK P.L., 5 Washington St., Newark,
N.J. 07102. Tel: 201-624-7100
NEWBERRY L., 60 W. Walton St., Chicago,
Ill. 60610. Tel: 312-943-9090
NORFOLK P.L., 301 E. City Hall Ave.,
Norfolk, Va. 23510. Tel: 703-441-2429
UNIV. OF NORTH CAROLINA, SCHOOL OF L.
SCIENCE, Chapel Hill, N.C. 27514.
Tel: 919-933-8361
UNIV. OF NORTH CAROLINA, LOUIS ROUND
WILSON L., Chapel Hill, N.C. 27514.
Tel: 919-933-1301
NORTH CAROLINA STATE L., Box 27727,
Raleigh, N.C. 27601. Tel: 919-829-7172. TWX: 510-928-1830
NORTH COUNTRY L. SYSTEM, 1050 Arsenal
St., Watertown, N.Y. 13602. Tel: 315-SU2-5540. Teletype: 315-788-4491

UNIV. OF NORTH DAKOTA L., Grand Forks, N. Dakota 58201. Tel: 701-777-2617

NORTH DAKOTA STATE L. COMM., Capitol Grounds, Bismarck, N.D. 58501. Tel: 701-224-2490

NORTHEASTERN UNIV., ROBERT G. DODGE L., 360 Huntington Ave., Boston, Mass. 02115. Tel: 617-437-2350

NORTHERN ILLINOIS UNIV., DEPT. OF L. SCIENCE, DeKalb, Ill. 60115. Tel: 815-753-1000

NORTHWESTERN UNIV., CHARLES DEERING L., Evanston, Ill. 60201. Tel: 312-492-3741; Chicago Campus, Tel: 312-649-8649

NOTRE DAME, UNIV. OF, L., P.O. Notre Dame, South Bend, Ind. 46556. Tel: 219-283-7317

OAKLAND P.L., 125 14th St., Oakland, Calif. 94612. Tel: 415-273-9000

OBERLIN COLL. L., Oberlin, Ohio 44074. Tel: 216-774-1221

OHIO STATE L., State Office Bldg., Columbus, Ohio 43215. Tel: 614-469-2694

OHIO STATE UNIV., Main L., 1858 Neil Ave., Columbus, Ohio 43210. Tel: 614-293-6152. Teletype: 614-759-0349

OHIO UNIV. L., Athens, Ohio 45701. Tel: 614-594-5228. Teletype: 614-249-0704

UNIV. OF OKLAHOMA, WILLIAM B. BIZZELL MEM. L. & SCHOOL OF L. S., Norman, Okla. 73069. Tel: 405-325-2611

OKLAHOMA COUNTY L., N.W. 3rd at Robinson St., Oklahoma City, Okla. 73102. Tel: 405-CE5-0574

OKLAHOMA STATE DEPT. OF LS., 109 State Capitol, Oklahoma City, Okla. 73105. Tel: 405-521-3658. TWX: 910-831-3178

OMAHA P.L., 19th & Harney Sts., Omaha Nebr. 68102. Tel: 402-342-4766

UNIV. OF OREGON L., Eugene, Oregon 97403. Tel: 503-686-3063

OREGON STATE UNIV. L., Corvallis, Oregon 97331. Tel: 503-754-3411

OREGON STATE L., State L. Bldg., Salem, Oregon 97310. Tel: 503-364-2448. Ext. 448

GEORGE PEABODY COLLEGE FOR TEACHERS, PEABODY L. SCHOOL, Nashville, Tenn. 37203. Tel: 615-327-8154

UNIV. OF PENNSYLVANIA L., Central Bldg., 34th & Walnut Sts., Philadelphia, Pa. 19104. Tel: 215-594-7091

PENNSYLVANIA STATE L., Education Bldg Harrisburg, Pa. 17126. Tel: 717-78 2646. Teletype: 717-564-4184

PENNSYLVANIA STATE UNIV., FRED LEW PATTEE L., University Park, Pa. 1680 Tel: 814-865-0401. TWX: 510-69 2664

PHOENIX P.L., 12 E. McDowell Rd., Pho nix, Ariz. 85004. Tel: 602-262-64

UNIV. OF PITTSBURGH L., 5th Ave., Pit burgh, Pa. 15213. Tel: 412-621-35

L. ASSN. OF PORTLAND, (P.L. for Po land & Multnomah County) 801 S. 10th Ave., Portland, Oregon 972 Tel: 503-223-7201

PRATT INSTITUTE L. SCHOOL, 215 Ryer St., Brooklyn, N.Y. 11205. Tel: 2 MA2-2200

PRINCETON UNIV. L., Princeton, N 08540. Tel: 609-452-3000

PROVIDENCE P.L., 150 Empire St., Pr dence, R.I. 02903. Tel: 401-521-7

PUERTO RICO STATE L. DIV., Box 3127, Juan, Puerto Rico 00936. Tel: 8 765-0540

PURDUE UNIV. L., Lafayette, Ind. 47 Tel: 317-749-2571. Teletype: 810-1892

QUEENS BOROUGH P.L., 89-11 Me Blvd., Jamaica, N.Y. 11432. Tel: RE9-7828. Telex: 710-582-2625

QUEENS COLL., PAUL KLAPPER L., 6 Kissena Blvd., Flushing, N. Y. 1 Tel: 212-HI5-7500. Telex: 212 4994

RHODE ISLAND DEPT. OF STATE L. SERV 95 Davis St., Providence, R.I. 0 Tel: 401-277-2726

UNIV. OF RHODE ISLAND L., Kingston 02881. Tel: 401-792-2666. 710-381-1589

UNIV. OF ROCHESTER L., River C Station, Rochester, N.Y. 14627. 716-275-4461

ROSARY COLLEGE, DEPARTMENT OF ENCE, 7900 Division St., River F Ill. 60305. Tel: 312-FO9-6320

RUTGERS—THE STATE UNIV., GRA SCHOOL OF L. SERVICE, New Brun N.J. 08901. Tel: 201-CH7-176

ST. LOUIS P.L., 1301 Olive St., St. Mo. 63103. Tel: 314-241-2288

SAINT PAUL P.L., 90 W. 4th St., St Minn. 55102. Tel: 612-224-338

LIBRARY ADDRESSES AND TELEPHONE NUMBERS / 7

AN FRANCISCO P.L., Civic Center, San Francisco, Calif. 94102. Tel: 415-KL 8-4235

N JOSE STATE COLLEGE, DEPT. OF LIBRARIANSHIP, San Jose, Calif. 95114. Tel: 408-294-6414

MMONS COLLEGE, SCHOOL OF L. SCIENCE, Fenway, Boston, Mass. 02115. Tel: 617-738-2226

IITHSONIAN INSTITUTION LIBRARIES, Constitution Ave. at Tenth St. N.W., Washington, D.C. 20560. Tel: 202-381-5382

JTH CAROLINA STATE L., 1500 Senate St., P.O. Box 11469, Columbus, S.C. 29201. Tel: 803-758-3181

IV. OF SOUTH CAROLINA, MC KISSICK MEMORIAL L., Columbia, S.C. 29208. Tel: 803-777-3142. Telex: 810-666-118

TH DAKOTA STATE L. COMMISSION, 322 outh Fort St., Pierre, S.D. 57501. el: 605-CA4-3519. Ext. 219

V. OF SOUTHERN CALIFORNIA L. & CHOOL OF L. SCIENCE, University Park, os Angeles, Calif. 90007. Tel: 213-46-2543

IAL LIBRARIES ASSN. L., 235 Park ve. S., New York, N.Y. 10003. Tel: 2-777-8136

ANE P.L., W. 906 Main Ave., Spo-ne, Wash. 99201. Tel: 509-MA4-01

IGFIELD CITY L., 220 State St., Springld, Mass. 01103. Tel: 413-739-3871

FORD UNIVERSITY L., Stanford, Calif. 305. Tel. (Palo Alto): 415-321-2300

OLK COOPERATIVE L. SYSTEM, 627 N. arise Service Rd., Box 187, Bellport, Y. 11713. Tel: 516-924-8200. Telex:)-228-1310

USE P.L., 335 Montgomery St., Syra-e, N.Y. 13202. Tel: 315-473-4489

USE UNIV. L. & SCHOOL OF L. SCI-E, Syracuse, N.Y. 13210. Tel: 315-6-5541

ERS COLL. L., 525 West 120th St., v York, N.Y. 10027. Tel: 212--4222

E UNIV., SAMUEL PALEY L., Berks 3th Sts., Philadelphia, Pa. 19122. 215-787-8231

UNIV. OF TENNESSEE L., Knoxville, Tenn. 37916. Tel: 615-974-2441. Telex: 810-583-0176

TENNESSEE STATE L. & ARCHIVES, STATE LIBRARY DIV., Nashville, Tenn. 37219. Tel: 615-741-2683. Telex: 77-6453. TWX: 910-874-1304

UNIV. OF TEXAS, MIRABEAU B. LAMAR L. & GRADUATE SCHOOL OF L. SCIENCE, Austin, Texas 78712. Tel: 512-GR1-3811

TEXAS A & M UNIV., LS., College Sta., Texas 77843. Tel: 713-845-6111. Telex: 901-880-4425

TEXAS STATE L., Library Bldg., Box 12927, Capitol Sta., Austin, Texas 78711. Tel: 512-475-2166

UNIV. OF TOLEDO L., 2801 W. Bancroft St., Toledo, Ohio 43606. Tel: 419-531-5711

TOLEDO-LUCAS COUNTY P. L., 325 Michigan St., Toledo, Ohio 43624. Tel: 419-241-3133

TOPEKA P.L., 1515 W. Tenth St., Topeka, Kans. 66604. Tel: 913-CE5-2307. TWX: 910-744-6700

UNIV. OF TORONTO, SCHOOL OF LIBRARY SCIENCE, College of Education, Toronto, Zone 181, Ontario. Tel: 416-928-2294. Telex: 06-219-515

TUCSON P.L., 200 S. 6th Ave., Tucson, Ariz. 85701. Tel: 602-791-4393

TUFTS UNIV. L., NILS YNGE WESSELL LIBRARY, Medford, Mass. 02155. Tel: 617-628-5000

TULANE UNIV. OF LOUISIANA. HOWARD-TILTON MEMORIAL L., Audubon Pl. at Freret St., New Orleans, La. 70118. Tel: 504-865-7711. Ext. 7624

UNIV. OF TULSA, MC FARLIN L., Tulsa Okla. 74104. Tel: 918-WE9-6351. Ext. 351

TULSA CITY-COUNTY L. SYSTEM, 400 Civic Center, Tulsa, Okla. 74103. Tel: 918-581-5154

UNION COLL. L., Schenectady, N.Y. 12308. Tel: 518-346-8751. Teletype: 710-442-2992

U.S. AIR UNIV. L., Maxwell Air Force Base, Montgomery, Ala. 36112. Tel: 205-265-5621. Ext. 2888

U.S. DEPT. OF THE AIR FORCE LIBRARIES, Personnel Services Div., Washington D.C. 20330. Tel: 202-981-3551

U.S. DEPT. OF THE ARMY L., The Pentagon, Washington, D.C. 20310. Tel: 202-OX5-5346. Ext. 74301; Special Services Div. Ext. 55400

U.S. DEPT. OF COMMERCE L., Washington, D.C. 20230. Tel: 202-967-3611

U.S. DEPT. OF HEALTH, EDUC., AND WELFARE L., 330 Independence Ave. S.W., Washington, D.C. 20201. Tel: 202-963-3631

U.S. DEPT. OF THE NAVY L., 18th & Constitution Ave., N.W., Washington, D.C. 20360. Tel: 202-LI5-6700; Bureau of Naval Personnel, L. Servs. Branch, Special Servs. Dir. Tel: 202-OX2-0969

U.S. NATIONAL AGRICULTURAL L., Beltsville, Md. 20250. Tel: 301-345-6200

U.S. NATIONAL INSTS. OF HEALTH L., Bethesda, Md. 20014. Tel: 301-496-2447

U.S. NATIONAL L. OF MEDICINE, Bethesda, Md. 20014. Tel: 301-496-6221

U.S. VETERANS ADMINISTRATION L. SERVICE, Veterans Administration Bldg., Rm. 976, Washington, D.C. 20420. Tel: 202-DU9-2781

UNIV. OF UTAH L., Salt Lake City, Utah 84112. Tel: 801-322-6741. Telex: 910-925-5172

UTAH STATE L. COMMISSION, 2150 S. Second West, Salt Lake City, Utah 84115. Tel: 801-328-5875

UNIV. OF VERMONT & STATE AGRICULTURE COLL., GUY W. BAILEY L., Burlington, Vermont 05401. Tel: 802-864-4511. Ext. 213. TWX: 710-224-6437

VERMONT DEPT. OF LS., State Library Bldg., Montpelier, Vermont 05602. Tel: 802-223-2311. Ext. 548

UNIV. OF VIRGINIA, ALDERMAN L., Charlottesville, Va. 22901. Tel: 703-924-3026. Teletype: 510-587-5453

VIRGINIA STATE L., Capital St., Richmond Va. 23219. Tel: 703-770-2300

UNIV. OF WASHINGTON L., Seattle, Wash. 98105. Tel: 206-543-1760; SCHOOL OF LIBRARIANSHIP, Seattle, Wash. 98105. Tel: 206-543-2100

WASHINGTON STATE UNIV. L., Pullman, Wash. 99163. Tel: 509-325-4557

WASHINGTON STATE L., Olympia, Wash. 98501. Tel: 206-753-5590

WASHINGTON UNIV. L., Skinker & Lindell Blvds., St. Louis, Mo. 63130. Tel: 314-VO3-0100

WAYNE STATE UNIV. L., 5210 2 St., Detro Mich. 48202. Tel: 313-833-1400

WELLESLEY COLL. L., Wellesley, Ma 02181. Tel: 617-235-0320

WESLEYAN UNIV., OLIN MEM. L., Midd town, Conn. 06457. Tel: 203-DI7-44

WEST VIRGINIA L. COMMISSION, 20 Quarrier St., Charleston, W. 25300. Tel: 304-348-2041. TW 710-930-1801

WEST VIRGINIA UNIV. L., Morgantown, Va. 26506. Tel: 304-293-0111

WESTERN MICHIGAN UNIV., DEPARTME OF LIBRARIANSHIP, Kalamazoo, Mi 49001. Tel: 616-383-1847. TW 810-277-2505

UNIV. OF WESTERN ONTARIO, SCHOOL L. & INFORMATION SCIENCE, Lond Ont. Tel: 519-679-2111

WICHITA P. L., 223 S. Main St., Wich Kansas 67202. Tel: 316-265-528

H. W. WILSON CO., 950 Univ. Ave., Bro N.Y. 10542. Tel: 212-LU8-8400

STATE OF WISCONSIN, DIV. FOR L. SERVIC Dept. of Public Instruction, Wisco Hall, 126 Langdon St., Madison, 53703. Tel: 608-266-2205

UNIV. OF WISCONSIN L., 728 State Madison, Wis. 53706. Tel: 608-3521; L. SCHOOL. Tel: 608-262-123

UNIV. OF WISCONSIN-MILWAUKEE L., 2 E. Hartford Ave., Milwaukee, 53201. Tel: 414-228-4785

UNIV. OF WYOMING, WILLIAM ROBERT COE L., Box 3334, University Sta., I mie, Wyo. 82070. Tel: 307-766-3 Telex: 910-949-4946

WYOMING STATE L., Supreme Court B Cheyenne, Wyo. 82001. Tel: 307-7281. TWX: 910-949-4787

YALE UNIV., STERLING MEMORIAL L. High St., New Haven, Conn. 0 Tel: 203-436-8335

YESHIVA UNIV. L., Amsterdam Av 186th St., New York, N.Y. 10033 212-LO8-8400. Ext. 378–81

YONKERS P.L., S. Broadway, Yon N.Y. 10701. Tel: 914-DE7-1500

BRIGHAM YOUNG UNIV., GRADUATE OF L. AND INFORMATION SCI Provo, Utah 84601. Tel: 801-374

P.L. OF YOUNGSTOWN & MAHONING TY, 305 Wick Ave., Youngstown, 44503. Tel: 216-744-8636